THE PLANTAGENET ROLL

OF THE

𝔅lood 𝔏oyal

ANNE (PLANTAGENET) DUCHESS OF EXETER
AND HER SECOND HUSBAND SIR THOMAS ST LEGER
THE COMMON ANCESTORS OF ALL IN THIS VOLUME
FROM THE MONUMENTAL BRASS IN THE RUTLAND CHAPEL
WINDSOR CASTLE.

THE
PLANTAGENET
ROLL

OF THE

𝔅lood 𝔯oyal

BEING A COMPLETE TABLE OF
ALL THE DESCENDANTS NOW LIVING OF

𝔈dward 𝔍𝔍𝔍., 𝔎ing of 𝔈ngland

BY

THE MARQUIS OF RUVIGNY AND RAINEVAL

AUTHOR OF "THE BLOOD ROYAL OF BRITAIN," "THE JACOBITE PEERAGE,
BARONETAGE, AND KNIGHTAGE," "THE MOODIE BOOK," ETC.

𝔗he 𝔄nne of 𝔈xeter 𝔙olume

CONTAINING THE DESCENDANTS OF ANNE (PLANTAGENET)
DUCHESS OF EXETER

Originally published: London, 1907
Reprinted by Genealogical Publishing Co., Inc.
Baltimore, 1994
Library of Congress Catalogue Card Number 93-81361
International Standard Book Number 0-8063-1433-8
Set Number 0-8063-1436-2
Made in the United States of America

PREFACE

THE Descendants of King Edward IV. and of George, Duke of Clarence, having been given in the two preceding volumes, the present volume of THE PLANTAGENET ROLL OF THE BLOOD ROYAL contains those of their sister Anne, Duchess of Exeter.

The plan followed is identical with that adopted in the Clarence Volume. The lines from Duchess Anne are traced out in a series of Tables until about the middle of last century; then in the body of the book the descendants of the various persons last named in the Tables are set out in the order of primogeniture. The full dates of birth, marriage, and death are given, and in the cases of married persons the names of the husband and wife, &c.

In the Tables the dates of birth, marriage, and death are given whenever possible, but as the object of the writer has been merely to trace out the living descendants of Edward III., and in order to keep the work within bounds, he has been obliged to omit (except in some few cases, where it has been thought desirable to show the descent of a title) the names of persons who died without issue, or whose issue subsequently failed, and also the parentage of the wives.

In the case of a person having been married more than once, only the name of the wife or wives (or husband or husbands) by whom he (or she) had had issue are given, the figure in round brackets immediately following the marriage mark = signifying whether she (or he) is first, second, or third wife (or husband). Similarly, if the figure precedes the marriage mark, it signifies that he (or she) married as first or second wife (or husband) as the case may be. Wherever the compiler has been able to give the dates of birth and marriage, he has considered this sufficient indication of whether the children are by the first or second marriage; but where these dates have not been obtainable, the figure before the names shows of which marriage they are the issue.

When a name in the Tables is in italics, it signifies that they have a previous descent which has been already shown.

In the Roll itself considerations of space have again rendered it necessary to adopt the briefest possible description, and the words "and had issue" must be held to refer only (with the exceptions mentioned above) to those children who are now living, or whose issue now survives, or those concerning whose issue, or possible issue, the author has been unable to obtain particulars.

Each Section is headed by the name of the person last named in the Tables, and their children are 1a, 2a, &c. The issue of the a's, grandchildren of the head of the line, are b's, and the children of these last, great-grandchildren of the head of the line, are similarly c's, and so on, the d's being children of the c's, and great-great-grandchildren of the head of the line, &c.

The dates of birth and death immediately follow the names of the persons to whom they refer. In the cases of births, marriages, and deaths outside the United Kingdom, the author has endeavoured to give the place as well as the date.

vii b

Preface

The surnames of noblemen are given in round brackets after their Christian names, and the nationality of their titles is indicated by the initials and names within square brackets immediately following them.[1]

Anne (Plantagenet), Duchess of Exeter, whose descendants are here set out, was the eldest sister of Kings Edward IV. and Richard III. She was born at Fotheringay Castle, 10 Aug. 1439,[2] and died 14 Jan. 1475/6, having married before 30 July 1447, 1st, Henry (Holland), 2nd Duke of Exeter [E.], Admiral of England, Ireland, and Aquitaine, who having remained loyal to King Henry VI., was attainted on the accession of his brother-in-law, King Edward IV., 4 Nov. 1461, and afterwards joining the Earl of Warwick, was severely wounded and left for dead on the field of Barnet from seven o'clock in the morning until four o'clock in the afternoon, when he was conveyed to the house of one of his servants, called Ruthland, and from thence secretly carried for sanctuary to Westminster. From him the Duchess was divorced at her own suit, 12 Nov. 1472,[3] and his body was found cast upon the shore near Dover the following year, but by what means he came by his death has never been ascertained.[4]

She remarried Sir Thomas St. Leger, K.G., and they are both buried in the Rutland Chapel at Windsor, where there is a memorial on a plate of brass affixed to the wall, containing their picture kneeling, arms and epitaph (see Frontispiece).

Anne St. Leger, her only daughter and heiress,[5] married about 1490, Sir George Manners, 12th Lord Roos, "who with his said wife, lieth intombed in the North Cross of St. George's Chappel in Windsor Castle, with this Epitaph: 'Here lyethe buried George Manners, Knight, Lord Roos, who deceased the xxiii day of Octobre in the yere of our Lord God MVCXIII and Ladye Anne his wife, daughter of Anne, Duchess of Exetur, suster unto Kyng Edward the fourthe and of Thomas Sentlynger, Knight. The whyche Anne decessed the xxii day of April, in the yere of our Lord God MVCXXVI on whose soulls God have mercy, Amen.'"[6]

Their eldest son, Thomas, was created Earl of Rutland by King Henry VII. by letters patent, dated at Bridewell, 18 June 1526, and had an augmentation to his arms granted to show his descent from Anne Plantagenet, viz.: *Or, two bars azure, a chief of the last and gules, in the 1st and 4th quarters, two fleur-de-lys (for France), and in the 2nd and 3rd, a lion passant (for England), all or.* This coat, with the necessary differences, can be used by all his male descendants, and can be quartered by all those descended from him through armigerous heiresses or co-heirs.

---

[1] The initials E., S., I., G.B., U.K., F., H.R.E., and P.S., standing for England, Scotland, Ireland, Great Britain, the United Kingdom, France, the Holy Roman Empire, and the Papal States. With regard to foreign titles of nobility it was the original intention of the author to give them in the language of their nationality, but it would have appeared absurd to have written *Herzog von Teck* or to have referred to the *Freiherr Henrich von Worms, M.P.*; after much consideration, therefore, he decided to give them in English, adding the foreign equivalent in brackets immediately following so, " 3rd Baron of Hugel (Freiherr von Hugel)"—"7th Count of Salis (Graf von Salis)" after the plan recently adopted in the *Almanach de Gotha*. It is to be wished that some settled rule might be adopted by the press. To take one case which might be multiplied without end *Duc d'Orleans* or *Duke of Orleans* are both equally correct, but the *Duke d'Orleans*, which one constantly sees, is surely a misnomer. All the older writers used to translate the names and titles into English, and this appears the only way if any uniform plan is to be attempted.

[2] G. E. C.'s " Complete Peerage," iii. p. 298.

[3] Sandford's " Genealogical History of the Kings of England," &c., p. 394.

[4] Comines reports that he saw this unhappy nobleman in such deep distress that he ran on foot, bare-legged, after the Duke of Burgundy's train, begging his bread for God's sake, but that he uttered not his name; and that when he was known, the duke conferred upon him a small pension.

[5] Sandford in his " Genealogical History of the Kings and Queens of England," p. 394, says that she had, by her first husband, another daughter, also called Anne, wife of Thomas (Grey), Marquis of Dorset, but if so, this daughter must have died *s.p.* soon after her marriage.

[6] Sandford, p. 395.

Preface

His male representative is the present Duke of Rutland, but the heir of line of the Lady Anne Plantagenet is Lord De L'Isle and Dudley.

The Exeter Volume contains the names of some 25,052 living (or very lately living) descendants of the Duchess of Exeter,[1] having between them 59,360 lines of descent, being an average of a little over two descents each. It will thus be seen that the descendants of the Duchess Anne are much more numerous than those of either Edward IV. or of the Duke of Clarence, and with very few exceptions nearly all these lines of descent have now been worked out for the first time.[2] The great majority of her descendants have but one line of descent, but a number have two and more.

Three hundred and thirteen peers[3] are descended from the Duchess, the Duke of Westminster coming first with twenty-two descents, and the Earl of Ellesmere second with fifteen, while the Index contains over 3200 different surnames.

Like those of her brothers, Duchess Anne's descendants include persons in every station of life, and it is interesting to be able to record that now for the first time since her death 430 years ago, her blood is united with that of her brother Edward's royal descendants, in the persons of the grandchildren of another King Edward, viz. their Highnesses, the Princesses Alexandra and Maud of Great Britain and Ireland,[4] they being descended from Edward IV. through their mother, H.R.H. the Princess Royal, Duchess of Fife, and from Duchess Anne through their father the Duke of Fife.

This volume completes the Roll of the descendants of that Richard, Duke of York, whose claim to the throne led to the Wars of the Roses, and summarising the three volumes now published, we have here a single pedigree containing the names of from thirty to thirty-five thousand of his living descendants,[5] and showing 128,031 separate lines of descent from him. Included in the Roll are the names of all the crowned heads of Europe, with the exception of the Kings of Sweden and Servia, and the Prince of Montenegro [6]—of 371 [7] of our hereditary legislators; of the members of all the

---

[1] Where in consequence of an inter-marriage between the descendants of the Duchess of Exeter and of her brothers Edward IV. and the Duke of Clarence, the lines have merged, the author has not, in the majority of cases, unless he was able to give additional information, repeated the names, but has given a reference to the numbers in, and the page of the volume wherein the names will be found. The Index, however, contains the names of all the Duchess of Exeter's living descendants, whether or not they are set out in full in the body of the work.

[2] Of the previously published works on this subject, the two principal are "The Royal Families of England, Scotland, and Wales, and their Descendants, Sovereigns and Subjects," by John Burke and Sir J. Bernard Burke, Ulster King of Arms, 2 vols., 1847–1851, and "Our Noble and Gentle Families of Royal Descent," by Joseph Foster, M.A., 3 vols., 1885. The former contains some fourteen descents from the Duchess Anne, and the latter one only.

[3] This number includes Peeresses in their own right and English Bishops.

[4] Through the courtesy of the Duke of Fife, the author has been enabled to make here what he believes is the first authoritative statement regarding the correct designation of these Princesses.

[5] The Tudor Roll contains the names of 11,723 living descendants of Edward IV. and the Clarence Volume those of 17,625 of Duke George, while the present volume gives 25,052 of their sister. In consequence of intermarriages, however, a considerable number are descended from all three, while others again are descended from two of them. The author has not had time to work out the exact number, but a rough estimate fixes the number of the Duke of York's living descendants as above.

[6] The Prince of Monaco, excepted in the Preface to the Tudor Roll as not being descended from Edward IV., is descended from both the Duke of Clarence and Duchess Anne.

[7] In the Table of Peers given in the Clarence Volume two, the 3rd B. Raglan, Nos. 176 and 228, and the 5th B. Foley, Nos. 124 and 233, have been accidentally given twice, while eight others should be added, viz., [153a] 5th B. Ashburton [U.K.], who has two descents from Edward IV., and [210a] 6th E. of Mount Cashell [I.], [215a] 2nd B. Sackville [U.K.], [219a] 3rd B. Gerard [U.K.], [220a] 9th E. of Airlie [S.], [236a] 16th B. Lovat [S.], [247a] 4th B. Stanley of Alderley [U.K.], and [268a] 4th B. Dunally [I.], with one, one, three, eight, one, and one descents respectively from Clarence, making the total 280 or 281 with the Count della Catena, No. 227. Of the total of 371 Peers descended from the Duke of York, 114 are descended from all three of his children, ten from Edward IV. and the Duke of Clarence, fifty-four from Edward IV. and the Duchess of Exeter, fifty-five from the Duke of Clarence and the Duchess of Exeter, eleven from Edward IV. alone, thirty-seven from Clarence, and ninety from the Duchess Anne.

Preface

royal and princely houses of Europe; of many of the higher nobility of France, Germany, Austria, Hungary, Poland, Bohemia, Italy, Spain, Portugal, Russia, Belgium; and of the old aristocracy of the Southern States of America, together with those of many of our baronets and county families with their cadets, who so largely go to make up the professional classes; but with one or two trifling exceptions among the descendants of Edward IV., none of Duke Richard's descendants will be found in the lower walks of life.

The next volume will deal with the descendants of his sister, the Lady Isabel Plantagenet, wife of Henry (Bourchier), Count of Eu and Earl of Essex, while future volumes will deal with those of Lady Elizabeth Mortimer, wife of Henry, Lord Percy, called "Hotspur"; of John (Plantagenet, called of Gaunt), Duke of Lancaster; of Edmund (Plantagenet, called of Langley), Duke of York; of Thomas (Plantagenet, called of Woodstock), Duke of Gloucester; and of the Lady Isabel Plantagenet, wife of Ingleram (de Coucy), Earl of Bedford.

There are, of course, many who affect to laugh at any work treating of Royal Descents, and a volume which is devoted to setting forth the individual descent of various more or less obscure personages is naturally of purely personal interest to those whose descent it sets forth, but the present series approaches the subject from a totally different point—from the historical, not from the personal, and aims at treating in a fairly exhaustive manner of all the descendants of, and descents from, the greatest of our Plantagenet kings. While preparing this work the author has received some hundreds of letters from persons in every quarter of the globe, descended not only from Edward III., but in many cases our early Norman and Saxon Sovereigns, requesting that their descents may be included, and surprise has in some cases been expressed because the writer, while casting no doubt on the genuineness of the particular descent, has been obliged to explain, either that it did not come within the scope of his work, or else that a descent, from say John of Gaunt, could not be included in the volume dealing with those from Anne of Exeter.

The author is always glad to receive copies of all royal descents. They are all carefully arranged, and those coming from Edward III. will, if found correct, be duly included in their proper order. It is, however, impossible for him to say off-hand whether such and such a descent is correct. The work is not an easy one to prepare, and it is absolutely necessary for him to confine himself to the particular line of descent upon which he may for the moment be engaged.

Others say that a Royal descent is of no interest, since so many enjoy it, but allowing that there are some 60,000 descendants of Edward III. now living, what is that out of a total of say 100,000,000 persons of British descent, and even if Edward I. may be justly termed the father of the British people, it is quite a different thing to be able to trace the line. Let it be remembered that while a word from the King can put one in "the Peerage," or a successful financial speculation in the "Landed Gentry," birth alone entitles one to a place in the Plantagenet Roll, for on one side at least there must be a strain of gentle blood, through which it is possible to trace ancestry[1] to the feudal and crusading days.

Embracing as this work does all classes, from the sovereign to the peasant, it serves to unite all in a common interest in the traditions of the past. Who studying history, or visiting the tombs of the Edwards in Westminster Abbey, or reading Lytton's "Last of the Barons," could fail

[1] It should be remembered that any one whose name occurs in this Roll can trace an ancestry back in an unbroken line to William the Conqueror and Alfred the Great, to St. Louis and to the Emperor Charlemagne.

Preface

to feel a better citizen, knowing that step by step, and link by link, he is descended in a clear unbroken line from those who built up the foundations of our mighty empire, and is united by blood to our common sovereign.

Every effort has been made to make the Roll as complete as possible, and to thoroughly revise and bring the particulars up to date, and for this purpose proofs have been submitted to all those named therein, whose addresses the writer was able to ascertain, and he desires to return his most grateful thanks for the courtesy and assistance which have been extended to him on all hands. It is sometimes invidious to particularise, but he must especially acknowledge his indebtedness to G. E. Cokayne, Esq., Clarenceux King of Arms, Sir Arthur Vicars, K.C.V.O., Ulster King of Arms, H. Murray Lane, Esq., Chester Herald, G. D. Burtchaell, Esq., H. Houston Ball, Esq., Rev. the Hon. Hugh Courtenay, Col. J. G. Hicks, D. Upham Reynell-Upham, Esq., R. J. Kennedy of Cultra, Esq., C.M.G., C. W. Kennedy, Esq., F. E. Ball, Esq., the Rev. A. S. Hartigan, M.A., the late Duke of Rutland, Lady Victoria Manners, Sir Kenneth Matheson, Bart., Arthur F. G. Leveson-Gower, Esq., Maj.-Gen. J. J. Heywood, Mrs. Robert Noel, the Lady Elizabeth Cust, Major T. R. F. B. Hallowes, C. C. Lacaita, Esq., the Hon. A. N. Curzon, the Editor of *Notes and Queries*, Mrs. Wharton of Skelton Castle, the Rev. W. G. D. Fletcher, Luke G. Dillon, Esq., Mrs. Steuart Erskine, the Rev. E. H. Fellowes, A. Cary Elwes, Esq., Miss Maud G. Satterthwaite, Lord Bathurst, B. T. Fanshawe, Esq., Mrs. Ridout, Miss Martin, the Rev. A. de Vlieger, C. H. Talbot of Lacock, Esq., Malcolm Low of Clatto, Esq., Mrs. R. F. Maitland, the Rev. Canon Moor, W. M. How, Esq., the Hon. Mrs. Palny, Col. B. G. Davies-Cooke, Sir George Armytage, Bart., Francis Worsley, Esq., L. C. Forestier-Walker, Esq., W. Jackson Pigott, Esq., Philip J. C. Howard of Corby, Esq., Col. Philip Saltmarshe, and many others, who have not only assisted him with particulars concerning their own families, but have gone to considerable trouble in assisting him to trace out other lines of descent, in searching parish registers, and in obtaining dates.

In compiling this work the author can truthfully say that he has made every effort to make it as complete as possible—each descent is treated on its own merits, and no distinction is made, whether it be that of the peer or the yeoman—and *absolutely no charge or condition has been made for the insertion of any name or descent in this book.*

There are, of course, many lines which the writer has been unable to trace, the very magnitude of the task making all the conclusions arrived at of a more or less tentative nature—and he is only too fully aware of the number of other errors and imperfections, which must, almost of necessity, occur in a first attempt of this kind; but he asks for the kind indulgence of his readers —and he will be most grateful to all those who will point out to him omissions or other errors which may come under their notice. They will all be included in a supplementary volume with which the series will close.

CHERTSEY, *December* 1906.

LIST OF ILLUSTRATIONS

TABLE I

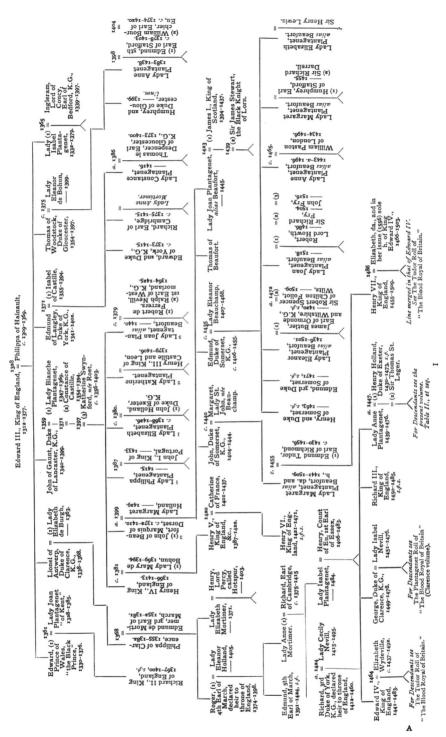

TABLE II

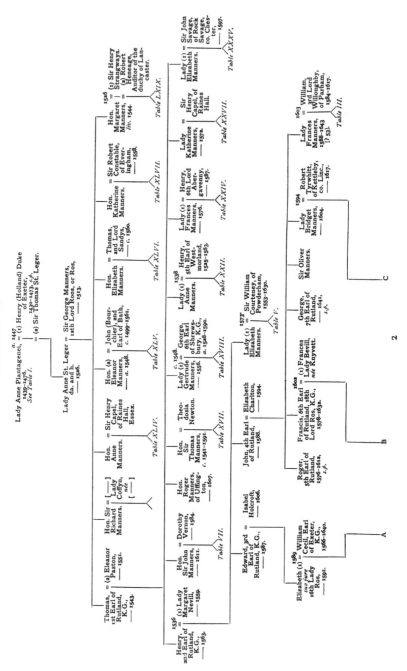

2

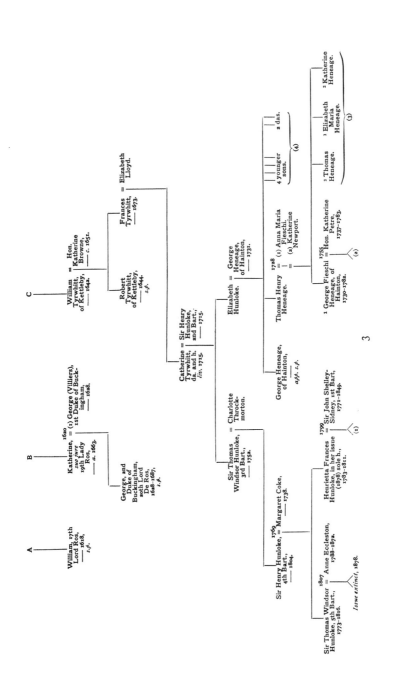

A

William, 17th
Lord Ros,
——— 1618,
s.p.

B

Katherine, = (1) George (Villiers),
1620
sua jure   1st Duke of Buck-
19th Lady   ingham,
Ros,   ——— 1628.
——— a. 1663.

George, 2nd
Duke of
Buckingham,
20th Lord
De Ros,
1628-1687,
s.p.

C

William   = Hon.
Tyrwhitt,   Katherine
of Kettleby,   Browne,
——— 1644.   —— c. 1651.

Robert   Frances   = Elizabeth
Tyrwhitt,   Tyrwhitt,   Lloyd.
of Kettleby,   1673.
——— 1644,
s.p.

Catherine = Sir Henry
Tyrwhitt,   Hunloke,
da. and h.   2nd Bart.,
liv. 1715.   ——— 1715.

Elizabeth = George
Hunloke.   Heneage,
              of Hainton,
              ——— 1731.

Sir Thomas   = Charlotte
Windsor Hunloke,   Throck-
3rd Bart.,   morton.
——— 1752.

George Heneage,   Thomas Henry   = (1) Anna Maria
of Hainton,   Heneage.   Fieschi,
                       1728   (a) Katherine
app. s.p.   =   Newport.
                       =

Sir Henry Hunloke, = Margaret Coke,
4th Bart.,   ——— 1738.
——— 1804.

1 George Fieschi = Hon. Katherine
Heneage, of   Petre,
Hainton,   1737-1783.
1730-1782.   1755

⟨a⟩

Henrietta Frances   = Sir John Shelley-
Hunloke, in her issue   Sidney, 1st Bart,
(1878) sole h.,   1771-1849.
1783-1811.   1799

⟨1⟩

4 younger   2 das.
sons.

⟨4⟩

2 Thomas   1 Elizabeth
Heneage.   Maria
                  Heneage.

⟨3⟩

1 Katherine
Heneage.

Sir Thomas Windsor = Anne Eccleston,
Hunloke, 5th Bart.,   1788-1872.
1773-1816.   1807

Issue extinct, 1878.

3

TABLE III

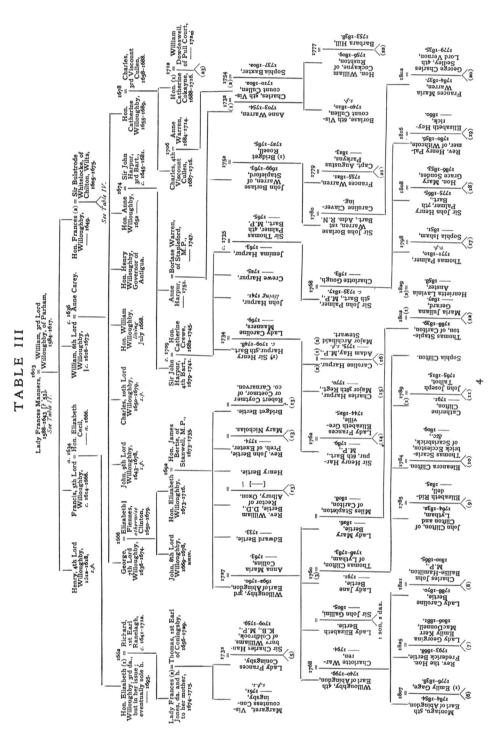

4

TABLE IV

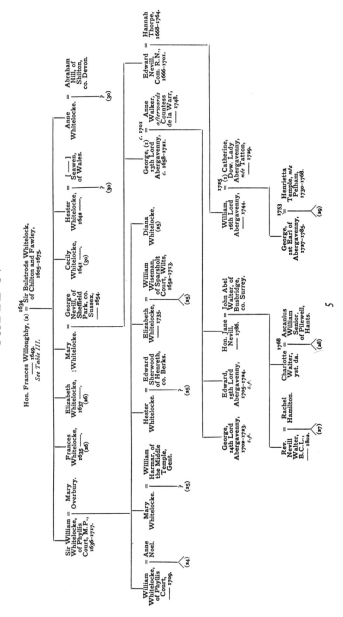

Hon. Frances Willoughby, (a) = Sir Bulstrode Whitelock, of Chilton and Fawley, 1605–1675. 1634. 1649.
See Table III.

5

TABLE V

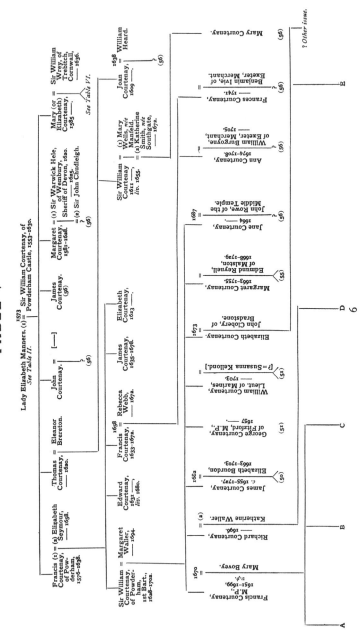

Lady Elizabeth Manners, (1) = Sir William Courtenay, of
                    1573   Powderham Castle, 1553–1630.
See Table II.

? Other issue.

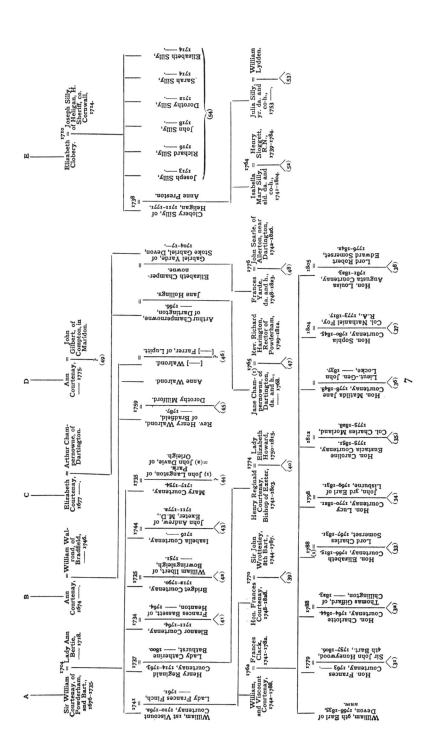

TABLE V

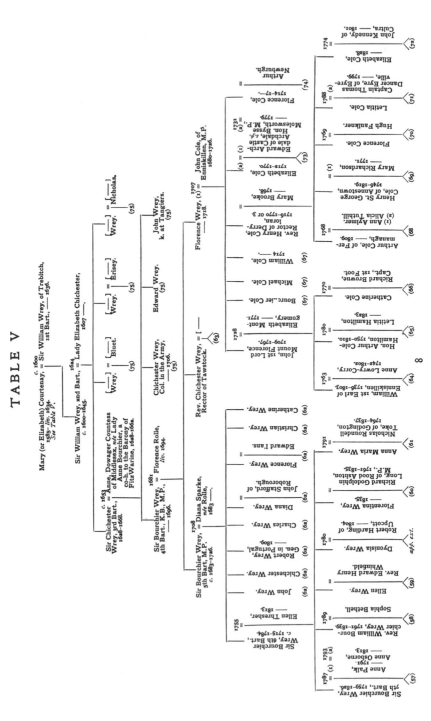

TABLE VII

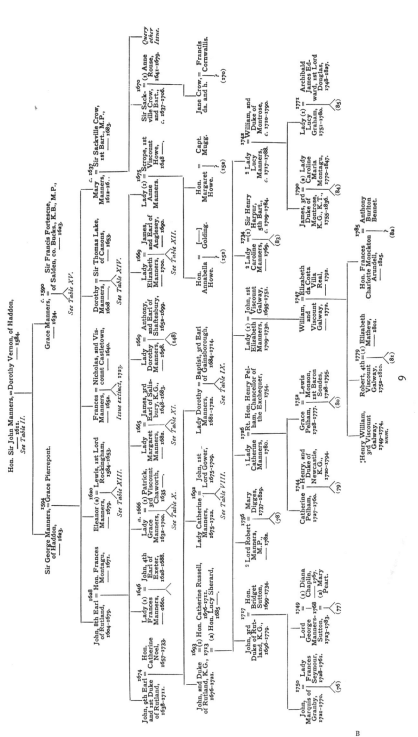

Hon. Sir John Manners, = Dorothy Vernon, of Haddon, ——1584.
See Table II.

9

TABLE VIII

Lady Catherine Manners, 1695-1722, *See Table VII.* =[169a] John, 1st Lord Gower, 1675-1709.

Hon. Jane Leveson-Gower, 1716. =[1718(2o)] John Proby, of Elton Hall, Hants, M.P., 1760.

Hon. William Leveson-Gower, M.P., — 1756. =[1720] Anne Grosvenor.

Very Rev. Baptist Proby, Dean of Lichfield, 1807. = Mary Russell.

Charles 1758 Proby, Capt. R.N. = Sarah Pownell.

Rev. Charles Proby. [110] = Catherine Proby. [110]

Baptist Leveson Proby. [110]

Thomas James Storer, of Purley Park, — 1792. = das. [110]

Hon. Elizabeth Proby, 1754-1808. [111]

Frances Storer, 1780-1821. [102]

Rev. Richard Hutchins Whitelock, 1778-1833. [103]

Anne Katherine Hill, 1908. [101] =[1800] Anthony Gilbert Storer, of Purley Park, 1784-1818. [102]

John, 1st Lord Carysfort, 1720-1772. =[1750] Hon. Elizabeth Allen, 1783.

John Joshua, 1st Earl of Carysfort, K.P., 1751-1828. [107] =[1774] (1) Elizabeth Osborne, 1783. =[1787] (2) Elizabeth Gren-ville, 1756-1842.

George, 2nd Earl of Warwick and Brooke, 1746-1816. [906] =[1776] (2) Henrietta Vernon, 1760-1838.

William, 1st Marquis of Lansdowne, 1737-1805. [905] =[1779] (2) Lady Louisa Fitz-Patrick, 1755-1789.

Stephen, 2nd Lord Holland, 1745-1774. =[1766] Lady Mary Fitz-Patrick, — 1778.

John, 2nd Earl of Upper Ossory, 1745-1818, *s.p.l.s.*

Henry Richard, 3rd Lord Holland, 1773-1840. [904] =[1797] Elizabeth Vassall, c. 1770-1845.

William, 8th Earl Waldegrave, 1788-1859. [902] =[181] Elizabeth Whitbread, c. 1792-1843.

John James, 6th Earl Waldegrave, 1785-1835. [901] =[1815] Anne King, c. 1790-1852.

Catherine Leveson Gower.

Richard Vernon, 1754 (a) of Hilton, co. Staf-ford, M.P., 1756-1800. =[1754] (1) John, 1st Earl of Upper Ossory, 1719-1758.

Cornelia Van Lennap, 1833. [903] =[1785]

William, 1st Lord Radstock, G.C.B., 1753-1825. =

George, 9th Earl Waldegrave, 1784-1794. [901]

George, 4th Earl Waldegrave, 1751-1789. = Lady Elizabeth Laura Waldegrave, 1760-1816. [184]

Henry Pytches Boyce. [99] =[181]

1 Lady Evelyn Leveson Gower, 1718-1764. =[1744] John, 3rd Earl Waldegrave, 1763.

1 Lady Elizabeth Leveson Gower, 1784. =[175] George, 4th Duke of Marlborough, K.G., 1762-1817. [100]

Lord John Philip Sackville, 1713-1765. =[1744] 1 Lady Frances Leveson Gower, 1788.

Lady Caroline Russell, 1743-1811. [100] =[1762]

Lady Amelia Spencer, 1785-1829. [99]

Cropley Ashley, 6th Earl of Shaftesbury, 1768-1851. [98] =[1796]

John, 4th Duke of Bedford, K.G., 1710-1771. =[1737] 1 Lady Elizabeth Keppel, 1739-1768.

Francis, Marquis of Tavistock, 1739-1767. [100] =[1764]

Lady Anne Spencer. [97] =[1797] Rev. Edward Nares, D.D.

1 Lady Gertrude Leveson Gower, c. 1720-1794. =[1737] (2)

John Tillie Coryton, of Pentille Castle, 1773-1843. [90] =[1803]

Lady Charlotte Spencer, 1769-1802. [97]

Sir Richard Wrot-tesley, 7th Bart., Dean of Worcester, 1721-1769. =[1739] 1 Lady Mary Leveson Gower, — 1778.

Elizabeth Leveson Gower, 1784-1844. [90]

John Spencer, 1767-1831. [96]

Katherine Maria Gresham, — 1808. =[1804] William Leveson Gower, 1779-1851. [96]

Henry Welbore, and Viscount Clifden, 1761-1836. [95] =[1792] Lady Elizabeth Spencer, 1764-1812. [96]

Frances Boscawen, 1813. =[1773] Hon. John Leveson Gower, Admiral R.N., 1740-1792.

Charlotte Elizabeth Mount, — 1846. =[182] Edward Leveson Gower, Rear-Ad. of the Blue, 1776-1853. [88]

Lady Caroline Spencer, 1763-1813. [95] =[1791] Francis Almeric, 1st Lord Churchill, 1779-1845. [94]

(2) Lady Louisa Egerton, 1723-1761, (3) Lady Susannah Stewart, — 1805. =[1748][1768] John, 1st Earl Gower, 1694-1754. =[1712] (1) Lady Evelyn Pierrepont, — 1727. =[1736] (3) Mary, Dow., Countess of Harold, *née* Lady Mary Tufton, 1701-1785.

Isabella Mary Broke, 1774-1816. — 1817. =[1796] John Leveson Gower, Gen. in the Army, 1 Granville, 1st Mar-quis of Stafford, K.G., 1721-1803. [86]

Lady Frances Fitz-Roy, 1774-1849. [94] =[181]

George, 5th Duke of Marlborough, 1766-1840. [93] =[1791] Lady Susan Stewart, 1767-1841. [93]

10

TABLE IX

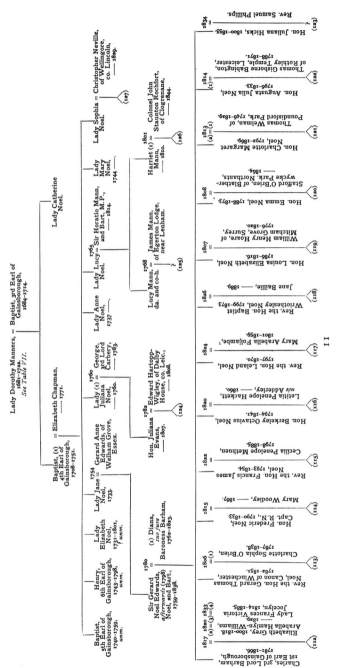

Lady Dorothy Manners, = Baptist, 3rd Earl of
1681–1722. | Gainsborough,
See Table VII. | 1684–1714.

TABLE X

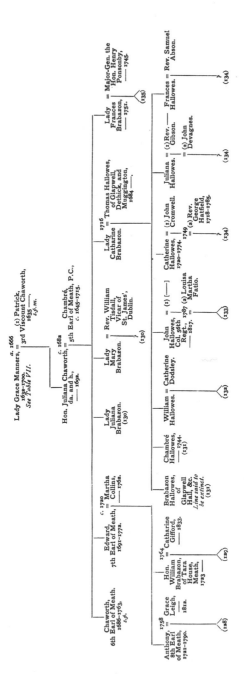

TABLE XI

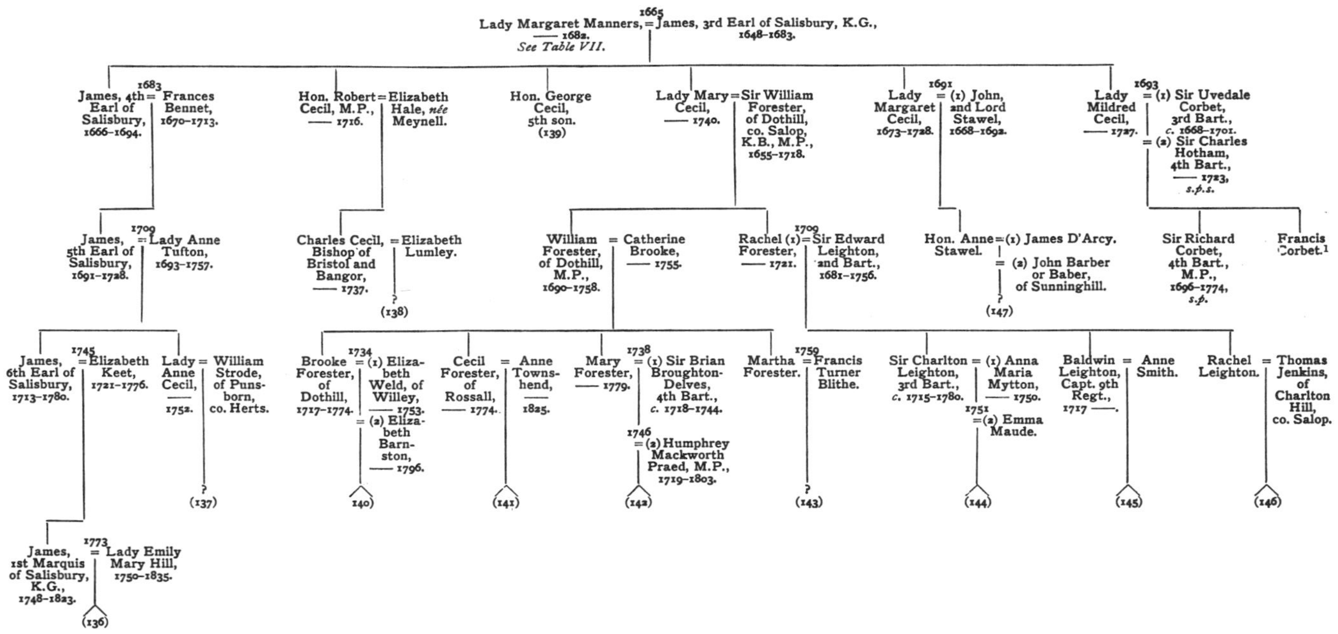

1665
Lady Margaret Manners, = James, 3rd Earl of Salisbury, K.G.,
—— 1682. See Table VII.
1648–1683.
1683
James, 4th Earl of Salisbury, 1666–1694.
= Frances Bennet, 1670–1713.
Hon. Robert Cecil, M.P., —— 1716.
= Elizabeth Hale, née Meynell.
Hon. George Cecil, 5th son. (139)
Lady Mary Cecil, —— 1740.
= Sir William Forester, of Dothill, co. Salop, K.B., M.P., 1655–1718.
1691
Lady Margaret Cecil, 1673–1728.
= (1) John, 2nd Lord Stawel, 1668–1692.
1693
Lady Mildred Cecil, —— 1727.
= (1) Sir Uvedale Corbet, 3rd Bart., c. 1668–1701.
= (2) Sir Charles Hotham, 4th Bart., —— 1723, s.p.s.
1709
James, 5th Earl of Salisbury, 1691–1728.
= Lady Anne Tufton, 1693–1757.
Charles Cecil, Bishop of Bristol and Bangor, —— 1737.
= Elizabeth Lumley.
? (138)
William Forester, of Dothill, M.P., 1690–1758.
= Catherine Brooke, —— 1755.
1709
Rachel (1) Forester, —— 1721.
= Sir Edward Leighton, 2nd Bart., 1681–1756.
Hon. Anne Stawel.
= (1) James D'Arcy.
= (2) John Barber or Baber, of Sunninghill.
? (147)
Sir Richard Corbet, 4th Bart., M.P., 1696–1774, s.p.
Francis Corbet.[1]
1745
James, 6th Earl of Salisbury, 1713–1780.
= Elizabeth Keet, 1721–1776.
Lady Anne Cecil, —— 1752.
= William Strode, of Punsborn, co. Herts.
? (137)
1734
Brooke Forester, of Dothill, 1717–1774.
= (1) Elizabeth Weld, of Willey, —— 1753.
= (2) Elizabeth Barnston, —— 1796.
(140)
Cecil Forester, of Rossall, —— 1774.
= Anne Townshend, —— 1825.
(141)
1738
Mary Forester, —— 1779.
= (1) Sir Brian Broughton-Delves, 4th Bart., c. 1718–1744.
1746
= (2) Humphrey Mackworth Praed, M.P., 1719–1803.
(142)
1759
Martha Forester.
= Francis Turner Blithe.
? (143)
Sir Charlton Leighton, 3rd Bart., c. 1715–1780.
= (1) Anna Maria Mytton, —— 1750.
1751
= (2) Emma Maude.
(144)
Baldwin Leighton, Capt. 9th Regt., 1717 ——.
= Anne Smith.
(145)
Rachel Leighton.
= Thomas Jenkins, of Charlton Hill, co. Salop.
(146)
1773
James, 1st Marquis of Salisbury, K.G., 1748–1823.
= Lady Emily Mary Hill, 1750–1835.
(136)

[1] This Francis Corbet, b. 11th June 1701, is generally supposed to have died s.p. in Scotland, but according to other accounts he was identical with the Francis Corbet (d. 1775) who became Dean of St. Patrick's, Dublin, and was ancestor of the Corbet Singletons, of Aclare, co. Meath.

TABLE XII

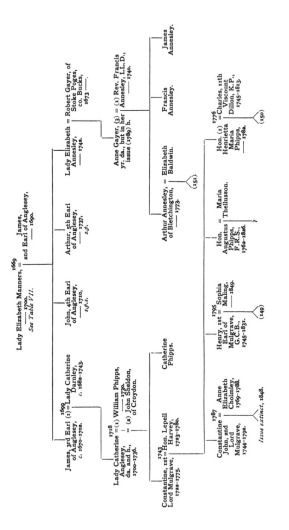

Lady Elizabeth Manners, = James,
—— 1700. | and Earl of Anglesey,
See Table VII.   —— 1690.

James, 3rd Earl = (1) Lady Catherine
of Anglesey,   Darnley,
c. 1670–1702.   c. 1682–1743.

Lady Catherine = (1) William Phipps,
Anglesey,   = (2) John Sheldon,
da. and h.,   of Croydon.
1700–1736.

John, 4th Earl
of Anglesey,
—— 1710,
s.p.s.

Arthur, 5th Earl
of Anglesey,
—— 1737,
s.p.

Lady Elizabeth = Robert Gayer, of
Annesley,   Stoke Poges,
—— 1742.   co. Bucks,
                   1673 ——

Anne Gayer, (3) = (1) Rev. Francis
yr. da., but in her   Annesley, LL.D.,
issue (1789) h.   —— 1740.

Catherine
Phipps.

Constantine, 1st = Hon. Lepell
Lord Mulgrave,   Harvey,
1722–1775.   1723–1780.

Henry, 1st = Sophia
Earl of   Maling,
Mulgrave,   —— 1849.
G.C.B.,
1745–1831.

Constantine = Anne
John, and   Elizabeth
Mulgrave,   Cholmley,
1744–1792.   1769–1788.

Issue extinct, 1848.

Hon.   = Maria
Augustus   Thellusson.
Phipps,
F.R.S.,
1762–1826.

Arthur Annesley, = Elizabeth
of Bletchington,   Baldwin.
—— 1773.

Francis
Annesley.

James
Annesley.

Hon. (1) = Charles, 11th
Henrietta   Viscount
Maria   Dillon, K.P.,
Phipps,   1745–1813.
1782.

(149)   ?   (151)   (150)

TABLE XIII

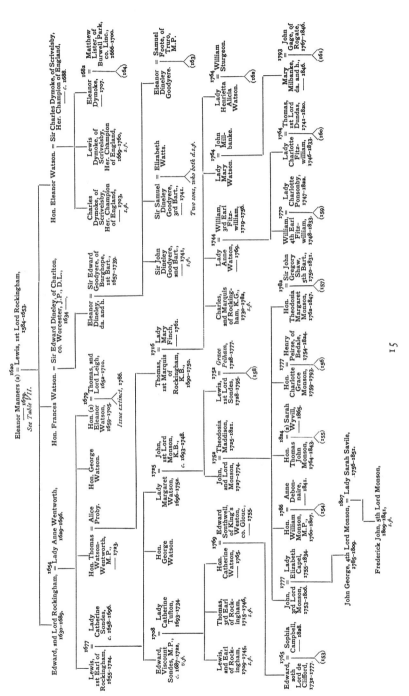

15

TABLE XIV

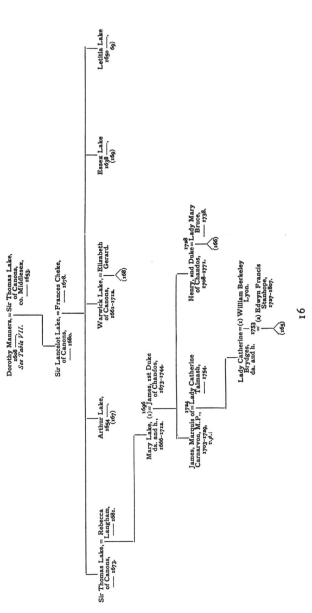

Dorothy Manners, = Sir Thomas Lake,
1608   of Canons,
See Table VII.   co. Middlesex,
                         —— 1653.

Sir Lancelot Lake, = Frances Cheke,
of Canons,   —— 1678.
—— 1680.

Sir Thomas Lake, = Rebecca
of Canons,   Langham,
—— 1673.   —— 1681.

Arthur Lake,
1654 ——
(167)

Warwick Lake, = Elizabeth
of Canons,   Gerard.
1661–1712.   (168)

Essex Lake
1658 ——
(169)

Letitia Lake
1650 ——
(69)

Mary Lake,   1696
da. and h., (1)=James, 1st Duke
1666–1712.   of Chandos,
                    1673–1744.

James, Marquis of=Lady Catherine
Carnarvon, M.P., 1724   Talmash,
1703–1729,   —— 1754.
v.p.¹

Henry, 2nd Duke=Lady Mary
of Chandos,   1728   Bruce,
1708–1771.   —— 1738.
                            (166)

Lady Catherine=(1) William Berkeley
Brydges,   Lyon.
da. and h.   1753 (2) Edwyn Francis
                        Stanhope,
                        1727–1807.
                        (165)

16

TABLE XV

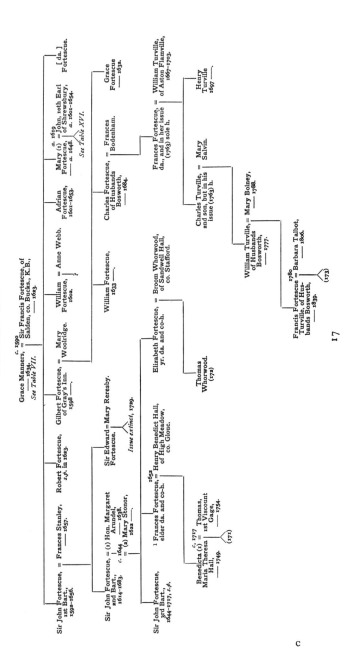

c. 1590
Grace Manners, = Sir Francis Fortescue, of
— 1634. | Salden, co. Bucks., K.B.,
See Table VII. | — 1623.

[da.]
Fortescue.

a. 1619
Mary (1) = John, 10th Earl
Fortescue, | of Shrewsbury,
| *a.* 1648. | *d.* 1601-1654.
See Table XVI.

William = Anne Webb,
Fortescue, | ?
1621.

Adrian
Fortescue,
1601-1653.

Grace
Fortescue,
1632.

Sir John Fortescue, = Frances Stanley,
1st Bart., | — 1657.
1592-1656.

Robert Fortescue,
s.p. in 1623.

Gilbert Fortescue, = Mary
of Gray's Inn. | Woolridge.
1598.

William Fortescue,
1633.

Charles Fortescue, = Frances
of Husbands | Bodenham.
Bosworth,
— 1684.

Sir Edward = Mary Rereaby.
Fortescue.

Issue extinct, 1789.

Frances Fortescue, = William Turville,
da., and in her issue | of Aston Flamville,
(1763) sole h. | 1667-1703.

Sir John Fortescue, = (1) Hon. Margaret
2nd Bart., | Arundel,
1614-1683. | — 1658.
| *c.* 1644. = (2) Mary Stonor,
| 1622 — .

1654
Frances Fortescue, = Henry Benedict Hall,
elder da. and co-h. | of High Meadow,
| co. Glouc.

Elizabeth Fortescue, = Broom Whorwood,
yr. da. and co-h. | of Sandwell Hall,
| co. Stafford.

Charles Turville, = Mary
2nd son, but in his | Salvin.
issue (1763) h.

Henry
Turville,
1697.

Sir John Fortescue,
3rd Bart.,
1644-1717, *s.p.*

Thomas
Whorwood.
(17?)

William Turville, = Mary Bolney,
of Husbands | 1788.
Bosworth,
— 1777.

c. 1717
Benedicta (1) = Thomas,
Maria Theresa | 1st Viscount
Hall; | Gage,
— 1749. | — 1754.

(17?)

1780
Francis Fortescue = Barbara Talbot,
Turville, of Hus- | 1806.
bands Bosworth,
— 1839.

(17?)

(17?)

17

C

TABLE XVI

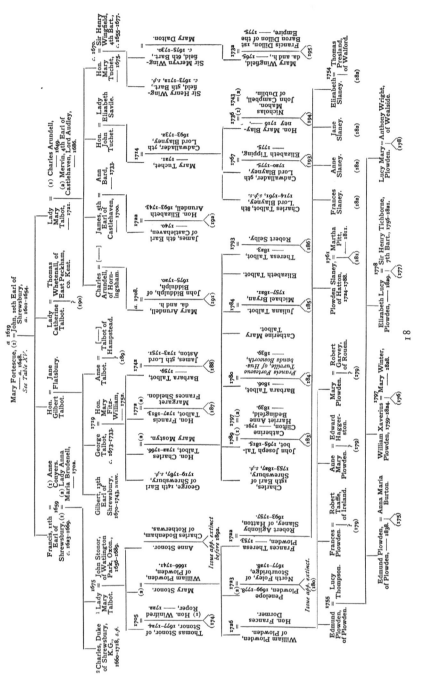

18

TABLE XVII

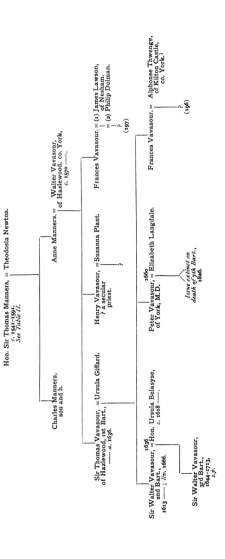

Hon. Sir Thomas Manners, = Theodosia Newton.
c. 1541-1591.
See Table II.

Charles Manners,
son and h.

Anne Manners, = Walter Vavasour,
of Hazlewood, co. York,
c. 1570 ——.

Sir Thomas Vavasour, = Ursula Giffard.
of Hazlewood, 1st Bart,
—— *d.* 1636.

Henry Vavasour, = Susanna Plant.
? a secular | ?
priest.

Frances Vavasour. = (1) James Lawson,
of Nesham.
= (2) Philip Dolman.
|
?
(197)

1636
Sir Walter Vavasour, = Hon. Ursula Belasyse,
and Bart., | *c.* 1618 ——.
1613 —— ; *liv.* 1666.

1660
Peter Vavasour, = Elizabeth Langdale.
of York, M.D.
|
Issue extinct on
death of 7th Bart.,
1826.

Frances Vavasour. = Alphonse Thwenge,
of Kilton Castle,
co. York.[1]
|
?
(196)

Sir Walter Vavasour,
3rd Bart.,
1644-1713.
s.p.

[1] A partial Pedigree of the family is in Ord's "Cleveland," p. 269, but this match is not recorded.

19

TABLE XVIII

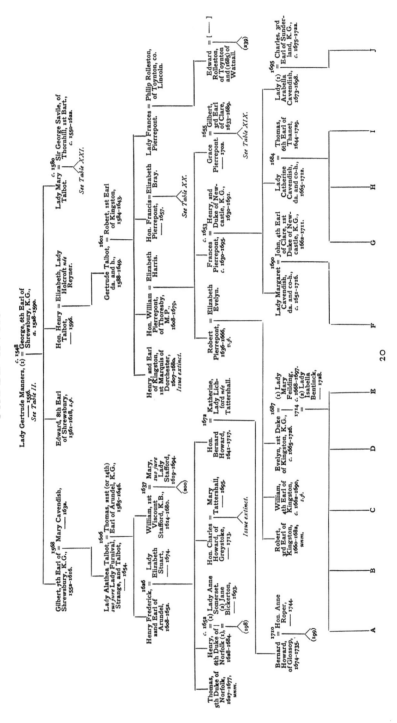

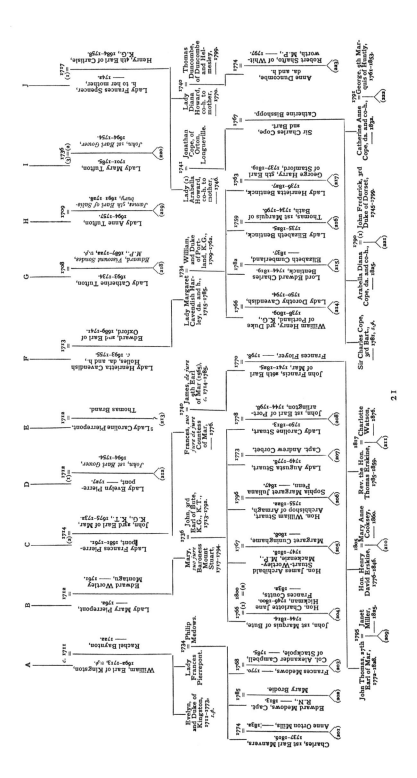

21

TABLE XIX

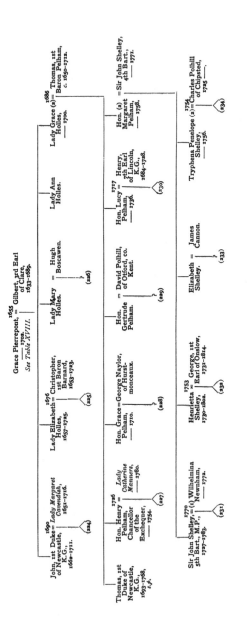

Grace Pierrepont, [655] = Gilbert, 3rd Earl
of Clare,
1702.   1633–1689.
See Table XVIII.

TABLE XX

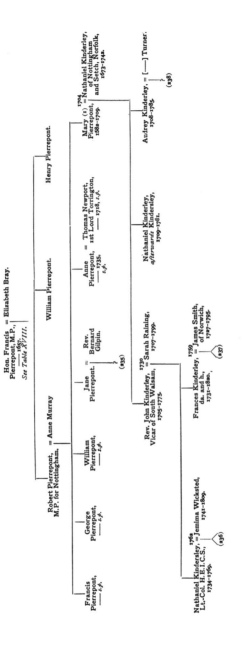

Hon. Francis Pierrepont, M.P., = Elizabeth Bray.
1657.
See Table XVIII.

Robert Pierrepont, M.P. for Nottingham. = Anne Murray.

William Pierrepont.

Henry Pierrepont.

Francis Pierrepont, s.p.

George Pierrepont, s.p.

William Pierrepont, s.p.

Jane Pierrepont. = Rev. Bernard Gilpin.
(x35)

Anne Pierrepont, —— 1735, s.p. = Thomas Newport, 1st Lord Torrington, —— 1718, s.p.

Mary (1) = Nathaniel Kinderley, of Nottingham and Setch, Norfolk, 1673-1742.
1704.
1582-1709.

Nathaniel Kinderley, afterwards Kinderley, 1709-1781.

Audrey Kinderley, = [——] Turner.
1708-1785.
(x38)

Rev. John Kinderley, Vicar of South Walsam, 1705-1775. = Sarah Raining, 1707-1799.
1730.

Frances Kinderley, da. and h., 1731-1820, = James Smith, of Norwich, 1727-1795.
1759.
(x37)

Nathaniel Kinderley, Lt.-Col. H.E.I.C.S., 1734-1769. = Jemima Wicksted, 1741-1809.
1762.
(x36)

23

TABLE XXI

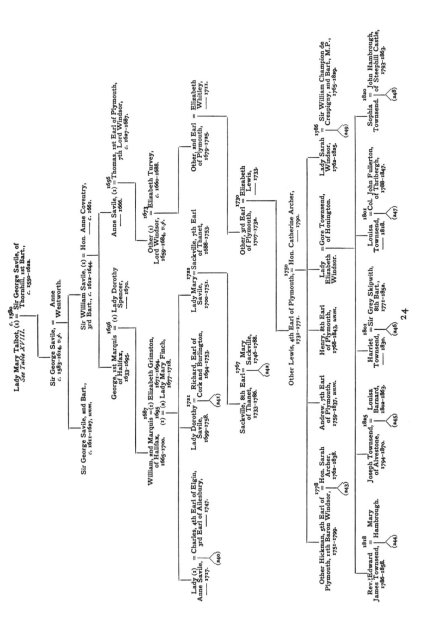

24

TABLE XXII

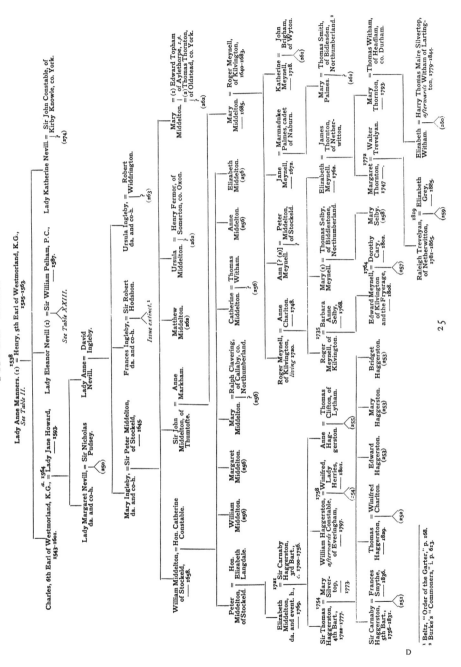

[1] Betz, "Order of the Garter," p. 168.
[2] Burke's "Commoners," i. p. 613.

25

D

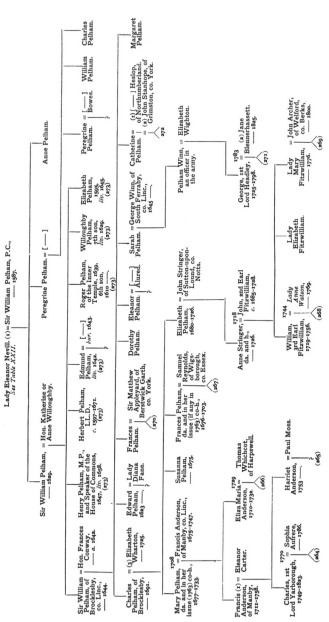

TABLE XXIII

Lady Eleanor Nevill (1) = Sir William Pelham, P.C., —— 1587.
See Table XXII.

Sir William Pelham, = Hon. Katherine or Anne Willoughby. —— 1629.

Peregrine Pelham. = [——]

Anne Pelham.

Sir William Pelham, of Brocklesby, co. Linc., —— 1644. = Hon. Frances Conway, —— d. 1642.

Henry Pelham, M.P., and Speaker of the House of Commons, 1647, liv. 1658. (273)

Herbert Pelham, L.L.D., c. 1597-1671. (273)

Edmund Pelham, liv. 1642. = [——] bur. 1643. (273)

Roger Pelham, of the Inner Temple, 1639, 6th son, 1610 (273)

Willoughby Pelham, 7th son, 1595, liv. 1649. (273)

Elizabeth Pelham, 1595, liv. 1645. (273)

Peregrine Pelham. = [——] Bowes.

William Pelham.

Charles Pelham.

Margaret Pelham.

Charles Pelham, of Brocklesby. —— 1691. = (2) Elizabeth Wharton, —— 1725.

Edward Pelham, 1663. = Lady Diana Fane. ?

Frances Pelham. = Sir Matthew Appleyard, of Berstwick Garth, co. York. (270)

Dorothy Pelham.

Eleanor Pelham. = [——] Alured. ?

Sarah Pelham. = George Winn, of South Ferraby, co. Linc., —— 1645.

Catherine Pelham = (1) [——] Heslop, of Northumberland. (2) John Stanhope, of Grimston, co. York. 272

Mary Pelham, da. and in her issue (1763) co-h., 1697-1733. = 1708 Francis Anderson, of Manby, co. Linc., 1675-1747.

Susanna Pelham. —— 1675.

Frances Pelham = Samuel Reynolds, of Wigborough, co. Essex. (267)

Elizabeth Pelham, 1680-1726. = John Stringer, of Sutton-upon-Lound, co. Notts.

Pelham Winn, an officer in the army.

Francis (1) Anderson, of Manby, 1711-1758. = Eleanor Carter.

Eliza Maria Anderson, 1710-1732. = 1729 Thomas Whichcot, of Harpswell. (266)

Anne Stringer, da. and h., —— 1726. = 1718 John, 2nd Earl Fitzwilliam, c. 1685-1728.

George, 1st Lord Headley, 1725-1798. = 1783 (a) Jane Blennerhassett, 1805. (271)

Charles, 1st Lord Yarborough, 1749-1843. = 1770 Sophia Aufrere, —— 1786. (264)

Harriet Anderson, 1753- = Paul Moss. (265) ?

William, 3rd Earl Fitzwilliam, 1719-1756. = 1744 *Lady Anne Watson*, —— 1769. (268)

Lady Elizabeth Fitzwilliam.

Lady Mary Fitzwilliam, 1776. = John Archer, of Welford, co. Berks., —— 1800. (269)

TABLE XXIV

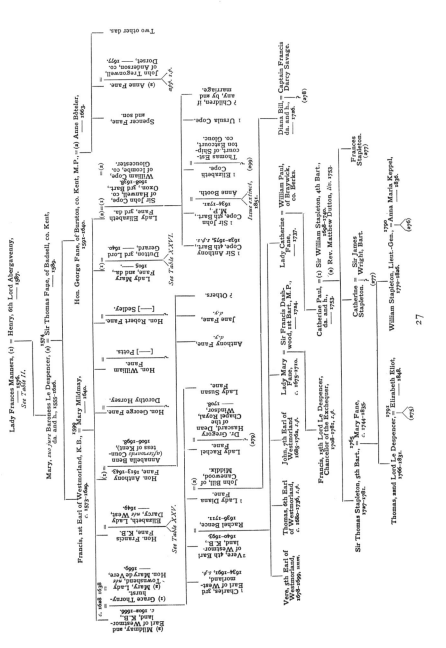

Lady Frances Manners, (1) = Henry, 6th Lord Abergavenny, 1587.
——— 1576.
See Table II.

Mary, *suo jure* Baroness Le Despencer, (2) = [1574] Sir Thomas Fane, of Badsell, co. Kent,
da. and h., 1555–1626. ——— 1589.

Hon. George Fane, of Burston, co. Kent, M.P., = (2) Anne Bôteler,
1591–1640. ——— 1663.

(2) Anne Fane, = (2) John Tregonwell,
of Anderson, co.
Dorset, ——— 1677. *aff. s.p.*

Two other das.

Spencer Fane, and son.

1 Ursula Cope.

Diana Bill, = Captain Francis
da. and h., ——— 1726. Darcy Savage.
? (278)

Sir John Cope, = Lady Elizabeth
of Hanwell, co. Fane, 3rd da.
Oxon., 3rd Bart., 1668–1638.
See Table XXXVI.

Dutton, 3rd Lord
Gerard, ——— 1640.

Lady Mary
Fane, 4th da.,
——— 1605.

1 Elizabeth
Cope. = Thomas Est-
court, of Ship-
ton Estcourt,
co. Glouc.
(299)

1 Sir Anthony
Cope, 5th Bart.,
1632–1675, *s.p.s.*

Anne Booth.
*Issue extinct,
1851.*

1 Sir John
Cope, 6th Bart.,
1634–1721.
M.P.,

Lady Catherine = William Paul,
Fane, ——— 1737. of Braywick,
co. Berks.

Catherine Paul, = (1) Sir William Stapleton, 4th Bart.,
da. and h., 1698–1740.
——— 1753. (2) Rev. Matthew Dutton, *liv.* 1753.

Frances
Stapleton.
(277)

Catherine = Sir James
Stapleton. Wright, Bart.
(277)

William Stapleton, Lieut.-Gen., = Anna Maria Keppel,
1770–1826. ——— 1836.
(276)

William Fane. = [——] Potts.

Hon. Robert Fane. = [——] Sedley.

Hon. William
Fane.

Hon. George Fane. = Dorothy Horsey.

Anthony Fane,
d.y.

Jane Fane,
d.y.

? Others.

Lady Mary = Sir Francis Dash-
Fane, wood, 1st Bart. M.P.,
c. 1675–1710. ——— 1724.

Francis, 15th Lord Le Despencer,
Chancellor of the Exchequer,
1708–1781, *s.p.*

Lady Susan
Fane.

Dr. Gregory = Lady Rachel
Hascard, Dean Fane,
of the (279)
Chapel Royal,
Windsor,
——— 1708.

John, 7th Earl of = Mary Fane,
Westmorland c. 1744–1835.
1685–1762, *s.p.* 1765

Sir Thomas Stapleton, 5th Bart., = Mary Fane,
1727–1781. c. 1744–1835.

Thomas, 2nd Lord Le Despencer, = Elizabeth Eliot,
1766–1831. ——— 1848. 1791
(275)

Francis, 1st Earl of Westmorland, K.B., = [1599] Mary Mildmay,
c. 1573–1629. ——— 1640.

Hon. Anthony = Annabella Benn
Fane, 1613–1643. (*afterwards* Countess of Kent),
1606–1698.

Hon. Francis = Elizabeth, Lady
Fane, K.B., Darcy, *née West*,
——— 1649. *See Table XXV.*

Rachel Bence,
1636–1711.

1 Lady Diana = John Bill, of
Fane. Canewood,
Middx.

Thomas, 6th Earl
of Westmorland,
c. 1680–1736, *s.p.*

Vere, 5th Earl of
Westmorland,
1678–1699, *unm.*

1 Charles, 3rd
Earl of West-
morland,
1634–1691, *s.p.*

3 Vere, 4th Earl
of Westmor-
land, K.B.,
1693–1693.

(2) Mildmay, 2nd
Earl of Westmor-
land, K.B.,
c. 1602–1666.

(1) Grace Thorny-
hurst,
c. 1628 1638.

(2) Mary, Lady
'Townshend, *née*
Hon. Mary *de Vere*,
1669.

27

TABLE XXV

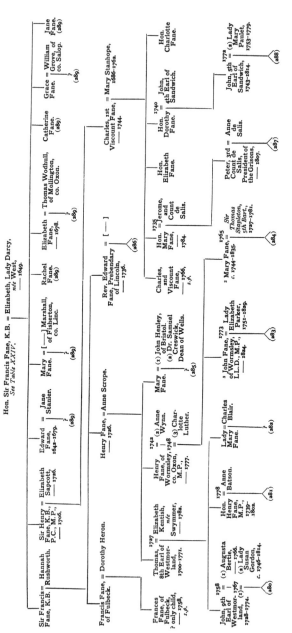

TABLE XXVI

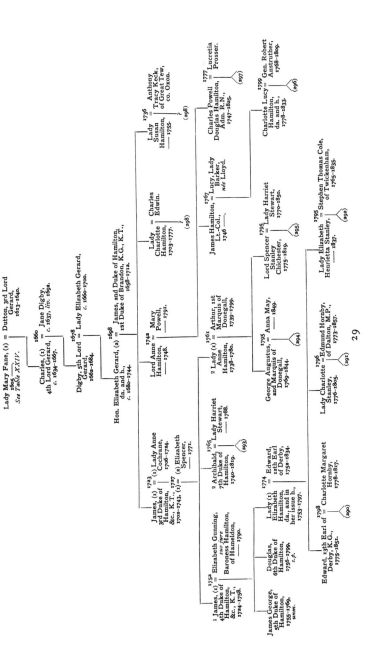

Lady Mary Fane, (1) = Dutton, 3rd Lord
1665   Gerard,
See Table XXIV.   1613-1640.

Charles, (1) = Jane Digby,
4th Lord Gerard,   *c.* 1637, *liv.* 1692.
c. 1634-1667.

1678
Digby, 5th Lord = Lady Elizabeth Gerard,
Gerard,   *c.* 1660-1700.
1662-1684.

1698
Hon. Elizabeth Gerard, (2) = James, 2nd Duke of Hamilton,
da. and h.,   1st Duke of Brandon, K.G., K.T.,
c. 1680-1744.   1658-1712.

1744
Lord Anne = Mary
Hamilton,   Powell,
— 1748.   — 1791.

Lady   = Charles
Charlotte   Edwin.
Hamilton,
1703-1777.

(298)

1736
Lady   = Anthony
Susan   Tracy Keck,
Hamilton,   of Great Tew,
— 1755.   co. Oxon.

?
Charles Powell = Lucretia
Douglas Hamilton,   Prosser.
Adm. R.N.,
1747-1825.

(298)

1777
(297)

1723   1777
James, (1) = (1) Lady Anne
3rd Duke of   Cochrane,
Hamilton,   1706-1724.
&c., K.T.,   (2) Elizabeth
1702-1743, (1) =   Spencer,
         — 1771.

1765
2 Archibald, = Lady Harriet
7th Duke of   Stewart,
Hamilton,   — 1788.
1740-1819.

(293)

1761
2 Lady (1) = Arthur, 1st Marquis of
Anne   Donegall,
Hamilton,   1739-1799.
1738-1780.

1795
George Augustus, = Anna May,
2nd Marquis of   — 1849.
Donegall,
1769-1844.

(294)

1767
James Hamilton, = Lucy, Lady
Lt.-Col.,   Barker,
1746 — .   *née* Lloyd.

1795
Lord Spencer = Lady Harriet
Stanley   Stewart,
Chichester,   1770-1850.
1775-1819.

(295)

1799
Charlotte Lucy = Gen. Robert
Hamilton,   Anstruther,
da. and h.,   1768-1809.
1778-1833.

(296)

1752a
1 James, (1) = Elizabeth Gunning,
4th Duke of   *suo jure*
Hamilton,   Baroness Hamilton,
&c., K.T.   of Hameldon,
1724-1758.   — 1790.

1774
Lady (1) = Edward,
Elizabeth   12th Earl
Hamilton,   of Derby,
da., and in   1752-1834.
her issue h.,
1753-1797.

James George,   Douglas,
5th Duke of   6th Duke of
Hamilton,   Hamilton,
1755-1769,   1756-1799,
unm.   *s. p.*

1798
Edward, 13th Earl of = Charlotte Margaret
Derby, K.G.,   Hornby,
1775-1851.   1778-1817.

(290)

1796
Lady Charlotte = Edmund Hornby,
Stanley,   of Dalton, M.P.,
1776-1805.   1773-1857.

(293)

1795
Lady Elizabeth = Stephen Thomas Cole,
Henrietta Stanley,   of Twickenham,
— 1837.   1765-1835.

(292)

29

TABLE XXVII

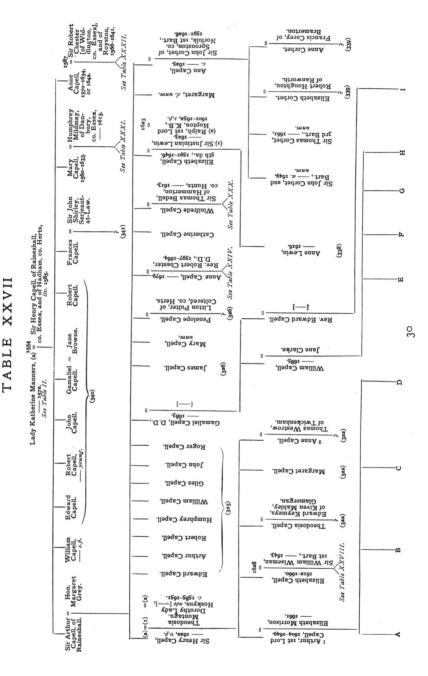

Sir Henry Capell, of Raineshall, 1554 Lady Katherine Manners, (2) = co. Essex, and of Hadham, co. Herts, 1572. *See Table II.* liv. 1585.

30

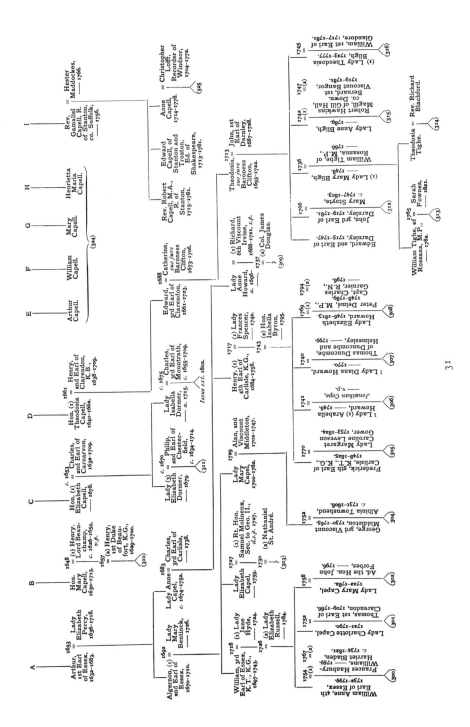

TABLE XXVIII

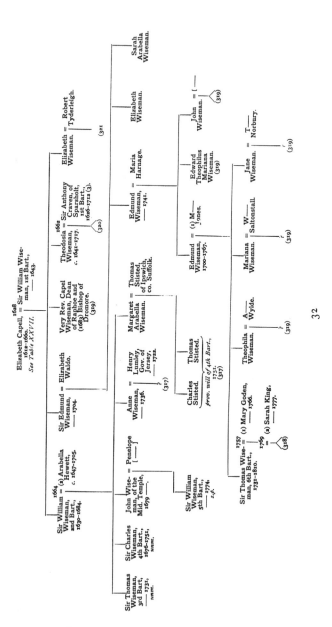

32

TABLE XXIX

Anne Capell, = Robert Chester, D.D.,[1]
— 1679. | Professor of Theology,[1]
See Table XXVIII. | 1599-1664.

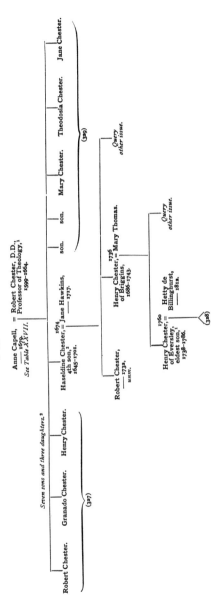

Seven sons and three daughters.[2]

Robert Chester. Granado Chester. Henry Chester.
(327)

Haseldine Chester,[1674] Jane Hawkins,
4th son,[2] — 1717.
1645-1701.

son. son. Mary Chester. Theodosia Chester. Jane Chester.
(329)

Robert Chester,
— 1734,
unm.

Henry Chester,[1726] Mary Thomas.
of Briggins,
1686-1743.

Query
other issue.

Henry Chester,[1760] Hetty de
of Eversley, Billinghurst,
eldest son,[1] — 1812.
1738-1786.

Query
other issue.

(328)

[1] In the Pedigree at the Heralds' College (c. 28, pt. i. p. 12) he is called Rector of Stevenedge.
[2] Burke's "Landed Gentry," 1900, p. 286.

33

E

TABLE XXX

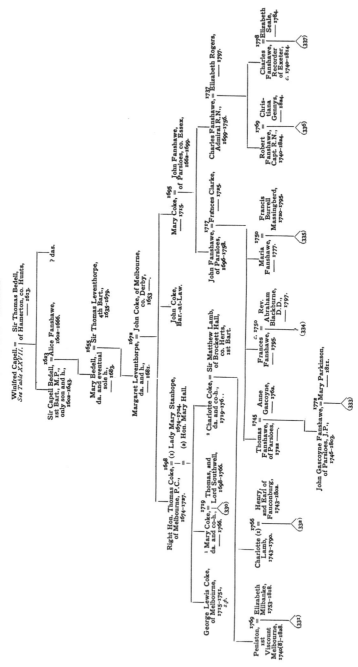

Winifred Capell. = Sir Thomas Bedell,
See Table XXVII. | of Hamerton, co. Hunts,
—— 1613.

Sir Capell Bedell, = Alice Fanshawe,   ? das.
1st Bart., M.P., | 1602–1666.
only son and h.,   1613
1602–1643.

Mary Bedell, = Sir Thomas Leventhorpe,
da. and eventual | 4th Bart,
sole h.,   1635–1679.
—— 1683.   1655

Margaret Leventhorpe, = John Coke, of Melbourne,
da. and h., | co. Derby,
—— 1681.   1672   1653.

Mary Coke, = John Fanshawe,
—— 1715. | of Parsloes, co. Essex,
1695   1662–1699.

John Coke,
Bar.-at-Law.

John Fanshawe, = Frances Clarke,
of Parsloes, | 1715.
1696–1758.   1717

Charles Fanshawe, = Elizabeth Rogers,
Admiral R.N., | 1797.
1699–1756.   1717

Robert   Chris-   Charles = Elizabeth
Fanshawe,   tiana   Fanshawe,   Seale,
Capt. R.N.,   Gennys,   Recorder   1784.
1740–1844.   —— 1844.   of Exeter,   1778
    c. 1740–1814.

(336)   (337)

Right Hon. Thomas Coke, = (1) Lady Mary Stanhope,
of Melbourne, P.C., | 1694–1734.
1675–1727.   =   (2) Hon. Mary Hall.
    1698

1 Mary Coke, = Thomas, and   ? Charlotte Coke,
da. and co-h., | Lord Southwell,   da. and co-h.,
—— 1766.   1698–1766.   1719–176..

(330)   1719

Charlotte (1) = Henry,   Anne   Thomas
Lamb,   and Earl of   Gascoyne,   Fanshawe,
1743–1790.   Fauconburg,   1762.   of Parsloes,
1756   1743–1802.   1722–
            1745

(332)

George Lewis Coke,
of Melbourne,
1715–1751,
s.p.

Peniston, = Elizabeth   Maria = Francis   Frances = Rev.
1st   Milbanke,   Fanshawe,   Burrell   Fanshawe,   Abraham
Viscount   1753–1818.   1777.   Massingberd,   1795.   Blackburne,
Melbourne,   1769   1720–1795.   D.D.,
1740(8)–1848.   1750   1797.
                1750   c. 1759

(331)   (335)   (334)

John Gascoyne Fanshawe, = Mary Parkinson,
of Parsloes, J.P., | 1811.
1746–1803.   1772

(333)

34

TABLE XXXI

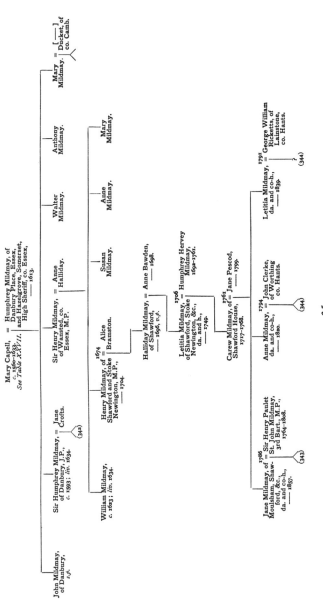

TABLE XXXII

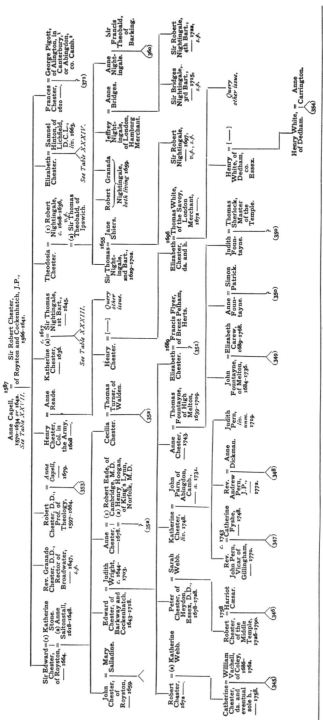

¹ Pedigree in the Heralds' College, c. 28, pt. 1, p. 12.
² See Clutterbuck's "Herts," iii. p. 363.

TABLE XXXIII

Katherine Chester, (a) = Sir Thomas Nightingale,
1696.   1st Bart.,
See Table XXXII.   1645.

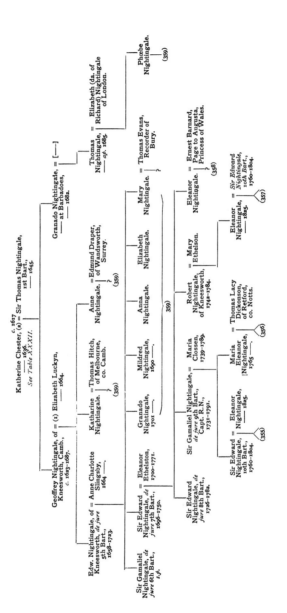

Geoffrey Nightingale, of = (1) Elizabeth Luckyn,   Granado Nightingale, = Elizabeth (da. of
Kneesworth, Camb.,   1664.   at Barbadoes,   Richard) Nightingale
c. 1643-1687.   1682.   of London.

Edw. Nightingale, of = Anne Charlotte   Katharine = Thomas Hitch,   Anne = Edmund Draper,   Thomas = [——]   Phebe
Kneesworth, *de jure*   Slingsby,   Nightingale, of Melbourne, Nightingale, of Wandsworth,   Nightingale,   Nightingale.
5th Bart.,   1664.   1701.   co. Camb.   Surrey.   *ob.* 1685.   (359)
1698-1723.   (359)   (359)   ?

Sir Gamaliel   Sir Edward = Eleanor   Granado   Mildred   Anna   Elizabeth   Mary = Thomas Evans,
Nightingale, *de Nightingale, *de Ethelston,   Nightingale, Nightingale, Nightingale. Nightingale.   Nightingale.   Recorder of
jure* 6th Bart., jure* 7th Bart., 1700-1771.   1701.   1690-,   Bury.
s.p.   1696-1750.   ?

                  Sir Edward   Sir Gamaliel Nightingale, = Maria   Robert   Mary   Eleanor = Ernest Barnard,
                  Nightingale, *de *de jure* 9th Bart.,   Clossen, Nightingale, Ethelston. Nightingale. Page to Augusta,
                  jure* 8th Bart., Capt. R.N.,   1739-1789. of Kneesworth,   Princess of Wales.
                  1726-1784.   1731-1791.   1744-1784.   (358)

                  Sir Edward = Eleanor   Maria = Thomas Lacy   Eleanor = Sir Edward
                  Nightingale, Nightingale, Eleanor   Dickenson,   Nightingale, Nightingale,
                  10th Bart.,   1845.   [Nightingale] of Retford, 1845.   10th Bart.,
                  1760-1804.   1765.   co. Notts.   1760-1804.
                  (355)   (356)   (357)

37

TABLE XXXIV

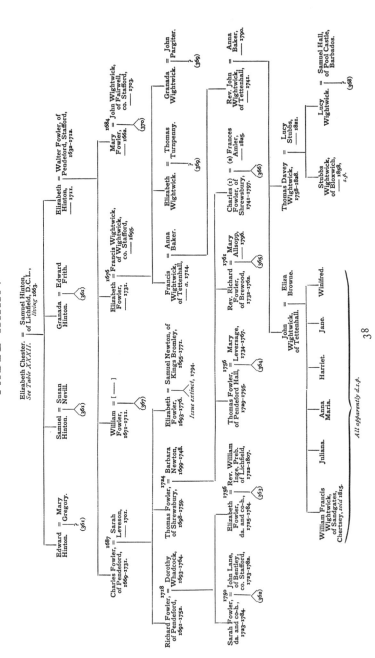

All apparently d.s.p.

38

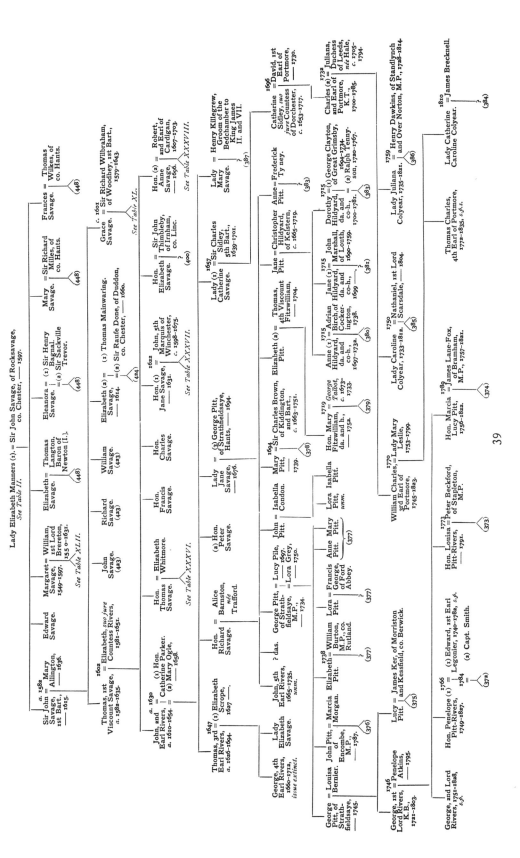

TABLE XXXVI

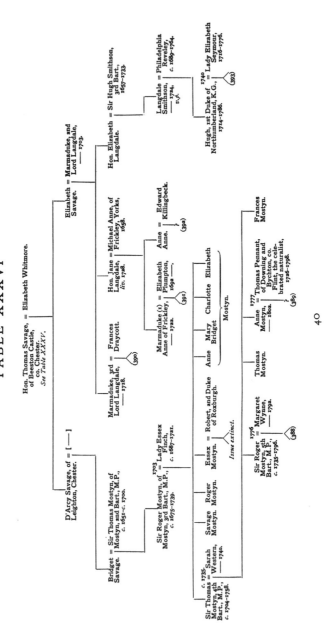

Hon. Thomas Savage, = Elizabeth Whitmore.
of Beeston Castle,
co. Chester.
See Table XXXV.

D'Arcy Savage, = [——]
Leighton, Chester.

Elizabeth = Marmaduke, 2nd
Savage. | Lord Langdale,
—— 1703.

Bridget = Sir Thomas Mostyn, of
Savage. | Mostyn, and Bart., M.P.,
c. 1651–*c.* 1700.

Sir Roger Mostyn, of = Lady Essex
Mostyn, 3rd Bart., M.P., | Finch,
c. 1675–1739. | *c.* 1687–1721.

Savage Roger
Mostyn. Mostyn.

Essex = Robert, 2nd Duke
Mostyn. | of Roxburgh.

Issue extinct.

Sir Thomas = Sarah
Mostyn, 5th | Western,
Bart., M.P., | —— 1740.
c. 1704–1758.

Sir Roger = Margaret
Mostyn, 6th | Wynne,
Bart., M.P., | —— 1792.
c. 1735–1796.
(388)

Thomas
Mostyn.

Anne = Thomas Pennant,
Mostyn, | of Downing and
—— 1802. | Brychton, co.
| Flint, the cele-
| brated naturalist,
| 1726–1798.
(389)

Frances
Mostyn.

Marmaduke, 3rd = Frances
Lord Langdale, | Draycott.
—— 1718.
(390)

Hon. Jane = Michael Anne, of
Langdale, | Frickley, Yorks,
liv. 1728. | 1658.

Marmaduke (?) = Elizabeth
Anne of Frickley, | Plumpton,
—— 1722. | 1692–,
(391)

Anne = Edward
Anne. | Killingbeck.
(392)

Anne Mary Charlotte Elizabeth
Bridget
Mostyn.

Hon. Elizabeth
Langdale.

Hon. Elizabeth = Sir Hugh Smithson,
Langdale. | 3rd Bart.,
| 1657–1733.

Langdale = Philadelphia
Smithson, | Reveley,
—— 1724, | *c.* 1685–1764.
v.p.

Hugh, 1st Duke of = Lady Elizabeth
Northumberland, K.G., | Seymour,
1714–1786. | 1716–1776.
(393)

40

TABLE XXXVII

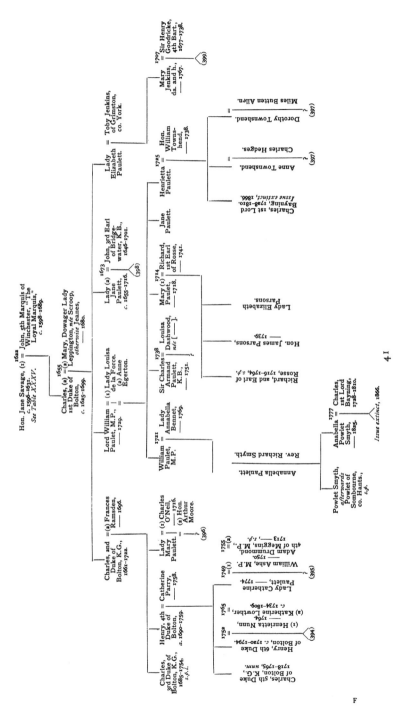

TABLE XXXVIII

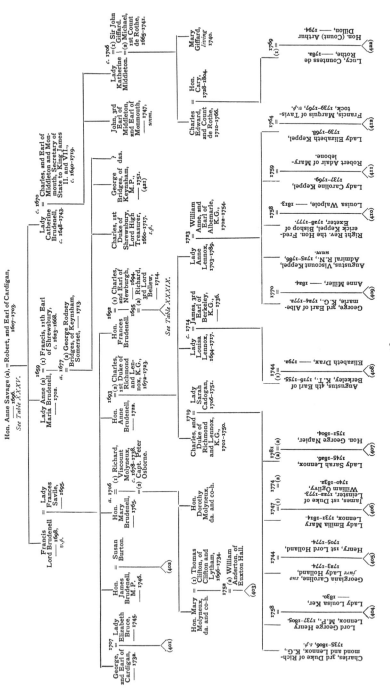

Hon. Anne Savage (a) = Robert, and Earl of Cardigan, 1696. 1607-1703.
See Table XXXV.

TABLE XXXIX

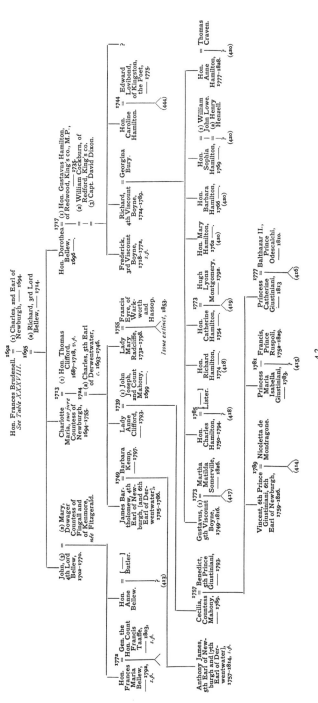

43

TABLE XL

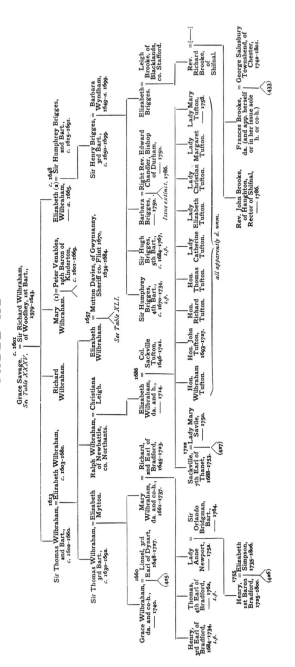

44

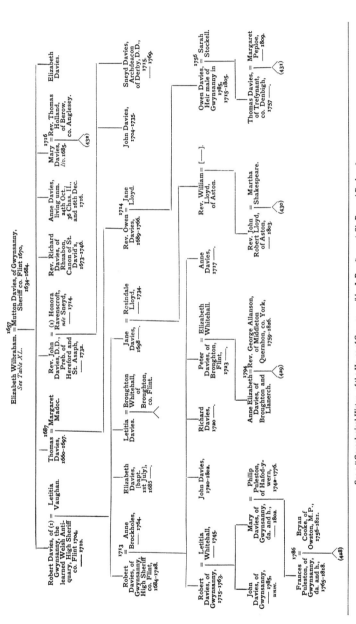

TABLE XLI

Elizabeth Wilbraham. = Mutton Davies, of Gwynsanny, [1665] Sheriff co. Flint 1670, 1634-1684.

See a "Genealogical History of the House of Gwynsanny," by J. B., *afterwards* Sir Bernard Burke, 1847.

45

TABLE XLII

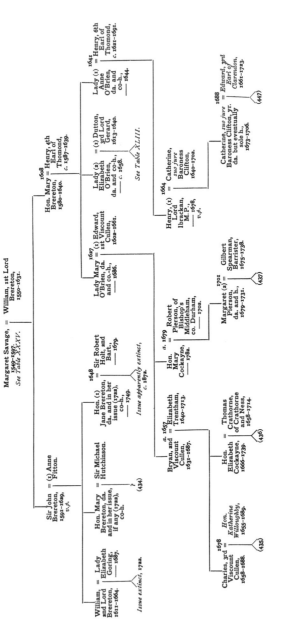

Margaret Savage, = William, 1st Lord Brereton,
1549-1597. 1550-1631.
See Table XXXV.

Sir John Brereton, 1591-1649, v.p. = (1) Anne Fitton.

Hon. Mary Brereton, da. and in her issue, if any (1722), co-h. = Sir Michael Hutchinson.

Hon. Mary Brereton, 1580-1640. = Henry, 4th Earl of Thomond, c. 1587-1639. 1608

Lady (1) Anne O'Brien, da. and co-h., —— 1644. = Henry, 6th Earl of Thomond, c. 1621-1691. 1641

Lady (2) Elizabeth O'Brien, da. and co-h., c. 1658. = (1) Dutton, 3rd Lord Gerard, 1613-1640.

See Table XLIII.

Lady Mary O'Brien, da. and co-h., —— 1686. = (1) Edward, 1st Viscount Cullen, 1602-1661. 1627

Henry, (1) Lord Ibrackan, M.P., —— 1678, v.f. = Catherine, suo jure Baroness Clifton, 1640-1702. 1664

Catherine, suo jure Baroness Clifton, yr. da. but eventually sole h., 1673-1706. = Edward, 3rd Earl of Clarendon, 1661-1723. 1688 (447)

Hon. (1) Jane Brereton, da. and in her issue (1722), co-h., —— 1749. = Sir Robert Holt, Bart., —— 1679. 1648

Issue apparently extinct, c. 1872.

(434)

William, 2nd Lord Brereton, 1611-1664. = Lady Elizabeth Goring, —— 1687.

Issue extinct, 1722.

Bryan, 3rd Viscount Cullen, 1631-1687. = Elizabeth Trentham, 1640-1713. a. 1657

Hon. Mary Cockayne, —— 1782. = Robert Pierson, of Bishop's Middleham, co. Durham, —— 1702. a. 1679

Margaret (2) Pierson, da. and h., 1679-1731. = Gilbert Spearman, Barrister, 1675-1738. 1701 (437)

Hon. Elizabeth Cockayne, 1666-1739. = Thomas Crathorne, of Crathorne and Ness, 1658-1714.

(436)

Charles, 3rd Viscount Cullen, 1698-1688. = Hon. Katherine Willoughby, 1655-1689. 1678

(435)

46

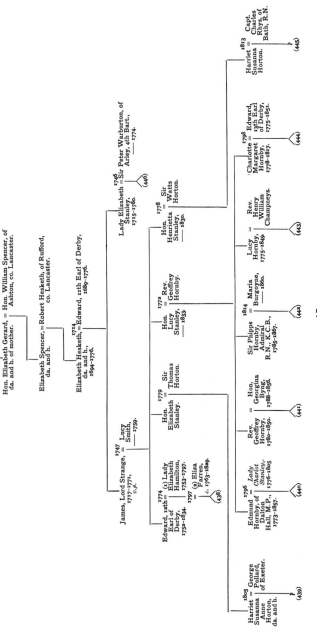

TABLE XLIII

47

Lady Elizabeth O'Brien (a), =(1) Dutton, 3rd Lord Gerard, c. 1698. 1613-1640. *See Table XLII.*

Hon. Elizabeth Gerard, = Hon. William Spencer, of da. and h. of mother. Ashton, co. Lancaster.

Elizabeth Spencer, = Robert Hesketh, of Rufford, da. and h. co. Lancaster.

Elizabeth Hesketh, = Edward, 11th Earl of Derby, 1714. da. and h, 1689-1776. 1694-1776.

Lady Elizabeth = Sir Peter Warburton, of Stanley, 1746. Arley, 4th Bart., 1715-1780. 1774. (446)

James, Lord Strange, 1717-1771, = Lucy Smith, 1747. v.p. 1759.

Edward, 12th Earl of =(1) Lady Elizabeth Derby, Hamilton, 1774. 1752-1834. 1753-1797. 1797. (2) Eliza Farren, c. 1763-1829. (436)

Hon. Elizabeth = Sir Thomas Stanley. 1779. Horton.

Hon. Lucy = Rev. Stanley, Geoffrey 1833. 1772. Hornby.

Hon. Henrietta = Sir Stanley, Watts — 1830. 1778. Horton.

Edmund Hornby, of Dalton Hall, M.P., 1773-1857. = Lady Charlot Stanley, 1796. 1776-1865. (440)

Rev. Geoffrey Hornby, 1780-1850. = Hon. Georgina Byng, 1788-1856. (441)

Sir Phipps Hornby, Admiral R.N., K.C.B., 1785-1867. = Maria Burgoyne, 1860. 1814. (442)

Lucy Hornby, 1775-1849. = Rev. Henry William Champneys. (443)

Charlotte Margaret Hornby, 1778-1817. = Edward, 13th Earl of Derby, 1775-1851. 1798. (444)

Harriet Susanna Horton. = Capt. Charles Rhys, of Bath, R.N. 1813. (445)

Harriet Susanna Anne Horton, da. and h. = George Pollard, of Exeter. 1805. (439)

TABLE XLIV

Hon. Anne Manners, = Sir Henry Capel, of London
and Raineshall.
See Table 11.

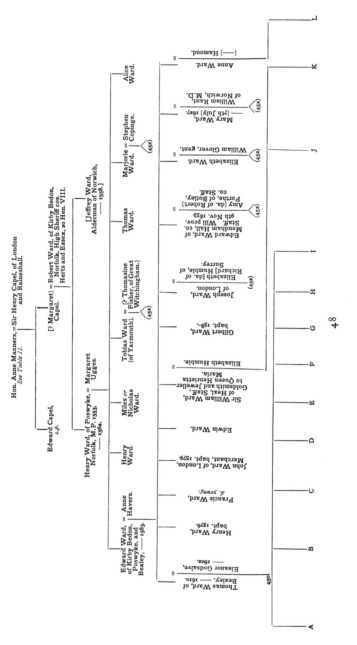

48

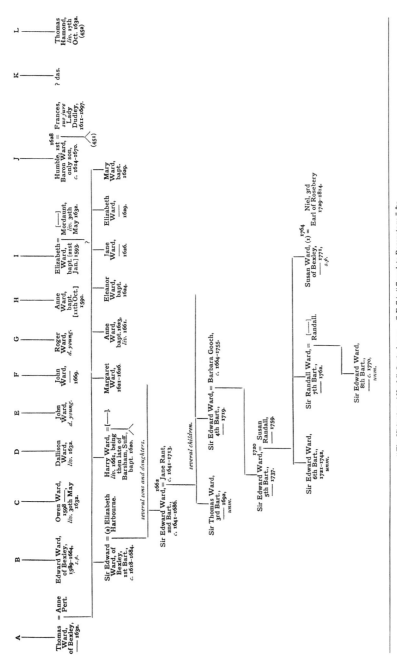

	A	B	C	D	E	F	G	H	I	J	K	L

Thomas Ward, of Bexley, —1632. = Anne Pert.

Edward Ward, of Bexley, 1589-1664, s.p.

Owen Ward, 1598 —30th May 1632. *liv.* 30th May 1632.

Dallison Ward, *liv.* 1632.

John Ward, d. young.

John Ward, 1669.

Roger Ward, d. young.

Anne Ward, bapt. [11th Oct.] 1590.

Elizabeth Ward, bapt. [21st Jan.] 1593. = [—] Mordaunt, *liv.* 30th May 1632.

Humble, 1st Baron Ward, only son, c. 1614-1670. = 1628 Frances, *suo jure* Lady Dudley, 1611-1697. (451)

? das.

Thomas Hamond, *liv.* 17th Oct. 1632. (452)

Sir Edward Ward, of Bexley, 1st Bart., c. 1618-1684. = (2) Elizabeth Harbourne.

Harry Ward, *liv.* 1661, being then late of Barsham, Suff., bapt. 1620. = [—].

Margaret Ward, 1621-1626.

Anne Ward, bapt.1623, *liv.* 1661.

Eleanor Ward, bapt. 1624.

Jane Ward, 1626.

Elizabeth Ward, 1629.

Mary Ward, bapt. 1629.

several sons and daughters.

Sir Edward Ward, 1662 = Jane Rant, and Bart., c. 1641-1713. c. 1641-1713.

several children.

Sir Thomas Ward, 3rd Bart., —1692, *unm.*

Sir Edward Ward, 4th Bart., = Barbara Gooch, —1719. c. 1664-1755.

Sir Edward Ward, 1720 = Susan Randall, 5th Bart., —1759. —1737.

Sir Randall Ward, 7th Bart., —1762. = [—] Randall.

Susan Ward, (1) = 1764 Niel, 3rd of Bexley, —1771, Earl of Rosebery s.p. 1729-1814.

Sir Edward Ward, 6th Bart., 1721-1742, *unm.*

Sir Edward Ward, 8th Bart., —c. 1770, *unm.*

"The Visitation of Norfolk," 1563, i. p. 3; G.E.C.'s "Complete Baronetage," &c.

49

G

TABLE XLV

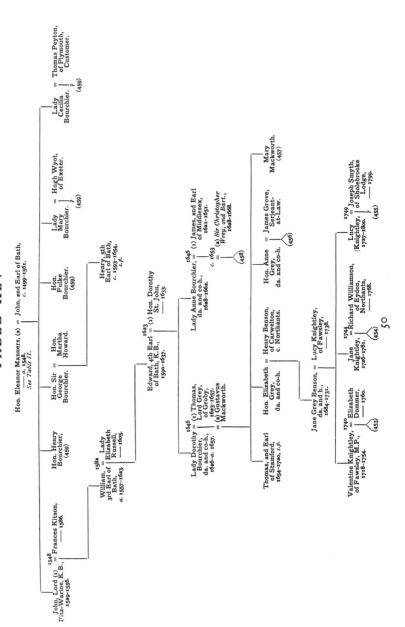

Hon. Eleanor Manners, (2) = John, and Earl of Bath,
a. 1548. *c.* 1499-1561.
See Table II.

Lady Cecila Bourchier. = Thomas Peyton, of Plymouth, Customer. (459)

John, Lord (1) = Frances Kitson, Fitz-Warine, K.B., 1586. 1529-1556. 1548

Hon. Henry Bourchier, (459)

Hon. Sir George Bourchier.

Hon. Martha Howard.

Hon. Fulke Bourchier. (459)

Lady Mary Bourchier. = Hugh Wyot, of Exeter. (459)

William, = Lady Elizabeth 3rd Earl of Russell, Bath, — 1605. a. 1557-1623. 1582

Henry, 5th Earl of Bath, *c.* 1593-1654, *s.p.*

Edward, 4th Earl = (1) Hon. Dorothy of Bath, K.B., St. John, 1590-1637. 1623 — 1623.

Lady Anne Bourchier, = (1) James, and Earl da. and co-h., of Middlesex, 1608-1662. 1621-1651. *c.* 1653 (2) *Sir Christopher Wray, 2nd Bart.,* 1648-1668. 1646

Lady Dorothy = (1) Thomas, Bourchier, Lord Grey, da. and co-h., of Groby, 1646-*a.* 1657. 1623-1657. = (2) Gustavus Mackworth. 1646

Thomas, and Earl of Stamford, 1654-1720, *s.p.*

Hon. Elizabeth = Henry Benson, Grey, of Carwelton, da. and co-h. *c.* Northants.

Hon. Anne = James Grove, Grey, Serjeant- da. and co-h. at-Law. (456)

Mary Mackworth. (457)

(458)

Jane Grey Benson, = Lucy Knightley, da. and h., of Fawsley, 1684-1731. — 1738.

Valentine Knightley, = Elizabeth of Fawsley, M.P., Dummer, 1718-1754. — 1760. 1740 (453)

Jane = Richard Williamson, Knightley, of Eydon, 1726-1781. Northants, — 1768. 1744 (454)

Lucy = Joseph Smyth, Knightley, of Stokebrooke 1727-1800. Lodge, — 1799. 1749 (455)

50

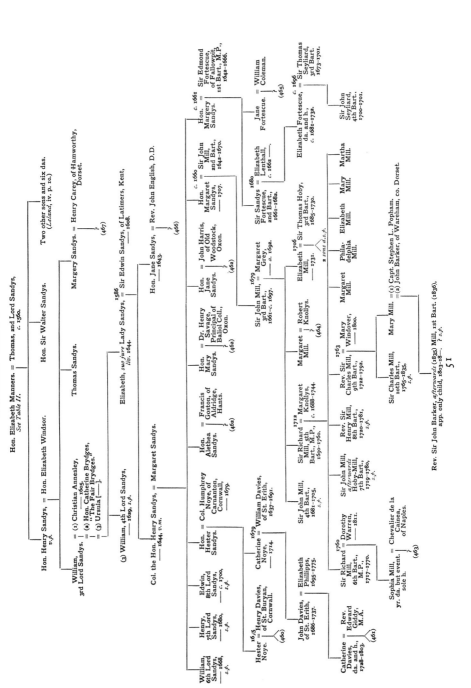

TABLE XLVI

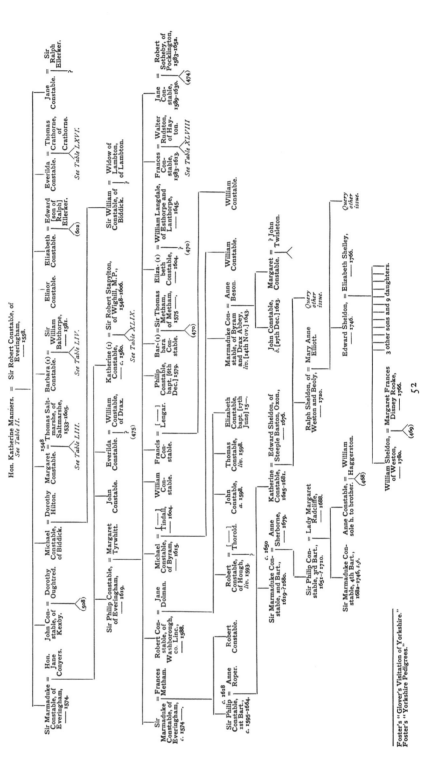

TABLE XLVII

Foster's "Glover's Visitation of Yorkshire."
Foster's "Yorkshire Pedigrees."

52

TABLE XLVIII

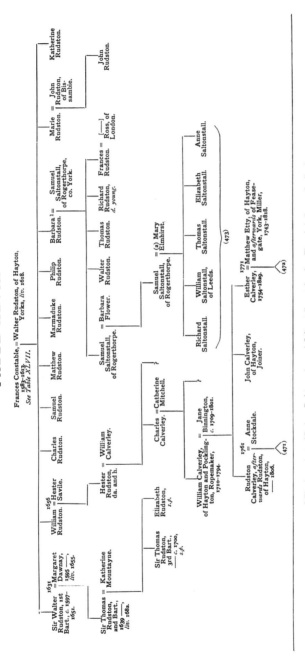

Frances Constable, = Walter Rudston, of Hayton, 1583-1613, Yorks, liv. 1618. See Table XLVII.

1 The descendants of Barbara Rudston, *afterwards* Saltonstall, are taken from Thoresby's *Ducatus Leodiensis*.

53

TABLE XLIX

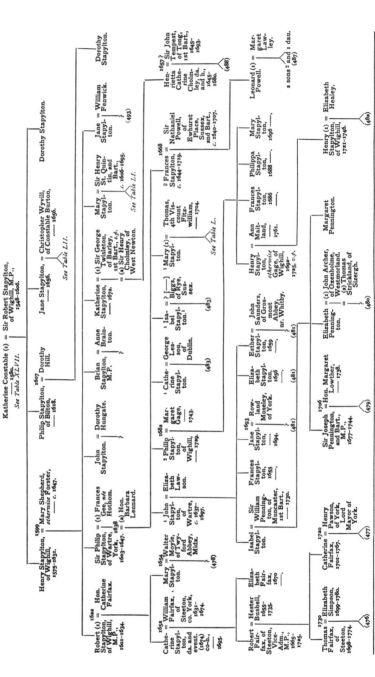

¹ See *The Genealogist*, xii. p. 194. Isabel is sometimes said to have died unmarried 6 Sept. 1644, and her sister Mary to have married 1st [—] Biggs of Rye, and 2ndly Viscount Fitzwilliam.

² The sons at least must have been dead, *s.p.m.*, before July 5, 1742, when the Baronetcy became extinct.

TABLE L

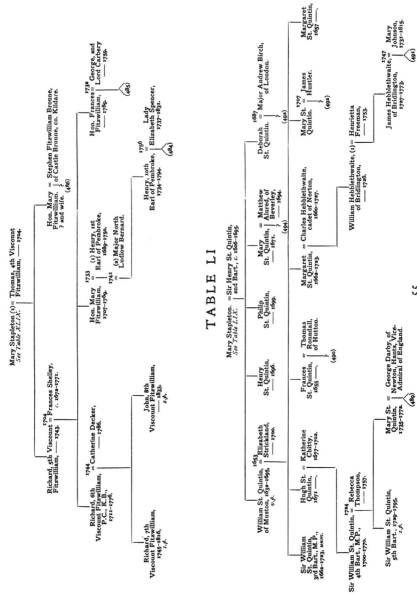

Mary Stapleton (1) = Thomas, 4th Viscount
See Table XLIX. | Fitzwilliam, —— 1704.

Hon. Mary = Stephen Fitzwilliam Bronne,
Fitzwilliam. | of Castle Bronne, co. Kildare.
? and wife. (496)

1704
Richard, 5th Viscount = Frances Shelley,
Fitzwilliam, 1743. (c. 1672-1771)

1733
Hon. Mary = (1) Henry, 1st
Fitzwilliam, | Earl of Pembroke,
1707-1769. | 1689-1750.
1741
= (2) Major North
Ludlow Bernard.

1738
Hon. Frances = George, and
Fitzwilliam. | Lord Carbery.
—— 1769. —— 1759.
(485)

1756
Henry, 10th = Elizabeth Spencer,
Earl of Pembroke, | 1737-1831.
1734-1794.
(484)

1744
Richard, 6th = Catherine Decker,
Viscount Fitzwilliam, | —— 1786.
P.C., K.B.,
1711-1776.

John, 8th
Viscount Fitzwilliam,
—— 1833.
s.p.

Richard, 7th
Viscount Fitzwilliam,
1745-1816,
s.p.

TABLE LI

Mary Stapleton. = Sir Henry St. Quintin,
See Table LIX. | and Bart., c. 1666-1695.

1653
William St. Quintin, = Elizabeth
of Muston, 1663-1695. | Strickland,
s.p. —— 1700.

Henry
St. Quintin,
—— 1696.

Frances = Thomas
St. Quintin, | Roundall,
1655 | of Hutton.
?
(490)

Philip,
St. Quintin,
—— 1699.

Mary = Matthew
St. Quintin, | Alured, of
—— 1671. ? | Beverley,
= —— 1694.

Margaret = Charles Hebblethwaite,
St. Quintin, | cadet of Norton,
1660-1723. | 1660-1797.

Deborah = Major Andrew Birch,
St. Quintin. | of London.
1689

Margaret
St. Quintin,
1657

Hugh St. = Katherine
Quintin, | Chitty,
1671- —. 1677-1702.

1724
Sir William = Rebecca
St. Quintin, | Thompson,
3rd Bart., M.P., —— 1757.
1662-1723, unm.

Mary St. = George Darby of
Quintin, | Newton, Hants, Vice-
1735-1772. | Admiral of England.
(486)

Sir William St. Quintin,
4th Bart., M.P.,
1700-1770.

Sir William St. Quintin,
5th Bart., 1729-1795,
s.p.

William Hebblethwaite, (1) = Henrietta
of Bridlington, | Freeman,
1726. —— 1753.

1747
James Hebblethwaite,
of Bridlington,
1727-1773.

Mary St. = James
Quintin. | Hustler.
1707
(492)

Mary
Johnson,
1731-1815.
(491)

TABLE LII

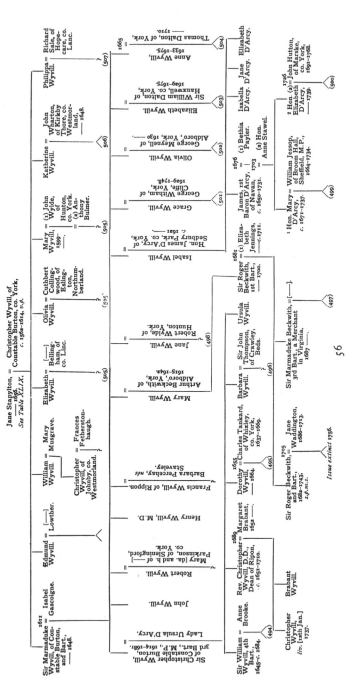

Jane Stapylton, = Christopher Wyvill, of
1656.   Constable Burton, co. York,
See Table XLIX.   c. 1562-1614, v.p.

Sir Marmaduke = Isabel
Wyvill, of Con- Gascoigne.
stable Burton,
and Bart.,
—— 1648.

1611

John Wyvill.

Robert Wyvill.

Mary [da. and h. of ——]
Parkinson, of Sleningford,
co. York.
=

Rev. Christopher = Margaret
Wyvill, D.D.,   Brabant,
Dean of Ripon, —— 1654.
c. 1651-1710.

1689

Henry Wyvill, M.D.

Francis Wyvill, of Rippon.

Barbara Percehay, née
Staveley.
=

Dorothy = Charles Tankard,
Wyvill,   of Whixley,
—— 1664.   co. York,
           1637-1669.

1655

Christopher = Frances
Wyvill, of Fetherston-
Johnby, co. haugh.
Westmorland.

William = Mary
Wyvill.   Musgrave.

Edmund = [——]
Wyvill. Lowther.

Lady Ursula D'Arcy,
=

Sir Christopher Wyvill,
3rd Bart., M.P., 1614-1681.

Sir William = Anne
Wyvill, 4th   Brooke.
Bart.,
1645-c. 1684.

Brabant
Wyvill.

Christopher
Wyvill.
liv. [12th Jan.]
1737.

494

Sir Roger Beckwith, = Jane
2nd Bart.,   Waddington,
1685-1743;   1686-1713.
s.p.m.f.

1705

Issue extinct 1756.

495

Sir Marmaduke Beckwith, = [——].
3rd Bart., a Merchant
in Virginia,
1687.

497

Mary Wyvill.
= Arthur Beckwith, of
  Aldboro', York,
  1615-1642.

Jane Wyvill.
= Robert Wylde, of
  Hunton, York.

498

Barbara = Sir John
Wyvill.   Thompson,
          of Crawley,
          Beds.

Ursula
Wyvill.

496

Elizabeth
Wyvill.
= [——] Belling-
  ham, of
  co. Linc.

Olivia
Wyvill.
= Cuthbert
  Collings-
  wood, of
  Esling-
  ton,
  Northum-
  berland.

505

Mary = (1) John
Wyvill, Wylde,
1599-.   of
         Hutton,
         co. York.
       (2) An-
         thony
         Bulmer.

Katherine = John
Wyvill.   Wharton,
            of Kirkby
            Thore, co.
            Westmor-
            land.
            —— 1648.

506

Philippa = Richard
Wyvill.   Sale, of
           Hope-
           care, co.
           Lanc.

507

Isabel Wyvill.
= Hon. James D'Arcy, of
  Sedbury Park, co. York,
  c. 1621.

1681

Grace Wyvill.
= George Witham, of
  Cliffe, York,
  1629-1748.

501

Olivia Wyvill.
= George Meynell, of
  Aldboro', York, 1630.

502

Elizabeth Wyvill.
= Sir William Dalton, of
  Hauxwell, co. York,
  1629-1675.

503

Anne Wyvill,
1633-1675.
= Thomas Dalton, of York.
  —— 1710.

504

Sir Roger = (1) Eliza-
Beckwith,   beth
1st Bart., Jennings,
1700.   c.-1711.

James, 1st = (1) Bethia
Baron D'Arcy, Payler.
of Navan,   (2) Hon.
c. 1650-1731. Anne Stawel.

1676   1703

1 Hon. Mary = William Jessop,
  D'Arcy,   of Broom Hall,
  c. 1671-1737. Sheffield, M.P.,
               1664-1734.

499

Isabella Jane   Elizabeth
D'Arcy. D'Arcy.   D'Arcy.

2 Hon. (1) = John Hutton,
  Elizabeth   of Marske,
  D'Arcy,   co. York,
  —— 1739.   1691-1768.

1726

500

56

TABLE LIII

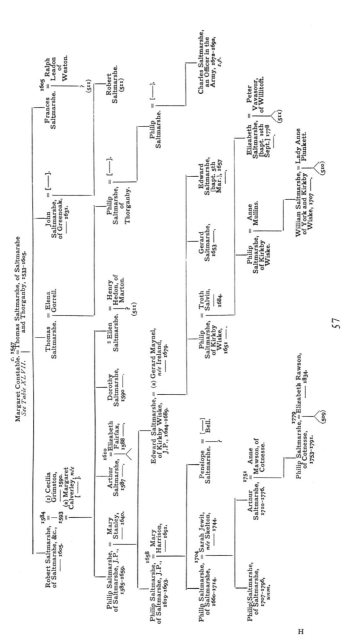

Margaret Constable. = Thomas Saltmarshe, of Saltmarshe
See Table XLVII. | and Thorganby, 1533–1605.
c. 1547.

Robert Saltmarshe, = (1) Cecilia Grimston, — 1590.
of Saltmarshe, &c., | (2) Margaret Calverley, *née* [—].
— 1605. | 1593.

Thomas = Elena Gorrell.
Saltmarshe. |

Frances = Ralph Leadon of Weston.
Saltmarshe. | 1605.
(511)

Philip Saltmarshe, = Mary Stanley,
of Saltmarshe, J.P., | — 1651.
1585–1659. | 1610.

Arthur = Elizabeth Fairfax,
Saltmarshe, | 1588.
1597. |

Dorothy Saltmarshe,
1590.

² Ellen = Henry Hedon, of Marton.
Saltmarshe. |
(511)

John = [—].
Saltmarshe,
of Greenoak,
1631.

Robert
Saltmarshe.
(511)

Philip = [—].
Saltmarshe,
of Thorganby.

Philip = [—].
Saltmarshe.

Charles Saltmarshe,
an Officer in the
Army, 1672–1692,
s.p.

Philip Saltmarshe, = Mary Harrison,
of Saltmarshe, J.P., | — 1661.
1619–1693. | 1658.

Edward Saltmarshe, = (2) Gerard Maynel,
of Kirkby Wiske, | *née* Ireland,
J.P., 1624–1689. | 1679.

Penelope = [—]
Saltmarshe. | Bell.
|
?

Philip, = Troth Salvin,
Saltmarshe, | 1684.
of Kirkby
Wiske,
1651– .

Gerard
Saltmarshe,
1653 — .

Edward
Saltmarshe,
[bapt. 5th
Mar.], 1657

Philip Saltmarshe, = Sarah Jewit,
of Saltmarshe, | *née* Skelton,
1660–1714. | — 1744.
1704.

Arthur = Anne Mawson, of
Saltmarshe, | Cotnesse.
1710–1776. | 1751.

Philip = Anne Mullins.
Saltmarshe, |
of Kirkby
Wiske.

William Saltmarshe, = Lady Anne
of York and Kirkby | Plunkett.
Wiske, 1707.
(510)

Elizabeth = Peter
Saltmarshe, | Vavasour,
[bapt. 10th | of Willitoft.
Sept.] 1778.
(511)

Philip Saltmarshe,
of Saltmarshe,
1707–1796,
unm.

Philip Saltmarshe, = Elizabeth Rawson,
of Cotnesse, | — 1834.
1753–1791.
(509)

57

H

TABLE LIV

Barbara Constable (1). = Sir William Babthorpe, —— 1581.
See Table XLVII.

Ralph Babthorpe, = Grace Byrnand, —— 1617. —— 1623.

Sir William = Grace [or Ursula] Babthorpe, | Tyrwhitt.
1580-16—.

= [——] Hamilton.

Katherine = (1) George Vavasour, Babthorpe. | of Spaldington, *liv.* 15-4.
= (2) John Ingleby, of Ripley, —— 1647.

Margaret = Sir Henry Cholmley, of Whitby Babthorpe, | and Roxby, York, —— 1628. | —— 1616.
See Table LVIII.

Robert Babthorpe.

Thomas Babthorpe. –

Ralph Babthorpe.

Katherine = (1) Sir George Babthorpe. | Palmes, of | Naburn, | —— 1654.
See Table LVII.

Elizabeth = John Constable, Babthorpe. | of Caythorpe, | —— 1621.
(542)

Barbara Babthorpe.

Anne = Thomas Dalton, of Ingleby. | Myton, in Holderness, | 1583-1639.
(543)

Ralph Babthorpe.
[——] Hamilton.
William Babthorpe, *s.p.*
Robert Babthorpe.
Richard Babthorpe.
John Babthorpe, *s.p.*
Thomas Babthorpe.
Frances Babthorpe. = (2) Thomas York, of Gowthwaite, *v.p.*
Grace Babthorpe, *s.p.*
Ursula Babthorpe.
Elizabeth Babthorpe.

John Yorke, of = (1) Florence Sharp.
Gowthwaite, co. York, | = (2) Catherine Daniell.
1638.
(512)

William Babthorpe.
Francis Babthorpe.
John Babthorpe.
Albert Babthorpe.

John Constable.
Thomas Constable.
William Constable, = Elizabeth Dolman.
1634.
Elizabeth Constable.
Katherine Constable.
Ursula Constable.

Ralph Constable.
Francis Constable.
Peter Constable.
Grace Constable.
Barbara Constable.
Frances Constable.

Barbara Constable.
Grace Constable.

A   B   C   D

58

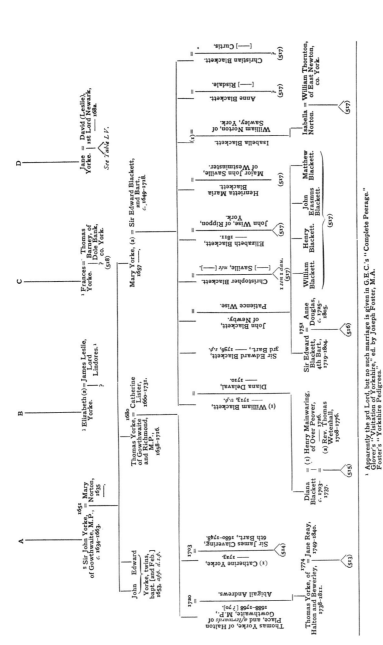

See Table LV.

¹ Apparently the 3rd Lord, but no such marriage is given in G.E.C.'s "Complete Peerage."
Glover's "Visitation of Yorkshire," ed. by Joseph Foster, M.A.
Foster's "Yorkshire Pedigrees."

TABLE LV

Jane Yorke. = David (Leslie), 1st Lord Newark, 1682.
See Table LIV.

David, and Lord Newark, 1694. $=$ Elizabeth Stewart. — 1670

Hon. Elizabeth Leslie, liv. 1693. $=$ Sir Archibald Kennedy, of Culzean, 1st Bart., 1710. — c. 1680

Hon. Mary Leslie, 1696–1748. $=$ (1) Sir Francis Kinloch, of Gilmerton, and Bart., — 1699 and 1708. (2) Sir Alexander Ogilvie, of Forglen, 1st Bart., M.P., — 1727.
See Table LVI.

Jean, styled Lady Newark, 1740. $=$ Sir Alexander Anstruther, — 1743. — 1694

Hon. (2) Christian Leslie, c. 1697–1752. $=$ Thomas Graham, of Balgowan, — 1735. — 1716 — A. lib. s.p.

Hon. Grizel Leslie. $=$ Thomas Drummond, of Logiealmond. (523)

Sir John Kennedy, and Bart., — 1742. $=$ Jane Douglas, — 1767. — 1706

James Kennedy, Architect, — 1754.

Jean Kennedy. $=$ Sir Gilbert Kennedy, of Girvanmains. (525)

Susan (3) $=$ Alexander, 9th Earl of Eglinton, c. 1660–1729.

Lady Susannah Montgomerie, — 1754. $=$ John Renton, of Lamberton. (527)

Lady Margaret Montgomerie, — 1799. $=$ (1) Sir Alexander Macdonald, 7th Bart., — 1746. — 1739 (528)

Lady Christian Montgomerie, c. 1689, — 1780. $=$ James Moray, of Abercairney. — 1737 (599)

Alexander, 10th Earl of Eglinton, 1723–1769, s.p.

Archibald, 11th Earl of Eglinton, 1726–1796. $=$ (2) Frances Twysden, — 1783. (926)

Elizabeth Kennedy. $=$ Sir John Cathcart, of Carleton, and Bart., d. 1765. — 1799 (525)

Jane Kennedy. $=$ John Blair, of Dunskey. (525)

Clementina Kennedy. $=$ George Watson, of Belton Park. (525)

William Bethune Chalmers, of Edinburgh, W.S. (522)

William, styled 4th Lord Newark, — 1773, unm.

Alexander, styled 5th Lord Newark, 1711–1791, unm.

Elizabeth Prince, — 1799. — 1740 [or 6]

Hon. Helen Anstruther, — 1787. — 1743

Rev. John Chalmers, of Radery, Minister of Kilconquhar, 1711–1791.

Sir John Kennedy, 3rd Bart., M.P., — 1744, unm.

Thomas, 9th Earl of Cassillis, — 1775, unm.

David, 10th Earl of Cassillis, — 1794, unm.

John, styled 5th Lord Newark, c. 1743–1818, s.p.

Alexander Manners Leslie, 1778–1803, unm.

Lady Frances Manners, 1753–1792. $=$ Hon. Philip Leslie, of Boulogne, Merchant, — 1747. — 1777

Hon. David Leslie, of Huntsmere Park, Berks. $=$ [—] Donaldson, of Allachie, Aberdeen. (519)

Hon. William Leslie, — 1759. $=$ [—] Senior. — 1791 (520)

Hon. Elizabeth Leslie, — 1787. $=$ [—] Magnus, of London, Merchant. (520)

Hon. Jane Leslie, — 1790. $=$ John Sanford, of Nynehead, — 1779. (521)

[—] Watson. $=$ Hugh Cathcart, Capt., Indian Navy, — 1770. (524)

Sir Andrew Cathcart, 4th Bart., c. 1742–1826, s.p.

Sir John Cathcart, 3rd Bart., c. 1735–1783, s.p.

60

TABLE LVI

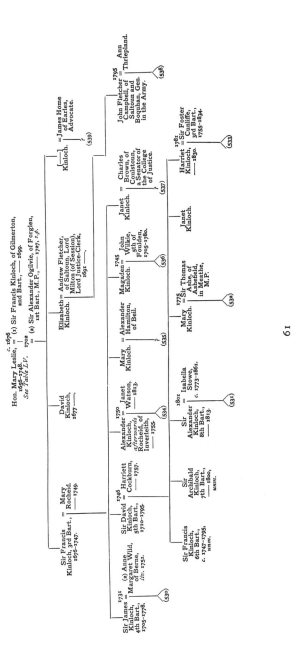

TABLE LVII

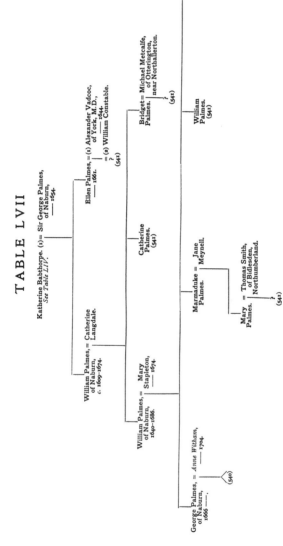

Katherine Babthorpe. (1)= Sir George Palmes,
See Table LIV.   of Naburn,
                              ——1654.

Ellen Palmes,= (1) Alexander Vadcoc,
——1661.   of York, M.D.,
                      ——1644.
              = (2) William Constable.
                   ?
                  (541)

Bridget= Michael Metcalfe,
Palmes. | of Otterington,
        | near Northallerton.
           ?
          (541)

Catherine
Palmes.
(541)

William Palmes, = Catherine
of Naburn,   Langdale.
c. 1609-1674.

Catherine
Palmes.
(541)

William
Palmes.
(541)

William Palmes, = Mary
of Naburn,   Stapleton,
1640-1686.   ——1674.

Marmaduke = Jane
Palmes.   Meynell.

Mary = Thomas Smith,
Palmes. of Biddlesden,
          Northumberland.
           ?
          (541)

George Palmes, = *Anne Witham,*
of Naburn,   ——1704.
1666 ——.
(540)

62

TABLE LVIII

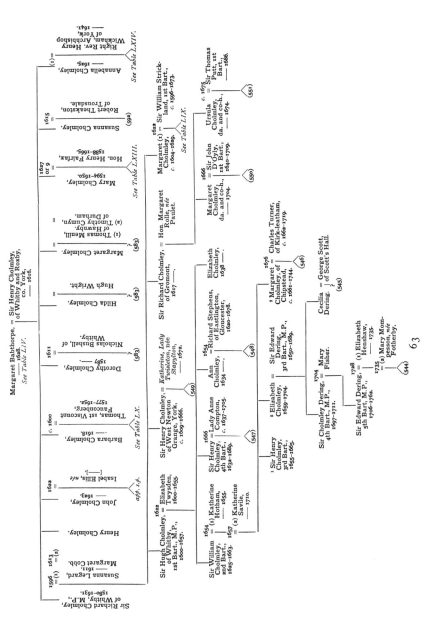

TABLE LIX

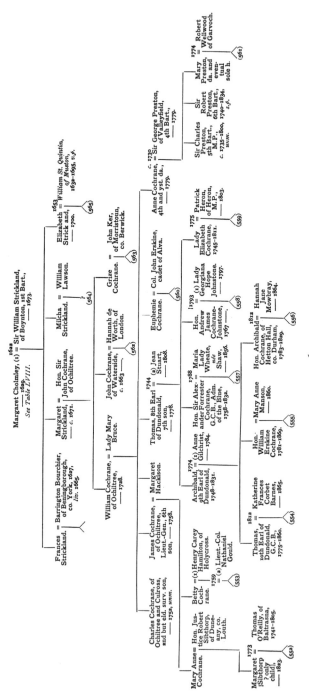

Margaret Cholmley, (1) = Sir William Strickland,
of Boynton, 1st Bart.,
See Table LVIII.

64

TABLE LX

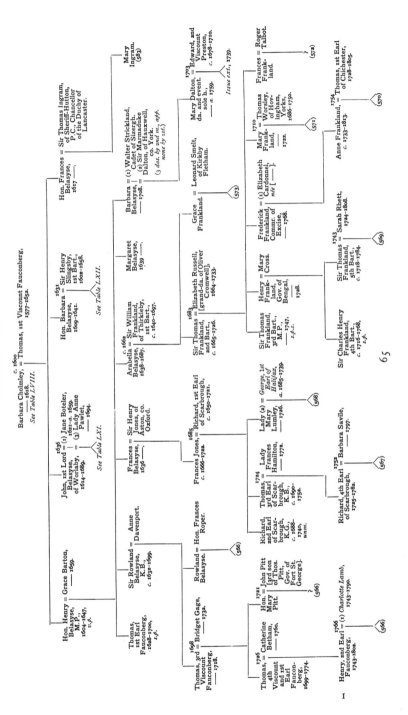

Barbara Cholmley, *c.* 1600. = Thomas, 1st Viscount Fauconberg, 1618. | 1577-1652.

See Table LVIII.

TABLE LXI

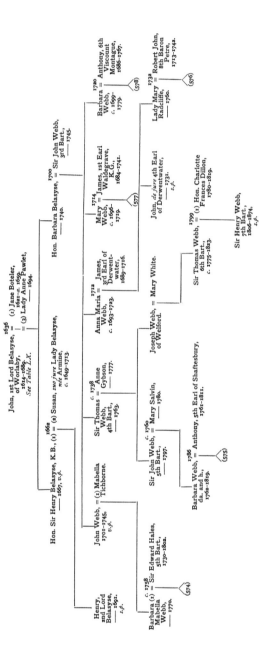

TABLE LXII

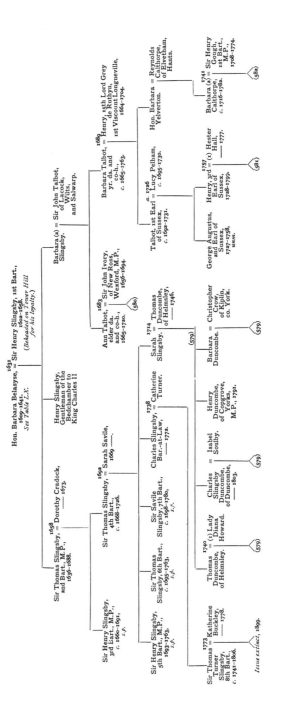

67

TABLE LXIII

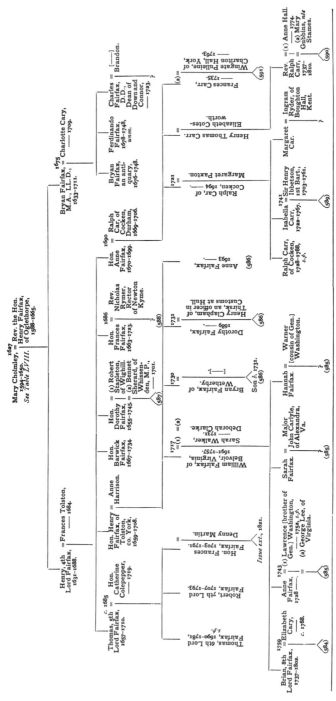

Mary Cholmley, = Rev. the Hon.
1594-1650. | Henry Fairfax,
See Table LVIII. | of Oglethorpe,
1588-1665.

1627

68

See Surtees' Durham, i. p. 209, for Car pedigree.

TABLE LXIV

Annabella Cholmley, (1) = Right Rev. Henry Wickham,
Archdeacon of York,
—— 1641.

1625.

See Table LVIII.

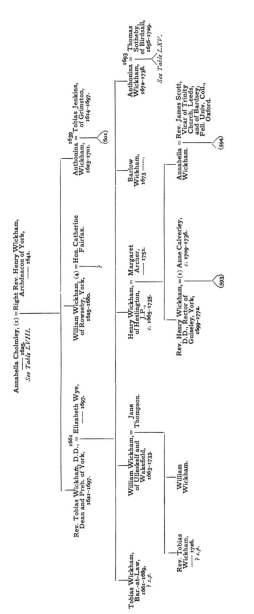

Rev. Tobias Wickham, D.D., = Elizabeth Wye,
Dean and Preb. of York, —— 1697.
1621-1697.

1661.

William Wickham, (4) = Hon. Catherine
of Rowseby, York, Fairfax.
1625-1680. ?

Anthonina = Tobias Jenkins,
Wickham, of Grimston,
1623-1701. 1614-1697.

1639.

(601.)

Tobias Wickham,
Bar.-at-Law,
1661-1689,
? *s.p.*

William Wickham, = Jane
of Ulleskelf and Thompson.
Wakefield,
1663-1733.

Henry Wickham, = Margaret
of Heslington, Archer,
J.P., —— 1751.
c. 1665-1735.

Barlow
Wickham,
1673 ——.

Rev. Tobias
Wickham,
? *s.p.*

1726.

William
Wickham.

Rev. Henry Wickham, = (1) Anne Calverley,
D.D., Rector of c. 1709-1736.
Guiseley, York,
1699-1772.

(593.)

Annabella = Rev. James Scott,
Wickham. Vicar of Trinity
Church, Leeds,
and of Bardsey,
Fell. Univ. Coll.,
Oxford.

(594.)

Anthonina = Thomas
Wickham, Sotheby,
1672-1738. of Birdsall,
1656-1729.

1693.

See Table LXV.

69

TABLE LXV

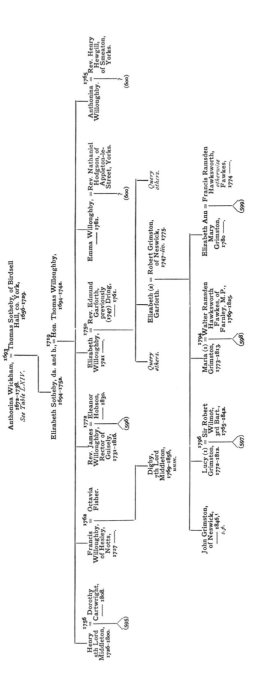

TABLE LXVI

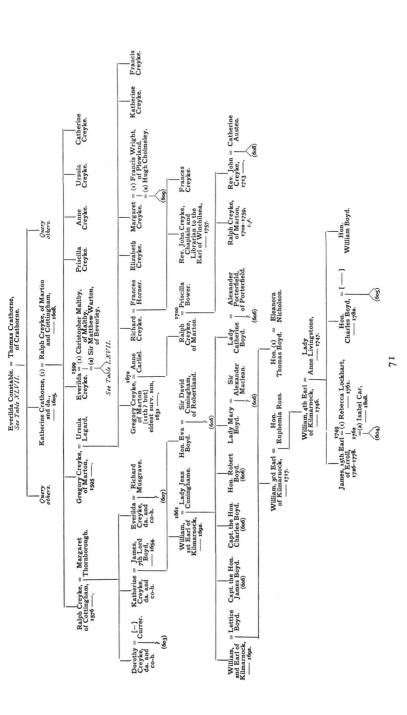

TABLE LXVII

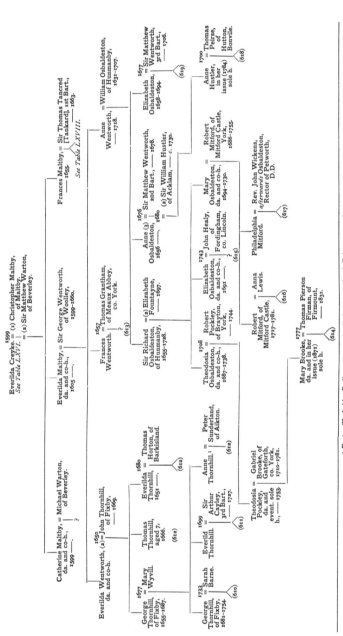

Everilda Creyke. 1599 = (1) Christopher Maltby, of Maltby. *See Table LXVI.* = (2) Sir Matthew Warton, of Beverley.

Frances Maltby, 1655 = Sir Thomas Tancred [Tankard], 1st Bart., 1663. *See Table LXVIII.*

Catherine Maltby, = Michael Warton, da. and co-h., of Beverley. 1599 ——, ?

Everilda Maltby, da. and co-h., 1605 ——,

Everilda Maltby, = Sir George Wentworth, da. and co-h., of Woolley, 1605 ——, 1599-1660.

Everilda Wentworth, (2) = John Thornhill, da. and co-h. of Fixby, 1659 —— 1669.

Frances Wentworth, 1657 = Thomas Grantham, of Meaux Abbey, co. York. (613)

Anne Wentworth, —— 1718. = William Osbaldeston, of Hunmanby, 1651-1707.

Sir Richard Osbaldeston, of Hunmanby, 1655-1728. = (2) Elizabeth Fountayne, 1697.

Anne (2) Osbaldeston, 1656 —— = Sir Matthew Wentworth, and Bart., —— 1698. 1696 = (2) Sir William Hustler, of Acklam, —— c. 1730.

Elizabeth Osbaldeston, 1658-1694. = Sir Matthew Wentworth, 3rd Bart., —— 1706. 1697 (619)

Anne Hustler, in her issue (1764) sole h. 1700 = Thomas Peirse, of Hutton, Bonvile. (618)

Mary Osbaldeston, da. and co-h., 1694-1730. = Robert Mitford, of Mitford Castle, York, 1686-1755.

Elizabeth Osbaldeston, da. and co-h., 1691 —— = John Healy, of Fordingham, co. Lincoln. 1743 (615)

Philadelphia Mitford. = Rev. John Wickens, *afterwards* Osbaldeston, Rector of Petworth, D.D. (617)

Everilda Thornhill, 1651 —— = Thomas Horton, of Barkisland. 1680 (612)

Anne Thornhill.[1] = Peter Sunderland, of Aikton. (612a)

Thomas Thornhill, aged 7, 1666. (612)

Everild Thornhill. = Sir Arthur Cayley, 3rd Bart., —— 1747. 1699 (611)

George Thornhill, of Fixby, 1655-1687. = Mary Wyvill. 1677

George Thornhill, of Fixby, 1681-1754. = Sarah Barne. 1733 (610)

Theodosia Pockley, da. and event. sole h., 1753. = Gabriel Brooke, of Gateforth, co. York, 1710-1781.

Theodosia Osbaldeston, da. and co-h., 1687-1738. = Robert Pockley, of Brayton, York, —— 1744. 1708

Robert Mitford, of Mitford Castle, 1717-1781. = Anna Lewis. (616)

Mary Brooke, da. and in her issue (1871) sole h. = Thomas Pierson Firman, of Firmount, —— 1831. 1777 (614)

[1] Foster (Yorkshire Pedigrees) says she died unmarried 11th Feb. 1755, aged 68.

72

TABLE LXVIII

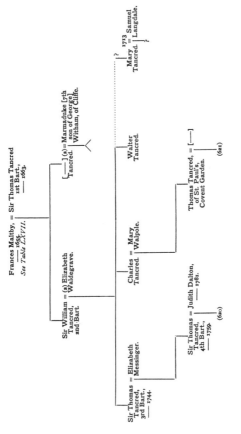

73

K

TABLE LXIX

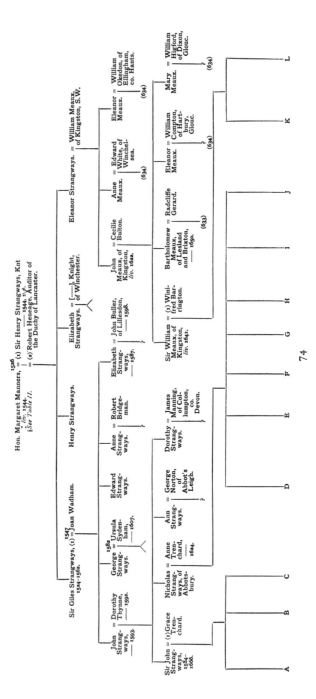

74

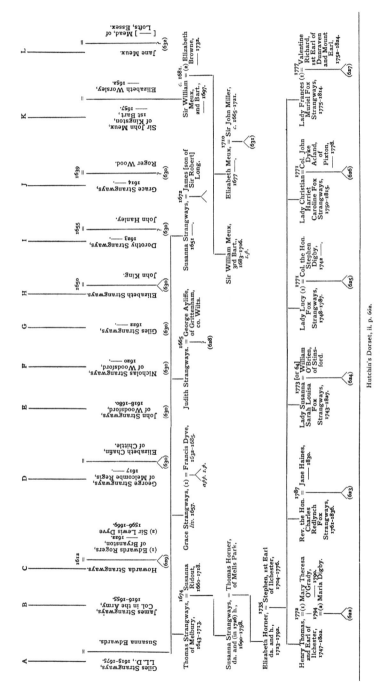

Hutchins's Dorset, ii. p. 602.

75

PHILIP, 3RD LORD DE L'ISLE AND DUDLEY.

THE PRESENT REPRESENTATIVE OF ANNE (PLANTAGENET), DUCHESS OF EXETER.

Photo, Lafayette, London.

THE PLANTAGENET ROLL

OF THE

BLOOD ROYAL OF BRITAIN

𝔇escendants of the Lady Anne Plantagenet (sister to Kings Edward IV. and Richard III.), b. 10 Aug. 1439; d. 14 Jan. 1476; wife, 1st, of Henry (Holland), 2nd Duke of Exeter [E.], b. 27 June 1430; d.s.p. (being found dead in the sea between Calais and Dover) 1473; 2ndly, of Sir Thomas St. Leger, Knight.

1. Descendants of HENRIETTA FRANCES HUNLOKE (see Table II.), b. 13 Jan. 1783; d. 5 Feb. 1811; m. 29 Ap. 1799, Sir JOHN SHELLEY, afterwards (R.L. 6 Mar. 1793) SHELLEY-SIDNEY, 1st Bart. [U.K.], bapt. 10 Nov. 1771; d. 14 Mar. 1849; and had issue 1a.

1a. Philip Charles (Shelley-Sidney, afterwards Sidney), 1st Baron De L'Isle and Dudley [U.K.], b. 11 Mar. 1800; d. 4 Mar. 1851; m. 13 Aug. 1825, Lady Sophia, da. of George (FitzClarence), 1st Earl Munster, d. 10 Ap. 1837; and had issue 1b to 3b.

1b. Philip (Sidney), 2nd Baron De L'Isle and Dudley [U.K.], b. 29 Jan. 1828; d. 17 Feb. 1898; m. 1st, 23 Ap. 1850, Mary, da. and h. of Sir William Foulis, 8th Bart. [E.], d. 14 June 1891; and had issue 1c to 3c.

1c. Philip (Sidney), 3rd Baron De L'Isle and Dudley [U.K.] (Penhurst Place, Tonbridge, Kent; Ingleby Manor, Middlesbrough; Carlton), b. 14 May 1853; m. 12 July 1902, the Hon. Elizabeth Maria, widow of William Harvey Astell, J.P., D.L., da. of Standish Prendergast (Vereker), 4th Viscount Gort [I.].

2c. Hon. Algernon Sidney, Lieut.-Col. and Brevet-Col. R.A. (Marlborough), b. 11 June 1854.

3c. Hon. William Sidney, Bar. Inner Temple (8 Lennox Gardens, S.W.), b. 19 Aug. 1859; m. 5 Dec. 1905, Winifred, da. of R. Yorke Bevan.

2b. Hon. Ernestine Wellington Sidney (Holmwood, West Cowes, I.W.), b. 9 Jan. 1834; m. as 2nd wife, 9 Jan. 1868, Philip Perceval, D.L., d. 1 Ap. 1897; and has issue 1c to 4c.

1c. Philip Perceval, now Hunloke, b. 26 Nov. 1868; m. 17 Feb. 1892, Silvia, da. of John Postle Haseltine of Walhampton, Lymington.

2c. Ernest Perceval, b. 19 Nov. 1871.

3c. Kathleen Sophy Perceval, b. (twin) 26 Nov. 1868.

4c. Ernestine Perceval.

3b. Hon. Sophia Philippa Sidney, m. 20 Ap. 1871, Alexander, Count Kielman-segg (Gulzow, bei Lauenburg, a.d. Elbe, Germany).

[Nos. 1 to 9.

The Plantagenet Roll

2. Descendants of GEORGE FIESCHI HENEAGE of Hainton (see Table II.), *b.* 7 Aug. 1730 ; *d.* 21 Mar. 1782; *m.* 18 Sept. 1755, the Hon. KATHERINE, da. of Robert James (PETRE), 8th Baron Petre [E.], *b.* 1737 ; *d.* 1783 ; and had issue.

See the Clarence Volume, pp. 425–427, Nos. 16639–16735.

[Nos. 10 to 106.

3. Descendants, if any, of THOMAS, ELIZABETH MARIA, and KATHERINE HENEAGE (see Table II.), brother and sisters of the above-named George Fieschi Heneage of Hainton.

4. Descendants, if any, of the four younger sons and two daughters of ELIZABETH HUNLOKE and her husband, GEORGE HENEAGE of Hainton[1] (see Table II.).

5. Descendants of Lady FRANCES CONINGSBY (see Table III.), *m.* 1732, Sir CHARLES HANBURY, *afterwards* WILLIAMS of Coldbrook, K.B., M.P., *b.* 8 Dec. 1709 ; *d.* 17 Nov. 1759 ; and had issue.

See the Clarence Volume, Table LXXV., p. 605, Nos. 26609–26696.

[Nos. 107 to 145.

6. Descendants of MONTAGU (BERTIE), 5th EARL OF ABINGDON [E.] (see Table III.), *b.* 30 Ap. 1784; *d.* 16 Oct. 1854; *m.* 1st, 27 Aug. 1807, EMILY, da. of Gen. the Hon. Thomas GAGE, *b.* 25 Ap. 1776; *d.* 28 Aug. 1838 ; and had issue 1*a*.

1*a. Montagu (Bertie), 6th Earl of Abingdon* [E.], b. 19 *June* 1808; d. 8 *Feb.* 1884; m. 7 *Jan.* 1835, *Elizabeth Lavinia, da. and h. of George Granville Vernon Harcourt, M.P., d. 16 Oct.* 1858 ; *and had issue* 1b *to* 9b.

1*b.* Montagu Arthur (Bertie), 7th Earl of Abingdon [E.] (*Wytham Abbey, Oxford ; Travellers' ; Carlton*), *b.* 13 May 1836; *m.* 1st, 10 July 1858, Caroline Theresa, da. of Charles Towneley of Towneley, Lancashire, *d.* 4 Sept. 1873 ; 2ndly, 16 Oct. 1883, Gwendeline Mary, da. of Lieut.-Gen. the Hon. Sir James Charlemagne Dormer, K.C.B. ; and has issue 1*c* to 7*c*.

1*c.*[1] Montagu Charles Francis Towneley-Bertie, Lord Norreys, J.P., D.L., formerly 3rd Batt. Princess Charlotte of Wales's (Berkshire Regt.), (2 *Norfolk Crescent, Hyde Park, W.*), *b.* 3 Oct. 1860; *m.* 25 July 1885, Hon. Rose Riversdale, sister of Frederick (Glyn), 4th Lord Wolverton [U.K.], da. of Vice-Ad. the Hon. Henry Carr Glyn ; and has issue 1*d* to 2*d*. [Nos. 146 to 147.

---

[1] Elizabeth, their second da., *m.* as 2nd wife, Cuthbert Tunstall, *afterwards* Constable, of Burton-Constable and Halsham, co. York (nephew and h. of the last Viscount Dunbar), *bur.* 20 Mar. 1747, and had issue Marmaduke Cuthbert Constable, *afterwards* Tunstall, *bapt.* 20 July 1743 (see Foster's "Yorkshire Pedigrees"). James Windsor Heneage of Cadeby, co. Linc., was probably a son of theirs. He *m.* 23 Sept. 1761, Elizabeth, da. of John Browne of Gatcombe, I.W., and had two das. and co-heirs, Mary, *b.* 21 Nov. 1762, *m.* 1791, William Fitzherbert, *afterwards* (5 Jan. 1783) Brookholes of Claughton, and had issue (see the Clarence Volume, p. 384, Nos. 14616–14617); and Elizabeth, *b.* 9 Dec. 1764, *m.* 22 Nov. 1799, Basil Fitzherbert of Norbury and Swynnerton, and had issue (see the Clarence Volume, p. 384, Nos. 14592–14615).

# of The Blood Royal

1*d*. Hon. Montagu Henry Edmund Cecil Towneley-Bertie, *b*. 2 Nov. 1887.

2*d*. Hon. Alexandra Rose Alice Towneley-Bertie, *b*. 17 Oct. 1886.

2*c*.[2] Hon. Arthur Michael Bertie, *b*. 29 Sept. 1886.

3*c*.[2] Hon. James Willoughby Bertie, *b*. 22 Sept. 1901.

4*c*.[1] Lady Mary Caroline Bertie, *b*. 11 Aug. 1859, *m*. 5 Aug. 1879, Lieut.-Col. Lord Edmund Bernard Talbot, M.V.O., D.S.O., M.P. (1 *Buckingham Palace Gardens, S.W.*) ; and has issue 1*d* to 2*d*.

    1*d*. Henry Edmund Talbot, *b*. 30 Oct. 1883.

    2*d*. Mary Caroline Magdalen Talbot, *b*. 24 Aug. 1880.

5*c*.[1] Lady Alice Josephine Bertie, *b*. 2 Mar. 1865 ; *m*. 1st, 1 Feb. 1890, Sir Gerald Herbert Portal, K.C.M.G., C.B., *d*. 25 Jan. 1894 ; 2ndly, 5 Oct. 1897, Comdt. Reyntiens, Belgian Artillery and A.D.C. to King of the Belgians (*Brussels*) ; and has issue 1*d*.

    1*d*. Priscilla Reyntiens, *b*. 1899.

6*c*.[2] Lady Gwendeline Theresa Mary Bertie, *b*. 20 Nov. 1885.

7*c*.[2] Lady Elizabeth Constance Bertie, *b*. 12 Mar. 1895.

2*b*. Right Hon. Sir Francis Leveson Bertie, P.C., G.C.M.G., G.C.V.O., K.C.B., H.B.M.'s Ambassador to France (*British Embassy, Paris ; Brooks's, &c.*), *b*. 17 Aug. 1844 ; *m*. 11 Ap. 1874, Lady Feodorowna Cecilia, da. of Henry (Wellesley), 1st Earl Cowley [U.K.] ; and has issue 1*c*.

    1*c*. Vere Frederick Bertie (13 *Hyde Park Mansions, N.W.*), *b*. 20 Oct. 1878 ; *m*. 1901, Nora, da. of Frederick Webb.

3*b*. Rev. the Hon. Alberic Edward Bertie, M.A. (Oxon.), Rector of Gedling (*Gedling Rectory, Nottingham ; United University*), *b*. 14 Nov. 1846 ; *m*. 27 Ap. 1881, Lady Caroline Elizabeth, da. of Mark (McDonnell), 5th Earl of Antrim [I.] ; and has issue 1*c* to 7*c*.

    1*c*. Aubrey Charles Bertie, *b*. 22 Jan. 1882.

    2*c*. Schomberg Montagu Bertie, *b*. 12 Aug. 1888.

    3*c*. Alberic Willoughby Bertie, *b*. 10 Jan. 1891.

    4*c*. Ninian Mark Kerr Bertie, *b*. 19 Nov. 1896.

    5*c*. Irene Elsie Bertie, *b*. 25 Dec. 1883.

    6*c*. Lavinia May Bertie, *b*. 10 Mar. 1887.

    7*c*. Olivia Bridget Bertie, *b*. 5 Nov. 1900.

4*b*. Hon. George Aubrey Vere Bertie, *formerly* Major and Lieut.-Col. 1st Batt. Coldstream Guards (*Maresfield, East Cowes, Isle of Wight; Travellers'*), *b*. 1 May 1850 ; *m*. 13 Oct. 1885, Harriet Blanche Elizabeth, da. of Sir Walter Rockcliff Farquhar, 3rd Bart. [G.B.] ; and has issue 1*c* to 3*c*.

    1*c*. Claude Peregrine Bertie, *b*. 13 July 1890.

    2*c*. Vere Mary Bertie, *b*. 30 Sept. 1886.

    3*c*. Margaret Adine Bertie, *b*. 29 Ap. 1888.

5*b*. Hon. Charles Claude Bertie, *late* Lieut. Berks Militia and 47th Regt., *b*. 31 Aug. 1851 ; *m*. 29 Ap. 1890, Adelaide, da. of the Rev. Jeremiah Borroughes of Lingwood Lodge, Norfolk ; *d*. 28 Aug. 1903.

6*b*. Hon. Reginald Henry Bertie, C.B., Col. (ret.) *formerly* Comdg. 2nd Batt. Royal Welsh Fusiliers (*Ebworth Park, Stroud ; Naval and Military*), *b*. 26 May 1856 ; *m*. 18 Oct. 1892, Lady Amy Evelyn, da. of Henry Reginald (Courtenay), Lord Courtenay.

7*b*. Lady Elizabeth Emily Bertie (*Florence, Italy*).

8*b*. Lady Lavinia Louisa Bertie, *m*. 16 Jan. 1883, Robert Bickersteth (70 *Cromwell Road, S.W.*).

9*b*. Lady Frances Evelyn Bertie, a nun (*Convent of the Visitation, Harrow-on-the-Hill*).   [Nos. 148 to 177.

The Plantagenet Roll

7. Descendants of Rev. the Hon. FREDERIC BERTIE (see Table III.), b. 12 Feb. 1793 ; d. 4 Mar. 1868 ; m. 17 Oct. 1825, Lady GEORGIANA EMILY, da. of Vice-Admiral Lord Mark Robert KERR, by his wife Charlotte M'Donnell, suo jure Countess of Antrim [I.], b. 3 July 1806 ; d. 20 May 1881 ; and had issue.

See the Clarence Volume, p. 633, Nos. 28381-28394.   [Nos. 178 to 191.

8. Descendants of Lady CAROLINE BERTIE (see Table III.), b. 17 Oct. 1788 ; d. 12 Mar. 1870 ; m. 23 Jan. 1821, CHARLES JOHN BAILLIE-HAMILTON, M.P., b. 4 Jan. 1800 ; d. 25 Aug. 1865 ; and had issue 1a to 3a.

1a. Peregrine Charles Baillie-Hamilton, b. 23 May 1823 ; d. 21 Feb. 1860 ; m. 12 July 1848, Mary, da. of Edward Way, d. 30 July, 1875 ; and had issue 1b to 2b.

1b. Rev. George James Baillie-Hamilton, B.A. (Camb.), Vicar of Waverton, Cheshire, b. 1 Mar. 1851 ; d. 14 July 1904 ; m. 6 July 1875, Eliza (Ruabon Road, Wrexham), da. of the Rev. Lucius Fry of Croft, Leicestershire, and had issue 1c to 11c.

1c. George Leslie Baillie-Hamilton, b. 13 Aug. 1877.
2c. Charles Douglas Baillie-Hamilton, b. 30 Oct. 1880.
3c. Arthur Vivian Baillie-Hamilton, b. 24 Nov. 1881.
4c. Lucius Hugh Noel Baillie-Hamilton, b. 30 Jan. 1886.
5c. Patrick Stephen Baillie-Hamilton, b. 27 Feb. 1890.
6c. Edith Mary Baillie-Hamilton, b. 7 July 1876.
7c. Aline Melrose Baillie-Hamilton, b. 5 Sept. 1879.
8c. Nora Constance Baillie-Hamilton, b. 1 Aug. 1883.
9c. Ethel Gordon Baillie-Hamilton, b. 25 July 1885.
10c. Madeline Baillie-Hamilton, b. 15 Mar. 1888.
11c. Helen Margaret Baillie-Hamilton, b. 7 June 1896.

2b. Lesa Baillie Baillie-Hamilton, m. 5 Aug. 1874, John Ball Ball (Ashburton Cottage, Putney Heath, S.W.; Brookmeadow, the Holmwood, Dorking); and has issue 1c to 6c.

1c. Leslie Hamilton Ball, b. 5 Feb. 1879.
2c. Kenneth Melrose Ball, b. 15 Oct. 1880.
3c. Basil Des Geneys Ball, sometime Midshipman R.N., b. 10 May 1883.
4c. Sylvia Sybil Ball, b. 14 Sept. 1875.
5c. Gladys Mary Ball, b. 8 Feb. 1882 ; m. 4 June 1903, Horace Milman Haves (Sunt, Edenbridge); and has issue 1d.
1d. Mary Isabella Hayes, b. 4 Mar. 1904.
6c. Lesa Beryl Ball, b. 16 Oct. 1887.

2a. Caroline Sophia Elizabeth Baillie-Hamilton, b. 27 Jan. 1822 ; d. 8 Mar. 1854 ; m. 28 Sept. 1844, Francis Caissotti, Count de Roubion, d. 10 Ap. 1882 ; and had issue 1b.

1b. Delphine Caissotti, Countess de Roubion (Villa Rozy, Alpes Maritimes, France; Boulevard Czarevitch, Nice), b. (at Nice) 13 Oct. 1845 ; m. (there) 1st, Viscount Francis de Constantin (2nd son of Marquis de Constantin de Chateauneuf), d.s.p.s. (there) ; 2ndly (at the same place), Leonard Rozy.

3a. Emily Eleanor Baillie-Hamilton, b. (in London) 3 May 1824 ; d. (at Chiswick) 10 Oct. 1904 ; m. (at Florence) 10 Mar. 1847, George, Count and Baron Agnès-

[Nos. 192 to 211.

80

# of The Blood Royal

Des Geneys, b. (*at Genoa*) 4 *July* 1828; d. (*there*) 22 *Ap.* 1864; *and had issue* 1*b to* 4*b.*

    1*b.* George Emanuel Charles Augustus, *Count and Baron Agnès-Des Geneys*, b. (*at Torquay*) 10 *Feb.* 1848; d. (*at Gosport*) 25 *June* 1891, *unm.*

    2*b.* Countess Alice-Emily Caroline Des Geneys, *b.* (at Nice) 12 Oct. 1849; *m.* (at Genoa) 29 Ap. 1872, Cavaliere Eugenio Figoli, 1st Count Figoli des Geneys (1892) [Italy], a Senator since 1900, *b.* (in Genoa) 1 July 1845; and has issue 1*c* to 2*c.*

    1*c.* Georgina Emily Carla Maria Figoli, *b.* (in Genoa) 12 Jan. 1873; *m.* (in Arenzano, Liguria) 27 Oct. 1897, Marquis (Marchese) Giacomo Pinelli Gentile Tabrago (*Castello Tagliolo, Monferrato*); and has issue 1*d* to 4*d.*

    1*d.* Marchesino Agastino Pinelli Gentile Tabrago, Conte di Tagliolo, *b.* (at Tagliolo) 29 Aug. 1898.

    2*d.* Marchesino Constantino Emilio Pinelli Gentile Tabrago, *b.* (at Tagliolo) 3 Sept. 1904.

    3*d.* Marchesina Eugenia Isabella Pinelli Gentile Tabrago, *b.* (at Genoa) 21 Mar. 1900.

    4*d.* Marchesina Carla Alberta Pinelli Gentile Tabrago, *b.* (at Genoa) 2 Ap. 1902.

    2*c.* Mariquita Augusta Figoli, *b.* (at Arenzano) 19 May 1878; *m.* 19 Jan. 1905 (in Arenzano), Signor Lorenzo Quartara of Genoa and Quarto Mare, *b.* (at Genoa) 1865.

    3*b.* *Countess Beatrice Christine Helene Des Geneys,* b. (*at Nice*) 14 *Jan.* 1851; d.s.p. (*at Passy, Paris*) 7 *Dec.* 1888; m. (*in Paris*) 20 *June* 1885, *Monsieur Antoine De La Barre Duparcq.*

    4*b.* Countess Carolina Louisa Maria Des Geneys (*Il Boulal, Pinerolo, Piemonte*), *b.* (at Turin) 12 Ap. 1856, *unm.*   [Nos. 212 to 219.

9. Descendants of JOHN CLIFTON of Clifton and Lytham, co. Lancaster (see Table III.), *b.* 25 Jan. 1764; *d.* 23 Mar. 1832; *m.* 23 Nov. 1785, ELIZABETH, da. of Thomas RIDDELL of Felton Park and Swinburne Castle, *d.* 19 Nov. 1825; and had issue 1*a* to 5*a.*

    1*a.* *Thomas Clifton of Clifton and Lytham, J.P., D.L.,* b. 29 *June* 1788; d. 1851; m. 17 *Mar.* 1817, *Hetty, widow of David Campbell of Kildalloig, da. of Peregrine Treves, Postmaster-General of Calcutta; and had issue* 1*b to* 3*b.*

    1*b.* *John Talbot Clifton of Clifton and Lytham, J.P., D.L., M.P., Col.* 1*st Royal Lancashire Militia,* b. 5 *Mar.* 1819; d. 16 *Ap.* 1882; m. 16 *Ap.* 1844, *Lady Eleanor Cecily, da. of the Hon. Henry Cecil Lowther and sister to Henry (Lowther),* 3*rd Earl of Lonsdale* [*U.K.*], b. 20 *Dec.* 1822; d. 24 *Mar.* 1894; *and had issue.*
    See the Clarence Volume, p. 602, Nos. 26503–26509.

    2*b.* *Charles Frederick (Clifton, afterwards* (1859) *Abney-Hastings),* 1*st Baron Donington* [*U.K.*], b. 17 *June* 1822; d. 24 *July* 1895; m. 30 *Ap.* 1853, *Edith Mary,* suo jure *Countess of Loudoun* [*S.*], *Baroness Botreaux, Hungerford, De Molyens and Hastings* [*E.*], d. 22 *Jan.* 1874; *and had issue.*
    See the Clarence Volume, pp. 71–72, Nos. 1–12.

    3*b.* Augustus Wykeham Clifton, *late* Capt. Rifle Brigade (*Warton Hall, Lytham*), *b.* 2 Mar. 1829; *m.* 11 Dec. 1855, Bertha Lelgarde, suo jure Baroness Grey de Ruthyn [E.], *d.* 15 Dec. 1887; and has issue.
    See the Clarence Volume, p. 72, Nos. 13–17.

    2*a.* *John Clifton of Lincoln's Inn,* b. 2 *May* 1790; d. 28 *Sept.* 1843; m. 28 *Ap.* 1817, *Maria, da. of John Trafford of Trafford,* d. 28 *Sept.* 1844; *and had issue.*
    See the Clarence Volume, p. 325, Nos. 9444–9449.

    3*a.* *William Clifton,* b. 13 *June* 1791.   [Nos. 220 to 250.

The Plantagenet Roll

4a. *Edward Clifton of Dorset Square, London, Capt. Coldstream Guards, b.*
17 *Feb.* 1794; d. 23 *Jan.* 1850; m. 15 *Jan.* 1819, *Elizabeth, da. of Thomas*
Scarisbrick, Eccleston of Eccleston, Scarisbrick and Wrightington, d. 9 *Nov.* 1862;
and had issue.
See the Clarence Volume, p. 431, Nos. 16898–16915.

5a. *Harriet Jane Clifton.* [Nos. 251 to 268.

10. Descendants of ELEANORA CLIFTON (see Table III.), *d.* (-);
m. 19 Ap. 1784, THOMAS SCARISBRICK, sometime Eccleston
of Eccleston, Wrightington and Scarisbrick, *d.* 1 Nov. 1809;
and had issue.

See the Clarence Volume, p. 431, Nos. 16898–16915.
[Nos. 269 to 286.

11. Descendants of CATHERINE CLIFTON (see Table III.), *d.* May 1791;
m. as 1st wife, 29 May 1789, JOHN JOSEPH TALBOT, *b.* 9 June
1765; *d.* 8 Aug. 1815; and had issue 1*a.*

1a. *John (Talbot), 16th Earl of Shrewsbury [E.] and Waterford [I.], b.* 18 *Mar.*
1791; d. 9 *Nov.* 1852; m. 27 *June* 1814, *Maria Theresa, da. of William Talbot of*
Castle Talbot, d. 8 *June* 1856; *and had issue* 1*b* to 2*b.*

1b. *Lady Maria Alathea Beatrix Talbot, b.* 26 *May* 1815; *d.* 18 *Dec.* 1858;
m. 9 *Ap.* 1839, *Philip Andrew (Doria-Pamphilj-Landi), Prince Doria-Pamphilj-*
Landi (1854), *Prince of Torriglia* (13 *May* 1760), *Prince of Melfi* (1531) *and*
Valmontone, Duke of Avigliano, &c., &c., b. 28 *Sept.* 1813; *d.* 19 *Mar.* 1876; *and*
had issue 1*c* to 5*c.*

1c. *John Andrew (Doria-Pamphilj-Landi), Prince Doria-Pamphilj-Landi* (1854),
&c., b. 4 *Aug.* 1843; *d.s.p.* 7 *Ap.* 1890.

2c. Alfonso (Doria-Pamphilj-Landi), Prince Doria-Pamphilj-Landi (1854), &c.,
&c. [Rome], *b.* (at Rome) 25 Sept. 1851; *m.* 24 June 1882, Lady Emily Augusta
Mary, da. of Henry Pelham Alexander (Pelham-Clinton), 6th Duke of Newcastle
[G.B.], &c.; and has issue 1*d* to 2*d.*

1d. Prince Philip Andrew Doria-Pamphilj-Landi, *b.* (at Rome) 1 Mar. 1886.

2d. Princess Orietta Doria-Pamphilj-Landi, *b.* (at Rome) 25 May 1887.

3c. Theresa Doria-Pamphilj-Landi, *b.* (at Rome) 1 Mar. 1840; *m.* (there)
14 Jan. 1858, Emilio (Massimo), 2nd Duke of Rignano (1828) [Rome] (*Rome,*
30 *Piazza Aracoeli*); and has issue 1*d.*

1d. Maria Massimo, *b.* (at Rome) 30 July 1859; *m.* (there) 26 Nov. 1884,
Prospero (Colonna), 12th Prince of Sonnino, Syndic of Rome and a Senator [Italy]
(*Rome, Villino, Massimo, Via S. Basilio*); and has issue 1*e* to 3*e.*

1e. Mario Colonna, *b.* (at Rome) 28 Feb. 1886.

2e. Piero Colonna, *b.* (at Rome) 23 May 1891.

3e. Fabrizio Colonna, *b.* (at Rome) 12 Oct. 1893.

4c. Guendalina Doria-Pamphilj-Landi (*Milan*), *b.* (at Pegli) 1 Aug. 1846; *m.*
(at Rome) 24 Feb. 1868, Gian Luca Cavazzi, Count and Baron della Somaglia (3 Feb.
1452) [Milan], Knight of Malta, *b.* 8 Feb. 1841; *d.* (at Naples) 6 Mar. 1896; and
has issue 1*d* to 3*d.*

1d. Gian Giacomo (Cavazzi), Count and Baron della Somaglia (1452) [Milan],
Patrician of Milan (*Milan, Corso Porta Romana* 13), *b.* (in Milan) 16 July 1869;
m. (at Oleggio Castello) 5 July 1899, Virginia, da. of Claude (Dal Pozzo), Marquis of
Annone, &c.; and has issue 1*e.*

1e. Guendalina Cavazzi, *b.* 23 Aug. 1904.

2d. Maria Cavazzi, *b.* 19 May 1871; *m.* 1 July 1895, Carlo (Castelbarco-Albani-
Nos. 287 to 298.

82

# of The Blood Royal

Visconti-Simonetta), 2nd Prince of Montignano (1848) [Italy] (*Milan, Via Prince Umberto* 6); and has issue 1e to 5e.

1e. Count Cæsar Castelbarco-Albani-Visconti-Simonetta, *b.* (at Milan) 1 June 1896.

2e. Count Francis Castelbarco-Albani-Visconti-Simonetta, *b.* (at Milan) 30 Mar. 1900.

3e. Count William Castelbarco-Albani-Visconti-Simonetta, *b.* (at Casciago) 14 Aug. 1901.

4e. Giovanna Castelbarco-Albani-Visconti-Simonetta, *b.* (at Casciago) 12 Aug. 1897.

5e. Elena Castelbarco-Albani-Visconti-Simonetta, *b.* (at Casciago) 18 Oct. 1898.

3d. Magdalena Cavazzi, *b.* 26 Mar. 1873; *m.* 3 June 1894, Louis Alberigo (Trivulzio), 2nd Prince of Musocco (1885) [Italy] (*Milan, Piazza S. Alessandro* 4); and has issue 1e to 2e.

1e. Gian Giacomo Trivulzio, Marquis of Sesto Ulteriano, *b.* (at Milan) 25 Oct. 1896.

2e. Marianna Trivulzio, *b.* (at Bellagio) 27 Sept. 1895.

5c. Olimpia Doria-Pamphilj-Landi, *b.* (at Rome) 21 Oct. 1854; *m.* (there) 20 May 1878, Fabrizio (Colonna), 3rd Prince of Avella, and a Senator [Italy] (*Rome*); and has issue 1d to 4d.

1d. Marco Antonio Colonna, *b.* (at Rome) 25 July 1881.

2d. Ascanio Colonna, *b.* (at Naples) 8 Aug. 1883.

3d. Marozia Colonna, *b.* (at Rome) 13 Mar. 1885.

4d. Margherita Colonna, *b.* (at Rome) 5 June 1890.

2b. *Lady Gwendoline Catherine Talbot,* b. 3. Dec. 1817; d. 27 Oct. 1840; m. *as 1st wife,* 11 May 1835, Mark Anthony (Borghèse), *Prince of Sulmona* (10 Nov. 1605) [Rome], *commonly called Prince Borghèse,* b. 23 Feb. 1814; d. 5 Oct. 1886; *and had issue* 1c.

1c. Princess Agnes Borghèse, *b.* (at Rome) 5 May 1836; *m.* 31 May 1854, Rodolph (Boncompagni Ludovisi), Prince of Piombino (1594) [H.R.E.], &c., &c. (*Rome, Palais Piombino*); and has issue 1d to 6d.

1d. Ugo, Duke of Sora (*Rome*), *b.* (at Rome) 8 May 1856; *m.* (at Rome) 1st, 7 Oct. 1877, Victoria, da. of Francis (Patrigi-Naro-Montoro), Marquis of Paganico, &c., *b.* 27 Ap. 1857; *d.* 22 Jan. 1883; 2ndly (at Rome), 6 July 1884, Laura, da. of Emilio, Prince Altieri, *b.* 29 Jan. 1858; *d.* 4 May 1892; and has issue 1e to 5e.

1e. Prince Anthony Frances Maria Boncompagni-Ludovisi, *b.* (at Rome) 20 Oct. 1886.

2e. Princess Guendalina Boncompagni-Ludovisi (*Roma, Via S. Eustachio* 31), *b.* (at Rome) 26 Nov. 1878; *m.* (at Rome) 25 Nov. 1897, Marquis Antonio Pio Vincenzo Malvezzi-Campeggi, *b.* (in Rome) 13 Aug. 1870; *d.* 9 Ap. 1900.

3e. Princess Wilhelmina Boncompagni-Ludovisi, *b.* (at Rome) 4 July 1881; *m.* (at Foligno) 24 Oct. 1900, Pompeo, Count di Campello della Spina.

4e. Princess Eleanor Boncompagni-Ludovisi, *b.* (at Rome) 25 Ap. 1885.

5e. Princess Theresa Boncompagni-Ludovisi, *b.* (at Rome) 24 Jan. 1889.

2d. Prince Louis Boncompagni-Ludovisi (*Rome*), *b.* (at Rome) 21 June 1857; *m.* (at Florence) 24 Oct. 1881, Isabella, da. of Andrew (Rondinelli-Vitelli), Marquis of Bucine; and has issue 1e to 4e.

1e. Prince Andrew Boncompagni-Ludovisi, *b.* (at Rome) 3 Feb. 1884.

2e. Prince Paul Boncompagni-Ludovisi, *b.* (at Rome) 19 Dec. 1886.

3e. Prince Louis Boncompagni-Ludovisi, *b.* (at Florence) 16 Feb. 1890.

4e. Prince Baldassarre Boncompagni-Ludovisi, *b.* (at Rome) 30 Oct. 1900.

3d. Prince Joseph Boncompagni-Ludovisi (*Rome*), *b.* (at Rome) 22 Mar. 1865; *m.* (at Rome) 15 Jan. 1891, Arduina, da. of Guy, Count of San Martino Valperga; and has issue 1e to 2e. [Nos. 299 to 324.]

83

The Plantagenet Roll

1e. Prince Boncompagno Boncompagni-Ludovisi, b. (at Rome) 26 Oct. 1896.
2e. Princess Rosalia Boncompagni-Ludovisi, b. (at Rome) 26 Feb. 1893.
4d. Princess Guendalina Boncompagni-Ludovisi (Genoa), b. (at Rome) 17 July 1859; m. (at Rome) 23 Ap. 1879, Marquis Giambattista Cattaneo della Volta, d. 2 Sept. 1897.
5d. Princess Magdalen Boncompagni-Ludovisi, a nun, b. (at Rome) 23 Nov. 1861.
6d. Princess Maria Boncompagni-Ludovisi, b. (at Rome) 10 Mar. 1869; m. (there) 24 Oct. 1888, Francis Negroni, Duke Caffarelli, Knt. of Malta (Rome, Via Condotti 61); and has issue 1e to 3e.
1e. Joseph Caffarelli, b. (at Rome) 3 Ap. 1890.
2e. Philip Caffarelli, b. (at Rome) 5 June 1891.
3e. Charles Caffarelli, b. (at Rome) 12 June 1893.   [Nos. 325 to 332.

12. Descendants of THOMAS STAPLETON of Carlton (see Table III.), b. 28 Ap. 1788; d. 4 July 1839; m. 1st, 3 Nov. 1802, MARIA JULIANA, da. of Sir Robert Cansfield GERARD, 9th Bart. [E.], d. 9 Feb. 1827; 2ndly, 29 Sept. 1829, HENRIETTA LAVINIA, da. of Richard Fitzgerald ANSTER, H.E.I.C.S., d. 14 Nov. 1858; and had issue 1a to 5a.

1a. Miles Thomas (Stapleton), 8th Baron Beaumont [E.], b. 4 June 1805; d. 16 Aug. 1854; m. 9 Sept. 1844, the Hon. Isabella Anne, da. of John Cavendish (Browne), 3rd Baron Kilmaine [I.]; and had issue 1b to 2b.
1b. Henry (Stapleton), 9th Baron Beaumont [E.], b. 11 Aug. 1848; d.s.p. 23 Jan. 1892.
2b. Miles (Stapleton), 10th Baron Beaumont [E.], b. 17 July 1850; d. 16 Sept. 1895; m. 7 Nov. 1893, Ethel Mary (Carlton Towers, Yorks), da. and h. of Sir Charles Henry Tempest, 1st Bart. [U.K.]; and had issue 1c to 2c.
1c. Mona Josephine Tempest (Stapleton), 11th Baroness Beaumont [E.], b. 1 Aug. 1894.
2c. Hon. Ivy Mary Stapleton, b. 4 Oct. 1895.

2a. John Stapleton, Bar.-at-Law, M.P., b. 11 Ap. 1816; d. 25 Dec. 1891; m. 26 Ap. 1860, Frances Dorothea, da. of Edward Bolton King of Chadshunt, co. Warwick, d. 8 May 1899; and had issue 1b to 9b.
1b. Rev. Gilbert Stapleton, M.A. (Oxon.), Rector of Rotherwick (Rotherwick Rectory, Hants), b. 11 May 1862; m. 1st, 21 Ap. 1891, Anna Mary Katherine, da. of the Rev. Thomas Langshaw, d.s.p. 18 June 1891; 2ndly, 3 Jan. 1894, Eleanor Sarah, da. and h. of the Rev. Gibbes Jordan; and has issue 1c to 2c.
1c. Katharine Anna Stapleton.
2c. Margaret Alianora Stapleton.

2b. Cuthbert Stapleton (Gilbert River, N. Queensland), b. 25 April 1863; m. Dec. 1899, Amelia, widow of [——] Frank, da. of [——] Grainer.
3b. Thomas Stapleton (Batstones, Natal), b. 31 May 1869.
4b. Bryan Stapleton of the Indian Public Works Dept., b. 20 Aug. 1871.
5b. Louis Henry Stapleton (Kimberley, South Africa), b. 25 July 1874.
6b. Monica Stapleton (27 Edwardes Square, Kensington, W.).
7b. Frances Stapleton, m. 27 Feb. 1894, T. W. Lush (Silchester Manor, Reading).
8b. Georgiana Maria Stapleton, m. 9 Dec. 1891, the Rev. Edwin John Frayling, Vicar of Harwich (Harwich Vicarage); and has issue 1c to 5c.
1c. Bryan Edwin Frayling, b. 5 Aug. 1893.
2c. Michael Stapleton Frayling, b. 20 Ap. 1898.   [Nos. 333 to 346.

3c. John Cuthbert Frayling, *b.* 12 July 1899.
4c. Gerard Dunstan Warren Frayling, *b.* 19 Sept. 1900.
5c. Eve Georgiana Frayling.
9b. Joan Henrietta Stapleton (27 *Edwardes Square, Kensington, W.*).

3a. Bryan John Stapleton, D.L., b. 6 *Jan.* 1831; d. 21 *Mar.* 1903; m. 24 *June* 1857, *Mary Helen Alicia* (30 *Leckford Road, Oxford*), *da. of John Thomas Dolman of Souldern House, Oxon., M.D.; and had issue* 1b *to* 9b.
1b. Nicholas Stapleton, *b.* 30 Mar. 1861; *m.* 25 Oct. 1886, Mary Magdalene, da. of Lieut.-Col. A. A. Douglas, R.M.A.; and has issue 1c to 2c.
1c. Gwendoline Lavinia Stapleton.
2c. Ruth Magdalena Stapleton.

2b. Gregory Stapleton, Lieut. R.N., *b.* 30 Jan. 1864; *m.* 29 Feb. 1904, Marie, da. of Anthony MacDermott of the Park, Killarney, R.M.; and has issue 1c.
1c. Marie Josephine Stapleton, *b.* 4 May 1905.
3b. Christopher Stapleton, *b.* 20 May 1870.
4b. Rev. Philip Stapleton, S.J., *b.* 28 Jan. 1874.
5b. Helen Stapleton, *m.* 23 Jan. 1893, Wilfrid Ignatius Wilberforce (59 *Kingston Road, Oxford*); and has issue 1c to 2c.
1c. Arthur Richard Anthony Wilberforce, *b.* 4 Dec. 1899.
2c. Everilda Helen Mary Bertrand Wilberforce, *b.* 22 Dec. 1903.

6b. Winifred Stapleton, a nun, O.S.B.
7b. Sibyl Stapleton, *m.* 27 Feb. 1899, Charles Myles O'Reilly, Capt. I.S.C.; and has issue 1c to 3c.
1c–3c. See the Clarence Volume, p. 449, Nos. 19093–19095.
8b. Mary Elizabeth Stapleton, a nun.
9b. Veronica Stapleton.

4a. Catharine Stapleton, d. 27 *Ap.* 1872; m. 1 *July* 1830, *Edward Widdrington Riddell of Bootham House, co. York,* b. 4 *Sept.* 1803; d. 30 Oct. 1870; *and had issue* 1b *to* 3b.
1b. Very Rev. Canon Edward Widdrington Riddell (*Redcar, Yorks*), *b.* 10 May 1831.
2b. John Gerard Riddell, b. 8 *Aug.* 1835; d. 27 *Nov.* 1905; m. 15 *Ap.* 1863, *Katherine Flora, da. of Edward Chaloner of Hermeston and Hodsock,* d. 16 *July* 1898; *and had issue* 1c *to* 5c.
1c. Edward Charles Riddell (*Hermeston Hall, Notts; Hodsock Park, Notts*), *b.* 27 June 1867; *m.* 24 Sept. 1896, Edith Mary Catherine, da. and h. of Capt. Frederic Gerard of Kinwarton House; and has issue 1d to 3d.
1d. Arthur Frederick Riddell, *b.* 27 July 1897.
2d. Ralph Gerard Riddell, *b.* 13 Aug. 1899.
3d. Grace Mary Riddell, *b.* 12 Nov. 1902.

2c. Gerard Joseph Riddell (*Cannon House, Picton, N.Z.*), *b.* 22 Sept. 1868; *m.* Mary, da. of [——] Seymour.
3c. Mary Katherine Riddell, *m.* 20 Ap. 1898, John Joseph Weld; and has issue 1d.
1d. See the Clarence Volume, p. 369, No. 12625.

4c. Helen Frances Mary Riddell, *m.* 30 Ap. 1895, Harold Philip Harold-Barry (*Ballyvonare, Buttevant, co. Cork*); and has issue 1d to 4d.
1d. John Gerard Harold-Barry, *b.* 28 Jan. 1896.
2d. Charles William Harold-Barry, *b.* 21 May 1897.
3d. Edward Basil Harold-Barry, *b.* 1 Sept. 1901.
4d. Hilda Mary Harold-Barry, *b.* 25 May 1900.
5c. Teresa Mary Riddell.

[Nos. 347 to 381.

Ⅽhe Plantagenet Roll

3b. Right Rev. Arthur Grange Riddell, (R.C.) Lord Bishop of Northampton (*Bishop's Palace, Northampton*), *b.* 15 Sept. 1836.

5a. *Lavinia Mary Stapleton,* d. 30 *Sept.* 1855; m. as 2nd wife, 19 *July* 1853, *Sir Alexander Matheson, 1st Bart.* (1882) [*U.K.*], *M.P.,* b. 16 *Jan.* 1805; d. 27 *July* 1886; *and had issue 1b to 2b.*

1b. Sir Kenneth James Matheson, 2nd Bart. [U.K.] (*Duncraig Castle, Lochalsh; Gledfield House, Ardgay; 15 Hyde Park Gardens, W., &c.*), *b.* 12 May 1854.

2b. Mary Isabella Matheson, *m.* 30 Ap. 1881, Wallace Charles Houstoun (8 *Stanhope Terrace, Hyde Park, W.*); and has issue 1c to 2c.

1c. Hugo Henry Houstoun, *b.* 14 July 1883.

2c. Lavinia Mary Houstoun, *m.* 12 Dec. 1905, Sir Duncan Edwyn Hay, 10th Bart. [S.] (*King's Meadows, Haystown, Peebles*). [Nos. 382 to 386.

13. Descendants, if any surviving, of EDWARD BERTIE,[1] *d.* 21 Sept. 1733; of the Rev. WILLIAM BERTIE,[1] D.D., Rector of Albury, co. Oxon., who *m.* and had issue James, Richard, Frances, Sophia, and Anne; of HENRY BERTIE[1]; of the Rev. JOHN BERTIE,[1] Prebendary of Exeter and Rector of Ken, co. Devon, who *d.* 1 Feb. 1774; and had issue Willoughby, Anne, Mary, Bridget, Elizabeth, Frances Mary, Eleanora, Isabella, Mary, and Sophia Eustacia[2]; and of BRIDGET BERTIE,[1] wife of ROBERT COYTMOR (or COETMOR) of Coytmor, co. Carnarvon (see Table III.).

14. Descendants of Sir HENRY HARPUR, 6th Bart. [E.], M.P. (see Table III.), *d.* 10 Feb. 1789; *m.* 17 July 1762, Lady FRANCES ELIZABETH, da. of Francis (GREVILLE), 1st Earl Brooke, and of Warwick [G.B.], *b.* 11 May 1744; *d.* 6 Ap. 1825; and had issue.

See the Tudor Roll of "The Blood Royal of Britain," pp. 200–201, Nos. 21342–21377.   [Nos. 387 to 422.

15. Descendants, if any, of CHARLES HARPUR, Major 38th Regt. (see Table III.), *d.* 9 July 1770.

16. Descendants, if any surviving, of CAROLINE HARPUR (see Table III.), *m.* 1st, as 2nd wife, ADAM HAY, M.P. co. Perth, *d.s.p.* 15 Nov. 1775; 2ndly, Major ARCHIBALD STEWART; and had issue (at least [3]) 1a.

1a. *Caroline Stewart,* m. *William Jenny.*

---

[1] Brothers and sister to Willoughby, 2nd Earl of Abingdon.

[2] One of these married Samuel Ryder Weston, D.D., Canon Residentiary of St. Paul's. Brydges' "Collins," iii. p. 631.

[3] Glover's "Derby," ii. p. 217.

# of The Blood Royal

17. Descendants of THOMAS PALMER (see Table III.), *b.* 1771;
d.v.p. 4 June 1810; *m.* Dec. 1798, SOPHIA, da. of Sir Justinian
ISHAM, 7th Bart. (1627) [E.]; *d.* 1851; and had issue 1*a*
to 2*a*.

1*a*. *Sir Thomas Palmer, 6th Bart.* [*E.*], d. *unm.* 16 *Ap.* 1817.

2*a*. *Caroline Sophia Palmer*, d. *Nov.* 1874; m. 21 *July* 1827, *Col. Robert
Close, H.E.I.C.S.*, d. *Jan.* 1857; *and had issue* 1*b to* 3*b*.
1*b*. *Barry Maxwell Close*, d. 1873.
2*b*. Vere Henry Close, *late* Capt. 90th Regt.
3*b*. Sophia Caroline Close (*The Close, Lichfield*), m. 23 Dec. 1856, Henry
Orlando Bridgeman; *b.* 26 Jan. 1825; *d.s.p.* 14 June 1879.

[Nos. 423 to 424.

18. Descendants of Sir JOHN HENRY PALMER, 7th Bart. [E.] (see
Table III.), *b.* 11 Ap. 1775; *d.* 26 Aug. 1865; *m.* 3 May 1808,
the Hon. MARY GRACE, da. of Lewis (Thomas) WATSON, 2nd
Baron Sondes [G.B.], *b.* 29 Dec. 1786; *d.* 24 Nov. 1853; and
had issue 1*a* to 4*a*.

1*a*. *Sir Geoffrey Palmer, 8th Bart.* [*E.*], b. 9 *June* 1809; d. *unm.* 10 *Feb.*
1892.

2*a*. Rev. Sir Lewis Henry Palmer, 9th Bart. [E.], sometime (1843–1878) Rector
of East Carlton (*Carlton Park, near Rockingham; Carlton Curlieu, co. Leicester*),
b. 16 Aug. 1818.

3*a*. *Grace Palmer*, d. 21 *Oct.* 1890; m. *as 1st wife*, 30 *Sept.* 1846, *the Right
Rev. Edward Trollope, Lord Bishop Suffragan of Nottingham, D.D.*, b. 15 *Ap.* 1817;
d. 11 *Dec.* 1893; *and had issue* 1*b to* 2*b*.
1*b*. Mary Grace Trollope (*Woodford, Thrapston*), m. 10 Oct. 1867, Sir Richard
Lewis De Capell-Brooke, 4th Bart. (1803) [U.K.], *b.* 7 Ap. 1831; *d.* 3 Feb. 1892;
and has issue 1*c* to 4*c*.
1*c*. Sir Arthur Richard De Capell-Brooke, 5th Bart. [U.K.], J.P., C.C., High
Sheriff, co. Rutland, 1899 (*Great Oakley Hall, Kettering, &c.*), *b.* 12 Oct. 1869; *m.*
25 Feb. 1897, Fanny Cecil Talbot, da. of Capt. Duncan McNeill of Dransay Park.
2*c*. Edward Geoffrey De Capell-Brooke, *b.* 31 Jan. 1880.
3*c*. Mary Charlotte De Capell-Brooke.
4*c*. Caroline Sophia De Capell-Brooke.

2*b*. Caroline Julia Trollope, *m.* 27 June 1871, Wyrley Peregrine Birch (*Cranford, co. Northants*); and has issue 1*c* to 3*c*.
1*c*. Lewis Henry Peregrine Birch, *b.* 22 Ap. 1873.
2*c*. Geoffrey Cecil Peregrine Birch, *b.* 1884.
3*c*. Evelyn Audrey Grace Birch.

4*a*. *Theodosia Mary Palmer*, d. 27 *Sept.* 1868; m. *as 1st wife*, 19 *Feb.* 1846,
the Rev. George Edmond Maunsell of Thorpe Malsor, b. 6 *Ap.* 1816; d. 29 *Oct.*
1875; *and had issue*[1] 1*b*.
1*b*. Rev. Cecil Henry Maunsell, M.A. (Oxon.), Lord of the Manor and Patron
of Thorpe Malsor (*Thorpe Malsor Hall, Kettering*), *b.* 9 Jan. 1847.

[Nos. 425 to 435.

---

[1] See the Clarence Volume, p. 50, No. 24022.

The Plantagenet Roll

19. Descendants of the Rev. HENRY PALMER of Withcote Hall, co. Leicester (see Table III.), *b.* 4 Jan. 1780; *d.* 14 Aug. 1856; *m.* 27 June 1816, ELIZABETH, da. of the Rev. Samuel HEYRICK, *d.* 8 Nov. 1860; and had issue 1*a* to 6*a*.

1*a.* Frederick Palmer of Withcote Hall, co. Leicester, J.P., D.L., *late* Capt. 27th Regt. and Col. Comdt. Leicestershire Yeo. Cav. (*Withcote Hall, Oakham; 30 Beaufort Gardens, S.W.*), *b.* 15 July 1825; *m.* 14 Nov. 1850, Mary, da. of William Henry Harrison of Ripon and Ainderby, Yorks, M.P., and sister of the late William Henry Harrison-Broadley, M.P.; and has issue 1*b* to 4*b*.

1*b.* Edward Geoffrey Broadley Palmer, J.P., *formerly* Major 3rd Batt. Leicestershire Regt. (*Burrough, Melton Mowbray; Junior Carlton*), *b.* 14 June 1864; *m.* 8 Jan. 1891, Sibyll Caroline, da. of Capt. William James Smith Neill, R.A., of Barneweill and Swindridge Muir, Ayrshire; and has issue 1*c* to 3*c*.

1*c.* Geoffrey Frederick Neill Palmer, *b.* 20 Sept. 1893.

2*c.* Lewis Henry Palmer, *b.* 27 Jan. 1903.

3*c.* Sibyll Alice Bridget Palmer, *b.* 27 Nov. 1891.

2*b.* Mary Sophia Palmer.

3*b.* Hester Alice Palmer, *m.* 1886, Charles Henry Vane Holder.

4*b.* Emily Heyrick Palmer.

2*a.* Rev. Charles Samuel Palmer, Rector of Eardisley, Rural Dean of Weobley, Canon Residentiary of Hereford and Proctor in Convocation (*Eardisley Rectory, Hereford; The Residence House, Hereford*), *b.* 29 May 1830; *m.* 16 Nov. 1854, Ellen, da. of the Rev. Henry Douglas, Canon of Durham, *d.* 23 July 1905; and has issue 1*b* to 2*b*.

1*b.* Mabel Jane Palmer, *m.* 15 Feb. 1881, Richard Crawshay Bailey (*Pigeon House, Bodenham, Leominster*); and has issue 1*c* to 2*c*.

1*c.* Charles Henry Bailey, *b.* 16 Ap. 1882.

2*c.* Richard Fitzroy Bailey, *b.* 27 Nov. 1883.

2*b.* Margaret Eleanor Palmer, *m.* 23 Ap. 1891, Charles Henry Fehlar Christie (*Chipping Ongar, Essex*); and has issue 1*c* to 4*c*.

1*c.* Alexander Henry Christie, *b.* 20 Mar. 1892.

2*c.* Charles Peroame Christie, *b.* 16 Aug. 1893.

3*c.* Arthur Christie, *b.* 1 Mar. 1896.

4*c.* John Traill Christie, *b.* 19 Oct. 1899.

3*a.* Thomas Palmer, Capt. 47th Regt. and Hon. Major Auxiliary Forces (*Brook House, Eardisley*), *Hereford*, *b.* 8 Dec. 1832; *m.* 20 Sept. 1860, Harriet Elizabeth, da. of Edward Dawson of Whatton House, Leicestershire.

4*a.* Herrick Augustus Palmer, *formerly* Capt. 62nd Regt. and Major Glamorganshire Militia (12 *Grand Parade, St. Leonards-on-Sea, Sussex*), *b.* 23 Sept. 1835; *m.* 21 Nov. 1861, Dorothy Susan, da. of Sir Arthur Grey Hazlerigg, 12th Bart.; and has issue 1*b* to 9*b*.

1*b.* Heyrick Arthur Palmer, *b.* 23 May 1864.

2*b.* Frederick Charles Palmer, Capt. 2nd Vol. Batt. Manchester Regt., *b.* 21 Nov. 1866; *m.* 15 Sept. 1897, Eleanor Annie, da. of Henry Wilson Sharpin, F.R.C.S., of 34 Sillwood Road, Brighton; and has issue 1*c* to 2*c*.

1*c.* Dorothy Esther Palmer, *b.* 1898.

2*c.* Eleanor Evelyn Joan Palmer, *b.* 1904.

3*b.* Robert Henry Palmer, *b.* 19 Feb. 1868.

4*b.* Charles Palmer, *b.* 21 June 1869.

5*b.* Francis Hubert Palmer, *b.* 6 Aug. 1877.

6*b.* Thomas Martival Palmer, *b.* 13 May 1880.

7*b.* Elizabeth Ethel Palmer.

[Nos. 436 to 463.

88

# of The Blood Royal

8b. Barbara Gwendoline Mary Isabel Palmer, *m*. 10 Feb. 1904, Fort Greenwood; and has issue 1c.

1c. Francis Basil Fort Greenwood, *b*. 3 Dec. 1904.

9b. Henrietta Dorothy Palmer.

5a. *Barbara Catherine Palmer, d.* 19 *Feb.* 1895 ; m. 2 *Feb.* 1843, *Lieut.-Col. Joseph Walker Pease of Hesslewood, East Riding, York, J.P., D.L.,* b. 24 *May* 1820 ; d. 22 *Nov.* 1882; *and had issue* 1b *to* 5b.

1b. *Henry Joseph Robinson Pease of Hesslewood, J.P., D.L.,* b. 29 *Dec.* 1843 ; d. 6 *May* 1892 ; m. 15 *Ap.* 1869, *Dora Elizabeth, da. of John Boulderson Barkworth of Raywell, East Yorkshire ; and had issue* 1c *to* 4c.

1c. Joseph Robinson Pease of Hesslewood (*Hesslewood, near Hull*), *b*. 27 Jan. 1873 ; *m*. Aug. 1899, Isabel, da. of [——] Colville.

2c. William Henry Barkworth Robinson Pease, *b*. 21 Sept. 1874 ; *m*.

3c. Godfrey Barton Robinson Pease, *b*. 15 May 1887.

4c. Dora Mary Robinson Pease, *m*. Feb. 1895, Vere D'Oyley Noble.

2b. *Francis Richard Pease, J.P., D.L.,* b. 25 *May* 1848 ; b. 5 *Aug.* 1904 ; m. 15 *Dec.* 1885, *Isabel Mary* (*St. Mary's House, Beverley ;* 17 *Lancaster Gate, S.W.*), *da. of Capt. William Claude Cole-Hamilton of Beltrim, co. Tyrone,* 80*th Regt. ; and had issue* 1c *to* 4c.

1c. Francis Claud Pease, *b*. Nov. 1886.

2c. William Geoffrey Pease, *b*. Jan. 1888.

3c. Isabel Catherine Pease.

4c. Elizabeth Pease.

3b. Barbara Mary Pease (*Thornbury, Shanklin, Isle of Wight*), *m*. 20 Ap. 1876, Rev. William Greville Hazlerigg, Vicar of Billesdon, *b*. 8 June 1847 ; *d*. 1 Nov. 1893 ; and has issue 1c to 5c.

1c. Roger Greville Hazlerigg, *b*. 22 Jan. 1877.

2c. Guy Maynard Hazlerigg, *b*. 1887.

3c. Charlotte Isabel Hazlerigg.

4c. Barbara Henrietta Hazlerigg.

5c. Eleanor Frances Hazlerigg.

4b. Eleanor Louisa Pease, *m*. 29 Jan. 1874, Arthur Hancock Edwards of Pye Nest, Halifax, and Castle Ruins, Fowey, J.P., D.L. (*Pye Nest, Halifax ; Undercliff, Fowey*) ; and has issue 1c to 5c.

1c. Geoffrey Otho Charles Edwards, B.A., *b*. 2 Oct. 1876.

2c. Henry Arthur Rolleston Edwards, *b*. 1881.

3c. Eleanor Churchill Edwards, *m*. 25 June 1900, William Boger of St. Willon, Fowey.

4c. Barbara Florence Edwards.

5c. Winifred Delia Edwards, *m*. 1902, Com. Spencer Allen Hickley, R.N.

5b. Charlotte Emily Pease, *m*. 17 July 1879, Henry Willoughby Trevelyan, late Col. 4th Batt. Duke of Wellington's West Riding Regt. (*Wentworth, Parkstone-on-Sea, Dorset ; Army and Navy*).

6a. *Mary Jemima Palmer, d.* 14 *June* 1898; m. 7 *Oct.* 1847, *Francis Leslie Pym of The Hasels, Beds., and Radwell House, Herts,* b. 14 *Sept.* 1818; d. 23 *Ap.* 1860; *and had issue* 1b *to* 7b.

1b. Francis Pym of The Hasels, Beds., and Radwell House, Herts, J.P., D.L. (*The Hasels, Sandy, Beds.*), *b*. 6 Dec. 1849 ; *m*. 19 July 1891, Alice Conway, da. of Sir George Colthurst, 5th Bart. [I.], M.P.

2b. Frederick William Pym, *b*. 27 Jan. 1859.

3b. Jane Elizabeth Pym (*The Warrens, Feering, Kelvedon, Essex*), *m*. 7 Jan. 1869, the Rev. William Cornish Hunt, Rector of Odell, Beds. ; *d*. 7 Feb. 1891 ; and has issue 1c to 10c. [Nos. 464 to 490.]

89

The Plantagenet Roll

1c. Francis Thomas Hunt, b. 6 Dec. 1879.

2c. Frederick William Hunt, b. 22 Dec. 1881.

3c. Caroline Ethel Jane Hunt, b. 30 Oct. 1869; m. Mar. 1896, Eustace Alban Kenyon, Indian Telegraph Dept.; and has issue 1d to 3d.

1d. William Patrick Kenyon, b. 16 Mar. 1898.

2d. Dorothy Ethel Kenyon, b. 1897.

3d. Violet Mary Kenyon, b. 11 June 1899.

4c. Ida Lucy Hunt, b. 4 Nov. 1870; m. Aug. 1895, Charles Edmund Ashfield.

5c. Florence Mary Hunt, b. 16 July 1872.

6c. Katherine Louisa Hunt, b. 3 Nov. 1873.

7c. Mabel Hunt, b. 14 Aug. 1875.

8c. Isabel Hunt, b. 22 Ap. 1877.

9c. Dorothy Harriet Hunt, b. 25 Oct. 1883.

10c. Ruth Margaret Hunt, b. 24 Ap. 1886.

4b. *Lucy Jemima Pym, d. 16 Sept. 1892; m. 9 Ap. 1874, Lieut.-Col. Harry Godfrey Thornton, late Grenadier Guards; and had issue 1c to 2c.*

1c. Lucy Eleanor Thornton, b. 23 July 1879.

2c. Mary Caroline Thornton, b. 3 Aug. 1880.

5b. Alice Mary Pym.

6b. Eleanor Constance Pym.

7b. Catherine Rose Pym, *m.* 18 June 1890, Rev. Edward Frank Hill, M.A. (Oxon.), Vicar of Shrivenham (*Shrivenham Vicarage, Berks*), s.p.

[Nos. 491 to 508.

20. Descendants of FRANCES MARIA WARREN (see Table III.), b. 6 May 1784; d. 17 Sept. 1837; m. 5 Aug. 1802, George Charles (VENABLES-VERNON), 4th BARON VERNON [G.B.], b. 4 Dec. 1779; d. 18 Nov. 1835; and had issue 1a.

1a. *George John (Venables-Vernon, afterwards (14 Oct. 1837) Warren), 5th Baron Vernon [G.B.], b. 22 June 1803; d. 31 May 1866; m. 1st, 30 Oct. 1824, Isabella Caroline, da. of Cuthbert Ellison of Hebburn, M.P., d. 14 Oct. 1853; and had issue 1b to 5b.*

1b. *Augustus Henry (Venables-Vernon), 6th Baron Vernon [G.B.], b. (at Rome) 1 Feb. 1829; d. 1 May 1883; m. 7 June 1851, Lady Harriet Frances Maria, da. of Thomas William (Anson), 1st Earl of Lichfield [U.K.], b. 26 Dec. 1827; d. 15 Feb. 1898; and had issue 1c to 7c.*

1c. *George William Henry (Venables-Vernon), 7th Baron Vernon [G.B.], b. 25 Feb. 1854; d. 15 Dec. 1898; m. 14 July 1885, Frances Margaret (Pau, France), da. of Francis Lawrance of New York; and had issue 1d to 3d.*

1d. George Francis Augustus (Venables-Vernon), 8th Baron Vernon [G.B.] (*Sudbury Hall, Derby; The Towers, Poynton, Stockport*), b. 28 Sept. 1888.

2d. Hon. Francis William Lawrance Venables-Vernon, R.N., b. 6 Nov. 1889.

3d. Hon. Fanny Lawrance Venables-Vernon.

2c. Hon. William Frederick Cuthbert Venables-Vernon (*Bath; Travellers'*), b. 18 July 1856; *m.* 17 Ap. 1884, Louise, da. of Gen. Daniel Marsh Frost of St. Louis City, U.S.A.; and has issue 1d to 2d.

1d. Richard Henry Venables-Vernon, b. 27 Jan. 1885.

2d. William Walter Venables-Vernon, b. 1890.

3c. Hon. Diana Venables-Vernon, b. 22 Feb. 1852; *m.* 4 May 1896, Charles Edmund Newton (*Mickleover Manor, Derby*).

4c. Hon. Mildred Venables-Vernon, *m.* 2 Nov. 1878, Hon. Henry Augustus Stanhope (*Ashe Warren, Overton, Hants*); and has issue 1d to 3d.

[Nos. 509 to 516.

90

# of The Blood Royal

1d. Hester Stanhope, *b.* 10 Dec. 1879.

2d. Ghita Stanhope, *b.* 26 Nov. 1881.

3d. Cicely Stanhope, *b.* 29 Oct. 1884.

5c. Hon. Margaret Venables-Vernon, *b.* 15 *May* 1865; *d.* 27 *Dec.* 1888; *m.* as 1*st* wife, 4 *Aug.* 1887, *Rev.* Frederick Tufnell, *M.A., Rector of Sudbury (Sudbury Rectory, Derby); and had issue* 1*d.*

1d. Honoria Margaret Tufnell, *b.* 21 Dec. 1888.

6c. Hon. Alice Venables-Vernon, *m.* 1 Feb. 1896, the Rev. Somerset Corry Lowry (*St. Augustin's Vicarage, Bournemouth*); and has issue 1*d.*

1d. Hugh Vernon Lowry, *b.* 3 Feb. 1897.

7c. Hon. Adela Venables-Vernon, *m.* 9 Ap. 1896, Capt. Algernon Horatio Anson, R.N., J.P. (*United Service*); and has issue 1*d* to 2*d.*

1d. John Henry Algernon Anson, *b.* 13 Jan. 1897.

2d. Edward Reynell Anson, *b.* 31 Jan. 1902.

2b. Hon. William John Borlase-Warren-Venables-Vernon, J.P., D.L., Knt. of the Italian Order of St. Maurice and St. Lazarus, and of the Norwegian Order of St. Olaf, Accademico Correspondente della Crusca at Florence, *late* Lieut. Stafford Militia (75 *Eccleston Square, S.W.*), *b.* 1 Ap. 1834; *m.* 1st, 8 May 1855, Agnes Lucy, da. of Sir John Peter Boileau, 1st Bart. [U.K.], *d.* 30 Sept. 1881; 2ndly, 25 Feb. 1884, Annie Georgiana, da. of Charles Eyre of Welford Park, Newbury; and has issue 1*c* to 3*c.*

1c¹. Reginald William Borlase-Warren-Venables-Vernon, *b.* 27 Jan. 1856; *m.* 20 May 1879, Edith Georgiana, da. of William Smith Cowper Cooper of Toddington Park, Harlington, Beds.; and has issue 1*d* to 2*d.*

1d. Agnes Ida Borlase-Warren-Venables-Vernon, *b.* 16 Jan. 1882.

2d. Mabel Eveline Borlase-Warren-Venables-Vernon, *b.* 17 Feb. 1883.

2c². Arnold Borlase-Warren-Venables-Vernon, Midshipman R.N., *b.* 18 Oct. 1887.

3c². Mary Anne Alice Borlase-Warren-Venables-Vernon, *b.* 23 Mar. 1885.

3b. Hon. Caroline Maria Venables-Vernon (*Carfax, Windsor*), *m.* 7 May 1845, the Rev. Frederick Anson, M.A., Canon of Windsor, *b.* 28 Mar. 1811; *d.* 9 Sept. 1885; and has issue 1*c* to 11*c.*

1c. Frederick Henry Anson, M.A., C.E. (72 *St. George's Square, S.W.*), *b.* 3 Dec. 1848; *m.* Aug. 1885, Agnes Henrietta, da. of the Right Hon. Sir Thomas Dyke Acland, 11th Bart.; and has issue 1*d* to 2*d.*

1d. Mary Acland Anson, *b.* 27 Oct. 1886.

2d. Frances Gertrude Acland Anson, *b.* 23 Dec. 1890.

2c. George Edward Anson, M.D., M.R.C.S., L.R.C.P. (*Wellington, New Zealand*), *b.* 20 Sept. 1850; *m.* 1891, Margaret Emily, da. of [———] Greenstreet of Christchurch, New Zealand; and has issue 1*d* to 4*d.*

1d. George Frederick Vernon Anson, *b.* 1892.

2d. Hugo Vernon Anson, *b.* 1894.

3d. Thomas Vernon Anson, *b.* 18—.

4d. Janet Margaret Anson, *b.* 1897.

3c. Rev. Alfred William Anson, Rector of Martinsville, Henry Co., Virginia, U.S.A., *b.* 13 May 1852; *m.* 1st, 29 Ap. 1876, Georgiana Frances, da. of the Rev. W. Greene of Oaklands, Virginia, U.S.A., *d.* 1892; 2ndly, 1894, Ellena, widow of Augustus Greene; and has issue 1*d* to 8*d.*

1d. William Frederick Alfred Anson, *b.* 7 Aug. 1878.

2d. Caroline Frances Anson, *b.* 15 Mar. 1877.

3d. Mary Ellen Anson, *b.* 1880.

4d. Lucy Georgiana Anson, *b.* 1882.

5d. Ethel Laura Anson, *b.* 1884.

6d. Grace Godyn Anson, *b.* 1888.

7d. Hilda Anson, *b.* 1896.

8d. Edith Vernon Anson, *b.* 1898.

The Plantagenet Roll

4c. Walter Vernon Anson, Capt. (ret.) R.N., Sup. of Greenwich Royal Hospital Schools (*United Service*), b. 3 Oct. 1855; m. 1892, Minna Spencer Cowper, da. of Capt. Cowper Coles, C.B., R.N.

5c. Arthur Anson (*Carfax, Hatton, Ceylon*), b. 2 Oct. 1857.

6c. Charles Eustace Anson, M.V.O., Capt. R.N. (*Needwood, The Avenue, Bournemouth*), b. 3 Dec. 1859; m. 17 Oct. 1888, Maria Evelyn, da. of Horatio Senftenberg John Ross, of Portsmouth, d. 11 Feb. 1905; and has issue 1d to 4d.

1d. Frederick Charles Anson, b. 1889.

2d. Horatio St. George Anson, b. 1903.

3d. Edith Anson, b. 1893.

4d. Rachel Anson, b. 1894.

7c. Ernest Anson, M.A., M.I.C.E., b. 26 Sept. 1864; m. 12 Dec. 1903, Katherine, da. of John MacFarlan, *formerly* I.C.S.; and has issue 1d to 2d.

1d. Joan Caroline Anson } twins.
2d. Katharine Anson

8c. Rev. Harold Anson, M.A. (Oxon.), *late* Warden of St. John's College, Auckland, and Chaplain to Bishops of Wellington and Auckland, N.Z. (*Carfax, Windsor*), b. 4 Dec. 1867; m. 6 Oct. 1894, Gwenllian Maud, da. of Henry Langridge, of 54 Victoria Street, S.W.; and has issue 1d to 2d.

1d. Bernard John Evelyn Anson, b. 21 Mar. 1899.

2d. Christine Anson.

9c. Rev. Hugh Richard Anson, M.A. (Oxon.), Vicar of Sandridge (*Sandridge, Herts*), b. 5 Ap. 1869.

10c. Laura Anson.

11c. Adelaide Mary Anson.

4b. Hon. Adelaide Louisa Vernon (*Mount Vernon, Torquay*), m. 12 June 1855, Adm. Sir Reginald John Macdonald of Clanranald, 26th Capt. and Chief of his Clan, K.C.B., K.C.S.I., b. 7 Oct. 1819; d. 15 Dec. 1899; and has issue 1c to 4c.

1c. Allan Douglas Macdonald of Clanranald, 27th Capt. and Chief of his Clan, *late* Capt. R.A., b. Ap. 1856.

2c. Angus Roderick Macdonald, b. Ap. 1858; m. 1884, Leucoline Helen, da. of the Rev. Henry Clarke, M.A.

3c. Adelaide Effrida Macdonald.

4c. Maud Macdonald.

5b. *Hon. Louisa Warren Vernon, b. 12 Aug. 1838; d. 11 Feb. 1894; m. 16 Ap. 1873, the Rev. Thomas Parry Garnier, Canon of Norwich and Rector of Cranworth, d. 17 March 1898; and had issue.*

See the Clarence Volume, p. 509, Nos. 22042–22045.   [Nos. 550 to 574.

21. Descendants of FRANCES WARREN (see Table III.), *bapt.* 17 Nov. 1755; *d.* (at Derby) 22 June 1821, considering herself a widow;[1] *m.* (at Risley, co. Derby) 9 Sept. 1779, Captain AUGUSTUS PARKYNS (who was considered dead in 1814, but who in reality)[1] *d.* (at Lexington, U.S.A.) Nov. 1823; and had issue 1a to 2a.

1a. *Augustus Parkyns, Lieut. R.N., b. c. 1787; d. unm. (at Trowell, co. Notts)* 3 *Jan.* 1811.

2a. *Anne Catherine Parkyns, d. after 1824; m. (at the Bermudas) 13 Jan.*

---

[1] *Ex inform.* G. E. Cokayne, Esq., Clarenceux King of Arms, to whom the Editor is indebted for the particulars relating to her descendants.

# of The Blood Royal

1810, William (not Samuel) Territt of Chilton Hall, co. Suffolk, LL.B. (Trin. Hall, Camb., 1792), LL.D. (1797), Barrister Lincoln's Inn (1791), Advocate Doctors' Commons (8 July 1797), and a Judge of the Vice-Admiralty Court in the Bermudas (1802–1815), b. c. 1769; d. 11 Aug. 1836; and had issue 1b.

1b. Frances Mary Territt, a great beauty, and sometime Bedchamber Woman to Queen Victoria, d. 25 Dec. 1877 ; m. 1st, 4 Oct. 1832, George John Forbes, styled Viscount Forbes, d.v.p. 13 Nov. 1836 ; 2ndly, 15 Dec. 1838, Thomas Nugent Vaughan, J.P., d. (in Dublin) 14 Sept. 1847 ; and had issue 1c to 4c.

1c. } Sons by 1st husband. See the Clarence Volume, pp. 74–75, Nos. 60–85.
2c. }

3c. [——] Vaughan, b. 28 Nov. 1844.

4c. Frances Edith Vaughan, younger da., m. (at Hove) 15 Jan. 1873, Thomas Guy Paget, only son of John Paget of The Boltons, Kensington.

[Nos. 575 to 602.

22. Descendants of the Hon. WILLIAM COCKAYNE of Rushton Hall, co. Northants (see Table III.), b. 16 Ap. 1756 ; d. 8 Oct. 1809 ; m. 11 Oct. 1777, BARBARA (afterwards (1801) COCKAYNE-MEDLYCOTT), da. and eventually sole heir of George HILL of Rothwell Manor, co. Northants, the King's most ancient Ser-jeant-at-Arms, b. 19 May 1753 ; d. 2 June 1838 ; and had issue 1a to 5a.

1a. Hon. (R.W. 23 Sept. 1836) Matilda Sophia Cockayne, b. 13 Feb. 1779 ; d. 23 Feb. 1869 ; m. 31 Dec. 1804, the Rev. Robert Austen of Hadwell Lodge, co. Cork, LL.D., Prebendary of Cloyne and Rector of Midleton, co. Cork, b. Oct. 1771 ; d. 4 Nov. 1854 ; and had issue 1b to 3b.

1b. Frances Matilda Austen, b. 2 Ap. 1807 ; d. 5 Jan. 1892 ; m. 14 Feb. 1830, Robert Uniacke Penrose, afterwards (1834) Penrose-FitzGerald of Corkbeg and Lisquinlan, co. Cork, b. 1 July 1800 ; d. 11 June 1857 ; and had issue 1c to 4c.

1c. Sir Robert Uniacke Penrose-FitzGerald, now (R.L. 26 June 1896) Uniacke-Penrose-FitzGerald, 1st Bart. (1896) [U.K.], M.P., J.P., D.L., Hon. Col. 9th Batt. King's Roy. Rifle Corps (Corkbeg Island, Whitegate, co. Cork ; 35 Grosvenor Road, S.W.), b. 9 July 1839 ; m. 13 Sept. 1867, Jane Emily, da. of Gen. Sir William John Codrington, G.C.B., M.P.

2c. Charles Cooper Penrose-FitzGerald, now (R.L. 26 June 1896) Uniacke-Penrose-FitzGerald, Admiral R.N., b. 30 Ap. 1841 ; m. 29 Nov. 1882, Henrietta Elizabeth, da. of the Rev. Francis Hewson of Lunganstown ; and has issue 1d to 4d.

1d. Robert Francis Uniacke Uniacke-Penrose-FitzGerald, b. 8 Sept. 1886.

2d. John Uniacke Penrose-FitzGerald, b. 27 July 1888.

3d. Mary Elizabeth Uniacke-Penrose-FitzGerald.

4d. Laura Frances Uniacke-Penrose-FitzGerald.

3c. James Henry Brabazon Penrose-FitzGerald (Midleton, co. Cork), b. 1 July 1843 ; m. 1 May 1886, Louisa Josephine, da. of the Rev. John Dennis Penrose of Woodhill; and has issue 1d to 5d.

1d. Charles Bryan Penrose-FitzGerald, b. 3 Dec. 1887.

2d. Edward Uniacke-Penrose-FitzGerald, b. 18 Dec. 1888.

3d. Herbert James Cooper Penrose-FitzGerald, b. 15 Aug. 1891.

4d. Maurice John Penrose-FitzGerald, b. 8 Ap. 1894.

5d. Nesta Fanny Harriet Penrose-FitzGerald.

4c. Fanny Louisa Geraldine Penrose-FitzGerald, b. 27 Jan. 1846, unm.

2b. Anna Matilda Austen (Ballynoe, Queenstown, Cork), m. 4 Aug. 1845, Gen. Edmund Roche of Ballymonis, J.P., 3rd Light Dragoons, d. Ap. 1897 ; and has issue 1c.

[Nos. 603 to 616.

93
N

₩ₕₑ Plantagenet Roll

1c. Caroline Matilda Georgiana Roche (8 *Raby Place, Bath*), *m.* 2 Dec. 1874, Lieut.-Col. Joseph Edward Lucas Thackwell of Aghada Hall, J.P., *b.* 23 Jan. 1853; *d.* 16 Dec. 1886; and has issue 1*d* to 5*d*.

1d. Walter Joseph de Rupe Thackwell, B.A. (T.C.D.), Capt. Tipperary Art. (*Aghada Hall, Rostellan, co. Cork; Coneragh, near Youghal*), *b.* 12 July 1876.

2d. Noel Edmund Osbert Thackwell, Lieut. R.G.A., *b.* 16 Dec. 1878.

3d. Edward Hillyar Roche Thackwell, *late* Lieut. East Lancashire Regt., *b.* 15 Nov. 1879.

4d. Arthur Charles Austen Thackwell, Lieut. Indian Army, *b.* 17 Nov. 1882.

5d. Violet Caroline Josephine Thackwell, *m.* 3 June 1902, Major Sinclair Francis Kirkwood.

3b. Caroline Sophia Austen, *unm.*

2a. Hon. (*R.W.* 4 *Sept.* 1838) *Mary Anne Cockayne*, b. 11 *Dec.* 1781; d. 16 *June* 1873; m. 6 *Ap.* 1811, *William Adams of Thorpe, co. Surrey, LL.D., Advocate in Doctors' Commons*, b. 13 *Jan.* 1772; d. 11 *June* 1851; *and had issue* 1*b* to 6*b*.

1b. Borlase Hill Adams, M.A. (Oxon.), Bar.-at-Law, J.P., *b.* 4 Ap. 1817; *m.* 2ndly, 18 Aug. 1874, Mary Anne, da. of the Rev. William Brown Staveley, B.A., Rector of High Halden; and has issue 1*c* to 4*c*.

1c. James Edwin Cokayne Adams, Bar.-at-Law, *b.* 3 Dec. 1876

2c. Violet Eleanor Cokayne Adams, *b.* 6 June 1875.

3c. Lettice Mary Cokayne Adams, *b.* 10 Sept. 1878.

4c. Patience Georgiana Cokayne Adams, *b.* 6 Dec. 1879.

2b. Rev. Henry Willoughby Adams, M.A. (Oxon.), sometime (1863–1891) Rector of Great Parndon, *b.* 15 June 1820.

3b. George Edward Adams, now (R.L. 15 Aug. 1873) Cokayne, M.A. (Oxon.), Clarenceux King of Arms, 1894, &c., &c. (*Exeter House, Roehampton*), *b.* 29 Ap. 1825; *m.* 2 Dec. 1856, Mary Dorothea, sister of Henry, 1st Baron Aldenham [U.K.], da. of George Henry Gibbs of Aldenham House, co. Herts, &c., *d.* 11 Mar. 1906; and has issue.

See the Clarence Volume, p. 158, Nos. 2445–2448.

4b. Georgiana Catherine Adams, b. 29 *Jan.* 1815; d. 27 *Sept.* 1879; m. 4 *June* 1839, *the Rev. George Adams, B.D.* (*Oxon.*), *Rector of Farndon, Northants*, 1838–1855, b. Oct. 1805; d. 17 *Jan.* 1855; *and had issue* 1*c* to 4*c*.

1c. Edward Willoughby Adams, Lieut.-Col. (ret.) R.A., *b.* 20 Nov. 1844, *unm.*

2c. George Hill Adams, B.A. (Camb.), *b.* 4 Dec. 1845, *unm.*

3c. Mary Anne Adams, *b.* 10 Aug. 1847, *unm.*

4c. Margaret Eliza Adams, *b.* 30 May 1850, *unm.*

5b. Louisa Anne Adams, b. 10 *Sept.* 1818; d. 17 *Ap.* 1897; m. 6 *May* 1845, *Henry Hucks (Gibbs), 1st Baron Aldenham [U.K.], F.S.A., &c., &c.* (*Aldenham House, co. Herts; St. Dunstan's, Regent's Park*); *and had issue.*

See the Clarence Volume, pp. 156–157, Nos. 2401–2424.

6b. Eliza Adams, *b.* 31 Aug. 1833, *unm.*

3a. Hon. (*R.W.* 23 *Sept.* 1836) *Caroline Eliza Cockayne*, b. 17 *Oct.* 1787; d. 12 *Mar.* 1860; m. 6 *Ap.* 1811, *Thomas Philip Maunsell of Thorpe Malsor, M.P.*, d. 4 *Mar.* 1866; *and had issue.*

See the Clarence Volume, p. 570, Nos. 24022–24041.

4a. Frances Annabella Cockayne, b. 21 *July* 1795; d. 25 *July* 1835; m. 9 *Aug.* 1816, *William Assheton of Downham Hall and Cuerdale, J.P., D.L.*, d. 8 *Aug.* 1858; *and had issue.*

See the Clarence Volume, p. 123, Nos. 1411–1426.

5a. Elizabeth Charlotte Cockayne (*tenth and youngest da.*), b. 9 *June* 1798; d. 21 *Ap.* 1883; m. 14 *Feb.* 1825, *the Hon. Edmund Sexton Pery*, d. 31 Dec. 1860; *and had issue.*

See the Clarence Volume, pp. 560–561, Nos. 23736–23748.   [Nos. 617 to 712.

# of The Blood Royal

23. Descendants of the Hon. CATHERINE COKAYNE (see Table III.), b. 5 Jan. 1688; bur. 26 Nov. 1716; m. as 1st wife, 13 Mar. 1712, WILLIAM DOWDESWELL of Pull Court, High Sheriff co. Worcester 1726, bur. 30 Aug. 1728; and had issue 1a.[1]

1a. *Frances Dowdeswell, only surv. ch. of her mother*, bapt. (*at St. James', Westminster*) 9 Nov. 1713; d. *about* 1775, *will dated* 9 *Aug., proved* 2 *Dec. that year*; m. *in or before* 1736, *William Basil, previously Ball*[2] *of Wilton Park, co. Bucks, and Drumboe Castle, co. Donegal*, d. 4 *Oct.* 1755, *will dated* 4 *Mar.* 1752, *proved* 1 *Oct.* 1755; *and had issue* 1b *to* 13b.

  1b. *Martin Basil, Capt. 18th Dragoons* (1759), bapt. *Jan.* 1737; *matric. St. Edmund's Hall, Oxon.*, 5 *Mar.* 1754, *aged* 17; d. *unm.* (*in Germany*); *admon.* 28 *Aug.* 1760 *to mother.*

  2b. [*son*] *Basil*, b. (*at Wilton*) 19 *Mar.* 1742.

  3b. *William Basil*, bapt. (*at St. James', Westm.*) 27 *Sept.* 1743.

  4b. *Gilbert Basil*, b. (*at St. James', Westm.*) 15 *Feb.* 1745.

  5b. *Edmund Basil of Newhouse, co. Bucks, twin*, b. (*at St. James', Westm.*) 14 *Nov.* 1746; d. (*app. s.p.*) 14 *Dec.* 1779.[3]

  6b. *Gabriel Basil, twin*, b. (*at St. James', Westm.*) 14 *Nov.* 1746; *matric. Pembroke Coll., Oxon.*, 21 *Mar.* 1765, *aged* 18; *living* 9 *Aug.* 1775.

  7b. *Thomas Basil*, bapt. 11 *Aug.* 1748.

  8b. *George Basil*, bapt. 20 *Oct.* 1749, *living* 12 *Ap.* 1779.

  9b. *Frances Basil*, b. 26 *June* (*and bapt. at St. James'* 13 *July*) 1738; *living* 9 *Aug.* 1775, *and then wife of Charles Byne, by whom she is believed to have had issue.*

  10b. *Mary Basil, called da. and h. by Burke and Foster*, b. 11 (*and bapt. at St. Ann's, Soho,* 26) *July* 1739; d. *before* 9 *Aug.* 1775; m. 17 *Ap.*[4] 1768, *Sir Samuel Hayes, 1st Bart.* [I.], d. 21 *July* 1807; *and had issue* 1c *to* 3c.

    1c. *Sir Samuel Hayes, 2nd Bart.* [I.], d. 16 *Sept.* 1827; m. *Aug.* 1803, *Elizabeth, da. of Sir Thomas Lighton, 1st Bart.* [I.], d. 18 *Jan.* 1848; *and had issue* 1d *to* 4d.

      1d. *Sir Edmund Samuel Hayes, 3rd Bart.* [I.], *M.P.*, b. 2 *July* 1806; d. 30 *June* 1860; m. 3 *July* 1837, *Emily, da. of the Hon. Sir Hercules Pakenham, K.C.B.*, d. 21 *Ap.* 1883; *and had issue* 1e *to* 9e.

        1e. *Sir Samuel Hercules Hayes, 4th Bart.* [I.], b. 3 *Feb.* 1840; d. 7 *Nov.* 1891; m. 25 *July* 1878, *the Hon. Alice Anne, da. of James* (*Hewitt*), *4th Viscount Lifford* [I.]; *and had issue* 1f.

          1f. *Alice Emily Hayes* (*Drumboe Castle, Stranorlar, co. Donegal*), b. 29 *June* 1879.

        2e. *Sir Edmund Francis Hayes, 5th Bart.* [I.] (*Como, Sydney, New South Wales; Drumboe Castle, Stranorlar, co. Donegal*), b. 1850; m. 1900, *Alice, da. of Judge Wilkinson of Sydney, N.S.W.*

        3e. *Emily Anne Hayes* (*Purbrook Lodge, Cosham, Hants*). [Nos. 713 to 715.]

---

[1] The Editor is indebted to G. E. Cokayne, Esq., Clarenceux King of Arms, and to H. Houston Ball, Esq., for the above information concerning the descendants (other than those of Mrs. Hayes *née* Basil) of the Hon. Catherine Dowdeswell *née* Cokayne.

[2] He was devisee of the estate of Martin Caulfield Basil of Wilton Park, Treasurer to King James II. and VII., in whose will, dated 24 Sept. 1730, proved 20 Nov. 1735, he is styled "his dear Godson William Basil, whose name by a late Act of Parliament is changed from William Ball."

[3] His will, dated 13 Ap. 1779, was proved 22 Dec. 1779, and mentions his brother George B., "who has lived an extravagant life for several years," and his dear sister Anne (? if it should not be Amy). Samuel Hayes of Leicester Fields, husband of his late sister Mary, is an executor. The residue to be divided between his said sister Anne and the said Samuel Hayes and their heirs.

[4] On Monday, Samuel Hayes of Lincoln's Inn Fields, Surgeon, to Miss Basil of Henrietta Street, Cavendish Square. *Gazetteer*, Saturday, 22 Ap. 1768.

The Plantagenet Roll

4e. *Mary Frances Hayes*, d. 1876 ; m. 17 *Ap.* 1872, *James Paterson of Whitelee, Roxburgh ; and had issue.*

5e. Catherine Hayes, ⎫
6e. Alice Caroline Hayes, ⎬ *(Purbrook Lodge, Cosham, Hants).*

7e. Emma Agnes Hayes, *m.* 20 Sept. 1879, Lieut.-Col. William Woods, *formerly* Comdg. Hants Imp. Yeo. *(Warnford Park, Bishops Waltham ; Whitley Hall, Wigan ;* 10 *Ashley Gardens, S.W.*); and has issue 1*f* to 2*f*.

    1*f.* Henry Charles Woods, Lieut. Grenadier Guards, *b.* 1881.

    2*f.* Edmund William Woods, *b.* 1886.

8e. Georgina Mary Anne Hayes, ⎫
9e. Louisa Lydia Hayes, ⎬ *(Purbrook Lodge, Cosham, Hants).*

2d. *Anne Hayes*, m. 11 *Feb.* 1829, *the Rev. Robert Traill, Rector of Skull, co. Cork,* b. 15 *July* 1793 ; *d.* 1847 ; *and had issue.*

3d. *Harriet Hayes.*

4d. *Mary Hayes*, d. 1874 ; m. 6 *Ap.* 1832, *Francis Mansfield of Castle Wray and Ardrummon House, co. Donegal, J.P.,* b. 9 *Nov.* 1796 ; *d.* 1884 ; *and had issue* 1*e to* 5*e.*

1e. Francis Stewart Mansfield of Castle Wray, B.A., J.P., D.L., Lieut.-Col. 5th Batt. Royal Inniskilling Fusiliers *(Castle Wray, Letterkenny, co. Donegal),* b. 26 Feb. 1833 ; *m.* 1861, Anna Philippa, da. of George Simon Harcourt, M.P. ; and has issue 1*f* to 7*f*.

    1*f. Francis Harcourt Mansfield, b.* Sept. 1861.

    2*f. Ralph Chandos Henniker Mansfield, b.* Sept. 1862.

    3*f. Henry Bevan Mansfield, b.* May 1865.

    4*f. Robert Mansfield, b.* Nov. 1869.

    5*f. Jessy Gertrude Anne Mansfield, m.* 1887, George Rawdon Maurice Hewson, J.P.

    6*f. Isabel Mary Mansfield, m.* 12 Aug. 1896, Sir Harry Jocelyn Urquhart Stewart, 11th Bart. [I.] *(Fort Stewart, Ramelton, co. Donegal);* and has issue 1*g* to 6*g*.

        1*g.* William Francis Stewart, *b.* 6 Oct. 1901.

        2*g.* Jocelyn Harry Stewart, *b.* 1903.

        3*g.* Isabel Stewart.

        4*g.* Kathleen Mary Stewart.

        5*g.* Hester Anna Lilian Stewart.

        6*g.* Violet Mary Stewart.

    7*f.* Emily Anna Philippa Mansfield.

2e. *James Charles Henry Mansfield,* b. *May* 1841 ; *d. (? s.p.)* 28 *Feb.* 1889 ; *m. Jane, da. of Dr. Coates, M.D.*

3e. Edmund Christopher Mansfield, J.P., *b.* May 1851 ; *m.* 1890, Minnie Frances, da. of Surg.-Major Ovens of Aghnagaddy House, co. Donegal, J.P., 5th Dragoon Guards ; and has issue 1*f*.

    1*f. Edmund Francis Hayes Mansfield, b.* 1891.

4e. Eliza Mansfield.

5e. Mary Jane Mansfield.

2c. *Mary Hayes*, d. (−) ; m. *the Rev. Andrew Thomas Hamilton, brother of Gen. Sir John James Hamilton, 1st Bart.* (1814) [*U.K.*].

3c. *Frances Hayes*, d. (−); m. 26 *Jan.* 1799, *John Boyd of Ballymacool, co. Donegal,* b. 20 *Aug.* 1769 ; *d.* 1836 ; *and had issue* 1*d to* 3*d.*

    1d. *Mary Boyd*, d. 1886 ; m. *William H. Porter*, d. 1883 ; *and had issue* 1*e.*

    1e. William Henry Porter, now (R.L. 1891) Boyd, J.P., D.L. *(Ballymacool, Letterkenny, co. Donegal),* b. 1843 ; *m.* 1879, Charlotte Agnes, da. of Col. James Henry Dopping, J.P. ; and has issue 1*f* to 7*f*.

[Nos. 716 to 741.

# of The Blood Royal

1*f*. John Dopping Boyd, *b*. 14 Feb. 1886.
2*f*. William Henry Ker Porter Boyd, *b*. 4 Feb. 1890.
3*f*. Charles Knox Basil Boyd, *b*. 2 June 1892.
4*f*. Mary Rosalie Boyd, *b*. 8 June 1880.
5*f*. Helen Boyd, *b*. 17 Ap. 1882.
6*f*. Agnes Boyd, *b*. 18 Ap. 1888.
7*f*. Haidee Boyd, *b*. 4 June 1891.
   2*d*. *Anna Maria Boyd*, d. (–); m. *William Stewart Ross of Sheep Hill, co.
Derry.*
   3*d*. *Isabella Boyd*, d. (–); m. *John Robinson.*
   11*b*. *Honour Charlotte Basil*, b. 19 *Mar*. (*and* bapt. *at St. Anne's, Soho*, 12 *Ap.*)
1742.
   12*b*. *Amy Basil*, b. 11 *May* (*and* bapt. *at St. James', Westm.*, 20 *June*) 1751.
   13*b*. *Anne Basil*,[1] *living* 13 *Ap.* 1779.   [Nos. 742 to 748.

24. Descendants, if any, of WILLIAM WHITELOCKE of Phyllis Court,
co. Oxon., M.P. (see Table IV.), *d*. 27 July 1709; *m*. ANNE,
da. and co-h. of Edward NOEL (? NOWELL), of the Inner
Temple, Secretary to the Excise Commissioners; and had
issue 1*a*.

   1*a*. *Anne Whitelocke*,[2] d. *Ap.* 1699; m. *G. Cooper; and had issue* (*at least*) 1*b*.
   1*b*. *Rev. Edward Cooper of Phyllis Court, D.C.L., Preb. of Bath and Wells and
Vicar of Sonning*, d. [–]; m. 1769, *Jane, da. of* [———] *Leigh* (*a younger son of
Theophilus L. of Adlestrop*); *and had issue* (*at least*) 1*c*.
   1*c*. *Rev. Edward Cooper, Fellow of All Souls, as founder's Kin, Rector of
Hamstall Ridward*, d. (–); m. *Caroline Isabella, only da. of Philip Lybbe Powys
of Hardwick, co. Oxon.; and had issue* 1*d*.
   1*d*. *Rev. Edward Philip Cooper, Vicar of Little Dalby, co. Leicester*, d. (–);
m. 1825, *Caroline Louisa, eld. da. of Philip Lybbe Powys of Hardwick; and had
issue* 1*e to* 2*e*.
   1*e*. *Edith Cassandra Cooper*, ? d. *unm.*
   2*e*. *Sophia Mary Leigh Cooper*, ? d. *unm.*

25. Descendants, if any, of MARY WHITELOCKE, wife of WILLIAM
HARMAR of the Middle Temple; HESTER WHITELOCKE, wife
of EDWARD SHERWOOD of Henreth, co. Bucks; of ELIZABETH
WHITELOCKE,[3] *d*. 1735, wife of WILLIAM WISEMAN of
Sparsholt Court, co. Bucks, *b*. 1652; *d*. 1713; and of DIANA
WHITELOCKE, das. of Sir William WHITELOCKE of Phyllis
Court, Oxon., M.P. (see Table IV.).

---

   [1] Query, if she was not identical with 12*b*.
   [2] In Burke's "Irish Landed Gentry" (1899, p. 268) she is stated to have *d.v.p.*
(and app. *unm.*) Ap. 1699, but in the same author's "Visitation of the Seats and
Arms of the Nobility," &c. (1855, p. 72), she is said to have married and had issue
as above.
   [3] She had issue a da. and h. Mary, who *d*. 1740, having *m*. Edward Clarke of
Ardington, and had issue a son, William Wiseman Clarke, who *m*. twice and had
issue, William Nelson (by 2nd wife), and Dorothy Maria (by 1st wife).

The Plantagenet Roll

26. Descendants, if any, of FRANCES WHITELOCKE, *bapt.* 30 Dec. 1635, and of ELIZABETH WHITELOCKE, *bapt.* 11 Jan. 1637 (see Table IV.), elder sisters of the above-named Sir William Whitelocke of Phyllis Court.

27. Descendants of the Rev. NEVILL WALTER, Rector of Burgh Apton and the Mediety of Holveston, Norfolk, B.C.L. (Oxon.) (see Table IV.), *d.* 1802; *m.* RACHEL, da. of George HAMILTON, M.P. (sixth son of James, 6th Earl of Abercorn [S.]), *d.* (–); and had issue 1*a*.[1]

1*a*. *Jane Walter*, d. 11 *May* 1848; m. *the Rev. Walter Robert Churchman Kellet, afterwards Long, P.C. and Patron of Dunston* 1796–1841; b. 1762; d. 4 Feb. 1841; *and had issue* 1*b* *to* 2*b*.

1*b*. *Robert Kellet Long of Dunston Hall, J.P., D.L., M.A. (Camb.)*, b. 4 *May* 1804; d. 26 *Feb.* 1874; m. 16 *Mar.* 1843, *Maria Louisa, da. of William Fortescue of Writtle Lodge, Essex*, d. 26 Oct. 1846; *and had issue* 1*c* *to* 3*c*.

1*c*. Fortescue Walter Kellet Long, Lord of the Manor of Dunston, M.A. (Oxon.) (*Dunston Hall, near Norwich*), b. 11 Dec. 1843.

2*c*. Rev. Charles Hamilton Kellet Long, B.A. (Camb.), Vicar of Swinderby (*Swinderby Vicarage, co. Lincoln*), b. 19 Ap. 1845; *m.* 11 Mar. 1873, Edith Mary, da. of Edward Lyon of Johnen Hall, Eccleshall; and has issue 1*d* to 7*d*.

1*d*. Ernest Kellet Long, b. 15 Jan. 1874.
2*d*. Edward Fortescue Long, b. 4 Dec. 1876.
3*d*. *Walter Neville Long*, b. 2 *Mar.* 1882; d. (–).
4*d*. Ethel Long.
5*d*. Mary Long.
6*d*. Alice Dormer Long.
7*d*. Dorothy Long.

3*c*. Rev. Ernest Henry Kellet Long, M.A. (Oxon.), Rector of Newton Flotman (*Newton Flotman Rectory, Norfolk*), b. 7 Oct. 1846; *m.* 31 Jan. 1877, Elizabeth Margaret Beresford, da. of the Rev. John George Beresford of Bedale; and has issue 1*d* to 7*d*.

1*d*. Basil Kellett Long, b. 28 Feb. 1878.
2*d*. John Beresford Long, b. 20 Feb. 1879.
3*d*. William Fortescue Long, b. 24 May 1880.
4*d*. Walter Denman Long, b. 22 Sept. 1881.
5*d*. Charles Ernest Long, b. 21 Nov. 1882.
6*d*. Margaret Marie Long, b. 27 Feb. 1884.
7*d*. Nellie Nevill Long, b. 25 Aug. 1886.

2*b*. *Rev. Henry Churchman Long, B.A. (Camb.), Vicar of Dunston* 1841–1884, b. 10 *Jan.* 1809; d. 21 *Ap.* 1884; m. 18 *Sept.* 1838, *Charlotte Emma, da. of Gen. Sir Robert John Harvey, K.C.B.*, d. (–); *and had issue* 1*c* to 6*c*.

1*c*. Octavius Nevill Long, b. 30 Dec. 1857.
2*c*. Emma Julia Long, b. 10 July 1839.
3*c*. Beatrice Jane Long, b. 26 Mar. 1849.
4*c*. Alma Long, b. 28 Oct. 1855.
5*c*. Cecilia Long, b. 22 Feb. 1860.
6*c*. Magdelena Long, b. 6 Mar. 1863.   [Nos. 749 to 770.

---

[1] Foster's "Our Noble and Gentle Families and Royal Descent," i. p. 18.

# of The Blood Royal

28. Descendants of CHARLOTTE WALTER (see Table IV.), *d.* (-);
m. as 2nd wife, 1768, ASCANIUS WILLIAM SENIOR of Pilewell,
Hants, and Cannon Hill House, Berks; and had issue 1*a*
to 2*a*.[1]

1*a*. *Nevillia Senior,* d. 17 Dec. 1842; m. 2 *Jan.* 1792, *Lieut.-Gen. William
Thomas of Brockhill, Devon, Col.* 41*st Regt.,* b. 1760; d. 20 *Jan.* 1848; *and had
issue* 1*b* to 3*b.*

1*b. William Nevill Thomas,* b. 28 *June* 1801; d. 3 *Mar.* 1878; m. 1 *July* 1846,
Frances Bent, da. of [——] *Smith of Bideford, M.D.; and had issue* 1*c* to 2*c.*

1*c.* Fleming Thomas, *b.* 3 Sept. 1851; *m.* 26 Feb. 1880, Annetta Moyse, da. of
John Walters Williams.

2*c.* Nevillia Thomas.

2*b. Rev. Charles Ascanius Nevill Thomas, curate of Chudleigh,* b. 4 *June* 1811;
d. 21 *Ap.* 1867; m. 19 *Nov.* 1850, *Elizabeth, da. of Adm. William Isaac Scott of
Chudleigh, R.N.,* d. *Nov.* 1854; *and had issue* 1*c.*

1*c.* Ascanius William Nevill Thomas, Capt. 20th Hussars, 1881, *b.* 5 Nov. 1853;
m. 1 May 1877, Rose Valentine, da. of Charles William Morice of Feltham; and
has issue 1*d.*

1*d.* Nevillia Thomas.

3*b. Charlotte Elizabeth Josephine Thomas,* b. 2 *Feb.* 1806; d. 12 *Jan.* 1876;
m. 31 *Aug.* 1836, *the Rev. Dashwood Lang, Vicar of Westleigh,* d. 19 *Mar.* 1874;
and had issue 1*c* to 5*c.*

1*c.* Rev. William Francis Dashwood Lang, M.A. (Oxon.) (*Lisburne, Torquay*),
b. 26 Ap. 1842; *m.* 19 May 1881, Anne Diana, da. of Adm. John William Montagu;
s.p.s.

2*c.* Edwin Arthur Lang (*Darara, India*), *b.* 2 Aug. 1845; *m.* 15 Jan. 1873,
Kathleen Evelyn, da. of Henry Gloster French of Roscommon; and has issue
1*d* to 3*d.*

1*d.* Arthur Nevill Dashwood Lang, *b.* 13 Oct. 1873.

2*d.* Donald Horace Lang, *b.* 13 Sept. 1875.

3*d.* Harold de Freyne Lang, *b.* 18 Aug. 1882.

3*c.* Charles Augustus Lang (*Vigo House, Weybridge*), *b.* 1 Oct. 1847; *m.*
30 Sept. 1871, Ellen Rhoda, da. of Frederick Jones of London; and has issue
1*d* to 5*d.*

1*d.* Charles Frederick Dashwood Lang, *b.* 22 Feb. 1874.

2*d.* Augustus Bernard Dashwood Lang, *b.* 9 Mar. 1881.

3*d.* Winifred Nevillia Lang.

4*d.* Theodora Josephine Lang.

5*d.* Agatha Phyllis Lang.

4*c.* Helen Nevillia Lang, *b.* 28 May 1839; *m.* 24 Oct. 1861, Charles Shea
Giles, R.N. (*South Hill Park, Hampstead*); and has issue 1*d* to 7*d.*

1*d.* Rev. Arthur Linzee Giles, Vicar of Okehampton, *b.* 25 Nov. 1864; *m.* 1902,
Dorothea Mary, widow of Michael Williams of Gnaton Hall, South Devon, J.P.,
da. of Edward S. Carus Wilson of Penmount, J.P.

2*d.* Ernest Nevill Giles, *b.* 19 Jan. 1866.

3*d.* Reginald Hood Giles, *b.* 5 Nov. 1871.

4*d.* Cecil Dashwood Giles, *b.* 29 Jan. 1875.

5*d.* Herbert Shea Giles, *b.* 2 Jan. 1879.

6*d.* Florence Nevillia Giles.

7*d.* Helen Frances Giles.   [Nos. 771 to 793.

---

[1] Foster's " Our Noble and Gentle Families and Royal Descent," i. pp. 17–18.

The Plantagenet Roll

5c. Mary Frances Dottin Lang, *b.* 19 Sept. 1840; *m.* 26 Ap. 1862, Sidney Higgs Craven (*Bickley, Kent*); and has issue 1*d* to 4*d*.

    1*d*. Sidney Dashwood Craven, *b.* 10 July 1863.

    2*d*. Arthur Nevill Craven, *b.* 22 Dec. 1866.

    3*d*. Gertrude Craven, *m.* 1904, Richard Valpy (*Kimberley, South Africa*).

    4*d*. Agnes Edith Josephine Craven.

2*a*. *Charlotte Maria Senior*, d. 29 *July* 1798; m. *as* 1*st wife*, 19 *Aug.* 1790, *Gen. Francis Fuller*, d. (*at Versailles*) 26 *May* 1841; *and had issue* 1*b to* 3*b*.

    1*b*. *Francis Fuller, Lieut.-Col. comdg.* 59*th Regt.* 1834, b. 28 *May* 1791; d. 27 *May* 1853; m. *Charlotte Matilda Finch*, d. (*in Canada*) 14 *Jan.* 1855; *and had issue* 1*c to* 3*c*.

        1*c*. Charles Travers Fuller.

        2*c*. Emilia Fuller, *m. s.p.*

        3*c*. *Frances Elizabeth Fuller*, d. 8 *Sept.* 1867; m. 12 *Jan.* 1855, *Charles Gifford of Coburg, Canada; and had issue* 1*d to* 2*d*.

            1*d*. Wearman Gifford of Montreal, in 1885.

            2*d*. Francis Gifford.

    2*b*. *Charlotte Fuller*, d. 19 *Ap.* 1865; m. 11 *Jan.* 1813, *Thomas Gunning, Surgeon-Gen. in the Army*, d. 30 *Nov.* 1849; *and had issue* 1*c to* 2*c*.

        1*c*. *Thomas Wyatt Gunning, Bar.-at-Law*, b. 29 *Nov.* 1813; d. (–); m. 1*st*, 10 *May* 1849, *Lucy, da. of John Jenkins*, d. 6 *July* 1858; 2*ndly*, 14 *Oct.* 1861, *Elizabeth, da. of Richard Lathburg; and had issue* 1*d to* 5*d*.

            1*d*. Francis Nevill Gunning, *b.* 8 Nov. 1852.

            2*d*. Montagu Wyatt Gunning, *b.* 15 Dec. 1862.

            3*d*. Charlotte Augusta Gunning, *m.* 15 Aug. 1874, Dr. Alfred Henry Buck.

            4*d*. Eveline Midora Gunning, *b.* 18 May 1865.

            5*d*. Lilian Hilda Gunning, *b.* 20 Dec. 1870.

        2*c*. *Nevillia Emilia Gunning*, d. 3 *June* 1878; m. 4 *Sept.* 1852, *Matthew Parker of Bath; and had issue* 1*d to* 3*d*.

            1*d*. Edward Nevill Parker, *b.* 24 June 1853.

            2*d*. Nevillia Charlotte Parker, *b.* 23 Dec. 1854.

            3*d*. Beatrice Frances Parker, *b.* 9 July 1856.

    3*b*. *Emilia Fuller*, b. 1798; d. 14 *Sept.* 1863; m. 10 *Jan.* 1818, *Lieut.-Col. Francis Fuller, C.B.*, b. 29 *Oct.* 1788; d. 19 *Ap.* 1868; *and had issue* 1*c to* 7*c*.

        1*c*. Francis Fuller, Capt. *late* 59th Regt., *b.* 31 Dec. 1820; *unm.* 1885.

        2*c*. *William Ross Fuller, Major, sometime* 53*rd Regt.*, b. 2 *Feb.* 1826; d. (–); m. 1*st*, 19 *Feb.* 1867, *Annie, da. and h. of Lieut.-Col. Radcliffe Stokoe, H.E.I.C.S.*, d. 6 *Dec.* 1868; 2*ndly*, 4 *Jan.* 1870, *Edith, da. of* [——] *Neale*, d. *Mar.* 1875; 3*rdly, July* 1876, *Florence Gascoigne, da. of* [——] *Williams; and had issue* 1*d to* 6*d*.

            1*d*.[1] Francis William Nevill Fuller.

            2*d*.[2] Henry Ross Fuller.

            3*d*.[3] Norman Frederick Fuller.

            4*d*.[1] Annie Fuller.

            5*d*.[3] Florence May Fuller.

            6*d*.[3] Irene Margaret Esperanza Fuller.

        3*c*. *John Fuller,* 71*st Regt.*, b. 7 *Jan.* 1827; d. 1867; m. 1*st*, *Alicia, da. of* [——] *Grasset*, d.s.p.s.; 2*ndly, Jane, da. of* [——] *Roberts; and had issue* (*now in New Zealand*).

        4*c*. Frederic Walter Fuller, of the Colonial Office, *b.* 29 Ap. 1838.

        5*c*. Charlotte Fuller.

        6*c*. Maria Fuller, *m.* George Leslie Lee of Avonside, Canterbury, New Zealand.

[Nos. 794 to 820.

# of The Blood Royal

7c. Mary Anne Fuller, b. 27 Jan. 1834; d. 13 Feb. 1875; m. 1 May 1858, the Rev. Richard Baxendale, Vicar of St. John's, Maidstone; and had issue 1d to 7d.
1d. Francis Richard Salisbury Baxendale, b. 6 Sept. 1860.
2d. Herbert Lloyd Salisbury Baxendale, b. 2 Mar. 1864.
3d. Arthur Salisbury Baxendale, b. 11 Jan. 1866.
4d. Cyril Edward Salisbury Baxendale, b. 26 Aug. 1870.
5d. May Ellen Baxendale.
6d. Ethel Maud Baxendale.
7d. Margaret Amabel Baxendale.　　　　　　　　　　　　　　[Nos. 821 to 827.

29. **Descendants of** GEORGE (NEVILL), 1st EARL [G.B.] and 17th BARON [E.] OF ABERGAVENNY (see Table IV.), b. 24 June 1727; d. 10 Sept. 1785; m. 5 Feb. 1753, HENRIETTA, widow of the Hon. Richard Temple of Romsey, sister of Thomas, 1st Earl of Chichester [G.B.], da. of Thomas PELHAM of Stanmere, b. 1 Aug. 1730; d. 31 Aug. 1768; and had issue 1a to 3a.

1a. Henry (Nevill), 2nd Earl [G.B.] and 18th Baron [E.] of Abergavenny, K.T., b. 22 Feb. 1755; d. 27 Mar. 1843; m. 3 Oct. 1781, Mary, da. and h. of John Robinson, of Wyke House, Midx., M.P., Secretary to the Treasury, d. 26 Oct. 1796; and had issue 1b to 2b.
1b. John (Nevill), 3rd Earl [G.B.] and 19th Baron [E.] of Abergavenny, b. 25 Dec. 1789; d. unm. 12 Ap. 1845.
2b. William (Nevill), 4th Earl [G.B.] and 20th Baron [E.] of Abergavenny, b. 28 June 1792; d. 17 Aug. 1868; m. 7 Sept. 1824, Caroline, da. of Ralph Leeke of Longford Hall, d. 19 May 1873; and had issue.
See the Tudor Roll of "The Blood Royal of Britain," pp. 352-354, Nos. 27115-27167.

2a. Rev. the Hon. George Henry Nevill, of Flower Place, Surrey, b. 6 Dec. 1760; d. 7 Aug. 1844; m. 11 May 1787, Caroline, da. of the Hon. Richard Walpole, M.P., d. 21 Dec. 1841; and had issue 1b.
1b. Reginald Henry Nevill of Dangstein, co. Sussex, J.P., D.L., b. 14 Sept. 1807; d. 11 Sept. 1878; m. 12 Dec. 1847, Lady Dorothy Fanny (45 Charles Street, Berkeley Square, W.), da. of Horatio (Walpole), 3rd Earl of Orford [U.K.]; and had issue 1c to 4c.
1c. Edward Augustus Nevill, J.P. (Trotton Place, Petersfield, Hants), b. 28 Feb. 1851; m. 7 Aug. 1877, Edith Fanny Owen, da. of Lieut.-Gen. Edward Owen Leggatt, I.S.C.
2c. Horace John Nevill, late Lieut. King's Royal Rifles (26 Warwick Square, S.W.), b. 22 Oct. 1855; m. 2 Jan. 1880, Annie Harriet Martha, da. of Henry Dickson Rowe; and has issue 1d to 2d.
1d. Frederick Reginald Nevill, b. 27 Sept. 1880.
2d. John Henry Adrian Nevill, b. 17 Mar. 1882.
3c. Ralph Henry Nevill, b. 4 Feb. 1865.
4c. Meresia Dorothy Augusta Nevill, b. 14 Dec. 1849.

3a. Lady Henrietta Nevill, b. 24 May 1756; d. (at Auderlecht, near Brussels) 2 Ap. 1833; m. 9 Sept. 1779, Sir John Berney, 7th Bart. [E.], b. 1757; d. (at Bruges) 4 Sept. (or Oct.) 1825-68; and had issue 1b.
1b. Sir Hanson Berney, 8th Bart. [E.], b. 3 Dec. 1780; d. Sept. 1870; m. 2ndly, 10 Oct. 1843, Agnes, da. of Thomas Peck, d. 6 Oct. 1870; and had issue 1c.
1c. Sir Henry Hanson Berney, 9th Bart. [E.], LL.B. (Burncrook, Moffat, N.B.), b. 30 Nov. 1843; m. 31 Jan. 1866, Jane Dorothy, da. of the Rev. Andrew Bloxam, M.A.; and has issue 1d to 9d.　　　　　　　　[Nos. 828 to 887.

The Plantagenet Roll

1d. *Thomas Hugh Berney, Capt. 2nd Batt. Prince of Wales' Own West Yorkshire Regt.*, b. 17 Oct. 1866; d. (*being killed at Monte Cristo, Natal*) 18 Feb. 1900; m. 2 *July* 1892, *Fridzwede Katherine, da. of Lieut.-Col. Frederic W. Bell*; *and had issue* 1e *to* 2e.

    1e. Thomas Reedham Berney, b. 6 July 1893.

    2e. Richard Geoffrey Gordon Berney, b. 19 Jan. 1897.

2d. Richard William Berney (*Brakfontein, Orange River Colony*), b. 20 Dec. 1867.

3d. John Hanson Berney (*Tawatai, Eketuhuna, Wellington, N.Z.*), b. 22 Nov. 1868; m. Ap. 1900, Margaret, da. of Sinclair George of New Zealand; and has issue 1e.

    1e. Hugh Barton Berney, b. 11 Jan. 1902.

4d. Robert Henry Berney, B.A. (Camb.), b. 5 May 1871.

5d. Andrew James Berney, B.A. (Camb.), Assistant Commissioner, Sierra Leone, b. 23 Sept. 1873.

6d. Alexander David Berney, b. 20 Sept. 1877.

7d. Mary Agnes Berney, b. 30 Mar. 1876.

8d. Jane Dorothy Elizabeth Berney, b. 28 Nov. 1878.

9d. Catherine Ann Berney, b. 19 June 1880; m. 24 Aug. 1904, Robert William Thomas Ewart, M.B. (4 *Wandsworth Bridge Road, Fulham, S.W.*); and has issue 1e.

    1e. Robert Charles Berney Ewart, b. 26 June 1905.

[Nos. 888 to 899.

30. Descendants, if any surviving, of CECILY WHITELOCKE, *bapt.* 9 Jan. 1641; of HESTER WHITELOCKE, *bapt.* Aug. 1642, wife of [——] SEAWEN of Wales; and of ANNE WHITELOCKE, wife of ABRAHAM HILL of Shilton, co. Devon, younger sisters to Sir William Whitelocke of Phyllis Court, Oxon. (see Table IV.).

31. Descendants of the Hon. FRANCES COURTENAY (see Table V.), *b.* Jan. 1763; *d.* (–); *m.* 13 Dec. 1779, Sir JOHN HONYWOOD, 4th Bart. [E.], M.P., *b. c.* 1757; *d.* 29 Mar. 1806; and had issue 1a to 6a.

1a. *Sir John Courtenay Honywood, 5th Bart. [E.]*, b. 1787; d. 12 *Sept.* 1832; m. 27 *July* 1808, *Mary Anne, da. of the Rev. Sir William Henry Cooper, 4th Bart. [E.]*, d. 10 *Mar.* 1841; *and had issue* 1b *to* 4b.

1b. *Sir John Edward Honywood, 6th Bart. [E.]*, b. 16 *Mar.* 1812; d. 17 *July* 1845; m. 17 *Ap.* 1834, *Mary, da. of the Rev. Charles Hughes Hallett of Higham;* *and had issue* 1c *to* 4c.

1c. *Sir Courtenay Honywood, 7th Bart. [E.]*, D.L., b. 5 *Mar.* 1835; d. 17 *Ap.* 1878; m. 23 *Aug.* 1855, *Annie Maria, da. of William Paynter of Camborne House, Richmond; and had issue* 1d *to* 6d.

1d. *Sir John William Honywood, 8th Bart. [E.]*, J.P. (*Evington Place, Ashford*), b. 15 *Ap.* 1857; *m.* 22 Aug. 1877, Zaidee Emily Isuelte, da. of John Bodychan Sparrow of Gwyndu, co. Anglesea, d. 15 Oct. 1893; and has issue 1e to 5e.

    1e. Courtenay John Honywood, b. 29 May 1880.

    2e. William Honywood, b. 7 Ap. 1891.

    3e. Philip Sydney Honywood, b. 5 Sept. 1893.

    4e. Zaidee Violet Honywood, b. 8 June 1878.

    5e. Hilda Catharine Honywood, b. 23 Ap. 1886.

[Nos. 900 to 905.

# of The Blood Royal

2*d*. Cecil Robert Honywood, *b*. 27 Dec. 1862.

3*d*. Reginald Ernest Honywood, *b*. 14 Dec. 1863.

4*d*. Guy Honywood, *b*. 7 Nov. 1871.

5*d*. Annie Mabel Honywood.

6*d*. Violet Constance Evelyn Honywood, *m*. 24 Dec. 1902, William Reginald Welsford Mumby.

2*c*. *Frances Hallett Honywood*, d. 7 *Oct.* 1890; m. 22 *Jan.* 1861, *the Rev. Thomas Stone Carnsew of Flexbury, Vicar of Constantine, Cornwall ; and had issue* 1*d to* 6*d*.

1*d*. Walter Henry Carnsew, *b*. 27 Oct. 1862.

2*d*. John Honywood Carnsew, *b*. 10 Dec. 1872.

3*d*. Frances Carnsew.

4*d*. Emma Marion Carnsew.

5*d*. Mary Gertrude Carnsew.

6*d*. Florence Hilda Carnsew.

3*c*. Marion Grace Honywood, *m*. 9 Feb. 1869, the Rev. John Theed Watson, Rector of Woodford (*Woodford Rectory, near Thrapstone*); and has issue 1*d* to 11*d*.

1*d*. Rev. John Edward Watson, M.A. (Camb.), Curate of St. Philip's, Clerkenwell (25 *Wharton St., W.C.*), *b*. 26 Jan. 1872.

2*d*. Charles Joseph Watson, Natal Mounted Police (*Pietermaritzburg*), *b*. 8 Ap. 1874.

3*d*. Arthur Edmund Honywood Watson, Natal Mounted Police (*Pietermaritzburg*), *b*. 22 Mar. 1884.

4*d*. Alexander Henry St. Croix Watson, *b*. 3 May 1885.

5*d*. Mary Caroline Watson.

6*d*. Dorothy Elizabeth Watson.

7*d*. Cicely Magdalene Bawtree Watson.

8*d*. Etheldreda Lilian Watson.

9*d*. Florence Jacoba Watson.

10*d*. Geraldine Isabel Watson.

11*d*. Constance Mary Watson.

4*c*. Florence Elizabeth Honywood, *m*. 22 Aug. 1867, the Rev. Edward William Northey, *late* Vicar of Chaddesden (*Woodcote House, Epsom*); and has issue 1*d* to 9*d*.

1*d*. Edward Northey, Major 3rd Batt. King's Royal Rifle Corps, *b*. 28 May 1868; *m*. 30 Ap. 1897, Evangeline, da. of Daniel Cloete of Montebello, Newlands, S.A.; and has issue 1*e* to 2*e*.

1*e*. Florence Evangeline Cloete Northey, *b*. 17 Mar. 1898.

2*e*. Renee Muriel Northey, *b*. 24 Dec. 1902.

2*d*. Charles Henry Northey, *b*. 26 Ap. 1873.

3*d*. William Northey, D.S.O., Capt. Durham Light Infantry, *b*. 29 Jan. 1876 ; *m*. 6 Mar. 1905, Violet, da. of J. Ferguson.

4*d*. Francis Vernon Northey, *b*. 8 Ap. 1881.

5*d*. Florence Isabel Northey, *m*. July 1889, Frank Richardson.

6*d*. Mildred Louisa Northey, *m*. 20 July 1892, Major Archie Stewart Buckle, R.F.A.

7*d*. Mary Northey, *m*. 1 Mar. 1905, C. Malcolm Cumming (*Negri Sembilan, Malay States*).

8*d*. Gwendolen Northey.

9*d*. Muriel Northey, *m*. 23 Ap. 1903, Capt. Oswald Birley Harter, Durham Light Infantry.   [Nos. 906 to 940.

The Plantagenet Roll

2b. *Mary Anne Elizabeth Honywood*, d. 18 June 1890 ; m. 4 Feb. 1834, *Capt. Frederick Barne of Sotterley and Dunwich, M.P.*, d. 15 Mar. 1886 ; and had issue. See the Clarence Volume, pp. 610–611, Nos. 26804–26810.

3b. *Louisa Lucy Honywood*, d. 18 Oct. 1870 ; m. 4 June 1844, *the Rev. James Whyte, Rector of King's Nymton, Devon.*

4b. Elizabeth Josepha Honywood.

2a. *Frances Elizabeth Honywood*, d. (–) ; m. *Aubone Surtees of Pigdon, Northumberland, J.P.*, 11th Light Dragoons, b. 14 Dec. 1777 ; d. (–) ; and had issue.[1]

3a. *Annabella Christiana Honywood*, d. 4 Ap. 1814 ; m. as 1st wife, 25 Aug. 1806, *the Right Hon. Sir Edward Knatchbull, 9th Bart. [E.]*, b. 20 Dec. 1781 ; d. 24 May 1849 ; and had issue 1b to 2b.

1b. *Sir Norton Joseph Knatchbull, 10th Bart. [E.]*, b. 10 July 1808 ; d. 2 Feb. 1868 ; m. 31 May 1831, *Mary, da. of Jesse Watta Russell of Ham Hall, co. Stafford*, d. 3 Sept. 1874 ; and had issue 1c to 5c.

1c. *Sir Edward Knatchbull, 11th Bart. [E.]*, b. 26 Ap. 1838 ; d.s.p. 30 May 1871.

2c. Sir Wyndham Knatchbull, 12th Bart. [E.], J.P. (*Mersham Hatch, near Ashford*), b. 9 June 1844 ; m. 18 Mar. 1902, Margaret Elizabeth, widow of John Dillon-Browne, da. of Charles Taylor.

3c. *Mary Louisa Knatchbull, m.* 29 Mar. 1856, Major-Gen. Charles Stirling Dundas, Bengal Art., b. 9 Sept. 1824 ; d. 28 May 1895 ; and has issue 1d to 3d.

1d. Malcolm James Russell Dundas, Major 3rd Batt. The Buffs, b. 24 Jan. 1859 ; m. 8 Feb. 1893, Margaret Ann, da. of Thomas Holford of Castle Hill.

2d. *Amy Mary Dundas, m.* 22 July 1902, Henry Swainson Cowper, J.P., F.S.A. (*High House, Hawkshead, Lancashire*) ; and has issue 1e.

1e. Christopher Swainson Cowper, b. 13 June 1903.

3d. *Alice Norton Dundas, m.* 26 July 1898, John Maurice Edward Lloyd, M.A., Bar.-at-Law (*Plâs Trefaldwyn, Montgomery*) ; and has issue 1e to 2e.

1e. John Davies Knatchbull Lloyd, b. 28 Ap. 1900.

2e. Wyndham Edward Buckley Lloyd, b. 13 July 1901.

4c. Eleanor Grace Knatchbull, *m.* as 2nd wife, 29 Aug. 1857, Robert John O'Reilly of Mill Castle, co. Westmeath, b. 9 July 1813 ; d. 18 Dec. 1879 ; and has issue 1d.

1d. Kathleen Mary O'Reilly.

5c. Beatrice Johanna Knatchbull (15 *Rosary Gardens, S.W.*), *m.* as 4th wife, 1 Dec. 1874, Charles Edmund (Law), 3rd Baron Ellenborough [U.K.], b. 17 Nov. 1820 ; d. 9 Oct. 1890.

2b. *Mary Dorothea Knatchbull*, d. 22 Feb. 1838 ; m. as 1st wife, May 1826, *Edward Knight of Godmersham Park and Chawton House, J.P., D.L.*, b. 1794 ; d. 5 Nov. 1879 ; and had issue 1c to 4c.

1c. Wyndham William Knight, *late* Capt. Royal E. Kent Mounted Rifles, J.P. (*Bilting House, Wye, Kent*), b. 5 Dec. 1828 ; *m.* 1849, Henrietta Frances, da. of Lieut.-Col. Armstrong, d. 1891 ; and has issue 1d to 2d.

1d. Edward Knight, b. 1852 ; *m.* 20 Ap. 1882, Mary Augusta Repps, da. of the Rev. Henry Evans Lombe of Bylaugh Park ; and has issue 1e.

1e. Mary Dorothea Knight.

2d. Mary Georgina Knight.

2c. *Philip Henry Knight, Major Royal Welsh Fusiliers*, b. 25 Aug. 1835 ; d. 4 Jan. 1882 ; m. 18—, [——], da. of [——] ; and had issue 1d.

1d. Fanny Knight, *m.* 18 Feb. 1897, Charles Cecil Howard Gore, *late* of Linwood, Hants ; and has issue 1e.

1e. Cecil Beryl Katherine Gore, b. 1898.   [Nos. 941 to 965.

---

[1] A numerous family, of which the sons, Villiers Charles Villiers and Honeywood Graham, died 1876. Burke's "Landed Gentry," 1900, p. 1525.

# of The Blood Royal

3c. *William Brodnax Knight, Capt. Queen's Bays,* b. 3 *Feb.* 1838 ; d. 4 *Nov.*
1896 ; m. 1863, *Louisa Octavia Charlotte, da. of Courtenay Stacey of Sandling
Place ; and had issue* 1d *to* 5d.

1d. Wyndham Charles Knight, Capt. 4th Bengal Cavalry, b. 30 Nov. 1863 ;
m. 1896, Harriet Monica, da. of Francis J. Johnston.

2d. Reginald Brodnax Knight, b. 16 Feb. 1867 ; m. 1889, Marian, da. of Major
Calvert.

3d. Dorothea Maud Knight.

4d. Violet Laura Amherst Knight.

5d. Irene Constance Louisa Knight.

4c. *Georgina Elizabeth Knight,* d. 26 *May* 1864 ; m. 31 *Aug.* 1858, *the Rev.
Frederic Pretyman, B.D., J.P., Hon. Canon of Lincoln Cathedral and Rector of
Great Carlton,* b. 1819 ; d. [——] ; *and had issue* 1d.

1d. Ernest George Pretyman, J.P., D.L., M.P., Hon. Col. 1st Suffolk Vol. Art.,
late Capt. R.A. (Orwell Park, Ipswich ; Riby Grove, Stallingboro), b. 13 Nov. 1859 ;
m. 28 June 1894, Lady Beatrice Adine, da. of Cecil George Orlando (Bridgeman),
4th Earl of Bradford [U.K.], &c. ; and has issue.

See the Clarence Volume, p. 212, Nos. 4233-4237.

4a. *Caroline Honywood,* d. (–) ; m. 1807, *Edward Temple (only son of the
Rev. Thomas William Temple, D.D.) ; and had issue* 1b *to* 3b.

1b. Courtenay George Henry Temple.

2b. Anne Eliza Temple.

3b. *Mary Eliza Temple,* d. 1 *July* 1881 ; m. 1*st,* 27 *Nov.* 1843, *Robert
(Sherard), 6th Earl of Harborough [G.B.], 8th Baron Sherard [I.],* d.s.p. 28 *July*
1859 ; 2*ndly,* 20 *Ap.* 1864, *Major Thomas William Claggitt,* d. 16 *May* 1885.

5a. *Eliza Augusta Honywood.*

6a. *Louisa Catherine Honywood,* d. 1822 ; m. 1820, *the Rev. Henry R. Quartly.*
[Nos. 966 to 978.

32. Descendants of the Hon. CHARLOTTE COURTENAY (see Table V.),
b. 14 July 1764 ; *d.* 22 Nov. 1844 ; *m.* 23 June 1788, THOMAS
GIFFARD of Chillington, co. Stafford, *d.* 1 Aug. 1823 ; and
had issue.

See the Clarence Volume, pp. 395-396, Nos. 15077-15122.
[Nos. 979 to 1024.

33. Descendants of the Hon. ELIZABETH COURTENAY (see Table V.), *b.*
2 Sept. 1766 ; *d.* 11 Sept. 1815 ; *m.* as first wife, 7 June 1788,
Lord CHARLES HENRY SOMERSET, *b.* 12 Dec. 1767 ; *d.* 20 Feb.
1831 ; and had issue.

See the Clarence Volume, pp. 328-330, Nos. 9749-9835.
[Nos. 1025 to 1111.

34. Descendants of the Hon. LUCY COURTENAY (see Table V.), *b.*
13 June 1770 ; *d.* 17 Dec. 1821 ; *m.* 2 Aug. 1798, JOHN
(VAUGHAN), 3rd EARL OF LISBURNE [I.], *b.* 3 Mar. 1769 ; *d.*
18 May 1831 ; and had issue 1*a* to 4*a.*

1a. *Ernest Augustus (Vaughan), 4th Earl of Lisburne [I.],* b. 30 *Oct.* 1800 ; d.
8 *Nov.* 1873 ; m. 1*st,* 27 *Aug.* 1835, *Mary, da. of Sir Lawrence Palk, 2nd Bart.*
[G.B.], d. 23 *July* 1851 ; 2*ndly,* 5 *Ap.* 1853, *the Hon. Elizabeth Augusta Harriet,
da. of Col. Hugh Henry Mitchell,* d. 13 *Dec.* 1883 ; *and had issue* 1b *to* 2b.

The Plantagenet Roll

1b. Ernest Augustus Malet (*Vaughan*), 5th Earl of Lisburne [*I.*], b. 26 *June* 1836; d. 31 *Mar.* 1888; m. 1*st,* 24 *June* 1858, Gertrude Laura, *da. of Edwyn Burnaby of Baggrave Hall, co. Leicester,* d. 29 *Mar.* 1865; 2*ndly,* 15 *May* 1878, *Alice D'Alton (who re-m. as* 2*nd wife,* 25 *Sept.* 1889, *William (Amherst),* 3*rd Earl Amherst), da. of Edmund Probyn of Huntley Manor; and had issue 1c to* 3*c.*

1c. Arthur Henry George (*Vaughan*),ˉ 6th Earl of Lisburne [*I.*], b. 20 *July* 1862; d. 4 *Sept.* 1899; m. 24 *Oct.* 1888, Evelyn (*Crosswood, Aberystwith ;* 13 *Embankment Gardens, S.W.*), *da. of Edmund Probyn of Huntley Manor, co. Gloucester; and had issue* 1*d to* 2*d.*

1d. Ernest Edmund Henry Malet (Vaughan), 7th Earl of Lisburne [I.] (*Crosswood, Aberystwith ; Birchgrove, Aberystwith*), b. 8 Feb. 1892.

2d. Lady Enid Evelyn Vaughan, b. 27 Sept. 1889.

2c. Lady Ida Constance Vaughan, *m.* 4 Dec. 1886, Brig.-Gen. Seymour Charles Hale Monro, C.B., Comdg. 1st Batt. Seaforth Highlanders ; and has issue 1*d* to 3*d.*

1d. Charles Henry Hale Monro, b. 1887.

2d. Ian Alistair Seymour Monro, b. 1897.

3d. Aline Enid Elma Monro, b. 1889.

3c. Lady Lucy Vaughan, *m.* 17 Oct. 1883, Capt. Martin Albert Silber; and has issue 1*d* to 2*d.*

1d. Esme Malet Silber, b. 1889.

2d. Enid Violet Silber, b. 1884.

2b. Lady Elizabeth Malet Vaughan (58 *Park Street, Grosvenor Square, W.*), *m.* 6 Aug. 1860, John Inglis Jones of Derry Ormond, co. Cardigan, J.P., D.L., *d.* 15 Dec. 1879 ; and has issue 1*c* to 2*c.*

1c. Wilmot Inglis-Jones, J.P., D.L., High Sheriff co. Cardigan 1891 (*Derry Ormond, co. Cardigan*), b. 28 Mar. 1868 ; *m.* 27 Nov. 1897, Eva Winifred Selina, da. of Alfred Ker of Montalto ; and has issue.

See the Clarence Volume, p. 342, Nos. 11006–11008.

2c. Mary Gwendolen Inglis Jones, *m.* 3 Aug. 1887, Sir Henry Hamilton Erroll Chamberlain, 4th Bart. [U.K.] (16 *Chester Street, S.W.*) ; and has issue 1*d* to 2*d.*

1d. Henry Wilmot Chamberlain, b. 17 May 1899.

2d. Ursula Elizabeth Chamberlain, b. 20 Feb. 1897.

2a. Hon. George Lawrence Vaughan, *Capt. in the Army,* b. 8 *Feb.* 1802; d. 19 *Aug.* 1879; m. 4 *Oct.* 1830, *Mary Josephine Roche, da. of Henry O'Shea of Madrid,* d. 10 *June* 1895 ; *and had issue* 1*b to* 2*b.*

1b. George Augustus Vaughan, *formerly Capt. in the Army* (*Lapley, Penkridge*), *b.* 7 Sept. 1833 ; *m.* 12 Aug. 1862, Laura Mary, da. of Charles Moore of Mooresfoot, co. Tipperary, *d.* 9 Jan. 1898 ; and has issue 1*c* to 2*c.*

1c. Wilmot Charles Vaughan, *formerly Capt.* 20th Hussars (*Union ; United Service*), *b.* 21 Dec. 1863 ; *m.* 1895, Nora, da. of Frederick Fane ; and has issue (a da.) 1*d.*

1d. Muriel Vaughan, b. 10 Aug. 1897.

2c. Christine Mary Vaughan, b. 17 Aug. 1866 ; d. 5 *Nov.* 1897 ; m. *as* 1*st wife,* 2 *June* 1890, *John Charles Matthias Ogilvie-Forbes of Boyndlie, J.P., D.L. (Boyndlie, Fraserburgh, co. Aberdeen); and had issue* 1*d to* 2*d.*

1d. George Arthur Drostan Ogilvie-Forbes, b. 6 Dec. 1891.

2d. Rebecca Edith Mary Ogilvie-Forbes.

2b. Mary Celeste Vaughan (*Lapley, Stafford*), *m.* 26 Ap. 1877, Edmund Malet Vaughan, D.L., *b.* 12 Feb. 1840 ; *d.* 10 May 1882 ; and has issue 1*c* to 3*c.*

1c. Eugene Napoleon Ernest Malet Vaughan (sponsors H.M. the Empress Eugenie and the Prince Imperial), Capt. Grenadier Guards, b. 19 Nov. 1878.

2c. George Edmund Vaughan, Lieut. Coldstream Guards, b. 1 Mar. 1881.

3c. Louise Mary Vaughan, b. 15 Nov. 1879. [Nos. 1112 to 1137.

# of The Blood Royal

3a. *Hon. John Shafto Vaughan*, b. 13 Oct. 1803; d. Ap. 1881.

4a. *Hon. William Malet Vaughan*, b. 18 May 1807; d. 13 Dec. 1867; m. 21 June 1838, Louisa, da. of Edmund Wigan of Lapley, co. Stafford, d. 11 Jan. 1842; and had issue 1b.

1b. *Edmund Malet Vaughan, D.L.*, b. 12 Feb. 1840; d. 10 May 1882; m. 26 Ap. 1877, Mary Celeste, da. of the Hon. George Lawrence Vaughan; and had issue 1c to 3c.

1c-3c. See p. 30, Nos. 1135-1137.   [Nos. 1138 to 1140.

35. Descendants of the Hon. CAROLINE EUSTACIA COURTENAY (see Table V.), b. 26 Mar. 1775; d. 6 Mar. 1851; m. 5 Jan. 1812, Col. CHARLES MORLAND, b. 1775; d. 13 June 1828; and had issue 1a.

1a. *William Courtenay Morland, M.A., J.P., D.L.*, High Sheriff, co. Sussex, 1876 (*The Court Lodge, Lamberhurst, Kent*), b. 13 Mar. 1818; m. 27 June 1843, Margaretta Eliza, da. of Gen. Sir William Cator, K.C.B., R.A., d. 16 Jan. 1897; and has issue 1b to 2b.

1b. *Charles William Morland*, Major and Hon. Lieut.-Col. 5th Kent R.V., J.P., b. 6 Feb. 1849; m. 14 June 1882, Ada Mary, da. of H. G. W. Sperling of Edgeworth Manor.

2b. *Henry Courtenay Morland*, Major *late* 9th Lancers (*The Punt, Rye*), b. 21 Mar. 1855; m. 30 Sept. 1884, Lady Alice Maud, da. of William (Nevill), 1st Marquis of Abergavenny [U.K.], &c., d. 19 Feb. 1898; 2ndly, 29 July 1902, Bessie Josephine, da. of John Laird of Birkenhead; and has issue 1c to 3c.

1c. *William Morland*, b. 28 May 1903.

2c. *John Courtenay Morland*, b. 18 Dec. 1904.

3c. *Violet Alice Morland*, b. 12 Nov. 1886.   [Nos. 1141 to 1146.

36. Descendants of the Hon. MATILDA JANE COURTENAY (see Table V.), b. 7 July 1778; d. 4 Aug. 1848; m. Lieut.-Gen. JOHN LOCKE, d. 1837; and had issue 1a to 3a.

1a. *Rev. Charles Courtenay Locke, Rector of Newcastle, co. Limerick*, d. 16 Feb. 1848; m. 1st, [——], da. of [——]; 2ndly, 9 Dec. 1845, Blanche, da. of Lord Robert Edward Henry Somerset, d.s.p. 14 Oct. 1879; and had issue 1b.

1b. *Matilda Locke*, m. Baron [——] of Brussels.

2a. *John Locke*, m.; and had issue 1b to 2b.

1b. *William Locke*, Col. in the Army (*Army and Navy*), m.; and has issue 1c.

1c. *Lucy Locke*, m. an Italian gentleman.

2b. *Caroline Locke*, m. lately in Germany.

3a. *Matilda Harriet Elizabeth Locke*, b. 12 May 1804; d.s.p. 29 Dec. 1877; m. 5 Nov. 1834, Henry LXIX., Prince of Reuss Kœstritz, b. 19 May 1792: d.s.p. 1 Feb. 1878.   [Nos. 1147 to 1150.

37. Descendants of the Hon. SOPHIA COURTENAY (see Table V.), b. 25 Jan. 1780; d. 11 Jan. 1845; m. Dec. 1804, Col. NATHANIEL FOY, R.A., b. 1773; d. (at Woolwich) 28 Mar. 1817; and had issue 1a.

1a. *Sophia Elizabeth Foy*, b. Oct. 1806; d. 16 May 1857; m. 6 Nov. 1834, Richard Matthews Poulden, R.A., b. 30 May 1803; d. 21 Aug. 1885; and had issue 1b to 2b.

The Plantagenet Roll

1b. Edward Courtenay Poulden, b. 18 *Oct.* 1839; d. *July* 1885; m. *Catherine,* da. of [——] *Bland; and had issue* 1c *to* 2c.

 1c. Richard Henry Courtenay Poulden (*Australia*), b. 4 Ap. 1875; m.; and has issue (3 children).

 2c. Sophia Elizabeth Poulden, m. Broke Bland, Solicitor (*Bega, New South Wales*); and has issue (a da.) 1d.

  1d. [——] Bland, b. June 1904.

 2b. Sophia Harriet Poulden, b. 9 Feb. 1855; m. 27 Nov. 1888, Henry Charles Arundell Day (*Oriel Lodge, Walton Clevedon*); and has issue 1c.

  1c. Henry Chesmer Poulden Day, b. 28 Ap. 1889.   [Nos. 1151 to 1155.

38. Descendants of the Hon. Louisa Augusta Courtenay (see Table V.), b. 25 Dec. 1781; d. 9 Feb. 1823; m. 17 Oct. 1805, Lord Robert Henry Edward Somerset, G.C.B., b. 19 Dec. 1776; d. 1 Sept. 1842; and had issue.

See the Clarence Volume, p. 331, Nos. 9836–9860.   [Nos. 1156 to 1180.

39. Descendants of the Hon. Frances Courtenay (see Table V.), b. 10 Mar. 1748; d. 24 Feb. 1828; m. 7 June 1770, Sir John Wrottesley, 8th Bart. [E.], b. 22 Dec. 1744; d. 23 Ap. 1787; and had issue.

See the Tudor Roll of "The Blood Royal of Britain," pp. 333–334, Nos. 26544–26587.   Nos. 1181 to 1224.

40. Descendants of the Right Rev. Henry Reginald Courtenay, Lord Bishop of Exeter, LL.D. (see Table V.), b. 27 Nov. 1741; d. 9 June 1803; m. 26 Jan. 1774, Lady Elizabeth, da. of Thomas (Howard), 2nd Earl of Effingham [U.K.], b. 10 Nov. 1750; d. 31 Oct. 1815; and had issue 1a to 2a.

 1a. William (*Courtenay*), 10*th Earl of Devon* [*E.*], b. 19 *June* 1777; d. 19 *Mar.* 1859; m. 1*st,* 29 *Nov.* 1804, *Lady Harriet, da. of Sir Lucas Pepys,* 1*st Bart.* [*G.B.*], *M.D., F.R.S., and his wife Jane Elizabeth,* suo jure 12*th Countess of Rothes* [*S.*], b. 1 *June* 1777; d. 16 *Dec.* 1839; *and had issue* 1b *to* 2b.

  1b. William Reginald (*Courtenay*), 11*th Earl of Devon* [*E.*], P.C., b. 19 *Ap.* 1807; d. 18 *Nov.* 1888; m. 27 *Dec.* 1830, *Lady Elizabeth, da. of Hugh* (*Fortescue*), 1*st Earl Fortescue* [*G.B.*], K.G., b. 10 *July* 1801; d. 27 *Jan.* 1867; *and had issue* 1c *to* 2c.

   1c. Edward Baldwin (*Courtenay*), 12*th Earl of Devon* [*E.*], b. 7 *May* 1836; d. *unm.* 15 *Jan.* 1891.

   2c. Lady Agnes Elizabeth Courtenay, m. 22 Ap. 1869, Charles Lindley (Wood), 2nd Viscount Halifax [U.K.], 4th Bart. [G.B.], President of the English Church Union, &c. &c. (*Hickleton, near Doncaster; Garrowby, near Stamford Bridge;* 79 *Eaton Square, S.W.*); and has issue 1d to 3d.

    1d. Hon. Edward Frederick Lindley Wood, Lieut. Yorks Dragoons Imp. Yeo., b. 16 Ap. 1881.

    2d. Hon. Alexandra Mary Elizabeth Wood, b. 25 Aug. 1871 (Queen Alexandra sponsor), m. as 2nd wife, 15 Sept. 1898, Hugh Clement Sutton, Major Coldstream Guards, D.A.A.G., Cape Colony; and has issue 1e to 2e.

     [Nos. 1225 to 1227.

# of The Blood Royal

1e. Margaret Agnes Sutton, b. 26 Sept. 1899.
2e. Mary Frances Sutton, b. 12 June 1904.
3d. Hon. Mary Agnes Emily Wood, b. 25 Mar. 1877; m. 17 Sept. 1903, George Richard Lane-Fox, M.P. (*Hope Hall, Boston Spa, Yorks*); and has issue 1e to 2e.
1e. Marcia Agnes Mary Lane-Fox, b. 4 Sept. 1904.
2e. Mary Kathleen Lane-Fox, b. 19 Aug. 1905.

2b. *Henry Hugh (Courtenay), 13th Earl of Devon [E.], Rector of Powderham, Prebendary of Exeter,* b. 15 July 1811; d. 29 Jan. 1904; m. 6 Jan. 1835, Lady Anna Maria, da. of George Gwyther, afterwards Leslie, by his wife Henrietta Anne, suo jure 14th Countess of Rothes [S.], b. 19 July 1815; d. 18 Feb. 1897; and had issue 1c to 2c.
1c. Henry Reginald Courtenay, Lord Courtenay, b. 20 Jan. 1836; d. 27 May 1898; m. 12 June 1862, Lady Evelyn (Kenton, Exeter), da. of Charles Christopher (Pepys), 1st Earl of Cottenham [U.K.]; and had issue 1d to 5d.
1d. Charles Pepys (Courtenay), 14th Earl of Devon [E.] (*Powderham Castle, near Exeter; The Castle, Newcastle, co. Limerick, &c. &c.*), b. 14 July 1870.
2d. Rev. the Hon.¹ Henry Hugh Courtenay, Rector of Powderham (*Powderham Rectory, Exeter*), b. 1 Aug. 1872.
3d. Rev. the Hon.¹ Frederick Leslie Courtenay, M.A. (Oxon.), Curate of Cheriton-with-Tichborne (*Tichborne Rectory, Alresford*), b. 31 Aug. 1875.
4d. Lady¹ Amy Evelyn Courtenay, b. 22 Feb. 1865; m. 18 Oct. 1892, Col. the Hon. Reginald Henry Bertie, C.B.
5d. Lady¹ Caroline Elizabeth Courtenay, b. 3 Jan. 1867.
2c. Hon. Hugh Leslie Courtenay, M.A. (Oxon.), (*Knighton, Old Tiverton Road, Exeter*), b. 1 Aug. 1852; m. 31 Mar. 1880, Laura Georgina (divorced 1884), da. of Major George Henry Courtenay; and has issue 1d.
1d. Anna Maria Laura Courtenay, b. 26 Feb. 1881.

2a. *Right Hon. Thomas Peregrine Courtenay, M.P.,* b. 31 May 1782; d. 7 July 1841; m. 5 Ap. 1805, Anne, da. of Mayow Wynell-Mayow of Sydenham, d. Dec. 1860; and had issue 1b to 7b.
1b. *Right Rev. Reginald Courtenay, D.D., sometime (1856–1879) Lord Bishop of Kingston, Jamaica,* b. 26 Feb. 1813; d. 13 Ap. 1906; m. 23 July 1842, Georgiana, da. of Adm. Sir John de la Poer Beresford, 1st Bart. [U.K], d. 7 Sept. 1870; and had issue 1c to 3c.
1c. Georgiana Harriet Anne Courtenay, b. 31 Jan. 1846; m. 11 Aug. 1869, the Rev. George Thomas Ryves, M.A., Vicar of Upper Tean, d. 30 Jan. 1897; and has issue 1d to 6d.
1d. Reginald Arthur Ryves, b. 9 Feb. 1873.
2d. George Bernard Ryves, b. 19 Nov. 1874.
3d. Percy Mayow Ryves.
4d. Miriam Georgiana Beresford Ryves.
5d. Evangeline Ryves.
6d. Constance Ryves.
2c. Evangeline Claudette Courtenay, m. 20 May 1880, Lieut.-Col. Charles John Blake, late R.A.; and has issue.
3c. Mabel Courtenay.

2b. George Henry Courtenay, late Major 60th Rifles (*Southtown House, Kenton, Exeter*), b. 23 Dec. 1814; m. 22 Sept. 1852, Laura, da. of David Samuda, d. 28 June 1892; and has issue 1c to 6c.
1c. Edward Reginald Courtenay, Col. and A.A.G., N.-W. District, formerly Comdg. 11th Hussars, b. 27 June 1853; m. 1st, 1878, Kathleen Ruth (div. 1881), da. of Major-Gen. Hugh Augustus Crofton; 2ndly, 5 Aug. 1891, Mary Emily, da. of Major-Gen. Frederick Hammersley; and has issue 1d.
1d. Mary Catherine Natalie Courtenay, b. 14 Dec. 1892. [Nos. 1228 to 1251.

The Plantagenet Roll

2c. Rev. Thomas Peregrine Courtenay, Vicar of Shaugh Prior (*Shaugh Prior Vicarage, Devon*), *b.* 21 Feb. 1856; *m.* 24 Jan. 1883, Elizabeth, da. of William Gittoes.

3c. Catherine Laura Courtenay, *b.* 13 Mar. 1857.

4c. Anne Henrietta Courtenay, *b.* 12 Nov. 1858.

5c. Elizabeth Frances Courtenay, *b.* 5 Jan. 1860.

6c. Laura Georgina Courtenay, *b.* 26 Ap. 1861; *m.* 1st, 31 Mar. 1880, the Hon. Hugh Leslie Courtenay (who divorced her, May 1884); 2ndly, 7 Feb. 1885, Reginald Workman (? Reginald Latham Wenham).

3b. Henry Reginald Courtenay, Major-Gen. *late* R.A. (*Belgrave Mansions, S.W.*), *b.* 11 Mar. 1823; *m.* 17 Jan. 1893, Elizabeth, da. of Thomas Booth of Plas Madoc.

4b. Josceline Courtenay (*The Whim, Weybridge*), *b.* 22 Dec. 1824.

5b. Elizabeth Howard Courtenay, b. 1 Aug. 1808; d. 23 Dec. 1883; m. 18 Aug. 1853, the Rev. John Hughes, M.A., Vicar of Longcot, Berks.

6b. Mary Courtenay, b. 27 Aug. 1811; d. 8 Feb. 1902; m. 1st, the Rev. Henry James Wharton, Vicar of Mitcham, d. 1858; 2ndly, Major Charles Agnew, d. 8 June 1874; and had issue (four sons by 1st marriage, now all dead; one of them, however, having m. and had issue a son).

7b. Catherine Courtenay (Kenton, Torquay), b. 17 Feb. 1827; m. 3 June 1851, the Rev. George Carter, M.A., Rector of Compton Beauchamp, d. 14 Mar. 1890; and has issue 1c to 5c.

1c. Charles William Carter, b. 20 Aug. 1855; d. (–).

2c. Rev. Ernest Courtenay Carter, Vicar of St. Jude's, Whitechapel, E., b. 17 Feb. 1858; m. 1890, Lilian, da. of His Honour Judge (Thomas) Hughes of Uffington House, Chester.

3c. Rev. Wynell Henry Carter, Rector of St. Mary Arches, Exeter, b. 9 July 1869.

4c. Evelyn Howard Carter, m. 1879, Henry Edmund Carlisle.

5c. Catherine Carter.   [Nos. 1252 to 1263.

41. Descendants of ELEANOR COURTENAY (see Table V.), *b.* 4 Feb. 1711; *d.* 1764; *m.* 10 June 1734, FRANCIS BASSET of Heanton Court, Umberleigh, co. Devon, *d.* 1764; and had issue 1*a* to 3*a*.

1a. Francis Basset of Heanton Court and Umberleigh, d. unm. 1802.

2a. Elizabeth Eustacia Basset, d. (–); m. 31 Aug. 1762, John Hooke Campbell-Hooke of Bargeston, co. Pembroke, Lord Lyon King of Arms, d. 1 Sept. 1795; and had issue 1b to 2b.

1b. Charlotte Campbell-Hooke, m. Sir Thomas Gage.

2b. Caroline Campbell-Hooke, m. William Halton.

3a. Eleanora Basset, b. 9 June 1741; d. (–); m. 18 Aug. 1763, John Davie of Orleigh, Buckland Brewer, co. Devon, d. (–); and had issue 1b to 9b.

1b. Joseph Davie, afterwards (1803) Basset of Watermouth and Umberleigh, b. 18 May 1764; d. 10 Dec. 1846; m. 1799, Mary, da. of Christopher Irwin of Barnstaple, d. 21 Ap. 1862; and had issue 1c to 4c.

1c. Arthur Davie Basset of Watermouth, b. 14 May 1801; d. 8 Dec. 1870; m. 4 Dec. 1828, Harriet Sarah, da. of Thomas Smith Crawfurth, b. 14 July 1806; d. 18 Dec. 1863; and had issue 1d to 2d.

1d. Rev. Arthur Crawfurth Davie Basset, M.A. of Watermouth, b. 11 Aug. 1830; d. unm. 23 Ap. 1880.

2d. Harriet Mary Basset of Umberleigh and Watermouth, m. 7 Jan. 1858, Charles Henry Williams, now (R.L. 11 Oct. 1880) Basset, J.P., D.L., Major N.
[No. 1264.

# of The Blood Royal

Devon Hussars (son of Sir William Williams, 1st Bart. [U.K.]) (*Watermouth Castle, Ilfracombe; Umberleigh, Atherington, &c.*); and has issue 1e to 2e.

1e. Walter Basset, Lieut. R.N., b. 20 Sept. 1863; m. 18 Nov. 1890, Ellen Caroline Charlotte, da. of Adm. Sir William Montagu Dowell, G.C.B.

2e. Edith Basset Basset, m. 18 Oct. 1882, Capt. Ernest Charles Penn Curzon, *late* 18th Hussars; and has issue 1f to 2f.

1f. Charles Ernest Basset Lothian Curzon, b. 10 May 1885.

2f. Lorna Katherine Curzon, b. 10 Sept. 1887.

2c. Rev. Francis William Davie Basset, Rector of Heanton Punchardon, Devon, m. Mary, da. of William Cartwright of Teignmouth.

3c. *Augusta Mary Basset,* d. (–); m. 17 Ap. 1827, *the Rev. William Bickford Coham of Coham and Dunsland, LL.B.,* bapt. 6 Ap. 1792; d. 2 July 1843; *and had issue* 1d *to* 2d.

1d. *William Holland Bickford Coham of Coham and Dunsland, J.P., D.L.,* b. 28 July 1828; d. 22 Sept. 1880; m. 3 Sept. 1857, *Dora Elizabeth Louisa, da. of Gen. Sir Hopton Stratford Scott, K.C.B.; and had issue* 1e.

1e. Elinor Mary Bickford Coham of Coham, m. 5 June 1883, John Blyth Fleming, now (R.L. 1883) Coham-Fleming, J.P., D.L., High Sheriff, co. Devon, 1887 (*Coham, co. Devon; Upcot Avenal, Sheepwash, co. Devon*); and has issue 1f.

1f. Blyth Bickford Coham-Fleming, b. 5 Sept. 1885.

2d. *Augusta Christiana Davie Coham of Dunsland and Arscott,* d. 13 July 1901; m. 29 Ap. 1858, *Major Harvey George Dickinson,* d. Nov. 1866; *and had issue* 1e *to* 3e.

1e. Arscott William Harvey Dickinson, M.A. (Oxon.), J.P., Bar.-at-Law (*Dunsland, Brandis-Corner, N. Devon; The Tower, Compton Gifford, S. Devon*); b. 23 Ap. 1859; m. 11 Jan. 1893, Mary, da. of the Rev. Sabine Baring-Gould of Lew Trenchard; and has issue 1f to 3f.

1f. Arscott Sabine Harvey Dickinson, b. 28 Nov. 1893.

2f. Edward Dabernon Dickinson, b. 27 June 1895.

3f. Bickford Holland Coham Dickinson, b. 16 July 1900.

2e. *Augusta Frances Courtenay Dickinson,* d. 14 Oct. 1892; m. 3 Nov. 1883, *Henry Morton Tudor Tudor, Comm. R.N.; • and had issue* 1f *to* 2f.

1f. Douglas Courtenay Tudor, b. 1891.

2f. Alice Irene Tudor, b. Oct. 1887.

3e. Elinor Mary Coham Dickinson, m. 14 Ap. 1884, Capt. William M'Coy Fitz-Gerald Castle, R.N.; and has issue 1f to 2f.

1f. Basil Langford Harvey Castle, b. Sept. 1892.

2f. Violet Eleanor M'Coy Castle, b. Sept. 1888.

4c. *Mary Davie Basset,* d. (–); m. 1826, *Gen. Sir Hopton Stratford Scott of Woodville, Lucan, co. Dublin, K.C.B.; and had (with other) issue* 1d.

1d. Dora Elizabeth Louisa Scott (youngest da.), m. 3 Sept. 1857, William Holland Bickford Coham of Coham and Dunsland, J.P., D.L., d. 22 Sept. 1880; and has issue.
See p. 111, Nos. 1270–1271.

2b. Rev. Charles Davie, Rector of Heanton Punchardon, Devon, m. Bridget, da. of [——] Boyfield of Lee, co. Kent; and has issue 1c to 2c.

1c. Charles Christopher Davie, Capt. 67th Regt.

2c. Mary Jane Davie, m. John May of Broadoak, near Barnstaple, J.P., D.L.

3b. John Davie, Post-Capt. R.N., m. and had issue (a son and a da.).

4b. *Peregrine Davie, H.E.I.C.S.,* d. (*in India*); m. *and had issue.*

5b. *Eleanora Davie,* d. (–); m. 22 *Sept.* 1802, *the Rev. Lewis Lewis of Gwynfé, J.P., D.L., Rector of Clovelly,* d. 1826; *and had issue* 1c *to* 3c.

1c. *Lewis Lewis of Gwynfé, J.P., D.L.,* b. 23 Dec. 1805; d. 9 Jan. 1859; m. 9 *Mar.* 1830, *Sarah Simmons Barnes, da. of William Colbourne of Colbourne,* d. (–); *and had issue* 1d *to* 7d. [Nos. 1265 to 1287.

III

The Plantagenet Roll

1*d*. Charles Bassett Lewis of Gwinfé, J.P., D.L., Major late 44th and 25th Regt., &c. (*Gwinfé House, near Llangadock, co. Carmarthen; Hillside Hatherley, Cheltenham*), *b*. 13 Dec. 1831; *m*. 29 Jan. 1863, Sarah Amelia, da. of Samuel Brown of Clifton; and has issue 1*e*.

    1*e*. Eleanora Constance Lewis, *m*. 9 Feb. 1898, Col. James Henry Worthington Pedder.

    2*d*. Lewis Gwyn Lewis, Lieut. Indian Navy, *b*. 21 Sept. 1834.

    3*d*. Frank Davie Lewis, *b*. 31 May 1838.

    4*d*. George Septimus Lewis, *b*. 21 Sept. 1848.

    5*d*. Eleanora Jane Lewis.

    6*d*. Eustatia Harriette Lewis, *m*. the Rev. Henry Alison; and has issue (1 son and 4 das.).

    7*d*. *Augusta Blanche Lewis*, d. 31 Oct. 1890; m. *Ap*. 1890, *James Maddan*.

  2*c*. *Thomas Lewis*, d. (–) ; m. 19 *Ap*. 1836, *Victoire Maria*, *da. of Andrew Houston of Grenada, W.I.; and had issue* 1*d* to 3*d*.

    1*d*. Andrew Courtenay Lewis, *b*. 31 Jan. 1837.

    2*d*. Charles Houston Lewis, *b*. 17 Feb. 1844.

    3*d*. Eleanora Harriette Lewis.

  3*c*. *Eleanora Elizabeth Lewis*, d. (–) ; m. *Oct*. 1827, *Charles Bishop of Dolgarrey, co. Carmarthen*.

  6*b*. *Julia Davie*, m. the Rev. *J. W. Beadon*.

  7*b*. *Eustachia Davie*, m. Capt. *Shairp, 29th Regt.*

  8*b*. *Charlotte Davie*, m. Gen. *Debrisay*.

  9*b*. *Mary Davie*, m. 1st, [——] *Lumsden, H.E.I.C.S.*; 2ndly, [——] *Jones*.
                                              [Nos. 1288 to 1297.

42. Descendants of BRIDGET COURTENAY (see Table V.), *b*. 1 May 1712; *d*. 7 Mar. 1790; *m*. 29 Jan. 1735, WILLIAM ILBERT of Bowringsleigh, co. Devon, *d*. Dec. 1751; and had issue 1*a* to 8*a*.

  1*a*. *William Ilbert of Bowringsleigh, High Sheriff co. Devon* 1768; d. *Feb.* 1785; m. 1761, *Frances, da. and h. of William Roope of Horswell House, co. Devon*, d. 9 *Feb*. 1812; *and had issue* 1*b* to 7*b*.

    1*b*. *Rev. Roope Ilbert of Bowringsleigh*, b. 1763; d.s.p. 1823.

    2*b*. *Peter Ilbert of Bowringsleigh*, b. 1765; d.s.p. Nov. 1825.

    3*b*. *Courtenay Ilbert, Capt. R.A.*, b. 1780; d. 14 *Jan*. 1816; m. 1804, *Anne*, *da. of Geoffrey Taylor of Sevenoaks*, d. 17 *June* 1859; *and had issue* 1*c* to 2*c*.

    1*c*. *William Roope Ilbert of Bowringsleigh, J.P., D.L.*, b. 15 *Ap*. 1805; d. 30 *June* 1862; m. 31 *Mar*. 1830, *Augusta Jane, da. of James Somerville Fownes Somerville of Dinder House*, d. 1 Oct. 1884; *and had issue* 1*d* to 3*d*.

      1*d*. *William Roope Ilbert of Bowringsleigh, M.A., J.P., &c.*, b. 2 *Ap*. 1833; d.s.p. 30 *Ap*. 1902.

      2*d*. Frances Anne Ilbert, *m*. 14 Nov. 1866, the Right Rev. Alfred Earle, Lord Bishop Suffragan of Marlborough, Dean of Exeter, D.D. (*The Deanery, Exeter*); and has issue 1*e* to 3*e*.

        1*e*. Francis Alfred Earle, Lieut.-Col. Royal Warwickshire Regt. (*Bowringsleigh, Kingsbridge*), *b*. 18 Ap. 1869; *m*. 1 Dec. 1898, Margaret Henrietta, da. of Henry H. Nugent Bankes; and has issue 1*f*.

          1*f*. Timothy Earle Earle, *b*. 8 Ap. 1905.

        2*e*. Katherine Louisa Ilbert Earle, *m*. 19 Jan. 1899, the Rev. Robert Jones, M.A., Rector of Banham (*Banham Rectory, Norfolk*).

        3*e*. Henrietta Sophia Earle, *m*. 1904, Edward Ashburne Manisty (64 *Palace Gardens Terrace, Kensington*); and has issue 1*f*.

          1*f*. Mary Katharine Manisty.   [Nos. 1298 to 1303.

# of The Blood Royal

3*d.* Augusta Charlotte Ilbert, *unm.*

2*c.* Rev. Peregrine Arthur Ilbert, *Rector of Thurlestone,* b. 18 *Ap.* 1810; d. 10 *Nov.* 1894; m. 30 *Ap.* 1840, *Rose Anne, da. of George Welsh Owen of Lowman Green, Tiverton; and had issue* 1*d* to 8*d.*

1*d.* Sir Courtenay Peregrine Ilbert, K.C.S.I., C.I.E., M.A. (Oxon.), Clerk of the House of Commons, *formerly* Member of the Council of the Viceroy of India, and *afterwards* Parliamentary Counsel to the Treasury (*Speaker's Court, Westminster Palace, S.W.*), *b.* 12 June 1841; *m.* 27 June 1874, Jessie, da. of the Rev. Charles Bradley; and has issue 1*e* to 5*e.*

1*e.* Lettice Ilbert, *m.* 6 July 1899, Herbert Albert Laurens Fisher, Fellow and Tutor of New College, Oxford, *s.p.*

2*e.* Olive Ilbert, *unm.*

3*e.* Jessie Helen Ilbert, *m.* 24 Nov. 1904, George Young, Second Secretary of Legation, Madrid.

4*e.* Mora Peregrina Ilbert, *unm.*

5*e.* Joyce Violet Ilbert, *unm.*

2*d.* Arthur Ilbert, *b.* 23 Mar. 1843; *d.* 3 *June* 1899; *m.* 8 *May* 1886, *Beatrice* (*Enmore, East Sheen*), *da. of Rev. G. Porter; and had issue* 1*e* to 2*e.*

1*e.* Courtenay Adrian Ilbert, *b.* 22 Ap. 1888.

2*e.* Evelyn Rosemary Ilbert.

3*d.* Owen Ilbert, *b.* 13 *Jan.* 1846; *d.* 12 *Dec.* 1896; *m.* *Mar.* 1875, *Mary Elizabeth Elder, da. of Rev. E. Elder, D.D., Headmaster of Charterhouse; and had issue* 1*e* to 4*e.*

1*e.* Peregrine Edward Ilbert (*New Zealand*), *b.* 19 Oct. 1878, *unm.*

2*e.* Owen Lewis Ilbert (*Shanghai*), *b.* 13 Jan. 1880, *unm.*

3*e.* Geoffrey Arthur Ilbert (*Canada*), *b.* 5 June 1883, *unm.*

4*e.* Rose Dorothy Ilbert, *m.* 19 July 1904, George Gordon Coulton (42 *Mill Road, Eastbourne*).

4*d.* Willoughby Ilbert (12 *South Square, Gray's Inn, W.C.*), *b.* 22 Feb. 1848; *unm.*

5*d.* Donald Ilbert (*Thurlestone, Kingsbridge, Devon*), *b.* 8 June 1850, *unm.*

6*d.* Lewis George Ilbert (*Moran, Sibsagur, Assam*), *b.* 7 Dec. 1857; *m.* 30 *Nov.* 1898, Annie Hector, da. of the Rev. John Barrack; and has issue 1*e.*

1*e.* Margaret Annie Ilbert.

7*d.* Marian Lucy Ilbert, *m.* 25 Ap. 1867, Robert Campbell, Bar.-at-Law (*Bantham, Kingsbridge*); and has issue 1*e* to 3*e.*

1*e.* Ilbert Lewis Campbell.

2*e.* Hugh Elphinstone Campbell, *m.* 10 Oct. 1905, Ethel Marion, da. of Sir Pelham Warren, H.B.M.'s Consul-General at Shanghai.

3*e.* Helen Constantia Campbell.

8*d.* Helen Ilbert, *unm.*

4*b.* Bridget Mary Ilbert, *d.* 1834; *m.* *Francis Cross of Great Duryard, co. Devon.*

5*b.* Frances Ilbert, *d.* 24 *July* 1824; *m.* 17 *Feb.* 1800, *James Somerville Fownes, afterwards* (*R.L.* 15 *Jan.* 1831) *Somerville of Dinder House, J.P.,* b. 19 *Jan.* 1769; d. Oct. 1848; *and had issue* 1*c* to 2*c.*

1*c.* James Curtis Somerville of Dinder, *M.A., J.P., D.L., High Sheriff co. Somerset* 1854, b. 26 *Dec.* 1807; *d.* 13 *June* 1876; *m.* 23 *June* 1846, *Emily Periam, da. of Sir Alexander Hood, 2nd Bart.* [*U.K.*], *M.P., d.* 1 *Jan.* 1900; *and had issue* 1*d* to 4*d.*

1*d.* Arthur Fownes Somerville of Dinder, LL.B., J.P., Bar.-at-Law (*Dinder House, Wells*), *b.* 23 Ap. 1850; *m.* 4 Aug. 1880, Ellen, da. of W. Stanley Sharland of New Norfolk, New Zealand; and has issue 1*e* to 3*e.*

1*e.* Harold Fownes Somerville, *b.* 25 May 1881.

2*e.* James Fownes Somerville, Mid. R.N., *b.* 17 July 1882.

3*e.* Marjorie Fownes Somerville, *b.* 7 Sept. 1883.   [Nos. 1304 to 1329.

113

The Plantagenet Roll

2*d*. William Fownes Somerville (*Gisborne, New Zealand*), *b*. 4 June 1851; *m*. 23 Oct. 1878, Bertha Eveline, da. of Sir Thomas Tancred, 7th Bart. [E.]; and has issue 1*e* to 3*e*.

    1*e*. William Tancred Somerville, *b*. 18 July 1879.

    2*e*. Ernest Selby Somerville, *b*. 1882.

    3*e*. Aenid Bertha Somerville.

3*d*. Frances Fownes Somerville, *m*. 3 Jan. 1871, Sir Henry Churchill Maxwell-Lyte, K.C.B., F.S.A., Deputy Keeper of the Public Records since 1886, one of the Royal Commissioners on Historical MSS., &c. &c. (3 *Portman Square, W.*); and has issue.

4*d*. Emily Fownes Somerville, *m*. 5 July 1877, the Ven. Edward Leighton Elwes, Archdeacon of Chichester (*Woolbeding Rectory, Midhurst*); and has issue.

2*c*. *Augusta Jane Somerville*, d. 1 Oct. 1844; m. 31 Mar. 1830, *William Roope Ilbert of Bowringsleigh, J.P., D.L.*, d. 30 June 1862; and had issue 1d to 3d. See p. 112, Nos. 1298–1304.

6*b*. *Sophia Maria Ilbert*, d. 1 Jan. 1836; m. 31 Aug. 1810, *Robert John Harrison, Major Royal Montgomery Militia, b.* 6 Dec. 1779; d. 16 Mar. 1844; and had issue 1c to 3c.

    1*c*. *Rev. Robert John Harrison of Caerhowel, b.* 5 Ap. 1813; d. 4 Sept. 1872; m. 26 Aug. 1841, *Eliza, da. of the Rev. Devereux Mytton of Penylan, d.* 19 May 1858; and had issue 1d to 2d.

        1*d*. *Robert John Harrison of Caerhowel, J.P., D.L., High Sheriff co. Montgomery* 1880, *Lieut.-Col. 4th Batt. South Wales Borderers, b.* 27 Sept. 1852; d. 6 June 1896; m. 2 June 1874, *Charlotte Henrietta Emily, da. of Hugh Montgomery of Grey Abbey; and had issue 1e to 3e.*

            1*e*. Hugh Robert Edward Harrison of Caerhowel, Capt. 4th Batt. South Wales Borderers (*Caerhowel, co. Montgomery*), *b*. 16 Ap. 1875; *m*. 1899, Evelyn Hester, da. of Alfred Edward Miller Mundy of Shipley Hall.

            2*e*. Cecil Pryce Harrison, *b*. 25 July 1880.

            3*e*. Gwendolen Lucy Elizabeth Harrison.

        2*d*. Elizabeth Sophia Mytton Harrison, *m*. as 2nd wife, 4 Dec. 1895, William Henry Anthony Wharton of Gilling Wood and Skelton, J.P. (*Skelton Castle, co. York*).

    2*c*. *Pryce Ilbert Harrison, Hon. Col. and Lieut.-Col. Comdg. Stafford Militia, b.* 15 Nov. 1814; d. 7 May 1887.

    3*c*. *Sophia Mary Harrison*, b. 16 June 1816; d. 5 Sept. 1872; m. 6 June 1839, *Erasmus Saunders*, b. 20 Sept. 1812; d. 10 July 1872; and had issue 1d to 3d.

        1*d*. Robert Erasmus Saunders, *b*. 7 Ap. 1852; *m*. 17 Sept. 1880, Edith Marion, da. of Col. Graves; and has issue 1*e* to 3*e*.

            1*e*. Francis Percival Saunders, Lieut. R.N., *b*. 18 Sept. 1881.

            2*e*. Arthur Courtenay Saunders, Lieut. Duke of Cornwall's L.I., *b*. 29 May 1883.

            3*e*. Hilda Gladys Saunders, *b*. 8 Nov. 1884.

        2*d*. Sophia Mary Saunders (*Rosehill, Lymington*), *b*. 6 July 1842; *unm*.

        3*d*. Emily Augusta Saunders, *b*. 26 Aug. 1846; *m*. 11 Jan. 1866, Capt. Nowell Salmon, R.N., V.C.; and has issue 1*e* to 2*e*.

            1*e*. Geoffrey Nowell Salmon, Capt. Rifle Brig., *b*. 26 Nov. 1897.

            2*e*. Eleanor Nowell Salmon.

7*b*. *Augusta Ilbert*, d. 1848; m. 1869, *John Lort Phillips of Haverfordwest, d.* 18 Oct. 1839; and had issue 1c to 4c.

    1*c*. *Richard Ilbert Lort Phillips (3rd son)*, b. 1819; d. 1860; m. 1851, *Frederica Isabella, da. of Charles (de Rutzen), Baron de Rutzen; and had issue 1d to 4d.*

        1*d*. John Frederick Lort Phillips of Lawrenny, J.P., High Sheriff co. Pembroke 1880 (*Lawrenny Park, co. Pembroke*), *b*. 27 Nov. 1854; *m*. 30 July 1895, the Hon. Maude (sometime Maid of Honour to Queen Victoria), widow of Sir Andrew Barclay Walker, 1st Bart. [U.K.], da. of Haughton Charles Okeover of Okeover.

[Nos. 1330 to 1355.

# of The Blood Royal

2d. Ethelbert Edward Lort Phillips (79 *Cadogan Square, S.W.*), b. 23 Feb. 1857; *m.* 7 Feb. 1891, Louisa Jane, da. of George Gunnis.

3d. Frederica Isabella Augusta Lort Phillips (9 *Wilbraham Place, Sloane Street, S.W.*); *m.* 27 Ap. 1871, Alfred Gillett, b. 4 June 1834; d. 27 Aug. 1894; and has issue 1e to 4e.

1e. Frederick William Alfred Herbert Gillett, *late* Lieut. Pembrokeshire Yeo. Cav. (28 *Beaufort Gardens, S.W.*), b. 21 Mar. 1872; *m.* 14 Sept. 1897, Cecily Mary, da. of Henry Lamplugh Wickham of Wootton, J.P.; and has issue 1f to 2f.

1f. Raymond Gillett, b. 25 Sept. 1903.

2f. Eira Teresa Gillett, b. 1 Feb. 1901.

2e. Frederica Florence Elizabeth Gillett, b. 9 Oct. 1873; *m.* 23 Oct. 1895, Ynyr Richard Patrick Burges (*Parkanaur, Castle Caulfield, co. Tyrone*); and has issue 1f to 4f.

1f. Ynyr Alfred Burges, b. 16 Ap. 1900.

2f. Richard Ynyr Burges, b. 21 Aug. 1901.

3f. Patrick Claud Burges, b. 14 June 1905.

4f. Margaret Elizabeth Burges, b. 18 Sept. 1903.

3e. Florence Emmeline Phillippa Gillett, b. 29 Oct. 1874.

4e. Ethel Frances Gillett, b. 9 Aug. 1882.

4d. Emmeline Charlotte Louisa Lort Phillips, *m.* 5 Mar. 1885, Herbert Crowe Dugdale, Capt. *late* 16th Lancers (*Dunsinea, Phœnix Park, Dublin*); and has issue 1e to 2e.

1e. Constance Gladys Dugdale.

2e. Sybil Eldrydd Kathleen Dugdale.

2c. *Arthur Lort Phillips, d. 1867; m. Frances, da. of Morgan Jones of Pennylan, co. Cardigan; and had issue 1d to 2d.*

1d. John Phillips.

2d. Peregrine Phillips.

3c. *Frances Elizabeth Lort Phillips, d. Sept. 1867; m. 22 Oct. 1836, Henry George Fownes, Bar.-at-Law,* b. 26 *Nov.* 1809; d. 14 *Feb.* 1875; *and had issue* 1d *to* 7d.

1d. Rev. John Edward Curtis Fownes, b. 1 Oct. 1841.

2d. Henry Lort Fownes, b. 20 Nov. 1844.

3d. Augusta Fownes.

4d. Frances Maria Fownes, *m.* Nov. 1865, Thomas Percival Beckwith, and has issue.

5d. Charlotte Catherine Fownes.

6d. Sophia Fownes.

7d. Margaret Wilhelmina Fownes.

4c. *Augusta Lort Phillips, d. 6 Mar. 1880; m. 1 May 1845, Sir John Henry Scourfield, 1st Bart. [U.K.], M.P.,* d. 3 *June* 1876; *and had issue* 1d.

1d. Sir Owen Henry Philipps Scourfield, 2nd Bart. [U.K.], J.P., D.L., High Sheriff co. Pembroke 1881, Hon. Col. Pembroke Yeo. Cav., &c. (*Williamston, Neyland, R.S.O.; The Mote, Haverfordwest*), b. 10 Mar. 1847; *m.* 1st, 6 Mar. 1877, Gertrude Katherine, da. of Seymour Philipps Allen of Cresselly, d. 2 Nov. 1894; 2ndly, 29 Jan. 1896, Frances Katharina Harriet, da. of the Rev. Josiah Turner Lea of Orchardlea, Droitwich.

2a. *William Elford Ilbert, Col. South Devon Militia.*

3a. *Henry Ilbert.*

4a. *Peregrine Ilbert.*

5a. *Henry Ilbert.*

6a. *Catherine Ilbert, m. Richard Prideaux of Kingsbridge.*

7a. *Bridget Anne Ilbert, m. William Birdwood of Totnes, M.D.*

8a. *Jane Ilbert, m. J. G. Pearse of South Molton.*   [Nos. 1356 to 1380.

The Plantagenet Roll

43. Descendants of the Hon. ISABELLA COURTENAY (see Table V.), *b.* 16 July 1716; *d.* (–); *m.* 14 May 1744, JOHN ANDREW of Exeter, M.D., *b. c.* 1711; *d.* Mar. 1772; and had issue 1*a.*

1*a.* *John Andrew, Rector of Powderham* (5 *May* 1784) *and Archdeacon of Exeter,* b. 1750; d. 3 *July* 1799; m. 24 *Oct.* 1775, *Isabella, da. of the Rev. John Pitman, Rector of Alphington,* b. *c.* 1754; d. 29 *Aug.* 1825; *and had issue* 1b *to* 7b.

1*b.* *Charles Andrew, R.A.,* b. 19 *Aug.* 1792; d. *June* 1871; m. *May* 1831, *Frances, da. of William Deedes of Sandling, co. Kent, M.P.,* d. *Jan.* 1869; *and had issue* 1c *to* 2c.

1*c.* Charles Andrew, R.N.

2*c.* Isabella Andrew, *m.* the Rev. C. Nutt.

2*b.* *Isabella Andrew,* b. 26 *Aug.* 1776; d. 10 *Nov.* 1861; m. 1812, *Edward Lloyd Sanders of Stoke Hill, Exeter,* d. 1839; *and had issue* 1c *to* 2c.

1*c.* *Edward Andrew Sanders of Stoke Hill, J.P., D.L.,* b. 2 *Mar.* 1813; d. 20 *Mar.* 1905; m. 13 *June* 1848, *Marianne, da. of the Rev. James Ford* (*son of Sir Richard Ford*); *and had issue* 1d.

1*d.* Isabella Jane Sanders (*Stoke House, Exeter*), *unm.*

2*c.* *Rev. Lloyd Sanders, Rector of Whimple,* b. 3 *Ap.* 1814; d. 23 *Dec.* 1898; m. 1 *Nov.* 1854, *Emily, da. of Major Hugh Northcote; and had issue* 1d *to* 4d.

1*d.* Lloyd Charles Sanders, *b.* 3 June 1857.

2*d.* Hugh Sanders, *b.* 31 Oct. 1861; *m.* 16 Ap. 1901, Mary, da. of Henry Lowry of Havelock, N.Z.

3*d.* Rev. Arthur A. Sanders, Rector of Whimple (*Whimple Rectory, Exeter*), *b.* 26 May 1863; *m.* 13 Feb. 1905, Eva Madeline, da. of the Rev. John Lamb.

4*d.* Frances Sanders, *b.* 23 Aug. 1859.

3*b.* *Mary Anne Andrew,* b. 14 *Dec.* 1777; m. [——] *Wright; and had issue* 3 *sons.*

4*b.* *Frances Andrew,* b. 10 *Oct.* 1779; d. 1816; m. *as 2nd wife,* 1809, *William Speke of Jordans, D.L., High Sheriff co. Somerset* 1819, b. 1771; d. 17 *Ap.* 1839; *and had issue* 1c *to* 2c.

1*c.* *Francis Speke,* d. 30 *Mar.* 1845; m. *as 1st wife,* 23 *June* 1838, *the Rev. John Thomas Pine-Coffin of Portledge, co. Devon, Preb. of Exeter,* b. 8 *Jan.* 1807; *and had issue* 1d.

1*d.* *John Richard Pine-Coffin of Portledge, J.P., D.L.,* b. 3 *June* 1842; d. 16 *Mar.* 1890; m. 27 *June* 1865, *Matilda, da. of William Speke of Jordans; and had issue* 1e *to* 10e.

1*e.* John Edward Pine-Coffin, J.P., Lieut. N. Lancashire Regt. (*Portledge, near Bideford, co. Devon*), *b.* 24 Dec. 1866; *m.* 22 Aug. 1894, Louisa Gertrude Douglas, da. of John Barre Beresford of Learmont, J.P., D.L.; and has issue 1*f.*

1*f.* Edward Claude Pine-Coffin, *b.* 25 May 1895.

2*e.* William Geoffrey Pine-Coffin, *b.* 8 May 1870.

3*e.* Richard Pine-Coffin, *b.* 24 Sept. 1872.

4*e.* Tristram James Pine-Coffin, *b.* 4 Aug. 1885.

5*e.* Miriam Matilda Pine-Coffin, *m.* 18 Jan. 1888, Russell James Kerr (*The Haie, Newnham-on-Severn*); and has issue 1*f* to 4*f.*

1*f.* William John Kerr, *b.* 23 Ap. 1890.

2*f.* Ralph Kerr, *b.* 16 Aug. 1892.

3*f.* Helen Mary Kerr, *b.* 21 Oct. 1898.

4*f.* Joan Kerr, *b.* 15 May 1897.

6*e.* Winifred Georgina Pine-Coffin.

7*e.* Linda Sybil Pine-Coffin, *m.* 6 June 1894, James Rynd Brisco; and has issue 1*f.*

1*f.* Kathleen Brisco, *b.* 6 July 1895. [Nos. 1381 to 1400.

116

# of The Blood Royal

8e. Lettice Emily Pine-Coffin, m. 21 Mar. 1905, Mark Kerr, Capt. Scottish Rifles.

9e. Dorothy Isabella Pine-Coffin.

10e. Helen Gladys Pine-Coffin.

2c. Charlotte Speke, m. Marwood Mules.

5b. Charlotte Andrew, b. 23 May 1781; m. [——] Kitson; and had issue 2 sons, who d.s.p.

6b. Elizabeth Andrew, b. 23 Sept. 1783; d. 1 Mar. 1836; m. 22 July 1806, Gen. Edward William Leyborne, afterwards Leyborne-Popham of Littlecote and Hunstrete Park, J.P., b. 27 June 1764; and had issue 1c to 6c.

1c. Edward William Leyborne-Popham of Littlecote, &c., b. 6 Sept. 1807; d.s.p. 1881.

2c. Francis Leyborne-Popham, M.A., J.P., D.L., b. 14 Oct. 1809; d. 30 July 1880; m. 3 Sept. 1857, Elizabeth, da. of James Block of Charlton, co. Wilts, d. 21 Aug. 1865; and had issue 1d to 5d.

1d. Francis William Leyborne-Popham, J.P., &c. (Littlecote Park, Ramsbury, Wilts; Hunstrete Park, Pensford, Bristol), b. 8 Mar. 1862; m. 12 Nov. 1890, Maud Isabel, da. of Harry Howard of Greystoke Castle.

2d. Francis Hugh Arthur Leyborne-Popham, b. 4 Mar. 1864.

3d. Francis Alexander Compton Leyborne-Popham, b. 31 Mar. 1865; d. 3 June 1899; m. 2 Jan. 1890, Ethel, da. of J. Kent Nye of Montpelier Lodge, Sussex; and had issue 1e to 2e.

1e. Hugh Alexander Leyborne-Popham, b. Oct. 1890.

2e. Violet Leyborne-Popham, b. 1896.

4d. Elizabeth Susan Leyborne-Popham, m. as 1st wife, 9 Feb. 1882, Louis George de Hale Ponsonby, d. 6 Nov. 1887; 2ndly, 9 Sept. 1899, George Augustus Bligh Livesay (Ardmore, Parkstone, Dorset); and has issue 1e to 3e.

1e. Mabel Elizabeth Ponsonby, b. 27 Ap. 1883.

2e. Eileen Cecilia Ponsonby, b. 24 Mar. 1886.

3e. Joan Ponsonby, b. 3 July 1887.

5d. Elinor Louisa Leyborne-Popham, m. 17 Dec. 1891, Arthur Tremayne Buller (Sopwell, St. Albans); and has issue 1e to 6e.

1e. Mowbray Louis Buller, b. 11 Dec. 1892.

2e. Eric Tremayne Buller, b. 3 Jan. 1894.

3e. Michael Francis Buller, b. 13 Sept. 1896.

4e. Millicent Elinor Buller, b. 30 May 1898.

5e. Audrey Margaret Buller, b. 4 Mar. 1900.

6e. Elizabeth Gwendolen Buller, b. 7 Sept. 1902.

3c. Rev. John Leyborne-Popham, Rector of Cholton Foliatt, Wilts, b. 19 Feb. 1811; d. 24 Sept. 1872; m. 1st, Frances, da. of Edward Lloyd Sanders of Stoke House, Devon, b. 1811; d. 1839; 2ndly, Ann (Winterbourne, Bournemouth), da. of Dr. Meyrick of Ramsbury, Wilts; and had issue (by both marriages, of whom) 1d.

1d. Dorothy Leyborne-Popham, m. as 2nd wife, 11 Aug. 1887, Thomas Tyrwhitt Drake of Shardeloes, d. 24 July 1888.

4c. Alexander Hugh Leyborne-Popham, b. 27 Nov. 1821; d. 24 May 1866; m. 1854, Anne Georgiana, da. of George Dodwell of Kevinsford, co. Sligo; and had (with other) issue 1d to 2d.

1d. Alexander Hugh Leyborne-Popham, b. 1855.

2d. Annie Elizabeth Leyborne-Popham, m. 11 Nov. 1886, Charles James Phillips.

5c. Mary Anne Leyborne-Popham, d. 12 Mar. 1855; m. as 1st wife, 12 May 1835, Charles Eyre, previously Archer Houblon, of Welford Park, J.P., D.L., d. 22 July 1886; and had issue 1d to 3d.

1d. George Bramston Eyre, now (R.L. 6 Oct. 1891) Archer-Houblon, J.P.,
[Nos. 1401 to 1422.

The Plantagenet Roll

Lieut.-Col. Comdg. 3rd Royal Berks Regt., High Sheriff co. Essex 1898 (*Hallingbury Place, Bishop Stortford; Welford Park, co. Berks; 73 Upper Berkeley Street, W.*), *b.* 26 June 1843; *m.* 17 Ap. 1872, Lady Alice Frances, da. of Alexander William Crawford (Lindsay), 25th Earl of Crawford and 8th Earl of Balcarres [S.]; and has issue.

See the Clarence Volume, p. 228, Nos. 4632–4639.

2*d.* Isabella Mary Eyre, *b.* 31 Jan. 1845; *m.* 15 July 1865, Sir Archibald Hamilton Dunbar of Northfield, 7th Bart. [S.], J.P., D.L. (*Duffus House, Elgin*).

3*d.* Annie Georgina Eyre, *b.* 12 July 1849; *m.* as 2nd wife, 25 Feb. 1884, the Hon. William John Borlase-Warren-Venables-Vernon, J.P., D.L. (75 *Eccleston Square, S.W.*); and has issue.

See p. 91, Nos. 530–531.

6*c.* Isabella Leyborne-Popham (*Hollybank, Emsworth, Hants*), *m.* 16 Oct. 1841, Sir Robert Miller Mundy, K.C.M.G., *b.* 12 Oct. 1813; *d.* 1892; and has issue 1*d.* to 10*d.*

1*d.* Marian Catherine Mundy, *m.* Lieut.-Col. Charles R. Pearson, 3rd Buffs.

2*d.* Isabella Emily Mundy, *m.* as 1st wife, 28 Sept. 1872, Com. the Hon. Horatio Nelson Sandys Hood, R.N., *d.* 3 Feb. 1881; 2ndly, 1888, Percy James Edward Leveson, *d.* 1898.

3*d.* Millicent Mundy, *m.* Lieut.-Col. Frederick W. Gore.

4*d.* *Maria Georgiana Mundy, d.* 23 *Ap.* 1876; m. *as 1st wife,* 27 *Oct.* 1859, *Admiral the Hon. William Cecil Carpenter (R.L.* 1868), *previously Chetwynd-Talbot, d.* 13 *May* 1904; *and had issue* 1*e.*

1*e.* Sarah Marie Talbot-Carpenter, *unm.*

5*d.* Eleanor Mundy.

6*d.* Elizabeth Mundy.

7*d.* Emmeline Mundy.

8*d.* Constance Mundy, *m.* 9 Aug. 1881, William Webb Spencer Follett; and has issue 1*e.*

1*e.* Robert Mundy Follett.

9*d.* Rose Mundy, *m.* as 1st wife, 1890, Godfrey Henry Basil Mundy, Lieut. R.N.

10*d.* Maude Mundy, *m.* 18 Sept. 1880, Turner Collin.

7*b. Augusta Charlotte Andrew, b.* 12 *Aug.* 1787; *d.* 28 *June* 1847; *m.* 1 *June* 1809, *Ralph Barnes of Exeter, b.* 14 *July* 1781; *d.* 22 *Feb.* 1869; *and had issue* 1*c to* 2*c.*

1*c.* Rev. *Reginald Henry Barnes, Vicar of Heavitree and Preb. of Exeter, b.* 12 *Feb.* 1831; *d.* 29 *Sept.* 1889; *m.* 14 *Aug.* 1866, *Frances Mary Emily, da. of William Nation* (*she re-m.* 6 *Ap.* 1895 *T. Stevens*); *and had issue* 1*d to* 6*d.*

1*d.* Reginald Barnes, D.S.O., Capt. 4th Hussars, *b.* 13 Ap. 1871.

2*d.* Kenneth Barnes, *b.* 11 Sept. 1878.

3*d.* Violet Augusta Mary Barnes, *commonly called* Violet Vanbrugh, the well-known Actress, *b.* 11 June 1867; *m.* 9 Dec. 1894, Arthur Bourchier, M.A. (Oxon.), Actor-Manager (*The Albany, Piccadilly, W.; Otway Cottage, Bushey Heath*).

4*d.* Edith Helen Barnes, *b.* 30 Sept. 1868; *m.* as 2nd wife, 27 Sept. 1894, Sir Hugh Shakespear Barnes, K.C.S.I., K.C.V.O., Member of H.M.'s India Council (8 *Hyde Park Terrace, W.*).

5*d.* Angela Anne Barnes, *b.* 24 Feb. 1870; *m.* 8 Ap. 1898, Capt. Digby L. Mallaby, R.E., *d.* 11 Oct. 1902.

6*d.* Irene Barnes, *commonly called* Irene Vanbrugh, the well-known Actress, *b.* 2 Dec. 1872; *m.* 3 July 1901, Dion Boucicault (29B *Wimpole Street, W.*).

2*c.* Anne Barnes (7 *Alma Place, Falmouth*), *m.* 4 Oct. 1860, the Rev. William Rogers, M.A., Rector of Mawnan, *b.* 13 Jan. 1817; *d.* 28 Dec. 1889; and has issue 1*d.*

1*d.* Ralph Baron Rogers, M.A. (Oxon.), *b.* 6 Feb. 1862; *m.* 7 Sept. 1899, Edith Mary, da. of the Rev. Saltern Rogers. [Nos. 1423 to 1454.

# of The Blood Royal

44. Descendants, if any, of Lady MARY COURTENAY (see Table V.), *b.* 19 Nov. 1717; *d.* 1754; *m.* 1st, 11 Oct. 1735, JOHN LANGSTON of Park; 2ndly, JOHN DAVIE of Orleigh.

45. Descendants of the Rev. HENRY WALROND of Bradfield (see Table V.), *bur.* 8 June 1787; *m.* 22 Jan. 1759, DOROTHY, *da.* of [——] MILLFORD; and had issue 1*a* to 2*a*.

    1*a.* *William Henry Walrond of Bradfield,* b. 28 *Jan.* 1762; d. 20 *Feb.* 1845; m. *Mary, da. of* [——] *Alford of Sandford ; and had issue* 1b *to* 2b.

    1*b.* *Frances Walrond of Bradfield,* b. 1796; d. 1866; m. 6 *July* 1815, *Benjamin Bowden Dickinson, afterwards* (*R.L.* 22 *Ap.* 1845) *Walrond, J.P., D.L.,* b. 26 *Dec.* 1793; d. 15 *July* 1851; *and had issue* 1c *to* 2c.

    1*c.* *Sir John Walrond Walrond, 1st Bart.* [*U.K.*]*, J.P., D.L., M.P.,* b. 1 *Mar.* 1818; d. 23 *Ap.* 1889; m. 20 *May* 1845, *Hon. Frances Caroline, da. of Samuel* (*Hood*)*, 2nd Lord Bridport* [*G.B.*]*; and had issue* 1d *to* 7d.

    1*d.* The Right Hon. Sir William Hood Walrond, 2nd Bart. [U.K.], P.C., M.P., J.P., D.L. (*Bradfield, Cullompton, Devon ; 9 Wilbraham Place, S.W.*), b. 26 Feb. 1849 ; *m.* 11 Ap. 1871, Elizabeth Katharine, da. and h. of James Pitman of Dunchideock House, Devon ; and has issue 1*e* to 3*e*.

    1*e.* William Lionel Charles Walrond (*Tidcombe, Tiverton*), *b.* 22 May 1876 ; *m.* 18 June 1904, Lottie, da. of George Coats of 39 Park Lane, W., and Belleisle, co. Ayr.

    2*e.* Evelyn Maud Walrond, *m.* 27 Aug. 1901, George Russell Northcote (15 *Tite Street, Chelsea, S.W.*).

    3*e.* Dorothy Katharine Walrond, *m.* 28 Oct. 1897, Arthur Robert Pyers (Southwell), 5th Viscount Southwell [I.] (*Knolton Hall, Ellesmere*) ; and has issue 1*f* to 4*f*.

    1*f.* Hon. Robert Arthur William Joseph Southwell, *b.* 5 Sept. 1898.

    2*f.* Hon. Francis Joseph Southwell, *b.* 31 Mar. 1900.

    3*f.* Hon. John Michael Southwell, *b.* 17 Dec. 1901.

    4*f.* Hon. Elizabeth Katharine Mary Southwell, *b.* 2 June 1904.

    2*d.* Arthur Melville Walrond, *formerly* Sub.-Lieut. R.N. (*Redhayes, Pinhoe, Exeter ; Naval and Military*), *b.* 17 Mar. 1861 ; *m.* 27 Dec. 1888, Marion, da. of William Ronnell Coleridge of Salston House, Ottery, Devon ; and has issue 1*e* to 2*e*.

    1*e.* Victor Walrond, *b.* 1889.

    2*e.* Nancy Walrond, *b.* 9 Sept. 1891.

    3*d.* Katherine Mary Walrond (*Bickleigh, Tiverton*), *m.* 21 June 1864, Charles Arthur Williams Troyte of Huntsham Court, Devon, D.L., *b.* 11 May 1842 ; *d.* 11 Ap. 1896 ; and has issue 1*e* to 5*e*.

    1*e.* Hugh Leonard Acland-Troyte, J.P., *formerly* Lieut. 20th Hussars, Major 3rd Vol. Batt. Devonshire Regt. (*Huntsham Court, Bampton, N. Devon ; National*), *b.* 18 Dec. 1870 ; *m.* 3 June 1899, Helen Jessie, da. of Henry Chapman of Wanstead, Essex.

    2*e.* Gilbert John Acland-Troyte, Capt. King's Royal Rifle Corps, *b.* 4 Sept. 1876.

    3*e.* Herbert Walter Acland-Troyte, *b.* 13 Sept. 1882.

    4*e.* Frances Lucy Acland-Troyte, *m.* 8 May 1897, Col. Francis Sudlow Garratt, C.B., D.S.O., 6th Dragoon Guards ; and has issue 1*f* to 2*f*.

    1*f.* Gertrude Mary Garratt.

    2*f.* Esther Frances Garratt.

    5*e.* Cicely Mary Acland Troyte.   [Nos. 1455 to 1473.

The Plantagenet Roll

4d. Margaret Walrond (41 *Portland Place, W.*), *m.* 30 Mar. 1875, Charles Henry Rolle (Hepburn-Stuart-Forbes-Trefusis), 20th Baron Clinton [E.], *d.* 20 Mar. 1904; and has issue.
See the Tudor Roll of " The Blood Royal of Britain," p. 170, Nos. 20192–20195, and Nos. 20199–20201.

5d. Gertrude Walrond, *m.* 1 Nov. 1879, Sir Charles Thomas Dyke Acland, 12th Bart. [E.], J.P., D.L., sometime (1882–1892) M.P. (*Holnicote, Taunton ; Killerton, Exeter*).

6d. Mary Caroline Walrond (*Farnborough, Banbury*), *m.* 1st, as 2nd wife, 5 Oct. 1876, Lieut.-Col. Sir George Clay, 3rd Bart. [U.K.], *b.* 14 Aug. 1831; *d.* 30 June 1878; 2ndly, 28 Feb. 1881, Lieut.-Col. Walter Henry Holbech, *b.* 11 May 1845; *d.* 6 Mar. 1901; and has issue 1*e* to 5*e*.

1e. William Hugh Holbech, *b.* 18 Aug. 1882.

2e. Ronald Herbert Acland Holbech, *b.* 5 Jan. 1887.

3e. Sybil Mary Clay, *b.* 18 Jan. 1878.

4e. Olive Ruth Holbech, *b.* 31 Ap. 1893.

5e. Marjorie Walrond Holbech, *b.* 20 Oct. 1897.

7d. Edith Isabel Walrond, *m.* 29 July 1875, Herbert James Benyon, *formerly* Fellowes, J.P., D.L., High Sheriff co. Dorset 1892, and Lord-Lieut. co. Berks (*Englefield House, near Reading ; Kingston House, near Dorchester*); and has issue 1*e* to 4*e*.

1e. Henry Arthur Benyon, *b.* 9 Dec. 1884.

2e. Gertrude Fellowes, *b.* 29 Aug. 1876; *m.* Jan. 1897, the Rev. Francis Edward Rooke, B.A. (Oxon.), Vicar of Mortimer West End (*Mortimer West End Vicarage, Berks*); and has issue 1*f* to 2*f*.

1f. Henry Wallace Rooke, *b.* 17 Nov. 1897.

2f. Marjorie Lilian Rooke, *b.* 24 Feb. 1900.

3e. Edith Marion Benyon, *b.* 19 Jan. 1880.

4e. Winifred Benyon, *b.* 28 Mar. 1893.

2c. Margaret Louisa Walrond (*Eastbourne House, Teignmouth*), *m.* 25 Aug. 1863, Edward Drewe, Capt. 1st Devon Militia, *b.* 26 Feb. 1834; *d.* 27 June 1883.

2b. Margaret Walrond.

2a. Peggy Walrond, bapt. 25 *Sept.* 1765; *m. Tristram Whitter, Comm. R.N. ;* and had issue. [Nos. 1474 to 1497.

46. Descendants, if any, of [——] WALROND, da. of William WALROND of Bradfield, who *d.* 1746 (see Table V.), wife of [——] FARRER of Lupitt.

47. Descendants of JANE CHAMPERNOWNE of Dartington, co. Devon (see Table V.), *bur.* 16 Jan. 1768; *m.* as 1st wife, 31 Oct. 1765, the Rev. RICHARD HARINGTON, Rector of Powderham, *b.* 11 Ap. 1729; *d.* June 1812; and had issue 1*a*.

1a. *Arthur Harington, afterwards* (*R.L.* 13 *May* 1774) *Champernowne of Dartington, M.P., High Sheriff co. Devon* 1811, b. 30 *Dec.* 1767; d. 7 *June* 1819; m. 11 *Sept.* 1806, *Louisa, da. of John Buller of Morval, co. Devon, d.* 31 *Dec.* 1870; *and had issue* 1*b to* 5*b*.

1b. *Henry Champernowne of Dartington, b.* 14 *Sept.* 1815; *d.* 24 *May* 1851; *m.* 24 *Ap.* 1838, *Charlotte, da. of Sir Antony Buller of Pound, d.* 28 *Oct.* 1899; *and had issue* 1*c to* 5*c*.

RICHARD (PLANTAGENET), 3RD DUKE OF YORK, K.G.

THE COMMON ANCESTOR OF ALL THOSE NAMED IN THIS AND THE TWO
PRECEDING VOLUMES.

In the South Window of Penrith Church, Cumberland.

# of The Blood Royal

1c. *Arthur Champernowne of Dartington, M.A., J.P.,* b. 19 *Mar.* 1839; d. 1887; m. 11 *Oct.* 1870, *Helen Elizabeth Caroline (Hood Manor, Dartington, Totnes),* da. *of Michael Linning Melville of Hartfield Grove ; and had issue* 1*d to* 9*d.*

    1*d.* Arthur Melville Champernowne of Dartington, B.A. (Oxon.), Bar.-at-Law (*Dartington Hall, Totnes*), *b.* 16 Aug. 1871.

    2*d.* Amyas Walter Champernowne; *b.* 19 Sept. 1873.

    3*d.* Robert Antony Champernowne, *b.* 6 Jan. 1882.

    4*d.* Gilbert Raleigh Champernowne, *b.* 1884.

    5*d.* Edward Buller Champernowne, *b.* 1885.

    6*d.* Charlotte Elizabeth Champernowne.

    7*d.* Elinor Marcia Champernowne.

    8*d.* Helen Frances Champernowne, *b.* 11 Jan. 1878; *m.* Ap. 1905 [——].

    9*d.* Agnes Dorothy Champernowne, *b.* 20 Dec. 1880.

2c. Henry Champernowne, Col. *late* R.E. (44 *Draycott Place, S.W. ; Pound Yelverton*), *b.* 21 May 1840 ; *m.* 30 Aug. 1880, Elizabeth Charlotte, da. of Major-Gen. Thomas Andrew Lumsden Murray, R.E.

3c. Rev. Walter Champernowne, M.A. (Oxon.), Rector of Northleigh (*Northleigh Rectory, Honiton*), *b.* 3 Sept. 1848; *m.* 14 Nov. 1905, Elizabeth Mary, da. of George Andrew Spottiswoode of Chatton, J.P.

4c. Caroline Champernowne.

5c. Margaret Champernowne.

2b. *Rev. Richard Champernowne, M.A., Rector of Dartington,* b. 4 *Sept.* 1817 ; d. 22 *Oct.* 1890 ; m. 2 *May* 1848, *Elizabeth, da. of the Rev. Thomas Keble, Vicar of Bisley, co. Gloucester,* d. 6 *Mar.* 1870 ; *and had issue* 1c *to* 9c.

    1c. Philip Henry Champernowne, B.A. (Oxon.), *formerly* Major 5th Vol. Batt. Rifle Brig. (Prince Consort's Own) (*Seale Lodge, Farnham, Surrey*), *b.* 17 Oct. 1859 ; *m.* 6 Ap. 1893, Katharine Theresa Vidal, da. of John Alexander Radcliffe of 39 Cambridge Terrace, Hyde Park, W. ; and has issue 1*d* to 2*d.*

        1*d.* Richard Harington Radcliffe Champernowne, *b.* 7 Oct. 1897.

        2*d.* Doris Champernowne, *b.* 1895.

    2c. Francis Gawayne Champernowne, B.A. (Oxon.), Bar.-at-Law (*New University*), *b.* 22 Ap. 1866.

    3c. Thomas Arthur Champernowne, Lieut. 38th Batt. Imp. Yeo., *b.* 3 Ap. 1868.

    4c. Rev. John Edward Champernowne, M.A. (Oxon.), Curate of St. Stephen and St. Lawrence's, Exeter (11 *College Road, Exeter*), *b.* 5 Mar. 1870 ; *m.* 30 Sept. 1902, Audrey Eliza, da. of Joseph Russell Evans of 3 Christ Church Road, Winchester.

    5c. *Mary Elizabeth Champernowne,* b. 1 *July* 1853 ; d. 22 *Feb.* 1882 ; m. 28 *Ap.* 1881, *the Rev. Thomas Woodman, Rector of Down St. Mary, formerly Canon of Bloemfontein, &c. (Down St. Mary Rectory, Bow, North Devon).*

    6c. Sarah Louisa Champernowne, *m.* 1885, the Rev. George Kestell Kestell-Cornish, M.A. (Oxon.), Archdeacon of Madagascar (*Ambinanindrano, Mahanoro, Madagascar*).

    7c. Agnes Charlotte Champernowne.

    8c. Edith Alicia Champernowne, *m.* 20 Dec. 1895, James Frederic Williams (*The Cottage, Dartington*); and has issue 1*d* to 2*d.*

        1*d.* Frederic Williams, *b.* (at Roma, Queensland) 14 Ap. 1898.

        2*d.* Jane Champernowne Williams, *b.* (at Toowoomba, Queensland) 7 Feb. 1900.

    9c. Cecilia Margaret Champernowne, *m.* 9 Jan. 1890, Charles Wigan, M.A. (Oxon.) (*Lynbrook, Knaphill, Surrey ; Athenæum*); and has issue 1*d* to 5*d.*

        1*d.* Charles Richard Wigan, *b.* (twin) 29 Dec. 1890.

        2*d.* Thomas Keble Wigan, *b.* 1892.   [Nos. 1498 to 1524.

The Plantagenet Roll

3d. Mary Cecilia Wigan, *b.* (twin) 29 Dec. 1890.

4d. Gwendolen Akers Wigan, *b.* 1897.

5d. Margaret Harington Wigan, *b.* 1898.

3b. *Jane Champernowne,* d. *22 Jan.* 1892; m. *12 Aug.* 1828, *the Rev. William Martin, Vicar of Staverton, b.* 8 *Feb.* 1798; d. *10 Ap.* 1850; *and had issue 1c to 7c.*

1c. Rev. *William Martin, b.* 11 *Jan.* 1831; d. *7 Sept.* 1890; m. *10 Feb.* 1886, *Mary Tucker, da. of Richard Luxton; and had issue 1d.*

1d. William Arthur Martin, *b.* 2 Dec. 1886.

2c. Rev. Richard Martin, Vicar of Ilfracombe, Prebendary of Exeter *(Ilfracombe Vicarage, Devon), b.* 1 Mar. 1836; *m.* 30 June 1863, Eliza Rose, da. of the Rev. Daniel Rose Fearon, Vicar of St. Mary Church, Devon.

3c. Rev. Charles Martin, Rector of Dartington, *formerly* Warden of Radley College *(Dartington Rectory, Totnes), b.* 17 Oct. 1840; *m.* 14 Sept. 1869, Dora Frances, da. of George Moberly, sometime Lord Bishop of Salisbury ; and has issue *1d* to *9d.*

1d. Charles Selwyn Martin *(The Lydes, Toddington, Winchcombe, Gloucestershire), b.* 1 Feb. 1873, *m.* 29 Jan. 1902, Cynthia Mildred, da. of Arthur Herbert Savory of Merry Gardens, Burley ; and has issue *1e.*

1e. Charles Christopher Martin, *b.* 24 Dec. 1902.

2d. Rev. John Sturges Martin, Curate of Dartington *(Meads, Dartington), b.* 2 May 1874 ; *m.* 9 Ap. 1902, Anne Mildred Llewelyn, da. of the Rev. Jerome John Mercier, Rector of Kemerton ; and has issue *1e.*

1e. Dorothy Palma Martin, *b.* 5 Ap. 1903.

3d. Arthur Campbell Martin, *b.* 20 Aug. 1875.

4d. William Keble Martin, *b.* 9 July 1877.

5d. Richard Harington Martin, *b.* 11 Sept. 1881.

6d. Edith Renira Martin, *b.* 5 Aug. 1870.

7d. Dora Caroline Martin, *b.* 21 Aug. 1871.

8d. Margaret Eleanor Martin, *b.* 16 May 1879.

9d. Mary Katharine Martin, *b.* 27 Ap. 1880.

4c. Caroline Martin, *b.* 17 June 1829 *(Longcause, Totnes).*

5c. *Frances Martin,* b. *13 July* 1834; d. *13 May* 1891; m. *24 June* 1852, *the Rev. Joseph Lloyd Brereton, Preb. of Exeter, Rector of Little Massingham, d.* 15 *Aug.* 1901; *and had issue 1d to 11d.*

1d. *William Lloyd Brereton, Lieut.-Col. 1st Batt. Royal Munster Fusiliers, b.* 4 *Jan.* 1856; d. *1 Aug.* 1898; m. *16 Ap.* 1890, *Ethel Alice, da. of Gen. Bertie Clay, Bengal Staff Corps; and had issue 1e.*

1e. William Munster Lloyd Brereton, *b.* 29 Nov. 1894.

2d. Rev. Francis Lloyd Brereton, Head Master of the North-Eastern County School, Barnard Castle, *b.* 27 Aug. 1859 ; *m.* 9 Aug. 1900, Maud Louise, da. of Samuel Dixon, Esq. ; and has issue *1e* to *2e.*

1e. Joseph Lloyd Brereton, *b.* 2 Sept. 1901.

2e. Henry Lloyd Brereton, *b.* 19 Ap. 1903.

3d. Rev. Henry Lloyd Brereton, Rector of Little Massingham *(Little Massingham Rectory, Norfolk), b.* 13 Jan. 1864.

4d. David Lloyd Brereton, Capt. 2nd Batt. Durham Light Infantry, *b.* 11 Sept. 1875.

5d. Rev. Philip Harington Lloyd Brereton, Fellow of St. Augustine's College, Canterbury, *b.* 15 May 1877.

6d. Anna Frances Brereton, *b.* 21 June 1854 ; *m.* 6 Jan. 1892, the Rev. Joseph Hugill Thompson, Rector of Romansleigh and late Headmaster of the Devon County School *(Romansleigh Rectory, Devon)* ; and has issue *1e.*

1e. Arthur Brereton Thompson, *b.* 6 Dec. 1892. [Nos. 1525 to 1551.

# of The Blood Royal

7d. Henrietta Mary Brereton, b. 7 July 1858.
8d. Margaret Brereton, b. 7 Aug. 1862.
9d. Jane Brereton, b. 12 Dec. 1867.   (*Little Massingham Rectory,*
10d. Eleanor Brereton, b. 12 Feb. 1869.   *Norfolk.*)
11d. Cicely Brereton, b. 14 Nov. 1873.

6c. Anne Martin, b. 16 Aug. 1842.
7c. Louisa Renira Martin, b. 27 Jan. 1844.   (*Longcause, Totnes.*)

4b. Caroline Champernowne, b. 21 Nov. 1810; d. 1 Feb. 1886; m. 22 *June* 1842, the Rev. Isaac Williams of Stinchcombe, co. Gloucester, Fellow of Trin. Coll. (*Oxon.*), b. 12 Dec. 1802; d. 1 *May* 1865; and had issue 1c to 4c.

   1c. Rev. John Edward Williams (15 *Westbourne Gardens, W.*), b. 9 June 1843; m. 31 Aug. 1881, Emily Mary, da. of Rev. R. Wade-Gery; and has issue 1d.

      1d. Robert Henry Isaac Williams, b. 26 May 1885.

   2c. Rev. George Arthur Williams (18 *Rusper Road, Horsham*), b. 30 June 1844; m. 11 Jan. 1871, Emily, da. of Rev. E. Bullock Webster; and has issue 1d.

      1d. Gertrude Louisa Williams, b. 28 Mar. 1872; m. 21 Ap. 1903, William A. Hubert (*Rosehill, Billingshurst*); and has issue 1e.

         1e. William Henry Hubert, b. 5 Mar. 1904.

   3c. Antony Champernowne Williams (*Meadowlands, Dursley*), b. 28 Oct. 1848; m. 27 Sept. 1884, Mabel Austen, da. of Col. Edward Thornbrough Parker Shewen, R.M.L.I.

   4c. James Frederic Williams (*The Cottage, Dartington*), b. 12 Jan. 1852; m. 20 Dec. 1895, Edith Alicia Champernowne, da. of Rev. Richard Champernowne of Dartington; and has issue.
See p. 121, Nos. 1520–1521.

5b. Maria Champernowne, d. 29 Ap. 1893; m. 8 Mar. 1836, Charles Herbert Mallock of Cockington, J.P., b. 28 May 1802; d. 20 Ap. 1873; and had issue 1c to 7c.

   1c. Richard Mallock of Cockington, J.P., D.L., sometime (1886–1895) M.P., b. 28 Dec. 1843; d. 29 June 1900; m. 1st, 18 Ap. 1876, Mary Jones, da. of Thomas Ashton Hodgson Dickson of Liverpool, d. 2 June 1878; 2ndly, 19 June 1880, Elizabeth Emily,[1] da. of George Maconchy of Rathmore; and had issue 1d to 4d.

      1d. Charles Herbert Mallock, Capt. R.A. (*Cockington Court, Torquay*), b. 15 May 1878.

      2d. Roger Champernowne Mallock, b. 21 Sept. 1881.

      3d. Rawlyn Richard Maconchy Mallock, b. 18 Mar. 1885.

      4d. Helen Mary Mallock, b. 7 Mar. 1877.

   2c. Rev. John Jervis Mallock, M.A., Rector of East Allington (*East Allington Rectory, Devon*), b. 10 June 1856; m. 8 Aug. 1888, Alice Deborah,[1] da. of George Maconchy of Rathmore.

   3c. Charlotte Sophia Mallock.

   4c. Harriet Mallock.

   5c. Frances Mallock, m. 28 July 1880, the Rev. Josiah Newman, M.A., Rector of West Buckland (*West Buckland Rectory, Devon*); and has issue 1d to 6d.

      1d. Charles Herbert Alfred Newman, b. 3 July 1887.

      2d. Mary Louisa Newman, b. 10 May 1881.

      3d. Frances Agnes Newman, b. 20 Sept. 1882.

      4d. Joan Olive Anastasia Newman, b. 31 Jan. 1884.

      5d. Ruth Ellen Newman, b. 23 Aug. 1885.

      6d. Rachel Jaquete Newman, b. 15 Oct. 1892.

   6c. Elizabeth Mallock.

   7c. Catherine Mallock.   [Nos. 1552 to 1583.

---

[1] For their descent from George, Duke of Clarence, see the Clarence Volume, pp. 283–284.

The Plantagenet Roll

48. Descendants of FRANCES YARDE (see Table V.), *b.* 18 June (and *bapt.* at Stoke Gabriel 17 July) 1748; *d.* 7 Aug. 1823; *m.* (at Dartington) 8 Ap. 1776, JOHN SEARLE of Allerton, co. Devon, *b.* 19 Jan. 1742; *d.* 13 Sept. 1826; and had issue 1*a.*

1*a.* *Frances Searle (eventual heiress),* b. 25 Nov. 1784 *(and bapt.* 21 *July* 1786); d. 23 *Mar.* 1856; m. 1 *Aug.* 1809, *the Rev. James Champion Hicks, B.A. (Oxon.) (son of Adm. Thomas Hicks, R.N.), Chaplain R.N.* 1807–8, *Master of Launceston Grammar School, and Chaplain to the Duke of Northumberland* 1821, *and afterwards* (1834–1855) *Perpetual Curate of Rangeworthy, co. Gloucester, bapt.* 23 *Oct.* 1781; d. 6 *Sept.* 1855; *and had issue* 1*b to* 5*b.*

1*b.* *Rev. James Hicks, B.A. (Oxon.), Vicar of Pydle-trenthide, co. Dorset, author of "The Teaching of the Church," "Prayer Book Leaflets," &c., b.* 21 *July* 1810; d. 28 Dec. 1889; m. 16 *July* 1845, *Emma, da. of William Barry, d.* 3 *June* 1895; *and had issue* 1*c to* 8*c.*

1*c. William Searle Hicks of Newcastle-on-Tyne, b.* 6 *Mar.* 1849; *d.* 21 *Nov.* 1902; *m.* 29 *Ap.* 1875, *Anne Alice* (3 *Roseworth Villas, Gosforth, Newcastle-on-Tyne), da. of the Rev. Edward Hussey Adamson, M.A., Vicar of St. Alban's, Heworth; and had issue* 1*d to* 9*d.*

1*d.* James Edward Hicks (3 *Roseworth Villas, Gosforth, Newcastle-on-Tyne*).

2*d.* Henry Leicester Hicks, *b.* 5 Feb. 1883.

3*d.* George Adamson Hicks, *b.* 29 Sept. 1884.

4*d.* Francis William Hicks, *b.* 18 May 1886.

5*d.* John Searle Hicks, *b.* 1 Feb. 1888.

6*d.* Charles Herbert Hicks, *b.* 2 Nov. 1890.

7*d.* Frances Anne Hicks, *b.* 21 Feb. 1876.

8*d.* Eleanor Mary Hicks, *b.* 1 Ap. 1877.

9*d.* Margaret Hicks, *b.* 16 July 1878.

2*c.* John George Hicks, Col. *late* 2nd Northumberland (Percy) Vol. Artillery *(Oakfield, Benwell, Newcastle-on-Tyne), b.* 4 June 1850; *m.* 1st, 20 July 1883, Mary Jane, da. of Anthony Carr of London, *d.* 7 May 1884; 2ndly, 18 Ap. 1892, Mary, da. of the Rev. William Proctor, M.A., Vicar of Doddington, Hon. Canon of Durham and Rural Dean of Bamburgh; and has issue 1*d.*

1*d.* Hilda Mary Hicks, *b.* 23 Ap. 1884.

3*c.* Rev. Edward Barry Hicks, M.A. (Trin. Col., Dublin), Vicar of Killingworth 1890–1895, *afterwards* of St. Mary's, Newcastle-on-Tyne (*St. Mary's Vicarage, Newcastle-on-Tyne), b.* 27 June 1858; *m.* 4 Aug. 1886, Mary, da. of Robert Middlemas; and has issue 1*d to* 6*d.*

1*d.* Gilbert Hicks, *b.* 24 July 1887.

2*d.* Henry Charlewood Hicks, *b.* 2 June 1891.

3*d.* Walter Edward Hicks, *b.* 23 Jan. 1893.

4*d.* William Barry Hicks, *b.* 18 Jan. 1897.

5*d.* Mary Isabel Hicks, *b.* 18 Aug. 1889.

6*d.* Gertrude Middlemas Hicks, *b.* 19 Nov. 1894.

4*c.* Emma Frances Hicks, Sister Superior Clewer Sisterhood, *b.* 22 July 1847.

5*c.* Margaret Hicks, *b.* 17 Ap. 1853.

6*c.* Louisa Mary Hicks, *b.* 28 Feb. 1855; *m.* 28 May 1885, Henry Clement Charlewood (3 *Bentinck Terrace, Newcastle-on-Tyne*); and has issue 1*d to* 5*d.*

1*d.* Clement James Charlewood, *b.* 27 Mar. 1888.

2*d.* George Edward Charlewood, *b.* 26 Mar. 1890.

3*d.* William Henry Charlewood, *b.* 18 Feb. 1893.

4*d.* Alfred Charlewood, *b.* 14 Mar. 1894.

5*d.* Catherine Rosamond Charlewood, *b.* 15 Feb. 1891.

[Nos. 1584 to 1609.

# of The Blood Royal

7c. Sarah Hicks, b. 2 Sept. 1859 ; d. 14 Feb. 1891 ; m. 14 Ap. 1883, Charles Herbert Elliot (Kirk Braddon, Croydon Road, Beckenham) ; and had issue 1d to 4d.

1d. William Faber Elliot, b. 11 Mar. 1884.

2d. Charles Barry Elliot, b. 2 Sept. 1886.

3d. Herbert Benbow Elliot, b. 28 Jan. 1890.

4d. Amy Mary Elliot, b. 4 Aug. 1885.

8c. Ellen Elizabeth Hicks, b. 8 Jan. 1861.

2b. Francis Yarde Hicks (5 Rolle Villas, Exmouth), b. 26 June 1821.

3b. Amelia Mary Hicks, b. 11 Mar. 1826.

4b. Ellen Hicks, b. 1 Dec. 1828.

5b. Louisa Hicks (5 Rolle Villas, Exmouth), b. 12 Jan. 1829 ; m. the Rev. William Henry Leicester, M.A. (Camb.), Vicar of Marthall, Cheshire, and afterwards of St. Juliot, Cornwall, d. 12 May 1901. [Nos. 1610 to 1618.

49. Descendants, if any, of ANNE COURTENAY (see Table V.), *d.* 1775 (*bur.* in St. Paul's, Exeter) ; *m.* JOHN GILBERT of Compton in Marldon.

50. Descendants, if any surviving, of JAMES COURTENAY of Walredon, Whitchurch, co. Devon (see Table V.), *b. c.* 1655 ; *bur.* (at Powerham) 7 Jan. 1727 ; *m.* (lic. dated 27 Mar.) 1682, ELIZABETH, da. of [——] BOURDON of Cheverston, Kenton, *bur.* (at Whitchurch) 19 Jan. 1703 ; and had issue 1*a* to 3*a*.

1a. James Courtenay, 2nd son, bapt. 12 Mar. 1787.

2a. George Courtenay, b. 7 May 1699 ; d. 15 June 1751, m. 25 May 1738, Mary, da. of John Keysor Ipplepen ; and had issue 1b to 5b.

1b. George Courtenay, b. 28 Sept. 1746 ; liv. unm. 1768 ; d.s.p.

2b. Mary Kay Courtenay, b. 1 Oct. 1740.

3b. Elizabeth Courtenay, b. 31 Mar. 1742.

4b. Isabella Courtenay, b. 16 July 1744.

5b. Eleanora Courtenay, b. 9 Feb. 1749.

3a. Ann Courtenay, bapt. 14 Aug. 1690 ; bur. (at Whitchurch) 19 July 1762 ; m. John Jope of Buckland and Monachorum.

51. Descendants, if any, of GEORGE COURTENAY of Fitzford, M.P., *b.* 24 Dec. 1657 ; and of WILLIAM COURTENAY, Lieut. of Marines, will dated 30 Jan. 1702, proved 15 Mar. 1703 [? *m.* SUSANNA, da. of John KELLOND of Painsford, Ashprington] (see Table V.).

52. Descendants of ISABELLA MARY SILLY (see Table V.), *b.* 5 May 1741 ; *d.* 3 Dec. 1804 ; *m.* (at Bodmin) 24 Aug. 1764, HENRY SLOGGETT, R.N., *b.* 12 Nov. 1739 ; *d.* 1 Dec. 1784 ; and had issue 1*a* to 2*a*.

1a. Rev. Charles Sloggett of the Mansion, Saltash, co. Cornwall, b. 3 Dec. 1766 ; d. 6 Dec. 1826 ; m. 7 Mar. 1788, Mary, da. of Capt. Jesse Barlow, R.N. ; and had issue 1b.

The Plantagenet Roll

1b. Jesse Henry Sloggett of the Mansion, Saltash, R.N., b. 7 *Feb.* 1790; d.
20 *Feb.* 1849; m. (*at Digby, Canada, being then an Officer of H.M.S. "Wye"*),
28 *June* 1818, *Sarah Anne, da. and co-h. of Edward Benjamin Lee of Digby,
Canada,* d. 8 *Mar.* 1842; *and had issue* 1c *to* 2c.

1c. *Rev. Charles Sloggett, Rector of Chiddingfold, co. Surrey,* b. 21 *Ap.* 1819;
d. 26 *Nov.* 1903; m. 8 *Mar.* 1855, *Mary, da. of Æneas Cannon, M.D.,* d. *May*
1867; *and had issue* 1d *to* 4d.

1d. Henry Maxwell Sloggett, Lieut.-Col. R.A.M.C. (*Malta*), b. 21 July 1858;
m. 23 Sept. 1890, Louisa Monica, da. of Nicholas Coulthurst of Southsea.

2d. Mary Isobel Roquier Sloggett, *m.* 20 Ap. 1881, John Henry Miles (*Green-
mount, Ballydehob, co. Cork*); and had issue 1e to 3e.

1e. Robert Charles Miles, b. 2 Nov. 1883.

2e. George Henry Miles, b. 18 June 1885.

3e. Gladys Mary Miles.

3d. Alice Emma Sloggett, *m.* 26 Nov. 1882, the Rev. Thomas Stephen Cooper,
M.A., F.S.A. (*Chaleshurst, Chiddingfold, co. Surrey*); and has issue 1e to 6e.

1e. Osbert Stephen Cooper, b. 2 May 1887.

2e. Alice Maud Evelyn Cooper.

3e. Brenda Cecil Cooper.

4e. Joan Marion Cooper.

5e. Audrey Legh Cooper.

6e. Marjorie Aldham Cooper.

4d. Editha Gertrude Sloggett, *m.* 19 Feb. 1901, Llewellyn Thomas Manly Nash,
Lieut.-Col. R.A.M.C. (*Totland Bay, Freshwater, Isle of Wight*); and has issue 1e
to 2e.

1e. Charles Montgomery Llewellyn Nash, b. 18 Mar. 1902.

2e. Thomas Arthur Manly Nash, b. 18 June 1905.

2c. *William Henry Sloggett of Tremabyn, Paignton, Inspector-General R.N.,* b.
30 *Aug.* 1820; d. 9 *June* 1902; m. 22 *June* 1848, *Elizabeth Clarke, da. of Thomas
Cornish Crossing, J.P.,* d. 30 *Nov.* 1892; *and had issue* 1d *to* 3d.

1d. *Henry Charles Sloggett, Lieut. R.N.,* b. 15 *Jan.* 1852; d. (*at Honolulu*)
24 *Mar.* 1905; m. 1 *June* 1875, *Annie, da. of Richard Ellery of Wearde House,
Saltash, co. Cornwall,* d. (*at Honolulu*) 29 *May* 1900; *and had issue* 1e *to* 2e.

1e. Henry Digby Sloggett (naturalised American) (*Lihue, Kauai, Hawaii*), b.
18 Sept. 1876; m. 3 June 1903, Lucy Etta, da. of Senator S. W. Wilcox of Kauai,
Hawaii; and has issue 1f.

1f. Richard Henry Sloggett, b. 31 May 1904.

2e. Myra Sloggett, *m.* 5 July 1898, J. F. Humburg of Honolulu, German
Merchant.

2d. Arthur Thomas Sloggett, Col. R.A.M.C., C.M.G., F.Z.S., Knt. of Grace of
St. John of Jerusalem, &c. (*Tremabyn, Paignton; 26 Inverness Terrace, W.*), b.
24 Nov. 1857; m. 25 June 1881, Helen, da. of John Robert Boyson, *late* Solicitor-
General, Madras; and has issue 1e to 3e.

1e. Arthur John Henry Sloggett, Lieut. Rifle Brigade, b. 4 May 1882.

2e. Minnie Margaret Sloggett.

3e. Dorothy Carmynow Sloggett.

3d. Christiana Mary Sloggett, *m.* 28 July 1870, Malcolm McNeile, Capt. R.N.
(*Admiralty House, Lewes, Susex*); and has issue 1e to 3e.

1e. Malcolm Douglas McNeile, Lieut. R.N., b. 15 June 1880.

2e. Herman Cyril McNeile, b. 28 Sept. 1888.

3e. Minnie Mabel McNeile (*The Boltons, Lewes, Sussex*), *m.* 26 Sept. 1895,
John Raymond Barkworth, Capt. R.E., d. 2 Jan. 1898; and has issue 1f.

1f. Evelyn Hilda Barkworth. [Nos. 1619 to 1645.

126

# of The Blood Royal

2a. *Isabella Mary Sloggett*, b. 1768; d. (−); m. 1787, *John Wallis of Bodmin, Mayor and Deputy-Recorder of Bodmin, Vice-Warden of the Stannaries; and had issue 1b to 6b.*

1b. *Rev. John Wallis, Vicar of Bodmin*, b. 1789.
2b. *Henry Wallis, Capt. 1st Madras N.I.*, b. 1789.
3b. *Christopher Wallis, Attorney*, b. 1799.
4b. *Preston Wallis, Attorney.*
5b. *Frances Wallis*, m. *Major-Gen. J. Darby, R.A.*
6b. *Louisa Wallis*, m. *the Rev. W. Morshead, Clerk in Holy Orders.*

53. Descendants, if any, of JULIA SILLY (see Table V.), b. 1753; m. WILLIAM LYDDEN; and had issue.

54. Descendants, if any, of JOSEPH SILLY (see Table V.), b. 1713; RICHARD SILLY, b. 1716; JOHN SILLY, b. 1718; DOROTHY SILLY, b. 1712; SARAH SILLY, b. 1714: and ELIZABETH SILLY, b. 1714 (see Table IX.).

55. Descendants, if any surviving, of MARGARET COURTENAY (see Table V.), bapt. 17 Sept. 1663; bur. (at Powderham) 23 Mar. 1755;[1] m. EDMUND[2] REYNELL of Malston, b. 1668 (being aged 6 in 1674); d. 1729; and had issue 1a to 6a.

1a. *William Reynell of Malston, son and h., proved father's will 21 May 1729; living 26 July 1739.*

2a. *George Reynell, bapt. (at Wolborough) 17 June 1693; matric. Wadham Coll. Oxon., 1711, and was drowned same year.*

3a. *Francis Reynell, living 1729.*

4a. *Edmund Reynell, living 1729;* m. *(lic. 10 Aug.) 1739, Elizabeth Rennard.*

5a. *Anne Reynell, eldest da.,* m. *(lic. Bishop of Exeter's Act Books, 6 Sept.) 1726, being then "of Sherford," Abraham Searle of Buckland Monachorum, and afterwards of London, Gentleman; and had issue 1b.*

1b. *Dorothy Searle,* m. *Francis Prior of Sparkwell, co. Devon; and had issue 1c to 7c.*

---

[1] This date, together with the particulars concerning the daughter Anne and her family, is taken from an old MS. Pedigree prepared by the late John William Upham, Esq., when he was collecting family data about 1840.

[2] Called "George" by Vivian, who has apparently translated the Latin entry of the birth of his son George in 1693 into a marriage between a George Reynell and Margaret Courtenay. Vivian, following Lysons, says Giles Reynell, the last of this line, died 1735. Giles is presumably an error, for the Registers show that it was a *George* Reynell, who was bur. 8 Ap. 1735. This George may have been Edmund's younger brother George, who was aged 3 in 1674, and was living in 1726. Mr. W. Upham Reynell-Upham, Hon. Sec. of the Devon and Cornwall Record Society, to whom I am indebted for the loan of the Pedigree mentioned above, remarks, "It also appears from 'Trans. Exeter Archit. Soc.' that William Reynell of Malston, Esq., sold two-thirds titles of Broadclist, 26 July 1739."

The Plantagenet Roll

1c. *Francis Prior, Purser of the "* Hussar *" frigate* 1769; m. (*lic.* 19 *Oct.*) 1769, *Sarah, da. of Charles Ragland of Plymouth.*
2c. *John Prior,* m. *Eliza Bridget Gawler of Chudleigh.*
3c. *Henry Holland Prior.*
4c. *William Prior.*
5c. *Martha Ann Prior,* m. *Richard Strong of Exeter.*
6c. *Elizabeth Prior,* m. *William Forord of Totness.*
7c. *Dorothy Prior,* m. *William Knight of London.*
6a. *Lucy Reynell,* m. *before* 1726, *Jonathan Ford, Gentleman.*

56. Descendants, if any, of JANE COURTENAY, *bapt.* 2 Feb. 1664;[1] *m.* (lic. dated 5 May) 1687, JOHN ROWE of the Middle Temple; of ANNE COURTENAY, *bapt.* 27 Oct. 1674; *d.* 6 May 1708; *m.* WILLIAM BOURGOYNE of Exeter, Merchant, *d.* 10 June 1705; and of FRANCES COURTENAY, *d.* 13 Feb. 1741; *m.* BENJAMIN IVIE of Exeter, Merchant; of MARY COURTENAY; of JOAN COURTENAY, *bapt.* 17 July 1609; *m.* (at St. Martin's, Exeter) 4 Sept. 1638, WILLIAM HEARD; of JOHN COURTENAY; of JAMES COURTENAY; and of MARGARET COURTENAY, *bapt.* 23 Jan. 1581; *d.* 17 July 1628; *m.* 1st, Sir WARWICK HELE of Wembury, Sheriff co. Devon 1620, *d.* 1625; 2ndly, Sir JOHN CHUDLEIGH.

57. Descendants of Sir BOURCHIER WREY, 6th Bart. (1628) [E.] (see Table VI.), *b.* 1759; *d.* 20 Nov. 1826; *m.* 1st, 14 Mar. 1786, ANNE, da. of Sir Robert PALK, 1st Bart. [G.B.], *d.* 1791; 2ndly, 1793, ANNE, da. of John OSBORNE, *d.* 26 Jan. 1813; and had issue 1*a* to 5*a*.

1a. *Sir Bourchier Palk Wrey, 7th Bart.* [*E.*], b. 10 *Dec.* 1788; d. 11 *Sept.* 1879; m. 1*st,* 1818, *Ellen, widow of* [——] *Riddle, da. of* [——], d. 23 *July* 1842; *and had issue* 1b.

1b. *Ellen Caroline Wrey,* d. 13 *Oct.* 1866; m. 9 *Aug.* 1838, *Edward Joseph Weld of Lulworth, J.P., D.L.,* d. 8 *Dec.* 1877; *and had issue.*
See the Clarence Volume, pp. 367–368, Nos. 12553–12578.

2a. *Rev. Sir Henry Bourchier Wrey, 8th Bart.* [*E.*], b. 5 *June* 1797; d. 23 *Dec.* 1882; m. 1*st,* 27 *Sept.* 1827, *Ellen Maria, da. of Nicolas Roundall Toke of Godington,* d. 1 *Mar.* 1864; *and had issue* 1b *to* 3b.

1b. *Sir Henry Bourchier Toke Wrey, 9th Bart.* [*E.*], b. 27 *June* 1829; d. 10 *Mar.* 1900; m. 6 *July* 1854, *the Hon. Marianne Sarah, da. and h. of Philip Castell (Sherard), 9th Baron Sherard* [*I.*], d. 16 *Feb.* 1896; *and had issue* 1c *to* 13c.

1c. *Sir (Robert) Bourchier Sherard Wrey of Trebitch, 10th Bart.* [*E.*], Capt. (ret.) R.N., Major Royal N. Devon Hussars Imp. Yeo., J.P., &c., and a co-heir to the Barony of Fitzwarine [*E.*] (*Tawstock Court, Barnstaple*), b. 23 May 1855.

2c. *Philip Bourchier Sherard Wrey (Union),* b. 28 June 1858; m. 14 Aug. 1889, *Alice Mary, da. of Capt. Barton, R.H.A.*; *and has issue* 1d.

1d. *Florence Muriel Phyllis Wrey.*   [Nos. 1646 to 1674.

---

[1] These dates are taken from a Pedigree of the family of Courtenay by the Rev. George Oliver, D.D., and Pitman Jones, privately printed, for a loan of which the Editor has to thank the Rev. and Hon. Henry H. Courtenay, Rector of Powderham.

3*c*. Rev. Albany Bourchier Sherard Wrey, M.A. (Oxon.), Rector of Tawstock with Harracott (*Corffe, Barnstaple*), *b.* 4 Jan. 1861; *m.* 5 Aug. 1896, Isabel Frances Sophia, da. of Thomas Horn Fleet of Darenth Grange, J.P., D.L.

4*c*. William Bourchier Sherard Wrey, late Comm. R.N. (*Naval and Military*), *b.* 2 Ap. 1865; *m.* 3 June 1897, Flora Bathurst, da. of Vice-Adm. W. S. Grieve of Ord House.

5*c*. Arthur Henry Wrey (64 *Fitzjohn's Avenue, N.W.*), *b.* 18 June 1872; *m.* 11 Dec. 1897, Florence, da. of Thomas Radmall.

6*c*. Edward Castell Wrey (*Gualequay, Argentina*), *b.* 9 Feb. 1875; *m.* 1901, Katharine Joan, da. of the Rev. John Dene; and has issue 1*d* to 2*d*.

1*d*. Richard Castel Bourchier Wrey, *b.* 1903.

2*d*. Katharine Augusta Wrey, *b.* 27 Mar. 1902.

7*c*. Reginald Charles Wrey, Lieut. 1st Batt. Devonshire Regt., *b.* 17 June 1876.

8*c*. Annie Marian Wrey.

9*c*. Emma Henrietta Wrey.

10*c*. Augusta Eleanor Wrey.

11*c*. Florence Amelia Wrey.

12*c*. Beatrice Alexandra Wrey.

13*c*. Isabel Maria Wrey.

2*b*. Rev. Bourchier William Toke Wrey, S.C.L. (Camb.), Rector of Combeinteignhead (*Combeinteignhead Rectory, Teignmouth*), *b.* 7 Aug. 1830; *m.* 8 Sept. 1859, Anne Caroline, da. of Thomas Crosthwait of Fitzwilliam Square, Dublin, *d.* 19 Feb. 1896; and has issue 1*c* to 6*c*.

1*c*. Rev. Henry Bourchier Wrey, Curate-in-charge of Christchurch Rushall (*St. Mary's Rushall, near Walsall*), *b.* 1863; *m.* 1895, Helen Esmé, da. of Frederick Charles Ernest Griffin of Gorsty Hayes Manor; and has issue 1*d* to 3*d*.

1*d*. Mary Caroline Bourchier Wrey.

2*d*. Helen Edith Bourchier Wrey.

3*d*. Dorothy Esmé Bourchier Wrey.

2*c*. Ellen Caroline Wrey.

3*c*. Evelyn Maria Wrey, *b.* 12 Nov. 1865.

4*c*. Mary Blanche Wrey.

5*c*. Alice Constance Frances Wrey, *b.* 18 Jan. 1873.

6*c*. Henrietta Sophia Wrey, *b.* 11 Aug. 1875.

3*b*. Anna Maria Toke Wrey, *d.* 7 Mar. 1867; *m. as 1st wife, 3 Sept. 1857, the Very Rev. Isaac Morgan Reeves, D.D., Dean and Rector of Ross (Glandore House, co. Cork); and had issue 1c.*

1*c*. Helen Wrey Reeves, *m.* 12 Jan. 1882, Joseph Wrixon Leycester (*Ennismore, co. Cork*).

3*a*. *Robert Bourchier Wrey, d. (–).*

4*a*. *Anna Eleanor Wrey, d.* 25 *Jan.* 1846; *m.* 1*st*, 19 *July* 1806, *Edward Hartopp of Little Dalby, d.* 5 *Feb.* 1813; 2*ndly*, 9 *Dec.* 1815, *Sir Lawrence Vaughan Palk, 3rd Bart.* [*G.B.*], *M.P., b.* 24 *Ap.* 1793; *d.* 16 *May* 1860; *and had issue* 1*b to* 4*b*.

1*b*. *Edward Bourchier Hartopp of Dalby Hall, M.P., J.P., D.L., High Sheriff co. Leicester* 1832, *b.* 14 *Dec.* 1808; *d.* 31 *Dec.* 1884; *m.* (*at Naples*) 18 *Feb.* 1834, *Honoria, da. of Gen. William Gent; and had issue* 1*c to* 7*c*.

1*c*. *William Wrey Hartopp, Capt. R.H. Guards, d.* 1874; *m.* 20 *June* 1861, *Lina, da. of Thomas Howie; and had issue* 1*d to* 2*d*.

1*d*. Florence Honoria Hartopp, of Dalby, *b.* 18 Oct. 1866; *m.* 4 June 1894, James Burns, now (R.L. 1894) Burns-Hartopp, J.P., Capt. R.H. Guards (*Dalby Hall, Melton Mowbray; Scraptoft Hall, co. Leicester*); and has issue 1*e* to 2*e*.

1*e*. Lætitia Honoria Burns-Hartopp.

2*e*. Helen Dorothy Lina Burns-Hartopp.   [Nos. 1675 to 1701.

2d. Dorothy Hartopp, *b.* 16 Mar. 1871 ; *m.* 23 Nov. 1898, Capt. Edward Bell, Worcester Regt.

2c. *Edward Hartopp, Lieut.* 10*th Hussars,* d. (–).

3c. Maria Georgina Hartopp, *m.* 2 Sept. 1865, Francis Bramley Baker.

4c. Anna Eleanor Hartopp, *m.* 9 Dec. 1880, the Hon. Alan Joseph Pennington (*Burleigh Hall, Loughborough*).

5c. Honoria Hartopp, *m.* 1864, Charles Arkwright.

6c. Juliana Evans Hartopp, *m.* 1st, 28 July 1863, Charles Shuttleworth Holden, *b.* 16 July 1838 ; *d.* 6 Aug. 1872 ; 2ndly, 1876, George Balfour Traill, Major-Gen. *late* R.A. ; and has issue 1*d.*

1d. Edward Charles Shuttleworth Holden, J.P., Major Derbysh. Yeo. Cav. (*The Cottage, Doveridge, Derby*), *b.* 7 Jan. 1865.

7c. Elizabeth Hartopp (*Corso Hill, co. Ayr ; Kirktonholm, co. Lanark*), *m.* 22 Ap. 1869, Sir William James Montgomery Cuninghame of Glenmore, 9th Bart. (1672) [S.], V.C., M.P., *b.* 20 May 1834 ; *d.* 11 Nov. 1897 ; and has issue 1*d.*

1d. Sir Thomas Andrew Alexander Cuninghame, 10th Bart. [S.], D.S.O., Capt. 4th Batt. Rifle Brigade (*Corse Hill, co. Ayr ;* 19 *Wilton Street, S.W.*), *b.* 30 Mar. 1877 ; *m.* 1 Nov. 1904, Alice Frances Denison, da. of Sir (George) William Des Vaux, G.C.M.G.

2d. Edward William Montgomery Cuninghame, Lieut. R.H.A. (*Southfield, Renfrewshire, N.B.*), *b.* 30 May 1878.

3d. Edith Honoria Cuninghame, *b.* 26 Ap. 1870 ; *m.* 7 Sept. 1901, John Anthony Cecil Tilley (son of Sir John Tilley, K.C.B.) (12 *Chester Square, S.W.*).

4d. Marjorie Eva Charlotte Cuninghame.

5d. Violet Jessie Cuninghame.

6d. Bridget Ann Cuninghame.

2b. *Robert Palk Hartopp, b.* Oct. 1812 ; d. (–).

3b. *Lawrence* (*Palk*), 1*st Baron Haldon* [U.K.], *b.* 5 *Jan.* 1818 ; *d.* 22 *Mar.* 1883 ; m. 15 *Nov.* 1845, *Maria Harriet, da. of Sir Thomas Henry Hesketh, 4th Bart.* [G.B.] ; *and had issue* 1*c to* 4*c.*

1c. *Lawrence Hesketh* (*Palk*), 2*nd Baron Haldon* [U.K.], *b.* 6 *Sept.* 1846 ; d. 31 *Dec.* 1903 ; m. 7 *Oct.* 1868, *the Hon. Constance Mary, da. of George William* (*Barrington*), 7*th Viscount Barrington* [I.] ; *and had issue.*

See the Clarence Volume, pp. 93–94, Nos. 676–691.

2c. Hon. Edward Arthur Palk, Lieut.-Col. Comdg. and Hon. Col. 4th Batt. Devonshire Regt. (*Little Testwood, Totton, Hants*), *b.* 26 June 1854 ; *m.* 18 July 1883, Charles Frances, da. of the Rev. Sir Frederick Shelley, 8th Bart. [E.].

3c. Hon. *Annette Maria Palk,* d. 21 *May* 1884 ; m. 16 *July* 1873, *Sir Alexander Baird of Urie, 1st Bart.* (1897) [U.K.], *Lord-Lieut. co. Kincardine* (*Urie, Stonehaven, N.B.*) ; *and had issue* 1*d to* 6*d.*

1d. John Lawrence Baird, C.M.G., D.L., 2nd Sec. in Diplo. Ser., *b.* 27 Ap. 1874.

2d. Alexander Walter Frederick Baird, D.S.O., Capt. and Brevet-Major Gordon Highlanders, *b.* 2 Oct. 1876.

3d. Evelyn Margaret Baird.

4d. Janet Norah Baird, *m.* 1 Oct. 1902, Major Arthur George Ferguson, *late* Rifle Brig., Inspector of Constabulary for Scotland ; and has issue 1*e* to 2*e.*

1e. Angus Arthur Ferguson.

2e. Alexander Ferguson.

5d. Nina Isabel Baird.

6d. Muriel Jane Baird.

4c. Hon. Evelyn Elizabeth Palk, *m.* 26 Ap. 1882, Major Ernest Gambier Parry, *late* 23rd Royal Welsh Fusiliers (*Elmcroft, Goring-on-Thames*) ; and has issue 1*d* to 2*d.* [Nos. 1702 to 1740.

# of The Blood Royal

1*d*. Thomas Robert Gambier Parry, *b*. 13 Feb. 1883.
2*d*. Thomas Mark Gambier Parry, *b*. 29 May 1884.

4*b*. *Isabella Palk*, d. 10 Dec. 1865 ; m. 10 *Aug*. 1848, *Samuel Weare Gardiner of Combe Lodge, J.P., D.L., High Sheriff co. Oxon.*, b. 2 Feb. 1821 ; d. 13 *Mar*. 1866 ; *and had issue* 1*c to* 2*c*.

1*c*. Charles Lawrence Weare Gardiner (*Elmcroft, Goring ; Crossways, Lympstone, Devon*), *b*. 15 Nov. 1849 ; *m*. 26 Aug. 1891, Amelia Lucy, da. of Walter Yates.

2*c*. *Isabella Laura Elizabeth Gardiner*, d. 23 *July* 1886 ; m. 18 *Ap*. 1877, *Sir Thomas Johnson Dancer, 7th Bart* (1662) [*I*.] ; *and had issue* 1*d to* 2*d*.
1*d*. Grace Helen Dancer.
2*d*. Barbara Jane Dancer.

5*a*. *Eleanora Elizabeth Wrey*, b. 1795 ; d. 12 *Jan*. 1882 ; m. 1*st*, 2 *Mar*. 1815, *Albany Savile of Oaklands, Devon, D.C.L., M.P.*, d. *Feb*. 1831 ; 2*ndly, the Rev. Richard Fayle of Torquay*, d. 1872 ; *and had issue* (*with possibly others by* 2*nd marriage*) 1*b to* 8*b*.

1*b*. Rev. *Bourchier Wrey Savile, M.A.*, b. 11 *Mar*. 1817 ; d. 1889 ; m. *Ap*. 1842, *Mary Elizabeth, da. of James Whyte of Pilton House, Devon ; and had issue* 1*c to* 6*c*.
1*c*. Walter Albany Savile.
2*c*. Bourchier Beresford Savile, Paymaster R.N.
3*c*. Henry Savile, Lieut. R.N., *b*. 2 Mar. 1854.
4*c*. Blanche Eleanor Bourchier Savile, *m*. 7 Ap. 1869, John du Terreau Bogle, Major R.E. ; and has issue.
5*c*. Emma Elizabeth Adelaide Savile, *b*. 2 Dec. 1847 ; *m*. 22 Aug. 1866, Major-Gen. John Beresford ; and has issue.
6*c*. Augusta Fanny Savile, *b*. 28 Ap. 1851.

2*b*. Henry Bourchier Osborne Savile, C.B., Hon. Col. 1st Gloucester A.V., *late* R.A., J.P., High Sheriff (3 *Rodney Place, Clifton, Bristol*), *b*. 5 May 1819 ; *m*. 1st, July 1842, Catherine, da. and h. of the Rev. Thomas Law, *d*. 1846 ; 2ndly, 1848, Mary, da. of Cornelius O'Callaghan of Ballynahinch, *d*. 1870 ; 3rdly, 1872, Ellen Lucy, da. of Richard Sisson Darling of Trinidad ; and has (with other) issue 1*c*.

1*c*. Albany Robert Savile, Lieut.-Col. Royal Irish Regt. Professor, Royal Mil. Coll., Sandhurst, *b*. 12 Mar. 1844 ; *m*. 1869, Sybilla, da. of Gen. George Twemlow, Bengal Artillery.

3*b*. Rev. Frederick Alexander Savile, now (1874) Stewart-Savile, M.A. (Camb.), J.P., *formerly* Rector of Kings Nympton and Torwood (*Hollanden Park, Hildenborough ; Tonbridge, Kent*), *b*. 4 July 1820 ; *m*. Sept. 1852, Sophia Stewart, da. of Thomas Dykes of Oatlands, Lanark ; and has issue 1*c to* 6*c*.

1*c*. Walter Stewart Stewart-Savile, *late* Capt. The Buffs, *b*. July 1855 ; *m*. 1885, Mildred, da. of Capt. Campbell, R.E. ; and has issue 1*d to* 2*d*.
1*d*. Doreen Stewart-Savile.
2*d*. Esmé Stewart-Savile.

2*c*. Robert Dykes Stewart Stewart-Savile, A.D.C. to the Governor of New Zealand (Lord Onslow) 1888 (*Pilcaple Castle, Aberdeen*), *b*. Jan. 1863 ; *m*. Katherine, da. of Henry Lumsden ; and has issue 1*d to* 2*d*.
1*d*. Derrick Stewart-Savile.
2*d*. Gladys Stewart-Savile.

3*c*. Marion Louisa Stewart-Savile, *m*. 1 June 1886, Lodovick Edward Bligh, J.P., Major *late* The Buffs (*Cambria House, Minehead, Somerset*); and has issue 1*d* to 3*d*.
1*d*-3*d*. See the Clarence Volume, p. 288, Nos. 7779–7781.

[Nos. 1741 to 1764.

131

The Plantagenet Roll

4c. Eleanor Sophia Stewart-Savile, *m.* 27 June 1882, Robert Jamieson (*The Wells, Epsom*); and has issue 1*d*.

1*d*. Margaret Jamieson.

5c. Adelaide Margaret Stewart-Savile.

6c. Alice Stewart Margaret Stewart-Savile.

4b. Edward Bourchier Savile, Recorder of Okehampton (53 *Eccleston Square, S.W.*), *b.* 16 Oct. 1823; *m.* 1st, 1853, Cornelia, da. of D. O'Callaghan of Ballynahinch, *d.* 1857; 2ndly, 13 Sept. 1860, Margaret Marion, da. of the Rev. John Stevenson of Patrixbourne, Hon. Canon of Canterbury; and has issue 1*c* to 6*c*.

1*c*. Rev. Edward Stevenson Gordon Savile, M.A. (Oxon.), *b.* 24 Feb. 1866.

2*c*. Henry Montague Savile, *b.* 5 Sept. 1867.

3c. Frances Eleanora Savile, *m.* 1890, the Rev. William Osborn Bird Allen, M.A. (Camb.), Secretary S.P.C.K.

4c. Evelyn St. Leger Savile, *m.* 27 Ap. 1895, Joseph Randolph Randolph (*Eastcourt, Malmesbury*).

5c. Ida Gwendoline Savile.

6c. Lilian Marion Estille Savile, *m.* 16 Dec. 1897, Lionel Charles Whitehead Phillips (*Unsted Park, Godalming*); and has issue 1*d* to 3*d*.

1*d*. John Savile Phillips, *b.* 24 Jan. 1902.

2*d*. Mary Gwendolen Phillips.

3*d*. Rachel Margaret Phillips.

5b. John Walter Savile of Ballendrick, co. Perth, &c., Lieut.-Col. 1st Devon Militia, formerly Indian Army, b. 24 Jan. 1825; d. 1894; m. 25 Jan. 1859, Sarah Emma, da. of George Stodart of Ballendrick; and had issue 1c to 6c.

1*c*. George Walter Wrey Savile, Capt. 2nd Batt. Middlesex Regt., *b.* 14 Mar. 1860; *m.* Ellen Louisa, da. of Col. A. D. Parsons.

2*c*. Philip Bourchier Savile, *b.* 9 June 1861.

3*c*. Reginald Vernon Savile, *b.* 22 Oct. 1864.

4c. Leopold Halliday Savile, *b.* 31 Aug. 1870; *m.* 1904, Evelyn, da. of [——] Styleman; and has issue (a da.)

5c. Lorina Augusta Savile, *m.* 1895, Charles Cornelius Savile; and has issue 1*d* to 3*d*.

1*d*. Marcella Savile.

2*d*. Gwendolen Savile.

3*d*. Joan Savile.

6c. Mildred Eleanor Savile.

6b. Robert Bourchier Savile, b. 2 Oct. 1829; d. 1866; m. 11 Sept. 1860, Eliza, da. of [——] Mackenzie; and had issue 1c to 2c.

1*c*. Gordon Mackenzie Savile.

2*c*. Frank Holt Savile.

7b. Eleanor Maria Savile (*Calverly Mount, Tunbridge Wells*), *m.* Rev. G. A. Rogers; and has issue.

8b. Henrietta Anna Savile, b. 21 Nov. 1830; d. 1 May 1893; m. 1st, 7 Ap. 1853, Capt. Wallace Buchanan, d.s.p. 1855; 2ndly, 26 Ap. 1859, Gerald de Courcy Hamilton; and had issue 1c.

1*c*. Constantine de Courcy Hamilton (*Ringrone, Woking*), *b.* 17 Nov. 1861; *m.* 7 Sept. 1887, Eliza Susan Eccles, da. of Capt. Robert Hepburne Swinton, R.N.; and has issue 1*d* to 2*d*.

1*d*. Gerald de Courcy Hamilton, *b.* 1 Aug. 1899.

2*d*. Evelyn de Courcy Hamilton, *b.* 8 Oct. 1890.   [Nos. 1765 to 1793.

132

# of The Blood Royal

58. Descendants of the Rev. WILLIAM BOURCHIER WREY of Melksham, Rector of Tawstock and Combeinteignhead, Devon (see
Table VI.), *bapt.* 6 May 1761; *d.* 27 Aug. 1839; *m.* Nov.
1789, SOPHIA, da. and co.-h. of George BETHELL of Bradford,
Wilts; and had issue 1*a* to 5*a*.

1*a*. *William Long Wrey, Lieut.* 19*th Dragoons*, b. 1792.

2*a*. *Edward Wrey, Judge, H.E.I.C.S.*, b. 7 *Jan.* 1794; d. 30 *May* 1840; *m.*
9 Feb. 1818, *Juliana, da. of the Rev. George Wilson*, d. 11 *Mar.* 1892; *and had
issue* 1*b* *to* 2*b*.

1*b*. *George Bourchier Wrey*, b. 4 *Jan.* 1820; d. 9 *Mar.* 1854; m. 8 *July* 1848,
Sarah, da. of Col. John Cuninghame of Caddel and Thornton, d. 29 *July* 1869; *and
had issue* 1*c*.

1*c*. George Edward Bourchier Wrey of Thornton and Caddel, B.A. (Camb.)
(131 *Ashley Gardens, S.W.*), *b.* 9 Mar. 1851; *m.* 24 Feb. 1886, Anne Maud, da. of
the Rev. Arthur Bourchier Wrey; and has issue 1*d*.

1*d*. Charles Edward Wrey, R.N., *b.* 30 Mar. 1889.

2*b*. *Florence Eliza Wrey*, d. (−); *m.* 31 *July* 1845, *the Rev. George Leroux
Wilson of Hermosa, Southsea; and had issue* 1*c* *to* 2*c*.

1*c*. Edward Leroux Wilson, Lieut. R.N., *b.* 1 Sept. 1852.

2*c*. Ellen Wilson.

3*a*. *Rev. John Wrey*, b. *Sept.* 1797; d. 20 *Oct.* 1872; *m.* 1*st*, 1826, *Anne
Burnett, da. of the Rev. Thomas Yeomans*, d. 15 *Sept.* 1860; *and had issue* 1*b*
to 4*b*.

1*b*. *Charles Joseph Wrey, Capt. R.N.*, b. 20 *Dec.* 1828; d. 23 *Aug.* 1891;
m. 1*st*, 9 *May* 1867, *Caroline Rashleigh, da. and h. of the Rev. Charles Howard
Archer of Lewannick*, d. 16 *Dec.* 1870; 2*ndly*, 21 *Mar.* 1875, *Henrietta Jane, da.
of Admiral Charles Aldridge; and had issue* 1*c*.

1*c*. Douglas Edward Archer Bourchier Wrey (*Stoodley Knowle, Torquay*), b.
25 Mar. 1869; *m.* 1888, Mary Thomasine, da. of Henry Archdale Owen, d. 18 Aug.
1905.

2*b*. Rev. Arthur Bourchier Wrey, M.A. (Camb.), Vicar of St. Mary Church
1876–1905 (*Trebigh, Torquay*), b. 17 Ap. 1831; *m.* 1st, 18 Jan. 1859, Helen, da. of
the Rev. Thomas Phillpotts, Hon. Canon of Truro, *d.* 10 May 1878; 2ndly, 24 Aug.
1881, Claudine Maud, da. of Charles Twinning, Q.C., *d.* 6 Jan. 1904; and has issue
1*c* to 6*c*.

1*c*. Wilfred Arthur Bourchier Wrey, Lieut. 1st Batt. Duke of Cornwall's L.I.,
b. 20 Mar. 1885.

2*c*. Hugh Bourchier Wrey, Mid. R.N., *b.* 19 July 1888.

3*c*. Emily Florence Wrey.

4*c*. Cicely Helen Wrey, *m.* 20 Ap. 1893, the Rev. Henry Charles Wilder, M.A.,
Rector of Farnham Royal (*Farnham Royal Rectory, Bucks*); and has issue 1*d* to 4*d*.

1*d*. Henry Arthur John Wilder, *b.* 26 May 1894.

2*d*. Frederick Wrey Wilder, *b.* 23 Sept. 1899.

3*d*. Augusta Helen Mary Wilder, *b.* 29 Aug. 1895.

4*d*. Alice Victoria Wilder, *b.* 20 Mar. 1897.

5*c*. Anne Maud Wrey, *m.* 24 Feb. 1886, George Edward Bourchier Wrey
(131 *Ashley Gardens, S.W.*); and has issue.
See p. 133, No. 1795.

6*c*. Mary Claudine Wrey.

3*b*. *Henrietta Maria Wrey*, d. 30 *Jan.* 1886; *m.* 15 *Aug.* 1861, *the Rev. Charles
Baring Gardiner* (9 *Lorne Villas, Preston Park, Brighton*); *and had issue* 1*c* *to* 7*c*.

[Nos. 1794 to 1810.

The Plantagenet Roll

1c. George Charles Gardiner (20 *Warwick Avenue, W.*), *b.* 10 Oct. 1862; *m.* 8 Aug. 1894, Beatrice Mary, da. of [——] Peck; and has issue 1*d* to 4*d*.

1*d*. Geoffrey Baring Gardiner, *b.* 8 Oct. 1896.

2*d*. Paul Wrey Gardiner, *b.* 13 Ap. 1898.

3*d*. Margaret Eleanor Gardiner, *b.* 15 May 1895.

4*d*. Elizabeth Beatrice Gardiner, *b.* 22 Jan. 1902.

2c. John Rawson Gardiner (4140 *Dorchester Street, Montreal*), *b.* 14 Mar. 1866; *m.* 22 Sept. 1897, Emma Elsie, da. of [——] Evans; and has issue 1*d*.

1*d*. Gerald Rawson Gardiner, *b.* 3 Sept. 1898.

3c. *William Arthur Gardiner,* b. 20 *May* 1869; d. 18 *Mar.* 1903; m. 5 *July* 1900, *Ethel Mary* (3 *Clifton Terrace, Southsea*), *da. of* [——] *Cunningham Scott; and had issue* 1*d*.

1*d*. Charles Francis Wrey Gardiner, *b.* 30 June 1901.

4c. Herbert Allen Gardiner, *b.* 26 Ap. 1871.

5c. Henry Bourchier Wrey Gardiner, *b.* 1 May 1876.

6c. Marianne Louisa Gardiner, *b.* 13 Mar. 1864.

7c. Isabel Maria Gardiner, *b.* 28 Sept. 1867.

4b. Eleanor Mary Wrey, *m.* 3 Ap. 1873, Eugene John Alexander, *late* of 21 St. James' Square, Bath.

4a. Eleanor Wrey, d. (? unm.).

5a. Elizabeth Wrey, d. (–); m. 19 *Dec.* 1851, *the Rev. John Clare Pigot.*

[Nos. 1811 to 1823.

59. Descendants, if any, of ELLEN WREY (see Table IV.), wife of the Rev. EDWARD HENRY WHINFIELD.

60. Descendants of FLORENTINA WREY (see Table IV.), *d.* 1835; *m.* RICHARD GODOLPHIN LONG of Rood Ashton, M.P., *bapt.* 12 Nov. 1761; *d.* 1835; and had issue 1*a* to 3*a*.

1a. *Walter Long of Rood Ashton, Wraxall and Whaddon, M.A., J.P., D.L., &c.,* b. 10 *Oct.* 1793; d. 31 *Jan.* 1867; m. 1*st,* 3 *Aug.* 1819, *Mary Anne, da. of the Right Hon. Archibald Colquhoun of Killermont, Lord Registrar of Scotland,* d. 15 *Mar.* 1856; *and had issue* 1*b to* 3*b*.

1b. *Richard Penruddocke Long of Rood Ashton, &c., M.P., J.P., D.L.,* b. 19 *Dec.* 1825; d. 16 *Feb.* 1875; m. 4 *Oct.* 1853, *Charlotte Anna, da. of the Right Hon. William Wentworth Fitzwilliam Dick, formerly Hume of Humewood, M.P.,* d. 18 *Dec.* 1899; *and had issue* 1*c to* 8*c*.

1c. Right Hon. Walter Hume Long, P.C., M.P., *late* Chief Secretary for Ireland, and President of the Local Government Board, Col. Comdg. Royal Wilts. Imp. Yeo., &c. &c. (*Rood Ashton, Trowbridge; Chitterne Lodge, Codford; 57 Cadogan Gardens, S.W., &c.*), *b.* 13 July 1854; *m.* 1 Aug. 1878, Lady Dorothy Blanche, da. of Richard Edmund (Boyle), 9th Earl of Cork and Orrery [I.], K.P.; and has issue 1*d* to 4*d*.

1*d*. Walter Long, D.S.O., Lieut. 2nd Dragoons, *b.* 26 July 1879.

2*d*. Robert Eric Onslow Long, *b.* 22 Aug. 1892.

3*d*. Victoria Florence de Burgh Long, *m.* 26 Nov. 1901, George Abraham Gibbs, J.P. (35 *Wilton Place, S.W.; Tyntesfield, near Bristol*).

4*d*. Lettice Margaret Long, *m.* 18 Ap. 1904, William George Daniel Cooper, *late* 7th Hussars (*Whittlebury Lodge, Towcester*).

2c. Richard Godolphine Walmesley Long, now (R.L. 14 Jan. 1888) Chaloner, M.P., J.P., Capt. *late* 3rd Hussars (*Gisborough Hall, Yorks*), *b.* 13 Oct. 1856; *m.* 18 Nov. 1882, Margaret, da. of the Rev. W. Brocklesby Davis, M.A., Vicar of Ramsbury; and has issue 1*d* to 6*d*.   [Nos. 1824 to 1829.

154

# of The Blood Royal

1*d*. Richard Godolphine Hume Chaloner, *b*. 29 June 1883.

2*d*. Thomas Weston Peel Long Chaloner, *b*. 6 May 1889.

3*d*. Margaret Bruce Esmé Chaloner.

4*d*. Ursula Violet Chaloner.

5*d*. Cynthia Frances Charlotte Chaloner.

6*d*. Honoria Elizabeth Dundas Chaloner.

3*c*. Robert Chaloner Critchley Long, *b*. (–); *m*. 6 Feb. 1884, Maud Felicia Frances, da. of Capt. Willis Johnson, R.N.; and has issue 1*d* to 2*d*.

1*d*. Muriel Millesaintes Lilian Long.

2*d*. Margaret Bruce Long.

4*c*. William Hoase Bourchier Long, Capt. 2nd Batt. Royal W. Kent Regt., *b*. 22 Mar. 1868.

5*c*. Florence Frideswide Long, *m*. 5 July 1882, Sir Arthur Henderson Fairburn, 3rd Bart. (1869) [U.K.] (45 *Brunswick Square, Hove*).

6*c*. Margaret Henrietta Georgiana Long, *m*. 6 Aug. 1887, Hugh Frank Clutterbuck (*Middlewick, Corsham*).

7*c*. Charlotte Ethel Long, *m*. John E. H. Martin.

8*c*. Frances Laura Arabella Long, *m*. 18 July 1882, Harry Willis Darell de Windt (whom she div. 1888); 2ndly, 1892, Arthur George Lyster.

2*b*. Flora Henrietta Long, *m*. 26 Ap. 1853, Charles Penruddocke of Compton Park, J.P., D.L., High Sheriff co. Wilts, *b*. 30 Sept. 1828; *d*. 30 Oct. 1899; and has issue 1*c* to 6*c*.

1*c*. Charles Penruddocke, J.P. (*Compton Park, Salisbury, Wilts; Bratton Lodge, Wincanton, Somerset*), *b*. 26 Sept. 1858; *m*. 30 Ap. 1890, Annie Elizabeth Dickinson Maria Carew Brampford, da. of the Rev. William Speke of Sheldon Court; and has issue 1*d* to 6*d*.

1*d*. Charles Penruddocke, *b*. 16 Jan. 1893.

2*d*. George William Penruddocke, *b*. (twin) ?? July 1894.

3*d*. Thomas Penruddocke, *b*. 2 Sept. 1??7.

4*d*. Flora Mary Elizabeth Penruddocke, *b*. 27 Feb. 1891.

5*d*. Sybil Frances Penruddocke, *b*. (twin) 31 July 1894.

6*d*. Lætitia Constance Penruddocke, *b*. 26 Oct. 1895.

2*c*. Agnes Flora Penruddocke, *m*. 2 June 1880, Reginald Gambier Long, *s.p.*

3*c*. Lætitia Blanche Penruddocke, *m*. 10 Feb. 1880, John Stuart Lindsay Long, Comm. (ret.) R.N. (*The Firs, Walburton, Arundel*); and has issue 1*d* to 3*d*.

1*d*. John Victor Tylney Long, *b*. 5 June 1883.

2*d*. Robert Penruddocke Tylney Long, *b*. 23 Feb. 1889.

3*d*. Dorothy Long, *b*. 24 Dec. 1881.

4*c*. Constance Henrietta Lowther Penruddocke.

5*c*. Amy Elizabeth A'Court Penruddocke, *m*. 22 July 1879, Charles Garnet Richardson (*Beechcroft, Englefield Green*); and has issue.

6*c*. Sybil Katharine Long.

3*b*. Jane Agnes Long, *m*. 26 Aug. 1860, Charles Forbes of Moriack Castle, N.B.

2*a*. *Ellen Long*, d. (–); *m. as 2nd wife*, 1812, *John Walmesley of the Hall of Ince, co. Lancaster*, b. 28 *Dec.* 1775; *d.* 1860; *and had issue* 1*b to* 2*b*.

1*b*. *Richard Walmesley of the Hall of Ince and Lucknam, J.P.*, b. 1816; *d.* 1893; *m.* 1849, *Ann Eliza, da. of William Donaldson; and had issue* 1*c*.

1*c*. John Walmesley of Lucknam, J.P. (*Lucknam, co. Wilts*), *b*. July 1861.

2*b*. *Florentine Walmesley*, d. 1872; *m.* 1834, *John Hawkesworth of Forest, Queen's Co.; and had issue* 1*c*.

1*c*. Walter Hawkesworth, *m*. and has issue a large family.

[Nos. 1830 to 1862.

135

The Plantagenet Roll

3a. Dionysia Meliora Long, d. (–); m. 6 Dec. 1838, *the Rev. Joseph Medlicott, Vicar of Potterne, Wilts*, d. 1860; *and had issue 1b to 2b.*

1b. Henry Edmonstone Medlicott, `M.A. (Oxon.), J.P., C.C. (*Sandfield, co. Wilts*), b. 18 Jan. 1840; m. Ap. 1874, Kate D'Oyly, da. of Alexander Robinson Gale of Stanton Lodge, Bury St. Edmunds; and has issue 1c to 4c.

    1c. Walter Sandfield Medlicott, b. Aug. 1879.
    2c. Henry Edward Medlicott.
    3c. Stephen Medlicott.
    4c. Kate Josephine Medlicott.

2b. Rev. Walter Edward Medlicott, M.A., Vicar of Swanmore (*Swanmore Vicarage, Hants*), b. 184–; m. June 1868, Edith Louisa, da. of the Rev. Robert Sumner (son of the Lord Bishop of Winchester); and has issue (with 1 other son and 2 das.) 1c.

    1c. Robert Sumner Medlicott.   [Nos. 1863 to 1869.

---

61. Descendants of ANNA MARIA WREY (see Table IX.), d. (–); m. 1791, NICOLAS ROUNDELL TOKE of Godington, co. Kent, b. 19 May 1764; d. 19 Feb. 1837; and had issue 1a.

    1a. Ellen Maria Toke, d. 1 Mar. 1864; m. *as 1st wife, the Rev. Sir Henry Bourchier Wrey, 6th Bart.* [E.], d. 23 Dec. 1882; *and had issue 1b to 3b.*

    1b.–3b. See pp. 128–129, Nos. 1672–1698.   [Nos. 1870–1896.

---

62. Descendants, if any, of JOHN; CHICHESTER; ROBERT, a Gen. in the Portuguese Service, d. 1809; CHARLES; DIANA, wife of JOHN STAFFORD of Roborough; FLORENCE, wife of EDWARD I'ANS; CHRISTIAN and CATHERINE WREY, brothers and sisters of Sir BOURCHIER WREY, 5th Bart. [E.] (see Table VI.).

---

63. Descendants of the Rev. CHICHESTER WREY, Rector of Tawstock, Devon (see Table VI.), m. and had issue.

---

64. Descendants of WILLIAM (COLE), 1st EARL OF ENNISKILLEN [I.] (see Table VI.), b. 1736; d. 22 May 1803; m. 3 Nov. 1763, ANNE, sister of Armar, 1st Earl of Belmore [I.], da. of Galbraeth Lowry CORRY of Ahenis, b. 24 June 1742; d. Sept. 1802; and had issue 1a to 6a.

    1a. *John Willoughby (Cole), 2nd Earl of Enniskillen* [I.], *1st Baron Grinstead* [U.K.], *K.P.*, b. 23 Mar. 1768; d. 31 Mar. 1840; m. 15 Oct. 1805, Lady Charlotte, da. of Henry (Bayly, afterwards Paget), 1st Earl of Uxbridge [G.B.], b. 26 Oct. 1781; d. 26 Jan. 1817; and had issue 1b.

    1b. *William Willoughby (Cole), 3rd Earl of Enniskillen* [I.], *2nd Baron Grinstead* [U.K.], *D.C.L., F.R.S., F.G.S., &c.*, b. 25 Jan. 1807; d. 12 Nov. 1886; m. 1st, 16 Jan. 1844, Jane, da. of James A. Casamaijor, d. 13 May 1855; *and had issue 1c to 6c.*

136

1c. Lowry Egerton (Cole), 4th Earl of Enniskillen [I.], 3rd Baron Grinstead [U.K.], K.P. (*Florence Court, Enniskillen*), b. 21 Dec. 1845; m. 12 July 1869, Charlotte Marion, da. and co.-h. of Douglas Baird of Closeburn; and has issue 1d to 5d.

    1d. John Henry Michael Cole, Viscount Cole, Major North Ireland Imp. Yeo., *late* 7th Hussars, b. 10 Sept. 1876.

    2d. Hon. Galbraith Lowry Egerton Cole, Lieut. 10th Hussars, b. 8 Mar. 1881.

    3d. Hon. Reginald Berkeley Cole, Lieut. 9th Lancers, b. 26 Nov. 1882.

    4d. Lady Kathleen Mary Cole, b. 25 Nov. 1873; m. 1 Aug. 1903, Charles Walter Villiers.

    5d. Lady Florence Ame Cole, b. 3 Feb. 1878; m. 11 July 1899, Hugh (Cholmondeley), 3rd Baron Delamere [U.K.] (*Vale Royal, Northwich*); and has issue 1e.

        1e. Hon. Thomas Pitt Hamilton Cholmondeley, b. 19 Aug. 1900.

2c. Hon. Arthur Edward Casamaijor Cole, J.P., *late* Rifle Brigade (*Keswick Lodge, Norwich*), b. 9 Mar. 1851; m. 24 Ap. 1877, Adelaide, da. of James Blackwood of Melbourne, Victoria; and has issue 1d.

    1d. Lowry Arthur Casamaijor Cole, b. 10 Ap. 1878.

3c. Lady Charlotte Jane Cole, m. 1 Dec. 1874, James Hugh Smith-Barry of Fola Island, co. Cork (*Stowell, Pewsey, Wilts*); and has issue.

4c. Lady Florence Mary Cole, m. 28 Dec. 1870, John Henry (Crichton), 4th Earl of Erne [I.], K.P., P.C. (*Crom Castle, Newtown Butler, co. Fermanagh; 21 Knightsbridge, S.W.*); and has issue 1d to 6d.

    1d. Henry William Crichton, Viscount Crichton, D.S.O., an Equerry-in-Ordinary to H.R.H. the Prince of Wales, Capt. R.H. Guards (*Turf; Marlborough*), b. 30 Sept. 1872; m. 10 June 1903, Lady Mary Cavendish, da. of Hugh Lupus (Grosvenor), 1st Duke of Westminster [U.K.]; and has issue 1e.

        1e. Hon. Mary Kathleen Crichton.

    2d. Hon. George Arthur Charles Crichton, Capt. 2nd Batt. Coldstream Guards (*Guards'; Bachelors'*), b. 6 Sept. 1874.

    3d. Hon. Arthur Owen Crichton, Lieut. 3rd Batt. Gordon Highlanders (*Bachelors'; Carlton*), b. 15 Aug. 1876.

    4d. Hon. James Archibald Crichton, *late* Capt. Rifle Brigade (*Bachelors'*), b. 8 Dec. 1877.

    5d. Lady Evelyn Louisa Selina Crichton, b. 21 July 1879; m. 7 Nov. 1899, the Hon. Gerald Ernest Frances Ward, M.V.O., 1st Life Guards (15 *Hyde Park Street, W.*).

    6d. Lady Mabel Florence Mary Crichton, b. 31 Mar. 1882.

5c. Lady Alice Elizabeth Cole, m. 30 June 1891, the Right Hon. Evelyn Ashley, P.C. (*Broadlands, Romsey; 13 Cadogan Square, S.W.*); and has issue 1d.

    1d. Anthony Henry Evelyn Ashley, b. 25 Feb. 1894.

6c. Lady Jane Evelyn Cole (14 *Brechin Place, S.W.*).

2a. *Hon. Sir Galbraith Lowry Cole, G.C.B., Gen. in the Army, Governor of the Cape of Good Hope, &c.,* b. 1 *May* 1772; d. 4 *Oct.* 1842; m. 15 *June* 1815, *Lady Frances, da. of James (Harris), 1st Earl of Malmesbury, d. 1 Nov. 1847; and had issue.*

    See the Tudor Roll of "The Blood Royal of Britain," p. 431, Nos. 31112–31123.

3a. *Lady Sarah Cole, d. 14 Mar. 1833; m. Jan. 1790, Owen Wynne of Hazelwood, M.P., d. 12 Dec. 1841; and had issue 1b to 5b.*

    1b. *Right Hon. John Arthur Wynne of Hazelwood, M.P., High Sheriff, cos. Sligo and Leitrim,* b. 20 *Ap.* 1801; d. 19 *June* 1865; m. 7 *Ap.* 1838, *Lady Anne Wandesforde, da. of James (Butler), 1st Marquis of Ormonde [I.], K.P., d. 27 Nov. 1849; and had issue 1c to 3c.*   [Nos. 1897 to 1929.

1c. Owen Wynne of Hazelwood, J.P., D.L., High Sheriff, co. Sligo, 1875; co. Leitrim, 1880 (*Hazelwood, co. Sligo ; Lurgan Lodge, Manor Hamilton*), b. 5 Feb. 1843; m. 1 Nov. 1870, Stella Fanny, da. of Sir Robert Gore-Booth, 4th Bart. [I.], d. 1 Mar. 1887; and has issue 1d to 4d.

1d. Muriel Caroline Louisa Wynne, m. 22 June 1892, Philip Dudley Perceval.

2d. Evelyn Mary Wynne.

3d. Madeline Mary Wynne.

4d. Dorothy Adelaide Wynne.

2c. Sarah Wynne.

3c. Grace Florence Wynne.

2b. *Rev. William Willoughby Wynne*, b. 6 Sept. 1802; d. Sept. 1860; m. Sophia, da. of Alexander Perceval of Temple House, co. Sligo, J.P.

3b. *Anne Wynne*, d. 22 Oct. 1829; m. *as 1st wife*, 1 Sept. 1811, Somerset Richard (Butler), 3rd Earl of Carrick [I.], b. 28 Sept. 1779; d. 4 Feb. 1838; and had issue 1c.

1c. Lady Sarah Juliana Butler (*Coorheen House, Loughrea*), b. 29 July 1812; m. 8 Oct. 1832, William Thomas (Le Poer-Trench), 3rd Earl [I.] and 2nd Viscount [U.K.] Clancarty, 2nd Marquis of Heusden [Netherlands], G.C.B., b. 21 Sept. 1803; d. 26 Ap. 1872; and has issue.

See the Tudor Roll of "The Blood Royal of Britain," pp. 255–256, Nos. 23325–23349.

4b. *Sarah Anne Wynne*, d. 1862; m. *as 2nd wife, Edward Joshua Cooper of Markree Castle, co. Sligo*, M.P., d. 23 Ap. 1863; and had issue 1c to 5c.

1c. Laura Frances Cooper, m. 1860, Arthur Warre.

2c. Charlotte Sophia Cooper.

3c. Emma Maria Cooper, m. 8 Sept. 1870, Henry Eastwood.

4c. Selina Elizabeth Cooper.

5c. Cecily Florence Cooper, m. 8 May 1866, Col. Richard Augustus Cooper, d. 1890.

5b. *Elizabeth Wynne*, d. 1855; m. *the Rev. Luke Fowler (son of Robert Fowler, Lord Bishop of Ossory and Ferns*).

4a. *Lady Elizabeth Anne Cole*, d. 26 May 1807; m. *as 1st wife*, 1788, Col. Richard Magenis of Chanter Hill, co. Fermanagh, b. 1763; d. 6 Mar. 1831; and had issue 1b to 6b.

1b. *Henry Arthur Magenis (3rd son), Lieut.-Col. 87th Royal Irish Fusiliers*, b. July 1795; d. 14 Nov. 1852; m. 11 June 1828, Joseph Urusle Elise, da. of M. J. Damain de Kerostan of Brittany, d. 25 Dec. 1887; and had issue 1c to 3c.

1c. Henry Cole Magenis, Major-Gen., *late* R.H.A., J.P., D.L. (*Finvoy Lodge, Ballymoney ; 9 Great Marlborough Street, Regent Street, W.*), b. 10 Sept. 1838.

2c. Edward Cole Magenis (*Drumdoe, Boyle, Roscommon*), b. 18 Oct. 1841; m. 22 Dec. 1885, Cicily, da. of Joseph Hornby Birley of Brookside, Newton-le-Willows, J.P., d. 15 Nov. 1894; and has issue 1d to 4d.

1d. Richard Henry Cole Magenis, b. 20 Ap. 1888.

2d. Marjorie Elsie Magenis, b. 1 Jan. 1886.

3d. Sheila Frances Magenis, b. 13 May 1901.

4d. Cicily Magenis, b. 13 Oct. 1894.

3c. Elizabeth Anne Florence Magenis, m. 1863, Col. Edward Meurant, *late* 83rd Regt, s.p.

2b. *Rev. John Balfour Magenis*, d. 1862; m. *Frances Margarette, widow of George Ede of Merry Oak, Southampton, da. of Judge Moore of Lamberton Park ; and had issue 1c.* [Nos. 1930 to 1974.

# of The Blood Royal

1c. Geraldine Magenis, d. 1882 ; m. *as 1st wife,* 1864, *Col. Leonard Howard Lloyd Irby of Boyland Hall, Long Stratton, co. Norfolk, and 18 Chester Square, S.W.; and had issue.*

3b. Sir Arthur Charles Magenis, G.C.B., H.B.M.'s Minister at the Court of Lisbon, d. 4 Feb. 1867.

4b. Anne Louise Magenis, d. Nov. 1855 ; m. 19 *May* 1821, *David Albemarle Bertie Dewar of Doles, co. Hants, and Great Cumberland Place, London,* d. 25 Nov. 1859 ; *and had issue* 1c *to* 2c.

1c. Albemarle Dewar of Doles, co. Hants, Capt. 87th *and* 20th *Regts.,* b. 1822 ; d. *June* 1862 ; m. 30 *June* 1854, *Jane, da. and h. of Felix O'Beirne,* d. 10 *Mar.* 1905 ; *and had issue* 1d *to* 3d.

1d. Albemarle O'Beirne Willoughby Dewar (*Doles, Andover ; The Dean, Hurstbourne Tarrant, Andover*), b. 15 June 1855 ; m. 29 Ap. 1882, Florence Wilhelmina Rose, da. of Lieut.-Col. Marriott Matthew, D.L. ; and has issue 1e to 2e.

1e. Albemarle Willoughby David Dewar, b. 16 Sept. 1886.

2e. Hubert Stephen Lowry Dewar, b. May 1892.

2d. George Albemarle Bertie Dewar, b. 3 Nov. 1862.

3d. Adeliza Mary Bertie Dewar, b. 8 May 1861.

2c. Elizabeth Dewar, d. (-) ; m. [——], *Marquis Taliacarne of Levanto, near Genoa, Italian Diplo. Serv. ; and had issue* 1d *to* 2d.

1d. Arthur Bertie, Marquis Taliacarne, d. (*in New Zealand*) 1891 ; m. *and had issue.*

2d. Georgina Taliacarne, a nun.

5b. Elizabeth Anne Magenis, d. Ap. 1882 ; m. *July* 1824, *Capt. James Wilmot Williams of Herringston,* d.v.p. 4 *May* 1845 ; *and had issue* 1c *to* 5c.

1c. Edward Wilmot Williams, J.P., D.L., *late* Bengal Cavalry (*Herringston House, Dorchester*), b. 24 Nov. 1826 ; *m.* 6 Feb. 1862, the Hon. Sophia, da. of Standish (O'Grady), 2nd Viscount Guillamore [I.] ; and has issue 1d to 4d.

1d. Berkeley Cole Wilmot Williams, Capt., *late* P.W.O. Yorkshire Regt., b. 4 May 1865.

2d. Ashley Paget Wilmot Williams, D.S.O., Capt. 21st Lancers, b. 7 Jan. 1867.

3d. Meriel Gertrude Wilmot Williams, *m.* 8 Aug. 1885, Capt. Cecil Howard Degby Fetherstonhaugh, J.P., *late* 1st Dragoons (*Bracklyn Castle, Killucan*); and has issue 1e to 2e.

1e. Ashby Elliot Herbert Fetherstonhaugh, b. 3 July 1886.

2e. Meriel Eleanor Fetherstonhaugh, b. 12 Feb. 1897.

4d. Huldah Gwladys Wilmot Williams.

2c. Sir Albert Henry Wilmot Williams, K.C.V.O., Gen. R.A. (22 *Chesham Place, S.W.*), b. 8 Feb. 1832.

3c. Ashley George Wilmot Williams (*Cadlington, Blendworth, Horndean, co. Hants*), b. 24 Nov. 1834 ; *m.* Aug. 1871, Emily Louisa, da. of Morgan Treherne ; and has issue 1d to 3d.

1d. Percy Alexander Williams, b. 30 Sept. 1873.

2d. Florence Elizabeth Williams, b. 25 May 1872 ; *m.* 4 Oct. 1895, John Pepys Cockerell ; and has issue 1e to 2e.

1e. Andrew Pepys Cockerell.

2e. John Arthur Pepys Cockerell.

3d. Ellery Laura Williams, b. 22 Oct. 1875.

4c. Florence Elizabeth Wilmot Williams, d. 14 *Sept.* 1887 ; m. 5 *June* 1855, *the Hon. St. Leger Richard Glyn,* b. 3 Oct. 1825 ; d. 16 Ap. 1873 ; *and had issue* 1d *to* 5d.

1d. Constance Gertrude Glyn, *m.* 5 June 1889, George Henry Eyre-Matcham, J.P., Capt. *late* Wiltshire Regt. (*Bramble Hill, Lyndhurst, Hants*) ; and has issue 1e to 4e.

[Nos. 1975 to 1995.

The Plantagenet Roll

1e. John St. Leger Eyre-Matcham, b. 28 Mar. 1890.

2e. Florence Ellery Mary Eyre-Matcham, b. 7 Feb. 1893.

3e. Joyce Horatia Eyre-Matcham, b. 4 Oct. 1895.

4e. Constance Valentine Eyre-Matcham, b. 14 Feb. 1897.

2d. Florence Elizabeth Mary Glyn, m. 23 June 1880, William Wyndham Portal J.P. (*Southington, Overton, Hants*); and has issue.
See the Clarence Volume, p. 216, Nos. 4354–4357.

3d. Edith Theodosia Glyn, m. 25 July 1896, Henry Thomas Timson (*St. Vincents, Grantham ; Thatchbury Mount, Totton, Hants*); and has issue 1e to 2e.

1e. Florence Timson, b. 25 June 1897.

2e. Dorothy Timson, b. 20 Dec. 1898.

4d. Mabel Glyn, m. 2 June 1890, Capt. Robert Henry Fowler, *late* The King's Shropshire L. I. (*Rahinston, Enfield, co. Meath*); and has issue 1e to 2e.

1e. Robert St. Leger Fowler, b. 7 Ap. 1891.

2e. George Glyn Fowler, b. 4 Jan. 1896.

5d. Beatrice Ellerlie Glyn, m. 11 Oct. 1888, Capt. Frederick Howard Wingfield Fetherstonhaugh, *late* The Cameronians ; and has issue (a da.).

5c. Gertrude Mary Wilmot Williams, m. 5 June 1855, Major-Gen. Sir Alexander James Hardy Elliot, K.C.B. (36 *Ennismore Gardens, S.W.*).

6b. *Florence Catherine Magenis, d. 1837 ; m. 9 June 1823, John Ashley Warre of Cheddon, co. Somerset and West Cliffe House, Ramsgate ; and had issue (3 sons and 1 da.).*

5a. *Lady Florence Cole, b. 1779 ; d. 1 Mar. 1862 ; m. 17 Oct. 1797, Blayney Townley Balfour of Townley Hall, M.P., J.P., D.L., b. 28 May 1769 ; d. 22 Dec. 1856 ; and had issue 1b.*

1b. *Blayney Townley Balfour of Townley Hall, J.P., High Sheriff co. Louth 1841, Lieut.-Governor of the Bahamas 1833, b. 2 July 1799 ; d. 5 Sept. 1882 ; m. 12 Jan. 1843, Elizabeth Catherine, da. and h. of Richard Molesworth Reynell of Reynella ; and had issue 1c to 4c.*

1c. Blayney Reynell Townley Balfour, J.P., D.L., High Sheriff co. Louth 1885 (*Townley Hall, near Drogheda, co. Louth*), b. 15 Ap. 1845.

2c. Rev. Francis Richard Townley Balfour, M.A. (Camb.), Canon of Bloemfontein, b. 21 June 1846.

3c. Catherine Florence Agnes Townley Balfour, b. 17 Jan. 1858.

4c. Mary Henrietta Townley Balfour, b. 23 Oct. 1860.

6a. *Lady Henrietta Frances Cole, d. 2 July 1848 ; m. 20 July 1805, Thomas Philip (Weddell, previously Robinson, and afterwards (1833) De Grey), 2nd Earl De Grey [U.K.], 5th Baron Lucas [E.], 3rd Baron Grantham [G.B.], K.G., b. 8 Dec. 1781 ; d. 14 Nov. 1859 ; and had issue 1b to 2b.*

1b. *Anne Florence, suo jure 6th Baroness Lucas [E.], b. 8 June 1806 ; d. 23 July 1880 ; m. 7 Oct. 1833, George Augustus Frederick (Cowper), 6th Earl Cowper [G.B.], 6th Baron Cowper and Butler, and Baron Dingwall [S.], 4th Prince Cowper [H.R.E.], &c., b. 26 June 1806 ; d. 15 Ap. 1856 ; and had issue 1c to 4c.*

1c. *Frances Thomas de Grey (Cowper), 7th Earl Cowper [G.B.], 7th Baron Lucas and Cowper, and 3rd Baron Butler [E.], 4th Baron Dingwall [S.], 5th Prince Cowper [H.R.E.], K.G., P.C., &c., b. 11 June 1834 ; d. 18 July 1905 ; m. 25 Oct. 1870, Lady Katrine Cecilia (Panshanger, Hertford ; 4 St. James' Square, S.W.), da. of William (Compton), 4th Marquis of Northampton [G.B.].*

2c. *Lady Florence Amabell Cowper, b. 4 Dec. 1840 ; d. 28 Ap. 1886 ; m. 9 Aug. 1871, the Hon. Auberon Herbert, D.C.L., late M.P. (Old House, Berryhood, Ringwood) ; and had issue 1d to 2d.*

1d. Auberon Thomas (Herbert), 11th Baron Dingwall [S.] and 8th Baron Lucas [E.], b. 25 May 1876 (*Wrest Park, Ampthill*).

2d. Nan Ino Herbert, b. 13 June 1880. [Nos. 1996 to 2018.

140

# of The Blood Royal

3c. Lady Adine Eliza Anne Cowper, b. 17 Mar. 1843; d. 20 Oct. 1868; m. 29 Sept. 1866, *the Hon. Julian Fane*, b. 10 Oct. 1827; d. 19 Ap. 1870; *and had issue* 1d.

    1d. Ethel Anne Priscilla Fane, *b.* 27 June 1867; *m.* 17 Feb. 1887, William Henry Grenfell, M.P. (*Taplow Court, Maidenhead; 4 St James' Square, S.W.*); and has issue 1e to 4e.

        1e–4e. See the Clarence Volume, p. 352, Nos. 11474–11494.

    4c. Lady Amabel Cowper, *m.* 18 Nov. 1873, Lord Walter Talbot Kerr, Admiral of the Fleet, G.C.B. (*58 Cromwell Road, S.W.*); and has issue 1d to 6d.

        1d–6d. See the Clarence Volume, p. 630, Nos. 28202–28207.

  2b. Lady Mary Gertrude Robinson, b. 5 Feb. 1809; d. 11 July 1892; m. 6 July 1839, *Henry Vyner of Newby Hall, Ripon*, d. 22 Jan. 1861; *and had issue* 1c to 2c.

    1c. Robert Charles de Grey Vyner of Gautby, Capt. *late* Grenadier Guards, High Sheriff co. Cheshire 1893 (*Fairfield, York; Newby Hall, Ripon; Coomb Hurst, Kingston Hill*), b. 13 Feb. 1842; m. 10 July 1865, Eleanor Margaret, da. of the Rev. Slingsby Duncombe Shafto; and has issue 1d to 2d.

        1d. Mary Evelyn Vyner, *m.* 31 July 1886, Lord Alwyne Frederick Compton, D.S.O., M.P. (*7 Balfour Place, W.; Torloisk, Tobermory, N.B.*); and has issue.

        See the Clarence Volume, p. 199, Nos. 3931–3932.

        2d. Violet Aline Vyner, *m.* 1st, 19 July 1890, James Francis Harry (St. Clair-Erskine), 5th Earl of Rosslyn [S.] and Baron Loughborough [G.B.], divorced 1902; 2ndly, 12 Aug. 1903, Charles Jarrett; and has issue 1e to 2e.

            1e. Francis Edward Scudamore St. Clair-Erskine, Lord Loughborough, *b.* 16 Nov. 1892.

            2e. Lady Rosabelle Millicent St. Clair-Erskine, *b.* 30 Oct. 1891.

    2c. Henrietta Anne Theodosia Vyner, C.I., *m.* 8 Ap. 1851, George Frederick Samuel (Robinson), 1st Marquis of Ripon [U.K.], 4th Baron Grantham [G.B.], K.G., P.C., G.S.C.I., sometime (1880–1884) Viceroy of India; (1892–1895) Secretary of State for the Colonies, &c. (*Studley Royal, near Ripon; 9 Chelsea Embankment, S.W.*); and has issue 1d.

        1d. Frederick Oliver Robinson, Earl de Grey, K.C.V.O., Treasurer of the Household to H.M. Queen Alexandra (*Coombe Court, Kingston Hill*), b. 29 Jan. 1852; m. 7 May 1885, Constance Gladys, Dowager-Countess of Lonsdale [U.K.], da. of Sidney (Herbert), 1st Lord Herbert of Lea [U.K.], P.C.

                                    [Nos. 2019 to 2056.

65. Descendants of the Hon. ARTHUR COLE, *afterwards* COLE-HAMILTON of Skea, co. Fermanagh, M.P. (see Table VI.), *b.* 8 Aug. 1750; *d.* 1810; *m.* 1780, LETITIA, da. and h. of Claude HAMILTON of co. Tyrone, *d.* 7 Feb. 1823; and had issue 1*a* to 4*a*.

  1a. Claude William Cole-Hamilton, b. 7 July 1781; d. 25 Ap. 1822; m. *as* 1st *husband*, 10 Oct. 1805, *Nichola Sophia*, da. of *Richard Chaloner of Kingsfort*, d. 31 Jan. 1863; *and had issue* 1b.

    1b. Arthur Willoughby Cole-Hamilton of Beltrim, J.P., D.L., b. 23 Nov. 1806; d. 16 Dec. 1891; m. 16 Dec. 1831, *Emily Catherine*, da. of *the Rev. Charles Cobbe-Beresford*, d. 19 Nov. 1869; *and had issue* 1c to 9c.

      1c. William Claude Cole-Hamilton of Ballitore House, High Sheriff co. Tyrone 1867, *Capt.* 88th *Regt.*, b. 8 Aug. 1833; d. 25 Ap. 1882; m. 10 June 1858, *Caroline Elizabeth Josephine*, da. of *the Hon. Andrew Godfrey Stuart of Lisdhu; and had issue* 1d to 4d.

        1d. Arthur Richard Cole-Hamilton, D.L., Lieut.-Col. 6th Royal Irish Rifles (*Beltrim, co. Tyrone; Bellewstown House, Drogheda*), b. 29 Ap. 1859; *m.* 1st, 2 Jan.

                                        [No. 2057.

1882, Jeannette, da. of Samuel Moore of Moorlands, *d.* 7 Ap. 1883; 2ndly, 18 Feb. 1884, Florence Alice, da. of James Duke Hughes of Burntwood, Surrey; and has issue 1*e.*

1*e.* William Moore Cole-Hamilton, *late* Lieut. King's Royal Rifle Corps (*The Elms, Ongar, Essex*), *b.* 3 Ap. 1883; *m.* Oct. 1903, Ada Beatrice, da. of William Peter Huddle of Dover; and has issue 1*f.*

1*f.* Nora Kathleen Cole-Hamilton, *b.* 1904.

2*d.* *William Andrew Thomas Cole-Hamilton, Capt. Royal Irish Fusiliers,* b. 6 *July* 1864; d. 16 *May* 1903; m. 1891, *Lizzie Alexander, widow of Capt. Ashton Rendle, M.S.C., da. of Christopher S. Penny; and had issue* 1*e to* 2*e.*

1*e.* Con William Eric Cole-Hamilton, *b.* 7 Mar. 1894.

2*e.* Clodagh Madeline Janie Cole-Hamilton, *b.* 13 Nov. 1897.

3*d.* Claud George Cole-Hamilton, D.S.O., Capt. 6th Batt. Royal Irish Rifles (*Santa Lucia, Rosaris, Argentina*), *b.* 27 Jan. 1869; *m.* 4 Ap. 1893, Lucy Charlewood, da. of Reginald Henry Thorold; and has issue 1*e* to 3*e.*

1*e.* Isabel Katherine Cole-Hamilton, *b.* 8 Jan. 1894.

2*e.* Lucy Alice Cole-Hamilton, *b.* 21 Feb. 1896.

3*e.* Norah Elizabeth Cole-Hamilton, *b.* Mar. 1899.

4*d.* Isabel Mary Cole-Hamilton, *m.* 15 Dec. 1885, Francis Richard Pease, J.P., D.L. (*Forestmere, Liphook, Hants*).

2*c.* Claude Cole-Hamilton, now Chaloner, J.P. (*King's Fort, Mognalty, Kells, co. Meath*), *b.* 20 Nov. 1838; *m.* 2 June 1875, Henrietta Anne, da. of Alexander Montgomery of Kilmer; and has issue 1*d* to 5*d.*

1*d.* Claud Willoughby Chaloner, Capt. Inniskilling Fusiliers and Instructor of Musketry, *b.* 22 Jan. 1882.

2*d.* John Cole-Chaloner, *b.* 28 May 1889.

3*d.* Sophia Elizabeth Chaloner, *b.* 22 Feb. 1877.

4*d.* Emily Chaloner, *b.* 11 May 1878.

5*d.* Henrietta Frances Chaloner, *b.* 2 Jan. 1881.

3*c.* Charles Richard Cole-Hamilton, Comm. (ret.) R.N., *b.* 6 Dec. 1842.

4*c.* *Rev. Arthur Henry Cole-Hamilton,* b. 17 *Ap.* 1846; d. 15 *Dec.* 1889; m. 17 *Ap.* 1873, *Harriet Elizabeth* (*Hertingfordbury, Herts.*), *da. of John Tisdall of Charlesfort, co. Meath; and had issue* 1*d to* 5*d.*

1*d.* Henry Arthur Cole-Hamilton, Hon. Capt. in Army and Capt. Reserve of Officers (*Beltrim, Wolverhoek, O.R.C.*), *b.* 30 Ap. 1874.

2*d.* George William Cole-Hamilton, B.A. (Camb.) (*Gortin, O.R.C.*), *b.* 12 Sept. 1875.

3*d.* Rev. Richard Mervyn Cole-Hamilton, M.A. (Oxon.), Curate of Alfreton, *b.* 14 Dec. 1877.

4*d.* John Claude Cole-Hamilton, B.A., Lieut. R.N., *b.* 24 Mar. 1879.

5*d.* Charles Cole-Hamilton, B.A., *b.* 15 Jan. 1885.

5*c.* John Isaac Cole-Hamilton (*Sutton Hall, Ferrybridge, Yorkshire*), *b.* 12 July 1851; *m.* 22 Feb. 1884, Elinor Bourne, da. of Henry Royds of Elm House, Wavertree; and has issue 1*d* to 3*d.*

1*d.* Hugh Arthur Willoughby Cole-Hamilton, *b.* 10 Oct. 1887.

2*d.* John Beresford Cole-Hamilton, *b.* 1 Dec. 1894.

3*d.* Margaret Selina Cole-Hamilton, *b.* 1884.

6*c.* *Emily Harriet Cole-Hamilton,* b. 6 *Jan.* 1835; d. 28 *Sept.*, 1885; m. 29 *Ap.* 1858, *John Gordon Bowen of Burt House, co. Donegal; and had issue* 1*d to* 6*d.*

1*d.* Edward Ferguson Bowen, *b.* 5 July 1860.

2*d.* George John Bowen, *b.* 23 Aug. 1861.

3*d.* Emily Jane Louisa Bowen.

4*d.* Frances Charlotte Bowen.

5*d.* Katherine Maud Bowen.

6*d.* Selina Bowen.

[Nos. 2058 to 2088.

# of The Blood Royal

7c. Frances Sophia Cole-Hamilton, *unm.*

8c. Selina Cole-Hamilton (*Brookman's Park, Hatfield*); *m.* 31 Dec. 1870, Robert George Gaussen, Capt. *late* Grenadier Guards, *d.* 10 Jan. 1906; and has issue 1*d* to 2*d*.

1*d*. Emilia Christian Gaussen, *m.* 2 Mar. 1898, H. L. Tottenham; and has issue 1*e* to 4*e*.

1*e*. Arthur Robert Tottenham, *b.* June 1900.

2*e*. Charles Casamajor Tottenham, *b.* Nov. 1901.

3*e*. Patrick Tottenham, *b.* Mar. 1904.

4*e*. Christian Nichola Tottenham, *b.* Jan. 1903.

2*d*. Cicily Anne Gaussen.

9c. *Letitia Grace Cole-Hamilton*, b. 2 Oct. 1844; d. 13 *Jan.* 1888; m. 17 *Aug.* 1869, *Col. the Hon. Henry George Louis Crichton, A.D.C. to H.M. the King, &c.* (*Netley Castle, Netley Abbey, Hants*); *and had issue 1d to 7d.*

1*d*. Charles William Harry Crichton, Capt. 10th Hussars, *b.* 7 July 1872.

2*d*. Reginald Louis Crichton, Lieut. R.N., *b.* 23 Dec. 1874; *m.* 1902, Hester Beatrice, da. of the Rev. Richard Allen White.

3*d*. Frederick Marcus Crichton, B.A. (Oxon.), *b.* 10 Aug. 1877.

4*d*. Richard Edward Crichton, Lieut. King's Royal Rifle Corps, *b.* 21 June 1879.

5*d*. John Arthur Crichton, *b.* 19 Aug. 1883.

6*d*. Emily Florence Crichton, *m.* 9 July 1895, Major Edward Bernard John Seely, D.S.O., M.P., J.P., D.L. (*Berwick Lodge, Ryde, I.W.*); and has issue 1*e* to 5*e*.

1*e*. Frank Reginald Seely, *b.* 26 June 1896.

2*e*. Henry John Alexander Seely, *b.* 1 May 1899.

3*e*. Arthur Patrick William Seely, *b.* 18 Aug. 1905.

4*e*. Emily Grace Seely, *b.* 18 Jan. 1898.

5*e*. Irene Florence Seely, *b.* 22 June 1902.

7*d*. Louisa Charlotte Crichton.

2a. *Letitia Cole-Hamilton*, d. (-) 1853; *m. Aug.* 1815, *Major Randall Stafford of Tully, co. Cavan.*

3a. *Elizabeth Ann Cole-Hamilton*, d. (-) 1849; *m.* 1820, *Henry Slade.*

4a. *Isabella Cole-Hamilton*, d. 1827; *m. James Hamilton.*

[Nos. 2089 to 2108.]

66. Descendants, if any, of the Hon. CATHERINE COLE (see Table VI.), *m.* 6 Oct. 1770, RICHARD BROWNE, Capt. 1st Regt. of Foot.

67. Descendants, if any surviving, of BOURCHIER COLE; MICHAEL COLE; and WILLIAM COLE, *bapt.* 21 Ap. 1714, younger brothers to JOHN (COLE), 1st BARON MOUNT FLORENCE [I.](see Table VI.).

68. Descendants of ARTHUR COLE of Fermanagh (see Table VI.), *d.* 1809 (will dated 18 Feb. 1806, proved 4 Jan. 1810); *m.* 1st, 28 Oct. 1768, ANN, da. of James AYLMER of Croagh; 2ndly, ALICIA, da. of [——] TUTHILL; and had issue 1*a* to 5*a*.

1a.² *Thomas Cole.*

2a.¹ *Maria Cole*, d. (-); m. [——] *Gabbitt; and had issue 1b.*

1b. [——] *Gabbitt*, m. [——] *Bailey.*

The Plantagenet Roll

3a.[2] *Anna Wilford Cole*, b. 1790; d. 4 *June* 1856; m. 12 *Nov.* 1808, *David Verner of Derryesker, co. Armagh*, b. 5 *Sept.* 1780; d. 6 *Dec.* 1826; *and had issue* 1b *to* 6b.

1b. *Arthur Cole Verner, Mayor of Sandwich, Essex co., Canada* 1878, b. 28 *Mar.* 1811; d. 2 *Ap.* 1890; m. *Ap.* 1835, *Harriet, da. of William Eayrs of Jersey*, d. 2 *Ap.* 1890; *and had issue* 1c *to* 7c.

1c. Frederick Arthur Verner, b. 26 Feb. 1836.

2c. James William David Verner, b. 14 Mar. 1844; m. 10 Jan. 1893, Helen Erskine, da. of [——] Spiers.

3c. *John Edward Verner*, b. 9 *Jan.* 1852; d. (? *unm.*).

4c. Anna Victoria Verner, m. 6 June 1855, J. S. Donaldson of Toronto; d. (–).

5c. *Alicia Verner*, d. (–); m. *Dr. J. Coventry of Windsor, Ontario*, d. (–).

6c. Clara Verner, m. [——].

7c. Isabel Octavia Verner, m. 20 June 1871, S. M. Goddard of Sandwich, Canada; and has issue.

2b. *William John Verner, Col. Royal Antrim Rifles, formerly 53rd and 21st Regts.*, b. 1 *Feb.* 1819; d. 21 *Sept.* 1902; m. 27 *May* 1850, *Mary Anne, da. of John Rogers of London*, d. 15 *Feb.* 1901; *and had issue* 1c *to* 4c.

1c. William Willoughby Cole Verner, Col. *late* Rifle Brigade, b. 22 Oct. 1852; m. 30 Nov. 1881, the Hon. Elizabeth Mary Emily, da. of Henry William (Parnell), 3rd Baron Congleton [U.K.]; and has issue 1d to 2d.

1d. Rudolf Henry Cole Verner, R.N., b. 16 Jan. 1883.

2d. Dorothy May Verner.

2c. *Wilfred Cole Verner*, b. 15 *May* 1863; d. 21 *Nov.* 1889; m. 13 *Ap.* 1885, *Geraldine Beatrice, da. of Reginald Kempe ; and had issue* 1d.

1d. Cecil Reginald Verner, b. 12 Ap. 1886.

3c. Constance Ida Verner (2 *Victoria Terrace, Hove, Brighton*).

4c. Evelyn Diana Verner, m. 22 Sept. 1885, Hugh Verner Dobson.

3b. *John Willoughby Verner, Collector of Customs, Canada*, b. 13 *Jan.* 1821 ; d. *Aug.* 1887 ; m. 7 *May* 1846, *Charlotte Sherwood, da. of Paul Gassford of Brockville, Canada ; and had issue* 1c *to* 5c.

1c. *John Arthur Cole Verner*, d. (? *unm.*).

2c. *Norah Pauline Verner*, d. (–); m. 1st, *James Wyld ;* 2ndly, *George Wyld ; and had issue* 1d.

1d. *Verner Wyld.*

3c. *Anna Wingfield Verner*, d. (? *unm.*).

4c. *Sarah Verner*, d. (? *unm.*).

5c. Mary Isabel Verner, m. Archer Baker.

4b. *Alicia Verner*, b. 16 *Nov.* 1812; d. 8 *Aug.* 1859; m. 1st, 23 *May* 1838, *Handcock Montgomery of Beesmont Park, co. Monaghan*, d. 8 *May* 1839 ; 2ndly, 20 *July* 1846, *Langford Kennedy of Cultra*, d. 2 *Feb.* 1850 ; *and had issue* 1c *to* 3c.

1c. Alexander Nixon Montgomery, J.P., Comdt. I.N.N.G., *late* Capt. Royal Fusiliers (*Ismont, Mid-Ilovu, Natal*), b. 23 Mar. 1839; *m.* 4 Jan. 1861, Istere Alicia, da. of Señor Solomon Atrutl of Gibraltar, *d.* 14 May 1900; and has issue 1d to 9d.

1d. John Willoughby Verner Montgomery, Capt. Natal Carabineers, b. 18 May 1867.

2d. Quintin Hogg Montgomery (*Beaumont, Natal*), b. 26 June 1877 ; m. 29 Oct. 1903, Adeline Maud, da. of John Arend de Waal Berning ; and has issue 1e.

1e. Dulcia Maud Montgomery, b. 28 Aug. 1904. [Nos. 2109 to 2124.

144

# of The Blood Royal

3d. Alethe Sylva Montgomery, *m.* 13 Dec. 1880, Leonard Guise Wingfield-Stratford (*Powerscourt, Natal*); and has issue 1*e* to 5*e*.

    1*e.* Mervyn Edward John Wingfield-Stratford, *b.* 17 Sept. 1883.

    2*e.* Maud Frances Jane Wingfield-Stratford.

    3*e.* Agnes Mary Wingfield-Stratford.

    4*e.* Murielle Victoria Alethe Wingfield-Stratford.

    5*e.* Hermione Wingfield-Stratford.

4d. Blanche Lucia Montgomery, *m.* 8 Ap. 1891, Edward Henry Hayes (*Hardington, Beaumont, Natal*); and has issue 1*e.*

    1*e.* Virginia Lucia Hayes.

5d. Grace Dorothea Montgomery, *m.* 16 Dec. 1891, Richard Nevill Wingfield-Stratford (*Wingfield, Beaumont, Natal*); and has issue 1*e.*

    1*e.* Esmé John Richard Wingfield-Stratford, *b.* 12 Feb. 1897.

6d. Istere Octavia Montgomery, *m.* 25 Jan. 1897, Reginald Dewhurst (*Asply, Beaumont, Natal*); and has issue 1*e.*

    1*e.* Istere Dewhurst.

7d. Alexandra Rogeria Louisa Montgomery, *m.* 23 Feb. 1905, Frank Foxton Beaumont.

8d. Edith Lavinia Decima Montgomery.

9d. Irene Sibyl Theresa Montgomery.

2c. Charles William Kennedy (*Scots Hill House, Croxley Green, R.S.O., Herts*), *b.* 6 July 1850; *m.* 8 July 1884, Florence Eliza, da. of Rowland Hunt of Borcatton, co. Salop.

3c. Henrietta Frances Alicia Kennedy (*Erlimont, Erley, Reading*), *b.* 24 Jan. 1849; *m.* 1 Aug. 1871, Francis Weldon, Capt. Madras Staff Corps; and has issue 1*d* to 4*d.*

    1*d.* Walter Langford Weldon, *b.* 30 July 1872; *m.* 1 Dec. 1904, Emma Anne, da. of [——] Tod, *d.* 25 May 1905.

    2*d.* Ernest Stuart Weldon, *b.* 6 Jan. 1877.

    3*d.* Ethel Olive Weldon, *b.* 13 Feb. 1875.

    4*d.* Winifred Edith Weldon, *b.* 19 Oct. 1883.

5b. *Grace Anna Dorothea Verner*, b. 17 *July* 1815; d. 6 *Ap.* 1864; m. 1*st*, 12 *Aug.* 1843, *the Rev. Charles Ross de Havilland of Havilland Hall, Guernsey*, d. 6 *Oct.* 1851; *2ndly, George Bell of Guernsey; and had issue* 1*c.*

    1*c.* John Thomas Ross de Havilland, Jurat of the Royal Court of Guernsey 1881 (*Havilland Hall, Guernsey*), *b.* 11 Ap. 1852; *m.* 1879, Louisa Lathann, da. of Charles B. Young of Washington, U.S.A.; and has issue 1*d* to 4*d.*

        1*d.* Piers de Havilland, *b.* 15 Aug. 1883.

        2*d.* Grace de Havilland.

        3*d.* Kathleen de Havilland.

        4*d.* Dulce de Havilland.

6b. *Olivia Verner*, d. 29 Dec. 1890; m. 20 *May* 1846, *the Rev. Robert Aldridge, Incumbent, Knowle Hill, Berks* 1859–1862, *previously Capt.* 60*th Rifles*, d. 29 *Oct.* 1896; *and had issue* 1*c* to 4*c.*

    1*c.* Reginald Aldridge, *b.* 2 Jan. 1850; *m.* 12 Ap. 1893, Louisa, da. of [——] Aldridge.

    2*c.* Robert Aldridge, *b.* 12 Ap. 1853.

    3*c.* Alfred Aldridge, *b.* 13 June 1857; *m.* 26 Jan. 1903, Alice Gaston, da. of [——] Peasegood.

    4*c.* Olivia Aldridge.

4a.[2] *Theresa Benoit Cole*, d. 6 *Ap.* 1863; m. *Mar.* 1815, *Capt. Alexander Kennedy, R.N.*, d. 1 *Ap.* 1849; *and had issue* 1*b to* 2*b.*   [Nos. 2125 to 2154.

1*b*. John Alexander Kennedy, Major-Gen. R.M.L.I., *b.* 1823; *m.* 1st, 1872, Amy, da. of Lieut.-Col. Malcolm M'Gregor, 21st Scottish Fusiliers, *d.* 1875; 2ndly, 1879, Marion, da. of Robert Wether of Kew, Surrey.

2*b*. Charles Stewart Kennedy, *formerly* a Clerk in the Admiralty, *b.* 1825.

5*a*.² *Alicia Cole*, m. *Hugh Tuthill; and had issue (a son)* 1*b*.

1*b*. *W. Tuthill, who went to New Orleans in* 1855. [Nos. 2155 to 2156.

69. Descendants of HENRY ST. GEORGE COLE of Annestown, co. Waterford, High Sheriff of that county 1798–1799, Captain and Brevet-Major in the Army (see Table VI.), *b.* 17 Mar. 1746; *d.* 15 May 1819; *m.* 1st, MARY, da. of Henry RICHARDSON of Belturbet, co. Cavan, M.D., *d.* 12 Mar. 1771; 2ndly, 30 Jan. 1772, ELIZABETH, widow of WILLIAM THOMPSON of Dublin, da. of James MACROBERTS of Castleroe, co. Kildare; and had issue 1*a*.

1*a*. *Henry Cole of Frescati Lodge, co. Dublin, Bar.-at-Law, one of the Police Magistrates of Dublin,* b. 1768; d. 14 *Nov.* 1840; m. *Jan.* 1812, *Frances Arabella, da. of Henry La Nauze of Aubawn, co. Cavan,* d. 4 *Mar.* 1859; *and had issue* 1*b to* 2*b*.

1*b*. *John Willoughby Cole, Sub-Inspector Royal Irish Constabulary, Balbriggan,* b. 1813; d. (–); m. 3 *June* 1850, *Elizabeth Hariette, da. of John Hamilton Brown of Cumber House, co. Londonderry,* d. 8 *Aug.* 1881; *and had issue* 1*c*.

1*c*. *Jane Matilda Cole,* d. 21 *Mar.* 1889; m. 3 *Aug.* 1872, *Captain Robert Lefroy (Aubrey, Shankill, co. Dublin); and had issue* 1*d to* 3*d*.

1*d*. Rev. Robert Willoughby Lefroy, B.A. (*St. Michael's, Blackrock, co. Cork*), *b.* 8 Nov. 1877.

2*d*. Francis Buchanan Lefroy, *b.* 12 June 1885.

3*d*. Sydney Maud Lefroy.

2*b*. *Henrietta Catherine Cole,* d. 29 *Sept.* 1897; m. 10 *Jan.* 1849, *the Rev. William Alfred Hamilton, D.D., Rector of Taney and Canon of Christ Church Cathedral, Dublin,* b. 19 *Mar.* 1824; d. 13 *Feb.* 1897; *and had issue* 1*c to* 9*c*.

1*c*. Rev. Henry Balfour Hamilton, M.A. (T. C. Dublin), Rector of West Leake and Kingston-on-Suir (*West Leake Rectory, co. Notts.*), *b.* 18 Dec. 1849; *m.* 24 Aug. 1875, Hannah Sophia, da. of John Hubert Moore; and has issue 1*d* to 3*d*.

1*d*. Alfred Henry John Hamilton, Lieut. Royal Indian Marine.

2*d*. Rev. John Cole Hamilton, B.A. (Oxon.).

3*d*. Cicely Henrietta Augusta Hamilton.

2*c*. Alfred St. George Hamilton, B.A. (T. C. Dublin) (*Cluan-na-Greine, Foxrock, co. Dublin*), *b.* 5 Dec. 1851; *m.* 24 Nov. 1896, Emeline Caroline, da. of Richard Atkinson of Gortmore, co. Dublin.

3*c*. William Drummond Hamilton, M.A. (Oxon.), J.P. (*Lennan Park, Ramelton, co. Donegal*), *b.* 4 Aug. 1859; *m.* 5 Aug. 1891, Alice Josephine, da. of George Kinahan of Roebuck Park, co. Dublin, D.L.; and has issue 1*d* to 2*d*.

1*d*. Margaret Henrietta Hamilton.

2*d*. Dorothy Alice Hamilton.

4*c*. Willoughby James Hamilton (*Sydenham House, Dundrum, co. Dublin*), *b.* 9 Dec. 1864; *m.* 31 May 1894, Sophia Jane, da. of Charles Thompson of Herbert Hill, co. Dublin, J.P.

5*c*. Rev. Francis Cole Lowry Hamilton, M.A. (Durham), Rector of Northenden (*Northenden Rectory, co. Chester*), *b.* 26 Ap. 1869; *m.* 28 Ap. 1898, Maria Georgina, da. of George Kinahan of Roebuck Park, co. Dublin, D.L. [Nos. 2157 to 2169.

# of ᵀᵍᵉ Blood Royal

6c. Blayney Hamilton (*Lakelands, Dundrum, co. Dublin*), b. 13 June 1872; m. 1 June 1898, Irene Kirkwood, da. of Commissary-General James Long of Manor House, Dundrum, co. Dublin, J.P.; and has issue 1d to 2d.

    1d. Blayney Hamilton, b. 4 May 1902.

    2d. Arthur Hamilton, b. 29 Jan. 1905.

7c. Gertrude May Hamilton, b. 29 Ap. 1853; m. 1st, 1 Sept. 1875, Erskine Wilmot-Chetwode of Woodbrook, Queen's Co.; 2ndly, 13 Mar. 1890, the Rev. Edward Mewburn Walker, Fellow, Librarian, and Senior Tutor of Queen's College, Oxford, and sometime Proctor of that University, and Rector of Besselsleigh (*Besselsleigh Rectory, Abingdon ; 9 Merton Street, Oxford*); and has issue 1d to 4d.

    1d. John Drummond Walker, b. 4 Jan. 1891.

    2d. Gertrude Florence Evelyn Wilmot-Chetwode, m. 30 Nov. 1899, Captain Arthur Henry Marindin, 42nd Royal Highlanders (Black Watch) (*Woodfield, Worcestershire*).

    3d. Rita Kathleen Wilmot-Chetwode, m. 25 Sept. 1901, Arthur Kinahan (*Moyglare, co. Meath*).

    4d. Henrietta Frances Walker.

8c. Florence Eglantine Hamilton, b. 29 Ap. 1853; m. 9 Dec. 1897, Frances Elrington Ball (6 *Wilton Place, Dublin*).

9c. Catherine Henrietta Hamilton, b. 4 May 1858; m. 28 Oct. 1886, Robert Pollock Hamilton (*Manor Lodge, Donaghadee, co. Down*); and has issue 1d to 4d.

    1d. Charles Pollock Hamilton.

    2d. Hugh Alfred Hamilton.

    3d. Kathleen Emma May Hamilton.

    4d. Eva Maud Hamilton.   [Nos. 2170 to 2183.

70. Descendants, if any, of THOMAS COLE (see Table VI.), d. 20 Dec. 1771, and of FLORENCE COLE, m. Aug. 1769, HUGH FAULKNER.

71. Descendants of LETITIA COLE (see Table VI.), d. (–); m. 1st, Ap. 1770, Major ROBERT JOHNSON of Lettyville, King's Co.,[1] d. 3 July 1787; 2ndly, 6 Jan. 1788, Capt. THOMAS DANCER EYRE of Eyreville, co. Galway, d. Oct. 1799; and had issue 1a to 2a.

    1a. Thomas Stratford Eyre of Eyreville, co. Galway, J.P., b. 8 Dec. 1788; d. Feb. 1877; m. Feb. 1822, Grace Lynar, da. of the Rev. William Lynar Fawcett of Dublin, d. May 1834; and had issue 1b to 3b.

    1b. Thomas Stratford Eyre of Eyreville, b. 30 Oct. 1822; d. 20 Feb. 1898; m. 13 Mar. 1860, Marion Dallas (*Eyreville, Kiltormer, Ballinasloe, co. Galway*), da. of Alexander Russel ; and had issue 1c to 5c.

    1c. Lionel Hedges Eyre (*Vancouver, British Columbia*), b. 27 May 1863.

    2c. Willoughby Cole Eyre (*Vancouver, British Columbia*), b. 20 June 1865; m. 1890, Minnie, da. of [——] Heywood ; and has issue 1d.

    1d. Arthur Lowry Cole Eyre, b. 1891.

    3c. Marion Letitia Eleanor Eyre (*Eyreville, Kiltormer, Ballinasloe*), b. 15 Dec. 1860; m. 10 Sept. 1901, Frederick Haydon Horsey of St. Margaret's, Twickenham, d.s.p. 6 Ap. 1903.

    4c. Grace Geraldine Eyre, b. 27 June 1870; m. 13 Aug. 1890, William Ingram Worthington now (R.L. 12 Ap. 1902) Worthington-Eyre (12 *Tivoli Terrace, South Kingstown, co. Dublin*); and has issue 1d to 7d.   [Nos. 2184 to 2188.

---

[1] By whom she had issue a son and da. who both d. unm.

The Plantagenet Roll

1d. William Stratford Eyre Worthington-Eyre, b. 9 May 1891.

2d. Lionel George Worthington-Eyre, b. 15 Sept. 1893.

3d. Robert Worthington-Eyre, b. 4 Aug. 1895.

4d. Hedges Eyre Worthington-Eyre, b. 8 Sept. 1899.

5d. Marion Grace Worthington-Eyre, b. 3 July 1892.

6d. Olive Geraldine Worthington-Eyre, b. 1 Dec. 1900.

7d. Florence Mary Worthington-Eyre, b. 20 May 1904.

5c. Olive Kathleen Eyre, b. 26 June 1873.

2b. Grace Elizabeth Eyre (Eyreville, Kiltormer, Ballinasloe), b. 24 Oct. 1824.

3b. Amelia Eyre, b. 22 Sept. 1827; d. 1872; m. 1856, Capt. Phayre, 24th Regt.; and had issue two sons and a da.[1]

2a. Elizabeth Florence Eyre, b. 1794; d. 19 Feb. 1871; m. 1816, Rev. Edward Hartigan, Vicar of Kiltormer, co. Galway, b. 15 June 1789; d. 19 July 1850; and had issue 1b to 8b.

1b. William Henry Hartigan, Bar.-at-Law (Belmont, Monkstown, co. Dublin), b. 16 Jan. 1819; m. 10 Ap. 1866, Ellen, da. of the Rev. Henry Martin of Aughrim, co. Galway, s.p.

2b. Charles Stewart Hartigan, b. Feb. 1828; d. 12 June 1896; m. 5 Mar. 1857, Anna Maria (Clandon, Clarence Road, Mottingham, Kent), da. of the Rev. Allen Mitchell, Vicar of Drumsnatt, co. Monaghan; and had issue 1c to 6c.

1c. Rev. Allen Stewart Hartigan (Wroughton, Wilts), b. 22 July 1858; m. 2 Aug. 1881, Florence Mary, da. of Samuel Henry Cleaver of Woodford, Essex; and has issue 1d to 3d.

1d. Allen Stewart Cleaver Hartigan (Witwatersrand Deep, Box 5, Knight's, Johannesburg), b. 13 May 1882.

2d. Kenneth Leslie Stewart Hartigan, b. 2 July 1899.

3d. Gladys Florence Stewart Hartigan, b. 25 Mar. 1888.

2c. Edward Ross Hartigan, Major 112th Regt. Indian Army (Nasirabad, India), b. 2 Ap. 1860; m. 2 Sept. 1896, Edith Frances Rosina, da. of Major-Gen. Edward Joseph Ridgeway Connolly of Lee, Kent, R.M.L.I.; and has issue 1d.

1d. Guy Edward Ross Stewart Hartigan, b. 13 Sept. 1898.

3c. Arthur Edwin Stewart Hartigan, Major Sind Horse (Quetta, India), b. 1 July 1862; m. 19 Jan. 1894, Emmeline Agnes, da. of Major White, R.M.L.I.

4c. Elizabeth Florence Cole Hartigan, b. 11 Ap. 1864.

5c. Hester Maria Corry Hartigan, b. 11 Feb. 1868; m. 16 Oct. 1899, Herbert Crichton McDouall, M.R.C.S. [Eng.] (The Hospital, Gladesville, Sydney, N.S.W.); and has issue 1d to 4d.

1d. Edith Isabella Stewart McDouall, b. 25 July 1900.

2d. Barbara Crichton McDouall, b. 25 Jan. 1902.

3d. Penelope Crichton McDouall, b. 23 Ap. 1903.

4d. [da.] McDouall, b. 1905.

6c. Edith Cecil Stewart Hartigan, b. 1 Dec. 1878.

3b. Robert Stratford Hartigan, d. Sept. 1871.

4b. Chichester Cole Hartigan, m. 7 Nov. 1883, Elizabeth Westrop, da. of Berkeley Vincent of Summer Hill, co. Clare.

5b. Thomas Dancer Hartigan, d. 24 Jan. 1862.

6b. Letitia Hartigan, b. 6 Ap. 1817; d. 30 Jan. 1897; m. 18 Dec. 1855, William Ryves Croker, J.P.; and had issue 1c.

1c. Edith Mabella Croker (Fir Grove, East Hoathly, Sussex), b. 15 Aug. 1857; m. 22 Nov. 1882, John Love Vincent, Col. 5th Northumberland Fusiliers, d.s.p. 16 Sept. 1894.

[Nos. 2189 to 2214.

148

# of The Blood Royal

1c. Edward Downes *Panter, afterwards (c.* 1854) *Downes*, b. 5 *July* 1834; d. 23 Dec. 1878; m. 5 *July* 1869, Maud, da. of [——] *Bally*, d. 28 *Nov.* 1901; *and had issue.*

2c. Frederick Kennedy Panter, b. 1836; d. (? *unm.*) (*at Perth, W. Australia*) 14 *May* 1878.

3c. Herbert Gauntlet *Panter, Inspector-Gen. of Recruiting*, b. 24 *Jan.* 1838; d. 18 *Ap.* 1888; m. *Emily Augusta, da. of* [——] *Adderley.*

4c. William Henry Panter, R.N., *b.* 9 May 1841; *m.* Alice, da. of [——] Mansfold.

5c. Frances Grace Constance Panter, *b.* (in Prince Edward's Island) 13 Sept. 1844; *m.* 24 Sept. 1873, John Ford Bally, Lieut. R.H.A.

8b. *Emily Jane Kennedy*, b. 3 *Ap.* 1817; d. 11 *Mar.* 1886; m. 5 *Aug.* 1847, *Donald Mackenzie Douglas*, d. 30 *Sept.* 1883; *and had issue.*

9b. *Grace Kennedy*, b. 14 *Oct.* 1819; d. 9 *May* 1900; m. 18 *July* 1844, *Arthur Woodgate*, b. 13 *Dec.* 1813; d. 20 *June* 1899; *and had issue* 1c *to* 3c.

1c. Arthur George Kennedy Woodgate, Factory Inspector, *b.* 24 June 1845; *m.* 22 Sept. 1881, Sylvia, da. of Thomas Henry Barton, Metropolitan Police Magistrate, Dublin (by his wife the Hon. Charlotte *née* Plunket); *and has issue* 1d *to* 3d.

1d. Henry Plunket Woodgate, *b.* 1888.

2d. Sybil Grace Charlotte Woodgate.

3d. Mildred Violet Woodgate.

2c. Florence Grace Woodgate, *m.* 1871, William Hill.

3c. Marion Frederika Douglas Woodgate, *m.* as 2nd wife, 1871, Robie Uniacke, Bar.-at-Law (*Gorsebrook, Halifax*); *and has issue* 1d *to* 2d.

1d. Cecil Dudley Woodgate Uniacke.

2d. Grace Uniacke.

10b. Sophia Janet Kennedy, *b.* 5 May 1827; *m.* 1853, the Rev. Joseph Marshall of Baronne Court, J.P., *b.* 1801; *d.* 25 Dec. 1865; and has issue 1c to 4c.

1c. William Kennedy Marshall, J.P., D.L., High Sheriff King's Co. 1886 (*Baronne Court, Parsonstown*), *b.* 12 Mar. 1858; *m.* 27 May 1881, Ada Elizabeth, da. of Michael Don Keatinge of Woodsgift, D.L.; *and has issue* 1d *to* 5d.

1d. Gilbert Kennedy Marshall, *b.* 28 May 1888.

2d. William George Marshall (twin), *b.* 13 May 1899.

3d. Eva Josephine Marshall.

4d. Esmé Georgina Ermyntrude Marshall.

5d. Ada Iris Marshall (twin), *b.* 13 May 1899.

2c. Josephine Marshall, *m.* 9 July 1874, Lieut.-Col. Thomas Bernard Hackett of Riverstown, J.P., *b.* 15 June 1836; *d.* 5 Oct. 1880.

3c. Georgina Marshall, *m.* 1st, 28 Ap. 1877, Col. William Grogan Graves of Cloghan Castle, J.P., D.L., High Sheriff King's Co., *b.* 14 Feb. 1836; *d.* 17 Feb. 1890; 2ndly, 17 Oct. 1891, James Kingston Barton, J.P. (*Green Hill, co. Kilkenny*); and has issue 1d to 3d.

1d. Robert Kennedy Grogan Graves (*Cloghan Castle, Banagher, King's Co.*), *b.* 1 Jan. 1878.

2d. William Geoffrey Plantagenet Graves, R.N., *b.* 22 May 1881.

3d. Michael Kennedy Barton, *b.* 3 Oct. 1895.

4c. *Sophia Margaret Marshall*, d. 2 *Nov.* 1884; m. 11 *July* 1883, A. R. *Hutchinson, late Major R.W.F., R.M.* (*Kiltorkan, co. Kilkenny*); *and had issue* 1d.

1d. Murielle Eleanor Sophia Hutchinson.

11b. Florence Kennedy (*Monkstown*), *m.* S. H. Morton, 6th Dragoon Guards.

12b. Augusta Kennedy (*Ealing*), *m.* 1st, Robert Manderson, H.E.I.C.; 2ndly, Gen. Cuseley; and has issue (1 da.).   [Nos. 2267 to 2291.

151

The Plantagenet Roll

2a. John Kennedy of Dunbrody, co. Wexford, J.P., b. 14 *July* 1780; d. 3 *Feb.* 1852; m. 1st, *Maria, da. of Col. Call,* d. 25 *Mar.* 1841; *and had issue* 1b.

1b. Henrietta Maria Kennedy, d. 14 *Dec.* 1849; m. *as* 1st *wife,* 18 *Nov.* 1841, *Philip Jocelyn Newton of Dunleckney, co. Carlow, J.P., D.L.,* b. 23 *Mar.* 1818; d. 20 *Ap.* 1895; *and had issue.*
See the Clarence Volume, pp. 297–298, Nos. 8307–8311.

3a. Arthur Kennedy, Lieut.-Col. 18th *Hussars,* b. 21 *July* 1781; d. 15 *Sept.* 1855; m. 17 *Oct.* 1835, *Mabella, widow of Kenrick Morres Hamilton-Jones of Moneyglass House, da. of Major Charles Hill of Bellaghy Castle,* d. 9 *May* 1868; *and had issue* 1b *to* 2b.

1b. Elizabeth Caroline Thomasina Kennedy (*Kilmorony, Athy, co. Kildare*), m. 12 June 1862, Sir Anthony Crossdill Weldon, 5th Bart. [I.]; b. 16 Mar. 1827; d. 14 Jan. 1900; and has issue 1c to 6c.

1c. Sir Anthony Arthur Weldon, 6th Bart. [I.], D.S.O., J.P., D.L. (*Kilmorony, Athy, co. Kildare ; Rahinderry, Queen's Co.*), b. 1 Mar. 1863; m. 11 Feb. 1902, Winifred, da. of Col. Varty-Rogers of Broxmore Park, co. Hants; and has issue 1d to 2d.

1d. Anthony Edward Wolseley Weldon, b. 1 Dec. 1902.

2d. Thomas Brian Weldon, b. 19 May 1905.

2c. Bertram de Weltden Weldon, Capt. Leicester Regt., b. 16 Nov. 1872.

3c. Ralphe Lewen Weldon, *late* Imp. Yeo., b. 17 June 1875.

4c. Henry Walter Weldon, Capt. P.W. Leinster Regt., b. 2 Nov. 1878.

5c. Mabelle Harriet Lucy Weldon, b. 25 Dec. 1867.

6c. Murielle Nina Eva Weldon, b. 17 Feb. 1877.

2b. Louisa Emily Georgina Kennedy, b. 13 Jan. 1842; m. 11 Nov. 1902, Robert Edward Percy Winton.

4a. Alexander Kennedy, Capt. R.N., b. 18 *Feb.* 1783; d. 1 *Ap.* 1849; m. *Mar.* 1815, *Therese Benoit, da. of Arthur Cole,* d. 6 *Ap.* 1863; *and had issue* 1b *to* 2b.
1b–2b. See p. 146, Nos. 2155–2156.

5a. William Kennedy, Deputy Military Auditor-General of Bengal, b. 14 *Feb.* 1784; d. 8 *Jan.* 1836; m. 22 *Dec.* 1822, *Charlotte, da. of Sir R. Blair,* d. 11 *Sept.* 1846; *and had issue* 1b.

1b. Robert Blair Kennedy, Lieut.-Col. Public Works Department, Madras, b. 14 Dec. 1824; d. 13 Oct. 1886; m. 1st, 30 Nov. 1848, *Alicia Emily Margaretta, da. of Col. Chichester Cruickshank ; 2ndly,* 28 Nov. 1877, *Emily Elizabeth Mackenzie, da. of Donald Mackenzie Douglas,* d. 17 Nov. 1892; *and had issue* 1c *to* 3c.

1c. Claude Kennedy, Col. in the Army, *late* 12th Foot, b. 21 July 1852; m. 28 Nov. 1882, Ethel, da. of Col. Miles; and has issue 1d.

1d. Miles Arthur Claude Kennedy, b. 12 Aug. 1885.

2c. Lucy Margarita Kennedy.

3c. Kathleen Douglas Kennedy, b. 27 Oct. 1878; m. 7 July 1902, Capt. Douglas Patton Bethune, Rifle Brigade.

2b. Eliza Herenlina Kennedy, d. 17 Aug. 1880.

6a. Robert Kennedy, Colonial Secretary (of Bermuda), b. 24 *Mar.* 1785; d. 17 *Oct.* 1864; m. [——], *widow of* [——], *da. of* [——].

7a. Langford Kennedy, b. 18 *May* 1787; d. 2 *Feb.* 1850; m. 20 *July* 1846, *Alicia, widow of Handcock Montgomery, da. of David Verner,* d. 8 *Aug.* 1859; *and had issue* 1b *to* 2b.

1b. Charles William Kennedy (*Scot's Hill House, Croxley Green, R.S.O.*), b. 6 July 1850; m. 8 July 1884, Florence Eliza, da. of Rowland Hunt of Boreatton, Salop.

2b. Henrietta Frances Alicia Kennedy, b. 24 Jan. 1849; m. 1 Aug. 1871, Francis Weldon, Capt. in Madras Staff Corps; and has issue 1c to 4c.

[Nos. 2292 to 2318.

# of The Blood Royal

1*c.* Walter Langford Weldon, *b.* 30 July 1872; *m.* 1 Dec. 1904, Emma Anne, da. of [——] Tod, *d.* 25 May 1905.

2*c.* Ethel Olive Weldon, *b.* 13 Feb. 1875.

3*c.* Ernest Stuart Weldon, *b.* 6 Jan. 1877.

4*c.* Winifred Edith Weldon, *b.* 19 Oct. 1883.

8*a.* **Charles Pratt Kennedy,** *Lieut.-Col. Bengal Horse, and for many years Political Agent at Simla,* b. 15 Nov. 1789; d. (? s.p.) 25 May 1875; m. 20 Dec. 1838, Charlotte, da. of Henry Unett of Freens Court, d. 19 Ap. 1903.

9*a.* *Thomas Kennedy,* b. 21 Oct. 1791; d. (being drowned in the St. Lawrence River, Canada) 14 Sept. 1853; m. 1*st,* 1817, Deborah, da. of [——] Camp, d. 1847; 2ndly, Mildred, da. of [——] Ellison, d. (being drowned with her husband) 14 Sept. 1853; and had issue 1b to 5b.

1*b.* Rev. John Kennedy, M.A., *b.* 31 Jan. 1820; *m.* 20 Nov. 1850, Sarah Bunnell.

2*b.* Elizabeth Selina Kennedy, *b.* 22 Sept. 1823; *m.* 31 Jan. 1845, D. Pease; and has issue.

3*b.* *Mary Jane Kennedy,* b. 27 *June* 1828; d. 5 *Sept.* 1858; m. *Henry Rogers;* and had issue.

4*b.* Cornelia Kennedy, *b.* 30 Aug. 1832; *m.* 24 Jan. 1854, Enos Bunnell of Brantford, Canada; and has issue.

5*b.* Phoebe Maria Kennedy, *b.* 12 Jan. 1839; *m.* Robert Rogers; and has issue.

10*a.* *Mabella Kennedy,* b. 5 *Dec.* 1777; d. 27 *Oct.* 1810; m. 4 *Sept.* 1807, [——] Lunell.

11*a.* *Maria Kennedy,* b. 30 *Mar.* 1779; d. (–); m. 23 *Mar.* 1801, Marcus McCausland; and had issue 1b to 4b.

1*b.* *Marcus Langford McCausland, Rector of Birr, King's Co.,* b. 27 *Jan.* 1802; d. 6 Dec. 1881; m. 24 *Aug.* 1832, Fanny Georgina, da. of the Right Rev. the Hon. Edmund Knox, Lord Bishop of Limerick, D.D., d. 31 Dec. 1894; and had issue 1c to 8c.

1*c.* Marcus Langford McCausland, Col. *late* 11th Foot, *b.* 14 Aug. 1834.

2*c.* Edmund Bacon McCausland, *b.* 21 Aug. 1836.

3*c.* William Henry McCausland, Lieut.-Col. *late* Madras S.C., *b.* 11 Aug. 1838.

4*c.* John Kennedy McCausland, Major A.P.D., *late* Capt. King's Own Borderers, *b.* 26 May 1846.

5*c.* Francis Harry Ernest McCausland.

6*c.* Charlotte Ann McCausland.

7*c.* Mary Caroline McCausland, *m.* [——] Wright.

8*c.* Jessy Elizabeth McCausland, *m.* [——] Dunbar.

2*b.* *John Kennedy McCausland, C.B., Gen. Indian Army,* b. 1 *June* 1803; d. 23 *July* 1879; m. 26 *June* 1834, Emma, da. of [——] Faithfull, d. 28 *July* 1889; and had issue 1c to 5c.

1*c.* William Henry McCausland, Major-Gen. in the Army, *b.* 11 May 1836; *m.* 10 Aug. 1861, Mary, da. of [——] Briggs; and has issue.

2*c.* *John Kennedy McCausland,* b. 20 *Ap.* 1840; d. (in India) 3 *Sept.* 1865.

3*c.* Arthur Kennedy McCausland, *b.* 14 Oct. 1850; *m.* [——].

4*c.* Chester Stanley McCausland, *b.* 10 Aug. 1854; *m.* Patience, da. of [——] Homer; and has issue.

5*c.* Clara Lumley McCausland, *b.* 3 Mar. 1848; *m.* 10 Aug. 1871, Turner Poulter Clarke, *d.* 13 Jan. 1903.

3*b.* *Dominick McCausland, Q.C.,* b. 20 *Aug.* 1806; d. 28 *June* 1873; m. *and had issue.*

4*b.* *Rev. William Henry McCausland,* b. 5 *Nov.* 1808; d. (–); m. *and had issue.*   [Nos. 2319 to 2334.

153

Tbe Plantagenet Roll

12a. *Elizabeth Selina Kennedy,* b. *9 June* 1796; d. 3 *Dec.* 1868; m. *Dec.* 1824 (? 1822), *William Unett, Capt.* 43*rd Regt.,* d. 26 *June* 1880; *and had issue* 1b.

1b. *Thomasine Unett,* d. 21 *May* 1852; m. *John Pryce Williams, Bar.-at-Law; and had issue* 1c.

1c. John Unett Williams.   [No. 2335.

73. Descendants of ELIZABETH COLE (see Table VI.), b. 27 Oct. 1712; d. Jan. 1770; m. 1st as 2nd wife, EDWARD ARCHDALE of Castle Archdale, High Sheriff co. Fermanagh 1722, d.s.p.; 2ndly, 7 Dec. 1731, the Hon. BYSSHE MOLESWORTH, M.P., d. 1779; and had issue 1a to 12a.

1a. *Arthur Molesworth of Fairlawn, co. Armagh, Major* 14*th Dragoons,* d. 20 *Aug.* 1803; m. 1*st, Sept.* 1764, *Catherine, sister of Sir Lionel Wright Fletcher-Vane,* 1*st Bart.* [*G.B.*], *da. of Walter Fletcher-Vane;* 3*rdly, Elizabeth, da. of* [——] *Ledingham,* d. 14 *Dec.* 1816; *and had issue* 1b *to* 3b.

1b. *Arthur Nepean Molesworth of Fairlawn,* b. 27 *Aug.* 1799; d. 25 *May* 1877; m. 18 *Jan.* 1820, *Harriet, da. of Capt. Charles Hawkins,* d. 6 *Oct.* 1880; *and had issue* 1c *to* 4c.

1c. *Arthur Molesworth of Fairlawn,* b. 11 *Oct.* 1821; d. 1892; m. *July* 1855, *Elizabeth Urquhart, da. of Dr. King, R.N.,* d. 1889; *and had issue* 1d *to* 2d.

1d. Arthur Nepean Molesworth of Fairlawn (*Hillsboro', Monkstown, co. Dublin*), b. 28 Nov. 1856; m. 5 Oct. 1898, Kathleen, da. of John De la Cour Cornwall of Janeville, co. Cork; and had issue 1e.

1e. Arthur William Bysshe Nepean Molesworth, b. 30 Jan. 1902.

2d. Frances Elizabeth Ives Molesworth, b. 10 Sept. 1858.

2c. *Thomas Nepean Molesworth,* b. 24 *June* 1824; d. 24 *Ap.* 1878; m. 11 *Oct.* 1846, *Sarah Georgina, da. of William Kertland of Dublin,* d. 18 *Dec.* 1884; *and had issue* 1d *to* 6d.

1d. Arthur Nassau Molesworth, District Engineer Canadian Trans-Continental Railway, *late* Ch. Engineer and Sup. of Ohio River and Charleston Railway (*Corry Buildings, Ottawa*), b. 14 Aug. 1851; m. 1st, 17 Jan. 1878, Sophia, da. of the Hon. John Sifton of Canada, d. 11 Ap. 1892; 2ndly, 18 Dec. 1894, Edith, da. of W. B. Whiteside of Johnson City; and has issue 1e.

1e. Kate Molesworth, b. 14 Aug. 1887.

2d. *Balfour Nepean Molesworth, C.E.,* b. 6 *Dec.* 1853; d. 15 *Nov.* 1896; m. 10 *June* 1882, *Louisa Agnes, da. of H. H. Thompson of the Hudson's Bay Co., Penetangursheen.*

3d. William Ponsonby Molesworth (*99 St. Joseph Street, Toronto*), b. 11 May 1856; m. 5 May 1883, Bathurst Georgina, da. of Edward Fitzgerald of Toronto, Q.C.; and has issue 1e to 4e.

1e. George Nepean Molesworth, b. 19 Nov. 1885.

2e. John Christian Ponsonby Molesworth, b. 26 Jan. 1888.

3e. Fitzgerald William Molesworth, b. 7 Nov. 1892.

4e. Margaret Louisa Molesworth, b. 24 Feb. 1895.

4d. Lucy Mary Molesworth.

5d. Eva Sarah Molesworth.

6d. Maud Marion Molesworth, *m.* 3 June 1896, James Hastings Carter (*Toronto*), s.p.

3c. Caroline Molesworth, *m.* 21 May 1873, Ralph M'Grough Bond-Shelton (*The Argosy, Moy, co. Tyrone*).

4c. Harriet Molesworth, *m.* 1st, 3 Jan. 1850, the Rev. Richard Wrightson, Vicar of Lusk, d. 10 July 1875; 2ndly, 27 Nov. 1877, William Symms; and has issue 1d to 2d.   [Nos. 2336 to 2350.

154

# of The Blood Royal

1*d.* Richard Blaney Wrightson, *b.* 22 May 1851.

2*d.* Arthur Nepean Wrightson, C.E., *b.* 23 July 1852; *m.* 1880, Gertrude Mary, da. of Christopher Domville Savage of Dublin; and has issue 1*e* to 2*e.*

1*e.* Richard Francis Wrightson.

2*e.* Caroline Wrightson.

2*b. Thomas William Ponsonby Molesworth,* b. 10 *Dec.* 1800; d. 11 *Jan.* 1881; *m.* 16 *Ap.* 1827, *Anne,* da. *of the Rev. Thomas Fawcett of Green Nortons; and had issue* 1*c to* 4*c.*

1*c.* Rev. Thomas Molesworth, B.A. (Camb.), *formerly* Chaplain to the Forces (*Alton, Hants*), *b.* 31 Dec. 1829; *m.* 13 June 1854, Carolina Mary, da. of William Bowles of Abingdon; and has issue 1*d* to 5*d.*

1*d.* Montague Pulteney Molesworth, *b.* 4 June 1856.

2*d.* Rev. Hugh Thomas Molesworth, Rector of Allora (*Allora Rectory, Queensland*), *b.* 30 Mar. 1860; *m.* 11 Dec. 1889, Alice Marian, da. of Edward Deshon, Auditor-Gen. of Queensland; and has issue 1*e.*

1*e.* Bevil Hugh Molesworth, *b.* 13 Jan. 1891.

3*d.* Constance Maud Caroline Molesworth.

4*d.* Agnes Mary Molesworth.

5*d.* Alice Sophia Molesworth.

2*c.* Rev. Walter Molesworth, M.A. (Camb.), Vicar of Bishopsworth (*Bishopsworth Vicarage, Bristol*), *b.* 6 Feb. 1831.

3*c.* Lucy Molesworth.

4*c.* Mary Molesworth.

3*b. Elizabeth Molesworth,* d. Nov. 1827; *m. Feb. 1789, Richard Reynell of Reynella, co. Westmeath,* b. 1759; *d.* 28 *Jan.* 1807; *and had issue* 1*c to* 2*c.*

1*c. Richard Molesworth Reynell of Reynella,* b. Dec. 1791; *d.* 13 *Sept.* 1824; *m. May* 1819, *Catherine,* da. *of the Hon. Ponsonby Moore,* d. 17 *Dec.* 1859; *and had issue* 1*d.*

1*d. Elizabeth Catherine Reynell,* d. (–); *m.* 12 *Jan.* 1843, *Blayney Townley Balfour, of Townley Hall, J.P.,* d. Sept. 1882; *and had issue* 1*e to* 4*e.*

1*e*–4*e.* See p. 140, Nos. 2013–2016.

2*c. Frances Reynell,* d. 3 *Ap.* 1827; *m.* 14 Feb. 1814, *Gen. John Nugent, C.B.*

2*a. Robert Molesworth, Capt.* 38*th Regt.,* d. (–); *m.* 1770, [——], *da. of* [——] *Rose of Linerick; and had issue* 1*b to* 7*b.*

1*b. Arthur Molesworth, Major-Gen. H.E.I.C.S.,* d. 7 *Jan.* 1843; *m. Mary,* da. *of Matthew Kearney,* d. 3 *Feb.* 1860; *and had issue* 1*c.*

1*c. Hickman Thomas Molesworth of Kenwith, co. Devon, Major-Gen. R.A.,* b. 7 *Aug.* 1820; *d.* 27 *Jan.* 1896; *m.* 15 *Ap.* 1857, *Marianne,* da. *of Robert Lindsay; and had issue* 1*d to* 10*d.*

1*d.* Hickman Crawford Molesworth, Lieut.-Col. R.A., *b.* 12 Feb. 1858; *m.* 1883, Margaret Amelia, widow of Serg.-Major M'Lean, da. of John Hopper; and has issue 1*e* to 4*e.*

1*e.* Arthur Crawford Valentine Molesworth, *b.* 1885.

2*e.* Guy Lindsay Molesworth, *b.* 1887.

3*e.* Violet Marguerite Molesworth.

4*e.* Ivy Frederica Molesworth.

2*d.* Arthur Ludovic Molesworth, Major R.A. and Brig. Major at Sch. of Gunnery, *b.* 12 July 1860; *m.* 1896, Beatrice Emma, da. of Fourney Adams of Augusta, U.S.A.

3*d.* Robert Everard Molesworth, M.R.C.S. Eng., M.R.C.P. Lond., Major Royal Army Med. Corps., *b.* 7 July 1861; *m.* 1889, Catherine Isabella, da. of J. Allen.

[Nos. 2351 to 2375.

155

The Plantagenet Roll

4d. Rev. Thomas Charles Underwood Molesworth, M.A. (Camb.), Chaplain to Indian Govt., b. 27 Oct. 1866; m. 1895, Mary Rosamond, da. of the Rev. John Richard Turner Eaton, Hon. Canon of Worcester; and has issue 1e to 2e.

1e. Richard Cecil Molesworth, b. 31 May 1898.

2e. Margaret Theodora Molesworth.

5d. Richard Piggot Molesworth, Capt. R.A., b. 25 Jan. 1868.

6d. Herbert Ellicombe Molesworth, Lieut. R.A., b. 15 Dec. 1872.

7d. Walter Guy Molesworth, Assist. Engineer Public Works Dept., Madras, b. 18 Feb. 1874; m. 1903, Ethel Vernon, da. of Thomas Richard Jessop, F.R.C.S.

8d. Alec Lindsay Mortimer Molesworth, Lieut. Bedfordshire Regt., b. 24 Mar. 1881.

9d. Gertrude Molesworth, m. 15 July 1855, the Rev. Robert Walpole Sealy, Vicar of Abbotsham (Abbotsham Vicarage, Bideford); and has issue 1e to 4e.

1e. Edward Molesworth Walpole Sealy, b. 1889.

2e. Avice Mary Sealy.

3e. Gertrude Silvia Sealy.

4e. Violet Inez Sealy.

10d. May Molesworth, m. 3 June 1891, Charles John Didham, late Comm. R.N.; and has issue 1e to 2e.

1e. Deborah Gertrude Mary Didham.

2e. Joyce Alisamond May Didham.

2b. Rev. Robert Francis Molesworth, formerly Capt. 5th Madras N.I., b. 30 June 1826; d. 8 May 1877; m. 7 Feb. 1852, Gertrude Marie le Normand (57 Queen's Gate, S.W.), da. and co.-h. to George Bagot Gosset, 4th Dragoon Guards; and had issue 1c to 3c.

1c. George Bagot Gosset Francis Richard Pigot Molesworth, M.A. (Camb.), Bar. Lincoln's Inn (57 Queen's Gate, S.W), b. 23 Jan. 1853.

2c. Henry Lempriere Molesworth, b. 26 Sept. 1862; d. 22 June 1881; m. 10 June 1878, Katherine, da. of [——] Barstow; and had issue 1d.

1d. Hugh Molesworth, b. 19 June 1879.

3c. Algernon Francis Molesworth, b. 26 June 1873.

3b. Gertrude Molesworth, d. 6 Dec. 1864; m. 7 Feb. 1824, Francis Lascelles, Madras C.S.; and had issue 1c to 3c.[1]

1c. Francis Henry Lascelles of Mayfield, Surrey, F.S.A., b. 16 Jan. 1825; d. (-); m. 1850, Mary, da. of Samuel N. Ward of Baston.

2c. Arthur Rowley William Lascelles, b. 30 Nov. 1828; m. twice.

3c. Mary Catherine Lascelles, m. 12 Ap. 1842, Samuel Neville Ward, Madras C.S.; and has issue 1d to 7d.

1d. Arthur Edward Ward, Capt. Bengal Staff.

2d. Henry Branson Ward.

3d. William Neville Ward.

4d. Rowley Lascelles Ward.

5d. Mary Gertrude Ward, m. Col. Hankin.

6d. Elizabeth Emmeline Ward.

7d. Alice Molesworth Ward.

4b. Mary Molesworth, d. 25 May 1881; m. as 2nd wife, 23 June 1832, Nathaniel William Kindersley, Madras C.S., d. 3 Dec. 1844; and had issue 1c to 4c.

1c. Edward Nassau Molesworth Kindersley, Capt. late 19th Regt. (Pencarron, Sherborne, Dorset), b. 28 Aug. 1836; m. 4 Feb. 1868, Ada Good, da. of John Murray of London; and has issue 1d to 8d.   [Nos. 2376 to 2403.

---

[1] "Foster Peerage," 1880, p. 44.

# of The Blood Royal

1*d.* John Molesworth Kindersley, *b.* 24 Nov. 1868; *m.* 23 Ap. 1898, Olive Montagu, da. of [——] Walford; and has issue 1*e.*
1*e.* Nancy Kindersley, *b.* 18 Sept. 1899.

2*d.* Robert Molesworth Kindersley, *b.* 21 Nov. 1871; *m.* 3 Nov. 1896, Gladys Margaret. da. of [——] Beadle; and has issue 1*e* to 4*e.*
1*e.* Lionel Nepean Kindersley, *b.* 6 Aug. 1897.
2*e.* Hugh Kenyon Kindersley, *b.* 7 May 1899.
3*e.* Richard Francis Kindersley, *b.* 5 Feb. 1905.
4*e.* Margaret Mary Anne Kindersley, *b.* 18 Ap. 1902.

3*d.* Guy Molesworth Kindersley, *b.* 28 Feb. 1876; *m.* 30 July 1903, Kathleen Agnes Rhoda, da. of [——] Elton; and has issue 1*e.*
1*e.* Edmund Murray Kindersley, *b.* 21 Jan. 1905.

4*d.* Emily Molesworth Kindersley, *b.* 24 Nov. 1870; *m.* 27 Nov. 1901, Arthur Maxwell Quill; and has issue 1*e* to 2*e.*
1*e.* Enid Dorothy Maxwell Quill, *b.* 31 Aug. 1902.
2*e.* Lois Quill, *b.* 20 June 1904.

5*d.* Ada Molesworth Kindersley, *b.* 3 Sept. 1879.
6*d.* Muriel Molesworth Kindersley, *b.* 11 Nov. 1880.
7*d.* Beatrice Molesworth Kindersley, *b.* 20 Ap. 1883.
8*d.* Agnes Molesworth Kindersley, *b.* 4 Feb. 1886.

2*c.* Henry Wasey Kindersley, H.M.'s Inspector of Factories, late 29th and 99th Regts. (*Drumcardin, North Queensferry*), *b.* 29 May 1841; *m.* 6 June 1867, Helen Maria, da. of Lieut.-Col. John Doyle O'Brien; and has issue 1*d* to 4*d.*
1*d.* Archibald Ogilvie Lyttelton Kindersley, Major 3rd Batt. Highland L.I., *b.* 7 Ap. 1869.
2*d.* Ronald Charles Murray Kindersley, *b.* 11 Aug. 1870.
3*d.* Douglas Cumming Paget Kindersley, *b.* 8 Aug. 1873.
4*d.* Helen Florence Athole Kindersley.

3*c.* Septimus Wigran Kindersley (*Sydney*), *b.* 21 Dec. 1844; *unm.*
4*c.* Mary Agnes Kindersley, *m.* 1 Feb. 1866, James Blake Maurice, F.R.C.S. (*Lloran House, Marlborough*); and has issue 1*d* to 12*d.*
1*d.* George Thelwall Kindersley Maurice, Capt. R.A.M.L., *b.* 23 Mar. 1867; *m.* 1 Feb. 1905, Olive, da. of Sir Henry Burdett of The Lodge, Porchester Square, W., K.C.B.
2*d.* Rev. Robert Baskerville Maurice, Assist. Master at Stone House, Broadstairs, *b.* 13 Aug. 1868.
3*d.* Oliver Calley Maurice, M.R.C.S., *b.* 13 Dec. 1869; *m.* 5 Oct. 1901, Violet, da. of H. Rycroft Gifford of Locheridge House, Overton, J.P.; and has issue (2 sons).
4*d.* Ernest Coddrington Maurice, Estate Agent, *b.* 1 Jan. 1871.
5*d.* Walter Byron Maurice, Surgeon, *late* R.N. (*Marlborough*), *b.* 5 Sept. 1872.
6*d.* Henry Gascoigne Maurice, Bar.-at-Law, *b.* 24 May 1874.
7*d.* Charles James Kindersley Maurice, C.E., *b.* 28 Oct. 1875; *m.* 23 Mar. 1904, Sylvia, da. of Walter Pennington Creyke; and has issue (a son).
8*d.* Thomas Hector Molesworth Maurice, Lieut. R.N., *b.* 3 May 1877; *m.* 27 Dec. 1904, Cicely, da. of H. Rycroft Gifford of Locheridge House, Overton, J.P.
9*d.* John Kindersley Maurice, *b.* 20 May 1883.
10*d.* Godfrey Kindersley Maurice, *b.* 15 Jan. 1887.
11*d.* Agnes Mary Caroline Maurice, *b.* 3 Oct. 1878.
12*d.* Helen Mary Kindersley Maurice, *b.* 20 Aug. 1881.

5*b.* *Emma Molesworth*, d. 22 *May* 1858; m. 23 *July* 1836, *George Macartney Ogilvie, H.E.I.C.S.*, d. *Feb.* 1878; *and had issue* 1c *to* 6c. [Nos. 2404 to 2438.

The Plantagenet Roll

1c. George Macartney Ogilvie, b. 13 Sept. 1841.

2c. Osmuna Ogilvie, b. 10 Jan. 1851.

3c. Zena Margaret Ogilvie.

4c. Emma Mary Ogilvie.

5c. Ada Molesworth Ogilvie.

6c. Inez Selina Ogilvie.

6b. *Selena Hase Molesworth*, d. 22 *Jan.* 1891; m. 9 *Mar.* 1844, *Hickman Kearney*, d. 27 *Oct.* 1869; *and had issue* 1c *to* 2c.

1c. Hickman Thomas Kearney, b. 14 Dec. 1844, unm. 1880.

2c. Rev. Arthur Henry Kearney, Vicar of Ixworth, Suffolk, b. 16 Jan. 1852.

7b. *Agnes Molesworth*, d. 2 *Dec.* 1862; m. *as* 1st *wife*, 12 *Oct.* 1847, *the Rev. Charles Richard de Havilland, late Vicar of Downside, Somerset; and had issue* 1c *to* 9c.

1c. Saumarez de Havilland, b. 14 Ap. 1850.

2c. Arthur Molesworth de Havilland, b. 14 Aug. 1851.

3c. Rev. Charles de Havilland, Curate of Woobam, Bucks, b. 29 May 1854; m. 8 May 1878, Alice Jannette, da. of Jason Saunders of Medley Manor.

4c. Cecil James de Havilland, b. 13 Jan. 1856.

5c. Algernon de Havilland, b. 1 Jan. 1859.

6c. Eustace Richard de Havilland, b. 27 Mar. 1861.

7c. [——] de Havilland, b. 9 Ap. 1879.

8c. Alice Martha de Havilland.

9c. Agnes Carteret Clara de Havilland.

3a. *Hickman Blayney Molesworth*, d. 3 *May* 1844; m. 1st, *Wilhelmina Dorothea, da. of Brindley Hone; and had issue* 1b.

1b. *Sir Robert Molesworth, Chief Justice at Melbourne*, b. 3 *Nov.* 1806; d. 1890; m. 2 *Jan.* 1840, *Henrietta, da. of the Rev. Joseph England Johnson*, d. 1879; *and had issue* 1c *to* 4c.

1c. Hickman Molesworth, *formerly* Puisne Judge of the Supreme Court of Victoria (*Edlington, Auburn, Melbourne*), b. 23 Feb. 1842; m. 1st, 9 July 1868, Elizabeth Emily, da. of William Rudledge; 2ndly, 15 June 1882, Alice Henrietta, da. of Dr. Ffloyd Minter Peck of Sale, Gippsland, Australia; and has issue 1d to 8d.

1d. Robert Arthur Molesworth, b. 6 July 1871.

2d. William Farnham Molesworth, b. 7 Mar. 1874.

3d. Hickman Walter Lancelot Molesworth, b. 1892.

4d. Enid Josephine Molesworth, b. 1869.

5d. Emily Maude Molesworth, b. 1871.

6d. Margaret Alice Elaine Molesworth, b. 1883.

7d. Lynette Emily Ffloyd Molesworth, b. 1886.

8d. Enone Florence Mary Molesworth, b. 1888.

2c. Robert Arthur Molesworth, b. 15 Ap. 1843; m. 10 June 1874, Flora Macdonald, da. of John Matheson; and has issue 1d to 3d.

1d. John Matheson Molesworth, b. 16 Feb. 1878.

2d. Robert Hickman Molesworth, b. 24 Nov. 1879.

3d. William Edwin Molesworth, b. 1887.

3c. [a son] Molesworth, b. Sept. 1851.

4c. Elizabeth Josephine Molesworth, b. 3 Mar. 1846; m. 10 Mar. 1869, George Edmeades Tolhurst.

2b. *Theophilus Molesworth*, d. *Ap.* 1851.

3b. *Caroline Molesworth*, m. *Col. Gurnell, H.E.I.C.S.*

4a. *St. George Molesworth*, d. (−); m. *and had issue* (*at least*) 1b.

1b. *William St. George Molesworth.*   [Nos. 2439 to 2470.

158

JOHN JAMES ROBERT (MANNERS), 7TH DUKE OF RUTLAND, K.G., P.C.

HEIR MALE OF LADY ANNE ST. LEGER, THE ONLY CHILD OF ANNE
(PLANTAGENET), DUCHESS OF EXETER.

Photo, Lafayette, London.

# of The Blood Royal

5a. *Richard Molesworth.*

6a. *Ponsonby Molesworth, Capt. 29th Regt., d. (–); m. Susanna, sister to Sir Roger Hale Sheaffe, 1st Bart. [U.K.], da. of William Sheaffe, Deputy Collector of Customs at Boston, U.S.A., d. 7 Aug. 1834.*

7a. *William Molesworth.*

8a. *John Cole Molesworth.*

9a. *Caroline Molesworth, d. (–); m. Charles Walker.*

10a. *Florence Molesworth, d. (–); m. as 1st wife, 1 July 1757, the Rev. Thomas Colclough of Kilmagee, co. Kildare, D.D.; and had issue [1] 1b to 3b.*

1b. *Cæsar Colclough, 36th Regt., d.s.p. Admon. 19 Jan. 1792.*

2b. *Florence Colclough, d. unm.*

3b. *Harriet Colclough, m. Col. Jonas Watson, d. (being killed by the Rebels on the Three Rock Mountains) May 1798.*

11a. *Alice Molesworth.*

12a. *Caroline Amelia Molesworth.*

74. Descendants, if any, of FLORENCE COLE (see Table VI.), b. 1714; m. ARTHUR NEWBURGH.

75. Descendants, if any, of Col. CHICHESTER WREY, d. 1706; EDWARD WREY and JOHN WREY (killed at Tangier), younger sons of Sir CHICHESTER WREY, 3rd Bart. [E.], also of the said Sir Chichester's three sisters, who m. respectively [——] BLUET, [——] ERISEY, and [——] NICHOLAS (see Table VI.).[1]

76. Descendants of JOHN MANNERS, MARQUIS OF GRANBY (see Table VII.), b. 2 Jan. 1721; d.v.p. 18 Oct. 1770; m. 3 Sept. 1750, Lady FRANCES, da. of Charles (SEYMOUR), 6th Duke of Somerset [E.], b. 8 July 1728; d. 25 Jan. 1761; and had issue.

See the Tudor Roll of "The Blood Royal of Britain," pp. 292–304, Nos. 25350–25716.   [Nos. 2471 to 2824.

77. Descendants of Lord GEORGE MANNERS, *afterwards* (1762) MANNERS SUTTON (see Table VII.), b. 8 Mar. 1723; d. 7 Jan. 1783; m. 1st, 5 Dec. 1749, DIANA, da. of Thomas CHAPLIN of Blankney, d. 13 May 1767; 2ndly, 5 Feb. 1768, MARY, da. of Joshua PEART; and had issue 1a to 7a.

1a. *John Manners, Capt. in the Guards, b. 29 July 1752; d. 17 Feb. 1826; m. Anne, natural da. of John Manners, Marquis of Granby, d. 17 Feb. 1826; and had issue 1b to 3b.*

1b. *Rev. Frederick Manners, b. 1784; d. 30 Aug. 1826; m. 2 Sept. 1821, Lady Henrietta Barbara, da. of John (Lumley), 7th Earl of Scarbrough [E.], d. 27 July 1864; and had issue 1c to 2c.*

---

[1] Burke's "Irish Landed Gentry," p. 76.

159

The Plantagenet Roll

1c. John Henry Manners of Kelham, M.P., b. 4 *Aug.* 1822; d. 5 *July* 1898; m. 21 *Ap.* 1853, *Mary Jemima, da. of the Rev. Gustavus Andrew Burnaby; and had issue* 1*d.*

    1*d.* Edith Mary Manners, *m.* 25 Aug. 1877, Robert Heathcote, J.P. (*Lobthorpe, Grantham; Manton, Oakham*); and has issue 1*e* to 2*e.*

    1*e.* Robert Evelyn Manners Heathcote, *b.* 1884.

    2*e.* Sybil May Dominica Heathcote, *m.* 16 Sept. 1903, John Francis Hamilton Sinclair Cunliffe Brookes Forbes Goodeve-Erskine, Lord Garioch.

    2*c. Rev. William Manners,* b. 27 *Dec.* 1824; d. 29 *Dec.* 1899; m. *Sarah Anne, da. of* [——] *Williams,* d. 9 *Feb.* 1875; *and had issue* 1*d* to 3*d.*

    1*d.* Frederick William Manners, *late* Lieut. 4th Batt. East Surrey Regt., *b.* 19 Aug. 1865.

    2*d.* Henry Manners, *b.* 1867.

    3*d.* Violet Henrietta Manners.

    2*b. George Manners, Comm. R.N.,* d. 13 *Jan.* 1836.

    3*b. Mary Georgiana Manners,* d. 8 *Nov.* 1846; m. 20 *May* 1812, *Robert Nassau Sutton, Capt.* 7*th Fusiliers,* b. 1 *Aug.* 1776; d. 7 *Ap.* 1833; *and had issue* 1*c to* 4*c.*

    1*c. Rev. Robert Sutton of Scawby, J.P.,* b. 1 *Mar.* 1813; d. 1885; m. 4 *May* 1847, *Charlotte, sister and h. of Sir John Nelthorpe,* 8*th (and last) Bart.* [*E.*], d. 11 *Nov.* 1872; *and had issue* 1*d to* 8*d.*

    1*d.* Robert Nassau Sutton, now (R.L. 13 Oct. 1884) Sutton-Nelthorpe of Scawby, J.P., D.L., *late* Major 8th Hussars (*Scawby Hall, Brigg*), *b.* 13 May 1850; *m.* 1 Jan. 1885, the Hon. Dulcibella, da. of William (Eden), 4th Baron Auckland [I.]; and has issue 1*e* to 4*e.*

    1*e.* Oliver Sutton Nelthorpe, *b.* 1888.

    2*e.* Christopher Sutton Nelthorpe, *b.* 1890.

    3*e.* Griffith Sutton Nelthorpe, *b.* 1892.

    4*e.* Ursula Sutton Nelthorpe.

    2*d.* Henry John Sutton, *late* Lieut. Royal Irish Fusiliers, *b.* 9 Dec. 1851.

    3*d.* Francis Richard Sutton, *b.* 27 Mar. 1853; *m.* 1881, Edith Louisa, da. of Arthur Pryor of Highlands; and has issue 1*e* to 4*e.*

    1*e.* Richard Coningsby Sutton, *b.* 1882; *m.* 1904, Katherine, da. of Francis Foljambe Anderson.

    2*e.* Francis Arthur Sutton, *b.* 1884.

    3*e.* Olinda Emily Sutton.

    4*e.* Sylvia Katherine Sutton.

    4*d.* Hugh Nelthorpe Sutton, *b.* 3 May 1857.

    5*d. Mary Georgiana Sutton,* d. 19 *Feb.* 1902; m. 8 *Feb.* 1876, *Coningsby Charles Sibthorp, High Sheriff co. Lincoln* 1877 (*Canwick Hall, Lincoln*).

    6*d.* Evelyn Charlotte Sutton (*Eldon Villa, Ryde, I.W.*), *m.* 16 Dec. 1884, Major Paul Swinburne, *d.* 19 Jan. 1905.

    7*d.* Mabel Albinia Sutton, *m.* 29 June 1876, Montagu Richard Waldo-Sibthorp (*Canwick Hall, Lincoln*); and has issue 1*e* to 3*e.*

    1*e.* Mabel Janetta Waldo-Sibthorp, *m.* 18 Ap. 1903, Sir Montague Aubrey Rowley Cholmeley, 4th Bart. [U.K.], Capt. Grenadier Guards (*Easton Hall, Grantham, &c.*); and had issue 1*f.*

    1*f.* Rosamond Mary Edith Cholmeley.

    2*e. Esther Mary Waldo-Sibthorp,* d. 27 *Sept.* 1905; m. 22 *July* 1902, *John St. Vigor-Fox* (*Girsby Manor, co. Lincoln*); *and had issue* 1*f.*

    1*f.* Mirabel Esther Mary Fox, *b.* 2 Sept. 1905.

    3*e.* Evelyn Elizabeth Waldo-Sibthorp.

    8*d.* Janetta Nina Sutton, *m.* 10 Feb. 1886, the Rev. Geoffrey Barrington Simeon (*Beaconsfield, Graham Road, Malvern*); and has issue.

See the Clarence Volume, p. 477, Nos. 21007–21009.   [Nos. 2825 to 2852.

# of The Blood Royal

2c. *Frederick Sutton, Capt.* 11th Hussars, b. 26 Feb. 1817; d. 2 June 1900; m. 1st, 12 May 1841, Eliza, da. of the Rev. W. M. Jones, d. 1844; 2ndly, 19 Oct. 1847, Georgiana, da. of the Ven. Archdeacon Croft, d. 20 Mar. 1898; and had issue 1d to 6d.

1d. Algernon Charles Sutton (*Hampstead House, Chidham, Chichester*), b. 6 Feb. 1852; m. 20 Oct. 1886, Winifred Alice, da. of William Edwin Cotton Fell of Lochrin; and has issue 1e to 4e.

1e. Frederick Nassau Sutton, b. 18 Ap. 1888.

2e. Fergus Algernon Sutton, b. 26 Aug. 1891.

3e. Oliver Manners Sutton, b. 15 Mar. 1896.

4e. Irene Winifred Sutton, b. 18 Oct. 1893.

2d. Herbert Arthur Sutton (*Kelham House, Notts*), b. 4 Ap. 1853; m. 8 Sept. 1893, Josephine Constance Stanley, da. of Joshua Verney Lovett Lace of Christleton Old Hall, d. 1 June 1905; and has issue 1e.

1e. Roland Manners Verney Sutton, b. 9 Dec. 1895.

3d. Rev. Charles Nassau Sutton, Rector of Withyham (*Withyham Rectory, Sussex*), b. 9 Feb. 1859; m. 27 Sept. 1883, Edith Mary, da. of Lieut.-Col. H. Cafe; and has issue 1e.

1e. Charles Lexington Manners Sutton, b. 26 Ap. 1891.

4d.[1] Ruth Isabella Sutton, m. 2 Ap. 1866, Lieut.-Col. Frederick Lockwood Edridge, late 20th Regt.; and has issue 1e to 4e.

1e. Charles Sutton Edridge, b. 11 Feb. 1867.

2e. *Frederick Bertram Edridge,* b. 8 Feb. 1870; d. (–).

3e. Hugh Lockwood Edridge, b. 28 Feb. 1872.

4e. Mary Isabella Edridge.

5d.[2] Amy Georgiana Sutton, m. 9 June 1875, Comm. Francis Hay Chapman, R.N. (107 *Shooter's Hill Road, Blackheath, S.E.*); and has issue 1e to 9e.

1e. Cecil Sutton Chapman, Lieut. R.A., b. 1880.

2e. Francis Arthur Chapman, Lieut. R.N., b. 1881.

3e. Charles Manners Sutton Chapman, b. 1889.

4e. Lyon Greenwood Croft Chapman, b. 1895.

5e. Richard Keppel George Sutton Chapman, b. 1898.

6e. Eva Catherine Drummond Chapman.

7e. Miriam Amy Georgina Chapman.

8e. Marie Auriol de Vismes Chapman.

9e. Vera Frederica Chapman.

6d.[2] Eva Pulteney Marguerite Sutton, m. 2 June 1881, Lieut.-Col. John Warre Sill, R.E.; and has issue 1e to 3e.

1e. John Sutton Sill, b. 1886.

2e. Eva Johanna Sill.

3e. Winifred Edith Harriet Sill.

3c. *Mary Isabella Sutton,* d. 6 May 1855; m. as 1st wife, 2 June 1840, Sir George Baker, 3rd Bart. [G.B.], b. 16 June 1816; d. 27 Aug. 1872; and had issue 1d to 5d.

1d. Sir Frederick Edward Rhodes (R.L. 1878), formerly Baker, b. 12 July 1843.

2d. George Barrington Baker, now (R.L. 14 July 1900) Baker-Wilbraham, M.A. (Oxon.), Bar.-at-Law (*Rode Hall, Scholar Green, Cheshire, &c.*), b. 26 Jan. 1845; m. 4 Ap. 1872, Katharine Frances, da. and h. of Gen. Sir Richard Wilbraham, K.C.B.; and has issue 1e to 4e.

1e. Philip Wilbraham Baker-Wilbraham, M.A., Fellow of All Souls' Coll. (Oxon.), Bar.-at-Law (5 *Lancaster Street, W.*), b. 17 Sept. 1875; m. 8 Aug. 1901, Joyce Christabel, da. of the Right Hon. Sir John Henry Kennaway, 3rd Bart., P.C., C.B., M.P.; and has issue 1f to 2f.   [Nos. 2853 to 2882.

161

The Plantagenet Roll

1f. Joyce Katharine Baker-Wilbraham, b. 29 June 1902.

2f. Mary Frances Baker-Wilbraham, b. 19 Aug. 1904.

2e. Katharine Mary Baker, m. 25 July 1899, the Rev. Piers John Benedict Ffoulkes, Rector of Odd Rode (*Odd Rode Rectory, Stoke-on-Trent*).

3e. Margaret Isabel Baker-Wilbraham.

4e. Sibylla Frances Baker-Wilbraham.

3d. Isabella Maria Baker (44 *Green Street, W.*), m. 14 Dec. 1865, Charles Oliver Frederick Cator of Beckenham, d. 10 Dec. 1876; and has issue 1e.

1e. Charles George Lumley Cator, M.A. (Camb.), b. 26 Jan. 1872; m. [———].

4d. *Alice Emily Jane Baker*, d. 1 *June* 1901; m. 11 Nov. 1885, *the Right Rev. Charles Waldegrave Sandford, 4th Lord Bishop of Gibraltar, D.D.*

5d. *Evelyn Nina Frances Baker*, d. 19 Aug. 1904; m. 23 Aug. 1877, *Herbert Perrott Murray (Pakington), 3rd Baron Hampton* [*U.K.*] (*Waresley Court, Kidderminster*); and had issue.

See the Tudor Roll of "The Blood Royal of Britain," p. 450, Nos. 31712–31719.

4c. Anna Maria Sutton, m. 12 Dec. 1853, Joost Peter, Baron van Aerssen Beyeren van Voshol [Netherlands], Chamberlain to the King of the Netherlands, d. 20 Aug. 1857.

2a. *The Most Rev. Charles Manners-Sutton, Lord Archbishop of Canterbury*, b. 17 Feb. 1755; d. 21 *July* 1828; m. 3 *Ap.* 1778, *Mary, da. of Thomas Thoroton of Sereveton, co. Notts.*, d. 10 *Mar.* 1832; *and had issue 1b.*

1b. *Charles (Manners-Sutton), 1st Viscount Canterbury* [*U.K.*], *G.C.B.*, b. 29 *Jan.* 1780; d. 21 *July* 1845; m. 1st, 8 *July* 1811, *Lucy Maria Charlotte, da. of John Denison of Ossington, co. Notts*, d. 7 *Dec.* 1815; 2ndly, 6 *Dec.* 1828, *Ellen, widow of John Home Purves, da. of Edmund Power of Curragheen, co. Waterford*, d. 16 *Nov.* 1845; *and had issue 1c to 4c.*

1c. *Charles John (Manners-Sutton), 2nd Viscount Canterbury* [*U.K.*], b. 17 *Ap.* 1812; d. *unm.* 13 *Nov.* 1869.

2c. *John Henry Thomas (Manners-Sutton), 3rd Viscount Canterbury* [*U.K.*], *K.C.B., G.C.M.G.*, b. 27 *May* 1814; d. 23 *June* 1877; m. 5 *July* 1838, *Georgiana, da. of Thomas Tompson of Witchingham Hall, Norfolk*, d. 14 *Sept.* 1899; *and had issue 1d to 5d.*

1d. Henry Charles (Manners-Sutton), 4th Viscount Canterbury [U.K.], J.P., D.L. (*Brooke House, Norwich; White's; Marlborough, &c.*), b. 12 July 1839; m. 16 Ap. 1872, Amye Rachel, da. of the Hon. Frederick Walpole, M.P., and sister to Robert Horace (Walpole), 5th Earl of Orford [U.K.]; and has issue 1e.

1e. Hon. Henry Frederick Manners-Sutton, D.L., b. 8 Ap. 1879.

2d. *Hon. Graham Edward Henry Manners-Sutton, D.L.*, b. 7 *Feb.* 1843; d. 30 *May* 1888; m. 12 *Feb.* 1867, *Charlotte Laura, da. of Lieut.-Col. Francis L'Estrange Astley of Burgh Hall, Norfolk* (12 *Sloane Terrace Mansions, Chelsea, S.W.*); *and had issue 1e to 2e.*

1e. Francis Henry Astley Manners-Sutton (*White's*), b. 10 Feb. 1869.

2e. Charles Graham Manners-Sutton, Lieut. R.E. (*Larkin Hall, near Rochester; Junior United Service*), b. 23 Jan. 1872; m. 15 June 1903, Ethelwyn, da. of Charles Hindle; and has issue 1f.

1f. Charlotte Ethelwyn Manners-Sutton, b. 22 Ap. 1904.

3d. *Hon. Robert Henry Manners-Sutton, Bar.-at-Law*, b. 12 *Ap.* 1854; d. 26 *Feb.* 1899.

4d. Hon. Anna Maria Georgiana Manners-Sutton, m. 25 Aug. 1868, Charles Edward Bright, C.M.G. (98 *Cromwell Road, S.W.*); and has issue 1e to 4e.

1e. Alfred Ernest Bright (sponsor H.R.H. the Duke of Edinburgh), b. 16 Mar. 1869; m. 1898, Edith Kate, da. of James Tully, d. 1902; and has issue 1f to 2f.

1f. Hilary Georgina Bright, b. 1899.

2f. Edith Rachel Bright, b. 1902.

[Nos. 2883 to 2907.

162

# of The Blood Royal

2e. Charles Henry Manners-Sutton Bright (4 *Barkston Gardens, S.W.*), *b.* 18 June 1870; *m.* 18 Nov. 1896, Ada Madeline, da. of Alfred Christian Garrick of Holcombe, Dorking.

3e. Richard George Tyndall Bright, C.M.G., Capt. and Brevet-Major Rifle Brigade (*Windham ; Naval and Military*), *b.* 5 Feb. 1872.

4e. Georgina Amye Blanche Bright, *m.* June 1903, Major Gerald Marmaduke de Langport Dayrell, 3rd Batt. Bedfordshire Regt. ; and has issue 1*f*.

1*f*. Joan Ada Georgina Dayrell, *b.* 1904.

5d. Hon. Mabel Georgiana Manners-Sutton (*Lowestoft, Suffolk*).

3c. *Hon. Charlotte Matilda Manners-Sutton*, b. 30 Nov. 1815; d. 14 *May* 1898; m. 12 *Feb.* 1833, *Richard Sanderson*, M.P., b. 1784; d. 29 *Oct.* 1857 ; *and had issue* 1d to 7d.

1d. Richard Manners Sanderson, *b.* 11 July 1835; *m.* 6 Sept. 1870, Matilda Anne Adelaide Eliza, da. of William James Walker ; and has issue 1*e* to 3*e*.

1e. Richard Edward Henry Sanderson, *b.* 11 Ap. 1875.

2e. Maud Alice Isobel Sanderson.

3e. Eveline Mary Jane Sanderson.

2d. Thomas Henry Sanderson, *b.* 11 June 1841.

3d. Percy Sanderson, Consul at Galatz, *late* Royal (Madras) Artillery, *b.* 7 July 1842.

4d. Rev. Edward Manners Sanderson, Vicar of Weston St. Mary, co. Linc., *b.* 2 Oct. 1847 ; *m.* 23 June 1875, Eveline, da. of the Rev. G. Venables ; and has issue (a son and da.).

5d. Charlotte Louisa Gertrude Sanderson.

6d. Lucy Fanny Mary Sanderson.

7d. Maud Amy Frances Sanderson.

4c. *Hon. Frances Diana Manners-Sutton*, b. 17 Dec. 1829; d. 2 *June* 1874; m. 8 *Aug.* 1848, *Delaval Loftus* (*Astley*), 18*th Baron Hastings* [*E.*], b. 24 *Mar.* 1825 ; d. 28 *Sept.* 1872; *and had issue* 1d *to* 4d.

1d. *Bernard Edward Delaval* (*Astley*), 19*th Baron Hastings* [*E.*], b. 9 *Sept.* 1855 ; d. *unm.* 22 *Dec.* 1875.

2d. *George Manners* (*Astley*), 20*th Baron Hastings* [*E.*], b. 4 *Ap.* 1857 ; d. 18 Sept. 1904 ; m. 17 *Ap.* 1880, *the Hon. Elizabeth Evelyn* (*Melton Constable, Norfolk ; Delaval, Newcastle-on-Tyne ; 9 Seymour Street, Portman Square, W.*), da. of Charles (*Harbord*), 5*th Baron Suffield* [*E.*] ; *and had issue* 1e *to* 6e.

1e. Albert Edward Delaval (Astley), 21st Baron Hastings [E.] (*Melton Constable, Norfolk ; Seaton Delaval, Newcastle-on-Tyne*), *b.* 24 Nov. 1882 (King Edward sponsor).

2e. Hon. Jacob John Astley, Lieut. 16th Lancers, *b.* 5 Mar. 1884.

3e. Hon. Charles Melton Astley, *b.* 5 May 1885.

4e. Hon. Alexandra Rhoda Astley (Queen Alexandra sponsor), *b.* 28 Sept. 1886.

5e. Hon. Bridget Astley, *b.* 8 Mar. 1889.

6e. Hon. Hester Astley, *b.* 17 May 1899.

3d. Hon. Henry Jacob Astley, *formerly* Lieut. Norfolk Artillery, E. Div. R.A., and Suffolk Yeo. Cav. (*Sedgeford, King's Lynn*), *b.* 2 Mar. 1867 ; *m.* 8 July 1891, Sybil, da. of Charles George Fountaine.

4d. Hon. Agneta Frances Delaval Astley, *m.* 22 Oct. 1891, Roland le Strange, J.P., D.L. (*Hunstanton Hall, Norfolk*) ; and has issue 1*e* to 2*e*.

1e. Charles Alfred le Strange (H.R.H. Duke Alfred of Saxe-Coburg sponsor), *b.* 9 Dec. 1892.

2e, Bernard le Strange, *b.* 23 Aug. 1900.   [Nos. 2908 to 2932,

163

The Plantagenet Roll

2*b. Mary Manners-Sutton*, b. 2 *Mar.* 1779; d. 4 *Sept.* 1831; m. *as 1st wife, 17 May 1806, the Right Rev. and Hon. Hugh Percy, Lord Bishop of Carlisle, D.D.,* b. 29 *Jan.* 1784; d. 5 *Feb.* 1856; *and had issue* 1*c to* 7*c*.

1*c. Algernon Charles Percy, afterwards* (1847) *Heber-Percy, of Hodnet Hall, J.P., D.L.,* b. 29 *June* 1812; d. 24 *Jan.* 1901; m. 29 *July* 1839, *Emity, da. and co-h. of the Right Rev. Reginald Heber, Lord Bishop of Calcutta, D.D.,* d. 8 *Nov* 1902; *and had issue*.

See the Tudor Roll of "The Blood Royal of Britain," pp. 188–189, Nos. 20997–21044; also the Clarence Volume, pp. 266–267, Nos. 7094–7142.

2*c. Rev. Henry Percy of Greystoke, Canon of Carlisle,* b. 5 *June* 1813; d. 6 *Sept.* 1870; m. 1 *Feb.* 1841, *Emma Barbara, da. of Capt. Benjamin Baker Galbraith of Old Derrig,* d. *Nov.* 1877; *and had issue*.

See the Tudor Roll of "The Blood Royal of Britain," p. 189, Nos. 21045–21067.

3*c. Hugh Josceline Percy of Eskrigg, J.P., D.L.,* b. 9 *Dec.* 1817; d. 9 *Feb.* 1882; m. 24 *Oct.* 1859, *Anne, da. of Joseph Story*.

See the Tudor Roll of "The Blood Royal of Britain," pp. 189–190, Nos. 21068–21072.

4*c. Mary Isabella Percy,* b. 18 *Feb.* 1808; d. *Mar.* 1878; m. 21 *July* 1840, *the Rev. Frederick Vernon Lockwood, Preb. of Canterbury,* d. 1 *July* 1851; *and had issue*.

See the Tudor Roll of "The Blood Royal of Britain," p. 190, Nos. 21073–21075.

5*c. Lucy Percy,* b. 28 *Ap.* 1811; d. *Jan.* 1887; m. 13 *Feb.* 1832, *Henry William Askew of Glenridding and Conishead Priory,* b. 1808; d. 1890; *and had issue*.

See the Tudor Roll of "The Blood Royal of Britain," p. 190, Nos. 21076–21093.

6*c. Gertrude Percy,* b. 30 *Aug.* 1814; d. 27 *Ap.* 1890; m. 12 *July* 1834, *William Pitt (Amherst), 2nd Earl* [U.K.] *and 3rd Baron* [G.B.] *Amherst,* b. 3 *Sept.* 1805; d. 26 *Mar.* 1886; *and had issue*.

See the Tudor Roll of "The Blood Royal of Britain," pp. 190–191, Nos. 21094–21113.

7*c. Ellen Percy,* b. 7 *Nov.* 1815; d. 1899; m. 5 *Ap.* 1836, *the Rev. Edward Thompson,* d. 3 *Ap.* 1838; *and had issue*.

See the Tudor Roll of "The Blood Royal of Britain," p. 191, Nos. 21114–21121.

3*b. Charlotte Manners-Sutton,* b. 4 *Dec.* 1786; d. 14 *Feb.* 1825; m. 5 *Oct.* 1812, *the Ven. James Croft, Archdeacon of Canterbury,* d. 9 *May* 1869.

4*b. Isabella Manners-Sutton,* b. 5 *Dec.* 1791; d. *Nov.* 1855; m. 30 *Nov.* 1830, *Henry William Chichester*.

5*b. Caroline Manners-Sutton,* b. 12 *May* 1797; d. (–); m. *Sept.* 1830, *the Rev. Charles Chichester, Rector of Barton, co. Suffolk,* b. 1798; d. 4 *Feb.* 1858.

3*a. Thomas (Manners), 1st Baron Manners* [U.K.], b. 24 *Feb.* 1756; d. 31 *May* 1842; m. 1st, 4 *Nov.* 1803, *Anne, da. of Sir Joseph Copley, formerly Moyle of Sprotborough, 1st Bart.* [G.B.], d. 5 *Aug.* 1814; 2ndly, 1815, *the Hon. Jane, da. of James (Butler), 9th Baron Caher* [I.], d. 2 *Nov.* 1846; *and had issue* 1*b*.

1*b. John Thomas (Manners), 2nd Baron Manners* [U.K.], b. 17 *Aug.* 1818; d. 14 *Nov.* 1864; m. 28 *Sept.* 1848, *Lydia Sophia, da. of Vice-Adm. William Bateman Dashwood; and had issue* 1*c to* 5*c*.

1*c. John Thomas (Manners), 3rd Baron Manners* [U.K.] (*Avon Tyrrell, Christchurch, Hants; Mansfield House, 18 New Cavendish Street, W.*), b. 15 *May* 1852; m. 12 *Aug.* 1885, *Constance Edwina Adeline, da. of Col. Henry Edward Hamlyn Fane of Clovelly, M.P.; and has had issue* 1*d to* 4*d*.

1*d. Hon. John Nevile Manners,* b. 6 *Jan.* 1892.

2*d. Hon. Francis Henry Manners,* b. 21 *July* 1897.

3*d. Hon. Betty Constance Manners,* } (twins), b. 15 *June* 1889.
4*d. Hon. Angela Margaret Manners,* }

[Nos. 2933 to 3421.

164

2c. Hon. Claud Henry Manners, b. 15 Sept. 1856.

3c. Hon. Mildred Jane Manners.

4c. Hon. Mary Theresa Manners, m. 6 Dec. 1881, Col. Ralph Leeke, *late* Grenadier Guards, J.P. (*Longford Hall, Newport, Salop*); and has issue 1d to 2d.

1d. Ralph Henry Leeke, b. 6 Dec. 1883.

2d. Charles Leeke, b. 26 Mar. 1887.

5c. Hon. Etheldreda Mary Manners, m. 29 Oct. 1891, Lieut.-Col. Bertram Reveley Mitford, D.S.O.; and has issue 1d to 3d.

1d. Etheldreda Josceline Mitford.

2d. Enid Constance Mitford.

3d. Stella Gladys Mitford.

4a. *Diana Manners-Sutton*, d. (–); m. 21. *Ap*. 1778, *Francis Dickins of Branches Park, co. Suffolk.*

5a. *Louisa Bridget Manners-Sutton*, d. 5 Feb. 1800; m. 15 June 1790, *Edward Lockwood-Perceval*, d. 1794.

6a. *Charlotte Manners-Sutton*, d. 1827; m. 16 June 1789, *Thomas Lockwood.*

7a. *Mary Manners-Sutton*, b. 4 Aug. 1771; d. 20 Nov. 1829; m. 1799, *the Rev. Richard Lockwood of Fifield, Essex*, d. 1830.   [Nos. 3422 to 3430.

78. Descendants of Col. Lord ROBERT MANNERS, M.P. (see Table VII.), d. 31 May 1782; m. 1 Jan. 1756, MARY, da. of [——] DIGGES of Roehampton, b. 1737; d. 22 Feb. 1829; and had issue 1a to 2a.

1a. *Robert Manners, Lieut.-Gen. and Col. 30th Regt., M.P.*, b. 2 Jan. 1758; d. 9 June 1823.

2a. *Mary Manners*, b. 20 Nov. 1756; d. 1834; m. 31 Jan. 1877, *William Hamilton Nisbet of Dirleton and Belhaven*, d. July 1822; and had issue 1b.

1b. *Mary Nisbet*, d. July 1855; m. 1st, 11 Mar. 1799, *Thomas (Bruce), 7th Earl of Elgin and 11th Earl of Kincardine* [S.], *P.C. (marriage dissolved by Act of Parl. 1808)*, b. 20 July 1766; d. 14 Nov. 1841; and had issue 1c to 2c.

1c. *Lady Mary Bruce*, b. 28 Aug. 1801; d. 21 Dec. 1883; m. 28 Jan. 1828, *the Right Hon. Robert Adam Dundas, afterwards (1835) Christopher, and subsequently (1855) Nisbet-Hamilton of Dirleton and Belhaven, and also of Bloxholm, &c., co. Lincoln, P.C., M.P., Chancellor of the Duchy of Lancaster, &c.*, b. 9 Feb. 1804; d. 9 June 1877; and had issue.

1d. Mary Georgiana Constance Nisbet-Hamilton of Belhaven and Dirleton, &c., m. 11 Sept. 1888, Henry Thomas Ogilvey, now Nisbet-Hamilton-Ogilvey, J.P., D.L. (*Biel, Prestonkirk; Archerfield, Dirleton; Winton Castle, Pencaitland; Bloxholm Hall, Lincoln*).

2c. *Lady Lucy Bruce*, b. 20 Jan. 1806; d. 4 Sept. 1881; m. as 2nd wife, *John Grant of Kilgraston and Pitkeathly, co. Perth, J.P., D.L.*, b. 13 June 1798; d. 20 Jan. 1873; and had issue 1d to 7d.

1d. *Charles Thomas Constantine Grant of Kilgraston, J.P., D.L.*, b. 2 July 1831; d. 8 May 1891; m. 8 Oct. 1856, *Janet Matilda, da. of William Hay of Duns Castle; and had issue 1e to 6e.*

1e. John Patrick Grant of Kilgraston and Pitkeathly, Capt. *late* Seaforth Highlanders (*Kilgraston, co. Perth; Drummonie House, Bridge of Earn*), b. 18 July 1872.

2e. Lucy Blanche Cordilia Grant, b. 5 Aug. 1857; m. 20 Ap. 1882, Sir Uthred James Hay Dunbar, 8th Bart. [S.], b. 26 Feb. 1843; d.s.p. 4 Sept. 1904 (*Galloway Lodge, Boscombe, Bournemouth*).

3e. Annie Grant, b. 3 Feb. 1860.

4e. Constance Mary Grant, b. 15 May 1862.

5e. Margaret Grant, b. 2 May 1864.

6e. Beatrice Grant, b. 7 May 1866.   [Nos. 3431 to 3437.

The Plantagenet Roll

2d. Alan Rudolph Grant, *late* Indian Forest Dept., *b.* 28 Feb. 1843; *m.* 17 July 1884, Florence, da. of James Cuffe St. George.

3d. Alaric Frederick Grant, Comm. (ret.) R.N. (12 *Evelyn Mansions, Carlisle Place, S.W.*), *b.* 17 Aug. 1844; *m.* 6 May 1884, the Hon. Victoria, Maid of Honour to Queen Victoria, da. of Evan Baillie of Dochfour.

4d. Mary Grant.

5d. *Anne Grant, d.* 25 *Nov.* 1858; m. 9 *Sept.* 1856, *John Brooke Johnson, afterwards Brooke, Rajah Mudak of Sarawak (eldest nephew and heir of Sir James Brooke, 1st Rajah of Sarawak), d.* 1868; *and had issue 1e.*

1e. John Charles Evelyn Hope Brooke (*The Hill, Thorpe Mandeville, Banbury), b.* 15 Nov. 1858; *m.* 27 Ap. 1892, the Hon. Violet Mary, da. of Walter Bulkeley (Barrington), 9th Viscount Barrington [I.]; and has issue.

See the Clarence Volume, p. 94, Nos. 702–707.

6d. *Lucy Grant, d.* 16 *Jan.* 1875; m. *as 1st wife,* 27 *Sept.* 1866, *Rev. the Hon. Charles William Alexander Feilding, b.* 28 *Ap.* 1833; *d.* 30 *Nov.* 1893; *and had issue 1e to 4e.*

1e. John Basil Feilding, J.P. (*Upper Downing, Holywell, N. Wales), b.* 27 Dec. 1868-; *m.* 24 Feb. 1897, Emily Margaret, da. of Ewen Montieth Tod; and has issue 1f.

1f. Charles Rudolph Feilding, *b.* 16 Jan. 1902.

2e. Rowland Charles Feilding (*White's*), *b.* 18 May 1871; *m.* 29 Ap. 1903, Edith Mary, da. of Frederick Stapleton-Bretherton of The Hall, Rainhill; and has issue 1f.

1f. Joan Mary Feilding, *b.* 13 Ap. 1904.

3e. Adelaide Mary Feilding, ⎫
4e. Lucy Constance Feilding, ⎬ (8 *Tite Street, Chelsea*).

7d. Charlotte Augusta Grant, Sister of the Community of the Ascension.

[Nos. 3438 to 3454.

79. Descendants of CATHERINE PELHAM (see Table VII.), *b.* 24 July 1727; *d.* 27 July 1760; *m.* 3 Oct. 1744, HENRY (CLINTON), 9th EARL OF LINCOLN [E.], 2nd DUKE OF NEWCASTLE [G.B.], K.G., *b.* 16 Ap. 1720; *d.* 22 Feb. 1794; and had issue.

See the Clarence Volume, pp. 174–176, Nos. 2876–2937.

[Nos. 3455 to 3516.

80. Descendants of GRACE PELHAM (see Table VII.), *b.* 18 Aug. 1728; *d.* 31 July 1777; *m.* 12 Oct. 1752, LEWIS (MONSON, *afterwards* (R.L. 31 Jan. 1751) WATSON), 1st BARON SONDES [G.B.], *b.* 28 Nov. 1728; *d.* 30 Mar. 1795; and had issue 1*a* to 3*a*.

1a. *Lewis Thomas (Watson), 2nd Baron Sondes* [G.B.], b. 18 *Ap.* 1754; d. 20 *June* 1806; m. 30 *Nov.* 1785, *Mary Elizabeth, da. and h. of Richard Milles of North Elmham;* (re-m. *as 1st wife,* 23 *Jan.* 1809, *Lieut.-Gen. Sir Henry Montresor, K.C.B.; and*) d. 29 *Sept.* 1818; *and had issue 1b to 5b.*

1b. *Lewis Richard (Watson), 3rd Baron Sondes* [G.B.], b. 24 *May* 1792; d. *unm.* 14 *Mar.* 1836.

2b. *George John (Watson), afterwards* (R.L. 27 Dec. 1820) *Milles, 3rd Baron Sondes* [G.B.], b. 20 *Jan.* 1794; d. 17 *Dec.* 1874; m. 24 *July* 1823, *Eleanor, da. of Sir Edward Knatchbull, 8th Bart.* [E.], d. 30 *Oct.* 1883; *and had issue 1c to 5c.*

1c. *George Watson (Milles), 5th Baron Sondes* [G.B.], 1st *Earl Sondes* [U.K.], b. 2 *Oct.* 1824; d. 10 *Sept.* 1894; m. 25 *Jan.* 1859, *Charlotte* (99 *Eaton Place, S.W.*), *da. of Sir Henry Stracey, 5th Bart.* [U.K.]; *and had issue 1d to 7d.*

# of The Blood Royal

1*d*. George Edward (Milles), 2nd Earl Sondes [U.K.], &c., 6th Baron Sondes [G.B.] (*Less Court, Faversham ; Nacklington, Canterbury, &c.*), *b*. 11 May 1861.

2*d*. Hon. Lewis Arthur Milles, Major 3rd Batt. King's Own (*Cavalry*), *b*. 3 Oct· 1866.

3*d*. Hon. Henry Augustus Milles, now (R.L. 1 Mar. 1900) Milles-Lade, *late* Capt. R.E. Kent Yeo. (*Nash Court, Boughton, Kent*), *b*. 24 Nov. 1867.

4*d*. Lady Mary Georgina Milles, *m*. 24 June 1884, the Rev. Leslie Ellis Goodwin (son of the late Lord Bishop of Carlisle) ; and has issue 1*e* to 3*e*.

1*e*. George Gonville Wycliffe Goodwin, *b*. 1890.

2*e*. Mary Agneta Wycliffe Goodwin, *b*. 1885.

3*e*. Blanche Geraldine Wycliffe Goodwin, *b*. 1887.

5*d*. Lady Lily Geraldine Milles.

6*d*. Lady Constance Grace Milles, *m*. 1 Oct. 1885, Francis William George Gore (18 *Norfolk Street, Park Lane, W.*) ; and has issue 1*e* to 3*e*.

1*e*. George Rous Temple Gore, *b*. 1889.

2*e*. Christopher Gerald Gore, *b*. 1903.

3*e*. Violet Gladys Gore, *b*. 1887.

7*d*. Lady Violet Elizabeth Milles.

2*c*. Hon. *Lewis Richard Watson Milles, Lieut.-Col. Rifle Brigade, b.* 5 *Aug.* 1829 ; *d.* 7 *June* 1871 ; *m.* 12 *Nov.* 1861, *Georgina, da. of Robert Turle of Armagh, d.* 9 *Oct.* 1869 ; *and had issue* 1*d*.

1*d*. Inna Georgiana Milles (*Money Hall, Rickmansworth*), *m*. 21 Feb. 1885, the Hon. Louis Guy Scott, *b*. 23 Ap. 1850 ; *d*. 23 Ap. 1900 ; and has issue 1*e*.

1*e*. Inna Vera Evelyn Scott.

3*c*. Hon. *Mary Julia Milles, b.* 8 *Oct.* 1825 ; *d.* 10 *Ap.* 1901 ; *m.* 22 *July* 1845, *Edward* (*Fellowes*), 1*st Baron de Ramsay* [*U.K.*], *b.* 14 *Ap.* 1809 ; *d.* 9 *Aug.* 1887 ; *and had issue.*

See the Tudor Roll of "The Blood Royal of Britain," pp. 433–434, Nos. 31222–31234.

4*c*. Hon. *Elizabeth Frances Milles, b.* 26 *Aug.* 1827 ; *d.* 12 *Mar.* 1894 ; *m.* 3 *Sept.* 1846, *James George Henry* (*Stopford*), 5*th Earl of Courtown* [*I.*], 4*th Baron Saltersford* [*G.B.*] (*Courtown House, Gorey, Wexford*) ; *and had issue.*

See the Tudor Roll of "The Blood Royal of Britain," pp. 158–159, Nos. 19778–19814.

5*c*. Hon. *Jemima Townshend Milles, b.* 5 *Oct.* 1830 ; *d.* 17 *July* 1890 ; *m.* 1 *Mar.* 1859, *Frederick* (*son of the Right Hon. Henry*) *Goulbourn, C.B., Chairman of Customs, b.* 8 *Ap.* 1818 ; *d.* 10 *May* 1878.

3*b*. Hon. *Richard Watson, M.P., b.* 6 *Jan.* 1800 ; *d.* 24 *July* 1852 ; *m.* 21 *Dec.* 1839, *Lavinia Jane, da. of Lord George Quin, previously Taylour, b.* 21 *Mar.* 1816 ; *d.* 20 *Feb.* 1888 ; *and had issue.*

See the Tudor Roll of "The Blood Royal of Britain," p. 225, Nos. 22105–22124.

4*b*. Hon. *Mary Grace Watson, b.* 29 *Dec.* 1786 ; *d.* 24 *Nov.* 1853 ; *m.* 3 *May* 1808, *Sir John Henry Palmer of Carlton, 7th Bart.* [*E.*], *d.* 26 *Aug.* 1865 ; *and had issue.*

See p. 87, Nos. 425–435.

5*b*. Hon. *Catherine Watson, b.* 10 *June* 1802 ; *d.* 24 *Nov.* 1884 ; *m.* 23 *Ap.* 1829, *Sir William De Capell-Brooke, 3rd Bart.* [*U.K.*], *b.* 12 *June* 1801 ; *d.* 4 *Mar.* 1886 ; *and had issue* 1*c to* 3*c*.

1*c*. *Sir Richard Lewis De Capell-Brooke, 4th Bart.* [*U.K.*], *b.* 7 *Ap.* 1831 ; *d.* 3 *Feb.* 1892 ; *m.* 10 *Oct.* 1867, *Mary Grace* (*Woodford, Thrapston*), *da. of the Right Rev. Edward Trollope, Lord Bishop Suffragan of Nottingham ; and had issue* 1*d to* 4*d*. [Nos. 3517–3612.

The Plantagenet Roll

1d. Sir Arthur Richard De Capell-Brooke, 5th Bart. [U.K.], J.P. (*Great Oakley Hall, Kettering, &c.*), *b.* 12 Oct. 1869; *m.* 25 Feb. 1897, Fanny Cecil Talbot, da. of Capt. Duncan McNeill.

 2d. Edward Geoffrey De Capell-Brooke, *b.* 31 Jan. 1880.

 3d. Mary Charlotte De Capell-Brooke.

 4d. Caroline Sophia De Capell-Brooke.

 2c. Arthur Watson De Capell-Brooke of Loddington, J.P., Capt. 4th Hussars, b. 7 *May* 1836; *d.* 5 *Ap.* 1896; *m.* 3 *Aug.* 1865, *Eleanor Frances* (11 *Hyde Park Square, W.*), *da. of Thomas Thornhill of Fixby Hall; and had issue* 1*d to* 3*d.*

 1d. Catherine Honoria De Capell-Brooke, *m.* 31 July 1902, Hugh Arthur Paget (*Carfax, Englefield Green, Surrey*).

 2d. Edith Julia De Capell-Brooke, *m.* 21 Sept. 1899, Duncan Macpherson, Comm. (ret.) R.N. (*Westlake, West Coker, Yeovil*); and has issue 1*e* to 3*e.*

 1e. Francis Cameron Macpherson, *b.* 3 Oct. 1901.

 2e. Sheila Honoria Macpherson, *b.* 14 Dec. 1902.

 3e. Rosemary Catherine Macpherson, *b.* 3 June 1905.

 3d. Eleanor Grace De Capell-Brooke, *m.* 5 Aug. 1897, Gerald Seymour Guinness, J.P. (*Edenmore, Raheny, co. Dublin*); and has issue 1*e* to 3*e.*

 1e. Gerald Richard De Capell-Brooke Guinness, *b.* 1899.

 2e. Hermione Grace Guinness, *b.* 1898.

 3e. Georgina Elizabeth Guinness, *b.* 1903.

 3c. Charles Edward De Capell-Brooke, B.A. (Camb.), *b.* 5 Dec. 1842.

 2a. Hon. Henry Watson, b. 20 *Ap.* 1755; *d.* (–).

 3a. Hon. George Watson, M.P., b. 20 *Feb.* 1768; *d.* (–).

[Nos. 3613 to 3626.

81. Descendants of ROBERT (MONCKTON-ARUNDELL), 4th VISCOUNT GALWAY [I.], K.B., P.C. (see Table VII.), *b.* 4 July 1752; *d.* 23 July 1810; *m.* 1st, Mar. 1779, ELIZABETH, da. of Daniel MATTHEW of Felix Hall, *d.* 19 Nov. 1801; and had issue 1*a* to 2*a.*

 1a. William George Monckton-Arundell), afterwards (1826) *Monckton, 5th Viscount Galway* [*I.*], *b.* 28 *Mar.* 1782; *d.* 2 *Feb.* 1834; *m.* 4 *June* 1804, *Catherine Elizabeth, da. and h. of Capt. George Handfield, d.* 7 *Ap.* 1862; *and had issue* 1*b to* 4*b.*

 1b. George Edward (Monckton-Arundell), 6th Viscount Galway [*I.*], *b.* 1 *Mar.* 1805; *d.* 6 *Feb.* 1876; *m.* 25 *Ap.* 1838, *Henrietta Eliza, sister to Richard, 1st Baron Houghton* [*U.K.*], *da. of Robert Pemberton Milnes of Fryston Hall, M.P., d.* 10 *Sept.* 1891; *and had issue* 1*c.*

 1c. George Edmund Milnes (Monckton-Arundell), 7th Viscount Galway [I.], 1st Baron Monckton [U.K.], C.B., D.L., C.A., J.P., Hon. Col. (formerly Comdg.) Sherwood Rangers Imp. Yeo. (*Serlby Hall, Bawtry, Yorks; 9 Stratford Place, W.*), *b.* 18 Nov. 1844; *m.* 24 July 1879, Vere, a Lady of Justice of the Order of St. John [E.], da. of Ellis Gosling of Beesbridge Hall; and has issue 1*d* to 2*d.*

 1d. Hon. George Vere Arundell Monckton-Arundell, Lieut. 1st Life Guards, *b.* 24 Mar. 1882.

 2d. Hon. Violet Frances Monckton, *b.* 14 May 1880; *m.* 7 July 1904, Capt. Geoffrey Henry Julian Skeffington Smyth, D.S.O.; and has issue 1*e.*

 1e. Terence George Randal Smyth, *b.* 31 May 1905.

 2b. Hon. Edmund Gambier Monckton, Col. West York Militia, b. 21 *Dec.* 1809; *d.* 7 *Oct.* 1872; *m.* 10 *June* 1845, *Arabella Martha, da. of the Rev. John Robinson, M.A., d.* 25 *July* 1880; *and had issue.*

 See the Clarence Volume, pp. 608–609, Nos. 26763–26782.

[Nos. 3627 to 3650.

168

# of The Blood Royal

3b. Hon. *Horace Manners Monckton, Lieut.-Col. Comdg. 3rd Hussars,* b. 8 *May* 1824; d. 14 *Jan.* 1904; m. 1*st,* 16 *Oct.* 1856, *Georgina, da. of Sir Thomas Wollaston White, 2nd Bart.* [*U.K.*], d. 7 *July* 1879; 2*ndly,* 11 *Nov.* 1885, *Emily Sarah, widow of T. Till of Waingates, Thornton Heath, da. of James Cooper; and had issue* 1*c to* 2*c.*

1*c.* Horace Woollaston Monckton, Barrister I.T. (*Whitecairn, Wellington College Station, R.S.O., Berks*), b. 18 Aug. 1857.

2*c.* Catherine Elizabeth Monckton, b. 27 Mar. 1862.

4b. Hon. *Caroline Isabella Monckton* (*Ashlyn, Leighton Buzzard*) b. 5 Mar. 1831; m. 25 Mar. 1856, the Rev. Thomas John Monson, M.A., Rector of Kirby-under-Dale, b. 28 Ap. 1825; d. 23 July 1887; and had issue 1*c* to 8*c.*

1*c.* George John Monson, A.M.I.C.E., b. 28 Jan. 1857.

2*c.* Alfred John Monson, b. 30 May 1860; m. 27 Oct. 1881, Agnes Maude, da. of William Day of Eversley Garth; and has issue 1*d* to 4*d.*

1*d.* Philip Evelyn John Monson, b. 1887.

2*d.* Florence Edmone Monson.

3*d.* Margaret Rosamond Monson.

4*d.* Violet Theodosia Monson.

3*c.* Henry John Monson, *late* Comptroller of the Estates of Boghas Pasha (*The Brand, Loughborough*), b. 24 Sept. 1862; m. 21 Aug. 1901, Theodosia Anne Emily, da. of the Rev. George Howard Wright of White Hill House, West Liss; and has issue 1*d* to 3*d.*

1*d.* Thomas Debonnaire Monson, b. 14 Feb. 1905.

2*d.* Edome Theodosia Monson, b. 3 May 1903.

3*d.* [da.] Monson, b. 1904.

4*c.* Gilbert John Monson, F.R. Hist. Soc., F.R. Society of Literature (*Ashlyn, Leighton Buzzard*), b. 17 Sept. 1870.

5*c.* Beatrice Grace Monson.

6*c.* Florence Mary Monson.

7*c.* Alice Edome Monson (*St. Andrew's House, W.*).

8*c.* Constance Adelaide Monson (*Netley House, Cavendish Square, W.*).

2a. Hon. *Henrietta Maria Monckton-Arundell,* d. 1 *May* 1847; m. 22 *Aug.* 1808, *Robert Pemberton Milnes of Fryston House, co. York,* b. 20 *May* 1784; d. *Nov.* 1858; *and had issue* 1*b to* 2*b.*

1*b.* *Richard Monckton* (*Milnes*), 1*st Baron Houghton* [*U.K.*], *D.C.L., F.R.S.,* b. 19 *June* 1809; d. 11 *Aug.* 1885; m. 31 *July* 1851, *Annabella Hungerford, da. of John* (*Crewe*), 2*nd Baron Crewe* [*G.B.*], d. 24 *Feb.* 1874; *and had issue.*

See the Tudor Roll of "The Blood Royal of Britain," pp. 311–312, Nos. 26007–26013; also the Clarence Volume, pp. 360–361, Nos. 12323–12328.

2*b.* *Henrietta Eliza Milnes,* d. 10 *Sept.* 1891; m. 25 *Ap.* 1838, *George Edward* (*Monckton-Arundell*), 6*th Viscount Galway* [*I.*], d. 6 *Feb.* 1876; *and had issue* 1*c.*

1*c.* See p. 168, Nos. 3627–3630. [Nos. 3651 to 3686.

82. Descendants, if any, of the Hon. FRANCES CHARLOTTE MONCKTON-ARUNDELL (see Table VII.), *d.* 12 Sept. 1825; *m.* 15 Feb. 1785, ANTHONY BURLTON BENNETT.

83. Descendants of Lady CAROLINE MANNERS (see Table VII.), *d.* 10 Nov. 1769; *m.* 1st (Spec. Lic. Fac. 2 Oct.), 1734, Sir HENRY HARPUR, 5th Bart. [E.], *b. c.* 1709; *d.* 7 June 1784; and had issue.

See p. 86, Nos. 387–422. [Nos. 3687 to 3722.

The Plantagenet Roll

84. Descendants of JAMES (GRAHAM), 3rd DUKE OF MONTROSE [S.], 3rd EARL GRAHAM [G.B.], K.G. (see Table VII.), *b.* 8 Feb. 1755; *d.* 30 Dec. 1836; *m.* 2ndly, 24 July 1790, Lady CAROLINE MARIA, da. of George (MONTAGU), 4th Duke of Manchester [G.B.], *b.* 10 Aug. 1770; *d.* 26 Mar. 1847; and had issue 1*a* to 3*a*.

1*a*. *James (Graham), 4th Duke of Montrose [S.], and Earl Graham [G.B.], K.T.,* b. 16 *July* 1799; d. 30 *Dec.* 1874; m. 15 *Oct.* 1836, *the Hon. Caroline Agnes, da. of John (Horsley-Beresford), 2nd Baron Decies [I.],* b. 1818 (re-m. 2ndly, 22 *Jan.* 1876, W. S. Stirling-Crawford of Milton, d. 23 Feb. 1883; and 3rdly, 26 *July* 1888, Marcus Henry Milner), d. 16 Nov. 1894; and had issue 1b to 3b.

1*b*. Douglas Beresford Malise Ronald (Graham), 5th Duke of Montrose [S.], and Earl Graham [G.B.], K.T., Lord Clerk Register of Scotland, &c. (*Buchanan Castle, near Glasgow*), *b.* 7 Nov. 1852; *m.* 24 July 1876, Violet Hermione, da. of Sir Frederic Graham of Netherby, 3rd Bart. [G.B.]; and has issue 1*c* to 5*c*.

1*c*. James Graham, Marquis of Graham, D.L., *b.* 1 May 1878.

2*c*. Lord Douglas Malise Graham, Lieut. R.A., *b.* 14 Oct. 1883.

3*c*. Lord Alastair Mungo Graham, Mid. R.N., *b.* 12 May 1886.

4*c*. Lady Helen Violet Graham, *b.* 1 July 1879.

5*c*. Lady Hermione Emily Graham, *b.* 22 Feb. 1882.

2*b*. Lady Beatrice Violet Graham, *m.* 15 Dec. 1863, Algernon William Fulke (Greville), 2nd Baron Greville [U.K.] (*Clonhugh, Mullingar, Ireland*); and has issue. See the Clarence Volume, p. 356, Nos. 12176–12180.

3*b*. Lady Alma Imogine Leonora Charlotte Graham, Lady of Grace of the Order of St. John of Jerusalem [E.], *m.* 27 July 1872, Gavin (Campbell), 1st Marquis [U.K.] and 7th Earl [S.] of Breadalbane, K.G., P.C., sometime (1892–1895) Treasurer of the Household to Queen Victoria, &c., &c. (*Taymouth Castle, Aberfeldy, Armaddy Castle, Argyll ; 68 Ennismore Gardens, S.W.*).

2*a*. *Lady Georgiana Charlotte Graham,* b. 3 *June* 1791; d. 13 *Feb.* 1835; m. as 1st wife, 26 *July* 1814, George William (Finch-Hatton), 10th Earl of Winchilsea and 5th Earl of Nottingham [E.], b. 22 *May* 1791; d. 8 *Jan.* 1858; and had issue 1b to 2b.

1*b*. *George James (Finch-Hatton), 11th Earl of Winchilsea and 6th Earl of Nottingham [E.],* b. 31 *May* 1815; d. 9 *June* 1887; m. 1st, 6 *Aug.* 1846, Lady Constance Henrietta, da. of Henry (Paget), 2nd Marquis of Anglesey [U.K.], b. 22 *Jan.* 1823; d. 5 *Mar.* 1878; and had issue 1c to 2c.

1*c*. Lady Constance Eleanora Caroline Finch-Hatton (9 *St. George's Road, S.W.*), *m.* 3 June 1871, Capt. the Hon. Frederick Charles Howard, *d.* 26 Oct. 1893; and has issue. See the Clarence Volume, p. 386, Nos. 14685–14686.

2*c*. *Lady Hilda Jane Finch-Hatton,* b. 3 *Mar.* 1856; d. 8 *Feb.* 1893; m. 23 *Ap.* 1877, *Henry Vincent Higgins, 1st Life Guards ; and had issue* 1d to 2d.

1*d*. Cecil Matthew Stanley Higgins, *b.* 14 Feb. 1878.

2*d*. Rupert Henry Higgins, *b.* 5 Jan. 1879.

2*b*. *Lady Caroline Finch-Hatton,* b. 6 *July* 1816; d. 13 *Mar.* 1888; m. 2 *Feb.* 1837, *Christopher Turnor of Stoke Rochford, M.P., J.P., D.L., High Sheriff co. Lincoln* 1833, b. 4 *Ap.* 1809; d. 7 *Feb.* 1886; and had issue 1c to 7c.

1*c*. *Edmund Turnor of Stoke Rochford, J.P., D.L., High Sheriff co. Lincoln* 1894, and sometime M.P., b. 24 *Mar.* 1838; d.s.p.; m. 17 *Ap.* 1866, *Lady Mary Catherine, da. of Charles (Gordon), 10th Marquis of Huntly [S.]; d.* 15 Dec. 1903.

[Nos. 3723 to 3740.

170

# of The Blood Royal

2c. Christopher Hatton Turnor (*Stoke Rochford, Grantham*), *b.* 16 Dec. 1840 ; *m.* (at Toronto) 4 May 1871, Alice, da. of the Hon. Hamilton H. Killaly ; and has issue 1d.

    1d. Christopher Turnor, *b.* (at Toronto) 23 Nov. 1873.

3c. Algernon Turnor, C.B., J.P. (*Goadby Hall, Melton Mowbray*), *b.* 14 Nov. 1845 ; *m.* 3 Aug. 1880, the Lady Henrietta Caroline, da. of Randolph (Stewart), 9th Earl of Galloway [S.] ; and has issue 1d to 5d.

    1d. Herbert Broke Turnor, *b.* 22 Aug. 1885.

    2d. Christopher Randolph Turnor, *b.* 16 Aug. 1886.

    3d. Marjorie Caroline Isabel Turnor.

    4d. Algitha Blanche Turnor.

    5d. Verena Henrietta Turnor.

4c. Graham Augustus Turnor (*Australia*), *b.* 13 Sept. 1853 ; *m.* 1st (in Australia), 18 July 1880, Annie, da. of [——] Riddell, *d.* 12 Mar. 1889 ; 2ndly (in Australia), 26 May 1897, Beatrice, da. of [——] Cranstone ; and has issue 1d to 6d.

    1d. Edmund Turnor, *b.* 29 Dec. 1899.

    2d. Effie Caroline Turnor, *b.* 30 Ap. 1882.

    3d. Constance Yolande Turnor, *b.* 14 June 1883.

    4d. Charlotte Octavia Turnor, *b.* 28 Mar. 1885.

    5d. Bertha Kathleen Turnor, *b.* 4 Mar. 1889.

    6d. Edmunda Lilia Turnor, *b.* 22 Nov. 1903.

5c. Edith Georgina Turnor, *m.* 16 Sept. 1868, Frederick Archibald Vaughan (Campbell), 3rd Earl [U.K.], and 4th Baron [G.B.] Cawdor (*Stackpole Court, Pembroke ; Cawdor Castle, Nairn*) ; and has issue.

See the Tudor Roll of "The Blood Royal of Britain," pp. 214–215, Nos. 21735–21746.

    6c. Bertha Kathleen Turnor.

7c. *Dora Agnes Caroline Turnor*, d. 7 *Ap.* 1899 ; m. 27 *July* 1889, *Benjamin Bloomfield Trench of Loughton Moneygall, King's co.* (41 *Onslow Square, S.W.*) ; *and had issue* 1d to 2d.

    1d. Sheelah Georgiana Bertha Trench, *b.* 28 May 1890.

    2d. Theodora Caroline Trench, *b.* 17 July 1891.

3a. *Lady Lucy Graham*, b. 25 *Sept.* 1793 ; d. 16 *Sept.* 1875 ; m. 9 *Feb.* 1818, *Edward (Herbert), 2nd Earl of Powis [U.K.], K.G.,* b. 22 *Mar.* 1785 ; d. 17 *Jan.* 1848 ; *and had issue.*

See the Tudor Roll of "The Blood Royal of Britain," pp. 431–432, Nos. 31124–31162.   [Nos. 3741 to 3810.

85. Descendants of Lady LUCY GRAHAM (see Table VII.), *b.* 9 Aug. 1751 ; *d.* 13 Feb. 1780 ; *m.* as 1st wife, 13 June 1771, ARCHIBALD (DOUGLAS, previously STEWART), 1st BARON DOUGLAS of Douglas Castle [G.B.] ; *b.* (in Paris) 28 July 1784 ; *d.* 26 Dec. 1827 ; and had issue 1a to 3a.

1a. *Archibald (Douglas), 2nd Baron Douglas of Douglas Castle [G.B.],* b. 25 *Mar.* 1773 ; d. *unm.* 27 *Jan.* 1844.

2a. *Charles (Douglas), 3rd Baron Douglas of Douglas Castle [G.B.],* b. 26 *Oct.* 1775 ; d. *unm.* 11 *Sept.* 1848.

3a. Hon. *Jane Margaret Douglas,* b. 21 *Dec.* 1799 ; d. 10 *Jan.* 1859 ; m. 22 *Nov.* 1804, *Henry James (Scott-Montagu), 2nd Baron Montagu [G.B.],* b. 16 *Dec.* 1776 ; d. 30 *Oct.* 1845 ; *and had issue.*

See the Tudor Roll of "The Blood Royal of Britain," pp. 162–163, Nos. 19900–19934.   [Nos. 3811 to 3845.

The Plantagenet Roll

86. Descendants of GRANVILLE (LEVESON-GOWER), 1st MARQUIS OF STAFFORD [G.B.], 3rd BARON GOWER [E.], K.G. (see Table VIII.), *b.* 4 Aug. 1721; *d.* 26 Oct. 1803; *m.* 2ndly, 28 Mar. 1784, Lady LOUISA, da. and eventual co-h. of Scrope (EGERTON), 1st Duke of Bridgewater [G.B.], *b.* 30 Ap. 1723; *d.* 14 Mar. 1761; 3rdly, 23 May 1768, Lady SUSANNAH, da. of Alexander (STEWART), 6th Earl of Galloway [S.], *d.* 15 Aug. 1805; and had issue.

See the Tudor Roll of "The Blood Royal of Britain," pp. 371–376, Nos. 28030–28392; p. 516, Nos. 34692–34726; pp. 376–382, Nos. 28393–29129; and pp. 516–526, Nos. 34727–35195. [Nos. 3846 to 5448.

87. Descendants of Gen. JOHN LEVESON-GOWER (see Table VIII.), *b.* 25 June 1774; *d.* 3 Sept. 1816; *m.* 27 Dec. 1796, ISABELLA MARY, da. of Philip Bowes BROKE of Broke Hall, co. Suffolk, *d.* 28 May 1817; and had issue 1*a* to 2*a*.

1*a. John Leveson-Gower of Bill Hill, co. Berks, b. 5 Ap. 1802; d. 18 Nov. 1883; m. 18 Ap. 1825, Charlotte Gertrude Elizabeth, da. of Col. Henry Hugh Mitchell, 26th Regt. (by Lady Harriet Isabella née Somerset), d. 4 Aug. 1876; and had issue 1b to 4b.*

1*b.* John Edward Leveson-Gower of Bill Hill, J.P., Capt. 68th Foot, *b.* 20 Mar. 1826; *m.* 2ndly, 1 May 1879, Katherine Elizabeth (*Bill Hill, Wokingham*), da. of Basil Edward Arthur Cochrane; and has issue 1*c* to 2*c*.

1*c.* John Henry Leveson-Gower, Lieut. Grenadier Guards, *b.* 20 Sept. 1880.

2*c.* Idonea Gertrude Leveson-Gower.

2*b. Hugh Broke Boscawen Leveson-Gower, Capt. 56th Regt., b. 12 Aug. 1836; d. 25 May 1890; m. 20 June 1865, Janet Elizabeth, da. of the Rev. Henry Curtis Cherry, d. 6 June 1904; and had issue 1c to 5c.*

1*c.* Charles Cameron Leveson-Gower, Major 31st Lancers (*Cavalry*), *b.* 30 June 1866; *m.* 17 Aug. 1892, Beatrice, da. of Henry Francis Makins; and has issue 1*d* to 2*d*.

1*d.* Harold Boscawen Leveson-Gower, *b.* 2 July 1905.

2*d.* Janet Leveson-Gower, *b.* 19 May 1893.

2*c.* Philip Leveson-Gower, Capt. Sherwood Foresters (*Army and Navy*), *b.* 6 Feb. 1871; *m.* 2 Oct. 1899, Eleanor Maria, da. of Christopher R. Nugent of the Hall, Pinner, J.P.; and has issue 1*d*.

1*d.* Hugh Nugent Leveson-Gower, *b.* 1 July 1900.

3*c.* Edith Leveson-Gower.

4*c.* Mabel Leveson-Gower.

5*c.* Gertrude Leveson-Gower.

3*b. Sackville Leveson-Gower, b. 27 Aug. 1839; d. 3 May 1874.*

4*b.* Cecil Henrietta Maria Leveson-Gower (*West Lodge, Wokingham*).

2*a. Isabella Leveson-Gower, b. 13 Aug. 1803; d. 24 Sept. 1858; m. 8 Sept. 1825, Sir John Thomas Ibbetson-Selwin, 6th Bart. [G.B.], d. 20 Mar. 1869; and had issue 1b to 3b.*

1*b. Sir Henry John (Selwin-Ibbetson), 1st Baron Rookwood [U.K.], b. 26 Sept. 1826; d. 15 Jan. 1902.*

2*b. Isabella Mary Selwin, b. 4 Jan. 1827; d. 5 June 1895; m. 14 Ap. 1852, Edmund Calverley of Oulton Hall, co. York, J.P., D.L., b. 14 Aug. 1826; d. 15 Sept. 1897; and had issue 1c to 4c.* [Nos. 5449 to 5460.

172

# of The Blood Royal

1c. John Selwin Calverley of Oulton Hall, Leeds, J.P., D.L., b. 4 July 1855;
d. 30 Dec. 1900; m. 24 Ap. 1888, Sybil Isabella (8 Cromwell Place, S.W.), da. of
Ralph Disraeli; and had issue 1d to 3d.
> 1d. Sybil Horatia Calverley, b. 13 Sept. 1889.
> 2d. Katharine Isabella Calverley, b. 7 Mar. 1895.
> 3d. Frances Mary Calverley, b. 16 May 1896.

2c. Horace Walter Calverley, late Capt. 5th Dragoons (Oulton Hall, Leeds;
18 Chesham Place, S.W.), b. 3 Sept. 1862; m. 6 Jan. 1891, Louisa Mary, da. of Sir
Brydges Powell Henniker, 4th Bart. [U.K.]; and has issue 1d.
> 1d. Joyce Eden Calverley, b. 17 Jan. 1895.

3c. Edmond Leveson Calverley, Govt. Librarian O.R.C. (Calverley Hall,
Bloemfontein), b. 7 June 1864; m. 19 July 1893, Sybil Maitland, da. of Osbert
Salvin of Hawksfold, Haslemere, F.R.S.; and has issue 1d to 4d.
> 1d. Hugh Salvin Calverley, b. 30 Aug. 1894.
> 2d. Osbert Leveson Calverley, b. 6 July 1899.
> 3d. Amice Mary Calverley, b. 9 Ap. 1896.
> 4d. Caroline Bettina Calverley, b. July 1904.

4c. Gertrude Mabel Calverley, m. 4 Jan. 1883, Arthur Ernest Brooke-Hunt
(Piers Court, Dursley); and has issue 1d.
> 1d. Godfrey Leveson Brooke-Hunt, b. 26 Oct. 1885.

3b. Gertrude Louisa Jane Selwin (Villa Borghese, Torquay), m. 17 June 1863,
the Rev. Edward Capel Cure, M.A., Rector of St. George's, Hanover Square, Canon
of Windsor and Chaplain in Ordinary to H.M., b. 6 Nov. 1828; d. 30 Nov. 1890;
and has issue 1c to 4c.

1c. Edward Henry Capel Cure (Isola S. Giovanni, Lago Maggiore, Italy), b.
27 June 1866; m. 16 July 1889, Muriel Elizabeth Anna Louisa, da. of Sir Percy
Dixwell Nowell Dixwell-Oxenden, 10th Bart. [E.]; and has issue 1d.
> 1d. Bettina Eleanora Zoe Capel Cure, b. 27 July 1898.

2c. Rev. Walter Robert Capel Cure, M.A. (Oxon.), Vicar of St. John's, Oulton
(St. John's Vicarage, Oulton, Leeds), b. 6 Oct. 1870; m. 4 Sept. 1900, Mary Lorenza,
da. of Algernon Dauglish of 45 The Avenue, Kew; and has issue 1d.
> 1d. Walter Edward Capel Cure, b. 20 May 1902.

3c. Denzil James Capel Cure (Old House Farm, Sevenoaks, Weald), b. 13 June
1872; m. 15 July 1893, Helena Maud, da. of L. Taylor.

4c. Gertrude Isabella Capel Cure, m. 2 July 1895, the Rev. Henry Eden
Olivier, M.A. (Oxon.), Vicar of St. Michael's (St. Michael's Vicarage, Maidstone);
and has issue 1d to 3d.
> 1d. Jasper George Olivier, b. 20 Ap. 1896.
> 2d. Arthur Eden Olivier, b. 6 July 1898.
> 3d. Martin John Olivier, b. 20 Feb. 1900.   [Nos. 5461 to 5482.

88. Descendants of EDWARD LEVESON-GOWER, Rear-Admiral of the
Blue (see Table VIII.), b. 8 May 1776; d. 6 Dec. 1853; m.
13 Nov. 1822, CHARLOTTE ELIZABETH, da. of Harry MOUNT of
Wasing Place, Reading, d. 18 July 1826; and had issue 1a to 2a.

1a. Elizabeth Leveson-Gower, b. 13 Ap. 1824; d. 4 Ap. 1875; m. 28 Aug. 1854,
Charles Patton Keele (8 Prospect Place, Southampton); and had issue 1b to 5b.
> 1b. Charles Edward Keele, b. 6 July 1855; m. 4 Oct. 1892, Ella, da. of Lawford
Acland of Langdown; and has issue 1c.
> 1c. Charles Acland Keele, b. 23 Jan. 1894.   [Nos. 5483 to 5484.

The Plantagenet Roll

2b. John Rushworth Keele, b. (twin) 2 Dec. 1860; m. 11 Nov. 1896, Mildred Emily, da. of Francis Sanders of the Terrace, Oaken.

3b. Granville George Keele, b. (twin) 2 Dec. 1860.

4b. Mary Elizabeth Keele, b. 6 Sept. 1856; m. 5 Nov. 1879, Capt. Edward Pilkington, R.N.

5b. Alice Frances Keele, b. 7 Dec. 1857; m. 2 Aug. 1882, Trelawny Giles (Horsell, Woking); and has issue 1c to 4c.

1c. Granville Charles Trelawny Giles, b. 9 May 1891.

2c. Alfred Edward Boscawen Giles, b. 6 Mar. 1895.

3c. Ada Maud Keele Giles, b. 11 Ap. 1884.

4c. Amy Frances Giles, b. 1 Jan. 1894.

2a. Frances Charlotte Leveson-Gower (2 Rue Carnot, Versailles), b. 13 Dec. 1825; m. 7 Nov. 1854, the Viscount Papillon de la Ferté, d. 7 Jan. 1883; and had issue 1b to 3b.

1b. Jeanne Elizabeth Louise de la Ferté, b. 2 Feb. 1857; m. 25 Oct. 1880, Frederic Delbruck.

2b. Suzanne Louise Charlotte de la Ferté, b. 5 Dec. 1858.

3b. Gabrielle Fanny de la Ferté, b. 11 Dec. 1865; m. 5 June 1883, Robert Delbruck. [Nos. 5485 to 5496.

89. Descendants of WILLIAM LEVESON-GOWER (see Table VIII.), b. 6 Aug. 1779; d. 3 Oct. 1851; m. 20 Aug. 1804, KATHERINE MARIA, da. and h. of Sir John GRESHAM, 6th Bart. [E.], d. 7 Oct. 1808; and had issue 1a to 2a.

1a. William Leveson-Gower of Titsey Place, co. Surrey, b. 23 Nov. 1806; d. 15 Dec. 1860; m. 17 June 1834, Emily Josephine Eliza, da. of Sir Francis Hastings Doyle, 1st Bart. [U.K.], d. 16 Ap. 1872; and had issue.
See the Clarence Volume, pp. 272–274, Nos. 7276–7328.

2a. Katharine Frances Leveson-Gower, b. 19 Aug. 1805; d. 26 Feb. 1880; m. as 2nd wife, 23 Ap. 1845, Capt. George Hope, R.N., b. 30 May 1801; d. 1 Ap. 1893; and had issue 1b.

1b. Frances Katherine Hope (Ormonde Lodge, Southborough, Tunbridge Wells). [Nos. 5497 to 5550.

90. Descendants of ELIZABETH LEVESON-GOWER (see Table VIII.), b. 19 Nov. 1784; d. 24 Mar. 1824; m. (at St. James', Westminster) 15 Aug. 1803, JOHN TILLIE CORYTON of Pentillie Castle, co. Cornwall, b. 4 Ap. 1773; d. 10 Sept. 1843; and had issue 1a to 5a.

1a. William Coryton of Pentillie Castle, co. Cornwall, b. 17 Feb. 1807; d. 17 May 1836; m. 30 Jan. 1834, Harriet (who re-m., 1 Mar. 1842, Edmund (Parker), 2nd Earl of Morley [U.K.]), da. of Montagu Edmund Parker of Whiteway, Devon ; and had issue 1b.

1b. Frances Harriet Coryton, d. 30 Oct. 1862; m. as 1st wife, 30 Oct. 1862, (afterwards Sir) Thomas Villiers Lister of Armitage Hill, co. Berks, K.C.M.G., Under-Secretary of State for Foreign Affairs, d. 26 Feb. 1902; and had issue 1c to 6c.

1c. George Coryton-Lister, Major King's Royal Rifle Corps, b. 18 Nov. 1863; d. 30 May 1903; m. 18 June 1898, Lady Evelyn Selina (50 Warwick Square, S.W.;

174

# of The Blood Royal

Armytage Hill, Ascot), da. of Allen Alexander (Bathurst), 6th Earl Bathurst [*G.B.*] ; *and had issue* 1*d to* 2*d.*

    1*d.* Martin Douglas Bathurst Coryton-Lister, *b.* 6 May 1899.

    2*d.* Stella Evelyn Coryton-Lister, *b.* 22 Jan. 1901.

    2*c.* Edmund Algernon Coryton-Lister, *b.* 2 Ap. 1870.

    3*c.* Harry Coryton-Lister.

    4*c.* Maria Theresa Lister, *m.* 21 May 1890, Edward Farquhar; and has issue 1*d* to 2*d.*

    1*d.* Harold Lister Farquhar, *b.* 15 Ap. 1884.

    2*d.* Rupert Lister Farquhar, *b.* 7 July 1897.

    5*c.* Katherine Lister, *m.* 3 Aug. 1899, the Hon. Harold Albert Denison, Lieut. R.N. (30 *St. James' Square, S.W.*) ; and has issue 1*d.*

    1*d.* John Albert Lister Denison, *b.* 30 May 1901.

    6*c.* Constance Mary Lister, *m.* 20 Ap. 1892, James Frederick Maximilian Hartmann ; and has issue 1*d* to 3*d.*

    1*d.* James Frederick Lister-Hartmann, *b.* 25 Feb. 1893.

    2*d.* Robert Alexander Lister-Hartmann, *b.* 5 Jan. 1896.

    3*d.* Henry Felix Lister-Hartmann, *b.* 29 May 1901.

    2*a. Augustus Coryton of Pentillie Castle, J.P., D.L., b.* 30 Jan. 1809 ; d.s.p. 17 *Sept.* 1891.

    3*a. Henry Coryton, Capt. R.N., b.* (*at Crocodon*) 26 *Mar.* 1810 ; d. (? s.p.) 17 *Sept.* 1879.

    4*a. Rev. Granville Coryton, b.* (*at Pentillie Castle*) 30 *May* 1816 ; *d.* (? s.p.) 11 *Ap.* 1876 ; m. *Oct.* 1845, *Jessie, da. of F. King of Burreton, Hants, d.* 3 *Sept.* 1881.

    5*a. George Edward Coryton of Liss Place, Hants, J.P., b.* (*at Pentillie Castle*) 2 *Feb.* 1819 ; d. 22 *Mar.* 1886 ; m. 20 *Aug.* 1844, *Mary Louisa, da. of the Rev. Charles Phillot, Rector of Frome, d. Oct.* 1883 ; *and had issue* 1*b to* 2*b.*

    1*b.* William Coryton, J.P., D.L., Capt. Royal Cornwall Rangers Militia (*Pentillie Castle, St. Mellion, R.S.O., Cornwall*), *b.* 30 Oct. 1847 ; *m.* 16 Feb. 1887, Evelyn Annie, da. of Vice-Admiral George Parker of Delamere, Devon ; and has issue 1*c* to 6*c.*

    1*c.* John Tillie Coryton, *b.* 25 Aug. 1888.

    2*c.* Edmund George Coryton, *b.* 15 Dec. 1889.

    3*c.* William Alec Coryton, *b.* 16 Feb. 1895.

    4*c.* Ruth Evelyn Coryton, *b.* 11 May 1891.

    5*c.* Mary Louisa Coryton, *b.* 7 Oct. 1893.

    6*c.* Joan Elizabeth Loveday Coryton, *b.* 2 June 1900.

    2*b.* Frederick Coryton, J.P. (*Liss Place, Hants*), *b.* 1 Mar. 1850 ; *m.* 9 Aug. 1888, Augusta Margaret Elizabeth, da. of R. Manders of Dublin ; and has issue 1*c* to 3*c.*

    1*c.* Augustus Frederick Coryton, *b.* 13 May 1892.

    2*c.* Georgiana Charlotte Coryton, *b.* 6 May 1889.

    3*c.* Isolda Louisa Coryton, *b.* 28 Sept. 1890.   [Nos. 5551 to 5574.

91. Descendants of Lady MARY LEVESON-GOWER (see Table VIII.), *d.* 30 Ap. 1778 ; *m.* 1739, the Very Rev. Sir RICHARD WROTTESLEY, 7th Bart. [E.], M.P., Dean of Worcester, *b.* 1721 ; *d.* 29 July 1769 ; and had issue.

    See the Tudor Roll of " The Blood Royal of Britain," pp. 333–341, Nos. 26544–26793.   [Nos. 5575 to 5824.

The Plantagenet Roll

92. Descendants of FRANCIS RUSSELL, *styled* MARQUIS OF TAVISTOCK, M.P. (see Table VIII.), *b.* 27 Sept. 1739 ; *d.v.p.* 22 Mar. 1767 ; *m.* 8 June 1764, Lady ELIZABETH, da. of William Anne (KEPPEL), 2nd Earl of Albemarle [E.], *b.* 15 Nov. 1739 ; *d.* (at Lisbon) 2 Nov. 1768 ; and had issue 1*a* to 3*a*.

1*a*. *Francis (Russell), 5th Duke of Bedford [E.], b. 23 July 1765 ; d. unm. 2 Mar. 1802.*

2*a*. *John (Russell), 6th Duke of Bedford [E.], b. 6 July 1766 ; d. 20 Oct. 1839 ; m. 1st (at Brussels), 21 Mar. 1786, the Hon. Georgiana Elizabeth, da. of George (Byng), 4th Viscount Torrington [G.B.], d. 11 Oct. 1801 ; 2ndly, 23 June 1803, Lady Georgiana, da. and eventual (1836) co-h. of Alexander (Gordon), 4th Duke of Gordon [S.], d. (at Nice) 24 Feb. 1853 ; and had issue.*
See the Tudor Roll of "The Blood Royal of Britain," pp. 426–428, Nos. 30609–30661 (for children by 1st wife); and pp. 480–484, Nos. 33383–33561 (for children by 2nd wife).

3*a*. *Lord William Russell, b. (posthumous) 20 Aug. 1767 ; d. 6 May 1840 ; m. 11 July 1789, Lady Charlotte Anne, da. of George (Villiers), 4th Earl of Jersey [E.], b. 2 May 1771 ; d. 31 Aug. 1808 ; and had issue.*
See the Tudor Roll of "The Blood Royal of Britain," pp. 359–360, Nos. 27569–27604. [Nos. 5825 to 6091.

93. Descendants of GEORGE (SPENCER, *afterwards* (1807) SPENCER-CHURCHILL), 5th DUKE OF MARLBOROUGH [E.] (see Table VIII.), *b.* 6 Mar. 1776 ; *d.* 5 Mar. 1840 ; *m.* 15 Sept. 1791, Lady SUSAN, da. of John (STEWART), 7th Earl of Galloway [S.], *b.* 10 Ap. 1767 ; *d.* 2 Ap. 1841 ; and had issue.

See the Tudor Roll of "The Blood Royal of Britain," pp. 510–511, Nos. 34417–34504. [Nos. 6092 to 6179.

94. Descendants of FRANCIS ALMERIC (SPENCER), 1st BARON CHURCHILL [U.K.] (see Table VIII.), *b.* 26 Dec. 1779 ; *d.* 10 Mar. 1845 ; *m.* 25 Nov. 1801, Lady FRANCES, da. of Augustus Henry (FITZROY), 3rd Duke of Grafton, K.G., *b.* 1 June 1780 ; *d.* 7 Jan. 1866 ; and had issue.

See the Tudor Roll of "The Blood Royal of Britain," pp. 338–341, Nos. 26703–26793. [Nos. 6180 to 6270.

95. Descendants of Lady CAROLINE SPENCER (see Table VIII.), *b.* 27 Oct. 1763 ; *d.* 23 Nov. 1813 ; *m.* 19 Mar. 1792, HENRY WELBORE (AGAR-ELLIS), 2nd VISCOUNT CLIFDEN [I.] and BARON MENDIP [G.B.], *b.* 22 Jan. 1761 ; *d.* 13 July 1836 ; and had issue 1*a*.

1*a*. *George James Welbore (Agar-Ellis), 1st Baron Dover [U.K.], F.R.S., F.S.A., b. 17 Jan. 1797 ; d.v.p. 10 July 1833 ; m. 7 Mar. 1822, Lady Georgiana, da. of George (Howard), 6th Earl of Carlisle [E.], b. 16 May 1804 ; d. 17 Mar. 1860 ; and had issue.*
See the Tudor Roll of "The Blood Royal of Britain," pp. 228–229, Nos. 22213–22234. [Nos. 6271 to 6292.

# of The Blood Royal

96. Descendants of Lady ELIZABETH SPENCER (see Table VIII.), *b.* 20 Dec. 1764; *d.* 13 Jan. 1812; *m.* 5 Feb. 1790, JOHN SPENCER (eldest son of Lord Charles Spencer, M.P.), *b.* 21 Dec. 1767; *d.* 17 Dec. 1831; and had issue 1*a* to 2*a*.

1*a.* *Rev. Frederick Charles Spencer, Rector of Wheatfield, b.* 18 *Mar.* 1796; d. 2 *Oct.* 1831; m. 6 *Oct.* 1823, *Mary Anne, da. of Sir Scrope Bernard-Tyringham-Morland, 4th Bart.* [G.B.], *M.P.* (*who* re-m. 1835, *the Rev. Edward Fanshawe Glanville*), d. 21 Jan. 1882; *and had issue* 1*b.*

1*b.* *Rev. Charles Vere Spencer, M.A., Rector of Wheatfield, b.* 17 *May* 1827; d. 27 *May* 1898; m. 22 *June* 1852; *Emma Frederica* (*Wheatfield, Tetsworth, Oxon.*), *da. of John Robert A'Court Gray of Kingweston; and had issue* 1*c* to 7*c.*

1*c.* Aubrey John Spencer, M.A. (Oxon.), J.P., Barrister Lincoln's Inn, *late* Assist. Comr. to Royal Com. on Agriculture (*Wheatfield, Tetsworth; 19 Old Buildings, Lincoln's Inn*), *b.* 18 June 1853; *m.* 9 Ap. 1885, Florence Mary, da. of Frederick Halsey Janson of 8 Fourth Avenue, Hove; and has issue 1*d* to 4*d.*

    1*d.* Aubrey Vere Spencer, *b.* 4 Ap. 1886.

    2*d.* Ethel Frances Spencer, *b.* 16 Dec. 1887.

    3*d.* Frederica Elizabeth Spencer, *b.* 31 Mar. 1892.

    4*d.* Caroline Mildred Spencer, *b.* 26 Nov. 1898.

2*c.* George Trevor Spencer, R.N., *b.* 6 Feb. 1855.

3*c.* Edmund Vere Spencer, Capt. 1st Midx. R.E. (Vol.), *b.* 13 Nov. 1866.

4*c.* Charles Gordon Spencer, I.C.S. (*Rajahmundry, India*), *b.* 23 Feb. 1869; *m.* 13 Jan. 1903, Edith Mary, da. of Col. Hugh Pearce Pearson, C.B.; and has issue 1*d.*

    1*d.* Cynthia Mary Spencer, *b.* Mar. 1904.

5*c.* Rev. Frederick Augustus Morland Spencer (*Bishop Monckton, Ripon*), *b.* 23 July 1878.

6*c.* Mildred Frances Spencer.

7*c.* Frederica Marion Spencer.

2*a.* *Elizabeth Spencer, b.* 6 *Jan.* 1799; d. 2 *June* 1870; m. 22 *Ap.* 1823, *Lacy Rumsey, Clerk of the Bills in H.M.'s Treasury, b.* 11 *Jan.* 1787; d. *Sept.* 1872; *and had issue* 1*b* to 3*b.*

1*b.* Rev. Lacy Henry Rumsey (*The Vicarage, Llanstadwell, co. Pembroke*), *b.* 17 Nov. 1824; *m.* 9 Dec. 1856, Anne Nowell, da. of the Rev. William John Bussell; and has issue 1*c* to 7*c.*

    1*c.* Lacy Llewellyn Ninian Churchill Rumsey (27 *Estelle Road, London, N.W.*), *b.* 3 Nov. 1857.

    2*c.* Almaric Aubrey Herbert Rumsey (3 *Mayflower Road, London, S.W.*), *b.* 20 Sept. 1863; *m.* 29 Aug. 1891, Amelia, widow of W. A. Clements, da. of James Brown; and has issue 1*d* to 5*d.*

        1*d.* Clement Herbert Bradley Rumsey, *b.* 18 Feb. 1901.

        2*d.* Gerald Henry Churchill Rumsey, *b.* 2 May 1904.

        3*d.* Alma Winifred Constance Rumsey, *b.* 10 June 1892.

        4*d.* Olive Mary Gwendolen Rumsey, *b.* 10 Feb. 1894.

        5*d.* Gwladys Emily Nowell Rumsey, *b.* 3 Ap. 1897.

    3*c.* Herbert William Lacy Rumsey, a Master at the Wolverhampton Grammar School (10 *Horsman Street, Wolverhampton*), *b.* 24 May 1865.

    4*c.* Athelstane Aubrey Cecil Rumsey (*Freemantle, Western Australia*), *b.* 19 Aug. 1866.

    5*c.* Vere de Mentque Osmund Rumsey, *b.* 18 Ap. 1873.

    6*c.* Constance Ada Nowell Rumsey (10 *Hyde Road, Eastbourne*), *b.* 9 Nov. 1860.

    7*c.* Gwendolen Ella Helena Rumsey, *b.* 27 Oct. 1872.   [Nos. 6293 to 6317.

The Plantagenet Roll

2b. *Almaric Rumsey*, b. 31 Dec. 1825; d. 8 *Ap.* 1899; m. 11 *Jan.* 1872, *Caroline Montagu, da. of Thomas John Pittar; and had issue* 1c.

1c. Charles Almeric Rumsey, Principal Mathematical Master at Dulwich College (33 *Hawke Road, London, S.E.*), b. 26 Dec. 1872.

3b. *Caroline Rumsey*, b. 11 Dec. 1830; d. 10 *Ap.* 1857; m. 13 *May* 1856, *the Rev. James Chesterton Bradley* (8 *Cardigan Road, Richmond, Surrey*); *and had issue* 1c.

1c. Caroline Spencer Bradley, *b.* 10 Ap. 1857; *m.* 11 June 1890, William H. Blake, M.D. (*Bedford Lodge, West Wickham, Kent*); and has issue 1d to 3d.

1d. John Churchill Blake, b. 30 May 1894.

2d. Patrick Ethelbert Blake, b. 2 Dec. 1902.

3d. Rose Spencer Blake, b. 15 May 1891. [Nos. 6318 to 6322.

97. Descendants of Lady CHARLOTTE SPENCER (see Table VIII.), *b.* 18 Oct. 1769; *d.* 10 Jan. 1802; *m.* 16 Ap. 1797, the Rev. EDWARD NARES, D.D., Regius Professor of Modern History and Languages in the University of Oxford; and had issue.[1]

98. Descendants of Lady ANNE SPENCER (see Table VIII.), *b.* 5 Nov. 1773; *d.* 7 Aug. 1865; *m.* 10 Dec. 1796, CROPLEY-ASHLEY (ASHLEY-COOPER), 6th EARL OF SHAFTESBURY [E.], *b.* 27 Dec. 1768; *d.* 2 June 1851; and had issue.

See the Tudor Roll of "The Blood Royal of Britain," pp. 428–430, Nos. 31029–31073. [Nos. 6323 to 6367.

99. Descendants, if any, of Lady AMELIA SOPHIA SPENCER (see Table VIII.), *b.* 8 Sept. 1785; *d.* 30 Jan. 1829; *m.* 1812, HENRY PYTCHES BOYCE.[2]

100. Descendants of Lady FRANCES LEVESON-GOWER (see Table VIII.), *d.* 26 June 1788; *m.* 1744, Lord JOHN PHILIP SACKVILLE, *b.* 12 June 1713; *d.* 1765; and had issue.

See the Clarence Volume, pp. 223–224, Nos. 4502–4535.
[Nos. 6368 to 6401.

101. Descendants of JOHN JAMES (WALDEGRAVE), 6th EARL WALDE-GRAVE [G.B.], 7th BARON WALDEGRAVE [E.] (see Table VIII.), *b.* 30 July 1785; *d.* 30 July 1835; *m.* 30 Oct. 1815, ANNE, da. of John William KING of Hastings (who re-m. 1839, Algernon Hicks), *d.* 23 Aug. 1852; and had issue 1a to 3a.

1a. *George Edward* (*Waldegrave*), 7th Earl [G.B.] and 8th Baron [E.] Walde-grave, b. 8 Feb. 1816; *.* d.s.p. 28 *Sept.* 1846.

---

[1] Brydges' "Collins," i. p. 452.

[2] They had at least one da., Frances Augusta Boyce, *d.* 4 Feb. 1893; *m.* 24 July 1849, Sir George Lewis Horton-Wilmot, 5th Bart. [G.B.], *d.s.p.* 24 Oct. 1887.

# of The Blood Royal

2a. Lady Annette Laura Maria Waldegrave, b. 23 Mar. 1818 ; d. 28 Feb. 1856 ;
m. 27 Feb. 1841, *Lieut.-Gen. Archibald Money of Crown Point, co. Norfolk, C.B.,*
d. 25 Aug. 1858.

3a. Lady Horatia Elizabeth Waldegrave, b. 2 Nov. 1823 ; d. 24 June 1884 ; m.
1st, *17 May 1847, John Joseph Webbe-Weston of Sutton Place, co. Surrey, d.s.p.*
24 *Sept.* 1849 ; 2ndly, *28 Nov. 1854, John (4th son of Lieut.-Gen. John and the*
Hon. Anne née Lake) Wardlaw of 44 Princes Gardens.

102. Descendants of WILLIAM (WALDEGRAVE), 8th EARL [G.B.] and
9th BARON [E.] WALDEGRAVE, C.B. (see Table VIII.), *b.*
27 Oct. 1788 ; *d.* 24 Oct. 1859 ; *m.* 1st, 10 Aug. 1812, ELIZA-
BETH, da. of Samuel WHITBREAD of Cardington (by his wife
Lady Elizabeth *née* Gray), *d.* 1 Mar. 1843 ; and had issue 1*a*
to 5*a*.

1*a. William Frederick (Waldegrave), Viscount Chewton, b. 29 June 1816 ;*
d.v.p. *(being mortally wounded at the Alma) 7 Oct.* 1854 ; m. 2 *July* 1850, *Frances,*
V.A., *da. of Capt. John Bastard, R.N. ; and had issue 1b to 2b.*

1*b.* William Frederick (Waldegrave), 9th Earl [G.B.] and 10th Baron [E.]
Waldegrave, P.C., Chief Conservative Whip in the House of Lords and *formerly*
(1886–1892 and 1895–1896) a Lord-in-Waiting to Queen Victoria (*Chewton Priory,*
Bath ; 20 Bryanston Square, W.), *b.* 2 Mar. 1851 ; *m.* 5 Aug. 1874, Lady Mary
Dorothea, da. of Roundell (Palmer), 1st Earl of Selborne [U.K.]; and has issue 1*c*
to 3*c.*

1*c.* William Edward Seymour Waldegrave, Viscount Chewton, *b.* 20 Oct. 1882.

2*c.* Lady Mary Wilfreda Waldegrave, *b.* 3 Sept. 1875 ; *m.* 15 May 1900, the
Rev. Richard Aubrey Chichester Bevan, Rector of Hurstpierpoint (*The Red House,*
Hurstspierpoint, Sussex) ; and has issue 1*d* to 3*d.*

1*d.* Michael Lee Bevan, *b.* 12 July 1903.

2*d.* Favell Margaret Bevan, *b.* 31 Oct. 1901.

3*d.* Katherine Mildred Bevan, *b.* 26 Sept. 1904.

3*c.* Lady Laura Margaret Waldegrave, *b.* 25 June 1880 ; *m.* 1st, 19 July 1899,
Alfred Millington Knowles, *d.* (being killed in action near Buffelshock) 9 Aug. 1900 ;
2ndly, 7 June 1904, Reginald Nicholson (40 *Lennox Gardens, S.W.*) ; and has
issue 1*d.*

1*d.* Gerald Hugh Nicholson, *b.* 24 Ap. 1905.

2*b.* Rev. the Hon. Henry Noel Waldegrave, M.A. (Camb.), Rector of Marston
Bigot (*Marston Bigot Rectory, Frome*), *b.* (posthumous) 14 Oct. 1854 ; *m.* 27 Oct.
1892, Anne Katherine, da. of the Rev. William Pollexfen Bastard ; and has issue
1*c* to 3*c.*

1*c.* Dorothy Caroline Frances Waldegrave, *b.* 1 Mar. 1894.

2*c.* Irene Grace Waldegrave, *b.* 14 June 1895.

3*c.* Elizabeth Katharine Waldegrave, *b.* 7 May 1897.

2*a. Right Rev. the Hon. Samuel Waldegrave, Lord Bishop of Carlisle, D.D., b.*
13 *Sept.* 1817 ; d. 1 Oct. 1869 ; m. 23 *Jan.* 1845, *Jane Anne, da. of Francis Pym of*
The Hasells, Beds, d. 6 *June* 1877 ; *and had issue 1b.*

1*b.* Rev. Samuel Edmund Waldegrave, B.A. (Camb.), Rector of Oborne
(*Oborne Rectory, Sherborne, Dorset*), *b.* 21 May 1856 ; *m.* 14 Jan. 1886, Alice, da.
of Charles D. Millett of the London and Westminster Bank ; and has issue 1*c* to 4*c.*

1*c.* Samuel Charles Waldegrave, *b.* 14 May 1887.

2*c.* George Turner Waldegrave, *b.* 18 Mar. 1889.

3*c.* Frederick Arthur Waldegrave, *b.* 2 Ap. 1892.

4*c.* Edmund John Waldegrave, *b.* 10 May 1899.   [Nos. 6402 to 6418.

The Plantagenet Roll

3a. Lady Laura Waldegrave, b. 17 Mar. 1821; d. 10 Ap. 1885; m. 2 Feb. 1848, Roundell (Palmer), 1st Earl of Selborne [U.K.], P.C., sometime (1872–1874) Lord High Chancellor, &c., b. 27 Nov. 1812; d. 4 May 1895; and had issue 1b to 5b.

  1b. William Waldegrave (Palmer), 2nd Earl of Selborne [U.K.], P.C., High Commissioner of South Africa and Governor of the Transvaal (Blackmoor, Liss, Hants), b. 17 Oct. 1859; m. 27 Oct. 1883, Lady Beatrix Maude, da. of Robert Arthur Talbot (Gascoyne-Cecil), 3rd Marquis of Salisbury [G.B.], K.G.; and had issue 1c to 4c.

    1c. Roundell Cecil Palmer, Viscount Wolmer, b. 15 Ap. 1887.

    2c. Hon. Robert Stafford Arthur Palmer, b. 26 Sept. 1888.

    3c. Hon. William Jocelyn Lewis Palmer, b. 15 Sept. 1894.

    4c. Lady Mabel Laura Georgiana Palmer, b. 6 Oct. 1884.

  2b. Lady Laura Elizabeth Palmer (The Old House, Wonston, Hants), m. 26 Oct. 1876, the Right Rev. George Ridding, D.D., 1st Lord Bishop of Southwell, d. 30 Aug. 1904.

  3b. Lady Mary Dorothea Palmer, m. 5 Aug. 1874, William Frederick (Waldegrave), 9th Earl [G.B.] and 10th Baron [E.] Waldegrave (Chewton Priory, Bath); and has issue.

  See p. 179, Nos. 6403–6409.

  4b. Lady Sophia Matilda Palmer, m. 16 Feb. 1903, Count Amable Charles Franquet de Franqueville, LL.D., D.Lit. (Château de la Muette, Passy, Paris; Château de Bourbilly, par Semur en Auxois Côté d'Or).

  5b. Lady Sarah Wilfreda Palmer, m. 3 Oct. 1883, George Tournay Biddulph (Douglas House, Petersham, Surrey; 43 Charing Cross, S.W.); and has issue 1c.

    1c. Victor Roundell George Biddulph, b. 24 May 1897.

4a. Lady Maria Waldegrave (46 Victoria Road, Kensington, W.), m. 2 Oct. 1844, the Rev. William Brodie, Vicar of East Meon, b. 8 Oct. 1821; d. 5 June 1882; and has issue 1b to 5b.

  1b. Alfred Waldegrave Brodie, b. 13 Nov. 1851; m. 26 Sept. 1878, Catherine Elizabeth, da. of Major-Gen. Francis Applegath.

  2b. Edgar Waldegrave Brodie, J.P., late Capt. King's R. Rifle Corps (9 Embankment Gardens, Chelsea), b. 19 Nov. 1857; m. 28 Ap. 1886, Nora Kathleen, da. and h. of Capt. C. G. O'Callaghan of Ballinahinch, J.P., D.L.; and has issue 1c to 3c.

    1c. Malcolm William O'Callaghan Brodie, b. 30 Jan. 1887.

    2c. Donald Francis O'Callaghan Brodie, b. 1 Ap. 1888.

    3c. Angus George O'Callaghan Brodie, b. 11 July 1902.

  3b. Wilfred Leslie Waldegrave Brodie (19 Holland Villas Road, Kensington), b. 5 Jan. 1866; m. 1 June 1892, Sidonie Anna Franziska, da. of H.E. Field-Marshal Gen. von Neuber; and has issue 1c.

    1c. Franziska Maria Sidonie Brodie, b. 7 Nov. 1900.

  4b. Elizabeth Maria Brodie, d. 1 May 1868; m. 3 Ap. 1866, the Rev. Sidney George Gillum, Vicar of Pucklechurch, Bristol, formerly (1875–1891) Rector of Pentridge, Dorset; and had issue 1c.

    1c. Mary Gillum, m. 1889, the Rev. J. H. A. Law, Rector of West Felton (West Felton Rectory, Salop); and has issue 1d to 3d.

      1d. Charles Law, b. 19 June 1890.

      2d. Harry Law, b. 17 Mar. 1892.

      3d. Victor Patrick Law, b. 14 Mar. 1901.

  5b. Mary Arabella Brodie, m. 15 Ap. 1890, the Rev. William Monro Wollaston, Canon of Gibraltar (Villa Montboissier, Cannes).

5a. Lady Mary Waldegrave (9 Park Road, Southborough, Tunbridge Wells).

[Nos. 6419 to 6449.

180

# of The Blood Royal

103. Descendants of WILLIAM (WALDEGRAVE), 1st BARON RADSTOCK [I.], G.C.B. (see Table VIII.), *b.* 9 July 1753; *d.* 20 Aug. 1825; *m.* 28 Dec. 1785, CORNELIA, da. of David VAN LENNAP, Chief of the Dutch Factory at Smyrna, *d.* 10 Oct. 1839; and had issue 1*a* to 3*a*.

1*a.* Granville George (*Waldegrave*), 2nd Baron Radstock [*I*.], b. 24 *Sept.* 1786; *d.* 11 *May* 1857; m. 7 *Aug.* 1823, *Esther Caroline, da. of James Puget of Totteridge,* *d.* 16 *Mar.* 1874; *and had issue* 1*b to* 2*b.*

1*b.* Granville Augustus William (Waldegrave), 3rd Baron Radstock [I.], &c. (*Mayfield, Woolston, Hants*), *b.* 10 Ap. 1833; *m.* 16 July 1858, Susan Charlotte, da. of John Hales Calcraft of Runpstone (by the Lady Caroline Montagu), *d.* 8 Dec. 1892; and has issue 1*c* to 6*c.*

1*c.* Hon. Granville George Waldegrave (4 *Park Square West, Regent's Park*), *b.* 1 Sept. 1859.

2*c.* Hon. Montagu George Waldegrave (*Peshawar, India*), *b.* 15 July 1867; *m.* 15 July 1898, Constance Marian, da. of James C. J. Brodie of Lethen.

3*c.* Hon. Edith Caroline Waldegrave, *m.* 10 Ap. 1889, Alister Gilian Fraser (13 *Harley House, Regent's Park, N.W.; Nalderswood, Leigh, Reigate*).

4*c.* Hon. Mabel Waldegrave.

5*c.* Hon. Constance Waldegrave.

6*c.* Hon. Mary Waldegrave, *m.* 25 Ap. 1896, Edwyn Robert Bevan (*Banwell Abbey, Somerset*).

2*b. Hon. Caroline Esther Waldegrave, b.* 24 *May* 1826; *d.* 3 *July* 1898; m. 15 *June* 1852, *Sir Thomas William Brograve Beauchamp-Proctor, afterwards (R.L. 9 July* 1852) *Proctor-Beauchamp, 4th Bart. [G.B.], b.* 2 *July* 1815; *d.* 7 Oct. 1874; *and had issue* 1*c to* 7*c.*

1*c.* Sir Reginald William Proctor-Beauchamp, 5th Bart. [G.B.], J.P., D.L. (*Langley Park, Norwich; 27 Hill Street, Berkeley Square*), *b.* 23 Ap. 1853; *m.* 7 June 1880, Lady Violet (div. 1901), da. and h. of John Strange (Jocelyn), 5th Earl of Roden [I.]; and has issue 1*d* to 2*d.*

1*d.* Ginévra Sheila Hilda Mary Sophie Proctor-Beauchamp.

2*d.* Nadine Proctor-Beauchamp.

2*c.* Horace George Proctor-Beauchamp, C.B., Lieut.-Col. and Brevet-Col. (*formerly* Comdg.) 20th Hussars (5 *Hans Place, S.W.*), *b.* 3 Nov. 1856; *m.* 15 Nov. 1892, Florence, da. and h. of H. M. Leavitt of New York.

3*c.* Montagu Harry Proctor-Beauchamp, B.A. (Camb.), a Missionary in China (*Szechuen, China*), *b.* 19 Ap. 1860; *m.* 20 Ap. 1892, Florence, da. of Robert Barclay of Reigate; and has issue 1*d* to 3*d.*

1*d.* Montagu Barclay Granville Proctor-Beauchamp, *b.* 4 Aug. 1893.

2*d.* Ivor Cuthbert Beauchamp Proctor-Beauchamp, *b.* 19 Aug. 1900.

3*d.* Muriel Esther Dornie Proctor-Beauchamp, *b.* 23 Jan. 1897.

4*c.* Ida Caroline Proctor-Beauchamp, *m.* 6 Oct. 1891, Col. Robert Henry Curzon Drury-Lowe, *late* Gren. Guards.

5*c.* Hilda Proctor-Beauchamp, *m.* 10 Dec. 1884, J. E. Kynaston Studd (67 *Harley Street, W.*); and has issue 1*d* to 5*d.*

1*d.* Eric Studd, *b.* 1887.

2*d.* Ronald Granville Studd, *b.* 1889.

3*d.* Lionel Fairfax Studd, *b.* 1891.

4*d.* Bernard Cyril Studd, *b.* 1892.

5*d.* Vera Constance Victoria Studd, *b.* 1897. [Nos. 6450 to 6471.

181   2 A

The Plantagenet Roll

6c. Constance Proctor-Beauchamp, *m.* 30 July 1889, William Douglas Robinson-Douglas (*Orchardton, Castle Douglas*).

7c. Maude Proctor-Beauchamp, *m.* 7 May 1889, the Rev. William Thomas Baring Hayter, Vicar of Westbury (*Westbury Vicarage, Wilts*); and has issue 1*d* to 3*d*.

1*d*. Dorothea Hayter, *b.* 1891.

2*d*. Mary Ethel Hayter, *b.* 1892.

3*d*. Hilda Ruth Hayter, *b.* 1895.

2*a*. *Hon. Emily Susanna Laura Waldegrave*, b. 6 *Nov.* 1787; d. 12 *Ap.* 1870; m. 25 *Aug.* 1815, *Nicolas Westby of Thornhill*, b. 23 *Oct.* 1787; d. 24 *Aug.* 1860; *and had issue* 1*b to* 3*b*.

1*b*. *Edward Perceval Westby of Roebuck Castle, &c., and High Sheriff co. Clare* 1854, d. 23 *Ap.* 1893; m. 1*st*, 13 *Oct.* 1853, *Elizabeth Mary, da. of the Right Hon. Francis Blackburne, Lord Chancellor of Ireland*, d. 1863; *and had issue* 1*c to* 2*c*.

1*c*. Francis Vandeleur Westby, J.P., High Sheriff co. Clare 1895 (*Roebuck Castle, co. Dublin; Kilballyowen, co. Clare*), *b.* 15 June 1859; *m.* 1888, Janet Louisa, da. of George Orme of Castle Lacken, co. Mayo; and has issue 1*d* to 3*d*.

1*d*. Perceval St. George Charles Westby, *b.* 20 Nov. 1888.

2*d*. Horace William Turner Westby, *b.* 22 Dec. 1891.

3*d*. Granville Nicholas Frances Westby, *b.* 18 Mar. 1894.

2*c*. Emily Jane Laura Westby.

2*b*. *Emily Elizabeth Westby*, d. (–); m. *the Rev. F. Braithwaite*.

3*b*. *Louisa Isabella Westby*, d. 3 *Oct.* 1894; m. 9 *Nov.* 1847, *Marcus Keane of Beech Park, J.P.*, b. 7 *Feb.* 1815; d. 29 *Oct.* 1883; *and had issue* 1*c to* 4*c*.

1*c*. Percival William Keane, *b.* 12 Sept. 1848; *m.* 25 Sept. 1873, Mary Frances, da. of the Rev. Robert Ellis of Rash House, co. Tyrone; and has issue 1*d*.

1*d*. Isabella Louisa Keane.

2*c*. Marcus Thomas Francis Keane, J.P., D.L. (*Beech Park, Ennis; Doon Dahlin, Carrigaholt, co. Clare*), *b.* 31 July 1854; *m.* 28 July 1903, Henrietta Mary, da. of Major William Mills Malony of Kiltanon, co. Clare, D.L.; and has issue 1*d*.

1*d*. Helen Louise Keane, *b.* 17 Jan. 1905.

3*c*. Frederick Colpoys Keane, Lieut. Carmarthen Artillery, *b.* 11 Mar. 1868; *m.* 1 June 1898, Rose Dorothy, da. of Major-Gen. William Robert Farmer of Bloomfield; and has issue 1*d* to 4*d*.

1*d*. Anthony Colpoys Keane, *b.* 6 July 1899.

2*d*. Marcus Hugh Keane, *b.* 23 Nov. 1901.

3*d*. Granville Keane, ⎫
4*d*. John Colpoys Keane, ⎰ *b.* (twins) 24 July 1905.

4*c*. Louisa Caroline Keane.

3*a*. *Hon. Caroline Waldegrave*, b. 4 *Oct.* 1798; d. 7 *Jan.* 1878; m. 16 *Dec.* 1830, *the Ven. Carew Anthony St. John Mildmay, M.A., Archdeacon of Essex*, b. 2 *Feb.* 1800; d. 13 *July* 1878; *and had issue* 1*b to* 2*b*.

1*b*. *Augusta Jane St. John Mildmay*, d. 14 *July* 1892; m. 1*st*, *William Coesvelt Kortright*, d. *July* 1863; 2*ndly*, *as* 2*nd wife*, 14 *May* 1867, *Edmond Henry St. John Mildmay, Capt. in the Austrian Army, K.C. of the Danebrogh Order, &c. &c.* (131 *Cromwell Road, S.W.*); *and had issue by* 2*nd marriage*.

See the Clarence Volume, p. 468, Nos. 20789–20791.

2*b*. *Evelyn Mary St. John Mildmay*, d. 11 *Jan.* 1881; m. 17 *Oct.* 1878, *the Rev. William Quennell*.   [Nos. 6472 to 6494.

182

# of The Blood Royal

104. Descendants of HENRY RICHARD (FOX, *afterwards* VASSALL), 3rd BARON HOLLAND [G.B.], F.R.S., F.S.A. (see Table VIII.), *b.* 21 Nov. 1773 ; *d.* 22 Oct. 1840 ; *m.* 9 July 1797, ELIZABETH, sometime wife of Sir Godfrey WEBSTER, 4th Bart. [E.], da. and h. of Richard Vassall of Jamaica, *d.* 17 Nov. 1845 ; and had issue 1*a* to 2*a*.

1*a*. Henry Edward (*Fox*), 4th Baron Holland [G.B.], b. 7 Mar. 1802 ; d.s.p.s. (*at Naples*) 18 Dec. 1859.

2*a*. Hon. Mary Elizabeth Fox, b. 19 Feb. 1806 ; d. 7 Dec. 1891 ; m. 24 May 1830, Thomas Atherton ,(Powys), 3rd Baron Lilford [G.B.], b. 2 Dec. 1801 ; d. 15 Mar. 1861 ; and had issue 1b to 7b.

1*b*. Thomas Littleton (*Powys*), 4th Baron Lilford [G.B.], b. 18 Mar. 1833 ; d. 17 June 1896 ; m. 1st, 14 June 1859, Emma Elizabeth, da. of Robert William Brandling of Low Gosforth, d. 9 July 1884 ; and had issue 1c to 2c.

1*c*. John (Powys), 5th Baron Lilford [G.B.] (*Lilford Hall, Oundle ; Ban Hall, Preston*), b. 12 Jan. 1863 ; m. 9 Aug. 1894, Milly Louisa Isabella, da. of George William Culme Soltan-Symons of Chaddlewood, co. Devon ; and has issue 1d.

1*d*. Hon. Thomas Atherton Powys, b. 8 May 1896.

2*c*. Hon. Stephen Powys (92 *Mount Street*, W. ; *St. Ann's Hill, Chertsey*), b. 8 Mar. 1869.

2*b*. Hon. Leopold William Henry Powys, now (*R.L.* 1890) Fox-Powys of Bewsey Hall, D.L., b. 17 Sept. 1837 ; d. 18 July 1893 ; m. 27 Feb. 1862, Lady Mary, da. of Archibald (*Acheson*), 3rd Earl of Gosford [I.], K.P., b. 21 Mar. 1835 ; d. 30 Jan. 1892 ; and had issue 1c to 6c.

1*c*. Edith Galfrida Fox-Powys, m. 1st, 9 Aug. 1888, Capt. Charles Blood Mulville, Dragoon Guards, d. 28 Mar. 1901 ; 2ndly, 12 July 1904, Edward Chenevix Austen-Leigh (80 *Cadogan Square, S.W.*).

2*c*. Emily Marion Emma Fox-Powys, m. 1 Dec. 1892, Major Ellis Houlton Ward, late 60th Rifles (17 *The Circus, Bath*).

3*c*. Maud Blanche Fox-Powys (2 *Harewood Place, Hanover Square, W.*).

4*c*. Mary Theresa Gwendolen Fox-Powys, m. 15 Ap. 1896, Mervyn Owen Wayne Powys (*Haygrass House, Taunton*).

5*c*. Hilda Geraldine Fox-Powys.

6*c*. Louise Christine Fox-Powys.

3*b*. Rev. the Hon. Edward Victor Robert Powys, LL.B. (*Camb.*), formerly Vicar of Thorpe Abchurch (*Windham*), b. 11 Feb. 1839 ; m. 8 June 1865, Elizabeth Gwenllian, da. and h. of William Watkyn-Wayne of Plas Newydd ; d. 21 Nov. 1870 ; and had issue 1c to 2c.

1*c*. Mervyn Owen Wayne Powys, M.A. (Camb.), late Lieut. Northants Regt. (*Haygrass House, Taunton*), b. 5 Nov. 1866 ; m. 15 Ap. 1896, Mary Theresa Gwendoline, da. of the Hon. Leopold Fox-Powys.

2*c*. Edward William Wayne Powys.

4*b*. Hon. Edith Galfrida Powys, b. 2 July 1834 ; d. 10 Feb. 1864 ; m. as 1st wife, 20 Ap. 1858, Thomas Henry Burroughes (*Ketton Cottage, Stamford ; 16 Lower Berkeley Street, W.*) ; and had issue 1c to 2c.

1*c*. Edward Robert Burroughes, b. 7 May 1862.

2*c*. Rachel Georgiana Burroughes, m. 11 Ap. 1893, George William Whitmore Green-Price, J.P. (*The Gables, Norton, R.S.O., Radnor*).

5*b*. Hon. Mary Elizabeth Frances Powys (42 *Montagu Square, W.*).

6*b*. Hon. Constance Emma Augusta Powys (73 *Belgrave Road, S.W.*), m. 7 May 1867, Arthur William Crichton of Broadwood Hall, Salop, d. 4 Feb. 1882 ; and has issue 1c.

1*c*. Gwyneth Eva Crichton.

7*b*. Hon. Caroline Mary Powys, m. 19 Oct. 1897, Frederic George Dawtrey Drewitt, M.D. (14 *Palace Gardens Terrace, Kensington, W.*).

[Nos. 6495 to 6511.

105. Descendants of Lady LOUISA FITZPATRICK (see Table VIII.), *b.* 1755; *d.* 7 Aug. 1789; *m.* as 2nd wife, 19 July 1779, WILLIAM (FITZMAURICE). 1st MARQUIS OF LANSDOWNE [G.B.], 2nd EARL OF SHELBURNE [I.], *bapt.* 13 May 1737; *d.* 7 May 1805; and had issue 1*a.*

1*a. Henry Petty (Fitzmaurice), 3rd Marquis of Lansdowne [G.B.], 4th Earl of Shelburne [I.], and (in 1818) 4th Earl of Kerry, &c. [I.], K.G., P.C.,* b. 2 *July* 1780; d. 31 *Jan.* 1863; m. 30. *Mar.* 1808, *Lady Louisa Emma, da. of Henry Thomas (Fox-Strangeways), 2nd Earl of Ilchester [G.B.],* b. 27 *June* 1785; d. 3 *Ap.* 1851; *and had issue* 1b *to* 3b.

1*b. William Thomas Fitzmaurice, Earl of Kerry, M.P.,* b. 30 *Mar.* 1811; d.v.p. 21 *Aug.* 1836; m. 18 *Mar.* 1834, *Lady Augusta Lavinia Priscilla, da. of John (Ponsonby), 4th Earl of Bessborough [I.], and (by her, who* m. 2ndly, 2 *Ap.* 1845, *the Hon. Charles Alexander Gore) had issue* 1c.

1*c. Lady Mary Fitzmaurice (Styche, Market Drayton),* m. 4 Oct. 1860, Gen. the Right Hon. Sir Percy Egerton Herbert, K.C.B., M.P., *b.* 15 Ap. 1822; *d.* 7 Oct. 1876; and has issue.

See the Tudor Roll of "The Blood Royal of Britain," p. 238, Nos. 22472–22478.

2*b. Henry (Fitzmaurice), 4th Marquis of Lansdowne [G.B.], 5th Earl of Kerry and Shelburne [I.], K.G.,* b. 5 *Jan.* 1816; d. 5 *July* 1866; m. 2ndly, 1 *Nov.* 1843, *Emily Jane,* suo jure 8th *Baroness Nairne* [S.], d. 25 *June* 1895; *and had issue.*

See the Tudor Roll of "The Blood Royal of Britain," pp. 532–533, Nos. 35512–35529.

3*b. Lady Louisa Fitzmaurice,* b. 21 *Jan.* 1813; m. 10 *Feb.* 1845, *the Hon. James Kenneth Howard, M.P.,* b. 5 *Mar.* 1814; d. 7 *Jan.* 1882; *and had issue.*

See the Clarence Volume, p. 625, Nos. 28017–28021.

[Nos. 6512 to 6542.

106. Descendants of HENRIETTA VERNON (see Table VIII.), *b.* Aug. 1760; *d.* 22 Ap. 1838; *m.* as 2nd wife, 14 July 1776, GEORGE (BROOKE), 2nd EARL OF WARWICK AND BROOKE [G.B.], 9th BARON BROOKE [E.], K.T., *b.* 16 Sept. 1746; *d.* 2 May 1816; and had issue.

See the Tudor Roll of "The Blood Royal of Britain," pp. 196–199, Nos. 21230–21323. [Nos. 6543 to 6636.

107. Descendants of JOHN JOSHUA (PROBY), 1st EARL OF CARYSFORT [I.] and BARON [U.K.], K.P. (see Table VIII.), *b.* 12 Aug. 1751; *d.* 7 Ap. 1828; *m.* 1st, 19 Mar. 1774, ELIZABETH, da. of the Right Hon. Sir William OSBORNE, 8th Bart. [I.], *d.* Nov. 1783; 2ndly, 12 May 1787, ELIZABETH, sister to George, 1st Marquis of Buckingham [G.B.], da. of the Right Hon. George GRENVILLE, *b.* 24 Oct. 1756; *d.* 2 Dec. 1842; and had issue 1*a* to 3*a.*

1*a. John (Proby), 2nd Earl of [I.] and Baron [U.K.] Carysfort,* b. 1780; d. unm. 11 *June* 1855.

2*a. Granville Leveson (Proby), 3rd Earl of [I.] and Baron [U.K.] Carysfort,*

# of The Blood Royal

Admiral R.N., b. 1782; d. 3 *Nov.* 1868; m. 5 *Ap.* 1818, *Isabella, da. of the Hon. Hugh Howard*, d. 22 *Jan.* 1836 ; *and had issue* 1*b to* 4*b.*

1*b.* Granville Leveson (*Proby*), 4*th Earl of* [*I.*] *and Baron* [*U.K.*] *Carysfort, K.P., P.C.,* b. 14 *Sept.* 1824 ; d.s.p. 18 *May* 1872.

2*b.* William (Proby), 5th Earl [I.] and Baron [U.K.] Carysfort, K.P., &c. (*Elton Hall, Peterborough ; Glen Art Castle, Arklow ; 10 Hereford Gardens, W.*), b. 18 Jan. 1836 ; *m.* 11 Ap. 1860, Charlotte Mary, da. of the Rev. Robert Boothby Heathcote of Friday Hill, co. Essex.

3*b.* Lady Emma Elizabeth Proby, d. 24 *June* 1900 ; m. 7 *Aug* 1844, *the Right Hon. Lord Claud Hamilton, P.C., M.P.,* b. 27 *July* 1813 ; d. 3 *June* 1884; *and had issue* 1*c to* 4*c.*

1*c.* Douglas James Hamilton, now (R.L. 1904) Proby, Lieut.-Col. Irish Guards (2 *Draycott Place, S.W.*), b. 23 Sept. 1856 ; *m.* 6 July 1882, Lady Margaret Frances, da. of Richard John (Hely-Hutchinson), 4th Earl of Donoughmore [I.]; and has issue 1*d to* 4*d.*

1*d.* Granville Proby, *b.* 13 Sept. 1883.

2*d.* Richard George Proby, *b.* 21 July 1886.

3*d.* Jocelyn Campbell Patrick Proby, *b.* 3 Mar. 1900.

4*d.* Betty Alice Adeline Proby, *b.* 17 May 1889.

2*c.* Louisa Charlotte Hamilton (*Hind Head House, Haslemere*), *m.* 29 Feb. 1876, Professor John Tyndall, D.C.L., LL.D., F.R.S., *d.* 4 Dec. 1893.

3*c.* Emma Frances Hamilton (117 *Church Street, Chelsea, S.W.*).

4*c.* Mary Stuart Hamilton, *m.* as 2nd wife, 2 Oct. 1878, Wilbraham Frederic (Tollemache), 2nd Baron Tollemache [U.K.] (*Peckforton Castle, Tarporley, Cheshire ; 61 Cadogan Gardens, S.W.*).

4*b.* Lady Theodosia Gertrude Proby, d. 21 *Oct.* 1902; m. 10 *Sept.* 1859, *William Montagu Baillie, J.P., High Sheriff, Bristol,* 1860 (*Southmoor, Dean Park, Bournemouth*) ; *and had issue* 1*c to* 4*c.*

1*c.* Granville Hugh Baillie, *b.* 28 May 1873 ; *m.* 6 Mar. 1897, Eleni, da. of Pericles Acatos of Galatz ; and has issue 1*d.*

1*d.* Hilda Ina Baillie, *b.* 26 Nov. 1899.

2*c.* Isabella Georgiana Baillie.

3*c.* Caroline Mary Baillie.

4*c.* Eva Baillie.

3*a.* Lady Elizabeth Proby, b. 19 *Ap.* 1792 ; d. 17 *Oct.* 1869; m. 2 *Feb.* 1816, *William Wells of Holme Wood, co. Hunts, Capt. R.N.,* d. 3 *Aug.* 1826 ; *and had issue.*

See the Tudor Roll of "The Blood Royal of Britain," p. 280, Nos. 24950–24955.   [Nos. 6637 to 6656.

108. Descendants of ANTHONY GILBERT STORER of Purley Park, co. Berks (see Table VIII.), *b.* 1782 ; *d.* 1818 ; *m.* 18 Jan. 1806, ANNE KATHERINE, da. of Thomas HILL of co. Salop, *d.* 7 May 1855 ; and had issue 1*a* to 2*a.*

1*a.* Anthony Morris Storer of Purley Park, J.P., b. 25 *Sept.* 1816 ; d. 5 *Ap.* 1902 ; m. 15 *Nov.* 1860, *Cicely Barr* (*Purley Park, Reading*), *da. of Sir John Pollard Willoughby, 4th Bart.* [*G.B.*]; *and had issue* 1*b.*

1*b.* Leila Minna Gertrude Storer, *m.* 15 Jan. 1889, George Frederick Downing Fullerton (*Sherfield Hall, Basingstoke*) ; and has issue 1*c to* 4*c.*

[No. 6657.

The Plantagenet Roll

1c. George Cecil Downing Fullerton, b. 7 May 1891.

2c. Richard Alexis Downing Fullerton, b. 12 Oct. 1893.

3c. Ivy Leila Fullerton, b. 4 Oct. 1889.

4c. Myra Acida Violet Downing Fullerton, b. 30 June 1896.

2a. *Margaret Storer*, b. 30 *Nov.* 1819; d. 17 *Mar.* 1902; m. 14 *Ap.* 1847, *the Rev. William Edward Sellon, M.A., Rector of Langua and Kentchurch*, b. 19 *May* 1819; d. 23 *Feb.* 1885; *and had issue 1b to 5b.*

1b. Rev. William Storer Sellon, Rector of Kettlebaston (*Kettlebaston Rectory, Ipswich*), b. 23 Sept. 1848; m. 11 June 1889, Margaret Anne, da. of Harry Turner of Leominster, s.p.

2b. Stephen Prescott White D'Alte Sellon (36 *Victoria Street, Westminster*), b. 24 Feb. 1853; m. 13 Sept. 1884, Wine Field Mary Alice, da. of Charles Evan MacDougall of Dunolly Castle; and has issue 1c to 2c.

1c. Stephanie May Sellon, b. 24 Aug. 1885.

2c. Cicely Sellon, b. 28 Sept. 1886.

3b. Anthony Gilbert Sellon (*Heimat, Chatham*), b. 8 May 1855; m. 24 Nov. 1898, Hortense, da. of [———] Deidesheim of Switzerland; and has issue 1c.

1c. Hugh Gilbert René Sellon, b. 22 Sept. 1902.

4b. Anne Katherine Fanny Sellon, b. 2 Jan. 1850.

5b. Priscilla Lydia Sellon, b. 20 Mar. 1851.   [Nos. 6658 to 6669.

109. Descendants of FRANCES STORER (see Table VIII.), b. 1780; d. 8 Ap. 1821; m. 19 Sept. 1800, the Rev. RICHARD HUTCHINS WHITELOCKE, M.A., Vicar of Skillington, co. Lincoln, b. 11 May 1772; d. 14 Aug. 1833; and had issue 1a to 3a.

1a. *Hugh Anthony Whitelocke, Custos of Hanover, Jamaica*, b. 24 Feb. 1804; d. 14 *Sept.* 1869; m. 19 *Aug.* 1846, *Helen Campbell, da. of Thomas Tate; and had issue 1b to 5b.*

1b. Frederick William Moncrieffe Whitelocke (*Moreland, Jamaica*), b. 9 Oct. 1859; m. 27 Ap. 1899, Gertrude Henslowe, da. of Frederick Wilmot Taylor; and has issue 1c to 3c.

1c. Leslie Wilmot Stewart Whitelocke, b. 13 June 1901.

2c. Helen Anglin Whitelocke, b. 27 Jan. 1900.

3c. Evelyn Constance Whitelocke, b. 26 Jan. 1903.

2b. Richard Henry Anglin Whitelocke, M.D., F.R.C.S. (6 *Banbury Road, Oxford*), b. 13 Aug. 1861; m. 3 July 1889, Barbara, da. of George Lowe Reid; and has issue 1c to 5c.

1c. Hugh Anthony Bulstrode Whitelocke, b. 9 June 1891.

2c. Gilbert Charles Anglin Whitelocke, b. 13 Aug. 1893.

3c. Madeline Lowe Reid Whitelocke, b. 24 May 1898.

4c. Mary Anglin Whitelocke, } b. (twins) 8 July 1901.
5c. Nora Helen Whitelocke, }

3b. Thomas Edward Whitelocke, b. 11 Mar. 1864.

4b. Charles Oliver Tate Whitelocke (*Bulstrode Park, Jamaica*), b. 18 Oct. 1866; m. 27 Sept. 1900, Esther Beatrice, da. of Philip Hart; and has issue 1c.

1c. Roland Winston Bulstrode Whitelocke, b. 16 Oct. 1905.

5b. Fanny Anglin Whitelocke, b. 5 Aug. 1851; m. 30 Sept. 1880, Thomas Stewart McNeel (*Petersville, Jamaica*).

2a. *Frances Elizabeth Whitelocke*, b. 15 *July* 1808; d. 23 *Sept.* 1881; m. 27 *Oct.*
           [Nos. 6670 to 6683.

186

# of The Blood Royal

1830, *James Heywood of Brooksbank, Chorlton, Lancashire,* b. 15 *Ap.* 1805; d. 17 *Ap.* 1836; *and had issue* 1b *to* 3b.

1b. John James Heywood, Major-General in the Army (*Pinewood, Tunbridge Wells*), b. 24 July 1832; *m.* 27 Oct. 1860, Anna, da. of Major-Gen. East Apthorp, C.B.

2b. Frances Ann Heywood, b. 9 Aug. 1831; *m.* 19 Feb. 1851, Hugh Hughes of Hoddesdon, Herts.

3b. Charlotte Heywood (3 *Rusthall Mansions, Bedford Park, London, W.*), b. 27 Jan. 1834; *m.* 26 Aug. 1856, the Rev. Frederick Ripley, M.A., b. 18 Feb. 1827; d. 6 Aug. 1899; *and has issue* 1c *to* 4c.

1c. Rev. Reginald John Ripley, sometime (1900–1904) Rector, Cathedral Church, Spanishtown, Jamaica, Organising Secretary S.P.G. (131 *Hurst Grove, Bedford*), b. 6 Nov. 1863; *m.* 13 May 1893, Ella Maud, da. of Edmund Brown Stephenson; and has issue 1d to 5d.

1d. Reginald Charles Proby Ripley, b. 6 Oct. 1894.

2d. Robert Lionel Apthorp Ripley, b. 18 Ap. 1889.

3d. Dorothy Ruth Heywood Ripley, b. 22 Ap. 1896.

4d. Hilda Monica Ripley, b. 23 Ap. 1902.

5d. Florence Margaret Ripley, b. 17 Aug. 1903.

2c. *Frederick Arthur Ripley of Manaqua, Nicaragua,* b. 17 *Aug.* 1867; d. (? *unm.*) *July* 1905.

3c. Emily Margaret Ripley, b. 7 Dec. 1865.

4c. Florence Mary Ripley, b. 24 Nov. 1869.

3a. *Charlotte Julia Whitelocke,* b. 1 *Jan.* 1818; d. 28 *June* 1884; *m.* 26 *May* 1846, *the Rev. John Bowman Turner, M.A., Rector of Barford, Norfolk,* b. 6 *July* 1816; d. 7 *Feb.* 1892; *and had issue* 1b *to* 2b.

1b. Francis Bowman Turner (*Syston, Leicestershire*), b. 31 Aug. 1849; *m.* 8 June 1871, Barbara Lucy, da. of the Rev. William Grigson, M.A.; and has issue 1c to 2c.

1c. Katharine Mary Turner, b. 21 Dec. 1871.

2c. Mabel Frances Turner, b. 3 Mar. 1875; *m.* 24 June 1902, Lawrence Rea (*Boscombe, Bournemouth*).

2b. Henry Whitelocke Turner, M.A., Rector of North Runcton, Norfolk (*North Runcton Rectory, Norfolk*), b. 31 Aug. 1851; *m.* 20 July 1887, Blanche Beatrice, da. of Isaac Bugg Coaks; and has issue 1c to 2c.

1c. Anthony Whitelocke Turner, b. 15 Ap. 1890.

2c. Leila Whitelocke Turner, b. 12 May 1888. [Nos. 6684 to 6700.

110. Descendants, if any, of the Rev. CHARLES PROBY, Rector of Stanwich, co. Northants (see Table VIII.), *m.* CATHERINE, da. of the Rev. Baptist PROBY, Dean of Lichfield; · BAPTIST LEVESON PROBY; and of their sisters.

111. Descendants of the Rev. BAPTIST PROBY, Dean of Lichfield, D.D. (see Table VIII.), d. 18 Jan. 1807; *m.* MARY, da. of the Rev. John RUSSELL, Rector of Fisherton; and had issue.

See the Clarence Volume, pp. 611–613, Nos. 26811–26885.

[Nos. 6701 to 6776.

The Plantagenet Roll

112. Descendants of CHARLES (NOEL), 1st EARL OF GAINSBOROUGH, 3rd BARON BARNHAM [U.K.] (see Table IX.), b. 2 Oct. 1781; d. 10 June 1866; m. 2ndly, 13 May 1817, ELIZABETH, da. of the Hon. Sir George GREY, 1st Bart. [U.K.], d. 20 Sept. 1818; 3rdly, 29 June 1820, ARABELLA, da. of Sir James Hamlyn WILLIAMS, 2nd Bart. [G.B.], d. 4 Oct. 1829; 4thly, 25 July 1833, Lady FRANCES, V.A., da. of Robert (JOCELYN), 3rd Earl of Roden [I.], b. 20 Nov. 1814; d. 12 May 1885; and had issue 1a to 7a.

1a. *Charles George (Noel), 2nd Earl of Gainsborough [U.K.]*, b. 5 Sept. 1818; d. 13 Aug. 1881; m. 1 Nov. 1841, Lady Adelaide Harriet Augusta, da. of William George (Hay), 16th Earl of Erroll [S.], K.T., b. 18 Oct. 1821; d. 22 Oct. 1867; and had issue 1b to 4b.

1b. Charles William Francis (Noel), 3rd Earl of Gainsborough [U.K.], &c. (*Exton Park, Oakham; Campden House, co. Chester*), b. 20 Oct. 1850; m. 1st, 9 May 1876, Augusta Mary, da. of Robert Berkeley of Spetchley, d. 5 Nov. 1877; 2ndly, 2 Feb. 1880, Mary Elizabeth, da. of James Arthur Dease of Turbotston; and has issue 1c to 6c.

1c. Arthur Edward Joseph Noel, Viscount Campden, b. 30 June 1884.

2c. Hon. Charles Hubert Francis Noel, b. 22 Oct. 1885.

3c. Hon. Robert Edmund Thomas More Noel, b. 10 Ap. 1888.

4c. Lady Agnes Mary Catherine Noel, b. 9 Oct. 1877.

5c. Lady Norah Ida Emily Noel, b. 4 Jan. 1881.

6c. Lady Clare Mary Charlotte Noel, b. 3 Mar. 1882.

2b. Hon. Edward Noel, Lieut.-Col. *late* Rifle Brigade, sometime D.A.A.G., Ceylon (*Junior United Service*), b. 28 Ap. 1852; m. 7 Oct. 1884, Ruth, da. of W. H. Lucas of Treniffle; and has issue 1c to 3c.

1c. Edward William Charles Noel, b. 14 Ap. 1886.

2c. Hubert Lewis Clifford Noel, b. 19 Oct. 1888.

3c. Baptist Lucius Noel, b. 26 Feb. 1890.

3b. *Lady Blanche Elizabeth Mary Annunciata Noel*, b. 25 Mar. 1845; d. 21 Mar. 1881; m. 6 Mar. 1870, Thomas P. Murphy, d. 11 Oct. 1890.

4b. *Lady Constance Julia Eleanor Georgiana Noel*, b. 19 Oct. 1847; d. 8 Ap. 1891; m. as 1st wife, 13 Jan. 1874, Sir Alan Henry Bellingham, 4th Bart. [G.B.], a Senator of the Royal University, J.P., D.L. (*The Castle, Castle Bellingham, co. Louth*); and had issue 1c to 4c.

1c. Edward Henry Charles Patrick Bellingham, *late* Lieut. Royal Scots, b. 26 Jan. 1879; m. 11 June 1904, Charlotte Elizabeth, widow of Frederick Gough, da. of Alfred Payne.

2c. Roger Charles Noel Bellingham, b. 28 Ap. 1884.

3c. Ida Mary Elizabeth Agnes Bellingham, a nun.

4c. Augusta Mary Monica Bellingham, m. 6 July 1905, John (Crichton-Stuart), 4th Marquis of Bute [G.B.], 9th Earl of Dumfries, and 7th Earl of Bute [S.], Hereditary Keeper of Rothesay Castle, &c. (*Mount Stuart, Rothesay; Cardiff Castle, co. Glamorgan; St. John's Lodge, Regent's Park, N.W.; Dumfries House, Ayrshire; 5 Charlotte Square, Edinburgh*).

2a. Right Hon. and Hon. Gerard James Noel of Catmose, Oakham, P.C., M.P., J.P., D.L., sometime (1876–1880) First Commr. of Works, &c. (*Catmose, Oakham*), b. 28 Aug. 1823; m. 30 June 1863, Lady Augusta Mary, sister to Henry, 3rd Earl of Lonsdale [U.K.], da. of the Hon. Henry Cecil Lowther, M.P.; and has issue 1b to 2b.   [Nos. 6777 to 6792.

188

# of The Blood Royal

1b. Gerard Cecil Noel, *late* Capt. Northants Regt., *b.* 4 Dec. 1864; *m.* 10 Feb. 1897, Madeline Edith, da. of Thomas Henry Clifton of Lytham; and has issue 1c to 2c.

  1c. Tom Cecil Noel, *b.* 12 Dec. 1897.

  2c. Charles Cecil Noel, *b.* 27 Nov. 1904.

2b. Henry Cecil Noel, Capt. *late* 17th Lancers, *b.* 23 May 1868; *m.* 2 Ap. 1902, Frances Mary, da. of Frederick Pepys Cockerill.

3a. *Hon. Henry Lewis Noel*, b. 30 *Nov.* 1824; d. 7 *June* 1898; m. 1*st*, 27 *May* 1852, *Emily Elizabeth, da. of Rev. the Hon. Baptist Wriothesley Noel*, d. 3 *Oct.* 1890; *and had issue 1b to 6b.*

  1b. Gerard Thomas Noel, J.P., *late* Major Durham L.I. (*Wyld Court, Axminster*), *b.* 13 May 1856; *m.* 19 Jan. 1888, Edith Mary, da. of Rev. the Hon. William Byron; and has issue 1c to 4c.

    1c. John Byron Noel, *b.* 6 Ap. 1891.

    2c. William Henry Middleton Noel, *b.* 11 Sept. 1898.

    3c. Mary Cecily Noel, *b.* 15 Nov. 1888.

    4c. Audrey Noel, *b.* 7 May 1894.

  2b. Hugh Middleton Noel (*Langley Lodge, Hants*), *b.* 3 Ap. 1862; *m.* 20 June 1901, Helen Winifred, da. of Robert Gibbs of The Cedars, Yardley, Hastings; and has issue.

    1c. Geoffrey Francis Middleton Noel, *b.* 1902.

  3b. Henry Hamlyn Noel (*Handford, King's co., California*), *b.* 8 June 1874; *m.* 28 Ap. 1897, Mary, da. of John Lauer Oliver; and has issue 1c to 3c.

    1c. Edward Frances Hamlyn Noel, *b.* 4 Jan. 1899.

    2c. Gerard Hamlyn Noel, *b.* Feb. 1900.

    3c. Mildred Mary Hamlyn Noel.

  4b. Evelyn Mary Noel, *m.* 10 Nov. 1880, Herbert Robinson Arbuthnot (76 *Westbourne Terrace, W.*); and has issue 1c to 4c.

    1c. Ashley Herbert Arbuthnot, *b.* 1884

    2c. Evelyn Marion Arbuthnot, *b.* 1881

    3c. Mary Sybil Arbuthnot, } *b.* (twins) 1883.
    4c. Frances Emily Arbuthnot, }

  5b. Gertrude Arabella Noel, *m.* 3 Dec. 1891, Thomas Cheney Garfit (*Kenwick Hall, Louth, co. Lincoln*); and has issue 1c to 4c.

    1c. Thomas Noel Cheney Garfit, *b.* 1892.

    2c. Edward Christopher Cheney Garfit, *b.* 1899.

    3c. Mary Elizabeth Garfit, *b.* 1893.

    4c. Violet Emily Garfit, *b.* 1894.

  6b. Emilia Frances Noel (*Leybourne, Lincoln*).

4a. (Son by 4th wife and his children.) See the Clarence Volume, p. 291, Nos. 8140–8142.

5a. *Lady Mary Arabella Louisa Noel*, b. 16 *Mar.* 1822; d. 27 *June* 1883; m. *Aug.* 1846, *Sir Andrew Agnew of Lochnaw, 8th Bart.* [S.], *M.P.*, b. 2 *Jan.* 1818; d. 25 *Mar.* 1892; *and had issue 1b to 12b.*

  1b. Sir Andrew Noel Agnew of Lochnaw, 9th Bart. [S.], M.P., &c. (*Lochnaw Castle, Stranraer, co. Wigtown; 21 Abingdon Street, Westminster*), *b.* 14 Aug. 1850; *m.* 15 Oct. 1889, Gertrude, da. of the Hon. Gowran Charles Vernon.

  2b. Henry de Courcy Agnew, J.P. (13 *Southwark Crescent, Hyde Park, W.; Kenward, Yalding, Maidstone*), *b.* 1 Nov. 1851; *m.* 23 Dec. 1885, Ethel, da. of Capt. Thomas Goff of Oakport; and has issue 1c to 2c.

    1c. Dorothea Alma Agnew.

    2c. Hazel Louisa Agnew.

         [Nos. 6793 to 6825.

                                    2 B

The Plantagenet Roll

3b. Charles Hamlyn Agnew, J.P., Major 4th Hussars (*Naval and Military, Cavalry, &c.*), b. 21 June 1859; m. 30 June 1897, Lilian Anne, da. of Major-Gen. Sir James Wolfe Murray, K.C.B.; and has issue 1c.

    1c. Fulque Melville Gerald Noel Agnew, b. 5 Oct. 1900.

4b. Quentin Graham Kinnaird Agnew, M.V.O., D.S.O., J.P., Major Manchester Regt., and Assist. Mil. Sec. to Com.-in-Chief at Gibraltar, &c. (*Naval and Military*), b. 8 Jan. 1861; m. 9 Feb. 1899, Evelyn Mary, da. of Capt. John Hobhouse Lugles Alexander, R.N., C.B.; and has issue 1c.

    1c. Quentin David Hope Agnew, b. 7 Feb. 1900.

5b. Gerard Dalrymple Agnew, *late* Lieut. The Buffs, b. 24 Ap. 1862.

6b. Madeline Diana Elizabeth Agnew, m. 1st, 7 Feb. 1867, Thomas Henry Clifton of Lytham, M.P., d. 31 Mar. 1880; 2ndly, 30 Jan. 1889, Sir James Hamlyn Williams Williams-Drummond, 4th Bart. [U.K.] (*Edwinsford, Llandilo; Hawthornden, Midlothian*); and has issue 1c to 7c.

    1c. John Talbot Clifton of Clifton (*Lytham Hall, Lytham*), b. 1 Dec. 1868.

    2c. Harry Arthur Clifton, Lieut. 7th Dragoons, b. 5 Sept. 1874; m. Jan. 1903, Gladys, da. of Sir Griffith Humphrey Hugh Evans, K.C.I.E.

    3c. Charles Caryl Clifton, Lieut. 2nd Batt. Royal Scots Fusiliers, b. 25 Ap.1877.

    4c. James Hamlyn Williams Williams-Drummond, b. 25 May 1891.

    5c. Madeline Edith Clifton, m. 10 Feb. 1897, Capt. Gerald Cecil Noel; and has issue 1d.

        1d. See p. 189, Nos. 6794–6795.

    6c. Constance Gertrude Cecily Clifton, m. 8 Dec. 1891, Capt. the Hon. James Frederick Hovell-Thurlow-Cumming-Bruce, d.s.p., v.p. (at Magersfontein) 11 Dec. 1899.

    7c. Frances Victoria Clifton, m. 25 June 1903, the Hon. Kenneth Fitz-Gerald Kinnaird (*Orchard House, Bickley, Kent*); and has issue 1d.

        1d. Anne Barbara Kinnaird, b. 1904.

7b. Arabella Frances Georgiana Agnew, } twins.
8b. Caroline Charlotte Agnew,

9b. Louisa Lucia Agnew, m. 10 July 1877, Duncan Macneill; and has issue 1c to 6c.

    1c. Andrew Duncan Macneill, b. 1881.

    2c. William Mackinnon Macneill, b. 1890.

    3c. Alma Louisa Macneill, m. 17 Ap. 1902, the Rev. Cyril Percival Heywood, Vicar of Titley (*Titley Vicarage, co. Hereford*).

    4c. Elizabeth Evelyn Macneill.

    5c. Cecilia Christian Macneill.

    6c. Constance Isabella Macneill.

10b. Mary Alma Victoria Agnew, m. 19 Aug. 1875, Arthur Fitzgerald (Kinnaird), 11th [S.] and 3rd [U.K.] Baron Kinnaird (*Rossie Priory, Inchture; 10 St. James's Square, S.W.*); and has issue 1c to 5c.

    1c. Douglas Arthur Kinnaird, Master of Kinnaird, Lieut. Scots Guards, b. Aug. 1879.

    2c. Hon. Kenneth Fitzgerald Kinnaird (*Orchard House, Bickley, Kent*), b. 31 July 1880; m. 25 June 1903, Frances Victoria, da. of Thomas Henry Clifton of Lytham, M.P.; and has issue 1d.

        1d. See p. 190, No. 6841.

    3c. Hon. Arthur Middleton Kinnaird, b. 20 Ap. 1885.

    4c. Hon. Patrick Charles Kinnaird, b. 4 Dec. 1898.

    5c. Hon. Margaret Alma Kinnaird, b. 27 Jan. 1892.

11b. Rosina Constance Agnew, m. 14 Ap. 1898, the Rev. James Davidson, M.A. (*Blackadder Manse, North Berwick*); and has issue 1c to 2c.

                                           [Nos. 6826 to 6858.

# of The Blood Royal

1c. Andrew Nevile Davidson, b. 13 Feb. 1899.

2c. Louisa Margaret Constance Davidson, b. 26 Feb. 1901.

12b. Marguerite Violet Maud Agnew, m. 23 July 1890, Francis Dudley Williams-Drummond, J.P., D.L., Capt. Carmarthen Art. (Portiscliff, Ferryside, South Wales); and has issue 1c to 3c.

1c. William Hugh Dudley Williams-Drummond, b. 13 Feb. 1901.

2c. Eleanor Mary Williams-Drummond, b. 16 June 1891.

3c. Constance Marie Katherine Williams-Drummond, b. 3 June 1893.

6a. *Lady Catherine Hamilton Noel*, b. 29 *Sept.* 1829; d. 9 *Mar.* 1855; m. as *first wife*, 19 *June* 1849, *James* (Carnegie), 9th *Earl of Southesk and* 6th *Bart.* [S.], 1st *Baron Balinhard* [U.K.], K.T., d. 21 *Feb.* 1905; *and had issue* 1b *to* 4b.

1b. Charles Noel (Carnegie), 10th Earl of Southesk and 7th Bart. [S.], 2nd Baron Balinhard [U.K.] (Kinnaird Castle, Brechin, N.B.; Crimonmogate, Lonmay; Elsick, Kincardine), b. 20 Mar. 1854; m. 1 Aug. 1891, Ethel Mary Elizabeth,[1] da. and heir of Sir Alexander Bannerman, 10th Bart. [S.]; and has issue 1c to 4c.

1c. Charles Alexander Carnegie, Lord Carnegie, b. 23 Sept. 1893.

2c. Hon. Alexander Bannerman Carnegie, b. 30 Dec. 1894.

3c. Lady Katherine Ethel Carnegie, b. 12 June 1892.

4c. Lady Mary Elizabeth Carnegie, b. 4 Nov. 1898.

2b. Lady Arabella Charlotte Carnegie, m. 7 Feb. 1878, Samuel Henry Romilly, J.P., D.L. (56 Eccleston Square, S.W.; Huntington Park, Kington, co. Hereford); and has issue 1c to 5c.

1c. Bertram Henry Samuel Romilly, D.S.O., Capt. Scots Guards, b. 6 Nov. 1878.

2c. Frederic Carnegie Romilly, b. 10 Sept. 1886.

3c. Cicely Elisabeth Romilly.

4c. Dorothea Katharine Romilly.

5c. Constance Felicity Romilly.

3b. Lady Constance Mary Carnegie, C.I., m. 9 Nov. 1876, Victor Alexander (Bruce), 9th Earl of Elgin, 13th Earl of Kincardine [S.], 2nd Baron Elgin [U.K.], K.G., P.C., G.C.S.I., G.C.I.E., &c. (Broomhall, Dunfermline; 29 Hyde Park Gate, S.W.); and has issue 1c to 10c.

1c. Edward James Bruce, Lord Bruce (Bachelors'), b. 8 June 1881.

2c. Hon. Robert Bruce, Lieut. 11th Hussars, b. 18 Nov. 1882.

3c. Hon. Alexander Bruce, b. 29 July 1884.

4c. Hon. David Bruce, b. 11 June 1888.

5c. Hon. John Bernard Bruce, b. 9 Ap. 1892.

6c. Hon. Victor Alexander Bruce, b. 13 Feb. 1897.

7c. Lady Elizabeth Mary Bruce, b. 11 Sept. 1877; m. 22 Sept. 1898, Henry Babington Smith, C.B., C.S.I. (29 Hyde Park Gate, S.W.); and has issue 1d to 3d.

1d. Michael James Babington Smith, b. 20 Mar. 1901.

2d. Henry George Babington Smith, b. 13 Oct. 1902.

3d. Bernard Babington Smith, b. 26 Oct. 1905.

8c. Lady Christian Augusta Bruce, b. 25 Jan. 1879, m. 15 Dec. 1904, Herbert Kinnaird Ogilvy (Auchterhouse, Forfar).

9c. Lady Constance Veronica Bruce, b. 24 Feb. 1880.

10c. Lady Rachel Catherine Bruce, b. 23 Feb. 1890.

4b. Lady Beatrice Diana Cecilia Carnegie, m. 28 July 1874, the Rev. Henry Holmes Stewart, Rector of Porthkerry (The Rectory, Barry, Cardiff); and has issue 1c to 5c. [Nos. 6859 to 6890.

---

[1] See the Clarence Volume, p. 224, for her descent from George of Clarence.

The Plantagenet Roll

1*c*. Gilbert Carnegie Stewart, *b.* 27 June 1875.
2*c*. Charles Montgomery Stewart, *b.* 8 Oct. 1876.
3*c*. Herbert Noel Stewart, Lieut. R.N., *b.* 9 Ap. 1881.
4*c*. Catherine Elizabeth Stewart, *b.* 11 Dec. 1877.
5*c*. Mabel Constance Stewart, *b.* 12 Sept. 1879.
7*a*. (Da. by 4th wife and her children.) See the Clarence Volume, pp. 291–292, Nos. 8143–8174.   [Nos. 6891 to 6927.

113. Descendants of Rev. the Hon. GERARD THOMAS NOEL, Canon of Winchester (see Table IX.), *b.* 2 Dec. 1782; *d.* 24 Feb. 1851; *m.* 1st, 1 Feb. 1806, CHARLOTTE SOPHIA, da. of Sir Lucius O'BRIEN, 3rd Bart. [I.], *d.* 31 Aug. 1838; and had issue 1*a* to 3*a*.

1*a*. Anna Sophia Noel, b. 6 Nov. 1806; d. 17 Feb. 1857; m. 10 Oct. 1832, the Ven. Philip Jacob, Archdeacon and Canon of Winchester, Rector of Crawley, d. 1885; and had issue [1] 1b to 6b.
1*b*. Augustus Jacob, *b.* 20 Aug. 1839.
2*b*. Ernest Henry Jacob, *b.* 5 Ap. 1849.
3*b*. Cecil Jacob, *b.* 29 Aug. 1851.
4*b*. Edith Sophia Jacob.
5*b*. Gertrude Louisa Jacob.
6*b*. Isabel Margaret Jacob, *m.* 2 Oct. 1862, the Rev. William Henry Castleman, Vicar of The Edge, co. Gloucester; and has issue 1*c* to 4*c*.
1*c*. Margaret Ellen Castleman.
2*c*. Lilian Gertrude Castleman.
3*c*. Mabel Sophia Castleman.
4*c*. Grace Emma Castleman.

2*a*. Charlotte Christiana Noel, d. 19 Dec. 1848; m. as 1st wife, 10 Oct. 1832, the Rev. James Drummond Money, Vicar of Sternfield, co. Suffolk, b. 26 Ap. 1805; d. 20 Ap. 1875; and had issue (7 sons and 4 das.[1]).
3*a*. Elizabeth Welman Noel, b. Ap. 1817; d. 26 Sept. 1868; m. 7 Ap. 1853, the Rev. George Augustus Seymour, Rector of Holy Trinity and Master of St. Mary Magdalene, Winchester; and had issue [1] 1b.
1*b*. Geraldine Mary Seymour.   [Nos. 6928 to 6938.

114. Descendants of the Hon. FREDERIC NOEL, Capt. R.N. (see Table IX.), *b.* 26 Ap. 1790; *d.* 27 Dec. 1833; *m.* 7 Sept. 1815, MARY, da. of William WOODLEY (who re-m. 1838 Lieut.-Gen. Sir Thomas Hawker, K.C.H.), *d.* 24 Jan. 1867; and had issue 1*a* to 2*a*.

1*a*. Rev. Augustus William Noel, Rector of Stanhoe, b. 30 July 1816; d. 1884; m. 16 June 1841, Lucy Elizabeth, da. of Capt. Norris William Tonge of Alveston, R.N., d. 1874; and had issue 1b to 3b.
1*b*. Rev. Frederic Augustus Douglas Noel, sometime (1863–1893) in the Exchequer and Audit Office, and afterwards Rector of Staunton, *b.* 28 Aug. 1843.
2*b*. Sir Gerard Henry Uctred Noel, K.C.B., K.C.M.G., Vice-Admiral R.N., a Naval Lord of the Admiralty, *formerly* A.D.C. to H.M. Queen Victoria (5 *Chester*
                                                                    [Nos. 6939 to 6940.

---

[1] Foster's " Peerage," 1880, p. 272.

# of The Blood Royal

Place, S.W.), *b.* 5 Mar. 1845; *m.* 11 Aug. 1875, Charlotte Rachel Frederica, da. of Francis Joseph Cresswell of King's Lynn; and has issue 1c to 3c.

1c. Francis Arthur Gerard Noel, *b.* 3 Dec. 1880.

2c. Charlotte Ida Frederica Noel, *b.* 11 Mar. 1878.

3c. Constance Ida Diana Noel, *b.* 21 June 1879.

3b. Ida Lucy Noel (*Staunton, near Coleford, co. Gloucester*).

2a. *Fanny Louisa Noel*, b. 16 *Oct.* 1820; d. *Ap.* 1901; m. 28 *June* 1843, *Henry Victor Malan de Merindol, of St. Catherine's Hill, Guildford, M.A., M.D.,* d. 23 *Jan.* 1879 ; *and had issue* [1] *1b to 5b.*

1b. Henry Noel de Merindol, *b.* 4 July 1850; *m.* 6 Sept. 1876, Mary Louisa, da. of the Rev. H. F. Brook, Canon of York; and has issue 1c.

1c. Leslie Noel de Merindol, *b.* 21 July 1877.

2b. Cæsar Frederic de Merindol, *b.* 1 Nov. 1852.

3b. Ernest de Merindol, *b.* 18 Aug. 1858.

4b. Emma Louisa Maud de Merindol.

5b. Gertrude Alice de Merindol, *m.* as 2nd wife, 4 Oct. 1876, Benjamin de Montmorency Dowson.   [Nos. 6941 to 6950.

115. Descendants of Rev. the Hon. FRANCIS JAMES NOEL, M.A. (see Table IX.), *b.* 4 May 1793; *d.* 30 July 1854; *m.* 24 Ap. 1822, CECILIA PENELOPE, da. of Paul Cobb METHUEN of Corsham, M.P., *b.* 1 June 1798; *d.* 27 June 1885; and had issue 1*a* to 4*a*.

1a. *Edward Andrew Noel, J.P., D.L., one of H.M. Corps of Gentlemen-at-Arms, &c., b.* 2 *Jan.* 1825; d. 18 *Feb.* 1899; m. 24 *Aug.* 1848, *Sarah Gay, da. of W. B. Darwin of Elston Hall, d.* 15 *June* 1889; *and had issue 1b to 7b.*

1b. William Frederick Noel (*The Great House, North Nibley, co. Gloucester*), sometime (1899–1901) Col. on the Staff, R.E., in Natal, Col. R.E., J.P., *b.* 8 Aug. 1849; *m.* 1st, 4 Feb. 1879, Josephine Annie (div. 26 June 1883), da. of Joseph Watts Halliwell of Stratford Park, Stroud, *d.* Mar. 1904; 2ndly, 21 Jan. 1885, Beatrice Elizabeth, da. of the Rev. Joseph Christopher Bradney, M.A., *d.* 16 Oct. 1889; 3rdly, 2 Sept. 1896, Laura Carolina, da. of Charles Henry Beilby, *d.* 5 July 1897; and has issue 1c to 4c.

1c. Cecil Gerard Frederick Noel, *b.* 22 Dec. 1880.

2c. Maurice Waldegrave Noel, *b.* 30 Dec. 1888.

3c. Sarah Dorothy Beatrice Noel, *b.* 2 July 1886.

4c. Audrey Noel, *b.* 17 June 1897.

2b. Francis Charles Methuen Noel, Capt. R.N. (*Junior United Service*), *b.* 5 June 1852; *m.* 27 Oct. 1886, Wilmot Juliana, da. of Thomas Maitland Snow of Cleve House, Exeter; and has issue 1c to 3c.

1c. Francis Methuen Noel, *b.* 28 Dec. 1888.

2c. Montague Wriothesley Noel, R.N., *b.* 12 Nov. 1892.

3c. Mary Penelope Noel, *b.* 10 Aug. 1887.

3b. Robert Lascelles Gambier Noel, Capt. (ret.) R.N. (80 *Colherne Court, South Kensington, S.W.*), *b.* 27 June 1855; *m.* 23 Mar. 1887, Letitia Louisa Carmela, da. of the Rev. S. W. Koelle, D.Ph.; and has issue 1c to 3c.

1c. Gambier Baptist Edward Noel, *b.* 24 June 1888.

2c. Norman Philpot Robert Noel, *b.* 15 July 1891.

3c. John Andrew Vernatti Noel, *b.* 23 May 1893.   [Nos. 6951 to 6963.

---

[1] Foster's "Peerage," 1880, p. 272.

193

The Plantagenet Roll

4b. James Wriothesley Noel (*Junior Carlton*), b. 3 Oct. 1861.

5b. Anne Noel Noel, b. 31 Oct. 1853; d. 10 Dec. 1887; m. 5 Aug. 1873, Col. Thomas Hamilton Forsyth, 62nd Regt. (*Northwold, Bournemouth*); and had issue 1c to 3c.

    1c. Ronald Graham Hamilton Forsyth, b. 1 Dec. 1875; m. 1904, Helen Crosbie, da. of [——] Sawyer of St. Barbara, California; and has issue 1d.

    1d. Thomas Hamilton Forsyth, b. 1 Sept. 1905.

    2c. Annie Cecilia Noel Forsyth.

    3c. Mary Beatrice Gertrude Forsyth.

6b. Matilda Catherine Noel, m. 19 Sept. 1893, John Charles Griffith, J.P., Col. Comdg. 2nd Vol. Batt. Gloucester Regt., three times Mayor of Cheltenham (*Deanwood House, Pitville, Cheltenham*); and has issue 1c to 2c.

    1c. Edward Noel Griffith, b. 14 Oct. 1896.

    2c. Mary Catherine Griffith, b. 25 July 1894.

7b. Eleanor Agnes Noel, m. 31 Dec. 1889, Francis Joseph Cade, M.A., Head Master Junior Department, Cheltenham College (*Teighmore, Cheltenham*).

2a. Rev. Montague Henry Noel, M.A. (Oxon.), b. 18 Dec. 1840.

3a. Matilda Catherine Emma Noel, m. 4 Aug. 1849, Sir Edward Leigh-Pemberton, K.C.B. (5 *Warwick Square, S.W. ; Torry Hill, Sittingbourne, Kent*); and has issue 1b to 4b.

    1b. Robert Leigh-Pemberton, J.P., late Capt. 3rd Batt. Queen's Own (*Army and Navy*), b. 25 Dec. 1852; m. 5 June 1883, Edith Selina Hay, da. of Robert Hay Murray; and has issue 1c to 3c.

        1c. Robert Douglas Pemberton, b. 27 Ap. 1896.

        2c. Nora Edith Pemberton, b. 12 Mar. 1884.

        3c. Elsie Alice Pemberton, b. 29 Dec. 1889.

    2b. Wilfred Leigh-Pemberton, Bar.-at-Law (*Wrinsted Court, Sittingbourne ; 21 Old Square, Lincoln's Inn*), b. 19 June 1854; m. 1 Jan. 1891, Alice Augusta, da. of Capt. David Holland Erskine ; and has issue 1c.

        1c. Thomas Edward Geoffrey Pemberton, b. 15 Nov. 1893.

    3b. Mary Beatrice Pemberton.

    4b. Maud Cicely Pemberton.

4a. Millicent Mary Noel, m. 8 June 1852, Berkeley Plantagenet Guilford Charles Noel, J.P., D.L.; and has issue 1b to 4b.

    1b. Charles Francis Adderley Noel, late 2nd Dragoon Guards, b. 30 Aug. 1854.

    2b. Rev. Edward Henry Noel, M.A. (Oxon.), Rector of Frinsted (*Frinsted Rectory, near Sittingbourne*), b. 12 Feb. 1859.

    3b. James Harington Noel, b. 17 Feb. 1861.

    4b. Louisa Letitia Millicent Noel.   [Nos. 6964 to 6987.

116. Descendants of the Hon. BERKELEY OCTAVIUS NOEL (see Table IX.), b. 3 Dec. 1794; d. 28 Mar. 1841; m. 22 June 1820, LETITIA PENELOPE, widow of ANDREW HACKET of Moxhull Park, da. of Ralph ADDERLEY of Coton, co. Stafford, d. 18 Jan. 1860 ; and had issue 1a.

1a. Berkeley Plantagenet Guilford Charles Noel, J.P., D.L., late of Moxhull Park, co. Warwick, b. 29 July 1821 ; m. 8 June 1852, Millicent Mary, da. of Rev. the Hon. Francis James Noel ; and has issue 1b to 4b.

See p. 194, Nos. 6984–6987.   [Nos. 6988 to 6992.

# of The Blood Royal

117. Descendants of Rev. the Hon. LELAND NOEL (see Table IX.), *b.* 21 Aug. 1797; *d.* 10 Nov. 1870; *m.* 30 Dec. 1824, MARY ARABELLA, da. of John Savile FOLJAMBE of Osberton, *b.* 27 Nov. 1801; *d.* 2 May 1859; and had issue 1*a* to 2*a*.

See the Clarence Volume, p. 608, Nos. 26754–26757. [Nos. 6993 to 6996.

118. Descendants of Rev. the Hon. BAPTIST WRIOTHESLEY NOEL (see Table IX.), *b.* 10 July 1799; *d.* 19 Jan. 1873; *m.* 17 Oct. 1826, JANE, da. of Peter BAILLIE of Dochfour, *d.* 13 May 1889; and had issue 1*a* to 7*a*.

1*a*. *Wriothesley Noel, Judge of Insolvency and Land Tax Commr., Melbourne,* b. 15 *Aug.* 1827; d. 19 *May* 1886; m. 1858, *Margaret, da. of John M'Kenzie of Tain,* d. 6 *June* 1869; *and had issue* 1*b to* 2*b*.

1*b*. Guy Noel, Solicitor (*Lynton House,* 11 *Adamson Road, Hampstead*), b. 28 Dec. 1860; *m.* 2 June 1883, Blanche Mabel Mayne, da. of James Hatch Gibbs of Glenroy Park, Brighton, Victoria; and has issue 1*c* to 2*c*.

1*c*. Eleanor Baillie Noel, *b.* 21 Aug. 1885.

2*c*. Valerie Winifred Wriothesley Noel, *b.* 26 Oct. 1888.

2*b*. Eleanor Noel, *b.* 10 Nov. 1858; *m.* 1884, Alfred Cornish (*Dunraven, Toorak, Melbourne*).

2*a*. Ernest Noel, J.P., D.L., sometime (1874–1886) M.P. (*Hingham Hall, Norfolk;* 51 *South Street, Mayfair*), *b.* 18 Aug. 1831; *m.* 1st, 24 June 1857, Louisa Hope, da. of Thomas Milne of Warley House, co. York, *d.s.p.* 23 Aug. 1870; 2ndly, 15 Oct. 1873, Lady Augusta, da. of George Thomas (Keppel), 6th Earl Albemarle [E.], *d.* 1902.

3*a*. Albert Leland Noel (*St. Lawrence, Canterbury*), *b.* 4 Nov. 1835; *m.* 21 June 1859, Ella, da. of the Rev. Capel Molyneux; and has issue 1*b* to 3*b*.

1*b*. Barham Molyneux Noel (*Johannesburg*), *b.* 8 Feb. 1868; *m.* 4 Dec. 1895, Dorothy, da. of Spencer Brunton; and has issue 1*c*.

1*c*. Audrey Baillie Noel, *b.* 30 Dec. 1896.

2*b*. Dorothy Manners Noel.

3*b*. Ina Katharine Noel.

4*a*. Eugene Frederic Noel, J.P. (15 *Craven Hill Gardens, Hyde Park*), *b.* 18 Sept. 1839; *m.* 1 Aug. 1865, Ethel Maria, da. of Thomas Chapman, F.R.S.; and has issue 1*b* to 5*b*.

1*b*. Evan Baillie Noel, *b.* 23 Jan. 1879.

2*b*. Hilda Mary Noel.

3*b*. Margaret Eugenia Noel.

4*b*. Cicely Jane Noel.

5*b*. Inula Edith Noel.

5*a*. *Mary Jane Noel,* d. 16 *May* 1887; *m.* 23 *Ap.* 1868, *Thomas Anthony Denny of Beeding Wood, co. Sussex; and had issue.*

6*a*. *Emily Elizabeth Noel,* d. 3 *Oct.* 1890; m. *as* 1*st wife,* 27 *May* 1852, *the Hon. Henry Lewis Noel,* d. 7 *June* 1898; *and had issue.*

See p. 189, Nos. 6797–6818.

7*a*. Edith Louisa Noel. [Nos. 6997 to 7035.

195

The Plantagenet Roll

119. Descendants of the Hon. LOUISA ELIZABETH NOEL (see Table IX.), *b.* 20 Jan. 1786; *d.* 5 Jan. 1816; *m.* 10 Feb. 1807, WILLIAM HENRY HOARE of Mitcham Grove, co. Surrey, *b.* 2 Mar. 1776; *d.* 18 Sept. 1820; and had issue 1*a* to 5*a*.

1*a*. Henry Hoare *of Staplehurst, High Sheriff co. Kent* 1842, b. 27 *Dec.* 1807; *d.* 16 *Ap.* 1866; m. 3 *May* 1836, *Lady Mary, da. of Charles (Marsham), 2nd Earl of Romney [G.B.], b.* 15 *Ap.* 1811; *d.* 23 *Feb.* 1871; *and had issue* 1*b to* 9*b.*

1*b*. Henry Hoare *of Staplehurst,* b. 6 *Aug.* 1838; *d.* 5 *Aug.* 1898; m. 31 *Jan.* 1865, *Beatrice Ann, da. of the Rev. George Barber Paley of Langcliffe, co. York; and had issue* 1*c to* 9*c.*

1*c*. Henry Hoare, Capt. Loyal Suffolk Hussars (*Barking Hall, Needham Market, Suffolk*), *b.* 25 Dec. 1866; *m.* 28 Dec. 1898, Geraldine Mariana, da. of Lord Augustus Hervey; and has issue 1*d* to 3*d*.

1*d*. Henry Peregrine Hoare, *b.* 1901.

2*d*. Rollo Hoare, *b.* 1903.

3*d*. Angela Hoare, *b.* 1903.

2*c*. Frederick Henry Hoare, *b.* 13 Nov. 1871.

3*c*. Edward Henry Hoare, Lieut. The Buffs, *b.* 8 Oct. 1872.

4*c*. Robert Henry Hoare, *b.* 6 Nov. 1872.

5*c*. Eric Henry Hoare, *b.* 16 Dec. 1878.

6*c*. Beatrice Mary Hoare, *m.* 18 Dec. 1883, Arthur Edward Hollond (*Great Ashfield House, Bury St. Edmunds*); and has issue 1*d* to 7*d*.

1*d*. Henry Arthur Hollond, *b.* 14 Oct. 1884.

2*d*. Victor Andrew Hollond, *b.* 7 Oct. 1894.

3*d*. Gladys Margaret Beatrice Hollond.

4*d*. Phyllis Caroline Pansy Hollond.

5*d*. Muriel Matilda Hollond.

6*d*. Ivy Iseult Hollond.

7*d*. Elspeth Enid Hollond.

7*c*. Evangeline Hoare, *m.* as 3rd wife, 2 June 1900, Percy Brodrick Bernard, J.P., D.L. (*Castle Hacket, Tuam*); and has issue 1*d*.

1*d*. Morrogh Wyndham Percy Bernard, *b.* 5 Feb. 1902.

8*c*. Linda Hoare, *m.* 8 Ap. 1897, the Rev. Sydney Rhodes James, Headmaster of Malvern College (*The School House, Malvern*); and has issue 1*d* to 3*d*.

1*d*. Sydney Herbert Rhodes James, *b.* 13 Oct. 1901.

2*d*. Evelyn Zoe Rhodes James, *b.* 1 Mar. 1898.

3*d*. Linda Margery Rhodes James, *b.* 28 Jan. 1900.

9*c*. Violet Hoare.

2*b*. Rev. Walter Marsham Hoare, M.A., Rector of Colkirk (*Colkirk Rectory, co. Norfolk*), *b.* 13 Aug. 1840; *m.* 3 Jan. 1867, Jessie, da. of James Robertson; and has issue 1*c* to 7*c*.

1*c*. Walter Robertson Hoare (*Daneshill, Basingstoke*), *b.* 27 Oct. 1867; *m.* 28 Oct. 1897, Constance Gertrude, da. of Sir Edward Stock Hill, K.C.B., sometime M.P.; and has issue 1*d* to 6*d*.

1*d*. Michael Walter Hoare, *b.* 8 Feb. 1900.

2*d*. Bertram Walter Hoare, *b.* 19 June 1901.

3*d*. Nigel Walter Hoare, *b.* 29 Sept. 1902.

4*d*. David Walter Hoare, *b.* 10 Mar. 1904.

5*d*. Jocelyn Walter Hoare, *b.* 26 Aug. 1905.

6*d*. Veronica Constance Hoare, *b.* 11 Aug. 1898. [Nos. 7036 to 7066.

# of The Blood Royal

2c. Rev. Arthur Robertson Hoare, Chaplain to the Forces, b. 17 Oct. 1871 m. 7 Aug. 1902, Mabel Penelope, da. of Rev. the Hon. John Marsham; and has issue 1d.

    1. Gladys Hoare, b. June 1904.

3c. Vincent Robertson Hoare, Lieut. Suffolk Yeo. Cav., b. 15 Mar. 1873; m. 5 Nov. 1901, Elsie, da. of Quintin Hogg; and has issue 1d to 2d.

    1d. Margaret Elspeth Hoare, b. Nov. 1902.

    2d. Isabel Hoare, b. July 1904.

4c. Alice Mary Hoare, m. 19 Sept. 1903, Francis John Kingdon Hull (Limpsfield); and has issue 1d to 2d.

    1d. Robert Hoare Hull, b. 18 Oct. 1905.

    2d. Rachel Hull, b. 12 Sept. 1904.

5c. Mary Hoare.

6c. Jessie Katherine Hoare.

7c. Winifred Ina Hoare.

3b. *Charles Hoare, b. 1 Aug. 1844; d. 30 Mar. 1898; m. 9 Ap. 1872, Katharine Patience Georgiana (Purbrook Park, Cosham, Hants), da. of the Right Rev. Lord Arthur Charles Hervey, Lord Bishop of Bath and Wells; and had issue 1c to 7c.*

    1c. Charles Hervey Hoare, Capt. Glamorgan Imp. Yeo. Cav., b. 16 Dec. 1875.

    2c. Arthur Hervey Hoare, b. 25 July 1877.

    3c. Guy Sydenham Hoare, b. 16 Oct. 1879.

    4c. Reginald Hervey Hoare, b. 25 July 1882.

    5c. Patience Mary Hoare.

    6c. Constance Sarah Hoare.

    7c. Katherine Angelina Adeliza Hoare.

4b. William Hoare, M.A. (Iden Manor, Staplehurst, Kent), b. 13 Sept. 1847; m. 2 May 1878, Laura, da. of Col. Sir John Farnaby Lennard, 1st Bart. [U.K.]; and has issue 1c to 4c.

    1c. Geoffrey Lennard Hoare, Capt. Kent Art., b. 10 Ap. 1879.

    2c. Lionel Lennard Hoare, Lieut. R.F.A., b. 24 Aug. 1881.

    3c. Richard Lennard Hoare, b. 27 Mar. 1886.

    4c. Mary Laura Hoare, b. 27 Mar. 1886.

5b. Alfred Hoare (Charlesrod Farm, East Grinstead), b. 4 Nov. 1850; m. 22 Dec. 1881, Beatrice Pollard, da. of E. Bond of Hampstead; and has issue 1c to 5c.

    1c. John Edward Alford Hoare, b. 2 Aug. 1895.

    2c. Joanna Beatrice Hoare, b. 6 Oct. 1882.

    3c. Olive Mary Hoare, b. 25 Jan. 1884.

    4c. Helen Lucy Hoare, b. 14 July 1885.

    5c. Sybil Frances Hoare, b. 12 Feb. 1887.

6b. Hugh Edward Hoare, sometime (1892–1895) M.P. (Danbury Palace, Chelmsford; Hurley House, Marlow; 117 Piccadilly, W.), b. 1854; m. 1886, Elizabeth Katharine Mary, da. of James Wolfe Murray of Cringletie, co. Peebles, d. Ap. 1905; and has issue 1c to 2c.

    1c. Percival Hugh Trench Hoare, b. 17 Jan. 1888.

    2c. Evelyn Melville Shovel Hoare, b. 9 June 1889.

7b. Mary Sophia Hoare (Dolloways Bank, Buxted, Sussex), m. 1 May 1863, the Rev. Thomas William Onslow Hallward, Rector of Frittenden, b. 1827; d. 24 June 1899; and has issue 1c to 9c.

    1c. Rev. John Hallward, Rector of Bulawayo (Bulawayo, South Africa), b. 1870.

    2c. Henry Hallward, b. 1870.

    3c. Hubert Charles Hallward, b. 1873.

    4c. Walter Toke Hallward, b. 1878.

[Nos. 7067 to 7103.

The Plantagenet Roll

5c. Bernard Marsham Hallward, b. 1882.

6c. Mary Gertrude Hallward, b. 1867.

7c. Margaret Emily Hallward, b. 1868.

8c. Kathleen Leslie Hallward, b. 1875.

9c. Dorothy Hallward, b. 1881; m. 1905, William Jenkyns.

8b. Caroline Charlotte Hoare.

9b. Sophia Louisa Hoare.

2a. Rev. William Henry Hoare of Oakfield, b. 31 Oct. 1809; d. 22 Feb. 1888; m. 17 July 1834, Ariminta Anne, da. (and in her issue (1876) co-h. of Lieut.-Gen. Sir John James Hamilton, 1st Bart. [U.K.], d. 10 June 1875; and had issue 1b to 3b.

1b. Hamilton Noel Hoare, now (R.L. 1884) Hamilton-Hoare, formerly a member of Hoare's Bank (Oakfield Lodge, Three Bridges; 3 Draycott Place, S.W.).

2b. Henry William Hoare (96 Ebury Street, S.W.), b. 1 Ap. 1843; m. 6 Sept. 1877, Mary, da. of William Owen of Withybush; and has issue 1c to 3c.

1c. Evelyn Hoare, m. 1902, the Rev. Gerald Gurney Richards, Vicar of St. Peter and St. Paul, Teddington; and has issue 1d to 2d.

1d. Anthony Richards, b. 1903.

2d. Ursula Richards, b. 1905.

2c. Muriel Hoare.

3c. Sybil Hoare.

3b. Araminta Louisa Hoare, m. 28 Ap. 1870, John Webb Probyn (Abbenhall Lodge, co. Gloucester); and has issue 1c to 3c.

1c. Rev. Hubert Edmund Hamilton Probyn, b. 11 Feb. 1871; m. 28 Ap. 1904, Emily Mabel, da. of E. Cropper; and has issue 1d.

1d. Emily Araminta Probyn, b. 12 Feb. 1905.

2c. Rev. Wilfred Julian Noel Probyn, b. 29 June 1872.

3c. Juliana Probyn, m. John W. Gooch (Esher Place, Surrey).

3a. Gerard Noel Hoare, J.P., R.N., b. 4 May 1811; d. 23 Nov. 1901; m. 11 Mar. 1834, Sophia Lilias, da. of Stafford O'Brien of Blatherwycke, co. Northants, d. 1892; and had issue 1b to 8b.

1b. Rev. Ernest Villars Hoare, Vicar of Fenny Stratford (Fenny Stratford Vicarage, co. Berks), b. 6 Oct. 1837; m. 18 June 1861, Georgina Elizabeth, da. of the Rev. William Purdon; and has issue 1c.

1c. Percy Henry Villars Hoare, b. 22 Feb. 1870.

2b. Stafford O'Brien Hoare, now (Deed Poll, 1897) Hoare-Stafford-O'Brien, J.P., D.L., High Sheriff co. Bucks 1893; b. 23 Feb. 1843; m. 19 Ap. 1876, Frances Matilda Anne, da. of the Rev. Charles Henry Ramsden of Chilham; and has issue 1c.

1c. Lilias Frances Matilda Stafford O'Brien, b. 29 Feb. 1880.

3b. Gerard Noel Hoare (Greenstead Rectory, Ongar, Essex), m. 1 June 1871, Lucy, da. of the Rev. Charles Cotterill of Glanford Bridge; and has issue 1c to 3c.

1c. Charles Gerard Noel Hoare, b. 9 Mar. 1872; m. 6 May 1903, Marion, da. of Walter Sargent of Rugby, M.A.; and has issue 1d.

1d. Julian Hoare, b. 25 Ap. 1905.

2c. Henry Stafford Noel Hoare, b. 3 May 1877.

3c. Lilias Sophia Noel Hoare, b. 20 May 1873.

4b. Charles Middleton Hoare.

5b. Emma Louisa Hoare, m. June 1859, the Rev. Edward Salmon Bagshawe of Bulwick, co. Notts; and has issue.

6b. Agatha Sophia Hoare, m. 14 May 1861, Digby W. G. Fairfield, d.s.p. 22 July 1872.

7b. Sophia Lilias Hoare, m. 29 May 1877, the Rev. Algernon Charles Stafford-O'Brien, d.s.p. (-).   [Nos. 7104 to 7135.

# of The Blood Royal

8b. Jane Celestria Hoare, *m.* 1 June 1865, Francis Rodney Murray (*Walton House, Walton, near Ipswich*); and has issue 1c to 3c.

1c. Rodney Montolieu Murray, b. 22 *June* 1869; d. 19 *Jan.* 1900; m. 21 *Aug.* 1893, *Violet, da. of* [——] *Jones; and had issue* 1d.

1d. Violet Murray, b. 15 Aug. 1895.

2c. Frances Jane Murray, *m.* 14 Sept. 1892, Harry Shuldham Shuldham-Lye, M.V.O., Col. (ret.) *late* Comdg. 2nd Batt. R. Irish Regt.; and has issue 1d to 2d.

1d. Murray Shuldham-Lye, b. 4 Dec. 1895.

2d. Frances Valencia Shuldham-Lye, b. 4 Ap. 1894.

3c. Mary Celestria Murray, *m.* 1893, Conyers Lang, Comm. (ret.) R.N.; and has issue 1d.

1d. Winifred Mary Conyers Lang, b. 1894.

4a. *Louisa Elizabeth Hoare,* b. 1813; d. 21 *July* 1884; m. 22 *Mar.* 1836, *the Hon. Peter John Locke King, M.P., J.P., D.L.,* b. 25 *Jan.* 1811; d. 12 *Nov.* 1885; *and had issue* 1b *to* 4b.

1b. Hugh Fortescue Locke King, J.P., Bar.-at-Law (*Brooklands, Weybridge; 4 Mount Street, W.*), b. 7 Oct. 1848; *m.* 3 Jan. 1884, Ethel, da. of Sir Thomas Gore-Browne, K.C.M.G., C.B.

2b. Hester Fortescue King.

3b. Anna Clementina King.

4b. Eleanor Elizabeth King.

5a. *Mary Jane Hoare,* b. 14 *Mar.* 1816; d. 1 *Dec.* 1888; m. 28 *June* 1843, *Arthur (Kinnaird),* 10th [S.] *and* 2nd [*U.K.*]*.Baron Kinnaird,* b. 8 *July* 1814; d. 26 *Ap.* 1887; *and had issue* 1b *to* 6b.

1b. Arthur Fitzgerald (Kinnaird), 11th [S.] and 3rd [U.K.] Baron Kinnaird, &c. (*Rossie Priory, Inchture, &c.*), b. 16 Feb. 1847; *m.* 19 Aug. 1875, Mary Alma Victoria, da. of Sir Andrew Agnew, 8th Bart. [S.]; and has issue.
See p. 190, Nos. 6852–6857.

2b. Hon. Frederica Georgiana Kinnaird (*Park Riding, Bickley, Kent*), b. 4 May 1845; *m.* 27 Dec. 1870, Alfred Orlando Jones, M.D., *d.* 1896; and has issue 1c to 4c.

1c. Alfred Ivan Noel Jones, b. 6 Dec. 1871.

2c. Arthur Mervyn Jones, b. 13 Oct. 1874.

3c. Charles Ruthven Jones, b. 14 Oct. 1882.

4c. Frederica Olivia Jones, b. 24 Jan. 1881.

3b. Hon. Louisa Elizabeth Kinnaird (115 *Mount Street, W.*), b. 1 Nov. 1848.

4b. Hon. Agneta Olivia Kinnaird, b. 5 June 1850; *m.* 7 Jan. 1874, Roland Yorke Bevan (9 *Rutland Gate, S.W.*); and has issue 1c to 2c.

1c. Winifred Agneta Yorke, b. 30 Oct. 1874; *m.* 5 Dec. 1905, the Hon. William Sidney.

2c. Olivia Mary Yorke, b. 23 Dec. 1875; *m.* 23 June 1905,· Lancelot St. George Rathborne.

5b. Hon. Gertrude Mary Kinnaird (5¹ *Bickenhall Mansions, Baker Street, W.*), b. 29 Nov. 1853.

6b. Hon. Emily Cecilia Kinnaird (115 *Mount Street, W.*), b. 20 Oct. 1855.

[Nos. 7136 to 7164.]

120. Descendants of the Hon. EMMA NOEL (see Table IX.), *b.* 26 Feb. 1788; *d.* 19 Nov. 1873; *m.* 7 June 1808, Stafford O'BRIEN of Blatherwycke Park, co. Northants, High Sheriff, co. Rutland, 1809; *d.* 3 Mar. 1864; and had issue 1*a* to 4*a*.

1a. *Henry Stafford O'Brien, afterwards Stafford O'Brien of Blatherwycke Park, J.P., D.L., High Sheriff co. Northants* 1868, b. 22 *Feb.* 1814; d. 1880; m. 31 *Aug.* 1841, *Lucy, da. of the Rev. Henry W. Nevile of Walcot Park; and had issue* 1b *to* 3b.

The Plantagenet Roll

1*b*. Horace Stafford Stafford O'Brien of Blatherwycke Park, J.P., D.L., High Sheriff co. Clare 1875 (*Blatherwycke Park, near Wansford; Cratloe Woods, co. Clare*), *b*. 1842; *m*. 21 Oct. 1869, Eleanor Elizabeth Georgiana, da. and h. of John Kent Egerton Holmes; and has issue 1*c* to 2*c*.

    1*c*. Egerton Augustus Stafford O'Brien, *b*. 1872.

    2*c*. Horace Henry Stafford O'Brien, *b*. 1883.

    2*b*. Lucy Violet O'Brien.

    3*b*. Alianore Emma Matilda O'Brien.

    2*a*. Algernon Stafford O'Brien, *b*. 1815.

    3*a*. *Angelina Mary O'Brien*, d. 29 *Ap*. 1836; *m*. *as 1st wife, 7 May 1833, the Rev. Augustus FitzRoy, b. 9 Dec.* 1809; *d. 12 Feb.* 1869; *and had issue.*

See the Tudor Roll of "The Blood Royal of Britain," p. 336, Nos. 26622–26625.

    4*a*. *Sophia Lilias O'Brien*, d. 1892; *m*. 11 *Mar*. 1834, *Gerard Noel Hoare, J.P., R.N.; and had issue.*

See p. 198, Nos. 7123–7142.   [Nos. 7165 to 7194.

121. Descendants of the Hon. CHARLOTTE MARGARET NOEL (see Table IX.), *b*. 6 May 1792; *d*. 18 Aug. 1869; *m*. 1st, as 2nd wife, 22 Jan. 1813, THOMAS WELMAN of Poundisford Park, co. Somerset, *b*. 14 June 1746; *d*. 28 Jan. 1829; 2ndly, 1 Jan. 1839, THOMAS THOMPSON of Vanbrugh House, *d*. 8 Dec. 1865; and had issue 1*a*.

    1*a*. Charles Noel Welman, J.P., D.L., late of Norton Manor (*Southern Leigh, Minehead*), *b*. 4 Dec. 1814; *m*. 1 May 1835, Annette Elizabeth, da. of Cornelius Henry Bolton, *d*. 1 May 1887; and has issue 1*b* to 9*b*.

    1*b*. Charles Cæsar Welman, J.P., *late* 49th Regt. (*Norton Manor, co. Somerset*), *b*. 5 Mar. 1840; *m*. 26 Nov. 1862, Eugenia Mary, da. of Charles Henry Stonor of Lostock; and has issue 1*c* to 7*c*.

1*c*–7*c*. See the Clarence Volume, p. 419, Nos. 15855–15861.

    2*b*. Arthur Nelson Welman, Major Somerset Imp. Yeo., *b*. 26 Nov. 1845; *m*. 1 Aug. 1878, Katherine Fearing, da. of Charles Strong of New York.

    3*b*. Frederick Tristram Welman, *b*. 19 Feb. 1849; *m*. 28 Aug. 1883, Mary, da. of Briscoe Ray of Torquay; and has issue 1*c*.

    1*c*. Agnes Mary Stella Welman.

    4*b*. Gerard Wilfred Welman (*The Tower, Newquay, Cornwall*), *b*. 4 July 1854; *m*. 5 Sept. 1888, Katharine Maud Morwenna, da. of Sir Paul Molesworth, 10th Bart. [E.]; and has issue 1*c* to 2*c*.

    1*c*. Blanche Mary Welman.

    2*c*. Hilda Katherine Welman.

    5*b*. Henry Acton Welman (*72 Rue des Pierres, Bruges*), *b*. 11 Ap. 1856; *m*. 15 June 1882, Mary Letitia, da. of Sir Paul Molesworth, 10th Bart. [E.]; and has issue 1*c* to 6*c*.

    1*c*. Gilbert Molesworth Welman, *b*. 16 Sept. 1888.

    2*c*. Paul Arundell Welman, *b*. 22 Jan. 1890:

    3*c*. Henry Bolton Welman, *b*. 20 May 1893.

    4*c*. Frances Morwenna Welman.

    5*c*. Adela Mary Welman.

    6*c*. Loveday Margaret Welman.   [Nos. 7195 to 7216.

# of The Blood Royal

6b. Augusta Charlotte Welman.

7b. Mary Maude Welman, m. 3 Oct. 1865, Charles Joseph Stonor, J.P. (*Llanvair, Ascot, Berks*) ; and has issue.

See the Clarence Volume, pp. 418–419, Nos. 15841–15851.

8b. Frances Agnes Welman, m. 9 June 1874, Cyril James Wilson; and has issue.

9b. Annette Josephine Welman. [Nos. 7217 to 7231.

122. Descendants of the Hon. AUGUSTA JULIA NOEL (see Table IX.), b. 7 Jan. 1796; d. 19 June 1833; m. as 1st wife, 27 Ap. 1814, THOMAS GISBORNE BABINGTON of Rothley Temple, co. Leicester, J.P., D.L., b. 24 July 1788; d. 19 Jan. 1871 ; and had issue 1a to 3a.

1a. *Rev. Thomas Arthur Babington of Cossington, co. Leicester, M.A. (Camb.),* b. 25 Nov. 1820; d. 30 Nov. 1896; m. 19 Aug. 1847, *Katherine Mary, da. of Cornelius Henry Bolton of Faithlegg, d. 23 Nov. 1881 ; and had issue 1b to 3b.*

1b. Mary Augusta Babington.

2b. Eleanor Katharine Babington.

3b. Emily Frances Babington, m. 8 July 1886, Arthur Edward Wellington Fox, M.B., F.R.C.P. (*Ennox Lodge, Hinton, Charterhouse, Bath*).

2a. *Augusta Diana Babington, d. 25 Mar. 1856; m. 9 Ap. 1839, Frederic Lewin of The Hollies, Kent, d. 17 June 1877.*

3a. Louisa Jean Babington, m. 3 Feb. 1842, the Ven. Francis C. P. Reynolds, Archdeacon of Bombay. [Nos. 7232 to 7235.

123. Descendants, if any, of the Hon. JULIANA HICKS NOEL (see Table IX.), b. 4 Oct. 1800 ; d. 4 Jan. 1855 ; m. 20 June 1834, the Rev. SAMUEL PHILLIPS.

124. Descendants of the Hon. JULIANA EVANS (see Table IX.), d. 20 May 1807 ; m. 1782, EDWARD HARTOPP, *afterwards* HARTOPP-WIGLEY of Little Dalby, co. Leicester, d. 20 June 1808 ; and had issue 1a to 2a.

1a. *Edward Hartopp of Little Dalby, d. 5 Feb. 1813 ; m. 19 July 1806, Anna Eleanor, da. of Sir Bourchier Wrey, 6th Bart. [E.], who re-m. 9 Dec. 1815, Sir Lawrence Vaughan Palk, 3rd Bart. [G.B.], d. 25 Jan. 1846 ; and had issue.*

See p. 129, Nos. 7236–7251.

2a. *Rev. William Evans Hartopp, Rector of Harby, d. (–) ; m. Eliza Georgiana, da. of George Stamer Gubbins of Kilfrush ; and had issue 1b.*

1b. *Edward Samuel Evans Hartopp of Clepsham Hall, co. Rutland, b. 7 Feb. 1820 ; d. 5 Oct. 1894 ; m. Jan. 1852, Mary, da. of Henry Goode of Claremount, d. 27 Nov. 1875 ; and had issue 1c.*

1c. William Evans Hartopp, Bar.-at-Law, *late* of Moor Park, King's Co., b. 12 June 1855 ; m. 12 Oct. 1886, Janet Georgina, da. of George Bogle of Rosemount, co. Ayr. [Nos. 7236 to 7252.

125. Descendants, if any, of LUCY MANN (see Table IX.), m. 1768, JAMES MANN of Egerton Lodge, near Lenham.

The Plantagenet Roll

126. Descendants of HARRIET MANN (see Table IX.), d. Ap. 1810 ; m. as first wife, 29 July 1801, Col. JOHN STAUNTON ROCHFORT of Clogrenane, co. Carlow, d. 6 May 1844 ; and had issue 1a.

1a. *Horace William Noel Rochfort of Clogrenane, J.P., D.L., High Sheriff co. Carlow 1839, and for Queen's Co.* 1845, b. 5 Nov. 1809 ; d. 16 May 1891 ; m. 1st, 6 Aug. 1837, Frances Elizabeth, da. of Thomas Phillips Cosby of Stradbally Hall, d. 25 Mar. 1841 ; 2ndly, 4 Sept. 1845, the Hon. Charlotte, da. of Samuel (Hood), 2nd Baron Bridport [I.], b. 8 Aug. 1813 ; and had issue 1b to 6b.

1b. John Burgh Rochfort, late Lieut. R.A. (*Clogrenane, co. Carlow*), b. 28 June 1838 ; m. 29 Dec. 1863, Hilare Charlotte, da. of Henry Hall of Barton Abbey ; and has issue 1c to 6c.

1c. Horace Cosby Rochfort, b. 16 May 1877.

2c. Oswald John Rochfort, b. 25 Jan. 1883.

3c. Catherine Frances Rochfort, b. 2 June 1867 ; m. 3 Jan. 1895, Joseph Henry Garratt (*Herberton, Blackrock, co. Dublin*).

4c. Eva Blanche Rochfort, b. 10 June 1871.

5c. Hilare Gertrude Rochfort, b. 12 Aug. 1873.

6c. Grace Rochfort, b. 20 Aug. 1879.

2b. Horace William Rochfort, Capt. R.N. (ret.) (9 *Hatherley Place, Cheltenham*), b. 20 Aug. 1839 ; m. 1882, Elizabeth, da. and heir of Marriott R. Dalway, M.P. ; and has issue 1c to 2c.

1c. Horace Marriott Thomas Rochfort, b. 21 Jan. 1883.

2c. Dorothy Frances Elizabeth Rochfort, b. 1 Jan. 1886.

3b. *Thomas Francis Cosby Rochfort, Col. 4th European Light Cav.*, b. 8 Feb. 1841 ; d. 14 Oct. 1901 ; m. 1889, Alice, widow of Col. Daunt, da. of [——].

4b. William Rochfort, J.P. (*Cahir Abbey, co. Tipperary*), b. 29 Dec. 1847 ; m. 14 Ap. 1875, Helen Blanche, da. of R. S. Palmer of Dromquinna, co. Kerry.

5b. Alexander Nelson Rochfort, Lieut.-Col. R.A., b. 3 June 1850.

6b. Amelia Catherine Rochfort (48 *Stephen's Green, Dublin*), m. 14 Dec 1871, Thomas Pakenham Law, K.C., d. 29 May 1905 ; and has issue 1c to 4c.

1c. Samuel Horace Law, M.D., F.R.C.S.I. (49 *Merrion Square, Dublin*), b. 22 Oct. 1873 ; m. 18 July 1905, Sybil Mary, da. and co-h. of Sir George Clay, 3rd Bart. [U.K.].

2c. Alexander Henry Law, B.A., b. Feb. 1878.

3c. Thomas Pakenham Law, b. May 1879.

4c. Mabel Harriet Law, b. Nov. 1880.   [Nos. 7253 to 7269.

127. Descendants of Lady SOPHIA NOEL (see Table IX.), d. (–) ; m. CHRISTOPHER NEVILE of Wellingore, co. Lincoln, d. 1829 ; and had issue 1a to 3a.

1a. *Christopher Henry Nevile, afterwards* (*R.L.* 7 *June* 1798) *Noel, of Walcot and Wellingore, co. Lincoln, Col. Rutland Fencible Cavalry*, b. 1774; d. 27 Feb. 1838 ; m. Dec. 1818, [——], da. of [——] Abbot, d. (–) ; and had issue 1b.

1b. *Sophia Mary Noel, d.* (–) ; m. 30 May 1844, Frederick William Allix of Willoughby Hall, co. Lincoln, J.P., D.L., b. 11 Ap. 1816 ; d. 13 Oct. 1894 ; and had issue 1c to 2c.

1c. Noel Charles Noel Allix, J.P., D.L., Knight of the Orders of the Medjidie and Osmanieh, *late* Gren. Guards, and Equerry to the Khedive (*Willoughby Hall, Grantham*), b. 15 May 1846 ; m. 11 Mar. 1871, Helen, da. of Edwin Taunton of Bromborough, d. 10 Aug. 1889 ; and has issue 1d.

1d. Muriel Lilian Helen de Burgh Allix.

2c. Helen Harriet Elizabeth Allix, m. 16 July 1870, Abel Humphrey Ram, *late* of Ramsfoot, co. Wexford.   [Nos. 7270 to 7272.

# of The Blood Royal

2a. Henry William Nevile, *Rector of Cottesmore,* b. *Mar.* 1775; d. 8 *Nov.* 1843; m. 1807, *Amelia, da. of James Mann of Hallow Park, co. Worcester,* d. 25 *Oct.* 1822; *and had issue* 1b *to* 7b.

  1b. *Henry Nevile of Walcot and Wellingore,* J.P., D.L., *High Sheriff co. Lincoln* 1849; b. 31 *Dec.* 1809; d. 7 *Dec.* 1862; m. 29 *Ap.* 1847, *Ellen, da. of the Rev. Charles Bryan of Woolastone; and had issue* 1c *to* 2c.

    1c. Ralph Henry Christopher Nevile, J.P., *High Sheriff co. Lincoln* 1883 (*Wellingore Hall, co. Lincoln*), b. 15 *Nov.* 1850; m. 30 *Nov.* 1871, Mildred Frances, da. of Charles Robert Scott-Murray of Danesfield, J.P., M.P.; and has issue.

    See the Clarence Volume, p. 448, Nos. 19031–19037.

    2c. Cicely Mary Sophia Nevile, m. 24 *Ap.* 1879, Edward Weston Cracroft, *formerly* Cracroft-Amcotts, J.P. (*Hackthorn Hall, Lincoln*).

  2b. *Charles James Nevile,* b. 1812; d. (*? unm.*) 1 *Feb.* 1878.

  3b. *Rev. Gerard Nevile,* M.A., *Vicar of Tilton,* b. 1815; d. 11 *May* 1881; m. 18 *Aug.* 1842, *Rosamond, da. of Sir Matthew Blakiston, 3rd Bart.* [G.B.], d. 10 *May* 1862; *and had issue* 1c *to* 2c.

    1c. Henry Nevile, b. 31 May 1845; d. (*? s.p.*); m. 8 *Aug.* 1876, Lucy, da. of [——] Roberts of Edinburgh.

    2c. Amelia Nevile.

  4b. George Nevile, J.P., D.L., *High Sheriff co. Lincoln* 1858, *late Lieut.* R.A. (*Stubton Hall, co. Lincoln*), b. 25 *Oct.* 1822; m. 29 *Dec.* 1846, Madalene Elizabeth, da. of Capt. George M. Glasgow, R.A.

  5b. *Emily Nevile,* d. *Aug.* 1879; m. 1830, *James Harris Veale of Passaford, J.P.,* D.L., b. 1800; d. 1876; *and had issue* 1c.

    1c. *Henry Mallett Veale,* J.P., b. 1831; d. 1905 *or* 1906; m. 1*st,* 1854, *Elizabeth, da. of Aaron Saunders of King's Nympton,* d. *Mar.* 1883; 2*ndly,* 1886, *Ellen, widow of Christopher Edmonds, Ceylon C.S., da. of* [——]; *and had issue* (*by* 1*st wife*) 1d *to* 10d.

      1d. Henry Veale (*Passaford, Hatherleigh, co. Devon*).

      2d. James Veale.

      3d. Westcott Harris Veale.

      4d. Arthur James Veale.

      5d. Lucy Veale.

      6d. Caroline Veale.

      7d. Elizabeth Veale.

      8d. Emily Veale, m. 17 Oct. 1894, Lionel Frederick West, M.R.C.S., L.R.C.P. (*Marlboro' House, Queen Street, Morley, Leeds*).

      9d. Mary Veale.

      10d. Sophia Eleanor Veale.

  6b. *Sophia Nevile,* d. 29 *Dec.* 1868; m. 13 *Ap.* 1842, Rev. the Hon. John Fortescue, b. 5 *May* 1796; d. 3 *Jan.* 1869; *and had issue.*

    See the Tudor Roll of "The Blood Royal of Britain," pp. 282–283, Nos. 25005–25019.

  7b. *Lucy Nevile,* d. (–); m. 31 *Aug.* 1841, *Henry Stafford O'Brien Stafford of Blatherwycke, &c.,* J.P., D.L., d. 1880; *and had issue.*

  3a. *Sophia Charlotte Neville,* m. *Gen. Ainslie.*   [Nos. 7273 to 7309.

128. Descendants of ANTHONY (BRABAZON), 8th EARL OF MEATH [I.] (see Table X.), b. 1721; d. 4 Jan. 1790; m. 20 May 1758, GRACE, da. of John LEIGH of Rosegarland, co. Wexford; d. 23 Oct. 1812; and had issue 1a to 6a.

  1a. *William (Brabazon), 9th Earl of Meath* [I.], b. 9 *July* 1769; d. *unm.* 26 *May* 1797.

The Plantagenet Roll

2a. *John Chambre (Brabazon), 10th Earl of Meath [I.], 1st Baron Chaworth [U.K.], K.P., b. 9 Ap. 1772; d. 15 Mar. 1851; m. 31 Dec. 1801, Lady Melosina Adelaide, da. of John (Meade), 1st Earl of Clanwilliam [I.], d. 26 Mar. 1866; and had issue 1b to 2b.*

1b. *William (Meade), 11th Earl of Meath [I.], 2nd Baron Chaworth [U.K.],* b. 25 Oct. 1803; d. 26 *May* 1887; m. 23 *Nov.* 1837, *Harriot, da. of Sir Richard Brooke, 6th Bart. [E.], d.* 16 *July* 1898; *and had issue 1c to 2c.*

1c. Reginald (Brabazon), 12th Earl of Meath [E.], 3rd Baron Chaworth [U.K.], P.C., Chancellor of the Royal University of Ireland, &c. (*Kellruddery House, near Bray; Ottermead, near Chertsey; 83 Lancaster Gate, W*.), b. 31 July 1841; m. 7 Jan. 1868, Lady Mary Jane, da. and h. of Thomas (Maitland), 11th Earl of Lauderdale [S.]; and has issue 1d to 6d.

1d. Reginald le Normand Brabazon, Lord Ardee, Capt. 2nd Batt. Grenadier Guards, b. 24 Nov. 1869.

2d. Hon. Arthur Lauderdale le Normand Brabazon, *late* Capt. Royal Dublin Fusiliers, b. 28 Sept. 1872.

3d. Hon. Claud Maitland Patrick Brabazon, Lieut. Irish Guards, b. 16 July 1874.

4d. Hon. Ernest William Maitland Molyneux Brabazon, b. 22 Mar. 1884.

5d. Lady Mary Florence Brabazon, b. 16 Ap. 1877.

6d. Lady Violet Constance Maitland Brabazon, b. 26 Sept. 1886.

2c. Lady Kathleen Harriot Brabazon (40 *Eaton Square, S.W.*).

2b. *Lady Theodosia Brabazon,* b. 15 *July* 1808; d. 13 *Feb.* 1876; m. 22 *June* 1832, *Archibald (Acheson), 3rd Earl of Gosford [I.], 2nd Baron Worlingham [U.K.], 9th Bart. [S.], K.P.,* b. 20 *Aug.* 1806; d. 15 *June* 1864; *and had issue 1c to 6c.*

1c. Archibald Brabazon Sparrow (Acheson), 4th Earl of Gosford [I.], 3rd Baron Worlingham [U.K.], 10th Bart. [S.], K.P., &c. (*Gosford Castle, Market Hill; 22 Mansfield Street, Portland Place*), b. 19 Aug. 1841; m. 10 Aug. 1876, Lady Louisa, Lady of the Bedchamber to H.M. the Queen, da. of William Drogo (Montagu), 7th Duke of Manchester [G.B.], K.P.; and has issue 1d to 5d.

1d. Archibald Charles Montagu Brabazon Acheson, Viscount Acheson, Lieut. Reserve of Officers, late Coldstream Guards, b. 26 May 1877.

2d. Hon. Patrick Charles George Cavendish Acheson, M.V.O., Lieut. R.N., b. 30 June 1883.

3d. Lady Alexandra Louise Elizabeth Acheson (H.M. the Queen sponsor), m. 17 June 1905, Capt. Hon. Frederick Stanley, 10th Hussars.

4d. Hon. Lady Mary Acheson.

5d. Lady Theodosia Louisa Augusta Acheson.

2c. Hon. Edward Archibald Brabazon Acheson, Major-Gen., *late* Col. Coldstream Guards (*Guards'; Travellers'*), b. 22 May 1844; m. 1869, Clementina, da. of Gen. Sir Gaspard le Marchant, K.C.B., G.C.S.I.; and has issue 1d to 4d.

1d. Theodosia Margaret Hilda Acheson, b. 5 Feb. 1870; m. 7 Dec. 1898, Lancelot Squarey (*Egerton Park, Rock Ferry, Cheshire*); and has issue 1e to 2e.

1e. Arthur de Coligny Acheson Squarey, b. 1904.

2e. Audrey Theodosia Madeleine Squarey, b. 1900.

2d. Edith Maude Acheson, b. 2 Mar. 1871.

3d. Norah Sybelle Acheson, b. July 1874; m. 7 Nov. 1894, Frank Ramsden of Hexthorpe, J.P., D.L., b. 1 Jan. 1840; d.s.p. 1903.

4d. Gladys Acheson, b. 5 Dec. 1875.

3c. Lady Gertrude Emily Acheson, m. 20 Feb. 1856, the Right Hon. Francis John Savile Foljambe, P.C. (*Osberton, co. Notts*); and has issue.

See the Clarence Volume, p. 271, Nos. 7241–7249.

4c. *Lady Mary Acheson,* b. 21 *Mar.* 1835; d. 5 *Mar.* 1898; m. 27 *Feb.* 1862,
[Nos. 7310 to 7340.

# of The Blood Royal

the Hon. Leopold William Henry Powis, afterwards (R.L. Nov. 1890) *Fox-Powys of Bewsey Hall, D.L.,* b. 17 *Sept.* 1837 ; d. 30 *Jan.* 1892 ; *and had issue.* See p. 183, Nos. 6498–6503.

5c. Lady Edith Acheson.

6c. *Lady Katharine Acheson,* b. 24 *June* 1839 ; d. 5 *Mar.* 1898 ; m. 28 *July* 1868, *Capt. Frederick William Duncombe, Gren. Guards,* b. 28 *Jan.* 1842 ; d. 6 *Feb.* 1878 ; *and had issue* 1d *to* 3d.

1d. Basil Archibald Charles Duncombe (*Ampthill, St. John's, Ryde, I.W.*), b. 12 Jan. 1870 ; m. 12 Jan. 1896, Ida, da. of Alfred Hope Doeg ; and has issue 1e to 3e.

1e. Hubert Basil Elliot Duncombe, b. 21 May 1901.

2e. Phyllis Gertrude Duncombe, b. 25 June 1897.

3e. Katharine Duncombe, b. 24 Aug. 1898.

2d. Wilfred Arthur Duncombe, now Duncombe Anderson (*Lea Hall, Gainsborough*), b. 30 Sept. 1871 ; m. 7 June 1905, Margaret Louise, da. and co-h. of Francis Foljambe Anderson (son of Sir Charles Henry John Alexander, 9th and last Bart. [E.]).

3d. Ethel Coralie Duncombe, b. 6 Nov. 1872 ; m. 11 July 1900, John Quayle (*New Valley, Norwood, Ceylon*).

3a. *Lady Mary Brabazon,* b. 18 *Mar.* 1759 ; d. 29 *Aug.* 1851 ; m. 23rd *June* 1781, *Arthur Knox of Castlerea, co. Mayo, and Woodstock, co. Wicklow, J.P.,* b. 13 *Sept.* 1759 ; d. 23 *Oct.* 1798 ; *and had issue* 1b *to* 3b.

1b. *John Knox of Castlerea and Woodstock, J.P., D.L.,* b. 13 *May* 1783 ; d. 31 *Dec.* 1861 ; m. 12 *Mar.* 1808, *Maria Anne, da. of Major John Knox of Mount Falcon,* d. 1 *June* 1861 ; *and had issue* 1c *to* 4c.

1c. *Arthur Edward Knox of Castlerea, and of Trolton, co. Sussex,* b. 28 *Dec.* 1808 ; d. 26 *Sept.* 1886 ; m. 12 *Dec.* 1835, *Lady Jane, da. of Laurence (Parsons), 2nd Earl of Rosse* [*I.*], b. *Oct.* 1813 ; d. 31 *Dec.* 1883 ; *and had issue* 1d *to* 4d.

1d. Arthur Henry Knox, R.N., b. Mar. 1852.

2d. Maria Jane Knox, m. 30 Nov. 1875, William Henry Irvine, Capt. 3rd Buffs ; and has issue 1e to 2e.[1]

1e. Edith Irvine.

2e. Ethel Irvine.

3d. Alice Knox, m. 31 Mar. 1864, Col. Horace Parker Newton, R.A., *formerly* Col. on Staff, Comdg. R.A. Western District ; and has issue 1e to 6e.[2]

1e. Horace Edward Newton, b. 10 June 1868.

2e. Cecil John Newton, b. 2 July 1872.

3e. Robert Algernon Newton, b. 23 July 1874.

4e. Alice Jane Newton.

5e. Evelyn Helen Newton.

6e. Blanch Caroline Newton.

4d. Helen Knox, m. 26 Ap. 1870, Charles John Fletcher, J.P., High Sheriff co. Sussex 1894 (*Dale Park, near Arundel*) ; and has issue 1e to 5e.

1e. Charles Arthur Fletcher, *late* Lieut. Royal Sussex Regt., b. 15 May 1871.

2e. Alan Francis Fletcher, Lieut. 4th Batt. Warwickshire Regt., b. 21 Ap. 1876.

3e. Eleanor Susan Fletcher, m. 23 Jan. 1899, Ronald Aubrey Freemantle (22 *Sloane Court, S.W.*) ; and has issue 1f.

1f. Maurice Alan Freemantle, b. 31 July 1900.

4e. Evelyn Elizabeth Fletcher, b. 22 June 1879.

5e. Ethel Florence Fletcher, b. 7 Ap. 1883.

2c. Ernest Knox of Castlerea, Major N. Mayo Militia, m. 12 July 1836, Charlotte Catherine, da. of James Knox-Gore of Broadlands Park, M.P. ; and had issue.
[Nos. 7341 to 7372.

---

[1] Foster's " Peerage," 1880.   [2] Ibid., 1880.

2 D

The Plantagenet Roll

3c. Edward William John Knox, Capt. 75th Regt., d. *(being killed at the Siege of Delhi)* 1857 ; m. 1854, *Charlotte Emily, da. of Major Gardiner of Farm Hill, co. Mayo ; and had issue.*

4c. Alfred Charles Knox, Capt. 73rd Regt., d. *25 June* 1893 ; m. 1855, *Victoria Anne, da. of Col. Arthur Hunt; R.A. ; and had issue.*

2b. Rev. Arthur Knox, b. 22 Nov. 1793 ; d. (? s.p.) ; m. *Nov.* 1810, *Mary, sister to James,* 1st *Baron Dunsandle and Clan-Conal* [*I.*], *da. of the Right Hon. Dennis Daly, M.P.,* d. *24 Ap.* 1885.

3b. Anne Knox, d. (–) ; m. *William Edward Scott, Bar.-at-Law.*

4a. Lady Martha Brabazon, b. 20 Nov. 1761 ; d. (–) ; m. *Maurice Bagenal St. Leger Keating,* d. *Dec.* 1835.

5a. Lady Catherine Brabazon, b. 19 Aug. 1770 ; d. *24 Dec.* 1847 ; m. *6 Aug.* 1799, *the Rev. Francis Brownlow, Rector of Upper Comber, co. Derry, b. 12 June* 1779 ; d. *20 Oct.* 1847 ; *and had issue* 1b *to* 3b.

1b. *William Brownlow of Knapton House, Queen's co., and Loughderry, co. Monaghan, J.P., D.L.,* b. 1802 ; d. *18 July* 1881 ; m. 1835, *Charlotte, da. of William Browne o Browne's Hill, co. Carlow ; and had issue (with das.)* 1c.

1c. William Vesey Brownlow, C.B., Major-Gen. *late* 1st Dragoon Guards (*Army and Navy*), *b.* 12 June 1841 ; *m.* 1st, 19 Nov. 1881, Lady Anne Henrietta, da. of John Hamilton (Dalrymple), 10th Earl of Stair [S.], *b.* 10 Nov. 1855 ; *d.* 18 Feb. 1898 ; 2ndly, 1 June 1904, Lady Kathleen Susan Emma, da. of John Stuart (Bligh), 6th Earl of Darnley [I.].

2b. Rev. John Brownlow, Dean of Clonmacnoise, b. 10 Oct. 1804 ; d. *24 May* 1882 ; m. *19 July* 1833, *Lady Elizabeth, da. of John (Bligh),* 4th *Earl of Darnley* [*I.*], b. *7 Aug.* 1800 ; d. *13 Nov.* 1872 ; *and had issue* 1c *to* 2c.

1c. Rev. Duncan John Brownlow, Incumbent of Donoghpatrick, co. Meath, b. *4 Mar.* 1842 ; d. *29 Sept.* 1904 ; m. *28 Mar.* 1883, *Margaret Stuart, da. of John James Verschoyle ; and had issue* 1d *to* 2d.

1d. Elizabeth Bligh Brownlow, } (*Lurgan, Greystones, co. Wicklow*).
2d. Helen Isabel Brownlow, }

2c. Elizabeth Catherine Brownlow (*Egremont, Monkstown, co. Dublin*), b. 22 June 1834 ; *unm.*

3b. James Brownlow of Killynether Castle, J.P., b. *17 Dec.* 1811 ; d. *11 Sept.* 1894 ; m. *23 May* 1849, *Maria Harriet, da. of Major Rainey of Mount Panther, co. Down ; and had issue* 1c *to* 9c.

1c. William Claude Brabazon Brownlow (*Coolderry, Carrickmacross*), b. 11 Nov. 1850 ; *m.* 14 Feb. 1882, Janet, da. of Robert Orme of Owenmore ; and has issue 1d to 7d.

1d. Guy James Brownlow, b. 26 Dec. 1883.

2d. Andrew Brownlow, twin, b. 22 Jan. 1894.

3d. Gwendolen Sydney Brownlow.

4d. Eileen Anne Brownlow.

5d. Marjorie Violet Brownlow.

6d. Geraldine Maria Brownlow.

7d. Nina Emily Brownlow, twin.

2c. Charles James Rainey Brownlow, b. 2 May 1860.

3c. Rev. Harold Arthur Brownlow, B.A. (Camb.), Rector of Cheriton (*Cheriton Rectory, Alresford, Hants*), b. 27 July 1864 ; *m.* Jan. 1894, Katharine, da. of Thomas Elliot Harrison of Whitburn ; and has issue 1d to 2d.

1d. Patrick Maurice Elliot Brownlow, b. 17 Ap. 1896.

2d. Renée Esmé Jean Brownlow, b. 9 Oct. 1894.

4c. Catherine Frances Brownlow, *m.* 7 Oct. 1874, the Rev. Henry Robert Arthur Johnson, Vicar of Tugby, co. Leic., d. 19 Feb. 1894 ; and has issue (with 2 das.) 1d to 3d.

[Nos. 7373 to 7389.]

# of The Blood Royal

1d. Henry Stafford Brownlow Johnson, *b.* 12 Jan. 1876.

2d. Evelyn Brownlow Johnson, *b.* 1 Jan. 1880.

3d. Cecil Wilson Johnson, *b.* 19 July 1881.

5c. Caroline Grey Brownlow, *m.* 18 Mar. 1880, James Edward Blair (*Drumpark, Dumfries, N.B.*), son of Gen. Blair, V.C., C.B. ; and has issue 1*d* to 3*d*.

1d. Duncan James Nugent Blair, *b.* 11 Sept. 1882.

2d. Elsie Blair.

3d. Marjorie Blair.

6c. Maria Isabella Brownlow.

7c. Emily Louisa Brownlow, *m.* 15 July 1879, the Rev. Feilding Arthur Wolfe Hamilton-Gell, *lately* Rector of Staunton in Peak, co. Derby (*Winslade, Clyst St. Mary, Exeter*) ; and has issue 1*d* to 2*d*.

1d. Doreen Emily Hamilton-Gell, *m.* 5 July 1899, Nathaniel Robert Radcliffe, D.S.O., Capt. Devon Regt. ; and has issue 1*e*.

1e. Robert Derwent Hamilton Radcliffe, *b.* 14 May 1902.

2d. Kathleen Effie Hamilton-Gell, *m.* 25 Ap. 1905, P. Randall-Johnson (*Finiton, Devon*) ; and has issue 1*e*.

1e. Philip Hamilton Randall-Johnson, *b.* 29 Mar. 1906.

8c. Margaret Ethel de Vesci Brownlow.

9c. Esme Bligh Brownlow, *m.* 31 Aug. 1905, Edmund Lovell Copleston (*Offwell, Devon*).

6a. *Lady Arabella Barbara Brabazon, b.* 15 *Nov.* 1774 ; *d.* (-) ; *m.* 21 *Mar.* 1803, *the Rev. John Middleton Scott of Ballygannon, co. Wicklow ; and had (with other) issue 1b.*

1b. Elizabeth Ruth Scott (10 *Cambray, Cheltenham*), *m.* as 2nd wife, 30 Jan. 1849, William (Courtenay), 10th Earl of Devon [E.], *d.* (*s.p.* by her) 19 Mar. 1859.

[Nos. 7390 to 7405b.

129. Descendants of the Hon WILLIAM BRABAZON of Tara House, co. Meath (see Table X.), *b.* Aug. 1723 ; *d.* (-) ; *m.* 10 May 1764, CATHARINE, da. and h. of Arthur GIFFORD of Aghern, co. Cork, *d.* 11 Feb. 1833 ; and had issue 1*α*.

1a. *Barbara Brabazon, d.* (-) ; *m. as 1st wife,* 24 *May* 1788, *John Moore of New Lodge, co. Herts, b.* 20 *Sept.* 1763 ; *d. Ap.* 1842 ; *and had issue 1b to 3b.*

1b. *William John Moore, afterwards* (1845) *Moore-Brabazon of Tara House, b.* 29 *Ap.* 1789 ; *d.s.p.* 1866.

2b. *John Arthur Moore, C.I.E., Major and a Director H.E.I.C., b.* 24 *Sept.* 1791 ; *d.* (-) ; *m.* 31 *July* 1827 ; *and had issue 1c to 5c.*

1c. John Arthur Henry Moore, now (since 1866) Moore-Brabazon, Hon. Lieut.-Col. in the Army, *late* B.S.C., High Sheriff co. Louth 1872 (*Tara House, co. Meath ; Tallyallen, co. Louth*), *b.* 13 June 1828 ; *m.* Feb. 1879, Emma Sophia, da. of Alfred Richards of Forest Hill ; and has issue 1*d* to 4*d*.

1d. William Lockhart Chambré Moore-Brabazon, *b.* 3 Jan. 1880.

2d. John Theodore Cuthbert Moore-Brabazon, *b.* 1884.

3d. Kathleen Barbara Sophia Moore-Brabazon.

4d. Hebe Crystabel Frideswide Moore-Brabazon.

2c. Charles William Moore, B.C.S.

3c. *Adolphus Warburton Moore, India Office,* d. (? unm.).

4c. Martin James Moore, Bengal Cavalry.

5c. *Frances Stewart Moore, d.* 21 *Feb.* 1895 ; *m.* 23 *Jan.* 1866, *Capt. Richard Charles Acton Throckmorton, heir-presumptive to Baronetcy* (1642) [*E.*] (*Coughton Court, Redditch*) ; *and had issue 1d to 7d.*

1d–7d. See the Clarence Volume, p. 382, Nos. 14521–14527.

3b. *Charles Henry Moore, b.* 31 *Mar.* 1798 ; *d.* (-).   [Nos. 7406 to 7419.

207

The Plantagenet Roll

130. Descendants, if any, of Lady JULIANA BRABAZON and Lady MARY BRABAZON, wife of the Rev. WILLIAM TISDALL, B.A., Vicar of St. James', Dublin (see Table X.).

131. Descendants, if any surviving, of BRABAZON HALLOWES of Glapwell, High Sheriff co. Derby; and of his brother, CHAMBRÉ HALLOWES, d. Sept. 1744 (see Table X.).

132. Descendants of WILLIAM HALLOWES (see Table X.), d. (–); m. CATHERINE, da. of [——] DODSLEY; and had issue 1a to 4a.

    1a. Thomas Hallowes of Glapwell, b. 16 Ap. 1771; d. unm. Dec. 1861.
    2a. William Hallowes, d. (in the East Indies).
    3a. Catharine Hallowes, m. [——] Coupe.
    4a. Anne Hallowes, m. 1st, Joseph Bilbie of Blidworth, co. Notts; 2ndly, [——] Heathcote; and had issue (with possibly others by 2nd husband) 1b.
    1b. Mary Anne Bilbie, d. 31 July 1877; m. 1 Mar. 1832, Francis Hall of Park Hall, co. Notts, J.P., D.L., b. 8 Dec. 1805; d.s.p. 1888.

133. Descendants of Col. JOHN HALLOWES, 56th Regt. (see Table X.), d. 24 May 1817; m. 1st, [——], da. of [——]; 2ndly, 2 Oct. 1787, LOUISA MARTHA, da. of Francis FATIO of St. Augustine, Florida; and had issue 1a to 11a.

    1a. Francis Hallowes of Glapwell Hall, J.P., Capt. R.N., b. 27 July 1788; d. 1 Dec. 1869; m. 7 Oct. 1818, Mary, da. of John Haffenden of Ashford; and had issue 1b to 5b.
    1b. Rev. Brabazon Hallowes of Glapwell Hall, M.A. (Oxon.), b. 10 Sept. 1819; d. 1 Sept. 1892; m. 1st, 16 June 1852, Jane Catherine Maria, da. of the Rev. Richard Howard of Llanrhiadr, D.D., d. 12 June 1853; 2ndly, 3 Sept. 1856, Elinor, da. of Thomas Green of Wilby and Athelington, d. 28 Dec. 1862; and had issue 1c to 5c.
    1c. Thomas Richard Francis Brabazon Hallowes, J.P., late Major 6th Dragoon Guards (Glapwell Hall, Chesterfield), b. 18 May 1853; m. 20 Oct. 1887, Fanny, da. of William Parish Robertson of Valparaiso; and has issue 1d to 3d.
    1d. Ronald Brabazon Hallowes, b. 18 July 1888.
    2d. John Chaworth Hallowes, b. 23 June 1894.
    3d. Gwendolyn Maud Hallowes, b. 15 July 1889.
    2c. Herbert Chaworth Hallowes (Ulverstone, Tasmania), b. 23 June 1857; m. 28 Mar. 1883, Elizabeth Duncan, da. of James Garroway of Glasgow; and has issue 1d to 5d.
    1d. Brabazon James Hallowes, b. 22 Aug. 1885.
    2d. Herbert Hallowes, b. 1897.
    3d. Geraldine Hallowes, b. 1890.
    4d. Dorothy Hallowes, b. 1892.
    5d. Louisa Hallowes, b. 1897.
    3c. Rev. Brabazon Chambré Hallowes, Rector of Eastnor (Eastnor Rectory, near Ledbury), b. 9 Ap. 1861; m. 18 Jan. 1894, Constance Emily, da. of the Rev. W. Sanders, Rector of Guildford; and has issue 1d to 2d.
    1d. Geoffrey Francis Brabazon Hallowes, b. 16 Mar. 1895.
    2d. Muriel Constance Hallowes, b. 31 July 1897.
    4c. Mary Elinor Hallowes, m. 20 Jan. 1886, the Rev. Gerald Henry Colvile, Rector of Weston (Weston Rectory, Shifnal); and has issue 1d to 3d.

[Nos. 7420 to 7433.

# of The Blood Royal

1*d*. Mansel Brabazon Fiennes Colvile, R.N., *b*. 19 Jan. 1887.

2*d*. Marjory Elinor Colvile.

3*d*. Evelyn May Colvile, *b*. 5 May 1899.

5*c*. Georgiana Catherine Hallowes, *m*. 21 Dec. 1892, Capt. William Birkenhead Mather Jackson, J.P. (*Ringwood, Chesterfield*); and has issue 1*d* to 3*d*.

1*d*. William Brabazon Mather Jackson, *b*. 7 Oct. 1893.

2*d*. George Christopher Mather Jackson, *b*. 12 Mar. 1896.

3*d*. Anthony Henry Mather Jackson, *b*. 9 Nov. 1899.

2*b*. *Francis Hallowes, Capt.* 2*nd Derby Militia*, b. 28 *Ap*. 1821; d. (*? unm.*) 9 *Dec*. 1883.

3*b*. *William Hallowes, Lieut.-Col.* 85*th Light Infantry*, b. 21 *Mar*. 1832; d. 9 *Sept*. 1879; m. 22 *June* 1861, *Louisa Coleman, da. of Lieut. Thomas Hallowes, R.N. ; and had issue* 1*c to* 6*c*.

1*c*. Francis William Hallowes, Major Indian Army, *b*. 28 May 1866; *m*. 26 Jan. 1891, Martha Musgrave, da. of Major-Gen. E. M. Beadon, *late* 85th King's L.I. ; and has issue 1*d* to 3*d*.

1*d*. William Edward Hallowes, *b*. 19 Dec. 1891.

2*d*. Jack Walter Hallowes, *b*. 15 July 1895.

3*d*. Martha Frances Hallowes, *b*. 3 Oct. 1903.

2*c*. Rev. Bernard Hallowes, Vicar of Brackenfield (*Brackenfield Vicarage, Alfreton, Derby*), *b*. Oct. 1869.

3*c*. Walter Haffenden Hallowes, Missionary in South Africa, *b*. June 1873.

4*c*. Beatrice Hallowes, *b*. 8 Feb. 1863.

5*c*. Agnes Wilhelmina Hallowes.

6*c*. Katherine Brabazon Hallowes.

4*b*. *Julian Hallowes*, d. (–); m. 3 *Feb*. 1848, *William Henry Addison of Addington, near Malling, Kent, M.D.*, d. 19 *June* 1892; *and had issue* 1*c to* 12*c*.

1*c*. Friend Addison (*Hirwen, New Guelderland, Natal*), *b*. Dec. 1848.

2*c*. William Henry Addison, *m*. and has issue (3 sons).

3*c*. Richard Addison, *m*. and has issue.

4*c*. Walter Addison, *m*. and has issue.

5*c*. Charles Addison, *unm*.

6*c*. *Victor Addison*, d. (–).

7*c*. Francis Addison, *unm*.

8*c*. Emily Addison, *m*. Archdeacon Robinson (*Bulawayo, Rhodesia*).

9*c*. *Margaret Addison*, d. *Oct. or Nov*. 1905; m. *Percy Field; and had issue* (1 *son and* 2 *das.*).

10*c*. Grace Addison, *m*. Neville Harrison (*Durban, Natal*), *s.p.*

11*c*. Juliet Addison, *unm*.

12*c*. Constance Addison, *unm*.

5*b*. Louisa Hallowes, *m*. 14 Sept. 1853, the Rev. David Phillips Lewis, Rector of Llandrino, co. Montgomery (8 *Gloucester Street, Belgrave Road, S.W.*); and has issue 1*c* to 7*c*.

1*c*. David Francis Lewis, C.B., A.D.C. to H.M. the King, Col. *late* The Buffs and Cheshire Regt., sometime (1899–1900) Governor of Sennaler, *b*. 21 Oct. 1855; *unm*.

2*c*. William Henry Phillips Lewis, Major R.A.M.C., *b*. 17 June 1859; *unm*.

3*c*. Charles Edward Llewellyn Lewis, *b*. 6 May 1865; *unm*.

4*c*. Cecil Hallowes Lewis, Major A.S.C., *b*. 9 Mar. 1869; *unm*.

5*c*. Ernest Richard Hallowes Lewis, *b*. 30 Oct. 1873; *unm*.

6*c*. Caroline Mary Lewis, *b*. 14 July 1854; *m*. 21 June 1892, Richard Egerton, Bar.-at-Law, Resident Magistrate Jamaica, *b*. 10 July 1844; *d.s.p.s.* 6 Oct. 1900.

[Nos. 7434 to 7466.]

209

The Plantagenet Roll

7c. Amy Louisa Lewis, b. 21 May 1867; m. 26 Ap. 1900, Edward Stanley Lloyd (*Ludlow*); and has issue 1d to 2d.

    1d. Evan John Stanley Lloyd, b. 2 Mar. 1902.

    2d. George Hallowes Lloyd, b. 22 Nov. 1904.

2a. John Hallowes of Milton, co. Hants, Admiral R.N., b. 21 Dec. 1791; d. 11 Jan. 1883; m. 3 Jan. 1822, *Margaret Lydia*, da. of Col. Nicholas Ramsay of Banff; d. (–); and had issue 1b to 4b.

    1b. George Skene Hallowes, Hon. Major-Gen., formerly Comdg. 25th King's Own Borderers (27 *Hogarth Road, S.W.*), b. 1830; unm.

    2b. Frederick William Hallowes, Admiral R.N., K.L.H., b. 1833; d. 1901; m. Georgiana, da. of [——] Haie; and had issue.

    3b. Henry Jardine Hallowes, Major-Gen. in the Army (47 *Lower Belgrave Street, Eaton Square, S.W.*), b. 1838; m. Charlotte Elizabeth, da. of the Hon. J. H. Gray, a Judge in British Columbia; and has issue 1c.

        1c. Beatrice Ramsay Hallowes.

    4b. Catherine Louisa Hallowes, b. 1835; m. Capt. John Low; and has issue.

3a. Thomas Hallowes, Lieut. R.N., d. (–); m. 1st, *Anne*, da. of [——] Tilbe, d. (–); 2ndly, *Mary Ann*, da. of [——] Coleman, d. (–); and had (with other) issue 1b to 2b.

    1b. Louisa Coleman Hallowes, b. 1 July 1832; m. 22 June 1861, Lieut.-Col. William Hallowes, d. 9 Sept. 1879; and has issue.

    See p. 209, Nos. 7441–7449.

    2b [——] Hallowes, m. Thomas Vaughan (19 *Newport, Lincoln*).

4a. Miller Hallowes, served 11 years in Army of Gen. Simon Bolivar, b. 19 Feb. 1799; d. 21. Sept. 1877; m. *Caroline*, da. of [——] Nicoll of Florida; and had issue.

5a. Price Brabazon Hallowes, d. (–); m. *Charlotte*, da. of [——] Bond; and had (with other) issue 1b.

    1b. Edward Price Blackwood Hallowes (91 *Onslow Gardens, South Kensington, S.W.*).

6a. William Hallowes, d. (–); m. *Elizabeth*, da. of [——] Tooke; and had (with other) issue 1b.

    1b. William Alexander Tooke Hallowes, M.A., Solicitor, of Messrs. Hallowes, Carter, & Ellis, 39 .Bedford Row, E.C. (*Heath Fern Lodge, East Heath Road, Hampstead*).

7a. Keith Hallowes, m. *Emily*, da. of [——] Bourne; and had issue.

8a. ⎫

9a. ⎬ 3 das. by 1st wife.

10a. ⎭

11a. Juliana Hallowes, m. 1st, [——] Pratt; 2ndly, James Booth.

                                           [Nos. 7467 to 7486.

134. Descendants, if any, of CATHERINE HALLOWES (see Table X.), b. c. 1720; d. 4 Sept. 1774; m. 1st, JOHN CROMWELL; 2ndly, 2 Nov. 1749, the Rev. GEORGE HATFIELD, Vicar of Doncaster,[1] b. c. 1718; d. 25 May 1785; of JULIANA HALLOWES, m. 1st, the Rev. [——] GIBSON; 2ndly, JOHN DEVAGNES; and of FRANCES HALLOWES, wife of the Rev. SAMUEL ABSON.

---

[1] By whom she had issue an only da. and h. Susannah, who d. 30 June 1780, aged 28, having m. 1st, 1777, John Sontag of the Hague, and 2ndly, Soloman Belshasar. *Ex inform.* Miss Hatfeild of Ickham, Wingham, Dover.

# of The Blood Royal

135. Descendants of Lady FRANCES BRABAZON (see Table X.), *d.*
4 Nov. 1751; *m.* Major-Gen. the Hon. HENRY PONSONBY,
M.P., *d.* (being slain at Fontenoy) 11 May 1745; and had
issue 1*a* to 2*a*.

1*a.* *Chambre Brabazon Ponsonby, M.P., d.* 20 *Dec.* 1762; m. *1st,* 28 *Sept.*
1846, *Elizabeth, da. and h. of Edward Clarke of Rouske, co. Meath; 3rdly, Mary,
da. of Sir William Barker of Kilcooly, 3rd Bart.* [*I.*], *who re-m. as 2nd wife,
c.* 1771, *Sir Robert Staples, 7th Bart.* [*I.*], *d.* 1773; *and had issue* 1*b to* 3*b.*

1*b.* *Chambre Brabazon Ponsonby, afterwards Ponsonby-Barker of Kilcooly, b.*
12 *June* 1762; *d.* 13 *Dec.* 1834; m. 4 *June* 1791, *Lady Henrietta, da. of Thomas
(Taylour), 1st Earl of Bective* [*I.*], *d.* 12 *Jan.* 1838; *and had issue* 1*c to* 2*c.*

1*c.* *Thomas Henry Ponsonby of Kilcooly, Capt. 6th Dragoons, b.* 21 *Feb.* 1807;
d. 10 *Feb.* 1880; m. 21 *Feb.* 1838, *Fanny Mary, da. of Major R. L. Dickson, d.*
4 *Feb.* 1893; *and had issue* 1*d to* 3*d.*

1*d.* *Chambre Brabazon Ponsonby of Kilcooly, b.* 14 *Dec.* 1839; *d.* 9 *Dec.* 1884;
m. 22 *Oct.* 1873, *the Hon. Mary Eliza Sophia (Kilcooly Abbey, Thurles), da. of
Edward (Plunkett), 16th Baron Dunsany* [*I.*]; *and had issue* 1*e to* 4*e.*

1*e.* Thomas Brabazon Ponsonby, *late* Lieut. 10th Hussars (*Kilcooly Abbey,
Thurles), b.* 29 *Dec.* 1878.

2*e.* Henry Chambre Ponsonby, *b.* 8 *Ap.* 1883.

3*e.* Dorothy Constance Ponsonby.

4*e.* Alice Isabel Ponsonby.

2*d.* Kathleen Louisa Georgiana Ponsonby.

3*d.* Blanche Mary Ponsonby (*Ryevale, Leixlip, co. Kildare*).

2*c.* *Catherine Jane Ponsonby, d. July* 1861; m. 25 *May* 1819, *Col. Edward
Michael Pakenham, afterwards Conolly, M.P., b.* 23 *Aug.* 1786; *d.* 4 *Jan.* 1848;
and had issue 1*d to* 5*d.*

1*d.* *Thomas Conolly of Castletown, co. Kildare, M.P., b.* 23 *Feb.* 1823; *d.* 10
Aug. 1876; m. 1 *Sept.* 1868, *Sarah, da. of Joseph Shaw of Celbridge; and had issue*
1*e to* 2*e.*

1*e.* Edward Michael Conolly, Capt. R.A. (*Castletown, Celbridge*), *b.* 20 Feb.
1874.

2*e.* Catherine Conolly, *m.* Ap. 1904, Gerald Shapland Carew (*Tedworth Square,
Chelsea, S.W.*).

2*d.* *John Angustus Conolly, V.C.,* Lieut.-Col. Coldstream Guards, *b.* 30 *Nov.*
1829; *d. Dec.* 1888; m. 4 *Aug.* 1864, *Ida Charlotte, da. of Edwyn Burnaby of
Baggrave Hall, d.* 17 *Mar.* 1886; *and had issue* 1*e to* 5*e.*

1*e.* John Richard Arthur Conolly, *b.* 22 July 1870.

2*e.* Aileen Geta Katherine Conolly, *m.* 10 Nov. 1891, Eustace Abel Smith
(*Longhills, co. Lincoln*); and has issue 1*f to* 4*f.*

1*f.* Edward Michael Conolly Abel Smith, *b.* 3 Dec. 1899.

2*f.* Desmond Abel Smith, *b.* 2 Sept. 1902.

3*f.* Emmeline Smith.

4*f.* Alethea Smith.

3*e.* Oonah Edwina Conolly, *m.* 22 Jan. 1891, Major John McNeile, *late* Coldstream Guards (9 *West Eaton Place, S.W.*); and has issue 1*f* to 4*f.*

1*f.* John Henry McNeile, *b.* 2 Aug. 1892.

2*f.* Aileen Charlotte McNeile, *b.* 6 Oct. 1893.

3*f.* Mary Bridget McNeile, *b.* 4 Nov. 1896.

4*f.* Rose Oonah McNeile, *b.* 10 June 1898.

4*e.* Louisa Augusta Conolly, } (*Hampton Court Palace*).
5*e.* Irene Beatrice Conolly, }   [Nos. 7487 to 7507.

The Plantagenet Roll

3d. Louisa Augusta Conolly, b. 12 *June* 1822; d. 4 *Nov.* 1854; m. 28 *July* 1846, *Clotworthy Wellington William Robert (Rowley), 3rd Baron Langford [I.],* b. 24 *July* 1825; d. 19 *July* 1854; *and had issue 1e to 4e.*

1e. Hercules Edward (Rowley), 4th Baron Langford [I.], a Rep. Peer, K.C.V.O., sometime (1886–1892) State Steward to the Viceroy, and (1895–1902) Comptroller of the Household, &c. (*Summerhill House, Enfield, co. Meath*), b. 1 June 1848; *m.* 11 July 1889, Georgina Mary, da. of Sir Richard Sutton, 4th Bart. [G.B.]; and has issue 1f to 3f.

1f. Hon. John Hercules William Rowley, b. 16 Dec. 1894.

2f. Hon. George Cecil Rowley, b. 18 Aug. 1896.

3f. Hon. Noel Maud Rowley, b. 25 Dec. 1893.

2e. Hon. William Chambre Rowley, *late* Major R.A., one of H.M.'s Hon. Corps of Gentlemen-at-Arms (*4 Cadogan Mansions, S.W.*), b. 30 Aug. 1849; *m.* 27 July 1889, the Hon. Mabel Maud, da. of William John (Legh), 1st Baron Newton [U.K.].

3e. Hon. Randolfe Thomas Rowley (*Tuparipari, Wanganui, N.Z.*), b. 22 Dec. 1852; *m.* 4 Oct. 1883, Rosetta, da. of Thomas Henry Fletcher of Homewood, New Zealand; and has issue 1f.

1f. Clotworthy Wellington Thomas Edward Rowley, b. 1 June 1885.

4e. Hon. Catharine Frances Rowley, b. 24 May 1847; d. 13 *Jan.* 1879; m. 5 *Ap.* 1877, *James Lenox Naper, J.P., D.L., High Sheriff co. Meath* 1853; d. (*Loughcrew, near Oldcastle, R.S.O., co. Meath*); *and had issue 1f.*

1f. William Lenox Naper, b. 4 Jan. 1879.

4d. Henrietta Conolly, b. 1827; d. (–); m. 29 *May* 1880, *the Rev. Edward Montgomery Moore.*

5d. Mary Margaret Conolly, b. *Aug.* 1834; d. 13 *May* 1894; m. 6 *June* 1854, *the Right Hon. Henry Bruen, P.C. [I.], M.P., J.P., D.L., &c. (Oak Park, co. Carlow, &c.); and had issue.*

See the Clarence Volume, pp. 623–624, Nos. 27963–27985.

2b. Frances Ponsonby, b. 6 *Nov.* 1749; d. 19 *Nov.* 1802; m. 28 *July* 1767, *Gorges Lowther of Kilrue, co. Meath,* d. 1785; *and had issue 1c to 4c.*

1c. *Gorges Lowther of Kilrue and Hampton Hall, co. Somerset, M.P.,* b. 1769; d. 23 *Feb.* 1854; m. *1st, July* 1794, *Julia, da. of the Rev. Thomas Huntingford,* d. 1830; *and had issue 1d to 7d.*

1d. St. George Lowther of Brading, I.W., d. 10 *Mar.* 1871; m. *2ndly, Mina, da. of Edward Golding of Maiden Erlegh, co. Berks; and had issue 1e to 2e.*

1e. Gorges St. George Beresford Lowther.

2e. Lancelot Lowther.

2d. Brabazon Lowther of Shrigley Park, J.P., d. 1877; m. *Jan.* 1847, *Ellen Jane (Shrigley Park, Macclesfield), da. of Thomas Legh of Lyme Park, LL.D., F.A.S.; and had issue 1e to 3e.*

1e. William Gorges Lowther, Lieut.-Col. and Hon. Col. Devon Artillery, *late* R.A., b. 20 Feb. 1850; *m.* 1874, Harriet Agnes, da. of the Rev. Edward Leigh Bennett of Long Sutton; and has issue 1f to 3f.

1f. Edward St. George Lowther, Lieut. R.A., b. 10 Dec. 1878.

2f. John Brabazon Lowther, b. 19 Ap. 1883.

3f. Thomas Beresford Lowther, b. 4 Ap. 1890.

2e. Henry Crofton Lowther, b. 26 Mar. 1856.

3e. Eleanor Constance Lowther.

3d. Marcus Lowther, Rear-Ad. R.N. (*2 Ependen Road, St. Leonards*), m. 1st, Emily Lutwidge, widow of Count Maximilian de Lercherfeld Brennberg, da. of Isaac Cookson of Mildon Park, J.P., d. 15 Jan. 1893; 2ndly, May 1897, Isabel, da. of J. Pletts of Newcastle, C.E. [Nos. 7508 to 7547.

212

# of The Blood Royal

4d. Julia Lowther, d. (-) ; m. 1831, *the Rev. Henry Lee of Kingsgate House, Winchester.*

5d. Maud Lowther, d. (-) ; m. 1*st, Thomas Legh of Lyme, co. Chester ; 2ndly, A. J. Deschamps de la Tour of Milford, co. Hants.*

6d. Blanche Lowther, d. (-) ; m. *Allen Dent.*

7d. Sophia Lowther, d. (-) ; m. *W. M. Bridger of Halnaker House, co. Sussex, and The Chantry, Bradford-on-Avon.*

2c. Frances Lowther, d. (-) ; m. *C. Apthorp.*

3c. Sophia Jane Lowther, d. (-) ; m. *J. Alcock.*

4c. Juliana Lowther, d. 15 Dec. 1847 ; m. 1803, *Capt. Thomas Penruddocke*, 3rd Guards, b. 6 Feb. 1781 ; d. 4 Ap. 1867 ; *and had issue* 1d *to* 5d.

1d. John Hungerford Penruddocke, b. 6 Aug. 1805 ; d. 23 Ap. 1900 ; m. 29 May 1856, *Elizabeth, da. of William Heald Ludlow Bruges of Seend, Wilts,* d. 24 Nov. 1897 ; *and had issue* 1e *to* 6e.

1e. John Hungerford Penruddocke, Chief Engineer Uganda Railway (*Nairobi, British East Africa*), b. 23 Feb. 18—.

2e. Edmund Long Penruddocke (*P.O. Box 715, Birmingham, Alabama, U.S.A.*), b. 5 July 18—; m. Norvelle, da. of [——] Bragge ; *and has issue* 1f.

1f. Norvelle Isabella Penruddocke, b. (at Montgomery, Alabama, U.S.A.) Nov. 1902.

3e. Annie Elizabeth Penruddocke, m. John Bell (*Hong-Kong*).

4e. Arundel Augusta Penruddocke, m. 1882, Joshua Reynolds Gascoigne Gwatkin, J.P., Major R.W.Y. Cavalry (*The Manor House, Potterne, Devizes*); and has issue 1f *to* 2f.

1f. Robert Torrington Gwatkin, Lieut. 6th Dragoon Guards, b. 10 Sept. 1885.

2f. Arundel Theophila Gwatkin, b. 2 Dec. 1886.

5e. Mary Albinia Penruddocke (*Tellisford, near Bath*).

6e. Helen A'Court Penruddocke.

2d. George Penruddocke, b. 6 June 1807 ; d. (-).

3d. Juliana Letitia Penruddocke, d. 6 Feb. 1890 ; m. 15 Feb. 1827, *Charles Penruddocke, Bar.-at-Law,* b. 21 Jan. 1779 ; d. 15 Dec. 1839 ; *and had issue* 1e *to* 5e.

1e. Charles Penruddocke *of Compton Chamberlayne, &c., J.P., D.L., High Sheriff co. Wilts* 1861, b. 30 Sept. 1828 ; d. 30 Oct. 1899 ; m. 26 Ap. 1853, *Flora Henrietta, da. of Walter Long of Rood Ashton, M.P. ; and had issue.*

See p. 135, Nos. 1845–1859.

2e. Rev. John Hungerford Penruddocke, M.A. (*Camb.*), late Rector of Baverstock, and previously for thirty-five years Vicar of South Newton, b. 23 Oct. 1829 ; d. 27 Sept. 1905 ; m. 14 Jan. 1858, *Emma* (*Baverstock, St. Swithin's Road, Bournemouth*), da. of John Powys of Westwood, co. Stafford ; *and had issue* 1f *to* 6f.

1f. John Powys Penruddocke, M.A. (Oxon.) (*Winchester House, Eastbourne*), b. 6 Sept. 1861 ; m. 1st, 17 Ap. 1897, Clara Albertina, da. of Major R. A. Kane, 71st Highland L.I., d. 20 Oct. 1901 ; 2ndly, 8 Jan. 1903, Margaret, da. of Canon E. Fiennes Trotman of Marshfield ; *and has issue* 1g *to* 3g.

1g. Cyril Powys Penruddocke, b. 12 Feb. 1896.

2g. Norman Feilding Penruddocke, b. 27 Sept. 1897.

3g. Lorna Mary Penruddocke, b. 29 May 1899.

2f. Edward Wyndham Penruddocke (*Bransgore, near Christchurch*), b. 19 Nov. 1863 ; m. 8 Aug. 1901, Muriel Turner, da. of [——] Newcomen of Kirkleatham Hall, Redcar ; *and has issue* 1g.

1g. Joan Teresa Powys Penruddocke, b. 3 Mar. 1903.

3f. Henry Beresford Penruddocke, Lieut. R.N.R., b. 26 June 1865 ; m. 20 Ap. 1899, Ada, da. of [——] White-White ; *and has issue* 1g.

1g. Dorothea Penruddocke, b. 16 June 1903.   [Nos. 7548 to 7579.

The Plantagenet Roll

4f. Rev. William Feilding Penruddocke, M.A. (Oxon.), Curate of St. Augustine's, Kilburn (4 *Bolton Road, N.W.*), *b.* 8 Oct. 1866; *unm.*

5f. Arthur Lowther Penruddocke, *b.* 20 Dec. 1872; *unm.*

6f. Catherine Letitia Penruddocke, *m.* 23 Aug. 1883, Edmund Maurice Sautter of Beauregard, Rolle, Geneva, *d.* (at Beauregard) 22 July 1887; and has issue 1g to 2g.

1g. Guy Alexander Sautter, *b.* 30 Dec. 1886.

2g. Marcelle Gertrude Sautter, *b.* 14 May 1885.

3e. Anna Wyndham Penruddocke, Deaconess, Bishop of Worcester's Deaconess Association (*Northfield House, Rugby*), *m.* 29 Sept. 1853, David Buchanan, M.A. (Camb.), *b.* 16 Jan. 1830; *d.* 30 May 1900; and has issue 1f to 9f.

1f. David Penruddocke Buchanan (*Mayfield Cunninghams, Manawater, New Zealand*), *b.* 18 Oct. 1856; *m.* 1st (at Wanganui, N.Z.), 14 Dec. 1887, Marianne Alice, da. of Gen. George Mein, *d.* 24 Mar. 1898; 2ndly (in Wanganui District), 31 Jan. 1900, Florence, da. of William Clarke Watkin; and has issue 1g to 5g.

1g. Robert Wyndham Buchanan, *b.* 17 June 1902.

2g. John Penruddocke Buchanan, *b.* 28 June 1903.

3g. Hilda Penruddocke Buchanan, *b.* 17 July 1890.

4g. Grace Buchanan, *b.* 11 Feb. 1901.

5g. Catherine Helen Buchanan, *b.* 8 Dec. 1904.

2f. John Penruddocke Buchanan, *b.* 16 Aug. 1864.

3f. George Penruddocke Buchanan, *b.* 21 Mar. 1877.

4f. Annie Letitia Buchanan, *b.* 6 Oct. 1854.

5f. Adeline Wyndham Buchanan, *b.* 19 Aug. 1855.

6f. Helen Rokeby Buchanan, *b.* 16 Sept. 1857; *m.* Nov. 1886, Charles Arthur John Levett (*Ratanui, Feilding, New Zealand*); and has issue 1g to 3g.

1g. Charles Edward Levett, *b.* 17 May 1888.

2g. Maud Helen Levett, *b.* 10 July 1889.

3g. Catherine Lissey Levett, *b.* 30 Dec. 1894.

7f. Gertrude Louisa Buchanan, *b.* 13 Mar. 1866.

8f. Margaret Henrietta Buchanan, *b.* 10 Aug. 1869.

9f. Jessie Lowther Buchanan, *b.* 30 July 1872.

4e. Letitia Grant Penruddocke (*Fyfield Lodge, Milton Silbourne, Pewsey, co. Wilts*).

5e. Charlesanna Posthuma Penruddocke, *m.* 26 Sept. 1865, Col. William Graydon, *d.s.p.* 11 Feb. 1895.

4d. Agnes Penruddocke, d. 1 (*or 3*) *Dec.* 1889; *m.* as 2nd wife, 8 *July* 1834, William Heald Ludlow-Bruges *of Seend, M.P., J.P., D.L.,* bapt. 25 *May* 1796; *d.* 25 *Sept.* 1855; and had issue 1e to 5e.

1e. Richard Heald Ludlow-Bruges, Lord of the Manor of Sandridge (*Seend, near Melksham ; Sandridge, near Chippenham*), *b.* 29 June 1845; *m.* 15 Sept. 1881, Lisette, da. of Col. Digby St. Vincent Hamilton.

2e. Henry Hungerford Ludlow-Bruges, J.P., *b.* 10 June 1847; *d.* (–).

3e. Juliana Ludlow-Bruges, *m.* Rev. Neston Heathcote of Shaw Hill, co. Wilts.

4e. Bertha Ludlow-Bruges.

5e. Eleanor Ludlow-Bruges.

5d. *Priscilla Sophia Penruddocke, b.* 31 *Dec.* 1822; *d.* 22 *Sept.* 1882; *m.* 10 *Jan.* 1843, Capt. *Robert Harris, R.N., b.* 1811; *d.* 16 *Jan.* 1865; *and had issue* 1e to 3e.

1e. Sir Robert Hastings Harris, K.C.B., K.C.M.G., Admiral R.N., President of the Royal Naval College (*Royal Naval College, Greenwich*), *b.* Oct. 1843; *m.* 25 Aug. 1875, Florence Cordelia, da. of Comm. William Edmund Henn-Gennys, R.N.; and has issue 1f to 8f.   [Nos. 7580 to 7610.

214

CECELY (NEVILE), DUCHESS OF YORK.

# of The Blood Royal

1f. Robert Henry Thomas Penruddocke Harris, *b.* 1881.

2f. William Vesey Hamilton Harris, *b.* 1891.

3f. Malcolm Alfred Milner Harris, *b.* 1900.

4f. Florence Catherine May Harris, *b.* 1876.

5f. Violet Blanche Josephine Harris, *b.* 1877.

6f. Dorothy Agnes Henn-Gennys Harris, *b.* 1879.

7f. Priscilla Sophia Harris, *b.* 1883.

8f. Winifred Mary Letitia Harris, *b.* 1885.

2e. Agnes Lucy Harris, b. 11 *Jan.* 1848; d. 6 *Feb.* 1900; m. *Oct.* 1886, *Rear-Admiral Robert Boyle, R.N.*, d. 12 *June* 1892; and had issue 1f to 2f.

1f. Archibald Boyle, *b.* 1887.

2f. David Boyle, *b.* 1889.

3e. Blanche Priscilla Harris, *b.* Mar. 1857; *m.* 13 Dec. 1877, Count Frederick Cosmeto Metaxa, Vice-Admiral R.N., late Naval A.D.C. to H.M. the King (*Brentry, Lansdowne, Weymouth*); and has issue 1f.

1f. Count Frederick Robert Wyndham Metaxa, Lieut. Royal Scots Fusiliers, *b.* 12 Sept. 1878.

3b. Mary Ponsonby, d. (−); m. *Thomas Barton of Grove, M.P.*, d. 1820; and had issue 1c to 4c.

1c. William Barton of Grove, J.P., D.L., High Sheriff co. Tipperary, b. 21 June 1790; d. 7 *Feb.* 1857; m. *Ap.* 1815, *Catherine, da. of Samuel Perry of Woodroffe (by the Hon. Deborah, da. of Henry Sadlier (Prittie), 1st Baron Dunalley [I.]),* d. 6 *Ap.* 1872; and had issue 1d to 7d.

1d. Samuel Henry Barton of Grove, J.P., D.L., b. 26 *Oct.* 1817; d. 27 *Nov.* 1891; m. 26 *Dec.* 1862, *Mary Elizabeth (15 Lansdown Place, Cheltenham), da. of Major Thomas Frobisher, J.P., D.L.; and had issue 1e to 3e.*

1e. William Henry Hugh Barton (*Grove, near Fethard*), *b.* 26 Feb. 1871.

2e. Charles Robert Barton (*Marlfield Cottage, Clonmel, co. Tipperary*), *b.* 4 Mar. 1877; *m.* 15 Oct. 1904, Ethel Mary, da. of George Cobden, J.P.

3e. Rose Catherine Florence Barton.

2d. William Hugh Barton, b. 1820; d. 1897; m. *Mary, da. of Capt. Blakeney; and had issue (five sons and four das.).*

3d. Deborah Barton, d. (−); m. *John Wade of St. Canices Cottage, Kilkenny,* d. (−); *and had issue 1e to 3e.*

1e. William Barton Wade, Col. Army Pay Dept. (*St. Canices Cottage, Kilkenny*), *b.* 11 July 1840; *m.* and has issue.

2e. John Wade.

3e. Catherine Anne Villiers Wade, *m.* as 2nd wife, 1874, Sir William Fitzmaurice Josiah Hort of Castle Strange, 4th Bart. [G.B.], *b.* 20 Jan. 1827; *d.s.p.* 18 Sept. 1887.

4d. Mary Frances Barton, d. 17 *Mar.* 1865; m. 4 *Oct.* 1845, *Charles Shaw, Q.C. (son of Sir Robert Shaw, 1st Bart. [U.K.]),* b. 27 *July* 1817; d. 9 *Dec.* 1870; *and had issue 1e to 10e.*

1e. Robert Barton Shaw (50 *Morpeth Mansions, S.W.*), *b.* 2 Dec. 1847; *m.* Dec. 1895, Caroline, da. of S. de la Cherois-Crommelin of Carrowdere.

2e. Charles Shaw, *b.* 24 June 1853.

3e. William Shaw, *b.* 5 Jan. 1857; *m.* and has issue 1f.

1f. William Shaw.

4e. Thomas Barton Shaw, Inspector, Board of Education, *late* Capt. R.E. (*Kildare Street, Dublin; United Service*), *b.* 27 May 1858.

5e. Catherine Shaw,
6e. Caroline Shaw,
7e. Maria Shaw,
8e. Emily Shaw,
9e. Alice Shaw,
10e. May Shaw,
} (*Mount Saville, Terenure, co. Dublin*).

[Nos. 7611 to 7639.

215

5*d. Catherine Grace Barton*, d. 15 Dec. 1902; m. 10 *June* 1852, *Sir Robert Shaw*, *4th Bart.* [*U.K.*], b. 3 *Aug.* 1821; d. 16 *May* 1895; *and had issue.*
See the Clarence Volume, p. 298, Nos. 8324–8330.

6*d.* Anne Margaret Barton, *m.* George Gough of Rathronan, co. Tipperary, *s.p.*
7*d.* Emily Martha Barton.

2*c. Chambré Brabazon Barton, Lieut.-Col. 2nd Life Guards*, d. (? *unm.*) 1834.
3*c. Grace Barton*, d. (–); m. 1*st, as 2nd wife, Lieut.-Col. Kingsmill Pennefather of New Park*, d.v.p. 1819; 2*ndly, Major Michael Angelo Galliazzi, Austrian Service; and had issue 1d to 2d.*
1*d.* Mary Pennefather, *unm.*
2*d. Catherine Pennefather*, d. 1 *Jan.* 1843; m. 17 *Aug.* 1840, *the Hon. Henry Alexander Savile*, b. 12 *Dec.* 1811; d. 1 *Mar.* 1850; *and had issue 1e.*
1*e. William Savile, D.L., Capt. 9th Lancers*, b. 8 *Oct.* 1841; d. 4 *Ap.* 1903; m. 12 *June* 1865, *Emily* (20*a St. James's Place, S.W.*), *da. of Capt. Delme Seymour Davies of Highmead; and had issue 1f to 2f.*
1*f.* John Herbert Drax Savile, late Capt. Rifle Brigade, b. 29 Mar. 1866.
2*f.* Beatrice Anne Louisa Savile.
4*c. Catherine Barton, m. Edmund Staples of Dunmore, Queen's Co.*
2*a. Juliana Ponsonby*, m. 1743, *William Southwell.*

[Nos. 7640 to 7651.

136. Descendants of JAMES (CECIL), 1st MARQUIS [G.B.] and 7th EARL [E.] OF SALISBURY, K.G., sometime (1783–1804) Lord Chamberlain to King George III. (see Table XI.), *b.* 14 Sept. 1748; *d.* 13 June 1823; *m.* 2 Dec. 1773, Lady MARY AMELIA, da. of Wills (HILL), 1st Marquis of Downshire [I.], *b.* 16 Aug. 1750; *d.* 28 Nov. 1835; and had issue 1*a* to 2*a*.

1*a. James Brownlow William (Cecil, afterwards (R.L. 22 Mar. 1821) Gascoyne-Cecil), 2nd Marquis [G.B.] and 9th Earl [E.] of Salisbury, K.G.*, b. 17 *Ap.* 1791; d. 12 *Ap.* 1868; m. 1*st,* 2 *Feb.* 1821, *Frances Mary, da. and h. of Bamber Gascoyne*, d. 15 Oct. 1839; 2*ndly,* 29 *Ap.* 1847, *Lady Mary Catherine, da. of George John (Sackville-West), 5th Earl De La Warr [G.B.] (who re-m. 5 July 1870, Edward Henry (Stanley), 15th Earl of Derby [E.], K.G.*), d. 6 *Dec.* 1900; *and had issue 1b to 6b.*
1*b. Robert Arthur Talbot (Gascoyne-Cecil), 3rd Marquis [G.B.] and 9th Earl [E.] of Salisbury, K.G., P.C., three times* (1885–1886, 1886–1892, *and* 1895–1902) *Prime Minister, &c. &c.*, b. 3 *Feb.* 1830; d. 22 *Aug.* 1903; m. 11 *July* 1857, *Georgina, V.A., C.I., da. of the Hon. Sir Edward Hall Alderson, a Baron of the Exchequer,* d. 20 *Nov.* 1899; *and had issue 1c to 7c.*
1*c.* James Edward Herbert (Gascoyne-Cecil), 4th Marquis [G.B.] and 10th Earl [E.] of Salisbury, P.C., C.B, *late* Lord Privy Seal (*Hatfield House, Hatfield; 20 Arlington Street, S.W., &c.*), b. 23 Oct. 1861; m. 17 May 1887, Lady Cicely Alice, da. of Arthur (Gore), 5th Earl of Arran [I.]; and has issue 1*d* to 4*d*.
1*d*–4*d.* See the Clarence Volume, p. 291, Nos. 8124–8127.
2*c.* Rev. Lord William Rupert Ernest Gascoyne-Cecil, Rector of Bishop's Hatfield, and Rural Dean of Hertford (*St. Audrey's, Hatfield*), b. 9 Mar. 1863; m. 16 Aug. 1887, Lady Florence Mary, da. of Edward (Bootle-Wilbraham), 1st Earl of Lathom [U.K.]; and has issue 1*d* to 6*d*.
1*d.* Randle William Gascoyne-Cecil, b. 28 Nov. 1889.
2*d.* Victor Alexander Gascoyne-Cecil, b. 21 May 1891.
3*d.* John Arthur Gascoyne-Cecil, b. 28 Mar. 1893.
4*d.* Rupert Edward Gascoyne-Cecil, b. 20 Jan. 1895.
5*d.* Eve Alice Gascoyne-Cecil, }
6*d.* Mary Edith Gascoyne-Cecil, } (twins), b. 13 Jan. 1900. [Nos. 7652 to 7663.

216

# of The Blood Royal

3c. Lord Edgar Algernon Robert Gascoyne-Cecil, K.C. (25 *Grove End Road*, *N.W.*), *b.* 14 Sept. 1864 ; *m.* 22 Jan. 1889, Lady Eleanor, da. of George (Lambton), 2nd Earl of Durham [U.K.].

4c. Lord Edward Herbert Gascoyne-Cecil, D.S.O., Major and Brevet Lieut.-Col. Grenadier Guards and Director of Intelligence and Agent for Sudan at Cairo (*Cairo, Egypt ; Junior Carlton*), *b.* 12 July 1867 ; *m.* 18 June 1894, Violet Georgina, da. of Admiral Frederick Augustus Maxse ; and has issue 1*d* to 2*d*.

1*d*. George Edward Gascoyne-Cecil, *b.* 9 Sept. 1895.

2*d*. Helen Mary Gascoyne-Cecil, *b.* 11 May 1901.

5c. Lord Hugh Richard Heathcote Gascoyne-Cecil, M.P. (20 *Arlington Street*, *S.W. ; Junior Carlton*), *b.* 14 Oct. 1869.

6c. Lady Beatrix Maud Gascoyne-Cecil, *m.* 27 Oct. 1883, William Waldegrave (Palmer), 2nd Earl of Selborne [U.K.], P.C. (*Blackmoor, Liss, Hants*) ; and has issue. See p. 180, Nos. 6420–6423.

7c. Lady Gwendolen Gascoyne-Cecil.

2b. Lord Eustace Brownlow Henry Gascoyne-Cecil, J.P., *late* Lieut.-Col. Coldstream Guards and sometime (1874–1800) Surveyor-Gen. of Ordnance, and (1865–1885) an M.P. (*Lychett Heath, Poole ;* 111 *Eaton Square, S.W.*), *b.* 24 Ap. 1834 ; *m.* 18 Sept. 1860, Lady Gertrude Louisa, da. of John (Scott), 2nd Earl of Eldon [U.K.] ; and has issue 1*c* to 3*c*.

1c. Evelyn Gascoyne-Cecil, M.P. (10 *Eaton Place, S.W.*), *b.* 30 May 1865 ; *m.* 16 Feb. 1898, the Hon. Alicia Margaret, da. of William Amherst (Tyssen-Amherst), 1st Baron Amherst of Hackney [U.K.] ; and has issue 1*d* to 3*d*.

1*d*. Robert William Evelyn Gascoyne-Cecil, *b.* 28 Feb. 1901.

2*d*. Margaret Gertrude Gascoyne-Cecil, *b.* 27 Nov. 1898.

3*d*. Maud Katharine Alicia Gascoyne-Cecil, *b.* 20 Oct. 1904.

2c. Algernon Gascoyne-Cecil, *b.* 31 Jan. 1879.

3c. Blanche Louisa Gascoyne-Cecil, *b.* 2 Ap. 1872.

3b. Lord Arthur Cecil (*The Mount, Lymington, Hants*), *b.* 3 July 1851 ; *m.* 1st, 8 Jan. 1874, Elizabeth Ann, da. of Joseph Wilson of Woodburn Manor, *d.* 11 Oct. 1901 ; 2ndly, 4 Nov. 1902, Baroness Frederica, da. of Otto, Baron Von Klenck [Austria] ; and has issue 1*c* to 2*c*.

1*c*–2*c*. See the Clarence Volume, p. 224, Nos. 4527–4529.

4b. Lady Mildred Arabella Charlotte Gascoyne-Cecil, *b.* 24 *Oct.* 1822 ; *d.* 18 *Mar.* 1881 ; *m.* 7 *July* 1842, *the Right Hon. Alexander James Beresford Hope, afterwards* (R.L. 1854) *Beresford-Hope of Bedgebury Park and Beresford Hall, P.C., M.P., President of the Royal Institute of British Architects, &c., b.* 25 *Jan.* 1820 ; *d. Oct.* 1887 ; *and had issue* 1*c to* 8*c*.

1c. Philip Beresford Beresford-Hope, J.P., Capt. and Hon. Major *late* W. Kent Yeo. (*Bedgebury Park, Cranbrook, Kent ; Beresford Hall, Ashbarne ;* 3 *Park Place, St. James'*), *b.* 16 May 1851 ; *m.* 1883, Evelyn, da. of Gen. Frost of St. Louis, U.S.A., *d.* 27 May 1900 ; and has issue.

2c. Charles Thomas Beresford-Hope (6 *Gledhow Gardens, S.W.*), *b.* 3 Nov. 1855 ; *m.* 18 June 1879, Julia Margaret, da. of Harold Augustus Ernuin ; and has issue 1*d* to 2*d*.

1*d*. Harold Thomas Beresford-Hope, *b.* 13 June 1882.

2*d*. Mildred Catherine Irene Beresford-Hope, *b.* 18 May 1881.

3c. Louisa Mary Beresford-Hope, *m.* 24 Aug. 1865, Hallyburton George (Campbell), 3rd Baron Strath.eden and Campbell [U.K.] (*Hartrigge, Jedburgh ;* 17 *Bruton Street, W.*) ; and has issue 1*d* to 4*d*.

1*d*. Hon. John Beresford Campbell, J.P., D.L., Capt. Reserve of Officers, *late* Coldstream Guards (*Moycullen House, co. Galway*), *b.* 20 June 1866 ; *m.* 15 Jan.

[Nos. 7664 to 7691.

The Plantagenet Roll

1895, the Hon. Alice Susan, da. of John (Hamilton), 1st Baron Hamilton of Dalzell [U.K.]; and has issue 1e to 4e.

1e. Donald Campbell, b. 16 Ap. 1896.

2e. Alastair Campbell, b. 21 Nov. 1899.

3e. Gavin Campbell, b. 28 Aug. 1901.

4e. Jean Campbell, b. 19 May 1904.

2d. Hon. Cecil Arthur Campbell (White's), b. 3 Ap. 1869.

3d. Hon. Kenneth Hallyburton Campbell (Bachelors'; White's), b. 21 May 1871; m. May 1905, Rosalinda, da. of Henry Oppenheim of 16 Bruton Street, W.

4d. Hon. Mildred Louisa Campbell, b. 29 Nov. 1867.

4c. Etheldreda Beresford-Hope, m. as 2nd wife, 19 Ap. 1876, Marwood Tucker (Coryton Park, near Axminster).

5c. Margaret Beresford-Hope, d. Sept. 1900; m. the Rev. Newton Mant, M.A. (Camb.), Vicar of Hendon.

6c. Agnes Beresford-Hope.

7c. Bridget Beresford-Hope, d. 27 Feb. 1896; m. 8 Feb. 1873, the Hon. Alban George Henry Gibbs, M.P., J.P., D.L. (82 Portland Place, W.); and had issue 1d to 3d.

1d–3d. See the Clarence Volume, p. 157, Nos. 2402–2404.

8c. Mary Frances Beresford-Hope, m. 1 Mar. 1886, the Right Hon. James William Lowther, P.C., M.P., F.R.G.S., Speaker of the House of Commons (Speaker's House, Westminster; 16 Wilton Crescent, S.W.); and has issue 1d to 3d.

1d–3d. See the Clarence Volume, p. 602, Nos. 26495–26497.

5b. Lady Blanche Mary Harriet Gascoyne-Cecil, b. 5 Mar. 1825; d. 16 May 1872; m. 15 Aug. 1843, James Maitland Balfour of Whittingehame, b. 5 Jan. 1820; d. 23 Feb. 1856; and had issue 1c to 6c.

1c. Right Hon. Arthur James Balfour of Whittingehame, P.C., M.P., sometime (1902–1905) Prime Minister and First Lord of the Treasury, &c. (Whittingehame, near Prestonkirk; 10 Downing Street, S.W.), b. 15 July 1848.

2c. Right Hon. Gerald William Balfour, P.C., sometime (1902–1905) President of the Board of Trade, formerly (1895–1900) Chief Secretary [I.] (3 Whitehall Court, S.W.; Fisher's Hill, Woking), b. 9 Ap. 1853; m. 21 Dec. 1887, Lady Elizabeth Edith, da. of Edward Robert (Bulwer-Lytton), 1st Earl of Lytton [U.K.]; and has issue 1d to 5d.

1d–5d. See the Clarence Volume, p. 97, Nos. 786–790.

3c. Eustace James Anthony Balfour, M.A., F.S.A., Lieut.-Col. London Scottish V.R. (32 Addison Road, W.), b. 8 June 1854; m. 12 May 1879, Lady Frances, da. of George Douglas (Campbell), 8th Duke of Argyll [S.], K.G., K.T.; and has issue 1d to 5d.

1d. Francis Cecil Campbell Balfour, b. 1884.

2d. Oswald Herbert Campbell Balfour, b. 1894.

3d. Blanche Elizabeth Campbell Balfour, b. 1880; m. 18 Nov. 1902, Edgar Trevelyan Stratford Dugdale (Merivale Hall, Atherstone); and has issue 1e.

1e. [——] Dugdale, b. 1903.

4d. Joan Alice Campbell Balfour, b. 1889.

5d. Alison Katherine Campbell Balfour, b. 1891.

4c. Eleanor Mildred Balfour, Principal of Newnham Coll., Cambridge, b. 11 Mar. 1855; m. 4 Ap. 1876, Professor Henry Sidgwick, M.A., Litt.D., Professor of Moral Philosophy at Cambridge, d. 1900.

5c. Evelyn Georgiana Mary Balfour, m. 19 July 1871, John William (Strutt), 3rd Baron Rayleigh [U.K.], O.M., D.C.L., LL.D., D.Sc., F.R.S. (Terling Place, Witham, Essex); and has issue 1d to 3d.

1d. Hon. Robert John Strutt, M.A. (Camb.), b. 28 Aug. 1875.

2d. Hon. Arthur Charles Strutt, Lieut. R.N. (Sunnyside, Chesterton Road,

[Nos. 7692 to 7725.

218

# of The Blood Royal

Cambridge), *b.* 2 Oct. 1878; *m.* 6 July 1905, Lady Mary Hilda, da. of Robert Bermingham (Clements), 4th Earl of Leitrim [I.].

    3*d.* Hon. William Maitland Strutt, *b.* 20 July 1886.

    6*c.* Alice Blanche Balfour (*Whittingehame, Prestonkirk, N.B.*).

    6*b.* Lady Margaret Elizabeth Cecil (*Oakdown, Burwash*).

    2*a. Lady Emily Anne Bennet Elizabeth Cecil, b.* 13 *July* 1789; d. 21 *Jan.* 1858; m. *as* 1st *wife*, 29 *May* 1812, *George Thomas John* (*Nugent*), 1st *Marquis of Westmeath* [*I.*], *b.* 17 *July* 1785; q.s.p. 5 *May* 1871; *and had issue* 1*b.*

    1*b. Lady Rosa Emily Mary Anne Nugent, b. May* 1814; *d.* 17 *Jan.* 1883; m. 28 *Ap.* 1840, *Fulke* (*Greville, afterwards* [*R.L.* 8 *Aug.* 1866] *Greville-Nugent*), 1st *Baron Greville* [*U.K.*], *b.* 17 *Feb.* 1821; *d.* 25 *Jan.* 1883; *and had issue.*

    See the Clarence Volume, p. 356, Nos. 12176–12185.   [Nos. 7726 to 7738.

137. Descendants, if any, of Lady ANNE CECIL (see Table XI.), *d.* 1752; *m.* WILLIAM STRODE of Punsborn, co. Herts.

138. Descendants, if any, of CHARLES CECIL, Lord Bishop of Bristol and Bangor (see Table XI.), *d.* 29 May 1737; *m.* ELIZABETH, da. of Sir Martin LUMLEY of Bradfeild, Bart.

139. Descendants, if any, of the Hon. GEORGE CECIL (see Table XI.).

140. Descendants of BROOKE FORESTER of Dothill, co. Salop (see Table XI.), *b.* 7 Feb. 1717; *d.* 8 July 1774; *m.* 1st, 4 May 1734, ELIZABETH, da. and h. of George WELD of Willey Park, co. Salop, *bur.* 28 May 1753; 2ndly, ELIZABETH, da. of Robert BRANSTON of Chester, *d.* 1 Nov. 1796; and had issue (with four sons by 1st wife who all *d. unm.*) a da. (by 2nd wife).

141. Descendants of Lieut.-Col. CECIL FORESTER of Rossall, near Shrewsbury (see Table XI.), *d.* 22 Aug. 1774; *m.* ANNE, da. and co-h. of Robert TOWNSHEND, *d.* 24 May 1825; and had issue 1*a* to 4*a.*

    1*a. Cecil Weld* (*Forester, afterwards* (*R.L.* 15 *Aug.* 1811) *Weld-Forester*), 1st *Baron Forester* [*U.K.*], bapt. 7 *April* 1767; *d.* 23 *May* 1828; m. 16 *June* 1800, *Lady Katherine Mary, da. of Charles* (*Manners*), 4th *Duke of Rutland* [*E.*], *b.* 29 *Ap.* 1779; *d.* 1 *May* 1829; *and had issue.*

    See the Tudor Roll of "The Blood Royal of Britain," pp. 301–304, Nos. 25593–25716.

    2*a. Francis Forester, Major R.H. Guards Blue and* 15th *Hussars, b.* 19 *Aug.* 1774; *d.* 21 *Oct.* 1861; *m.* 22 *July* 1813, *Lady Louisa Catherine Barbara, da. of William Henry* (*Vane*), 1st *Duke of Cleveland* [*U.K.*], *d.* 8 *Jan.* 1821; *and had issue.*

    See the Clarence Volume, pp. 581–582, Nos. 24444–24466.

    3*a. Catherine Forester, d.* 1 *Mar.* 1828; *m.* 28 *Mar.* 1793, *Capt. Stewart.*

    4*a. Arabella Belinda Forester, d.* (*–*); *m.* 11 *June* 1795, *Lieut.-Gen. George Kennaird Dana, Capt.* 34th *Regt., d.* 23 *June* 1837.   [Nos. 7739 to 7885.

The Plantagenet Roll

142. Descendants of MARY FORESTER (see Table XI.), *d.* 26 Sept. 1779; *m.* 1st, 2 May 1738, Sir BRIAN BROUGHTON, *afterwards* BROUGHTON-DELVES, 4th Bart. [E.], *b.* 9 Jan. 1717–1719; *d.* 11 Aug. 1744; 2ndly, 1746, HUMPHREY MACKWORTH-PRAED of Trevethoe, co. Cornwall, M.P., *b.* 1719; *d.* 1803; and had (with other issue by 2nd husband) issue 1*a* to 3*a*.

1*a*. Sir Brian Broughton-Delves, 5th Bart. [E.], b. A*p*. 1740; d.s.p. 16 *Jan.* 1766.

2*a*. Rev. Sir Thomas Broughton, 6th Bart. [E.], b. c. 1744; d. 23 *July* 1813; m. 1*st*, 31 *Mar.* 1768, Mary, da. and h. of John Wicker of Horsham, co. Sussex, d. 7 *June* 1785; and had issue 1*b* to 9*b*.

1*b*. Sir John Delves Broughton, 7th Bart. [E.], bapt. 17 *Aug.* 1769; d.s.p. 9 *Aug.* 1747.

2*b*. Rev. Sir Henry Delves Broughton, 8th Bart. [E.], b. 10 *Jan.* 1777; d. 3 *Nov.* 1851; m. 15 *June* 1807, Mary, da. of John Pigott of Capard, d. 26 *Dec.* 1863; and had issue 1*c* to 8*c*.

1*c*. Sir Henry Delves Broughton, 9th Bart. [E.], b. 22 *June* 1808; d. 26 *Feb.* 1899; m. 25 *Feb.* 1857, Eliza Florence Alexandrina, da. of Louis Rosenzweig, d. 14 *Nov.* 1882; and had issue 1*d* to 5*d*.

1*d*. Sir Delves Louis Broughton, 10th Bart. [E.], J.P. (*Doddington Park, Nantwich; Broughton Hall, Eccleshall*), b. 1 June 1857; *m.* 1st, 26 Ap. 1881, Rosamond, da. of John Lambert Broughton of Almington Hall, *d.* 11 Oct. 1885; 2ndly, 21 Dec. 1887, Mary Evelyn, da. of Rowland Hugh Cotton of Etwall Hall; and has issue 1*e* to 4*e*.

1*e*. Henry John Delves Broughton, *b.* 10 Sept. 1883.

2*e*. Brian Evelyn Delves Broughton, *b.* 1898.

3*e*. Violet Evelyn Delves Broughton, *b.* 10 Ap. 1894.

4*e*. Amice Ivy Delves Broughton, *b.* 23 Oct. 1902.

2*d*. Brian Broughton, *b.* 16 Ap. 1865.

3*d*. Zoë Angelique Broughton, *b.* 9 Ap. 1859; *m.* 5 July 1881, Neville Thursby (*Harleston, Northants*); and has issue 1*e* to 2*e*.

1*e*. Audley Delves Thursby, *b.* 24 Jan. 1888.

2*e*. Honor Zoë Thursby.

4*d*. Rhoda Delves Broughton, *b.* 28 Sept. 1860; *m.* 7 Nov. 1885, Vernon Lamonnerie Delves Broughton (*Fernhurst, The Park, Cheltenham*); and has issue 1*e* to 2*e*.

1*e*. Rhoda Mary Delves Broughton, *b.* 27 Jan. 1894.

2*e*. Nancy Delves Broughton, *b.* 15 Jan. 1896.

5*d*. Saba Maud Broughton, *b.* 25 June 1874; *m.* 10 Nov. 1896, Lionel Charles Molesworth (*Hough Hall, Nantwich*); and has issue 1*e* to 2*e*.

1*e*. Roger Bevil Molesworth, *b.* 7 Feb. 1901.

2*e*. Violet Saba Molesworth, *b.* 10 Aug. 1897.

2*c*. Rev. Delves Broughton of Broughton Hall, b. 23 *Jan.* 1812; d. *May* 1863; m. 22 *June* 1835, Jane, da. of George Bennet of Dublin, Q.C., d. 22 *Sept.* 1860; and had issue 1*d* to 3*d*.

1*d*. Delves Broughton, Lieut.-Col. (ret.) *late* East Yorkshire Regt., *b.* 17 May 1846; *m.* 16 Oct. 1872, Edith May Marion, da. of Phineas Riall of Old Conna Hill, Bray; and has issue 1*e* to 3*e*.

1*e*. Bryan Delves Broughton, Capt. East Yorkshire Regt., *b.* 14 Sept. 1873.

2*e*. Geoffrey Delves Broughton, Lieut. Royal Warwick Regt., *b.* 10 May 1880.

3*e*. Mary Edith Broughton. [Nos. 7886 to 790.-.

220

# of The Blood Royal

2*d*. *Eleanor Mary Broughton*, d. (–) ; m. 21 *July* 1864, *William Charles New-combe of Upper Eyarth, near Ruthin*, d. 1877 ; *and had issue* 1*e to* 2*e*.

1*e*. Richard Francis Mainwaring Newcombe, b. 5 Dec. 1865 ; d. 14 *Ap*. 1882.

2*e*. Harold Broughton Newcombe, b. 3 Nov. 1866.

3*d*. Rhoda Broughton.

3*c*. *Alfred Delves Broughton*, b. 20 Nov. 1826 ; d. 10 *Mar*. 1895 ; m. 16 *Mar*. 1858, *Clemence, da. of C. L. D. Fattorini of Sydney, M.D. ; and had issue* 1*d to* 2*d*.

1*d*. Vernon Lamonnerie Delves Broughton (*Fernherst, The Park, Cheltenham*), b. 27 Oct. 1859 ; *m*. 7 Nov. 1885, Rhoda, da. of Sir Henry Delves Broughton, 9th Bart. [E.] ; and has issue 1*e* to 2*e*.

1*e*–2*e*. See p. 220, Nos. 7896–7897.

2*d*. Ernest Clement Vernon Broughton, a member of the New South Wales Parliament, J.P., &c. (*Sydney, New South Wales*), b. 29 Jan. 1865 ; *m*. 15 Feb. 1890, Amelia Lockyer, da. of William Newcombe of New South Wales, J.P.

4*c*. *Mary Broughton*, d. 23 *Sept*. 1844 ; m. 9 *Jan*. 1838, *the Rev. Walter Clarke, Vicar of Swinderby, co. Lincoln ; and had issue* 1*d*.

1*d*. *Agnes Mary Clarke*, d. 16 *Mar*. 1894 ; m. 28 *Ap*. 1870, *Sir Adelbert Cecil Chetwynd-Talbot, K.C.I.E., Lieut.-Col. Indian Army, lately* (1896–1900) *Resident in Kashmir, &c.* (*East India United Service*) ; *and had issue* 1*e to* 4*e*.

1*e*. Adelbert William James Chetwynd-Talbot, I.C.S., *b*. 6 Feb. 1876.

2*e*. *Guendolen Beatrix Nesta Chetwynd-Talbot*, b. 20 Jan. 1873 ; *m*. 24 Sept. 1896, Capt. Stuart Hill Godfrey, Political Agent at Dir, Swat, and Chitral ; and has issue 1*f* to 3*f*.

1*f*. John Talbot Godfrey, b. 8 July 1897.

2*f*. Jane Vivian Agnes Godfrey, b. 4 Dec. 1900.

3*f*. Margaret Ella Godfrey, b. 15 Sept. 1903.

3*e*. Muriel Agnes Eleanora Chetwynd-Talbot, b. 5 Mar. 1874.

4*e*. *Esmé Mary Dorothea Chetwynd-Talbot*, b. 6 Mar. 1880 ; *m*. 15 Sept. 1900, Capt. Armine Brereton Dew, Political Dept. of Govt. of India.

5*c*. *Henrietta Broughton*, b. 18 *June* 1815 ; d. 15 *May* 1883 ; m. 23 *May* 1848, *the Rev. William Grice, Vicar of Sherborne, co. Warwick*, b. *Aug*. 1813 ; d. 10 *Jan*. 1885 ; *and had issue* 1*d*.

1*d*. *Louisa Elizabeth Mary Grice*, *m*. 4 Oct. 1876, George William Hutchinson, now Grice-Hutchinson, *late* Capt. 90th Light Infantry (*The Boynes, Upton-on-Severn*) ; and has issue 1*e* to 5*e*.

1*e*. George William Grice-Hutchinson, b. 18 Sept. 1877.

2*e*. Claude Broughton Grice-Hutchinson, b. 28 Feb. 1881.

3*e*. Charles Grice Grice-Hutchinson, b. 30 June 1884.

4*e*. Rowan Ernest Grice-Hutchinson, b. 29 June 1885.

5*e*. Cecily Anne Grice-Hutchinson.

6*c*. *Caroline Broughton*, d. 28 *July* 1863 ; m. 27 Feb. 1851, *the Rev. Archibald Paris, Rector of Ludgvan, co. Cornwall*, d. *Oct*. 1861 ; *and had issue* 1*d to* 6*d*.

1*d*. *Herbert George Paris*, R.N., b. 25 *Ap*. 1854 ; d. 19 *Sept*. 1900 ; m. 14. *Jan*. 1891, *Marie, da. of Jörgen Henrich Keiding of Bergen* ; *and had issue* 1*e to* 2*e*.

1*e*. Charles Nicolay Paris, b. 26 Sept. 1892.

2*e*. Mildred Olga Paris, b. 12 June 1894.

2*d*. *Archibald Paris*, Lieut.-Col. R.M.A. (*Royal Military Academy, Woolwich*), b. 9 Nov. 1861 ; *m*. 3 Sept. 1885, Lilian Jean, da. of Gen. Henry Melvill ; and has issue 1*e*.

1*e*. Archibald Charles Melvill Paris, b. 28 May 1885.

3*d*. *Edith Laura Paris* (*Leahurst, Tickhill, co. York*), *m*. 5 July 1876, William Knight Hamilton Ramsay White of Leahurst, b. 23 Jan. 1834 ; d. 11 June 1900 ; and has issue 1*e* to 5*e*. [Nos. 7905 to 7928.

221   2 F

The Plantagenet Roll

1e. Archibald Woollaston White, Capt. Yorkshire Art., heir-presumptive to Baronetcy (1802) [U.K.] (*Leahurst, Tickhill, co. York*), *b.* 14 Oct. 1877 ; *m.* 12 Aug. 1903, Gladys Becher Love, da. of the Rev. Edward Augustus Bracken Pitman of Stonegrave ; and has issue 1*f*.

    1*f*. Thomas Astley Woollaston White, *b.* 13 May 1904.

2e. William Taylor White, *b.* 9 Feb. 1880.

3e. Charles Ramsay White, Capt. 3rd Batt. P.W.O. Yorkshire Regt., *b.* 11 May 1881.

4e. John Broughton White, *b.* 8 Mar. 1889.

5e. Bridget White.

4d. *Helen Constance Paris*, d. 15 *Oct.* 1900 ; m. 5 *Ap.* 1883, *Sir Francis Elliott Walker, 3rd Bart.* [U.K.] (*Swansfield, Alnwick*) ; *and had issue* 1*e* to 2*e*.

    1e. Baldwin Charles Walker, *b.* 11 Jan. 1884.

    2e. Helen Marjorie Walker, *b.* 18 Ap. 1885.

5d. Mildred Caroline Paris, *m.* 1 Jan. 1880, Rowland Comyns Berkeley (*Cotheridge Court, Worcester*) ; and has issue 1*e* to 6*e*.

    1e. Rowland Broughton Berkeley, *b.* 1883.

    2e. Harold Sale Berkeley, *b.* 1886.

    3e. Egbert Paris Berkeley, *b.* 1888.

    4e. Wilfred Nichols Berkeley, *b.* 1889.

    5e. Evelyn Mary Berkeley.

    6e. Mildred Sybil Berkeley.

6d. Rhoda Mary Paris, *m.* 5 Aug. 1884, Charles William D'Albiac (*Burton House, Twickenham*) ; and has issue 1*e* to 4*e*.

    1e. Herbert Charles D'Albiac, *b.* 14 July 1888.

    2e. John Henry D'Albiac, *b.* 28 Jan. 1894.

    3e. Archibald Francis D'Albiac, *b.* 2 Nov. 1898.

    4e. Cordelia Mary D'Albiac.

7c. *Jane Broughton*, d. 30 *June* 1873 ; m. 7 *Oct.* 1847, *the Rev. Charles Henry Mainwaring, Rector of Whitmore*, b. 22 Nov. 1819 ; d. 3 *Ap.* 1878 ; *and had issue* 1*d* to 8*d*.

1d. Rowland Broughton Mainwaring, C.M.G., Col. *late* Comdg. Royal Welsh Fusiliers (*Wrexham ; The Lodge, Bembridge, I.W.*), *b.* 11 Sept. 1850 ; *m.* 4 Aug. 1880, Evelyn Louisa Jane, da. of Mervyn Edward Archdale of Castle Archdale.

2d. Gerald Mainwaring, *b.* 5 Ap. 1854.

3d. Rev. Percy Edward Mainwaring, M.A. (Oxon.), Rector of Whitmore (*Whitmore Rectory, Newcastle-under-Lyme*), *b.* 14 Dec. 1857.

4d. *Gordon Lewis Mainwaring*, b. 30 *Mar.* 1860 ; d. (? *unm.*) 1903.

5d. Ethel Mary Mainwaring, *m.* 24 July 1877, William Robert Parker Jervis, J.P. (*Meaford Stone, and Park Hall, Longton, co. Stafford*) ; and has issue 1*e* to 4*e*.

    1e. William Swynfen Whitehall Jervis, *b.* 27 Aug. 1879.

    2e. Edward Mainwaring Jervis, *b.* 15 Oct. 1880.

    3e. Evelyn St. Vincent Jervis, *b.* 8 Nov. 1883.

    4e. Ethel Mary Jervis, *b.* 6 May 1878.

6d. Maude Mainwaring (*Park Hall, Longton*), *m.* as 2nd wife, 15 July 1886, the Hon. Edward Swynfen Parker-Jervis, *d.* 3 Jan. 1896.

7d. Pauline Jane Mainwaring, *m.* 10 Sept. 1891, the Rev. Robert Lingen Burton, Vicar of Little Aston.

8d. Sophie Henrietta Julia Mainwaring, *m.* 19 Ap. 1879, Col. Walter Niel Jervis, R.A. (*Gendercott, Clupton, Devon*) ; and has issue 1*e*.

    1e. Gordon Mainwaring Jervis, *b.* 13 Dec. 1882.

8c. *Laura Broughton*, d. (−) ; m. 28 *Oct.* 1849, *John Compton Maul, Bar.-at-Law*, d. 1 *Feb.* 1880 ; *and had issue* 1*d* to 6*d*.   [Nos. 7929 to 7960.

222

# of The Blood Royal

1*d*. Henry Compton Maul, J.P., *late* Major 3rd Batt. Oxfordshire L.I. (*Horley House, Banbury*), *b*. 6 Oct. 1850; *m*. 5 Ap. 1883, Mary Essex, da. of Capt. Henry William Selby-Lowndes, 15th Hussars; and has issue 1*e* to 3*e*.

    1*e*. Henry Compton Maul, Lieut. 3rd Batt. Oxfordshire L.I., *b*. 11 Sept. 1885.

    2*e*. Richard Selby-Lowndes Maul, *b*. 14 Aug. 1886.

    3*e*. Gerald Broughton Maul, *b*. 19 Sept. 1891.

2*d*. John Broughton Maul.

3*d*. Spencer Duncan Maul, *late* Capt. York and Lancaster Regt.

4*d*. Laura Maul.

5*d*. Evelyn Ester Maul.

6*d*. Alice Mary Maul.

3*b*. *Thomas Delves Broughton, b. 26 Aug. 1878; d. 24 Jan. 1846; m. 28 Mar. 1800, Elizabeth Hester Rowlls, da. and h. of John Rowlls Legh of Adlington Hall, d. 15 Nov. 1821; and had issue 1c to 7c.*

    1*c*. *Rev. Thomas Delves Broughton, Rector of Bletchley, b. 18 Feb. 1801; d. 10 Aug. 1859; m. 2 Ap. 1834, Frances, da. of Lewis Corkran, member of Bombay Council; and had issue 1d to 5d.*

    1*d*. *Vernon Delves Broughton, Dept. Master of the Royal Mint, Melbourne, b. 6 Dec. 1834; d. 25 Feb. 1886; m. 4 July 1861, Augusta Mary Anne, da. of George Arbuthnot of Norbiton; and had issue 1e.*

    1*e*. Vernon Warburton Broughton, *b*. 25 Nov. 1864.

    2*d*. *Lewis Pryce Delves Broughton, Puisne Judge of the High Court of Judicature of Calcutta, and Admin.-Gen. of Bengal, b. 10 May 1836; d. 3 Jan. 1902; m. 26 Dec.* 1867, *Mary Elizabeth Randall, da. of Gen. Sir Frank Turner, K.C.B., d. 9 Sept.* 1890; *and had issue 1e to 3e.*

    1*e*. Cicely Broughton, *m*. 30 Jan. 1894, William Barrow-Simonds, Bar.-at-Law (*Waterside, Abbott's Barton, Winchester*); and has issue 1*f* to 5*f*.

    1*f*. John Barrow-Simonds, *b*. 1896.

    2*f*. Robert William Barrow-Simonds, *b*. 13 Oct. 1905.

    3*f*. Mary Barrow-Simonds, *b*. 1894.

    4*f*. Joan Barrow-Simonds, *b*. 1896.

    5*f*. Ivy Barrow-Simonds, *b*. 1901.

    2*e*. Margaret Broughton, *m*. 16 Ap. 1904, Robert Dabney Heinemann (*Durfold Farm, Warnham, Sussex*); and has issue 1*f*.

    1*f*. Peter Dabney Heinemann, *b*. 22 Feb. 1905.

    3*e*. Joan Broughton, *m*. 19 Oct. 1901, Capt. John Stebbing Corlett, 15th Lancers (*Charlton Court, near Maidstone*); and has issue 1*f* to 2*f*.

    1*f*. Ivan Archibald Lewis Corlett, *b*. 3 Ap. 1904.

    2*f*. Mary Delves Corlett, *b*. 16 Oct. 1902.

    3*d*. *Cecil Delves Broughton, Comm. R.N., b. 19 June 1837; d. 1 May 1899; m. 1 June 1871, Marion Honora, da. of the Rev. Theodore Bouwens; and had issue 1e to 6e.*

    1*e*. Theodore Delves Broughton, Capt. R.E., *b*. 25 Dec. 1872; *m*. 1897, Marion Julia, da. of Charles Augustus Theodore Bouwens; and has issue 1*f* to 2*f*.

    1*f*. Brian Charles Broughton, *b*. 1903.

    2*f*. Ruth Marion Broughton, *b*. 29 Oct. 1898.

    2*e*. Hugo Delves Broughton, *late* Lieut. Cheshire Regt., *b*. 25 Aug. 1878.

    3*e*. Lewis Percy Broughton, *b*. 1881.

    4*e*. Marjory Frances Broughton.

    5*e*. Ruth Broughton.

    6*e*. Dorothy Julia Broughton.   [Nos. 7961 to 7989.

The Plantagenet Roll

4d. Francis Sullivan Delves Broughton, Comm. R.N., b. 6 *Sept.* 1838 ; d. 27 *Feb.* 1878 ; m. 14 *Aug.* 1872, *Josephine Harriet (who* m. 2*ndly, Cressett Thursby Pelham), da. of William Whaley Billyard of N.S.W.; and had issue* 1e *to* 2e.

1e. Frances Broughton, b. 28 June 1878.

2e. Marion Ida Broughton.

5d. Frances Katharine Josepha Broughton, 1st Class Order of the Chefekat, m. 4 Ap. 1866, Admiral Sir John Arbuthnot Fisher, G.C.B. (16 *Bolton Street, Piccadilly ; Marlborough ; United Service*) ; and has issue 1e to 4e.

1e. Cecil Fisher, M.A. (Oxon.), a Judge in I.C.S. (*Diragepier, Bengal*), b. 18 July 1868.

2e. Beatrix Alice Fisher, b. 7 Jan. 1867 ; m. 28 Jan. 1896, Capt. Reginald Rundell Neeld, R.N., Heir presumptive to Baronetcy (1859) [U.K.] (*Twatley Farm, Malmesbury*).

3e. Dorothy Sybil Fisher, 2nd Class of the Chefekat, b. 5 Nov. 1873.

4e. Parnela Mary Fisher, 2nd Class of the Chefekat, b. 18 Ap. 1876.

2c. William Edward Delves Broughton, R.E., b. 30 *Ap.* 1802 ; d. 5. *Ap.* 1880 ; m. 15 *Sept.* 1830, *Anne, da. of* [——] *Nugent,* d. 17 *Jan.* 1879 ; *and had issue* 1d *to* 5d.

1d. John Delves Broughton, Col. R.M.L.I., b. 15 *Aug.* 1836 ; d. (-) ; m. 15 *Ap.* 1876, *Lucy, da. of William Sudlow Roots,* d. 1887 ; *and had issue* 1e *to* 3e.

1e. Brian Delves Broughton, b. 22 June 1879.

2e. Alfred William Delves Broughton, Lieut. R.M.L.I., b. 16 Dec. 1880.

3e. Cecilia Mary Delves Broughton, m. 7 June 1904, Ferdinand William Smallpiece (*Browning's Down, Guildford*) ; and has issue 1f.

1f. Cecilia Lucy Smallpiece, b. 29 June 1905.

2d. William Edward Delves Broughton, Major-Gen. Bengal Army, b. 3 *Jan.* 1837 ; d. 15 Mar. 1895 ; m. 28 *Ap.* 1870, *Laura Margaret Buchan (Aspenden Hall, Buntingford, co. Herts), da. of Stephen Lawson ; and has issue* 1e *to* 6e.

1e. Legh Harley Delves Broughton, Capt. R.F.A., b. 28 Oct. 1875 ; m. 3 June 1903, Constance, da. of George Randall Johnson of Feniton Court ; and has issue 1f.

1f. Legh Randall Delves Broughton, b. Ap. 1904.

2e. William Edward Delves Broughton, Lieut. R.A., b. 13 Aug. 1879.

3e. Edith Laura Anna Broughton, m. Sept. 1896, Robert McLeod Richardson ; and has issue 1f to 4f.

1f. Robert John Broughton Richardson, } b. (twins) 1903.
2f. Edward Hugh Lawson Richardson, }

3f. Edith Marjorie Frances Richardson, b. 6 July 1897.

4f. Enid Ethel Penelope Richardson, b. 1900.

4e. Louisa Fanny Broughton, m. 1899, Arthur Buckwald Edgar Gibson ; and has issue 1f to 2f.

1f. Alwyne Gibson, b. 1900.

2f. Edgar Brian Gibson, b. 1902.

5e. Ethel Georgiana Delves Broughton.

6e. Florence Lucy Delves Broughton, m. 7 Ap. 1904, Roger Gordon Thomson, Lieut. R.F.A. ; and has issue 1f.

1f. Florence Margaret Gordon Thomson, b. 6 Feb. 1905.

3d. Francis Delves Broughton, b. 6 Mar. 1847.

4d. Harriot Magdalen Delves Broughton, } (*The Cottage, Warnham, near*
5d. Elizabeth Hester Maria Delves Broughton, } *Horsham*).

3c Mary Magdalene Broughton, b. 31 *May* 1803 ; d. 19 *Oct.* 1881 ; m. 10 *Ap.* 1834, *Archibald William Blane, Member of Council and Foreign Sec. to Govt. of the Mauritius,* b. 29 *Mar.* 1788 ; d. 2 *Nov.* 1852 ; *and had issue* 1d *to* 3d.

[Nos. 7990 to 8017.

# of The Blood Royal

1*d*. Robert Arthur Blane, Col., *formerly* Capt. 22nd Regt. (*Folkestone*), *b*. 23 June 1844; *m*. 14 Feb. 1870, Frances Smith, da. of Alexander Wrightson Lawe of Glanmire, J.P., D.L.; and has issue 1*e*.

1*e*. Archibald Rodney Alexander Blane, *b*. 7 *Jan*. 1879; *d*. 24 *Jan*. 1897.

2*d*. Maria Lydia Blane, b. 1 *Mar*. 1835; *d*. 27 *Jan*. 1889; *m*. 1*st*, 22 *May* 1856, *Capt. Archibald Oliver Wood, Bengal Army*; 2*ndly*, 15 *Mar*. 1875, *Col. Beville Grenville Vyvyan* (*Junior United Service*); and had issue 1*e* to 4*e*.

1*e*. Cecil Archibald Harry Wood, *late* Indian Postal Service (*Melrose, Dalhousie, Punjaub, India*), *b*. 1 May 1857; *m*. 21 Oct. 1886, Harriet Rawlings, da. of J. B. Collins of Bodmin; and has issue 1*f*.

1*f*. Dorothy Scobell Wood, *b*. 20 Dec. 1888.

2*e*. Percy Arthur Everest Wood, *late* 1st Batt. York and Lancaster Regt. (*Portland House, The Park, Buxton*), *b*. 17 Aug. 1858; *m*. 1st, 9 Oct. 1884, Sophia Mary Frances, da. of the Rev. Alan Cheales, *d*. 6 Mar. 1885; 2ndly, 22 Feb. 1890, Sophia Dorathea, da. of John Turnley of Drumnasole, co. Antrim, J.P., D.L.; and has issue (by 2nd marriage) 1*f* to 2*f*.

1*f*. Violet Dorathea Pauline Seymour Wood.

2*f*. Kathleen Charlotte Ottiwell Wood.

3*e*. Seymour Charles Gore Wood, District Traffic Supt. Govt. State Railways (*Cawnpore, United Provinces, India*), *b*. 4 Ap. 1860; *unm*.

4*e*. Ada Jessie Stewart Wood, *m*. 28 Jan. 1904, James Henry Howard Iles, *s.p.*

3*d*. Cecilia Elizabeth Blane, *m*. 16 Aug. 1860, William James McGrigor Dawn, 1st Royal Dragoons; and has issue 1*e* to 5*e*.

1*e*. Walter Archibald William Dawn (*Rangoon*), *b*. 5 July 1863; *unm*.

2*e*. Harold Frederick Legh Dawn (*Rangoon*), *b*. 28 July 1868; *m*. 16 Dec. 1901, Adeline Violet Marie, da. of Capt. Kerby, R.N.

3*e*. Laura Eveline Dawn, *unm*.

4*e*. Frances Muriel Dawn, *m*. 9 Oct. 1886, Major Archibald McLachlan, Royal Scots.

5*e*. Rachel Margaret Dawn, *unm*.

4*c*. Louisa Broughton, b. 9 *Sept*. 1815 (? 1816); *d*. 3 *July* 1871; *m*. 9 *Sept*. 1823, *Col. James McAlpine of Wyndsor, co. Mayo, 15th Hussars, d*. 7 *Feb*. 1857; *and had issue* 1*d* to 2*d*.

1*d*. Sarah Margaret Louisa McAlpine, b. 25 Dec. 1840; *d*. 30 *Mar*. 1863; m. *Capt. Arthur Masterton Robertson of Inshes, co. Inverness, 4th Dragoons; and had issue* 1*e*.

1*e*. Arthur Keith Stewart M'Alpine Robertson, *b*. 18 Dec. 1859.

2*d*. Elizabeth Hester Rosetta McAlpine (*Argrennan, co. Kirkcudbright*), *m*. 21 Sept. 1858, Robert Ker of Argrennan; and has issue 1*e*.

1*e*. Louisa Elizabeth Innes Ker, *b*. 18 June 1859; *m*. 17 Mar. 1885, Capt. Archer John William Musgrave, R.N., *d*. 20 May 1892; and has issue 1*f*.

1*f*. Tom Musgrave, *b*. 23 Aug. 1889.

5*c*. Emma Delves Broughton, b. 29 *Nov*. 1807; *d*. 15 *Nov*. 1842; m. 24 *July* 1830, *Henry Smith of Richmond, co. Surrey, Attorney-at-Law, d*. 25 *Jan*. 1868; *and had issue* 1*d* to 2*d*.

1*d*. Emma Broughton Smith, *m*. 22 July 1857, John Charles Sharpe (*Granville House, Richmond ; Longhope, Gloucestershire*); and has issue 1*e* to 6*e*.

1*e*. Charles Henry Sharpe, *b*. 11 Ap. 1858.

2*e*. Wilfred Stanley Sharpe, *b*. 29 Ap. 1860.

3*e*. Arthur Granville Sharpe, *b*. 5 Nov. 1862; *m*. 4 Oct. 1893, Eleanor Nona, da. of Samuel Ridley.

4*e*. Aubrey Lyster Sharpe, *b*. 26 Ap. 1868.   [Nos. 8018 to 8040.

225

The Plantagenet Roll

5e. Grace Emma Mary Sharpe, *b.* 11 Mar. 1866; *m.* William Charles Beasley Robinson; and has issue 1*f* to 2*f*.

1*f*. Aubrey Claude Beasley Robinson, *b.* 1 Ap. 1893.

2*f*. Grace Eleanor Monica Robinson, *b.* 31 May 1900.

6e. Ella Beatrice Sharpe, *b.* 31 May 1872; *m.* 9 Jan. 1901, John Archer.

2d. Laura Broughton Smith, *m.* 13 Mar. 1863, the Rev. George Carew Reynell, M.A. Camb., *late* Snr. Chaplain Bombay Eccles. Estab. (60 *West Cromwell Road, S.W.*); *s.p.*

6c. Laura Anne Broughton, d. 21 Mar. 1865; m. as 1st wife, 2 Nov. 1840, the Rev. Charles William Selby-Lowndes, d. 22 Sept. 1899; and had issue.

See the Clarence Volume, p. 476, Nos. 20971–20981.

7c. Fanny Maria Broughton, d. 19 Mar. 1897; m. 23 May 1839, Stephens Lawson, Surgeon, 87th Regt.; and had issue 1d.

1d. Laura Margaret Buchan Lawson (*Aspenden Hall, Buntingford, co. Herts*), *m.* 28 Ap. 1870, Major-Gen. William Edward Delves Broughton, *d.* 15 Mar. 1895; and has issue.

See p. 224, Nos. 8001–8014.

4b. Edward Delves Broughton, b. 11 Dec. 1782; d. 24 Ap. 1825; m. 25 Oct. 1808, Elizabeth, da. of John Batt of Moditonham Hall, co. Cornwall, d. 13 Mar. 1857; and had issue 1c.

1c. Edward Delves Broughton of Wistaston Hall, b. 6 Oct. 1816; d. 6 Oct. 1889; m. 22 Sept. 1847, Penelope, da. and eventual h. of James Walthall-Hammond of Wistaston Hall, d. 5 July 1883; and had issue 1d.

1d. Edward Walthall Delves Broughton, afterwards (R.L. 1887) Walthall, of Wistaston Hall, D.L., b. 20 Oct. 1848; d. 11 Sept. 1897; m. 8 Sept. 1870, Caroline Marion (The Cottage, St. Asaph), da. of Charles Augustus Stuart of West Hall, High Leigh; and had issue 1e to 7e.

1e. Edward Charles Walthall Delves Walthall, D.S.O., Capt. R.F.A. (*Wistaston Hall, Nantwich*), *b.* 24 Ap. 1874; *m.* 11 Nov. 1902, Isabel Sybil, da. of Lieut.-Gen. Sir James Bevan Edwards, K.C.M.G., C.B.

2e. Brian James Delves Walthall, Capt. Reserve of Officers, *late* R.M.L.I. (*Sports*), *b.* 17 May 1876.

3e. Henry Douglas Delves Walthall, Lieut. Denbigh Imp. Yeo., *b.* 7 Feb. 1880.

4e. Gilbert Alexander Delves Walthall, *b.* 26 June 1890.

5e. Helen Louisa Delves Walthall.

6e. Rhoda Janet Delves Walthall.

7e. Alice Dorothy Delves Walthall.

5b. Maria Broughton, d. 16 June 1841; m. Thomas Langford Brooke of Mere Hall, co. Chester, d. 21 Dec. 1815; and had issue 1c to 4c.

1c. Thomas Langford Brooke of Mere, b. 3 Sept. 1794; d. 24 Jan. 1848; m. 3 June 1817, Eliza, da. of John William Clough of Oxton Hall, co. York, d. 6 Ap. 1877; and had issue 1d to 7d.

1d. Thomas John Langford Brooke of Mere, b. 16 Mar. 1820; d. 2 Ap. 1865, having m. and had issue one son, who d. unm. 16 Sept. 1872.

2d. Frederick Langford Brooke.

3d. Charles Langford Brooke, m. and had issue.

4d. Eliza Maria Brooke.

5d. Henrietta Langford Brooke, m. William Smallcombe.

6d. Charlotte Brooke.

7d. Julia Brooke.

2c. Jonas Langford Brooke.

3c. Maria Elizabeth Brooke, d. 1 Ap. 1850; m. as 2nd wife, 1810, Meyrick Holme, afterwards Bankes, of Winstanley Hall, b. 12 Aug. 1768; d. 1 Mar. 1827; and had issue.

See the Clarence Volume, pp. 163–164, Nos. 2596–2610. [Nos. 8041 to 8093.

226

# of The Blood Royal

4c. *Jemima Brooke*, m. *Sir Jeremiah Dickson, K.C.B.*

6b. *Emma Broughton*, d. 22 *Mar.* 1820; m. *Lieut.-Gen. Coghlan.*

7b. *Henrietta Broughton*, d. (–); m. *Trafford Trafford (R.L.* 5 *Dec.* 1791), *previously Leigh, of Oughtrington Hall, co. Chester*, b. 1 *Dec.* 1770; d. 1859; *and had issue* 1c *to* 3c.

1c. *Richard Leigh Trafford of Oughtrington Hall, J.P., D.L., County Court Judge*, b. 30 *Ap.* 1800; d. 27 *Jan.* 1864; m. 26 *Ap.* 1832, *Eliza Frances, da. of Thomas Tarleton*, d. 10 *June* 1859; *and had issue* 1d *to* 11d.

1d. *George Leigh Trafford of Oughtrington Hall, Bar-at-Law, Lord Chief-Justice of St. Vincent*, b. 3 *Feb.* 1833; d. 15 *Feb.* 1901.

2d. *John Leigh Trafford, Solicitor*, b. 21 *July* 1834; d. 22 *Oct.* 1904.

3d. *Rev. William Trafford, Rector of St. Lawrence, Newland, co. Essex*, b. 16 *Nov.* 1835; d. 16 *May* 1901.

4d. *Thomas Henry Trafford, Lieut. R.A.*, b. 29 *Oct.* 1839; d. 1863.

5d. *Edward Leigh Trafford, Lieut. R.N.*, b. 6 *Feb.* 1841; d. 22 *Oct.* 1883.

6d. Richard Wylme Trafford, Comr. I.C.S., *b.* 6 Nov. 1843.

7d. *Frederic Trafford, a Clerk in the Admiralty*, b. 21 *Ap.* 1845.

8d. *Frances Maria Trafford*, b. 23 *Mar.* 1837; d. 30 *May* 1898; m. *H. H. Millett.*

9d. *Eliza Trafford*, b. 30 *May* 1842; d. 29 *Oct.* 1857.

10d. Henrietta Trafford (1 *Oppidant Road, Primrose Hill, London*), b. 9 Nov. 1846; m. John W. Hales, *late* Professor of English Literature, London Univ.

11d. *Mary Trafford*, b. 6 *Ap.* 1848; d. 1 *Nov.* 1856.

2c. *Augusta Trafford.*

3c. *Henrietta Trafford*, d. 5 *Jan.* 1892; m. *as 2nd wife*, 7 *June* 1836, *the Rev. George Mallory* (1832), *previously Leigh, Rector of Mobberley*, d. 26 *July* 1885; *and had issue* 1d *to* 6d.

1d. Wilfred Leigh Mallory (*Bowmanville, Ontario*), b. 23 Aug. 1853; m. 1887, Alice, da. of J. G. Clarke of Paris, Ont.; and has issue 1e.

1e. George Edward Leigh Mallory, *b.* 1 Dec. 1889.

2d. Rev. Herbert Leigh Mallory of Mobberley, Lord of the Manor and Patron of that place, Vicar of St. John's, Birkenhead (*The Manor House, Mobberley, co. Chester*), b. 26 July 1856; m. 20 June 1882, Annie Beridge, da. of the Rev. J. Jebb of Walton Lodge, co. Derby; and has issue 1e to 4e.

1e. George Herbert Leigh Mallory, *b.* 18 June 1886.

2e. Trafford Leigh Mallory, *b.* 11 July 1892.

3e. Mary Henrietta Mallory, *b.* 3 Feb. 1885.

4e. Annie Victoria Mallory, *b.* 19 Nov. 1887.

3d. Ellen Mallory, *b.* 28 Dec. 1839.

4d. *Edith Mallory*, d. 26 *Sept.* 1891; m. 1st, 28 *Ap.* 1875, *W. Wood Blake*, d.s.p. 1 *Aug.* 1881; 2ndly, *Ap.* 1883, *T. G. Kerans, M.D.* (*Cheltenham*); *and had issue* 1e *to* 3e.

1e. William Leigh Kerans, *b.* 21 July 1884.

2e. Edith Kerans, *b.* 1886.

3e. Violet Kerans, *b.* 1888.

5d. Alice Mallory, *m.* 1st, 10 Dec. 1868, James Walker, *d.* 2 Oct. 1871; 2ndly, as 2nd wife, 6 Sept. 1876, Thomas Watson Greig, J.P., D.L., Lord of the Barony of Glencarse, *late* Capt. Royal Perth Militia (*Glencarse House and Lassintullich, co. Perth*).

6d. Emma Mallory, *b.* 27 Nov. 1851.

8b. *Eliza Broughton*, d. *Feb.* 1856; m. *William Clough of Oxted Hall, co. Yorks.* [Nos. 8094 to 8109.

227

The Plantagenet Roll

9b. Jemima Broughton, d. 15 *Jan.* 1863; m. *Capt. William Robert Broughton, C.B., R.N., Col. R.M.*, d. 12 *Mar.* 1821; *and had issue* 1c *to* 3c.

1c. *William Broughton, Capt. R.N.*, b. 23 *Oct.* 1804; d. 17 *Aug.* 1849; m. 3 *Jan.* 1833, *Eliza, da. of John Perfect of Pontefract, Banker*, d. 1896; *and had issue* 1d *to* 6d.

1d. Eliza Jemima Broughton (*The Thorton, Tenbury, South Wales*), m. 1860, the Rev. Henry Morris of Withcall, d. 1888; and has issue 1e to 10e.

1e. Arthur Henry Morris, C.M.G., D.S.O., Major and Brevet Lieut.-Col. Royal Irish Regt., b. Jan. 1861; m. 1902, Dorothy Rhoda, da. of [——] Wilkie.

2e. Nevile Morris, b. Nov. 1861.

3e. Gerald Morris, b. Jan. 1863.

4e. Cecil Morris, b. Dec. 1863.

5e. Herbert Morris, b. 1869.

6e. Ethel Morris, m. 1897, Archibald Wybergh How (son of the 1st Bishop of Wakefield).

7e. Maud Morris.

8e. Alice Broughton Morris.

9e. Rhoda Morris.

10e. Grace Morris.

2d. Helen Broughton (*Winchester*), m. 16 Nov. 1867, Capt. Arthur Willoughby Crewe-Read, b. 18 June 1833; d. 6 May 1874; and has issue 1e.

1e. Muriel Bridget Crewe-Read, m. 1892, Herbert Lindsay Scott.

3d. Dora Broughton, m. 2 July 1857, Capt. Henry Reveley Mitford, *late* King's Own L.I. (*Winchester*); and has issue 1e to 6e.

1e. Bertram Reveley Mitford, D.S.O., Col. E. Surrey Regt. (*Naval and Military*), b. 6 Feb. 1863; m. 29 Oct. 1891, the Hon. Etheldreda Mary, da. of John Thomas (Manners), 2nd Baron Manners [U.K.]; and has issue.

See p. 165, Nos. 3428–3430.

2e. Percy Nugent Mitford, b. 25 May 1871.

3e. Sybil Constance Mitford, m. 30 Dec. 1902, Arthur John Montefiore-Brice, Bar.-at-Law (4 *Artillery Mansions, Victoria Street, S.W.*).

4e. Dora Florence Mitford.

5e. Evelyn Bertha Mitford, m. 22 July 1891, Lieut.-Col. Francis Joseph Lambkin, Royal Army Med. Corps; and has issue 1f.

1f. Evelyn Aileen Lambkin, b. 1892.

6e. Violet Nina Mitford, m. 11 Feb. 1904, T. W. A. Daman, M.A., M.B., C.M. (*Minster Yard, Lincoln*).

4d. Florence Mercedes Broughton (*River View, Heddington Hill, Oxford*).

5d. Rhoda Broughton, m. 7 Feb. 1877, Arthur Frederick Gurney.

6d. Alice Broughton (*River View, Heddington Hill, Oxford*), m. 25 Aug. 1869, Capt. William Thomson, 78th Highlanders, d. 1893; and has issue 1e to 6e.

1e. Henry Broughton Thomson, b. 1870.

2e. Thomas Weldon Thomson, b. 1872.

3e. Edward Vernon Thomson, b. 1873.

4e. William Montgomery Thomson, b. 1877.

5e. Norah Florence Thomson.

6e. Eleanor Ann Thomson.

2c. *Jemima Broughton*, d. 7 *Ap.* 1883; m. 11 *Jan.* 1827, *Thomas de Moleyns, Q.C.*, b. 24 *Jan.* 1807; d. 5 *Mar.* 1900; *and had issue* 1d *to* 3d.

1d. Townsend Aremberg de Moleyns, Major-Gen., *late* Col. R.A. (5 *Brechin Place, South Kensington*), b. 20 June 1838; m. 5 June 1866, Selina Harriet, da. of Henry Sneyd French; and has issue 1e to 2e.

1e. Richard Philip Aremberg de Moleyns, Lieut. Rifle Brigade, b. 13 Dec. 1881.

2e. Véra de Moleyns, b. 30 May 1880.   [Nos. 8110 to 8145.

228

# of The Blood Royal

2*d*. *Rose Gertrude de Moleyns*, b. 28 *Sept*. 1832; d. 1 *Feb*. 1869; m. *as* 1*st wife*, 24 *Nov*. 1864, *Col. George Eyre Massy of Riversdale*, b. 23 *Nov*. 1822; d. 26 *Ap*. 1885; *and had issue* 1*e*.

1*e*. Hugh Hammon George Massy (*Riversdale, co. Limerick*), *b*. 17 Mar. 1867; *m*. 7 Nov. 1894, Hortense, da. of Thomas Pennefather of Marlow; and has issue 1*f*.

1*f*. Hugh Hammon de Moleyns Massy, *b*. 20 Aug. 1895.

3*d*. Emmeline Theodora de Moleyns (*Tudor Hall, Monkstown, co. Dublin*), *m*. 6 Dec. 1872, Major Loftus Corbet Singleton, 92nd Highlanders, *d*. 1 May 1881; and has issue.

See the Clarence Volume, p. 198, Nos. 3442–3443.

3*c*. *Penelope Broughton*, d. 18 *June* 1888; m. 1829, *the Rev. William Spencer Phillips*, d. *May* 1863; *and had issue* 1*d* *to* 2*d*.

1*d*. Rev. Henry Frederick Phillips, Canon of Rochester (*Rochester*), *b*. 1832; *m*. Emma, da. of [——] Wade, *s.p.*

2*d*. *Rev. Spencer William Phillips, Vicar of Wateringbury*, b. 1 *Jan*. 1834; d. 14 *Dec*. 1894; m. 3 *July* 1866, *Emily Julia*, *da. of the Ven. Anthony Grant, Archdeacon of Rochester and St. Albans ; and had issue* 1*e* *to* 3*e*.

1*e*. Rev. Ernest Spencer Phillips, R.N., *b*. 5 Mar. 1869.

2*e*. Irene Edith Phillips, *b*. 6 July 1867.

3*e*. Gladys Cicely Mary Phillips, *m*. 10 Nov. 1904, Capt. Edwin Philip Le Mesurier, Royal Jersey Militia.

3*a*. *William Mackworth-Praed of Trevethoe and (j. u.) of Tyringham, M.P.*, b. 24 *June* 1749; d. 9 *Oct*. 1833; m. 19 *June* 1778, *Elizabeth Tyringham, da. and eventual h. of Barnaby Backwell of Tyringham and St. Clement Danes, Banker*, d. 25 *Feb*. 1811; *and had issue* 1*b* *to* 2*b*.

1*b*. *James Blackwell Praed of Tyringham, &c., M.P., High Sheriff co. Bucks* 1807, b. 30 *May* 1779; d. 13 *Jan*. 1837; m. 22 *Feb*. 1823, *Sophia, da. of Charles Chaplin of Blankney*, d. 6 *Mar*. 1854 ; *and had issue*.

See the Tudor Roll of "The Blood Royal of Britain," pp. 417–418, Nos. 30315–30323.

2*b*. *Sarah Arabella Praed*, d. 13 *June* 1834; m. 17 *Jan*. 1822, *the Rev. Henry Wrey Whinfield, Rector of Tyringham*, bur. 3 *Jan*. 1847.   [Nos. 8146 to 8163.

143. Descendants, if any, of MARTHA FORESTER (see Table XI.), *m*. 19 Mar. 1759, FRANCES TURNER BLITHE.

144. Descendants of Sir CHARLTON LEIGHTON, 3rd Bart. [E.], co. Shropshire Militia, and High Sheriff for that co. 1749 (see Table XI.), *d*. 1780; *m*. 1st, ANNA MARIA (in her issue 1867 a co-h. to the Barony of Powys of Charleton), da. of Richard MYTTON of Halston and (*jure uxoris*) of Condover; *d*. 1750; 2ndly, 22 Oct. 1751, EMMA, da. of Sir Robert MAUDE, 1st Bart. [I.], *d*. (–); and had issue (with possible others by 2nd wife) 1*a* to 4*a*.

1*a*. *Sir Charlton Leighton, 4th Bart. [E.], M.P.*, d. *unm*. 9 *Sept*. 1784.

2*a*. *Sir Robert Leighton, 5th Bart. [E.]*, b. 1752; d.s.p. *Feb*. 1819.

3*a*. *Anna Maria Leighton of Condover, co. Salop*, d. (–); m. *Nicholas Smythe of North Nibley, co. Gloucester, High Sheriff co. Salop* 1772; d. *and had issue* 1*b* *to* 5*b*.

The Plantagenet Roll

1b. Nicholas Owen Smythe, *afterwards* (R.L. 4 Feb. 1790) Smythe Owen of Condover, d.s.p. 30 *Jan.* 1804.

2b. Anna Maria Smythe, d. (–) ; m. *Feb.* 1792, *Edward Pemberton of Longnor, co. Salop ; and had issue* 1c *to* 3c.

1c. Edward William Smythe Pemberton, *afterwards* (R.L. 24 Dec. 1814) Owen of Condover, *High Sheriff co. Salop* 1819, b. 28 Dec. 1793 ; d. 1863 ; m. 10 *Feb.* 1844, Charlotte Maria, da. of John Edward Madocks, M.P.

2c. Harriet Maria Pemberton, d. 16 *Ap.* 1831 ; m. 7 *Nov.* 1814, Sir John Salusbury Salusbury (1813), *previously Piozzi of Brynbella, High Sheriff co. Flint* 1816, b. 9 *Sept.* 1793 ; d. 1858 ; *and had issue* 1d *to* 6d.

1d. Rev. George Augustus Salusbury *of Brynbella, LL.B.,* b. 16 *June* 1822 ; d. 24 Dec. 1893 ; m. 15 *Ap.* 1852, Fanny, *da. of Luke T. Crossly of Olive Mount, Liverpool ; and had issue* 1e *to* 2e.

1e. Edward Pemberton Salusbury, *late Capt. and Hon. Major* 3rd Batt. Shropshire [I.] (*Bachygraig, near St. Asaph*), b. 2 Nov. 1854 ; m. 2 Jan. 1884, Julia Melville, of James White Smith of Kathali, Bengal ; *and has issue* 1f *to* 2f.

1f. Edward Clare Frederic Salusbury, b. 10 May 1886.

2f. Rosamund Victoria Salusbury.

2e. Frederic Hamilton Salusbury, *LL.B., M.A.* (Camb.), Barrister (*Richmond, Edgecliffe Road, Sydney, N.S.W.*), b. 15 Ap. 1856 ; m. 28 Dec. 1892, Isabel Adelaide, da. of the Hon. William Henry Suttor of Bathurst, N.S.W. ; *and has issue* 1f.

1f. Frederick George Hamilton Salusbury, b. 17 Nov. 1895.

2d. Frederick Octavius Salusbury, *C.B., Major-Gen. late* 101st *Fusiliers,* b. 18 *Jan.* 1825 ; d. (? s.p.) 22 *June* 1905.

3d. Rev. Augustus Pemberton Salusbury, *M.A., Vicar of Wrockwardine, Salop ;* b. 25 Aug. 1826 ; d. 24 Mar. 1896 ; m. 20 *Ap.* 1852, Henrietta Sophia, da. of John Perkins of Norris Lodge, Herts ; *and had issue* 1e *to* 8e.

1e. Rev. Norman Salusbury, Vicar of Preston Patrick (*Preston Patrick Vicarage, Milnthorpe*), b. 5 Mar. 1859 ; m. 9 Ap. 1890, Helen Louisa, da. of Horace A. Coates of Stanley House, Andover ; *and has issue* 1f *to* 3f.

1f. Norman Horace Pemberton Salusbury, b. 23 Nov. 1893.

2f. Helen Winifred Salusbury.

3f. Gwendolen Mary Salusbury.

2e. Charles Pemberton Salusbury, b. 10 Ap. 1861.

3e. Rev. Francis Russell Salusbury, M.A. (Oxon.), Vicar of Purbrook (*Purbrook Vicarage, Cosham, Hants*), b. 12 Nov. 1865 ; m. 1 June 1893, Mabel Constance, da. of Charles Warner of Northlands.

4e. Amy Hester Salusbury.

5e. Maud Salusbury.

6e. Marion Salusbury.

7e. Edith Salusbury.

8e. Dora Salusbury.

4d. Hester Maria Salusbury, d. 1854 ; m. 16 *July* 1841, *the Rev.* Arthur Downes Gardner, *M.A., Vicar of Holywell, co. Flint.*

5d. Angelina Salusbury, d. 1872 ; m. 27 *Ap.* 1837, *John William Harden of the Inner Temple, Judge of the County Court for co. Chester.*

6d. Caroline Mary Salusbury, m. 25 *July* 1856, *the Rev.* Watkin Williams, *M.A., Rector of Nannerch, co. Flint.*

3c. Letitia Caroline Pemberton.

3b. Letitia Sophia Smythe, d. 21 Nov. 1812 ; m. 16 Feb. 1791, *Henry Augustus Leicester of Ashton Hayes, co. Chester,* b. 1 *June* 1765 ; d. 18 *July* 1816 ; *and had issue* 1c.

1c. Rev. Charles Leicester, *Rector of Westbury, co. Salop,* b. 29 Sept. 1795 ; d.

[Nos. 8164 to 8181.

230

# of The Blood Royal

16 *Mar.* 1858; m. 1*st*, 5 *July* 1821, *Sally, da. of Richard Topp of Whitton,* d. 10 *Sept.* 1843; *and had issue* 1*d to* 2*d.*

1*d. Letitia Philippa Leicester, co-heir* (1863) *to her father,* b. 14 *Nov.* 1822; d. (–); m. 17 *Jan.* 1851, *the Rev. David James Paterson, Vicar of Chilford, co. Chester; and had issue* 1*e to* 4*e.*

2*e.* Louisa Letitia Paterson.

3*e.* Helen Paterson.

4*e.* Georgina Ann Paterson.

    2*d. Augusta Sophia Leicester,* b. 19 *Dec.* 1824; m. 29 *Jan.* 1859, *Hippolyte la Bienvenue,* d. 27 *Dec.* 1890.

    4*b. Caroline Elizabeth Smythe,* d. 3 *Dec.* 1818; m. 13 *Jan.* 1794, *Charles Cholmondeley of Overleigh and Knutsford, co. Chester,* b. 6 *June* 1770; d. 5 *Dec.* 1846; *and had issue.*
See the Clarence Volume, pp. 494–495, Nos. 21553–21692.

    5*b. Louisa Harriet Smythe,* b. 1774; d. 12 *Oct.* 1888; m. *as* 2*nd wife, May* 1798, *Charles Leicester of Stanthorne Hall, co. Chester,* b. 9 *Sept.* 1766; d. 1815; *and had issue* 1*c to* 4*c.*

1*c. Rev. Frederic Leicester, M.A.,* b. 17 *July* 1802; d. 16 *Ap.* 1873; m. 2*ndly,* 17 *Oct.* 1861, *Amelia Susannah, da. of Lieut.-Col. John Campbell; and had issue* 1*d to* 3*d.*

1*d.* Sir Peter Fleming Frederic Leicester, 8th Bart. [E.], b. 25 Jan. 1863; *m.* 18 Ap. 1904, Kate Patten, da. of Edward M. Warren of New York.

2*d.* Byron Leicester, Capt. 1st Batt. Cheshire Regt., b. 23 Jan. 1868; *m.* 6 June 1895, Gwendolen Margaret, da. of John Brooke of Hockliffe Grange, co. Bedford; and has issue 1*e.*

1*e.* Meriel Gwendolen Leicester.

3*d.* Meriel Ammelia Caroline Leicester.

    2*c. Charles Byrne Leicester, E.I.C.S.,* b. 16 *Mar.* 1807; d. 21 *Sept.* 1831; m. 8 *Sept.* 1827, *Emily, da. of William Leicester, B.C.S. (who re-m.* 1832, *Lieut.-Col. John Campbell,* d. 21 *Nov.* 1875); d. 11 *Jan.* 1871; *and had issue* 1*d.*

1*d.* William Frederic Leicester, *late* Major Bengal S.C. (*Wenonah, Bournemouth,* b. 11 July 1831; *m.* 1st, 10 June 1871, Louisa Helen, da. of Daniel Godfrey, *d.s.p.* 1886; 2ndly, 1894, Mary Lilian, da. of George William Young of Branksome Manor, Bournemouth; and has issue 1*e* to 2*e.*

1*e.* George William Frederic Leicester, b. 24 Ap. 1895.

2*e.* Charles Byrne Warren Leicester, b. 30 Mar. 1896.

    3*c. Emily Elizabeth Leicester,* d. 23 *June* 1863; m. 1839, *Joseph Tongue Sharington Davenport,* b. 25 *Aug.* 1813; d. 23 *May* 1848.

    4*c. Lavinia Sophia Leicester,* d. 25 *Feb.* 1847; m. 14 *July* 1840, *Robert John St. Aubyn, R.N.*

    4*a.*[1] *Annabella Leighton,* d. 21 *Jan.* 1816; m. (*at Gretna Green*) 20 *Nov.* 1775, *William Baldwyn, afterwards Childe of Kinlet Hall, co. Salop, J.P., D.L.,* d. 3 *Feb.* 1824; *and had issue* 1*b.*

1*b. William Lacon Childe alias Baldwyn, afterwards (R.L.* 1849) *Childe of Kinlet Hall, and Kyre Park, co. Worcester, M.P., J.P., D.L., High Sheriff co. Salop* 1828, *&c.,* b. 3 *Jan.* 1786; d. 1880; m. 13 *Aug.* 1807, *Harriet, da. of William Cludde of Orleton; and had issue* 1*c to* 4*c.*

1*c. William Lacon Childe of Kinlet Hall, J.P.,* b. 6 *June* 1810; d.s.p.s. *Oct.* 1881.

2*c. Charles Orlando Childe, afterwards (R.L.* 1849) *Childe-Pemberton of Kinlet Hall and Millichope Park, J.P., D.L., High Sheriff co. Salop* 1859, b. 27 *Dec.* 1812;

[Nos. 8182 to 8232.

231

The Plantagenet Roll

d. 1 *May* 1883; m. 21 *Aug.* 1849, *Augusta Mary, da. of Henry Davenport Shake-spear, Senior Member of the Supreme Council of India and a Master in Chancery; and had issue* 1d *to* 4d.

1d. Charles Baldwyn Childe-Pemberton, *afterwards* (1884) *Childe of Kinlet Hall and Millichope Park, J.P., D.L., Capt. Salop Yeo. Cav., formerly R.H.G.,* b. 27 *Sept.* 1853; d.s.p. (*being killed at Potietter's Drift*) 20 *Jan.* 1900; m. 30 *Nov.* 1884, *Carlotten Amalia, widow of Arnold Crossley of Halifax, da. of C. Montgomery of Gothenburg.*

2d. William Shakespear Childe-Pemberton, a co-h. to the Baronies of Grey de Powys, Wake, Woodstock, and Holland [E.] (11 *Granville Place, Portman Square, W.*), *b.* 14 Jan. 1867; *m.* 28 June 1894, Lady Constance Violet, da. of John Stuart (Bligh), 6th Earl of Darnley [I.]; and has issue 1e to 2e.

1e. Edmund William Baldwyn Childe-Pemberton, *b.* 21 June 1895.

2e. Roland Ivo Lacon Childe-Pemberton, *b.* 29 Sept. 1898.

3d. Augusta Harriet Childe-Pemberton.

4d. Harriet Louisa Childe-Pemberton.

3c. Rev. Edward George Childe, *afterwards* (1880) *Baldwyn-Childe of Kyre, M.A., J.P., Preb. of Wareham, &c., b.* 23 *Dec.* 1818; d.s.p. 22 *Feb.* 1898; m. 23 *Ap.* 1862, *Francis Christina (Kyre Park, Tenbury, Worcester), da. of Sir Baldwin Leighton, 7th Bart. [E.].*

4c. Rev. Arthur Childe, *afterwards* (1878) *Childe-Freeman of Gaines Court, co. Hereford, b.* 2 *Ap.* 1820; d. 15 *Feb.* 1882; m. 1 *June* 1852, *Mary Harriet (Gaines, co. Hereford; Fernie, Whitbourne, near Worcester), da. and co-h. of John Freeman of Gaines, J.P., D.L., High Sheriff co. Hereford* 1832; *and had issue* 1d *to* 7d.

1d. Arthur John Childe-Freeman, *J.P., b.* 24 *Mar.* 1863; d. 1891; m. 1887, *Harriet, da. of Richard Alexander Shaw; and had issue* 1e *to* 3e.

1e. John Arthur Childe-Freeman, *b.* (twin) 17 Aug. 1890.

2e. Mary Abigail Childe-Freeman, *b.* 17 May 1888.

3e. Olive Childe-Freeman, *b.* (twin) 17 Aug. 1890.

2d. Rev. Edward Leonard Childe-Freeman, M.A., Rector of Edwyn Ralph (*Edwyn Ralph Rectory, Bromyard, co. Hereford*), *b.* 24 Feb. 1855; *m.* 15 June 1880, Edith, da. of George Mercer of Deal; and has issue 1e to 3e.

1e. Leonard George Childe-Freeman, *b.* 13 Mar. 1881.

2e. Arthur Harold Childe-Freeman, *b.* 10 July 1882.

3e. Dorothy Edith Childe-Freeman, *b.* 30 Dec. 1886.

3d. Cecil Edwyn Childe-Freeman, *b.* 11 Feb. 1861; m. 1887, Amy, da. of Alexander MacDougall of Vancouver; and has issue 1e.

1e. Édwyn Ralph Childe-Freeman, *b.* 27 Sept. 1897.

4d. Rowland Lacon Childe-Freeman, *b.* 19 Feb. 1870; *unm.*

5d. Alice Mary Childe-Freeman, *b.* 23 Dec. 1857; *m.* 20 Aug. 1879, William James Sandford-Thompson, J.P. (*The Villa, Montrose*); and has issue 1e to 5e.

1e. William Arthur Cecil Sandford-Thompson, *b.* 20 Oct. 1880.

2e. Lionel Edwyn Baldwyn Sandford-Thompson, *b.* 18 Feb. 1884.

3e. Reginald Keith Garioch Sandford-Thompson, *b.* 26 May 1889.

4e. Daisy Gwendoline Mary Sandford-Thompson, *b.* 9 Jan. 1883.

5e. Kathleen Muriel Sandford Thompson, *b.* 11 July 1885.

6d. Ida Lucy Childe-Freeman, *b.* 23 July 1859; *m.* the Rev. Evelyn Henry Hill, M.A., Vicar of Brereton (*Brereton Vicarage, near Rugeley, co. Stafford*), s.p.

7d. Katherine Jessie Childe-Freeman, *b.* 7 Ap. 1865; *m.* 2 May 1888, the Rev. George Christopher Battiscombe, Vicar of Uxbridge (*Uxbridge Vicarage, co. Middlesex*); and has issue 1e.

1e. Katherine Myra Faith Battiscombe, *b.* 26 Mar. 1897.

[Nos. 8233 to 8256.

# of The Blood Royal

145. Descendants of BALDWIN LEIGHTON, Capt. 9th Regt. (see Table XI.), *b.* 1717; *d.* (-); *m.* ANNE, da. of Capt. SMITH; and had issue 1*a* to 3*a.*

1*a.* Sir Baldwin Leighton, 6th Bart. [*E.*], *Governor of Jersey, b.* 15 *Jan.* 1747; *d.* 13 *Nov.* 1828; *m.* 2*ndly, Nov.* 1802, *Margaretta Louisa Anne, da. of Sir John Thomas Stanley, 6th Bart.* [*E.*], *d.* 8 *Jan.* 1842; *and had issue* 1*b.*

1*b.* Sir Baldwin Leighton, 7th Bart. [*E.*], *M.P., b.* 14 *May* 1805; *d.* 26 *Feb.* 1871; *m.* 9 *Feb.* 1832, *Mary, da. and eventual h. of Thomas Netherton Parker of Sweeney Hall, d.* 5 *Mar.* 1864; *and had issue* 1*c* to 5*c.*

1*c.* Sir Baldwin Leighton, 8th Bart. [*E.*], *M.P., b.* 27 *Oct.* 1836; *d.* 22 *Jan.* 1897; *m.* 30 *Jan.* 1864, *the Hon, Eleanor Leicester, now Leighton-Warren (Tabley House, Knutsford), da. of George (Warren, previously Leicester), 2nd Baron De Tabley* [*U.K.*]; *and had issue* 1*d* to 4*d.*

1*d.* Sir Bryan Baldwin Mawddwy Leighton, 9th Bart. [*E.*], Major Westmoreland and Cumberland Imp. Yeo. (*Loton Park, Shrewsbury*), *b.* 26 Nov. 1868; *m.* 3 Dec. 1890, Margaret Frances, da. of Major John Fletcher Fletcher of Saltoun Hall; and has issue 1*e* to 2*e.*

1*e.* John Burgh Talbot Leighton, *b.* 1892.

2*e.* Richard Tihel Leighton, *b.* 1893.

2*d.* Cuthbert Leighton, now (R.L. 9 Feb. 1899) Leicester-Warren, J.P. (*Nant-y-gaer, Gresford, Wrexham*), *b.* 6 Nov. 1877; *m.* 21 Aug. 1904, Hilda, da. of Capt. Edmund Henry Davenport of Davenport.

3*d.* Catharine Barbara Leighton.

4*d.* Meriel Gundrede Leighton, *m.* 9 Ap. 1890, Algernon Edward Perkins (*Sundorne Castle, Shrewsbury*); and has issue 1*e* to 3*e.*

1*e.* George Algernon Perkins, *b.* 1896.

2*e.* Meriel Elizabeth Perkins.

3*e.* Cynthia Gundrede Perkins.

2*c.* Stanley Leighton of Sweeney Hall, M.P., J.P., D.L., b. 13 Oct. 1837; d. 4 May 1901; m. 28 Aug. 1873, Jessie Marie (70 Chester Square, S.W.), da. and co-h. of Henry Bertie Watkin Williams-Wynn of Nantymeihed and Howbery Park; and had issue 1d to 2d.

1*d.* Bertie Edward Parker Leighton, Capt. 1st Dragoons (*Sweeney Hall, Oswestry*), *b.* 26 Nov. 1875.

2*d.* Rachel Frances Marion Leighton.

3*c.* Frances Christina Leighton (*Kyre Park, Tenbury, Worcester*), *m.* 23 Ap. 1862, the Rev. Edward George Baldwyn Childe of Kyre, *d.s.p.* 22 Feb. 1898.

4*c.* Isabella Leighton (*Knoyle House, Hindon; Norton Hall, Daventry*), *m.* 1st, 28 Oct. 1857, Beriah Botfield of Norton Hall, M.P., *d.* 7 Aug. 1863; 2ndly, 18 Aug. 1866, Alfred Seymour of Knoyle, D.L., M.P., *b.* 11 Nov. 1824; *d.* 15 Mar. 1888; and has issue 1*d.*

1*d.* Jane Margaret Seymour, *b.* 14 Mar. 1873.

5*c.* Charlotte Leighton (19 *Wilton Place, S.W.*), *m.* 7 Ap. 1893, Gen. the Hon. William Henry Adelbert Feilding, *d.s.p.* 25 Mar. 1895.

2*a.* Thomas Leighton, Major-Gen. H.E.I.C.S., b. 1751; d. 22 May 1808; m. Mary Louisa, da. of Capt. Everett, H.E.I.C.S.; and had issue 1b.

1*b.* Rev. Francis Leighton, b. 5 Dec. 1801; d. 15 Dec. 1870; m. 12 Feb. 1829, Catherine, da. of Samuel Amy Severne of Thenford, d. 22 Ap. 1884; and had issue 1c to 3c.

1*c.* Edward William Forester Leighton, *late* Capt. 9th Foot (29 *Parsons Green, S.W.; Naval and Military*), *b.* 20 Dec. 1839; *m.* 28 Aug. 1886, Beatrice

[Nos. 8257 to 8272.

233

The Plantagenet Roll

Jane, da. of John Eyre of Eyrecourt Castle, co. Galway; and has issue 1d to 2d.

1d. Charlton Dudley Forester Leighton, b. 17 June 1887.
2d. Olga Beatrice Leighton.
2c. Louisa Ann Leighton,
3c. Emma Victoria Leighton, } (41 *Buckingham Palace Mansions, S.W.*).
3a. Rev. *Francis Leighton, Vicar of Condover*, b. 1757 ; d. 1809.
[Nos. 8273 to 8276.

146. Descendants of RACHEL LEIGHTON (see Table XI.), *m*. THOMAS JENKINS of Charlton Hill, co. Salop; and had (with other) issue 1a to 2a.

1a. *Edward Jenkins of Charlton Hill*, d. 20 *May* 1820; m. *Sarah, da. of the Rev. Richard Boycott ; and had issue 1b to 2b.*

1b. *Robert Boycott Cressett Leighton Jenkins of Charlton Hill, Major in the Army*, b. 13 *Mar.* 1781 ; d. 2 *May* 1836 ; m. 26 *Feb.* 1808, *Elizabeth, da. of Richard Jenkins of Bicton Hall*, d. 29 Nov. 1857 ; *and had issue* 1c.

1c. *Charles Vanbrugh Jenkins of Charlton Hill and Cruckton, J.P., Major-Gen., Lieut.-Col. Comdg.* 19th *Hussars*, b. 4 *Mar.* 1822 ; d. 10 *Dec.* 1892 ; m. 24 *Mar.* 1847, *Annette Louisa Robertina, da. of Horace Aylward*, d. 1 *Feb.* 1887 ; *and had issue* 1d *to* 7d.

1d. *Robert Edward Arthur Jenkins, Lieut. B.S.C.*, b. 5 *Feb.* 1848 ; d.v.p. 28 *Feb.* 1876 ; m. 27 *Feb.* 1873, *Hannah, da. of S. Turnbull ; and had issue* 1e *to* 2e.

1e. Charles Edward Jenkins (*Cruckton Hall, and Broseley Hall, co. Salop*), b. 6 *Mar.* 1875.

2e. Rose Edith Annette Jenkins.

2d. *Edgar Francis Jenkins of Charlton Hill, D.L.*, b. 17 *Dec.* 1850 ; d. 18 *Jan.* 1898 ; m. 2ndly, 22 *Sept.* 1887, *Edith Helen* (*who re-m.* 24 *Feb.* 1900, *Edward John Williams Jeudwine*), *da. of William Shearman Turner of Gloucester Place, W. ; and had issue* 1e *to* 2e.

1e. Edgar Kynnersley Jenkins (*Charlton Hill, near Wroxeter*), b. 18 Mar 1891.

2e. Robert Charles Jenkins, b. 1 Jan. 1896.

3d. Charles Bradford Harries Jenkins, now (R.L. 1894) Wolseley-Jenkins, Lieut.-Col. 19th Hussars (*Abbotsfield, Shrewsbury*), b. 17 Mar. 1856 ; *m.* 16 June 1885, Ada Frances Alice, da. of Sir John Richard Wolseley, 6th Bart. [I.]; and has issue 1e to 2e.

1e. Charles Wolseley Jenkins, b. 11 Feb. 1890.
2e. Ada Frances Blennerhasset Jenkins.

4d. Mary Louisa Jenkins, *m.* 20 July 1886, Alfred Napier (4 *Marlborough Terrace, Taunton*) ; and has issue 1e to 2e.

1e. Donald Charles Napier, b. 8 Mar. 1893.
2e. Mary Katharine Napier, b. 26 Ap. 1887.

5d. Annette Geraldine Jenkins.
6d. Edith Augusta Jenkins.
7d. Eleanor Maud Jenkins.

2b. *Emma Gertrude Jenkins*, d. (-) ; m. *Francis Blithe Harries of Benthall Hall and Cruckton Hall ; and had issue* (*at least*) 1c *to* 2c.

1c. *Frances Harries of Cruckton and Broseley Hall*, d. *presumably* s.p.
2c. *Thomas Harries of Allesley, co. Warwick*, d. *presumably* s.p. 12 *Oct.* 1879.[1]
[Nos. 8277 to 8289.

---

[1] They devised their estates to their maternal cousin, Charles Vanbrugh Jenkins. Burke's " Landed Gentry," 1900, p. 860.

234

# of The Blood Royal

2a. *Emma Jenkins*, d. 1764; m. 16 *Ap.* 1759, *John Jenkins of Bicton Hall*, b. 16 *July* 1740; d. 28 *June* 1771; *and had issue* 1b *to* 2b.

1b. *Richard Jenkins of Bicton Hall*, b. 6 *Mar.* 1760; d. 3 *Nov.* 1797; m. *Oct.* 1781, *Harriet Constantina, da. of George Ravensworth of Wrexham, co. Denbigh*, d. 4 *Ap.* 1832; *and had issue* 1c *to* 3c.

1c. *Sir Richard Jenkins of Bicton Hall, G.C.B., D.C.L., J.P., D.L., a Director* H.E.I.C., b. 18 *Feb.* 1785; d. 30 *Dec.* 1853; m. 31 *Mar.* 1824, *Elizabeth Helen, da. of Hugh Spottiswoode, H.E.I.C.C.S.; and had issue* 1d *to* 8d.

1d. *Richard Jenkins of Bicton Hall, Col.* 1st *Bengal Cavalry*, b. 8 *Sept.* 1828; d. 9 *Sept.* 1880; m. *Sophia, widow of* [——] *Mayne, da. of Horace Aylward; and had issue* 1e.

1e. Rev. Richard Jenkins, Rector of Talaton, Ottery St. Mary, b. 27 July 1865; *m.s.p.*

2d. Charles Jenkins, b. 20 May 1831.

3d. Arthur Jenkins, b. 20 Jan. 1833.

4d. Edward Gordon Jenkins, b. 11 Mar. 1838.

5d. *Emily Jenkins*, d. (-); m. 12 *Nov.* 1845, *William Frederick Baring*, b. 12 *Aug.* 1822; d. 1903; *and had issue* 1e.

1e. Mary Emily Baring.

6d. *Cecilia Harriot Theophila Jenkins*, b. (*at Bombay*) 5 *Feb.* 1825; d. 21 *Dec.* 1895; m. *John Archibald Pym, 2nd Bombay Light Cavalry*, b. 6 *Feb.* 1830; d. (*at Bombay*) *Nov.* 1862; *and had issue* 1e.

1e. Charles Archibald Pym, b. 1854.

7d. Helen Jenkins, *m.* 21 July 1864, William Shearman Turner (*Gloucester Place, Hyde Park*); *and has issue* 1e *to* 2e.

1e. Percy Shearman Turner, M.A., Bar.-at-Law, b. 5 Mar. 1874; *m.* Oct. 1899, Blanche Edith, da. of [——] Kessler, *s.p.*

2e. Edith Helen Turner (*Charlton Hill, near Wroxeter*), *m.* 1st, as 2nd wife, 22 Sept. 1887, Edgar Francis Jenkyns of Charlton Hill, *d.* 18 Jan. 1898; 2ndly, 24 Feb. 1900, Edward John William Jeudwine; and has issue.

See p. 234, Nos. 8279–8280.

8d. *Melanie Jenkins*, d. 1891; m. *as* 3rd *wife*, 6 *Feb.* 1866, *William Vansittart of Brunswick Square, Brighton, D.L., M.P.*, b. 2 *May* 1813; d. 15 *Jan.* 1878; *and had issue* 1e.

1e. Charles Edward Bexley Vansittart, *m.* 28 July 1888, Constance Frances, da. of Sir Thomas Macdonald Miller, 4th Bart. [G.B.]; and has issue 1f to 2f.

1f. Constance Hilda Maude Bexley Vansittart.

2f. Melanie Bexley Vansittart.

2c. *Elizabeth Jenkins*, d. 29 *Nov.* 1857; m. 26 *Feb.* 1808, *Robert Boycott Cressett Leighton Jenkins of Charlton Hill*, d. 2 *May* 1836; *and had issue*.

See p. 234, Nos. 8277–8289.

3c. *Emma Jenkins*, d. 19 *Dec.* 1863; m. 27 *Jan.* 1829, *the Rev. Charles Wingfield of The Gro, co. Montgomery, M.A.*, b. 24 *Aug.* 1770; d. 1 *May.* 1850; *and had issue* 1d.

1d. *Charles George Wingfield of Onslow, J.P., D.L., High Sheriff co. Salop* 1873, b. 21 *Ap.* 1833; d. 5 *May* 1891; m. 1 *Feb.* 1865, *Jane Mary Anne, da. and h. of Clopton Lewis Wingfield of Rhysnant; and had issue* 1e *to* 2e.

1e. Charles Ralph Borlase Wingfield, J.P., Capt. Shropshire Militia (*Onslow Hall, near Shrewsbury*), b. 27 Oct. 1873.

2e. Constance Adela Wingfield, b. 25 Ap. 1878.

2b. *Edward Jenkins*, d. (-); m. *Elizabeth, da. of George Ravenscroft of Wrexham; and had (with other issue, an eldest son)* 1c.

1c. *Richard Boycott Jenkins, Col. in the Army*, d. (-); m. [——], *da. of* [——] *Ord; and had issue (two sons and two das.).*[1]   [Nos. 8290 to 8318.

---

[1] Burke's "Landed Gentry," 1900, p. 860.

The Plantagenet Roll

147. Descendants, if any, of the Hon. ANNE STAWEL (see Table XI.), wife 1st of JAMES DARCY, and 2ndly of JOHN BARBER or BABER of Sunning Hill.

148. Descendants of Lady DOROTHY MANNERS (see Table VII.), *d.* June 1698 ; *m.* 22 Sept. 1669, ANTHONY (ASHLEY COOPER), 2nd EARL OF SHAFTESBURY [E.], *b.* 1752 ; *d.* 2 Nov. 1699 ; and had issue.

See the Tudor Roll of "The Blood Royal of Britain," Table XCVIII., pp. 428–431, Nos. 30995-31123. [Nos. 8319 to 8447.

149. Descendants of HENRY (PHIPPS), 1st EARL OF MULGRAVE [U.K.], 3rd BARON MULGRAVE OF NEW ROSS [I.], and 1st BARON MULGRAVE [G.B.], G.C.B. (see Table XII.), *b.* 14 Feb. 1745 ; *d.* 7 Ap. 1831 ; *m.* 20 Oct. 1795, SOPHIA, da. of Christopher THOMPSON MALING of West Herrington, co. Durham, *d.* 17 Mar. 1849 ; and had issue 1*a* to 4*a*.

1*a. Constantine Henry (Phipps), 1st Marquis of Normanby [U.K.], 4th [I.] and 2nd [G.B.] Baron Mulgrave, K.G., &c., b.* 15 *May* 1797 ; *d.* 28 *July* 1863 ; m. 12 Aug. 1818, the Hon. Maria, da. of Thomas Henry (Liddell), 1st Baron Ravensworth [U.K.],* d. 20 Oct. 1882 ; *and had issue.*
See the Clarence Volume, pp. 92–93, Nos. 631–661.

2*a. Hon. Sir Charles Beaumont Phipps, K.C.B., Keeper of H.M.'s Privy Purse, and Treasurer of the Household to H.R.H. the Prince Consort, &c., b.* 27 *Dec.* 1801 ; d. 24 Feb. 1866 ; m. 25 June 1835, Margaret Anne, da. of the Ven. Henry Bathurst, Archdeacon of Norwich,* d. 13 *Ap.* 1874 ; *and had issue* 1*b to* 3*b.*

1*b.* Charles Edmund Phipps, *late* Major 18th Foot, sometime a Groom in Waiting to Queen Victoria (287 *Yate Street, Victoria, British Columbia*), *b.* 11 June 1844 ; *m.* 2 June 1868, Susan Stewart, da. of the Very Rev. John Gamble Geddes, Dean of Niagara, &c. ; and has issue 1*c* to 8*c.*

1*c.* Charles Stewart Phipps, *b.* 12 Dec. 1871.
2*c.* Albert Edmund Phipps, *b.* 1 May 1873.
3*c.* William Henry Gamble Phipps, *b.* 11 Jan. 1880.
4*c.* Augustus Henry Constantine Phipps, *b.* 1882.
5*c.* Alice Lepel Phipps, *b.* 26 Sept. 1870.
6*c.* Katherine Mary Phipps, *b.* 17 Jan. 1875.
7*c.* Victoria Alexandrina Phipps (Queen Victoria sponsor), *b.* 30 Mar. 1877.
8*c.* Mary Susan Frances Phipps, *b.* 26 Aug. 1878.

2*b.* Maria Henrietta Sophia Phipps, Keeper of the State Apartments, Kensington Palace, *m.* 1st, Jan. 1856, Capt. Frederick Sayer, *d.* 29 Feb. 1868 ; 2ndly, 4 Dec. 1872, Lieut.-Col. William Chaine, M.V.O. (*Kensington Palace, W.*) ; and has issue 1*c* to 6*c.*

1*c.* Frederic Charles Robert Sayer, *b.* 1859.
2*c.* Robert Dhuleep E. Sayer, *b.* 1861.
3*c.* William Robert Algernon Chaine, *b.* 1874.
4*c.* Evelyn Julia Marguerite Sayer, *m.* 29 Mar. 1879, Harry Hubert de Merve Slade (71 *Elizabeth Street, Eaton Square, S.W.*).
5*c.* Mabel Sayer, *m.* 1889, Francis Saville Barton.
6*c.* Harriet Lepel Dorothea Sayer, *m.* 25 July 1889, Harry Claude Frederick Hay (77 *Cadogan Place, S.W.*). [Nos. 8448 to 8494.

# of The Blood Royal

3*b*. Hon. Harriet Lepel Phipps, V.A., sometime (1862–1889) Maid of Honour and (1889–1901) as Bedchamber Woman in Ordinary to Queen Victoria.

3*a*. Hon. *Edmund Phipps, Recorder of Scarborough*, b. 7 *Dec*. 1808 ; d. 28 *Oct*. 1857 ; m. 15 *May* 1838, *Maria Louisa, widow of the Hon. Charles Francis Norton, da. of Lieut.-Gen. Sir Colin Campbell, K.C.B.*, d. 1888 ; *and had issue* 1*b*.

1*b*. Sir Constantine Edmund Henry Phipps, K.C.M.G., C.B., H.B.M.'s Envoy Extraor. and Min. Plen. at Brussels (*British Legation, Brussels*), b. 15 Mar. 1840 ; *m*. 1st, 7 Oct. 1863, Maria Jane, da. of Alfred Miller Mundy of Shipley, *d*. 30 Aug. 1902 ; 2ndly, 20 Jan. 1904, Alexandra Wassilewna, widow of Gomès Brandão, da. of Wassili de Schorrnacker of St. Petersburg ; and has issue 1*c*.

1*c*. Eric Clare Edmund Phipps, 3rd Sec. in Diplo. Ser. at Washington, *b*. 27 Oct. 1875.

4*a*. Rev. *Augustus Frederick Phipps, Chaplain in Ordinary to Queen Victoria, Hon. Canon of Ely, &c.*, b. 18 *Oct*. 1809 ; d. 27 *Jan*. 1896 ; m. 7 *Nov*. 1837, *Lady Mary Elizabeth Emily, da. of Henry (FitzRoy), 5th Duke of Grafton* [*E.*], d. 22 *Aug*. 1887 ; *and had issue*.

See the Clarence Volume, p. 339, Nos. 10864–10871.　　[Nos. 8495 to 8505.

150. Descendants of the Hon. HENRIETTA MARIA PHIPPS (see Table XII.), *d*. 1 Sept. 1782 ; *m*. as 1st wife, 19 Aug. 1776, CHARLES (DILLON, *afterwards* LEE-DILLON), 11th VISCOUNT DILLON [I.], K.P., *b*. 6 Nov. 1745 ; *d*. 9 Nov. 1813 ; and had issue.

See the Clarence Volume, pp. 440–445, Nos. 18777–18974.

[Nos. 8506 to 8702.

151. Descendants of ARTHUR ANNESLEY of Bletchington, co. Oxford (see Table XII.), *d*. Feb. 1773 ; *m*. ELIZABETH, da. of William BALDWIN of Aqualate ; and had issue 1*a*.

1*a*. Arthur *Annesley of Bletchington*, b. 1760 ; d. 20 *Jan*. 1841 ; m. 1 *Feb*. 1785, *Catherine, da. and h. of Admiral Sir Charles Hardy ; and had issue* 1*b* to 6*b*.

1*b*. Arthur (*Annesley*), 10*th Viscount Valentia* [*I.*], b. 30 *Nov*. 1785 ; d. 30 *Dec*. 1863 ; m. 12 *Aug*. 1808, *Eleanor, da. of Henry Stafford O'Brien of Blatherwycke Park*, d. 10 *June* 1843 ; *and had issue* 1*c* to 7*c*.

1*c*. Hon. Arthur Annesley, b. 14 *Sept*. 1809 ; d. 27 *Oct*. 1844 ; m. 18 *Jan*. 1836, *Flora Mary, da. of Lieut.-Col. James Macdonald of Clanranald* (*who* re-m. 3 *Mar*. 1847, *the Hon. George Talbot Devereux*), d. 5 *Nov*. 1884 ; *and had issue* 1*d* to 3*d*.

1*d*. Arthur (*Annesley*), 11th Viscount Valentia [I.], C.B., M.V.O., M.P., Comptroller of the Household to H.M. King Edward VII., also Premier Bart. [I.] (*Bletchington Park, Oxon. ; Eydon Hall, Banbury*), b. 22 Aug. 1843 ; *m*. 30 Jan. 1878, Laura Sarah, widow of Sir Algernon William Peyton, 4th Bart. [G.B.], da. of Daniel Hall Webb of Wykham Park ; and has issue 1*e* to 8*e*.

1*e*. Hon. Arthur Annesley, Lieut. 10th Hussars, *b*. 24 Aug. 1880.

2*e*. Hon. Caryl Arthur James Annesley, Lieut. Oxfordshire L.I.

3*e*. Hon. Vere Annesley, *b*. 8 Mar. 1879 ; *m*. 23 July 1901, the Rev. Guy Ronald Campbell (*Cranfield Rectory, Woburn Sands*) ; and has issue 1*f*.

1*f*. Hester Maud Vere Campbell.

4*e*. Hon. Violet Kathleen Annesley, *b*. 18 Mar. 1882.

5*e*. Hon. Helen Annesley, *b*. 30 July 1884 ; *m*. 3 Oct. 1905, John Pemberton Heywood Heywood-Lonsdale (*Stratton Audley, Bicester*).　　[Nos. 8703 to 8709.

The Plantagenet Roll

6e. Hon. Lettice Annesley, b. 24 Sept. 1885.

7e. Hon. Hilda Cecil Annesley, b. 19 Ap. 1889.

8e. Hon. Dorothy Annesley, b. 11 May 1892.

2d. Hon. Mary Annesley, b. 4 Oct. 1836; d. 27 Sept. 1879; m. 24 Feb. 1855, Lieut.-Col. Walter Chidiock Nangle, late R.A.; and had issue 1e to 7e.

1e. Arthur Gerald Tichborne Nangle, b. 9 Nov. 1861; d. (? unm.) Oct. 1895.

2e. Ronald Chidiock Macdonald Nangle, b. 15 June 1871.

3e. Jasper Chidiock Nangle, b. 1 May 1872.

4e. Chidiock Nangle, b. 16 Mar. 1874.

5e. Nea Arthur Nangle, m. 12 Oct. 1807, Arthur Leoni Glover, d. 20 Sept. 1905; and has issue 1f to 2f.

1f. Valerie Arthur Glover, b. 27 Mar. 1892.

2f. Hazel Reavely Glover, b. Ap. 1893.

6e. Gwendoline Nangle.

7e. Ismay Nangle.

3d. Hon. Flora Annesley (140 Sloane Street, S.W.), m. 23 June 1863, Col. Francis Lyon, R.A.; d. 26 Feb. 1885; and has issue 1e to 6e.

1e. Charles Lyon, Major R.F.A. (Naval and Military), b. 7 Ap. 1865; m. 1894, Rachel Mary Fearne, da. of Capt. Sir Arthur Elibank Havelock, G.C.M.G.; and has issue 1f to 2f.

1f. Francis Charles Lyon, b. 1895.

2f. Margaret Grace Lyon, b. 1899.

2e. Francis Lyon, D.S.O., Major R.A., b. 10 July 1867.

3e. Arthur Lyon, late Capt. Border Regt., b. 25 Jan. 1869.

4e. Henry Lyon, b. 10 Aug. 1872.

5e. Mary Lyon, m. 1895, the Rev. Percy Stewart, Rector of West Derby (West Derby Rectory, Liverpool); and has issue 1f to 5f.

1f. Ellinor Stewart, b. 1896.

2f. Mary Stewart, b. 1898.

3f. Phyllis Stewart, b. 1899.

4f. Agnes Stewart, b. 1901.

5f. Betty Stewart, b. 1903.

6e. Florence Lyon, m. 18 Oct. 1905, Charles Speke.

2c. Hon. Algernon Sydney Arthur Annesley, J.P., Hon. Col., late Commdt. 4th Batt. Oxfordshire L.I., formerly 16th Lancers (5 Leinster Gardens, Hyde Park, W.), b. 25 May 1829; m. 11 Oct. 1864, Helen Sydney, da. of Griffith Richards, Q.C.; and has issue 1d to 3d.

1d. Arthur Sydney Evelyn Annesley, late Capt. Rifle Brig. (Naval and Military; Wellington), b. 16 July 1865.

2d. Helen Sydney Martha Annesley, b. 14 Nov. 1867.

3d. Mabel Sydney Augusta Katharine Annesley, b. 12 May 1869; m. 20 Ap. 1893, William James Yorke Scarlett, J.P. (Gigha, co. Argyll; Fyfield House, Andover, co. Hants); and has issue 1e to 3e.

1e. Peter William Yorke-Scarlett, b. 1905.

2e. Katherine Mabel Helen Yorke-Scarlett, b. 1894.

3e. Sheila Mildred Yorke-Scarlett, b. 1896.

3c. Hon. Frances Arthur Charlotte Annesley, d. 13 May 1904; m. 17 Oct. 1852, Capt. William Linskill of Tynemouth Lodge, Northumberland; and had issue 1d.

1d. William Thomas Linskill (17 Murray Park, St. Andrews), b. 25 June 1855; m. 7 Mar. 1881, Jessie Munro, da. of James Stewart; and has issue 1e to 2e.

1e. Violet Frances Linskill.

2e. Nora Douglas Linskill.

[Nos. 8710 to 8744.

238

# of The Blood Royal

4c. Hon. Matilda Arthur Marina Annesley, d. 23 *May* 1894 ; m. 18 *July* 1845, *John Kent Egerton Holmes,* d. 16 *June* 1848 ; *and had issue.*
See the Tudor Roll of "The Blood Royal of Britain," p. 398, Nos. 29688–29690.

5c. Hon. Eva Arthur Henry Medora Annesley, d. 1894 ; m. 12 *Jan.* 1853, *Sir Henry Robinson, K.C.B., Vice-President Local Govt. Board [I.],* b. 1823 ; d. *Mar.* 1893 ; *and had issue* 1d *to* 3d.

1d. Hercules Francis Robinson, b. 1853 ; d. 1900 ; m. 4 *Nov.* 1879, *Eleanor Edith, da. of George Wilkinson of Killiney ; and had issue.*

2d. Sir Henry Augustus Robinson, P.C., K.C.B., Vice-President Local Govt. Board [I.] (*Lisnacarig, Foxrock, co. Dublin*), b. 1857 ; m. 6 June 1883, Harriet, da. of Sir Robert Lynch-Blosse, 10th Bart. [I.].

3d. Eva Eleanora Robinson, d. 1892 ; m. 8 *Feb.* 1882, *Joseph Hone.*

6c. Hon. Nea Arthur Ada Rose d'Amour Annesley, d. 13 Jan. 1894 ; *m.* 24 *Ap.* 1846, *Hercules George Robert (Robinson), 1st Baron Rosmead [U.K.], P.C., G.C.M.G.,* b. 19 Dec. 1824 ; d. 28 Oct. 1897 ; *and had issue* 1d *to* 4d.

1d. Hercules Arthur Temple (Robinson), 2nd Baron Rosmead [U.K.], Major 6th Batt. Lancashire Fusiliers (10 *Kensington Gardens Terrace, W.*), b. 6 Nov. 1866 ; *m.* 10 Oct. 1891, the Hon. Edith Louisa, da. of Richard (Handcock), 4th Baron Castlemaine [I.] ; and has issue 1e to 3e.

1e. Hon. Hercules Edward Joseph Robinson, b. 1 Sept. 1895.

2e. Hon. Norah Edith Florence Robinson, b. 16 Oct. 1893.

3e. Hon. Nea Kathleen Elizabeth Clare Robinson, b. 27 Nov. 1898.

2d. Eleanor Frances Alti Maria Robinson, d. 24 Nov. 1893 ; m. 9 *June* 1870, *Col. Edward Beauchamp St. John ; 2ndly,* 1883, *Major George Stevenson, late Argyll and Sutherland Highlanders ; and had issue.*

3d. Hon. Nora Augusta Maud Robinson, *m.* 1st, 7 Aug. 1878, Alexander Kirkman Finlay, *d.s.p.* 1883 ; 2ndly, 2 Sept. 1887, Charles Richard Durant (13 *Egerton Gardens, S.W.*) ; and has issue 1e to 7c.

1e. Noel Henry Colin Fairfax Durant, b. 1888.

4d. Hon. Nérèdah Leeta Robinson, *m.* 26 Ap. 1887, Lieut.-Col. Charles Tyrwhitt Dawkins, C.M.G. ; and has issue 1e.

1e. Charles George Hereward Dawkins, b. 1888.

7c. Hon. Altisidora Arthur Victoria Annesley (7 *St. George's Square, S.W.*).

2b. Rev. Charles Annesley Francis Annesley of Eydon Hall, co. Northants, b. 26 *Dec.* 1787 ; d. 26 *Sept.* 1863.

3b. James Annesley, d. (*? unm.*) 1828.

4b. George Martin Annesley, d. (*in India*) (*? unm.*) 1824.

5b. Catherine Elizabeth Annesley, b. 21 Oct. 1791 ; d. 30 *July* 1759 ; m. 4 *May* 1814, *Rev. the Hon. John Evelyn Boscawen, Canon of Canterbury,* b. 11 *Ap.* 1790 ; d. 12 *May* 1851 ; *and had issue* 1c *to* 7c.

1c. Evelyn (Boscawen), 6th Viscount Falmouth [G.B.], b. 18 *Mar.* 1819 ; d. 6 *Nov.* 1889 ; m. 29 *July* 1845, *Mary Frances Elizabeth (Stapleton), suo jure* 17*th Baroness Le Despencer [E.],* b. 24 *Mar.* 1822 ; d. 20 *Nov.* 1891 ; *and had issue* 1d *to* 6d.

1d. Evelyn Edward Thomas (Boscawen), 7th Viscount Falmouth [G.B.], 18th Baron Le Despencer [E.], C.B., M.V.O., &c., &c. (*Tregothnan, Truro ; Mereworth Castle, Maidstone ; 2 St. James' Square, S.W.*), b. 24 July 1847 ; *m.* 19 Oct. 1886, the Hon. Kathleen, da. of George (Douglas-Pennant), 2nd Baron Penrhyn [U.K.] ; and has issue.
See the Clarence Volume, p. 220, Nos. 4446–4450.

2d. Hon. Hugh Le Despencer Boscawen, J.P., D.L. (20 *South Street, Park Lane, W.*), b. 28 Feb. 1849 ; *m.* 23 May 1872, Lady Mary, da. of William (Fitzwilliam), 6th Earl Fitzwilliam [G.B.], K.G.   [Nos. 8745 to 8764.

The Plantagenet Roll

3d. Hon. John Richard De Clare Boscawen, J.P., D.L., *late* Capt. and Hon. Major Oxfordshire L.I. (*Tregye, Perranwell, Cornwall*), *b.* 19 Dec. 1860; *m.* 11 June 1890, Lady Margaret Florence Lucy, da. of George (Byng), 2nd Earl of Strafford [U.K.]; and has issue 1*e.*

    1*e.* Catherine Margaret Boscawen, *b.* 29 May 1891.

    4*d.* Hon. Mary Elizabeth Frances Catherine Boscawen, *m.* 26 June 1894, the Rev. Arthur Murray Dale, Rector of Tingrith (*Tingrith Rectory, Woburn*).

    5*d.* Hon. Edith Maria Boscawen (6 *Queen Anne Street, Cavendish Square, W.*).

    6*d.* Hon. Mabel Emma Boscawen, *m.* 18 Ap. 1882, Charles Henry Bennet Williams, J.P. (son of Sir Hugh Williams, 3rd Bart.) [G.B.] (*Eryl, St. Asaph, N. Wales*); and has issue 1*e* to 2*e.*

    1*e.* Evelyn Hugh Watkin Williams, Lieut. 10th Hussars, *b.* 21 Mar. 1884.

    2*e.* Mary Nesta Harriet Williams, *b.* 31 Jan. 1883.

    2*c. Hon. John Townshend Boscawen, M.A., Rector of Lamorran, b.* 30 *Oct.* 1820; d. 7 *July* 1889; m. 13 *Feb.* 1851, *Mary, da. of John Hearle Tremayne of Heligan, d.* 25 *Nov.* 1895; *and had issue* 1*d to* 7*d.*

    1*d.* John Hugh Boscawen (*Auckland, New Zealand*), *b.* 2 Dec. 1851; *m.* 1st, 1876, Katherine Isabel, da. of the Rev. John Williams Conway-Hughes of Nydd Vicarage, M.A., *d.* 1884; 2ndly, 15 Sept. 1886, Ellen, da. of Henry Parker of Louth, co. Lincoln, *d.* 21 Jan. 1895; and has issue 1*e* to 6*e.*

    1*e.* Hugh Townshend Boscawen, *b.* 1880.

    2*e.* [——] Boscawen, *b.* 1887.

    3*e.*[1] Valentia Maud Boscawen, *m.* 29 Jan. 1899, James Skitt Matthews (*Vancouver, British Columbia*); and has issue 1*f* to 3*f.*

    1*f.* James Evelyn Huia Boscawen Matthews,   } *b.* (twins) 22 June 1899.
    2*f.* Herbert Llewelyn Terna Boscawen Matthews,

    3*f.* Edward Hugh Pryce Boscawen Matthews, *b.* 31 July 1900.

    4*e.*[1] Gwladys Evelyn Boscawen.

    5*e.*[1] Gladys Boscawen.

    6*e.*[2] [——] Boscawen.

    2*d.* Rev. Arthur Townshend Boscawen, J.P., Rector of Ludgvan (*Ludgvan Rectory, Cornwall*), *b.* 9 July 1862; *m.* 1902, Christian, da. of Chapell Hodge of Pounds.

    3*d.* Townshend Evelyn Boscawen, *b.* 10 Dec. 1864; *m.* 1902, Mary Sophia, da. of Thomas Algernon Dorrien-Smith of The Abbey, Trescoe.

    4*d.* Percevale Noel Boscawen, *b.* 25 Dec. 1870.

    5*d.* Ethel Boscawen.

    6*d.* Blanche Boscawen.

    7*d.* Margaret Boscawen.

    3*c. Hon. Charlotte Boscawen, b.* 29 *Mar.* 1815; d. 28 *Aug.* 1851; m. 6 *Aug.* 1838, *the Rev. George Brydges Moore, Rector of Tunstall, d.* (–); *and had issue.*

    4*c. Hon. Frances Boscawen, b.* 13 *June* 1816; d. 23 *Oct.* 1882; m. 12 *Feb.* 1850, *Arthur Edward Somerset, d.* 9 *Sept.* 1853; *and had issue.* See the Clarence Volume, p. 332, Nos. 9868–9870.

    5*c. Hon. Anne Boscawen, b.* 14 *Feb.* 1824; d. 27 *Feb.* 1899; m. 13 *July* 1854 *the Rev. Leveson Cyril Randolph, M.A., Vicar of St. Luke's, Lower Norwood, d.* 1876; *and had issue.*

    6*c.* Hon. Gertrude Elizabeth Boscawen (*Flaneswood, Sevenoaks*).

    7*c. Hon. Lucy Boscawen, b.* 29 *May* 1827; d. 25 *Mar.* 1886; m. 26 *July* 1864, *Col. Bonar Millett Deane, d.* 1881.

    6*b. Barbara Caroline Annesley, b.* 17 *July* 1797; d. 5 *Nov.* 1883; m. 15 *Oct.* 1814, *Thomas Tyrwhitt-Drake of Shardeloes, M.P., J.P., D.L., b.* 16 *Mar.* 1783; d. 21 *Mar.* 1852; *and had issue* 1*c to* 9*c.*   [Nos. 8765 to 8791.

# of The Blood Royal

1c. Thomas Tyrwhitt-Drake of Shardeloes, J.P., D.L., High Sheriff co. Bucks 1859, b. 14 July 1817; d. 24 July 1888; m. 1st, 8 Aug. 1843, Elizabeth Julia, widow of Col. Wedderburn, da. of John Stratton, b. 1815; d. July 1885; and had issue 1d to 9d.

1d. Thomas William Tyrwhitt-Drake of Shardeloes, J.P., D.L., b. 28 Nov. 1849; m. 4 Aug. 1874, Frances Anne Isabella, da. of Col. Smith Dorrien of Haresfoot, co. Herts.

2d. William Wykeham Tyrwhitt-Drake (Shardeloes, Amersham, co. Bucks), b. 27 Sept. 1851; m. 22 Nov. 1883, Augusta, da. of the Rev. Herbert Richard Peel of Thornton House, co. Bucks; and has issue (a son) 1e.

1e. [——] Tyrwhitt-Drake, b. 7 Ap. 1887.

3d. Edward John Tyrwhitt-Drake, b. 6 Mar. 1855.

4d. Guy Percival Tyrwhitt-Drake, b. 26 Oct. 1859.

5d. Elizabeth Caroline Tyrwhitt-Drake, d. 22 Jan. 1901; m. as 1st wife, 5 July 1865, William Frederick Hicks-Beach (Witcombe Park, co. Gloucester); and had issue 1e to 8e.

1e. William Hicks-Beach, late Capt. 4th Batt. Gloucester Regt., b. 12 July 1866.

2e. Michael Hicks-Beach, b. 8 Aug. 1872.

3e. Ellis Hicks-Beach (Imber Cottage, Byfleet), b. 22 Ap. 1874; m. 24 Sept. 1903, Nancy, da. of Spencer Whitehead, a Master of the Supreme Court; and has issue 1f.

1f. Rachel Hicks-Beach, b. 17 July 1904.

4e. Edward Howe Hicks-Beach (Hazleton, Skeema River, British Columbia), b. 7 Dec. 1875; m. 1902, Louise, da. of [——] Jeynes of Vancouver, B.C.; and has issue (a da.) 1f.

1f. [——] Hicks-Beach, b. 12 Dec. 1905.

5e. Charles Hicks-Beach, b. 5 Jan. 1878.

6e. Violet Elizabeth Hicks-Beach.

7e. Margaret Agnes Hicks-Beach.

8e. Myrtle Ardina Hicks-Beach.

6d. Susan Emily Tyrwhitt-Drake, m. 23 Ap. 1868, George Shippon Willes, J.P., Lieut.-Col. Berks Yeo. Cav., late 3rd Hussars (Hungerford Park, co. Bucks; Cippenham House, Slough); and has issue 1e to 9e.

1e. George Coe Thomas Willes, b. Aug. 1870; m. 5 May 1900, Ethel A., da. of W. Sheppard of San José; and has issue 1f.

1f. Ethel Joan Willes, b. 10 May 1901.

2e. John Shippen Willes, b. 1 Feb. 1877.

3e. William Freke Willes, b. 26 June 1878.

4e. Florence Susan Willes, m. 1 Nov. 1899, Francis Robert Harding-Newman, late of Nelmes, Hornchurch, Essex; and has issue 1f to 2f.

1f. Francis Warren Andrew Harding-Newman, b. 30 Nov. 1903.

2f. Susan Fayth Harding-Newman, b. 11 Aug. 1900.

5e. Charlotte Mary Willes.

6e. Agnes Helena Willes.

7e. Margaret Floyer Willes.

8e. Joan Mabel Willes.

9e. Maud Julia Willes.

7d. Florence Georgina Tyrwhitt-Drake, m. Nov. 1873, Ernest Matthews (Little Shardeloes, Amersham); and has issue 1e to 3e.

1e. Diana Matthews.

2e. Muriel Olwyn Matthews.

3e. Olave Margery Matthews.

8d. Julia Diana Tyrwhitt-Drake.

9d. Agnes Louisa Tyrwhitt-Drake.

[Nos. 8792 to 8825.

241

The Plantagenet Roll

2c. Rev. John Tyrwhitt-Drake (*Malpas, co. Chester*), *m.* Emily Charlotte, da. of Nathaniel Micklethwaite of Taverham Hall, co. Norfolk, by Lady Charlotte *née* Rous; and has issue.

3c. Rev. *Edward Tyrwhitt-Drake, M.A., J.P., Rector of Amersham, b. 15 May 1832;* d. (*? unm.*) 1904.

4c. George Tyrwhitt-Drake.

5c. Frances Isabella Tyrwhitt-Drake.

6c. Augusta Charlotte Tyrwhitt-Drake, *m.* Aug. 1853, the Rev. James Annesley Dawkins; and has issue.

See the Clarence Volume, pp. 177–178, Nos. 2950–2959.

7c. *Elizabeth Catherine Tyrwhitt-Drake*, d. 21 *Ap.* 1899; m. 1862, *Wager Townley Allix*, b. 1 *Mar.* 1825; d. 18 *June* 1878; *and had issue* (2 *das.*).

8c. Charles Diana Tyrwhitt-Drake, *m.* 18 July 1860, Edward Chapman Clayton *late* Capt. Bucks Yeo. Cav. (*Bradford Abbas, near Sherborne; Cottesmore Grange, Oakham*); and has issue 1*d*.

1d. Greville William Clayton (*White's*), *b.* 19 Feb. 1868.

9c. Agnes Agatha Tyrwhitt-Drake.   [Nos. 8826 to 8842.

152. Descendants, if any, of the Hon. Annabella Howe, wife of [——] Golding, and of the Hon. Margaret Howe, wife of Capt. [——] Mugg (see Table VII.).

153. Descendants of Edward (Southwell), 20th Baron de Clifford [E.] (see Table XIII.), *b.* 6 June 1732; *d.* (at Auveny, near Nice) 1 Nov. 1777; *m.* 29 Aug. 1765, Sophia, da. of Samuel Campbell of Mount Campbell, co. Leitrim, *d.* 3 Aug. 1828; and had issue 1*a* to 4*a*.

1a. Edward (*Southwell*), 21st *Baron de Clifford* [*E.*], b. 23 *June* 1767; d.s.p. 30 *Sept.* 1832.

2a. *Hon. Catherine Southwell*, b. 19 *Sept.* 1768; d. 19 *July* 1801; m. 13 *Nov.* 1790, *Col. Kein Hayward George Coussmaker*, d. 11 *July* 1801; *and had issue* 1*b*.

1b. Sophia (*Coussmaker*), suo jure 22*nd Baroness de Clifford* [*E.*], b. 4 *Nov.* 1791; d. 3 *Jan.* 1874; m. 21 *Aug.* 1822, *Capt. John Russell, R.N.,* b. 10 *July* 1796; d. 27 *Ap.* 1835; *and had issue.*

See the Tudor Roll of "The Blood Royal of Britain," pp. 359–360, Nos. 27569–27580.

3a. *Hon. Sophia Southwell*, b. 10 *June* 1771; d. 9 *Nov.* 1795; m. *as* 1*st wife*, 12 *Ap.* 1790, *John Thomas (Townshend), 2nd Viscount Sydney* [*G.B.*], b. 21 *Feb.* 1764; d. 20 *Jan.* 1831; *and had issue* 1*b*.

1b. *Hon. Mary Elizabeth Townshend*, b. 6 *Mar.* 1794; d. 25 *Dec.* 1847; m. 1*st*, *as* 3*rd wife*, 4 *Oct.* 1825, *George James Cholmondeley*, b. 22 *Feb.* 1752; d. 5 *Nov.* 1830; 2*ndly, as* 2*nd wife*, 9 *Feb.* 1832, *Charles (Marsham), 2nd Earl of Romney* [*U.K.*], b. 22 *Nov.* 1777; d. 29 *Mar.* 1845; *and had issue* 1*c* to 2*c*.

1c. Hon. Robert Marsham, now (R.L. 27 Mar. 1893) Marsham-Townshend, M.A. (Oxon.), J.P., D.L., F.S.A., F.R.G.S., F.G.S., &c. (*Frognal, Kent; 5 Chesterfield Street, W.*), *b.* 15 Nov. 1834; *m.* 5 Ap. 1877, Clara Catherine, da. of the Rev. George Barber Paley, Rector of Freckenham; and has issue 1*d* to 2*d*.

1d. Hugh Sydney Marsham-Townshend, J.P., *late* Lieut. 4th Batt. Gloucestershire Regt., *b.* 9 Feb. 1878; *m.* 19 Ap. 1904, Cecilia Frances Laura, da. of Sir Henry Charles John Bunbury, 10th Bart. [E.]; and has issue 1*e*.

1e. John Marsham-Townshend, *b.* 17 Jan. 1905.

2d. Ferdinand Marsham-Townshend, B.A. (Oxon.), *b.* 17 Ap. 1880.

[Nos. 8843 to 8858.

242

# of The Blood Royal

2c. *Frances Sophia Cholmondeley*, b. 18 *July* 1826; d. 23 *Dec.* 1887; m. 16 *Ap.* 1846, *the Rev. John Charles Buchanan Riddell, M.A.*, d. 2 *Mar.* 1879; *and had issue.*

See the Tudor Roll of "The Blood Royal of Britain," p. 181, Nos. 20513-20522, and the Clarence Volume, p. 130, Nos. 1604-1613.

4a. *Hon. Elizabeth Southwell*, b. 11 *Jan.* 1776; d. 14 *Nov.* 1817; m. *as 1st wife, 9 Ap.* 1792, *William Charles (Keppel), 4th Earl of Albemarle [E.], G.C.H.*, b. 14 *May* 1772; d. 30 *Oct.* 1849; *and had issue.*

See the Clarence Volume, pp. 512-515, Nos. 22136-22365.

[Nos. 8859 to 9108.

154. Descendants of the Hon. WILLIAM MONSON, Col. in the Army, M.P. (see Table XIII.), b. 15 Dec. 1760; d. 26 Dec. 1807; m. 10 Jan. 1786, ANNE, da. of John DEBONNAIRE, d. 26 Feb. 1841; and had issue 1a.

1a. *William John (Monson), 6th Baron Monson [G.B.]*, b. 14 *May* 1796; d. 17 *Dec.* 1862; m. 8 *May* 1828, *Eliza, da. of Edmund Larken of Bedford Square*, d. 22 *Jan.* 1863; *and had issue 1b to 4b.*

1b. *William John (Monson), 7th Baron Monson [G.B.], 1st Viscount Oxenbridge [U.K.], P.C., K.C.V.O.*, b. 18 *Feb.* 1829; d.s.p. 16 *Ap.* 1898.

2b. *Debonnaire John (Monson), 8th Baron Monson [G.B.], C.V.O.*, b. 7 *Mar.* 1830; d. 18 *June* 1900; m. 25 *Dec.* 1861, *Augusta Louisa Caroline, da. of Lieut.-Col. the Hon. Augustus Frederick Ellis; and had issue 1c to 4c.*

1c. Augustus Debonnaire John (Monson), 9th Baron Monson [G.B.], Hon. Attaché to British Embassy in Paris and Private Secretary to H.B.M.'s Ambassador (*Burton Hall, co. Lincoln; Chart Lodge, Sevenoaks*), b. 22 Sept. 1868; m. 1 July 1903, Romaine, widow of Laurence Turnure of New York, da. of Gen. Roy Stone of the U.S.

2c. Hon. Edomé Eliza Theodosia Monson, *m.* 14 June 1890, Capt. Walter Hill Chetwynd (34 *Sloane Gardens, S.W.*); and has issue 1d.

1d. Phyllis Marion Chetwynd, *b.* 5 Ap. 1893.

3c. Hon. Mary Evelyn Mina Monson

4c. Hon. Adelaide Violet Cicely Monson, *m.* 9 June 1898, George Granville Leveson-Gower, *late* M.P., sometime (1894-1895) Comptroller of the Household to Queen Victoria, and (1880-1885) Private Sec. to the Right Hon. W. E. Gladstone, M.P. (13 *Seymour Street, Portman Square, W.*); and has issue 1d to 2d.

1d. Iris Irma Leveson-Gower, *b.* 20 Aug. 1899.

2d. Margaret Rosemary Leveson-Gower, *b.* 13 Mar. 1903.

3b. Right Hon. Sir Edmund John Monson, P.C., G.C.B., G.C.M.G., G.C.V.O., *lately* (1896-1904) H.B.M.'s Ambassador at Paris, &c. (*Brooks'; Reform*), b. 6 Oct. 1834; *m.* 6 July 1881, Eleanor Catherine Mary, da. of Major James St. John Munro, H.B.M.'s Consul at Monte Video; and has issue 1c to 3c.

1c. Maxwell William Edmund John Monson, Hon. Attaché British Embassy at Paris, *b.* 21 Sept. 1882.

2c. Edmund St. John Debonnaire John Monson, *b.* 9 Sept. 1883.

3c. George Louis Esmé John Monson, *b.* 28 Oct. 1888.

4b. *Rev. the Hon. Evelyn John Monson, M.A.*, b. 7 *May* 1838; d. 13 *Sept.* 1892; m. 10 *July* 1872, *Anne Grace Hynde (Croft Lodge, The Park, Newark-on-Trent), da. of James Kinnear of Edinburgh, W.S.; and had issue 1c to 4c.*

1c. William John Monson, Assist. Sec. to Administrator British E. Africa Protectorate (*Mombasa, British East Africa*), b. 12 Sept. 1873.

2c. Charles Evelyn John Monson, *late* Sherwood Foresters, b. 4 May 1878.

3c. Christopher John Monson, *b.* 8 Oct. 1881.

4c. Rachel Mary Eliza Monson, *b.* 21 Mar. 1875.   [Nos. 9109 to 9123.

Ⅎⅇ 𝔓𝔩𝔞𝔫𝔱𝔞𝔤𝔢𝔫𝔢𝔱 𝔕𝔩𝔞𝔫𝔱𝔞𝔤𝔢𝔫𝔢𝔱 𝔕𝔩𝔞𝔫𝔱

The Plantagenet Roll

155. Descendants of Rev. the Hon. THOMAS MONSON (see Table XIII.), *b.* 10 May 1764; *d.* 3 Ap. 1843; *m.* 2ndly, 11 Aug. 1824, SARAH, da. of the Rev. Christopher WYVILL, *d.* 25 June 1865; and had issue 1*a* to 2*a*.

1*a*. Rev. *Thomas John Monson, M.A.*, b. 28 *Ap.* 1825; d. 23 *July* 1887; m. 25 *Mar.* 1856, *Caroline Isabella, da. of William George (Monckton-Arundell), 5th Viscount Galway [I.]; and had issue.*
See p. 169, Nos. 3654–3668.

2*a*. Henrietta Anne Theodosia Monson (*The Grange, Bedale*), *m.* 2 Mar. 1848, Henry William De La Poer Beresford-Peirse of Bedale and Hutton Bonville, *b.* 27 Sept. 1820; *d.* 24 July 1859; and has issue 1*b* to 4*b*.

1*b*. Sir Henry Monson De La Poer Beresford-Peirse, 3rd Bart. [U.K.], J.P., D.L. (*Aiskew House, Bedale, co. Yorks*), *b.* 25 Sept. 1850; *m.* 1st, 11 Nov. 1873, Lady Adelaide Mary Lucy, da. of Francis (Bernard), 3rd Earl of Bandon [I.], *d.* 29 Sept. 1884; 2ndly, 23 Jan. 1886, Henrietta, da. of Sir Matthew Smith-Dodsworth, 4th Bart. [G.B.]; and has issue 1*c* to 6*c*.

1*c*. Henry Bernard De La Poer Beresford-Peirse, D.S.O., Major *late* Imp. Yeo., *b.* 9 Jan. 1875; *m.* 7 July 1904, Lady Mabel Marjorie, da. of Frederick (Campbell), 3rd Earl Cawdor [U.K.].

2*c*. Rev. Richard Windham De La Poer Beresford-Peirse, M.A. (Oxon.), *b.* 6 Aug. 1876.

3*c*. Evelyn Frances De La Poer Beresford-Peirse, *b.* 3 Sept. 1877.

4*c*. Ernest Arthur De La Poer Beresford-Peirse, *b.* 2 Oct. 1879.

5*c*. John William De La Poer Beresford-Peirse, *b.* 12 June 1883.

6*c*. Dorothy Harriet Julia Beresford-Peirse, *b.* 3 July 1894.

2*b*. *William John De La Poer Beresford-Peirse, Lieut.-Col. Berks Regt.*, b. 8 *Nov.* 1852; d. (–); m. 22 Feb. 1887, *Mary, da. of Thomas Chambers of Aberfoyle, Londonderry; and had issue* 1*c to* 2*c*.

1*c*. Noel Monson De La Poer Beresford-Peirse, *b.* 22 Dec. 1887.

2*c*. Thomas Chambers De La Poer Beresford-Peirse, *b.* 9 Oct. 1891.

3*b*. Rev. Windham De La Poer Beresford-Peirse, M.A. (Oxon.), Rector of Bedale (*Bedale Rectory, Yorks*), *b.* 1 Nov. 1858; *m.* 17 July 1889, Ethel Milman Proctor, da. of William Proctor Baker of Sandhill Park, Taunton; and has issue 1*c* to 3*c*.

1*c*. Arthur Cecil Proctor De La Poer Beresford-Peirse, *b.* 20 Oct. 1890.

2*c*. Raymond Windham De La Poer Beresford-Peirse, *b.* 4 July 1896.

3*c*. Mary Ethel Beresford-Peirse, *b.* 10 June 1893.

4*b*. Charlotte Grace Beresford-Peirse (*Hampton Court Palace*), *m.* 8 Oct. 1874, Capt. Maximilian Dudley Digges Dalison, Scots Guards, *b.* 5 Feb. 1852; *d.* (being killed "whilst gallantly leading his men" at Hasheen, near Suakim) 20 Mar. 1885; and has issue 1*c* to 2*c*.

1*c*. Maximilian Dudley Peirse Dalison (*Hamptons, near Tonbridge; Greetwell Hall, near Scawby, Lincoln*), *b.* 1 Nov. 1881.

2*c*. Joan Mary Dalison, *b.* 28 Ap. 1878.

[Nos. 9124 to 9155.

156. Descendants of the Hon. CHARLOTTE GRACE MONSON (see Table XIII.), *b.* 29 Mar. 1759; *d.* 19 July 1793; *m.* 16 Aug. 1777, HENRY PEIRSE of Bedale Hall, *b.* 1754; *d.* 1824; and had issue 1*a*.

1*a*. *Harriet Elizabeth Peirse*, d. 28 Feb. 1825; m. *as 2nd wife, Admiral Sir John Poo Beresford, 1st Bart.* [U.K.], *K.C.B., G.C.H.K.T.S., b. 2 Oct. 1844; and had issue* 1*b to* 5*b*.

# of The Blood Royal

1b. *Henry William De La Poer Beresford, afterwards (R.L.* 15 *Sept.* 1851) *Beresford-Peirse of Bedale Hall,* b. 27 *Sept.* 1820; d. 24 *July* 1859; m. 2 *Mar.* 1848, *Henrietta Anne Theodosia, da. of Rev. the Hon. Thomas Monson; and had issue.*

See p. 244, Nos. 9139–9155.

2b. *Rev. John George Beresford, M.A.,* b. 28 *Sept.* 1821; d. 17 *July* 1899; m. 3 *Feb.* 1848, *the Hon. Caroline Amelia (Ash Tree Cottage, Mirfield, Yorks), da. of Thomas (Denman),* 1st *Baron Denman [U.K.]; and had issue* 1c *to* 10c.

1c. *John Peirse De La Poer Beresford, Lieut. South Wales Borderers,* b. 2 *Dec.* 1846; d. 30 *Oct.* 1902; m. 25 *Aug.* 1881, *Mary Elizabeth Thomasina, da. of Col. Henry Stewart Beresford Bruce of Ballyscullion House; and had issue* 1d *to* 3d.

1d. George Wilfred Bruce De La Poer Beresford, b. 1888.

2d. Mary Caroline Helen Beresford.

3d. Marion Evelyn Beresford.

2c. *Charles Windham De La Poer Beresford, Capt. Mexican Navy, formerly R.N.,* b. 2 *June* 1858; d. 1896; m. 27 *Aug.* 1891, *Mary (Southsea), da. of John Warrington Rogers of Brighton, Melbourne, K.C.; and had issue* 1d *to* 2d.

1d. Charles Zaragosa De La Poer Beresford, b. 1893.

2d. Mary Caroline Laura Beresford, b. 1895.

3c. Henry William De La Poer Beresford, *late* Indian Marine, b. 27 Ap. 1862.

4c. Rev. Walter Vevers De La Poer Beresford, Chaplain to H.B.M.'s Forces in Pietermaritzburg, b. 22 June 1864; *m.* 3 Sept. 1902, Eleanor Mary, da. of W. R. Staveley of Harrogate; and has issue 1d.

1d. Eleanor Caroline Frederica Beresford, b. 19 June 1903.

5c. Caroline Theodosia Beresford, *m.* as 2nd wife, 3 Dec. 1866, Thomas Hood Cockburn-Hood of the Upper Houses of Legislature in New South Wales and Queensland, b. 1820; d. 1889.

6c. Marion Harriet Beresford.

7c. Gertrude Georgiana Beresford (*Dulverton, Granville Square, Scarborough*), *m.* 19 Ap. 1876, the Rev. John Shapland Eliott Cockburn-Hood, M.A. (Camb.), Vicar of Kirby Fleetham, b. 15 Jan. 1844; d. 1902; and has issue 1d to 6d.

1d. Claud Beresford Cockburn-Hood, b. 5 Aug. 1878.

2d. Marion Cockburn-Hood.

3d. Gertrude Cecilia Cockburn-Hood.

4d. Caroline Charlotte Cockburn-Hood, *m.* 1904, George Grant Daubeny.

5d. Mary Margaret Cockburn-Hood.

6d. Adelaide Anne Cockburn-Hood.

8c. Frances Anne Beresford, *m.* 8 Aug. 1888, the Rev. Edgar Carr, Rector of Kirkby Wiske (*Kirkby Wiske Rectory, Thirsk*); and has issue 1d to 3d.

1d. Guy Beresford Carr, b. 5 Nov. 1889.

2d. John Carr, b. 22 Ap. 1895.

3d. Frances Evangeline Carr, b. 27 Sept. 1891.

9c. Elizabeth Margaret Beresford, *m.* 31 Jan. 1877, the Rev. Ernest Henry Kellett Long, Rector of Newton Flotman (*Newton Flotman Rectory, Norwich*); and has issue.

See p. 98, Nos. 758–764.

10c. Catherine Emily Beresford, *m.* 1 Sept. 1894, the Rev. Joseph Frederick Griffiths, Rector of St. Paul's, Chippenham, and of Hardenhuish (*St. Paul's Rectory, Chippenham*); and has issue 1d to 5d.

1d. Thomas Denman Griffiths, b. 12 Dec. 1896.

2d. Frederick Charles Beresford Griffiths, b. 14 Nov. 1900.

3d. Catherine Comfort Griffiths, b. 31 July 1895.   [Nos. 9156 to 9205.

245   2 I

The Plantagenet Roll

4*d*. Emily Elizabeth Favell Griffiths, *b*. 31 July 1898.

5*d*. Rosa March Griffiths, *b*. 16 June 1903.

3*b*. *Harriet Charlotte Beresford*, d. 1893; m. 12 *June* 1843, *the Rev. Anthony Hammond, formerly Chaplain B.C.S.; and had issue* 1*c* to 7*c*.[1]

1*c*. Anthony Marcus Hammond, *b*. 17 Sept. 1849.

2*c*. Frederick Arthur Hammond, *b*. 22 Sept. 1853; *m*. 20 Ap. 1876, Laura Trew, da. of the Rev. William Gray.

3*c*. Alfred Charles Hammond, *b*. 29 May 1856.

4*c*. Harriet Marianne Eliza Hammond, *m*. 23 Ap. 1868, the Rev. Charles Cary Bull (*The Hall, Stoke Ash, Eye*); and has issue 1*d* to 3*d*.

1*d*. Ashley Ernest Bull, *b*. 30 July 1869.

2*d*. Alfred Charles Bull, *b*. 17 Aug. 1873.

3*d*. Evangeline Constance Bull.

5*c*. Constance Mary Hammond, *m*. 18 Aug. 1874, Edmund Percival Wilford, Lieut.-Col. Gloucestershire Regt.; and has issue 1*d* to 2*d*.

1*d*. Edmund Ernest Wilford, Lieut. Indian Army, *b*. 13 Jan. 1876.

2*d*. Hugh Anthony Wilford.

6*c*. Alice Georgina Hammond, *m*. 31 Jan. 1878, Lieut.-Col. John Meade Sherard (*Broomhouse Road, Parson's Green, S.W.*).

7*c*. Marion Isabel Hammond.

4*b*. *Georgiana Beresford*, d. 7 *Sept.* 1870; m. 23 *July* 1842, *the Right Rev. Reginald Courtenay, Lord Bishop of Kingston, Jamaica; and had issue.*

See p. 109, Nos. 1240–1248.

5*b*. *Marianne Katharine Emily Beresford*, b. 1 *Jan.* 1824; d. 14 *Ap.* 1865; m. *as* 1st *wife*, 1 *Mar.* 1849, *Lieut.-Gen. Sir Charles Ash Windham, K.C.B.*, d. 2 *Feb.* 1870; *and had issue* 1*c* to 4*c*.

1*c*. Charles Windham, Admiral R.N., C.V.O. (*Naval and Military*), *b*. 1 Mar. 1851.

2*c*. John Windham (140 *Cromwell Road, S.W.*), *b*. 24 Mar. 1854; *m*. 15 Aug. 1899, Alice Caroline, da. of Lieut.-Col. the Hon. Richard Hare.

3*c*. Reginald Windham (*Yarrow, Pincher Creek, Alberta, Canada*), *b*. 11 Ap. 1864; *m*. 14 Dec. 1885, Martha Ellen, da. of Thomas Gregory Wright, M.D., M.R.C.S.; and has issue 1*d* to 7*d*.

1*d*. Charles Ash Windham, *b*. 28 Ap. 1890.

2*d*. William Doughty Thelluson Windham, *b*. 2 July 1898.

3*d*. Richard Howe Windham, *b*. 19 Ap. 1903.

4*d*. Mary Breresford Windham, *b*. 17 Dec. 1886.

5*d*. Dorothy Windham, *b*. 5 May 1888.

6*d*. Alice Windham, *b*. 6 Oct. 1894.

7*d*. Katherine Hare Windham, *b*. 29 Dec. 1904.

4*c*. Mary Windham, *m*. 4 Nov. 1875, Richard Charles Hare, C.B., Col. *late* 2nd Batt. Cheshire Regt. (*Reymerston Hall, Attleboro', Norfolk; United Service*); and has issue 1*d* to 5*d*.

1*d*. Richard Hare, Capt. Royal Fusiliers, *b*. 20 Mar. 1877.

2*d*. Francis Hare, *b*. 15 Mar. 1884.

3*d*. Charles Beresford Hare, *b*. 5 Aug. 1889.

4*d*. Mary Windham Hare, *b*. 20 Mar. 1880.

5*d*. Dorothy Hare, *b*. 21 Dec. 1885.　　　　　　[Nos. 9206 to 9244.

---

[1] Foster's "Baronetage," 1880, p. 41.

# of The Blood Royal

157. Descendants of the Hon. THEODOSIA MARGARET MONSON (see Table XIII.), *b.* 20 Sept. 1762; *d.* 24 Oct. 1847; *m.* 9 Mar. 1782, Sir JOHN GREGORY SHAW, 5th Bart. [E.], *b.* 25 July 1750; *d.* 28 Oct. 1831; and had issue 1*a* to 9*a*.

1*a*. Sir John Kenward Shaw, 6th Bart. [E.], b. 15 Mar. 1783; d.s.p. 17 Mar. 1857.

2*a*. Charles Shaw, Capt. R.N., b. 18 Aug. 1785; d. 2 May 1829; m. 20 Ap. 1822, Frances Anne, da. of Sir Henry Hawley, 1st Bart. [G.B.], d. 11 Dec. 1872; and had issue 1b to 6b.

1*b*. Sir John Charles Kenward Shaw, 7th Bart. [E.], J.P. (*Kenward, Tonbridge, Kent*), *b.* 8 June 1829; *m.* 1st, 19 June 1860, Maria, da. and h. of Henry Sparkes of Shalford, *d.* 4 Sept. 1863; 2ndly, 15 Oct. 1868, Sophia Emma Anne Maria, da. of Capt. John William Finch, R.N.

2*b*. Rev. Charles John Kenward Shaw, M.A., b. 8 June 1829; d. 20 June 1875; m. 22 Nov. 1859, Julia Elizabeth, da. of Capt. John Harvey Boteler, R.N.; and had issue 1c to 7c.

1*c*. Rev. Charles John Monson Shaw, M.A. (Oxon.), Vicar of Margate (*The Vicarage, Margate*), *b.* 24 Nov. 1860; *m.* 1 June 1893, Elizabeth Louisa Whatman Best, da. of J. W. Bosanquet of Pennendon; and has issue 1*d*.

1*d*. John James Kenward Shaw, b. 11 June 1895.

2*c*. Henry Hawley Shaw, b. 4 Sept. 1862; d. 8 Mar. 1897; m. 3 Jan 1893, Agneta Maud, da. of the Rev. Robert Stamer Tabor, M.A.; and had issue 1d to 2d.

1*d*. John Charles Hawley Shaw, b. 1895.

2*d*. Henrietta Frances Lilian Shaw.

3*c*. Barnardiston Edward Boteler Shaw, b. 10 Sept. 1873.

4*c*. Lilian Adelaide Shaw, *m.* 11 July 1893, Charles Robert Tyser, Bar.-at-Law, late of 7 Fig Tree Court, Temple, E.C.

5*c*. Julia Emma Frances Shaw, *m.* 1894, Thomas Reginald Colquhoun Dill, Bar.-at-Law (26 *Drayton Gardens, S.W.; 1 New Square, Lincoln's Inn, W.C.*); and has issue 1d to 2d.

1*d*. Victor Robert Colquhoun Dill, b. 1897.

2*d*. Ivy Adelaide Margaret Dill, b. 1900.

6*c*. Annie Maria Shaw.

7*c*. Dorothy Emily Augusta Shaw, *m.* 14 Jan. 1897, Alexander Murray Ashmore, C.M.G. (*Colombo, Ceylon*); and has issue 1d to 2d.

1*d*. Dorothy Julia Ashmore, b. 1897.

2*d*. Isabel Lilian Shaw Ashmore, b. 1899.

3*b*. Alicia Frances Shaw, d. Feb. 1905; m. 22 Sept. 1846, Charles Woodgate, late Madras C.S.; and had issue 1c to 4c.

1*c*. Hardinge Briscoe Woodgate, b. 17 Mar. 1855; d. 6 Mar. (? unm.) 1900.

2*c*. Gertrude Frances Woodgate, d. 3 Dec. 1879; m. 21 Ap. 1870, Grey Sollery Grey; and had issue 1d to 2d.

1*d*. Georgiana Russell Grey, b. 2 Dec. 1871; d. (–).

2*d*. Gertrude Lilian Grey, m. 27 Ap. 1904, Ernest Sworder, M.B.; and has issue 1e.

1*e*. Dorina Lilian Sworder.

3*c*. Helena Constance Woodgate.

4*c*. Charlotte Alice Nina Woodgate.

4*b*. Gertrude Anne Shaw, d. (–); m. 2 Dec. 1847, Rupert Henry Warre, d. 25 Dec. 1855; and had issue 1c to 5c.   [Nos. 9245 to 9262.

247

1c. *Rupert Thomas Dennes Warre,* b. 1854; d. abt. 1879 (*? unm*).

2c. Louisa Madeline Warre, *m.* F. Falle of Jersey.

3c. Alice Mary Warre.

4c. Florence Warre, *m.* Louis Druce.

5c. Millicent Gertrude Warre.

5b. *Harriet Augusta Shaw,* d. 26 *Ap.* 1896; m. 2 *Ap.* 1850, *the Rev. John Beauvoir Dalison, M.A., J.P., Rector of Upwell St. Peter; and had issue.* See the Tudor Roll of "The Blood Royal of Britain," p. 392, Nos. 29496–29512.

6b. Louisa Margaret Shaw (*Gimble Grove, Pembury, co. Kent*), *m.* 22 Sept. 1846, the Rev. George Stephen Woodgate of Pembury, *b.* 22 June 1810; *d.* 14 Ap. 1871; and has issue *1c* to *13c.*

1c. Reginald Stephen Shaw Woodgate (*Pembury Hall, co. Kent; Pembury Lodge, St. Leonards-on-Sea*), *b.* 30 June 1849; *m.* 29 June 1880, Lydia Elizabeth, da. of Col. Walter Meller of Broadlands, co. Surrey, M.P., J.P., D.L.; and has issue *1d* to *2d.*

1d. Elisabeth Frances Shaw Woodgate.

2d. Rosamond Stephanie Meller Woodgate.

2c. George Hardinge Woodgate (*Slayton, Minn., U.S.A.*), *b.* 14 Sept. 1860; *m.* 19 May 1892, Margaret, da. of Robert Bruce Ronald of Pembury Grange, co. Kent; and has issue *1d.*

1d. Rose Woodgate.

3c. Mary Maud Woodgate.

4c. Agnes Louisa Woodgate, *m.* 12 Nov. 1872, Arthur Callender (*Ashfield, Lymm, co. Chester*); and has issue *1d* to *5d.*

1d. Geoffrey Arthur Romaine Callender, *b.* 25 Nov. 1875.

2d. Mildred Agnes Romaine Callender.

3d. Cecil Margaret Romaine Callender.

4d. Evelyn Grace Romaine Callender.

5d. Esme de Brune Romaine Callender.

5c. Mary Grace Woodgate (*24 Regency Square, Brighton*), *m.* 17 Aug. 1875, Thomas Plantagenet Bigg-Wither, *d.* 19 July 1890; and has issue *1d* to *4d.*

1d. Guy Plantagenet Bigg-Wither, R.N., *b.* 1 June 1878; *m.* Nov. 1904, Gladys Sylvie, da. and h. of Count F. d'Asparato.

2d. Harold Stephen Bigg-Wither, *b.* 21 Nov. 1887.

3d. Ralph Woodgate Bigg-Wither, *b.* 31 Jan. 1890.

4d. Dorothy Grace Bigg-Wither.

6c. *Frances Woodgate,* d. 16 *Mar.* 1903; m. 18 *May* 1886, *Henry William Vipond Barry* (*25 Waterloo Place, Dublin*); *and had issue* 1d.

1d. William Francis Vipond Barry, *b.* 22 Jan. 1890.

7c. Georgiana Katherine Woodgate.

8c. Isabel Mary Woodgate.

9c. Anne Evelyn Woodgate, *m.* 15 Ap. 1884, Arthur Sydney Tabor (*The Manor House, Cheam, co. Surrey*); and has issue *1d* to *4d.*

1d. Arthur Robert Tabor, *b.* 6 Feb. 1893.

2d. Sydney Evelyn Tabor.

3d. Joan Mary Tabor.

4d. Rhona Margaret Tabor.

10c. Ethel Margaret Woodgate.

11c. Beatrice Woodgate.

12c. Angela Mary Woodgate, *m.* 8 June 1893,▽ Bernard Edward Dalison,[1] M.B. (6 *Molineux Park, Tunbridge Wells*); and has issue *1d* to *2d.* [Nos. 9263 to 9312.

---

[1] See the Tudor Roll of "The Blood Royal of Britain" for his descent from Kings Henry VII. and Edward IV., p. 392, No. 29498.

# of The Blood Royal

1d. John Bernard Dalison, b. 30 Mar. 1898.

2d. Mary Eleanor Dalison.

13c. Cecily Blanche Woodgate, m. 26 Ap. 1894, the Rev. George Louis Lachlan, Vicar of Tudeley (*Tudeley Vicarage, Tonbridge*); and has issue 1d to 6d.

1d. Cecil George Lachlan, b. 14 Jan. 1895.

2d. Hugh Robert Lachlan, b. 19 Ap. 1896.

3d. Kenneth Harry Lachlan, b. 9 Aug. 1900.

4d. Vere William Woodgate Lachlan, b. 2 June 1903.

5d. Noel Shaw Lachlan, b. 1 Jan. 1905.

6d. Monica Mary Lachlan.

3a. Rev. *Robert William Shaw, Rector of Cuxton*, b. 4 *Oct.* 1804; d. 28 *Dec.* 1873; m. 18 *Feb.* 1830, *Sophia, da. of John Cornwall of Hendon*, d. 14 *Mar.* 1875; *and had issue* 1b *to* 4b.

1b. Rev. *Robert John Shaw of Wendling Hall*, b. 31 *July* 1831; d. 30 *Oct.* 1903; m. 17 *Ap.* 1860, *Ella de Visme (Wendling Hall, East Dereham), da. of Richard Thomas of Eyhorne House, Hollingbourne; and had issue* 1c *to* 5c.

1c. Lewis Hugh de Visme Shaw (33 *London Road, Maldon, Essex*), b. 26 Aug. 1865; m. 30 Ap. 1901, Edith Mary, da. of Capt. John Smyth Nelson; and has issue 1d.

1d. Horatia Edith de Visme Shaw, b. 14 Mar. 1902.

2c. John Gerard Cornwall Shaw, b. 22 Feb. 1868.

3c. Henry Augustus Gregory Shaw, b. 30 Aug. 1875.

4c. Eleanor Marian Shaw, m. 27 Jan. 1904, Leopold Arthur Bingham Gipps (*Pilgrim's Way, Hollingbourne*); and has issue 1d.

1d. Leopold Henry Frewin Gipps, b. 28 Ap. 1905.

5c. Ella Florence Shaw.

2b. John Monson Shaw (*Lowestoft, Suffolk*), b. 1 Oct. 1832; m. 8 Feb. 1872, Sarah Pain, da. of Thomas Francklyn of Cobtree, d. 1887.

3b. Sophia Anna Shaw (11 *Grange Park, Ealing*), m. 27 Nov. 1857, the Rev. Harry Lancelot Wingfield, Rector of Market Overton, d. 25 Aug. 1891; and has issue 1c to 8c.

1c. Harry Robert Shaw Wingfield (*St. Stephen's*), b. 22 Aug. 1859; m. 6 Feb. 1904, Lucy Elizabeth, da. of John Wilkinson Eccles of Dacrelands.

2c. Edward Reginald Hugh Wingfield (*Junior Constitutional*), b. 22 Mar. 1866.

3c. Alfred Lancelot Wingfield, Transvaal Native Affairs Dept. (*Ticencote, Bellevue, Johannesburg*), b. 12 Jan. 1870; m. 22 Oct. 1902, Dorothy May, da. of Barnard H. Davidson of Tulloch; and has issue 1d.

1d. Richard Barnard Lowndes Wingfield, b. 26 June 1904.

4c. Rev. Lewis William Wingfield, Curate-in-Charge of Brafield (*Brafield, Northants*), b. 1 Dec. 1871; m. 10 Sept. 1901, Florence Eliza, da. of C. R. Hill; and has issue 1d to 2d.

1d. Muriel Edith Grace Wingfield, b. 3 Nov. 1902.

2d. Cynthia Adelaide Wingfield, b. 7 June 1904.

5c. Ellen Harriet Wingfield, m. 9 Oct. 1884, William Borrett Sayres (2 *Marlborough Road, N.W.*); and has issue 1d to 3d.

1d. Hugh Wingfield Sayres, b. 2 Dec. 1888.

2d. Millicent Anna Sayres, b. 23 Aug. 1885.

3d. Winifred Ethel Sayres, b. 20 May 1892.

6c. Cicely Margaret Wingfield, m. 29 Oct. 1879, the Rev. Folliott Lynch Salusbury, Rector of Market Overton (*Market Overton, Oakham*); and has issue 1d to 4d.

1d. Harry Thelwall Wingfield Salusbury, Transvaal C.S. (*Pretoria*), b. 16 Jan. 1880.   [Nos. 9313 to 9343.

The Plantagenet Roll

2d. Lancelot Cecil Wingfield Salusbury, b. 3 Sept. 1885.

3d. Roger Wingfield Salusbury, b. 26 May 1889.

4d. Cicely Clare Salusbury, b. 8 Sept. 1882.

7c. Lilian Sophia Wingfield, m. 1892, George Sanders Clarke, M.R.C.P. (Eng.), L.R.C.P. (Lond.), d. 1899; and has issue 1d.

1d. Barbara Clarke, b. 1894.

8c. Isabel Grace Wingfield, m. 21 Jan. 1905, Lewis Charles Powles (*The Highlands, Rye*).

4b. Margaret Augusta Shaw, m. 1st, 19 Feb. 1867, the Rev. Spencer Philip Harvey, d. Jan. 1868; 2ndly, 6 June 1877, William Shaw Brooke George; and has issue 1c to 3c.

1c. Spencer Philip Shaw Harvey, b. 28 June 1869.

2c. Violet George.

3c. Helen George.

4a. *Catherine Elizabeth Shaw, d. 15 Mar. 1862; m. 29 Nov. 1806, Sir Henry Hawley, 2nd Bart. [G.B.], b. 20 Oct. 1776; d. 29 Mar. 1831; and had issue 1b to 6b.*

1b. *Sir Joseph Henry Hawley, 3rd Bart. [G.B.], b. 27 Oct. 1814; d. 20 Ap. 1875; m. 18 June 1839, Sarah Diana, da. of Gen. Sir John Crosbie, G.C.H., d. 9 Mar. 1881; and had issue 1c to 2c.*

1c. *Mildred Catherine Hawley, d. 13 Aug. 1902; m. 7 July 1869, Barrington Bulkeley Douglas-Campbell, C.B., C.V.O., Lieut.-Gen. and Major-Gen. Comdg. troops in Channel Islands (Saumarez Hill, Guernsey; 13 Manchester Square, W.); and had issue 1d to 3d.*

1d. *Archibald Douglas-Campbell, J.P., Capt. Reserve of Officers (55 Montague Square, W.), b. 25 Ap. 1870; m. 25 July 1895, Evelyn, da. of John Fletcher of Saltoun; and has issue 1e.*

1e. *Olive Douglas-Campbell, b. 2 May 1896.*

2d. *Barrington Sholto Douglas-Campbell, b. 15 July 1877.*

3d. *Leopold Colin Henry Douglas-Campbell, b. 5 Mar. 1881.*

2c. *Morna Georgina Hawley, m. 25 June 1874, Percy Fitzhardinge Raymond-Barker of Fairford Park, J.P., b. 23 Feb. 1843; d. 25 Feb. 1895; and has issue 1d to 2d.*

1d. *Reginald Henry Raymond-Barker (Fairford Park, co. Gloucester), b. 8 Feb. 1875.*

2d. *Hugh William Heneage Raymond-Barker, b. 15 Sept. 1876.*

2b. *Sir Henry James Hawley, 4th Bart. [G.B.], b. 14 July 1815; d.s.p. 5 Oct. 1898.*

3b. *Rev. Henry Charles Hawley, Rector of Leybourne, b. 31 July 1823; d. 16 Feb. 1877; m. 21 Oct. 1845, Mary Elizabeth (West Dene, Hollington Park, St. Leonards-on-Sea), da. of Sir Michael Cusack Smith, 3rd Bart. [I.]; and had issue 1c to 10c.*

1c. *Sir Henry Michael Hawley, 5th Bart. [G.B.], J.P. (Leybourne Grange, near Maidstone; Tumby Lawn, Boston), b. 25 Mar. 1848; m. 24 Nov. 1875, Frances Charlotte, da. of John Wingfield-Stratford of Addington Park; and has issue 1d to 5d.*

1d. *Henry Cusac Wingfield Hawley, b. 23 Dec. 1876.*

2d. *Cyril Francis Hawley, Lieut. King's Royal Rifle Corps, b. 24 June 1878.*

3d. *Michael Charles Hawley, b. 6 June 1879.*

4d. *Gladys Florence Hawley.*

5d. *Olive Victoria Hawley.*

2c. *Rev. Charles Cusac Hawley, M.A. (Camb.), Rector of Leybourne (Leybourne Rectory, near Maidstone).*

3c. *Frederick William Hawley, b. 8 Nov. 1854.* [Nos. 9344 to 9368.

250

# of The Blood Royal

4c. Arthur Cecil Hawley, *b.* 6 Feb. 1862.
5c. Edith Catherine Hawley.
6c. Ada Mary Hawley.
7c. Kathleen Augusta Hawley.
8c. Mary Blanche Hawley.
9c. Ethel Maud Hawley.
10c. Nina Cicely Hawley.

4b. *Catherine Anne Hawley,* b. 4 *Jan.* 1809; d. 2 *June* 1861; m. 7 *Sept.* 1831, *Major George John Smart of Tumby Hall, Boston,* 76th *Regt.,* d. 6 *Mar.* 1877; *and had issue* 1c *to* 4c.

1c. George Joseph Smart, Major-Gen. R.A., b. Dec. 1833; d. 27 *June* 1897; m. 15 Feb. 1882, *Emily, da. of W. E. Matthews; and had issue* 1d.

1d. George Henry Smart, Lieut. West Riding Regt., *b.* 29 Ap. 1883.

2c. Charlotte Georgina Smart, *m.* 15 Oct. 1861, the Hon. Justice Sir John Compton Lawrence, J.P., D.L. (7 *Onslow Square, S.W.; Wytham-on-the-Hill, Bourne, Lincolnshire*); and has issue 1d *to* 2d.

1d. Thomas Dalton Lawrence, *b.* 26 June 1865; *m.* 17 Aug. 1898, Millicent Emma Rachel, da. of William Dashwood Fane of Fulbeck; and has issue 1f to 3f.

1f. Ruth Katharine Lawrence, *b.* 13 July 1899.
2f. Clare Millicent Lawrence, *b.* 29 July 1900.
3f. Audrey Grace Lawrence, *b.* 25 July 1904.

2d. Katharine Louisa Lawrence.

3c. Catherine Sara Smart, } (28 *Marine Parade, Dover*).
4c. Dora Jane Smart,

5b. *Augusta Harriet Hawley,* d. 11 *Jan.* 1904; m. 6 *Aug.* 1839, *the Rev. John Hamilton, Vicar of Linstead,* d. 25 *May* 1891; *and had issue* 1c *to* 7c.

1c. John Hamilton (*Sorbie, Broadwater Down, Tunbridge Wells; Sunningdale House, St. Leonards; Junior Carlton*), *b.* 5 Oct. 1850; *m.* 24 July 1883, Helen, da. of Gen. Charles Crutchley of Sunninghill Park; and has issue 1d to 5d.

1d. John Hamilton, *b.* 5 June 1884.
2d. Charles Eliott Hamilton, *b.* 27 Feb. 1888.
3d. George Frederick Hamilton, *b.* 30 Mar. 1890.
4d. Julia Helen Hamilton.
5d. Margaret Euphemia Hamilton.

2c. George Trayton Eliott Hamilton (*Rotherfield, Leamington*), *b.* 27 June 1854; *m.* 8 June 1878, Anne, da. of William Farrer; and has issue 1d to 4d.

1d. Henry Francis Trayton Hamilton, *b.* 14 Mar. 1882.
2d. Archibald George Fuller Hamilton, *b.* 10 June 1887.
3d. Elinor Grace Hamilton, *b.* 21 Ap. 1879.
4d. Anne Christina Hamilton, *b.* 4 Sept. 1884.

3c. *Elizabeth Anna Hamilton,* d. Nov. 1903; m. 1st, *as 2nd wife,* 20 *Sept.* 1870, *Major Walter James M'Grigor, Cameron Highlanders,* d. 7 *June* 1891; 2ndly, 1902, *Randolph* [*Richards Luscombe, late Capt.* 14th *Dragoons* (4 *Durwood House, Kensington Court, W.*).

4c. *Augusta Christina Hamilton,* d. 24 *Ap.* 1871; m. 1868, *William Gordon Trevor, Capt.* 80th *Regt. and B.S.C.,* d. 8 *Oct.* 1884; *and had issue* 1d.

1d. Adela Christina Trevor, *m.* 30 Oct. 1895, William Alexander Lane (*Lyons Farm House, Broadwater, Sussex*); and has issue 1e to 3e.

1e. William Leslie Trevor Lane, *b.* 23 Nov. 1905.
2e. Diana Christina Lane, *b.* 26 Oct. 1896.
3e. Vera Annie Lane, *b.* 16 Mar. 1902.   [Nos. 9369 to 9399.

The Plantagenet Roll

5c. Cordelia Eleanor Hamilton, *m.* 25 Oct. 1877, Major Robert Evans Montgomery, *late* R.M.L.I. (9 *Kensington Court Gardens, W.*); and has issue 1d to 4d.

    1d. Arnulf Montgomery, *b.* 16 Ap. 1882.

    2d. Robert Hamilton Montgomery, *b.* 1 Sept. 1883.

    3d. Nathaniel Montgomery, *b.* 26 July 1885.

    4d. Cordelia Helen Montgomery, *b.* 21 Dec. 1886.

6c. Mary Grace Hamilton, *m.* 3 Dec. 1874, Capt. Charles Sheldon Pearce Woodruffe, R.N. (*Old Roar House, Silver Hill, St. Leonards-on-Sea*); and has issue 1d to 3d.

    1d. Hamilton Augustus Woodruffe, *b.* 1876.

    2d. John Sheldon Woodruffe, *b.* 1879.

    3d. Mary Euphemia Woodruffe.

7c. Adela Louisa Hamilton, *m.* 14 May 1874, Octavius Roper Tyler; and has issue.

See the Clarence Volume, p. 397, Nos. 15132–15135.

6b. Ellen Catherine Hawley (64 *Gloucester Terrace, Hyde Park, W.*).

5a. *Anna Maria Shaw, d.* 13 Oct. 1871; *m.* 8 *May* 1819, *Maximilian Dudley Digges Hammond, afterwards* (10 *Mar.* 1819) *Dalison of Hamptons, J.P., D.L., b.* 3 *Sept.* 1792; *d.* 11 *May* 1870; *and had issue.*

See the Tudor Roll of "The Blood Royal of Britain," pp. 391–393, Nos. 29479–29553.

6a. *Horatia Shaw, d.* 24 *Dec.* 1862; *m. as* 1st *wife,* 31 *Jan.* 1825, *Walter* (*Forbes*), 18th *Baron Forbes* [S.], *b.* 29 *May* 1798; *d.* 2 *May* 1868; *and had issue* 1b to 2b.

    1b. Horace Courtenay Gammell (Forbes), 19th Baron Forbes, and Premier Baron, and a Rep. Peer [S.] (*Castle Forbes, Whitehouse, co. Aberdeen*).

    2b. Hon. Atholl Monson Forbes, D.L. (*Brux Lodge, Forbes*), *b.* 15 Feb. 1841; *m.* 19 Sept. 1876, Margaret Alice, da. of Sir William Hanmer Dick-Cunyngham, 8th Bart. [S.]; and has issue 1c to 3c.

        1c. Atholl Laurence Cunyngham Forbes, Grenadier Guards, *b.* 14 Sept. 1882.

        2c. Ivan Courtenay Forbes, *b.* 11 Dec. 1883.

        3c. Marjory Winifred Forbes, *b.* 18 Oct. 1879.

7a. *Charlotte Susan Shaw, d.* 25 *Feb.* 1874; *m.* 5 *Dec.* 1820, *Rear-Admiral John Cornwall of Elstead, co. Surrey; and had issue* (*a son and a da., of whom the former is married and has issue a son and da.*).

8a. *Caroline Alicia Shaw, d.* 4 *Aug.* 1881; *m. Edward George of Sandgate, M.M.; and had* (*with other*) *issue* 1b.

    1b. William Shaw Brooke George (youngest son), *m.* 6 June 1877, Margaret Augusta, widow of the Rev. Philip Spencer Harvey, da. of the Rev. Robert William Shaw; and has issue.

See p. 250, Nos. 9352–9353.

9a. *Harriet Grace Shaw, d.* 29 *Oct.* 1872; *m.* 30 *Mar.* 1842, *the Rev. Allen Cooper, M.A., Minister of St. Mark's, North Audley Street.*

[Nos. 9400 to 9497.

158. Descendants of LEWIS (MONSON, *afterwards* WATSON), 1st BARON SONDES [G.B.] (see Table XIII.), *b.* 28 Nov. 1728 ; *d.* 30 Mar. 1795 ; *m.* 12 Oct. 1752, GRACE, da. and co-h. of the Right Hon. Henry PELHAM, *b.* 18 Aug. 1728 ; *d.* 31 July 1777; and had issue.

See. p. 167–168, Nos. 3517–3626.   [Nos. 9498 to 9607.

# of The Blood Royal

159. Descendants of WILLIAM (FITZWILLIAM), 4th [I.] and 2nd
[G.B.] EARL FITZWILLIAM (see Table XIII.), b. 30 May 1748 ;
d. 8 Feb. 1833 ; m. 1st, 11 July 1770, Lady CHARLOTTE, da.
of William (PONSONBY), 2nd Earl of Bessborough [I.], b. 10
Dec. 1747 ; d. 13 May 1822 ; and had issue 1a.

1a. Charles William Wentworth (Fitzwilliam, afterwards (1856) Wentworth-
Fitzwilliam), 5th [I.] and 3rd [G.B.] Earl Fitzwilliam, b. 4 May 1786 ; d. 4 Oct.
1857 ; m. 8 July 1806, the Hon. Mary, da. of Thomas (Dundas), 1st Baron Dundas
[G.B.], d. 1 Nov. 1830 ; and had issue 1b to 4b.
  1b. William Charles Wentworth-Fitzwilliam, Viscount Milton, b. 18 Jan. 1812 ;
d.v.p. 8 Nov. 1835 ; m. 15 Aug. 1833, Lady Selina, da. of Charles (Jenkinson), 3rd
Earl of Liverpool [G.B.] (who re-m. 28 Aug. 1845, George Savile Foljambe of
Osberton, and) d. 24 Sept. 1883 ; and had issue 1c.
    1c. Hon. Mary Selina Charlotte Fitzwilliam, b. (posthumous) 9 Jan. 1836 ;
d. 4 Jan. 1899 ; m. 20 June 1855, William Henry Berkeley (Portman), 2nd
Viscount Portman [U.K.] (Bryanston, Blandford, Dorset ; 22 Portman Square,
W.) ; and had issue 1d to 8d.
      1d. Hon. Edward William Berkeley Portman, J.P., D.L. (Hestercombe,
Taunton ; 33 Great Cumberland Place, W.), b. 30 July 1856 ; m. 7 July 1892, the
Hon. Constance Mary, widow of Capt. the Hon. Eustace Vesey, da. of Beilby
(Lawley), 2nd Baron Wenlock [U.K.].
      2d. Hon. Henry Berkeley Portman, late Major Dorset Yeo. Cav. (Came House,
Dorchester ; Emo Park, Portarlington), b. 16 Feb. 1860 ; m. 25 Sept. 1901, Emma
Andalusia Frere, Dowager Countess of Portarlington [I.], da. of Lord Nigel
Kennedy ; and has issue 1e.
        1e. Selina Lusia Portman, b. 11 Sept. 1903.
      3d. Hon. Claud Berkeley Portman, J.P., late Capt. Dorset Imp. Yeo. (Child
Okeford, Blandford), b. 1 Nov. 1864 ; m. 1st, 9 Feb. 1888, Mary Ada, da. of Major
Francis Gordon-Cumming (who obtained a divorce 1897 and) d. 22 May 1900 ; 2ndly,
12 Mar. 1898, Harriette Mary, da. of William Stevenson ; and has issue 1e to 4e.
        1e. Edward Claud Berkeley Portman, b. 8 July 1898.
        2e. Guinevere Portman, b. 5 Jan. 1889.
        3e. Sylvia Grace Portman, b. 19 Mar. 1900.
        4e. Jocelyn Portman, b. 27 May 1903.

      4d. Hon. Seymour Berkeley Portman (Bryanston, Blandford), b. 19 Feb. 1868.
      5d. Hon. Gerald Berkeley Portman, late Capt. 10th Hussars (Healing Manor,
co. Lincoln), b. 23 Jan. 1875 ; m. 16 July 1902, Dorothy Marie Isolde, da. of Sir
Robert Sheffield, 5th Bart. [G.B.] ; and has issue 1e.
        1e. Gerald William Berkeley Portman, b. 20 Aug. 1903.

      6d. Hon. Emma Selina Portman, m. 7 May 1885, Ronald Ruthven (Leslie-
Melville), 10th Earl of Leven and 9th Earl of Melville [S.], P.C. and a Rep. Peer
(Glenferness, Dava ; Rockhampton House, Rockhampton, &c.) ; and has issue 1e
to 5e.
        1e. John David Leslie-Melville, Lord Balgonie, b. 5 Ap. 1886.
        2e. Hon. Archibald Alexander Leslie-Melville, b. 6 Aug. 1890.
        3e. Hon. David William Leslie-Melville, b. 23 May 1892.
        4e. Hon. Ian Leslie-Melville, b. 14 Aug. 1894.
        5e. Lady Constance Betty Leslie-Melville, b. 7 Aug. 1888.

      7d. Hon Susan Alice Portman, m. 8 Aug. 1893, Alan William Heber-Percy,
J.P. (Durweston, Blandford) ; and has issue.
      See the Clarence Volume, p. 266, Nos. 7108–7112.
      8d. Hon. Mary Isabel Portman.   [Nos. 9608 to 9631.

The Plantagenet Roll

*2b. William Thomas Spencer (Wentworth-Fitzwilliam), 6th [I.] and 4th [G.B.]
Earl Fitzwilliam, K.G.,* b. 12 *Oct.* 1815; d. 20 *Feb.* 1902; m. 10 *Sept.* 1838, *Lady
Frances Harriet, da. of Sholto (Douglas), 19th Earl of Morton* [S.], b. 29 *Sept.*
1819; d. 16 *June* 1895; *and had issue* 1c *to* 11c.

1c. *William Wentworth-Fitzwilliam, Viscount Milton, M.P.,* b. 27 *July* 1839;
d.v.p. 17 *Jan.* 1877; m. 10 *Aug.* 1867, *Laura Maria Theresa, da. of Lord Charles
Beauclerk,* b. 3 *Jan.* 1849; d. 20 *Mar.* 1886; *and had issue* 1d *to* 4d.

1d. William Charles de Meuron (Wentworth-Fitzwilliam), 7th [I.] and 5th
[G.B.] Earl Fitzwilliam, D.S.O. (*Wentworth Woodhouse, Rotherham; Coollattin, co.
Wicklow, &c.*), b. 25 July 1872; *m.* 24 June 1896, Lady Maud Frederica Elizabeth,
da. of Lawrence (Dundas), 1st Marquis of Zetland [U.K.]; and has issue.
See the Tudor Roll of "The Blood Royal of Britain," p. 296; also the Clarence
Volume, p. 212, Nos. 4256–4258.

2d. Lady Laura Mary Wentworth-Fitzwilliam, *m.* 30 Ap. 1889, Capt. George
Sholto Douglas (*Newtonairds, Dumfries; Army and Navy*); and has issue 1e to 4e.

1e. Archibald Sholto George Douglas, b. 17 Mar. 1896.

2e. David Sholto William Douglas, b. 26 Aug. 1899.

3e. Margaret Laura Douglas, b. 13 May 1890.

4e. Katharine Charlotte Douglas, b. 19 Mar. 1898.

3d. Lady Mabel Florence Harriet Wentworth-Fitzwilliam, *m.* 29 July 1899,
William Mackenzie Smith, Capt. Yorkshire Dragoons Yeo. Cav. (*Barnes Hall, near
Sheffield*).

4d. Lady Theresa Evelyn Vilunza Wentworth - Fitzwilliam (*Wentworth
Woodhouse, Rotherham*).

2c. Hon. William Henry Wentworth-Fitzwilliam, D.L., sometime (1868–1892)
M.P. (*Wigganthorpe, York*), b. 26 Dec. 1840; *m.* 11 July 1877, Lady Mary Grace
Louisa, da. of John (Butler), 2nd Marquis of Ormonde [I.]; and has issue 1d to 3d.

1d. Marie Albreda Blanche Wentworth-Fitzwilliam, b. 15 Nov. 1878; *m.* 1904,
Capt. Harold Maxwell Walker, 1st Life Guards.

2d. Isabel Elizabeth Mary Wentworth-Fitzwilliam, b. 20 May 1880.

3d. Irène Serga Alice Jane Mary Wentworth-Fitzwilliam, b. 5 Feb. 1883.

3c. *Hon. William Thomas Wentworth-Fitzwilliam,* b. 7 *Oct.* 1846; d. 23 *Mar.*
1896; m. 21 *Dec.* 1876, *Elgiva Mary, da. of Hamilton Kinglake of Taunton, M.D.,*
d. 2 *Dec.* 1888; *and had issue* 1d.

1d. Elgiva Mary Kathorn Wentworth-Fitzwilliam, b. 11 Dec. 1885.

4c. Hon. William Charles Wentworth-Fitzwilliam, D.L., High Sheriff co.
Rutland 1898, Master of the Stables, and an Extra Equerry in Waiting to H.R.H.
the Prince of Wales (*Barnsdale, Oakham*), b. 31 Mar. 1848; *m.* 31 Oct. 1882,
Constance Anne, da. of Henry Brocklehurst; and has issue 1d.

1d. Eric Spencer Wentworth-Fitzwilliam, b. 4 Dec. 1883.

5c. Hon. William Hugh Spencer Wentworth-Fitzwilliam, D.L. (*Patrick-
Brompton Hall, Bedale*), b. 10 Jan. 1860; *m.* 8 Oct. 1801, Lady Ada Charlotte, da.
of George Godolphin (Osborne), 9th Duke of Leeds [E.].

6c. Hon. William Reginald Wentworth-Fitzwilliam, b. 12 Ap. 1862; *m.* 2 Feb.
1893, Edith, da. of the Hon. Charles Lane Fox, *d.s.p.* 19 June 1902.

7c. *Lady Frances Mary Wentworth-Fitzwilliam,* b. 1 *Mar.* 1842; d. 28 *Sept.*
1904; m. 18 *Nov.* 1867, *Charles Mervyn Doyne, J.P., D.L., High Sheriff co. Wexford* 1873 *and co. Carlow* 1875 (*Wells, Gorey*); *and had issue* 1d *to* 5d.

1d. Robert Wentworth Doyne, Capt. *late* 4th Batt. Oxfordshire L.I. (*Ashton,
Gorey*), b. 30 Dec. 1868; *m.* 30 Ap. 1898, Lady Mary Diana, da. of Henry
(Lascelles), 4th Earl of Harewood [U.K.]; and has issue 1e.

1e. Robert Harry Doyne, b. 30 Jan. 1899.

2d. Dermot Henry Doyne (*St. Austin's Abbey, Tullow, co. Carlow*), b. 21 Nov.
1871, *m.* 26 Ap. 1905, Alice Gertrude, da. of Frank Brooke of Ardeen, Shillelagh,
D.L.   [Nos. 9632 to 9654.

254

# of The Blood Royal

3*d*. Kathleen Doyne, *b.* 29 Sept. 1870.

4*d*. Eveleen Margaret Doyne, *b.* 26 Jan. 1876.

5*d*. Bridget Frances Doyne, *b.* 5 Oct. 1879.

8*c*. Lady Mary Wentworth-Fitzwilliam, *m.* 23 May 1872, the Hon. Hugh Le Despencer Boscawen, J.P., D.L. (20 *South Street, Park Lane, W.*).

9*c*. Lady Alice Mary Wentworth-Fitzwilliam.

10*c*. Lady Albreda Mary Wentworth-Fitzwilliam (*Roseboro', Naas, co. Kildare*), *m.* 18 Dec. 1895, the Hon. Charles Fowler Bourke, C.B.; *d.s.p.* 4 Ap. 1899.

11*c*. Lady Charlotte Mary Wentworth-Fitzwilliam (*Homeside, Duffield, co. Derby*).

3*b*. *Hon. George Wentworth-Fitzwilliam of Milton, M.P.*, b. 3 *May* 1817; d. 4 *Mar.* 1874; m. 18 *Mar.* 1865, *Alice Louisa, da. of Gen. the Hon. George Anson,* d. 14 *Jan.* 1879; *and had issue* 1*c* to 3*c*.

1*c*. George Charles Wentworth - Fitzwilliam, D.L., J.P, High Sheriff co. Northants 1894, Capt. Northants Imp. Yeo. (*Milton Park, Peterborough*), *b.* 2 Jan. 1866; *m.* 28 Dec. 1886, Evelyn, da. of Charles Stephen Lyster; and has issue 1*d* to 2*d*.

1*d*. George James Charles Wentworth-Fitzwilliam, *b.* 19 May 1888.

2*d*. William Thomas George Wentworth-Fitzwilliam, *b.* 28 May 1904.

2*c*. Alice Mary Wentworth-Fitzwilliam, *m.* 23 July 1892, Major Arthur Watkin Williams-Wynn (71 *Eccleston Square, S.W.; Coedymaen, Welshpool*); and has issue 1*d* to 3*d*.

1*d*. Charles Watkin Williams-Wynn, *b.* 19 May 1896.

2*d*. Maud Annora Williams-Wynn, *b.* 10 Aug. 1893.

3*d*. Alice Nesta Margaret Williams-Wynn, *b.* 10 Nov. 1894.

3*c*. Maud Wentworth-Fitzwilliam, *m.* 18 July 1892, the Hon. Cospatrick Thomas Dundas, J.P., D.L. (*Ainderby Hall, Northallerton*); and has issue 1*d* to 4*d*.

1*d*. John George Lawrence Dundas, *b.* 3 Nov. 1893.

2*d*. Winifred Maud Dundas, *b.* 13 Ap. 1895.

3*d*. Elgiva Margaret Dundas, *b.* 9 Nov. 1897.

4*d*. Ida Victoria Alice Dundas, *b.* 24 May 1905.

4*b*. *Lady Frances Laura Wentworth-Fitzwilliam*, b. 22 *Oct.* 1813; d. 25 *Mar.* 1887; m. 23 *June* 1837, *the Rev. William Bridgeman-Simpson, Rector of Babworth,* b. 9 *Sept.* 1813; d. 1 *Ap.* 1895; *and had issue* 1*c* to 6*c*.

1*c*. Orlando John George Bridgeman Bridgeman-Simpson (*Wentbridge, Pontefract; Brooks'*), *b.* 27 Aug. 1838; *m.* 30 Ap. 1873, Catherine Maria, da. of John Cotes of Woodcote; and has issue 1*d* to 3*d*.

1*d*. Lilian Frances Bridgeman-Simpson, *m.* Dec. 1903, Capt. Henry Percy Thurnall, 1st Batt. York and Lancaster Regt.; and has issue.

2*d*. Evelyn Mary Bridgeman-Simpson, *m.* 30 Sept. 1902, Henry Grenville Barnett (141 *Lauderdale Mansions, Maida Vale*); and has issue 1*e*.

1*e*. Henry Evelyn William Barnett, *b.* 2 Ap. 1903.

3*d*. Olga Florence Bridgeman-Simpson.

2*c*. William Bridgeman Bridgeman-Simpson (*Rufforth Hall, Yorks*), *b.* 15 Aug. 1843.

3*c*. George Arthur Bridgeman-Simpson, now (since 1896) Bridgeman (*Woodlands, Doncaster*), *b.* 14 Nov. 1846; *m.* 26 Nov. 1896, Lady Mary Eleanor, da. of Hugh (Fortescue), 3rd Earl of Fortescue [G.B.].

4*c*. Francis Charles Bridgeman Bridgeman-Simpson, now (since 1896) Bridgeman, Rear-Admiral R.N., *formerly* a Naval A.D.C. to H.M. the King (*Copgrove, near Leeds*), *b.* 7 Dec. 1848; *m.* 6 Nov. 1889, Emily Charlotte, da. of Thomas Shiffner of Westgate, D.L.

5*c*. *Mary Bridgeman Bridgeman-Simpson*, b. 27 *July* 1851; d. 18 *Jan.* 1880;

[Nos. 9655 to 9681.

255

The Plantagenet Roll

m. *as 1st wife*, 22 Feb. 1876, *Major Walter Pleydell Bouverie*, b. 5 *July* 1848; d. 20 *May* 1893; *and had issue 1d to 2d.*

1*d*. Mildred Alice Pleydell Bouverie, b. 10 Feb. 1877; *m.* 6 Jan. 1903, Charles Hingston (*Cliff House, Radcliffe on Trent*); and has issue 1*e* to 2*e*.

1*e*. Walter George Hingston, *b.* 1905.

2*e*. Bridget Emily Hingston, *b.* 1903.

2*d*. Sybil Pleydell Bouverie, *b.* 13 Dec. 1878; *m.* 9 June 1903, Mervyn Richard (Wingfield), 8th Viscount [I.], and 2nd Baron [U.K.] Powerscourt, M.V.O. (*Powerscourt Castle, Enniskerry*); and has issue 1*e* to 2*e*.

1*e*. Hon. Mervyn Patrick Wingfield, *b.* 22 Aug. 1905.

2*e*. Hon. Doreen Julia Wingfield, *b.* 29 Mar. 1904.

6*c*. Beatrice Dorothy Mary Bridgeman Bridgeman-Simpson (*The Manor House, North Deighton, Wetherby*), *m.* 7 Dec. 1881, Adolphus Montagu Duncombe, J.P., d. Mar. 1904. [Nos. 9682 to 9688.

160. Descendants of Lady Charlotte Fitzwilliam (see Table XIII.), *b.* 14 July 1746; *d.* 11 Feb. 1833; *m.* 24 May 1764, Thomas (Dundas), 1st Baron Dundas [G.B.], *b.* 16 Feb. 1741; *d.* 14 June 1820; and had issue 1*a* to 8*a*.

1*a*. *Lawrence (Dundas), 1st Earl of Zetland* [U.K.], b. 10 *Ap.* 1766; d. 19 *Feb.* 1839; m. 2 *Ap.* 1794, *Harriet, da. of Gen. John Hale*, d. 18 *Ap.* 1834; *and had issue 1b to 4b.*

1*b*. *Thomas (Dundas), 2nd Earl of Zetland* [U.K.], K.T., b. 5 Feb. 1795; d.s.p. 6 *May* 1873.

2*b*. *Hon. John Charles Dundas of Woodhall, Wetherby, co. Yorks, M.P., Lord-Lieut. of Orkney and Shetland,* b. 21 *Aug.* 1808; d. (*at Nice*) 14 Feb. 1866; m. 27 *Mar.* 1843, *Margaret Matilda (Middleton Lodge, Richmond, co. York), da. of James Talbot of Maryville, co. Wexford; and had issue 1c to 9c.*

1*c*. Lawrence (Dundas), 3rd Earl and 1st Marquis of Zetland [U.K.], 4th Baron Dundas [G.B.], K.T., P.C., sometime (1889–1892) Lord-Lieut. of Ireland, &c. &c. (*Aske, Richmond, co. York; Kerse House, co. Stirling; 19 Arlington Street, S.W.*), b. 16 Aug. 1844; m. 3 Aug. 1871, Lady Lilian, da. of Richard George (Lumley), 9th Earl of Scarbrough [E.]; and has issue.

See the Clarence Volume, p. 212, Nos. 4250–4254.

2*c*. *Hon. John Charles Dundas, M.P., Lord-Lieut. Orkney and Shetland,* b. 21 *Sept.* 1845; d. 13 *Sept.* 1892; m. 2 Aug. 1870, *the Hon. Alice Louisa (The Barrows, Charles Hill, Farnham), da. of Charles (Wood), 1st Viscount Halifax* [U.K.]; *and had issue 1d to 5d.*

1*d*. Charles Lawrence Dundas, *b.* 18 Aug. 1871; *m.* 1896, Georgina, widow of Capt. C. M. Stevens, da. of [——]; and has issue 1*e*.

1*e*. Margaret Dundas.

2*d*. Frederick James Dundas, b. 9 Jan. 1877.

3*d*. Evelyn Mary Dundas, *m.* 26 June 1895, Herbert Peake (*Bawtry Hall, co. York*); and has issue 1*e* to 4*e*.

1*e*. Raymond Peake, *b.* 25 May 1896.

2*e*. Osbert Peake, *b.* 30 Dec. 1897.

3*e*. Harald Peake, *b.* 28 Oct. 1899.

4*e*. Maud Eileen Peake, *b.* 12 Aug. 1904.

4*d*. Margaret Dundas, *m.* 26 Sept. 1899, Capt. Edward Bunbury North, Roy. Fusiliers (*Newton Hall, Kirby Lonsdale*); and has issue 1*e* to 2*e*.

1*e*. Marjorie North, *b.* 1902.

2*e*. Sylvia Myra North, *b.* 1904.

5*d*. Alice Katharine Dundas, *b.* 21 Dec. 1883. [Nos. 9689 to 9706.

256

# of The Blood Royal

3c. Hon. William Fitzwilliam James Dundas, D.L. (*The Cottage, Goodwood, Chichester*), *b.* 8 May 1860; *m.* 20 June 1892, Mary Maud, da. of Lieut.-Col. H. A. Prinsep; and has issue 1*d* to 4*d*.

1*d.* Geoffrey William Seymour Dundas, *b.* 12 Jan. 1896.

2*d.* Robert Bruce Dundas, *b.* 11 Aug. 1900.

3*d.* Margaret Beryl Dundas, *b.* 27 Ap. 1893.

4*d.* Mary Gwendolen Dundas, *b.* 22 Nov. 1894.

4c. Hon. Cospatrick Thomas Dundas, D.L. (*Ainderby Hall, Northallerton*) *b.* 5 Nov. 1862; *m.* 18 July 1892, Maud, da. of the Hon. George Wentworth Fitz-william; and has issue.

See p. 255, Nos. 9670–9673.

5c. Lady Harriot Emily Dundas, *m.* 7 Ap. 1875, Col. Charles Thomas Bunbury, *late* Rifle Brigade (*Cotswold House, Winchester*); and has issue 1*d* to 6*d*.

1*d.* Charles Hamilton St. Pierre Bunbury, Lieut. Yorkshire Regt., *b.* 1877.

2*d.* Wilfred Joseph Bunbury, *b.* 1882.

3*d.* Bertram John Bunbury, *b.* 1887.

4*d.* Evelyn James Bunbury, *b.* 1888.

5*d.* Mary Beatrice Theresa Bunbury, *b.* 1879.

6*d.* Cecilia Mary Bunbury, *b.* 1892.

6c. Lady Mary Dundas, *m.* 12 Oct. 1874, William Francis Plowden, J.P., D.L. (*Plowden Hall, North Lydbury, co. Salop*); and has issue 1*d* to 3*d*.

1*d.* Francis Charles Plowden, *b.* 26 Sept. 1877.

2*d.* Roger Edmund Joseph Plowden, *b.* 5 June 1879.

3*d.* Godfrey Bruce Aloysius Plowden, *b.* 9 Feb. 1892.

7c. Lady Charlotte Jane Dundas.

8c. Lady Laura Octavia Dundas, b. 11 *Oct.* 1855; *d.* 19 *Jan.* 1881; *m. as* 1*st wife,* 8 *Feb.* 1877, *Arthur (French),* 4*th Baron De Freyne* [*U.K.*] (*French Park, co. Roscommon*); *and had issue* 1*d*.

1*d.* Hon. Arthur Reginald French, Lieut. Garrison Regt., *b.* 3 July 1879.

9c. Lady Alice Dundas.

3b. Lady Margaret Bruce Dundas, b. 29 *June* 1796; *d.* 13 *Sept.* 1860; *m.* 5 *Feb.* 1816, *Henry Walker Yeoman of Woodlands, co. York, J.P., D.L., b.* 13 *July* 1789; *d.* 14 *Sept.* 1875; *and had issue* 1*c to* 6*c*.

1*c. Ven. Henry Walker Yeoman of Woodlands, Archdeacon of Cleveland, &c., b.* 21 *Nov.* 1816; *d. unm.* 30 *Mar.* 1897.

2*c. Thomas Lawrence Yeoman of Woodlands, Capt. and Hon. Major* 1*st Vol. Batt. Yorks Regt., b.* 21 *Dec.* 1819; *d. unm.* 10 *Feb.* 1901.

3*c. Rev. Constantine Bernard Yeoman, M.A.* (*Camb.*), *J.P., b.* 29 *June* 1823; *d.* 4 *Ap.* 1889; *m. Ap.* 1858, *Margaret Laura, da. of the Rev. J. D. Preston of Askham Bryan; and had issue* 1*d to* 6*d*.

1*d.* Margaret Constance Yeoman.

2*d. Harriot Emily Yeoman, d.* 8 *Oct.* 1894; *m. as* 1*st wife,* 20 *July* 1888, *William Henry Anthony Wharton, J.P.* (*Skelton Castle, Skelton-in-Cleveland*); *and had issue* 1*e*.

1*e.* Margaret Winsome Wharton.

3*d.* Sophia Bruce Yeoman.

4*d.* Eva Dorothy Yeoman.

5*d.* Charlotte Yeoman, ⎫
6*d.* Mary Yeoman, ⎬ twins.

4*c.* George Dundas Yeoman, M.A. (Camb.) (*Lorne Villa, Whitby*), *b.* 4 Nov. 1835; *m.* 27 Oct. 1869, Lady Dorothea Frances, da. of Francis (Hastings), 13th Earl of Huntingdon [E.].   [Nos. 9707 to 9737.

257

The Plantagenet Roll

5c. Robert Charles Yeoman, M.A. (Camb.), J.P., D.L., C.A. (*Groves Hall, Sleights, R.S.O., co. York*), b. 7 July 1838.

6c. Charlotte Yeoman, d. 6 *Ap.* 1892; m. 7 *Dec.* 1854, *John Thomas Wharton of Skelton Castle, J.P., D.L.*, b. 9 *Mar.* 1809; d. 1 *Mar.* 1900; *and had issue* 1d.

1d. William Henry Anthony Wharton, J.P. (*Skelton Castle, Skelton-in-Cleveland*), b. 14 Nov. 1859; *m.* 1st, 20 July 1888, Harriot Emily, da. of the Rev. Constantine Bernard Yeoman, d. 8 Oct. 1894; 2ndly, 4 Dec. 1895, Elizabeth Sophia Mytton, da. of the Rev. Robert John Harrison of Caerhowell; and has issue.

See p. 257, No. 9732.

4b. Lady Harriott Frances Dundas, b. 27 Sept. 1801; d. 13 Oct. 1878; m. 8 Dec. 1825, Col. Henry Lane.

2a. Hon. Charles Lawrence Dundas, b. 18 July 1771; d. 25 Jan. 1810; m. 16 Feb. 1797, Lady Caroline, da. of Aubrey (Beauclerk), 5th Duke of St. Albans [E.], d. 23 Nov. 1838; and had issue 1b to 2b.

1b. Catherine Elizabeth Dundas, b. 17 Jan. 1805; d. 12 Feb. 1876; m. 21 Aug. 1832, Gen. George Freeman Murray, Col. 60th Regt., sometime (1854-1861) Governor of Bermuda, d. 14 Ap. 1885; and had (with other) issue 1c.

1c. Adelaide Thornton Murray, d. 1868; m. 1863, Edmund Jacob Whitbread; and had issue 1d.

1d. Edmund Murray Whitbread, b. 1865.

2b. Charlotte Amelia Dundas, b. 17 Ap. 1808; d. (at Tegernsee, Bavaria) 27 Jan. 1881; m. 14 May 1846, Ralph Thomas Fawcett, d. (-); and had issue 1c.

1c. Florence Caroline Mary Fawcett.

3a. Rev. the Hon. Thomas Lawrence Dundas, M.A., b. 12 Oct. 1775; d. 17 Mar. 1848; m. 25 July 1816, Mary Jane, da. of the Rev. James Bosanquet, d. 15 Dec. 1827; and had issue 1b to 5b.

1b. Rev. Robert Bruce Dundas, formerly Rector of Harpole, M.A. (Camb.), b. 1821.

2b. Charlotte Mary Dundas (4 St. James' Terrace, York), b. 15 July 1817; m. 6 July 1852, Capt. Frederick Thompson of Poppleton Hall, b. 12 Aug. 1812; d. 1886; and has issue 1c to 2c.

1c. Henry Frederick Dundas Thompson, late Lieut. Oxfordshire L.I., b. 24 July 1856.

2c. Charlotte Edith Mary Thompson.

3b. Margaret Bruce Dundas, b. 16 Dec. 1822.

4b. Louisa Dundas (Sedbury Hall, Gilling, Richmond, co. York; Scar House, Arkindale, co. York), b. 1824; m. 14 Dec. 1847, George Gilpin Brown of Sedbury Park, d. 28 Nov. 1889; and has issue 1c.

1c. George Thomas Gilpin-Brown, J.P., High Sheriff co. York 1893 (Sedbury Park, Richmond, co. York), b. 1848.

5b. Anne Dundas (Glencairn, Leamington), b. Sept. 1825; m. 24 Aug. 1854, the Hon. Charles William Wentworth-Fitzwilliam, d.s.p. 20 Dec. 1894.

4a. Hon. Margaret Dundas, d. 8 May 1852; m. 1794, Archibald Speirs of Elderslie, M.P., b. 10 Feb. 1758; d. 24 Nov. 1832; and had issue 1b to 6b.

1b. Alexander Speirs of Elderslie, M.P., Lord-Lieut. co. Renfrew, b. 1803; d. 5 Oct. 1844; m. 22 June 1836, Eliza Stuart, da. of Thomas Campbell Hagart of Bantaskine (who re-m. 1867, Edward Ellice of Invergarry, M.P.); and had issue 1c to 2c.

1c. Archibald Alexander Speirs of Elderslie, M.P., b. 5 June 1840; d. 30 Dec. 1868; m. 3 Sept. 1867, Lady Anne, da. of Jacob (Pleydell-Bouverie), 4th Earl of Radnor [G.B.]; and had issue 1d.

1d. Alexander Archibald Speirs, J.P., D.L., late Capt. Argyll and Sutherland Highlanders (Houston House, and Elderslie House, co. Renfrew) b. (posthumous) 3 June 1869.   [Nos. 9738 to 9751.

258

# of The Blood Royal

2c. Eliza Speirs (24 *Old Queen Street, S.W.*), *m.* 12 Feb. 1863, Major-Gen. Sir Claud Alexander, 1st Bart. [U.K.], M.P., *b.* 15 Jan. 1831; *d.* 23 May 1899; and has issue 1*d.*

  1*d.* Sir Claud Alexander, 2nd Bart. [U.K.], J.P. (*Ballochmyle, Mauchline, co. Ayr; Fay Gate Wood, co. Sussex*), *b.* 24 Feb. 1867; *m.* 1st, 14 Dec. 1889, Lady Diana (divorced 1894), da. of Archibald (Montgomerie), 14th Earl of Eglinton [S.], &c.; 2ndly, 28 Jan. 1896, Rachel Belasyse, da. of the Rev. Henry Holden, D.D.; and has issue 1*e* to 3*e.*

    1*e.* Wilfred Archibald Alexander, *b.* 6 Oct. 1892.

    2*e.* Claud Alexander, *b.* 4 June 1897.

    3*e.* Boyd Alexander, *b.* 3 Dec. 1902.

2*b. Lawrence Dundas Speirs,* d. (–).

3*b. Frances Laura Speirs,* d. 1877; *m.* 24 *June* 1824, *Robert Cunninghame Cunninghame-Graham of Gartmore, D.L., b.* 14 *Sept.* 1799; *d.* 23 *Jan.* 1863; *and had issue* 1*c to* 7*c.*

  1*c. William Cunninghame Bontine Cunninghame Graham of Gartmore, J.P., D.L., b.* 11 *Ap.* 1825; *d.* 6 *Sept.* 1883; *m.* 12 *June* 1851, *the Hon. Anne Elizabeth* (39 *Chester Square, S.W.*), *sister of John,* 14*th Baron Elphinstone* [S.], *da. of Adm. the Hon. Charles Elphinstone-Fleeming; and had issue* 1*d to* 2*d.*

    1*d.* Robert Bontine-Cunninghame Cunninghame Graham of Gartmore, claims to be Earl of Menteith and Airth [S.], J.P., D.L., *sometime* (1886–1892) M.P. (*Gartmore, in Menteith, co. Stirling*), *b.* 24 May 1852; *m.* 1878, Gabriella, da. of Don Francisco José de Le Balmondierè of Chili.

    2*d.* Charles Elphinstone Fleeming Cunninghame - Graham, Comm. R.N. (60 *Warwick Square, S.W.*), *b.* 1 Jan. 1854; *m.* 13 June 1882, Mildred Emily Barbara, da. of the Rev. Charles Walter Bagot; and has issue 1*e* to 2*e.*

      1*e.* Angus Edward Malise Cunninghame-Graham, R.N., *b.* 16 Feb. 1893.

      2*e.* Olave Barbara Clementina Cunninghame-Graham, *b.* 1 June 1885.

  2*c. Robert Cunninghame-Graham, Lieut.* 78*th Highlanders,* d. (? *unm.*).

  3*c.* Douglas Alexander Cunninghame-Graham.

  4*c. Charlotte Fitzwilliam Cunninghame-Graham,* d. (? *unm.*).

  5*c.* Anne Margaret Cunninghame-Graham.

  6*c.* Margaret Jane Cunninghame-Graham, *m.* William Hope, Attaché, H.B.M.'s Legation at the Hague; and has issue.

  7*c. Mary Helen Isabella Cunninghame-Graham,* d. (? *unm.*).

4*b. Dorothea Dundas Speirs.*

5*b. Harriot Octavia Isabella Speirs.*

6*b. Matilda Isabella Grace Speirs.*

5*a. Hon. Charlotte Dundas, b.* 1775; *d.* 5 *Jan.* 1855; *m.* 19 *Ap.* 1808, *the Rev. William Wharton, M.A., Vicar of Gilling,* 1768; *d.* 26 *May* 1842; *and had issue* 1*b to* 3*b.*

  1*b. John Thomas Wharton of Gillingwood and Skelton Castle, J.P., D.L., b.* 9 *Mar.* 1809; *d.* 1 *Mar.* 1900; *m.* 7 *Dec.* 1854, *Charlotte, da. of Henry Walker Yeoman of Woodlands,* d. 6 *Ap.* 1892; *and had issue.*

  See p. 258, Nos. 9739–9740.

  2*b. Rev. James Wharton, Vicar of Gilling,* d. (–); *m.* 2 *May* 1854, *Elizabeth Harriette Astley, da. of Sir Astley Paston Cooper,* 2*nd Bart.* [*U.K.*]; *and had issue* 1*c to* 6*c.*

    1*c.* Philip Thomas Wharton, *b.* 1859.

    2*c.* George Henry Lawrence Wharton, *b.* 1865.

    3*c.* Elizabeth Charlotte Wharton, *m.* 1885, Capt. Reginald Charles Freeman, *late* 3rd Hussars; and has issue 1*d* to 2*d.*

      1*d.* Claude Reginald Freeman, *b.* 1886.

      2*d.* Dorothy Dundas Freeman, *b.* 1891.

[Nos. 9752 to 9770.

259

The Plantagenet Roll

4c. Margaret Bruce Dundas Wharton, *m.* 1883, William Edward Utterson, Kelso; and has issue 1d to 3d.

1d. William Vernon Charles Kelso, *b.* 1886.

2d. Maximilian Kelso, *b.* 1889.

3d. Mary Astley Kelso, *b.* 1888.

5c. Frances Mary Isabel Wharton, *m.* 1890, Cuthbert Barmby; and has issue 1d.

1d. Marjorie Bruce Barmby, *b.* 1891.

6c. Susan Marian Wharton.

3b. Charlotte Wharton.

6a. *Hon. Frances Laura Dundas, d. 27 Nov.* 1843; *m. 24 Jan.* 1805, *Robert Chaloner of Guisboro', co. York, M.P., d. 7 Oct.* 1842; *and had issue 1b.*

1b. *Margaret Bruce Chaloner, d. 13 June* 1837; *m. as 1st wife, 8 June* 1829, *the Right Hon. William Wentworth FitzWilliam Hume, afterwards (R.L. 17 June* 1864) *Dick of Humewood, co. Wicklow, M.P., J.P., D.L., b. 28 Oct.* 1806; *d. 15 Sept.* 1892; *and had issue 1c to 2c.*

1c. *Frances Laura Dick, d. (–).*

2c. *Charlotte Anna Dick, d. 18 Dec.* 1899; *m. 4 Oct.* 1853, *Richard Penruddocke Long of Rood Ashton, M.P., J.P., D.L., d. 16 Feb.* 1875; *and had issue.*
See p. 134, Nos. 1824–1843.

7a. *Hon. Mary Dundas, d. 1 Nov.* 1830; *m. 8 July* 1806, *Charles William (Wentworth-Fitzwilliam), 5th [I.] and 3rd [G.B.] Earl Fitzwilliam, d. 4 Oct.* 1857; *and had issue.*
See p. 253, Nos. 9608–9688.

8a. *Hon. Isabella Dundas, b. 25 Feb.* 1790; *d. 6 Dec.* 1887; *m. 4 May* 1814, *John Charles Ramsden of Buckden and Newby Park, M.P., b. 30 Ap.* 1788; *d.v.p. 29 Ap.* 1836; *and had issue 1b.*

1b. Sir John William Ramsden of Byrom, 5th Bart. [E.], J.P., D.L., Hon. Col. 9th Vol. Brig. N. Div. R.A. (V.D.), High Sheriff co. York 1868, and sometime (1853–1865, 1868–1874, and 1880–1886) M.P. and (1857–1858) Under Secretary of State for War (*Byrom, Ferrybridge; Longley Hall, Huddersfield, &c.*), *b.* 14 Sept. 1831; *m.* 2 Aug. 1865, Lady Helen Guendolen, da. and co.-h. of Edward Adolphus (Seymour), 12th Duke of Somerset [E.]; and has issue 1c to 3c.

1c. John Frecheville Ramsden, D.L. (*Turweston Manor, Brackley*), *b.* 7 Jan. 1877; *m.* 15 May 1901, Joan, da. of Geoffrey Fowell Buxton of Dunston Hall; and has issue 1d to 2d.

1d. John St. Maur Ramsden, *b.* 26 Ap. 1902.

2d. Geoffrey William Ramsden, *b.* 28 Aug. 1904.

2c. Hermione Charlotte Ramsden, *b.* 17 June 1867.

3c. Rosamund Isabel Ramsden, *b.* 12 Dec. 1872.

[Nos. 9771 to 9885.

161. Descendants of MARY MILBANKE (see Table XIII.), *d.* 9 Nov. 1846; *m.* 1793, JOHN GAGE of Rogate, co. Hants, *b.* 23 Dec. 1767; *d.* 24 Dec. 1846; and had issue 1a to 3a.

1a. *Rev. Thomas Wentworth Gage, d. 19 Mar.* 1837; *m. 17 Feb.* 1831, *Lady Mary Elizabeth, da. and co-h. of Charles (Douglas), 5th Marquis of Queensberry [S.], b. 4 Nov.* 1807; *d. 16 May* 1888; *and had issue 1b to 2b.*

1b. *Charles Wentworth Gage, b. 28 Feb.* 1832; *d. 17 May* 1868; *m. June* 1862, *Georgina (Woodlands, Peterborough, Canada West), da. of C. Toker of Montreal; and had issue 1c.*

1c. *Charles Wentworth Gage, b. 1 June* 1868.

2b. *Fanny Gage (11 Downe Terrace, Richmond Hill).* [Nos. 9886 to 9887.

260

# of The Blood Royal

2a. *Charlotte Margaret Gage*, d. 9 *Sept.* 1855; m. 20 *Oct.* 1825, *John Hodgett Foley, afterwards Hodgetts-Foley of Prestwood, M.P., J.P., D.L.,* b. 17 *July* 1797; d. 13 *Nov.* 1861; *and had issue* 1b.

    1b. *Henry John Wentworth Hodgetts-Foley of Prestwood, M.P., J.P., D.L.,* b. 9 *Dec.* 1828; d. 1894; m. 12 *Dec.* 1854, *the Hon. Jane Frances Anne, da: of Richard (Vivian), 1st Baron Vivian [U.K.],* b. 20 *May* 1824; d. 2 *Dec.* 1860; *and had issue* 1c.

    1c. Paul Henry Hodgetts-Foley, now Foley, J.P., D.L., F.S.A. (*Prestwood, Stourbridge; Stoke Edith, Hereford*), b. 19 *Mar.* 1857; m. 9 Feb. 1904, Dora, da. and h. of Hamilton W. Langley of Stoke Edith Park.

3a. *Louisa Henrietta Gage*, b. 21 *Dec.* 1809; d. (–); m. 16 *Nov.* 1847, *Baron Ernest Rodolph Bertouch,*[1] b. 20 *Feb.* 1808; d. 8 *July* 1869; *and had issue* 1b.

    1b. Baron Montagu William Ferdinand Bertouch (*Las Palmas*), b. 24 Aug. 1851; m. 31 July 1882, Beatrice Caroline, da. of [——] Elmslie; and has issue 1c.

    1c. Baron Ernest Rudolph Ferdinand Julian Bertouch (*London*), b. 1 July 1884.

[Nos. 9888 to 9890.

162. Descendants of Lady HENRIETTA ALICIA WATSON (see Table XIII.), *d.* (–); *m.* Oct. 1764, WILLIAM STURGEON; and had issue[2] 1a to 4a.

    1a. *Charles Alexander Sturgeon of London,* m. *Ann, da. of George Smithwaite of West Hall, near Wakefield; and had issue* 1b *to* 3b.

    1b. *Charles Sturgeon, Bar.-at-Law, I.T.,* m. 1st, *Eleanor, da. of the Rev. Peter Geary,* d.s.p.; 2ndly, *Jane Sydney Louisa, da. of Col. George Pinckney; and had issue* 1c.

    1c. *Charles Wentworth Dillon Sturgeon,* m. 1st, *Caroline Seymour, da. of Jonathan Sadler of co. Tipperary,* d.s.p.; 2ndly, *Lucy May, da. of Joseph Lillie of Ardwick and Moss Side, Manchester.*

    2b. *Charlotte Sturgeon,* m. *Lieut. Forbes, R.N.*

    3b. *Harriet Alicia Sturgeon,* m. *Lieut. Roberts.*

    2a. *Henry Robert Sturgeon, R.E., Col. in the South Guides on the Duke of Wellington's Staff,* m. 1805, *Sarah, da. of the Right Hon. John Philpot Curran, Master of the Rolls, I.T.,* b. 1779; d.s.p. 5 *May* 1808.

    3a. *Charlotte Sturgeon,* m. 1789, *James Edwards (2nd son of James Edwards of Old Court, co. Wicklow).*

    4a. *Agnes Sturgeon,* m. *Peter James (Pierre Jacques) La Chesney of Rouen.*

163. Descendants, if any surviving, of ELEANOR DINELEY GOODYERE, da., and in her issue h. of Sir Edward GOODYERE, 1st Bart. [E.] (see Table XIII.), *d.* aged 80; *m.* SAMUEL FOOTE of Truro, co. Cornwall, M.P., J.P.; and had issue[3] 1a to 4a.

    1a. *Edward Foote.*

    2a. *John Dineley Foote, afterwards Foote-Dineley, heir to his cousin Sir John Dineley-Goodyere, 5th Bart.* [E.].

    3a. *Samuel Foote, Actor and Dramatist, called "the English Aristophanes,"* bapt. 27 *Jan.* 1720; d. 21 *Oct.* 1777.

    4a. *Eleanor Foote.*

---

[1] A cadet of the Barons von Bertouch of Denmark.
[2] Burke's " Extinct Peerage," p. 571. The above does not include those persons shown by Burke to have *d.s.p.*
[3] Nash's " Worcester," i. p. 272.

The Plantagenet Roll

164. Descendants of ELEANOR DYMOKE (see Table XIII.), *bur.* 28 Dec. 1707 ; *m.* 1682, MATTHEW LISTER of Burwell Park, co. Linc., *bapt.* 27 Ap. 1666 ; *bur.* 22 June 1700 ; and had issue 1*a* to 4*a*.[1]

1*a. Matthew Lister of Burwell Park*, bapt. 3 *Jan.* 1684; d. 1 *June* 1744; m. *Sarah, da. of* [——]; *and had issue* 1*b to* 4*b.*

1*b. Matthew Lister of Burwell Park*, bapt. 14 *Ap.* 1706; bur. 15 *Jan.* 1786; m. 9 *July* 1723, *Grace, widow of Sir Edward Boughton, ——th Bart.* [E.], *da. of Sir John Shuckburgh, 3rd Bart.* [E.], bur. 4 *Mar.* 1779; *and had issue* 1*c to* 4*c.*

1*c. Matthew Dymoke Lister of Burwell Park*, bapt. 30 *Aug.* 1729; d. 9 *Feb.* 1772; m. 9 *Aug.* 1764, *Lydia, da. of Joseph Bancroft of Manchester, Merchant (who re-m. Thomas Livesey of Sturton)* ; *and had issue* 1*d to* 3*d.*

1*d. Matthew Bancroft Lister of Burwell Park*, claimed the Barony of Kyme (1295) [E.], *High Sheriff co. Lincoln* 1800, bapt. 11 *June* 1766 ; d. 14 *Oct.* 1842 ; m. 7 *Feb.* 1799, *Sophia, da. of* [——] *Bolton of London,* d. 27 *Dec.* 1851 ; *and had issue* 1*e to* 5*e.*

1*e. Matthew Henry Lister of Burwell Park*, b. 17 *July* 1801 ; d. 2 *Jan.* 1876 ; m. 1823, *Arabella, da. of John Cracroft of Hackthorn, co. Linc.,* d. 1 *Sept.* 1873 ; *and had issue* 1*f to* 3*f.*

1*f. Matthew Henry Lister of Burwell Park*, b. 14 *Oct.* 1826 ; d. 29 *May* 1880 ; m. 1st, 1859, *Clara, da. of Horace Houston ;* 2ndly, 5 *Feb.* 1874, *Katherine Ruth, da. of Thomas John Manning of St. Osyth, co. Essex,* d. 8 *May* 1900 ; *and had issue* 1*g to* 5*g.*

1*g.* Matthew Henry Lister, *b.* 31 May 1877 ; *m.* 1900, Daisy, widow of [——] Sandilands, da. of Col. Saunders ; and has issue 1*h* to 2*h.*

1*h.* Matthew Henry Lister, *b.* (–).

2*h.* Edith Frances Lister, *b.* 14 Sept. 1901.

2*g.*[1] Florence Holroyd Ribblesdale Lister, *m.* 6 June 1876, Porter Wilson of The Lawn, Brackenborough, co. Linc.

3*g.*[1] Edith Violet Lister.

4*g.*[1] Muriel Ada Lister.

5*g.*[2] Constance Margaret Douglas Lister, *b.* 28 Oct. 1874 ; *m.* John Ellingham.

2*f. Emily Sophia Lister,* d. 5 *Mar.* 1886 ; m. *the Rev. William D. Marsden,* d. 1866 ; *and had issue* 1*g to* 4*g.*

1*g. Delabere Marsden,* b. 29 *July* 1849 ; d. (*? unm.*) 22 *May* 1903.

2*g.* Stephen Marsden.

3*g.* Louis Marsden.

4*g.* [——] Marsden.

3*f. Florence Arabella Lister,* d. 3 *June* 1896 ; m. *the Rev. John Durell Durell ; and had issue* 1*g to* 2*g.*

1*g.* John Percy Durell, now Stables, *b.* (–) ; *m.* 16 Feb. 1898, Charlotte M., da. of Arthur H. Welsted ; and has issue.

2*g.* Helen or Eleanora Durell, *m.* 1883, Dobree Wickham ; and has issue.

2*e. John Samuel Lister of Saleby Grange, co. Linc., J.P.,* b. 25 *Jan.* 1812 ; d. 8 *Ap.* 1901 ; m. 4 *May* 1842, *Elizabeth, da. of William Wilcock of Savile Hill, Halifax ; and had issue* 1*f to* 3*f.*

1*f.* Hannah Frances Lister, *m.* 1st, 21 May 1862, Charles Pearson Elliott, H.E.I.C.S., d. 1 July 1876 ; 2ndly, 5 June 1878, the Rev. Frederick Charles Littler, Chaplain at Alassio (*Casa San Giorgio, Alassio, Italy ; Hollywood Tower, Bristol*) ; and has issue 1*g* to 4*g.*   [Nos. 9891 to 9903.

---

[1] See Maddison's "Lincolnshire Pedigrees," Harl. Soc. Pub. LI., p. 596 ; Burke's "Landed Gentry," 7th ed. ; and Foster's "Peerage," 1880, for the earlier generations.

# of The Blood Royal

1*g.* Rev. Charles Lister Boileau Elliott, B.A. (Camb.), Rector of Tattingstone (*Tattingstone Rectory, Suffolk*), *b.* 31 Oct. 1864; *m.* 8 Ap. 1891, Katharine Peel, da. of the Rev. Philip Stephen O'Brien; and has issue 1*h* to 2*h.*

 1*h.* Charles Arthur Boileau Elliott, *b.* 9 Feb. 1893.

 2*h.* Katharine Frances Boileau Elliott, *b.* 6 Feb. 1896.

2*g.* Arthur Edward Elliott, *b.* 4 Aug. 1867; *m.* 3 July 1895, Janet Harriet, da. of the Rev. Boteler Chernocke Smith; and has issue 1*h* to 2*h.*

 1*h.* Charles Pynsent Elliott, *b.* 27 June 1896.

 2*h.* Honor Elliott.

3*g.* William Robert Elliott, *b.* 1 July 1871.

4*g.* Edith Mary Elliott, *b.* 6 Sept. 1869.

2*f.* Elizabeth Sophia Lister (51 *Pevensey Road, St. Leonard's-on-Sea*).

3*f.* *Katharine Ellen Maria Lister*, d. 19 *Ap.* 1874; m. 26 *Sept.* 1872, *John Herbert Bowman* (*eldest son of John Eddowes Bowman of King's Coll., London*); *and had issue* 1*g.*

 1*g.* Herbert Lister Bowman (*New College, Oxford*), *b.* 15 Mar. 1874.

3*e.* *Lydia Boughton Lister*, d. 13 *Sept.* 1873; m. 27 *June* 1834, *the Rev. George Jackson, Vicar of North Reston and Rector of South Reston, co. Linc.; and had issue* 1*f* to 3*f.*

 1*f.* *Maud Jackson*, d. (? *unm.*).

 2*f.* *Rosa Jackson*, d. (? *unm.*).

 3*f.* Bertha Jackson, *m.* [———].

4*e.* *Sophia Lister*, d. 18 *Mar.* 1888; m. 27 *Dec.* 1831, *the Rev. Francis Pickford, Rector of Hagworthingham*, *b.* 10 *June* 1801; d. 10 *Nov.* 1883; *and had issue* 1*f* to 3*f.*

 1*f.* *Sophy Emily Hannah Pickford* (*Northwood, Cumberland Road, Kew*), *b.* 15 *Sept.* 1832; d. 5 *June* 1906.

 2*f.* *Georgiana Mary Pickford*, *b.* 26 *Ap.* 1835; d. 10 *Aug.* 1888; *m.* 13 *Sept.* 1860, *Arthur Reginald St. Clair Radcliffe* (*The Old Hall, Stackhouse, Settle, Yorkshire*); *and had issue* 1*g* to 3*g.*

  1*g.* Arthur Charles Forbes Radcliffe, *b.* 30 June 1861.

  2*g.* Francis Joseph Radcliffe, *b.* 19 Feb. 1863.

  3*g.* Edith Georgiana Fannie Radcliffe.

 3*f.* *Katharine Elizabeth Edith Pickford*, *b.* 10 *July* 1842; d. 14 *Mar.* 1885; *m. as* 1st *wife*, 22 Oct. 1863, *Francis Worsley* (187 *Queen's Gate, S.W.*); *and had issue* 1*g* to 3*g.*

  1*g.* Francis Richard Coltman Worsley (155 *Sloane Street, London*), *b.* 10 July 1866; *m.* 10 Feb. 1906. Charlotte Elizabeth Jane, widow of Capt. S. Sykes, Royal Scots Fusiliers, da. of Major Barrett of Moredon, North Curry, Somerset, J.P., D.L.

  2*g.* Rev. Frederick William Worsley, Vicar of Corringham (*Corringham Vicarage, Gainsborough*), *b.* 26 June 1873; *m.* 23 Jan. 1901, Catherine Ethel, da. of Henry W. Payne; and has issue 1*h* to 2*h.*

   1*h.* Francis Frederick Worsley, *b.* 2 June 1902.

   2*h.* Mary Elizabeth Worsley, *b.* 15 Oct. 1904.

  3*g.* Frank Pickford Worsley, Capt. West Yorkshire Regt. (Prince of Wales' Own), *b.* 23 Aug. 1874; *m.* 28 Dec. 1898, Gertrude, da. of [———] Brookes; and has issue 1*h.*

   1*h.* Katharine Pickford Worsley, *b.* 5 Nov. 1900.

5*e.* *Mary Lister*, d. 9 *May* 1877; m. 17 *May* 1825, *George Marmaduke Alington of Swinhope, co. Linc., J.P., D.L.*, b. 17 Feb. 1798; d. 18 Feb. 1890; *and had issue* 1*f* to 4*f.*

 1*f.* Arthur Hildebrand Alington of Swinhope, Admiral (ret.) R.N. (*Swinhope*,
[Nos. 9904 to 9924.

The Plantagenet Roll

North Thoresby, Lincolnshire), b. 10 Oct. 1839; m. 9 June 1870, Charlotte Mary, da. of the Rev. Charles Moore of Garlenick; and has issue 1g to 4g.

1g. Arthur Cyril Marmaduke Alington, Capt. E. Lancashire Regt., b. 15 June 1872; m. 1 Dec. 1903, Gladys Evelyn, da. of Major Bramston Hamilton, R.H.A.; and has issue 1h.

    1h. William James Alington, b. 26 Mar. 1906.

2g. Argentine Hugh Alington, Lieut. R.N., b. 10 July 1876; m. Janet Marchant, da. of Howard H. Tooth, M.D., C.M.G.

3g. Charlotte Hildegarde Mary Alington, m. 8 Ap. 1899, Frederick Parkin (Truro, Cornwall); and has issue 1h to 3h.

    1h. John Winford Alington Parkin, b. 20 Oct. 1901.

    2h. Joyce Mary Parkin, b. 4 Sept. 1903.

    3h. Eleanor Vida Parkin, b. 11 June 1905.

4g. Sophy Ellen Elfrida Alington, m. 12 Aug. 1902, James Bonnell Ernest Hudson; and has issue 1h.

    1h. Thomas Alington Hudson, b. 13 June 1903.

2f. Albert Edward Alington, late of Canterbury, N.Z. (Binbrook, co. Lincoln), b. 24 Nov. 1841.

3f. Frederick William Alington (Stenigot, Broxbourne, Herts), b. (at Coblentz) 27 July 1845.

4f. Sophy Anne Alington (Nuthurst, Ealing), m. 11 June 1862, the Rev. William Charles Sharpe, B.D., Vicar of Holme-Spalding, d. 6 Mar. 1865; and has issue 1g.

    1g. Sophy Alice Mary Sharpe, b. 7 May 1864.

2d. Rev. John Joseph Lister, d. (–); m. and had issue 1c to 3c.

1c. Lydia Lister, m. William Wilson of Alford, co. Linc., Solicitor; and has issue 1d.

    1d. Lister Wilson, Solicitor.

2c. Olivia Lister, d. (–); m. Major-Gen. George Cautley, Bengal Cavalry; and had issue (with a son killed in the Indian Mutiny) 1d to 2d.

    1d. [——] Cautley, m. Reginald Saunders, I.C.S.; and has issue (2 das.).

    2d. Aline Maria Cautley, d. (–); m. 3 Oct. 1861, Gen. Sir William Olpherts, G.C.B., V.C., b. 8 Mar. 1822; d. 19—; and had issue 1e to 4e.

        1e. William Cautley Olpherts, Major Royal Scots.

        2e. Alice Olpherts, unm.

        3e. Mary Olpherts, m. James Campbell (12 Cornwall Gardens, S.W.); and has issue 1f to 3f.

            1f. [——] Campbell.

            2f. [——] Campbell.

            3f. [——] Campbell.

        4e. Emily Olpherts, unm.

3c. Alice Lister, m. Wharton Cavie of Alford, co. Linc., Surgeon; and has issue 1d.

    1d. Alice Maria Cavie.

3d. Lydia Boughton Lister, d. 25 Mar. 1850; m. 1st, 13 June 1793, John Tipping of St. Clement Danes, d.s.p.; 2ndly, 17 Mar. 1803, the Rev. Samuel Francis Dashwood of Stanford Hall, co. Notts, b. 1773; d. (–); and had issue 1e to 4e.

1e. Rev. Samuel Vere Dashwood of Stanford Park, b. 3 Nov. 1803; d. 10 Nov. 1876; m. 1st, 24 Oct. 1828, Caroline, da. of Philip Hamond of Westacre, co. Norfolk, d. 28 May 1840; 2ndly, 25 Jan. 1844, Edith Elizabeth, da. of Col. Hawkshaw of Clifton, d. (–); and had issue 1f to 13f.　　　　[Nos. 9925 to 9949.

264

# of The Blood Royal

1f. Robert Lewes Dashwood, M.A. (Camb.) (*The Mount, Yarmouth, I.W.*), *b.* 9 Feb. 1840; *m.* 15 Aug. 1866, Edith Theresa, da. of Rowland Edward Cooper of Pains Hill, Surrey; and has issue 1g to 7g.

1g. Rev. Robert Vere Lewes Dashwood, M.A. (Camb.) (*Glebe House, Coates, Gloucester*), *b.* 6 Sept. 1869; *m.* 8 Oct. 1901, Agnes, da. of William S. Nicholson of Eastmore, Yarmouth.

2g. Claude Burrard Lewes Dashwood, B.A. (Camb.) (*Constitutional*), *b.* 30 Oct. 1873.

3g. Cuthbert William Lewes Dashwood, B.A. (Oxon.), *b.* 29 Jan. 1874.

4g. Sidney Lewes Dashwood, *b.* 25 Nov. 1882.

5g. Theresa Emma Charlotte Dashwood.

6g. Edith Caroline Dashwood.

7g. Constance Alice Dashwood.

2f. Edward Vere Dashwood (*St. Cross Lodge, Winchester*), *b.* 25 June 1846; *m.* 24 May 1888, Laura Frederica Penelope, da. of Major Edmund Crofts; and has issue 1g to 3g.

1g. Vere Edmund Crofts Dashwood, *b.* 10 Mar. 1889.

2g. Diana Penelope Dashwood.

3g. Iris Laura Dashwood.

3f. Frederick Dashwood, *b.* 10 Oct. 1849.

4f. Francis Henry Dashwood (*Junin, Buenos Ayres*), *b.* 11 Feb. 1855.

5f. Alfred Henry Dashwood (*Stibbington House, Wansford, Northants*), *b.* 8 Sept. 1856; *m.* 19 May 1892, Evelyn Maydwell, da. of the Rev. John Henry Holdich of Stibbington House; and has issue 1g.

1g. John Maydwell Dashwood, *b.* 6 June 1893.

6f. Edmund William Dashwood, Lieut.-Col. and Brevet-Col. 1st Batt. Northumberland Fusiliers (*Constitutional; Naval and Military*), *b.* 9 Sept. 1858.

7f. Philip Wilmot Dashwood (*Griffin's Wood, Epping*), *b.* 1 Oct. 1862; *m.* 1904, Adelaide Katharine Mary, da. of the Rev. Edward Harford, Preb. and Canon Resid. of Wells.

8f.[1] Caroline Maria Dashwood (*Repton, Burton-on-Trent*), *m.* 2 Oct. 1849, the Rev. Richard Surtees of Holtby, *d.* 29 Oct. 1899; and has issue 1g to 13g.

1g. Richard Villiers Surtees, *b.* 8 Ap. 1853; *m.* 12 June 1879, Emily Charlotte, da. of George Vesey Stewart of Kati Kati, N.Z.; and has issue 1h to 6h.

1h. Scott Surtees, *b.* 28 Feb. 1886.

2h. Caroline Margaret Surtees.

3h. Ethel Surtees.

4h. Sybil Surtees.

5h. Sophy Elizabeth Evelyn Surtees.

6h. Almeric Surtees.

2g. Edward Alexander Surtees, *b.* 12 Mar. 1863.

3g. Francis Vere Surtees (*Banham, Renfrew*), *b.* 22 Dec. 1864; *m.* 2 July 1895, Elizabeth Stanley, da. of Henry Grey Faber of Stockton-on-Tees; and has issue 1h to 2h.

1h. Vere Nathaniel Faber Surtees, *b.* 20 Jan. 1897.

2h. Siward Faber Surtees, *b.* 16 Ap. 1899.

4g. Philip Scott Surtees (*Stuckley's Bank, Clifton, Bristol*), *b.* 29 June 1868; *m.* 11 May 1891, Georgina, da. of H. M. Kemmis of Bridgwater, J.P.

5g. Charles Henry Surtees, *b.* 7 Dec. 1870; *m.* 18 Ap. 1906, Dorothy, da. of H. Sale of Repton, Burton, co. Trent.

6g. Mary Anne Surtees, *m.* 4 Sept. 1877, the Rev. Thomas Robinson, Rector of Brettenham (*Rushford College, Thetford*).

7g. Almeira Caroline Surtees, *m.* 8 Feb. 1882, Robert Macgregor Campbell.

[Nos. 9950 to 9982.

265

The Plantagenet Roll

8g. Louisa Matilda Surtees, *m.* 15 June 1881, Edward Smith (*Birnam Wood, Marton, N.Z.*).

9g. Sophy Geraldine Surtees, *m.* 24 Ap. 1879, Arthur Western Fullerton Smith (*Thrybergh, Marton, N.Z.*).

10g. Laura Charlotte Surtees, *m.* 15 July 1880, Augustus Wood-Acton (*Acton Scott, Church Stretton, Salop*); and has issue 1h.

1h. Joyce Wood-Acton.

11g. Ethel Maud Surtees, *m.* 1 Dec. 1887, Horatio Packe, Comm. (ret.) R.N.

12g. Caroline Evelyn Surtees.

13g. Charlotte Rosabelle Surtees, *m.* 28 July 1892, Henry Syndercombe Bower (*Estancia, cos Chilenos, Tomquist, F. C. del Sul, Buenos Ayres; Mainhull, Sturminster, Newton, Dorset*); and has issue (4 sons).

9f.¹ Matilda Katherine Dashwood, *m.* 25 Oct. 1854, the Rev. Charles Snell, *formerly* Rector of Oulton (*Eton Lodge, Tunbridge Wells*); and has issue 1g.

1g. Katherine Mary Snell, *b.* 25 Aug. 1855; *m.* 29 Aug. 1876, the Rev. Henry Woodruffe Proctor-Beauchamp, Rector of Copdock (*Copdock Rectory, Ipswich*); and has issue 1h to 3h.

1h. Ronald Charles William Proctor-Beauchamp, *b.* 23 July 1877; *m.* 19 July 1905, Helen, da. of Edward Jerome Herbert, of Waveney Hill, Lowestoft.

2h. Maurice Henry Proctor-Beauchamp, *b.* 8 Sept. 1886.

3h. Sybil Katherine Proctor-Beauchamp, *b.* 8 July 1889.

10f.¹ Sophia Diana Dashwood, *m.* 6 Feb. 1866, the Rev. George Horatio Davenport (*Foxley, Hereford*); and has issue 1g.

1g. Ralph Tichborne Davenport, *b.* 28 Jan. 1873.

11f.¹ *Lydia Charlotte Dashwood, d.* 14 *Jan.* 1902; m. 19 *Sept.* 1871, *Capt. Hugh Osborne Bateman, late 43rd Regt., d. May* 1906; *and had issue* 1g *to* 4g.

1g. Emily Winifred Elinor Bateman
2g. Sophy Kathleen Bateman
3g. Edith Mary Sacheverell Bateman
4g. Muriel Bateman
⎫ (*The Cottage, Osmaston Park, Ashbourne*).

12f.² Alice Dashwood (*Bulwick, Wansford*), *m.* 15 July 1873, Col. Thomas Tryon, High Sheriff co. Northants 1875, *d.* 19 Dec. 1888; and had issue 1g to 3g.

1g. Eva Mildred Tryon, *m.* 12 July 1898, Ernest William Proby Conant (*Lyndon Hall, near Oakham*); and has issue 1h to 2h.

1h. Roger John Edward Conant, *b.* 28 May 1899.

2h. Rupert Thomas Conant, *b.* 3 Dec. 1891.

2g. Ouida Mary Tryon.

3g. Violet Alice Grace Tryon.

13f.² Emma Laura Dashwood, *m.* 1st, 1881, George Henry Colmore (whom she div.); 2ndly, 1890, Edward Gordon Linzee (*Brambridge Lodge, Bishopstoke, Hants*); and has issue 1g to 2g.

1g. Henry Colmore, *b.* 1882.

2g. George Cyril Colmore, *b.* 1885.

2e. *Sophia Dashwood, d.* (–); *m. the Rev. Banks Wright of Shelton, Notts.*

3e. *Lydia Diana Dashwood, d.* 10 *Jan.* 1837; *m.* 15 *June* 1831, *Major George Birch of Clare Park, H.E.I.C.S., d.* 23 *Feb.* 1855; *and had issue* 1f *to* 2f.

1f. George Francis Birch, J.P., D.L., Lieut.-Col. *late* 3rd Batt. Hampshire Regt. (*Clare Park, Crondall, Southampton*), *b.* 6 Jan. 1834; *m.* 29 Oct. 1861, Katherine Georgina, da. of Hugo Montgomery Campbell, *d.* 6 Oct. 1886; and has issue 1g to 4g.

1g. George Reginald Birch, *b.* 27 Aug. 1864.

2g. Francis Herrick Birch, *b.* 23 Feb. 1866.

3g. Arthur Charles Birch, Capt. R.F.A., *b.* 24 Sept. 1870.

4g. Lydia Mary Birch.

[Nos. 9983 to 10012.

# of The Blood Royal

2f. Lydia Caroline Birch, d. 5 *July* 1881; m. 8 *Dec.* 1857, *the Right Hon. George Sclater-Booth, M.P., afterwards* (1887) *1st Baron Basing* [*U.K.*], *P.C., F.R.S.,* b. 19 *May* 1826; d. 22 *Oct.* 1894; *and had issue* 1g *to* 8g.

    1g. George Limbrey (Sclater-Booth), 2nd Baron Basing [U.K.], C.B., Lieut.-Col. and Brevet-Col. 1st Royal Dragoons (*Hoddington House, Winchfield, Hants*), b. 1 Jan. 1860; *m.* 12 Dec. 1889, Mary, da. of John Hargreaves of Maiden Erleigh, co. Berks, and Whalley Abbey, co. Lanc.; and has issue 1h to 3h.

    1h. Hon. John Limbrey Robert Sclater-Booth, b. 3 Dec. 1890.

    2h. Hon. John Penelope Sclater-Booth, b. 19 Oct. 1892.

    3h. Hon. Lydia Joyce Sclater-Booth, b. 20 Feb. 1898.

    2g. Hon. Charles Lutley Sclater-Booth, Bar. I.T. (*Basing House, Basingstoke*), b. 6 May 1862; *m.* 18 Ap. 1900, Ellen Geraldine, widow of W. Tudor Frere, da. of George Jones of Mitton; and has issue 1h.

    1h. George Lutley Sclater-Booth, b. 1903.

    3g. Hon. Walter Dashwood Sclater-Booth, Major R.F.A. (*Army and Navy*), b. 15 Feb. 1869.

    4g. Hon. Theodora Mary Sclater-Booth, *m.* 11 Ap. 1889, Remington Walter White-Thomson, M.A. (Camb.), sometime an Assist. Master Eton Coll. (39 *Hans Place, S.W.*).

    5g. Hon. Penelope Magdalen Sclater-Booth, *m.* 3 Aug. 1886, Charles A. Bovill (*Smeeth Paddocks, Ashford, Kent*); and has issue 1h to 3h.

    1h. Anthony Charles Stevens Bovill, b. 17 Oct. 1888.

    2h. Magdalen Ellen Bovill, b. 2 July 1887.

    3h. Rosa Mary Bovill, b. 12 May 1895.

    6g. Hon. Lydia Katharine Sclater-Booth, *m.* 30 Dec. 1893, Frank Walkinshaw (*Hartley Grange, Winchfield, Hants*); and has issue 1h to 5h.

    1h. Esmond Walkinshaw, b. 1895.

    2h. David Walkinshaw, b. 1900.

    3h. Lydia Marion Walkinshaw.

    4h. Barbara Walkinshaw.

    5h. Olive Elizabeth Walkinshaw.

    7g. Hon. Eleanor Birch Sclater-Booth, *m.* 19 July 1898, Henry Wilson Fox (4 *Halkin Street, S.W.*); and has issue 1h.

    1h. George Hubert Wilson Fox, b. 11 May 1899

    8g. Hon. Amy Cecily Sclater-Booth, *m.* 6 Ap. 1893, Francis Marshall (2 *Chesham Place, S.W.*).

    3c. Grace Lister, bapt. 28 *July* 1730.

    4c. Barbara Jane Lister, bapt. 28 *Jan.* 1732.

    2b. John Lister, bapt. 11 *Ap.* 1705.

    3b. Mary Lister, bapt. 4 *Nov.* 1704; bur. 16 *June* 1737; m. 1st, 16 *Ap.* 1722, *Thomas Heardson of Claythorpe*; 2ndly, 29 *Oct.* 1732, *as 1st wife, Francis (Scott), 2nd Earl of Deloraine* [S.], d.s.p. 11 *Ap.* 1739.

    4b. Eleanor Lister, *dead in* 1751; m. *the Rev. William Bowes, Rector of Scrivelsby; will dated 25 June, prov. 9 Oct.* 1751.

    2a. Michael Lister, bapt. 15 *May* 1688.

    3a. Dymoke Lister, bapt. 20 *Oct.* 1689; d. (⁼); m. *Faith, da. of* [——]; bur. 16 *Ap.* 1759; *and had issue* 1b *to* 2b.

    1b. Eleanor Lister, bapt. 13 *Aug.* 1726.

    2b. Faith Lister, bapt. 29 *Nov.* 1729.

    4a. Eleanor Lister, m. *John Thorold of Lincoln.*   [Nos. 10013 to 10033,

The Plantagenet Roll

165. Descendants of Lady CATHERINE ¹BRYDGES (see Table XIV.),
m. 1st, WILLIAM BERKELEY LYON, Royal Horse Guards ; 2ndly,
9 Aug. 1753, EDWYN FRANCIS STANHOPE, b. 1727 ; d. 16 May
1807 ; and had issue (at least by 2nd husband).

See the Clarence Volume, pp. 109–114, Nos. 1104–1239.

[Nos. 10034 to 10169.

166. Descendants of HENRY (BRYDGES), 2nd DUKE OF CHANDOS
[G.B.], 10th BARON CHANDOS [E.], K.B. (see Table XIV.),
bapt. 1 Feb. 1708 ; d. 28 Nov. 1771 ; m. 1st, 21 Dec. 1728,
Lady MARY, da. and in her issue (1796) heir of Charles
(BRUCE), 3rd Earl of Aylesbury [E.], 4th Earl of Elgin [S.],
d. 14 Aug. 1738 ; and had issue.

See the Tudor Roll of " The Blood Royal of Britain," pp. 151–156, Nos. 19573–
19723. [Nos. 10170 to 10320.

167. Descendants, if any, of ARTHUR LAKE, bapt. 23 Feb. 1654 (see
Table XIV.).

168. Descendants of WARWICK LAKE of Canons (see Table XIV.),
bapt. 13 Ap. 1661 ; d. 1712 ; m. ELIZABETH, widow (?) of
MILES STAPLETON, da. and h. of Sir Charles GERARD, 3rd Bart.
[E.], M.P.; and had issue.

See the Tudor Roll of "The Blood Royal of Britain," pp. 312–313, Nos. 26014–
26027. [Nos. 10321 to 10334.

169. Descendants, if any, of ESSEX LAKE, bapt. 20 Aug. 1638, and of
LETITIA LAKE, bapt. 19 June 1650 (see Table XIV.).

170. Descendants, if any, of JANE CROW (see Table VII.), wife of
FRANCIS CORNWALLIS.

171. Descendants of BENEDICTA MARIA THERESA HALL, a co-h. to the
Baronies of Percy, Poynings, and Fitzpayne [E.] (see Table
XV.), d. 25 July 1749 ; m. as 1st wife, c. 1717, THOMAS (GAGE),
1st VISCOUNT GAGE [I.], d. 21 Dec. 1754 ; and had issue 1a
to 2a.

1a. William Hall (Gage), 2nd Viscount Gage [I.], 1st Baron Gage [G.B.], b. 1
Jan. 1718 ; d.s.p. 11 Oct. 1791.

2a. Hon. Thomas Gage, Governor and Com.-in-Chief of H.M.'s Forces in
North America, d. 2 Ap. 1788 ; m. 8 Dec. 1758, Margaret, da. of Peter
Kemble, President of the New Jersey Council, d. 9 Feb. 1824 ; and had issue
1b to 6b.

1b. Henry (Gage), 3rd Viscount Gage [I.], 2nd Baron Gage [G.B.], b. 4 Mar.
1761 ; d. 29 Jan. 1808 ; m. 11 Jan. 1789, Susannah Maria, da. and h. of Gen.
William Skinner, d. 29 Ap. 1821 ; and had issue 1c to 2c.

# of The Blood Royal

1c. Henry Hall (Gage), 4th Viscount Gage [I.], 3rd Baron Gage [G.B.], b. 14 Dec. 1791; d. 20 Jan. 1877; m. 8 Mar. 1813, Elizabeth Maria, da. of the Hon. Edward Foley of Stoke Edith, d. 13 June 1857; and had issue 1d to 4d.

    1d. Hon. Henry Edward Hall Gage, Lieut.-Col. Royal Sussex Militia, b. 9 Jan. 1814; d. 8 Sept. 1875; m. 31 Aug. 1840, Sophia Selina, da. of Sir Charles Knightley, 2nd Bart. [G.B.], d. 4 May 1886; and had issue 1e to 2e.

        1e. Henry Charles (Gage), 5th Viscount [I.] and 4th Baron [G.B.] Gage (Firle Place, Lewes), b. 2 Ap. 1854; m. 23 July 1894, Leila Georgiana, da. of the Rev. Frederick Peel; and has issue.
        See the Clarence Volume, p. 605, Nos. 26594–26597.

        2e. Selena Elizabeth Gage, m. 1st, 22 July 1862, Henry Cavendish Cavendish (1852, formerly Taylor) of Chyknell, co. Salop, J.P., D.L. (div. Jan. 1872); 2ndly, 1873, J. White; and has issue 1f to 3f.

            1f. Edith Selina Cavendish, m. 24 May 1893, Major Hubert Cornwall Legh, King's Royal Rifle Corps.

            2f. Ethel Julia Cavendish.

            3f. Elfrida Geraldine Cavendish.

    2d. Hon. Edward Thomas Gage, Lieut.-Gen. and Col. Comdg. R.H.A., C.B., b. 28 Dec. 1825; d. 21 May 1889; m. 1st, 17 Jan. 1856, Arabella Elizabeth, da. of the Hon. Thomas William Gage, d. 8 Nov. 1860; 2ndly, 17 Nov. 1862, Ella Henrietta (29 Clifton Crescent, Folkestone), da. of James Maxse (by his wife, Lady Caroline, née Berkeley); and had issue 1e to 8e.

        1e. William Henry St. Quintin Gage, b. 12 Feb. 1858.

        2e. Francis Edward Gage, b. 13 Oct. 1860.

        3e. Ella Molyneux Berkeley Gage, Major and Hon. Lieut.-Col. 3rd County of London Imp. Yeo., late 14th Hussars (Cavalry), b. 29 Sept. 1863; m. 30 Oct. 1888, Ethel Marion, da. of John Lysaght of Springfort, co. Gloucester; and has issue 1f.

            1f. John Fitzhardinge Berkeley Gage, b. 3 June 1901.

        4e. James Seton Drummond Gage, Lieut. 5th Dragoons, b. 28 June 1870.

        5e. Moreton Foley Gage, Capt. 7th Dragoons, b. 12 Jan. 1873; m. 1902, Annie Massie, da. of William Everard Strong of New York City, U.S.A.; and has issue 1f.

            1f. Berkeley Everard Foley Gage, b. 27 Feb. 1904.

        6e. Mary Cecil Elizabeth Wilhelmina Gage, b. 12 Sept. 1856; m. 28 Dec. 1882, the Rev. Henry Stewart Gladstone (Honingham Vicarage, Norwich); and has issue 1f to 2f.

            1f. Thomas Henry Gladstone, b. 21 Mar. 1889.

            2f. Kathleen Mary Gladstone, b. 15 Mar. 1887.

        7e. Georgiana Elizabeth Gage (5 Eaton Terrace, S.W.), b. 5 July 1859.

        8e. Mabel Maria Gage, b. 10 June 1866; d. 12 May 1901; m. 27 Ap. 1899, Lieut.-Col. William Eliot Peyton, D.S.O. 15th Hussars; and had issue.

    3d. Hon. Caroline Harriet Gage, b. 23 July 1823; d. 8 May 1888; m. 4 May 1847, Standish Prendergast (Vereker), 4th Viscount Gort [I.], b. 6 July 1819; d. 9 Jan. 1900; and had issue 1e to 8e.

        1e. John Gage Prendergast (Vereker), 5th Viscount Gort [I.], b. 28 Jan. 1849; d. 15 Aug. 1902; m. 28 Jan. 1885, Eleanor (Hamsterley Hall, co. Durham), da. and co-h. of Robert Smith Surtees of Hamsterley Hall; and had issue 1f to 2f.

            1f. John Standish Surtees Prendergast (Vereker), 6th Viscount Gort [I.] (East Cowes Castle, I.W.), b. 10 July 1886.

            2f. Hon. Standish Robert Gage Prendergast Vereker, b. 12 Feb. 1888.

        2e. Hon. Foley Charles Prendergast Vereker, Capt. R.N., b. 21 June 1850; d. 24 Oct. 1900; m. 25 Mar. 1876, Ellen Amelia (Ruhstein, Spring Grove, Isleworth), da. of the Rev. Henry Michael Myddelton Wilshere, Rector of Simon's Town, Cape .Colony; and had issue 1f to 8f. [Nos. 10335 to 10356,

        2 M

The Plantagenet Roll

1f. Standish Henry Prendergast Vereker, H.B.M.'s Vice-Consul at Cherbourg, *b.* 12 Nov. 1878.

2f. Leopold George Prendergast Vereker, Sub-Lieut. R.N.R. (H.R.H. the *late* Duke of Albany sponsor), *b.* 26 Jan. 1881.

3f. Maurice Charles Prendergast Vereker, *b.* 21 Aug. 1884.

4f. Foley Gerald Prendergast Vereker, *b.* 12 Ap. 1893.

5f. Violet Eva Vereker, *b.* 23 Mar. 1882.

6f. Lilian Isolda Vereker, *b.* 1 May 1883.

7f. Muriel Agnes Vereker, *b.* 19 Oct. 1886.

8f. Ivy Mary Vereker, *b.* 21 Feb. 1888.

3e. Hon. Jeffrey Edward Prendergast Vereker, *late* Major R.A. (*Naval and Military*), *b.* 27 Mar. 1858 ; *m.* 1902, Deno, da. of [——] Head.

4e. Hon. Isolda Caroline Vereker, *m.* 23 Nov. 1870, Sir Charles William Frederick Craufurd, 4th Bart. [G.B.] (10 *Warwick Square, S.W. ; The Crescent, Hayling*) ; and has issue 1*f* to 9*f*.

1f. George Standish Gage Craufurd, D.S.O., Capt. 1st Batt. Gordon Highlanders, *b.* 19 Nov. 1872.

2f. Quentin Charles Alexander Craufurd, Lieut. R.N., *b.* 11 Feb. 1875 ; *m.* 1 Oct. 1899, Ann, da. of Thomas Blackwell.

3f. Alexander John Fortescue Craufurd, *b.* 22 Mar. 1876.

4f. Charles Edward Vereker Craufurd, Sub-Lieut. R.N., *b.* 17 July 1885.

5f. Hester Jane Laline Craufurd, *b.* 19 Sept. 1871.

6f. Laline Isolda Craufurd, *b.* 7 Aug. 1877.

7f. Isolda Mabel Cecil Craufurd, *b.* 30 Sept. 1878.

8f. Eleanor Mary Dorothea Craufurd, *b.* 7 Mar. 1887.

9f. Margaret Elizabeth Maria Craufurd, *b.* 27 Feb. 1889.

5e. Hon. Mabel Elizabeth Vereker (10 *Wilton Street, S.W.*).

6e. Hon. Laline Maria Vereker.

7e. Hon. Elizabeth Maria Vereker, *m.* 1st, 7 Dec. 1886, William Harvey Astell, J.P., D.L., of Woodbury Hall, co. Beds., *b.* 26 Nov. 1860 ; *d.* 20 Ap. 1896 ; *m.* 2ndly, 12 June 1902, Philip (Sidney), 3rd Baron de L'Isle and Dudley [U.K.] (*Penshurst Place, Tonbridge ; Ingleby Manor, Middlesbrough*) ; and has issue 1*f* to 3*f*.

1f. Richard John Vereker Astell (*Woodbury Hall, Sandy, co. Beds. ; 16 Sloane Gardens, S.W.*), *b.* 7 Sept. 1890.

2f. Laline Annette Astell, *b.* 1 Oct. 1888.

3f. Cynthia Elizabeth Violet Astell, *b.* 10 Aug. 1893.

8e. Hon. Corinna Julia Vereker (*Holly Hill, Ditchingham, Norfolk*).

4d. Hon. Fanny Charlotte Gage, b. 8 *Nov.* 1830 ; *d.* 23 *Jan.* 1883 ; *m.* 15 *Feb.* 1853, *Capt. William Tomline, late* 10th *Hussars.*

2c. Hon. Thomas William Gage of Westbury, co. Hants, b. 4 *Aug.* 1796 ; *d.* 26 *Jan.* 1855 ; *m.* 12 *June* 1824, *Arabella Cecil, da. of Thomas William St. Quintin of Scampston Hall, co. York, d.* 25 *Feb.* 1840 ; *and had issue* 1*d.*

1d. Arabella Gage, d. 8 *Nov.* 1860 ; *m. as 1st wife,* 17 *Jan.* 1856, *Gen. the Hon. Edward Thomas Gage, C.B., d.* 21 *May* 1889 ; *and had issue.* See p. 269, Nos. 10344–10354.

2b. John Gage of Rogate, co. Hants, b. 23 *Dec.* 1767 ; *d.* 24 *Dec.* 1846 ; *m.* 20 *May* 1793, *Mary, da. and h. of John Milbanke, d.* 9 *Nov.* 1846 ; *and had issue.* See pp. 260–261, Nos. 9886–9890.

3b. Maria Theresa Gage, d. 21 *Ap.* 1832 ; *m.* 2 *Mar.* 1792, *Sir James Craufurd, afterwards* (*R.L.* 25 *June* 1812) *Gregan-Craufurd, 2nd Bart.* [G.B.], *b.* 11 *Oct.* 1861 ; *d.* 9 *July* 1839 ; *and had issue* 1*c* to 2*c.*

1c. Rev. Sir George William Craufurd, 3rd Bart. [G.B.], *b.* 10 *Ap.* 1797 ; *d.* [Nos. 10357 to 10398.

# of The Blood Royal

24 *Feb.* 1881; m. 1st, 15 *Feb.* 1843, the *Hon. Hester, sister to William, 1st Earl of Lovelace [U.K.], da. of Peter (King), 7th Baron King [G.B.],* b. 2 *May* 1806; d. (*at Pisa*) 18 *Mar.* 1848; *and had issue* 1d.

    1d. Sir Charles William Frederick Craufurd, 4th Bart. [G.B.], *late* Lieut. R.N. (10 *Warwick Square, S.W.; The Crescent, Hayling*), b. 28 *Mar.* 1847; m. 23 *Nov.* 1870, the *Hon.* Isolda Caroline, da. of Standish Prendergast (Vereker), 4th Viscount Gort [I.]; and has issue.

    See p. 270, Nos. 10367–10375.

    2c. *Jane Craufurd,* d. 25 *May* 1884; m. 1st, 12 *Oct.* 1823, *Gen. Christopher Chowne (R.L.* 3 *Dec.* 1811), *formerly Tilson,* d. 15 *July* 1834; 2ndly, 29 *Aug.* 1836, the *Rev. Sir Henry Richard Dukenfield, 7th Bart.* [E.], d.s.p. 24 *Jan.* 1858.

    4b. *Louisa Elizabeth Gage,* d. 21 *Jan.* 1832; m. 13 *Feb.* 1794, *St. James Henry Blake, 3rd Bart.* [G.B.], d. 21 *Feb.* 1832; *and had issue* 1c *to* 6c.

    1c. Sir Henry Charles Blake, *4th Bart.* [G.B.], b. 23 *Mar.* 1794; d. 20 *Ap.* 1841; m. 1st, 2 *Aug.* 1819, *Mary Anne, da. of William Whitter of Midhurst,* d. 20 *Ap.* 1841; *and had issue* 1d *to* 2d.

    1d. *Rev. Henry Bunbury Blake, Rector of Hessett,* b. 14 *May* 1820; d.v.p. 20 *Ap.* 1873; m. 1 *July* 1847, *Frances Marion, da. of Henry James Oakes of Nowton Court; and had issue* 1e *to* 5e.

    1e. Sir Patrick James Graham Blake, 5th Bart. [G.B.] (*Bardwell Manor, Ixworth*), b. 23 Oct. 1861; *m.* 18 Oct. 1883, Emma Gertrude, da. of Thomas Pilkington Dawson of Groton House, co. Suffolk; and has issue 1f to 2f.

    1f. Cuthbert Patrick Blake, b. 2 Jan. 1885.

    2f. Veronica Blake, b. 10 Feb. 1887.

    2e. Marion Louisa Blake, b. 17 Jan. 1848.

    3e. Emma Gage Blake, b. 20 June 1857; *m.* 24 Aug. 1892, George Henry Fillingham (*Syerston Hall, Newark*); and has issue 1f.

    1f. George Augusta Fillingham, b. 1893.

    4e. Julia Porteus Blake, b. 7 Oct. 1858.

    5e. Mary Anne Thellusson Blake, b. 19 Jan. 1860.

    2d. *William Gage Blake of Nowton Hall,* b. 14 *Nov.* 1821; d. 1889; m. 16 *June* 1859, *Mary, da. of the Rev. James T. Bennet of Cheveley; and had issue* 1e *to* 3e.

    1e. Constance Gage Blake, b. 20 Mar. 1860; *m.* 1883, Edward Charles Harrison Bennet, *formerly* of Copdock, Ipswich; and has issue 1f.

    1f. Judith Harrison Bennet, b. 1883.

    2e. Evelyn Gage Blake, b. 23 July 1861.

    3e. Henrietta Lillie Gage Blake, b. 27 Oct. 1864.

    2c. *Rev. William Robert Blake, Vicar of Great Barton, co. Suffolk,* b. 1800; d. 6 Dec. 1868.

    3c. *James Bunbury Blake of Thurston House, co. Suffolk,* b. 1802; d. *July* 1874; m. 1 *Nov.* 1831, *Catherine, da. and co-h. of Sir Thomas Pilkington, 7th Bart.* [S.], d. 1899; *and had issue* 1d.

    1d. George Pilkington Blake, J.P., Col. Suffolk Imp. Yeo., *formerly* 84th Regt. (*Willesboro, Ashford, Kent*), b. 23 Ap. 1835; *m.* 1st, 15th May 1860, Adeline, da. of James King King of Staunton Park, M.P., d. Ap. 1890; 2ndly, July 1893, Adela Mary, widow of Thomas Duffield, da. of Theobald Theobald of Sutton Courtney Abbey, J.P.; and has issue 1e to 4e.

    1e. Eustace James Pilkington Blake (*St. Leonards, East Sheen*), b. 26 Mar. 1865; *m.* 1889, Ethel Minna, da. of Col. P. B. Schrieber, Royal Scots; and has issue 1f to 2f.

    1f. Norman Pilkington Blake, } b. (twins) 1890.   [Nos. 10399 to 10424.
    2f. Violet Hilda Blake, }

The Plantagenet Roll

2e. Adeline Annie Blake, *m.* 1884, Hardinge Hay Cameron, Ceylon Civil Service.

3e. Kathleen Mary Blake, *m.* 1888, Francis Millett Richards (*Ashtead, near Epsom*); and has issue 1*f.*

1f. Thomas Millett Richards, *b.* 1889.

4e. Geraldine Blake.

4c. Thomas Gage Blake, *b.* 1805; *d.* (*? unm.*).

5c. Louisa Annabella Blake, *d.* (–); *m. May* 1827, *Francis King Eagle, Bencher M.T., County Court Judge, d.* 8 *June* 1856; *and had issue* 1*d.*

1d. Francis Blake Eagle, *14th Light Dragoons, b.* 6 *Dec.* 1833; *d.* 3 *Feb.* 1879; *m.* 1 *Nov.* 1865, *Emma Ellen, da. of Lieut. Henry Bond; and had issue* 1*e to* 8*e.*[1]

1e. Francis Elwyn Burbury Eagle, *b.* 29 Aug. 1866.

2e. Maude Campbell Eagle.

3e. Rose Eagle.

4e. Violet Eagle.

5e. Lilian Dundas Eagle.

6e. Kathleen Emma Louisa Eagle.

7e. Cecil Mary Eagle.

8e. Evelyn Gage Wing Eagle.

6c. Emily Eliza Blake, *d.* 26 *Jan.* 1859; *m. Michael Edwards Rogers, d.* 21 *Ap.* 1832; *and had issue* 1*d.*[1]

1d. Emily Louisa Merilena Rogers, *m.* 1863, the Rev. J. H. Marshall (*New Zealand*); and has issue (5 children).

5b. Charles Margaret Gage, *d. Sept.* 1814; *m. as* 1*st wife,* 22 *Ap.* 1802, *Admiral Sir Charles Ogle, 2nd Bart.* [*U.K.*], *b.* 24 *May* 1775; *d.* 16 *June* 1858; *and had issue* 1*c to* 3*c.*

1c. Sir Chaloner Ogle, 3rd Bart. [*U.K.*], *b.* 18 *July* 1803; *d.* (*at Brussels*) 3 *Feb.* 1859; *m.* 5 *Ap.* 1842, *Eliza Sophia Frances, da. and h. of William Thomas Roe of Withdean Court, co. Sussex, d.* 12 *May* 1886; *and had issue* 1*d to* 2*d.*

1d. Sir Chaloner Roe Majendie Ogle, 4th Bart. [*U.K.*], *b.* 2 *June* 1843; *d. unm.* 29 *Nov.* 1861.

2d. Hebe Emily Maritana Ogle, *d.* 28 *May* 1889; *m.* 19 *July* 1865, *Eldred Vincent Morris Curwen, J.P.* (*Withdean Court, co. Sussex*); *and had issue* 1*e to* 2*e.*

1e. Chaloner Frederick Hastings Curwen, *b.* 20 *July* 1866; *d.* 3 *Mar.* 1897; *m. Elizabeth, da. of Sir William Gordon Cameron, K.C.B.; and had issue* (*two children*).

2e. Edith Margaret Spence Curwen.

2c. Charlotte Arabella Ogle, *d.* 22 *July* 1840; *m.* (*at Paris*) 15 *Ap.* 1836, *Jules, Baron de Braidenbach of Darmstadt.*

3c. Sophia Ogle, *d.* 23 *Ap.* 1896; *m.* 17 *Aug.* 1830, *the Rev. Edward Chaloner Ogle of Kirkley Hall, Preb. of Salisbury, b.* 7 *Aug.* 1798; *d.* 7 *Nov.* 1869; *and had issue* 1*d to* 5*d.*

1d. Newton Charles Ogle, J.P., D.L. (*Kirkley Hall, near Newcastle-on-Tyne*), *b.* 19 Feb. 1850; *m.* 26 Nov. 1895, Lady Lilian Katharine Selina, da. of William (Denison), 1st Earl of Londesborough [U.K.], *d.* 31 July 1899; 2ndly, 12 Oct. 1903, Beatrice Anne, da. of Sir John William Cradock-Hartopp, 4th Bart. [G.B.]; and has issue 1*e* to 2*e.*

1e. John Francis Chaloner Ogle, *b.* 1 Dec. 1898.

2e. Hester Mary Ogle, *b.* 31 July 1904.

2d. Annie Charlotte Ogle.   [Nos. 10425 to 10442.

---

[1] Foster's " Baronetage," 1800, p. 45.

# of The Blood Royal

3d. Sophia Henrietta Ogle, *m.* 24 June 1879, the Most Rev. Hugh Willoughby Jermyn, D.D., Lord Bishop of Brechin and Primus of Scotland (*Brechin*).

4d. Isabel Ogle (*Chesters, Humshaugh, co. Northumberland*), *m.* 12 Dec. 1860, Nathaniel George Clayton of Chesters and Charlwood Park, J.P., D.L., *b.* 20 Sept. 1833; *d.* 5 Sept. 1895; and has issue 1*e* to 6*e.*

    1*e.* *John Bertram Clayton of Chesters and Charlwood Park,* b. 9 *Oct.* 1861; d. 8 *Ap.* 1900; m. 26 *Jan.* 1886, *Florence Octavia* (*Chesters, Humshaugh, co. Northumberland ; Charlwood Park, Surrey*), *da. of Cadogan Hodgson Cadogan of Brinkburn Priory ; and had issue* 1*f to* 2*f.*

        1*f.* Eleanor Clayton.

        2*f.* Diana Pauline Clayton.

    2*e.* Edward Francis Clayton, Major Scots Guards (78 *Portland Place, W.*), *b.* 21 Aug. 1864; *m.* 24 Feb. 1900, Jeanne Marie Renée, da. of [——], Baron de Fougères.

    3*e.* George Savile Clayton, *b.* 20 Oct. 1869.

    4*e.* Mary Sophia Clayton, *m.* 18 Jan. 1883, Mark Fenwick (*Abbotswood, Stow-on-the-Wold*).

    5*e.* Isabel Evelyn Clayton, *m.* 14 July 1891, Robert Lancelot Allgood (*Nunwick, co. Northumberland*).

    6*e.* Alice Pauline Clayton, *m.* 20 Sept. 1905, Herbert Swinburne, son and heir of Sir John Swinburne, 7th Bart. [E.]

5d. Alice Katherine Ogle, *m.* 21 Feb. 1874, George A. Fenwick ; and has issue.

6b. Emily Gage, b. 25 *Ap.* 1776; d. 28 *Aug.* 1838; m. *as* 1st *wife,* 27 *Aug.* 1807, *Montagu* (*Bertie*), 5th *Earl of Abingdon* [*E.*], b. 30 *Ap.* 1784; d. 16 *Oct.* 1854; *and had issue.*

See pp. 78–79, Nos. 146–177.   [Nos. 10443 to 10484.

172. Descendants, if any, of THOMAS WHORWOOD (see Table XV.).

173. Descendants of FRANCIS FORTESCUE TURVILLE of Husbands Bosworth, co. Leicester (see Table XV.), *d.* 13 July 1839 ; *m.* 9 Ap. 1780, BARBARA, sister to Charles, 15th Earl of Shrewsbury [E.] and Waterford [I.], *d.* 4 June 1806 ; and had issue 1*a.*

    1*a. George Fortescue Turville of Husbands Bosworth,* b. 5 *Feb.* 1782; d. 10 *Dec.* 1859; m. 9 *Oct.* 1826, *Henrietta, da. of Baron Adolph van der Lanckin of Galenbeck, Mecklenburg-Schwerin ; and had issue* 1*b to* 2*b.*

        1*b. Sir Francis Charles Fortescue Turville of Husbands Bosworth,* K.C.M.G., b. 31 *Jan.* 1832; d.s.p. 20 *Dec.* 1889; m. 3 *Aug.* 1878, *Adelaide Annabella, widow of John* (*Young*), 1st *Baron Lisgar* [*U.K.*], *P.C., da. of Edward Tuite Dalton,* d. 19 *July* 1895.

        2*b.* Mary Frances Charlotte Turville (*Husbands Bosworth, Leicester*).

                                        [No. 10485.

174. Descendants of THOMAS STONOR of Stonor, co. Oxon (see Table XVI.), *b.* 20 June 1677 ; *d.* 10 Aug. 1724 ; *m.* 2ndly, 14 July 1705, the Hon. WINIFRED, da. of Christopher (ROPER), 5th Baron Teynham [E.], *d.* 1722 ; and had issue.

See the Clarence Volume (Table XLVIII.), pp. 418–420, Nos. 15809–16222.

                                       [Nos. 10486 to 10899.

The Plantagenet Roll

175. Descendants of EDMUND PLOWDEN of Plowden (see Table XVI.), *d.* 4 Ap. 1838; *m.* ANNA MARIA, da. of Robert BURTON of Longner, co. Salop, *d.* (–); and had issue 1*a*.

1*a*. *Anna Maria Plowden*, d. 18 *Oct.* 1825; m. *the Rev. John Eyton, Vicar of Wellington and Rector of Eyton*, d. 10 *Jan.* 1823; *and had issue* 1*b to* 7*b*.

1*b. John Eyton*, d. 1836 (? *unm.*).

2*b. Rev. Robert William Eyton of Albury House, Guildford, Author of the "Antiquities of Shropshire,"* d. 8 *Sept.* 1881; m. 1839, *Mary E., da. of the Rev. J. G. Watts, Rector of Ledbury*, d. 18 *Feb.* 1883; *and had issue* 1*c to* 7*c.*

1*c.* William Henry Plowden Eyton, *b.* 18 Sept. 1843; *m.* 26 Aug. 1886, Marianne Elizabeth, widow of James Quinlan of Dublin, Barrister, da. of [——].

2*c.* Rev. Robert Eyton, Rector of St. Margaret's, Westminster, Preb. of St. Paul's and Sub-Almoner to H.M. the Queen (*St. Margaret's Rectory, Westminster, S.W.*), *b.* 21 June 1845; *m.* July 1886, Sarah Constantia, da. of Charles Manners Lushington, M.P.

3*c.* Philip Eyton, Lieut.-Col. *late* Border Regt., *b.* 3 Mar. 1847; *m.* 1888, Ethel, da. of the Rev. C. F. Seymour, Rector of Winchfield; and has issue (a son).

4*c.* Rose Margaret Eyton.

5*c.* Anna Maria Eyton.

6*c.* Mary Eyton.

7*c.* Edith Jane Eyton, *m.* Spencer Walpole Craigie.

3*b. Henry Eyton*, d. 30 *Sept.* 1841 (? *unm.*).

4*b. Joseph Eyton.*

5*b. Mary Eyton*, m. *William Henry Perry.*

6*b. Ann Rose Eyton*, d. 23 *July* 1891; m. 6 *Sept.* 1836, *Rev. Henry Beckwith, Rector of Eaton Constantine,* b. 29 *Nov.* 1806; d. 22 *Oct.* 1888; *and had issue* 1*c to* 2*c.*

1*c.* Henry John Beckwith, J.P., Capt. 53rd Regt. (*Millichope Park, Craven Arms, co. Salop; Silksworth House, co. Durham*), *b.* 24 Aug. 1840; *m.* 12 Oct. 1876, Kathleen Elizabeth, da. of Robert Craven Wade of Clonebraney, J.P., D.L.; and has issue 1*d* to 2*d.*

1*d.* William Malebisse Beckwith, Lieut. Coldstream Guards, *b.* 20 Aug. 1877; *m.* 30 Ap. 1904, Lady Muriel Beatrice, da. of Charles Henry (Gordon-Lennox), 7th Duke of Richmond [E.] and Lennox [S.], &c., K.G.; and has issue 1*e.*

1*e.* John Beckwith, *b.* 16 Mar. 1905.

2*d.* Kathleen Frances Malebisse Beckwith.

2*c.* Rose Caroline Beckwith.

7*b. Anna Maria Dorothea Eyton*, d. 1888; m. 6 *Oct.* 1838, *Richard Neave,* b. 31 *May* 1808; d. 12 *Sept.* 1877; *and had issue* 1*c to* 3*c.*

1*c.* Rev. Richard Lewis Irvine Neave (*St. Catherine's Catholic Church, Littlehampton*), *b.* 3 July 1851.

2*c.* Barbara Frances Mary Neave, *m.* 9 June 1886, Count Roger de Courson (5 *Rue Crevaux, Paris*).

3*c.* Mary Rose Neave, *m.* 4 Ap. 1883, Edward St. Jullien (*Montreuil-sur-Mer, Pas de Calais, France*); and has issue 1*d* to 2*d.*

1*d.* Marie Rose de St. Jullien, *b.* 1887.

2*d.* Anne Marie St. Jullien, *b.* 1889.　　　　　　　　　[Nos. 10900 to 10916.

176. Descendants of WILLIAM XAVIERIUS PLOWDEN (see Table XVI.), *b.* 11 Aug. 1759; *d.* (at Ghent) 1 Nov. 1824; *m.* 13 Nov. 1797, MARY, da. of Simon WINTER, *d.* 1828; and had issue 1*a* to 2*a.*

1*a. William Henry Francis Plowden of Plowden, High Sheriff co. Salop* 1848, b. 21 *Oct.* 1802; d. 23 *July* 1870; m. 23 *Jan.* 1834, *Barbara, da. of Francis Cholmeley of Brandsby Hall,* d. 26 *June* 1853; *and had issue* 1*b to.* 5*b.*

# of The Blood Royal

1*b*. William Francis Plowden, J.P., D.L. (*Plowden Hall, Lydbury North, co. Salop*), *b*. 3 June 1853; *m*. 12 Oct. 1874, Lady Mary, sister of Lawrence, 1st Marquis of Zetland [U.K.], da. of the Hon. John Charles Dundas; and has issue. See p. 257, Nos. 9725–9727.

2*b*. Ellinor Plowden.

3*b*. Constance Plowden, *m*. 28 Aug. 1877, Francis Froes; and has issue 1*c*.

    1*c*. Joseph Francis Gerard Froes, *b*. 19 Oct. 1881.

4*b*. Gertrude Mary Plowden.

5*b*. Laura Mary Plowden, *m*. 16 July 1873, James William Thomas Thunder, J.P. (*Bellowstown House, Drogheda*); and has issue 1*c* to 5*c*.

    1*c*. Cyril Joseph Thunder, *b*. 27 July 1875.

    2*c*. Bernard William Thunder, *b*. 15 Aug. 1877.

    3*c*. Wilfred Michael Thunder, *b*. 15 Nov. 1881.

    4*c*. Constance Maria Thunder, *b*. 29 June 1885.

    5*c*. Mary Annette Thunder, *b*. 10 Nov. 1887.

2*a*. *Charles Joseph Plowden of Rome*, b. (?) *Feb*. 1805; *d*. 28 *Feb*. 1884; *m*. 12 *July* 1847, *Eliza, da. of Capt. George Bryan, d. May* 1897; *and had issue* 1*b* *to* 3*b*.

1*b*. Charles William Plowden, of Messrs. Plowden & Co., Bankers (*Rome*), *b*. 13 Oct. 1849; *m*. 1878, Josephine, da. of Joseph Senior; and has issue 1*c* to 4*c*.

    1*c*. Edmund Charles Plowden, *b*. 24 Oct. 1879.

    2*c*. Richard Anthony Plowden, *b*. 24 May 1881.

    3*c*. Hugh Vincent Plowden, *b*. 26 Mar. 1883.

    4*c*. Dorothy Josephine Plowden, *b*. 29 Ap. 1885.

2*b*. Francis Hugh Plowden, C.B., Brigadier-General Comdg. Mandalay Brigade (*Mandalay*), *b*. 15 Aug. 1851; *m*. 14 Ap. 1885, Isabel, da. of Major John Augustus Fane of Wormsley; and has issue 1*c* to 3*c*.

    1*c*. Hugh Plowden, *b*. 24 Mar. 1886.

    2*c*. Geoffrey Plowden, *b*. 9 Dec. 1888.

    3*c*. Sybil Plowden, *b*. 1 Sept. 1887.

3*b*. Roger Herbert Plowden of Strachur (*Strachur, Loch Fyne Side, N.B.*), *b*. 12 Oct. 1853; *m*. 1st, 2 Aug. 1883, Minnie, da. of Henry Dump of Woodlands, Gateacre, near Liverpool, *d*. 4 Ap. 1899; 2ndly, 3 June 1901, Helen, da. of William Stanley Haselline of Palazzo Altieri, Rome; and has issue 1*c* to 3*c*.

    1*c*. Humphrey Roger Plowden, *b*. 23 Ap. 1889.

    2*c*. Piers Standich Plowden, *b*. 24 Mar. 1899.

    3*c*. Roger Stanley Plowden, *b*. 12 Mar. 1902.   [Nos. 10917 to 10943.

177. Descendants of ELIZABETH LUCY PLOWDEN (see Table XVI.), *d*. 24 Jan. 1829; *m*. 1778, Sir HENRY TICHBORNE, 7th Bart. [E.], *b*. 6 Sept. 1756; *d*. 14 June 1821; and had issue 1*a* to 4*a*.

1*a*. *Sir Henry Joseph Tichborne, 8th Bart*. [E.], b. 8 *Jan*. 1779; d. 3 *June* 1845; m. 23 *Ap*. 1806, *Anne, da. of Sir Thomas Burke, 1st Bart*. [I.], d. 12 *Aug*. 1853; *and had issue* 1*b to* 6*b*.

1*b*. *Eliza Anne Tichborne*, d. 4 *July* 1883; m. 5 *May* 1829, *Joseph Thaddeus* (*Dormer*), 11*th Baron Dormer* [E.], *b*. 1 *June* 1790; d. 5 *July* 1871; *and had issue* 1*c to* 4*c*.

1*c*. *John Baptist Joseph* (*Dormer*), 12*th Baron Dormer* [E.], *b*. 22 *May* 1830; d. 22 *Dec*. 1900; m. 1st, 14 *June* 1866, *Louisa Frances Mary, da. of Edward King Tenison of Kilronan Castle, d*. 9 *Sept*. 1868; *and had issue* 1*d*.

275

The Plantagenet Roll

1*d*. Hon. Louise Florence Edith Dormer, *b*. 4 Sept. 1868; *m*. 20 July 1892, Henry Charles Vicars Hunter of Kilbourne Hall, co. Derby (*Mawley Hall, Cleobury Mortimer, co. Salop*); and has issue 1*e* to 3*e*.

1*e*. Henry John Francis Hunter, *b*. 29 Dec. 1893.

2*e*. Thomas Vicars Hunter, *b*. 2 Ap. 1897.

3*e*. Clare Mary Hunter, *b*. 2 Oct. 1895.

2*c*. Sir *James Charlemagne Dormer*, *K.C.B., Lieut.-Gen., &c.*, b. 26 *Jan*. 1834; d. 3 *May* 1893; m. 8 *Oct*. 1861, *Ella Frances Catherine, widow of Robert Cutler Fergusson of Craigdarroch, da. of Sir Archibald Alison, 1st Bart.* [*U.K.*]; *and had issue 1d to 8d*.

1*d*. Roland John (Dormer), 13th Baron Dormer [E.] (*Peterley House, Amersham, Bucks*), *b*. 24 Nov. 1862.

2*d*.[1] Hon. Charles Joseph Thaddeus Dormer, Comm. R.N. (10 *William Street, Hyde Park, W.*), *b*. 24 Feb. 1864; *m*. 17 Feb. 1903, Marjorie, da. of Sir Robert Cavendish Spencer Clifford, 3rd Bart. [U.K.]; and has issue 1*e* to 2*e*.

1*e*. Charles Walter James Dormer, *b*. 20 Dec. 1903.

2*e*. Georgiana Mary Dormer, *b*. 1 Feb. 1906.

3*d*.[1] Hon. Gwendoline Mary Dormer, *b*. 1 July 1865; *m*. as 2nd wife, 16 Oct. 1883, Montagu Arthur (Bertie), 7th Earl of Abingdon [E.] (*Wytham Abbey, Oxford*); and has issue.

See p. 79, Nos. 150–151 and 157–158.

4*d*. Hon.[1] Eveline Mary Dormer (*Alltyrodyn, Llandyssil, S. Wales*), *b*. 30 July 1866; *m*. 18 May 1892, James Logan Stewart, *late* 7th Hussars, *d*. 1897 ; and has issue 1*e* to 2*e*.

1*e*. James Alexander Stewart, *b*. 1893.

2*e*. Douglas Dormer Stewart, *b*. 1897.

5*d*. Hon.[1] Mary Catherine Dormer, *b*. 13 Oct. 1867; *m*. 9 Sépt. 1891, John David Rees, C.I.E., M.P. (17 *Pall Mall, S.W.; Hillmedes, Harrow-on-the-Hill*); and has issue 1*e* to 2*e*.

1*e*. Richard Lodowick Rees, *b*. 4 Ap. 1900.

2*e*. Rosemary Rees, *b*. 22 Sept. 1901.

6*d*. Hon.[1] Ethel Mary Dormer, *b*. 31 May 1870.

7*d*. Leonie Mary Dormer, a nun, *b*. 2 Nov. 1872.

8*d*. Hon.[1] Constance Mary Dormer, *b*. 1 Dec. 1874.

3*c*. Hon. Hubert Francis Dormer, lately a Clerk in the Admiralty (10 *Wetherby Place, S.W.*), *b*. 4 Nov. 1837; *m*. 11 Nov. 1865, Mary Jane Elizabeth, da. of Kenelm Digby; and has issue 1*d* to 8*d*.

1*d*. Edward Henry Dormer, *b*. 13 Oct. 1870; *m*. 24 June 1903, Vanessa Margaret, da. of Sir Robert Hudson Borwick of 16 Berkeley Square and Eden Lacy; and has issue 1*e* to 2*e*.

1*e*. Robert Francis Edward Baptist Dormer, *b*. 27 June 1904.

2*e*. Cecilia Mary Margaret Dormer, *b*. 22 Nov. 1905.

2*d*. John Hubert Dormer (63*a Elizabeth Street, Eaton Square, S.W.; Courtenay Lodge, Hove, Sussex*), *b*. 13 Jan. 1874; *m*. 14 Aug. 1900, Virginia Sinclair, da. of Capt. Tankerville Chamberlaine; and has issue 1*e* to 2*e*.

1*e*. Olivette Ferdinande Mary Dormer, *b*. 21 June 1902.

2*e*. Mary Louisa Isabel Dormer, *b*. 11 May 1904.

3*d*. Kenelm Everard Dormer, *b*. 22 Feb. 1879.

4*d*. Robert Stanhope Dormer, *b*. 18 Aug. 1880.

5*d*. Cecil Francis Joseph Dormer, a Clerk in the Foreign Office, *b*. 14 **Feb**. 1883.   [Nos. 10944 to 10975.

---

[1] R.W. 7 May 1901.

# of The Blood Royal

6*d.* Gertrude Jane Mary Dormer, *m.* 28 May 1885 (annulled 1896), Edmund Granville Ward of Northwood Park, Cowes.

7*d.* Elizabeth Mary Dormer, *m.* 6 Feb. 1900, Luke Gerald Dillon, M.D. (*Tempest House, Seaham, Durham*) ; and has issue 1*e.*

1*e.* Gerald Dormer FitzGerald Dillon, *b.* Ap. 1901.

8*d.* Alice Mary Dormer.

4*c.* Hon. Mary Isabel Lucy Dormer, a nun.

2*b. Frances Catherine Tichborne,* d. 19 *Ap.* 1836 ; m. *as 2nd wife,* 22 *Sept.* 1829, *Henry Benedict (Arundell),* 11*th Baron Arundell of Wardour* [*E.*] *and Count Arundell* [*H.R.E.*], d. 19 *Oct.* 1862 ; *and had issue.*
See the Clarence Volume, p. 436, Nos. 18456–18457.

3*b. Julia Tichborne,* d. 4 *June* 1892 ; m. 1*st,* 1 *Feb.* 1830, *Lieut.-Col. Charles Thomas Talbot,* b. 24 *Nov.* 1782 ; d. 30 *Ap.* 1838 ; 2*ndly,* 10 *Jan.* 1839, *Capt. John Hubert Washington Hibbert of Bilton Grange,* d. 15 *June* 1875 ; *and had issue* 1*c to* 9*c.*

1*c. Bertram Arthur (Talbot),* 17*th Earl of Shrewsbury* [*E.*] *and Waterford* [*I.*], b. 11 *Dec.* 1832 ; d. *unm.* 10 *Aug.* 1856.

2*c.* Paul Edgar Tichborne Hibbert of Ashby St. Ledgers, J.P., High Sheriff co. Northants 1890 (*Braywick Lodge, Maidenhead*), *b.* 25 Jan. 1846 ; *m.* 24 Feb. 1876, Charlotte Julia, widow of Robert Curzon of Alvaston, da. of William Gerard Walmesley of Westwood House ; and has issue.
See the Clarence Volume, p. 324, Nos. 9415–9421.

3*c. Herbert Aloysius Tichborne Hibbert,* b. 2 *Nov.* 1849 ; d. 31 *Mar.* 1879 ; m. 28 *Nov.* 1871, *Mary, da. of John Vincent (Hornyold, previously Gandolfi),* 13*th Marquis Gandolfi* [*Genoa*], *&c., of Blackmore Park, J.P., D.L. ; and had issue.*
See the Clarence Volume, p. 317, Nos. 9184–9188.

4*c.*[1] *Lady Annette Mary Talbot,* d. 4 *May* 1886 ; m. 17 *Jan.* 1855, *Sir Humphrey De Trafford,* 2*nd Bart.* [*U.K.*], d. 4 *May* 1886 ; *and had issue.*
See the Clarence Volume, pp. 322–323, Nos. 9320–9348.

5*c.*[1] Lady Gwendaline Elizabeth Talbot (*Whitley Abbey, Coventry*), *m.* 29 Oct. 1857, Edward Petre of Whitley Abbey, *d.* 24 Nov. 1902 ; and has issue.
See the Clarence Volume, p. 376, Nos. 12955–12960.

6*c.* Winifred Julia Tichborne Hibber

7*c. Lydia Anne Tichborne Hibbert,* d. 27 *Feb.* 1888 ; m. 19 *Sept.* 1870, *Henry Joseph Stourton of Holme Hall, J.P.,* d. 19 *Oct.* 1896 ; *and had issue.*
See the Clarence Volume, p. 367, Nos. 12546–12550.

8*c. Cecilia Elizabeth Tichborne Hibbert,* d. 3 *Jan.* 1865 ; m. *as* 1*st wife,* 21 *May* 1862, *Sir Charles Henry Tempest,* 1*st Bart.* [*U.K.*], b. 5 *Jan.* 1834 ; d.s.p.m.s. 1 *Aug.* 1894 ; *and had issue* 1*d.*

1*d.* Ethel Mary Tempest (*Carlton Towers, co. York*), *m.* 7 Nov. 1893, Miles (Stapleton), 10th Baron Beaumont [E.], *d.* 16 Sept. 1895 ; and has issue.
See p. 84, Nos. 333–334.

9*c.* Emily Frances Tichborne Hibbert (*Worsbro' Hall, Barnsley, co. York*), *m.* 3 Aug. 1870, William Henry Michael Aloysius Martin-Edmunds of Worsbro' Hall, D.L., *b.* 8 May 1847 ; *d.* 6 Oct. 1899 ; and has issue 1*d* to 3*d.*

1*d.* Cecilia Elizabeth Mary Agnes Martin-Edmunds (*Worsbro' Hall, Barnsley, co. York*).

2*d.* Magdalen Mary Josephine Martin-Edmunds.

3*d.* Olyve Mary Evelyn Martin-Edmunds.

4*b. Catherine Caroline Tichborne,* d. (–) ; m. 22 *Ap.* 1847, *William Greenwood of Brookwood Park and Woodcote, Lieut.-Col. Grenadier Guards,* b. 10 *Ap.* 1798 ; d. 1872 ; *and had issue* 1*c to* 2*c.*

1*c.* Eveline Mary Greenwood (*Brookwood Park, co. Hants*), *m.* Charles Higgins.

2*c.* Emily Mary Annette Greenwood.   [Nos. 10976 to 11046.

The Plantagenet Roll

5b. *Lucy Ellen Tichborne,* d. 8 *Ap.* 1900; m. *Col. John Towneley of Towneley, M.P.,* b. 16 *Feb.* 1806; d. 21 *Feb.* 1878; *and had issue.*
See the Tudor Roll of "The Blood Royal of Britain," p. 537, Nos. 35781–35784.

6b. *Emily Blanche Tichborne,* d. (–); m. 1*st,* 25 *July* 1836, *John Benett; 2ndly,* 2 *July* 1850, *Matthew James Higgins of Lowndes Square.*

2a. *Sir Edward Tichborne, afterwards (R.L.* 29 *May* 1826) *Doughty,* 9*th Bart.* [*E.*], b. 27 *Mar.* 1782; d. 5 *Mar.* 1873; m. 26 *June* 1827, *the Hon. Katherine, da. of James Everard (Arundell),* 9*th Baron Arundell of Wardour* [*E.*], d. 12 *Dec.* 1878; *and had issue.*
See the Clarence Volume, p. 438, Nos. 18514–18533.

3a. *Sir James Francis Tichborne, afterwards (R.L.* 6 *Feb.* 1853) *Doughty Tichborne,* 10*th Bart.* [*E.*], b. 3 *Oct.* 1784; d. 11 *June* 1862; m. 1 *Aug.* 1837, *Henrietta Felicite, da. of* [——] *Seymour,* d. 12 *Mar.* 1868; *and had issue* 1b.

1b. *Sir Alfred Joseph Doughty Tichborne,* 11*th Bart.* [*E.*], b. 4 *Sept.* 1839; d. 22 *Feb.* 1866; m. 17 *Ap.* 1861, *the Hon. Teresa Mary, da. of Henry Benedict (Arundell),* 11*th Baron Arundell* [*E.*] *(who re-m.* 24 *Feb.* 1873, *Capt. Henry Lamplugh Wickham and),* d. 17 *Sept.* 1895; *and had issue.*
See the Clarence Volume, p. 364, Nos. 12436–12437.

4a. *Lucy Elizabeth Tichborne,* b. 1801; d. *Jan.* 1884; m. *George Nangle, son of Walter Nangle of Kildalkey, co. Meath.*   [Nos. 11047 to 11072.

178. Descendants of LUCY MARY PLOWDEN (see Table XVI.), d. (–); m. ANTHONY WRIGHT of Wealside, co. Essex, d. (–); and had issue 1a to 4a.

1a. *Anthony George Wright, afterwards* (1835) *Wright-Biddulph of Fitzwalters, co. Essex, and of Biddulph and Burton, co. Sussex,* d. (–); m. 15 *Jan.* 1827, *Catharine Dorothy, da. of Simon Thomas Scrope of Danby, de jure* 19*th Earl of Wilts* [*E.*], d. 4 *Ap.* 1884; *and had issue* 1b *to* 3b.

1b. *Anthony John Wright-Biddulph,* b. 27 *Jan.* 1830; d.s.p.

2b. *Clementina Maria Wright-Biddulph,* b. 2 *June* 1832; m. 2 *Aug.* 1860, *Charles John Radcliffe (Ordsall, Twyford, Berks);* and has issue 1c to 4c.

1c. *Joseph Anthony Radcliffe,* b. 30 *July* 1861.

2c. *Charles James Forbes Radcliffe (Whavelunga, Telewaite, New Zealand),* b. 8 *July* 1864; m. 20 *Mar.* 1901, *Caroline Emily Ann, da. of John Octavius Weston of the Lindens, Picton, N.Z.*

3c. *Arthur Ranald Macdonell Radcliffe,* b. 1 *June* 1867.

4c. *Gwendaline Amelia Mary Radcliffe.*

3b. *Geraldine Mary Wright-Biddulph,* b. 26 *Nov.* 1835; m. 14 *Ap.* 1863, *Capt. Godfrey Edward Allaster Radcliffe (Dan-y-Graig, Grosmont, co. Monmouth);* and has issue 1c to 2c.

1c. *Allaster Joseph Radcliffe,* b. 12 *June* 1867.

2c. *Mary Frances Radcliffe,* b. 28 *Mar.* 1864.

2a. *John Wright.*

3a. *Mary Wright,* d. 19 *Dec.* 1854; m. 1808, *Vincent Henry Eyre of Highfield and Newbold, High Sheriff co. Derby,* b. 20 *Jan.* 1775; d. 5 *June* 1851; *and had issue* 1b *to* 2b.

1b. *Vincent Anthony Eyre of Lindley Hall, co. Leicester, and Newbold, co. Derby,* b. 8 *Aug.* 1809; d. 22 *Mar.* 1887; m. 1*st,* 6 *Ap.* 1842, *Anne, da. of Edward Huddleston of Sawston Hall, co. Camb.,* d. 19 *Ap.* 1881; *and had issue* 1c *to* 6c.

1c. *Vincent Thomas Eyre of Lindley Hall, Capt.* 6*th Inniskilling Dragoons,* b. 29 *Jan.* 1843; d. 26 *Sept.* 1893; m. 8 *Sept.* 1873, *Barbara Agnes Caroline, da. of Thomas Giffard of Chillington; and had issue* 1d *to* 5d.   [Nos. 11073 to 11081.

278

# of The Blood Royal

1*d*. Vincent Thomas Joseph Eyre (*Lindley Hall, Nuneaton; Newbold, co. Derby*), *b*. 17 Nov. 1880.

2*d*. Reginald Francis Eyre, *b*. 5 June 1882.

3*d*. Valentine William Eyre, *b*. 16 Sept. 1888.

4*d*. Barbara Gertrude Mary Eyre.

5*d*. Muriel Frances Eyre.

2*c*. Arthur Henry Eyre, *b*. 13 Sept. 1851; *m*. 6 June 1874, Julia, da. of [——] O'Conor; and has issue 1*d*.

1*d*. Arthur Nevile Eyre, *b*. May 1876.

3*c*. Ferdinand John Eyre, J.P., High Sheriff co. Suffolk (*Moreton Hall, Suffolk; 5 Berkeley Square, W.*), *b*. 22 Aug. 1854; *m*. 21 June 1880, Mary Gabrielle, da. of Sir Henry Richard Paston-Bedingfeld, 6th Bart. [E.].

4*c*. *Isabella Mary Eyre*, d. (*at Rome*) 7 *Dec*. 1866; *m*. 9 *Sept*. 1865, *Major Henry John Darell of Calehill*, b. 25 *June* 1819; d. 9 *June* 1868.

5*c*. Julia Maria Eyre, *m*. 1st, Oct. 1868, Anthony Morris; 2ndly, 14 Feb. 1899, Charles H. Robarts; and has issue (by 1st husband).

6*c*. Matilda Eyre, *m*. 1884, Robert Pryor.

2*b*. *Anne Mary Eyre*, b. 1816; d. 22 *Oct*. 1842; *m*. 24 *Nov*. 1836, *John Errington of High Warden, J.P., D.L., High Sheriff co. Northumberland* 1865, b. 4 *Oct*. 1807; d. 11 *Dec*. 1878; *and had issue* 1*c*.

1*c*. Anne Lucy Errington, *m*. 13 Oct. 1862, John Francis (Arundell), 12th Baron Arundell of Wardour [E.], and Count Arundell [H.R.E.] (*Wardour Castle, Tisbury*).

4*a*. *Anne Wright*, d. 24 *Oct*. 1838; *m*. *as 2nd wife*, 2 *July* 1812, *Sir Charles Wolseley of Wolseley, 7th Bart*. [E.], b. 20 *July* 1769; d. 3 *Oct*. 1846; *and had issue* 1*b* to 3*b*.

1*b*. *Sir Charles Wolseley, 8th Bart*. [E.], b. 6 *May* 1813; d. 15 *May* 1854; *m*. 23 *Sept*. 1839, *Mary Anne, da. of Nicholas Selby of Acton House, co. Midx.*, d. 18 *Jan*. 1873; *and had issue* 1*c* to 3*c*.

1*c*. Sir Charles Michael Wolseley, 9th Bart. [E.], J.P., D.L. (*Wolseley Hall, Stafford*), *b*. 4 July 1846; *m*. 17 July 1883, Anita Theresa, da. of Daniel T. Murphy of New York and San Francisco; and has issue 1*d* to 2*d*.

1*d*. Edric Charles Joseph Wolseley, *b*. 7 Ap. 1886.

2*d*. William Ralph Wolseley, *b*. 1 July 1887.

2*c*. Edward Talbot Wolseley, *late* Capt. 3rd Stafford Militia (*Maryland, Ascot*), *b*. 13 Oct. 1848; *m*. 23 Jan. 1872, Frances Mary, da. of Edward Joseph Weld of Lulworth Castle; and has issue.

See the Clarence Volume, p. 368, Nos. 12570–12575.

3*c*. Rev. Robert Joseph Wolseley (R.L.) (*The Presbytery, Mount St. Ervan's, Grenville, Grenada, W.I.*).

2*b*. *Marianne Wolseley*, d. 1 *Nov*. 1884; m. 25 *Nov*. 1834, *Francis (de Lousada), 1st Marquis of San Miniato* (1846) [*Tuscany*], *H.B.M. Consul for Rhode Island and Massachusetts*, b. *Nov*. 1813; d. (*at Boston*) 17 *Mar*. 1870; *and had issue* 1*c* to 2*c*.

1*c*. *Horace Francis (de Lousada), 2nd Marquis of San Miniato* [*Tuscany*], *and* (20 *Feb*. 1880) *5th Duke of Losada and Lousada* (1759), *and a Grandee of the 1st Class* [*Spain*], *formerly Lieut.-Col. 5th Madras N.I.*, b. 29 *Sept*. 1837; d. *unm*. 26 *Dec*. 1905.

2*c*. Francis Clifford (de Lousada), 6th Duke of Losada and Lousada [Spain] and 3rd Marquis of San Miniato [Tuscany], Comm. (ret.) R.N. (*4 Lancaster Street, Hyde Park, W.*), *b*. 17 Oct. 1842; *m*. 20 Dec. 1879, Emily Florence, widow of Sir Eardley Gideon Culling Eardley, 4th Bart. [U.K.], da. and h. of James Somers Magee of New Orleans, and the Lodge, co. Antrim.   [Nos. 11082 to 11104.

279

ᚦe Plantagenet Roll

3b. *Caroline Wolseley*, d. 23 *Sept.* 1880 ; m. 22 *Aug.* 1845, *Marmaduke Charles Salvin of Burnhall, Durham, J.P., D.L.,* b. 11 *Feb.* 1812 ; d. 27 *Dec.* 1885 ; *and had issue* 1c *to* 6c.

1c. Marmaduke Henry Salvin (*Burn Hall, Durham ; Sarnesfield Court, co. Worcester*), b. 28 Mar. 1849 ; m. 24 Feb. 1897, Annette Mary, da. of Sir William Vavasour, 3rd Bart. [U.K.].

2c. Mary Salvin.

3c. Louisa Mary Salvin, m. 20 Aug. 1878, Philip Witham (*Sutton Place, Guildford*) ; and has issue.

4c. Teresa Mary Salvin, m. 28 Nov. 1876, Charles Ernest Bell, *late* of Park House, Durham ; and has issue.

5c. Agnes Mary Salvin, m. 21 Oct. 1886, Edward Cayley Worsley.

6c. Francesca Josephine Salvin, m. 25 Sept. 1877, George Oswald Sharples, *late* of Wavertree, Liverpool ; and has issue. [Nos. 11105 to 11110.

179. Descendants, if any, of FRANCES PLOWDEN, wife of ROBERT TAAFFE of Ireland ; ANNE MARY PLOWDEN, wife of EDWARD HAGGERSTON ; and of MARY PLOWDEN, wife of ROBERT GARVEY of Rouen (see Table XVI.).

180. Descendants, if any surviving, of PENELOPE PLOWDEN (see Table XVI.), b. 1699 ; d. 25 June 1778 ; m.[1] as 2nd wife, 1723, NORTH FOLEY of Stourbridge, *bapt.* 16 Sept. 1677 ; *bur.* 13 Feb. 1728.

181. Descendants of PLOWDEN SLANEY of Hatton Grange, co. Salop (see Table XVI.), b. 22 Aug. 1724 ; *bur.* 7 Feb. 1788 ; m. 15 June 1761, MARTHA, da. and co-h. of Humphrey PITT of Priors Lee, co. Salop, d. 9 Nov. 1811 ; and had issue 1a.

1a. *Robert Slaney of Hatton Grange,* b. 12 *June* 1764 ; d. 12 *Feb.* 1834 ; m. *Aug.* 1790, *Mary, da. of Thomas Mason of Shrewsbury ; and had issue* 1b.

1b. *Robert Aglionby Slaney of Hatton Grange and Walford Manor, M.P., J.P.,* b. 9 *June* 1791 ; d. 19 *May* 1862 ; m. 1*st,* 17 *Feb.* 1812, *Elizabeth, da. and h. of William Hawkins Muccleston of Walford Manor ; and had issue* 1c *to* 3c.

1c. *Elizabeth Frances Slaney,* d. 26 *Nov.* 1870 ; m. 13 *May* 1835, *Thomas Campbell Eyton of Eyton, J.P., D.L.,* b. 10 *Sept.* 1809 ; d. *Oct.* 1880 ; *and had issue* 1d *to* 7d.

1d. *Thomas Slaney Eyton of Eyton and Walford Hall, J.P., D.L., High Sheriff co. Salop* 1890, b. 19 *June* 1843 ; d. 25 *May* 1899 ; m. 10 *Mar.* 1866, *Isabel Sarah Dashwood, da. of John Henry Hay Ruxton of Broad Oak, Brenchley ; and had issue* 1e *to* 2e.

1e. *Ralph Aglionby Slaney Eyton Eyton, J.P., b. 28 Aug.* 1870 ; d. *unm.* 190–.

2e. Isabel Margaret Hay, m. 26 Ap. 1889, Charles Edward Morris, J.P., High Sheriff co. Salop 1905 (*Wood Eaton Manor, Stafford ; Calvington, Newport, co. Salop*) ; and has issue 1f to 7f. [No. 11111.

---

[1] Nash's " Worcester," ii. p. 468. Burke, " Landed Gentry," says she m. 1st, Thomas Foley of Stourbridge ; 2ndly, Richard Whitworth. By North Foley she had a son and 2 daughters, who all *d.s.p.*

# of The Blood Royal

1f. Charles Reginald Morris, *b.* 21 July 1890.
2f. Robert Edward Morris, *b.* 24 Jan. 1893.
3f. Constance Isabel Morris.
4f. Rose Margaret Eleanor Morris.
5f. Mary Penelope Morris.
6f. Violet Catherine Morris.
7f. Elizabeth Sarah Morris.

2d. Robert Henry Eyton, *b.* 7 Dec. 1845; *m.* 26 Aug. 1866, Eleanor Josephine, da. of Francis Fosbery of Currahbridge, co. Limerick; and has issue 1*e* to 5*e*.
1e. Hugh Eyton.
2e. Charles Eyton.
3e. Cecil Eyton.
4e. Alice Eyton.
5e. Vera Eyton.

3d. Elizabeth Charlotte Eyton, *b.* 7 July 1838.
4d. Rose Mary Eyton, *b.* 10 Feb. 1840.
5d. Frances Julia Eyton, b. *27 June* 1841; *d.* 28 *July* 1887; *m.* 3 *Ap.* 1866, *the Rev. Frederick Freeman O'Donoghue of Market Rasen, M.A.,* d. *May* 1887; *and had issue* 1*e*.
1e. Kathleen Maud O'Donoghue, *m.* 10 Oct. 1893, the Rev. Francis Wolferstan Toms (*Combe Martin Rectory, N. Devon*); and has issue 1*f* to 3*f*.
1f. Rose Mary Toms, *b.* 24 Aug. 1895.
2f. Sylvia Frances Toms, *b.* 18 May 1897.
3f. Honora Kathleen Toms, *b.* 23 Nov. 1898.

6d. Katharine Anne Eyton, *b.* 7 Nov. 1844; *m.* 7 Ap. 1869, the Rev. Daniel George Lysons, M.A. (Oxon.), Vicar of Rowsley (*Rowsley Vicarage, co. Derby*); and has issue 1*e* to 9*e*.
1e. Herbert Bertram Daniel Lysons, *b.* 6 May 1873.
2e. Noel Heldebrand Lysons, *b.* 16 Dec. 1875.
3e. Kenneth Campbell Lysons, *b.* 17 Oct. 1879.
4e. Beatrice Margaret Lysons, *b.* 23 Feb. 1870.
5e. Monica Frances Elizabeth Lysons, *b.* 20 Sept. 1874.
6e. Rhoda Mary Lysons, *b.* 26 Aug. 1877; *m.* 27 Sept. 1905, J. Wilfred Mather of Costa Rica.
7e. Muriel Alice Montgomery Lysons, *b.* 23 June 1881.
8e. Irene Agnes Lysons, *b.* 22 Jan. 1884.
9e. Esmé Katharine Lysons, *b.* 22 Dec. 1885.

7d. Mary Elizabeth Eyton.

2c. Mary Slaney, d. 17 *May* 1866; *m.* 8 *May* 1839, *William Watkin Edward Wynne of Peniarth, M.P., J.P., D.L., Constable of Harlech Castle,* b. 23 Dec. 1801; *d.* 9 *June* 1880; *and had issue* 1*d* to 2*d*.
1d. William Robert Maurice Wynne, Lord-Lieut. co. Merioneth, Constable of Harlech Castle, J.P., D.L., &c. (*Peniarth, Towyn, co. Merioneth*), *b.* Feb. 1840; *m.* 20 May 1891, Fanny, widow of R. T. Williamson, da. of William Kendall.
2d. Owen Slaney Wynne, J.P., D.L. (*Doluwcheogryd, Dolgelly, co. Merioneth*), *b.* 17 Oct. 1842; *m.* 1 Oct. 1870, Mary, widow of F. P. Davies of Barmouth, da. of Edward Owen of Garthyngharad, *d.* 23 May 1900.

3c. Frances Catherine Slaney of Hatton Grange, d. 18 *Oct.* 1896; *m.* 9 *Oct.* 1845, *Lieut.-Col. William Kenyon, afterwards* (*R.L.* 23 *July* 1862) *Kenyon-Slaney, J.P., D.L., High Sheriff co. Salop* 1871, *b.* 20 *Feb.* 1815; *d.* 10 *Dec.* 1884; *and had issue* 1*d to* 7*d*. [Nos. 11112 to 11143.

The Plantagenet Roll

1*d*. Right Hon. William Slaney Kenyon-Slaney, P.C., M.P., J.P., D.L., *late* Col. Grenadier Guards (*Hatton Grange, near Shifnal*), *b*. 24 Aug. 1847; *m*. 22 Feb. 1887, Lady Mabel Selena, da. of Orlando (Bridgeman), 3rd Earl of Bradford [U.K.]; and has issue 1*e* to 2*e*.

    1*e*. Robert Orlando Rodolph Kenyon-Slaney, *b*. 13 Jan. 1892.

    2*e*. Sybil Agnes Kenyon-Slaney, *b*. 26 Jan. 1888.

2*d*. Walter Rupert Kenyon-Slaney, Lieut.-Col. 3rd Batt. Rifle Brigade, *b*. 25 Sept. 1851; *m*. 4 Sept. 1878, May, da. of H. J. Schooles, M.D.; and has issue 1*e*.

    1*e*. Neville Aglionby Kenyon-Slaney, *b*. 26 July 1879.

3*d*. Francis Gerald Kenyon-Slaney, Major Durham L.I., *b*. 7 Nov. 1858; *m*. 19 July 1892, Edith Mary Sherwin, da. of Major Joseph Holt of Egbeare, co. Cornwall.

4*d*. Percy Robert Kenyon-Slaney (*Bratton Clovelly, Lew Down, R.S.O., North Devon, La Florida, Estacion Alvarez, Rosario, Argentina*), *b*. 9 June 1861; *m*. 25 Ap. 1895, Geraldine Ellen Georgina, da. of the Rev. George Whitmore; and has issue 1*e* to 3*e*.

    1*e*. Philip Percy Kenyon-Slaney, *b*. 12 Feb. 1896.

    2*e*. Gerald William Kenyon-Slaney, *b*. 20 July 1899.

    3*e*. Frances Diamond Sara Kenyon-Slaney, *b*. 19 July 1897.

5*d*. Agnes Charlotte Kenyon-Slaney.

6*d*. Katherine Maud Kenyon-Slaney.

7*d*. Violet Mabel Kenyon-Slaney.   [Nos. 11144 to 11156.

182. Descendants, if any surviving, of FRANCES SLANEY (see Table XVI.) and of her sisters ANNE, JANE, and ELIZABETH, *m*. 27 Feb. 1754, THOMAS PRESLAND of Walford.

183. Descendants of JOHN JOSEPH TALBOT (see Table XVI.), *b*. 9 June 1765; *d*. 8 Aug. 1815; *m*. 1st, 29 May 1789, CATHERINE, da. of Thomas CLIFTON of Lytham, *d*. May 1791; 2ndly, 4 May 1797, HARRIET ANNE, da. of the Rev. Bacon BEDINGFELD of Ditchingham Hall (who *re-m*. (at Paris) as 1st wife, 31 Dec. 1815, the Hon. HENRY ROPER CURZON, *afterwards* (1842) 15th BARON TEYNHAM [E.], and) *d*. 7 June 1839; and had issue 1*a* to 4*a*.

    1*a*. (Son by 1st wife.) See p. 82, Nos. 287–332.

    2*a*. George Henry Talbot, *d*. 11 *June* 1839; *m*. 6 *Ap*. 1829, *Augusta Jones, illegitimate da. of Sir Horace St. Paul, 1st Bart. [U.K.] (who re-m. as 1st wife, 10 Sept. 1839, the Hon. Craven Fitzhardinge Berkeley, and), d*. 25 *Ap*. 1841; *and had issue 1b*.

        1*b*. *Augusta Talbot* (*sole heir* 1846), *d*. 3 *July* 1862; *m*. *as 1st wife*, 22 *July* 1851, *Edward George* (*Fitzalan-Howard*), 1st *Baron Howard of Glossop* [U.K.], P.C., *b*. 20 *Jan*. 1818; *d*. 1 *Dec*. 1883; *and had issue.*

        See the Tudor Roll of "The Blood Royal of Britain," pp. 372–373, Nos. 28212–28233.

    3*a*. *Harriet Talbot*, *d*. (*at Brussels*) 9 *Oct*. 1866; *m*. 19 *Oct*. 1829, *John W. Searle*, *d*. 1861.

    4*a*. *Susan Margaret Talbot*, *d*. (? *unm.*).   [Nos. 11157 to 11225.

282

# of The Blood Royal

184. Descendants of BARBARA TALBOT (see Table XVI.), d. 4 June 1806; m. 9 Ap. 1780, FRANCIS FORTESCUE TURVILLE of Husbands Bosworth, co. Leicester, d. 13 July 1839; and had issue.

See p. 273, No. 10485.   [No. 11226.

185. Descendants of JULIANA TALBOT (see Table XVI.), d. (-); m. 7 June 1784, MICHAEL BRYAN, Connoisseur, author of " The Biographical and Critical Dictionary of Painters and Engravers," b. 9 Ap. 1757 ; d. 21 Mar. 1821 ; and had issue (with possible other issue) 1a.

1a. *Marianne Bryan*, b. (*at Bruges*) 23 *Jan.* 1796; d. 31 *Aug.* 1838; m. 7 *Ap.* 1818, *Thomas Peacock ; and had (with other) issue* 1b.

1b. Theresa Talbot Peacock (8th da.), *m.* as 2nd wife, 1855, Sir James Laing, J.P., D.L., High Sheriff co. Durham 1879 (*Thornhill, Sunderland ; Etal Manor, Cornhill, co. Northumberland*) ; and has issue 1c to 13c.

1c. *Arthur Laing*, b. 1856 ; d. 16 *Mar.* 1901 ; m. 1882, *Jean Arabella, da. of the Rev. John Scott Moncrieff ; and had issue* 1d.

1d. Colin Moncrieff Laing.

2c. *James Laing*, b. 7 *Mar.* 1858 ; d. 23 *Jan.* 1895 ; m. 12 *Jan.* 1886, *Emily Cecilia, da. of Thomas Elliot Harrison of Whitburn ; and had issue.*

3c. George Laing, *b.* 13 May 1866 ; *m.* 16 May 1890, Annie Mulholland, da. of the Rev. Henry Stobart of Wykeham Rise, Totteridge ; and has issue.

4c. Hugh Laing, b. 1871.

5c. Bryan Laing, *b.* 1875 ; *m.* 17 Oct. 1901, Eleanor, da. of Frederick John Leather of Middleton Hall, co. Northumberland, J.P.

6c. Florence Talbot Laing, *m.* 2 Feb. 1882, Alwyn de Blaquiere Valentine Paget, Lieut.-Col. *late* Durham L.I. (124 *Belgrave Road, S.W.*); and has issue 1d to 4d.

1d. Rupert Alwyn Paget, Lieut. Queen's Own, *b.* 14 Dec. 1882.

2d. Gladys Theresa Paget, *b.* 7 Sept. 1885.

3d. Florence Eleanor Paget, *b.* 25 Sept. 1887.

4d. Kathleen Louisa Paget, *b.* 6 June 1896.

7c. Theresa Talbot Laing.

8c. Mabel Talbot Laing, *m.* 30 Jan. 1894, Col. H. V. Cowan, R.H.A.

9c. Maud Talbot Laing, *m.* 18 Ap. 1900, the Rev. Cyril Robert Carter, Fellow of Magdalen College, Oxford.

10c. Sophia Talbot Laing, *m.* 28 July 1891, Percival Charles du Sautoy Leather, *late* Capt. 5th Batt. Northumberland Fusiliers (*Northumberland Estate, Ceylon*); and has issue 1d to 3d.

1d. Paul du Sautoy Leather, *b.* 3 Oct. 1900.

2d. Mabel Dorothy Leather, *b.* 30 Oct. 1892.

3d. Olive Margaret Leather, *b.* 16 Aug. 1896.

11c. Margaret Dunbar Laing, *m.* 11 Aug. 1891, Lieut.-Col. Alfred Stokes, D.S.O., R.H.A.

12c. Eleanor Stepney Laing.

13c. Louisa Harcourt Laing.   [Nos. 11227 to 11246.

The Plantagenet Roll

186. Descendants of Lady THERESA TALBOT (see Table XVI.), *d.* 1 Jan. 1823; *m.* 5 Feb. 1793, ROBERT SELBY (youngest son of Thomas Selby of Biddlestone), *d.* (–) ; and had issue 1*a*.

1*a*. *John Thomas Selby, Cameriere Segreto di Cappa Spada to H. H. Pope Pius IX., Com. St. Gregory the Great and Knight of Francis I. of Naples,* b. 1804; d. 1 *July* 1872; m. *Anna Maria, da. of John Searle of Molesworth, co. Hunts; and had issue* 1*b to* 3*b*.

1*b*. *Robert John Selby,* d. *(in Florence)* 19 *Mar.* 1875; m. 26 *July* 1858, *Caroline, da. of* [——], *Count di San Giorgio* (*by his wife Lady Anne,* née *Harley*); *and had issue* 1*c to* 3*c*.

1*c*. *William Selby,* d. (–) ; m. *Nov.* 1903; *and had issue (a son and da.).*

2*c*. Walter Selby.

3*c*. Robert Selby.

2*b*. *John George Falconberg de Selby,* d. 10 *Ap.* 1903; m. *Henrietta Maria, da. of Andrew John Maley of Merrion Square, Dublin; and had issue* 1*c to* 2*c*.

1*c*. Henrietta Maria Georgiana de Selby.

2*c*. Margaret Maria Hilda de Selby.

3*b*. *Anna Maria Theresa Selby,* d. 10 *June* 1872; m. 20 *Dec.* 1870, *Edward Walter Farrell; and had issue* 1*c*.

1*c*. Flavia Farrell (10 *Avenue MacMahon, Paris*).　　　[Nos. 11247 to 11251.

187. Descendants of the Hon. FRANCIS TALBOT of Witham Place, co. Essex (see Table XVI.), *b.* 1727; *d.* 1813; *m.* 2ndly, 18 May 1772, MARGARET FRANCES, da. of William SHELDON of Weston, co. Warwick; and had issue 1*a* to 2*a*.

1*a*. *Charles Thomas Talbot, Lieut.-Col. in the Army,* b. 24 *Nov.* 1782; d. 30 *Ap.* 1838; m. 1 *Feb.* 1830, *Julia, da. of Sir Henry Joseph Tichborne, 8th Bart.* [E.] (*who re-m.* 1839, *John Hubert Washington Hibbert of Bilton Grange and*), d. 4 *June* 1792; *and had issue.*
See p. 277, Nos. 10996–11031.

2*a*. *Maria Talbot,* d. (app. s.p.) 25 *Ap.* 1814; m. 22 *Sept.* 1802, *James Wheble of Woodley Lodge, co. Berks.*　　　[Nos. 11252 to 11287.

188. Descendants of BARBARA TALBOT (see Table XVI.), *d.* (in Paris) Oct. 1759; *m.* 30 June 1742, JAMES (ASTON), 5th LORD ASTON of Forfar [S.], *b.* 1723; *d.* 24 Aug. 1751; and had issue.

See the Clarence Volume, Table XL., pp. 377–381, Nos. 12970–13141.
[Nos. 11288 to 11446.

189. Descendants, if any, of ANNE TALBOT (see Table XVI.), wife of [——] TALBOT of Hampstead.

190. Descendants, if any, of Lady CATHERINE TALBOT (see Table XVI.), wife of THOMAS WHITENALL of East Peckham, co. Kent.

# of The Blood Royal

191. Descendants of MARY ARUNDELL (see Table XVI.), *d.* (–); *m.* about 1708, JOHN BIDDULPH of Biddulph Castle, co. Stafford, and Burton, co. Sussex, *b.* about 1675; *d.* May 1720; and had issue 1*a* to 4*a*.

1*a*. *Richard Biddulph of Burton, b. c. 1707; d. unm. 1767.*

2*a*. *Charles Biddulph of Burton, d. 17 May 1784; m. 1st, Elizabeth, da. of Sir Henry Arundell Bedingfeld, 3rd Bart. [E.], d. 1763; 2ndly, Frances Appollonia, widow of Henry Wells, da. of George Brownlow Doughty of Snarford; and had issue 1b.*

1*b*. *John Biddulph of Biddulph and Burton, d. unm. 2 Aug. 1835.*

3*a*. *Mary Biddulph, b. 1710; d. 14 June 1778; m. 19 Ap. 1732, Thomas Stonor of Stonor, co. Oxford, d. 2 Feb. 1772.*

See the Clarence Volume, Table XLVIII., pp. 418–419, Nos. 15809–15908.

4*a*. *Anne Biddulph, d.* (–); *m. Anthony Wright of Wealside, co. Essex; and had (with possibly other) issue 1b.*

1*b*. *Anthony Wright of Wealside, d.* (–); *m. Lucy Mary, da. of Edmund Plowden of Plowden; and had issue.*

See pp. 278–280, Nos. 11073–11110.   [Nos. 11447 to 11584.

192. Descendants of JAMES (TUCHET), 6th EARL OF CASTLEHAVEN [I.] and 16th BARON AUDLEY [E.] (see Table XVI.), *d.* (in Paris) 12 Oct. 1740; *m.* 24 May 1722, ELIZABETH, da. of HENRY (ARUNDELL), 4th BARON ARUNDELL of Wardour [E.], *b.* 15 Sept. 1693; *d.* July 1743; and had issue.

See the Clarence Volume, Table LVI., pp. 469–471, Nos. 20812–20851.
[Nos. 11585 to 11624.

193. Descendants of CADWALLADER (BLAYNEY), 9th LORD BLAYNEY, BARON OF MONAGHAN [I.] (see Table XVI.), *b.* 2 May 1720; *d.* 21 Nov. 1775; *m.* 22 Dec. 1767, ELIZABETH, da. of Thomas TIPPING of Beaulieu, co. Louth, *d.* 17 May 1775; and had issue 1*a* to 4*a*.

1*a*. *Cadwallader Davis (Blayney), 10th Lord Blayney, Baron of Monaghan [I.], b.1769; d. unm. 2 Ap. 1784.*

2*a*. *Andrew Thomas (Blayney), 11th Lord Blayney, Baron of Monaghan [I.], b. 30 Nov. 1770; d. 8 Ap. 1834; m. 5 July 1796, Lady Mabella, da. of James (Alexander), 1st Earl of Caledon [I.], b. 7 Aug. 1775; d. 4 Mar. 1854; and had issue 1b to 2b.*

1*b*. *Cadwallader Davis (Blayney), 12th and last Lord Blayney, Baron of Monaghan [I.], b. 19 Dec. 1802; d. unm. 18 Jan. 1874.*

2*b*. *Hon. Anne Blayney, d. 11 Dec. 1882; m. 20 Nov. 1818, Admiral Charles Gordon, R.N., C.B.; and had issue 1c.*

1*c*. *Jane Gordon, d.* (–); *m. 1st, 1840, the Rev. James Henry Scudamore Burr; 2ndly, as 2nd wife, 7 Jan. 1853, the Rev. Francis Lewis of St. Pierre, co. Monmouth, J.P., D.L., d. (s.p. by her) Feb. 1872; 3rdly, Capt. Rolland of Dibden Lodge, Hythe, Southampton; and had issue by 1st husband (a son and da., the latter of whom m. Francis Moggridge, and had an eldest da., Mary Eleanor, who m. recently (at St. James' Church, Piccadilly) Arthur Campbell Way of Spalding, co. Norfolk), yr. son of Charles Martin Wade of Spaynes Hall, Yeldham, Essex.*

3*a*. *Hon. Sophia Blayney, d.* (–); *m. 1788, John Armstrong of Lisgoole, co. Fermanagh; and had issue 1b.*

The Plantagenet Roll

1b. Elizabeth Armstrong, d. 12 *June* 1853 ; m. 8 *June* 1808, *Sir Charles Smith, afterwards (R.L.* 12 *Mar.* 1846) *Dodsworth, 3rd Bart.* [*G.B.*], b. 22 *Aug.* 1775 ; d. 28 *July* 1857 ; *and had issue* 1c *to* 7c.

1c. *Sir Matthew Smith-Dodsworth, 4th Bart.* [*G.B.*], b. 6 *Feb.* 1819 ; d. 30 *Ap.* 1858 ; m. 23 *Sept.* 1852, *Anne Julia, da. of Col. John Crowder of Brotherton, co. Yorks, K.H.,* d. 26 *Feb.* 1890 ; *and had issue* 1d *to* 4d.

1d. *Sir Charles Edward Smith-Dodsworth, 5th Bart.* [*G.B.*], b. 27 *June* 1853 ; d.s.p. 5 *Aug.* 1891 ; m. 5 *Mar.* 1889, *Blanche, da. of the Hon. George Edwin Lascelles.*

2d. Sir Matthew Blayney Smith-Dodsworth, 6th Bart. [G.B.], J.P., C.C. (10 *Upper Belgrave Road, Clifton, Bristol*), b. 26 Oct. 1856 ; m. 8 Nov. 1887, Agnes Eliza, da. of John Crowder ; and has issue 1e to 3e.

1e. Claude Matthew Smith-Dodsworth, b. 12 Aug. 1888.

2e. Violet Agnes Smith-Dodsworth, b. 17 Dec. 1889.

3e. Hilda Monica Smith-Dodsworth, b. 1903.

3d. *Frederick Cadwallader Smith-Dodsworth,* 11th *Foot,* b. 15 *Aug.* 1858 ; d. 1900 ; m. 1888, *Hannah Elizabeth, da. of* [——] *Harrison of Littlerock Farm, Osceola co., Iowa, U.S.A.; and had issue* 1e.

1e. Dorothy Smith-Dodsworth (*Thornton Watlass, near Bedale*), b. 5 Nov. 1891.

4d. Henrietta Smith-Dodsworth, m. as 2nd wife, 23 Jan. 1886, Sir Henry Monson de la Poer Beresford Peirse, 3rd Bart. [U.K.] (*Aiskew House, Bedale*) ; and has issue.

See p. 244, Nos. 9141–9146.

2c. *Frederick Smith Smith-Dodsworth,* b. *Feb.* 1822 ; d. 11 *Oct.* 1885 ; m. 4 *May* 1848, *Jane Rebecca, da. of John Young of Westridge, I.W.; and had issue* 1d.

1d. Rose Alexandrine Elizabeth Maria Smith-Dodsworth, m. 9 Feb. 1891, Aymar (de Seyssel), Marquis of Aix and Sommariva [? Italy], d. 1896.

3c. *Henrietta Maria Smith-Dodsworth,* d. 1882 ; m. 1 *Dec.* 1858, *the Rev. Robert Whytehead, M.A., Rector of All Saints, Yorks.*

4c. *Elizabeth Smith-Dodsworth,* d. 21 *Nov.* 1867 ; m. 15 *Feb.* 1849, *Joseph D. Tetley of Kilgram, co. York; and had issue* 1d.

1d. William Charles Tetley, b. 13 Feb. 1851 ; m. 11 Sept. 1877, Anastasia, da. of the Rev. Josiah J. Prickett, Incumbent of Markington, York.

5c. *Frances Charlotte Smith-Dodsworth* (*St. Stephen's House, Acomb, Yorkshire*), m. 4 Sept. 1857, the Rev. James Le Maistre, LL.D., D.C.L., Rector of Everingham, d. 1899 ; and has issue 1d to 4d.

1d. Charles Matthew Hutton Dodsworth Le Maistre, M.A. (Dublin), Bar. I.T. (3 *Essex Court, Temple, E.C.*), b. 1858.

2d. Rev. Sylvester John James Sullivan Le Maistre, M.A. (Oxon.), Rector of Everingham (*Everingham Rectory, York*), b. (–) ; m. 1891, Constance Gertrude, da. of the Rev. Frederick Henry M. Blaydes ; and has issue 1e to 2e.

1e. [——] Le Maistre, b. 1893.

2e. [——] Le Maistre, b. 1892.

3d. Mabella Williama Charlotte Lane Le Maistre.

4d. Alice Frances Esther Jeune Le Maistre.

6c. *Catherine Smith-Dodsworth,* d. 8 *Oct.* 1900 ; m. *as* 2nd *wife,* 15 *Ap.* 1844, *John Dalton of Sleningford Park,* d. 1 *July* 1864 ; *and had issue* 1d *to* 2d.

1d. *Charles Montagu Cecil Dalton,* d. (*in Canada*) ; m.; *and had issue, now resident in America.*

2d. *Catherine Elizabeth Dalton,* m. 13 *May* 1867, *William Driffield of Huntingdon, co. York; and had issue.*

7c. Charlotte Salisbury Smith-Dodsworth (*Wetton House, Bridlington Quay*).

[Nos. 11625 to 11646.

286

# of The Blood Royal

4a. *Hon. Mary Blayney, d. 1800; m. 1794, Edmund Tipping of Bellurgan Park, Dundalk, co. Louth; and had issue 1b.*

1b. *Catherine Tipping, d. (-); m. 1815, the Rev. Richard Hamilton, Rector of Culdaff and Cloncha, co. Donegal, d. 1842; and had issue 1c to 4c.*

1c. *Ven. Edward James Hamilton, Archdeacon of Derry,* b. 14 May 1819; d. 8 July 1896; m. 1844, *Georgina Susan, da. of Gen. George Vaughan Hart of Kilderry, M.P.,* d. 1882; *and had issue 1d to 7d.*

1d. *Edward Blayney Hamilton, Judge of Small Cause Court, Melbourne,* b. 1 Jan. 1845; d. 10 Sept. 1904; m. 1880, *Amy, da. of Judge Stephen, Melbourne; and had issue 1e to 3e.*

1e. Edward James Hamilton, *b.* 17 Oct. 1881.

2e. Catherine Charlotte Hamilton.

3e. Ida Hamilton.

2d. Richard Hart Hamilton (*Muralh, Locarno, Switzerland*), b. 22 Mar. 1846; m. 17 July 1876, Helen, da. of Stephen M'Gusty, s.p.

3d. George Vaughan Hamilton, C.B., Lieut.-Col. (ret.) Army Service Corps (*Taragh, London Road, Cheltenham*), b. 22 Oct. 1851; m. 11 June 1879, Clementina, da. of James Connell of Conheath, N.B., s.p.

4d. William John Lawrence Hamilton (*Dromore, South Salt Springs, British Columbia*), b. 13 Mar. 1859; m. 1 Dec. 1883, Louisa, da. of Charles Hayward; and has issue (6 sons and 5 das.).

5d. Charlotte Ellerker Hamilton (*Rathmore, Portrush, co. Antrim*).

6d. Catherine Emily Hamilton, m. 4 Jan. 1880, the Rev. William Fitzroy Garstin, Rector of Glendoorn, *formerly* of Christ Church, Londonderry (*Glendoorn Rectory, Letterkenny, co. Donegal*); and has issue 1e to 7e.

1e. Edward James Hamilton Garstin, ⎫ b. (twins) 21 Nov. 1881.
2e. William FitzRoy Hamilton Garstin, ⎭

3e. George Christophulus Garstin, b. 21 Sept. 1883.

4e. John Loftus Garstin, b. 23 Feb. 1885.

5e. Richard Hart Garstin, b. 25 Mar. 1886.

6e. Norman Garstin, b. 22 Sept. 1893.

7e. Georgina May Garstin, b. 30 May 1889.

7d. Frances Alicia Harriette Hamilton, m. 3 Dec. 1881, Richard Erris Hamilton (**35** *Aylesbury Road, Dublin*); and has issue 1e.

1e. Frances Charlotte Ellerker Hamilton, b. 11 Oct. 1886.

2c. *Richard Tipping Hamilton, Local Govt. Inspector,* b. 26 Nov. 1821; d. 16 Oct. 1904; m. 29 Dec. 1849, *Anna, da. of Latham Blacker,* d. 30 June 1904; *and had issue 1d to 6d.*

1d. Richard Erris Hamilton (35 *Aylesbury Road, Dublin*), b. 21 Nov. 1850; m. 3 Dec. 1881, Frances Alicia Harriette, da. of Rev. Edward James Hamilton; and has issue 1e.

1e. See p. 287, No. 11663.

2d. Latham Blacker Hamilton (*Calcutta, India*), b. 25 Oct. 1853; m. 22 Sept. 1881, Elizabeth, da. of Dr. Lynch.

3d. Edward Lawrence Hamilton (36 *The Cedar House, South Myms, Herts; Oriental*), b. 4 Mar. 1858; m. 2 May 1900, Helena Ann, da. of the Rev. T. A. Lindon; and has issue 1e to 2e.

1e. Arthur Hans Hamilton, b. 28 May 1901.

2e. Alexander Philip Hamilton, b. 17 June 1902.

4d. Catherine Isabella Alicia Hamilton (3 *Pakenham Villas, Monkstown, co. Dublin*), b. 9 Jan. 1852.

5d. Harriette Elizabeth Georgina Hamilton (*St. Thomas' Hospital, S.E.*), b. 8 Feb. 1855.   [Nos. 11647 to 11671.

287

The Plantagenet Roll

6d. Alice Flora Hamilton, *b.* 8 May 1862; *m.* 20 Oct. 1886, George Herbert Ewart (*Firmount, Belfast*); and has issue 1*e* to 5*e*.

1*e*. Grace Hamilton Ewart, *b.* 26 Feb. 1890.

2*e*. Alice Rosalind Ewart, *b.* 30 Dec. 1892.

3*e*. Anna Kathleen Ewart, *b.* 15 Mar. 1894.

4*e*. Frances Madeline Ewart, *b.* 12 Mar. 1896.

5*e*. Helen Flora Ewart, *b.* 8 May 1898.

3c. Alicia Hamilton, b. *Ap.* 1818; d. *28 Nov.* 1867; m. 21 *Ap.* 1835, *Evory Kennedy of Queensbury Place, London, and Belgard Castle, co. Dublin, M.D., D.L., b. 28 Nov.* 1811; *d. Good Friday* 1886; *and had issue* 1*d to* 6*d.*

1d. Richard George Kennedy, Lieut.-Col. Bengal Staff Corps, formerly Capt. 18th Hussars, b. 18 *Nov.* 1841; *d.* 30 *Aug.* 1881; *m.* 1871, *Agnes Fanny, da. of Aylmer Harris; and had issue* 1*e.*

1*e*. Rev. Evory Hamilton Kennedy, Rector of Bale (*Bale Rectory, Norfolk*), *b.* 7 Aug. 1872; *m.* 4 Mar. 1905, Violet, da. of the Ven. Basil Wilberforce, Archdeacon of Westminster.

2d. James Gilbert Kennedy, b. 1855; *d.* 1895; *m.* 1*st,* 16 *Feb.* 1887, *Linda, da. of Capt. Seaton, d.* 1890; *2ndly, Susan, widow of* [——] *White, da. of* [——]; *and had issue* 1*e.*

1*e*. Eilleen Kennedy (*Graystones, co. Dublin*), *b.* 24 July 1888.

3d. Georgina Mary Kennedy (1 *Sussex Place, Hyde Park, W.*), *b.* 24 Dec. 1837; *m.* 9 Nov. 1882, James Hack Tuke, Banker, a member of the Congested Districts Board, Dublin, &c. &c., *d.* 13 Jan. 1896.

4d. Alice Mary Kennedy, *m.* 1st, 28 Aug. 1862, Sir Alexander Hutchinson Lawrence, 1st Bart. [U.K.], *b.* (at Allahabad) 1838; *d.* (in India) 27 Aug. 1864; 2ndly, 10 Oct. 1871, Sir George Young, 3rd Bart. [U.K.] (*Formosa Place, Cookham*); and has issue 1*e* to 4*e*.

1e. Sir Henry Hayes Lawrence, 2nd Bart. [U.K.], b. (at Lahore) 26 *Feb.* 1864; *d.* 27 *Oct.* 1898; *m.* 10 *Nov.* 1890, *Victoria Margaret (who re-m.* 1904 *the Rev. James Berkeley Bristow), da. of Theodore Walrond of* 65 *Lancaster Gate, C.B.; and had issue* 1*f to* 3*f.*

1*f*. Norah Margaret Lawrence, *b.* 16 Dec. 1891,

2*f*. Alice Henrietta Lawrence, *b.* 6 May 1896,   } (*Belgard, Clondalkin, co. Dublin*).

3*f*. Margaret Eacy Lawrence, *b.* 8 Sept. 1896,

2*e*. George Young, 2nd Sec. Diplo. Ser., *b.* 25 Oct. 1872; *m.* 24 Nov. 1904, Jessie Helen, da. of Sir Courtenay Peregrine Ilbert, K.C., S.I.C.I.E.

3*e*. Geoffrey Winthorp Young (22 *Sussex Villas, South Kensington*), *b.* 25 Oct. 1876.

4*e*. Edward Hilton Young, Bar. I.T. (22 *Sussex Villas, Kensington, W.*), *b.* 20 Mar. 1879.

5d. Mary Harriet Mabel Kennedy (*Larkfield, Ballybrack, co. Dublin*), *b.* 16 July 1849; *m.* 2 Oct. 1867, the Very Rev. H. H. Dickinson, Dean of the Chapel Royal, Dublin, and Vicar of St. Ann's, *d.* 17 May 1905; and has issue 1*e* to 6*e*.

1*e*. Charles Dickinson, J.P., F.S.I., Land Agent (*Larkfield, Ballybrack, co. Dublin*), *b.* 23 Ap. 1869; *m.* 30 Ap. 1901, Olive, da. of Edward Rawson of Carlow, M.D.; and has issue 1*f* to 2*f*.

1*f*. Edward Charles Norman Dickinson, *b.* 3 Dec. 1903.

2*f*. Elizabeth Olive Dickinson, *b.* 15 July 1902.

2*e*. Harold Evory Dickinson (*Bloemfontein, S. Africa*), *b.* 26 June 1872; *m.* 1902, Florence, da. of Major Brodrick; and has issue 1*f*.

1*f*. Kathleen Dickinson.

3*e*. Cyril Henry Dickinson, Bar.-at-Law (*St. Roman's, Clondalkin, co. Dublin*), *b.* 1 July 1876; *m.* 12 Aug. 1902, Aileen, da. of Major C. E. H. Duckett Steuart of Steuart's Lodge, co. Carlow.   [Nos. 11672 to 11694.

288

# of The Blood Royal

4e. Frank Dickinson, Farming in South Africa, *b.* 27 Mar. 1878; *m.* 1902, Milly, da. of Gen. Charles Marais; and has issue 1*f.*

1*f.* Mary Dickinson.

5e. Page Lawrence Dickinson, Architect (*Larkfield, Ballybrack, co. Dublin*), *b.* 8 Sept. 1881.

6e. Mabel Dickinson.

6d. Constance Letitia Kennedy (51 *Gunterstone Road, West Kensington, W.*), *b.* 11 Aug. 1850; *m.* 15 Feb. 1887, Jemmitt Joseph Stopford (son of the Ven. Edward Stopford, Archdeacon of Meath), *d.* 18 Aug. 1902; and has issue 1*e* to 4*e.*

1*e.* Robert Jemmet Stopford, *b.* 19 May 1895.

2*e.* Alice Katherine Stopford, *b.* 26 Mar. 1888.

3*e.* Edith Mary Stopford, *b.* 12 Aug. 1889.

4*e.* Elinor Dorothy Stopford, *b.* 9 Sept. 1890.

4c. Harriette Catherine Hamilton, C.I. (5 *Egerton Place, S.W.*), *b.* 1820; *m.* 26 Aug. 1841, John Laird Mair (Lawrence), 1st Baron Lawrence [U.K.], G.C.B., G.C.S.I., P.C., *b.* 4 Mar. 1811; *d.* 27 June 1879; and has issue 1*d* to 9*d.*

1*d.* John Hamilton (Lawrence), 2nd Baron Lawrence [U.K.], a Lord-in-Waiting to H.M. the King, &c. (*Chetwode Manor, co. Bucks ; 66 Pont Street, S.W.*), *b.* 1 Oct. 1846; *m.* 22 Aug. 1872, Mary Caroline Douglas, da. and h. of Richard Campbell of Auchinbreck; and has issue 1*e* to 2*e.*

1*e.* Hon. Alexander Graham Lawrence, Lieut. 3rd Batt. Bedford Regt., *b.* 29 Mar. 1878.

2*e.* Hon. Anna Douglas Lawrence, *b.* 15 July 1876.

2d. Hon. Henry Arnold Lawrence, b. *17 Mar.* 1847; d. *16 Ap.* 1902; m. 6 *May* 1879, *Constance Charlotte* (*Box House, Minchinhampton*), da. *of the Rev. George Irving Davies of Kelsale ; and had issue* 1e *to* 5e.

1*e.* Malcolm Eyton Lawrence, *b.* 10 Mar. 1889.

2*e.* Christopher Hal Lawrence, *b.* 11 Nov. 1893.

3*e.* Constance Letitia Lawrence, *b.* 26 Jan. 1881.

4*e.* Phyllis May Lawrence, *b.* 4 May 1882.

5*e.* Mary Pauline Lawrence, *b.* 27 Jan. 1886.

3d. Hon. Charles Napier Lawrence (23 *Eaton Square, S.W.*), *b.* 27 May 1855; *m.* 22 June 1881, Catherine Sumner, da. of Frederick Wiggin of New York.

4d. Hon. Herbert Alexander Lawrence, Lieut.-Col. Comdg. and Hon. Col. 4th County of London Imp. Yeo. (10 *Sloane Gardens, S.W.*), *b.* 8 Aug. 1861; *m.* 26 Ap. 1892, the Hon. Isabel Mary, da. of Charles (Mills), 1st Baron Hillingdon [U.K.]; and has issue 1*e* to 3*e.*

1*e.* Oliver John Lawrence, *b.* 5 Aug. 1893.

2*e.* Michael Charles Lawrence, *b.* 6 Oct. 1894.

3*e.* Elizabeth Peace Lawrence.

5d. Hon. Katharine Letitia Lawrence, *m.* 28 Jan. 1868, Col. William Lowndes Randall, *late* Indian Army (6 *Egerton Mansions, S.W.*); and has issue 1*e* to 5*e.*

1*e. John* Randall, *Capt. Indian Army,* b. 16 *Oct.* 1838; d. 13 *Sept.* 1905; m. 20 *July* 1899, *Grace, da. of* [——] *Keats.*

2*e.* Henry Lowndes Randall, Capt. South African Constabulary, *b.* 12 Oct. 1870.

3*e.* William Lawrence Randall (*Johannesburg, Transvaal*), *b.* 28 Jan. 1873; *m.* 7 Mar. 1899, Lilian, da. of [——] Purcell.

4*e.* James Randall, Wine Merchant, *b.* 9 May 1876; *m.* 25 Jan. 1905, Elantine Noel Nieta, da. of Madame Nieta.

5*e.* Neville Randall, Clerk in Child's Bank, *b.* 21 Ap. 1881.

6d. Hon. Harriette Emily Lawrence, *m.* 28 July 1877, Sir Henry Stewart Cunningham, K.C.I.E., *formerly* Judge of the High Court of Judicature, Calcutta (83 *Eaton Place, S.W.*); and has issue. [Nos. 11695 to 11723.

The Plantagenet Roll

7d. Hon. Alice Margaret Lawrence, *m.* 14 July 1870, the Rev. Lancelot Charles Walford, Vicar of St. Saviour's, Chelsea (12 *Basil Mansions, S.W.*); and has issue.
See the Clarence Volume, p. 482, Nos. 21083–21085.

8d. Hon. Mary Emma Lawrence, *m.* 27 Feb. 1872, Francis William Buxton, M.A., J.P., *late M.P.* (42 *Grosvenor Gardens, S.W.*); and has issue 1*e* to 8*e*.

1e. John Lawrence Buxton, Capt. Rifle Brigade, *b.* 1 Dec. 1877.

2e. Hugh Forster Buxton, *b.* Ap. 1882.

3e. Robert Vere Buxton, *b.* Ap. 1883.

4e. Ruth Buxton, *m.* 17 May 1898, Jocelyn Brudenell (Pelham), 6th Earl of Chichester [U.K.], 7th Baron Pelham [G.B.] (*Stanmer, Lewes*); and has issue 1*f* to 2*f*.

1f. Francis Godolphin Henry Pelham, Lord Pelham, *b.* 23 Mar. 1905.

2f. Lady Elizabeth Jocelyn Pelham, *b.* 27 Mar. 1899.

5e. Madeline Buxton, *m.* 26 Mar. 1901, Capt. George Sidney Clive, Grenadier Guards (*Perrystone Court, co. Hereford*); and has issue.

6e. Hilda Buxton.

7e. Frances Mary Buxton.

8e. Cecil Buxton.

9d. Hon. Maude Agnes Lawrence (5 *Egerton Place, S.W.*).

[Nos. 11724 to 11739.

194. Descendants of the Hon. MARY BLAYNEY (see Table XVI.), *b.* 16 Mar. 1716; *d.* (–); *m.* 1st, Dec. 1736, NICHOLAS MAHON; 2ndly, 1743, JOHN CAMPBELL of Dublin (said to have been a member of the Argyll family); and had issue 1*a* to 8*a*.[1]

1a. Cadwallader Campbell, b. May 1744.

2a. John Campbell, Lieut. in the Army.

3a. Charles Blayney Campbell.

4a. Moutray Campbell.

5a. Elinora Caroline Mahon, m. Joseph Corry of co. Monaghan.

6a. Mary Anne Campbell.

7a. Margaret Campbell.

8a. Elizabeth Campbell.

195. Descendants of MARY WINGFIELD (see Table XVI.), *d.* 20 Feb. 1765; *m.* (at St. Botolph's, Bishopsgate) 1732, FRANCIS DILLON of Proudstown, co. Meath, 1st BARON DILLON (1767) [H.R.E.], *d.* 10 Sept. 1775; and had issue 1*a* to 3*a*.

1a. John (Dillon), 2nd Baron Dillon [H.R.E.], b. 1734; d. 19 Mar. 1806; m. 1st, [——], d. (at Liege) 1768; 2ndly, [——], da. of Henry Collins; 3rdly, [——]; and had issue (at least by 2nd wife) 1b.

1b. William Henry (Dillon), 3rd Baron Dillon [H.R.E.], K.C.H., Vice-Admiral, R.N.,[2] b. 8 Aug. 1779; d. 1857.

2a. Baron Francis Dillon, Lieut.-Gen. and Col. of Cavalry in the Imperial Service, created a Baron of the Empire, d. (at Rome) 1789; m. Elizabeth, da. of P. Spendlove; and had issue 1b to 4b.

---

[1] Lodge's "Irish Peerage," vi. pp. 317–319.
[2] According to some accounts he was illegitimate.

# of The Blood Royal

1b. Charles (Dillon), 2nd Baron Dillon [H.R.E.], living 1829, when he was a claimant for the Great Chamberlainship of England.[1]
2b. Baroness Mary Elizabeth Dillon.
3b. Baroness Antonia Dillon.
4b. Baroness Roselia Dillon.

3a. Baron William Mervyn Dillon, m. Sophia, da. of Austin Pack Goddard of Brampton, co. Kent, Knight of St. Stephen of Tuscany; and had issue 1b to 2b.
1b. Baron John Joseph Dillon of Hatch House, co. Wilts, Knight and Baron of the Holy Roman Empire, Bar.-at-Law, a well-known writer of the early part of the nineteenth century.
2b. Baroness Henrietta Sophia Isabella Dillon.

196. Descendants, if any, of FRANCES VAVASOUR (see Table XVII.), wife of ALPHONSO THWENGE of Kilton Castle, co. York.

197. Descendants of FRANCES VAVASOUR (see Table XVII.), m. 1st, JAMES LAWSON of Nesham; 2ndly, PHILIP DOLMAN.

198. Descendants of HENRY (HOWARD), 6th DUKE OF NORFOLK (see Table XVIII.), b. 12 July 1628; d. 11 Jan. 1684; m. 1st, c. 1652, Lady ANNE, da. of Edward (SOMERSET), 2nd Marquis of Worcester [E.], d. (-); 2ndly, JANE, da. of Richard BICKERTON (who re-m. Col. THOMAS MAXWELL, and) d. 28 Aug. 1693; and had issue 1a to 5a.

1a.[1] Henry (Howard), 7th Duke of Norfolk, K.G., b. 11 Jan. 1654; d.s.p. 2 Ap. 1701.
2a.[1] Lord Thomas Howard of Worksop, co. Notts, d. 9 Nov. 1689; m. 11 Oct. 1681, Mary Elizabeth, da. and h. of Sir John Savile of Copley, 1st Bart. [E.], b. c. 1663; and had issue.
See the Clarence Volume, pp. 363–381, Nos. 12397–13141.
3a.[1] Lady Elizabeth Howard, d. 16 July 1732; m. Oct. 1676, George (Gordon), 1st Duke of Gordon [S.], d. 7 Dec. 1716; and had issue.
See the Clarence Volume, p. 381, Nos. 13142–14420.
4a. Lady Frances Howard, m. 1680, [——] Marquis Valparesa of Flanders [Spain].
5a.[2] Lady Philippa Howard, b. 1678; d. 5 Ap. 1731; m. Ralph Standish of Standish; and had issue 1b.
1b. Cecilia Standish of Standish, d. (-); m. William Towneley of Towneley, b. 1714; d. 2 Feb. 1741; and had issue.
See the Clarence Volume, pp. 314–316, Nos. 9083–9126.

[Nos. 11740 to 13799.

---

[1] See "Epitome of the Case of the Claim of the Dillon Family of Proudstown to the Great Chamberlainship of all England," by Sir John Joseph Dillon, Knight, and Baron S.R.E. London, 1829. His grandmother, Mary, wife of Francis Dillon of Proudstown, 1st Baron Dillon (1767), was only da. and h. of Sir Mervyn Wingfield, 6th Bart., who was great great great grandson and heir male of Sir Anthony Wingfield of Letheringtram, co. Suffolk, K.G., by his wife Elizabeth, eldest sister and co-h. of John (de Vere), 14th Earl of Oxford [E.], Hereditary Lord Great Chamberlain, who d.s.p.

The Plantagenet Roll

199. Descendants of BERNARD HOWARD of Glossop (see Table XVIII.), b. 14 Mar. 1674; d. 22 Ap. 1735; m. 22 June 1710, the Hon. ANNE, da. of Christopher (ROPER), 4th Baron Teynham [E.], d. 1744; and had issue.

See the Clarence Volume, Table LII., pp. 432–435, Nos. 18017–18455.

[Nos. 13800 to 14237.

200. Descendants of WILLIAM (HOWARD), 1st VISCOUNT STAFFORD [E.], K.B. (see Table XVIII.), b. 30 Nov. 1614; d. (being most unjustly beheaded, the last victim of Titus Oates) 29 Dec. 1680; m. (lic. dated 11 Oct. 1637) MARY, suo jure (1688) COUNTESS OF STAFFORD [E.], sister and h. of Henry (STAFFORD), 5th Baron Stafford [E.], da. of the Hon. Edward STAFFORD, b. 1619; d. 23 Jan. 1694; and had issue.

See the Clarence Volume, Table XVII., p. 537, Nos. 22808–23151.

[Nos. 14238 to 14581.

201. Descendants of CHARLES (MEDOWS, afterwards (R.L. 17 Sept. 1788) PIERREPONT), 1st EARL MANVERS [U.K.] and VISCOUNT NEWARK [G.B.] (see Table XVIII.), b. 14 Nov. 1737; d. 17 June 1816; m. 14 Nov. 1774, ANNE ORTON, da. of William MILLS of Richmond, d. 24 Aug. 1832; and had issue 1a to 3a.

1a. Charles Herbert (Pierrepont), 2nd Earl Manvers [U.K.] and Viscount Newark [G.B.], b. 11 Aug. 1778; d. 27 Oct. 1860; m. 23 Aug. 1804, Mary Letitia, da. of Anthony Hardolph Eyre of Grove, d. 7 Sept. 1860; and had issue 1b to 3b.

1b. Sydney William Herbert (Pierrepont), 3rd Earl [U.K.] and Viscount Newark [G.B.], b. 12 Mar. 1812; d. 16 Jan. 1900; m. 15 June 1852, Georgina Jane Elizabeth Fanny (6 Tilney Street, Park Lane, W.), da. and co-h. of Augustin Louis Joseph Casimir Gustavus (de Franquetot), Duke of Coigny [F.]; and had issue 1c to 4c.

1c. Charles William Sydney (Pierrepont), 4th Earl Manvers [U.K.] and Viscount Newark [G.B.] (Holme Pierrepont, Nottingham; Thoresby Park, Ollerton), b. 2 Aug. 1854; m. 28 Sept. 1880, Helen, da. of Sir Michael Robert Shaw-Stewart, 7th Bart. [S.]; and has issue 1d to 4d.

1d. Evelyn Robert Pierrepont, Viscount Newark, b. 25 July 1888.

2d. Lady Cicely Mary Pierrepont, b. 4 Nov. 1886.

3d. Lady Alice Helen Pierrepont, b. 30 Aug. 1889.

4d. Lady Sibell Pierrepont, b. 19 May 1892.

2c. Hon. Evelyn Henry Pierrepont, J.P. (Higham Grange, Nuneaton), b. 23 Aug. 1856; m. 1 June 1880, Sophia, da. of William Arkwright of Sutton Scarsdale; and has issue 1d to 3d.

1d. Gervas Evelyn Pierrepont, b. 15 Ap. 1881.

2d. Eva Mary Pierrepont, b. 23 Oct. 1882.

3d. Clare Isma Pierrepont, b. 2 Sept. 1884.

3c. Lady Emily Annora Charlotte Pierrepont (13 Belgrave Square, S.W.), m. as 2nd wife, 24 Sept. 1878, Frederick (Lygon), 6th Earl Beauchamp [U.K.], P.C., b. 10 Nov. 1830; d. 19 Feb. 1891; and has issue 1d to 4d.

1d. Hon. Robert Lygon, Capt. Grenadier Guards (Guards'; Bachelors'), b.

[Nos. 14582 to 14592.

# of The Blood Royal

9 Aug. 1879; *m.* 10 Oct. 1903, Cecil Albinia, da. of Sir George Gough Arbuthnot; and has issue 1*e.*

    1*e.* Reginald Arthur Lygon, *b.* 28 July 1904.

    2*d.* Hon. Henry Lygon, *b.* 10 Ap. 1884.

    3*d.* Lady Agnes Lygon, *b.* 7 Dec. 1880.

    4*d.* Lady Maud Lygon, *b.* 5 July 1882.

    4*c.* Lady Mary Augusta Pierrepont, *m.* 4 Ap. 1899, John Peter Grant (*Rothiemurchus, Aviemore, co. Inverness; Culduthel House, co. Inverness*); and has issue 1*d* to 3*d.*

        1*d.* Patrick Charles Henry Grant, *b.* 5 Mar. 1900.

        2*d.* Alexander Ludovic Grant, *b.* 26 Mar. 1901.

        3*d.* Gregor James Grant, *b.* 11 Ap. 1902.

    2*b. Lady Mary Frances Pierrepoint, b. 16 Mar.* 1819; *d.* 12 *June* 1905; *m.* 21 *Aug.* 1845, *Edward Christopher Egerton, M.P., Under Secretary of State, b.* 27 *July* 1816; *d.* 27 *Aug.* 1869; *and had issue.*
See the Tudor Roll of "The Blood Royal of Britain," p. 389, Nos. 29300–29313.

    3*b. Lady Annora Charlotte Pierrepont, b.* 11 *Sept.* 1822 ; *d.* 22 *Mar.* 1888 ; m. 18 *Aug.* 1853, *Charles Watkin Williams-Wynn of Coed-y-Maen, M.P., b.* 4 *Oct.* 1822; *d.* 1896 ; *and had issue.*
See the Tudor Roll of "The Blood Royal of Britain," p. 276, Nos. 24824–24836.

    2*a. Hon. Henry Manners Pierrepont of Conholt Park, co. Hants, P.C., b.* 18 *Mar.* 1780; *d.* 10 *Nov.* 1851; *m.* 12 *May* 1818, *Lady Sophia, da. of Henry* (*Cecil*), *1st Marquis of Exeter* [*U.K.*], *b.* 4 *Feb.* 1792; *d.* 2 *Nov.* 1823; *and had issue.*
See the Tudor Roll of "The Blood Royal of Britain," pp. 415–416, Nos. 30252–30269.

    3*a. Lady Frances Augusta Pierrepont, b.* 19 *June* 1781; *d.* 10 *Feb.* 1847 ; *m.* 1*st,* 20 *Oct.* 1802, *Admiral William Bentinck, b.* 17 *June* 1764; *d.* 21 *Feb.* 1813; 2*ndly,* 30 *July* 1821, *Henry William Stephens; and had issue* (*at least by* 1*st husband*) 1*b* to 2*b.*

        1*b. Charles Aldenburg Bentinck of Indio, co. Devon, &c., b.* 22 *Mar.* 1810; *d.* 7 *Feb.* 1891; *m.* 1*st,* 10 *May* 1849, *Harriet, da. of Baldwin Fulford of Fulford, d.* 15 *Mar.* 1853; *and had issue* 1*c.*

            1*c.* Henry Aldenburg Bentinck, Bar.-at-Law, D.L. (60 *Cadogan Square, S.W.*), *b.* 7 Jan. 1852; *m.* 9 July 1890, Alma, da. of Lord Clarence Paget.

        2*b. Renira Henrietta Aldenburg Bentinck, b.* 18 *Mar.* 1811; *d.* 16 *Jan.* 1868 ; m. *as* 2*nd wife,* 21 *July* 1842, *the Rev. George Martin, Chancellor and Canon Resid. of Exeter, d.* 27 *Aug.* 1860.   Nos. 14593 to 14646.

202. Descendants, if any, of EDWARD MEDOWS, Capt. R.N. (see Table XVIII.), *d.* 1813 ; *m.* 1785, MARY, da. of John BRODIE.

203. Descendants of FRANCES MEDOWS (see Table XVIII.), *d.* 1770 ; *m.* 3 Sept. 1768, Lieut.-Col. ALEXANDER CAMPBELL of Stackpole, co. Pembroke, *d.* Nov. 1785 ; and had issue 1*a.*

    1*a. Sir Henry Frederick Campbell, K.C.B., G.C.H., a Gen. in the Army, b.* 10 *July* 1769; *d.* 2 *Sept.* 1856; *m.* 10 *Ap.* 1808, *Emma, widow of Col. Thomas Knox, da. of Thomas Williams, d.* 20 *Mar.* 1847 ; *and had issue* 1*b* to 3*b.*

        1*b. George Herbert Frederick Campbell, J.P., D.L., a Col. in the Army, b.* 19 *June* 1811; *d.* (–); *m.* 5 *Nov.* 1838, *Louisa, da. of Richard Henry Cox of Hillingdon House; and had issue* 1*c* to 7*c.*

              2 P

The Plantagenet Roll

1c. Walter Sidney Campbell, J.P. (*Evenley, co. Northants;* 125 *Mount Street, W.*), b. 1845.

2c. George Augustus Campbell (*The Market House, Brackley;* 46 *Wilton Crescent, S.W.*), b. 7 July 1847; m. 23 July 1868, the Hon. Alice, da. of Percy (Barrington), 8th Viscount Barrington [I.]; and has issue.
See the Clarence Volume, p. 95, Nos. 711–717.

3c. Henry Algernon Campbell, b. (–); m. Jan. 1873, Edith, da. of Prideaux Selby of Pawston; and has issue.

4c. Francis Alexander Campbell of the Foreign Office, b. (–); m. 1880, Dora Edith, da. of Hugh Hammersley.

5c. Arthur Charles Campbell, *late* Capt. Rifle Brigade, b. (–).

6c. Fanny Georgiana Campbell, m. 29 June 1859, Lieut.-Col. the Hon. Henry Walter Campbell, J.P. (44 *Charles Street, Berkeley Square*); and has issue.
See the Tudor Roll of "The Blood Royal of Britain," p. 216, Nos. 21771–21778.

7c. Mary Louisa Campbell, m. Arthur Charles Hammersley.

2b. *Frances Augusta Campbell,* d. 29 *May* 1878; m. 10 *Dec.* 1836, *Col. the Hon Charles James Fox Stanley,* b. 25 *Ap.* 1808; d. 13 *Oct.* 1884; *and had issue.*
See the Tudor Roll of "The Blood Royal of Britain," p. 493, Nos. 33765–33776.

3b. *Harriet Campbell,* d. (–); m. *Lieut.-Col. Robert Moorsom, Scots Guards.*
[Nos. 14647 to 14680.

204. Descendants of JOHN (STUART), 1st MARQUIS [G.B.] AND 4th EARL [S.] OF BUTE, F.R.S. (see Table XVIII.), *b.* 30 June 1744; *d.* (at Geneva) 16 Nov. 1814; *m.* 1st, 1 Nov. 1766, the Hon. CHARLOTTE JANE, da. and eventual h. of Herbert (HICKMAN-WINDSOR), 2nd VISCOUNT WINDSOR [I.], *b.* 7 May 1746; *d.* 28 Jan. 1800; 2ndly, 17 Sept. 1800, FRANCES, da. and co-h. of Thomas COUTTS of the Strand, Middlesex, Banker, *d.* 12 Nov. 1832; and had issue 1a to 6a.

1a. *John Stuart, Lord Mount Stuart,* b. 25 *Sept.* 1767; d.v.p. 22 *Jan.* 1794; m. 12 *Oct.* 1792, *Lady Elizabeth Penelope, da. and h. of Patrick (Mackdowall Crichton), 5th Earl of Dumfries* [S.], b. 25 *Nov.* 1772; d.v.p. 25 *July* 1797; *and had issue 1b to 2b.*

1b. *John (Stuart, afterwards (R.L. 26 Aug. 1805) Crichton-Stuart), 2nd Marquis* [G.B.] *and 5th Earl* [S.] *of Bute, also (in 1803) 7th Earl of Dumfries* [S.], K.T., b. 10 *Aug.* 1793; d. 18 *Mar.* 1848; m. 2ndly, 10 *Ap.* 1845, *Lady Sophia Frederica Christina, da. of Francis (Rawdon-Hastings), 1st Marquis of Hastings* [U.K.], b. 1 *Feb.* 1809; d. 28 *Dec.* 1859; *and had issue 1c.*

1c. *John Patrick (Crichton-Stuart), 3rd Marquis of Bute* [G.B.], 8th *Earl of Dumfries* [S.], K.T., b. 12 *Sept.* 1847; d. 9 *Oct.* 1900; m. 16 *Ap.* 1872, *the Hon. Gwendolen Mary Anne, da. of Edward George (Fitzalan Howard), 1st Baron Howard of Glossop* [U.K.]; *and had issue 1d to 4d.*

1d. John (Crichton-Stuart), 4th Marquis of Bute [G.B.], 9th Earl of Dumfries and 7th Earl of Bute [S.], Hereditary Keeper of Rothesay Castle, &c. (*Mount Stuart, Rothesay; Cardiff Castle, Glamorgan; St. John's Lodge, Regent's Park; 5 Charlotte Square, Edinburgh*), b. 20 June 1881; m. 6 July 1905, Augusta Mary Monica, da. of Sir Alan Henry Bellingham, 4th Bart. [G.B.].

2d. Lord Ninian Edward Crichton-Stuart (*Falkland House, Fife*), b. 15 May 1883.

3d. Lord Colum Edmund Crichton-Stuart, b. 3 Ap. 1886.

4d. Lady Margaret Crichton-Stuart, b. 24 Dec. 1875.

2b. *Hon. Lord (R.W. 28 May 1817) Patrick James Herbert Stuart, afterwards*
[Nos. 14681 to 14684.

294

# of The Blood Royal

(R.L. 21 Mar. 1817) Crichton-Stuart, M.P., b. (posthumous) 25 Aug. 1794; d. 7 Sept. 1859; m. 13 July 1818, Hannah, da. of William Tighe of Woodstock, co. Kilkenny, M.P., d. 5 June 1872; and had issue 1c to 2c.

1c. James Frederick Dudley Crichton-Stuart, M.P., Lieut.-Col. Grenadier Guards, b. 17 Feb. 1824; d. 24 Oct. 1891; m. 28 July 1864, Gertrude Frances (25 Wilton Crescent, S.W.), da. of the Right Hon. Sir George Hamilton Seymour, G.C.B.; and had issue.

See the Clarence Volume, p. 142, Nos. 1929–1933.

2c. Herbert Crichton-Stuart, D.L., b. 5 Aug. 1827; d. Dec. 1891; m. 28 Aug. 1860, Fanny Adelaide (Rockland, St. Mary, Bournemouth), da. of John Labouchere of Broome Hall, Surrey; and had issue 1d to 2d.

1d. James Fortescue Crichton-Stuart (Travellers'), b. 3 Mar. 1864; m. 29 Sept. 1894, Lilian Louisa, da. of Thomas Holdsworth Newman of Coryton; and has issue 1e.

1e. Joan Evelyn Crichton-Stuart.

2d. Margaret Adelaide Crichton-Stuart, m. 7 May 1892, the Rev. Harry Percy Grubb, Vicar of Hurdsfield (Hurdsfield Vicarage, Macclesfield); and has issue 1e to 4e.

1e. Harold Crichton-Stuart Grubb, b. 22 Feb. 1893.
2e. Norman Percy Grubb, b. 2 Aug. 1895.
3e. Kenneth George Grubb, b. 9 Sept. 1900.
4e. Violet Margaret Grubb, b. 7 Nov. 1898.

2a. Lord Henry Stuart, b. 7 June 1777; d. 19 Aug. 1809; m. 15 July 1802, Lady Gertrude Amelia, da. and h. of George (Mason-Villiers), 2nd Earl of Grandison [I.], d. 30 Aug. 1809; and had issue.

See the Clarence Volume, pp. 146–147, Nos. 2097–2105.

3a. Lord George Stuart, C.B., Rear-Admiral R.N., b. 4 Mar. 1780; d. 19 Feb. 1819; m. 7 Oct. 1800, Jane, da. of Major-Gen. James Stewart, d. 1 Feb. 1862; and had issue 1b to 3b.

1b. Henry Stuart of Montford, Bute, b. 1 Jan. 1808; d. 19 May 1880; m. 9 Nov. 1840, Cecilia, da. of Charles Hammersley of 25 Park Crescent, W., d. 28 Feb. 1890; and had issue 1c to 10c.

1c. Dudley Charles Stuart, Comm. R.N. (Lundie, Edgell, co. Forfar), b. 20 Nov. 1844; m. 31 Mar. 1875, Amy Clara, da. of Lieut.-Col. Charles Harrison Page of Llandaff, J.P.; and has issue 1d to 10d.

1d. Evelyn Charles Henry Stuart, late Lieut. R.N., b. 21 Dec. 1875.
2d. James Martin Stuart, b. 15 Jan. 1877.
3d. Dudley Stuart, b. 8 Nov. 1883.
4d. Henry Stuart, b. 1886.
5d. Eric Hoy Stuart, b. 1890.
6d. Kenneth Freemantle Stuart, b. 1895.
7d. Ethel Margaret Stuart, b. 4 Jan. 1878.
8d. Mary Cecilia Stuart, b. 1879.
9d. Lillis Amy Stuart, b. 1881.
10d. Heather Sybil Stuart, b. Feb. 1900.

2c. John Windsor Stuart, Col. Argyll and Bute Vol. Art. (Foley House, Rothesay), b. 3 Dec. 1846; d. 8 Dec. 1905; m. 30 Ap. 1873, Flora, da. of Capt. William James Campbell of Snettisham ; and had issue 1d to 3d.

1d. Henry Campbell Stuart (Rhubodach, Bute), b. 2 Mar. 1874; m. 20 Ap. 1904, Eileene Barbara, da. of Major H. G. Fenton Newall of The Links House, St. Andrews; and has issue 1e.

1e. Mary Barbara Stuart, b. 13 Jan. 1905.

2d. John Dudley Stuart (Twyn Andrew, Wenvoe, Glamorgan), b. 1 Sept. 1875; m. 30 Ap. 1902, Florence Emily, da. of Charles Hunter, Chief Engineer of the Bute Docks, Cardiff.   [Nos. 14685 to 14719.

The Plantagenet Roll

3d. Elizabeth Ada Mary Stuart, b. 25 May 1878.

3c. Evelyn Stuart, d. 3 Jan. 1867; m. 2 Aug. 1860, Charles Hallyburton Campbell, B.C.S. (64 Cromwell Road, S.W.); and had issue.

4c. Emily Catherine Stuart, d. 1882; m. 5 Nov. 1861, Martin Ridley Smith, one of H.M.'s Lieutenants for the City of London and Sheriff in 1891 (Warren House, Hayes Common, Kent); and had issue 1d to 4d.

    1d. Everard Reginald Martin Smith, b. 13 Oct. 1875.

    2d. Ethel Evelyn Martin Smith, m. 12 Dec. 1891, Stuart MacRae (Handley House, Newark-on-Trent); and has issue 1e to 3e.

        1e. Kenneth Stuart MacRae, b. 1892.

        2e. John Nigel MacRae, b. 1894.

        3e. Grace Emily MacRae, b. 1897.

    3d. Audrey Cecilia Martin Smith, m. 1899, Walter Heriot of C. J. Hambro et fils (53 Hans Place, S.W.); and has issue 1e to 2e.

        1e. James Eric Heriot, b. 1900.

        2e. Martin Heriot, b. 1904.

    4d. Sybil Emily Martin Smith, m. 17 July 1894, Charles Eric Hambro, M.P. (70 Princes Gate, S.W.); and has issue 1e to 2e.

        1e. Charles Jocelyn Hambro, b. 1897.

        2e. Richard Everard Hambro, b. 1900.

5c. Gertrude Mary Stuart, d. 4 June 1905; m. 23 Oct. 1866, Edward Alexander Hambro, J.P., D.L., a Director of the Bank of England, &c. (Hayes Place, co. Kent; Milton Abbey, Blandford); and had issue 1d to 5d.

    1d. Charles Eric Hambro, M.P. (70 Princes Gate, S.W.), b. 20 Sept. 1872; m. 17 July 1894, Sybil Emily Martin, da. of Martin Ridley Smith, D.L.; and has issue. See p. 296, Nos. 14730–14731.

    2d. Harold Everard Hambro, Lieut. R.H.A. (The Warrens, Farnham), b. 20 Jan. 1876; m. 29 Ap. 1902, Katharine Alethea, da. of William Charles Scott of Thorpe, Chertsey, J.P.

    3d. Angus Valdimar Hambro, b. 8 July 1883.

    4d. Olaf Hambro, b. 1 Dec. 1885.

    5d. Violet Mary Hambro, b. 24 Sept. 1884.

6c. Elizabeth Charlotte Stuart (Bray Manor, St. Germans, Cornwall), m. 21 Sept. 1880, George Edward Sneyd, M.A. (Oxon.), d. 14 Jan. 1894; and has issue 1d to 5d.

    1d. Ralph Sneyd, b. 1882.

    2d. George Stuart Sneyd, b. 1883.

    3d. Robert Stuart Sneyd, b. 1886.

    4d. Honora Sneyd, b. 1881.

    5d. Gwendolen Sneyd, b. 1888.

7c. Clara Georgina Stuart.

8c. Cecilia Stuart.

9c. Frederica Stuart, m. 22 Mar. 1877, Col. Michael Rowland Gray Buchanan (Ettrick Dale, Isle of Bute); and has issue 1d to 8d.

    1d. Claude Buchanan, b. 17 Feb. 1878.

    2d. Kenneth Buchanan, b. 25 Jan. 1880.

    3d. Ronald Buchanan, b. 1883.

    4d. Frederic Buchanan, b. 1887.

    5d. Marjory Buchanan, b. 27 July 1881.

    6d. Dorothy Buchanan, b. 1885.

    7d. Cecilia Mary Buchanan, b. 1891.

    8d. Emily Buchanan, b. 1893.

10c. Octavia Henrietta Mary Stuart.   [Nos. 14720 to 14756.

# of The Blood Royal

2b. *Elizabeth Jane Stuart,* b. 18 *July* 1803; d. 27 *Jan.* 1877; m. 18 *Aug.* 1825 *John (Townshend), 4th Marquis [G.B.] and 7th Viscount [E.] Townshend,* d. 10 *Sept.* 1863; *and had issue.*
See the Clarence Volume, pp. 194–195, Nos. 3333–3367.

3b. *Emily Frances Stuart,* b. 7 *Feb.* 1806; d. 16 *June* 1886; m. 9 *Jan.* 1834, *the Hon. Charles Abbott,* b. 8 *Aug.* 1803; d. 17 *Dec.* 1838; *and had issue* 1c.

1c. Charles Stuart Henry (Abbott), 4th Baron Tenterden [U.K.], *b.* 30 Oct. 1865.

4a. *Lady Maria Alicia Charlotte Stuart,* b. 28 *Oct.* 1768; d. 1841; m. *Charles Pinfold.*

5a. *Lady Charlotte Stuart,* b. 16 *July* 1771; d. 5 *Sept.* 1847; m. 13 *June* 1797, *Sir William Jackson Homan of Dunlum, 1st Bart. [U.K.],* b. 1771; d. (–); *and had issue* 1b.

1b. *Sir Philip George Stuart Homan, 2nd Bart. [U.K.],* b. 6 *Sept.* 1802; d. (? *unm.*).

6a. *Lady Frances Stuart,* d. 29 *Mar.* 1859; m. 15 *Sept.* 1823, *Dudley (Ryder), 2nd Earl of [U.K.] and 3rd Baron [G.B.] Harrowby, K.G.,* b. 19 *May* 1798; d. 19 *Nov.* 1882; *and had issue.*
See the Tudor Roll of "The Blood Royal of Britain," p. 523, Nos. 35036–35050.
[Nos. 14757 to 14807.

205. Descendants of the Hon. JAMES ARCHIBALD STUART, *afterwards* (Jan. 1795) STUART-WORTLEY, and finally (1803) STUART-WORTLEY-MACKENZIE, M.P. (see Table XVIII.), *b.* 19 Sept. 1747; *d.* 1 Mar. 1818; *m.* 8 June 1767, MARGARET, da. of Sir David CUNINGHAME, 3rd Bart. [S.], *d.* 13 Jan. 1808; and had issue 1α to 2α.

1a. *James Archibald (Stuart-Wortley-Mackenzie), 1st Baron Wharncliffe* [U.K.], b. 1 *Nov.* 1776; d. 19 *Dec.* 1845; m. 30 *Mar.* 1799, *Lady Elizabeth Caroline Mary, da. of John (Creighton), 1st Earl of Erne [I.],* d. 23 *Ap.* 1856; *and had issue* 1b *to* 4b.

1b. *John (Stuart-Wortley-Mackenzie), 2nd Baron Wharncliffe [U.K.],* b. 23 *Ap.* 1801; d. 22 *Oct.* 1855; m. 12 *Dec.* 1825, *Lady Georgiana Elizabeth, da. of Dudley (Ryder), 1st Earl of Harrowby [U.K.],* b. 23 *Ap.* 1804; d. 22 *Aug.* 1884; *and had issue.*
See the Tudor Roll of "The Blood Royal of Britain," p. 525, Nos. 35120–35148.

2b. *Hon. Charles Stuart Stuart-Wortley-Mackenzie,* b. 3 *June* 1802; d. 22 *May* 1844; m. 17 *Feb.* 1831, *Lady Emmeline Charlotte Elizabeth, da. of John Henry (Russell), 5th Duke of Rutland [E.],* b. 2 *May* 1806; d. 30 *Oct.* 1855; *and had issue* 1c.

1c. Hon. Victoria Alexandrina Mary Louisa Stuart Stuart-Wortley-Mackenzie[1] *(Duneaves, Harrow), m.* 4 July 1863, Sir William Earle Welby, *afterwards* (R.L. 27 *Dec.* 1875) Welby-Gregory, 4th Bart. [U.K.], M.P., J.P., D.L., *b.* 4 Jan. 1829; *d.* 26 Nov. 1898; and has issue 1d to 2d.

1d. Sir Charles Gynne Earle Welby, 5th Bart. [U.K.], C.B., M.P., *sometime* (1900–1902) Assist. Under Secretary of State for War (unpaid), &c. *(Denton Manor, Grantham ; 34 Hill Street, Berkeley Square, W.), b.* 11 Aug. 1865; *m.* 24 Nov. 1887, Maria Louisa Helen, da. of Lord Augustus Hervey; and has issue 1e to 5e.
[Nos. 14808 to 14838.

---

[1] See the Tudor Roll of "The Blood Royal of Britain," pp. 296, 377, and the Clarence Volume, p. 338, for her descents from King Edward IV. and George, Duke of Clarence, respectively. Lady Welby has also a senior maternal descent from Anne of Exeter.

The Plantagenet Roll

1e. Richard William Gregory Welby, b. 6 Oct. 1888.

2e. Oliver Charles Earle Welby, b. 26 Jan. 1902.

3e. Dorothy Geraldine Welby, b. 4 July 1890.

4e. Katharine Amothe Welby, b. 7 Ap. 1895.

5e. Joan Margaret Welby, b. 10 Ap. 1898.

2d. Emmeline Mary Elizabeth Welby, m. 11 Oct. 1893, Henry John Cockayne Cust, M.P. (St. James' Lodge, Delahay Street, Westminster, S.W.).

3b. Right Hon. and Hon. James Archibald Stuart-Wortley, P.C., K.C., M.P., Recorder of the City of London, b. 3 July 1805; d. 22 Aug. 1881; m. 6 May 1846, Jane, da. of Paul Beilby (Lawley, afterwards Lawley-Thompson), 1st Baron Wenlock [U.K.], b. 5 Dec. 1820; d. 4 Feb. 1900; and had issue.
See the Tudor Roll of "The Blood Royal of Britain," pp. 291–292, Nos. 25336–25349.

4b. Hon. Caroline Jane Stuart-Wortley-Mackenzie, b. 13 June 1809; d. 12 June 1876; m. 30 Aug. 1830, the Hon. John Chetwynd Talbot, Q.C., b. 31 May 1806; d. 26 May 1852; and had issue 1c to 2c.

1c. Right Hon. John Gilbert Talbot, P.C., M.P., D.C.L. (Falconhurst, Eden Bridge, Kent; 10 Great George Street, S.W.), b. 24 Feb. 1835; m. 19 July 1860, the Hon. Meriel Sarah, da. of George William (Lyttelton), 4th Baron Lyttelton [G.B.]; and has issue.
See the Tudor Roll of "The Blood Royal of Britain," pp. 223–224, Nos. 22056–22071.

2c. Right Rev. Edward Stuart Talbot, Lord Bishop of Southwark, formerly of Rochester, D.D. (Bishop's House, Kennington Park, S.E.), b. 19 Feb. 1844; m. 29 June 1870, the Hon. Lavinia, da. of George William (Lyttelton), 4th Baron Lyttelton [G.B.]; and has issue.
See the Tudor Roll of "The Blood Royal of Britain," p. 224, Nos. 22074–22078.

2a. Louisa Harcourt Stuart-Wortley-Mackenzie, b. Oct. 1781; d. 30 June 1848; m. 23 June 1801, George (Percy), 2nd Earl of Beverley, afterwards (12 Feb. 1865) 5th Duke of Northumberland [G.B.], b. 22 June 1778; d. 22 Aug. 1867; and had issue.
See the Tudor Roll of "The Blood Royal of Britain," pp. 186–188, Nos. 20954–20996.   [Nos. 14839 to 14925.

206. Descendants of the Most Rev. and Hon. WILLIAM STUART, Lord Archbishop of Armagh, D.D. (see Table XVIII.), b. Mar. 1755; d. 6 Mar. 1822; m. 3 May 1796, SOPHIA MARGARET JULIANA, da. of Thomas PENN of Stoke Pogis, d. Ap. 1847; and had issue 1a to 2a.

1a. William Stuart of Tempsford Hall, co. Beds, and Aldenham Abbey, co. Herts, J.P., D.L., b. 31 Oct. 1798; d. 7 July 1874; m. 1st, 8 Aug. 1821, Henrietta Maria Sarah, da. and h. of Adm. Sir Charles Morice Pole, 1st Bart. [U.K.], G.C.B., d. 26 July 1853; and had issue 1b to 5b.

1b. William Stuart of Tempsford Hall, and Aldenham Abbey, M.P., Hon. Col. 3rd Batt. Bedford Regt., b. 7 Mar. 1825; d. 21 Dec. 1893; m. 13 Sept. 1859, Katherine, da. of John Armytage Nicholson of Balrath, Bury, d. 16 Oct. 1881; and had issue 1c to 4c.

1c. William Dugald Stuart, J.P., Major and Hon. Lieut.-Col. 3rd Bedford Regt. (Tempsford Hall, Sandy, co. Beds; 36 Hill Street, W.), b. 18 Oct. 1860; m. 11 July 1893, Millicent Helen Olivia, da. of Capt. George W. Bulkeley Hughes; and has issue 1d.

1d. William Esmé Montagu Stuart, b. 22 Nov. 1895.   [Nos. 14926 to 14927.

298

# of The Blood Royal

2c. Henry Esmé Stuart, b. 12 July 1865.

3c. Mary Charlotte Florence Stuart.

4c. Elizabeth Frances Sybil Stuart.

2b. *Charles Pole Stuart of Sandymount House, Woburn, J.P.*, b. *7 May 1826* d. *26 Aug. 1896*; m. *20 Mar.* 1860, *Anne (Fryern, Chandlers Ford, co. Hants), da. of Robert Smyth of Gaybrook; and had issue* 1c *to* 7c.

1c. *Robert Alexander Stuart of Fryern*, b. 5 *July* 1862; d. *30 Mar.* 1899; m. 6 *Jan.* 1897, *Edith Margaret Nina, da. of the Rev. H. E. Stoker; and had issue* 1d.

1d. Enid Frances Anne Stuart, b. 28 Nov. 1897.

2c. Reginald Pole Stuart, Major 1st Batt. N. Staffordshire Regt., b. 22 July 1863; m. 29 June 1895, Hester Elizabeth, da. of Gerhard Myburgh of Orange Grove, Cape Town; and has issue 1d to 2d.

1d. Kathleen Anne Pole Stuart, b. 20 Aug. 1899.

2d. Rosalind Esmé Pole Stuart, b. 28 Oct. 1900.

3c. Charles Dudley Stuart, b. 26 Oct. 1864.

4c. Ralph Esmé Stuart, Capt. R.A., b. 9 Ap. 1869.

5c. Constance Mary Stuart.

6c. Florence Amabel Stuart.

7c. Grace Henrietta Stuart.

3b. *Mary Pole Stuart*, b. 23 *Sept.* 1822; d. 25 *Jan.* 1852; m. *as 1st wife,* 1 *Aug.* 1843, *Jonathan Rashleigh, J.P., D.L., High Sheriff co. Cornwall* 1877, d. *12 Ap.* 1905; *and had issue* 1c *to* 4c.

1c. *Jonathan Rashleigh*, b. 26 *May* 1845; d.v.p. *8 Dec.* 1872; m. 1 *Nov.* 1870, *Mary Frances, da. of John Labouchere of Broome Hall, co. Surrey; and had issue* 1d.

1d. John Cosmo Stuart Rashleigh (*Menabilly, co. Cornwall*), b. 2 July 1872.

2c. Evelyn William Rashleigh, J.P., C.A. (*Stockton, Saltash, co. Cornwall*), b. 6 Jan. 1850; m. 29 Ap. 1879, Jane Elizabeth, da. of Onley Savill Onley of Stisted Hall, Essex; and has issue 1d to 2d.

1d. William Stuart Rashleigh, b. 17 June 1882.

2d. Jane Henrietta Rashleigh.

3c. *Caroline Mary Stuart Rashleigh*, d. 3 *Jan.* 1880; m. 21 *Nov.* 1867, *Major Charles Poore Long, 13th Light Infantry*, d. 2 *Nov.* 1871; *and had issue* 1d *to* 2d.

1d. William Evelyn Long of Hurts Hall, J.P. (*Fairfield House, Saxmundham*), b. 10 Feb. 1871; m. 22 Feb. 1898, Muriel Hester,[1] da. of Thomas Frederick Charles Vernon Wentworth of Wentworth Castle; and has issue 1e.

1e. William George Long, b. 28 Mar. 1899.

2d. Mary Eleanora Long, m. John Longe (*Chillesford Lodge, Suffolk*).

4c. Alice Henrietta Rashleigh.

4b. *Henrietta Pole Stuart*, b. 10 *Feb.* 1824; d. 14 *Feb.* 1887; m. 4 *Feb.* 1845, *Reginald Thistlethwayte Cocks of London, Banker*, b. 6 *Oct.* 1816; d. 13 *Jan.* 1895; *and had issue* 1c *to* 2c.

1c. Agneta Henrietta Cocks.

2c. *Amabel Margaretta Cocks*, d. *Sept.* 1891; m. 15 *Dec.* 1874, *William Newcome Nicholson, M.A.*, b. 22 *May* 1833; d. 1889; *and had issue.*

5b. *Louisa Pole Stuart*, b. *Aug.* 1828; d. 7 *Jan.* 1858; m. *as 1st wife,* 3 *Aug.* 1852, *the Rev. Oliver Matthew Ridley, M.A.* (*Oxon.*) (*East Hill, Charminster*); *and had issue* 1c *to* 4c.

1c. Rev. Stuart Oliver Ridley, M.A. (Oxon.), Vicar of Scarisbrick (*Ormskirk Vicarage*), b. 8 June 1853.   [Nos. 14928 to 14949.

---

[1] See her descent from Kings Henry VII. and Edward IV. in the Tudor Roll of "The Blood Royal of Britain," p. 179.

The Plantagenet Roll

2c. Henry Nicholas Ridley, M.A. (Oxon.), b. 10 Dec. 1855.

3c. Mary Louisa Ridley.

4c. Fanny Louisa Pole Ridley.

2a. *Mary Juliana Stuart*, d. 11 *July* 1866 ; m. 28 *Feb.* 1815, *Thomas* (*Knox*), *2nd Earl of* [*I.*] *and Baron* [*U.K.*] *Ranfurly*, b. 19 *Ap.* 1786 ; d. 21 *Mar.* 1858 ; *and had issue.*
See the Clarence Volume, pp. 551–553, Nos. 23487–23534.

[Nos. 14950 to 15000.

207. Descendants, if any surviving, of Lady Augusta Stuart (see Table XVIII.), b. Feb. 1749 ; d. 5 Feb. 1778 ; m. Aug. 1773, Capt. Andrew Corbet of the Horse Guards (Blue) ; and had issue (a son, a clergyman).[1]

208. Descendants of Lady Caroline Stuart (see Table XVIII.), b. May 1750 ; d. 20 Jan. 1813 ; m. 1 Jan. 1778, John (Dawson), 1st Earl of Portarlington [I.], b. 23 Aug. 1744 ; d. 25 Nov. 1798 ; and had issue 1a to 7a.

1a. *John* (*Dawson*), *2nd Earl of Portarlington* [*I.*], b. 26 *Feb.* 1781 ; d. *unm.* 28 Dec. 1845.

2a. *Hon. Henry Dawson, afterwards* (*R.L. 14 Mar.* 1829) *Dawson-Damer*, b. 19 *July* 1786 ; d. 27 *May* 1841 ; m. 20 *May* 1813, *Eliza, da. of Capt. Edmund Joshua Moriarty, R.N.* (*and his wife Lady Lucy, née Luttrell*), d. 12 *June* 1857 ; *and had issue 1b to 2b.*

1b. *Henry John Reuben* (*Dawson-Damer*), *3rd Earl of Portarlington* [*I.*], K.P., b. 5 *Sept.* 1822 ; d.s.p. 1 *Mar.* 1889.

2b. *Lady* (*R.W. 13 Feb.* 1846) *Caroline Mary Dawson-Damer*, b. 3 *Oct.* 1818 ; d. 5 *Dec.* 1851 ; m. 16 *Dec.* 1847, *Admiral Sir George St. Vincent King, afterwards* (*R.L. 13 Feb.* 1888) *Duckworth-King, 4th Bart.* [*G.B.*], K.C.B., b. 15 *July* 1809 ; d. 18 *Aug.* 1891 ; *and had issue 1c to 2c.*

1c. Sir Dudley Gordon Alan Duckworth-King, 5th Bart. [G.B.], Lieut.-Col. Comdg. and Hon. Col. 1st Vol. Batt. Devonshire Regt., *late* Welsh Regt., J.P., D.L. (*Wear House, Countess Wear, R.S.O., Devon*), b. 28 Nov. 1851 ; m. 15 Ap. 1890, Eva Mary, da. of Major-Gen. Ralph Gore, R.H.A. ; and has issue 1d to 3d.

1d. George Henry James Duckworth-King, b. 8 June 1891.

2d. John Richard Duckworth-King, b. 11 June 1899.

3d. Violet Caroline Duckworth-King, b. 22 May 1894.

2c. Anne Louisa Caroline Duckworth King.

3a. *Hon. George Lionel Dawson, afterwards* (*R.L. 14 Mar.* 1829) *Dawson-Damer, P.C., C.B., Col. in the Army*, b. 28 *Oct.* 1788 ; d. 14 *Ap.* 1856 ; m. 20 *Aug.* 1825, *Mary Georgiana Emma, da. of Lord Hugh Seymour*, d. 30 *Oct.* 1848 ; *and had issue.*
See the Clarence Volume, pp. 139–141, Nos. 1847–1905.

4a. *Hon. Lionel Charles Dawson*, b. 7 *May* 1790 ; d. 25 *Sept.* 1842 ; m. 15 *Sept.* 1820, *Lady Elizabeth Emily, da. and co-h. of George Frederick* (*Nugent*), *7th Earl of Westmeath* [*I.*], d. 6 *Sept.* 1863 ; *and had issue.*
See the Clarence Volume, pp. 142–143, Nos. 1994–2016.

5a. *Lady Caroline Elizabeth Dawson*, b. 21 *Mar.* 1782 ; d. 16 *Feb.* 1861 ; m.

[Nos. 15001 to 15086.

---

[1] Brydges' " Collins' Peerage," ii. p. 579.

MONUMENT IN BATTESFORD CHURCH OF THOMAS (MANNERS),
1st EARL OF RUTLAND, K.G.

GRANDSON OF THE LADY ANNE PLANTAGENET, AND THE COMMON ANCESTOR OF NOS. 1-45906.

*From a Photo, W. E. Gray, Bayswater, by kind permission
the Editor of the " Art Journal."*

# of The Blood Royal

17 *Feb.* 1801, *Henry Brooke (Parnell), 1st Baron Congleton* [*U.K.*], d. 8 *June* 1842; *and had issue.*
See the Clarence Volume, pp. 286–289, Nos. 7689–7817.

6*a. Lady Louisa Mary Dawson,* b. 7 *Sept.* 1783; d. (app.s.p.) 18 *Aug.* 1845; m. *as 2nd wife, 2 Feb.* 1829, *the Rev. Walter (Davenport), afterwards Davenport-Bromley, of Wootton Hall and Bagenton,* d. 1 *Dec.* 1862.

7*a. Lady Harriet Dawson,* b. 9 *Oct.* 1784; d. 16 *Dec.* 1827; m. 4 *May* 1813, *Very Rev. the Hon. Henry David Erskine, Dean of Ripon,* b. 1786; d. 27 *July* 1859; *and had issue* 1*b to* 4*b.*

1*b.* Harriet Erskine, *b.* 30 Jan. 1814.

2*b.* Fanny Louisa Erskine (13 *Montagu Square, W.*), *b.* 6 Aug. 1822; *m.* 16 Sept. 1847, Henry Linwood Strong, Bar.-at-Law, Registrar Probate Court, *d.* 17 Nov. 1886; and has issue 1*c* to 5*c.*

1*c. Arthur Hugh Linwood Strong,* d. *Dec.* 1903.

2*c. Clement Erskine Linwood Strong,* d. 28 *Nov.* 1889.

3*c.* Alice Georgiana Caroline Linwood Strong, *m.* 27 June 1883, Godfrey Lewis Clark (*Tal-y-garn, Llantrisant, Glamorgan*); and has issue 1*d* to 3*d.*

1*d.* Wyndham Damer Clark, *b.* 27 Mar. 1884.

2*d.* Godfrey Henry Jocelyn Clark, *b.* 6 Aug. 1889.

3*d.* Lionel Clement Erskine Clark, *b.* 23 Dec. 1891.

4*c.* Zoë Sophia Barbara Linwood Strong, *m.* 18 July 1885, Francis Seymour Inglefield, D.S.O., Col. of the General Staff at Curragh Camp (*United Service*); and has issue 1*d.*

1*d.* Valentine Erskine Inglefield, 1st Batt. East Yorks Regt., *b.* 6 May 1886.

5*c.* Beatrice Caroline Linwood Strong, *m.* 7 Mar. 1899, Robert Steuart Erskine (22 *Stanford Road, Kensington Court, W.*).

3*b.* Anne Agnes Erskine, *b.* 1824; *m.* 29 Aug. 1859, Robinson Fowler, Bar.-at-Law, Stip. Mag. at Manchester, *d.* 1895.

4*b. Julia Henrietta Erskine,* d. 20 *Feb.* 1891; m. 17 *Feb.* 1856, *Lieut.-Gen. Broadley Harrison, 11th Hussars,* d. 30 *June* 1890; *and had issue* 1*c to* 6*c.*

1*c.* Henry Broadley Harrison, now Broadley, M.P. (*Walton House, Brough*), *b.* 12 Nov. 1853; *m.* Isabella, da. of John Tracy; and has issue 1*d* to 4*d.*

1*d.* John Harrison Broadley.

2*d.* Daisy Harrison Broadley, *m.* 1902, Capt. the Hon. Francis Stanley Jackson (*Junior Carlton*); and has issue 1*e.*

1*e.* [——] Jackson, *b.* 1903.

3*d.* Leola Harrison Broadley.

4*d.* Louisa Harrison Broadley.

2*c.* Broadley Harrison, Lieut. 1st Batt. East Yorks Regt., *b.* 1862; *m.* 28 Mar. 1889, Ada Gertrude, da. of K. R. Watkins; and has issue 1*d* to 2*d.*

1*d.* Francis Petros Broadley Harrison, *b.* 25 June 1905.

2*d.* Gertrude Broadley Harrison, *b.* 3 Sept. 1891.

3*c.* Mary Broadley Harrison, *m.* 13 Mar. 1876, Col. William Jackson Parker, B.C.S.; and has issue 1*d* to 5*d.*

1*d.* Arthur Parker, *b.* 11 Jan. 1882.

2*d.* Robert Parker, twin, *b.* 18 Dec. 1888.

3*d.* Eva Parker, *b.* 19 Ap. 1877; *m.* 18 Ap. 1900, Bernard Nunn.

4*d.* Louise Parker, *b.* 13 June 1885.

5*d.* Mabel Frances Parker, twin, *b.* 18 Dec. 1888.

4*c.* Eva Erskine Broadley Harrison.

5*c.* Louisa Sophia Broadley Harrison, *m.* 1880, William Wilfred Carey (*Villa Carey, Cairo*).

6*c.* Julia Henrietta Erskine Broadley Harrison, *m.* Capt. Godfrey Williams, 11th Hussars.   [Nos. 15087 to 15243.

The Plantagenet Roll

209. Descendants of JOHN THOMAS (ERSKINE), 31st EARL (*a.* 1014) and 11th EARL (1565) OF MAR [S.] (see Table XVIII.), *b.* 1772; *d.* 20 Sept. 1828; *m.* 17 Mar. 1795, JANET, da. of Patrick MILLER of Dalswinton, *d.* 25 Aug. 1825; and had issue 1*a* to 3*a*.

1*a.* *John Francis Miller (Erskine), 32nd Earl (a.* 1014) *and 12th Earl* (1565) *of Mar and 11th Earl of Kellie* [*S.*], b. 28 *Dec.* 1795; d.s.p. 19 *June* 1866.

2*a.* *Lady Frances Jemima Erskine, d.* 19 *June* 1842; *m.* 12 *Oct.* 1830, *William James Goodeve of Clifton, co. Gloucester, d.* 22 *Dec.* 1861; *and had issue* 1*b to* 5*b.*

1*b.* John Francis Erskine (Goodeve, now (1866) Goodeve-Erskine), 33rd Earl of Mar (*a.* 1014) [S.], Premier Earl of Scotland and a Rep. Peer, &c. (*Sunnington Rise, Bournemouth*), *b.* 29 Mar. 1836; *m.* 12 Sept. 1866, Alice Mary Sinclair, da. of John Hamilton of Hilston Park, Monmouth; and has issue 1*c.*

1*c.* John Francis Hamilton Sinclair Cunliffe Brooks Forbes Goodeve-Erskine, Lord Garioch (*Bachelors'; New (Edinburgh)*), *b.* 27 Feb. 1868; *m.* 15 Sept. 1903, Sybil May Dominica, da. of Robert Heathcote of Manton Hall.

2*b.* *Lady* [1] *Frances Jemima Erskine Goodeve, b.* 13 *Dec.* 1831; *d.* 11 *Aug.* 1887; *m.* 29 *Mar.* 1854, *Lieut.-Gen. James Nowell Young, late Judge Advocate-General, Bengal* (13 *Jevington Gardens, Eastbourne*); *and had issue* 1*c to* 3*c.*

1*c.* *Charles Walter Young, Major in the Army, b.* 1862; *d.* (–); *m.* 1885, *Constance Barnes, da. of the Rev.* [——] *Johnson; and had issue* 1*d to* 3*d.*

1*d.* Edward Nowell Goodeve Young, *b.* 1886.

2*d.* Oswald Walter Young, *b.* 1889.

3*d.* Lionel Erskine Young, *b.* 1891.

2*c.* Alice Young, *m.* James Lane; and had issue 1*d* to 3*d.*

1*d.* Charles Lane.

2*d.* Frank Lane.

3*d.* Mildred Lane.

3*c.* Isabel Young.

3*b.* *Charlotte Erskine Goodeve, b.* 27 *May* 1833; *d.* 9 *Sept.* 1859; *m.* 30 *Nov.* 1857, *Charles Bell of Bangkok, Siam, d.* 2 *Sept.* 1859; *and had issue* 1*c.*

1*c.* Amy Elizabeth Bell.

4*b.* Lady Eliza Philadelphia Erskine Goodeve, *m.* 14 Aug. 1862, the Rev. Edward Maule Cole, M.A., Vicar of Wetwang (*Wetwang Vicarage, York*); and has issue 1*c* to 7*c.*

1*c.* Seymour Hamilton Maule Cole, Storekeeper, State Railways of India (*Karachi, India*), *b.* 23 Aug. 1866; *m.* 27 June 1892, Lilian May Sullivan, da. of Robert Kerr Kerr; and has issue 1*d* to 6*d.*

1*d.* Douglas Seymour Francis Erskine Maule Cole, *b.* 11 Aug. 1898.

2*d.* Wilmot Edward Robert Erskine Maule Cole, *b.* 29 May 1903.

3*d.* Florence Violet Erskine Cole, *b.* 7 Nov. 1893.

4*d.* Crystal Mary Vera Erskine Cole, *b.* 17 Jan. 1895.

5*d.* Edna Beryl Mavis Erskine Cole, *b.* 29 July 1896.

6*d.* Lilian Maude Erskine Cole, *b.* 2 Dec. 1900.

2*c.* Edward Wilmot Maule Cole (*Mitcham, Surrey*), *b.* 11 Ap. 1868; *m.* 1898, Helen, da. of [——] Anderson.

3*c.* Maurice St. Michael Maule Cole, *b.* 29 Sept. 1872.

4*c.* John Francis Erskine Maule Cole, *b.* 28 May 1877.

5*c.* Beatrice Madeline Erskine Cole, *m.* 24 Dec. 1884, Henry Tanner Ferguson, M.I.C.E. (*Wolleigh, Bovey Tracey*); and has issue 1*d* to 8*d.* [Nos. 15244 to 15266.]

---

[1] R.W. 15 Oct. 1885.

# of The Blood Royal

1*d*. Donald Harry Ferguson, *b*. 8 Feb. 1890.

2*d*. Gerald William Ferguson, *b*. 27 Dec. 1891.

3*d*. George Hamilton Ferguson, *b*. 18 Mar. 1896.

4*d*. Roland Edward Stuart Ferguson, *b*. 22 Aug. 1899.

5*d*. Helen Evelyn Ferguson, *b*. 23 Feb. 1886.

6*d*. Kathleen Erskine Ferguson, *b*. 25 Mar. 1887.

7*d*. Mary Beatrice Erskine Ferguson, *b*. 3 May 1888.

8*d*. Violet Madeline Ferguson, *b*. 17 Nov. 1893.

6*c*. Edith Marguerite Erskine Cole.

7*c*. Mary Christian Janet Erskine Cole.

5*b*. Lady Madelina Erskine Goodeve-Erskine (2 *College Terrace, Kemp Town, Brighton*).

3*a*. Lady *Jean Janet Erskine*, d. 16 *May* 1861; m. 29 *Ap*. 1830, *Edward Wilmot-Chetwode of Woodbrooke, Queen's co.*, d. 9 *May* 1874; *and had issue* 1*b to* 4*b*.

1*b*. *Knightley Jonathan Wilmot-Chetwode*, b. 31 *May* 1831; d. (? s.p.) 12 *Jan*. 1887; m. 20 *Nov*. 1872, *Henrietta, widow of Count Kalling of Swarting, Sweden, and da. of Charles Uggla of Stora Djulö, Marshal of the (Swedish) Court*.

2*b*. *Edward Robert Erskine Wilmot-Chetwode*, b. 24 *Sept*. 1852; d. 1 *Ap*. 1886; m. 1 *Sept*. 1875, *Gertrude, da. of the Rev. Alfred Hamilton of Taney, co. Dublin; and had issue* 1*c to* 2*c*.

1*c*. Gertrude Florence Evelyn Wilmot-Chetwode, *m*. 30 Nov. 1899, Capt. Arthur Henry Marindin of Woodfield, co. Worcester (*Riverside, Palace Road, East Molesey*); and has issue (3 das.).

2*c*. Rita Kathleen Wilmot-Chetwode, *b*. 9 Nov. 1879; *m*. A. Kinahan; and has issue 1*d*.

1*d*. George Chetwode Kinahan.

3*b*. Alice Margaret Agnes Wilmot-Chetwode (*Woodbrook, Portarlington*).

4*b*. *Janet Philadelphia Wilmot-Chetwode*, d. 1880; m. *Thomas O'Donoghue; and had issue* 1*c to* 2*c*.

1*c*. Rev. [——] O'Donoghue, in Holy Orders of the Catholic Church.

2*c*. [——] O'Donoghue, a nun.   [Nos. 15267 to 15283.

210. Descendants of the Hon. HENRY DAVID ERSKINE (see Table XVIII.), *b*. 10 May 1776; *d*. 31 Dec. 1846; *m*. 22 Oct. 1805, MARY ANNE, da. of John COOKSEY, *d*. 4 Mar. 1860; and had issue 1*a* to 4*a*.

1*a*. *Walter Coningsby (Erskine), 10th Earl of Mar* (1565) *and 12th Earl of Kellie* [*S.*], *a Rep. Peer, C.B.*, b. 12 *July* 1810; d. 17 *Jan*. 1872; m. 11 *Sept*. 1834, *Elsie, da. of Col. Youngson of Bowscar, co. Cumberland*, d. 14 *July* 1895; *and had issue* 1*b to* 2*b*.

1*b*. *Walter Henry (Erskine), 11th Earl of Mar* (1565) *and 13th Earl of Kellie* [*S.*], *a Rep. Peer*, b. 17 *Dec*. 1839; d. 16 *Sept*. 1888; m. 14 *Oct*. 1863, *Mary Anne* (16 *Lowndes Square, S.W.*), *da. of William Forbes of Medwyn; and had issue* 1*c to* 7*c*.

1*c*. Walter John Francis (Erskine), 12th Earl of Mar (1565) *and* 14th Earl of Kellie (1619), 17th Lord Erskine (1429) [S.], Premier Viscount of Scotland and a Rep. Peer (*Alloa House, co. Clackmannan ; Kellie Castle, co. Fife*), b. 29 Aug. 1865 ; *m*. 14 July 1892, Lady Violet, da. of Anthony (Ashley-Cooper), 8th Earl of Shaftesbury [E.]; and has issue 1*d* to 2*d*.

1*d*. John Francis Ashley Erskine, Lord Erskine, *b*. 26 Ap. 1895.

2*d*. Hon. Francis Walter Erskine, *b*. 9 Jan. 1899.   [Nos. 15284 to 15286.

The Plantagenet Roll

2c. Hon. William Augustus Forbes Erskine, 3rd Sec. Diplo. Ser. (*Bachelors'*), b. 30 Oct. 1871.

3c. Hon. Alexander Penrose Forbes Erskine, b. 13 Aug. 1881.

4c. Lady Constance Elsie Erskine.

5c. Lady Louisa Frances Erskine.

6c. Lady Frances Elizabeth Erskine, *m.* as 2nd wife, 29 July 1899, the Rev. Frederick Tufnell, M.A., Rector of Sudbury (*Sudbury Rectory, Derby*); and has issue 1d to 2d.

　1d. Henry Frederick Erskine Tufnell, b. 5 May 1903.

　2d. Mary Louisa Victoria Tufnell, b. 15 May 1901.

7c. Lady Alice Maud Mary Erskine.

2b. Hon. Augustus William Erskine, J.P. (*Bowscar, Penrith*), b. 18 June 1841; *m.* 18 Ap. 1871, Harriet Susannah, da. of William Forbes of Medwyn, d. 23 Feb. 1884; and has issue 1c to 5c.

　1c. Henry Walter Coningsby Erskine, b. 11 May 1872.

　2c. Walter Augustus Erskine, Lieut. R.G.A., b. 22 July 1880.

　3c. Eveline Mary Elise Erskine, b. 25 Nov. 1874; *m.* 20 May 1896, Major Henry Lowther, Indian Army; and has issue 1d to 3d.

　　1d. Christopher Henry Erskine Lowther, b. 1897.

　　2d. Robert Lancelot Lowther, b. 1900.

　　3d. Francis William Forbes Lowther, b. 1904.

　4c. Agnes Helen Erskine, b. 16 Ap. 1876.

　5c. Dorothy Christian Erskine, b. 31 Mar. 1878.

2a. Hon. *James Augustus Erskine*, b. 27 *Mar.* 1812; d. 24 *July* 1885; m. 1st, 15 *June* 1837, *Fanny, da. of Gen. Henry Ivatt Delacombe, C.B.*, d. 17 *Sept.* 1851; 2ndly, 4th Nov. 1852, *Elizabeth Bogue, da. of George Brodie, Historiographer Royal* [S.], d. 9 *Feb.* 1882; *and had issue* 1b *to* 11b.

1b. Augustus Erskine, in H.M.'s Customs at Melbourne, *late* 108th Regt. (*Brighton, Victoria*), b. 15 May 1843; *m.* 1st, Anne, da. of [———], d. 1886; 2ndly, 6 Aug. 1888, Kathleen, da. of Edmund Lyons of North Melbourne; and has issue 1c to 2c.

　1c. Bushby Lyons Erskine, b. 21 Aug. 1890.

　2c. Fentoun Augustus Erskine, b. 29 June 1895.

2b. William Alexander Ernest Erskine, b. 24 Mar. 1857; *m.* 1st, 27 Dec. 1878, Edith Elizabeth, widow of C. A. Turner of Staplegrove, da. of William Frank Elliot of Wilton, Taunton, d. Dec. 1879; 2ndly, 4 Jan. 1881, Amelia Esther, da. of Capt. John Ovens, 57th Regt.; and has issue 1c to 2c.

　1c. Eva Edith Mar Erskine, b. 24 Dec. 1879.

　2c. Ernestine Marguerite Louisa Erskine, b. 14 Oct. 1881; *m.* 20 Oct. 1902, Richard M'Gusty (*3 Pier Street, Lee-on-Solent, Hants*); and has issue 1d.

　　1d. Frances Margot Erskine M'Gusty, b. Nov. 1904.

3b. Charles Henry Stuart Erskine (1 *Beaumont Mansions, West Kensington, W.*), b. 19 Sept. 1858; *m.* 7 Sept. 1880, Constance Claire, da. of William Frank Elliot of Wilton, Taunton; and has issue 1c to 3c.

　1c. Constance Gwendoline Erskine.

　2c. Marion Esmé Erskine.

　3c. Kathleen Nadine Erskine.

4b. Edmond Walterton Coningsby Erskine (*Johannesburg, Transvaal*), b. 9 Nov. 1860; *m.* 1st, 6 Dec. 1882, Evelina Florence, da. of George Jones of Cuper Grange, Trinidad (marriage dissolved on her petition 1894); 2ndly, 1894, Edith, da. of Major Alexander Crombie; and has (with other children by 2nd wife) issue 1c.

　1c. Lowiny Lita Arabella Erskine, b. 12 Oct. 1883. 　　[Nos. 15287 to 15316.

304

# of The Blood Royal

5*b*. Evelyn Pierrepont Erskine, H.M.'s Customs (*Bunbury, West Australia*), *b*. 7 Sept. 1870; *m*. 1898, Avis Maria, da. of Joseph Hough of Collie River, West Australia; and has issue 1*c* to 3*c*.

   1*c*. Augustus Evelyn Erskine, *b*. 1902.

   2*c*. Aimie Rhoda Wilhelmina Erskine, *b*. 1898.

   3*c*. Azelina Aileen Erskine, *b*. 1900.

6*b*. Hugh Bushby Erskine (*Bunbury, West Australia*), *b*. 16 Sept. 1872; *m*. 5 Jan. 1897, May, da. of John Valentine of Bunbury; and has issue 1*c* to 3*c*.

   1*c*. John Patrick William Erskine, *b*. 1899.

   2*c*. Kellie Edmond Erskine, *b*. 1902.

   3*c*. Hugh Pierrepont Erskine, *b*. 1903.

7*b*. *Caroline Erskine*, b. 1845; d. 21 *Nov*. 1865; m. 1 *Nov*. 1864, *Col. George Falconer Pearson, M.S.C.; and had issue* 1*c*.

   1*c*. Caroline Pearson, *b*. 26 Oct. 1865.

8*b*. Rachel Georgina Erskine, *b*. 21 June 1854; *m*. 3 Dec. 1882, the Rev. Edward Field Norman (*Watford Vicarage, Rugby*); and has issue 1*c* to 2*c*.

   1*c*. Muriel Rachel Elizabeth Norman, *b*. 10 Sept. 1883.

   2*c*. Mary Margaret Isabel Norman, *b*. 8 June 1890.

9*b*. Elizabeth Mai Erskine, *b*. 8 Dec. 1863; *m*. 16 June 1897, Alexander Cockburn McBarnet, Bar.-at-Law (*Cairo, Egypt*); and has issue 1*c* to 4*c*.

   1*c*. Alexander Augustus Erskine McBarnet, *b*. 28 Feb. 1899.

   2*c*. George Gordon Kellie McBarnet, *b*. 25 May 1901.

   3*c*. Donald Victor Charles McBarnet, *b*. 24 May 1902.

   4*c*. Elizabeth Sheila Pajetta McBarnet, *b*. 6 Dec. 1904.

10*b*. Lowiny Ida Erskine, *b*. 1 Ap. 1868; *m*. 16 Aug. 1892, Major Charles James Addison, *late* R.A.M.C. (*Kirkee*, 642 *Fulham Road, S.W.*); and has issue 1*c*.

   1*c*. Lowiny Ivy Nairne Dupré Addison, *b*. 14 Oct. 1895.

11*b*. Augusta Helen Erskine, *b*. 22 July 1875; *m*. 15 Mar. 1895, Thomas George Harkness (*Windett, Wimbledon*); and has issue 1*c* to 2*c*.

   1*c*. George Augustus Erskine Harkness, *b*. 5 Nov. 1902.

   2*c*. Christophine Audrey Erskine Harkness, *b*. 28 Feb. 1900.

3*a*. *Henry David Erskine, Capt. R.M.*, b. 15 *June* 1814; d. 7 *Dec*. 1852; m. 27 *June* 1846, *Eliza, da. of John Ingle*, d. 1881; *and had issue* 1*b*.

   1*b*. Coningsby James Erskine (*Junior Carlton*), *b*. 27 Ap. 1849; *m*. 3 July 1872, Louisa Jane, da. of Thomas Henry Baylis, K.C.; and has issue 1*c*.

     1*c*. Evelyn Erskine.

4*a*. Lady (*R.W.* 1866) *Anne Caroline Erskine*, b. 3 *Sept*. 1823; d. 4 *Dec*. 1891; m. 18 *June* 1856, *the Rev. Joseph Haskoll*, d. 26 *Feb*. 1871; *and had issue* 1*b to* 7*b*.

   1*b*. Thomas James Forbes Haskoll, B.A. (*Pelham House, West Folkestone*), *b*. 15 July 1857; *m*. 14 Ap. 1896, Violet Marion, da. of Henry Alfred James, M.A.; and has issue 1*c*.

     1*c*. Thomas James Erskine Haskoll, *b*. 4 Nov. 1898.

   2*b*. Charles Joseph Haskoll, *b*. 24 Feb. 1868.

   3*b*. Mary Harriet Erskine Haskoll (*Liliput Cottage, Parkstone, Dorset*), *b*. 15 June 1857.

   4*b*. Agnes Caroline Haskoll, *b*. 23 Dec. 1861.

   5*b*. Frances Helena Haskoll, *b*. 23 May 1863.

   6*b*. Edith Monica Haskoll, *b*. 5 May 1865.

   7*b*. Alice Neale Haskoll, *b*. 2 Oct. 1866.   [Nos. 15317 to 15348.

The Plantagenet Roll

211. Descendants of Rev. the Hon. THOMAS ERSKINE, M.A., Vicar of Beighton (see Table XVIII.), *b.* 10 July 1785 ; *d.* 1 Jan. 1859 ; *m.* 4 June 1817, CHARLOTTE, da. of Major WATSON, *d.* 1 Dec. 1876 ; and had issue 1*a* to 3*a*.

1*a*. *Thomas Floyer Erskine, of the Civil Service, b.* 10 *July* 1819; *d.* 30 *Sept.* 1872; *m.* 28 *Aug.* 1856, *Emma, da. of Boughhey Hepworth of York Place, Portman Square ; and had issue 1b to 2b.*

    1*b*. Alice Mary Erskine,   ⎫

    2*b*. Frances Anne Janet Erskine, ⎬ (37 *St. Martin's, Stamford*).

2*a*. Charlotte Mary Erskine (67 *St. Martin's, Stamford*).

3*a*. Mary Margaret Anna Erskine, now (R.L. 30 Aug. 1884) Zwilchenbart-Erskine (*Portway House, Warminster*), *m.* as 2nd wife, 27 Dec. 1864, Rodolph Zwilchenbart of Dean Wood, co. Berks, *d.* 2 Ap. 1883 ; and has issue 1*b*.

    1*b*. Gratney Rodolph Zwilchenbart-Erskine (*The Buries, Bishopstrow, Warminster*), *b.* 1871 ; *m.* 1896, Theodora, da. of W. H. Laverton of Leighton, Westbury ; and has issue 1*c*.

        1*c*. Helen Mary Zwilchenbart-Erskine, *b.* 1901.   [Nos. 15349 to 15354.

212. Descendants of Lady EVELYN PIERREPONT (see Table XVIII.), *d.* 26 June 1727 ; *m.* as 1st wife, 8 Mar. 1712, JOHN (LEVESON-GOWER), 1st EARL GOWER [G.B.], *b.* 10 Aug. 1694; *d.* 25 Dec. 1754 ; and had issue.

See pp. 172, 175–184, Nos. 3846–5448 and 5575–6636.

                                    [Nos. 15355 to 18031.

213. Descendants, if any, of Lady CAROLINE PIERREPONT (see Table XVIII.), *m.* 1712, THOMAS BRAND.

214. Descendants of WILLIAM HENRY CAVENDISH (BENTINCK), 3rd DUKE OF PORTLAND [E.], K.G. (see Table XVIII.), *b.* 14 Ap. 1738 ; *d.* 30 Oct. 1809 ; *m.* 8 Nov. 1766, Lady DOROTHY, da. of William (CAVENDISH), 4th DUKE OF DEVONSHIRE [E.], K.G., *b.* 27 Aug. 1750 ; *d.* 3 June 1794 ; and had issue.

See the Tudor Roll of "The Blood Royal of Britain" (Table XLII.), pp. 245–248, Nos. 23010–23115.   [Nos. 18032 to 18137.

215. Descendants of Lord EDWARD CHARLES BENTINCK (see Table XVIII.), *b.* 3 Mar. 1744 ; *d.* 8 Oct. 1819 ; *m.* 28 Dec. 1782, ELIZABETH, da. of Richard CUMBERLAND, the celebrated dramatist and writer, *d.* 1837 ; and had issue 1*a* to 2*a*.

1*a*. *Harriet Elizabeth Bentinck, b.* 9 *Ap.* 1787 ; *d.* 31 *Dec.* 1862 ; *m. as 2nd wife,* 28 *May* 1809, *Sir William Mordaunt Sturt Milner, 4th Bart.* [G.B.], *d.* 24 *Mar.* 1855 ; *and had issue.*

See the Clarence Volume, pp. 269–272, Nos. 7203–7220 and 7240–7270.

2*a*. *Charlotte Georgiana Sophia Bentinck, d.* 1819; *m.* 1814, *Lieut.-Gen. Sir Robert Garrett of Ellington, Isle of Thanet, K.C.B.*   [Nos. 18138 to 18186.

# of The Blood Royal

216. Descendants of Lady ELIZABETH CAVENDISH BENTINCK (see Table XVIII.), b. 27 June 1735 ; d. 12 Dec. 1825 ; m. 22 May 1759, THOMAS (THYNNE), 1st MARQUIS OF BATH [G.B.], b. 13 Sept. 1734 ; d. 19 Nov. 1796 ; and had issue.

See the Tudor Roll of "The Blood Royal of Britain," pp. 212–222, Nos. 21654–22022.   [Nos. 18187 to 18555.

217. Descendants of Lady HENRIETTA CAVENDISH BENTINCK (see Table XVIII.), b. 6 Mar. 1736 ; d. 4 June 1827 ; m. 28 May 1763, GEORGE HARRY (GREY), 5th EARL OF STAMFORD [E.] and 1st EARL OF WARRINGTON [G.B.], b. 1 Oct. 1737 ; d. 28 May 1819 ; and had issue.

See the Tudor Roll of "The Blood Royal of Britain," pp. 320–328, Nos. 26183–26404.   [Nos. 18556 to 18779.

218. Descendants of Lady CATHERINE TUFTON (see Table XVIII.), b. 24 Ap. 1693 ; d. 13 Feb. 1734 ; m. 23 Jan. 1708, EDWARD WATSON, styled VISCOUNT SONDES, M.P., b. c. 1687 ; d.v.p. 20 Mar. 1722 ; and had issue.

See pp. 242–243, Nos. 8843–9108.   [Nos. 18780 to 19045.

219. Descendants of Lady ANNE TUFTON (see Table XVIII.), b. 9 Aug. 1694 ; d. 22 Mar. 1757 ; m. 12 Feb. 1709, JAMES (CECIL), 5th EARL OF SALISBURY [E.], b. June 1691; d. 9 Oct. 1728 ; and had issue.

See pp. 216–219, Nos. 7652–7738.   [Nos. 19046 to 19132.

220. Descendants of Lady MARY TUFTON (see Table XVIII.), b. 6 July 1701 ; d. 12 Feb. 1785 ; m. 2ndly, as 3rd wife, 16 May 1736, JOHN (LEVESON-GOWER), 1st EARL GOWER [G.B.], P.C., b. 10 Aug. 1694 ; d. 25 Dec. 1754 ; and had issue.

See p. 172, Nos. 5449–5574.   [Nos. 19133 to 19258.

221. Descendants of ARABELLA DIANA COPE (see Table XVIII.), d. Aug. 1825 ; m. 1st, 4 Jan. 1790, JOHN FREDERICK (SACKVILLE, 3rd DUKE [G.B.] and 9th EARL [E.] OF DORSET, b. 25 Mar. 1745 ; d. 19 July 1799 ; 2ndly, 7 Ap. 1801, CHARLES (WHITWORTH), 1st (and only) EARL [U.K.] and BARON [I.] WHITWORTH, P.C., Viceroy of Ireland, bapt. 29 May 1752 ; d.s.p. 12 May 1825 ; and had issue 1a to 2a.

1a. *George John Frederick (Sackville), 4th Duke [G.B.] and 10th Earl [E.] of Dorset,* b. 15 Nov. 1793 ; d.s.p. 14 Feb. 1815.
2a. *Lady Elizabeth Sackville (in 1864 sole heir),* suo jure 1st *Baroness Buckhurst* (1864) [U.K.], b. 11 Aug. 1795 ; d. 9 Jan. 1870 ; m. 21 June 1813, *George John (West, afterwards (R.L. 6 Nov. 1843) Sackville-West), 5th Earl [G.B.] and 11th Baron [E.] De La Warr,* P.C., b. 26 Oct. 1791 ; d. 23 Feb. 1869 ; *and had issue.*
See the Clarence Volume, pp. 223–224, Nos. 4502–4535.
                                                        [Nos. 19259 to 19292,

The Plantagenet Roll

222. Descendants of CATHERINE ANNE COPE (see Table XVIII.), *d.* 16 Nov. 1832 ; *m.* 4 Ap. 1791, GEORGE (GORDON), 9th MARQUIS OF HUNTLY [S.], 1st BARON MELDRUM [U.K.], Premier Marquis of Scotland, K.T., *b.* 28 June 1761 ; *d.* 17 June 1853 ; and had issue.

See the Tudor Roll of " The Blood Royal of Britain," pp. 527–529, Nos. 35196–35318.   [Nos. 19293 to 19415.

223. Descendants of ANNE DUNCOMBE (see Table XVIII.), *d.* (–) ; *m.* 18 Ap. 1774, ROBERT SHAFTO of Whitworth, co. Durham, M.P., *d.* 24 Nov. 1797 ; and had issue 1*a* to 2*a*.

1*a*. *Robert Eden Duncombe Shafto of Whitworth, M.P.*, b. 23 *Mar.* 1776 ; d. 17 *Jan.* 1848 ; m. Nov. 1803, *Catherine, da. of Sir John Eden, 4th Bart.* [E.], b. 1770 ; d. 19 *Mar.* 1872 ; *and had issue* 1b *to* 5b.

1*b*. *Robert Duncombe Shafto of Whitworth, M.P., J.P., D.L.*, b. 7 *Ap.* 1806 ; d. 1889 ; m. 1838, *Charlotte Rosa, da. of William Baring, M.P.*, d. 20 *Nov.* 1898 ; *and had issue* 1c *to* 2c.

1*c*. Robert Charles Duncombe Shafto (*Whitworth Park, Ferryhill, co. Durham*), *b.* July 1843 ; *m.* 1884, Alice Vere, da. of Frederic Boucher of Sydney, N.S.W., and Frimley, co. Surrey.

2*c*. Edith Rose Shafto, *m.* 2 May 1867, the Rev. Edward Abercrombie Wilkinson, M.A., J.P., Vicar of Whitworth (*Whitworth Vicarage, Ferryhill*) ; and has issue 1*d* to 8*d*.

1*d*. Edward James Wilkinson, *b.* 25 July 1868 ; *m.* 22 Nov. 1898, Ethel, da. of Arthur F. Varley of Chiswick.

2*d*. Stephen Wilkinson, *b.* 31 Mar. 1872 ; *m.* June 1897, Constance Greta, da. of Edward Stout ; and has issue 1*e* to 2*e*.

1*e*. Michael Wilkinson, *b.* 14 May 1898.

2*e*. Christopher Denys Wilkinson, *b.* 8 Oct. 1901.

3*d*. George Robert Wilkinson, *b.* 30 Dec. 1875.

4*d*. Lancelot Wilkinson, *b.* 28 Nov. 1878.

5*d*. Edith Dorothea Wilkinson.

6*d*. Mary Katherine Wilkinson, *m.* 10 Oct. 1895, Alan Hutchinson, J.P. (*Tudhoe, co. Durham*) ; and has issue 1*e* to 3*e*.

1*e*. Alan Edward Hutchinson, *b.* 24 July 1896.

2*e*. Miles Middleton Hutchinson, *b.* 7 Sept. 1897.

3*e*. John Francis Baring Hutchinson, *b.* 9 Aug. 1902.

7*d*. Rachel Wilkinson, *m.* 20 Feb. 1895, Percy Somers Tyringham Stephens, J.P. (*Croxdale, Wood House, Durham*) ; and has issue 1*e* to 3*e*.

1*e*. Martin Tyringham Stephens.

2*e*. Joan Tyringham Stephens.

3*e*. Lettice Stephens.

8*d*. Cicely Wilkinson, *m.* 26 Aug. 1897, Charles Thurstan Fogg-Elliot, Capt 4th Batt. Durham L.I. (*Staindrop, Darlington*) ; and has issue 1*e* to 4*e*.

1*e*. Mark Fogg-Elliot, *b.* 30 Sept. 1898.

2*e*. Oliver Fogg-Elliot, *b.* 19 May 1901.

3*e*. Lancelot Fogg-Elliot, *b.* 17 Jan. 1903.

4*e*. Robin Fogg-Elliot, *b.* 9 Nov. 1904.

2*b*. *Rev. John Duncombe Shafto*, b. 16 *May* 1807 ; d. 6 *Aug.* 1863 ; m. *Catherine, da. of the Rev. Robert Moore (son of the Archbishop of Canterbury)*, d. 14 *July* 1888 ; *and had issue* 1c *to* 4c.   [Nos. 19416 to 19437.

308

# of The Blood Royal

1c. Catherine Mary Fitzwilliam Duncombe Shafto.

2c. Dulcibella Maria Shafto (*St. Martin's, Sevenoaks*), *m.* 11 Sept. 1866, the Rev. Arthur Majendie, Rector of Bladon, *d.* 15 Jan. 1895; and has issue 1*d* to 3*d*.

1*d*. Rev. Lionel Robert Majendie, Rector of Bladon with Woodstock (*Bladon Rectory, Oxford, b.* 17 Sept. 1871; *m.* 9 Oct. 1902, Marjorie, da. of the Rev. Canon Savage; and has issue 1*e* to 2*e*.

1*e*. Dorothy Elizabeth Majendie, *b.* 1 Aug. 1903.

2*e*. Margaret Dulcibella Majendie, *b.* 18 Oct. 1905.

2*d*. Bernard John Majendie, Capt. King's Royal Rifle Corps, *b.* 27 Ap. 1875; *m.* 22 Nov. 1904, Dorothy, da. of G. Davidson.

3*d*. Dulcie Shafto Majendie.

3c. *Amelia Harriet Shafto, d.* 26 *Jan.* 1900; *m.* 28 *Dec.* 1867, *Robert Norton, M.P., J.P., D.L.* (*Downs House, Yalding, Maidstone*); *and had issue* 1*d to* 4*d.*

1*d*. Robert Douglas Norton, of the Foreign Office, *b.* 17 Sept. 1868.

2*d*. Reginald Arthur Norton, R.N., *b.* 28 Oct. 1873.

3*d*. Gertrude Mary Norton, *b.* 1 Jan. 1870.

4*d*. Evelyn Norton, *b.* 31 July 1875.

4c. Emma Shafto (*Grey's Court, Henley-on-Thames*), *m.* 21 June 1877, Lieut.-Col. Richard Talbot Plantagenet Stapleton, 19th Hussars, *b.* 21 Ap. 1834; *d.* 28 Ap. 1899; and has issue 1*d* to 4*d*.

1*d*. Sir Miles Talbot Stapleton, 9th Bart. [E.] (*Grey's Court, Henley-on-Thames*), *b.* 26 May 1893.

2*d*. Marguérite Cecile Catherine Stapleton, *b.* 13 Dec. 1878; *m.* 6 Ap. 1904, Capt. Arthur Duncombe Shafto, D.S.O. (*Oakleigh, Scotby, Carlisle*); and has issue 1*e*.

1*e*. Mark Duncombe Shafto, *b.* 21 Aug. 1905.

3*d*. Olive Florence Stapleton, *b.* 22 June 1880.

4*d*. Hilda Alice Stapleton, *b.* 24 Feb. 1884.

3b. *Rev. Slingsby Duncombe Shafto, b.* 11 *Aug.* 1811; *d.* (–); *m.* 19 *July* 1838, *Frances, da. of Joseph Hunter of Walbottle; and had issue* 1*c to* 5*c.*

1c. Slingsby Duncombe Shafto, J.P., D.L., *b.* 1844; *m.* 30 Sept. 1876, Louisa Anne, da. of Frederick Newman Appleyard; and has issue 1*d* to 5*d*.

1*d*. Slingsby Duncombe Shafto, Lieut. 7th Batt. K.R.R.C., *b.* 17 Aug. 1877.

2*d*. Robert Charles Duncombe Shafto, *b.* 6 July 1879.

3*d*. Thomas Duncombe Shafto, *b.* 21 Ap. 1884.

4*d*. Rosa Louisa Eleanor Duncombe Shafto, *b.* 12 July 1878.

5*d*. Silvia Duncombe Shafto, *b.* 31 Dec. 1885.

2c. *Fanny Shafto, d.* 11 *Feb.* 1886; *m.* 1*st*, 23 *Nov.* 1863, *Major John Wynd Coates of Pasture House, Northallerton; 2ndly,* 26 *Ap.* 1873, *John Hawksworth Legard; and had issue* 1*d to* 2*d.*

1*d*. George Shafto Legard, *b.* 29 July 1874.

2*d*. Ralph Hawksworth Legard, *b.* 1875.

3c. Eleanor Margaret Shafto, *m.* 10 July 1865, Capt. Robert Charles de Grey Vyner, J.P., D.L. (*Newby Hall, Ripon ; Tupholme Hall, Lincoln, &c.*); and has issue.

See p. 141, Nos. 2049–2054.

4c. Rosa Shafto, *m.* 1871, Col. Arthur Wombwell.

5c. Georgiana Shafto, *m.* 3 Sept. 1860, Henry Cradock.

4b. *Rev. Arthur Duncombe Shafto, Rector of Brancepeth, J.P., b.* 11 *Jan.* 1815; *d.* 28 *Feb.* 1900; *m.* 1 *Sept.* 1842, *Dorothea Anne, da. of George Hutton Wilkinson of Harperley Park, d.* 18 *Feb.* 1866; *and had issue* 1*c to* 5*c.*

1c. Charles Ottiwell Duncombe Shafto, B.A. (Camb.), J.P., Bar.-at-Law, *b.* 1853; *m.* 4 June 1877, Helena Rosa, da. and co-h. of the Rev. George Pearson Wilkinson of Harperley Park, J.P.; and has issue 1*d* to 4*d*.   [Nos. 19438 to 19472.

The Plantagenet Roll

1*d*. Charles Duncombe Shafto, Lieut. Durham L.I., *b*. 27 June 1878 ; d. (*being killed at Spion Kop*) Jan. 1900.

2*d*. Arthur Duncombe Shafto, *b*. 8 Ap. 1880.

3*d*. George Duncombe Shafto, *b*. Feb. 1882.

4*d*. Kathleen Duncombe Shafto, *b*. May 1884.

2*c*. Susan Frances Duncombe Shafto, d. 1872 ; m. 20 Jan. 1870, *the Right Hon. John Lloyd Wharton, P.C., M.P., J.P., D.L., &c., Chairman Quarter Sessions, co. Durham, &c.* (*Dryburn, Durham ; Bramham, Tadcaster ; 1c King Street, St. James'*) ; and had issue 1*d*.

1*d*. Mary Dorothea Wharton, *m*. 23 Jan. 1894, Lieut.-Col. Charles Waring Darwin, Durham L.I. ; and has issue 1*e* to 3*e*.

1*e*. Charles John Wharton Darwin, *b*. 12 Dec. 1894.

2*e*. Francis Wharton Darwin, *b*. July 1896.

3*e*. Gilbert William Lloyd Darwin, *b*. 9 Nov. 1899.

3*c*. Dorothea Elizabeth Duncombe Shafto, *m*. 25 May 1870, the Rev. William Fawcett, Vicar of Somerford Keynes (*Somerford Keynes Vicarage, Wilts*) ; and has issue 1*d* to 9*d*.

1*d*. Arthur Fawcett, *b*. 4 Feb. 1871.

2*d*. Foyle Fawcett, *b*. 26 Ap. 1876.

3*d*. Edward Fawcett, *b*. 24 Mar. 1880.

4*d*. John Fawcett, *b*. 13 Mar. 1884.

5*d*. Winifred Fawcett.

6*d*. Dorothy Fawcett, *m*. 6 Ap. 1899, Col. Cuthbert George Collingwood, C.B. (*Glanton Pyke, Glanton R.S.O., Northumberland*) ; and has issue 1*e* to 4*e*.

1*e*. Edward Foyle Collingwood, *b*. 17 Jan. 1900.

2*e*. Cuthbert John Collingwood, *b*. 12 Jan. 1901.

3*e*. Arthur Christopher Collingwood, *b*. 21 Mar. 1902.

4*e*. Richard George Collingwood, *b*. 7 Oct. 1903.

7*d*. Marion Fawcett.

8*d*. Ruth Fawcett.

9*d*. Decima Fawcett.

4*c*. Margaret Duncombe Shafto, *m*. 13 Oct. 1886, the Rev. Arthur Evans.

5*c*. Edith Mary Duncombe Shafto, *m*. 4 Feb. 1891, Capt. Charles Foyle Randolph, J.P., Lancashire Fusiliers (*Kimpton Lodge, near Andover, co. Hants*).

5*b*. Catherine Shafto, d. (–) ; m. 1827, *William Charles Harland of Sutton Hall, co. York.*

2*a*. Thomas Shafto, b. 20 Aug. 1777 ; d. (–).   [Nos. 19473 to 19495.

224. Descendants of JOHN (HOLLES), 4th EARL OF CLARE and 1st DUKE OF NEWCASTLE [E.], K.G. (see Table XIX.), *b*. 9 Jan. 1662 ; *d*. 15 July 1711 ; *m*. Feb. 1690, Lady MARGARET, da. and co-h. of Henry (CAVENDISH), 2nd Duke of Newcastle [E.], *b. c.* 1651 ; *d*. 24 Dec. 1716 ; and had issue.

See p. 306, Nos. 15355–18778.   [Nos. 19496 to 22908.

225. Descendants of Lady ELIZABETH HOLLES (see Table XIX.), *b. c.* 1657 ; *d*. 9 Nov. 1725 ; *m*. (mar. lic. 4 May) 1676, CHRISTOPHER (VANE), 1st BARON BARNARD [E.], *b. c.* 1653 ; *d*. 28 Oct. 1723 ; and had issue.

See the Clarence Volume (Table LXXIII.), pp. 581–586, Nos. 24444–24573.

[Nos. 22909 to 23038.

# of The Blood Royal

226. Descendants, if any, of Lady MARY HOLLES (see Table XIX.), wife of HUGH BOSCAWEN, and of Lady ANNE HOLLES.

227. Descendants of the Right Hon. and Hon. HENRY PELHAM, Chancellor of the Exchequer (see Table XIX.), d. 6 Mar. 1754 ; m. 29 Oct. 1726, Lady CATHERINE, da. of John (MANNERS), 2nd Duke of Rutland [E.], K.G., d. 1780 ; and had issue.

See pp. 166–168, Nos. 3455–3626. [Nos. 23039 to 23210.

228. Descendants of the Hon. GRACE PELHAM (see Table XIX.), d. 1710 ; m. GEORGE NAYLOR of Hurstmonceaux Castle, co. Sussex.

229. Descendants, if any, of the Hon. GERTRUDE PELHAM (see Table XIX.), wife of DAVID POLHILL of Otford, co. Kent.

230. Descendants of the Hon. LUCY PELHAM (see Table XIX.), d. 20 July 1736 ; m. 16 May 1717, HENRY (CLINTON), 7th EARL OF LINCOLN [E.], K.G., b. 1684 ; d. 7 Sept. 1828 ; and had issue.

See the Clarence Volume, pp. 174–176, Nos. 2876–2937.

[Nos. 23211 to 23272.

231. Descendants of Sir JOHN SHELLEY, 5th Bart. [E.] (see Table XIX.), b. 1727 ; d. 11 Sept. 1783 ; m. 1st, 27 Aug. 1769, WILHELMINA, da. of John NEWNHAM of Maresfield Park, co. Sussex, d. 21 Mar. 1772 ; and had issue 1a.

1a. Sir John Shelley, 6th Bart. [E.], b. 3 Mar. 1771 ; d. 28 Mar. 1852; m. 4 June 1807, Frances, da. and h. of Thomas Winckley of Brockholes, co. Lancaster, d. 24 Feb. 1873 ; and had issue 1b to 6b.
2b. Sir John Villiers Shelley, 7th Bart. [E.], b. 18 Mar. 1808 ; d. 26 Jan. 1867 (leaving issue an only da., who m. and d.s.p. 12 Ap. 1898).
2b. Rev. Sir Frederick Shelley, 8th Bart. [E.], b. 5 May 1808 ; d. 19 Mar. 1869 ; m. 4 Feb. 1845, Charlotte Martha, da. of the Rev. Henry Hippisley of Lamborne Place, d. 20 May 1893 ; and had issue 1c to 3c.
1c. Sir John Shelley, 9th Bart. [E.], J.P., D.L., Hon. Col. 1st Devon Imp. Yeo., High Sheriff co. Devon 1895 (Shobrooke Park, Crediton), b. 31 Aug. 1848 ; m. 29 June 1882, Marion Emma, da. of Richard Benyon of Englefield House ; and has issue 1d to 4d.
1d. John Frederick Shelley, b. 14 Oct. 1884.
2d. Richard Shelley, b. 18 Jan. 1892.
3d. Elizabeth Marion Shelley, b. 14 June 1883.
4d. Constance Mary Shelley, b. 5 May 1890.
2c. Frederick Shelley, J.P. (Ambarrow Hill, Sandhurst, co. Berks), b. 31 Aug. 1849 ; m. 1 June 1882, Lady Margaret, da. of Stafford Henry (Northcote), 1st Earl of Iddesleigh [U.K.], G.C.B. ; and has issue 1d.
1d. Pastorella Cecilia Martha Shelley, b. 28 Jan. 1886.
3c. Charlotte Frances Shelley, b. 21 May 1855 ; m. 18 July 1883, the Hon. Edward Arthur Palk (Little Testwood, Totton, co. Hants). [Nos. 23273 to 23280.

The Plantagenet Roll

3b. *Adolphus Edward Shelley*, b. 2 *Mar.* 1812; d. 29 *May* 1854; m. 28 *Ap.* 1836, *Amelia, da. of Henry Hinchliffe; and had issue* 1c *to* 2c.

1c. Montagu Adolphus Shelley, b. 11 Feb. 1842.

2c. *Katharine Cecilia Shelley*, d. 5 *Sept.* 1902; m. 1*st*, 3 *Mar.* 1859, *James Bontein, Groom of the Privy Chamber and Clerk of the Robes to H.M. Queen Victoria* 1821, d. 16 Oct. 1884; 2*ndly, as* 2*nd wife,* 1885, *Major-Gen. Francis Edward Drewe of Grange, co. Devon*; d. 20 Feb. 1891; *and had issue* 1d *to* 2d.

1d. James Shelley Bontein, J.P., a member of the Roy. Co. of Archers (H.M.'s Scottish Body Guard) (*Glencruitten, Oban, co. Argyll*), b. 26 Nov. 1859; *m.* 14 Dec. 1889, Emilie Josephine, widow of Hans Sloane Stanley of Paulton's Park, da. of Francis Edwards of Pickerage, co. Bucks.

2d. Eva Louisa Bontein, *m.* 19 July 1883, the Hon. John Schomberg Trefusis, C.M.G. (*Hayne, Cullompton, Devon*); and has issue.

See the Tudor Roll of "The Blood Royal of Britain," p. 170, Nos. 20211–20214.

4b. Spencer Shelley, *late* a Principal Clerk in Treasury (37 *Bathwick Hill, Bath*), b. 24 Dec. 1813; *m.* 1 Feb. 1843, Susannah, da. of Stephen Martin Leake; and has issue 1c to 5c.

1c. Spencer Shelley (*The Beeches, Newnham on Severn*), b. 24 Oct. 1843; *m.* Mary Penny, da. of [——] Watson; and has issue 1d to 2d.

1d. Spencer Shelley, b. 1878.

2d. Margaret Ruth Shelley.

2c. Francis Heskett Shelley (*Monsava Estate, Galadera, Ceylon*), b. 2 Mar. 1854.

3c. Georgiana Fanny Shelley, *m.* 8 Aug. 1867, Richard Saul Ferguson, J.P., D.L., Chancellor of Carlisle, d. 1900; and has issue 1d to 2d.

1d. Spencer Charles Ferguson, b. 13 Aug. 1868.

2d. Margaret Josephine Ferguson.

4c. Florentia Shelley, *m.* 15 July 1870, James Henry Davidson (*Aldeburgh, co. Suffolk*); and has issue 1d to 6d.

1d. Florence May Davidson, b. 16 May 1871; *m.* 26 July 1897, John Gardiner, B.A. (Oxford Honours), M.R.C.S., L.R.C.P. (10 *Braidwood Terrace, Mutley, Plymouth*); and has issue 1e to 2e.

1e. John Spencer Hesketh Gardiner, b. 9 Ap. 1899.

2e. Joyce Enid Gardiner, b. 11 Aug. 1901.

2d. Violet Maude Davidson, b. 31 Dec. 1873.

3d. Daisy Shelley Davidson, b. 30 Mar. 1875; *m.* 12 Mar. 1898, Henry George Talbot Carr (*Bleak House, Aldeburgh, Suffolk*); and has issue 1e to 2e.

1e. John Henry Talbot Carr, b. 10 Mar. 1899.

2e. Audrey Violet Talbot Carr, b. 29 Sept. 1901.

4d. Dora Davidson, b. 18 Ap. 1876; *m.* 26 Nov. 1898, Ernest Allott (*Kincraig, 98 York Road, Southend-on-Sea*); and has issue 1e.

1e. Enid Phyllis Allott, b. 24 Dec. 1902.

5d. Barbara Augusta Davidson, b. 3 July 1878.

6d. *Gladys Edith Davidson*, b. 12 *Dec.* 1880; d. 18 *Ap.* 1905.

5c. *Rosamond Blanche Isabel Shelley*, *m.* 27 Jan. 1892, Herbert Fullarton Dent (*Chestnut Lodge, Surbiton, Surrey; Canton, China*); and has issue 1d.

1d. William Herbert Shelley Dent, b. 30 Jan. 1905.

5b. *Fanny Lucy Shelley*, b. 2 *Feb.* 1811; d. 11 *May* 1899; m. 19 *May* 1834, *the Hon. George Edgcumbe*, b. 23 *June* 1800; d. 18 *Feb.* 1882; *and had issue* 1c *to* 5c.

1c. Richard John Frederick Edgcumbe, J.P., one of H.M.'s Serjeants-at-Arms, Capt. Royal Bucks Militia (*Edgbarrow, Crowthorne, Berks; 33 Tedworth Square,*

[Nos. 23281 to 23309.

312

# of The Blood Royal

S.W.), b. 12 Aug. 1843; m. 26 Nov. 1872, Mary Louisa, da. of John Bligh Monck of Coley Park; and has issue 1d.

1d. Kenelm William Edward Edgcumbe, b. 9 Oct. 1873.

2c. Edward Mortimer Edgcumbe, Lieut. N.Z. Militia, b. 30 Aug. 1847; d. 29 June 1890; m. 30 Jan. 1868, Constance (Parnell, Auckland, N.Z.), da. of the Rev. Robert Burrowes of St. Stephen's, Auckland; and had issue 1d to 4d.

1d. George Valletort Edgcumbe (Valtersholme, Devonport, Auckland, N.Z.), b. 26 Jan. 1869; m. 1897, Georgina Mildred, da. of Thomas Aubrey Bell, of Auckland; and has issue (with 3 das.) 1e.

1e. Edward Piers Edgcumbe, b. 1903.

2d. Ernest Athole Valletort Edgcumbe (Cotehele, Parnell, Auckland, N.Z.), b. 25 July 1870; m. 1896, Louisa, da. of William Martin of Auckland; and has issue 1e.

1e. Florence Maye Edgcumbe, b. 1890.

3d. Gerald Richard Valletort Edgcumbe, b. 15 Aug. 1871.

4d. Florence Violet Edgcumbe.

3c. Caroline Cecilia Edgcumbe (3 Lowndes Square, S.W.), m. 19 May 1866, Athole Charles (Liddell), 3rd Earl of Ravensworth [U.K.], d.s.p. 7 Feb. 1904.

4c. Elizabeth Catharine Edgcumbe, m. 1 July 1874, Lieut.-Col. Albert Thornton Wodehouse, R.A. (4 Wingfield Villas, Stoke, Devonport).

5c. Emily Fanny Georgiana Edgcumbe (Heath Lodge, Bournemouth), m. 1st, 13 Ap. 1871, Major George Edward Earle, b. 29 Mar. 1843; d. 1 June 1878; 2ndly, 4 June 1879, Lieut.-Gen. James Sinclair Thomson, d. 20 Jan. 1893; and has issue 1d to 3d.

1d. Mabel Emily Patience Earle, m. 3 Oct. 1893, Capt. Vernon Henry Mellor, 3rd Batt. Sherwood Foresters.

2d. Marion Elizabeth Earle, m. 27 Ap. 1899, H. S. Bassett.

3d. Dorothy Georgiana Thomson, b. 17 June 1881.

6b. Cecilia Victoria Shelley, d. (–); m. 11 Aug. 1842, Thomas Fassett Kent, Bar.-at-Law.　　　　　　　　　　　　　　　　　　　　　　　[Nos. 23310 to 23322.

232. Descendants of HENRIETTA SHELLEY (see Table XIX.), b. Feb. 1730; d. May 1802; m. 26 June 1753, GEORGE (ONSLOW), 1st EARL OF ONSLOW [U.K.] and 4th BARON ONSLOW [G.B.], b. 13 Sept. 1731; d. 17 May 1814; and had issue 1a to 2a.

1a. Thomas (Onslow), 2nd Earl of Onslow [U.K.] and 5th Baron [G.B.] Onslow, b. 15 Mar. 1754; d. 22 Feb. 1827; m. 1st, 20 Dec. 1776, Arabella, da. and co-h. of Eton Mainwaring Ellerker of Risby Park, co. York, d. 11 Ap. 1782; and had issue 1b to 2b.

1b. Arthur George (Onslow), 3rd Earl of Onslow [U.K.] and 6th Baron [G.B.] Onslow, b. 25 Oct. 1777; d. 24 Oct. 1870; m. 21 July 1818, Mary, da. of George Fludyer of Ayston, co. Rutland, b. 18 Ap. 1793; d. 1 Mar. 1830; and had issue.
See the Tudor Roll of "The Blood Royal of Britain," p. 488, Nos. 33674–33675.

2b. Hon. Thomas Cranley Onslow of Stoke Park, co. Surrey, Col. 2nd Surrey Militia, &c., b. 7 Oct. 1778; d. 7 July 1861; m. 28 May 1812, Susannah Elizabeth, da. and co-h. of Nathaniel Hillier of Stoke Park, d. 26 Mar. 1852; and had issue 1c to 2c.

1c. George Augustus Cranley Onslow, b. 14 May 1813; d.v.p. 13 Ap. 1855; m. 11 July 1848, Mary Harriet Anne, da. of Lieut.-Gen. William F. B. Loftus of Kilbride, co. Wicklow, d. 13 Ap. 1855; and had issue 1d.

1d. William Hillier (Onslow), 4th Earl of Onslow [U.K.], 7th Baron Onslow [G.B.], P.C., G.C.M.G., Lord High Steward of Guildford, President of the Board of Agriculture, formerly (1888–1892) Governor and Commander-in-Chief of New
　　　　　　　　　　　　　　　　　　　　　　　[Nos. 23323 to 23325.

The Plantagenet Roll

Zealand, &c., &c. (*Clandon Park, Guildford; 7 Richmond Terrace, Whitehall, S.W.*), *b.* 7 Mar. 1853; *m.* 3 Feb. 1875, the Hon. Florence Coulston, da. and co-h. of Alan Legge (Gardner), 3rd Baron Gardner [I. and U.K.]; and has issue 1*e* to 4*e*.

    1*e*. Richard William Alan Onslow, Viscount Cranley, 3rd Sec. Diplo. Ser., *b.* 23 Aug. 1876.

    2*e*. Hon. Victor Alexander Herbert Huia Onslow, *b.* 13 Nov. 1890.

    3*e* Lady Gwendolen Florence Mary Onslow.

    4*e*. Lady Dorothy Evelyn Augusta Onslow.

  2*c*. *Arthur Edward Onslow, Lieut.-Col. Scots Fusiliers, b.* 13 Nov. 1815; *d.* 10 *July* 1897; *m.* 30 *April* 1846, *Margaret Anne,*[1] *da. of Edward Ferrers of Baddesley Clinton (by his wife Lady Harriet, née Townshend), d.* 11 *Ap.* 1892; *and had issue* 1*d to* 5*d.*

    1*d*. Charles Vere Townshend Onslow (now R.L. 2 May 1898) Mainwaring-Ellerker-Onslow (*Ingleby, Wimborne Road, Bournemouth*), *b.* 31 May 1848; *m.* 31 Oct. 1876, Amelia Tolson, da. of Frederick Roger Carter; and has issue 1*e* to 3*e*.

      1*e*. Arthur Guildford Mainwaring-Ellerker-Onslow, *b.* 8 July 1888.

      2*e*. Arabella Vere Gwendolen Mainwaring-Ellerker-Onslow, *b.* 21 Oct. 1885.

      3*e*. Minnie Margaret Matilda Mainwaring-Ellerker-Onslow, *b.* 23 July 1892.

    2*d*. Arthur Denzil Onslow, *b.* 25 Jan. 1856.

    3*d*. Arthur Edward Onslow (*Thorncliff, 22 Zetland Road, Redland, Bristol*), *b.* 1 Sept. 1862; *m.* 1888, Emma Elizabeth, da. of [——] Barnacott; and has issue 1*e*.

      1*e*. Vivian Isidore Onslow, *b.* 1888.

    4*d*. Ferrers Mainwaring Onslow (*2 Montrose Terrace, Plymouth*), *b.* 18 Oct. 1863; *m.* 28 Ap. 1892, Edith, da. of Alfred Broad.

    5*d*. Constance Henrietta Onslow (*Baddesley Clinton, Cleveland Road, Torquay*), *b.* 15 Nov. 1854; *m.* 27 July 1885, Isidore James Carter, Solicitor.

  2*a*. *Hon. Edward Onslow, b.* 9 *Ap.* 1858; *d.* 18 *Oct.* 1829; *m.* 6 *Mar.* 1783, *Marie Rosalie, da. of John (de Bourdeille), Seigneur de Couzance in France, d.* 20 *June* 1842; *and had issue* 1*b.*

    1*b*. *Arthur Onslow, K.L.H., an officer in the French Army, b.* 9 *May* 1788; *d.* 25 *Ap.* 1876; *m.* 26 *Mar.* 1819, *Emilia Charlotte, da. of R. Wetherell of Brighthelmstone, co. Sussex, d.* 1 *Nov.* 1843; *and had issue* 1*c.*

      1*c*. *Frederick Horace Onslow, b.* 3 *May* 1825; *d.* (–); *m.* 5 *Nov.* 1867, *Alexandrina Ogilvie (The Nest, Tamaris-sur-Mer, Var, France), da. of Capt. James Vetch, R.E.; and had issue* 1*d.*

        1*d*. Arthur Onslow, *b.* 7 June 1871; *m.* 25 Sept. 1893, Emily, da. of J. Howe; and has issue 1*e* to 2*e*.

          1*e*. George Shelley Onslow, *b.* 20 Ap. 1897.

          2*e*. Mary Alexandrina Onslow, *b.* 16 Sept. 1894.   [Nos. 23326 to 23341.

233. Descendants, if any, of ELIZABETH SHELLEY (see Table XIX.), wife of JAMES CANNON.

234. Descendants, if any surviving, of TRYPHENA PENELOPE SHELLEY (see Table XIX.), *d.* 1756; *m.* as 2nd wife, 1754, Charles POLHILL of Chipsted, *b.* 8 May 1725; and had issue.[2]

  1*a*. *Tryphena Penelope Polhill, b.* 25 *June* 1756; *d.* 25 *Feb.* 1795; *m. George Stafford; and had issue* 1*b to* 2*b.*

    1*b*. *Charles Stafford.*

    2*b*. *Thomas George Stafford.*

---

1 See the Clarence Volume, p. 192, for her descent from George, Duke of Clarence.
2 Berry's " Kent Genealogies," 1830, p. 336.

# of The Blood Royal

235. Descendants, if any, of JANE PIERREPONT, wife of the Rev. BERNARD GILPIN (see Table XX.).

236. Descendants of NATHANIEL KINDERSLEY, Lieut.-Col. H.E.I.C.S. Artillery (see Table XX.), *b.* 18 Oct. 1734; *d.* 20 Oct. 1769; *m.* 19 Ap. 1762, JEMIMA, Author of "Letters from the East Indies," 1777, da. of [——] WICKSTED, *b.* 2 Oct. 1741; *d.* 1809; and had issue 1*a.*

1*a.* *Nathaniel Edward Kindersley, H.E.I.C.S. Civil Service, b.* 2 *Feb.* 1762; *d. Feb.* 1831; *m. Hannah, widow of Capt. William Wasey, da. of* [——] *Butterworth ; and had issue* 1*b* to 4*b.*

1*b.* *Right Hon. Sir Richard Torin Kindersley, the last of the Vice-Chancellors, b.* 5 *Oct.* 1792; *d.* 27 *Oct.* 1879; *m.* 17 *Aug.* 1824, *Mary Ann, da. of the Rev. John Leigh Bennett of Thorpe Place, Chertsey, b.* 1797; *d.* 27 *Jan.* 1864; *and had issue* 1*c* to 4*c.*

1*c.* Edward Leigh Kindersley, J.P., Lord of the Manor and Patron of Borough Green, co. Camb. (*Clyffe, Dorchester*), *b.* 7 Mar. 1828; *m.* 22 Ap. 1852, Fanny Maitland, da. of Henry Wilson of Stowlangtoft Hall; and had issue 1*d* to 11*d.*

1*d.* Charles Porcher Wilson Kindersley, Capt. *late* Coldstream Guards, and sometime A.D.C. to the Gov.-Gen. of Canada, *b.* 3 Jan. 1857; *m.* 18 Sept. 1894, Jean Ramsay, da. of Robert Barr Brown of Ottawa; and has issue (with 2 younger das.) 1*e* to 3*e.*

1*e.* Geoffrey Charles Kindersley, *b.* 16 Jan. 1898.

2*e.* Charles Kindersley, *b.* 7 Ap. 1900.

3*e.* Elaine Agnes Jean Kindersley, *b.* 27 Aug. 1895.

2*d.* Edward Kindersley, *b.* 23 Sept. 1858; *m.* 8 Mar. 1886, Eleanor, da. of H. Tarrant, Barrister-at-Law; and has issue 1*e* to 3*e.*

1*e.* Doris Kindersley, *b.* 21 Dec. 1886.

2*e.* Phyllis Kindersley, *b.* 2 Oct. 1892.

3*e.* Meriel Kindersley, *b.* 20 Mar. 1899.

3*d.* Richard Kindersley, *b.* 3 Ap. 1862.

4*d.* Henry Redhead Kindersley, Barrister-at-Law, *b.* 8 Feb. 1864; *m.* 20 Oct. 1897, Mary Dorothea, da. of T. Evan Lees of Beaucroft, Wimborne; and has issue 1*e* to 2*e.*

1*e.* Nathaniel Kindersley.

2*e.* Dorothea Kindersley.

5*d.* Rev. Cyril Edwin Kindersley, M.A. (Camb.), Vicar of Colehill (*Colehill Vicarage, Wimborne*), *b.* 13 Sept. 1865; *m.* 11 June 1903, Maud Eleanor, da. of Major R. D. D. Hay.

6*d.* Maitland FitzRoy Kindersley, *formerly* Royal Scots Fusiliers, *b.* 12 July 1868; *m.* 21 Aug. 1891, Constance, da. of Col. Hamilton, Scottish Rifles; and has issue 1*e* to 2*e.*

1*e.* Audrey Hamilton Kindersley, *b.* Aug. 1892.

2*e.* Charles Leigh Kindersley, *b.* Aug. 1893.

7*d.* Ellinor Kindersley, *b.* 5 Mar. 1853.

8*d.* Fanny Kindersley, *b.* 16 July 1854.

9*d.* *Agnes Adela Kindersley, b.* 28 *Oct.* 1855; *d.* 23 *Feb.* 1902; *m.* 20 *Dec.* 1876, *Farrer (Herschell), 1st Baron Herschell* [*U.K.*], *P.C., G.C.B., Lord High Chancellor of Great Britain, b.* 1837; *d.* 1 *Mar.* 1899; *and had issue* 1*e* to 3*e.*

1*e.* Richard Farrer (Herschell), 2nd Baron Herschell [*U.K.*] (3 *Whitehall Court, S.W.*), *b.* 22 May 1878.

2*e.* Hon. Agnes Freda Herschell, *b.* 9 Oct. 1881.

3*e.* Hon. Muriel Fanny Herschell, *b.* 4 Ap. 1883.   [Nos. 23342 to 23363.

The Plantagenet Roll

10*d.* Audrey Mary Kindersley, *b.* 11 Mar. 1867; *m.* 19 June 1889, Montague Scott Williams, J.P., Hon. Lieut.-Col. Dorset Yeomanry, and High Sheriff co. Dorset 1894 (*Woolland House, Blandford, Dorset*) ; and has issue 1*e* to 8*e.*

1*e.* Charles Montague Williams, *b.* 9 June 1890.
2*e.* Edward Jeffery Williams, *b.* 28 Jan. 1892.
3*e.* Richard John Williams, *b.* 17 June 1893.
4*e.* Herbert Farrer Williams, *b.* 2 June 1895.
5*e.* Rashleigh Henry Williams, *b.* 2 June 1897.
6*e.* Robert Cyril Williams, *b.* 20 Jan. 1899.
7*e.* Eric George Williams, *b.* 16 Dec. 1900.
8*e.* Eustace Maitland Williams, *b.* 17 Oct. 1902.

11*d.* Katherine Kindersley, *b.* 30 Jan. 1870.

2*c. Rev. Richard Cockburn Kindersley, M.A. (Camb.), Vicar of Bramford Speke with Cowley, co. Devon,* b. *3 July* 1831 ; d. 16 *July* 1871 ; m. 10 *Nov.* 1857, *Georgina Anne, da. of Edward Cockburn Kindersley ; and had issue* 1*d to* 10*d.*

1*d.* Richard Kindersley, *b.* (–).
2*d.* Henry Kindersley, *b.* (–).
3*d.* Arthur Kindersley, *b.* (–).
4*d.* Walter Kindersley, *b.* (–).
5*d.* William Kindersley, *b.* (–) ; *m.* 26 May 1898, Alexandra Eugnica, da. of [——] Ferguson.
6*d.* Edmund Kindersley, *b.* (–).
7*d.* Georgina Kindersley.
8*d.* Katherine Kindersley.
9*d.* Emily Kindersley.
10*d.* Margaret Kindersley.

3*c. Agnes Caroline Kindersley,* b. 24 *Mar.* 1829; d. (–) ; m. 20 *Ap.* 1852, *Fuller Maitland Wilson of Stowlangtoft Hall, J.P., D.L., M.P., Lieut.-Col. West Suffolk Militia, and High Sheriff co. Suffolk* 1873 ; b. 27 *Aug.* 1825; d. 4 *Sept.* 1875 ; *and had issue* 1*d to* 10*d.*

1*d.* Arthur Maitland Wilson, J.P., D.L. (*Stowlangtoft Hall, near Bury St. Edmunds*), *b.* 16 June 1857 ; *m.* 21 July 1880, Harriet Maude Isabella, da. of Col. Sir Nigel Kingscote of Kingscote, K.C.B., *d.* 14 Mar. 1906; and has issue 1*e* to 3*e.*

1*e.* Henry Maitland Wilson, *b.* 5 Sept. 1881.
2*e.* Nigel Maitland Wilson, *b.* 6 Ap. 1884.
3*e.* Reginald Maitland Wilson, *b.* 17 Jan. 1889.

2*d.* Henry Fuller Maitland Wilson, Col. Rifle Brigade, *b.* 18 Feb. 1859 ; *m.* Feb. 1884, Charlotte Elise, da. of Gen. Sir Hugh Gough, K.C.B., V.C. ; and has issue 1*e* to 3*e.*

1*e.* Arthur Henry Maitland Wilson, *b.* 18 Jan. 1885.
2*e.* Hugh Maitland Wilson, *b.* 6 Ap. 1886.
3*e.* Muriel Maitland Wilson.

3*d.* Joseph Maitland Wilson, *b.* 22 Dec. 1868.
4*d.* Agnes Katherine Maitland Wilson, *m.* 25 Sept. 1894, the Rev. James Wilson Davy Brown, Rector of Stowlangtoft (*Stowlangtoft Rectory, Bury St. Edmunds*).
5*d.* Ethel Maitland Wilson.
6*d.* Ellen Maitland Wilson.
7*d.* Constance Maitland Wilson, *m.* 29 Nov. 1888, Henry Wilson Smith (*Colebrook Park, Tonbridge*) ; and has issue 1*e.*

1*e.* William Henry Wilson Smith, *b.* 26 Nov. 1889.   [Nos. 23364 to 23397.

316

# of The Blood Royal

8d. Ida Maitland Wilson, *m.* 25 Jan. 1898, Capt. John Alan Le Norreys Daniell, 11th Hussars.

9d. Amy Maitland Wilson.

10d. Alice Maitland Wilson.

4c. Mary Elizabeth Kindersley, b. 29 *Ap.* 1834; d. 20 *Ap.* 1877; m. *as 1st wife,* 4 *Jan.* 1857, Rev. the Hon. *William Byron, late Rector of Trowsell (United University)* ; *and had issue* 1d *to* 5d.

1*d.* George Anson Byron, M.A. (Oxon.), J.P., Barrister-at-Law (55 *Queen's Gardens, W.*), *b.* 3 Mar. 1858; *m.* 22 Aug. 1891, Georgiana Maie, da. of Sir Francis Burdett, 7th Bart. [E.]; and has issue 1*e* to 2*e*.

1*e.* Margaret Dorothy Byron, *b.* 30 June 1892.

2*e.* Rhona Mary Byron, *b.* 8 Aug. 1893.

2*d.* Wilfred Byron, Capt. Leicestershire Imp. Yeo., *b.* 31 Jan. 1871; *m.* 25 Sept. 1901, Sylvia Mary, da. of the Rev. Charles Thomas Moore, Rector of Appleby Magna.

3*d.* Eleanor Mary Byron, *m.* 21 Jan. 1885, Henry Seymour Hoare (*Morden, Surrey*) ; and has issue 1*e* to 3*e.*

1*e.* Algernon Seymour Hoare, *b.* Nov. 1886.

2*e.* Dorothy Mary Hoare, *b.* Nov. 1885.

3*e.* Olivia Katherine Hoare, *b.* Jan. 1889.

4*d.* Edith Mary Byron, *m.* 19 Jan. 1888, Capt. Gerard Thomas Noel, J.P. (*Wyld Court, Axminster ; Lamcote House, Notts*) ; and has issue. See p. 189, Nos. 6798–6801.

5*d.* Katherine Mary Byron, *m.* 5 July 1894, William Robert Campion (*Danny Park, Hurstpierpont, Sussex*) ; and has issue 1*e* to 2*e.*

1*e.* William Simon Campion, *b.* 1895.

2*e.* Dorothy Campion, *b.* 1897.

2*b.* Nathaniel William Kindersley, Madras C.S., b. 1 *June* 1794 ; d. 3 *Dec.* 1844 ; m. 1st, 1823, *Jane, da. of* [——] *Elliott,* b. 8 *June* 1805 ; d. (*at Tanjore, India, M.I.*) 9 June 1831 ; 2ndly, 23 June 1832, *Mary, da. of Major-Gen. Arthur Molesworth, H.E.I.C.S. ; and had issue* 1c *to* 6c.

1*c.* John Robert Kindersley, Madras C.S., Judge of the High Court at Madras, b. 8 *May* 1826 ; d. 27 *Aug.* 1901 ; m. 1*st,* 1 *Sept.* 1853, *Emma, da. of Ewan Christian of the Cape of Good Hope,* b. 9 *Oct.* 1832 ; d. 6 *July* 1875 ; 2ndly, 30 *Sept.* 1876, *Dora Jane, da. of Major-Gen. Fasken ; and had issue* 1d *to* 6d.

1*d.* Arthur Fasken Kindersley, *b.* 12 Feb. 1879.

2*d.* Robin Grenville Kindersley, *b.* 6 June 1880 ; *m.* 21 Jan. 1906, Maria, da. of V. O. von Baranoff.

3*d.* Emma Frances Kindersley, *b.* 16 July 1854 ; *m.* 13 Mar. 1875, Stewart R. Turnbull ; and has issue 1*e* to 8*e.*

1*e.* Stuart Kindersley Turnbull, *b.* 6 Mar. 1876.

2*e.* Richard Christian Turnbull, *b.* 26 Jan. 1879.

3*e.* William Joseph Ugo Turnbull, *b.* 24 Mar. 1885.

4*e.* Robertson Turnbull, *b.* 20 Jan. 1894.

5*e.* Frances Jessie Turnbull, *b.* 18 Aug. 1881.

6*e.* Cornelia May Turnbull, *b.* 7 June 1888.

7*e.* Dorothy Mary Turnbull, *b.* 22 Sept. 1891.

8*e.* Marjorie Aletta Turnbull, *b.* 4 Ap. 1897.

4*d.* Grace Kindersley, *b.* 18 Nov. 1862.

5*d.* May Kindersley, *b.* 27 July 1869 ; *m.* 20 Feb. 1894, H. L. T. Hansard ; and has issue 1*e* to 2*e.*

1*e.* John Henry Hansard, *b.* 13 Mar. 1895.

2*e.* Richard Luke Hansard, *b.* 2 Aug. 1898.

6*d.* Mary Kindersley, *b.* 14 July 1877. [Nos. 23398 to 23432.

The Plantagenet Roll

2c. Nathaniel Edward Bruce Kindersley, Capt. in the Army, b. 6 *Oct.* 1830 ; d. 30 *Mar.* 1893 ; m. 4 *Nov.* 1852, *Annie Sophia, da. of Capt. George Robinson, R.N. ; and had issue* 1d *to* 2d.

1d. Annie Nathalie Sophia Kindersley, m. 1889, Alfred Douglas Hensley, *s.p.*

2d. Eleanor Lucy Kindersley, *unm.*

3c–6c. Children by 2nd wife. See pp. 156–157, Nos. 2403–2438.

3b. Edward Cockburn Kindersley, M.A. (Camb.), Translator of " The History of Bayard," b. 1799 ; d. 6 *July* 1866 ; m. *Harriet, da. of* [——] *Torin ; and had issue* 1c *to* 7c.

1c. Benjamin Torin Kindersley, B.A. (Camb.), 1857.

2c. Francis Martin Kindersley, *m.* 28 Jan. 1860, Sidonie, da. of Judge G. H. Ellis of Madras.

3c. Jemima Harriet Kindersley, *m.* 24 Nov. 1853, the Rev. John Spearman Wasey, Vicar of Compton Parva ; and had issue (see p. 203).

4c. Mary Elizabeth Kindersley, *m.* 19 May 1859, Thomas Palmer Chapman.

5c. Georgiana Anne Kindersley, *m.* 10 Nov. 1857, the Rev. Richard Cockburn Kindersley, *d.* 16 July 1871 ; and has issue.

See p. 316, Nos. 23374–23383.

6c. Frances Augusta Kindersley.

7c. Caroline Agnes Kindersley.

4b. Henrietta Louisa Aurora Kindersley, d. (−) ; m. 1816, *the Ven. Henry Lloyd Loring, D.D., Archdeacon of Calcutta,* d. 4 *Sept.* 1823; *and had issue* 1c *to* 2c.

1c. Rev. Edward Henry Loring, Vicar of Cobham, Surrey, b. 1823 ; d. (−) ; m. 1st, 11 *May* 1853, *Hannah Adelaide, da. of Arthur Cuthbert Marsh of Caldwell,* d. 11 *Mar.* 1859 ; 2ndly, 5 *Aug.* 1863, *Charlotte, da. of* [——] *Watson of Chigwell ; and had issue* 10 *children.*

2c. Frances Louisa Loring, b. 1821.   [Nos. 23433 to 23488.

237. Descendants of FRANCES KINDERLEY (see Table XX.), b. 5 Nov. 1731 ; d. 4 Feb. 1820 ; m. 6 Feb. 1759, JAMES SMITH of Norwich, Gentleman, b. 15 June 1727 ; d. 8 Mar. 1795 ; and had issue 1a to 4a.

1a. Sir James Edward Smith, M.D., F.R.S., Founder and first President of the Linnæan Society, b. 2 Dec. 1759 ; d.s.p. 17 *Mar.* 1828.

2a. Francis Smith, bapt. 30 *Aug.* 1764; d. 11 *Sept.* 1815 ; m. 24 *June* 1795, *Sarah, da. of John Marsh,* b. 1765 ; d. 23 *May* 1850 ; *and had issue* 1b *to* 2b.

1b. Frances Catherine Smith, Authoress (eldest da. and co-h.), b. 7 *May* 1796 ; d. 20 *Jan.* 1869 ; m. 10 *Nov.* 1817, *Alfred Barnard of Norwich, Gentleman,* b. 15 *Nov.* 1793 ; d. 4 *July* 1835 ; *and had issue* 1c *to* 5c.

1c. Alfred Francis Barnard of Diss, Norfolk, b. 4 *Jan.* 1821; d. 14 *Sept.* 1894; m. 5 *Jan.* 1854, *Mary Hog, da. of Thomas Calvert Girtin, M.R.C.S.,* b. 20 *Jan.* 1829 ; d. 6 *July* 1899 ; *and had issue* 1d *to* 6d.

1d. Francis Pierrepont Barnard, M.A. (Oxon.), F.S.A. (Bilsby House, near Alford, Lincolnshire ; St. Mary's Abbey, Windermere), b. 27 Nov. 1854 ; m. 15 *Ap.* 1884, *Eliza, eldest da. and co-h. of William Pollard of St. Mary's Abbey, J.P., s.p.s.*

2d. Leonard Girtin Barnard, b. 6 Jan. 1860 ; m. 12 Dec. 1888, Edith Lucy Maria, da. of Col. F. W. Johnstone, 27th and 92nd Foot and Lanark Militia ; and has issue 1e to 3e.

1e. Francis Humphrey Pierrepont Barnard, b. 7 Ap. 1895.

2e. Dorothea Frances Maria Pierrepont Barnard, b. 27 July 1891.

3e. Barbara Alice Mary Pierrepont Barnard, b. 21 Sept. 1893.

3d. Walter Girtin Barnard, b. 17 Feb. 1862 ; m. 3 July 1887, Mary Helen, da. of W. G. Clifton of Canada West ; and has issue 1e.

1e. Helen Clifton Barnard, b. 1888.   [Nos. 23489 to 23495,

318

of The Blood Royal

4d. Catherine Rachel Barnard, *b.* 23 Jan. 1863; *m.* 22 Nov. 1892, Pastor Frederick von Anspach, sometime of Bochum, Westphalia, and now (?) of Wiesbaden; and has issue 1*e* to 3*e*.

1*e.* Walter von Anspach, *b.* 1891.
2*e.* Dorothea von Anspach.
3*e.* [da.] von Anspach.

5d. Mary Frances Barnard, *b.* 11 Oct. 1867; *m.* 1st, 5 Sept. 1894, Ludwig Roth of Wiesbaden (from whom she obtained a divorce); 2ndly, 18 Nov. 1903, Henry Stansbury Millett, Barrister-at-Law (*Penpol, Cornwall*); and has issue 1*e.*

1*e.* Stansbury Girtin Millett, *b.* 23 Oct. 1904.

6d. Ethel Kinderley Barnard, *b.* 31 Jan. 1869; *m.* F. Sutton (118 *Calabria Road, Highbury, N.W.*); and has issue (*a da.*).

2c. George Savile Barnard, b. 26 Dec. 1821; d. 4 *May* 1878; m. 19 *Oct.* 1847, *Jean, da. of* [——] *Hunter,* d. 21 *July* 1871; *and had issue* 1*d.*

1*d.* George Sydney Barnard, *b.* 8 Dec. 1849.

3c. Francis Barnard, J.P. (*Kew, Melbourne, Australia*), *b.* 16 Jan. 1823; *m.* 8 Ap. 1857, Elizabeth, da. of George Allman, *b.* 29 July 1823; and has issue 1*d* to 5*d.*

1*d.* Francis George Allman Barnard, M.A. (*Kew, Melbourne*), *b.* 26 Dec. 1857; *m.* 20 Aug. 1889, Mary Rachel, da. of Henry Watts; and has issue 1*e* to 2*e.*

1*e.* Norman Francis Watts Barnard, *b.* 1 Sept. 1893.
2*e.* Muriel Elizabeth Barnard, *b.* 10 Jan. 1891.

2d. Alfred Edward Allman Barnard (*Kew, Melbourne*), *b.* 31 Aug. 1861; *m.* 9 May 1888, Ellen, da. of James Kirby; and has issue 1*e.*

1*e.* Wilmer Mary Allman Barnard, *b.* 10 May 1891.

3d. Albert William Allman Barnard (*Sydney, N.S.W.*), *b.* 23 Ap. 1864; *m.* 8 Feb. 1898, Mary, da. of P. J. FitzGerald, J.P.; and has issue 1*e.*

1*e.* Kenneth Joseph Allman Barnard, *b.* 29 Jan. 1899.

4d. Robert James Allman Barnard, M.A., Lecturer of Mathematics at Ormond Coll., Melbourne Univ., *b.* 14 Ap. 1866; *m.* 22 Mar. 1895, Jessie, da. of James Macfarlan; and has issue 1*e.*

1*e.* Helen Macfarlan Barnard, *b.* 25 Dec. 1903.

5d. Elizabeth Frances Allman Barnard, *b.* 11 Sept. 1859, *unm.*

4c. Frederick William Barnard (*Hawthorn, Melbourne, Australia*), *b.* 2 Dec. 1829; *m.* 9 Sept. 1852, Elizabeth, da. of William Bardwell, *b.* 21 Sept. 1834; and has issue 1*d* to 3*d.*

1*d.* Frederick William Barnard (*Mossman, Queensland*), *b.* 29 June 1857; *m.* 18 Oct. 1888, Elizabeth Emily, da. of [——] Lock; and has issue 1*e.*

1*e.* Emily Frances Violet Barnard, *b.* 13 Jan. 1892.

2d. Francis Henry Barnard (*Melbourne, Australia*), *b.* 9 Aug. 1859; *m.* 18 Ap. 1889, Ada Louisa, da. of [——] Maskell; and has issue 1*e.*

1*e.* Francis William Pierrepont Barnard, *b.* 17 May 1899.

3d. George Samuel Barnard (*Perth, West Australia*), *b.* 27 July 1868; *m.* 18 July 1899, Ellen, da. of [——] Beeston; and has issue 1*e.*

1*e.* Violet Barnard, *b.* 22 Oct. 1904.

5c. Alicia Mildred Barnard, *b.* 22 Mar. 1825, *unm.*

2b. Harriet Smith, b. 21 *May* 1798; d. 1871; m. 27 *Aug.* 1820, *Charles Edwards of Wisbech, Cambs,* b. 24 *Mar.* 1797; d. 1868; *and had issue* 1*c* to 2*c.*

1*c.* John Pierrepont Edwards, sometime British Consul-General at Washington, U.S.A., *b.* 11 May 1833; *m.* 25 Oct. 1876, Antoinette Laurence, da. of Laurence Waterbury of New York; and has issue (2 children). [Nos. 23496 to 23523.

319

The Plantagenet Roll

2c. Frederick Stuart Edwards, b. 13 *Mar.* 1835; d. *Sept.* 1894; m. 23 *June* 1859, *Frances Jane Douglas, da. of Edward Power,* b. 27 *Ap.* 1838; d. 23 *June* 1892; *and had issue* 1*d to* 5*d.*

1*d.* Rev. Charles Pierrepont Edwards.

2*d.* Rev. Frederick Edwards.

3*d.* Janet Mabel Edwards.

4*d.* Edith Edwards.

5*d.* Florence Edwards.

3a. Frances Julia Smith, b. 19 *Nov.* 1776; d. 11 *Ap.* 1854; m. 17 *July* 1804, *Thomas Martin,* b. 1 *Feb.* 1769; d. 27 *Feb.* 1850; *and had issue* 1*b to* 2*b.*

1*b. Rev. Frederick Martin, Preb. of Lincoln,* b. 30 *Mar.* 1805; d. *unm.* 6 *Dec.* 1864.

2*b. Lucy Martin,* b. 25 *Ap.* 1814; d. 23 *Dec.* 1893; m. 6 *Mar.* 1849, *William Henry Martineau of Foxholes, Weybridge,* b. 26 *Mar.* 1812; d. 3 *May* 1892; *and had issue* 1*c to* 2*c.*

1*c.* Lucy Eliza Martineau (*Foxholes, Weybridge*), *b.* 8 June 1852.

2*c.* Frances Julia Martineau, *b.* 23 Oct. 1853; *m.* 1st, 7 Jan. 1879, the Rev. Joseph John Gurney of Bracondale Lodge, Norwich, *d.s.p.* 12 Ap. 1890; 2ndly, 24 July 1900, the Rev. John Bonham Croft, M.A. (Camb.).

4a. Esther Ann Smith, bapt. 8 *July* 1778; d. 29 *Nov.* 1851; m. 19 *June* 1800, *Charles Weston of Thorpe, near Norwich,* b. *Nov.* 1776; d. 16 *June* 1864; *and had issue* 1*b to* 2*b.*

1*b. Frances Bridget Pleasance Weston,* b. 7 *July* 1801; d. (–); m. 1834, *Neville Cunstance, Capt.* 11*th Hussars,* b. 28 *Feb.* 1790; d. 11 *Sept.* 1880; *and had issue* 1*c to* 2*c.*

1*c. Rev. Charles Neville Custance, Rector of Brampton, co. Norfolk,* b. 1835; d. (–); m. *Harriet Charlotte, da. and co-h. of Edward Salwey of The Lodge, co. Salop, and Elton Hall, co. Hereford,* d. 1870; *and had issue.*

2*c.* Henry Neville Custance, *b.* 1836.

2*b.* Elizabeth Weston, living 1899; *m.* Lieut.-Col. Edward George Cubitt, 7th Hussars, *d.* 1 Jan. 1888; and had issue 1*c* to 3*c.*

1*c.* Charles Percy Cubitt, *b.* 17 Dec. 1844.

2*c.* Edward Neville Cubitt, *b.* 1852.

3*c.* Georgiana Gertrude Cubitt, *b.* 31 Mar. 1850; *m.* as 2nd wife, 18 Nov. 1890, Charles Foster, Solicitor, Clerk of the Peace for co. Norfolk [brother to Sir William Foster, 2nd Bart. [U.K.]] (*Thorpe, Norwich*); and has issue 1*d.*

1*d.* Georgina Fanny Julia Foster, *b.* 1891.   [Nos. 23524 to 23536.

238. Descendants, if any, of AUDREY KINDERLEY (see Table XX.), *b. c.* 1708; *d.* 6 Mar. 1785, wife of [———] TURNER.

239. Descendants of EDWARD ROLLESTON of Toynton, co. Linc., and (on the death of his cousin Lancelot, *s.p.* 1685) of Watnall, co. Notts (see Table XVIII.), *d.* (–); m., and had issue.[1]

240. Descendants of Lady ANNE SAVILE (see Table XXI.), *d.* 18 July 1717; *m.* as 1st wife, CHARLES (BRUCE), 4th EARL OF ELGIN [S.] and 3rd EARL OF AILESBURY [E.], *d.s.p. m.* 10 Feb. 1747; and had issue.

See the Tudor Roll of "The Blood Royal of Britain," pp. 151–156, Nos. 19573–19723.   [Nos. 23537 to 23685.

# of The Blood Royal

241. Descendants of Lady Dorothy Savile (see Table XXI.), *b.* 13 Sept. 1699; *d.* 21 Sept. 1758; *m.* 21 Mar. 1721, Richard (Boyle), 4th Earl of Cork [I.] and 3rd Earl of Burlington [E.], K.G., *b.* 25 Ap. 1694, *d.s.p. m.* 3 Dec. 1753; and had issue 1*a*.

1*a*. *Charlotte (Boyle), suo jure 6th Baroness Clifford [E.], b. 27 Oct. 1731; d. 24 Dec. 1754; m. 27 Mar. 1748, William (Cavendish), 4th Duke of Devonshire [E.], K.G., b. 1720; d. 2 Oct. 1764; and had issue.*
See the Tudor Roll of "The Blood Royal of Britain," Table XLI., pp. 240–248, Nos. 22826–23115. [Nos. 23686 to 23948.

242. Descendants of Sackville (Tufton), 8th Earl of Thanet [E.] (see Table XXI.), *b.* Aug. 1733; *d.* 10 Ap. 1786; *m.* 30 Aug. 1767, Mary, da. of Lord John Sackville, *b.* 1 Ap. 1746; *d.* Sept. 1788; and had issue.

See the Clarence Volume, Table XXV., p. 224.

243. Descendants of Other Hickman (Windsor), 5th Earl of Plymouth and 11th Baron Windsor [E.] (see Table XXI.), *b.* 30 May 1751; *d.* 12 June 1799; *m.* 20 May 1788, the Hon. Sarah, da. and co-h. of Andrew (Archer), 2nd Baron Archer [G.B.], *b.* 19 July 1762 (re-m. as 1st wife, 24 July 1800, William Pitt (Amherst), 1st Earl Amherst [U.K.], and) *d.* 27 May 1838; and had issue 1*a* to 3*a*.

1*a*. *Other Archer (Windsor), 6th Earl of Plymouth and 12th Baron Windsor [E.], b. 2 July 1789; d.s.p. 10 July 1733.*

2*a*. *Lady Maria Windsor, b. 13 May 1790; d. 7 Ap. 1855; m. 25 Oct. 1811, Arthur Blundell Sandys Trumbull (Hill), 3rd Marquis of Downshire [I.] and Earl of Hillsborough [G.B.], K.P., b. 8 Oct. 1788; d. 12 Ap. 1845; and had issue 1b to 4b.*

1*b*. *Arthur Wills Blundell Sandys Trumbull Windsor (Hill), 4th Marquis of Downshire [I.] and Earl of Hillsborough [G.B.], K.P., b. 6 Aug. 1812; d. 6 Aug. 1868; m. 23 Aug. 1837, the Hon. Caroline Frances, da. of Stapleton (Stapleton-Cotton), 1st Viscount Combermere [U.K.], G.C.B., d. 10 May 1893; and had issue.*
See the Clarence Volume, pp. 357–358, Nos. 12214–12222.

2*b*. *Arthur Edwin Hill, afterwards (R.L. 9 Sept. 1862) Hill-Trevor, 1st Baron Trevor [U.K.], b. 4 Nov. 1819; d. 25 Dec. 1894; m. 1st, 27 June 1848, Mary Emily, da. of Sir Richard Sutton, 2nd Bart. [G.B.], d. 24 Jan. 1855; 2ndly, 15 Ap. 1858, the Hon. Mary Catherine (25 Belgrave Square, S.W.), sister to Alfred, 4th Baron Scarsdale [G.B.], da. of Rev. the Hon. Alfred Curzon; and had issue 1c to 8c.*

1*c*. Arthur William (Hill-Trevor), 2nd Baron Trevor [U.K.] (*Brynkinalt, Chirk, co. Denbigh*), *b.* 19 Nov. 1852; *m.* 1st, 30 Aug. 1894, the Hon. Annie Mary Eleanor (*previously* wife of Robert (Curzon), 15th Baron Zouche [E.]), da. of Alexander (Fraser), 17th Baron Saltoun [S.], *d.s.p.* 10 May 1895; 2ndly, 7 Dec. 1897, Rosamond, Dowager Countess of Bantry [I.], da. of the Hon. Edmund Petre; and has issue 1*d*.

1*d*. Hon. Mary Rosamond Hill-Trevor, *b.* 22 Feb. 1899.

2*c*. Hon. George Edwin Hill-Trevor (15 *Sloane Gardens, S.W.*), *b.* 15 Nov. [Nos. 23949 to 23961.

The Plantagenet Roll

1859; *m.* 26 Ap. 1893, Ethel Georgina Mary, da. of Hillyar Chapman of Kilhendre, Ellesmere; and has issue 1*d*.

1*d.* Hillyar George Edwin Hill-Trevor, *b.* 31 Dec. 1895.

3*c.* Hon. Charles Edward Hill-Trevor, *late* Capt. Royal Welsh Fusiliers and Priv. Sec. and A.D.C. to Governor of New Zealand (*White's*), *b.* 22 Dec. 1863.

4*c.* Hon. Marcus Richard Hill-Trevor, A.D.C. to Lieut.-Gov. of Transvaal (*Bachelors'*), *b.* 25 Sept. 1872.

5*c.* Hon. Arthur Eustace Hill-Trevor, Lieut. Montgomery Imp.Yeo. (*Bachelors'*), *b.* 15 July 1876.

6*c.* Hon. Edith Mary Hill-Trevor, *m.* 31 July 1890, Augustus William West (18 *Lowndes Square, S.W.*).

7*c.* Hon. Leila Sophy Hill-Trevor.

8*c.* Hon. Mary Hill-Trevor, *m.* 2 Jan. 1901, Capt. James Archibald Morrison, M.P., Grenadier Guards (*Fonthill, co. Wilts ;* 139 *Harley Street, W.*) ; and has issue 1*d* to 2*d*.

1*d.* Simon Archibald Morrison, *b.* 19 Sept. 1903.

2*d.* Mary Morrison, *b.* 6 Feb. 1902.

3*b. Lady Charlotte Augusta Hill, b.* 30 *June* 1815; *d.* 24 *Nov.* 1861; *m.* 2 *Aug.* 1843, *Sir George Chetwynd, 3rd Bart.* [*G.B.*], *b.* 6 *Sept.* 1809; *d.* 24 *Mar.* 1869 ; *and had issue* 1*c to* 4*c.*

1*c.* Sir George Chetwynd, 4th Bart. [G.B.], High Sheriff co. Warwick 1875 (1 *Carlos Place, W.*), *b.* 31 May 1849; *m.* 6 June 1870, Florence, Dowager Marchioness of Hastings [U.K.], da. of Henry (Paget), 2nd Marquis of Anglesey [U.K.]; and has issue 1*d* to 3*d*.

1*d.* Guy George Chetwynd, *b.* 6 Dec. 1874; *m.* 1902, Rosalind, da. of [——] Secor.

2*d.* Lilian Florence Maud Chetwynd, *b.* 10 Mar. 1876 ; *m.* 20 Jan. 1898, Henry Cyril (Paget), 5th Marquis of Anglesey [U.K.], 6th Earl of Uxbridge [G.B.], and 14th Baron Paget [E.], *d.* 1905.

3*d.* Olive Constance Sophia Chetwynd, *b.* 24 Feb. 1877.

2*c.* Walter Hill Chetwynd, *late* Capt. 16th Lancers (34 *Sloane Gardens, S.W.*), *b.* 13 Jan. 1856 ; *m.* 14 June 1890, the Hon. Edomé Eliza Theodosia, da. of Debonnaire John (Monson), 8th Baron Monson [G.B.]; and has issue.

See p. 243, No. 9111.

3*c.* Isabel Marion Chetwynd (*Chaseley House, Rugeley*), *m.* 1st, 24 May 1870, Cudworth Halsted Poole of Marbury Hall, co. Salop (who obt. a div. 1876); 2ndly, as 2nd wife, 22 June 1880, Robert Wellington (Stapleton-Cotton), 3rd Viscount Combermere [U.K.], *d.* 20 Feb. 1898 ; and has issue 1*d* to 2*d*.

1*d.* Francis Lyneh Wellington (Stapleton-Cotton), 4th Viscount Combermere [U.K.] (*Combermere Abbey, Whitchurch*), *b.* 29 June 1887.

2*d.* Florence Mary Charlotte Poole, *m.* 19 May 1903, Edward Francklin (12 *Southwick Street, W.*).

4*c.* Georgiana Chetwynd (4 *Lennox Gardens, S.W.*), *m.* 4 May 1874, Dudley Frances (North), 7th Earl of Guilford [G.B.], *b.* 14 July 1851 ; *d.* 19 Dec. 1885 ; and has issue 1*d* to 2*d*.

1*d.* Frederick George (North), 8th Earl of Guilford [G.B.] (*Waldershare Park, Dover ; Eythorne House, Dover, &c.*), *b.* 19 Nov. 1876 ; *m.* 25 June 1901, Mary Violet, da. of William Hargrave Pawson of Shawdon ; and has issue 1*e* to 2*e*.

1*e.* Francis George North, Lord North, *b.* 15 June 1902.

2*e.* Hon. John Montagu North, *b.* 28 Feb. 1905.

2*d.* Lady Muriel Emily North, *b.* 16 Ap. 1879.

4*b. Lady Mary Penelope Hill, b.* 3 *Sept.* 1817; *d.* 15 *July* 1884; *m.* 2 *Aug.* 1838, *Alexander Nelson (Hood), 1st Viscount* [*U.K.*], *and 3rd Baron* [*I.*] *Bridport, 5th Duke of Bronté* [*Sicily*], *G.C.B., b.* 23 *Dec.* 1814; *d.* 4 *June* 1904; *and had issue* 1*c to* 9*c.* [Nos. 23962 to 23984.

322

# of The Blood Royal

1c. Arthur Wellington Alexander Nelson (Hood), 2nd Viscount [U.K.] and 4th Baron [I.] Bridport, C.B. (*Sudley Lodge, Bognor ; Castello di Maniace, Bronté, Sicily*), *b.* 15 Dec. 1839 ; *m.* 4 Ap. 1872, Lady Maria Georgina Julia, sister to Henry Edward, 5th Earl of Ilchester [G.B.], da. of the Hon. John George Charles Fox-Strangways ; and has issue 1*d* to 3*d*.

    1*d*. Hon. Maurice Henry Nelson Hood, Sub-Lieut. R.N.R., *b*. 16 Jan. 1881.

    2*d*. Hon. Mary Hood, *b*. 19 Jan. 1873 ; *m*. 21 Ap. 1898, Herbert Frederick Cook, F.S.A., a member of the firm of Cook, Son, & Co., of St. Paul's Churchyard, author of "Giorgione," &c. (*Copseham, Esher, Surrey*) ; and has issue 1*e* to 2*e*.

        1*e*. Vera Mary Cook, *b*. 15 Feb. 1899.

        2*e*. Rachel Margaret Cook, *b*. 7 Ap. 1903.

    3*d*. Hon. Sybil Amy Hood, *b*. 10 Aug. 1874.

2c. Hon. William Nelson Hood, Lieut. (ret.) R.N., *b*. 6 Jan. 1848.

3c. Hon. Alexander Nelson (Hood), 6th Duke of Bronté [Two Sicilies], Comm. of the Crown of Italy, Private Sec. to H.R.H. the Princess of Wales (28B *Albemarle Street, W. ; Castello di Maniace, Bronté, Sicily*), *b*. 28 June 1854.

4c. Hon. Alfred Nelson Hood, *b*. 1 Oct. 1858.

5c. Hon. Victor Albert Nelson Hood (Queen Victoria sponsor), *b*. 14 Nov. 1863.

6c. Hon. Nina Maria Hood, V.A., sometime (1877–1901) a Woman of the Bed-chamber to H.M. Queen Victoria, *m*. 7 Feb. 1861, Lieut.-Col. George Arthur Ferguson of Pitfour, D.L. (*Pitfour, Mintlaw, co. Aberdeen*) ; and has issue 1*d* to 5*d*.

    1*d*. Arthur George Ferguson, Inspector of Constabulary for Scotland, *late* Major Rifle Brigade (*Bellwood, Perth*), *b*. 22 June 1862 ; *m*. 1 Oct. 1902, Janet Norah, da. of Sir Alexander Baird, 1st Bart. [U.K.] ; and has issue 1*e* to 2*e*.

        1*e*. Angus Arthur Ferguson, *b*. 26 July 1904.

        2*e*. Francis Alexander Ferguson, *b*. 3 Ap. 1895.

    2*d*. Rev. Edwin Augustus Ferguson, Vicar of St. Thomas, Eastville (*St. Thomas' Vicarage, Eastville, Bristol*), *b*. 24 Sept. 1864 ; *m*. 26 Ap. 1892, Madeline Isabella, da. of Col. William Chester Master, C.B. ; and has issue 1*e* to 4*e*.

        1*e*. Donald Francis Ferguson, *b*. 29 July 1896.

        2*e*. Nina Madeline Ferguson, *b*. 16 May 1893.

        3*e*. Dora Isabel Ferguson, *b*. 16 Jan. 1895.

        4*e*. Vera Victoria Ferguson, *b*. 6 Sept. 1897.

    3*d*. Charles Alexander Ferguson, *b*. 21 Oct. 1873.

    4*d*. Edith Rosa Ferguson, *b*. 7 Feb. 1867 ; *m*. 27 Oct. 1897, Francis Crawley (*Stockwood, Luton, co. Beds*) ; and has issue 1*e* to 2*e*.

        1*e*. Joan Crawley, *b*. 1900.

        2*e*. Julyan Frances Crawley, *b*. 1903.

    5*d*. Mary Georgiana Ferguson, *b*. 14 May 1877 ; *m*. 10 Sept. 1903, the Hon. Rupert Edward Selborne Barrington (*Potchefstroom, Transvaal*) ; and has issue 1*e*.

        1*e*. Eric Rupert Barrington, *b*. 13 Dec. 1904.

7c. Hon. Mary Hood, *m*. 16 Ap. 1868, Hugh de Grey (Seymour), 6th Marquis of Hertford [G.B.], 7th Baron Conway [E. and I.], P.C. (*Ragley Hall, Alcester*) ; and has issue.

    See the Clarence Volume, pp. 132–133, Nos. 1684–1697.

8c. Hon. Adelaide Fanny Hood, *m*. 16 Sept. 1879, Captain Herbert Frederick Gye, R.N., H.B.M.'s Consul at Brest (1 *Rue de Traverse, Brest*) ; and has issue 1*d* to 5*d*.

    1*d*. Alexander Hugh Gye, Lieut. R.N., *b*. 1884.

    2*d*. Evelyn Mary Gye, *b*. 1880.

    3*d*. Mabel Louisa Gye, *b*. 1882.

    4*d*. Nina Gye, *b*. 1883.

    5*d*. Irene Alice Gye, *b*. 1889.
[Nos. 23985 to 24030,

The Plantagenet Roll

9c. Hon. Rosa Penelope Hood, sometime (1886–1894) Maid of Honour to Queen Victoria, *m.* 31 July 1894, William Herbert Evans of Forde Abbey, co. Dorset, *d.s.p.* 18 Sept. 1900.

3a. *Harriet (Windsor, afterwards (R.L. 8 Nov. 1855) Windsor-Clive),* suo jure 13*th Baroness Windsor* [E.], b. 30 *July* 1797 ; d. 9 *Nov.* 1869 ; m. 19 *June* 1819, *the Hon. Robert Henry Clive of Oakly Park, co. Salop,* b. 15 *Jan.* 1789 ; d. 20 *Jan.* 1854 ; *and had issue* 1b *to* 4b.

1b. *Hon. Robert Windsor-Clive, M.P.,* b. 24 *May* 1824 ; d. 4 *Aug.* 1859 ; m. 20 *Oct.* 1852, *Lady Mary Selina Louisa, da. of George (Bridgeman), 2nd Earl of Bradford* [U.K.], d. 12 *July* 1889 ; *and had issue* 1c *to* 4c.

1c. Robert George (Windsor-Clive), 1st Earl of Plymouth (1905) [U.K.], 14th Baron Windsor [E.], P.C. (*Hewell Grange, Redditch ; St. Fagan's Castle, Cardiff ; 54 Mount Street, W.*), b. 27 Aug. 1857 ; m. 11 Aug. 1883, Alberta Victoria Sarah Caroline, da. of the Right Hon. Sir Augustus Berkeley Paget, P.C., G.C.B. ; and has issue 1d to 4d.

1d. Other Robert Windsor-Clive, Viscount Windsor, b. 23 Oct. 1884.

2d. Hon. Ivor Miles Windsor-Clive, b. 4 Feb. 1889.

3d. Hon. Archer Windsor-Clive, b. 6 Nov. 1890.

4d. Lady Phyllis Windsor-Clive, b. 28 Dec. 1886.

2c. Hon. (R.W. 1870) Georgina Harriet Charlotte Windsor-Clive (*Oakly Park, Bromfield, co. Salop*), b. 6 Oct. 1853.

3c. Hon. (R.W. 1870) Henrietta Lucy Windsor-Clive (*Oakly Park, Bromfield, co. Salop*), b. 1 Ap. 1855.

4c. Hon. (R.W. 1870) Mary Agnes Windsor-Clive (*Hildersham Hall, co. Cambridge*), b. 29 May 1856 ; *m.* 18 July 1892, John Knowsley Thornton, d. 3 Jan. 1904 ; and has issue 1d to 2d.

1d. Knowsley Thornton.

2d. Margery Gertrude Thornton, b. 7 Mar. 1896.

2b. Hon. George Herbert Windsor Windsor-Clive, J.P., D.L., sometime (1860–1885) M.P., Lieut.-Col. *late* Coldstream Guards (12 *Stratford Place, W.*), b. 12 Mar. 1835 ; *m.* 17 Oct. 1876, the Hon. Gertrude Albertina, da. of Charles Rudolph (Trefusis), 19th Baron Clinton [E.], b. 21 July 1845 ; *d.* 11 Ap. 1878 ; and has issue 1c.

1c. George Windsor-Clive, Capt. Coldstream Guards, b. 6 Ap. 1878.

3b. *Hon. Henrietta Sarah Windsor-Clive,* b. 28 *Mar.* 1820 ; d. 30 *Jan.* 1899 ; m. 24 *Nov.* 1853, *Edward Hassey of Scotney Castle, J.P., D.L.,* b. 13 *July* 1807 ; d. 3 *Sept.* 1894 ; *and had issue.*

See the Tudor Roll of "The Blood Royal of Britain," p. 433, Nos. 31174–31186.

4b. Hon. Victoria Alexandrina Windsor-Clive (Queen Victoria sponsor), *m.* 9 Ap. 1874, the Rev. Edward Ffarington Clayton, Rector of Ludlow (*Ludlow Rectory, co. Salop*) ; and has issue.

See the Tudor Roll of "The Blood Royal of Britain," p. 433, Nos. 31188–31190. [Nos. 24031 to 24060.

244. Descendants of the Rev. EDWARD JAMES TOWNSEND, Rector of Ilmington (see Table XXI.), *b.* 28 Aug. 1786 ; *d.* 19 Ap. 1858 ; *m.* 17 Mar. 1818, Mary, da. of John HAMBROUGH of Pipewell Hall, *d.* (–) ; and had issue 1*a* to 6*a*.

1a. *John Gore Townsend, d.* (?) *unm.*

2a. *Frederick Townsend, Lord of the Manor and Patron of Honington, J.P., D.L., sometime M.P.,* b. 5 *Dec.* 1822 ; d.s.p. 16 *Dec.* 1905 ; m. 21 *July* 1863, *Mary*

# of The Blood Royal

Elizabeth (Honington Hall, Shipston-on-Stour, co. Warwick), d. and h. of the Rev. John Butler of Kilkenny.

3a. *Elizabeth Caroline Townsend,* d. (?) *unm.*
4a. *Julia Townsend.*
5a. *Laura Townsend,* d. (-) ; m. 9 *Ap.* 1885, *Arthur Bigge.*
6a. *Emily Townsend,* d. (-) ; m. 1862, *Thomas Donald.*

245. Descendants of JOSEPH TOWNSEND of Alveston, J.P., D.L. (see Table XXI.), *b.* 25 Feb. 1794; *d.* 29 Ap. 1870; *m.* 9 June 1825, LOUISA, sister of Robert John, 9th Baron Willoughby de Broke [E.], da. of the Rev. Robert BARNARD, *b.* 24 July 1802; *d.* 22 Ap. 1863; and had issue 1a.

1a. *Charles John Townsend, J.P.,* b. *May* 1838; d. 1902; m. *Nov.* 1872, *Teresa Charlotte (Alveston Hall, co. Warwick), da. of the Rev. George Rudston-Read.*

246. Descendants of HARRIET TOWNSEND (see Table XXI.), *d.* 7 July 1830 ; *m.* 22 Ap. 1801, Sir GREY SKIPWITH, 8th Bart. [E.], *b.* 17 Sept. 1771 ; *d.* 13 May 1852; and had issue 1a to 15a.

1a. *Sir Thomas George Skipwith, 9th Bart.* [E.], b. 9 *Feb.* 1803; d. 30 *Nov.* 1863; m. 2ndly, 21 *May* 1853, *Jane, da. of Hubert Butler Moore of Shannon View, co. Galway,* d. 3 *May* 1862; *and had issue* 1b *to* 2b.

1b. *Sir Peyton d'Estoteville Skipwith, 10th Bart.* [E.], b. 12 *Feb.* 1857; d. 12 *May* 1891; m. 5 *Feb.* 1879, *Alice Mary (who re-m.* 1 *June* 1892, *Major John Hugh Ward-Boughton-Leigh (Ullesthorpe House, Rugby), da. of Major-Gen. Benjamin Bousfield Herrick, R.M., L.I. ; and had issue* 1c *to* 3c.

1c. Sir Grey Humberston d'Estoteville Skipwith, 11th Bart. [E.] (*Leamington Hastings, Rugby*), *b.* 4 Dec. 1884.

2c. Carrie d'Estoteville Skipwith, *b.* 16 Mar. 1880.

3c. Violet Jane Skipwith, *b.* 31 Oct. 1881.

2b. Grey Herbert Skipwith, *b.* 2 July 1860.

2a. William Skipwith, Capt. *late* 47th Regt., *b.* 2 Dec. 1807 ; m. 8 Sept. 1843, Louisa, da. of Edward Morant Gale of Upham House, co. Hants ; and has issue 1b.

1b. Ida Skipwith.

3a. *Fulwar Skipwith, a Judge H.E.I.C.S.,* b. 18 *Feb.* 1810 ; d. 22 *June* 1883 ; m. 2 *July* 1835, *Mary Philadelphia, da. of the Rev. Thomas Coker Adams,* b. 23 *June* 1895 ; *and had issue* 1b *to* 3b.

1b. *Grey Townsend Skipwith of Loversall Hall, Doncaster, J.P., Col. R.E.,* b. 2 *Nov.* 1838; d. 12 *Aug.* 1900; m. 1st, 3 *Dec.* 1867, *Elizabeth Helen, da. of Major James Wemyss,* d. 1878; 2ndly, 21 *Sept.* 1887, *Sophia Flora (Loversall Hall, Doncaster), da. of Col. Charles Cooke Yarborough, C.B. ; and had issue* 1c *to* 9c.

1c. Fulwar Estoteville Skipwith, *b.* 9 June 1874; *m.* 23 Aug. 1905, Kathleen Alice Georgina, da. of the Rev. John Adams.

2c. James Wemyss Skipwith, Capt. R.E., *b.* 25 Nov. 1875.

3c. Frederick Skipwith, Lieut. Indian Army, *b.* 23 Dec. 1877.

4c. Charles Grey Yule Skipwith, *b.* 20 Ap. 1890.

5c. Granville Arthur Skipwith, *b.* 17 June 1893.

6c. Mary Effie Skipwith, *b.* 16 Jan. 1872.

7c. Flora Blanche Skipwith, } *b.* (twins) 10 Feb. 1889.
8c. Helen Frances Skipwith, }

9c. Gertrude Esther May Skipwith, *b.* 25 Nov. 1891.   [Nos. 24061 to 24075.

The Plantagenet Roll

2b. *Mary Wilhelmina Skipwith*, d. 1881; m. *as 2nd wife*, 2 *June* 1877, *Col. Sir Henry Yule, K.C.S.I., R.E.*, d. 30 *Dec.* 1889.

3b. Frances Annabella Skipwith (11 *Lansdowne Road, Tunbridge Wells*).

4a. *Grey Skipwith, Capt. R.N.*, b. 10 *Ap.* 1811; d. 1894; m. 1*st*, 26 *Ap.* 1853, *Louisa Maria, sister to Sir Richard, 1st Bart. [U.K.], G.C.S.I., and da. of Richard Temple of The Nash, co. Ware*, d. 2 *Mar.* 1864; 2*ndly*, 27 *Ap.* 1867, *Fanny Elizabeth, da. of Henry Tudor of 12 Portland Place, London; and had issue* 1b *to* 4b.

1b. Grey Skipwith, Recruiting Staff Officer at Manchester, *late* Major and Brevet Lieut.-Col. R.M.L.I. (*Junior United Service*), b. 31 July 1855.

2b. Harry Louis d'Estoteville Skipwith, Comm. R.N., b. 23 Jan. 1868.

3b. Frederick George Skipwith, Capt. R. Warwick Regt., b. 31 Aug. 1870; *m.* 1903, Bertha Sylvia, da. of Charles Augustus Chapman, at Chicago.

4b. Sophia Mary Skipwith, *m.* as 2nd wife, 1897, the Rev. Gray Granville, Vicar of Wasperton (*Wasperton Vicarage, near Warwick*); and has issue 1c to 3c.

1c. Bernard D'Ewes Granville, b. 1899.

2c. Bevill Gray Granville, b. 1903.

3c. Mary Granville, b. 1901.

5a. *Lionel Skipwith of Doctors' Commons*, b. 5 *Aug.* 1816; d. 18 *Ap.* 1886; m. 9 *Nov.* 1852, *Nannette, da. of Thomas Walker of Ravenfield, co. York*, d. 1877; *and had issue* 1b *to* 9b.

1b. *Archibald Peyton Skipwith*, b. 27 *Aug.* 1853; d. *Jan.* 1884; m. 3 *June* 1880, *Edith (who re-m.* 31 *Jan.* 1888, *Capt. Reginald Curtis Toogood), da. of the Rev. Francis Coulman Royds; and had issue* 1c *to* 2c.

1c. Frank Peyton Skipwith, b. 28 Feb. 1881.

2c. Nora Skipwith, b. 30 Ap. 1882.

2b. Frederick Charles Skipwith (*Milton Road, Mount Roskill, Auckland, New Zealand*), b. 22 Sept. 1857; *m.* 16 Feb. 1893, Mary Annie, da. of George Frederick Cremer of New Zealand; and has issue 1c to 2c.

1c. Gore Peyton Lewis Skipwith, b. 2 Feb. 1894.

2c. Lionel Ernest Skipwith, b. 29 Aug. 1896.

3b. Robert Windsor Skipwith (*Garrick; Wellington*), b. 7 Jan. 1860; *m.* 1904, Mildred, widow of C. W. Parry, da. of Col. Thomas Edward Vickers, C.B.

4b. Francis Skipwith, *late* Lieut. Bedfordshire Regt. (14 *Curzon Park, Chester*), b. 10 Feb. 1861; *m.* 25 Ap. 1899, Marjory, da. of Capt. J. F. Rolt of Chrissleton; and has issue 1c to 3c.

1c. Robert Grey Skipwith, b. 2 Feb. 1900.

2c. Lionel Peyton Skipwith, b. 23 June 1902.

3c. William Estoteville Skipwith, b. 16 June 1904.

5b. Rev. Granville Gore Skipwith, Rector of Englefield (*Englefield Rectory, co. Berks*), b. 29 July 1865; *m.* 12 July 1899, Violet Mary, da. of Geo. Walter Tyser of Oakfield, J.P.; and has issue 1c to 3c.

1c. Philip Lionel d'Estoteville Skipwith, b. 1 May 1904.

2c. Osmund Humbertson Skipwith, b. 28 Feb. 1906.

3c. Barbara Nannette Skipwith, b. 21 Mar. 1902.

6b. Helen Skipwith, *m.* June 1878, Howard Gilliat (9 *Upper Belgrave Street*, S.W.; *Abbot's Ripton Hall, Huntingdon*); and has issue 1c to 5c.

1c. Otho Claude Skipwith Gilliat, Lieut. 4th Batt. Rifle Brigade, b. 7 Dec. 1881.

2c. John Francis Grey Gilliat, b. 1 May 1883.

3c. Frank Leslie Gilliat, b. 16 Mar. 1885.

4c. Margaret Nannette Helen Gilliat, b. 31 Jan. 1891.

5c. Giana Dorothea Gilliat, b. 3 Feb. 1892.   [Nos. 24076 to 24103.]

# of The Blood Royal

7b. Dora Mary Skipwith (13 Sussex Mansions, Sussex Place, S.W.).

8b. Mabel Georgina Skipwith, m. 17 June 1885, William Henry Perry Leslie (The Lodge, Hunstanton, co. Norfolk); and has issue 1c to 3c.

1c. Henry William Eyton Leslie.

2c. Nannette Mary Leslie.

3c. Patience Mary Leslie.

9b. Nannette Ida Skipwith.

6a. Rev. Randolph Skipwith, Rector of Whilton, b. 22 Nov. 1822; d. 11 Mar. 1899; m. 2 Sept. 1846, Mary Holden, da. of the Rev. Henry E. Steward; and had issue 1b.

1b. Constance Laura Skipwith, m. 5 Sept. 1872, the Rev. George Spencer Leigh-Bennett, Vicar of Long Sutton (Long Sutton Vicarage, co. Lincoln); and has issue 1c to 2c.

1c. Alfred Estoteville Leigh-Bennett, b. 23 Oct. 1873.

2c. Olliph Spencer Leigh-Bennett, b. 6 July 1881.

7a. Rev. Humberston Skipwith, late Rector of Hamstall Ridware (1 St. Mark's Road, Milverton, Leamington), b. 8 Dec. 1823; m. 1st, 26 Oct. 1865, Adelaide Emma, da. and h. of the Rev. Henry Biddulph, Rector of Birdinbury, d. 27 Mar. 1869; 2ndly, 18 Ap. 1871, Louisa Mary, da. of the Rev. Arthur Robert Kenney-Herbert, Rector of Burton-on-Dunsmore and Rural Dean; and has issue 1b.

1b.¹ Alice Louisa Skipwith.

8a. Sidmouth Stowell Skipwith, Comm. R.N., b. 29 Mar. 1825; d. 14 Sept. 1872; m. 10 Sept. 1861, Charlotte, da. of James Blackwell Praed of Tyringham, d. 18 Nov. 1897; and had issue.
See p. 229, Nos. 8159–8163.

9a. Anna Skipwith, d. Sept. 1878; m. 1st, 21 Dec. 1824, the Rev. John Thomas Parker, Vicar of Newbold-on-Avon, d. 26 Oct. 1852; and had issue (3 sons).

10a. Selina Skipwith, d. 12 Sept. 1880; m. 3 May 1824, James William Lennox Naper of Loughcrew, co. Meath, J.P., D.L., b. 18 Feb. 1791; d. 2 Sept. 1868; and had issue 1b to 4b.

1b. James Lennox Naper, J.P., D.L., High Sheriff co. Meath 1853, and Major Meath Militia (Loughcrew, near Old Castle, R.S.O.), b. 5 Dec. 1825; m. 5 Ap. 1877, the Hon. Katherine Frances, da. of Clotworthy (Rowley), 3rd Baron Langford [I.], d. 13 Jan. 1879; and has issue 1c.

1c. William Lennox Naper, b. 4 Jan. 1879.

2b. William Dutton Naper, Lieut.-Col. late Major 11th Foot (2B Dawson Street, Princess Street, W.), b. 13 Oct. 1830; m. 6 Dec. 1876, Jane, da. of Richard Wyatt Edgell of Milton Place, co. Surrey, and Lympstone, co. Devon.

3b. Lelia Naper, d. 1 Feb. 1879; m. as 1st wife, 1870, Lieut.-Col. John Nicholas Coddington, J.P., D.L. (Oldbridge, near Drogheda); and had issue 1c to 2c.

1c. Arthur Francis Coddington, b. 8 Nov. 1873.

2c. Hubert John Coddington, b. 16 Nov. 1877.

4b. Anna Selina Naper.

11a. Harriet Skipwith, d. 15 June 1858; m. as first wife, 24 June 1828, Henry Christopher Wise of Woodcote, co. Warwick, M.P., J.P., D.L., b. 7 Oct. 1806; d. June 1883; and had issue 1b to 3b.

1b. William Naper Wise, b. 10 Feb. 1832; d. (–).

2b. Frederick Grey Wise, b. 30 Sept. 1838; d. (–).

3b. Augustus Wise, b. 22 Aug. 1840.

12a. Louisa Skipwith, d. 19 Sept. 1875; m. 27 Mar. 1827, John Fullerton of Thribergh Park, &c., co. York, d. 6 Mar. 1871; and had issue 1b to 7b.

[Nos. 24104 to 24126.

The Plantagenet Roll

1b. Rev. Charles Garth Fullerton of Thribergh Park, M.A., b. 26 *Aug.* 1838 ;
d. 4 *Feb.* 1890; m. 18 *Sept.* 1862, *Catherine, da. of the Rev. Arthur Robert B.
Kenney-Herbert, M.A. ; and had issue* 1c *to* 4c.

1c. John Skipwith Herbert Fullerton, J.P. D.L. (*Thribergh Park, Rotherham ;
and Noblethorpe, Barnsley*), b. 21 Sept. 1865 ; m. 9 May 1893, Mary Gace, da. and h.
of Robert Couldwell Clarke of Noblethorpe ; and has issue 1d to 3d.

1d. John Robert Rankin Fullerton, b. 22 Aug. 1894.

2d. Charles Alan Clarke Fullerton, b. 14 Dec. 1895.

3d. David William Fullerton, b. 4 Ap. 1902.

2c. Grey d'Estoteville Herbert Fullerton, Capt. 4th Batt. Royal Warwickshire
Regt., *late* 13th Hussars, b. 19 Oct. 1867 ; m. 27 Oct. 1897, Gertrude Susan, da. of
Frederick Cazenove of Warfield Grove, Bracknell.

3c. Hildegarde Mary Fullerton, b. 13 Feb. 1870.

4c. Catherine Herbert Fullerton, b. 5 Sept. 1874.

2b. Arthur George Fullerton, Comm. R.N., b. 23 Sept. 1844 ; m. 29 Oct. 1872,
Isabella, da. of Col. St. Aubyn Molesworth of Stoke Davenport, R.E.

3b. Louisa Fullerton.

4b. Sophia Fullerton, d. (-), m. 14 *Nov.* 1871, *the Rev. Henry Taylor
Cordeaux, Rector of Boothby Graffoe (Boothby Graffoe Rectory, co. Lincoln).*

5b. Julia Frances Fullerton.

6b. Charlotte Fullerton.

7b. Ellin Fullerton.

13a. Marianne Skipwith, d. 21 *Oct.* 1878 ; m. 16 *Ap.* 1839, *the Rev. Granville
John Granville, Rector of Stratford-on-Avon,* d. 26 *Ap.* 1871; *and had issue* 1b
to 3b.

1b. Rev. Gray Granville, Vicar of Wasperton (*Wasperton Vicarage, near
Warwick*), b. 12 Aug. 1843 ; m. 1st, 1881, Josephine Dora, da. of [——] Lawrence,
d.s.p. 1884 ; 2ndly, 1897, Sophia Mary, da. of Capt. Grey Skipwith, R.N. ; and has
issue.

See p. 326, Nos. 24081–24083.

2b. Grace Granville, b. 31 Aug. 1848 ; m. 1 Aug. 1871, the Rev. Henry Leigh-
Bennett, *late* Rector of Thribergh, and Hon. Canon of Lincoln (*Bexhill-on-Sea*) ; and
has issue 1c to 7c.

1c. Granville Leigh - Bennett, b. 18 Sept. 1872 ; m. 1892, Mary, da. of
R. Wigley.

2c. Edward Leigh-Bennett, b. 25 Feb. 1874.

3c. Harold Grey Leigh-Bennett, b. 28 May 1879.

4c. Henry Skipwith Leigh-Bennett, b. 18 Ap. 1883.

5c. Maud Leigh-Bennett, b. 7 Dec. 1875.

6c. Mary Ellinor Leigh-Bennett, b. 17 Feb. 1877 ; m. 1898, Horace Savory,
M.R.C.S. (Eng.), L.R.C.P. (Lond.) (2 *Harpur Place, Bedford*).

7c. Grace Muriel Leigh-Bennett, b. 21 Nov. 1881.

3b. Gertrude Granville, m. as 2nd wife, 30 Ap. 1878, the Right Rev.
George Richard Mackarness, Lord Bishop of Argyle and the Isles, *d.s.p.*
Ap. 1883.

14a. Lelia Sophia Skipwith, d. 25 *Aug.* 1889 (*Burke*) or *Oct.* 1878 (*Foster*);
m. *as* 3rd *wife,* 3 *Jan.* 1855, *Admiral Robert Tryon of Heathfield House, Fareham,
R.N. ; and had issue* 1b *to* 2b.

1b. Henry William Tryon, *late* Gordon Highlanders, b. 1855 ; m. 1881, Fanny,
da. of Richard Turnor of Kingsworthy House, Winchester.

2b. Charles Robert Tryon, b. 1857.

15a. Elizabeth Skipwith.   [Nos. 24127 to 24154.

328

# of The Blood Royal

247. Descendants of LOUISA TOWNSEND (see Table XXI.), *d.* 4 May 1818 ; *m.* 10 Dec. 1801, Col. JOHN FULLERTON of Thribergh Park, co. York, *b.* 1788 ; *d.* 19 Jan. 1847 ; and had issue 1*a* to 7*a*.

1*a. John Fullerton of Thribergh Park, d.* 6 *Mar.* 1871 ; m. 1827, *Louisa, da. of Sir Grey Skipwith, 8th Bart. [E.], d.* 19 *Sept.* 1875 ; *and had issue.* See p. 328, Nos. 24127–24138.

2*a. Rev. Weston Fullerton, Rector of Thribergh, d.* (–) ; m. *Charlotte, da. of the Rev. T. Trebeck, Rector of Chirley ; and had issue* 1*b* to 3*b.*

1*b.* Sir John Reginald Thomas Fullerton, K.G., C.V.O., C.B., Vice-Admiral R.N., Groom-in-Waiting to H.M. the King, Knight of St. Anne of Russia, and of the Crown of Prussia, &c. (*Hamble, Southampton*), *b.* 10 Aug. 1840 ; *m.* 18 June 1874, Ada, da. of Col. Edward Samuel Capel ; and has issue 1*c* to 5*c.*

1*c.* Alan Edward Weston Fullerton, *b.* 1877.
2*c.* Eric John Arthur Fullerton, *b.* 1878.
3*c.* Judith Fullerton, *m.* 1901, Lieut. Sydney Julius Meyrick, R.N.
4*c.* Rachel Elizabeth Fullerton, *m.* 1901, Lieut. Henry Gerald Elliot Lane, R.N.
5*c.* Daisy Fullerton.

2*b.* Cecilia Louisa Anne Fullerton.
3*b.* Selina Fullerton.

3*a. Thomas Fullerton, d.* 1825 (?) *unm.*

4*a. Rev. Arthur Fullerton, Rector of Thribergh, d.* 1875 ; *and had* (*with others*) *issue* 1*b.*

1*b. Henry Howard Fullerton* (3*rd son*), *Lieut. Royal West Surrey Regt., d.* (*in Burmah*) 3 *Dec.* 1886.

5*a. Anna Fullerton, d.* 3 *Aug.* 1837 ; *m.* 6 *Jan.* 1825, *George Ramsden of the Priory, Conisbrough, b.* 13 *Jan.* 1796 ; *d.* (–) ; *and had issue* 1*b.*

1*b. Rev. Frederick John Ramsden, M.A., Rector of Uffington, b.* 5 *Aug.* 1836 ; *d.* 1903 ; *m.* 22 *Aug.* 1865, *Anna Cassandra* (58 *Cornwall Gardens, S.W.*), *da. of Rear-Admiral the Hon. Major Jacob Henniker ; and had issue* 1*c* to 4*c.*

1*c.* Frederick Frank Ramsden, *b.* 1867.
2*c.* Cassandra Ramsden, *m.* 1898, George William Staunton.
3*c.* Julia Selina Ramsden.
4*c.* Frances Georgina Ramsden.

6*a. Elizabeth Fullerton, d.* 1854 ; *m.* 1826, *Henry William Pickard of Newton House, Sturminster Marshall, co. Dorset, R.A., b. Oct.* 1794 ; *d.* 1873 ; *and had issue* (*with 3 other sons and 4 das.*) 1*b.*

1*b. Rev. Henry Adair Pickard of Sturminster Marshall, co. Dorset, M.A.*

7*a. Frances Fullerton, d.* 1896 ; *m. the Rev. Charles Smith, Rector of East Sarstone, co. Berks.* [Nos. 24155 to 24178.

248. Descendants of SOPHIA TOWNSEND (see Table XXI.), *d.* (–) ; *m.* 11 Feb. 1820, JOHN HAMBROUGH of Steephill Castle, Isle of Wight, and Pipewell Hall, co. Northants, J.P., *b.* 1793 ; *d.* 4 Feb. 1863 ; and had issue 1*a* to 2*a.*

1*a. Albert John Hambrough, J.P., D.L., F.L.S., b. Nov.* 1820 ; *d.* 6 *June* 1861 ; *m.* 1845, *Charlotte Jane* (*who re-m.* 1867, *Lieut.-Col. William Verner*), *da. of John Willis Fleming of Stoneham Park, M.P. ; and had issue* 1*b* to 7*b.*

1*b.* Dudley Albert Hambrough, J.P. (*Steephill, Isle of Wight*), *b.* 4 Feb. 1849 ; *m.* 1 Oct. 1871, Marion, da. of Thomas Matthews of Crewkerne, *d.* (–) ; 2ndly, 190–, [——], da. of [——] ; and has issue 1*c* to 3*c.* [No. 24179.

329

The Plantagenet Roll

1c. Ethel Amabel Hambrough.

2c. Millicent Violet Hambrough.

3c. Sybil Marion Hambrough.

2b. Otho Oldisworth Le Marchant Hambrough (23 *Eccleston Square, S.W.*), b. 9 Sept. 1858; *m.* 28 Nov. 1900, Isabel Emma Maria, da. of Henry Peach Keighley-Peach of Idlicote House, *s.p.s.*

3b. Kathleen Sophia Hambrough, *m.* J. H. Cheape; and has issue 1c to 4c.

1c. Albert John Cheape.

2c. Harry Windsor Cheape.

3c. Frederick Cheape.

4c. Dudley Cheape.

4b. Mary Elizabeth Hambrough.

5b. Gertrude Julia Hambrough, *m.* G. Booker; and has issue 1c to 2c.

1c. Windsor George Otho Booker.

2c. Mary Julia Booker.

6b. Catherine Louisa Hambrough, *m.* W. H. Verner, I.C.S.; and has issue 1c to 4c.

1c. Oliver William Verner.

2c. Frederick Charles Verner.

3c. Amy Alys Verner.

4c. Katherine Dorothy Verner.

7b. Norah Caroline Hambrough, *m.* May 1887, John Arthur Fyler of Woodlands, co. Surrey, *late* M.P. for Chertsey (*Cumber Lands, Kenley*), *s.p.*

2a. *Rev. Windsor Edmund Hambrough, M.A., Rector of Evenlode, co. Gloucester,* b. 1830; d. 3 Nov. 1899; m. *June 1853, Mary, da. of the Rev. Henry Worsley of Gatcombe, LL.D., d. Ap. 1895; and had issue 1b to 4b.*

1b. Beauchamp Windsor John Hambrough (45 *Selwyn Avenue, Richmond, Surrey*), b. 9 Nov. 1854; *m.* Louisa [da. of ——] Fisher; and has issue (3 children).

2b. Worsley Grey Hambrough (*Santa Cruz, California, U.S.A.*), b. 22 June 1857; *m.* 13 Feb. 1888, Susan Euphemia Charlotte, da. of the Rev. Henry Worsley, M.A.; and has issue 1c.

1c. Oscar Worsley Hambrough, b. 24 Mar. 1895.

3b. *Algernon Arthur Cyril Adam Hambrough,* b. 10 Nov. 1864; d. *June* 1894; m. *Harriet, da. of [——] Denny; and had issue (2 children).*

4b. Agnes Mary Hambrough, b. Jan. 1858; *m.* 1 Ap. 1887, Frank Gordon Wickham (*Avondale House, Fleet, Hants*); and has issue 1c to 6c.

1c. Arthur Frederic Gordon Wickham, b. 18 Feb. 1893.

2c. William Gordon Wickham, b. 2 June 1896.

3c. Sybil Mary Gordon Wickham, b. 15 Feb. 1888.

4c. Marion Primrose Gordon Wickham, b. 17 Jan. 1891.

5c. May Violet Gordon Wickham, b. 5 June 1894.

6c. Emily Dorothy Gordon Wickham, b. 7 Nov. 1901.

[Nos. 24180 to 24208.]

249. Descendants of Lady SARAH WINDSOR (see Table XXI.), b. 1762; d. 22 Dec. 1825; m. 4 Aug. 1786, Sir WILLIAM CHAMPION DE CRESPIGNY, 2nd Bart. [U.K.], M.P., b. 1 Jan. 1765; d. 28 Dec. 1829; and had issue 1a to 5a.

1a. *Augustus James Champion de Crespigny, Capt. R.N.,* b. (*at Nice*) *Ash Wednesday* 1791; d. (*on board H.M.S. " Scylla" off Port Royal, Jamaica*) 24 *Oct.* 1825; m. 22 *May* 1817, *Caroline, da. of Sir William Bowyer-Smijth, 7th Bart.* [E.] (*who re-m. her husband's brother, Herbert*), d. 25 *Jan.* 1876; *and had issue 1b.*

330

# of The Blood Royal

1b. *Sir Claude William Champion de Crespigny, 3rd Bart.* [*U.K.*], b. 25 *June* 1818; d. 11 *Aug*. 1868; m. 22 *Aug*. 1843, *Mary, da. of Sir John Tyssen Tyrrell, 2nd Bart.* [*U.K.*], *M.P.*, d. 11 *Jan*. 1876; *and had issue* 1c *to* 8c.

1c. Sir Claude Champion de Crespigny, 4th Bart. [U.K.], J.P. (*Champion Lodge, Maldon, co. Essex*), b. 20 Ap. 1847; m. 19 Sept. 1872, Georgiana Louisa Margaret, da. of Robert M'Kerrell ; and has issue 1d to 9d.

1d. Claude Champion de Crespigny, D.S.O., Capt. 2nd Life Guards (*Bachelors'*), b. 11 Sept. 1873.

2d. Claude Paul Champion de Crespigny, Lieut. Grenadier Guards, b. 19 Sept. 1878.

3d. Claude Philip Champion de Crespigny, Lieut. R.N., b. 3 Aug. 1880.

4d. Claude Vierville Champion de Crespigny, Lieut. Wilts Regt. and A.D.C. to Commr. E. African Protectorate, b. 25 Jan. 1882.

5d. Claude Norman Champion de Crespigny, b. 14 June 1888.

6d. Cicely Champion de Crespigny, b. 19 Oct. 1874 ; m. 19 Mar. 1896, George Granville Lancaster (6B *The Mansion, Albany, Piccadilly, W. ; Kilmarsh, Northampton*) ; and has issue 1e to 2e.

1e. Claude Granville Lancaster, b. 30 Aug. 1899.

2e. Cecily Valencia Lancaster, b. 26 Mar. 1898.

7d. Cérise Champion de Crespigny, b. 6 Dec. 1875 ; m. 3 Aug. 1899, Comm. the Hon. Robert Francis Boyle, R.N., M.V.O. ; and has issue 1e to 2e.

1e. Vivian Francis Boyle, b. 9 Jan. 1902.

2e. Moyra Blanche Boyle, b. 19 Feb. 1903.

8d. Crystal Champion de Crespigny, b. 9 May 1877 ; m. 18 Dec. 1901, Capt. Matthew Benjamin Dipnall Ffinch, *late* Prince of Wales Regt.

9d. Valerie Champion de Crespigny, m. 26 Nov. 1903, Capt. John Smiley, eldest son of Sir Hugh Houston Smiley, 1st Bart. [U.K.] ; and has issue 1e.

1e. Hugh Smiley, b. 14 Nov. 1905.

2c. Philip Augustus Champion de Crespigny, Lieut. R.N. (ret.) (*Round Hill, Lyndhurst*), b. 24 July 1850 ; m. 1 Oct. 1878, Rose, da. of Adm. the Right Hon. Sir Astley Cooper Key, G.C.B. ; and has issue 1d to 3d.

1d. Henry Champion de Crespigny, Lieut. 1st. Batt. Northampton Regt., b. 11 July 1882.

2d. Frederick Philip Champion de Crespigny, Mid. R.N., b. 30 Dec. 1884.

3d. Phyllis Rose Champion de Crespigny, b. 15 Sept. 1880 ; m. 8 Nov. 1904, William Watson Finny, Bar.-at-Law (36 *Merrion Square, Dublin*) ; and has issue 1e.

1e. Edmund John Champion Finny, b. 5 Aug. 1905.

3c. Tyrrell Other William Champion de Crespigny, Col. in Charge of Cavalry Records, *lately* Lieut.-Col. Comdg. 15th Hussars, b. 1 May 1859 ; m. 17 Aug. 1899, Kathleen Alice, da. of Henry James Wigram ; and has issue 1d to 2d.

1d. Rosalie Kathleen Champion de Crespigny, b. 2 June 1900.

2d. Eileen Ethel Champion de Crespigny.

4c. Eliza Mary Champion de Crespigny, m. 29 July 1871, Gen. Richard Temple Godman, *late* Lieut.-Col. Comdg. 5th Dragoon Guards (*Highden, Pulborough ; Ote Hall, Wivelsfield, co. Sussex*) ; and has issue 1d to 6d.

1d. Richard Temple Godman, b. 20 June 1873.

2d. Frederick Tyrell Godman, b. 26 Nov. 1875.

3d. Thomas Philip Godman, Capt. 1st Dragoons, b. 22 May 1877.

4d. George William Godman, b. 7 Oct. 1883.

5d. Cicely Mary Godman, m. 1899, George Broun Ibbetson.

6d. Sarah Rosalie Godman.

5c. *Emily Harriet Smith Champion de Crespigny, d.* 8 *Sept.* 1878 ; m. *as* 1*st*

[Nos. 24209 to 24238.

331

The Plantagenet Roll

wife, 25 *Oct.* 1876, *Lieut.-Col. Joseph Charles Smijth-Windham, R.A. (Ridgway, Farnham)*; *and had issue* 1d *to* 2d.

1d. Katharine Smijth-Windham.

2d. Mary Smijth-Windham.

6c. Sarah Anna Maria Gore Champion de Crespigny (*Warren Lodge, Wokingham*), *m.* 16 Sept. 1884, Lieut.-Col. Edmund Molyneux, *late* 7th Dragoons, *d.* 1898 ; and has issue 1d to 2d.

1d. Edmund Geoffrey Melling Molyneux, *b.* 1894.

2d. Emily Molyneux, *b.* 1892.

7c. Lucy Eugenie Bowyer Champion de Crespigny (21 *Rosemane Crescent, Battersea Park*), *m.* 1886, Arthur Macan, *d.* 17 Oct. 1898 ; and has issue 1d to 2d.

1d. Vivian Turner Wilford Macan, *b.* 24 Oct. 1892.

2d. Norah Macan, *b.* 24 Ap. 1889.

8c. Agnes Catherine Vierville Champion de Crespigny, *m.* 4 Nov. 1891, the Rev. John Prince Fallowes (*Heene Rectory, Worthing*); and has issue 1d to 4d.

1d. John Tyrell Champion Fallowes, *b.* 15 Aug. 1892.

2d. Richard Prince Fallowes, *b.* 11 Mar. 1901.

3d. Katharine Harriet Angela Fallowes, *b.* 9 Nov. 1894.

4d. Mary Agnes Fallowes, *b.* 18 Sept. 1899.

2a. *Rev. Heaton Champion de Crespigny, previously R.N., d. (at Ballarat, Australia)* 15 *Nov.* 1858 ; m. 19 *July* 1820, *Caroline, da. of the Right Rev. Henry Bathurst, Lord Bishop of Norwich,* d. (-) ; *and had issue* 1b *to* 2b.

1b. *Eyre Nicholas Champion de Crespigny, M.D., Bombay Medical Service, b. May* 1821 ; *d.* 15 *Feb.* 1895 ; *m.* ; *and had issue.*

2b. Claude Augustus Champion de Crespigny, R.N., *b.* 1829.

3a. *Hubert Joseph Champion de Crespigny, Bar.-at-Law, d.* 1 *July* 1881 ; m. *Caroline, widow of his brother Augustus James, da. of Sir William Smijth, 7th Bart.* [E.], *d.* 1 *July* 1881 ; *and had issue* 1b *to* 2b.

1b. *Caroline Julia Champion de Crespigny, d.* (-) ; *m.* 20 *Mar.* 1857, *William Clay, Capt.* 37th *Regt.*

2b. *Rosalie Julia Champion de Crespigny, d.* (-) ; *m.* 19 *Aug.* 1856, *Thomas Smith Badger-Eastwood, Bar.-at-Law, d.* 30 *May* 1866 ; *and had issue* 1c *to* 3c.

1c. Hugh Crespigny Badger-Eastwood, *b.* 25 Jan. 1863.

2c. Evelyn Mary Badger-Eastwood.

3c. Rosalie Josephine Badger-Eastwood.

4a. *Patience Anne Champion de Crespigny, d.* 22 *Mar.* 1843 ; m. *as* 1st *wife,* 2 *Dec.* 1814, *Rev. the Hon. Paul Anthony Irby, Rector of Cottesbrooke,* b. 16 *Dec.* 1784 ; *d.* 10 *Feb.* 1865 ; *and had issue* 1b *to* 2b.

1b. *Edward Irby, b.* 14 *May* 1821 ; *d.* 27 *July* 1900 ; *m.* 3 *Aug.* 1850, *Mary, da. of Archibald Windeyer of Kinross, Hunter River, New South Wales,* d. 20 *July* 1885 ; *and had issue* 1c *to* 5c.

1c. Edward de Crespigny Irby (*Narango Casino, Sydney*), *b.* 21 Sept. 1851 ; *m.* 1874, Edith, da. of Dr. Campbell ; and has issue 1d to 5d.

1d. Francis Edward Irby, *b.* 1877.

2d. Paul Anthony Irby, *b.* 1882.

3d. Llewelyn George Irby, *b.* 1883.

4d. Florence Margaret Irby, *b.* 1875.

5d. Winifred Edith Irby, *b.* 1880.

2c. Frederick William Irby, *b.* 21 Ap. 1859.

3c. Charles Augustus Irby (*Tenterfield, New South Wales*), *b.* 17 June 1861 ; *m.* 1888, Eva, da. of Richard Roberts of Sydney ; and has issue 1d to 6d.

[Nos. 24239 to 24263.

# of The Blood Royal

1*d*. Charles Edward Irby, *b.* 1889.
2*d*. Arthur Algernon Irby, *b.* 1890.
3*d*. Walter Leonard Irby, *b.* 1896.
4*d*. Beverley Keith Irby, *b.* 1899.
5*d*. Richard Wilfrid Irby, *b.* 1901.
6*d*. Eva Mary Irby.

4*c*. Mary Elizabeth Irby, *m.* 1876, Edward Carr (*Maitland, New South Wales*); and has issue 1*d* to 6*d*.
1*d*. Frederick Edward Carr, *b.* 1878.
2*d*. Gerald Ernest Carr, *b.* 1879.
3*d*. Noel Alfred Carr, *b.* 1881.
4*d*. William Irby Carr, *b.* 1883.
5*d*. Reginald Blakeney Carr, *b.* 1887.
6*d*. Grace Mary Carr, *b.* 1890.

5*c*. Fanny Australia Irby, *m.* 1886, Walter Windeyer Traill (*Wirépé, Turramurra, Sydney, N.S.W.*); and has issue 1*d* to 3*d*.
1*d*. Keith Rowland Traill, *b.* 1890.
2*d*. Stuart John Traill, *b.* 1892.
3*d*. Elsie Katharine Traill, *b.* 1888.

2*b. Caroline Irby,* d. (–) ; m. 1*st*, 27 *Feb.* 1849, *the Rev. Septimus Stockdale, Rector of Wilby,* d. 11 *May* 1849 ; 2*ndly*, 5 *May* 1859, *the Rev. Robert Gibbings, Vicar of Radley,* d. 3 *Jan.* 1865 ; *and had issue* 1*c to* 3*c*.[1]
1*c*. Agnes Fanny Gibbings.
2*c*. Caroline Mary Gibbings.
3*c*. Emma Louisa Gibbings.

5*a. Mary Catherine Champion de Crespigny,* d. 7 *June* 1858 ; m. 20 *July* 1830, *the Rev. John Brigstocke, Rector of Burton, co. Pembroke,* d. 1858 ; *and had issue (a son and* 5 *das.*). [Nos. 24264 to 24283.

250. Descendants, if any, of Lady MARGARET NEVILL (see Table XXII.), wife of Sir NICHOLAS PUDSEY.[2]

251. Descendants of Sir CARNABY HAGGERSTON, 5th Bart. [E.] (see Table XXII.) *b.* May 1756 ; *d.* 3 Dec. 1831 ; *m.* FRANCES,[3] da. of WALTER SMYTHE, *d.* 1836 ; and had issue 1*a*.

1*a. Mary Haggerston,* d. 20 *Aug.* 1857 ; m. *Jan.* 1805, *Sir Thomas Stanley-Massey-Stanley, 9th Bart.* [*E.*], d. 20 *Aug.* 1841 ; *and had issue* 1*b to* 4*b*.
1*b. Sir William Thomas Stanley-Massey-Stanley, 10th Bart.* [*E.*], bapt. 24 *Nov.* 1806 ; d. unm. (*in Paris*) 29 *June* 1867.
2*b. Sir Rowland Stanley-Massey-Stanley, afterwards* (*R.L.* 26 *June* 1820) *Errington, 11th Bart.* [*E.*], b. 4 *Ap.* 1809 ; d. 31 *Mar.* 1875 ; m. 7 *Jan.* 1839, *Julia, da. of Lieut.-Col. Sir John Macdonald, K.C.B.,* d. *Aug.* 1859 ; *and had issue* 1*c*.
1*c. Ethel Errington,* d. 16 *Oct.* 1898 ; m. *as* 1*st wife,* 28 *June* 1876, *Evelyn (Baring), 1st Earl of Cromer* [*U.K.*], *P.C., G.C.B., G.C.M.G., H.B.M.'s Agent and Consul-Gen. in Egypt, &c. (British Agency, Cairo); and had issue* 1*d to* 2*d*.
1*d. Rowland Thomas Baring, Viscount Errington, Diplo. Ser.* (*Bachelors' ; St. James'*), *b.* 29 *Nov.* 1877.
2*d. Hon. Windham Baring, b.* 29 *Sept.* 1880. [Nos. 24284 to 24285.

---

¹ Foster's " Peerage," 1880.   ² See Corrigenda.
³ Sister to Mrs. Fitzherbert.

The Plantagenet Roll

3b. Sir John Massey Stanley-Massey-Stanley, afterwards (R.L. 7 Aug. 1877) Errington, 12th Bart. [E.], bapt. 30 *Aug.* 1810; d.s.p. 19 *Mar.* 1893; m. 21 *Aug.* 1841, *Maria (Fernhill, Windsor; Villa L'Esterel, Cannes), only da. of* [——] *Baron de Tallyrand.*

4b. Maria Frances Stanley-Massey-Stanley, d. 4 *Mar.* 1889; m. *as 2nd wife,* 20 *Aug.* 1832, *Sir Richard Bulkeley Williams, afterwards (R.L. 26 June* 1827) *Williams-Bulkeley,* 10*th Bart.* [E.], *M.P.,* b. 23 *Sept.* 1801; d. 28 *Aug.* 1875; *and had issue* 1c.

1c. Sir Richard Lewis Mostyn Williams-Bulkeley, 11*th Bart.* [E.], b. 20 *May* 1833; d. 27 *Jan.* 1884; m. 1*st,* 18 *May* 1857, *Mary Emily (div. Nov.* 1864), *da. of Henry Bingham Baring;* 2*ndly,* 13 *Aug.* 1866, *Margaret Elizabeth, da. of Col. Peers Williams of Temple House, co. Berks, M.P.; and had issue* 1d *to* 2d.

1d. Sir Richard Henry Williams-Bulkeley, 12th Bart. [E.], Lord-Lieut. co. Anglesey, Lieut.-Col. and Hon. Col. Roy. Anglesey R.E. (Mil.) *(Baron Hill, Beaumaris;* 24A *Portland Place, W.),* b. 4 Dec. 1862; m. 10 Dec. 1885, Lady Magdalen, da. of Charles Philip (Yorke), 5th Earl of Hardwicke [G.B.]; and has issue.

See the Tudor Roll of "The Blood Royal of Britain," p. 177, Nos. 20392–20394.

2d. Bridget Henrietta Frances Williams-Bulkeley, b. 1871; m. 8 Dec. 1902, Benjamin Seymour Guinness (247 *Fifth Avenue, New York*).

[Nos. 24286 to 24290.

---

252. Descendants of Thomas Haggerston of Sandoe, co. Northumberland (see Table XXII.), *d.* 1829; *m.* Winifred, da. of Edward Charlton of Reedsmouth, co. Northumberland; and had issue 1*a* to 7*a*.

1a. Sir Thomas Haggerston, 6*th Bart.* [E.], b. 13 *July* 1785; d. 11 *Dec.* 1842; m. 24 *Jan.* 1815, *Margaret, da. and h. of William Robertson of Ladykirk, co. Berwick,* d. 26 *Oct.* 1823; *and had issue* 1b *to* 2b.

1b. Marianne Sarah Haggerston, d. 19 *Aug.* 1889; m. 10 *Sept.* 1834, *David (Marjoribanks, afterwards (R.L. 2 Sept.* 1834) *Robertson), 1st Baron Marjoribanks* [U.K.], b. 2 *Ap.* 1797; d. 19 *June* 1873; *and had issue* 1c *to* 2c.

1c. Hon. Sarah Robertson, m. 20 Aug. 1856, Watson Askew, now (R.L. 20 Sept. 1890) Askew-Robertson, J.P., D.L., High Sheriff co. Northumberland 1862, &c. &c. *(Pallinsburn, Cornhill, co. Northumberland; Ladykirk, co. Berwick);* and has issue 1d *to* 6d.

1d. David Hugh Watson Askew-Robertson, J.P., Bar.-at-Law Inner Temple, b. 21 Oct. 1863.

2d. William Haggerston Askew (55 *Albert Court, Princes' Gate, S.W.;* 1 *Queen's Gardens, Hove*), b. 4 Oct. 1868; m. 1903, Katherine Marjorie Strathearn, da. of the Hon. John Edward Gordon, M.P.

3d. John Bertram Askew, b. 16 Oct. 1869; m. 1 July 1893, Frederica, da. of Col. Dallon.

4d. Charles Marjoribanks Askew, b. 6 Sept. 1871.

5d. Mary Marjoribanks Askew, m. 6 Feb. 1894, James Bruce Wilkie, J.P., Capt. 3rd Batt. King's Own Scottish Borderers *(Foulden, co. Berwick);* and has issue 1e.

1e. Eleanor Isabel Wilkie, b. 3 Oct. 1895.

6d. Isabel Sarah Askew, m. 1903, the Rev. Robert Dixon Rosby Greene, Curate of Hexham Abbey *(West Park, Hexham).*

2c. Hon. Alicia Margaret Robertson, m. 26 June 1862, Sir Henry Day Ingilby, 2nd Bart. [U.K.] *(Ripley Castle, co. York; 9 Hereford Gardens, Park Lane, W., &c.).* [Nos. 24291 to 24299.

# of The Blood Royal

2b. *Margaret Frances Haggerston*, d. (–) ; m. **2** *July* 1850, *Lewis Joseph Eyre* (78 *Redcliffe Gardens, S.W.*); *and had (with other) issue* 1c.

1c. Marguerite Eyre (2nd da.), *m.* 11 Jan. 1887, Sir John de Marie Haggerston, 9th Bart. [E.] (*Ellington Hall, Chathill, co. Northumberland*).

2a. *Sir Edward Haggerston, 7th Bart.* [E.], d.s.p. 6 *May* 1857.

3a. *Sir John Haggerston, 8th Bart.* [E.], b. 18 *Aug.* 1798 ; d. 8 *Mar.* 1858 ; m. 5 *Aug.* 1851, *Sarah Anne, da. of H. Knight of Axminster, co. Devon*, d. 24 *Mar.* 1883 ; *and had issue* 1b *to* 4b.

1b. Sir John de Marie Haggerston, 9th Bart. [E.] (*Ellington Hall, Chathill, co. Northumberland*), b. 27 Nov. 1852 ; *m.* 11 Jan. 1887, Marguerite, da. of Lewis Joseph Eyre.

2b. Edward Charlton de Marie Haggerston (*Wellington ; Junior Carlton*), b. 8 Feb. 1857 ; *m.* 10 Oct. 1904, Florence, da. of William H. Perrin, C.E.

3b. Julia Mary Haggerston, *m.* 23 Ap. 1879, Lieut.-Col. Robert Lewis Arathoon, *late* Northamptonshire Regt., J.P. (*Court Lodge, Gillingham, co. Kent*) ; and has issue 1c to 6c.

1c. John Joseph Arathoon, b. 1880.

2c. Edward Benedict Arathoon, Sub-Lieut. R.N., b. 1884.

3c. Mary Cecilia Arathoon ; *m.* 1905, Lewis Edward Brown Greaves of Woodthorpe Hall, Yorks.

4c. Winifred Margaret Arathoon.

5c. Dorothea Arathoon.

6c. Roberta Arathoon.

4b. Winifred Josephine de Marie Haggerston (4 *Pembroke Road, Kensington,W.*).

4a. *George Haggerston.*

5a. *Mary Haggerston*, m. 1828, *H. S. Stephens.*

6a. *Frances Carnaby Haggerston*, d. 1870 ; m. 1824, *Henry John William Collingwood of Lilburn Tower and Cornhill House*, b. *Sept.* 1802 ; d. 14 *Ap.* 1840 ; *and had issue* 1b *to* 6b.

1b. *John Collingwood of Lilburn Tower and Cornhill House*, b. 25 Dec. 1826 ; d. 17 *Aug.* 1896 ; m. 8 *Jan.* 1861, *Jane, da. of John Lumsden of Learmouth, near Coldstream ; and had issue* 1c.

1c. John Carnaby Collingwood, J.P. (*Cornhill House, Cornhill-on-Tweed*), b. 1 Oct. 1870 ; *m.* 23 Oct. 1901, Katherine Winifred, da. of J. A. Swanston of Marshall Meadows, Berwick-on-Tweed ; and has issue 1d to 2d.

1d. John Henry Francis Collingwood, b. 4 May 1905.

2d. Nora Carnaby Collingwood, b. 26 Aug. 1902.

2b. *William Pole Collingwood, C.M.G., J.P., Major-Gen. in the Army*, b. 2 *Nov.* 1829 ; d. 11 *Ap.* 1898 ; m. 10 *Aug.* 1854, *Jane Constance, da. of Folliott Thornton Mostyn ; and had issue* 1c *to* 2c.

1c. Winefred Collingwood, *m.* Charles Lyon.

2c. Maude Collingwood, *m.* H. Hopkins.

3b. Clennell Collingwood, Major-Gen. *late* R.A. (*Ferndale, Central Hill, Norwood*), b. 16 Feb. 1836 ; *m.* 11 Aug. 1868, Annie, da. of Major J. H. Oakes Moore ; and has issue 1c to 8c.

1c. Percy Hildebrand Collingwood, b. 22 Ap. 1871.

2c. Clennell William Collingwood, b. 29 Ap. 1873.

3c. Cuthbert Collingwood, b. 15 Ap. 1878.

4c. Douglas Moore Collingwood, b. 4 Nov. 1887.

5c. Gordon Francis Collingwood, b. 23 June 1892.

6c. Rose Florence Collingwood.

7c. Dorothy May Collingwood.

8c. Winifred Mary Collingwood.   [Nos. 24300 to 24324.

335

The Plantagenet Roll

4*b*. Henry Collingwood, Col. Gloucester Regt., *b*. 7 Dec. 1839; *m*. 1868, Alice Mary, da. of [——] Oliver; and has issue 1*c*.

1*c*. Rebic Collingwood.

5*b*. *Frances Collingwood*, d. 14 *Sept*. 1867; m. 22 *July* 1852, *George Caldwell Dickins*, Major 46*th Regt*.

6*b*. *Mary Anne Collingwood*, d. 1894; m. 1859, *William Vaughan of Middleboro'*.

7*a*. *Winifred Haggerston*, d. 1878; m. *William Foster of Alnwick*.

[Nos. 24325 to 24326.

253. Descendants, if any, of EDWARD, MARY, and BRIDGET HAGGERSTON (see Table XXII.).

254. Descendants of WILLIAM HAGGERSTON, *afterwards* HAGGERSTON-CONSTABLE (see Table XXII.) of Everingham, *d*. 30 June 1797; *m*. 17 Oct. 1758, WINIFRED, *suo jure de jure* 11th BARONESS HERRIES [S.], da. and h. of William (MAXWELL), (but for the attainder 1715) 6th Earl of Nithsdale and 10th Lord Herries [S.], *d*. 13 July 1801; and had issue.

See the Clarence Volume, pp. 393–394, Nos. 14792–15000.

[Nos. 24327 to 24535.

255. Descendants, if any, of ANNE HAGGERSTON (see Table XXII.), wife [1] of THOMAS CLIFTON of Lytham, co. Lancaster.

256. Descendants, if any, of WILLIAM MIDDLETON, and of his sisters, MARGARET, wife of RALPH CLAVERING of Callaley, co. Northumberland; MARY; CATHERINE, wife of THOMAS WITHAM (4th son of William WITHAM of Sledwick, co. Durham); ANNE and ELIZABETH (see Table XXII.).

[2]57. Descendants of EDWARD MEYNELL of North Kilvington and The Fryerage, co. York, J.P. (see Table XXII.), *d*. 1808; *m*. 1764, DOROTHY, da. of William CARY of Torr Abbey, co. Devon, *d*. 1802; and had issue 1*a* to 3*a*.

1*a*. *Thomas Meynell of North Kilvington and The Fryerage, J.P., D.L.*, b. *Ap*. 1775; d. *July* 1854; m. 23 *Aug*. 1804, *Theresa Mary, da. of John Wright of Kelvedon, co. Essex*, d. *July* 1844; *and had issue* 1*b to* 4*b*.

1*b*. *Thomas Meynell of North Kilvington, &c., J.P., D.L.*, b. 1805; d.s.p. 24 *Mar*. 1863.

2*b*. *Edward Meynell, Bar.-at-Law*, b. 1811; d. 4 *Feb*. 1856; m. *May* 1840, *Katherine, da. of Joseph Michael, M.D.*, d. *Feb*. 1841; *and had issue* 1*c*.

1*c*. *Edward Thomas Meynell of North Kilvington, &c.*, b. 28 *Jan*. 1841; d.s.p. (*at Florence*) 17 *Mar*. 1879.

---

[1] Presumably the 1st or 2nd wife (both of whom *d.s.p.* Burke's "Landed Gentry," 1900, p. 310) of Thomas Clifton of Lytham, who *d*. 1783, having *m*. 3rdly, Lady Jane Bertie (see Table III.).

# of The Blood Royal

3b. Edgar John Meynell, J.P., Judge of County Courts and Recorder of Doncaster, b. 1 Feb. 1825; d. 15 Jan. 1901; m. 5 Aug. 1856, Maria Louisa, da. of Richard Samuel Short, previously Hassard of Edlington, co. Lincoln; and had issue 1c to 4c.

    1c. Edgar Meynell, Bar.-at-Law, b. 6 Sept. 1859 *(Kilvington Hall, near Thirsk; The Fryerage, near Yarm, co. York).*

    2c. Hugo Thomas Meynell, b. 6 Dec. 1862; d. 9 May 1898; m. 9 Ap. 1888, Mary Julia, da. of James Fleming, Q.C.; and had issue 1d to 5d.

        1d. Hugo Charles Meynell, b. 11 Feb. 1889.

        2d. Francis Edgar Meynell, b. 23 Sept. 1894.

        3d. Mary Louisa Maud Meynell.

        4d. Dorothy Mary Meynell.

        5d. Catherine Mary Meynell.

    3c. Louisa Mary Meynell.

    4c. Lucy Mary Meynell.

4b. Mary Theresa Meynell, d. 1 Sept. 1896; m. 14 Oct. 1862, Howard Downman Bedingfeld; and had issue 1c to 3c.

    1c. Howard Francis Bedingfeld, b. 9 Nov. 1865.

    2c. George Ernest Howard Bedingfeld, b. 17 Ap. 1867; m. 1894, Catherine, da. of [——] Loman of St. Louis, U.S.A.

    3c. Teresa Mary Bedingfeld, b. 1 June 1864; m. 2 June 1900, Ernest Gordon Bedingfeld, Capt. *late* 8th Hussars, a Military Knight of Windsor.

2a. George Meynell of Lincoln's Inn, Bar.-at-Law, d. 1844.

3a. Catharine Dorothy Meynell, b. 1 Dec. 1768; d. 19 Ap. 1839; m. 3 Mar. 1789, Simon Thomas Scrope of Danby, male representative of the House of Scrope and de jure 19th Earl of Wilts [E.], b. 29 Dec. 1758; d. 14 Aug. 1838; and had issue 1b to 3b.

    1b. Simon Thomas Scrope of Danby, b. 17 Ap. 1790; d. 1 Oct. 1872; m. 25 June 1821, Mary, da. of John Jones of Llanarth Court, co. Monmouth, d. 25 Ap. 1830; and had issue.

    See the Clarence Volume, p. 457, Nos. 19693–19707.

    2b. Henry Scrope, b. 13 Oct. 1798; d. 25 Oct. 1873; and had issue.

    3b. Catherine Dorothy Scrope, b. 4 Oct. 1791; d. 4 Ap. 1884; m. 15 Jan. 1827, Anthony George Wright of Wealside, co. Essex, afterwards Wright-Biddulph of Burton, co. Sussex; and had issue.

    See p. 278, Nos. 11073–11080.   [Nos. 24536 to 24569.

258. Descendants, if any, of MARY SELBY (see Table XXII.).

259. Descendants of RALEIGH TREVELYAN of Netherwitton (see Table XXII.), b. 6 Aug. 1781; d. 12 May 1865; m. 14 June 1819, ELIZABETH, da. of Robert GREY of Shorestone Hall, co. Northumberland, d. 16 Sept. 1885; and had issue 1a to 5a.

    1a. Thornton Raleigh Trevelyan, b. 18 Ap. 1820; d.v.p. 14 Feb. 1845; m. Dorothy, da. of Matthew Henderson of Galashiels; and had issue 1b to 2b.

    1b. Thornton Roger Trevelyan, J.P., b. 1843; d. 1904; m. 1864, Dobree Wilkinson (Netherwitton, near Morpeth), da. of J. W. Fraser of Bath; and had issue 1c to 6c.

        1c. John Spencer Trevelyan (Netherwitton, near Morpeth), b. 1864; m. 1897, Eleanor Margaret, da. of W. Brook Mortimer of Hay Car, co. Lancaster.

        2c. Walter Raleigh Trevelyan, b. 1866.   [Nos. 24570 to 24571.

The Plantagenet Roll

3c. Roger de Thornton Trevelyan, *b.* 1868.

4c. George Alfred Thornton Trevelyan, *b.* 1871.

5c. Freeman Blackett Thornton Trevelyan, *b.* 1874.

6c. Lilian Elizabeth Margaret Trevelyan, *m.* 1897, Ralph Spencer of Warbottle Hall.

2b. Constance Mary Trevelyan, *m.* 1st, 1864, James Jodel Mackie, Younger of Auchencairn, *d.v.p.;* 2ndly, 1869, Robert Benn; and has issue (and possibly others by 2nd husband) 1*c.*

1c. Constantia Florence Mackie, *b.* 1865.

2a. Walter Blackett Trevelyan, Bar.-at-Law, b. 17 *Mar.* 1821; *d.* 10 *Oct.* 1894; m. *Helena Caroline, widow of the Rev. Bryan Faussett, da. of Sir John Trevelyan, 5th Bart.* [*E.*], *d.* 14 *Mar.* 1898; *and had issue* 1*b to* 4*b.*

1b. Hubert Trevelyan, *late* Major Royal Inniskilling Fusiliers, *b.* 6 July 1847.

2b. Walter Trevelyan.

3b. Willoughby Fenwick Trevelyan, Capt. Army Pay Dept., *b.* 1 Aug. 1856.

4b. Constance Helena Trevelyan, *m.* as 2nd wife, 27 Dec. 1877, the Hon. Sir Arthur Moseley Channell, a Judge of the High Court of Justice, King's Bench Division, and a Member of the Council of Legal Education (1 *Bramham Gardens, South Kensington, S.W.*); and has issue 1*c.*

1c. Arthur Willoughby Trevelyan Channell, *b.* 14 July 1879.

3a. Raleigh Trevelyan, b. 15 *Aug.* 1833; *d.* 25 *Aug.* 1882; *m.* 1844, *Sarah Flora, da. of Capt. Macdonald.*

4a. Constance Trevelyan, d. (-); *m.* 7 *Aug.* 1850, *Robert Hawdon.*

5a. Helena Trevelyan, m. 3 Nov. 1852, Lieut.-Col. James Harrington Trevelyan, 60th Rifles, *b.* 9 Nov. 1811; *d.* 5 Nov. 1875; and has issue 1*b* to 5*b.*

1b. Charles Edgar Harrington Trevelyan, *b.* 27 Ap. 1856.

2b. Edmund James Willoughby Trevelyan, *b.* 7 Aug. 1859.

3b. Eugenie Arabella Trevelyan.

4b. Pauline Eulalia Louisa Trevelyan.

5b. Ada Bibiannah Emma Trevelyan. [Nos. 24572 to 24588.

260. Descendants of ELIZABETH WITHAM (See Table XXII.), *d.* (-); *m.* HENRY THOMAS MAIRE SILVERTOP, *afterwards* WITHAM of Lartington, co. Yorks, *b.* 28 May 1779; *d.* 28 Nov. 1844.

See the Clarence Volume, pp. 319–320, Nos. 9241–9266.

[Nos. 24589 to 24614.

261. Descendants, if any, of MARY PALMES (See Table XXII.), wife of THOMAS SMITH of Bidlesden, co. Northumberland; and of KATHERINE MEYNELL, *d.* 1718, wife of JOHN BRIGHAM of Wyton.

262. Descendants, if any, of MATTHEW MIDDLETON, and of his sisters, URSULA, wife of HENRY FERMOR of Somerton, co. Oxon., and MARY, wife 1st of EDWARD TOPHAM of Aylethorpe, who *d.s.p.*, and 2ndly, of THOMAS THORNTON of Oldstead, co. York (see Table XXII.).

263. Descendants, if any, of URSULA INGLEBY, wife of ROBERT WIDDRINGTON (See Table XXII.).

# of The Blood Royal

264. Descendants of CHARLES (ANDERSON, *afterwards* ANDERSON-PELHAM), 1st BARON YARBOROUGH [G.B.] (see Table XXIII.), *b.* 3 Feb. 1749; *d.* 22 Sept. 1823; *m.* 21 July 1770, SOPHIA, da. and h. of John AUFRERE of Chelsea, co. Middlesex, *d.* 25 Jan. 1786; and had issue 1*a* to 4*a*.

1*a*. *Charles (Anderson-Pelham), 2nd Baron* [G.B.] *and 1st Earl of* [U.K.] *Yarborough,* b. 8 *Aug.* 1781; d. 5 *Sept.* 1846; m. 11 *Aug.* 1806, *Henrietta Anna Maria Charlotte, da. of the Hon. John Bridgeman Simpson,* d. 30 *July* 1813; *and had issue.*
See the Tudor Roll of "The Blood Royal of Britain," pp. 421–422, Nos. 30415–30458.

2*a*. *Hon. Caroline Anderson-Pelham,* b. 18 *Jan.* 1777; d. *July* 1812; m. *as* 1st *wife,* 11 *Oct.* 1797, *Robert Cary Elwes of Great Billing, J.P.,* b. 28 *July* 1772; d. *Jan.* 1852; *and had issue* 1*b* to 5*b*.

1*b*. *Cary Charles Elwes of Great Billing, J.P., D.L.,* b. 2 *Nov.* 1800; d. 24 *Jan.* 1866; m. 1st, 17 *Aug.* 1826, *Elinor, da. of Rear-Adm. Peter Rye of Culworth, co. Northants,* d. 8 *Jan.* 1859; *and had issue* 1*c* to 4*c*.

1*c*. Valentine Dudley Henry Cary Elwes of Great Billing, &c., F.S.A., F.G.H.S., J.P., D.L., High Sheriff co. Lincoln 1873 *(Great Billing Hall, Northampton; The Manor House, Brigg, co. Lincoln),* b. 26 Nov. 1832; *m.* 1st, 28 Ap. 1856, Henrietta Catherine, da. of Charles Lane of Badgemore, *d.s.p.* 28 Ap. 1864; 2ndly, 30 Nov. 1865, Alice Geraldine, da. of Rev. the Hon. Henry Ward; and has issue.
See the Clarence Volume, p. 280, Nos. 7502–7512.

2*c*. *Eleanora Caroline Arabella Cary Elwes,* b. 12 *Feb.* 1828, d. *Jan.* 1890; m. 3 *Mar.* 1848, *Capt. Charles FitzGerald, R.N., C.B., Governor of Western Australia; and had issue.*

3*c*. Sophia Dorothea Cary Elwes *(Grange, Weston Favell, Northampton),* m. 1878, Jacob O'Connor, M.D., *d.s.p.* 3 Mar. 1886.

4*c*. Marian Georgina Cary Elwes, b. 1837; *d.* 1903; *m.* 16 July 1857, George F. Browning, *d.* 1872; and has issue.

2*b*. *Dudley Christopher Cary Elwes, 23rd Welsh Fusiliers and 1st King's Dragoon Guards,* b. 19 *Mar.* 1804; d. 25 *Oct.* 1852; m. 19 *May* 1829, *Mary Anne Sophia, da. of Rear-Adm. Peter Rye of Culworth, R.N.,* d. 9 *Dec.* 1847; *and had issue* 1*c* to 4*c*.

1*c*. Dudley George Cary Elwes, F.S.A., late 3rd Buffs *(Askham House, Conway, Florida),* b. 13 Nov. 1837; *m.* 3 Feb. 1863, Mary Georgina, da. of Frederick Mangles of Pendell Court, Bletchingley; and has issue 1*d* to 9*d*.

1*d*. Dudley Frederick Cary Elwes, M.A. (Oxon.) *(Bedford),* b. 14 Jan. 1864; *m.* 4 Sept. 1895, Mary Louisa, da. of Lieut.-Gen. George Thomas Field of Upton Park, co. Berks, R.A.; and has issue 1*e* to 2*e*.

1*e*. Dudley George Cary Elwes, *b.* 23 Nov. 1896.

2*e*. Edward Trevelyan Cary Elwes, *b.* 8 June 1901.

2*d*. Frank de Stuteville Cary Elwes, a naturalised U.S. citizen *(Jacksonville, Florida),* b. 7 Mar. 1865; *m.* 31 Oct. 1898, Susan, widow of [——] Law, da. of [——] Harper; and has issue 1*e* to 3*e*.

1*e*. Frederick Cary Elwes, *b.* Aug. 1899.

2*e*. Lewis Cary Elwes, *b.* 31 Oct. 1901.

3*e*. Mary Frances Cary Elwes, *b.* 2 Mar. 1905.

3*d*. Geoffrey Cary Elwes *(Dinsmore, Florida),* b. 14 Ap. 1866.

4*d*. Rev. Albert Cary Elwes, M.A. *(Finstock Vicarage, Oxon.),* b. 24 Oct. 1868.

5*d*. Alan Charles Cary Elwes *(Coronada, Florida),* b. 5 Dec. 1869.

6*d*. Herbert Cary Elwes, B.A. (Oxon.), *b.* 14 Feb. 1877.

7*d*. Walter Cary Elwes, *b.* 17 Sept. 1878.

8*d*. Lucy Marion Cary Elwes, *b.* 12 Jan. 1871.　　　　[Nos. 24615 to 24686.

The Plantagenet Roll

9d. Charlotte Cary Elwes, *b.* 27 Nov. 1872; *m.* 3 June 1905, Gerald Otway Hay Murray (*Northend Farm, Henley-on-Thames*).

2c. Eleanor Sophia Cary Elwes, *b.* 3 *Ap.* 1830; *d.* 5 *May* 1873; *m.* 1*st*, 12 *Mar.* 1853, *the Rev.* Charles Atkinson West, *d. Mar.* 1855; *2ndly*, 8 *Sept.* 1858, *the Rev.* Thomas Field, *B.D., Rector of Bigby, co. Lincoln, b.* 3 *Mar.* 1822; *d.* 15 *Aug.* 1896; *and had issue* 1*d* to 10*d*.

1d. Arthur Perrott Cary Field, M.A. (*Edgbaston, Birmingham*), *b.* 29 Mar. 1867; *m.* 27 Ap. 1897, Ethelwyn Mary, da. of Thomas Bullock; and has issue 1*e* to 3*e*.

1e. Dudley Thomas Cary Field, *b.* Feb. 1898.

2e. John Perrott Cary Field, *b.* May 1900.

3e. Margaret Ethelwyn Cary Field, *b.* June 1902.

2d. Rev. Francis George Elwes Field, M.A. (*Sheringham, Norfolk*), *b.* 2 Jan. 1869; *m.* 22 Ap. 1897, Alice Jane De Ville, da. of Charles Owen; and has issue 1*e* to 5*e*.

1e. Thomas Richard Owen Field, *b.* 9 Dec. 1899.

2e. George Arthur Charles Field, *b.* 17 July 1903.

3e. Robert Lionel Elwes Field, *b.* 29 July 1905.

4e. Joyce Mary Field, *b.* 6 July 1898.

5e. Alice Barbara Field, *b.* 1 Jan. 1902.

3d. Charles John Lionel Field (*Moosomin, Canada*), *b.* 16 Dec. 1869; *m.* 19 Feb. 1896, Lila, widow of H. Budge, da. of Samuel Foster.

4d. Robert Cecil Field (*Peak Hill, West Australia*), *b.* 31 May 1871; *m.* 8 Sept. 1902, Louisa, da. of Lawrence Eliot of Perth, West Australia; and has issue 1*e*.

1e. Lawrence Cecil Elwes Field, *b.* 13 June 1905.

5d. Rev. Lawrence Percy Field, B.A., Diocesan Inspector (*Leicester*), *b.* 14 Aug. 1872; *m.* 1st, 18 Ap. 1898, Alice Mary, da. of A. Darby, *d.* 21 Ap. 1902; 2ndly, 25 July 1905, Martha, widow of Capt. J. A. Williams, da. of T. J. Jones; and has issue 1*e*.

1e. Eleanor Lilian Field, *b.* 19 Feb. 1899.

6d. Charlotte Frances Harriet West, *b.* 29 June 1855; *unm.*

7d. Eleanor Margaret Field, *b.* 4 May 1860; *m.* 13 Aug. 1884, Francis Plumptre Beresford Osmaston, Bar.-at-Law (*Stoneshill, Limpsfield, Surrey*); and has issue 1*e* to 3*e*.

1e. Dudley Francis Osmaston, *b.* 12 Nov. 1892.

2e. Robert Shirley Osmaston, *b.* 17 Nov. 1894.

3e. Eleanor Dorothea Osmaston, *b.* 4 Oct. 1887.

8d. Edith Pelham Field, *b.* 30 Nov. 1861; *m.* 18 Sept. 1895, Charles William Tindall (*Wainfleet Hall, Lincolnshire*); and has issue 1*e*.

1e. Eleanor Winefride Tindall, *b.* 9 Mar. 1897.

9d. Beatrice Louisa Field, *b.* 24 Feb. 1863; *m.* 25 Nov. 1889, Walter John Underwood, R.A.; and has issue 1*e* to 3*e*.

1e. Cyril Lancelot Underwood, *b.* 6 Feb. 1892.

2e. Mabel Eileen Underwood, *b.* 23 Nov. 1895.

3e. Mary Underwood, *b.* 25 May 1898.

10d. Lilian Dudley Field, *b.* 25 May 1864; *unm.*

3c. Caroline Henrietta Cary Elwes, *b.* 4 *Aug.* 1832; *d.* 18 *Ap.* 1905; *m.* 17 Nov. 1859, *Gen.* George Thomas Field *of Upton Park, co. Berks, R.A., d.* 30 *Aug.* 1889; *and had issue* 1*d to* 8*d*.

1d. Thomas Perrott Field, Deacon, *b.* 16 Feb. 1876.

2d. Mary Louisa Field, *m.* 4 Sept. 1895, Dudley Frederick Cary Elwes (*The Crescent, Bedford*); and has issue.

See p. 339, Nos. 24675–24676.

3d. Gertrude Alice Field.

[Nos. 24687 to 24719.

# of The Blood Royal

4d. Caroline Elwes Field, *m.* 27 Jan. 1891, Rev. Edmund Mowbray, Vicar of St. Bartholomew's, Dover (*St. Bartholomew's Vicarage, Dover*) ; and has issue 1*e.*

1*e.* George Robert Mowbray, *b.* 15 July 1899.

5d. Eleanor Bonsquet Field.

6d. Sophy Annie Perrott Field.

7d. Charlotte Jessie Field.

8d. Cecilia Georgina Field.

4c. Charlotte Maria Cary Elwes, b. 30 Oct. 1835 ; d. 31 Oct. 1868 ; m. 16 Ap. 1857, Horatio Tennyson (brother to Alfred, 1st Baron Tennyson [U.K.]), d. 2 Oct. 1899 ; and had issue 1d to 3d.

1*d.* Cecilia Mary Tennyson, *m.* 2 *July* 1878, the Rev. Richard William Massey Pope, D.D. (*4 Keble Road, Oxford*), *s.p.*

2*d.* Eleanor Maud Tennyson, *unm.*

3*d.* Violet Dudley Tennyson, *unm.*

3b. George Cary Elwes, Fellow of All Souls, Oxford, b. 3 Feb. 1806 ; d. 13 Ap. 1859 ; m. 10 Feb. 1833, Arabella Elizabeth Sophia, da. of Thomas Fieschi Heneage, d. 9 Dec. 1853 ; and had issue.

See the Clarence Volume, p. 427, Nos. 16706–16735.

4b. Henry Robert Harrington Cary Elwes, 23rd Welsh Fusiliers, b. 1808 ; d. 1850 ; m. 1st, 1830, Harriet, da. of Charles Tennant, d. 1842 ; 2ndly, 1844, Caroline Eliza Cecil, da. of Col. Strode (who re-m. 1st, Dr. Seth Thompson ; 2ndly, Major Sidebottam Verner), d. 12 Oct. 1893 ; and had issue 1c.

1*c. Hugh William Henry Cary Elwes, Major (ret.) Durham Artillery Militia,* b. 2 July 1845 ; d. 16 Nov. 1904 ; m. 1st, May 1872, Emily Laura, da. of Capt. Henry Selby Lowndes, d. 14 Sept. 1876 ; 2ndly, 23 July 1891, Ann Sherson, da. of John Tawse ; and had issue 1d.

1*d.* Grace Isabella Laura Cary Elwes.

5b. Caroline Arabella Elizabeth Cary Elwes, d. 28 May 1866 ; m. 3 Feb. 1827, Rev. Charles James Barnard, Rector of Bigby and Roxby, co. Lincoln, previously R.N., b. 6 Nov. 1797 ; d. 29 Sept. 1868 ; and had issue 1c to 4c.

1*c. Charles Cary Barnard, J.P., formerly in Holy Orders,* b. 14 Dec. 1827 ; d. 28 Nov. 1905 ; m. 1st, 18 May 1854, Charlotte, da. of Henry Alington-Pye, d.s.p. 30 Jan. 1869, 2ndly, 27 Ap. 1870, Alice Rose, da. of Edward de Selvier Solis of Darro, Spain ; and had issue 1d to 4d.

1*d.* Gerard Charles Victor Barnard, *b.* 30 Mar. 1875 ; *m.* Daisy, da. of [———] Swainson ; and has issue (a da.).

2*d.* Cyril Darcy Vivian Cary Barnard, Wilts Regt., *b.* 11 Aug. 1876.

3*d.* Hubert Vyel Juan Barnard, *b.* 26 Mar. 1878.

4*d.* Muriel Vera Melosine Barnard.

2c. Caroline Georgina Barnard, b. 17 Aug. 1832 ; d. 1 Jan. 1903 ; m. 10 Ap. 1867, Major William Puckle, b. 13 Ap. 1835 ; d. 7 Ap. 1886 ; and had issue 1d to 2d.

1*d.* Pelham Cary Puckle (*Pittern Hill, Warwick ; Kineton, Warwickshire*), *b.* 8 July 1872 ; *m.* 2 Dec. 1899, Jessie Stanley, da. of Col. Stanley Arnold of Barton House, co. Warwick, C.B.

2*d.* Caroline Evelyn Puckle, *b.* 4 Ap. 1870 ; *m.* 14 Feb. 1903, Kenneth Trevor Stewart (*Hill Street House, 2 Hill Street, Knightsbridge, S.W.*) ; and has issue 1*e.*

1*e.* Charles John Raphael Barnewall Stewart, *b.* 17 July 1904.

3*c.* Adelaide Sophia Barnard (28 *St. James' Road, Tunbridge Wells*), *m.* as 2nd wife, 11 Sept. 1866, the Rev. Mordaunt Barnard, *d.* 29 Oct. 1885 ; and has issue 1*d.*

1*d.* Rev. Percy Mordaunt Barnard, *b.* 11 July 1868 ; *m.* 14 Feb. 1900, Alice Mary, da. of the Rev. Frederick Taunton ; and has issue 1*e* to 3*e.*

[Nos. 24720 to 24768.

2 X

The Plantagenet Roll

1e. Charles Mordaunt Barnard, b. 28 Feb. 1901.

2e. Osbert Howard Barnard, b. 28 Mar. 1903.

3e. Nea Everilda Barnard, b. 21 May 1905.

4c. Lucy Marion Barnard, m. 7 Aug. 1862, Edward Drummond, B.C.S. (13 St. James' Place, S.W.); and has issue.

See the Clarence Volume, p. 496, Nos. 21627–21629.

3a. Hon. Maria Charlotte Anderson Pelham, b. 6 July 1780; d. 1840; m. 1 June 1804, William Tennant of Aston Hall, b. 1783; d. 1835; and had issue 1b to 6b.

1b. Charles Edmund Tennant of Needwood House, co. Stafford, Comm. R.N., J.P., D.L., b. 28 Mar. 1811; d. 2 Jan. 1862; m. 1st, 21 May 1850, Sophia Amy, da. of Richard Temple of The Nash, co. Worc., d. (at Florence) 10 May 1857; 2ndly, 17 Feb. 1859, Constance Elizabeth, da. of Col. Cracroft Amcotts of Hackthorn, d. 26 Oct. 1898; and had issue 1c to 3c.

1c. Charles Richard Tennant, J.P., late Major 2nd Life Guards (St. Anne's Manor, Sutton, Loughborough), b. 9 Mar. 1851; m. 18 Nov. 1886, the Hon. Ruth Adamson, da. of Thomas (Brooks), 1st Baron Crawshaw [U.K.].

2c.[1] Charlotte Louisa Tennant (Kensington Palace Mansions, S.W.), m. 17 Dec. 1872, the Right Hon. Sir William Thackeray Marriott, P.C., K.C., M.P., Judge Advocate-Gen., d. 27 July 1903.

3c.[2] Constance Augusta Tennant, m. 27 June 1898, Sir Eric Alexander Buchanan, 3rd Bart. [U.K.] (Craigend Castle, Milngavie; 38 Sloane Court, S.W.); and has issue 1d to 2d.

1d. Charles James Buchanan, b. 16 Ap. 1899.

2d. Mary Constance Victoria Buchanan, b. 22 Jan. 1901.

2b. George Tennant of the Eades, co. Worc., Major 85th Regt., b. 3 Aug. 1812; d. 30 May 1872; m. 12 Feb. 1850, Mary, da. of William Symonds of Elsdon, co. Hereford, d. 30 Ap. 1903; and had issue 1c to 3c.

1c. Edmund William Tennant, J.P., Hon. Lieut.-Col., late Major 4th Batt. S. Staffordshire Regt. (The Eades, Upton-on-Severn), b. 9 Sept. 1859; m. 24 Nov. 1886, Mary Eliza, da. of James Lowe of Churchfield, Chorlton-cum-Hardy, M.A., J.P.; and has issue 1d to 2d.

1d. William George Tennant, R.N., b. 2 Jan. 1890.

2d. Roger Debonnaire Tennant, b. 28 Jan. 1902.

2c. Agnes Mary Tennant, m. 30 Aug. 1881, the Rev. William John Pinckney, late Vicar of Quatford (16 Upper Maze Hill, St. Leonards-on-Sea).

3c. Ethel Madeline Tennant, m. 6 Jan. 1886, the Rev. Henry Dealtry Thomas.

3b. Charlotte Anne Josephine Tennant, d. 3 Oct. 1874; m. 18 May 1830, Sir Richard Henry Charles Rycroft, 3rd Bart. [G.B.], b. 21 Dec. 1793; d. 21 Oct. 1864; and had issue 1c to 2c.

1c. Sir Nelson Rycroft, 4th Bart. [G.B.], b. 11 Mar. 1831; d. 30 Mar. 1894; m. 27 July 1858, Juliana, da. of Sir John Ogilvy of Inverquharity, 9th Bart. [S.]; and had issue.

See the Clarence Volume, p. 435, Nos. 18169–18178.

2c. Charles Alfred William Rycroft, b. 18 Sept. 1838; d. 23 Ap. 1884; m. 19 Jan. 1875, Edith Maude (28 Chester Square, S.W.), da. of Capt. Hugh Berners, R.N.; and had issue 1d to 4d.

1d. Alfred Richard Hugh Rycroft, Lieut. W. Kent Imp. Yeo., late Royal Welsh Fusiliers (Everlands, Sevenoaks), b. 21 Feb. 1876; m. 18 May 1901, Violet, da. of Capt. W. Kevill-Davies of Marsh Court, Leominster.

2d. Henry Frederick Rycroft, Lieut. 3rd Batt. York and Lancaster Regt., b. 26 Feb. 1879.

3d. Charlotte Maud Rycroft, m. 9 Nov. 1899, Fritz Ritter, Lieut. Royal Thuringian (6th Uhlan) Regt. [Nos. 24769 to 24798.

342

# of The Blood Royal

4d. Aurea Harriet Louisa Rycroft, *m.* 10 Feb. 1903, Major Edmund Stuart Eardley Wilmot Eardley-Russell, R.F.A. (41 *Eaton Square, S.W.*); and has issue 1*e.*

1*e.* Rupert Eardley-Russell, *b.* 1904.

4b. Harriet Tennant, d. 1842 ; m. *as* 1*st wife*, 1830, *Capt. Henry Robert Harrington Cary Elwes,* d. 1850 ; *and had issue.*
See p. 341, No. 24759.

5*b. Theodosia Mary Tennant,* d. (−) ; m. 1838, *the Rev. John James, Rector of Avington, co. Berks ; and had issue* 1*c.*

1*c. John Charles Horsey James, Commissioner of Land Titles and Chief Justice, Western Australia, b.* 30 *Jan.* 1841 ; d. 3 *Feb.* 1899 ; m. 1885, *Rebecca Catherine, da. of Charles Hippuff Clifton ; and had issue* 1*d to* 6*d.*

1*d.* Evelyn Harold Clifton James, *b.* 8 July 1886.
2*d.* Percival Arthur Clifton James, *b.* 23 Sept. 1887.
3*d.* Eustace Alfred Clifton James, *b.* 12 Jan. 1889.
4*d.* Meredith Charles Clifton James, *b.* 10 Dec. 1894.
5*d.* Meyrick Edward Clifton James, *b.* 30 Mar. 1897.
6*d.* Rosamond Clifton James, *b.* 10 Sept. 1892.

6*b. Lucy Tennant,* d. (−) ; m. 1850, *the Rev. Alfred Henry, Vicar of Coln St. Aldwin, co. Gloucester.*

4a. Hon. Arabella Anderson Pelham, b. 20 *Jan.* 1783 ; d. 16 *May* 1871 ; m. 19 *July* 1802, *Thomas Fieschi Heneage, b.* 28 *Sept.* 1771 ; d. Dec. 1854 ; *and had issue.*
See the Clarence Volume, pp. 426–427, Nos. 16701–16735.

[Nos. 24799 to 24842.

265. Descendants, if any, of HARRIET ANDERSON (see Table XXIII.), *b.* 9 June 1753 ; *d.* (−) ; *m.* PAUL MOSS.

266. Descendants, if any surviving, of ELIZA MARIA ANDERSON (see Table XXIII.), *b.* 3 May 1710 ; *d.* 1732 ; *m.* 27 Nov. 1729, THOMAS WHICHCOT of Harpswell ; and had issue 1*a* to 2*a.*

1*a. Frances Maria Whichcot, bapt.* 26 *Aug.* 1730 ; d. 22 *Aug.* 1750 ; m. *as* 2*nd wife, the Very Rev. John Fountayne, Dean of York, b. c.* 1715 ; d. 14 *Feb.* 1802 ; *and had issue* 1*b.*

1*b. Frances Maria Fountayne,* b. 8 *Mar.* 1750 ; d. 9 *Jan.* 1777 ; m. *as* 1*st wife,* 27 *Feb.* 1773, *William Tatton, afterwards Egerton of Wythenshawe, M.P., b.* 9 *May* 1749 ; d. 1806 ; *and had issue* 1*c.*

1*c. William Egerton of Wythenshawe, M.P., b.* 1774 ; d. *unm.* 9 *Feb.* 1799.

2*a. Catherine Whichcot, bapt.* 5 *Sept.* 1731 ; d. (?)

267. Descendants, if any surviving, of FRANCES PELHAM (see Table XXIII.), *bapt.* 3 May 1676 ; *d.* June 1703 ; *m.* SAMUEL REYNOLDS ; and had (with others who *d.s.p.*) issue 1*a.*

1*a. Samuel Reynolds, living* 1727.[1]

---

[1] Brydges' " Collins' Peerage," viii. p. 392.

343

The Plantagenet Roll

268. Descendants of WILLIAM (FITZWILLIAM), 3rd [I.] and 1st [G.B.] EARL FITZWILLIAM (see Table XXIII.), *b.* 15 Jan. 1719 ; *d.* 10 Aug. 1756 ; *m.* 22 June 1744, Lady ANNE, da. and in her issue (1782) co-h. of Thomas (WATSON-WENTWORTH), 1st Marquis of Rockingham [G.B.], *d.* 29 Aug. 1769 ; and had issue.

See pp. 253-260, Nos. 9608-9885. [Nos. 24843 to 25120.

269. Descendants of Lady MARY FITZWILLIAM (see Table XXIII.), *d.* 10 Sept. 1776 ; *m.* JOHN ARCHER of Welford, co. Berks, and Holme, co. Derby, *d.* 30 Sept. 1800 ; and had issue 1*a*.

1*a*. Susannah Archer (*sole h. in* 1819), *d.* 14 *Feb.* 1837; *m.* 18 *Sept.* 1770, *Jacob Houblon of Hallingbury Place, co. Essex, b.* 19 *Aug.* 1736 ; *d.* 14 *Oct.* 1783 ; *and had issue* 1*b to* 2*b.*

1*b. John Archer Houblon of Hallingbury and Welford, M.P., b.* 1 *Dec.* 1773 ; *d.* 1 *June* 1831 ; *m.* 29 *July* 1797, *Mary Anne, da. of Thomas Bramston of Skreens, co. Essex, M.P., d.* 4 *Ap.* 1865 ; *and had issue* 1*c to* 4*c.*

1*c. John Archer Houblon of Hallingbury, J.P., D.L., b.* 29 *Sept.* 1803 ; *d.s.p.* 6 *Oct.* 1891.

2*c. Charles Archer Houblon, afterwards* (1831) *Eyre of Welford Park, J.P., D.L., High Sheriff co. Berks* 1834, *b.* 13 *Oct.* 1806 ; *d.* 22 *July* 1886; *m.* 1*st,* 12 *May* 1835, *Mary Anne, da. of Gen. Leyborne Popham of Littlecote, d.* 12 *Mar.* 1855 ; *and had issue.*

See pp. 117-118, Nos. 1422-1434.

3*c. Rev. Thomas Archer Houblon, M.A., Rector of Peasemore, b.* 4 *Jan.* 1808 ; *d.* 21 *Dec.* 1874 ; *m.* 19 *July* 1839, *Eleanor, da. of the Rev. John Deedes of Willingale, d.* 11 *June* 1865 ; *and had issue* 1*d to* 5*d.*

1*d.* Rev. Thomas Henry Archer Houblon, M.A., D.D., Archdeacon of Oxford (*Christ Church, Oxford*), *b.* 9 Oct. 1849.

2*d.* Eleanor Archer Houblon, *b.* 24 Mar. 1843.

3*d.* Sophia Archer Houblon, *b.* 27 Dec. 1844.

4*d.* Louisa Archer Houblon, *b.* 19 July 1848.

5*d.* Maria Georgina Archer Houblon, *b.* 7 Nov. 1853.

4*c. Mary Anne Archer Houblon, b.* 21 *Oct.* 1811 ; *d.* 23 *May* 1896 ; *m.* 21 *Dec.* 1842, *William Forbes of Medwyn, J.P., D.L., d.* 12 *Mar.* 1891 ; *and had issue* 1*d to* 6*d.*

1*d.* John Houblon Forbes, J.P., D.L. (*Medwyn, West Linton, co. Peebles*), *b.* 22 Aug. 1852 ; *m.* 29 Mar. 1883, the Hon. Alexandra Katherine May, da. of Alexander (Fraser), 17th Lord Saltoun [S.] ; and has issue 1*e.*

1*e.* Dorothy Charlotte Mary Eleanor Forbes, *b.* 7 Jan. 1884.

2*d.* Mary Anne Forbes (16 *Lowndes Square, S.W.*), *m.* 14 Oct. 1863, Walter Henry (Erskine), 11th Earl of Mar and 13th Earl of Kellie [S.], *d.* 16 Sept. 1888 ; and has issue.

See p. 303, Nos. 15284-15294.

3*d. Louisa Forbes, d.* 12 *Sept.* 1878 ; *m. as 2nd wife,* 17 *Oct.* 1877, *Sir James Ranken Fergusson of Spitalhaugh, 2nd Bart.* [U.K.], *J.P., D.L., &c. (Spitalhaugh, West Linton, co. Peebles ; Bordlands, Dolphinton) ; and had issue* 1*e.*

1*e.* Louis Forbes Fergusson, B.A. (Oxon.), a Clerk in the Office of the Duchy of Lancaster (*Constitutional*), *b.* 5 Sept. 1878. [Nos. 25121 to 25153.

344

# of The Blood Royal

4d. *Harriet Susannah Forbes*, d. 23 Feb. 1884 ; m. 18 *Ap.* 1871, *the Hon. Augustus William Erskine (Bowscar, Penrith)* ; *and had issue.* See p. 304, Nos. 15296–15303.

5d. Helen Anne Forbes.

6d. Elizabeth Jane Forbes.

2b. *Maria Houblon*, b. 5 *July* 1771 ; d. 3 *Mar.* 1860 ; m. 16 *June* 1807, *the Rev. Alexander Ambrose Cotton of Girton*, d. 9 *Mar.* 1846 ; *and had issue* 1c *to* 2c.

1c. *Alexander Cotton of Landwade, co. Cambs., Lieut. R.N.*, b. c. 1808 ; d. 24 *May* 1860 ; m. 11 *Aug.* 1841, *Henrietta, da. of the Very Rev. Samuel Smith, D.D., Dean of Christ Church and Preb. of Durham ; and had issue* 1d.

1d. *Aline Cotton*, m. 1st, 12 Ap. 1864 (her cousin), the Rev. Charles Harrington, Rector of South Lacey, *d.s.p.* 9 Feb. 1868 ; 2ndly, Capt. Robert Biscoe, 19th Regt., *d.* 9 Jan. 1905.

2c. *Susanna Cotton*, d. (–) ; m. 17 *July* 1838, *John Gibbons ; and had issue.*

[Nos. 25154 to 25164.

270. Descendants, if any surviving, of FRANCES PELHAM (see Table XXIII.), *m.* Sir MATTHEW APPLEYARD of Berstwick Garth, co. York, Governor of Leicester ; and had issue 1*a* to 3*a*.[1]

1a. *Christopher Appleyard of Berstwick Garth, M.D.*, d. (*in London*).

2a. *Matthew Appleyard*, m. *Jane, da. of* [——] *Ramsden ; and had issue* 1b *to* 4b.

1b. *Matthew Appleyard*, bapt. (*at Berstwick*) 20 *July* 1684 ; d. (*there* 30 a.p.d. 1714).

2b. *Francis Appleyard, Captain,* bur. 18 *Dec.* 1751 ; m. *Anne, da. of* [——] *Taylor ; and had issue* 1c *to* 6c.

1c. *Francis Appleyard,* d.s.p.

2c. *Thomas Appleyard,* bapt. 25 *Feb.* 1730.

3c. *Matthew Appleyard,* bapt. 27 *Mar.* 1731.

4c. *William Appleyard,* bapt. 20 *Sept.* 1735.

5c. *Jane Appleyard,* bapt. 31 *Oct.* 1723 ; m. *George Laurence.*

6c. *Margaret Appleyard,* bapt. 17 *Mar.* 1728.

3b. *Jane Appleyard,* bapt. 23 *Aug.* 1792.

4b. *Anne Appleyard,* m. *the Rev. John Lambert, Rector of Leven ; and had issue* 1c *to* 2c.

1c. *Jane Lambert,* living unm. 1782.

2c. *Frances Lambert,* m. as 2nd wife, *the Rev. Thomas Jackson (son of the Vicar of Hedon) ; and had issue* 1d.

1d. *John Jackson,* d. 1781.

3a. *Anne Appleyard,* m. [——], *Sunderland.*

271. Descendants of GEORGE (WINN, *afterwards* (R.D. 20 Jan. 1777) ALLANSON-WINN), 1st Lord HEADLEY, BARON ALLANSON AND WINN [I.], and Baronet [G.B.] (see Table XXIII.), *b.* 1725 ; *d.* 9 Ap. 1798 ; *m.* 2ndly, 24 June 1783, JANE, da. and co.-h. of Arthur BLENNERHASSETT of Ballyseedy, co. Kerry, *d.* 25 Nov. 1825 ; and had issue 1*a* to 3*a*.

1a. *Charles (Allanson-Winn), 2nd Lord Headley, Baron Allanson and Winn* [I.], *and Baronet* [G.B.], also (*in* 1833) 8th Bart. [E.], b. 25 *June* 1784 ; d.s.p. 9 *Ap.* 1840.

---

[1] Poulson's "Holderness," ii. p. 364.

The Plantagenet Roll

2a. Hon. George Mark Arthur Way (Allanson-Winn), M.P., b. 14 Aug. 1785 ;
d. 5 Nov. 1827 ; m. 27 Ap. 1807, Elizabeth Mary, da. of. Lewis Majendie of Hed-
ingham Castle, co. Essex, d. 18 Ap. 1863 ; and had issue.
See the Clarence Volume, p. 117, Nos. 1300–1324.

3a. Hon. Jane Elizabeth Allanson-Winn, b. 8 July 1787 ; d. (at Rome) 12 Sept.
1841 ; m. as 2nd wife, 25 Sept. 1805, John Knight of Wolverley, co. Worcester, d. (at
Rome) 24 Jan. 1850 ; and had issue 1b to 3b.

1b. Sir Frederick Winn Knight, K.C.B., M.P., J.P., D.L., a Family Trustee
of the British Museum, &c., b. 1812 ; d.s.p.s. 3 May 1897 ; m. 1850, Mary Louisa
Couling (Wolverley House, Kidderminster), da. of E. Gibbs.

2b. Charles Allanson Knight, b. 1814 ; d. 26 Jan. 1879 ; m. 30 Ap. 1862,
Jessie Anne, widow of Count Alexander de Polignac, da. of William Ramsay ; and
had issue 1c to 2c.

1c. Charles Lewis William Morley Knight, Capt. late R.A., a Family Trustee
of the British Museum (24 *Charles Street, Berkeley Square, W. ; Villa Jessie,*
Cannes), b. 13 Feb. 1863.

2c. Margaret Elizabeth Knight, b. (at the Château de la Source, Loiret) ; m. as
2nd wife, 3 Mar. 1883, Prince Camille Armand Jules Marie de Polignac (*Villa*
Jessie, Cannes ; Chat. de Podwein, Radmannsdorf, Carniola); and has issue
1d to 3d.

1d. Prince Victor Mansfield de Polignac, b. 17 June 1899.

2d. Princess Constance Mabel de Polignac, b. 29 Jan. 1884.

3d. Princess Helen Agnes Anne de Polignac, b. (at Vienna) 30 June 1886.

3b. Edward Lewis Knight, Capt. 20th Foot, b. 1 Dec. 1817 ; d. 18 June 1882 ;
m. 2ndly, 1 Dec. 1856, Henrietta, da. of Edward Ayshford Sanford of Nynehead
Court, M.P., d. May 1876 ; and had issue 1c to 3c.

1c. Eric Ayshford Knight, J.P., Capt. Worcester Imp. Yeo. (Wolverley House,
Kidderminster), b. 18 Ap. 1863 ; m. 15 Sept. 1897, Constance Ida, da. of J. W. H.
Wilson of Winnipeg ; and has issue 1d to 3d.

1d. Frederick Knight, b. 22 Sept. 1899.

2d. Richard Knight, b. Dec. 1901.

3d. Ethel Mary Knight, b. 20 May 1903.

2c. Guy Cunninghame Knight, Major Loyal North Lancashire Regt., D.A.A.G.
Cairo, *b. 12 Dec. 1866 ; m. 11 June 1898, Menie E., da. of J. Cross Buchanan.*

3c. Isabella Dora Knight, m. 6 Aug. 1889, William Butler Wasbrough (13
Philbeach Gardens, W. ; Stockham, Wantage); and has issue 1d to 4d.

1d. William Lewis Wasbrough, b. 21 July 1891.

2d. Henry John Wasbrough, b. 29 Oct. 1898.

3d. Helen May Dora Wasbrough, b. 8 Dec. 1892.

4d. Dorothy Sydney Wasbrough, b. 29 Dec. 1895.   [Nos. 25165 to 25204.

272. Descendants, if any, of CATHERINE PELHAM (see Table XXIII.),
m. 1st [——] HESLOP of. co. Northumberland ; 2ndly, JOHN
STANHOPE of Grimston, co. York, and of MARGARET PELHAM.

273. Descendants, if any, of HENRY PELHAM, M.P., and (1647)
Speaker of the House of Commons, living 1658 ; of HERBERT
PELHAM, LL.D., *b. c.* 1597 ; *d.* 1671 ; of EDMUND PELHAM,
living 1642 ; of ROGER PELHAM, of the Inner Temple 1639,
b. 1610, living 1642 and 1647 ; of WILLOUGHBY PELHAM,
living 1629 ; and of their sister ELIZABETH, *bapt.* 3 Mar. 1595,
living 1645 (see Table XXIII.).

# of The Blood Royal

274. Descendants, if any, of Lady KATHERINE NEVILL (see Table XXII.), wife of Sir JOHN CONSTABLE of Kirby Knowle, co. York.

275. Descendants of THOMAS (STAPLETON), 22nd BARON LE DESPENCER, and 6th BARONET OF THE LEEWARD ISLANDS [E.] (see Table XXIV.), *b.* 10 Nov. 1766; *d.* 3 Oct. 1831; *m.* 29 July 1791, ELIZABETH, da. of Samuel ELIOT of Antigua, *d.* 3 July 1848; and had issue 1*a* to 7*a*.

1*a. Hon. Thomas Stapleton, b. 24 Ap. 1792; d.v.p. 1 June 1829; m. 2 Feb. 1816, Maria Wynne, da. of Henry Banks of Kingston House, co. Dorset, d. 15 Oct. 1823; and had issue 1b.*

1*b. Mary Frances Elizabeth (Stapleton), suo jure 23rd Baroness Le Despencer, b. 24 Mar. 1822; d. 20 Nov. 1891; m. 29 July 1845, Evelyn (Boscawen), 6th Viscount Falmouth [G.B.], b. 18 Mar. 1819; d. 6 Nov. 1889; and had issue 1c to 6c.*

1*c.* Evelyn Edward Thomas (Boscawen), 7th Viscount Falmouth [G.B.], 24th Baron Le Despencer [E.], C.B., M.V.O. (*Tregothnan, Truro ; Mereworth Castle, Maidstone ; 2 St. James' Square, S.W.*), *b.* 24 July 1847 ; *m.* 19 Oct. 1886, the Hon. Kathleen, da. of George (Douglas-Pennant), 2nd Baron Penrhyn [U.K.]; and has issue.

See the Clarence Volume, p. 220, Nos. 4446–4450.

2*c.* Hon. Hugh Le Despencer Boscawen, J.P., D.L. (20 *South Street, Park Lane, W.*), *b.* 28 Feb. 1849 ; *m.* 23 May 1872, Lady Mary, da. of William (Wentworth-Fitzwilliam), 6th [I.] and 4th [G.B.] Earl Fitzwilliam, K.G.

3*c.* Hon. John Richard De Clare Boscawen, J.P., D.L. (*Tregye, Perranwell, Cornwall*), *b.* 19 Dec. 1860 ; *m.* 11 June 1890, Lady Margaret Florence Lucy, da. of George (Byng), 2nd Earl of Strafford [U.K.]; and has issue 1*d.*

1*d.* Catherine Margaret Boscawen, *b.* 29 May 1891.

4*c.* Hon. Mary Elizabeth Frances Catherine Boscawen, *m.* 26 June 1894, the Rev. Arthur Murray Dale, Rector of Tingrith (*Tingrith Rectory, Woburn*).

5*c.* Hon. Edith Maria Boscawen (6 *Queen Anne Street, Cavendish Square, W.*).

6*c.* Hon. Mabel Emma Boscawen, *m.* 18 Ap. 1882, Major Charles Henry Bennett Williams, J.P. (*Eryl, St. Asaph, N. Wales*) ; and has issue 1*d* to 2*d.*

1*d.* Evelyn Hugh Walkin Williams, *b.* 21 Mar. 1884.

2*d.* Mary Nesta Harriet Williams, *b.* 31 Jan. 1883.

2*a. Rev. the Hon. Miles John Stapleton, Rector of Mereworth and Vicar of Tudeley-cum-Capel, b. 21 Mar. 1801 ; d.v.p. 11 June 1830 ; m. 29 Dec. 1820, Anne Byam, da. of Thomas Norbury Kerby of Antigua, d. 14 Jan. 1842 ; and had issue 1b to 2b.*

1*b. Adelaide Stapleton, d. 27 Aug. 1860 ; m. 23 Oct. 1851, Capt. Catesby Paget, d. 16 July 1878 ; and had issue 1c to 2c.*

1*c.* Maria Rachel Paget, *m.* 17 May 1888, Frederick Pratt-Barlow, *d.* 1893 ; and has issue 1*d.*

1*d.* Adelaide Grizel Pratt-Barlow, *b.* 1892.

2*c.* Adelaide Stapleton Paget.

2*b.* Jane Elizabeth Stapleton, *m.* 30 Ap. 1862, Archibald Godley, J.P., D.L. ; and has issue 1*c.*

1*c.* Anna Charlotte Adelaide Godley.

3*a. Rev. the Hon. Sir Francis Jarvis Stapleton, 7th Bart. [E.], b. 6 Aug. 1807 ; d. 11 Feb. 1874 ; m. 17 May 1830, Margaret, da. of Lieut.-Gen. Sir Arthur Aircy, K.C.H., d. 7 Feb. 1880 ; and had issue 1b to 7b.* [Nos. 25205 to 25223,

347

The Plantagenet Roll

1*b*. *Sir Francis George Stapleton, 8th Bart.* [*E*.], b. 19 *Mar.* 1831; d. 30 *Oct.* 1899; m. 5 *Sept.* 1878, *Mary Catherine* (*Fawley Court, Bucks*), *da. of Adam Steuart Gladstone of Hazelwood, co. Herts* (*who re-m.*, 1902, *William Dalziel Mackenzie of Farr, co. Inverness*); *and had issue* 1*c*.

    1*c*. Clare Florence Mary Stapleton, *b.* 2 Oct. 1879; *m.* 9 Ap. 1902, Capt. Geoffrey Charles Buxton; and has issue 1*d*.

        1*d*. Peter Stapleton Buxton, *b.* 1904.

2*b*. *Richard Talbot Plantagenet Stapleton, Lieut.-Col.* 19*th Hussars*, b. 21 *Ap.* 1834; d. 28 *Ap.* 1899; m. 21 *June* 1877, *Emma, da. of the Rev. John Duncombe Shafto*; *and had issue* 1*c to* 4*c*.

    1*c*. Sir Miles Talbot Stapleton, 9th Bart. (*Grey's Court, Henley-on-Thames*), *b.* 26 May 1893.

    2*c*. Marguerite Cecil Catherine Stapleton, *b.* 13 Dec. 1878; *m.* 6 Ap. 1904, Capt. Arthur Duncombe-Shafto, D.S.O.; and has issue 1*d*.

        1*d*. Mark Duncombe-Shafto, *b.* 1905.

    3*c*. Olive Frances Stapleton, *b.* 22 June 1880.

    4*c*. Hilda Alice Stapleton, *b.* 24 Feb. 1884.

3*b*. *Rev. Eliot Henry Stapleton, M.A., Rector of Mereworth*, b. 25 *Nov.* 1835; d. 28 *Sept.* 1892; m. 29 *Dec.* 1860, *Frances Mary, da. of Sir Walter Stirling of Faskine, 2nd Bart.* [*G.B.*], d. 13 *June* 1891; *and had issue* 1*c to* 5*c*.

    1*c*. Hugh Le Despencer Stapleton, Lieut. R.N. (*The Grange, Southam*), *b.* 30 Mar. 1863; *m.* 29 Ap. 1891, Bertha Gwendoline, da. of Major Edwin Adolphus Cook of Roydon Hall; and has issue 1*d* to 2*d*.

        1*d*. Gerald Stapleton.

        2*d*. Mary Augusta Blanche Stapleton.

    2*c*. Francis Harry Stapleton, Capt. Oxfordshire L.I., *b.* 13 Oct. 1876.

    3*c*. Eleanor Mary Caroline Stapleton.

    4*c*. Evelyn Stapleton, *m.* 9 June 1903, Alistair Hugh Forbes-Gordon (*Rathwade, co. Carlow*).

    5*c*. Florence Blanche Stapleton, *m.* 4 Oct. 1898, Alexander Collingwood Fownes Luttrell (*Edington, Bridgwater*); and has issue 1*d* to 2*d*.

        1*d*. Alexander Henry Luttrell, *b.* 6 Dec. 1902.

        2*d*. Romala Margaret Luttrell, *b.* 23 Oct. 1899.

4*b*. George Aircy Talbot Stapleton, *late* I.C.S. (87 *Onslow Square, S.W.*), *b.* 26 Feb. 1838; *m.* 1 Jan. 1873, Elizabeth Anne, da. of the Rev. George Somerset; and has issue 1*c*.

    1*c*. Mabyn Agnela Rose Stapleton.

5*b*. *Catherine Elizabeth Stapleton*, d. 18 *Mar.* 1905; m. 19 *Jan.* 1859, *Col. Charles George Tottenham, J.P. D.L., High Sheriff co. Wexford* 1874, *and for co. Wicklow* 1881, *late M.P. for New Ross* [1] (*Ballycurry, co. Wicklow*); *and had issue* 1*c to* 5*c*.

    1*c*. Charles Bosvile Tottenham, D.S.O., Major 14th Hussars, *b.* 19 Oct. 1869.

    2*c*. Catherine Isabelle Tottenham, *m.* 30 Aug. 1898, Major Roger Casement, *late* R.A. (*Cronroe, Wicklow*).

    3*c*. Florence Margaret Tottenham.

    4*c*. Lilian Emma Tottenham.

    5*c*. Mary Talbot Augusta Tottenham.

6*b*. *Florence Maria Stapleton*, d. Nov. 1902; *m.* 27 *Jan.* 1866, *Frederick Seymour, Governor of British Columbia*, d. 10 *June* 1869.

7*b*. *Margaret Mary Stapleton*, d. 20 *Jan.* 1876; *m.* 18 *Aug.* 1866, *Count Hubert de Stacpoole*, d. (*in France*) 26 *July* 1868; *and had issue* 1*c*.

        [Nos. 25224 to 25246.

---

[1] Being the sixth Charles Tottenham who has sat in Parliament in regular succession from father to son for that borough.

# of The Blood Royal

1c. Cecile de Stacpoole, m. 20 Aug. 1887, Galfrid Aloysius Cathcart de Trafford (St. Albans, Hampton-on-Thames); and has issue.
See the Clarence Volume, p. 323, Nos. 9355-9356.

4a. Hon. Maria Frances Catherine Stapleton, b. 22 Sept. 1794; d. 25 Feb. 1861; m. as 1st wife, 9 Jan. 1813, Robert (Jocelyn), 3rd Earl of Roden [I.], 1st Baron Clanbrassill [U.K.], K.P., d. 20 Mar. 1870; and had issue.
See the Clarence Volume, pp. 290-292, Nos. 8115-8174.

5a. Hon. Emma Stapleton, b. 27 Feb. 1796; d. 29 Dec. 1879; m. 5 May 1825 Charles (Brodrick), 6th Viscount Midleton [I.], 3rd Baron Brodrick [U.K.], d. 2 Dec. 1863; and had issue.
See the Clarence Volume, pp. 589-590, Nos. 24893-24914.

6a. Hon. Emily Stapleton, b. 8 Dec. 1798; d. 27 Jan. 1875; m. Nov. 1817, Lieut.-Gen. the Hon. Sir Hercules Robert Pakenham, K.C.B., b. 29 Sept. 1781; d. 7 Mar. 1850; and had issue 1b to 4b.

1b. Thomas Henry Pakenham, C.B., Lieut.-Gen. and Col. E. Lancashire Regt., late M.P. (10 Hertford Street, Mayfair, W.; Langford Lodge, Crumlin, co. Antrim), b. 26 June 1826; m. 25 Feb. 1862, Elizabeth Staples, da. of William Clarke of New York; and has issue 1c.

1c. Hercules Arthur Pakenham, Major 4th Batt. Royal Irish Rifles, late Capt. Grenadier Guards, and Private Sec. to Under Sec. for the Colonies, &c.; Pres. of Board of Agriculture, &c. &c.; High Sheriff co. Antrim (Langford Lodge, Crumlin, co. Antrim), b. 17 Feb. 1863; m. 16 Nov. 1895, Lilian Blanche Georgiana, da. of the Right Hon. Evelyn Ashley, P.C.; and has issue 1d to 2d.
1d. Hercules Dermot Wilfred Pakenham, b. 29 July 1901.
2d. Joan Esther Sybella Pakenham, b. 2 Feb. 1904.

2b. Emily Pakenham, d. 21 Ap. 1883; m. 3 July 1837, Sir Edmund Samuel Hayes, 3rd Bart. [I.], M.P., b. 2 July 1806; d. 30 June 1860; and had issue
See pp. 95-96, Nos. 713-722.

3b. Elizabeth Catherine Pakenham, d. 22 Jan. 1885; m. 6 Aug. 1850, Thomas Thistlethwayte of Southwick Park, High Sheriff co. Hants, b. 4 Dec. 1809; d. 1 Jan. 1900; and had issue 1c to 8c.

1c. Alexander Edward Thistlethwayte (Southwick Park, Fareham, Hants), b. 2 Mar. 1854.
2c. Arthur Henry Thistlethwayte, Capt. late Grenadier Guards, b. 25 Mar. 1857.
3c. Thomas George Thistlethwayte, Capt. late R.A., b. 17 Ap. 1859.
4c. Evelyn William Thistlethwayte, Capt. King's Royal Rifle Corps, b. 6 Ap. 1861.
5c. Robert Richard Thistlethwayte, b. 9 May 1863.
6c. Charles Michael Thistlethwayte, b. 9 Ap. 1865.
7c. Emily Thistlethwayte.

8c. Catherine Thistlethwayte, m. 20 July 1876, Lieut.-Col. Alexander Borthwick, M.V.O., Chief Constable of the Lothians and Peebles, late Rifle Brigade (35 Palmerston Place, Edinburgh); and has issue 1d to 5d.
1d. Hugh Frank Pakenham Borthwick, b. 23 July 1877.
2d. Arthur Sandilands Borthwick, b. 26 Dec. 1879.
3d. Evelyn Borthwick.
4d. Stanhope Borthwick.
5d. Grace Borthwick.

4b. Mary Frances Hester Pakenham, d. 4 Jan. 1898; m. 6 Aug. 1850, Sir William Verner, 2nd Bart. [U.K.], b. 4 Ap. 1822; d. 10 Jan. 1873; and had issue 1c to 3c.

1c. Sir William Edward Hercules Verner, 3rd Bart. [U.K.], b. 11 Jan. 1856; d.s.p. 8 June 1886.
2c. Alice Emily Verner, m. 1st, 8 Aug. 1875, Christopher Neville Bagot of Aughrane Castle, co. Galway, d. 23 May 1877; 2ndly, 30 Oct. 1879, Reginald Wynne Roberts Wynne (divorced 1895); and has issue 1d to 4d.

[Nos. 25247 to 25359

2 Y

The Plantagenet Roll

1*d*. William Hugh Neville Bagot, *b*. 187–.

2*d*. Reginald Evan Roberts Wynne, *b*. 1886.

3*d*. Ada Violet Edith Marguerite Roberts Wynne.

4*d*. Rose Constance Mary Roberts Wynne.

3*c*. Edith Verner.

7*a*. Hon. *Anna Frances Ester Stapleton*, d. 20 *Aug*. 1868; m. 3 *Dec*. 1828, *Henry* (*Maxwell*), 7th *Baron Farnham* [*I*.], *K.P*., b. 9 *Aug*. 1799; d.s.p. (*being killed with his wife in a railway accident near Abergele*) 20 *Aug*. 1868.

[Nos. 25360 to 25364.

276. Descendants, if any surviving, of Lieut.-Gen. WILLIAM STAPLETON (see Table XXIV.), *b*. 7 June 1770; *d*. 1826; *m*. 1790, ANNA MARIA, da. of the Most Rev. the Hon. Frederick KEPPEL, Lord Bishop of Exeter, *d*. 1836; and had issue 1*a*.

1*a*. *John Horace Thomas Stapleton*, d. 7 *Nov*. 1836; m. 1*st*, 2 *June* 1814, *the Hon. Georgiana Maria, da. of George* (*FitzRoy*), *2nd Baron Southampton* [*G.B.*], d. 8 *Aug*. 1830; 2ndly, 8 *July* 1834, *Charlotte Georgiana, da. of the Hon. Sir William Ponsonby*.

277. Descendants, if any, of CATHERINE STAPLETON (see Table XXIV.), *m*. Sir JAMES WRIGHT, (? 1st) Bart. [? G.B.], H.B.M.'s Resident Minister at Venice; and of FRANCES STAPLETON.

278. Descendants, if any, of DIANA BILL (see Table XXIV.), *d*. 23 May 1726; *m*. Capt. FRANCIS D'ARCY SAVAGE.

279. Descendants, if any, of Lady RACHEL FANE (see Table XXIV.), *m*. GREGORY HASCARD ASCARD, M.A. and D.D. Emm. Coll., Camb., Canon of Windsor 9 May 1671, Dean of the Chapel Royal 29 Sept. 1684, Rector of Bishopstoke and of Trinity, Queenhithe, and subsequently of St. Clement Danes, Strand, *d*. 1708; and of Lady SUSAN FANE.

280. Descendants of JOHN (FANE), 9th EARL OF WESTMORLAND [E.] (see Table XXV.), *b*. 5 May 1728; *d*. 26 Aug. 1774; *m*. 1st, 26 Mar. 1758, AUGUSTA, da. of Lord Montagu BERTIE, *d*. 4 Feb. 1766; 2ndly, 28 May 1767, Lady SUSAN, da. of Cosmo George (GORDON), 3rd Duke of Gordon [S.], *d*. 11 Dec. 1814.

See the Clarence Volume, Tables LXXIV. and XXVIII., pp. 599–603, Nos. 26282–26530; and p. 245, Nos. 5751–5866. [Nos. 25365 to 25728.

281. Descendants of the Hon. HENRY FANE, M.P. (see Table XXV.), *b*. 4 May 1739; *d*. 4 June 1802; *m*. 12 Jan. 1778, ANNE, da. of Edward Hickley BATSON of Avon Tyrrell, co. Southampton; and had issue 1*a* to 6*a*.

1*a*. *Rev. Edward Fane, Rector of Fulbeck, Preb. of Lincoln and Salisbury*, b. 7 *Dec*. 1783; d. 28 *Dec*. 1862; m. 7 *Oct*. 1816, *Maria, da. of Walter Parry Hodges of Dorchester*, d. 11 *Nov*. 1850; *and had issue 1b to 5b*.

# of The Blood Royal

1b. Henry Edward Fane, afterwards Hamlyn Fane of Clovelly Court, Avon Tyrrell, M.P., Lieut.-Col. 4th Light Dragoons, b. 5 Sept. 1817 ; d. 27 Dec. 1868 ; m. 9 Ap. 1850, Susan Hester, da. and co-h. of Sir James Hamlyn-Williams of Clovelly, 3rd Bart. [G.B.], d. 19 May 1869 ; and had issue 1c to 4c.

1c. Marion Elizabeth Hamlyn Fane, m. as 2nd wife, 5 Feb. 1879, Lieut.-Col. Sir (William) Lewis Stucley, 2nd Bart. [U.K.], J.P., D.L. (Affeton Castle, West Worlington ; Hartland Abbey, Bideford).

2c. Eveline Harriet Hamlyn-Fane (Avon Tyrrell, Ringwood ; 65 Cadogan Gardens, S.W.).

3c. Christine Louisa Hamlyn-Fane (Clovelly Court, N. Devon ; Langham Hall, Oakham), m. 11 June 1889, Frederick Gosling, afterwards (R.L. 1889) Hamlyn, J.P., D.L., d.s.p. 22 July 1904.

4c. Constance Edward Adeline Hamlyn-Fane, m. 12 Aug. 1885, John Thomas (Manners), 3rd Baron Manners [U.K.] (Mansfield House, 18 New Cavendish Street, W.; Avon Tyrrell, Hants); and has issue.
See p. 164, Nos. 3418–3421.

2b. Francis Augustus Fane of Fulbeck Hall, co. Lincoln, Col. in the Army, b. 22 Mar. 1824 ; d. 1 Feb. 1893 ; m. 10 Feb. 1863, Augusta, da. of William Fane, d. 14 June 1895 ; and had issue 1c to 2c.

1c. Hester Fane (52 Seymour Street, S.W.).

2c. Rachel Louisa Fane, m. 21 May 1889, Edmund Royds (Caythorpe, Grantham) ; and has issue 1d to 2d.

1d. Anthony Fane Royds, b. 1890.

2d. Jasper Frances Royds, b. 1896.

3b. Frederick Fane of Moyles Court, co. Hants, b. 11 July 1825 ; d. 22 Feb. 1902 ; m. 1st, 19 Aug. 1851, Elizabeth, da. of James Peel Cockburn, d. 11 May 1861 ; 2ndly, 28 Oct. 1864, Fanny Eliza, da. of Hollingworth Magniac ; and had issue 1c to 4c.

1c. Cicely Grace Augusta Fane, b. 22 June 1852 ; d. 4 Mar. 1877 ; m. as 1st wife, 2 Dec. 1875, William Robert Phelips, J.P., D.L. (Montacute House, Montacute, Somerset) ; and had issue 1d.

1d. Marjorie Cicely Phelips, m. 3 Aug. 1904, Capt. John Ingilby ; and has issue 1e.

1e. Cicely Eleanor Ingilby.

2c. Florence Mary Anne Fane, m. 10 Sept. 1873, Wynne Albert Bankes (Wolfeton House, Dorchester) ; and has issue 1d.

1d. Gladys Bankes, m. 1902, Hugh Nicholas Granville Stucley, late R.N (Pillhead, Bideford).

3c. Lilla Gertrude Fane (Shappen, Burley, Hants), m. 12 Jan. 1886, Capt. the Hon. Arthur Grenville Fortescue, b. (at Madura) 24 Dec. 1858 ; d. 3 Oct. 1895 ; and has issue 1d to 2d.

1d. Grenville Fortescue, b. 15 Mar. 1887.

2d. Joyce Margaret Fortescue, b. 13 Mar. 1892.

4c. Helen Violet Fane (Will Hall, Alton, Hants).

4b. Mary Eliza Caroline Fane, b. 13 Nov. 1820 ; d. 26 Jan. 1888 ; m. 24 June 1845, Anthony Peacock, afterwards (R.L. 1850) Willson of Rauceby Hall, M.P., b. 26 July 1811 ; d. 5 June 1866 ; and had issue 1c to 8c.

1c. Sir Mildmay Willson Willson, K.C.B., J.P., Major-Gen. late Col. Comdg. 1st Batt. Scots Guards (Rauceby Hall, Grantham), b. 13 July 1847.

2c. Rev. Vere Francis Willson, Rector of Fulbeck (Fulbeck Rectory, co. Lincoln), b. 13 Oct. 1855 ; m. 7 Aug. 1884, Rose, da. of the Rev. H. C. de St. Croix.

3c. Arthur Bruce Willson, late Lieut. R.N., b. 17 July 1857.

4c. Mary Georgiana Caroline Willson, b. 23 Ap. 1846 ; d. 5 Sept. 1889 ; m.
[Nos. 25729 to 25751.

351

The Plantagenet Roll

28 July 1869, Cecil Haffenden Hall, J.P., Capt. Scots Fusiliers, b. 10 Nov. 1843 ; d.v.p. 20 Aug. 1874 ; and had issue 1d.

    1d. Montagu Haffenden Hall, J.P., Capt. and Hon. Major 4th Batt. Lincolnsh. Regt., late Scots Guards (Whatton Manor, Nottingham), b. 11 Aug. 1870 ; m. 5 Feb. 1896, Mary Emily, da. of the Rev. Charles Daniel Crofts of Caythorpe.

    5c. Edith Harriet Willson.

    6c. Lucy Maria Willson (Eathorpe Hall, Leamington), m. 31 Mar. 1875, Beauchamp Henry John (Scott), 6th Earl of Clonmell [I.], b. 28 Dec. 1847 ; d. 2 Feb. 1898 ; and has issue 1d.

    1d. Rupert Charles (Scott), 7th Earl of Clonmell [I.] (Bishops' Court, Straffan, Kildare ; Eathorpe Hall, Leamington), b. 10 Nov. 1877 ; m. 8 Aug. 1901, Rachel Estelle, da. of Samuel Berridge of Toft Hill, Rugby ; and has issue 1e.

    1e. Lady Moira Estelle Norah Frances Scott, b. 6 Aug. 1902.

    7c. Laura Anne Willson.

    8c. Emily Grace Willson (Kettlethorpe Hall, Newark), m. 17 Feb. 1885, Major Frederick Augustus Cracroft Amcotts of Kettlethorpe, J.P., 5th Dragoons, b. 3 May 1853 ; d. 15 Ap. 1897 ; and has issue 1d to 3d.

    1d. Weston Cracroft-Amcotts (Kettlethorpe Hall, Newark), b. 7 Nov. 1888.

    2d. John Cracroft-Amcotts, b. 3 Jan. 1891.

    3d. Sylvia Cracroft-Amcotts, b. 22 Aug. 1886.

    5b. Augusta Cecily Fane (The Cottage, Fulbeck, Grantham).

    2a. Vere Fane of Little Penton Hall, b. 5 Jan. 1785 ; d. 18 Jan. 1863 ; m. 2 June 1815, Elizabeth, da. of Charles Chaplin of Blankney, d. 6 Jan. 1865 ; and had issue 1b to 3b.

    1b. Emily Fane, b. 21 Nov. 1822 ; d. 5 Mar. 1893 ; m. 5 Sept. 1849, Col. Edward Birch-Reynardson, C.B., J.P., b. 4 May 1812 ; d. 10 May 1896 ; and had issue 1c to 2c.

    1c. Vere Henry Birch-Reynardson, late Capt. 3rd Batt. Hants Regt. (Rushington Manor, Totton, Hants), b. 26 Mar. 1864 ; m. 4 Nov. 1892, Eva Annabella Jane, da. of Henry Morgan Earbery Crofton of Inchinappa ; and has issue 1d to 3d.

    1d. Edward Vere Birch-Reynardson, b. 28 Aug. 1894.

    2d. Morgan Henry Birch-Reynardson, b. 9 Dec. 1895.

    3d. Geraldine Rose Augusta Birch-Reynardson, b. 1 Aug. 1893.

    2c. Rose Catherine Birch-Reynardson (Elfordleigh, Plymouth, S. Devon), m. 14 Sept. 1875, John Hugh Bainbridge of Frankfield, Rear-Admiral R.N., J.P. ; b. 31 May 1845 ; and has issue 1d to 4d.

    1d. John Hugh Bainbridge (Frankfield, near Douglas, Cork), Lieut. R.N., b. 31 May 1879.

    2d. Kathleen Grace Fane Bainbridge.

    3d. Gwendolen Eleanor Bainbridge, m. Capt. A. B. Fox.

    4d. Dorothy Emily Bainbridge.

    2b. Emma Fane, b. 8 Sept. 1823 ; d. 14 Dec. 1847 ; m. 14 Aug. 1845, Westley Richads of Ashwell, co. Rutland, J.P., b. Aug. 1814 ; d. May 1897 ; and had issue 1c.

    1c. Adela Augusta Richards (Ashwell, Oakham), m. 23 Jan. 1873, Sir Henry Bromley, 5th Bart. [G.B.], d. 11 Mar. 1905 ; and has issue 1d to 5d.

    1d. Sir Robert Bromley, 6th Bart. [G.B.], J.P., Administrator and Treasurer of St. Kitts and Nevis (Government House, St. Kitts ; Stoke Newark, Notts), b. 6 Jan. 1874 ; m. 24 Feb. 1900, the Hon. Lilian, da. of Julian (Pauncefote), 1st Baron Pauncefote [U.K.] ; and has issue 1e to 2e.

    1e. Ruperta Sibyl Bromley, b. 15 Oct. 1901.

    2e. Esther Lilian Bromley, b. 11 Feb. 1905.   [Nos. 25752 to 25775.

352

# of The Blood Royal

2d. Maurice Bromley, now (R.L. 4 Feb. 1897) Bromley-Wilson, J.P., High Sheriff co. Westmorland 1901 (*Dallam Tower, Milnthorpe*), b. 27 June 1875.

3d. Arthur Bromley, Lieut. R.N., b. 8 Aug. 1876; m. 24 June 1904, Maye, da. of the Hon. James Dunsmuir, *formerly* Premier of British Columbia.

4d. Herbert Assheton Bromley, b. 16 Oct. 1879.

5d. Esther Bromley, m. 9 May 1905, Charles Robert Tryon.

3b. Georgiana Ellen Fane (*Ashwell, Oakham*), m. as 2nd wife, 20 Feb. 1856, Sir Henry Bromley, 4th Bart. [G.B.], b. 25 Dec. 1816; d. 21 Sept. 1895.

3a. *William Fane, H.E.I.C.S.*, b. 13 Ap. 1789; d. 7 Mar. 1839; m. 12 Jan. 1811, *Louisa Hay, da. of Thomas Dashwood*, d. 11 Nov. 1855; *and had issue* 1b *to* 7b.

1b. *William Dashwood Fane of Fulbeck Hall, J.P.*, b. 21 Oct. 1816; d. 29 Nov. 1902; m. 7 Aug. 1861, *Susan Millicent, da. of Gen. John Reeve by his wife, Lady Susan*, née *Sherard*, d. 12 Dec. 1877; *and had issue* 1c *to* 3c.

1c. William Vere Reeve Fane, Capt. and Hon. Major 3rd Batt. Lincolnshire Regt., *late* E. Surrey Regt. (*Fulbeck Hall, Grantham*), b. 29 Oct. 1868; m. 16 May 1895, Helen Beatrice, da. of Thomas Holdsworth Newman; and has issue 1d to 3d.

1d. Henry William Newman Fane, b. 6 Feb. 1897.

2d. Francis Christopher Fane, b. 9 June 1900.

3d. Charles William Fane, b. 2 Feb. 1904.

2c. Grace Susan Fane, m. 10 Feb. 1887, Col. Joseph Alexander Lambert, J.P., D.L., High Sheriff co. Mayo 1906, *late* Comdg. 2nd Dragoon Guards (*Brook Hill, co. Mayo*); and has issue 1d to 6d.

1d. Alexander Fane Lambert, b. 15 Nov. 1887.

2d. Guy William Lambert, b. 1 Dec. 1889.

3d. Francis John Lambert, b. 12 Mar. 1891.

4d. Jeffrey Maurice Lambert, b. 23 Jan. 1900.

5d. Grace Mary Blanche Lambert.

6d. Joan Millicent Lambert.

3c. Millicent Emma Rachel Fane, m. 17 Aug. 1898, Thomas Dalton Lawrance, Bar.-at-Law (43 *Montagu Square, W.*); and has issue 1d to 3d.

1d. Ruth Katharine Lawrance, b. 13 July 1899.

2d. Clare Millicent Lawrance, b. 29 July 1900.

3d. Audrey Grace Lawrance, b. 25 July 1904.

2b. *Louisa Anne Fleming Fane*, b. 7 Oct. 1814; d. 5 Dec. 1893; m. 26 Dec. 1840, *Capt. Henry Porter, afterwards* (1847) *Sherbrooke of Oxton Hall, J.P., D.L., High Sheriff co. Notts* 1859, b. 3 Sept. 1810; d. 12 June 1887; *and had issue* 1c *to* 5c.

1c. William Sherbrooke, J.P., Comm. (ret.) R.N. (*Oxton Hall, Southwell*), b. 23 Oct. 1844; m. 1 Sept. 1810, Margaret Macdonald, da. of Alexander Graham of Dunclutha; and has issue 1d to 5d.

1d. Henry Graham Sherbrooke, Lieut. R.N., b. 11 Feb. 1877; m. 19 Sept. 1899, Flora Maude, da. of John Liell Francklin of Gonalston.

2d. Robert Lowe Sherbrooke, b. 1885.

3d. Violet Sherbrooke, m. 23 July 1896, Hugh Bryans.

4d. Eva Caroline Sherbrooke, m. 1890, A. J. Popert.

5d. Gertrude Lilian Sherbrooke.

2c. Rev. Henry Nevile Sherbrooke, sometime (1891–1897) Vicar of Clifton, *previously* Capt. 43rd Foot, b. 3 Feb. 1846; m. 1st, 3 Feb. 1871, Lady Harriet Alice, da. and h. of George (Curzon-Howe), 2nd Earl Howe [U.K.], b. 17 June 1848; d. 13 Ap. 1875; 2ndly, 5 Mar. 1878, Lady Lilias Charlotte, da. of Hugh (Cairns), 1st Earl Cairns [U.K.], b. 1860; d. 5 Sept. 1889; 3rdly, Jan. 1892, Alice Maud, da. of Henry Abel Smith of Wilford House, co. Notts; and has issue 1d to 8d. [Nos. 25776 to 25802.

353

The Plantagenet Roll

1d. Penn Curzon Sherbrooke, Lieut. Notts Y.C., *b.* 28 Nov. 1871; *m.* 1893, Catherine Emily, da. of John Chaworth Musters of Annesley Park.

2d. Nevile Hugh Cairns Sherbrooke, Lieut. R.H.A., *b.* 8 Ap. 1880.

3d. Cuthbert Arthur Sherbrooke, *b.* 20 Jan. 1883.

4d. Sybil Mary Sherbrooke, *b.* 4 July 1873; *m.* 3 June 1905, Richard Francklin.

5d. Evelyn Alice Sherbrooke, *b.* 7 Ap. 1875; *m.* Feb. 1898, the Rev. N. Duncan.

6d.[2] Cicely Catherine Sherbrooke.

7d.[2] Marjorie Lilias Sherbrooke.

8d.[3] Louisa Constance Sherbrooke.

3c. Caroline Sherbrooke, *m.* 15 Mar. 1859, John Chaworth-Musters of Annesley Park, J.P., D.L., High Sheriff co. Notts 1864, *b.* 1838; *d.* 1887; and has issue *1d* to *4d.*

1d. John Patricius Musters, now (R.L. 6 Oct. 1888) Chaworth-Musters, J.P. (*Annesley Park, near Nottingham ; Wiverton Hall, near Bingham*), *b.* 13 Jan. 1860 ; *m.* Mary Anne, da. of George Sharpe ; and has issue *1e* to *11e.*

1e. George Patricius Chaworth-Musters, *b.* 14 June 1888.

2e. John Nevile Chaworth-Musters, *b.* 27 Nov. 1890.

3e. Anthony Chaworth-Musters, *b.* 3 Ap. 1892.

4e. John Mundy Chaworth-Musters, *b.* 9 Ap. 1895.

5e. Robert Chaworth-Musters, *b.* 24 July 1896.

6e. Douglas Chaworth-Musters, *b.* 2 June 1898.

7e. James Laurence Chaworth-Musters, *b.* 1 July 1901.

8e. Margarita Chaworth-Musters.

9e. Elsie Chaworth-Musters.

10e. Ruth Mary Chaworth-Musters.

11e. Catherine Lina Chaworth-Musters.

2d. Launcelot George Eden Michael Musters, *b.* 1868; *m.* 1893, Mabel Violet, da. of George Watson.

3d. Mary Catherine Musters, *b.* 1863.

4d. Catherine Emily Musters, *b.* 1864; m. 1893, Lieut. Penn Curzon Sherbrooke.

4c. Alice Louisa Sherbrooke, *m.* 17 Feb. 1863, George Eden Jarvis, J.P., D.L., *late* Capt. 18th Hussars, High Sheriff co. Lincoln 1878 (*Doddington Hall, co. Lincoln*).

5c. Mary Beresford Sherbrooke, *m.* as 3rd wife, 30 Ap. 1890, William (Forbes-Sempill), 17th Baron Sempill [S.] (*Craigievar Castle ; Whitehouse, Aberdeen*).

3b. Caroline Fane, b. 7 *July* 1818 ; d. 8 *Jan.* 1895 ; m. *as 2nd wife,* 22 *Jan.* 1838, *Gen. Marcus Beresford,* b. 28 *July* 1800 ; d. 16 *Mar.* 1876 ; *and had issue* 1c *to* 2c.

1c. Marcus De La Poer Beresford, *late* Capt. and Hon. Major 4th Batt. Roy. Warwickshire Regt., *b.* 20 Sept. 1847.

2c. Ethel Louisa Beresford, *m.* 7 Sept. 1880, Henry Montagu Spencer (*Blockley, Worcestershire*) ; and has issue *1d* to *3d.*

1d. Henry Beresford Spencer, Lieut. 2nd Vol. Batt. Gloucester Regt., *b.* 5 July 1881.

2d. Hilda Agnes Spencer, *b.* 25 June 1882.

3d. Eleanor Cicely Spencer, *b.* 5 Sept. 1883.

4b. Emily Maria Fane, b. 10 Dec. 1820 ; d. 11 *May* 1905 ; m. *as 3rd wife,* 26 *Ap.* 1859, *Bulkeley John Mackworth-Praed of Owsden Hall,* d. 12 *Mar.* 1876 ; *and had issue* 1c.

1c. Algernon Henry Mackworth-Praed, *b.* 7 Nov. 1861.

[Nos. 25803 to 25834.

354

# of The Blood Royal

5b. Julia Charlotte Fane, b. 21 *July* 1826 ; d. 20 *June* 1903 ; m. 23 *July* 1844, *Robert Alexander of Upavon,* b. 10 *Feb.* 1815 ; d. 23 *Oct.* 1863 ; *and had issue* 1c *to* 2c.

1c. *James Fane Alexander of Upavon, Wilts, Capt.* 17th *Lancers,* b. 1 *Jan.* 1846 ; d. (*? unm.*).

2c. *Emily Maude Alexander,* d. (*? unm.*).

6b. Adeline Fane, b. 6 *Sept.* 1830 ; d. 29 *June* 1897 ; m. 24 *Nov.* 1864, *William Earle Welby, J.P.* (*Bainton House, Stamford*) ; *and had issue* 1c.

1c. Louisa Felicia Welby.

7b. Augusta Fane, b. 3 *Nov.* 1831 ; d. 14 *June* 1895 ; m. 10 *Feb.* 1863, *Col. Francis Augustus Fane,* d. 1 *Feb.* 1893 ; *and had issue.*

See p. 351, Nos. 25737–25740.

4a. Robert George Cecil Fane, a Commissioner of the Court of Bankruptcy, b. 8 *May* 1796 ; d. 4 *Oct.* 1864 ; m. 2ndly, 7 *Sept.* 1841, *Harriette Anne, da. of Adm. the Hon. Sir Henry Blackwood,* 1st *Bart.* [*U.K.*], *K.C.B.,* d. (–) ; *and had issue* 1b *to* 3b.

1b. Cecil Francis William Fane, *late* Lieut. Grenadier Guards (*Old Lodge, Melton Mowbray*), b. 7 Oct. 1856 ; *m.* 8 May 1880, Lady Augusta Fanny (who obtained a div. 1904), da. of John Edward (Rous), 2nd Earl of Stradbroke [U.K.] ; and has issue 1c to 2c.

1c. Charles George Cecil Fane, *b.* 8 Ap. 1881.

2c. John Lionel Richards Fane, *b.* 2 Jan. 1884.

2b. Cicely Harriette Fane, } (23 *Charles Street, Berkeley Square, W.*).
3b. Blanche Anne Fane,

5a. Anne Fane, b. 19 *Jan.* 1780 ; d. *Mar.* 1831 ; m. *as* 2nd *wife,* 29 *Sept.* 1803, *Lieut.-Gen. John Michel of Dewlish and Kingston Russell,* b. 1765 ; d. 1844 ; *and had issue* 1b *to* 4b.

1b. *Right Hon. Sir John Michel of Dewlish, G.C.B., P.C., Field-Marshal Gen. Comdg. the Forces in Ireland, &c.,* b. 1 *Sept.* 1804 ; d. 24 *May* 1886 ; m. 15 *May* 1838, *Louisa Anne, da. of Major-Gen. C. H. Churchill, C.B. ; and had issue* 1c *to* 3c.

1c. John Horace Charles Michel, Major *late* Leicestershire Regt. (*Dewlish House, near Dorchester*), b. 12 Ap. 1843.

2c. Rachel Mary Lumley Godolphin Michel (56 *Warwick Square, S.W.*), m. 25 Ap. 1866, Raymond Hervey (de Montmorency), 3rd Viscount Frankfort de Montmorency [I.], K.C.B., *b.* 21 Sept. 1835 ; *d.* 7 May 1902 ; and has issue 1d to 3d.

1d. Willoughby John Horace (de Montmorency), 4th Viscount Frankfort de Montmorency [I.], Capt. Duke of Cornwall L.I., *b.* 3 May 1868.

2d. Hon. Kathleen Louisa Michel de Montmorency, *b.* 21 Sept. 1873.

3d. Hon. Lily Rachel Mary de Montmorency, *b.* 13 Ap. 1875.

3c. Louisa Augusta Michel, *m.* 16 Aug. 1881, Col. Charles Edward Beckett, 3rd Hussars.

2b. *Charles Edward Michel, J.P., Major-Gen. in the Army,* b. 24 July 1810 ; d. (–) ; m. 1851, *Emily, da. of Sir Robert Bowcher Clerk, C.B., Chief Justice at Barbados ; and had issue* 1c *to* 5c.

1c. Cecil Bowcher Duff Michel, *b.* 1854.

2c. Caroline Anne Michel, *m.* as 2nd wife, 2 June 1898, Charles Thorold Fane of Fulbeck Manor, J.P., *d.s.p.*

3c. Emily Charlotte Helen Michel.

4c. Helen Michel.

5c. Ada Rachel Michel.

3b. Henry Edward Michel.

[Nos. 25835 to 25855.

355

The Plantagenet Roll

4b. Charlotte Anne Michel, d. 1893 ; m. 5 *June* 1839, *Charles John Helyar of Poundisford Lodge, J.P., D.L.,* b. 15 *May* 1796; d. 19 *Jan.* 1858 ; *and had issue* 1c.

1c. *Charles Welman Hawker Helyar, J.P., late Lieut.-Col. 3rd Hussars,* b. 13 *Aug.* 1843 ; d. (–) ; m. 22 *Nov.* 1882, *Isabella, da. of Vincent Reynolds,* d. 24 *Sept.* 1899 ; *and had issue* 1d *to* 5d.

1d. Charles Vincent Hawker Helyar (*Poundisford Lodge, Pitminster, Taunton*), *b.* 8 Dec. 1883.

2d. Kenneth Carey Helyar, *b.* 17 Aug. 1886.

3d. Percival Helyar, *b.* 18 May 1888.

4d. Cecily Isabella Helyar, *b.* 6 Jan. 1885.

5d. Charlotte Jessie Helyar, *b.* 7 Jan. 1894.

6a. Harriet Fane, b. 10 *Sept.* 1793 ; d. 2 *Aug.* 1834 ; m. 31 *Jan.* 1814, *the Right Hon. Charles Arbuthnot,* d. 18 *Aug.* 1850. [Nos. 25856 to 25860.

282. Descendants, if any, of Lady MARY FANE (see Table XXV.), *m.* CHARLES BLAIR.

283. Descendants of JOHN FANE of Wormsley, LL.D., M.P. (see Table XXV.), *d.* 8 Feb. 1824 ; *m.* 16 Nov. 1773, Lady ELIZABETH, da. of Thomas (PARKER), 3rd Earl of Macclesfield [G.B.], *b.* 29 June 1751 ; *d.* 10 June 1829 ; and had issue 1*a* to 5*a*.

1a. *John Fane of Wormsley, High Sheriff co. Oxford* 1836, b. 9 *July* 1775 ; d. 4 *Oct.* 1850 ; m. 6 *June* 1802, *Elizabeth, da. of William Lowndes Stone of Brightwell Park,* d. 20 *Nov.* 1865 ; *and had issue* 1b *to* 6b.

1b. *John William Fane of Wormsley, M.P., J.P., D.L., D.C.L., Lieut.-Col. Oxford Militia,* b. 1 *Sept.* 1804 ; d. 19 *Nov.* 1875 ; m. 1*st,* 30 *Nov.* 1826, *Catherine, da. of Sir Benjamin Hobhouse, 1st Bart.* [U.K.], d. 6 *Nov.* 1828 ; 2*ndly,* 3 *Nov.* 1829, *Lady Ellen Catherine, da. of Thomas (Parker), 5th Earl of Macclesfield* [G.B.], d. 23 *Sept.* 1844 ; 3*rdly,* 18 *Nov.* 1845, *Charlotte, da. of Theodore Henry Broadhead,* d. 19 *May* 1855 ; 4*thly, Mar.* 1856, *Victoria* (88 *Eccleston Square, S.W.*), *da. of William Temple* (*who re.-m.* 1880, *Lieut.-Col. Sir John Terence O'Brien, K.C.M.G.*); *and had issue* 1c *to* 7c.

1c. John Augustus Fane, J.P., *late* Major Oxford Rifle Vol., *formerly* 46th Regt. (*Wormsley, Tetsworth, Oxon. ;* 9 *Belgrave Road, S.W.*), b. 23 Sept. 1830 ; *m.* 21 Jan. 1860, Eleanor, da. of Thomas Thornhill of Woodleys ; and has issue 1d *to* 6d.

1d. John Henry Scrope Fane, *late* Lieut. 3rd Batt. Oxfordshire L.I., *b.* 24 June 1861.

2d. Francis Luther Fane, *b.* 31 Mar. 1865.

3d. Sydney Algernon Fane (*Bentfield Bower, Stansted, Essex*), b. 27 Oct. 1867 ; *m.* 12 July 1894, Selina Violet, da. of Loftus FitzWygram ; and has issue 1e *to* 4e.

1e. Aubrey Francis Sydney Fane, *b.* 9 May 1895.

2e. Gerald William Reginald Fane, *b.* 7 Aug. 1898.

3e. Kenneth Cecil Fane, *b.* 16 Sept. 1902.

4e. Nigel Loftus Henry Fane, *b.* 25 July 1904.

4d. Catherine Elizabeth Agnes Fane, *b.* 30 Oct. 1862; *m.* 27 Aug. 1887, Albert Butler.

5d. Isabel Fane, *b.* 7 Ap. 1864 ; *m.* 14 Ap. 1885, Col. Brig.-Gen. Francis Hugh Plowden, C.B., Comdg. 1st Brig. Burmah Command (*Mandalay*) ; and has issue.

See p. 275, Nos. 10927–10939.

6d. Amy Eleanor Fane, *b.* 13 Nov. 1868. [Nos. 25861 to 25874.

# of The Blood Royal

2c. Henry George Fane, *late* Capt. 52nd Regt. (*Bicester House, Bicester*), *b.* 10 Sept. 1846; *m.* 5 July 1876, Blanche Louisa, da. of the Hon. Robert Charles Henry Spencer; and has issue 1*d* to 7*d*.

1*d*. Hubert William Fane, Associate Royal School of Mines, *b.* 9 Nov. 1878.

2*d*. Almeric Cecil Fane, A.M.I.C.E., *b.* 7 Jan. 1880.

3*d*. Arthur George Cecil Fane, I.P.W.D., *b.* 29 Dec. 1880.

4*d*. Robert Gerald Fane, Lieut. R.N., *b.* 8 Ap. 1882.

5*d*. Horatio Alfred Fane, *b.* 25 Feb. 1884.

6*d*. Francis John Fane, *b.* 13 Ap. 1885.

7*d*. Octavius Edward Fane, *b.* 15 Oct. 1886.

3c. Frederick William Fane (3 *Chesham Street, S.W.*), *b.* 26 July 1857; *m.* 30 Oct. 1880, Lady Annie Henrietta, da. of Col. the Hon. Charles Grantham Scott.

4c. Cecil Fane (*Malting Farm, Little Hallingsbury, Essex; Junior Carlton*), *b.* 27 June 1859; *m.* 25 Ap. 1892, Alice Mary, da. of the Rev. Thomas Ward Goddard, Vicar of Nazeing, *d.* 1 Feb. 1899; and has issue 1*d*.

1*d*. Valentine Cecil Fane, *b.* 30 Jan. 1893.

5c. *Sophia Fane*, b. 22 *Dec.* 1827; *d.* 24 Aug. 1886; m. 29 *July* 1851, *Arthur Henry Clerke Brown of Kingston Blount, J.P., D.L., High Sheriff co. Oxford* 1877, b. 9 *May* 1826; *d.* 20 *Mar.* 1889; *and had issue* 1*d* to 4*d*.

1*d*. Henry Clerke Brown, M.A., J.P., D.L. (*Kingston Blount, Tetsworth*), *b.* 8 May 1852; *m.* 1 May 1883, Mary Louisa Hester, da. of John Samuel Bowles of Milton Hill; and has issue 1*e*.

1*e*. John Clerke Brown, *b.* 16 July 1886.

2*d*. *George Clerke Brown*, b. 3 *May* 1855; *d.* 3 *Feb.* 1903; m. 16 *July* 1889, *Blanche Sophia Matilda*, da. of the Rev. Henry Bolton Power; and had issue 1*e* to 3*e*.

See the Clarence Volume, p. 455, Nos. 19651–19653.

3*d*. Mary Brown, *b.* 11 Aug. 1853; *m.* 9 May 1877, Col. John Fane Ballard (*Kingston Grove, Oxon.*); and has issue 1*e* to 4*e*.

1*e*. John Arthur Ballard, Capt. Oxford Regt., *b.* 10 Mar. 1878.

2*e*. Charles Frederick Ballard, R.N., *b.* 23 Mar. 1879.

3*e*. Muriel Frances Ballard.

4*e*. Alice Mary Ballard.

4*d*. *Catherine Sophia Brown*, b. 2 *Mar.* 1857; *d.* Mar. 1890; m. 8 *July* 1882, *William Henry Ashhurst, J.P., D.L., High Sheriff Oxford* 1891 (*Waterstock, Wheatley, Oxford*); *and had issue* 1*e* to 2*e*.

1*e*. Gladys Mary Ashhurst.

2*e*. Awdry Frances Ashhurst.

6c. *Ellen Fane*, b. 1833; *d.* 18 Nov. 1900; m. 24 Nov. 1853, *George Stratton of Wheler Lodge, Leicester, Bar.-at-Law, J.P.*, b. 15 *Feb.* 1827; *d. July* 1895; *and had issue* 1*d* to 3*d*.

1*d*. George Locke Stratton, *b.* 28 Oct. 1855; *m.* 1878, Sarah Elizabeth, da. of [——] Davidge; and has issue 1*e*.

1*e*. Ellen Louisa Stratton, *b.* June 1879; *m.* 19 Ap. 1900, Henry Herbert Lloyd (*Mornington Place, Wolverhampton*).

2*d*. Ellen Louisa Stratton, *b.* Sept. 1858.

3*d*. Emmeline Anne Madeline Stratton, *b.* Aug. 1860.

7c. Charlotte Elizabeth Fane, *m.* 2 Mar. 1871, George Henry Philpotts (15 *Warwick Road, Earl's Court, S.W.*); and has issue 1*d* to 5*d*.

1*d*. Adrian Ernest Fane Phillpotts, *b.* 1 Ap. 1877.

2*d*. Almeira Georgiana Mabel Phillpotts.

3*d*. Alice Helena Maud Phillpotts, a nun.

4*d*. Norah Gertrude Evelyn Phillpotts.

5*d*. Gertrude Violet Ada Phillpotts.

[Nos. 25875 to 25907.

2 z

The Plantagenet Roll

2b. Rev. Frederick Adrian Scrope Fane of Priors, Essex, b. 8 *Dec.* 1810; d. 5 *Oct.* 1894; m. 10 *June* 1834, *Joanna, da. of Sir Benjamin Hobhouse, 1st Bart.* [*U.K.*], d. 8 *Ap.* 1878; *and had issue* 1c *to* 4c.

1c. Frederick John Fane, Col. *late* Gloucester Regt. (*Priors, near Brentwood*), b. 30 Jan. 1840; *m.* 13 Nov. 1873, Annie Louisa, da. of Thomas Abbott of Halifax, N.S.; and has issue 1d.

1d. Frederick Luther Fane, B.A. (Oxon.), b. 27 Ap. 1875.

2c. Isabella Elizabeth Fane, *m.* 10 June 1857, the Rev. Almeric John Churchill-Spencer, b. 23 Jan. 1834; d. 3 May 1864; and has issue 1d to 2d.

1d. Henriette Churchill-Spencer.

2d. Adelaide Churchill-Spencer, *m.* 1st, 11 Feb. 1885, Major George Markham Davison, Durham L.I. (marr. dissolved 1902); 2ndly, 16 Sept. 1902, William Freeman O'Donoghue, Indian Public Works Dept.

3c. Georgiana Fane (*Brook Farm, Stondon, Essex*).

4c. Joanna Amelia Fane, *m.* 14 Mar. 1874, A. H. C. Waters (*Coopersale, Epping*); and has issue 1d.

1d. Georgiana Mary Joanna Waters.

3b. George Augustus Scrope Fane, b. 29 *Mar.* 1817; d. 14 *Aug.* 1860; *m.* 3 *June* 1843, *Frances Sophia Pole, da. of John Phillips of Culham ; and had issue* 1c *to* 3c.

1c. Charles Augustus Fane (*Carnarvon, West Australia*), b. 1846.

2c. Augustus Fane, Capt. (ret.) R.N. (*Constitutional*), b. 1847.

3c. Deborah Fane.

4b. Elizabeth Fane, b. 1 *June* 1802; d. 14 *May* 1885; m. 8 *Mar.* 1842, *the Rev. John Ballard*, d. 10 Oct. 1875; *and had issue* 1c.

1c. John Fane Ballard, Col. in the Army (*Kingston Grove, Oxon.*), b. 21 Nov. 1844; *m.* 9 May 1877, Mary, da. of Arthur Henry Clerke Brown of Kingston Blount, J.P., D.L.; and has issue.
See p. 357, Nos. 25892–25895.

5b. Anne Fane, b. 24 *Jan.* 1807; d. 21 *Nov.* 1829; m. 23 *Sept.* 1824, *John Billingsley Parry, Q.C.*, d. 28 *Mar.* 1876; *and had issue* 1c *to* 2c.

1c. Laura Parry (*Spencer Lodge, Ryde*), m. 1855, Capt. John Hamilton, R.N.; and has issue 1d to 2d.

1d. John Hamilton, Lieut.-Col. in the Army, b. 1859.

2d. Arthur Hamilton, Major 6th Dragoon Guards, b. 1861.

2c. *Annie Parry*, d. (–); m. [——] *Dewar ; and had issue* (2 das.).

6b. Charlotte Fane, b. 1 *Ap.* 1819; d. 1894; m. 16 *Nov.* 1852, *the Rev. Frederick Fyler*, b. 22 Feb. 1823; d. 10 *May* 1864; *and had issue* 1c *to* 3c.

1c. Frederick John Fane Fyler, *Capt.* 52nd Oxford L.I., b. 14 Nov. 1853; d. 19 *Aug.* 1886.

2c. John Arthur Fyler, *late* of Woodlands, co. Surrey, sometime M.P. for Chertsey (*United Universities*), b. Dec. 1855 ; *m.* May 1887, Caroline Norah, da. of Albert J. Hambrough of Steephill Castle, I.W., D.L.

3c. James l'Anson Fyler, d. 1875.

2a. Elizabeth Sarah Fane, b. 9 *Mar.* 1782; d. 1867; m. 12 *Dec.* 1813, *Col. Thomas Drake*, d. Dec. 1851.

3a. Charlotte Fane, b. 26 *July* 1787; d. 14 *Sept.* 1869; m. 28 *Dec.* 1813, *Col. John Potter Hamilton.*

4a. Georgiana Fane, b. 15 *Jan.* 1790; d. 15 *June* 1864; m. 9 *Dec.* 1816, *the Right Hon. Joseph Warner Henley of Waterperry, M.P., President of the Board of Trade*, b. 3 *Mar.* 1793; d. 9 Dec. 1884; *and had issue* 1b *to* 9b.

1b. Joseph John Henley, C.B., J.P., D.L., *late* General Inspector Local Govt.

[Nos. 25908 to 25928.

# of The Blood Royal

Board (*Waterperry Park, Oxford*), *b.* 29 Dec. 1821; *m.* 2 Oct. 1849, Agnes Welwyn, da. of Theodore Walrond of Calder Park, co. Lanark; and has issue 1c to 4c.

1c. Joseph Arthur Henley, *late* 82nd Regt., *b.* 7 Jan. 1856; *m.* 9 Jan. 1877, Kate Isabella, da. of Col. Graves; and has issue 1d to 2d.

1d. Joseph Charles Henley, R.N., *b.* 12 Sept. 1879.

2d. Violet Kate Henley.

2c. Georgina Caroline Henley, *m.* Sept. 1871, Philip James Digby Wykeham.

3c. Emma Augusta Henley, *m.* 18 July 1876, Ellis Frederick Dudgeon.

4c. Agnes Henley.

2b. Rev. *Francis George Henley, Rector of Lydlench, d. June* 1898.

3b. *Cecil Henley, d.* 1840.

4b. Arthur Henley, J.P. (*Eastwood, co. Carlow*), *b.* 1833; *m.* 27 Oct. 1868, Margaret, da. of Joseph John Gore of Derrymore; and has issue 1c to 4c.

1c. Francis Joseph Henley, Capt. Oxfordshire L.I., *b.* 28 Nov. 1869; *m.* Nov. 1903, Rose Minden, da. of [——] Rochfort.

2c. Cecil Henley, *b.* 3 Dec. 1880.

3c. Margaret Maria Henley.

4c. Georgiana Adelaide Henley.

5b. Georgiana Henley, *m.* 4 Sept. 1839, the Ven. G. Denison, Archdeacon of Taunton.

6b. *Grace Elizabeth Henley, d.* 28 *Aug.* 1898; m. 29 *Mar.* 1852, *the Rev.* (*Count*) [1] *Henry Jerome Augustine Fane De Salis, J.P.* (*Portnall Park, Virginia Water*); *and had issue* 1c *to* 5c.

1c. (Count) [1] Rodolph De Salis, B.A. (Camb.), Assoc. Mem. Inst. C.E., *b.* 1854; *m.* 27 June 1878, Edith Louisa Caroline, da. of Edwards Rousby; and has issue 1d.

1d. (Countess) [1] Edith Margaret De Salis, *b.* 12 July 1882.

2c. (Count) [1] Cecil Fane De Salis, B.A. (Oxon.), Bar.-at-Law (*Dawley Court, Uxbridge*), *b.* 1857; *m.* 3 Dec. 1889, Rachel Elizabeth Frances, da. of Edmund Waller of Farmington, co. Glouc.; and has issue 1d to 10d.

1d. (Count) [1] Henry Edmund Challoner Fane De Salis, *b.* 17 July 1891.

2d. (Count) [1] Edmund William Fane De Salis, *b.* 31 Dec. 1894.

3d. (Count) [1] Jerome Joseph Fane De Salis, *b.* 3 Jan. 1896.

4d. (Count) [1] John Peter Fane De Salis, *b.* 1897.

5d. (Count) [1] George Rodolph Fane De Salis, *b.* 1898.

6d. (Count) [1] Andrew Augustine Fane De Salis, *b.* 1901.

7d. (Count) [1] Stephen Hercules Fane De Salis, *b.* 1903.

8d. (Countess) [1] Barbara Grace Victoria Fane De Salis, *b.* 20 Jan. 1900.

9d. (Countess) [1] Grace Dorothea Fane De Salis, *b.* 1902.

10d. (Countess) [1] Judith Anna Fane De Salis, *b.* 1904.

3c. (Count) [1] William De Salis, M.V.O., Capt. R.N. (*Brookfield, Alverstoke*), *b.* 1858; *m.* 14 May 1889, Eliza Jesser, da. of Col. William Jesser Coope, *late* of Rouw Koop House, Rondebosch, Cape Colony; and has issue 1d to 3d.

1d. (Count) [1] Rodolph Henry De Salis, *b.* 25 May 1890.

2d. (Count) [1] Anthony De Salis, *b.* 11 May 1896.

3d. (Countess) [1] Ursula Eva De Salis, *b.* 21 Mar. 1892.

4c. Rev. (Count) [1] Charles De Salis, M.A. (Oxon.), Rector of Weston-super-Mare, Rural Dean of Locking, and Preb. of Wells (*Weston-super-Mare Rectory, Somerset*), *b.* 19 Mar. 1860; *m.* 21 July 1896, Lady Mary Alice, da. of Thomas (Parker), 6th Earl of Macclesfield [G.B.]; and has issue 1d to 3d.

1d. (Count) [1] Sydney Charles De Salis, *b.* 5 July 1898.

2d. (Countess) [1] Dorothy Mary De Salis, *b.* 25 June 1897.

3d. (Countess) [1] Ruth De Salis, *b.* 15 Dec. 1900.

5c. (Countess) [1] Georgiana De Salis, *m.* 19 Jan. 1883, the Rev. Robert Aber-

[Nos. 25929 to 25962.

---

[1] Title not used.

The Plantagenet Roll

cromby Hamilton, M.A. (Oxon.), Vicar of Cranbourne (*Cranbourne Vicarage, Berks*).

7b. Ellen Mary Henley, *m.* 1852, Capt. T. G. Drake, R.N., *d.* Dec. 1883.

8b. Ann Henley.

9b. Adelaide Charlotte Henley.

5a. *Augusta Fane*, b. 16 *Dec.* 1792 ; d. 24 *May* 1845 ; m. 25 *Ap.* 1815, *Benjamin Keene*, d. 1842.   [Nos. 25963 to 25965.

284. Descendants of MARY FANE (see Table XXV), *d.* 1835 ; *m.* 27 Nov. 1765, Sir THOMAS STAPLETON, 5th Bart. [E.], *b.* 24 Feb. 1727 ; *d.* 1781 ; and had issue.

See pp. 347–350, Nos. 25205–25364.   [Nos. 25966 to 26124.

285. Descendants, if any, of MARY FANE (see Table XXV.), *m.* 1st, JOHN HENLEY of Bristol ; 2ndly, the Rev. SAMUEL CRESWICK, D.D., Dean of Wells.

286. Descendants, if any surviving, of the Rev. EDWARD FANE, Prebendary of Lincoln (see Table XXV.), *d.* 1736 ; and had issue (at least) 1*a*.

1a. *Rev. Edward Fane, Rector of Fulbeck, co. Lincoln*, d. *Mar.* 1760.

287. Descendants of PETER (DE SALIS), 3rd COUNT OF SALIS (GRAF VON SALIS) [H.R.E.], President of the Grisons, J.P., D.L., Capt. Coldstream Guards (see Table XXV.), *d.* 20 Nov. 1807 ; *m.* ANNE, da. of [——] DE SALIS ; and had issue 1*a*.

1a. *Jerome (de Salis, afterwards (R.L. Dec. 1835) Fane de Salis), 4th Count of Salis (Graf von Salis)* [H.R.E.], *J.P., D.L.,* d. 2 Oct. 1836 ; m. 1st, *June* 1797, *Sophia, da. and h. of Admiral Francis William Drake of Buckland Abbey, co. Devon*, d. 1803 ; 2ndly, *Penelope, da. of R. Freeman of Uxbridge, M.D.,* d. 1807 ; 3rdly, *Henrietta, da. of the Right Rev. William Foster, D.D., Lord Bishop of Kilmore*, d. 27 Oct. 1856 ; and had issue 1b to 8b.

1b. *Peter John (Fane de Salis), 5th Count of Salis (Graf von Salis)* [H.R.E.], *Knight of Malta, Knight of the Red Eagle of Prussia, J.P., D.L., Lieut.-Col. in the Swiss Service,* b. 26 *Feb.* 1799 ; d. 24 *Dec.* 1870 ; m. 2ndly, 19 *July* 1824, *Cecilia Henrietta Margaret, da. of David Bourgioes of Neuchâtel,* d. ; and had issue 1c to 5c.

1c. *John Francis William (Fane de Salis), 6th Count of Salis (Graf von Salis)* [H.R.E.], b. 25 *Aug.* 1825 ; d.v.p. 7 *Aug.* 1871 ; m. 11 *Feb.* 1862, *Amelia Frances Harriet, da. of Christopher Tower of Huntsmore Park, co. Bucks,* d. 8 *Jan.* 1885 ; and had issue 1d to 3d.

1d. John Francis Charles (Fane de Salis), 7th Count of Salis (Graf von Salis) [H.R.E.], *J.P., D.L.,* 1st Sec. in Diplo. Ser. (*Loughgur, co. Limerick ; Château des Bondo, Canton of the Grisons, Switzerland*), b. 19 July 1864 ; *m.* (at Brussels) 6 Dec. 1890, the Countess Helen Marie, da. of Prince Eugene de Caraman-Chimay, b. (at Menars) 18 Aug. 1864 ; *d.* 1902 ; and has issue 1e to 3e.

1e. Count John Eugene Fane de Salis, b. 4 Oct. 1891.

2e. Count Anthony Rudolph Fane de Salis, b. 1897.

3e. Count Peter Francis Fane de Salis, b. 1902.

2d. Count Henry Rudolph de Salis, J.P., C.C., A.M.I.C.E., &c. (*Ivy Lodge, Iver Heath, co. Bucks*), b. 30 June 1866 ; *m.* 9 May 1893, Alice Mary, da. of Capt. Robert Lambert, 43rd L.I.   [Nos. 26125 to 26129.

# of The Blood Royal

3d. Countess Catharine Sophia de Salis, m. 24 July 1895, Thomas George Hare ; and has issue 1e to 2e.

1e. Adelaide Mary Hare, b. 1896.

2e. Frances Letitia Hare, b. 1904.

2c. Count Peter de Salis, late Austrian Army (La Plota, Neufchâtel), b. 22 Nov. 1827 ; m. 19 Nov. 1874, Agnes Louisa, da. of Charles Joseph La Trobe, C.B., 1st Governor of Victoria ; and has issue 1d.

1d. Countess Elizabeth de Salis, m. 1901, Baron Godfrey de Blonay.

3c. Count George Aloys de Salis, Capt. Austrian Army, b. 1 Dec. 1829 ; d. (? unm.) 22 Oct. 1866.

4c. Count Robert John Drake de Salis (Coire, Grisons), b. 13 Feb. 1837 ; m. 1870, Elsie, da. of J. B. de Tscharner ; and has issue (4 sons and 1 da.).

5c. Countess Anna Sophia Elizabeth de Salis, d. (−) ; m. Baron Gaudence de Salis, Senior Member of the Swiss Federal Council.

2b. Count Rudolph Leslie de Salis, C.B., Lieut.-Gen. and Col. 8th Hussars, b. May 1811 ; d. 13 Mar. 1880 ; m. 8 Nov. 1875, Augusta, widow of Gen. Derville, Indian Army, da. of [——].

3b. Count William de Salis of Dawley Court, co. Midx. and Teffont Manor, co. Wilts, J.P., b. 27 Oct. 1812 ; d. 3 Aug. 1896 ; m. 7 Mar. 1859, Emily Harriette, da. of J. T. Mayne of Teffont Manor.

4b. Hon. Count Leopold Fabius de Salis, a Member of the Upper House of New South Wales, b. 26 Ap. 1816 ; d. 20 Nov. 1898 ; m. 1844, Charlotte, da. of Capt. George Macdonald of Monar, 68th Regt., d. Feb. 1878 ; and had issue 1c to 4c.

1c. Count Leopold William Jerome Fane de Salis, late M.L.A. of New South Wales (Fleurs, St. Mary's, New South Wales), b. June 1845 ; m. 1895, Jeannette Caroline, da. of William Armstrong of Toowoomba, Queensland, M.A. ; and has issue 1d to 3d.

1d. Count Leopold William Jerome de Salis, b. 1896.

2d. Count John Peter Fabius de Salis, b. 1897.

3d. Countess Jeannette Nina Alexandra de Salis, b. 1901.

2c. Count George de Salis, formerly M.L.A. of New South Wales (Soglio-Micalago, Tharwa, New South Wales), b. Nov. 1852 ; m. Feb. 1878, Mary St. Lawrence Irving, da. of the Rev. Canon Pierce Galliard Smith of Canberre, New South Wales ; and has issue 1d to 7d.

1d. Count Rudolph Leopold Pierce de Salis, b. Aug. 1886.

2d. Count George William Irving de Salis, b. Feb. 1889.

3d. Count Charles Eric Fabius de Salis, b. May 1891.

4d. Countess Charlotte de Salis, b. 1880.

5d. Countess Mary de Salis, b. 1881.

6d. Countess Nina Emily Violet de Salis, b. 1883.

7d. Countess Emily Henrietta Georgina de Salis, b. 1885.

3c. Count Henry Gulbert Macdonald de Salis (Riversview, Umeralla, Cooma, New South Wales), b. Oct. 1858 ; m. Nov. 1884, Charlotte Maud, da. of Graham Macdonald of Balanagowan, Queensland ; and has issue 1d to 5d.

1d. Count Leopold Graham de Salis, b. Sept. 1885.

2d. Count Gulbert Leslie de Salis, b. 1887.

3d. Count Arthur Rodolph Neville de Salis, b. Nov. 1894.

4d. Count Edward George Farrar de Salis, b. 1899.

5d. Countess Charlotte Nina Vera de Salis, b. 1896.

4c. Countess Nina Henrietta de Salis, m. Sept. 1882, William Farrer, B.A. (Camb.) (Lambrigg, New South Wales).   [Nos. 26130 to 26154.

The Plantagenet Roll

5*b.* Count John Henry de Salis, b. 10 Dec. 1818; d. 11 *Feb.* 1894; m. 1848, *Julia Stanley Palmer, da. of John Shum, H.E.I.C.S.,* d. 8 *Sept.* 1890; *and had issue* 1*c* to 2*c.*

1*c.* Countess Georgina Henrietta de Salis, *m.* 28 Aug. 1867, Lieut.-Col. John Arthur Thomas Garratt, Grenadier Guards (*Bishops' Court, Exeter*); and has issue 1*d* to 4*d.*

1*d.* Lawrence Challoner Garratt, *late* Capt. and Brevet-Major Coldstream Guards (*Guards'*), *b.* 4 Oct. 1868; *m.* Jan. 1903, Violet Annie, da. of the Rev. Fitzwilliam Taylor of Ogwell, co. Devon; and has issue 1*e.*

1*e.* Rodulph John Garratt, *b.* May 1905.

2*d.* John Rodolph Francis Garratt (*New*), *b.* 16 July 1870; *m.* Nov. 1900, Grace Aylmer, da. of J. H. Ley of Trehill; and has issue 1*e.*

1*e.* Elizabeth Grace Garratt, *b.* Ap. 1902.

3*d.* Kathleen Henrietta Garratt.

4*d.* Sybil Edith Garratt, *m.* 1893, Mackworth Praed Parker; and has issue 1*e* to 2*e.*

1*e.* Gerard Parker, *b.* 1896.

2*e.* Sybil Muriel Parker.

2*c.* Countess Eva Letitia Mary de Salis (*Greenhalgh, Palace Road, Bangalore, India*).

6*b.* Rev. (Count) [1] Henry Jerome Augustine Fane de Salis, J.P. (*Portnall Park, Virginia Water*), *b.* 16 Feb. 1828; *m.* 29 Mar. 1853, Grace Elizabeth, da. of the Right Hon. Joseph Warner Henley of Waterperry, co. Oxon., D.C.L., *d.* 28 Aug. 1898; and has issue 1*c* to 5*c.*

See p. 359, Nos. 25941–25962.

7*b.* Countess *Sophia Juliana de Salis,* d. 5 *July* 1886; m. 27 *Oct.* 1831, *William Filgate of Lissrenny, J.P., High Sheriff co. Louth* 1832, b. 21 *July* 1781; d. 22 *Nov.* 1875; *and had issue* 1*c* to 7*c.*

1*c.* William de Salis Filgate, J.P., D.L., High Sheriff co. Louth 1879, *late* Capt. Louth Rifles (*Lissrenny, near Ardee, co. Louth*), *b.* 2 Dec. 1834; *m.* 4 Oct. 1870, Georgina Harriet, da. of William John French of Ardsallagh, co. Meath; and has issue 1*d* to 2*d.*

1*d.* Violet Evelyn Sophia Filgate.

2*d.* Eileen Georgina Filgate, *m.* 4 Aug. 1902, Richard Alexander Bailie Henry (*Rathnestin, Ardee*).

2*c.* Alexander Jerome Filgate, Col. *late* R.E. (106 *Jermyn Street, S.W.; St. James'; United Service*), b. 29 Aug. 1837.

3*c.* Rodolph *Townley Richard Filgate, H.M.'s Court of Probate, Ireland,* b. 18 Dec. 1839; d. 13 Dec. 1904.

4*c.* Leopold George Plantagenet Filgate, J.P. (*Ballycastle, co. Antrim*), *b.* 20 Aug. 1843.

5*c.* Townley Fane Filgate, Secretary Louth County Council (*Lissrenny, Ardee*), *b.* 26 Jan. 1846.

6*c.* Charles Roden Filgate, Bar.-at-Law, *b.* 16 Oct. 1849; *m.* Clare, da. of William Cooper of Coventry.

7*c.* Anne Harriet Penelope Eleanor Filgate, *m.* Sept. 1857, Thomas William Filgate of Tullykeel, co. Louth, J.P., *d.* 20 Feb. 1868.

8*b.* Countess *Catharina Barbara de Salis,* d. 20 *Feb.* 1869; m. 21 *June* 1832, *George* (*Leicester, afterwards* (*R.L.* 8 *Feb.* 1832) *Warren*), *2nd Baron De Tabley* [*U.K.*], b. 8 *Oct.* 1811; d. 19 *Oct.* 1887; *and had issue* 1*c* to 4*c.*

1*c.* John Byrne (*Leicester Warren*), *3rd Baron De Tabley* [*U.K.*], *7th Bart.* [*E.*], b. 26 *Ap.* 1835; d. *unm.* 22 Nov. 1895.　　　　　　[Nos. 26155 to 26195.

---

[1] Title not used.

# of The Blood Royal

2c. Hon. *Meriel Leicester Warren,* b. 25 Nov. 1839; d. 6 *July* 1872 ; m. *as 1st wife,* 31 *Jan.* 1862, *Allen Alexander (Bathhurst),* 6*th Earl Bathurst* [*G.B.*], d. 1 *Aug.* 1892 ; *and had issue.*
See the Clarence Volume, p. 637, Nos. 28837–28849.

3c. Hon. Eleanor Leicester Warren, *afterwards* (24 May 1900) Leighton-Warren *(Tabley House, Knutsford),* m. 30 Jan. 1864, Sir Baldwin Leighton, 8th Bart. [E.], d. 22 Jan. 1897 ; and has issue.
See p. 235, Nos. 8257–8265.

4c. Hon. Margaret Leicester Warren, m. 24 Aug. 1875, Sir Emile Algernon Arthur Keppel Cowell-Stepney, M.A., Bart. [U.K.] *(The Dell, Llanelly, co. Carmarthen ; Woodend, Ascot)* ; and has issue 1*d.*

1*d.* Katherine Meriel Cowell-Stepney, b. 12 Sept. 1876.   [Nos. 26196 to 26220.

288. Descendants of John (Montagu), 5th Earl of Sandwich [E.] (see Table XXV.), b. 26 Jan. 1743 ; d. 6 June 1814 ; m. 2ndly, 25 Ap. 1772, Lady Mary, da. of Henry (Paulet), 6th Duke of Bolton, b. Oct. 1753 ; d. 31 Mar. 1779 ; and had issue 1a to 2a.

1a. George John *(Montagu),* 6*th Earl of Sandwich* [*E.*], b. 5 *Mar.* 1773 ; d. 21 *May* 1818 ; m. 9 *July* 1804, *Lady Louisa Mary Anne Julia Harriet, da. of Armar (Lowry-Corry),* 1*st Earl of Belmore* [*I.*], b. 3 *Ap.* 1781 ; d. 19 *Ap.* 1862 ; *and had issue* 1*b to* 2*b.*

1*b.* John William *(Montagu),* 7*th Earl of Sandwich* [*E.*], b. 8 Nov. 1811 ; d. 3 *Mar.* 1884 ; m. 1*st,* 6 *Sept.* 1838, *Lady Mary, da. of Henry William (Paget),* 1*st Marquis of Anglesey* [*G.B.*], K.G., b. 16 *June* 1812 ; d. 20 *Feb.* 1859 ; *and had issue* 1*c to* 4*c.*

1*c.* Edward George Henry (Montagu), 8th Earl of Sandwich [E.] *(Hinchingbrooke, Huntingdon ; Hooke Court, Beminster, Dorset ;* 18 *Buckingham Gate, S.W.),* b. 13 July 1839.

2c. Hon. Victor Alexander Montagu, Rear-Adm. R.N., K.M. (43 *Rutland Place, S.W.),* b. 20 Ap. 1841 ; m. 28 Nov. 1867, Lady Agneta Harriet, da. of Charles Philip (Yorke), 4th Earl of Hardwicke, a Lady of the Bedchamber to H.R.H. Princess Christian ; and has issue.
See the Clarence Volume, p. 99, Nos. 8340–8343.

3c. Lady Emily Caroline Montagu, m. 30 May 1870, the Right Hon. Sir William Hart-Dyke, 7th Bart. [E.], P.C., M.P., J.P., D.L., Chairman L. C. & D. R. Co., *formerly* (1887–1892) Vice-Pres. of Council on Education *(Lullingstone Castle, Eynsford, Kent ; Horsham, Sussex)* ; and has issue 1*d* to 5*d.*

1*d.* Percival Hart-Dyke, J.P., Bar. Lincoln's Inn (3 *Berkeley Gardens, Kensington, W.),* b. 27 Oct. 1871.

2d. Oliver Hamilton Hart-Dyke, b. 4 Sept. 1885.

3d. Lina Mary Dyke, b. 24 Feb. 1873 ; m. 10 Feb. 1902, Alexander John Scott Scott-Gatty (son of Sir Alfred Scott-Gatty, H.M.'s Garter King of Arms) (18 *Buckingham Gate, S.W.)* ; and has issue 1*e.*

1*e.* Edward Comyn Scott-Gatty, b. 8 Jan. 1903.

4d. Hon. Mary Dyke, a Maid of Honour to H.M. the Queen, b. 19 Mar. 1875 ; m. 11 July 1905, Capt. Matthew Gerald Edward Bell, 3rd Batt. Rifle Brigade.

5d. Sydney Eleanor Margaret Dyke, b. 7 July 1881.

4c. Lady Anne Florence Adelaide Montagu, m. 5 Dec. 1876, Capt. Alfred Charles Duncombe, *late* 1st Life Guards *(Calwich Abbey, Osbourne, Derbyshire).*

2b. Lady Catherine Caroline Montagu, b. 7 Oct. 1808 ; d. 30 *Ap.* 1834 ; m. 1 Dec. 1831, *Count Alexander Adrian Florian Joseph Colonna Walewski, of Poland,* b. 4 *May* 1810 ; d. 26 *Sept.* 1868 ; *and had issue* (2 *children, who* d. *in infancy).*
[Nos. 26221 to 26234.

The Plantagenet Roll

2a. Lady Mary Montagu, b. 27 Feb. 1774; d. 4 Oct. 1824; m. 7 Oct. 1796, John Henry (Upton), 1st Viscount Templetown [I.], b. 8 Nov. 1771; d. 21 Sept. 1846; and had issue 1b to 4b.

  1b. Henry Montagu (Upton), 2nd Viscount Templetown [I.], b. 11 Nov. 1790; d. unm. 28 Mar. 1863.

  2b. George Frederick (Upton), 3rd Viscount Templetown [I.], G.C.B., b. 5 Aug. 1802; d.s.p. 4 Jan. 1890.

  3b. Hon. Edward John Upton, b. 18 Sept. 1816; d. 14 Mar. 1855; m. 14 Oct. 1843, Susan Moore, widow of William Wrighte Hewett, da. of the Rev. John Maddy, D.D., Preb. of Ely, d. (at Coblentz) July 1866; and had issue 1c.

    1c. Henry Edward Montagu Dorington Clotworthy (Upton), 4th Viscount Templetown [I.], a Rep. Peer (Castle Upton, Templepatrick, co. Antrim), b. 20 Ap. 1853; m. 28 Feb. 1883, Lady Evelyn Georgiana, da. of George William (Finch-Hatton), 10th Earl of Wilchilsea and Nottingham [E.]; and has issue 1d to 3d.

      1d. Hon. Eric Edward Montagu John Upton, b. 8 Mar. 1885.

      2d. Hon. Henry Augustus George Mountjoy Heneage Upton, b. 12 Aug. 1894.

      3d. Hon. Margaret Evelyn Upton, b. 5 Jan. 1884.

  4b. Hon. Mary Wilhelmina Upton, b. 19 June 1801; d. 20 Mar. 1876; m. 18 Aug. 1831, John Eden Spalding of the Holm (stepson of Lord Brougham), d. 29 Mar. 1869; and had issue 1c to 2c.

    1c. Augustus Frederick Montagu Spalding, J.P., D.L. (The Holme, New Galloway, Kirkcudbright; 11 Ashley Place, S.W.), b. 23 Oct. 1838.

    2c. Helen Mary Spalding (The Grove, Hillingdon, Uxbridge), m. as 2nd wife, 11 Ap. 1874, Rev. the Hon. John Grey, D.D., Canon of Durham, b. 6 Mar. 1812; d. 11 Nov. 1895.   [Nos. 26235 to 26240.

289. Descendants, if any, of EDWARD FANE, b. 1642; d. 1679; m. JANE, da. of James STANIER of London, Merchant; MARY FANE, wife of [——] MARSHALL of Fisherton, co. Lincoln; RACHEL FANE; ELIZABETH FANE, d. 2 May 1678, wife of THOMAS WODHULL of Mollington, co. Oxon.; CATHERINE FANE; GRACE FANE, wife of WILLIAM GROVE, co. Salop; and of JANE FANE (see Table XXV.).

290. Descendants of EDWARD (STANLEY), 13th EARL OF DERBY [E.], 1st BARON STANLEY of Bickerstaffe [U.K.], K.G. (see Table XXVI.), b. 21 Ap. 1775; d. 30 June 1851; m. 30 June 1798, CHARLOTTE MARGARET, da. of the Rev. Geoffrey HORNBY, b. 20 Oct. 1778; d. 16 June 1817; and had issue 1a to 5a.

1a. Edward Geoffrey (Stanley), 14th Earl of Derby [E.], b. 29 Mar. 1799; d. 23 Oct. 1869; m. 31 May 1825, the Hon. Emma Caroline, da. of Edward (Bootle-Wilbraham), 1st Baron Skelmersdale [U.K.], b. 17 Mar. 1805; d. 26 Ap. 1876; and had issue.

See the Tudor Roll of "The Blood Royal of Britain," pp. 491–492, Nos. 33734-33760.

2a. Hon. Henry Thomas Stanley, M.P., b. 9 Mar. 1803; d. 2 Ap. 1875; m. 1 Sept. 1835, Anne, da. of Richard Woolhouse.

See the Tudor Roll of "The Blood Royal of Britain," p. 492, Nos. 33761-33764.

3a. Hon. Charles James Fox Stanley, Col. in the Army, Col. Lancashire Militia,   [Nos. 26241 to 26271.

# of The Blood Royal

b. 25 *Ap.* 1808; d. 13 *Oct.* 1884; m. 10 *Dec.* 1836, *Frances Augusta, da. of Sir Henry F. Campbell, K.C.B.,* d. 29 *May* 1878; *and had issue.*

See the Tudor Roll of "The Blood Royal of Britain," p. 493, Nos. 33765–33776.

4*a. Lady Charlotte Elizabeth Stanley,* b. 11 *July* 1801; d. 15 *Feb.* 1853; m. 16 *Dec.* 1823, *Edward Penrhyn,* formerly *Leycester of East Sheen, J.P., D.L.,* b. 16 *Sept.* 1794; d. 6 *Mar.* 1861; *and had issue* 1*b* to 4*b.*

1*b.* Edward Hugh Leycester Penrhyn, J.P., D.L., Major 1st Royal Surrey Militia (*The Cedars, East Sheen, co. Surrey, &c.*), b. 7 June 1827; m. 21 Ap. 1853, Vere, da. of Robert Gosling of Botley's Park, near Chertsey, d. 16 Feb. 1900; and has issue.

See the Tudor Roll of "The Blood Royal of Britain," p. 493, Nos. 33778–33786; also the Clarence Volume.

2*b.* Rev. Oswald Henry Leycester Penrhyn, Vicar of Winwick, and Hon. Canon of Liverpool (*Winwick Vicarage, co. Lancaster*), b. 6 May 1828; m. 24 Ap. 1862, Charlotte Louisa Jane, da. of Edmund George Hornby of Dalton Hall, M.P.; and has issue 1*c* to 4*c.*

1*c.* Charles Windham Leycester Penrhyn, b. 5 Nov. 1873.

2*c.* Ethel Frances Penrhyn, b. 30 June 1864.

3*c.* Mary Charlotte Penrhyn, b. 12 Jan. 1868.

4*c.* Elizabeth Gertrude Leycester Penrhyn, b. 17 July 1869.

3*b.* Mary Charlotte Leycester Penrhyn (*Chiefden, Eltham, co. Kent*), b. 22 Nov. 1824; m. 1 Oct. 1850, Morgan Yeatman of Shawfield, Bromley, b. 7 Nov. 1824; d. 19 Aug. 1889; and has issue 1*c* to 7*c.*

1*c.* Morgan Edward Yeatman, b. 8 Aug. 1851; m. Blanche, da. of Jones Fullerton; and has issue 1*d* to 3*d.*

1*d.* Morgan John Yeatman, b. 1895.

2*d.* Edward Stanley Yeatman, b. 1905.

3*d.* Ellinor Mary Yeatman, b. 1890.

2*c.* Harry Oswald Yeatman, b. 1856; m. Benedicta, da. of [——] Page; and has issue 1*d* to 4*d.*

1*d.* Harry Morgan Yeatman, b. 1895.

2*d.* Robert Julian Yeatman, b. 1897.

3*d.* Edith Benedicta Mary Yeatman, b. 1898.

4*d.* Frances Alice Yeatman, b. 1900.

3*c.* Rev. Arthur William Yeatman, b. 1862.

4*c.* Frank Pym Stanley Yeatman, b. 1869.

5*c.* Ellinor Mary Yeatman, b. 1852.

6*c.* Florence Charlotte Yeatman, b. 1855; m. Charles E. Squire; and has issue 1*d* to 4*d.*

1*d.* Edward Arnold Squire, b. 1892.

2*d.* Stanley Charles Squire, b. 1893.

3*d.* Giles Frederick Squire, b. 1894.

4*d.* Cicely Beatrice Squire, b. 1896.

7*c.* Edith Vere Yeatman, b. 1864.

4*b.* Emma Catherine Leycester Penrhyn (23 *Friars Stile Road, Richmond, Surrey*).

5*a. Lady Ellinor Mary Stanley,* b. 3 *May* 1807; d. 11 *Sept.* 1887; m. 11 *June* 1835, *the Rev. Frank George Hopwood, Rector of Winwick, Canon of Chester,* b. 2 *Aug.* 1810; d. 11 *Mar.* 1890; *and had issue* 1*b* to 5*b.*

1*b.* Rev. Frank Edward Hopwood, b. 19 Oct. 1843; d. Oct. 1893; m. Helen F., da. of [——] Colvin; and has issue 1*c* to 7*c.*

1*c. Frank Colvin Hopwood,* b. 22 *Mar.* 1874; d. (–).

2*c.* Geoffrey Hopwood, b. May 1877.

3*c.* Hervey Hopwood, b. 23 Oct. 1884.

365   [Nos. 26272 to 26322.

3 A

4c. Ellinor Muriel Hopwood, b. 17 Feb. 1876.

5c. Mary Helen Hopwood, b. 7 Ap. 1879.

6c. Edith Vere Hopwood, b. May 1881.

7c. Evelyn Hopwood, b. 19 Oct. 1882.

2b. Arthur Robert Hopwood, Major in the Army, *late* Rifle Brigade, b. 18 Mar. 1845; *m.* 2 June 1887, Amy Gertrude, da. of Major Edward Hugh Leycester Penrhyn of East Sheen, J.P., D.L.; and has issue 1c.

1c. See p. 365, No. 26292. (Robert Hervey Hopwood, b. 29 Aug. 1890.)

3b. Charles Augustus Hopwood, C.B., *late* of the Foreign Office (18 *Beaufort Gardens, S.W.*), b. 27 Dec. 1847; *m.* 30 Oct. 1888, Georgie Florence Louisa, da. of George Lear Curtis.

4b. Susan Hopwood, b. 9 Aug. 1838; *unm.*

5b. Cecilia Catherine Hopwood, b. 12 Dec. 1839; *m.* 4 May 1871, the Very Rev. John Lionel Darby, Dean of Chester (*The Deanery, Chester*); and has issue 1c to 5c.

1c. Lionel Frank Christopher Darby, b. 30 Ap. 1873.

2c. Arthur John Lovett Darby, b. 9 Jan. 1876.

3c. Edward Henry d'Esterre Darby, b. 7 Mar. 1880.

4c. Mary Cecilia Darby, b. 15 Mar. 1872.

5c. Constance Ellinor Katharine Darby, b. 22 May 1882.

[Nos. 26323 to 26336.

291. Descendants of Lady CHARLOTTE STANLEY (see Table XXVI.), b. 17 Oct. 1776; d. 25 Nov. 1805; m. 22 Aug. 1796, EDMUND HORNBY of Dalton Hall, co. Westmoreland, M.P., b. 16 June 1773; d. 18 Nov. 1857; and had issue 1a.

1a. *Edmund George Hornby of Dalton Hall, M.P.*, b. 6 *Nov.* 1799; d. 27 *Feb.* 1865; m. 30 *Jan.* 1827, Sarah, *da. and co.-h. of Thomas Yates of Irwell House, co. Lancaster*, b. 21 *May* 1804; d. 17 *Aug.* 1886; *and had issue* 1b *to* 6b.

1b. Edmund Geoffrey Stanley Hornby, J.P., D.L., Major 3rd Batt. Royal Lancaster Regt. (*Dalton Hall, near Burton, co. Westmoreland*), b. 2 Jan. 1839, *unm.*

2b. Lucy Francesca Hornby, b. 12 Oct. 1829; *m.* 29 July 1851, Sir Charles Samuel Bagot, J.P., Hon. Commr. in Lunacy (*The Gables, East Sheen*), s.p.

3b. Ellinor Georgiana Katharine Hornby, b. 13 Ap. 1834; *m.* 18 Aug. 1857, the Rev. Henry Arbuthnot Feilden, Vicar of Kirkby Stephen (*Kirkby Stephen Vicarage, Westmoreland*); and has issue 1c to 2c.

1c. Helen Arbuthnot Feilden, b. 17 Mar. 1859; *m.* 28 Aug. 1890, Col. Henry Paul Mason, J.P., D.L. (*Eden Place, Kirkby Stephen*); and has issue 1d to 2d.

1d. Randle Paul Feilden Mason, b. 19 Nov. 1893.

2d. Marcia Helen Arbuthnot Mason, b. 23 July 1891.

2c. Katharine Maud Feilden, b. 3 Mar. 1861.

4b. Charlotte Louisa Jane Hornby, b. 12 Jan. 1836; *m.* 24 Ap. 1862, the Rev. Canon Oswald Henry Leycester Penrhyn, Rector of Winwick (*Winwick Rectory, Newton-le-Willows, Lancaster*); and has issue 1c to 4c.

1c–4c. See p. 365, Nos. 26296–26299.

5b. Victoria Susan Hornby, b. 23 July 1837; *m.* 22 Jan. 1861, the Rev. Canon Charles James Satterthwaite, Vicar of Disley (*Disley Vicarage, co. Chester*); and has issue 1c to 3c.

1c. Rev. Edmund James Satterthwaite, Vicar of Broadchalk (*Broadchalk Vicarage, Salisbury*), b. 1 Mar. 1866; *m.* 25 Jan. 1899, Adelaide Wynne, da. of Philip Pennant Pennant.

2c. Charles Geoffrey Satterthwaite, b. 15 Ap. 1873.   [Nos. 26337 to 26351.

# of The Blood Royal

3c. Gertrude Mary Charlotte Satterthwaite, *b.* 26 Oct. 1861; *m.* 5 Mar. 1889, John Sheridan Satterthwaite (*The Grange, Kenley, Surrey*); and has issue 1*d* to 4*d*.

   1*d.* Francis Edmund Sheridan Satterthwaite, *b.* 24 Sept. 1892.

   2*d.* Maud Gertrude Satterthwaite, *b.* 4 May 1891.

   3*d.* Evelyn Letitia Satterthwaite, *b.* 19 Nov. 1894.

   4*d.* Beatrice Mary Satterthwaite, *b.* 23 Mar. 1899.

  6*b.* Gertrude Mary Augusta Hornby, *b.* 15 July 1842.   [Nos. 26352 to 26357.

292. Descendants of Lady ELIZABETH HENRIETTA STANLEY (see Table XL.), *d.* Nov. 1837; *m.* 15 Jan. 1795, STEPHEN THOMAS COLE of Twickenham, co. Midx., and Stoke Lyne, co. Oxon., *b.* 26 Ap. 1765; *d.* 6 Sept. 1835; and had issue.

See the Tudor Roll of "The Blood Royal of Britain," pp. 495–497, Nos. 33851–33915.   [Nos. 26358 to 26422.

293. Descendants of ARCHIBALD (HAMILTON), 9th DUKE OF HAMILTON [S.], 6th DUKE OF BRANDON [E.], Premier Peer of Scotland (see Table XXVI.), *b.* 15 July 1740; *d.* 16 Feb. 1819; *m.* 25 May 1765, Lady HARRIET, da. of Alexander (STEWART), 6th Earl of Galloway [S.], *d.* 3 Dec. 1788; and had issue.

See the Tudor Roll of "The Blood Royal of Britain" (Table CXXIII.), and pp. 531–532, Nos. 35337–35441.   [Nos. 26423 to 26527.

294. Descendants of GEORGE AUGUSTUS (CHICHESTER, 2nd MARQUIS OF DONEGALL [I.] and BARON FISHERWICK [G.B.], K.P. (see Table XL.), *b.* 13 Aug. 1769; *d.* 5 Oct. 1844; *m.* 8 Aug. 1795, ANNA, da. of [——] MAY, *d.* 6 Feb. 1849; and had issue 1*a* to 5*a*.

  1*a. George Hamilton (Chichester), 3rd Marquis of Donegall [I.] and Baron Fisherwick [G.B.], 1st Baron Ennishowen and Carrickfergus [U.K.], K.P., G.C.H., b. 10 Feb. 1797; d. 20 Oct. 1883; m. 1st, 8 Dec. 1822, Lady Harriet Anne, da. of Richard (Butler), 1st Earl of Glengall [I.], b. 1 Jan. 1799; d. 14 Sept. 1860; and had issue 1b.*

   1*b. Lady Harriet Augusta Anna Seymourina Chichester, b. 30 Oct. 1836; d. 4 Ap. 1898; m. 22 Aug. 1857, Anthony (Ashley-Cooper), 8th Earl of Shaftesbury [E.], d. 13 Ap. 1886; and had issue.*

See the Tudor Roll of "The Blood Royal of Britain," pp. 428–429, Nos. 31029–31043.

  2*a. Edward (Chichester), 4th Marquis of Donegall [I.] and Baron Fisherwick [G.B.], b. 11 Jan. 1799; d. 20 Jan. 1889; m. 21 Sept. 1821, Amelia Spread Deane, da. of Henry Deane Grady of Lodge, co. Limerick, and Stillorgan Castle, co. Dublin, d. Mar. 1891; and had issue 1b to 4b.*

   1*b. George Augustus Hamilton (Chichester), 5th Marquis of Donegall [I.] and Baron Fisherwick [G.B.], Hereditary Lord High Admiral of Lough Neagh, b. 27 June 1822; d. 13 May 1904; m. 3rdly, 23 Dec. 1902, Violet Gertrude (Isle Magee, co. Antrim), da. of Henry St. George Twining of Halifax, Nova Scotia; and had issue 1c.*

    1*c.* Edward Arthur Donald St. George Hamilton (Chichester), 6th Marquis of Donegall [I.], and Baron Fisherwick [G.B.], Hereditary Lord High Admiral of Lough Neagh (*Isle Magee, co. Antrim*), *b.* 7 Oct. 1903.   [Nos. 26528 to 26543.

The Plantagenet Roll

2b. Lord Henry FitzWarrine Chichester, *late* Capt. Roy. Antrim Rifles (*Raleigh ; Hurlingham ; Sandown, &c.*), *b.* 11 Sept. 1834 ; *m.* 14 July 1860, Elizabeth Julia, da. and h. of Samuel Amy Severne of Poslingford, co. Suffolk, *d.* 15 June 1902 ; and has issue 1*c* to 6*c*.

1*c.* Severne Edward Spencer FitzWarrine Chichester, *b.* 16 Ap. 1861.

2*c.* FitzWarrine George Henry Washington Chichester, *b.* 15 Jan. 1863.

3*c.* Caroline Lizzie Henrietta Chichester.

4*c.* Louisa Jean Amelia Chichester, *m.* 22 June 1896, Samuel Pearson Yates, *late* Lieut. 11th Hussars.

5*c.* Lizzie Frances Augusta Chichester, *m.* 16 Dec. 1895, George Stanley Carey, Royal Irish Rifles, *d.* 4 Ap. 1896.

6*c.* Marie Jeannette Amelia Chichester, *m.* 21 Sept. 1897, William Henry Cleland (34 *Brunswick Square, Hove, Brighton*).

3b. Lord Adolphus John Spencer Churchill Chichester, b. 18 *Dec.* 1836 ; *d.* 5 *Mar.* 1901 ; *m.* 9 *Oct.* 1872, *Mary, da. and h. of Col. Robert Peel Dawson of Moyola Park, Castledawson, M.P. ; and had issue* 1*c to* 2*c.*

1*c.* Robert Peel Dawson Spencer Chichester, J.P., D.L., Capt. Reserve of Officers and Lieut.-Col. Comdg. 6th Batt. Midx. Regt., *late* Irish Guards (*Moyola Park, Castledawson, Londonderry ; Guards ; White's, &c.*), *b.* 13 Aug. 1873 ; *m.* 11 Dec. 1901, Debra Kerr, da. and h. of James Kerr Fisher of The Manor House, Kilrea, and Chicago, U.S.A. ; and has issue 1*d* to 2*d*.

1*d.* Robert James Spencer Chichester, *b.* 29 Sept. 1902.

2*d.* Marion Caroline Debra Chichester, *b.* 10 May 1904.

2*c.* Edward Brownlow Dawson Chichester, Capt. 4th Batt. Roy. Irish Rifles, *b.* 20 Mar. 1876.

4b. Lady Augusta Annabella Chichester, *m.* 1st, 23 Feb. 1844, Washington Sewallis (Shirley), 9th Earl Ferrers [G.B.], *b.* 3 Jan. 1822 ; *d.* 13 Mar. 1859 ; 2ndly, 15 June 1864, Capt. Frederick Henry Walsh, *late* 78th Highlanders (51 *Clarence Parade, Southsea*) ; and has issue 1*c* to 3*c*.

1*c.* Sewallis Edward (Shirley), 10th Earl Ferrers [G.B.], &c., (*Staunton Harold, Ashby-de-la-Zouch*), *b.* 24 Jan. 1847 ; *m.* 24 Oct. 1885, Lady Ina Maude, da. of William Henry Hare (Hedges White), 3rd Earl of Bantry [I.].

2*c.* Lady Augusta Amelia Shirley, *m.* 19 Aug. 1873, Sir Archdale Robert Palmer, 4th Bart. [G.B.] (*Wanlip Hall, Leicester*).

3*c.* Clara Augusta Walsh.

3a. Lord Hamilton Francis Chichester, b. 9 *Mar.* 1810 ; *d.* 1 *Jan.* 1854 ; *m.* 7 *Dec.* 1837, *Honoria Anastatia, da. of Col. Henry James Blake of Ardfry, co. Galway, d.* 7 *Feb.* 1878.

4a. Lord John Ludford Chichester, b. 12 *Nov.* 1811 ; *d.* 22 *Ap.* 1873 ; *m.* 27 *July* 1844, *Caroline, da. of Henry Bevan, d.* 11 *Dec.* 1883.

5a. Lord Stephen Algernon Chichester, b. 26 *Dec.* 1814 ; *d.* 14 *Jan.* 1890 ; *m.* 30 *Dec.* 1843, *Alphonsine Louise Laura, da. of* [——] *de Narboune, d.* 5 *July* 1881. [Nos. 26544 to 26558.

295. Descendants of Lord SPENCER STANLEY CHICHESTER (see Table XXVI.), *b.* 20 Ap. 1775 ; *d.* 22 Feb. 1819 ; *m.* 8 Aug. 1795, Lady HARRIET, da. of John (STEWART), 7th Earl of Galloway [S.], K.T., *d.* 30 Jan. 1850 ; and had issue.

See the Tudor Roll of "The Blood Royal of Britain," p. 511, Nos. 34505–34562. [Nos. 26559 to 26616.

# of The Blood Royal

296. Descendants of CHARLOTTE LUCY HAMILTON (see Table XXVI.), *b.* 1778 ; *d.* 2 Feb. 1833 ; *m.* 16 Mar. 1799, Gen. ROBERT ANSTRUTHER, *b.* 3 Mar. 1768 ; *d.v.p.* (at Corunna) 14 Jan. 1809 ; and had issue 1*a* to 4*a.*

1*a.* Sir Ralph Abercromby Anstruther, *4th Bart.* [*S.*], *b.* 1 *Mar.* 1804 ; *d.* 18 *Oct.* 1863 ; *m.* 2 *Sept.* 1831, Mary Jane, *da. of Major-Gen. Sir Henry Torrens, K.C.B. (who re-m.* 14 *Nov.* 1868, William Talbot Talbot Crosbie of Ardfert Abbey), *d.* 26 *Aug.* 1886 ; and had issue 1*b* to 3*b.*

1*b.* Sir Robert Anstruther, *5th Bart.* [*S.*], *M.P., b.* 28 *Aug.* 1834 ; *d.* 21 *July* 1886 ; *m.* 29 *July* 1857, Louisa Maria Chowne, *da. of the Rev. William Knox Marshall, Preb. of Hereford and Vicar of Wragby ;* and had issue 1*c* to 5*c.*

1*c.* Sir Ralph William Anstruther, 6th Bart. [S.], J.P., D.L., Lieut.-Col. Comdg. 6th Vol. Batt. Black Watch, *late* R.E. (*Balcaskie, Pittenweem, Fife ; Watten, Caithness*), *b.* 5 July 1858 ; *m.* 5 Aug. 1886, Mildred Harriet, da. of Edward Hussey of Scotney Castle ; and has issue 1*d* to 6*d.*

1*d.* Robert Edward Anstruther, *b.* 4 Ap. 1890.

2*d.* Margaret Christian Anstruther, *b.* 16 Aug. 1887.

3*d.* Magdalen Janet Anstruther, *b.* 19 Ap. 1889.

4*d.* Sarah Katharine Anstruther, *b.* 28 Sept. 1894.

5*d.* Elizabeth Mildred Louisa Anstruther, *b.* 29 Ap. 1896.

6*d.* Gertrude Mary Anstruther, *b.* 9 Mar. 1900.

2*c.* Henry Torrens Anstruther, British Director Suez Canal, *formerly* M.P. and (1895–1903) a Junior Lord of the Treasury (*Cowley House, Westminster, S.W.*), *b.* 27 Nov. 1860 ; *m.* 24 Aug. 1889, the Hon. Eva, da. of Charles Douglas (Hanbury Tracy), 4th Baron Sudeley [U.K.] ; and has issue 1*d* to 2*d.*

1*d.* Douglas Tollemache Anstruther, *b.* 15 July 1893.

2*d.* Joyce Anstruther, *b.* 6 June 1901.

3*c.* Robert Hamilton Anstruther, Comm. R.N. (*National*), *b.* 10 June 1862 ; *m.* 6 Jan. 1890, Edith Flora, da. of William Felton Peel of Hawley Hill, Blackwater ; and has issue 1*d.*

1*d.* Philip Noel Anstruther, *b.* 2 Sept. 1891.

4*c.* Arthur Wellesley Anstruther, Assist. Sec. Board of Agriculture (*Hook Heath, Woking*), *b.* 5 Mar. 1864 ; *m.* 1st, 26 Ap. 1893, the Hon. Mary Elma, da. of Thomas John Hovell-Thurlow (Cumming-Bruce), 5th Baron Thurlow [G.B.], *d.s.p.* 11 Feb.,1894 ; 2ndly, 21 Oct. 1901, Louisa Adele Rose, da. of W. H. Trapmann of Charleston, South Carolina, and 29 Roland Gardens, S.W. ; and has issue 1*d.*

1*d.* Alexander Meister Anstruther, *b.* 26 July 1902.

5*c.* Mary Evelyn Anstruther, *b.* 5 July 1859.

2*b.* Lucy Charlotte Anstruther, *d.* 14 Nov. 1903 ; *m.* 12 *Aug.* 1852, Sir Alexander Kinloch, 10th Bart. [S.], J.P., D.L. (*Gilmerton ; Haddington*) ; and had issue 1*c* to 4*c.*

1*c.* David Alexander Kinloch, C.B., M.V.O., J.P., D.L., Lieut.-Col. and Brevet-Col. *late* Comdg. 1st Batt. Grenadier Guards (20 *Eaton Place, S.W.*), *b.* 20 Feb. 1856 ; *m.* 25 Nov. 1897, Elinor Lucy, da. of Col. William Bromley-Davenport, M.P. ; and has issue 1*d* to 2*d.*

1*d.* Alexander Davenport-Kinloch, *b.* 17 Sept. 1902.

2*d.* Jean Mary Kinloch.

2*c.* Henry Anstruther Kinloch, Major King's Royal Rifle Corps, *b.* 7 Nov. 1859 ; *d.* 20 *Feb.* 1903 ; *m.* *June* 1891, Jane Agnes Maud (*Farm House, Old Windsor*), *da. of Sir Reginald Robert Bruce Guinness (who re-m.* 18 *July* 1905, Walter Traversari Legge ;* and had issue 1*d.*

1*d.* Harriet Patricia Constance Kinloch. [Nos. 26617 to 26635.]

The Plantagenet Roll

3c. Francis Kinloch, M.A. (Oxon.), LL.B. (Edin.), Barrister (71 *Great King Street, Edinburgh*), *b.* 6 Oct. 1863; *m.* 25 Mar. 1896, Marion Eva, da. of Charles Nairne Marshall of Curriehill, New Zealand; and has issue 1*d* to 3*d*.

 1d. Frederick Alexander Kinloch, *b.* 23 Nov. 1901.

 2d. Marjorie Catherine Kinloch.

 3d. Lucy Margaret Kinloch.

4c. Mary Anna Kinloch, d. Feb. 1898; m. 6 *Jan.* 1887, *Lothar Henry George de Bunsen of Berlin; and had issue* 1*d to* 2*d.*

 1d. Arnold George de Bunsen, *b.* 15 Dec. 1887.

 2d. Eric Henry de Bunsen, *b.* 24 Sept. 1889.

3b. Mary Anstruther, *m.* 20 June 1867, Charles Hugh Berners, J.P., D.L., High Sheriff co. Suffolk 1895 (*Woolverstone Park, Ipswich; 42 Lennox Gardens, S.W.*); and has issue 1*c* to 5*c*.

 1c. John Anstruther Berners, *late* 1st King's Dragoon Guards (*Kingscote Park, Wotton-under-Edge, Gloucestershire*), *b.* 23 Sept. 1869; *m.* 1 Feb. 1893, Ethel Charlotte, da. of Laurence James Baker of Ottershaw Park, Chertsey, J.P.; and has issue 1*d* to 3*d*.

  1d. Geoffrey Hugh Berners, *b.* 20 Nov. 1893.

  2d. ,Gwendoline Ethel Berners.

  3d. Olive Marjory Berners.

 2c. Ralph Abercrombie Berners, Capt. Royal Welsh Fusiliers (*Naval and Military*), *b.* 14 June 1871; *m.* 1 June 1898, Laura Gertrude, da. of Sir Robert Michael Laffan, K.C.M.G., R.E., Gov. of Bermuda.

 3c. Hamilton Hugh Berners, Irish Guards (*Guards'; Bachelors'*), *b.* 30 Sept. 1881.

 4c. Mary Alice Berners, *m.* Ap. 1889, Capt. Charles Spencer Warwick, Devonshire Regt.; and has issue 1*d* to 2*d*.

  1d. John Charles Spencer Warwick, *b.* 1890.

  2d. Gillian Mary Spencer Warwick, *b.* 1893.

 5c. Julia Katharine Berners, *m.* 3 Jan. 1895, Lieut.-Col. Steuart Bogle Smith, C.B., 1st King's Dragoon Guards; and has issue 1*d*.

  1d. James Anstruther Bogle Smith, *b.* 22 Aug. 1897.

2a. James Hamilton Anstruther, afterwards Lloyd-Anstruther of Hintlesham Hall, J.P., D.L., Col. in the Army, b. 20 Dec. 1806; d. 23 Dec. 1882; m. 1st, 6 Dec. 1838, *Georgiana Charlotte, da. of the Hon. Lindsay Merrick Burrell,* d. 21 *Sept.* 1843; 2ndly, 1 Nov. 1847, *the Hon. Georgiana Chri*.*tiana, da. of George (Barrington*), 5th *Viscount Barrington* [*I.*], d. 11 *July* 1881; *and had issue* 1*b to* 5*b.*

1b. Robert Hamilton Lloyd-Anstruther, J.P., D.L., Lieut.-Col. (ret.) Rifle Brigade, County Alderman for E. Suffolk, sometime (1886–1892), M.P. (*Hintlesham Hall, Ipswich; 37 Eccleston Square, S.W.*), *b.* 21 Ap. 1841; *m.* 5 July 1871, Gertrude Louisa Georgiana, da. of Francis Horatio FitzRoy; and has issue 1*c* to 2*c*.

 1c. FitzRoy Hamilton Lloyd-Anstruther, *b.* 5 July 1872; *m.* 11 Oct. 1898, the Hon. Rachel, da. of Augustus (Gough Calthorpe), 6th Baron Calthorpe [G.B.].

 2c. Rosalind Gertrude Lloyd-Anstruther, d. 2 June 1903; m. *as* 1st *wife,* 14 *Feb.* 1895, *Capt. Noel Armar Lowry-Corry, D.S.O. Grenadier Guards* (14 *Chester Square, S.W.*); *and has issue* 1*d to* 2*d.*

  1d. Armar Valentine Lowry-Corry, *b.* 25 Mar. 1896.

  2d. Rosemary Victoria Lowry-Corry, *b.* 24 May 1897.

2b. Francis William Lloyd-Anstruther, *late* Major and Hon. Lieut.-Col. 3rd Batt. Suffolk Regt. (*Wellington*), *b.* 20 Feb. 1849.

3b. James Lloyd-Anstruther (*Travellers'*), *b.* 9 Jan. 1852.

4b. Basil Lloyd-Anstruther, Lieut.-Col. and Brevet-Col. *formerly* Comdg. 1st Batt. Manchester Regt. (36 *Lennox Gardens, S.W.*), *b.* 1 Dec. 1852; *m.* 25 Ap. 1899, Adela Maria, widow of Major-Gen. the Hon. Alexander Stewart, da. of Sir Robert Loder, 1st Bart. [U.K.].   [Nos. 26636 to·26660.

# of The Blood Royal

5b. Cecil Lloyd Anstruther, Clerk of Printed Papers and Clerk attending the Table in the House of Lords (3 *Warwick Square, S.W.*), *b.* (twin) 1 Dec. 1852; *m.* 4 Aug. 1904, Bertha Mary, da. of John Capel Philips of The Heath House, Tean.

3a. *Jane Anstruther*, d. 13 *Mar.* 1865; m. 21 *Jan.* 1822, *John Dalyell of Lingo, co. Fife, and Ticknevin, D.L., Lieut.-Col. Fife Militia*, d. 7 *Oct.* 1843; *and had issue* 1b *to* 4b.

1b. Robert Anstruther Dalyell of Lingo, &c., C.S.I., LL.D., J.P., D.L., Vice Sec. Council of the Sec. of State, India, b. 5 *May* 1881; d.s.p.

2b. Ralph Dalyell of Lingo, C.B., J.P., D.L., in War Office, *formerly* (1875–1886) Private Sec. to Secs. of State for War (*Lingo, Fife; 21 Onslow Gardens, S.W.*), b. 29 June 1834; *m.* 1870, Annie Margaret Christina, da. of Algernon William Bellingham Greville of Granard; and has issue 1c to 4c.

1c. Ruth Margaret Dalyell.

2c. Violet Jane Dalyell, *m.* 29 July 1899, Horace Peel (41 *Ennismore Gardens, S.W.*); and has issue 1d to 2d.

1d. Pamela Georgiana Peel, *b.* 1 May 1900.

2d. Marjorie Violet Peel, *b.* 18 May 1902.

3c. Lilias Dalyell.

4c. Magdalene Dalyell.

3b. *Charlotte Lucy Hamilton Dalyell*, d. 28 *Ap.* 1902; m. 30 *June* 1853, the *Rev. Maurice William Ferdinand St. John, D.D., Proctor in Convocation and Canon of Gloucester* (*The Cloisters House, Gloucester*); *and has issue.* See the Clarence Volume, p. 489, Nos. 21257–21261.

4b. *Jane Melville Dalyell*, d. 1902 *or* 1903; m. 1852, *the Very Rev. William George Henderson, D.D., Dean of Carlisle*, d. 1905.

4a. ̈*Elizabeth Christian Anstruther*, d. 7 *Dec.* 1893; m. 2 *Nov.* 1837, *the Rev. W. H. Deane, Rector of Hintlesham*, d. 30 Nov. 1854.   [Nos. 26661 to 26675.

297. Descendants of Admiral CHARLES POWELL DOUGLAS HAMILTON, R.N. (see Table XL.), *b.* 26 Dec. 1747; *d.* 12 Mar. 1825; *m.* May 1777, LUCRETIA, da. of George Augustus PROSSER of Hampstead; and had issue 1*a.*

1a. *Augustus Barrington Price Hamilton, afterwards Douglas-Hamilton, Lieut. R.N.*, b. 22 *May* 1781; d. 27 *Aug.* 1849; m. 2 *Ap.* 1805, *Maria Catherine, da. of John Hyde, a Judge of the Supreme Court of Calcutta*, d. 1865; *and had issue* 1b *to* 9b.

1b. *Charles Henry Douglas-Hamilton, Capt. R.N.*, b. 7 *Oct.* 1808; d. 30 Nov. 1873; m. 2*ndly*, 31 *Jan.* 1860, *Elizabeth Ann, da. of the Ven. Justly Hill, Archdeacon of Bucks*, d. 27 *June* 1867; *and had issue* 1c to 4c.

1c. Alfred Douglas (Douglas-Hamilton), 13th Duke of Hamilton [S.], 10th Duke of Brandon [E.], Premier Peer of Scotland, Hereditary Keeper of Holyrood Palace (*Hamilton Palace, Lanarkshire*), b. 6 Mar. 1862; *m.* 4 Dec. 1901, Nina Mary Benita, da. of Major Robert Poore; and has issue 1d to 3d.

1d. Douglas Douglas-Hamilton, Marquis of Douglas and Clydesdale, *b.* 3 Feb. 1903.

2d. Lord George Nigel Douglas-Hamilton, *b.* 4 Jan. 1906.

3d. Lady Jean Douglas-Hamilton, *b.* 11 June 1904.

2c. Lady[1] Helena Augusta Charlotte Constance Sidney Douglas-Hamilton, *m.* 1 June 1899, the Rev. Robert Acland-Hood, M.A. (*Old Manor House, Sandgate*); and has issue 1d.

1d. *Elspeth Acland-Hood*, b. 23 *Ap.* 1900; d. 20 *Feb.* 1901.

[Nos. 26676 to 26681.

---

[1] R.W. 1896.

The Plantagenet Roll

3c. Lady[1] Isabel Frances Ulrica Iris Douglas-Hamilton, *m.* 8 July 1897, Capt. Cyril John Ryder (*Naval and Military*); and has issue 1*d* to 3*d*.

1*d*. Dudley Claud Douglas Ryder, *b.* 27 Ap. 1901.

2*d*. Iris Katharine Ryder, *b.* 10 Aug. 1899.

3*d*. Patience Ryder, *b.* 22 June 1905.

4c. Lady[1] Flora Mary Ida Douglas-Hamilton, *m.* 29 Sept. 1898, Major Robert Montagu Poore, D.S.O., 7th Hussars (*Old Lodge, Salisbury*).

2b. *Francis Seymour Douglas-Hamilton, Col. R.A.,* b. 19 *Jan.* 1811; d. 1 *June* 1874; m. 6 *Sept.* 1834, *Emma Catherine Frances, da. of Thomas Darby Coventry of Greenlands, Bucks,* d. 7 *Jan.* 1868; *and had issue* 1c *to* 7c.

1c. *Algernon Percy Douglas-Hamilton,* b. 22 *June* 1844; d. 31 *May* 1891; m. 4 *Nov.* 1874, *Idonia, da. of Capt. Douglas Ryves Douglas-Hamilton; and had issue* 1d *to* 4d.

1*d*. Percy Seymour Douglas-Hamilton (6 *Queen's Gate Gardens, S.W.*), *b.* 2 Oct. 1875; *m.* 20 July 1901, Edith Hamilton, da. of Sir Frederick Wills, 1st Bart. [U.K.], M.P.

2*d*. Constance Idonia Violet Douglas-Hamilton.

3*d*. Edith Lena Catherine Douglas-Hamilton, *m.* 8 Sept. 1903, the Rev. James Boyle (20 *Wesley Street, Waterloo, Liverpool*).

4*d*. Ethel Jessie Douglas-Hamilton.

2c. Aubrey Reginald Douglas-Hamilton, *late* 57th Regt. (*Broadlands, Broadstairs*), *b.* 21 Ap. 1851; *m.* 24 July 1878, Lucy, da. of the Hon. Robert Fitzgerald of Sydney, M.L.C., New South Wales; and has issue 1*d* to 5*d*.

1*d*. Kenneth Aubrey FitzGerald Seymour Douglas-Hamilton, Lieut. Royal Fusiliers, *b.* 22 Ap. 1879.

2*d*. Lesley Reginald Coventry Douglas-Hamilton, Lieut. Queen's Own Cameron Highlanders, *b.* 30 June 1881.

3*d*. Herbert Eustace Seymour Douglas-Hamilton, *b.* 2 June 1886.

4*d*. Claud Archibald Aubrey Douglas-Hamilton, *b.* 26 May 1889.

5*d*. Irene Lucy Douglas-Hamilton, *b.* 8 July 1883.

3c. Alexandrina Emma Ada Caroline Douglas-Hamilton.

4c. Rosabel Georgiana Maria Douglas-Hamilton, *m.* 21 Sept. 1876, Albert Charles Hadland (*Pen-y-Bryn, Swansea*).

5c. Constance Augusta Idonia Lorn Douglas-Hamilton.

6c. Rosalie Felicia Douglas-Hamilton.

7c. Blanche Annie Douglas-Hamilton.

3b. *Douglas Ryves Douglas-Hamilton,* b. 5 *Jan.* 1814; d. 1894; m. *Feb.* 1843, *Frances, da. of Hugh Ryves Graves of Fort William, Limerick,* d. 1897; *and had issue* 1c *to* 4c.

1c. Alexander Douglas-Hamilton.

2c. Frederick Douglas-Hamilton.

3c. Idonia Douglas-Hamilton (*Moreton, Horsham, Sussex*), *m.* 4 Nov. 1874, Algernon Percy Douglas-Hamilton, *d.* 31 May 1891; and has issue.
See p. 372, Nos. 26687–26690.

4c. Bertha Douglas-Hamilton, *m.* George Dawson.

4b. *Frederic Douglas-Hamilton, H.B.M.'s Minister-Resident and Consul-General to Ecuador,* b. 12 *May* 1815; d. 15 *May* 1887; m. 25 *Feb.* 1843, *Marina, da. of James Norton,* d. 15 *May* 1887; *and had issue* 1c *to* 5c.

1c. Frederick Robert Vere Douglas-Hamilton, *b.* 7 Dec. 1843; *m.* 1873, Josephine, da. of [——] Baumann.　　　　　[Nos. 26682 to 26710.

---

[1] R.W. 1896.

# of The Blood Royal

2c. Augustus Maitland Ronald Douglas-Hamilton, Lieut. R.N., *b.* 2 Sept. 1847 ; *m.* 1880 (dissolved 1895), Theresa Maude, da. of Capt. W. B. C. A. Parker Wentworth of Lawrence Town, Nova Scotia ; and has issue 1*d.*

    1*d.* Marina Norton Douglas Douglas-Hamilton.

3c. Archibald Douglas Schomberg Douglas-Hamilton, *late* Capt. 4th Batt. Royal Welsh Fusiliers, *b.* 1 Oct. 1861.

4c. *Annie Marina Augusta Douglas-Hamilton,* b. 23 Oct. 1845 ; d. (−) ; m. *4 Oct.* 1873, *Capt. Stephen Dix of Wickham, co. Kent, Gen. Superintendent R.M.S.P., C.A.,* d. 1883 ; *and had issue* 1*d to* 3*d.*

    1*d.* Charles Dix, *b.* Oct. 1876.

    2*d.* Stephen Hamilton Dix, *b.* 20 Aug. 1878.

    3*d.* Annie Hamilton Dix, *b.* Aug. 1874.

5c. Augusta Caroline Octavia Douglas-Hamilton, *b.* 12 Oct. 1856.

5*b. Rev. Adolphus Douglas-Hamilton, M.A.,* b. 5 *July* 1816 ; d. 12 *Sept.* 1893 ; m. 22 *May* 1847, *Henrietta Charlotte, da. of Admiral Sir Benjamin Hallowell-Carew, G.C.B.,* d. 6 *Jan.* 1901 ; *and had issue* 1*c to* 4*c.*

    1c. Edith Douglas-Hamilton.

    2c. Florence Anne Hallowell Douglas-Hamilton.

    3c. Mary Geraldine Douglas-Hamilton.

    4c. Eva Bertha Gwendoline Douglas-Hamilton.

6*b. Alfred Douglas-Hamilton of Gildea Hall, Essex, J.P., D.L., Bar.-at-Law,* b. 21 *Ap.* 1818 ; d. 25 *Mar.* 1895 ; m. 1st, 17 *July* 1845, *Adelaide, da. and co-h. of Alexander Black of Gildea Hall, d.* 17 *Ap.* 1870 ; 2*ndly,* 27 *Oct.* 1874, *Harriette Amy Blackburne, da. of W. H. Peters of Harefield, J.P. ; and had issue* 1*c to* 7*c.*

    1c. Alfred Hamilton Douglas-Hamilton, Bar.-at-Law (2 *Tanfield Court, Temple, E.C.*), *b.* 27 Jan. 1856.

    2c. Rev. William Arthur Douglas-Hamilton, B.A. (Camb.), Curate of St. Mary's, Monmouth.

    3c.[1] *Annie Laura Douglas-Hamilton,* d. 18 Oct. 1877 ; m. *as* 1*st wife,* 11 Nov. 1876, *Col. Everard Strangways Neave,* 18*th Bengal Cavalry, b.* 21 *Aug.* 1844 ; *d.* 18 *Oct.* 1896 ; *and had issue* 1*d.*

        1*d.* Everard Reginald Neave, B.A. (Oxon.), I.C.S., *b.* 21 July 1877.

    4c.[1] Nina Susannah Douglas-Hamilton, *m.* 30 July 1878, Sir William Cospatrick Dunbar of Mochrum, 9th Bart. [S.], C.B. (8 *Onslow Square, S.W. ; Mochrum Park, Kirkcowan, Wigtown, &c.*), J.P., D.L., Registrar-General for England and Wales.

    5c.[1] Laura Beatrice Douglas-Hamilton (8 *Onslow Square, S.W.*).

    6c.[2] Evelyn Mary Douglas-Hamilton.

    7c.[2] Amy Janet Douglas-Hamilton.

7*b. Octavius Hamilton, Major-Gen. in the Army, b.* 15 *Feb.* 1821 ; *d.* 14 *Aug.* 1904; m. 29 *June* 1852, *Katharine Augusta Westerera, da. of Capt. Donald Macleod, R.N., C.B.,* d. 30 *Nov.* 1902 ; *and had issue* 1*c to* 6*c.*

    1c. Rev. Hamilton Anne Hamilton, M.A. (Camb.), Rector of Arcadia, Pretoria, *late* Archdeacon of Kimberley (*Arcadia, Pretoria, South Africa*), *b.* 28 May 1853 ; *m.* 26 Oct. 1875, Lillie, da. of J. Bowles ; and has issue 1*d* to 4*d.*

        1*d.* Basil Sholto Anne Hamilton, *late* Capt. Army Service Corps (*Junior Constitutional*), *b.* 11 Aug. 1876.

        2*d.* James Angus Hamilton, *b.* 13 Aug. 1889.

        3*d.* Ilta Hamilton, *b.* 13 Aug. 1879.

        4*d.* Mary Hamilton Hamilton, *b.* 1 May 1885.

    2c. Augustus Maynard Hamilton, *late* Capt. 4th Batt. East Surrey Regt, *b.* 29 Nov. 1854.   [Nos. 26711 to 26734.

The Plantagenet Roll

3c. Charles Reginald Sydney Hamilton, *late* Capt. Gordon Highlanders (*Naval and Military*), *b.* 5 Oct. 1856 ; *m.* 10 Sept. 1890, Mary Isabel Hammond, da. of Capt. George Alexander Whitla of Ben Eaden ; and has issue 1*d.*

    1*d.* Elsie Muriel Hamilton, *b.* 21 Aug. 1891.

4c. Angus Falconar Hamilton, Major Queen's Own Cameron Highlanders, *b.* 20 Aug. 1863 ; *m.* 1 Aug. 1894, Anna Watson, da. of Capt. Alexander Watson Mackenzie of Ord, co. Ross ; and has issue 1*d.*

    1*d.* Camilla Beatrice Hamilton, *b.* 9 Aug. 1895.

5c. Camilla Alexandrina Lucy Hamilton.

6c. Katherine Seymour Hamilton (46 *Marylands Road, St. Peter's Park, Paddington, W.*).

8*b. Alexandrina Idonia Charlotte Susan Hamilton,* b. 31 *Aug.* 1824 ; d. (–) ; m. 29 *Mar.* 1851, *Robert Peel, Major* 13th *Prince Albert's L.I.,* b. 20 *Oct.* 1828 ; *and had issue* 1c *to* 5c.[1]

    1c. Robert Hamilton Charles James Peel, *b.* 9 Dec. 1853.

    2c. Edmund Arundel Lawrence Gerald Peel, *b.* 8 Feb. 1858.

    3c. Arthur Hugh Douglas Peel, *b.* 23 Nov. 1864.

    4c. Idonia Alice Maria Peel, *b.* 11 Mar. 1852.

    5c. Beatrice Rosa Maude Peel, *b.* 1 Dec. 1861.

9*b.* Lucretia Charlotte Susanna Hamilton, *m.*[2] Capt. Stephen Briggs, R.N. ; and has issue.   [Nos. 26735 to 26746.

298. Descendants, if any, of Lady CHARLOTTE HAMILTON (see Table XXVI.), *b.* 1703 ; *d.* 5 Feb. 1777 ; *m.* CHARLES EDWIN ; and of Lady SUSAN HAMILTON, *d.* 3 June 1755 ; *m.* 3 Aug. 1736, ANTHONY TRACY KECK of Great Tew, co. Oxon.

299. Descendants, if any, of ELIZABETH COPE (see Table XXIV.), wife of THOMAS ESTCOURT of Shipton Estcourt, co. Gloucester.

300. Descendants, if any, of WILLIAM ANNE (CAPEL), 4th EARL OF ESSEX [E.] (see Table XXVII.), *b.* 7 Oct. 1732 ; *d.* 5 Mar. 1799 ; *m.* 1st, 1 Aug. 1754, FRANCES, da. and co.-h. of Sir Charles HANBURY WILLIAMS, K.B., *d.* 19 July 1759 ; 2ndly, 3 Mar. 1767, HARRIET, da. of Col. BLADEN, *d.* 12 Mar. 1821 ; and had issue 1*a* to 3*a.*

1a. George (*Capel, afterwards Coningsby*), 5th *Earl of Essex* [E.], D.C.L., b. 13 *Nov.* 1857 ; d. 23 *Ap.* 1839.

    2a. Hon. *John Thomas Capel,* b. 2 *Mar.* 1769 ; d. 5 *Mar.* 1819 ; m. 2 *Ap.* 1792, *Lady Caroline, da. of Henry* (*Bayly, afterwards* (1770) *Paget*), 1st *Earl of Uxbridge* [G.B.], b. 6 *Feb.* 1773 ; d. 9 *July* 1847 ; *and had issue* 1b *to* 9b.

    1b. Arthur Algernon (*Capel, afterwards* (R.L. 23 *July* 1880) *Capell*), 6th *Earl of Essex* [E.], b. 27 *Jan.* 1803 ; d. 11 *Sept.* 1892 ; m. 1st, 14 *July* 1825, *Lady Caroline Janetta, da. of William* (*Beauclerk*), 8th *Duke of St. Albans* [E.], b. 28 *June* 1804 ; d. 22 *Aug.* 1862 ; 2ndly, 3 *June* 1863, *the Hon. Louisa Caroline Elizabeth, da. of Charles Boyle, Viscount Dungarvan,* b. 3 *June* 1833 ; d. 5 *May* 1876 ; *and had issue* 1c *to* 5c.

---

[1] Foster's "Baronetage," 1880, p. 461.
[2] Burke's "Peerage," 1902, p. 712. Both Foster and Lodge omit her.

374

Arthur 1ST Lord Capell and his Family

after C. Jansen

THE COMMON ANCESTORS OF Nos. 26747 - 33533.

# of The Blood Royal

1c. *Arthur de Vere Capell, Viscount Malden,* b. 22 *July* 1826; d.v.p. 10 *Mar.* 1879; m. 23 *Jan.* 1853, *Emma Mary (39 Loundes Street, S.W.), da. of Sir Henry Meux, 1st Bart.* [*U.K.*]; *and had issue* 1d *to* 5d.

1d. George Devereux de Vere (Capell), 7th Earl of Essex [E.] (*Cassioburg Park, Watford; 9 Mansfield Street, W.*), b. 24 Oct. 1857; m. 1st, 12 July 1882, Ellenor Harriet Maria, da. of William Henry Harford of Oldown House, Almondsbury, d. 31 Dec. 1885; 2ndly, 14 Dec. 1893, Adela, da. of Beach Grant of New York; and has issue 1e to 3e.

1e. Algernon George de Vere Capell, Viscount Malden, b. 21 Feb. 1884.

2e. Lady Iris Mary Athenais de Vere Capell, b. 8 June 1895.

3e. Lady Joan Rachel de Vere Capell, b. 28 Feb. 1899.

2d. Hon.[1] Randolph de Vere Capell, *formerly* Capt. 3rd Batt. Royal Scots, and A.D.C. to the Governor of Victoria, b. 1 Nov. 1865.

3d. Lady[1] Maud de Vere Capell.

4d. Lady[1] Evelyn de Vere Capell, m. 5 Sept. 1883, the Hon. Eustace Henry Dawnay, J.P., D.L. (*West Heslerton Hall, York*); and has issue 1e to 3e.

1e. Cuthbert Henry Dawnay, b. 4 Nov. 1891.

2e. Dorothy Maud Dawnay, b. 12 June 1884.

3e. Leila Mary Dawnay, b. 12 Mar. 1886.

5d. Lady[1] Sybil de Vere Capell, m. as 2nd wife, 18 Sept. 1890, Thomas (Brassey), 1st Baron Brassey [U.K.], K.C.B., D.C.L., *sometime* (1895–1900) Governor of Victoria, and (1884–1885) Lord-in-Waiting to Queen Victoria (*Normanhurst, Battle, Sussex; 24 Park Lane, W.*); and has issue 1e.

1e. Hon. Helen de Vere Brassey, b. 4 Sept. 1892.

2c. Hon. Reginald Algernon Capell, J.P., Dep. Chairman of Great Northern Railway (*26 Connaught Square*), b. 3 Oct. 1830; m. 24 Ap. 1858, Mary Eliza, da. of John Nicholas Fazakerly of Studleigh, J.P.

3c. Hon. Arthur Algernon Capell, Bar. I.T. (*23 Draycott Place, S.W.; Chorley Wood, Rickmansworth*), b. 27 July 1864; m. 23 Dec. 1890, Isabel Anne, da. of Col. Townshend Wilson; and has issue 1d to 2d.

1d. Constance Audrey Capell, b. 21 Oct. 1891.

2d. Rachel Julia Capell, b. 4 Ap. 1894.

4c. *Lady Adela Capell,* b. 4 *Mar.* 1828; d. 31 *Dec.* 1860; m. *as 2nd wife,* 3 *Nov.* 1858, *Archibald (Montgomery), 13th Earl of Eglinton* [S.], *1st Earl of Winton* [U.K.], *K.T.,* d. 4 *Oct.* 1861; *and had issue* 1d *to* 2d.

1d. Lady Sybil Amelia Adela Montgomery.

2d. Lady Hilda Rose Montgomery, m. 23 Feb. 1881, Tonman Mosley, J.P., a son of the 3rd Bart. [G.B.] (*Bangors Park, Iver, Bucks*); and has issue 1e to 4e.

1e. Nicholas Mosley, Lieut. Prince of Wales' Regt., b. 28 July 1882.

2e. Edward Hugh Mosley, b. 16 July 1884.

3e. Hildred Mosley.

4e. Sybil Hildegarde Mosley.

5c. Lady Beatrice Mary Capell (*26 Tedworth Square, Chelsea, S.W.*), b. 7 Dec. 1870.

2b. Hon.[2] *Algernon Henry Champagne Capel, Capt. R.N.,* b. 23 *Oct.* 1807; d. 21 *Nov.* 1886; m. 10 *Dec.* 1832, *Caroline, da. of Admiral the Hon. Sir Charles Paget, K.C.B.,* d. 11 *June* 1880; *and had issue* 1c *to* 3c.

1c. Reginald Ralph Algernon Capel, *late* Indian Navy (*Riverstone Park, Sydney, N.S. Wales*), b. 31 May 1841; m. 1875, Marion, da. of [——] Strathen of Riverstone; and has issue (2 sons).

2c. Charles Horatio Algernon Capel, b. 5 Aug. 1845; m. 28 June 1868, Alice Peel, da. of Frederick Bellairs; and has issue 1d to 2d.   [Nos. 26747 to 26771.]

---

[1] R.W., 6 Jan. 1893.   [2] R.W., May 1839.

The Plantagenet Roll

1*d*. Arthur Algernon de Vere Capel, *b*. 6 Ap. 1869.

2*d*. Gertrude Blanche Constance Capel.

3*c*. Millicent Florence Evelyn Capel, *m*. Ap. 1870, Richard Cole.

3*b*. Hon. *Adolphus Charles Frederick Molyneux Capell*, b. 28 *June* 1813; d. 13 *Aug*. 1899; m. 15 *Dec*. 1834, *the Hon. Charlotte Mary*, *da. of Henry (Maynard)*, *3rd Viscount Maynard* [*G.B.*], d. 27 *June* 1871; *and had issue* 1*c to* 3*c*.

1*c*. Rev. Horatio Bladon Capel, M.A., Rector of Great Easton (*Great Easton Rectory, Dunmow, Essex*), *b*. 10 Oct. 1839; *m*. 16 Aug. 1866, Ada Augusta, da. of Theophilus Hawkins of Newton Abbot; and has issue 1*d* to 4*d*.

1*d*. Horace Charles George Arthur Capel, *b*. 6 July 1868.

2*d*. Algernon Essex Capel, D.S.O., S. African Constabulary, *formerly* Capt. Cape Mounted Rifles, *b*. 1 Nov. 1869; *m*. 3 Mar. 1903, Lois Ethel, da. of William Slatter of Stratton, Cirencester; and has issue 1*e* to 2*e*.

1*e*. Algernon Arthur Capel, *b*. 7 Dec. 1903.

2*e*. Joan Lois Capel, *b*. 26 July 1905.

3*d*. Henry Addison Devereux Capel, *b*. 12 June 1873; *m*. 1 Aug. 1901, Olive Mary, da. of William Richardson-Bunbury.

4*d*. Mary Kathleen Capel, *m*. 1st, 3 Oct. 1893, Francis George West, *d*. (in South Africa) 1900; 2ndly, 1901, Edward Aubrey Courtauld Lowe of High Garratt, Braintree; and has issue 1*e* to 2*e*.

1*e*. George West, *b*. 18 Sept. 1894.

2*e*. Madeleine West, *b*. 10 July 1897.

2*c*. Rev. George Marie Capel, B.A. (Oxon.), Rector of Passenham and Dom. Chaplain to the Earl of Essex (*Passenham Rectory, Stony Stratford*), *b*. 11 Jan. 1845; *m*. 4 Jan. 1870, Annie, da. of Peter Stanley Lowe of Whitehall Churchstow; and has issue 1*d* to 6*d*.

1*d*. Arthur George Coningsby Capel, Lieut. 2nd Batt. Northants Regt., *b*. 28 June 1879.

2*d*. Dora Amy Isabel Capel.

3*d*. Marie Kathleen Capel, *m*. 21 Jan. 1897, D'Arcy Mackinnon Dawes (*The Manor House, Little Missenden, Bucks*).

4*d*. Léonie Annie Capel.

5*d*. Hilda Amalie Violet Capel.

6*d*. Bertha Sybil Capel.

3*c*. Florence Amelia Louisa Capel, *m*. 1st, 6 Oct. 1859, Francis Nevile Reade, 21st Fusiliers, *d*. 9 Nov. 1882; 2ndly, 1 Dec. 1883, Francis Maurice Drummond Drummond, Bar.-at-Law (20 *Marine Square, Brighton*); and has issue 1*d* to 4*d*.

1*d*. Francis Henry Horatio de Capel Reade (*Alexandria, Nebraska, U.S.A.*), *b*. 25 July 1860; *m*. 3 Feb. 1885, May, da. of James Hogg of Whitesbury, Kentucky, U.S.A.; and has issue 1*e* to 2*e*.

1*e*. Reginald Benton Capell Reade, *b*. 3 June 1901.

2*e*. Florence Maletta Capell Reade.

2*d*. Charles Nevil Molyneux de Capel Reade, *b*. 18 Dec. 1864.

3*d*. Henry Arthur Maynard Capell Reade (*High Beech, Parkstone, Dorset*), *b*. 10 Ap. 1866; *m*. 1st, 24 May 1887, Alice Mary, da. of George Baker of Broadlands, Petworth, *d*. 15 Aug. 1901; 2ndly, 26 Nov. 1902, Elizabeth Catherine, da. of Alfred Thomas of Chatham, co. Kent.

4*d*. Violet Mary Reade, *m*. 8 May 1879, Ernest Southgate Day (*Auckland, New Zealand*); and has issue 1*e* to 2*e*.

1*e*. Ernest Archibald Day, *late* Imp. Yeo., *b*. 5 Dec. 1881.

2*e*. Gordon Tyler Day, *b*. 20 Nov. 1883.

4*b*. *Harriet Jane Capel*, b. 19 *Feb*. 1793; d. (*apparently* s.p.) 24 *June* 1819; m. 26 *Dec*. 1817, *David Okeden Parry-Okeden of More Critchell, co. Dorset*, d. 28 *Oct*. 1833. [Nos. 26772 to 26799.

# of The Blood Royal

5b. Georgiana Capel, b. 13 *May* 1795; d. 19 *Oct.* 1835; m. 1*st,* 16 *Aug.* 1821, *Ralph Smyth of Gaybrook, co. Westmeath;* d.s.p. 1827; 2*ndly,* 18 *June* 1831, *Pierce O'Brien Butler of Dunboyne Castle, co. Meath.*

6b. Lady[1] *Maria Capel,* d. 30 *Dec.* 1856; m. 13 *Dec.* 1821, *Marquis Marius d'Espinasse de Fontanelle; and had issue.*

7b. Lady[1] *Louisa Anne Capel,* d. 28 *July* 1842; m. *Nov.* 1827, *Count Augustus d'Espinasse de Fontanelle.*

8b. Lady[1] *Horatia Capel,* b. 8 *May* 1805; d. 22 *May* 1864 (*being burnt to death at Cassiobury*); m. 16 *Oct.* 1851, *Col. the Count de Septeuil.*

9b. Lady Jane Capel, d. 2 *Nov.* 1849; m. *Nov.* 1833, *D. Macloughlin, M.D.*

3a. Rev. the Hon. William Robert Capel, M.A., b. 28 *Ap.* 1775; d. 3 *Dec.* 1854; m. 7 *June* 1802, *Sarah, da. of Samuel Salter of Rickmansworth,* d. 19 *Ap.* 1874; *and had issue* 1b *to* 5b.

1b. Edward Samuel Capel, Lieut.-Col. late Bengal Army, b. 16 *Jan.* 1811; d. 28 *May* 1896; m. 5 *June* 1838, *Elizabeth, da. of James Binnie of Demerara,* d. 19 *Nov.* 1851; *and had issue* 1c *to* 4c.

1c. Arthur William Capel, Col. *late* Bengal Cavalry, b. 23 Ap. 1840.

2c. Edward Capel, M.A., *formerly* in Holy Orders (29 *Member's Mansions, Victoria Street, I.W.*), b. 6 Sept. 1843.

3c. Ada Capel, *m.* 18 June 1874, Adm. Sir John Reginald Thomas Fullerton, G.C.V.O., C.B. (*Hamble, Southampton*); and has issue 1d *to* 5d.

1d. Alan Edward Weston Fullerton, b. 1877.

2d. Eric John Arthur Fullerton, b. 1878.

3d. Judith Fullerton, *m.* 1901, Sidney Julius Meyrick, Lieut. R.N.

4d. Rachel Elizabeth Fullerton, *m.* 1901, Henry Gerald Elliot Lane, Lieut. R.N.

5d. Daisy Fullerton.

4c. Edith Mary Capel (28 *Member's Mansions, Victoria Street, I.W.*).

2b. Jane Selina Capel, b. 25 *Oct.* 1805; d. 15 *June* 1892; m. 9 *May* 1826, *Thomas Truesdale Clarke of Swakeleys, co. Middlesex, J.P., D.L.,* b. 29 *Oct.* 1802; d. 5 *Ap.* 1890; *and had issue* 1c *to* 2c.

1c. William Capel Clarke, afterwards Clarke-Thornhill of Swakeleys, Fixby, and Rushton, J.P., D.L., High Sheriff co. Northants 1860, b. 8 *Ap.* 1832; d. 28 *June* 1898; m. 20 *Nov.* 1855, *Clara, da. and co-h. of Thomas Thornhill of Fixby Hall, co. Yorks.,* d. 16 *July* 1865; *and had issue* 1d *to* 3d.

1d. Thomas Bryan Clarke-Thornhill, M.A. (Oxon.), Sec. Diplo. Ser. (*Rushton Hall, Kettering, co. Northants; Fixby Hall, Huddersfield; Swakeleys, Middlesex; Binham, Norfolk*), b. 13 Mar. 1857.

2d. Clara Louisa Clarke-Thornhill, *m.* 27 Nov. 1884, Lieut.-Col. Francis Charles Carter, Berks Regt. (*Denoille House, Havant*); and has issue 1e *to* 2e.

1e. Herbert Francis George Carter, Lieut. King's Own Yorkshire L.I., b. 2 Aug. 1885.

2e. Gerald Ernest Berkeley Carter, Mid. R.N., b. 5 Aug. 1886.

3d. Gwendoline Blanche Clarke-Thornhill, *m.* 18 Dec. 1890, George Harrison Champion de Crespigny, J.P., Lieut.-Col. 3rd Batt. Northamptonshire Regt. (*Burton Latimer Hall, Kettering*); and has issue 1e *to* 3e.

1e. Arthur Oscar Champion de Crespigny.

2e. Mildred Frances Champion de Crespigny.

3e. Gwendoline Sybil Champion de Crespigny.

2c. Louisa Jane Selina Clarke, d. (–); m. 1851, *Vice-Adm. Thomas Cochrane of Buntings, Uxbridge,* d. 4 *June* 1889; *and had issue* 1d *to* 4d.

1d. Algernon Home Cochrane.

2d. Reginald Purves Cochrane.

3d. Helen Cochrane.

4d. Sybil Louise Cochrane.　　　　　　　　　　　　[Nos. 26800 to 26820.

---

[1] R.W., May 1839.

The Plantagenet Roll

3*b*. Louisa Capel (*Manor House, Long Wettenham, Berks*), *b.* 20 Ap. 1808 ; *m.* 21 Mar. 1831, the Rev. James Charles Clutterbuck, Vicar of Long Wittenham, *d.* 8 May 1885 ; and has issue 1*c* to 7*c*.

1*c*. Rev. Francis Capper Clutterbuck, M.A. (Oxon,), Vicar of Culham (*Culham Vicarage, Abingdon*), *b.* 20 Aug. 1842.

2*c*. William Robert Clutterbuck, Rear-Adm. R.N. (*Manor House, Long Wittenham, Berks*), *b.* 29 Dec. 1844 ; *m.* 30 June 1875, Catherine S., da. of C. I. Lambert.

3*c*. Louisa Marianne Clutterbuck, *d.* 17 *Ap.* 1903 ; *m.* 20 *Jan.* 1857, *the Rev. Robert Townsend Crawley, M.A. (Oxon.), Rector of North Ockendon* (*North Ockendon Rectory, Essex*) ; *and had issue*.

See the Clarence Volume, pp. 154–155, Nos. 2271–2276.

4*c*. Isabel Clutterbuck, *m.* 1875, J. S. Bowles of Milton Hill, co. Berks, *d.* 1884 ; and has issue 1*d*.

1*d*. Rev. John Erskine Bowles, Curate of Aston Brook, Birmingham, *b.* 1878.

5*c*. Ellen Hester Clutterbuck (*Fair Oak, Eastleigh, Hants*), *m.* 19 May 1868, J. G. Edwards of Fair Oak, *d.* 4 Mar. 1903 ; and has issue 1*d* to 6*d*.

1*d*. Lancelot Edwards, Capt. and Brevet-Major 2nd Batt. Lincoln Regt., *b.* 1870.

2*d*. James Edwards, *b.* 22 June 1872.

3*d*. Hugh Edwards, Comm. R.N., *b.* 14 Oct. 1873.

4*d*. Elinor Edwards, *b.* 12 Ap. 1869 ; *m.* 22 Feb. 1898, Robert Townshend Wickham (*West Mount, Chester ; Segrwyd, Denbigh*) ; and has issue 1*e* to 2*e*.

1*e*. Lancelot Townshend Wickham, *b.* 15 July 1902.

2*e*. Robert George Wickham, *b.* 14 June 1905.

5*d*. Hester Edwards, *b.* 29 May 1871 ; *m.* 8 June 1903, the Rev. Guy Cooper.

6*d*. Mary Edwards, *b.* 6 Nov. 1875.

6*c*. Mary Lucy Jane Clutterbuck, *m.* 1878, Lieut.-Col. J. H. Hamersley, *late* 22nd Regt.

7*c*. Emily Jemima Clutterbuck, *m.* 23 Aug. 1877, Thomas Marriott Davenport, Clerk of the Peace for Oxfordshire (*Headington Hill, Oxford*) ; and has issue 1*d* to 10*d*.

1*d*. Gilbert Capell Davenport, *b.* 17 Ap. 1881.

2*d*. Robert Clutterbuck Davenport, Lieut. R.N., *b.* 13 Ap. 1882.

3*d*. Hugh Nares Davenport, *b.* 18 July 1886.

4*d*. Leonard Marriot Davenport, *b.* 8 Ap. 1889.

5*d*. James Salter Davenport, *b.* 9 July 1890.

6*d*. Cecil Thornhill Davenport, *b.* 3 Feb. 1892.

7*d*. Lucy Catherine Davenport, *b.* 10 Nov. 1879.

8*d*. Norah Emily Davenport, *b.* 6 Oct. 1884.

9*d*. Evelyn Mary Davenport, *b.* 29 Mar. 1887.

10*d*. Rachel Margaret Davenport, *b.* 17 Ap. 1895.

4*b*. *Georgiana Capel*, b. 3 Oct. 1809 ; d. 1892 ; m. 28 *Sept.* 1829, *the Rev. Nathaniel Francis Wodehouse, Vicar of Dulverton*, b. 2 *Nov.* 1802 ; d. 23 *Oct.* 1870 ; *and had issue* 1*c* to 6*c*.

1*c*. Capel Wodehouse, Rear-Adm. R.N. (*The Grange, Waltham St. Lawrence, Twyford, Berks*), *b.* 25 Jan. 1841 ; *m.* 25 Ap. 1889, Portia Maria, da. of W. B. Rashleigh of The Manor House, Farningham ; and has issue 1*d* to 3*d*.

1*d*. Edmond Wodehouse, *b.* 25 Mar. 1894.

2*d*. Dulcibella Wodehouse, *b.* 2 Jan. 1891.

3*d*. Alice Wodehouse, *b.* 22 Mar. 1892.

2*c*. Georgina Sarah Wodehouse (*Waltham Dene, Twyford*), *m.* 26 Aug. 1863,

[Nos. 26821 to 26857.

378

# of The Blood Royal

the Rev. William Charles Fox of the Grange, Bristol, d. 1883; and has issue 1d to 4d.

    1d. Lionel Wodehouse Fox, *late* Capt. Somersetshire L.I., b. 21 Sept. 1865.

    2d. Armine Wodehouse Fox, b. 6 Ap. 1869.

    3d. Raymond Wodehouse Fox, b. 11 July 1873.

    4d. Eliza Frances Fox.

    3c. *Alice Jane Wodehouse*, d. (-); m. 12 *Oct.* 1865, *Bevil Granville, J.P., Major 23rd Royal Welsh Fusiliers* (*Wellesbourne Hall, near Warwick; Northchurch, Great Berkhamstead*); *and had issue 1d to 6d.*

    1d. Bernard Granville, Capt. 3rd King's Own Hussars, b. 21 July 1873; *m.* 1904, Edith, da. of the Right Hon. Thomas Frederick Halsey of Gaddesden Place, P.C., M.P.

    2d. Violet Granville, *m.* 1889, Walter Henry Maudslay.

    3d. Mary Olive Granville, *m.* Dec. 1893, Arthur Hubert Edward Wood, J.P., D.L., of Sudbourne Hall, Suffolk (*Browhead, Windermere*); and has issue 1e to 4e.

    1e. Edward Guy Wood, b. 30 Oct. 1894.

    2e. Richard Oliver Wood, b. 26 Mar. 1896.

    3e. Evelyn Sybil Wood, b. 12 Feb. 1900.

    4e. Alice Ava Wood, b. 1902.

    4d. Muriel Granville, *m.* 1895, Frederick Blomfield; and has issue (3 sons).

    5d. Grace Granville, *m.* 15 Nov. 1893, Harold M'Corquodale (*Forest Hall, Ongar*); and has issue (4 sons and 1 da.).

    6d. Morwenna Granville, *m.* 1905, Capt. Lionel Halsey, R.N.

    4c. Ellen Wodehouse.

    5c. Louisa Clara Wodehouse, *m.* 26 May 1864, Edmond Henry Wodehouse, C.B., *lately* a Comr. of Inland Revenue.

    6c. Francis Wodehouse, *m.* 1879, Francis Arthur Wodehouse, b. 18 June 1831; *d.* 30 Dec. 1891.

    5b. *Isabella Capel*, b. 15 *June* 1812; d. (-); m. 10 *May* 1854, *the Rev. Abiathar Hawkes, M.A., Rector of Rushton, Northants.*   [Nos. 26858 to 26874.

301. Descendants of Lady CHARLOTTE CAPEL, *afterwards* HYDE (see Table XXVII.), b. 2 Oct. 1721; d. 3 Sept. 1790; m. 30 Mar. 1752, THOMAS (VILLIERS), 1st EARL OF CLARENDON (1776) [G.B.] and BARON VILLIERS (1782) [Prussia], b. 1709; d. 11 Dec. 1786; and had issue 1a to 3a.

    1a. *Thomas* (*Villiers*), *2nd Earl of Clarendon* [*G.B.*] *and Baron Villiers* [*Prussia*], b. 26 *Dec.* 1753; d. *unm.* 7 *Mar* 1824.

    2a. *John Charles* (*Villiers*), *3rd Earl of Clarendon* [*G.B.*] *and Baron Villiers* [*Prussia*], b. 14 *Nov.* 1757; d.s.p.s. 22 *Dec.* 1838.

    3a. Hon. George Villiers, b. 23 Nov. 1759; d. 21 *Mar.* 1827; m. 17 *Ap.* 1798, *the Hon. Theresa, da. of John* (*Parker*), *1st Baron Boringdon* [*G.B.*], b. 22 *Sept.* 1775; d. 12 *Jan.* 1856; *and had issue 1b to 4b.*

    1b. *George William Frederick* (*Villiers*), *4th Earl of Clarendon* [*G.B.*] *and Baron Villiers* [*Prussia*], *K.G., G.C.B., P.C., sometime* (1847–1852) *Lord-Lieut. of Ireland and* (1853–1858, 1865–1866) *Chief Sec for Foreign Affairs, &c.,* b. 12 *Jan.* 1800; d. 27 *June* 1870; m. 4 *June* 1839, *Lady Katherine, widow of John Foster Barham of Stockbridge, M.P., da. of James Walter* (*Grimston*), *1st Earl of Verulam* [*U.K.*], b. 18 *Ap.* 1810; d. 4 *July* 1874; *and had issue 1c to 6c.*

    1c. Edward Hyde (Villiers), 5th Earl of Clarendon [G.B.] and Baron Villiers [Prussia], P.C., G.C.B., Lord Chamberlain of H.B.M.'s Household, &c. (*The Grove,*   [No. 26875.

The Plantagenet Roll

Watford, Herts; Stable Yard, St. James' Palace), b. 11 Feb. 1846; m. 6 Sept. 1876, Lady Caroline Elizabeth,[1] da. of Sidney James (Agar), 3rd Earl of Normanton [I.], b. 21 Mar. 1857; d. 9 May 1894; and has issue 1d to 2d.

1d. George Herbert Hyde Villiers, Lord Hyde, b. 7 June 1877, m. 5 Aug. 1905, Adeline Verena Isabel, sister to Arthur Herbert Tennyson (Cocks), 6th Baron Somers [G.B.].

2d. Lady Edith Villiers, b. 8 Nov. 1878.

2c. Hon. George Patrick Hyde Villiers, C.B., C.M.G., b. 27 Sept. 1847; d. 10 Jan. 1892; m. 9 Oct. 1884, Louisa Maria, da. of George Disney Magnay (who re-m. 28 June 1894, Major the Hon. Gilbert Legh of The Drove House, Thornham, King's Lynn); and had issue 1d to 3d.

1d. George John Theodore Villiers, b. 1 Oct. 1891.

2d. Katharine Alice Villiers, b. 16 Aug. 1885.

3d. Constance Barbara Villiers, b. 2 Aug. 1886.

3c. Hon. Francis Hyde Villiers, C.B., Assist. Under-Sec. of State for Foreign Affairs (103 Sloane Street, S.W.), b. 13 Aug. 1852; m. 28 June 1876, Virginia Katharine, da. of Eric Carrington Smith; and has issue 1d to 5d.

1d. Eric Hyde Villiers, b. 2 Feb. 1881.

2d. Gerald Hyde Villiers, b. 31 Aug. 1882.

3d. Algernon Hyde Villiers, b. 1 Feb. 1886.

4d. Dorothy Villiers, b. 20 Feb. 1879, m. 9 July 1904, Capt. Hugh Craufurd Keith Fraser, 1st Life Guards.

5d. Marjorie Mildred Villiers, b. 9 May 1890.

4c. Lady Constance Villiers, m. 31 May 1864, Frederick Arthur (Stanley), 16th Earl of Derby [E.], 1st Baron Stanley of Preston [U.K.], K.G., P.C., G.C.B., sometime (1888–1893) Gov.-Gen. of Canada, &c. (Knowsley, Prescot; Derby House, 33 St. James' Square, S.W., &c.); and has issue.
See the Tudor Roll of "The Blood Royal of Britain," p. 492, Nos. 33735–33746.

5c. Lady Alice Villiers, b. 17 Sept. 1841; d. 23 Nov. 1897; m. 16 Aug. 1860, Edward (Bootle-Wilbraham), 1st Earl of Lathom [U.K.], G.C.B., b. 12 Dec. 1837; d. 19 Nov. 1898; and had issue 1d to 6d.

1d. Edward George (Bootle-Wilbraham), 2nd Earl of Lathom [U.K.], &c., (Lathom House, Ormskirk, Lancashire; 1 Bryanston Square, W.), b. 26 Oct. 1864; m. 15 Aug. 1889, Lady Wilma, da. of William (Pleydell-Bouverie), 5th Earl of Radnor [G.B.]; and has issue 1e to 4e.

1e. Edward William Bootle-Wilbraham, Lord Skelmersdale, b. 16 May 1895.

2e. Lady Helen Alice Bootle-Wilbraham, b. 12 Aug. 1890.

3e. Lady Barbara Ann Bootle-Wilbraham, b. 2 May 1893.

4e. Lady Rosemary Wilma Bootle-Wilbraham, b. 12 Oct. 1903.

2d. Hon. Villiers Richard Bootle-Wilbraham, b. 17 Ap. 1867; m. 25 Oct. 1900, Violet Inez, da. of [——] de Romerio.

3d. Hon. Reginald Francis Bootle-Wilbraham, b. 26 July 1875; m. 18 Dec. 1903, Lilian Mary, da. of Major William Lyster Holt.

4d. Lady Alice Maud Bootle-Wilbraham (H.R.H. the late Princess Alice sponsor) (26 Lower Sloane Street, S.W.).

5d. Lady Florence Mary Bootle-Wilbraham, m. 16 Aug. 1887, the Rev. Lord William Rupert Ernest Gascoyne Cecil (St. Audrey's, Hatfield, Herts); and has issue.
See p. 216, Nos. 7658–7663.   [Nos. 26876 to 26914.

---

[1] For whose descent from George (Plantagenet), Duke of Clarence, see the Clarence Volume, Table VI. and p. 96.

# of The Blood Royal

6d. Lady Bertha Mabel Bootle-Wilbraham (77 *Cadogan Gardens, S.W.*), *m.* 9 May 1903, Major Arthur Frederick Dawkins, 1st Batt. Northumberland Fusiliers, *d.* (in Mauritius) Mar. 1905; and has issue 1e.

1e. Edith Dawkins, *b.* 24 May 1904.

6c. Lady Emily Theresa Villiers (19 *Stratford Place, W.; Ampthill Park, Ampthill*), *m.* 5 May 1868, Odo William Leopold (Russell), 1st Baron Ampthill [U.K.], H.B.M.'s Ambassador in Berlin 1871–18—, *d.* 25 Aug. 1884; and has issue. See the Clarence Volume, p. 74, Nos. 51–59.

2b. Hon. Edward Ernest Villiers, *b.* 23 Mar. 1806; *d.* 30 Oct. 1843; *m.* 1 Aug. 1835, the Hon. Elizabeth Charlotte, *da.* of Thomas Henry (*Liddell*), 1st Baron Ravensworth [U.K.], *d.* 15 Ap. 1890; and had issue. See the Clarence Volume, pp. 96–97, Nos. 763–799.

3b. Right Rev. the Hon. Henry Montagu Villiers, D.D., Bishop of Durham, *b.* 4 Jan. 1813; *d.* 9 Aug. 1861; *m.* 30 Jan. 1837, Amelia Maria, *da.* of William Hulton of Hulton Park, *d.* 5 Feb. 1871; and had issue 1c to 6c.

1c. Rev. Henry Montagu Villiers, M.A., Vicar of St. Paul's, Knightsbridge, and Preb. of St. Paul's, &c. (*St. Paul's Vicarage, Wilton Place, S.W.*), *b.* 13 Nov. 1837; *m.* 1st, 16 Ap. 1861, Lady Victoria, *da.* of John (Russell), 1st Earl Russell [U.K.], K.G., *b.* 20 Oct. 1838; *d.* 9 May 1880; 2ndly, 9 Jan. 1883, Charlotte Louisa Emily, *da.* of the Hon. Frederick William Cadogan; and has issue 1d to 15d.

1d. Henry Montagu Villiers, H.B.M.'s Consul in the Faroe Islands, Consul at Stockholm, Sweden (*Thorshaven, Faroe Islands*), *b.* 30 Mar. 1863; *m.* 7 Ap. 1896, Carmen, *da.* of Dr. Luhrsen, H.I.M.'s [German] Minister to Colombia; and has issue 1e to 3e.

1e. Cecil Montagu John Villiers, *b.* 24 Jan. 1897.

2e. George Dumba Villiers, *b.* 6 Mar. 1900.

3e. Victoria Mary Villiers, *b.* 1 Aug. 1903.

2d. John Russell Villiers (49 *Hans Place, S.W.*), *b.* 15 Jan. 1866; *m.* 19 Ap. 1893, Grace Elizabeth, *da.* of Major-Gen. William Earle, C.B., C.S.I.; and has issue 1e to 3e.

1e. Arthur Henry Villiers, *b.* 27 Mar. 1894.

2e. William Earle Villiers, *b.* 6 Jan. 1897.

3e. John Michael Villiers, *b.* 22 Oct. 1899.

3d. Thomas Lister Villiers (*Dickoya, Ceylon*), *b.* 31 Oct. 1869; *m.* 4 Nov. 1896, Evelyn, *da.* of William Higgin Walker of Newara Ellyia, Ceylon; and has issue 1e to 2e.

1e. Henry Lister Villiers, *b.* 21 July 1897.

2e. Thomas Hyde Villiers, *b.* 15 Jan. 1902.

4d. Godfrey Robert Randall Villiers (*Dickoya, Ceylon*), *b.* 22 Aug. 1877.

5d. Paul Frederick Villiers, 2nd Lieut. 14th Hussars, *b.* 8 July 1884.

6d. Gerald Berkeley Villiers, Sub.-Lieut. R.N., *b.* 14 June 1885.

7d. Oliver George Graham Villiers, *b.* 28 June 1886.

8d. Francis Edward Earle Villiers, *b.* 1 Jan. 1889.

9d. Frances Adelaide Villiers (44 *Great Cumberland Place, W.*), *b.* 19 Mar. 1862; *m.* 6 June 1893, Arthur Francis Walrond, *d.* 17 Jan. 1906.

10d. Gwendolen Mary Villiers, *b.* 25 Mar. 1864.

11d. Margaret Evelyn Villiers, *b.* 17 Feb. 1871.

12d. Dorothy Villiers, *b.* 28 Ap. 1872; *m.* 27 July 1898, the Rev. William Frederick Herbert Randolph, Vicar of Frome Selwood (*Frome Selwood Vicarage*).

13d. Mabel Agatha Villiers, *b.* 3 Jan. 1874.

14d. Katherine Helen Villiers, *b.* 30 Mar. 1875.

15d. Edith Mary Villiers, *b.* 24 Sept. 1887.

2c. Frederick Ernest Villiers, Major Herts Yeo. Cav., J.P., one of H.M.'s Body

[Nos. 26915 to 26989.

The Plantagenet Roll

Guard of Scottish Archers (*The Shieling, Ayr;* 18 *Cadogan Square, S.W.*), *b.* 16 Nov. 1840; *m.* 20 July 1869, Jane Isabella, da. and co-h. of Douglas Baird of Closeburn; and has issue 1*d* to 6*d*.

1*d*. George Frederick Montagu Villiers, Capt. 3rd Batt. Royal Scots Fusiliers (*Marlborough; New (Edinburgh)*), *b.* 13 Sept. 1870.

2*d*. Charles Walter Villiers, *late* Lieut. 3rd Batt. Royal Scots Fusiliers, *b.* 23 Sept. 1873; *m.* 1 Aug. 1903, Lady Kathleen Mary, da. of Lowry Egerton (Cole), 4th Earl of Enniskillen [I.]; and has issue (a da.).

3*d*. Reginald Hyde Villiers, D.S.O., *late* Lieut. 12th Lancers and Thornycroft's Mounted Inf., *b.* 4 Aug. 1876.

4*d*. Evelyn Charles Arthur Villiers, *b.* 15 July 1884.

5*d*. Florence Katherine Villiers, *b.* 6 Mar. 1872; *m.* 31 Aug. 1893, Henry Robert Baird (*Durris, Kincardine*); and has issue 1*e* to 3*e*.

1*e*. Robert Ian Baird, *b.* 1894.

2*e*. Douglas Montagu Baird, *b.* 1897.

3*e*. Kenneth Alexander Baird, *b.* 1899.

6*d*. Freda Ernestine Villiers, *b.* 8 May 1879.

3*c*. Amy Maria Villiers, *m.* 11 Ap. 1860, the Rev. Edward Cheese, M.A., Rector of Haughton-le-Skerne, *d.* 1886; and has issue 1*d* to 4*d*.

1*d*. Helen Maud Amy Cheese, *m.* 1883, Thomas Clennell Fenwick-Clennell, J.P., D.L. (*Harbottle Castle, Rothbury*); and has issue 1*e* to 6*e*.

1*e*. Thomas Percival Edward Fenwick-Clennell, *b.* 1886.

2*e*. Edward Clennell Fenwick-Clennell, *b.* 1892.

3*e*. Geoffrey Edward Fenwick-Clennell, *b.* 1896.

4*e*. Christopher Edward Fenwick-Clennell, *b.* 1900.

5*e*. Constance Maud Fenwick-Clennell.

6*e*. Frances Amy Fenwick-Clennell.

2*d*. Alice Helen Mary Cheese.

3*d*. Amy Theresa Edith Cheese, *m.* 14 July 1897, Edward A. Armfield-Marrow, Bar.-at-Law (70 *Evelyn Gardens, S.W.;* 2 *Garden Court, Temple, E.C.*); and has issue 1*e* to 2*e*.

1*e*. Edith Vera Armfield-Marrow, *b.* June 1900.

2*e*. Kinbarra Armfield-Marrow, *b.* Aug. 1904.

4*d*. Helena Gwendolen Evelyn Cheese, *m.* 1st, 25 July 1899, Denis Jerome Murch, Lieut. R.A., *d.* 27 Ap. 1900; 2ndly, 5 Aug. 1903, Arthur Harold Oscar Bliss (49 *Evelyn Gardens, S.W.*); and has issue 1*e*.

1*e*. Rupert Geoffrey Bliss, *b.* 9 June 1905.

4*c*. Gertrude Fanny Villiers, *m.* 22 Aug. 1865, Berkeley Paget (20 *Lexham Gardens, W.*); and has issue 1*d* to 8*d*.

1*d*. Leopold Cecil Paget (*Harewood, Leeds*), *b.* 26 Jan. 1871; *m.* 1 July 1897, Christina Jessie, da. of S. Mackenzie; and has issue 1*e* to 4*e*.

1*e*. Berkeley Paget, *b.* 1 Aug. 1898.

2*e*. Edward Catesby Paget, *b.* 7 Ap. 1903.

3*e*. Evelyn Mary Paget, *b.* 13 Feb. 1901.

4*e*. Rachel Paget, *b.* 14 Mar. 1906.

2*d*. Rev. Ernest Villiers Paget, B.A. (Camb.), Curate of St. Bartholomew, Brighton, *b.* 10 Ap. 1872.

3*d*. Algernon Berkeley Paget, *b.* 1 Nov. 1877.

4*d*. Eleanor Frances Paget, *b.* 12 Aug. 1866.

5*d*. Sybil Mary Paget, *b.* 9 Aug. 1869.

6*d*. Mildred Florence Paget, *b.* 3 Sept. 1873.   [Nos. 26990 to 27023.

7*d*. *Florinda Frances Paget*, b. 23 *July* 1875; d. 16 *Mar.* 1901; m. *as 1st wife*, 16 Nov. 1899, *John Kenneth Crawley, Lieut. R.N.; and had issue 1e.*

1*e*. Sybil Inez Crawley, *b*. 28 Aug. 1900.

8*d*. Inez Gertrude Paget, *b*. 26 July 1881, *m*. 12 Jan. 1905, Comm. Cole Cortlandt Fowler, R.N.; and has issue 1*e*.

1*e*. Florinda Gertrude Fowler, *b*. 12 Jan. 1906.

5*c*. Mary Agneta Villiers, *m*. 4 Ap. 1872, the Rev. James Hughes Cooper, Vicar of Cuckfield and Hon. Canon of Chester (*Cuckfield Vicarage, Sussex*); and has issue 1*d* to 2*d*.

1*d*. Wilbraham Villiers Cooper (*Chinthurst Hill, near Guildford*), *b*. 8 Mar. 1876; *m*. 2 Feb. 1902, the Hon. Rose Ellen, widow of Harry Chester Goodhart, Fellow of Trin. Coll., Camb., and Prof. of Humanity in Edin. Uni., da. of Stuart (Rendel), 1st Baron Rendel [U.K.].

2*d*. Marion Helen Cooper.

6*c*. Evelyn Theresa Villiers (21 *Lexham Gardens, S.W.*).

4*b*. *Lady Maria Theresa Villiers*, b. 8 *Mar.* 1803; d. 9 *Nov.* 1865; m. 6 *Nov.* 1830, *Thomas Henry Lister of Armetage Park, co. Stafford, Registrar-Gen. of Births, Marriages, and Deaths, author of "Granby," &c.*, b. 1800; d. 5 *June* 1842; 2*ndly*, 26 Oct. 1844, *the Right Hon. Sir George Cornewall Lewis, 2nd Bart.* [U.K.], M.P., b. 21 Oct. 1806; d. 13 *Ap.* 1863; *and had issue 1c to 3c.*

1*c*. *Sir Thomas Villiers Lister of Armitage Hill, co. Berks, K.C.M.G., Assist. Under-Sec. of State for Foreign Office,* b. 7 *May* 1832; d. 26 Feb. 1902; m. 1*st*, 30 Oct. 1862, *Fanny Harriet, da. of William Coryton of Pentillie, co. Cornwall,* d. 14 *Feb.* 1875; 2*ndly*, 10 *Jan.* 1877, *Florence Selina, sister of Alexander Charles, 10th Lord Belhaven and Stenton* [S.], *da. of Lieut.-Col. William John Hamilton, F.R.S., M.P.,* d. 6 *Aug.* 1904; *and had issue 1d to 11d.*

1*d*. *George Coryton-Lister, Major King's Royal Rifle Corps,* b. 18 Nov. 1863; d. 20 *May* 1903; m. 18 *June* 1898, *Lady Evelyn Selina* (50 *Warwick Square, S.W.; Armitage Hill, Ascot*), *da. of Allen Alexander* (*Bathurst*), 6*th Earl Bathurst* [G.B.]; *and had issue 1e to 2e.*

1*e*. Martin Douglas Coryton-Lister, *b*. 6 May 1899.

2*e*. Stella Evelyn Coryton-Lister, *b*. 27 Jan. 1901.

2*d*. Edmund Algernon Coryton-Lister, *b*. 2 Ap. 1870.

3*d*. Harry Coryton-Lister.

4*d*. Frederick Hamilton Coryton-Lister, Lieut. R.A., *b*. 5 Dec. 1880.

5*d*. Algernon Coryton-Lister, *b*. 9 Mar. 1887.

6*d*.[1] Maria Theresa Lister, *m*. 21 May 1890, Ernest Farquhar; and has issue 1*e* to 2*e*.

1*e*. Harold Lister Farquhar, *b*. 15 Ap. 1894.

2*e*. Rupert Lister Farquhar, *b*. 7 July 1897.

7*d*.[1] Katherine Lister, *m*. 3 Aug. 1899, the Hon. Harold Albert Denison, Lieut. R.N.; and has issue 1*e*.

1*e*. John Albert Lister Denison, *b*. 30 May 1901.

8*d*.[1] Constance Mary Lister, *m*. 20 Ap. 1892, James Frederick Maximilian Hartmann; and has issue 1*e* to 3*e*.

1*e*. James Frederick Lister Hartmann, *b*. 25 Feb. 1893.

2*e*. Robert Alexander Lister Hartmann, *b*. 5 Jan. 1896.

3*e*. Henry Felix Lister Hartmann, *b*. 29 May 1901.

9*d*. Mary Florence Lister, *b*. 12 July 1879.

10*d*. Christina Sybil Lister, *b*. 25 Dec. 1881.

11*d*. Margaret Evelyn Lister, *b*. 1 Ap. 1886.

2*c*. *Marie Theresa Lister*, d. 1 *Feb.* 1863; m. *as 1st wife*, 5 *Nov.* 1859, *the*
[Nos. 27024 to 27048.

The Plantagenet Roll

Right Hon. Sir William George Granville Venables-Vernon-Harcourt, P.C., M.P., b. 14 Oct. 1827; d. 1 Oct. 1904; *and had issue* 1d.

    1d. Right Hon. Lewis Harcourt, P.C., M.P., First Commissioner of Works (14 *Berkeley Square, W.; Nuneham Park, Oxford; Stanton Harcourt, Eynsham*), b. 1 Feb. 1863; m. 1 July 1899, Mary Ethel, da. of Walter H. Burns of New York, U.S.A., and North Mymms Park, Hatfield; and has issue 1e to 3e.

        1e. Doris Mary Theresa Harcourt, b. 30 Mar. 1900.

        2e. Olivia Vernon Harcourt, b. 5 Ap. 1902.

        3e. Barbara Vernon Harcourt, b. 28 Ap. 1905.

    3c. *Alice Beatrice Lister,* d. 28 *Mar.* 1898; m. 5 *Ap.* 1870, *Algernon* (*Borthwick*), 1st Baron Glenesk [U.K.], Proprietor of "The Morning Post" (139 *Piccadilly, W.; Château St. Michel, Cannes*); and had issue 1d.

        1d. Hon. Lilias Margaret Frances Borthwick, m. 15 Nov. 1893, Seymour Henry (Bathurst), 7th Earl Bathurst [G.B.], C.M.G. (*Cirencester House, Cirencester; 22 Bruton Street, W.*); and has issue 1e to 4e.

        1e–4e. See the Clarence Volume, p. 637, Nos. 28838–28841.

                                        [Nos. 27049 to 27057.

302. Descendants of Lady MARY CAPEL (see Table XXVII.), b. 13 Oct. 1722; d. 9 Ap. 1782; m. 26 Aug. 1758, Admiral the Hon. JOHN FORBES, d. 10 Mar. 1796; and had issue 1a.

    1a. *Catherine Elizabeth Forbes,* b. (*twin*) 1760; d. 23 *Oct.* 1851; m. 17 *May* 1784, *William* (*Wellesley, afterwards* (1778) *Wellesley-Pole*), 3rd Earl of Mornington [I.], 1st Baron Maryborough [U.K.], b. 20 May 1763; d. 22 Feb. 1845; *and had issue* 1b *to* 4b.

        1b. *William* (*Wellesley-Pole, afterwards* (R.L. 14 *Jan.* 1812) *Pole-Tylney-Long-Wellesley*), 4th Earl of Mornington [I.], 2nd Baron Maryborough [U.K.], b. 22 *June* 1788; d. 1 *July* 1857; m. 1st, 14 *May* 1812, *Catherine,* da. *and eventual h. of Sir James Tylney-Long,* 8th Bart. [E.], d. 12 Sept. 1825; *and had issue* 1c.

        1c. *William Richard Arthur* (*Tylney-Long-Wellesley*), 5th Earl of Mornington [I.], 3rd Baron Maryborough [U.K.], b. 7 Oct. 1813; d. unm. (at Paris) 25 July 1863.

        2b. *Lady Mary Charlotte Anne Wellesley-Pole,* b. 5 *May* 1786; d. 2 Feb. 1845; m. 22 July 1806, the Right Hon. Sir Charles Bagot, G.C.B., Gov.-Gen. of Canada, &c., b. 23 Sept. 1781; d. 19 May 1843; *and had issue.*

    See the Clarence Volume, p. 492, No. 21377.

        3b. *Lady Emily Harriet Wellesley-Pole,* b. 13 *Mar.* 1792; d. 6 *Mar.* 1881; m. 13 *Mar.* 1814, *FitzRoy James Henry* (*Somerset*), 1st Baron Raglan [U.K.], G.C.B., Field-Marshal, &c. &c., b. 30 Sept. 1788; d. (*before Sebastopol*) 28 *June* 1855; *and had issue.*

    See the Clarence Volume, p. 335, Nos. 9939–9952.

        4b. *Lady Priscilla Anne Wellesley-Pole,* b. 13 *Mar.* 1793; d. 18 Feb. 1879; m. 26 *June* 1811, *John* (*Fane*), 11th Earl of Westmorland [E.], G.C.B., b. 3 Feb. 1784; d. 16 Oct. 1859; *and had issue.*

    See the Clarence Volume, p. 599, Nos. 26282–26296.   [Nos. 27058 to 27087.

303. Descendants, if any, of Lady ELIZABETH CAPEL (see Table XXVII.), d. 21 Mar. 1759; m. 1st, 5 Ap. 1727, the Right Hon. SAMUEL MOLINEUX, Secretary to George, Prince of Wales, *afterwards* George II., *d.s.p.* 1727; 2ndly, 27 May 1730, NATHANIEL ST. ANDRÉ.

LADY ELIZABETH DELMÉ.
WITH HER TWO CHILDREN JOHN AND EMILIUS HENRY
AFTER SIR JOSHUA REYNOLDS
THE COMMON ANCESTORS OF Nº⁵ 28098 - 28169.

# of The Blood Royal

304. Descendants of GEORGE (BRODRICK), 3rd VISCOUNT MIDLETON [I.] (see Table XXVII.), *b.* 3 Oct. 1730; *d.* 22 Aug. 1765; *m.* 1 May 1752, Albinia, da. of the Hon. Thomas TOWNSHEND, M.P., *d.* 18 Sept. 1808; and had issue.

See the Clarence Volume, pp. 587–590, Nos. 24801–24984.

[Nos. 27088 to 27271.

305. Descendants of FREDERICK (HOWARD), 5th EARL OF CARLISLE [E.], K.G., K.T. (see Table XXVII.), *b.* 28 May 1748; *d.* 4 Feb. 1825; *m.* 22 Mar. 1770, Lady MARGARET CAROLINE, da. of Granville (LEVESON-GOWER), 1st Marquis of Stafford [G.B.], *b.* 2 Nov. 1753; *d.* 27 Jan. 1824; and had issue.

See the Tudor Roll of "The Blood Royal of Britain," Table LXXXV. and pp. 376–379, Nos. 28395–28982. [Nos. 27272 to 27860.

306. Descendants of Lady ARABELLA HOWARD (see Table XXVII.), *d.* 1746; *m.* as 1st wife, 14 Sept. 1741, JONATHAN COPE, *jure uxoris*, of Overton Longueville; and had issue.

See pp. 307–308, Nos. 19259–19415. [Nos. 27861 to 28019.

307. Descendants of Lady DIANA HOWARD (see Table XXVII.), *d.* 6 Mar. 1770; *m.* as 1st wife, 1740, THOMAS DUNCOMBE of Duncombe and Helmesley, co. York, *d.* 1799; and had issue.

See p. 308, Nos. 19416–19495. [Nos. 28020 to 28097.

308. Descendants of Lady ELIZABETH HOWARD, the beauty of the Court of Queen Charlotte (see Table XXVII.), *b.* 1746; *d.* June 1813; *m.* 1st, 16 Feb. 1769, PETER DELMÉ of Titchfield Place, co. Hants, M.P., *b.* 19 Dec. 1748; *d.* 5 Sept. 1789; 2ndly, 7 Jan. 1794, Capt. CHARLES GARNIER, R.N., *d.* 16 Dec. 1796; and had issue 1*a* to 2*a*.

1*a*. *John Delmé of Cams Hall*, b. 25 *July* 1772; d. 10 *May* 1809; m. 1791, *Frances, da. of George Charles Garnier of Rookesbury, co. Hants, d. 18 Aug. 1841; and had issue.*
See the Clarence Volume, pp. 511–512, Nos. 22103–22135.

2*a*. *Emilius Henry Delmé, afterwards* (1802) *Delmé-Radcliffe*, b. 28 *Mar.* 1774; d. 26 *Feb.* 1832; m. 27 *July* 1802, *Anne Melicent, da. and eventual h. of Charles Clarke of Addiscombe, by Anne, da. and eventual h. of John Radcliffe of Hitchin Priory, d. 1808; and had issue 1b to 2b.*

1*b*. *Frederick Peter Delmé-Radcliffe of Hitchin Priory, J.P., D.L.,* b. 18 *Dec.* 1804; d. 30 *Nov.* 1875; m. 14 *Ap.* 1831, *Emma, da. of John H. Waddington of Languish House, Petersfield, d. 25 Jan.* 1880; *and had issue 1c to 6c.*

1*c*. *Hubert Delmé-Radcliffe of Hitchin Priory, J.P.,* b. 27 *Mar.* 1839; d.s.p. 13 *Oct.* 1878.

2*c*. Francis Augustus Delmé-Radcliffe, J.P., Comm. R.N. (*Hitchin Priory, co. Herts*), *b.* 1 June 1845; *m.* 14 Ap. 1874, Georgy Melosina Mary Elizabeth, da. of Adm. Sir Charles Talbot, K.C.B., R.N. [Nos. 28098 to 28131.

385

The Plantagenet Roll

3c. Rev. Arthur Henry Delmé-Radcliffe, M.A., b. 21 June 1850; d. 11 Aug. 1896; m. 26 Jan. 1875, Beatrice Mary Frederica (4 Stanhope Gardens, S.W.), da. of the Hon. Frederick Dudley Ryder; and had issue 1d to 4d.

1d. Ralph Hubert John Delmé-Radcliffe, b. 11 Oct. 1877.

2d. Arthur Frederick Delmé-Radcliffe, b. 24 Jan. 1880.

3d. Beatrice Alice Delmé-Radcliffe, b. 22 Oct. 1875.

4d. Evelyn Penelope Delmé-Radcliffe, b. 22 Ap. 1873.

4c. Mellicent Delmé-Radcliffe, m. 11 Sept. 1858, Richard Rogers of Cottishall, co. Norfolk.

5c. Alice Delmé-Radcliffe, m. 24 Ap. 1862, Albert Frederic Hurt, J.P., D.L., Major and Hon. Lieut.-Col. (ret.) 3rd Batt. Derbyshire Regt. (Alderwasley, Matlock, Derby); and has issue 1d to 5d.

1d. Francis Cecil Albert Hurt, Lieut. Royal Welsh Fusiliers, b. 11 Mar. 1878; m. 16 Ap. 1903, Isabel Clara, da. of Herbert Strutt of Makemy, co. Derby; and has issue 1e.

1e. Francis George Hurt, b. 4 Jan. 1904.

2d. Seymour Frederic Auckland Albert Hurt, Lieut. Royal Scots Fusiliers, b. 18 Oct. 1879.

3d. Henry Albert le Fowne Hurt, Lieut. R.N., b. 5 Sept. 1881.

4d. Ralph Anthony Lowe Ponsonby Hurt, b. 1 Ap. 1885.

5d. Grace Emma Julia Hurt, m. 10 June 1902, Bertram Harry Godfrey Arkwright; and has issue 1e to 2e.

1e. Robert Harry Bertram Arkwright, b. 30 July 1903.

2e. Francis Godfrey Bertram Arkwright, b. 30 Jan. 1905.

6c. Constance Louisa Delmé-Radcliffe, m. 15 Jan. 1869, Charles William Talbot-Ponsonby, previously Talbot of Imokelly (Langrish House, Petersfield); and has issue.

See the Clarence Volume, p. 336, Nos. 9961–9967.

2b. Rev. Charles Delmé-Radcliffe, Rector of Holywell, co. Beds., b. 1 Feb. 1806; d. 1865; m. 14 Sept. 1831, Elizabeth, da. of John Delmé of Cams Hall, d. 31 Aug. 1879; and had issue.

See the Clarence Volume, p. 511, Nos. 22103–22118.   [Nos. 28132 to 28169.

309. Descendants, if any, of Lady ANNE HOWARD, the well-known poetess (see Table XXVII.), b. a. 1696; d. (–); m. 1st, RICHARD (INGRAM), 5th VISCOUNT IRVINE [S.], b. 6 Jan. 1688; d.s.p. 10 Ap. 1721; 2ndly, 11 June 1737, Col. JAMES DOUGLAS.

310. Descendants of the Hon. MARY CAPELL (see Table XXVII.), bapt. 16 Dec. 1630; d. 7 Jan. 1715; m. 1st, 28 June 1648, HENRY SEYMOUR, Lord BEAUCHAMP, b. c. 1626; d.v.p. bur. 30 Mar. 1654; 2ndly, 17 Aug. 1657, HENRY (SOMERSET), 1st DUKE OF BEAUFORT [E.], K.G., b. 1629; d. 21 Jan. 1700; and had issue 1a to 4a.

1a. William (Seymour), 3rd Duke of Somerset [E.], d. unm. 12 Dec. 1671.

2a. Charles Somersét, Marquis of Worcester, b. Dec. 1660; d.v.p. 13 July 1698; m. 5 June 1682, Rebecca, da. of Sir Josiah Child of Wanstead, Essex, d. 17 July 1712.

See the Clarence Volume, Table XXXV. and pp. 327–355, Nos. 9506–12162.
[Nos. 28170 to 30823.

# of The Blood Royal

3a. Lord Arthur Somerset, d. (–); m. *Mary, widow of Hugh Calveley Cotton, da. and h. of Sir William Russell, 1st Bart.* [E.]; *and had issue.*
See the Clarence Volume, Table XXXVIII. and pp. 355–362, Nos. 12163–12397.

4a. Lady (R.W. 28 *June* 1672) *Elizabeth Seymour,* d. 12 *Jan.* 1697; m. *as 1st wife,* 31 *Aug. or* 30 *Oct.* 1676, *Thomas (Bruce), 3rd Earl of Elgin* [S.], *2nd Earl of Ailesbury* [E.], b. 1656; d. *Nov.* 1741; *and had issue.*
See the Tudor Roll of "The Blood Royal of Britain," Table XIV. and pp. 151–186, Nos. 19573–20945. [Nos. 30824 to 32427.

311. Descendants of Lady ELIZABETH DORMER (see Table XXVII.), *d.* 1679; *m.* as 3rd wife, PHILIP (STANHOPE), 2nd EARL CHESTERFIELD [E.], *d.* 28 Jan. 1714.

See the Clarence Volume, Table VI. and pp. 102–106, Nos. 913–1036.
[Nos. 32428 to 32551.

312. Descendants of JOHN (BLIGH), 3rd EARL OF DARNLEY [I.], 12th BARON CLIFTON of Leighton Bromswold [E.] (see Table XXVII.), *b.* 28 Sept. 1719; *d.* 31 July 1781; *m.* 11 Sept. 1766, MARY, da. and h. of John STOYTE of Street, co. Westmeath, *d.* 27 Mar. 1803; and had issue 1*a* to 3*a*.

1a. John (Bligh), 4th Earl of Darnley [I.], *13th Baron Clifton* [E.], b. 30 *June* 1767; d. 17 *Mar.* 1831; m. 26 *Aug.* 1791, *Elizabeth, da. of the Right Hon. William Brownlow of Lurgan,* d. 22 *Dec.* 1831; *and had issue* 1*b* to 4*b*.

1b. Edward (Bligh), 5th Earl of Darnley [I.], *14th Baron Clifton* [E.], b. 25 *Feb.* 1795; d. 12 *Feb.* 1835; m. 26 *July* 1825, *the Hon. Emma Jane, da. of Henry (Parnell), 1st Baron Congleton* [I.], d. 15 *Mar.* 1884; *and had issue.*
See the Clarence Volume, p. 288, Nos. 7760–7817.

2b. Hon. Sir John Duncan Bligh, K.C.B., D.C.L., b. 11 *Oct.* 1798; d. 8 *May* 1872; m. 1*st,* 19 *Dec.* 1835, *Elizabeth Mary, da. of Thomas Gisborne, M.P.,* d. 22 *July* 1837; *and had issue* 1*c.*

1c. Elizabeth Mary Bligh (Enbrook, Sandgate), m. 18 June 1861, Walter John (Pelham), 4th Earl of Chichester [U.K.], 5th Baron Pelham [G.B.], *b.* 22 Sept. 1838; *d.s.p.* 28 May 1902.

3b. Lady Mary Bligh, b. 1 *June* 1796; d. 18 *June* 1823; m. *as 1st wife,* 1 *June* 1822, *Charles (Brownlow), afterwards 1st Baron Lurgan* [U.K.], b. 17 *Ap.* 1795; d. 30 *Ap.* 1847; *and had issue* 1*c.*

1c. Hon. Mary Elizabeth Brownlow, b. 27 *May* 1823; d. 30 *July* 1888; m. 8 *May* 1848, *Robert Peel Dawson of Castle Dawson, co. Londonderry, M.P.,* b. 2 *June* 1818; d. 2 *Sept.* 1877; *and had issue* 1*d.*

1d. Mary Dawson (Moyda Park, Castle Dawson, Londonderry), m. 9 Oct. 1872, Lord Adolphus John Spencer Churchill Chichester, *d.* 5 Mar. 1901; and has issue.
See p. 368, Nos. 26551–26554.

4b. Lady Elizabeth Bligh, b. 7 *May* 1800; d. 13 *Nov.* 1872; m. 19 *July* 1833, *the Rev. John Brownlow, Dean of Clonmacnoise,* d. 24 *May* 1882; *and had issue.*
See p. 206, Nos. 7374–7376.

2a. Hon. William Bligh, Col. in the Army, b. 25 *Sept.* 1775; d. 6 *Aug.* 1745; m. 21 *July* 1806, *Lady Georgiana Charlotte Sophia, da. of John (Stewart), 7th Earl of Galloway* [S.], d. *(at Madeira)* 1809; *and had issue.*
See the Tudor Roll of "The Blood Royal of Britain," p. 514, Nos. 34637–34660. [Nos. 32552 to 32641.

The Plantagenet Roll

3a. *Lady Theodosia Bligh*, b. 29 Feb. 1771; d. 21 Jan. 1840; m. 3 Nov. 1790, *Thomas Cherburgh Bligh of Brittas*, d. 17 Sept. 1830; *and had issue* 1b *to* 3b.

1b. *Edward Bligh of Brittas*, D.L., b. 1799; d. 11 Ap. 1872; m. 1827, Sophia, *da. of Charles Markwick Eversfield of Dene Park; and had issue* 1c *to* 2c.

1c. *Frederick Cherburgh Bligh of Brittas, Major 41st Regt.*, b. 23 Ap. 1829; d. 30 Nov. 1901; m. 14 Sept. 1858, *Emily Matilda, da. of Hinton East; and had issue* 1d *to* 4d.

1d. Frederick Arthur Bligh of Brittas, J.P., Capt. R.A., b. 3 July 1861; m. 22 June 1898, Mary Wentworth, da. of Lieut.-Gen. Wentworth Forbes; and has issue.

2d. Eva Sophia Bligh.

3d. Ada Theodosia Bligh.

4d. Eldina Mary Bligh.

2c. *Theodosia Bligh*, d. (-); m. 1850, *Edward Tredcroft, D.L., of Horsham, Sussex*, b. 15 Dec. 1828; *and had issue* 1d *to* 2d.

1d. Henry Edward Tredcroft, b. Mar. 1853; m. Dec. 1877, Mabel, da. of the Hon. Sir Gillery Pigott of Sherfield Hall, co. Hants; and has issue 1e to 4e.

1e. Lancelot Edward Bligh Tredcroft, b. Oct. 1878.

2e. Arthur Francis Drake Tredcroft, b. July 1880.

3e. Edith Barbara Tredcroft.

4e. Mabel Alice Tredcroft.

2d. Theodosia Isabella Tredcroft, m. 1870, Dennis Lambart Higgins.

2b. *Charles Bligh*, b. 15 Dec. 1808; d. 1892; m. 11 July 1837, *Fanny Catherine, da. of Vice-Adm. Sir William George Parker, 2nd Bart.* [G.B.], d. 7 Jan. 1894; *and had issue* 1c *to* 5c.

1c. William George Bligh.

2c. Elizabeth Bligh.

3c. Sophia Henrietta Bligh, m. 23 May 1866, John Gillett Livesay; and has issue (10 children).

4c. *Emily Rose Bligh*, d. 23 Oct. 1893; m. 1 May 1878, *Robert Vesey Stoney, J.P., D.L.* (*Rosturk Castle, co. Mayo; Knockadoo, Roscommon*).

5c. Georgina Theodosia Bligh.

3b. *Elizabeth Bligh*, d. 3 Jan. 1855; m. 1st, 1828, *John Cuming of Dublin, Bar.-at-Law*, d. 1 Aug. 1831; 2ndly, 10 May 1838, *John Fountain Elwin, F.R.C.P.; and had issue* (*with 2 sons by 2nd husband*) 1c.

1c. *Elizabeth Cuming*, m. 21 May 1850, *Capt. Edward Foley, R.N.*, b. 29 Oct. 1807; d. Sept. 1894; *and had issue* 1d *to* 9d.

1d. Ernest Edward Foley, Capt. Midx. Regt., b. 18 Jan. 1854; m. 30 Nov. 1879, Olivia Anna, da. of the Rev. John Fenlay of Corkagh, co. Dublin; and has issue.

2d. Arthur Paul Foley, B.A. (Oxon.), b. 1860.

3d. George Loftus Foley, b. 1861.

4d. Frank Wigram Foley, D.S.O., Capt. Royal Berks Regt., b. 24 June 1865; m. 5 Aug. 1903, Eva Mary Fitz-Hardinge (Milman), *suo jure* 21st Baroness Berkeley [E.] (*Martins Heron, Bracknell, Berks*); and has issue 1e.

1e. Hon. Mary Lalle Foley, b. 9 Oct. 1905.

5d. Fanny Isabella Foley.

6d. Elizabeth Bligh Foley, m. Nov. 1884, J. Henry Knight, *late* of Weybourne House, Surrey.

7d. Katherine Amelia Foley.

8d. Theodosia Sophia Foley.

9d. Margaret Alice Foley.

[Nos. 32642 to 32665.

388

# of The Blood Royal

313. Descendants of WILLIAM TIGHE of Rossana, co. Wicklow, M.P. (see Table XXVII.), *d.* 1782 ; *m.* 1765, SARAH, da. and h. of the Right Hon. Sir William FOWNES of Woodstock, co. Kilkenny (by his wife Lady Elizabeth, *née* Ponsonby), *d.* 1821 ; and had issue 1*a* to 3*a*.

1*a. William Tighe of Woodstock, M.P. [I. and U.K.],* b. 1766 ; d. 1816 ; *m.* 1793, *Marianne, da. and co-h. of Daniel Gahan of Coolquil, co. Tipperary, N.P. (by his wife Hannah, sister and co-h. of Matthew Bunbury of Kilfeache),* d. 1853 ; *and had issue 1b to 3b.*

1*b. Right Hon. William Frederick Fownes Tighe of Woodstock, P.C., M.P., Lord-Lieut. of Kilkenny, &c.,* d. 17 *Mar.* 1794 ; d.s.p. 1878.

2*b. Daniel Tighe of Rossana, J.P., D.L., High Sheriff co. Wicklow* 1827, d. 26 *Mar.* 1874 ; *m.* 3 *Mar.* 1825, *the Hon. Frances, da. of the Hon. Sir Edward Crofton, 3rd Bart.* [I.], d. 20 *Dec.* 1881 ; *and had issue.*

See the Tudor Roll of "The Blood Royal of Britain," p. 513, Nos. 34607–34633.

3*b. Hannah Tighe,* d. 5 *June* 1872 ; *m.* 13 *July* 1818, *Lord Patrick James Herbert Crichton-Stuart, M.P.,* d. 7 *Sept.* 1859 ; *and had issue.*

See p. 295, Nos. 14685–14696.

2*a. Elizabeth Tighe, m. the Rev. Thomas Kelly of Kellyville, Queen's co.*

3*a. Marianne Caroline Tighe,* b. c. 1777 ; d. 29 *July* 1861 ; *m.* 29 *Ap.* 1801, *Charles Hamilton of Hamwood, co. Meath,* b. 1772 ; d. 29 *Sept.* 1857 ; *and had issue 1b to 5b.*

1*b. Charles William Hamilton of Hamwood, J.P.,* b. 1 *Ap.* 1802 ; d. 16 *Feb.* 1880 ; *m.* 1 *June* 1841, *Letitia Charlotte, da. of William Henry Armstrong of Mount Heaton, M.P.,* d. 28 *June* 1872 ; *and had issue 1c to 3c.*

1*c.* Charles Robert Hamilton, J.P. (*Hamwood, Dunboyne, co. Meath*), *b.* 29 Aug. 1846 ; *m.* 10 Sept. 1874, Louisa Caroline Elizabeth, da. of Francis Brooke of Somerton, co. Dublin (by his wife the Hon. Henrietta, *née* Monck); and has issue 1*d* to 8*d.*

1*d.* Gerald Francis Charles Hamilton, *b.* 23 June 1877.

2*d.* Frederick Arthur Hamilton, *b.* 15 Dec. 1880.

3*d.* Eva Henrietta Hamilton, *b.* 28 June 1876.

4*d.* Letitia Marion Hamilton, *b.* 20 July 1878.

5*d.* Amy Kathleen Hamilton, *b.* 24 July 1879.

6*d.* Ethel Grace Hamilton, *b.* 1 Ap. 1882.

7*d.* Constance Louisa Hamilton, *b.* 27 June 1883.

8*d.* Lilian Mary Hamilton, *b.* 26 June 1884.

2*c.* Edward Chetwood Hamilton, J.P., Major *late* 5th Royal Dublin Fusiliers (*Mamree, Inistioge, Kilkenny*), *b.* 23 Aug. 1847 ; *m.* 4 Jan. 1870, Eleanor Georgina Anna Blanche, da. of Col. George Gladwin Denniss, 101st R. Bengal Fusiliers ; and has issue 1*d* to 4*d.*

1*d.* George Chetwood Digby Hamilton, *b.* 29 July 1874.

2*d.* Blanche Letitia Hamilton, *b.* 1 Nov. 1870.

3*d.* Eleanor Georgina Hamilton, *b.* 2 Oct. 1871.

4*d.* Kathleen Maud Albina Hamilton, *b.* 30 Sept. 1877.

3*c.* Arthur Hamilton, J.P., *late* Lieut. 12th Regt. (*Hollybrook, co. Dublin*), *b.* 16 Aug. 1848 ; *m.* 29 Oct. 1874, Alma Louisa Geraldine Isabella, da. of Edward Croker of Ballynagarde (by his wife Lady Georgiana, *née* Monck) ; and has issue 1*d* to 7*d.*

1*d.* Alick Edward Croker Hamilton, *b.* 14 Mar. 1879.

2*d.* Robin Arthur Vesey Hamilton, *b.* 29 Feb. 1884.

3*d.* Eric Richard Monck Hamilton, *b.* 19 Sept. 1888. [Nos. 32666 to 32722.

The Plantagenet Roll

4d. Geoffrey Cecil Monck Hamilton, b. 8 Dec. 1894.

5d. Dorothea Alice Letitia Hamilton, b. 12 Oct. 1876.

6d. Rosalie Alma Georgiana Hamilton.

7d. Elsie Marguerite Monck Hamilton.

2b. *William Tighe Hamilton*, b. 31 *Mar.* 1807 ; d. 1886 ; m. 27 *Sept.* 1832, *the* Hon. *Anne Louisa, sister and co-h. of William, 3rd Baron Ponsonby* [*U.K.*], *da. of Major-Gen.* Sir *William Ponsonby, K.C.B.*, d. 23 *Jan.* 1863 ; *and had issue* 1c.

1c. Frederick FitzRoy Hamilton, b. 1837.

3b. *Frederick John Henry Fownes Hamilton*, b. 27 *July* 1816 ; d. 1893 ; m. 22 *May* 1860, *Frances Catharine, da. of Richard Gethin of Earlsfield, co. Sligo ; and had issue* 1c.

1c. *Adela Maude Gethin Hamilton*, d. 1890 ; m. 10 *Feb.* 1885, Sir *William Cecil Godfrey, 5th Bart.* [*I.*] (*Kilcoleman Abbey, Milltown, Kerry*); *and had issue* 1d.

1d. Phyllis Maud Mary Godfrey.

4b. *Sarah Hamilton*, d. 15 *Mar.* 1892 ; m. *as 2nd wife*, 21 *June* 1836, *Rev. the* Hon. *Francis Howard, Vicar of Swords*, b. 12 *Jan.* 1797 ; d. 16 *Feb.* 1857 ; *and had issue* 1c *to* 5c.

1c. *Charles Francis Arnold* (*Howard*), *5th Earl of Wicklow* [*I.*], b. 5 *Nov.* 1839 ; d. *unm.* 20 *June* 1881.

2c. *Cecil Ralph* (*Howard*), *6th Earl of Wicklow* [*I.*], b. 26 *Ap.* 1842 ; d. 24 *July* 1891 ; m. 1st, 23 *Mar.* 1876, *Francesca Maria, da. of Thomas Chamberlayne of Cranbury Park, co. Hants*, d. 30 *Dec.* 1877 ; 2ndly, 2 *June* 1880, *Fanny Catherine, da. of Richard Robert Wingfield* (*who re-m.* 10 *Ap.* 1894, *Marcus Francis Beresford*) ; *and had issue* 1d *to* 2d.

1d. Ralph Francis (Howard), 7th Earl of Wicklow [I.], Capt. 2nd Life Guards (*Shelton Abbey, Arklow, Wicklow*), b. 24 Dec. 1877 ; *m.* 14 Jan. 1902, Lady Gladys Mary, da. of James (Hamilton), 2nd Duke of Abercorn [I.], K.G., P.C. ; and has issue 1e.

1e. William Cecil James Howard, Lord Clonmore, b. 30 Oct. 1902.

2d. Hon. Hugh Melville Howard, b. 28 Mar. 1883.

3c.¹ Lady Caroline Louisa Howard, ⎫
4c.¹ Lady Louisa Frances Howard, ⎬ (*Wingfield, Bray, Wicklow*).
5c. Lady Alice Mary Howard, ⎭

5b. Caroline Susan Hamilton, b. May 1812 ; *m.* 1st, Capt. Trevor Stannus, 97th Regt., b. 1798 ; d. May 1844 ; 2ndly, 1849, the Rev. John William Finley of Corkagh, b. 1805 ; d. (*s.p.* by her) 1879.　　　　　　　　[Nos. 32723 to 32735.

314. Descendants of THEODOSIA TIGHE (see Table XXVII.), d. (–) ; m. the Rev. RICHARD BLACHFORD, d. and had issue 1a to 2a.

1a. *John Blachford of Altadore, co. Wicklow.*

2a. *Mary Blachford, a distinguished poetess*, d. 1810 ; m. *Henry Tighe, M.P.*, d.s.p. 1836.

315. Descendants of Lady ANNE BLIGH (see Table XXVII.), d. Feb. 1789 ; m. 1st, 17 Sept. 1742, ROBERT HAWKINS MAGILL of Gill Hall, co. Down, M.P., d. (–) ; 2ndly, Dec. 1747, BERNARD (WARD), 1st VISCOUNT BANGOR [I.], b. Aug. 1719 ; d. 20 May 1781 ; and had issue 1a to 5a.

1a–3a. (Sons by 2nd husband.) See the Clarence Volume, Table XXXII., pp. 275–285, Nos. 7342–7661.　　　　　　　　[Nos. 32736 to 33053.

# of The Blood Royal

4a. Theodosia Magill (da. and h. of 1st husband), b. 5 *Sept.* 1743; d. 2 *Mar.* 1817; m. 29 *Aug.* 1765, *John (Meade), 1st Earl of Clanwilliam [I.]*, b. 21 *Ap.* 1744; d. 19 *Oct.* 1800; *and had issue 1b to 7b.*

1b. *Richard (Meade), 2nd Earl of Clanwilliam [I.]*, b. 10 *May* 1766; d. 3 *Sept.* 1805; m. 1st (*at Tehuschitz, Bohemia*), 6 *Oct.* 1793, *the Countess Caroline of Thunn, da. of Joseph (von Thunn), Count of Thunn [H.R.E.]*, b. 18 *May* 1789; d. (*in Vienna*) 8 *Aug.* 1800; *and had issue 1c to 3c.*

1c. *Richard (Meade), 3rd Earl of Clanwilliam [I.], 1st Baron Clanwilliam [U.K.], G.C.H.*, b. 15 *Aug.* 1795; d. 7 *Aug.* 1879; m. 3 *July* 1830, *Lady Elizabeth, da. of George (Herbert), 11th Earl of Pembroke [E.]*, b. 31 *Mar.* 1809; d. 20 *Sept.* 1858; *and had issue 1d to 4d.*

1d. Richard James (Meade), 4th Earl of [I.] and 2nd Baron [U.K.] Clanwilliam, G.C.B., K.C., M.G., Admiral of the Fleet (*Gill Hall, Dromore, co. Down; 32 Belgrave Square, S.W.*), b. 3 Oct. 1832; *m.* 17 June 1867, Elizabeth Henrietta, da. of Sir Arthur Edward Kennedy, G.C.M.G., C.B., Governor of Queensland; and has issue.

See p. 150, Nos. 2252–2262.

2d. Hon. Sir Robert Henry Meade, G.C.B., b. 16 Dec. 1835; d. 8 *Jan.* 1898; m. 2ndly, 13 *Ap.* 1880, *Caroline Georgiana, da. of Charles William Grenfell, M.P.,* d. 5 *Mar.* 1881; *and had issue 1e.*

1e. Charles Francis Meade, b. 25 Feb. 1881.

3d. Rev. the Hon. Sidney Meade, Canon of Salisbury, J.P. (*Frankleigh House, Bradford-on-Avon*), b. 29 Oct. 1839; *m.* 9 Dec. 1868, Lucy Emma, da. of J. H. Jacob of The Close, Salisbury; and has issue 1e to 3e.

1e. Francis Henry Meade, Barrister (*7 New Square, Lincoln's Inn, W.C.*), b. 6 Dec. 1870; *m.* Ap. 1900, Beatrice Mary, da. of Lord Esmé Stuart Gordon; and has issue 1f.

1f. Robert Sidney Stuart Meade, b. 16 Feb. 1901.

2e. Elizabeth Cecilia Meade, b. 5 Mar. 1872; *m.* 9 Aug. 1904, Capt. John Somerled Thorpe, *late* Scots Guards (*Coddington Hall, Newark; Ardbrecknish, Argyll*); and has issue 1f.

1f. James Ian Sidney Thorpe, b. 1905.

3e. Constance Selina Meade, b. 21 Sept. 1875; *m.* 19 Aug. 1902, Col. William Henry Sitwell, D.S.O. (*Frankleigh House, Bradford-on-Avon*).

4d. Lady Selina Catherine Meade, *m.* 1st, 23 Nov. 1854, Granville Edward Vernon, M.P., *b.* 23 Nov. 1816; *d.s.p.* 1 Feb. 1861; 2ndly, 8 July 1862, John Bidwell of the Foreign Office, d. 22 Aug. 1873; 3rdly, 14 Aug. 1880, Henry Arthur William Hervey, C.B. (*6 Egerton Place, S.W.*); and has issue.

2c. *Lady Caroline Meade,* b. 26 *Aug.* 1794; d. 29 *Aug.* 1820; m. *as 1st wife,* 10 *July* 1811, *Count Paul Szechenyi, Chamberlain to H.I.M. the Emperor of Austria,* b. 10 *Nov.* 1789.

3c. *Lady Selina Meade,* b. 2 *May* 1797; d. 29 *Aug.* 1872; m. 14 *June* 1821, *Charles John Nepomucenuss Gabriel, Count of Clam-Martinitz, a General in the Austrian Service and A.D.C. to H.I. and A.M.,* d. *Jan.* 1840.

2b. *Hon. Robert Meade, Gen. in the Army, Col. 12th Regt.,* b. 29 *Feb.* 1772; d. 11 *July* 1852; m. 29 *June* 1808, *Anna Louisa, da. of Gen. Sir John Dalling, 1st Bart. [G.B.],* d. 18 *Mar.* 1853; *and had issue 1c to 4c.*

1c. *John Meade of Burrenwood, co. Down, and Earsham Hall, co. Norfolk, Capt. late 43rd L.I.,* b. 23 *Mar.* 1812; d. 5 *May* 1886; m. 18 *June* 1846, *Elvira, da. of Robert Ibbetson, Governor of Penang; and had issue 1d to 4d.*

1d. John Percy Meade, *late* Capt. 2nd Batt. Oxfordshire L.I. (*Earsham Hall, Bungay; Burrenwood, co. Down*), b. 17 May 1847; *m.* 2 Jan. 1894, Helena Frances, da. of Sir Allen Johnson-Walsh, 4th Bart. [I.]; and has issue 1e to 3e.

1e. John Windham Meade, b. 28 Nov. 1894.

2e. Robert Percy Meade, b. May 1896.

3e. Helena Theodosia Kathleen Meade. [Nos. 33064 to 33077.

391

The Plantagenet Roll

2*d.* Robert Aubrey Meade, *b.* 12 July 1852.

3*d.* Rose Harriette Theodosia Meade, *m.* 28 Sept. 1880, Lieut.-Col. Edward Harris of the Shade, co. Leicester, *formerly* Comdg. 2nd Batt. Suffolk Regt.

4*d.* Elvira Adela Meade, *m.* 4 Feb. 1891, Capt. Roger Hall, *late* 2nd Batt. Royal Fusiliers (*Narrow Water, Warrenpoint, co. Down*).

2*c.* *Anne Meade,* d. 10 *June* 1864; m. *as 1st wife,* 15 *July* 1833, *Sir David Thurlow Cunynghame, 6th Bart.* [*S.*], *b.* 16 *Sept.* 1803; *d.* 12 *Nov.* 1869; *and had issue 1d to 3d.*

1*d.* *Sir Edward Augustus Cunynghame, 7th Bart.* [*S.*], *b. Jan.* 1839; *d.* 24 *Jan.* 1877.

2*d.* Mary Louise Cunynghame (*Kingham Lodge, Chipping Norton*), m. 25 Aug. 1858, Capt. Thomas Henry Evans of North Tuddenham, co. Norfolk, *d.s.p.s.* 1896.

3*d.* Augusta Theodosia Mary Cunynghame, d.s.p. 25 *Oct.* 1872; m. *as 1st wife,* 11 *Sept.* 1866, *H.H. Prince Edward of Ligne* (*La Meuville*).

3*c.* *Catherine Meade,* d. 1854; m. 18 *July* 1836, *Mortimer Ricardo, Capt. 2nd Life Guards,* d. 21 *Ap.* 1876; *and had issue 1d to 3d.*

1*d.* *David Ricardo, Capt. late 15th Hussars,* b. 16 *Aug.* 1841; *d. Ap.* 1876; m. 15 *July* 1872, *Annette, da. of Col. Walter Campbell of Skipness, co. Argyll.*

2*d.* *Frank Ricardo of Bromesberrow Place, M.P., J.P., D.L.,* b. 5 *June* 1850; *d.* 24 *May* 1897; m. 27 *Sept.* 1877, *Alice Henrietta* (*Bure Homage, Christchurch*), *da. of the Hon. Edmund Monckton; and had issue.*

See the Clarence Volume, p. 609, Nos. 26774–26779.

3*d.* Mabel Ada Ricardo, *unm.*

4*c.* *Caroline Meade,* d. 8 *July* 1890; m. 12 *July* 1854, *Sir William Compton Domvile, 3rd Bart.* [*U.K.*], *b.* 20 *May* 1825; *d.* 20 *Sept.* 1884; *and had issue 1d to 2d.*

1*d.* Sir Compton Meade Domvile, 4th Bart. [U.K.] (*Santry, near Dublin*), *b.* 24 Oct. 1857.

2*d.* Mary Adelaide Domvile, *m.* 21 Jan. 1886, Lieut.-Col. William Hutcheson Poë, C.B., J.P., D.L., High Sheriff Queen's Co. 1891 (*Heywood, Ballinakell, Queen's Co.; Slaghtfreedan Lodge, Cookstown, co. Tyrone*); and has issue 1e to 2e.

1*e.* Hugo Compton Poë, *b.* 1889.

2*e.* Isabel May Poë, *b.* 1893.

3*b.* Hon. John Meade, Lieut.-Gen., C.B., b. 1775; d. 6 *Aug.* 1849; m. 2 *Oct.* 1816, *Urania Caroline, da. of the Hon. Edward Ward,* d. 2 *Nov.* 1851; *and had issue.*

See the Clarence Volume, pp. 280–281, Nos. 7513–7516.

4*b.* Ven. Pierce Meade, *Archdeacon of Dromore,* b. 21 *Nov.* 1776; d. 22 *Nov.* 1834; m. 6 *Ap.* 1801, *Elizabeth, da. of the Right Rev. Thomas Percy, Lord Bishop of Dromore,* d. 26 *Sept.* 1823; *and had issue 1c to 2c.*

1*c.* *Edward Richard Meade,* b. 30 *Nov.* 1805; d. 19 *Jan.* 1890; m. 9 *Ap.* 1850, *Eleanor Eliza, da. of William George Ives Bosanquet, H.E.I.C.S.,* d. 4 *Ap.* 1880; *and had issue 1d to 3d.*

1*d.* Mary Frances Meade, *m.* 15 May 1873, Col. Arthur Broadwood, *late* Scots Guards (54 *Eaton Place, S.W.*); and has issue (5 das., of whom the eldest) 1*e.*

1*e.* Mary Eleanor Broadwood, *m.* 1903, Kenneth R. Balfour; and has issue 1*f* to 2*f.*

1*f.* Ronald Balfour, *b.* 1904.

2*f.* Margaret Balfour, *b.* 1906.

2*d.* Constance Isabel Meade.

3*d.* Helen Adelaide Meade (*Rocksoles, co. Lanark*), *m.* 1888, Gen. Sir Montagu Gilbert Gerard, K.C.B., K.C.S.I., *d.* July 1905; and has issue 1*e.*

1*e.* Gilbert Meade Gerard, *b.* 1889.

2*c.* *Theodosia Barbara Meade,* b. 24 *Mar.* 1804; *d.* 1890; m. 11 *Ap.* 1833, *the Rev. John Whalley of Ectom, co. Northants; and had issue.* [Nos. 33078 to 33103.

# of The Blood Royal

5b. Lady Anne Meade, b. 24 Ap. 1768; d. 20 Ap. 1826; m. 7 Ap. 1788, John Whaley of Whaley Abbey, co. Wicklow, d. 2 Jan. 1847; and had issue (with possibly others) 1c.

1c. Caroline Elizabeth Whaley, d. 11 Mar. 1871; m. 1814, Sir Charles Henry Coote, 9th Bart. [I.], d. 8 Oct. 1864; and had issue 1d to 4d.

1d. Sir Charles Henry Coote, 10th Bart. [I.], b. Sept. 1815; d. unm. 15 Nov. 1895.

2d. Rev. Sir Algernon Coote, 11th Bart. [I.], b. 20 Sept. 1817; d. 20 Nov. 1899; m. 1st, 12 Feb. 1847, Cecilia Matilda, da. of John Pemberton Plumptre of Fredville, M.P., d. 24 May 1878; 2ndly, 25 Sept. 1879, Constance (Wavertree, Stanbridge, Wilts), da. of T. H. Headlam of Wavertree; and had issue 1e to 8e.

1e. Sir Algernon Charles Plumptre Coote, 12th Bart. [I.], H.M.'s Lieut. and Custos Rotulorum of Queen's Co. (Ballyfin, Mountrath, Queen's Co.), b. 14 Dec. 1847; m. 1st, 28 Aug. 1873, Jean, da. of Capt. John Trotter of Dyrham Park, d. 15 Ap. 1880; 2ndly, 21 Ap. 1882, Ellen Melesina, da. of Philip Charles Chenevix Trench of Botleyhill; and has issue 1f to 8f.

1f. Ralph Algernon Coote, Capt. 17th Lancers, b. 22 Sept. 1874; m. 12 Ap. 1904, Alice, da. of Thomas Webber; and has issue 1g.

1g. John Ralph Coote, b. 10 Jan. 1905.

2f. John Methuen Coote, C.S. Uganda, late Diplo. Ser., b. 13 Mar. 1878.

3f. Bernard Trotter Coote, Lieut. R.N., b. 9 Ap. 1880.

4f. Charles Chenevix Coote, Lieut. Leinster Regt., b. 11 Sept. 1884.

5f. Arthur Philip Coote, b. 24 Jan. 1887.

6f. Maxwell Henry Coote, b. 1 June 1895.

7f. Ethel Jean Coote, b. 29 Ap. 1876; m. 14 July 1896, Ivor Bevan (58 Great Cumberland Place.).

8f. Mary Melesina Coote, b. 14 Sept. 1888.

2e. John Pemberton Plumptre Coote, Comm. (ret.) R.N., b. 15 Sept. 1850; m. 16 Dec. 1880, Eleanor Agnes, da. of John Osmaston of Hawkhurst Court; and has issue 1f to 3f.

1f. Mervyn Chidley Coote, 2nd Lieut. Durham L.I., b. 5 June 1885.

2f. Emily Cecilia Coote.

3f. Joyce Margaretta Coote.

3e. Orlando Robert Coote, J.P. (Umbria, Roehampton, S.W.), b. 14 Mar. 1855; m. 24 Aug. 1882, Edith Mary, da. of Adolphus William Hume of Ferndale, Tunbridge Wells; and has issue 1f.

1f. Nina Edith Coote, b. 23 Sept. 1883.

4e. Cecil Henry Coote (Wavertree, Feilding, New Zealand), b. 2 Oct. 1856; m. 28 Mar. 1888, Blanche Mabel, da. of John Oldham of New Zealand; and has issue 1f to 5f.

1f. John Cecil Coote, b. 20 Feb. 1889.

2f. Frederick Stanley Coote, b. 7 Mar. 1896.

3f. Eric Royds Methuen Coote, b. 1902.

4f. Ivy Mabel Coote.

5f. Myrtle Cecilia Coote.

5e. Rev. Herbert Chidley Coote, M.A. (Camb.), Rector of Trowbridge (Trowbridge Rectory, Wilts), b. 8 July 1861; m. 1 June 1886, Elizabeth Margaret, da. of Brenton Halliburton Collins of Tunbridge Wells, J.P.

6e.[1] Catharine Cecilia Coote, m. 30 Dec. 1896, the Rev. A. de Vlieger, D.Litt., Minister of the Presbyterian Church, Chorlton-cum-Hardy (Holmwood, Chorlton-cum-Hardy, Manchester); and has issue 1f to 2f.

1f. Raymond Algernon Coote de Vlieger, b. 15 Oct. 1897.

2f. Catharine Jean de Vlieger, b. 11 Aug. 1901.

7e.[2] Cecilia Constance Coote, m. 6 June 1900, Henry Western Plumptre, J.P. (Fredville, near Dover); and has issue 1f to 2f.   [Nos. 33104 to 33130.]

393

The Plantagenet Roll

1f. Eileen Cecilia Plumptre, *b.* 17 Ap. 1901.

2f. Evelyn Dora Plumptre, *b.* 6 Oct. 1903.

8e. Dora Maud Coote.

3d. Robert Coote, Admiral R.N., C.B., *b.* 1 *June* 1820; *d.* 17 *Mar.* 1898; *m.* 14 *Feb.* 1854, *Lucy, da. of Admiral Sir William Edward Parry, d.* 7 *Feb.* 1906; *and had issue 1e to 2e.*

1e. Stanley Victor Coote, M.A. (Oxon.), J.P., High Sheriff co. Roscommon 1900 (*Burley Manor, Ringwood*), *b.* 30 May 1862; *m.* 26 Oct. 1889, Louisa, *da.* of the Ven. Frederick Bathurst, Archdeacon of Bedford; and has issue 1*f.*

1f. Honor Dorothea Coote, *b.* 18 Nov. 1896.

2e. Caroline Maud Coote, *m.* 6 Aug. 1884, Brig.-Gen. Cecil William Park, C.B., Extra A.D.C. to H.M. the King; and has issue 1*f* to 3*f*.

1f. James Allan Park, *b.* 24 June 1885.

2f. Stella Margaret Park.

3f. Cecil Maud Vera Park.

4d. *Caroline Theodosia Grace Coote, b.* 2 *Mar.* 1819; *d.* (*at Nice*) *June* 1848; *m.* 1842, *Victor (de Massigy), Marquis of Massingy de la Pierre* [*F.*], *b.* (*at Lyons*) 1807; *d.* (*there*) 1889; *and had issue 1e.*

1e. *Caroline (de Massigy), suo jure Marchioness of Massingy de la Pierre* [*F.*], *b.* 1847; *d.* 28 *Ap.* 1891; *m. Louis Bernard Georges d'Auzac de Campagnac, of Villa Massingy d'Auzac, 2 Boulevard de Cimiez, Nice, b.* 1842; *d.* (*at Lourdes*) 3 *July* 1901; *and had issue 1f.*

1f. Marie Emmanuel John Maxime (d'Auzac), Marquis of Massingy d'Auzac [*F.*] (*Villa Massingy d'Auzac, 2 Boulevard de Cimiez, Nice*), *b.* 1869; *m.* (at Paris) 2 July 1895, Marie Ghislaine, *da.* of the Viscount de Vaulogé.

6b. Lady Catherine Meade, *b.* 7 Oct. 1770; *d.* 17 *Feb.* 1793; *m. as 1st wife,* 30 *June* 1789, Richard (*Wingfield*), 4*th Viscount Powerscourt* [*I.*], *b.* 29 Oct. 1762; *d.* 19 *July* 1809; *and had issue 1c to 2c.*

1c. *Richard (Wingfield), 5th Viscount Powerscourt* [*I.*], *b.* 11 *Sept.* 1790; *d.* 9 *Aug.* 1823; *m. 1st,* 6 *Feb.* 1813, *Lady Frances Theodosia, da. of Robert (Jocelyn), 2nd Earl of Roden* [*I.*], *K.P., d.* 10 *May* 1820; *and had issue.* See the Clarence Volume, p. 293, Nos. 8184–8196.

2c. *Rev. the Hon. Edward Wingfield, b.* 20 *Nov.* 1792; *d.* 6 *Sept.* 1825; *m.* 12 *Ap.* 1819, *Louisa Joan, da. of the Hon. George Jocelyn (who re-m.* 2 *Aug.* 1833, *Robert Richard Tighe), d.* 17 *June* 1874; *and had issue.* See the Clarence Volume, pp. 295–296, Nos. 8242–8285.

7b. Lady Melosina Adelaide Meade, *d.* 26 *Mar.* 1866; *m.* 31 *Dec.* 1801, *John Chambre (Brabazon), 10th Earl of Meath* [*I.*], *1st Baron Chaworth* [*U.K.*], *K.P., d.* 15 *Mar.* 1851; *and had issue.* See p. 204, Nos. 7310–7353.

5a. (Da. by 2nd husband.) See the Clarence Volume, Table XXXII., pp. 285–286, Nos. 7662–7688. [Nos. 33131 to 33268.

316. Descendants of Lady THEODOSIA BLIGH (see Table XXVII.), *b. c.* 1723; *d.* 20 May 1777; *m. as 1st wife, Nov.* 1745, WILLIAM (CROSBIE), 1st EARL OF GLANDORE [I.], *d.* 11 Ap. 1781; and had issue 1α to 3α.

1a. *John (Crosbie), 2nd Earl of Glandore* [*I.*], *b.* 25 *May* 1753; *d.s.p.* 20 *Ap.* 1815.

2a. *Lady Anne Crosbie, b.* 1 *Dec.* 1754; *d.* (–); *m. May* 1775, *John William Talbot of Mount Talbot, co. Roscommon; and had issue 1b to 3b.*

1b. *William Talbot of Mount Talbot, d.* (? s.p.) 1851.

2b. *Rev. John Talbot, afterwards (R.L.* 14 *Feb.* 1816) *Crosbie of Ardfert, M.P.,*

394

# of The Blood Royal

d. *Jan.* 1816; m. *Sept.* 1811, *Jane, da. of Lieut.-Col. Thomas Lloyd of Beech-mount, co. Limerick ; and had issue* 1c *to* 4c.

1c. **William Talbot Crosbie,** *afterwards (R.L.* 11 *Nov.* 1780) *Talbot-Crosbie,* J.P., D.L., *High Sheriff co.* Kerry 1848, b. 19 *Mar.* 1817; d. 4 *Sept.* 1899; m. 1st, 29 *July* 1839, Susan Anne, *da. of the Hon. Merrick Lindsey Peter Burrell,* b. 1816; d. 16 *Aug.* 1850; *and had issue* 1d *to* 7d.

1d. **John Talbot Darnley Talbot-Crosbie,** *Lieut.-Col. King's Royal Rifles,* J.P., b. 1 *May* 1843; d.s.p. 2 *Nov.* 1899.

2d. Lindsay Bertie Talbot-Crosbie, J.P., D.L., *late* R.N. (*Ardfert Abbey, co. Kerry*), b. 11 Aug. 1844; m. 29 Mar. 1871, Annie Crosbie, da. of Col. Edward Thomas Coke of Trusley and Debdale Hall, J.P., D.L. ; and has issue 1e to 9e.

See the Clarence Volume, p. 184, Nos. 3069–3077.

3d. William David Talbot-Crosbie (*Cloonca, Roscommon*), b. 17 June 1849 ; m. 3 Oct. 1874, Kathleen Sophia, da. of Col. Edward Thomas Coke of Trusley and Debdale Hall, J.P., D.L., *s.p.*

4d. Emily Jane Georgiana Talbot-Crosbie.

5d. Emma Anne Talbot-Crosbie, m. as 2nd wife, 9 July 1885, James Gordon-Oswald, *previously* Gordon of Scotstoun, co. Renfrew, d. (*s.p* by her) 3 Jan. 1897.

6d. Susan Elizabeth Talbot-Crosbie, m. 22 Nov. 1866, Owen Phibbs of Lisheen, J.P., D.L., High Sheriff co. Sligo 1884 (*Lisheen, Sligo*); and has issue 1e to 5e.

1e. Basil Phibbs, High Sheriff co. Sligo 1905 (*Corradoo, Boyle, co. Roscommon*), b. 22 Nov. 1867 ; m. 2 May 1899, Rebekah Wilbraham, da. of Herbert Wilbraham Taylor of Hadley Bourne, co. Herts, J.P. ; and has issue 1f to 2f.

1f. Geoffrey Basil Phibbs, b. 5 Ap. 1900.

2f. Denis William Phibbs, b. 15 May 1902.

2e. William Talbot Phibbs, b. 8 Nov. 1869 ; m. Phyllis, da. of [——] Princep of 46 Thurloe Square, S.W.

3e. Owen Lindsay Phibbs, b. 13 Nov. 1870.

4e. Darnley Phibbs (*Willow Grange, Potchefstroom, South Africa*), b. 22 Nov. 1873 ; m. 2 Sept. 1903, Laura Georgiana, da. of John Hewson of Tubrid, co. Kerry ; and has issue 1f.

1f. Henry Owen Phibbs, b. 7 July 1904.

5e. Catherine Anne Phibbs.

7d. Frances Charlotte Talbot-Crosbie, m. 25 May 1868, George Frederic Trench, J.P., B.A. (T.C.D.), F.S.I. (*Abbeylands, Ardfert*); and has issue 1e to 5e.

1e. Ernest Frederic Crosbie Trench, M.A. (T.C.D.), M.I.C.E. (*Drentagh, Hollycroft Avenue, Hampstead, N.W.*), b. 6 Aug. 1869 ; m. 3 Ap. 1895, Netta Wilbraham, da. of Herbert Wilbraham Taylor of Hadley Bourne, co. Herts ; and has issue 1f to 3f.

1f. Maurice Crosbie Trench, b. 29 Ap. 1896.

2f. Dermot George Crosbie Trench, b. 3 Jan. 1904.

3f. Noreen Charlotte Trench, b. 2 Nov. 1899.

2e. William Launcelot Crosbie Trench, b. 22 July 1881.

3e. Elizabeth Mary Trench, m. 24 Mar. 1896, William Edward Wingfield, Major, R.A. (*Wellington House, Cahir*) ; and has issue 1f to 4f.

1f. Richard James Trench Wingfield, b. 28 Dec. 1896.

2f. John Anthony David Wingfield, b. 2 July 1905.

3f. Charlotte Elfreda Wingfield, b. 5 Sept. 1898.

4f. Eveline Isabella Wingfield, b. 5 July 1903.

4e. Ruth Emma Trench, m. 30 Mar. 1904, Capt. Michael Biddulph, Army Pay Dept.

5e. Emily Olive Victoria Trench.

2c. **John Talbot of Mount Talbot,** J.P., D.L., *High Sheriff co. Roscommon, sometime* 35th *Regt.,* b. 4 *Oct.* 1818; d. 16 *July* 1859; m. 1st, 2 *Jan.* 1845,
[Nos. 33269 to 33303.

Ⲧⲏⲉ Ᵽlantagenet Ⲣoll

Marianne, da. of Marcus M'Causland of Fruit Hill, co. Londonderry (marriage dissolved by Act of Parliament 29 July 1856); 2ndly, 15 Oct. 1858, Gertrude Caroline, da. of Lieut.-Col. Edward Symes Bayly of Ballyarthur, J.P., D.L. (who re-m. 18 Aug. 1864, *the Hon. Francis George Crofton), d. 19 Aug.* 1869; *and had issue 1d to 2d.*

1d. William John Talbot, J.P., D.L., High Sheriff co. Roscommon 1883, and for co. Armagh 1903, *late* Capt. 7th Brigade S.I.D., R.A., 1886 *(Mount Talbot, Roscommon), b.* 1 July 1859 ; *m.* 14 Aug. 1897, Julia Elizabeth Mary, da. and h. of Sir Capel Molyneux of Castle Dillon, 7th Bart. [I.].

2d. *Marianne Jane Theodosia Talbot, d.* 3 *Jan.* 1894 ; *m.* 21 *Oct.* 1869, *Arthur Rickard Lloyd ; and had issue 1e to 4e.*

1e. John Lloyd.

2e. Henry Talbot Lloyd, Capt. R.M.L.I., d. *(being killed at Tientsin)* 1900.

3e. Arthur Lloyd.

4e. Diana Lloyd.

3c. *Anne Talbot, d.* 10 *Dec.* 1896 ; *m.* 27 *June* 1839, *the Rev. Maurice Atkin Cooke-Collis of Castle Cooke, co. Cork, D.D., Rector of Queenstown, b.* 24 *Mar.* 1812 ; *d.* 8 *Dec.* 1882 ; *and had issue 1d to 7d.*

1d. William Cooke-Collis, J.P., Lieut.-Col. Comdg. 9th Batt. King's Royal Rifle Corps, *late* Royal Irish Rifles *(Castle Cooke, Kilworth, co. Cork), b.* 1 Aug. 1847 ; *m.* 1st, 6 Nov. 1875, Katherine Maria, da. of Col. James Oliphant of Worlington Hall, co. Suffolk, R.E., *d.* 27 Jan. 1891 ; 2ndly, 4 Sept. 1894, Elizabeth Marian Shrubsole, da. of Edward Cunliffe of 66 The Drive, Brighton ; and has issue 1e to 7e.

1e. William James Norman Cooke-Collis, Lieut. Royal Irish Rifles, *b.* 7 May 1876.

2e. Maurice Talbot Cooke-Collis, *b.* 5 July 1879.

3e. Edward Cunliffe Cooke-Collis, *b.* 27 Oct. 1902.

4e.[1] Nora Cooke-Collis.

5e.[1] Katherine Sophia Cooke-Collis.

6e. Geraldine Cooke-Collis.

7e.[2] Elizabeth Susan Cooke-Collis.

2d. John Talbot Cooke-Collis, B.A. (Camb.), *b.* 30 May 1849 ; *m.* 2 Ap. 1891, Amalie Elizabeth, da. of John Conrad Reuss of Upper Long Ditton, co. Surrey.

3d. Maurice Crosbie Cooke-Collis, Col. *late* Bengal Staff Corps, *b.* 9 Oct. 1850.

4d. Jane Lloyd Cooke-Collis, *m.* 1st, 11 Dec. 1866, Nathaniel Cox Barton, R.N., *d.* May 1868 ; 2ndly, 23 Jan. 1877, James Erskine Oliphant, Bombay C.S.

5d. *Geraldine de Courcy Cooke-Collis, d. (at Bundaberg, Queensland)* 6 *Jan.* 1885 ; *m.* 9 *Feb.* 1869, *Augustus P. Barton.*

6d. Annie Talbot Crosbie Cooke-Collis.

7d. Emma Theodosia Cooke-Collis.

4c. *Diana Crosbie, d.* (–) ; *m.* 6 *Aug.* 1835, *Edward Thomas Coke of Trusley and Debdale Hall, J.P., D.L., d.* 26 *Feb.* 1888 ; *and had issue.*
See the Clarence Volume, pp. 183–184, Nos. 3042–3080.

3b. *Charles Talbot, Capt. 5th Fusiliers, d.s.p. (being killed at the battle of Walcheren).*

3a. *Lady Arabella Crosbie, b.* 21 *Oct.* 1757 ; *d.* 1813 ; *m.* 27 *Feb.* 1783, *the Hon. Edward Ward, M.P., b.* 1753 ; *d.* 1812 ; *and had issue.*
See the Clarence Volume, Table XXXII., pp. 275–281, Nos. 7342–7516.

[Nos. 33304 to 33533.

317. Descendants, if any, of ANNE WISEMAN (see Table XXVII.), *d.* 1736 ; *m.* HENRY LUMLEY, Governor of the Island of Jersey, *d.* 1722 ; and of MARGARET ARABELLA WISEMAN, *m.* THOMAS STISTED of Ipswich ; and had issue.

# of The Blood Royal

318. Descendants of Sir THOMAS WISEMAN, 6th Bart. [E.] (see Table XXVIII.), *b.* 30 Jan. 1731; *d.* 27 Jan. 1810; *m.* 1st, 1 Dec. 1757, MARY, da. of Michael GODEN, Master Attendant at Chatham Dockyard, *d.* 11 June 1766; 2ndly, 2 Dec. 1769, SARAH, da. of Thomas KING of Gravesend, *d.* 4 Dec. 1777; and had issue 1*a* to 4*a*.

1*a*. *Edmund Wiseman*, b. 2 *Dec.* 1758; d.v.p. 7 *May* 1787; m. 1783, *Jemima, da. of Michael Arne (who re-m.* 5 *Jan.* 1792, *Peter Reynolds of Chatham, d. Oct.* 1804; *and had issue* 1*b* to 2*b*.

  1*b*. *Sir William Saltonstall Wiseman, 7th Bart.* [E.], *Capt. R.N.*, b. **5** *Mar.* 1784; d. 1 *July* 1845; m. 1st (*dissolved* 1825), 8 *Jan.* 1812, *Catherine, da. of Sir James Mackintosh, Knt., Recorder of Bombay, d.* 27 *Oct.* 1862; *and had issue* 1*c*.

    1*c*. *Sir William Saltonstall Wiseman, 8th Bart.* [E.], *Rear-Admiral R.N., K.C.B.*, b. 4 *Aug.* 1814; d. 14 *July* 1874; m. 25 *Oct.* 1838, *Charlotte Jane, da. of Admiral Charles William Paterson of East Cosham House, R.N., d.* 23 *May* 1891; *and had issue* 1*d* to 2*d*.

      1*d*. *Sir William Wiseman, 9th Bart.* [E.], *Capt. R.R.*, b. 23 *Aug.* 1845; d. 11 *Jan.* 1893; m. 20 *Sept.* 1878, *Sarah Elizabeth, da. of Lewis Langworthy of Ellesmere House, Putney; and had issue* 1*e* to 5*e*.

        1*e*. Sir William George Eden Wiseman, 10th Bart. [E.] (15 *Nevern Square*, S.W.), *b.* 1 Feb. 1885.

        2*e*. Winifred May Wiseman, *b.* 26 Feb. 1880.

        3*e*. Dorothy Lilian Wiseman, *b.* 17 Oct. 1881.

        4*e*. Margery Elizabeth Wiseman, *b.* 3 Nov. 1883.

        5*e*. Joan Hilda Marion Wiseman, *b.* 13 Dec. 1890.

      2*d*. *Eliza Frances Charlotte Wiseman, d.* 1 *Ap.* 1875; m. *as 1st wife,* 22 *Oct.* 1865, *Rear-Admiral Henry M'Clintock Alexander of Dunduan, Coleraine,* b. 7 *Oct.* 1834; d. ; *and had issue* 1*e* to 3*e*.[1]

        1*e*. Robert William Wiseman Alexander, *b.* 11 Jan. 1870.

        2*e*. Charlotte Marion Alexander.

        3*e*. Agatha Frances Mary Alexander.

  2*b*. *Mary Anne Wiseman, d.* 21 *Nov.* 1828; m. 23 *Oct.* 1806, *Thomas Frid of Chatham, d.* 10 *Oct.* 1850; *and had issue* 1*c*.

    1*c*. *William Saltonstall Frid,* b. 14 *Oct.* 1811; d. (-); m. [——], *da. of* [——]; *and had issue* 1*d* to 3*d*.[1]

      1*d*. *William Saltonstall Frid,* m. ; *and had issue a son living in* 1878.

      2*d*. Mary Anne Frid, *m.* the Rev. George Maunder.

      3*d*. Eliza Jane Frid, *m.* Frederick Lockyer.

2*a*. *Thomas Wiseman of Northfleet, co. Kent,* b. 24 *Ap.* 1760; d. 1830; m. 13 *Jan.* 1778, *Susannah, da. of Alexander Bookham of Northfleet; and had issue* 1*b* to 11*b*.

  1*b*. *Thomas Wiseman,* b. 23 *Feb.* 1778; m. 30 *Aug.* 1813, *Sarah, da. of* [——] *Pink; and had issue.*

  2*b*. *Alexander Wiseman,* b. 30 *May* 1785; m. 28 *Aug.* 1807, *Anne, da. of* [——] *Stanley; and had issue.*

  3*b*. *Edmund Wiseman,* m.; *and had issue.*

  4*b*. *William Henry Wiseman,* m.; *and had issue.*

  5*b*. *Frederick Arthur Wiseman,* m.; *and had issue.* [Nos. 33534 to 33543.

---

[1] Foster's "Peerage," 1880.

The Plantagenet Roll

6b. *Charles Pierce Wiseman,* m.; *and had issue.*
7b. *Mariana Wiseman.*
8b. *Elizabeth Anne Wiseman.*
9b. *Susanna Frances Wiseman.*
10b. *Theophila Wiseman.*
11b. *Sarah Henrietta Wiseman.*

3a. *William Wiseman of Brompton, co. Kent,* b. 23 Ap. 1762 ; m. *Elizabeth, da.* of [——] *Robertson of London, and afterwards of Philadelphia ; and had issue* 1b.
1b. *George Augustus Wiseman,* b. (*at Portsea*) 20 Oct. 1808.

4a.[2] *Anne Wiseman,* m. *Joseph Langford.*

319. Descendants, if any surviving, of THEOPHILA WISEMAN, wife of A. WYLDE ; of MARIANA WISEMAN, wife of W. SALTONSTALL ; of JANE WISEMAN, wife of T. NORBURY ; of EDWARD THEOPHILUS MARIANA WISEMAN ; of JOHN WISEMAN, who *m.*, and had issue ; ELIZABETH MARY and SARAH ARABELLA WISEMAN ; and of the Right Rev. CAPEL WISEMAN, Lord Bishop of Dromore in 1683, *previously* Dean of Raphoe (see Table XXVIII.).

320. Descendants, if any surviving, of THEODOSIA WISEMAN (see Table XXVIII.), *b. c.* 1641 ; *d.* 2 Oct. 1717 ; *m.* (Lic. Fac.) 7 Ap. 1662, Sir ANTHONY CRAVEN of Sparsholt, co. Berks, 1st Bart. [E.], *bapt.* 5 Mar. 1626 ; *d.* 1712 (? 3) ; and had issue 1a to 2a.

1a.[1] *Elizabeth Craven,* b. 30 Sept. 1666 ; m. 30 Sept. 1692, *Samuel Palmer of All Hallows, Lombard Street,* a.p.d. 33 in 1692; *and had issue* 1b to 4b.
1b. *Samuel Palmer of Sparsholt, co. Berks,*
2b. *Elizabeth Palmer,*
3b. *Theodosia Palmer,* } *all living* 1712.
4b. *Anne Palmer,*

2a.[1] *Mary Craven,* m. *Edward Broughton ; and had issue* 1b.
1b. *Edward Broughton, living* 1712.

321. Descendants, if any, of ELIZABETH WISEMAN (See Table XXVIII.), wife of ROBERT TYDERLEIGH.

322. Descendants, if any, of THEODOSIA CAPELL, wife of EDWARD KEYMEYS of Kiven Mabley, co. Glamorgan ; of MARGARET CAPELL and of ANNE CAPELL, wife of THOMAS WESTROW of Twickenham (see Table XXVII.).

323. Descendants, if any, of EDWARD, ARTHUR, ROBERT, HUMPHREY, GILES, JOHN, and ROGER CAPELL (see Table XXVII.).

[1] They are named in their father's will, but it is not known which was the eldest.

# of The Blood Royal

324. Descendants, if any, of ARTHUR, WILLIAM, MARY, and HEN-RIETTA MARIA CAPEL (see Table XXVII.).

325. Descendants of ANNE CAPEL (see Table XXVII.), *b.* 1714; *d.* 9 Feb. 1778; *m.* CHRISTOPHER LOFFT, Bar.-at-Law, Recorder of Windsor and Private Secretary to Sarah, Duchess of Marlborough, *b.* 1704; *d.* 3 Feb. 1772; and had issue 1*a* to 5*a*.

1*a*. Lewis Capel Lofft, d. (? unm.).

2*a*. Capel Lofft of Troston Hall and Stanton, co. Suffolk, J.P., b. 14 Nov. 1751; d. (at Montcaliere) 8 Sept. 1824; m. 1st, 20 Aug. 1778, Anne, da. of Henry Emlyn of Windsor, F.S.A., Architect and restorer of St. George's Chapel, d. 1801; 2ndly, 1802, Sarah Watson, da. of Joseph Finch of Cambridge, d. 1855; and had issue 1b to 3b.

1*b*. Robert Emlyn Lofft of Troston Hall, &c., Capt. H.E.I.C.S., b. 9 Nov. 1783; d. 20 Sept. 1847; m. 1826, Letitia Niel, da. of Francis Richardson, Col. 1st Foot Guards (by his wife Letitia, da. of William Moseley of Owsden Hall), d. (at Ghent) 1832; and had issue 1c to 5c.

1*c*. Henry Capel Lofft, afterwards Moseley of Troston Hall, &c., J.P., b. 25 Feb. 1828; d. unm. 29 Dec. 1867.

2*c*. Robert Emlyn Lofft of Troston Hall, Bury St. Edmunds, J.P., High Sheriff co. Suffolk, 1881, b. 31 Aug. 1831; d. unm. 9 Oct. 1900.

3*c*. Letitia Lofft of Troston and Glenham conjointly with her sisters (35 Brunswick Square, Hove), b. 30 June 1829; m. 6 July 1854, the Rev. Hubert Ashton Holden, LL.D., Litt.D., Head Master Queen Elizabeth School, Ipswich, Fellow Trin. Coll., Cambridge, and Fellow and Member of Senate London Univ., &c. &c., b. 1822; d. 1 Dec. 1896; and has issue 1d to 8d.

1*d*. Henry Capel Lofft Holden, Col. R.A., F.R.S., Superintendent Royal Gun Factory, Woolwich, b. 23 Jan. 1856; m. 27 Mar. 1889, Elizabeth, da. of R. Farrant; and has issue 1e to 2e.

1*e*. Hubert Capel Lofft Holden, b. 24 Ap. 1890.

2*e*. Lætitia Muriel Lofft Holden, b. 25 Sept. 1895.

2*d*. Hubert Noel Lofft Holden, b. 28 Dec. 1865.

3*d*. Clara Lofft Holden, b. 24 Ap. 1858, unm.

4*d*. Lucy Pauline Lofft Holden, b. 2 Ap. 1859, unm.

5*d*. Ethel Lofft Holden, b. 6 Aug. 1860; m. 21 Jan. 1893, Stewart Douglas Wade; and has issue 1e to 2e.

1*e*. Emlyn Wade, b. 30 Aug. 1895.

2*e*. Douglas Ashton Wade, b. 13 Mar. 1898.

6*d*. Mildred Alexandra Lofft Holden, b. 14 May 1863, unm.

7*d*. Nona Capel Lofft Holden, b. 16 Ap. 1867; m. 27 Aug. 1903, John Herbert Bell; and has issue 1e.

1*e*. Arthur Capel Bell, b. 18 Sept. 1904.

8*d*. Hilda Beatrice Lofft Holden, b. 17 Jan. 1870; m. 27 Oct. 1896, Robert Hunt; and has issue 1e.

1*e*. Angela Beatrice Hunt, b. 27 Feb. 1898.

4*c*. Eliza Lofft of Troston and Glenham conjointly with her sisters (67 Earl's Court Square, S.W.), b. 20 Oct. 1832; m. 7 Aug. 1851, Frederick Robert Bevan of Weston Grove, Southampton, b. 27 Jan. 1824; d. 29 Aug. 1890; and has issue 1d to 8d.

1*d*. Francis Lofft Bevan (America), b. 23 Ap. 1854; m. 8 Aug. 1885, Lucy, da. of [——] Hooker; and has issue 1e to 10e.

[Nos. 33544 to 33560.]

399

The Plantagenet Roll

1*e*. Francis Capel Bevan, *b.* 4 Nov. 1889.
2*e*. Herbert Clarkson Bevan, *b.* 4 July 1892.
3*e*. Robert Douglas Bevan, *b.* 6 Oct. 1897.
4*e*. Frederick Edward Bevan, *b.* 26 Ap. 1903.
5*e*. Roella Elfrida Bevan, *b.* 2 July 1886.
6*e*. Nora Lofft Bevan, *b.* 17 Mar. 1888.
7*e*. Ethel Corina Bevan, *b.* 24 Mar. 1894.
8*e*. Bessie Sophia Bevan, *b.* 11 Aug. 1895.
9*e*. Edith Katharine Bevan, *b.* 8 July 1901.
10*e*. [——] Bevan, *b.* Mar. 1906.

2*d*. Frederick Capel Bevan, *b.* 4 Aug. 1860.

3*d*. Herbert Spencer Bevan, *b.* 15 Oct. 1866; *m.* 19 Nov. 1895, Jennie Douglas, da. of Gen. J. R. Williams of Memphis, Tennessee, *d.* 30 Sept. 1904; and has issue 1*e*.

1*e*. Laurence Emlyn Bevan, *b.* 7 Jan. 1903.

4*d*. Mary Constance Bevan, *b.* 20 Sept. 1852.
5*d*. Ellen Sylvia Bevan, *b.* 5 May 1864.
6*d*. Mabel Frederica Bevan, *b.* 2 May 1868.
7*d*. Rowena Dorothea Bevan, *b.* 13 Feb. 1870.
8*d*. Rachel Evelyn Bevan, *b.* 25 Oct. 1873.

5*c*. Annie Lofft of Troston and Glenham conjointly with her sisters.

2*b*. *Capel Lofft of Sucknush, co. Sussex and Millmead, Virginia, Fellow King's Coll., Cambridge, b.* 19 *Feb.* 1806; *d.* 1873; *m.* [——], *da. of* [——] *Anderson; and had issue* 1*c to* 2*c*.

1*c*. *Clara Lofft, d.* (*being drowned with her da.* [? *and only child*] *in the Lake of Geneva*); *m. the Rev.* [——] *Irving.*

2*c*. Minnie Lofft (*Socnersh Manor, Sussex*).

3*b*. *Annie Lofft, b.* 14 *Aug.* 1788; *d.* 14 *June* 1884; *m.* 1826, *the Rev. Walter John Spring Casborne of Newhouse, Pakenham, co. Suffolk, J.P., b.* 1790; *d.* 1881.

3*a*. *Christina Lofft, b.* 2 *Nov.* 1755.

4*a*. *Emma Louisa Lofft, b.* 1735.

5*a*. *Olivia Lofft, b.* 14 *Ap.* 1757.   [Nos. 33561 to 33580.

326. Descendants, if any, of JAMES CAPELL and PENELOPE CAPELL, wife of LITTON PULTER of Cottered, co. Herts (see Table XXVIII.).

327. Descendants, if any surviving, of ROBERT, GRENADO, and HENRY, the three eldest sons of ANNE, *née* CAPEL, *bur.* 26 Dec. 1679; and her husband, the Rev. ROBERT CHESTER, D.D., Professor of Theology, *bur.* 9 Ap. 1664 (see Table XXIX.).

328. Descendants of HENRY CHESTER of Eversley, co. Hants, and West Lavington, co. Wilts, one of the six Clerks in Chancery (see Table XXIX.), *b.* 26 Feb. 1738; *d.* 28 Oct. 1786; *m.* 24 June 1760, HETTY, da. of William DE BILLINGHURST of Mitchen Hall, co. Surrey (by his wife Lettice, sister to George Woodroffe of Poyle), *d.* 13 July 1812; and had issue (with das.) 1*a*.

1*a*. *Henry Chester, Solicitor, b.* 30 *May* 1762; *d.* 23 *July* 1832; *m.* 13 *Oct.* 1781, *Ann, da. of Joseph Higham of Pattishall, co. Northants,* d. 4 *Mar.* 1820; *and had (with other) issue* 1*b*.

400

MARY BEDELL, WIFE OF SIR THOMAS LEVENTHORPE
(TABLE XXX)
THE COMMON ANCESTOR OF Nᵒˢ 33585 - 34236
FROM THE ORIGINAL IN POSSESSION OF
BASIL T. FANSHAWE ESQ. AT BRATTON FLEMING.

# of The Blood Royal

1b. Henry Chester, afterwards (Jan. 1854) Woodroffe of Poyle, b. 29 Oct. 1783;
d. 22 July 1854; m. 20 Oct. 1810, Charlotte, da. of James Morris of Calcutta,
H.E.I.C.C.S., d. 25 Oct. 1871; and had issue 1c to 2c.

    1c. Henry Chester of Poyle, b. 7 Sept. 1811; d.s.p. 15 Sept. 1869.

    2c. Frederick James Chester of Poyle, b. 12 Nov. 1813; d. 24 May 1883; m.
25 Aug. 1847, Charlotte Ellen, da. of Charles Chester, d. (–); and had issue
1d to 4d.

    1d. Henry Morris Chester, Lord of the Manor of Wyke, co. Surrey, Bar.-at-
Law, C.C., LL.D. (Poyle Park, Tongham, Surrey), b. 13 Feb. 1852.

    2d. Ellen Charlotte Chester, m. 29 July 1869, G. O. Mellick Herron (Newdigate
Place, Surrey).

    3d. Alice Woodroffe Chester, m. 15 Jan. 1887, Col. Douglas Campbell de
Wend, Comdg. 15th Regl. District.

    4d. Frances Walter Chester, m. 7 Nov. 1896, Surg.-Col. A. C. Maunsell, Army
Medical Staff.   [Nos. 33581 to 33584.

329. Descendants, if any, of the three younger sons and three
daughters of the above-named ANNE CAPEL (see Section
327).

330. Descendants of MARY COKE (see Table XXX.), d. 17 Aug.
1766; m. Mar. 1719, THOMAS (SOUTHWELL), 2nd BARON
SOUTHWELL [I.], b. 7 Jan. 1698; d. 19/20 Nov. 1766; and
had issue.

See the Clarence Volume, Table VII., pp. 102–106, Nos. 913–1036.
                                              [Nos. 33585 to 33708.

331. Descendants of PENISTON (LAMB), 1st VISCOUNT MELBOURNE
[I.] and BARON MELBOURNE [U.K.] (see Table XXX.), b.
29 Jan. 1740 [or 48]; d. 22 July 1828; m. 13 Ap. 1769,
ELIZABETH, da. of Sir Ralph MILBANKE of Halnaby, 5th Bart.
[E.], d. 6 Ap. 1818; and had issue 1a to 3a.

    1a. William (Lamb), 2nd Viscount [I.] and Baron [U.K.] Melbourne, P.C.,
Prime Minister 1834–1841, b. 15 Mar. 1779; d.s.p.s. 24 Nov. 1848.

    2a. Frederick James (Lamb), 3rd Viscount [I.] and Baron [U.K.] Melbourne,
also 1st Baron Beauvale [U.K.], G.C.B., H.B.M.'s Ambassador to the Court of
Vienna, b. 17 Ap. 1782; d.s.p. 29 Jan. 1853.

    3a. Lady Emily Mary Lamb, d. 11 Sept. 1869; m. 1st, 20 July 1805, Peter
Leopold Louis Francis Nassau (Cowper), 5th Earl [G.B.] and Baron [E.] Cowper,
3rd Prince Cowper [H.R.E.], b. 6 May 1778; d. 27 June 1737; 2ndly, 16 Dec.
1839, Henry John (Temple), 3rd and last Viscount Palmerston [I.], K.G., G.C.B.,
b. 20 Oct. 1784; d.s.p. 18 Oct. 1865; and had issue 1b to 3b.

    1b. George Augustus Frederick (Cowper), 6th Earl [G.B.] and Baron [E.]
Cowper, 4th Prince Cowper [H.R.E.], b. 26 June 1806; d. 15 Ap. 1856; m. 7 Oct.
1833, Anne Florence, suo jure Baroness Lucas [E.], da. and co-h. of Thomas Philip
(Robinson), 2nd Earl de Grey [U.K.], d. 23 July 1880; and had issue.

    See p. 140, Nos. 2017–2047.

    2b. Lady Emily Caroline Catherine Frances Cowper, b. 6 Nov. 1810; d. 15 Oct.
                                      [Nos. 33709 to 33739.

The Plantagenet Roll

1872; m. 16 *June* 1830, *Anthony* (*Ashley-Cooper*), *7th Earl of Shaftesbury* [*E.*], *K.G.*, b. 28 *Ap.* 1801; d. 1 *Oct.* 1885; *and had issue*.

See the Tudor Roll of " The Blood Royal of Britain," pp. 428–429, Nos. 31029–31054.

3*b. Lady Frances Elizabeth Cowper*, b. 9 *Feb.* 1820; d. 26 *Mar.* 1880; m. 29 *Ap.* 1841, *Robert Jocelyn, Viscount Jocelyn, M.P.*, d.v.p. 12 *Aug.* 1854; *and had issue*.

See the Clarence Volume, pp. 290–291, Nos. 8115–8130.

[Nos. 33740 to 33781.

332. Descendants of Charlotte Lamb (see Table XXX.), b. 1 Nov. 1743; d. 1 Ap. 1790; m. as 1st wife, 29 May 1766, Henry (Belasyse), 2nd Earl of [G.B.] and 5th Viscount [E.] Fauconberg, b. 13 Ap. 1743; d. 23 Mar. 1802; and had issue 1a to 3a.

1*a. Lady Charlotte Belasyse*, b. 10 *Jan.* 1767; d. (–); m. *Thomas Edward Wynn, afterwards Belasyse, of Newburgh Hall, co. York*.

2*a. Lady Anne Belasyse*, b. 27 *Dec.* 1768; d. 7 *July* 1808; m. *as 1st wife*, 19 *July* 1791, *Sir George Wombwell, 2nd Bart.* [*G.B.*], b. 14 *Mar.* 1769; d. 28 *Oct.* 1846; *and had issue* 1*b*.

1*b. Sir George Wombwell, 3rd Bart.* [*G.B.*], b. 13 *Ap.* 1792; d. 14 *Jan.* 1855; m. 23 *June* 1824, *Georgiana, da. of Thomas Orby Hunter of Crowland Abbey, co. Linc.*, d. 10 *May* 1875; *and had issue* 1*c* to 4*c*.

1*c. Sir George Orby Wombwell, 4th Bart.* [*G.B.*], J.P., D.L., *late* 17th Lancers (*Newburgh Park, Easingwold, co. Yorks; 20 Wilton Crescent, S.W.*), b. 25 Nov. 1832; m. 3 Sept. 1861, Lady Julia Sarah Alice, da. of George Augustus Frederic (Villiers), 6th Earl of Jersey [E.]; *and has issue*.

See the Tudor Roll of " The Blood Royal of Britain," p. 358, Nos. 27554–27560.

2*c. Adolphus Ulick Wombwell, Lieut.-Col. late 12th Lancers*, b. 17 *May* 1834; d. 21 *June* 1886; m. 23 *Sept.* 1862, *Mary Caroline, da. of Col. Myddelton Biddulph of Chirk Castle, M.P.*, d. 20 *Sept.* 1890; *and had issue* 1*d*.

1*d. Mary Alexina Florence Wombwell*, b. 23 *Oct.* 1870; d. 1897; m. 19 *Nov.* 1890, *Louis St. Julien Prioleau; and had issue* 2 *children*.

3*c.* Henry Herbert Wombwell, *late* Capt. Royal Horse Guards (*3 Victoria Square, S.W.*), b. 24 Sept. 1840; m. 8 Feb. 1902, the Hon. Myrtle Mabel Muriel, sister of Hubert (Mostyn), 7th Baron Vaux of Harrowden [E.].

4*c. Frederick Charles Wombwell*, b. 12 *July* 1845; d. 7 *July* 1889; m. 12 *Jan.* 1868, *Marie, da. of* [——] *Boyer; and had issue* 1*d* to 2*d*.

1*d.* Frederick Adolphus Wombwell, Lieut. 16th Lancers (*20 Bruton Street, W.*), b. 8 Ap. 1869.

2*d.* Almina Victoria Maria Alexandra Wombwell, *m.* 26 June 1895, George Edward Stanhope Molyneux (Herbert), 5th Earl of Carnarvon [G.B.] (*Highclere Castle, Newbury; 13 Berkeley Square, W.*); and has issue 1*e* to 2*e*.

1*e.* Henry George Alfred Marius Victor Frances Herbert, Lord Porchester, b. 7 Nov. 1898.

2*e.* Lady Evelyn Leonora Almina Herbert, b. 15 Aug. 1901.

3*a. Lady Elizabeth Belasyse*, b. 17 *Jan.* 1770; d. 24 *Mar.* 1819; m. 1*st*, 23 *Ap.* 1789, *Bernard* (*Howard*) (*afterwards* 1815), *12th Duke of Norfolk* [*E.*], *marriage dissolved May* 1794; 2*ndly*, 26 *May* 1794, *Richard* (*Bingham*), *2nd Earl of Lucan* [*I.*], b. 4 *Dec.* 1764; d. 30 *June* 1839; *and had issue* 1*b* to 6*b*.

1*b. Henry Charles* (*Howard*), *13th Duke of Norfolk* [*E.*], *K.G.*, b. 12 *Aug.* 1791;

[Nos. 33782 to 33794.

402

# of The Blood Royal

d. 18 *Feb.* 1856; m. 26 *Dec.* 1814, *Lady Charlotte Sophia, da. of George Granville (Leveson-Gower), 1st Duke of Sutherland [U.K.]*, d. 7 *July* 1870; *and had issue.*
See the Tudor Roll of "The Blood Royal of Britain," pp. 371–373, Nos. 28179–28239.

2*b. George Charles (Bingham), 3rd Earl of Lucan [I.], G.C.B., Field-Marshal in the Army, &c.*, b. 16 *Ap.* 1800; d. 10 *Nov.* 1888; m. 29 *June* 1829, *Lady Anne, da. of Robert (Brudenell), 6th Earl of Cardigan [E.]*, b. 29 *June* 1809; d. 2 *Ap.* 1877; *and had issue.*
See the Tudor Roll of "The Blood Royal of Britain," pp. 177–178, Nos. 20395–20447.

3*b. Lady Elizabeth Bingham*, b. 1795; d. 9 *Sept.* 1838; m. *as 1st wife,* 27 *Mar.* 1815, *George Granville-Vernon-Harcourt of Nuneham Courtenay, Oxon., M.P.*, b. 6 *Aug.* 1785; d. 19 *Dec.* 1861; *and had issue* 1*c.*

1*c. Elizabeth Lavinia Granville-Vernon-Harcourt,* d. 16 *Oct.* 1858; m. 7 *Jan.* 1835, *Montagu (Bertie), 6th Earl of Abingdon [E.]*, d. 8 *Feb.* 1884; *and had issue.*
See p. 78, Nos. 146–177.

4*b. Lady Anne Bingham*, b. 22 *Feb.* 1797; d. 28 *Oct.* 1850; m. 18 *July* 1816, *Alexander Murray of Broughton, M.P.*, d. 15 *July* 1845.

5*b. Lady Louisa Bingham*, b. 1 *Mar.* 1798; d. 16 *Ap.* 1882; m. 22 *Aug.* 1817, *Francis (Wemyss-Charteris-Douglas), 9th Earl of Wemyss and 5th Earl of March [S.], 2nd Baron Wemyss [U.K.]*, d. 1 *Jan.* 1883; *and had issue.*
See the Clarence Volume, pp. 253–255, Nos. 6094–6143.

6*b. Lady Georgiana Bingham*, b. 19 *Ap.* 1799; d. 1 *July* 1849; m. 15 *June* 1821, *Charles Nevill of Neville Holt*, b. 1793; d. 18 *Oct.* 1848
[Nos. 33795 to 33990.

333. Descendants of JOHN GASCOYNE FANSHAWE of Parsloes, co. Essex, and Wyersdale, co. Lancaster, J.P. (see Table XXX.), *b.* 3 June 1746; *d.* 23 Dec. 1803; *m.* 19 May 1772, MARY, da. of Christopher PARKINSON of Prescott, co. Lancaster, *d.* 22 Mar. 1811; and had issue 1*a* to 2*a.*

1*a. Thomas Lewis Fanshawe of Parsloes and Wyersdale, M.A. (Oxon.), Vicar of Dagenham, 4th son, but h. in* 1843, b. 21 *Sept.* 1792; d. 5 *Mar.* 1858; m. 11 *Oct.* 1821, *Catherine Stephens, da. of Major-Gen. John Gaspard Le Marchant of Manor Le Marchant, Guernsey*, d. 1 *July* 1881; *and had issue* 1*b* to 3*b.*

1*b. John Gaspard Fanshawe of Parsloes and Wyersdale, late Clerk in the Board of Trade*, b. 27 *July* 1824; d. 27 *Dec.* 1903; m. 4 *Oct.* 1853, *Barbara Frederica Beaujolois, da. of the Hon. William James Coventry of Earl's Croome Court, J.P., D.L.*, d. 31 *Jan.* 1903; *and had issue* 1*c* to 5*c.*

1*c. Evelyn John Fanshawe, late* Capt. 4th Batt. Essex Regt. (132 *Ebury St.,* S.W.), b. 22 *July* 1854; *m.* 7 May 1887, Emily, da. of John Moore; and has issue 1*d.*

1*d.* Edgar Sydney Waldo Fanshawe, b. 29 Ap. 1891.

2*c.* Basil Thomas Fanshawe, *late* Capt. N. Devon Imp. Yeo. (*Holywell, Bratton Fleming, Devon ; The Park, Lunugala, Ceylon*), b. 28 July 1857; *m.* 19 Ap. 1890, Mary Georgina, da. of Sir William Henry Clerke, 10th Bart. [E.]; and has issue 1*d* to 6*d.*

1*d.* Aubrey Basil Fanshawe, *b.* 13 Nov. 1893.

2*d.* Evelyn Gascoyne Fanshawe, *b.* 16 Aug. 1903.

3*d.* Muriel Mary Fanshawe.

4*d.* Aline Barbara Fanshawe.

5*d.* Rachel Georgina Fanshawe.

6*d.* Vere Fanshawe.   [Nos. 33991 to 33999.

403

The Plantagenet Roll

3c. Lyonell Fanshawe, b. 6 *May* 1866; d. 31 *Oct.* 1904; m. 18 *Ap.* 1894, *Bessie Emily, da. of William Gibson Miller, d. 21 Oct. 1899; and had issue 1d.*

1*d.* Loftus Gaspard Lyonell William Fanshawe, *b.* 14 June 1896.

4*c.* Beaujolois Mabel Fanshawe, *m.* 12 Ap. 1887, Arthur George Ridout *(Condercum, Benwell, Northumberland)* ; and has issue 1*d.* to 3*d.*

1*d.* Lionel Arthur Christopher Ridout, *b.* 3 Ap. 1888.

2*d.* Gaspard Alured Evelyn Ridout, *b.* 1 Sept. 1898.

3*d.* Beaujolois Theresa Constance Ridout, *b.* 23 Aug. 1889.

5*c.* Violet Fanshawe, *m.* 24 Oct. 1899, the Hon. Huntley Douglas Gordon, Advocate (3 *Northumberland Street, Edinburgh*) ; and has issue 1*d.* to 2*d.*

1*d.* Douglas John Gordon, *b.* 14 Sept. 1900.

2*d.* Strathearn Gordon, *b.* 3 Sept. 1902.

2b. Thomas Basil Fanshawe, Col. late 33rd Regt., b. 3 *Dec.* 1829; d. 4 *May* 1905 ; m. 8 *Mar.* 1864, *Emily Catherine, da. of Gerard Lipyeatt Gosselin of Mount Ospringe, co. Kent ; and had issue* 1*c to* 5*c.*

1*c.* Herbert Cecil Fanshawe, Capt. Submarine Min. Mil. Eng., *b.* 9 Nov. 1867.

2*c.* Reginald Winnington Fanshawe, Capt. West Riding Regt., *b.* 2 Sept. 1871 ; *m.* 6 Dec. 1898, Susan Isabel, da. of R. F. MacTier, Bombay C.S. ; and has issue 1*d.*

1*d.* Nancy Peronell Fanshawe, *b.* 30 Sept. 1899.

3*c.* Frank Raymond Fanshawe, *b.* 5 Mar. 1874 ; *m.* 16 Ap. 1901, Henrietta Maude, da. of Adolphus John Carey of Guernsey ; and has issue 1*d.*

1*d.* Joan Fanshawe, *b.* 18 Dec. 1903.

4*c.* Helen Maude Fanshawe, *m.* 28 July 1890, Cecil Augustus Carey, Advocate and A.D.C. to the Governor of Guernsey *(Guernsey)* ; and has issue (2 das.).

5*c.* Lilian Emily Fanshawe.

3*b.* Helen Fanshawe *(Little Gaddesden, Herts)*, *m.* 7 May 1844, Edward Hanson Denison, Bar.-at-Law, *d.* 1 July 1864 ; and has issue 1*c* to 3*c.*

1*c.* Joseph Basil Denison, *b.* (–) ; *m.* 12 Mar. 1889, Annie Louisa, da. of Capt. Campbell of Glendarnel, Argyll ; and has issue (a son and da.).

2c. Helen Jemima Denison, d.s.p. 21 *May* 1889; m. 6 *Nov.* 1872, *William (Romilly), 2nd Baron Romilly [U.K.], d.* 23 *May* 1891.

3*c.* Katherine Alexandra Denison.

2a. Mary Annetta Fanshawe, b. 11 *Feb.* 1783; d. 13 *Sept.* 1840; m. 8 *June* 1803, *Henry Charles Boisragon of Walcot, co. Somerset, and of Cheltenham, M.D. ; and had issue* 1*b.*

1*b. Charles Henry Gascoyne Boisragon, Capt. in the Army, b.* 27 *Ap.* 1804 ; *d.* 7 *Feb.* 1837 ; m. 1827, *Ellen Gardiner, da. of Gen. Maxwell of Dalswinton, co. Dumfries ; and had issue* 1*c to* 4*c.*

1*c. Henry Francis Maxwell Boisragon, Major-Gen., b.* 27 *Mar.* 1828 ; d. 22 *Sept.* 1890 ; m. 16 *May* 1861, *Anna, da. of William Hudleston, I.C.S., d.* 9 *May* 1868 ; *and had issue* 1*d to* 2*d.*

1*d.* Guy Hudleston Boisragon, V.C., Major 5th Goorkha Rifles *(Junior Naval and Military)*, *b.* (at Kohat, Punjab) 5 Nov. 1864.

2*d.* Mabel Maxwell Boisragon, *b.* 7 Nov. 1862 ; *m.* 2 Nov. 1886, Capt. Herbert Wilkinson Dent, *late* The Queen's Regt. *(Broadleigh, Brockenhurst, Hants)* ; and has issue 1*e* to 3*e.*

1*e.* Robert Boisragon Dent, *b.* 25 Sept. 1887.

2*e.* Cecil Hudleston Dent, *b.* 7 July 1889.

3*e.* Guy Herbert Boisragon Dent, *b.* 30 May 1892.

2c. Theodore Walter Ross Boisragon, C.B., Major-Gen., b. 19 *May* 1830 ; d. 21 *Sept.* 1882 ; m. *Margaret, da. of [——] Gerrard ; and had issue* 1*d.*

[Nos. 34000 to 34022.

# of The Blood Royal

1*d.* Allan Maxwell Boisragon, Capt. in the Army, *late* Royal Irish Rifles, *b.* 22 Jan. 1860; *m.* Ethel, da. of [——] Roslyn; and has issue 1*e.*

   1*e.* Theodore A. Boisragon, *b.* 1897 or 1898.

3*c.* *Ellen Fanshawe Dundas Boisragon,* b. 25 *June* 1832; d. 3 *Oct.* 1899; m. 1*st,* 20 *Jan.* 1851, *Major James Drummond of Aberuchil Castle, Perthshire,* d. 26 *Ap.* 1852; 2*ndly,* 20 *Sept.* 1858, *Gen. Charles Simeon Thomason, R.E.; and had issue* 1*d to* 6*d.*

   1*d.* Rowland Maxwell Thomason (*Mhow, Central India*), *b.* 19 Ap. 1864, *m.* 28 Mar. 1894, Florence Ellen, da. of Dr. Lukis; and has issue 1*e.*

      1*e.* Maynard Grant Maxwell Thomason, *b.* 26 June 1897.

   2*d.* Archibald Fawcett Thomason, Major (*Lahore Fort, Punjab, India*), *b.* 31 Mar. 1866; *m.* 1st, 31 Mar. 1891, Lucy, da. of Gen. Charles Pollard, R.E.; 2ndly, 22 Mar. 1893, Charlotte, da. of Col. Charles Cantor; and has issue 1*e* to 3*e.*

      1*e.* James Maxwell Fawcett Thomason, *b.* 21 Sept. 1894.

      2*e.* Archibald David Fawcett Thomason, *b.* 25 Ap. 1898.

      3*e.* Lucy Mabel Maynard Thomason, *b.* 20 Dec. 1891.

   3*d.* Ellen Effie Drummond (103 *Warwick Road, Earl's Court, S.W.*), *b.* 18 Oct. 1851.

   4*d.* Annie Grant Thomason, *b.* 23 July 1859; *m.* 16 Oct. 1889, Edward Anster Neville (*Gorukour, United Provinces, India*); and has issue 1*e* to 2*e.*

      1*e.* John Noel Neville, *b.* 23 Dec. 1895.

      2*e.* Charles Neville, *b.* 18 Oct. 1897.

   5*d.* Ellen Farish Thomason, *b.* 9 May 1868; *m.* 2 Oct. 1892, Walter Jenkins (*The Pines, Shipbourne, Kent*), *s.p.*

   6*d.* Bessie Drummond Thomason, *b.* 3 Nov. 1870; *m.* 11 Dec. 1889, Clifford Beckett (*The Pines, Shipbourne, Kent*); and has issue 1*e* to 2*e.*

      1*e.* Clifford Thomason Beckett, *b.* 9 Nov. 1891.

      2*e.* Walter Napier Thomason Beckett, *b.* 25 Mar. 1893.

4*c.* *Annette Macpherson Boisragon,* b. 28 *Jan.* 1835; d. 13 *Aug.* 1905; m. 20 *Mar.* 1852, *Capt. Henry Drummond, R.E.,* d. 28 *Mar.* 1883; *and had issue* 1*d to* 6*d.*

   1*d.* Francis Henry Rutherford Drummond, Col. in Indian Army, *b.* 9 Sept. 1857; *m.* June 1890, Violet, da. of Col. Home, *s.p.*

   2*d.* Eric Grey Drummond, Capt. Indian Army, 4th Goorkha Rifles, *b.* 10 Sept. 1875; *unm.*

   3*d.* Alice Drummond, *b.* 14 May 1854; *m.* 21 Oct. 1875, Col. Crule Money, 9th Bengal Lancers; and has issue 1*e* to 3*e.*

      1*e.* Crule Frank Money, Lieut. 4th Goorkha Rifles, *b.* 18 June 1878; *unm.*

      2*e.* Henry Ironside Money, Lieut. 1st Goorkha Rifles, *b.* Sept. 1885.

      3*e.* Nettie Money, *b.* 19 Dec. 1880; *unm.*

   4*d.* Eva Drummond, *b.* 21 Oct. 1862; *m.* 25 Feb. 1888, Gordon Beatson; and has issue 1*e* to 2*e.*

      1*e.* Dorothy Beatson, *b.* 16 Oct. 1891.

      2*e.* Moira Beatson, *b.* 7 Dec. 1903.

   5*d.* Mayrie Maxwell Drummond, *b.* 26 Sept. 1864; *unm.*

   6*d.* Winifred Drummond, *b.* 30 Ap. 1867; *m.* 6 June 1899, the Rev. John Lister Coles (*Church Lodge, Stowting, near Hythe, Kent*); and has issue 1*e* to 4*e.*

      1*e.* John Lewis Drummond Coles, *b.* 28 Feb. 1903.

      2*e.* Beatrice Winifred Coles, *b.* 8 Dec. 1899.

      3*e.* Esmé Sylvia Maxwell Coles, *b.* 5 May 1901.

      4*e.* Joyce Annette Coles, *b.* 3 Sept. 1904.

[Nos. 34023 to 34053.

The Plantagenet Roll

334. Descendants, if any, of FRANCES FANSHAWE (see Table XXX.), d. 10 May 1795 ; m. a. 1750, the Rev. ABRAHAM BLACKBURNE of Hampton, co. Middlesex, M.A., D.D., Vicar of Dagenham, d. 26 Nov. 1797.

335. Descendants of MARIA FANSHAWE (see Table XXX.), d. 8 Ap. 1777 ; m. 14 June 1750, FRANCIS BURRELL MASSINGBERD of St. Michael's, Cornhill, bapt. 5 Mar. 1720 ; d. 6 May 1795 ; and had issue 1a.

1a. Rev. Francis Massingberd, Rector of Massingborough and Preb. of Lincoln, b. 24 Oct. 1755 ; d. 11 Ap. 1817 ; m. 14 Ap. 1795, Elizabeth, da. of William Burrell Massingberd of Ormsby, co. Lincoln, bur. 18 Ap. 1817 ; and had issue 1b.

1b. Rev. Francis Charles Massingberd, Rector of Ormsby and Chancellor of Lincoln Cathedral, b. 3 Dec. 1800 ; d. 5 Dec. 1872 ; m. 15 Jan. 1839, Fanny, da. of William Baring, M.P., d. 2 Ap. 1891 ; and had issue 1c.

1c. Rev. William Oswald Massingberd, Rector of Ormsby and Rural Dean of Hill, present male representative of the Massingberds of Ormsby (Ormsby Rectory, Lincoln), b. 23 Feb. 1848 ; m. 9 Dec. 1884, Emily Sophia, da. of the Rev. John Soper, Rector of Bag Enderby ; and has issue 1d.

1d. Dorothy Emily Massingberd, b. 6 Feb. 1886. [Nos. 34054 to 34055.

336. Descendants of ROBERT FANSHAWE, Capt. R.N., Commissioner Plymouth Dockyard (see Table XXX.), b. Jan. 1740 ; d. 4 Feb. 1824 ; m. 5 Dec. 1769, CHRISTIANA, da. of John GENNYS of Whitleigh Hall, co. Devon, d. 1824 ; and had issue 1a to 7a.

1a. Edward Fanshawe, C.B., Lieut.-Gen. R.E., b. 16 Oct. 1785 ; d. 22 Nov. 1858 ; m. 15 June 1811, Frances Mary, da. of Lieut.-Gen. Sir Hew Whiteford Dalrymple, 1st Bart. [U.K.], b. 3 Mar. 1790 ; d. 16 June 1865 ; and had issue 1b to 9b.

1b. Sir Edward Gennys Fanshawe, G.C.B., Adm. R.N., sometime (1878–1879) Commander-in-Chief at Portsmouth (74 Cromwell Road, S.W.), b. 27 Nov. 1814 ; m. 11 May 1843, Jane, sister of Edward, Viscount Cardwell [U.K.], and da. of John Cardwell, b. 17 Sept. 1815 ; d. 23 July 1900 ; and has issue 1c to 4c.

1c. Edward Cardwell Fanshawe, Major R.E., Col. 1st London Engineers Vol., b. 25 July 1844 ; m. 1st, 1874, [——], da. of [——] ; 2ndly, 6 Mar. 1900, Alice, da. of Col. George Drew, C.B. ; and has issue 1d to 4d.

1d. Edward Hew Fanshawe, South African Constabulary, late Lieut. 19th Hussars, b. 25 Ap. 1880.

2d. George Drew Fanshawe, b. 1902.

3d. Ethel Fanshawe, b. 22 Oct. 1881.

4d. Kathleen Maud Fanshawe, b. 28 Feb. 1904.

2c. Sir Arthur Dalrymple Fanshawe, K.C.B., Vice-Adm. R.N., late Commander-in-Chief on the Australian Station (United Service), b. 2 Ap. 1847 ; m. 21 Jan. 1874, Sarah Frances, da. of William Fox of Adbury Park ; and has issue 1d to 4d.

1d. Richard Dalrymple Fanshawe, 2nd Lieut. Scots Guards, b. 27 Aug. 1879 ; m. 19 Ap. 1906, Constance Kathleen, da. of W. J. S. Barber-Starkey of Knockshannock, co. Forfar.

2d. Guy Dalrymple Fanshawe, Lieut. R.N., b. 30 Mar. 1882.

3d. Winifred Edith Fanshawe, m. 18 Nov. 1902, the Rev. Edmund Hugh [Nos. 34056 to 34065.

# of The Blood Royal

Rycroft, Rector of Bishop's Waltham (*Bishop's Waltham Rectory, Hants*); and has issue 1e to 2e.

1e. Arthur John Rycroft.

2e. Barbara Frances Rycroft.

4d. Renea Leighton Fanshawe.

3c. Evelyn Leighton Fanshawe, B.A. Oxford, Bar.-at-Law (*Dalveagh, Aberfoyle*), b. 30 June 1854; m. 15 Oct. 1887, Frances Sophia, da. of Gen. Charles Alexander Fanshawe of Grodno, Russia, s.p.

4c. Alice Eliza Jane Fanshawe.

2b. *Hew Dalrymple Fanshawe, Lieut.-Col. 52nd Regt., J.P.*, b. (*twin*) 6 *July* 1817; d. 28 *Feb.* 1899; m. 30 *June* 1853, *Barbara, da. of Gen. Sir Thomas Bradford, G.C.H., G.C.B., K.T.S.*, d. 8 *Dec.* 1897; *and had issue* 1c *to* 3c.

1c. Rev. William Dalrymple Fanshawe, M.A., *late* Vicar of St. Clement's, Barnsbury, b. 19 Feb. 1856.

2c. Frederick Bradford Fanshawe, Capt. Royal Southern Reserve Regt., *late* Royal West Kent Regt. (*Hartwell, Reading*), b. 6 Jan. 1859; m. 10 July 1888, Marianne Ellen, da. of W. Arthur Fremlin of Court Lodge, Teston, co. Kent; and has issue 1d to 5d.

1d. Arthur Hew Bradford Fanshawe, b. 22 Oct. 1889.

2d. Leighton Dalrymple Fanshawe, b. 9 Jan. 1896.

3d. Frederick Fanshawe, b. 18 Nov. 1905.

4d. Barbara Evelyn Fanshawe, b. 5 Feb. 1891.

5d. Marianne Fanshawe, b. 11 Ap. 1892.

3c. Frances Elizabeth Fanshawe.

3b. *Charles Fanshawe, Gen. R.E.*, b. (*twin*) 6 *July* 1817; d. 9 *Dec.* 1901; m. 1st, 26 *Ap.* 1848, *Grizilda Emma, da. of Gen. Sir G. Harding, K.C.B.*, d. 1 *Nov.* 1852; 2ndly, 10 *Feb.* 1866, *Anne Williamina, da. of Capt. Charles Hope-Johnstone, R.N.*, b. 29 *Jan.* 1828; d. 11 *Jan.* 1899; *and had issue* 1c *to* 6c.

1c. George Dalrymple Fanshawe, Brig.-Gen. R.A. in command of the coast defences at Cork, b. 31 Aug. 1850; m. 7 Feb. 1899, Maud Mary, da. of Sir Frederick R. Saunders, K.C.M.G., Treasurer of Ceylon, s.p.

2c. Arthur Hope Fanshawe, Lieut. R.N., H.M. Coastguard at Salcombe, b. 4 Feb. 1867; m. 18 Ap. 1895, Agnes Elizabeth, da. of George Hustler Tuck, J.P., D.L.; and has issue 1d to 3d.

1d. Richard Arthur Fanshawe, b. 18 Feb. 1906.

2d. Stella Catherine Fanshawe, b. 22 Nov. 1898.

3d. Marjorie Hope-Johnstone Fanshawe, b. 30 July 1904.

3c. Basil Hew Fanshawe, Commander R.N., b. 18 May 1868; m. 16 Oct. 1899, Rosalie, da. of J. L. Adams of New York.

4c. Rev. Gerald Charles Fanshawe, Vicar of Godalming (*Godalming, Surrey*), b. 14 Nov. 1870; m. 30 Aug. 1904, Morforwyn Mary Leveson, da. of Lieut.-Col. George Hope Lloyd Hope-Verney; and has issue 1d.

1d. Mary Morforwyn Fanshawe, b. 12 Feb. 1906.

5c. John Edward Fanshawe, b. 15 Jan. 1873, Clerk in the British Linen Company Bank (2 *Coates Crescent, Edinburgh*).

6c. Zilla Mary Fanshawe, m. 12 Nov. 1885, Edward Foote Ward (*Salhouse Hall, Norfolk*), D.L.

4b. *Rev. Frederick Fanshawe, Fellow and Tutor of Exeter Coll., Oxford, Headmaster of Bedford School for nearly twenty years*, b. 14 *Feb.* 1821; d. 27 *Mar.* 1879; m. 20 *Dec.* 1855, *Mary Louisa, da. of Gen. Sir Henry Goldfinch, K.C.B.*; *and had issue* 1c *to* 3c.

1c. Katherine Mary Fanshawe, m. 19 Ap. 1894, Athelstan Arthur Baines.

2c. Anne Louisa Fanshawe.

3c. Frances Alice Fanshawe.   [Nos. 34066 to 34091.

407

The Plantagenet Roll

5b. Rev. Arthur Adolphus Fanshawe, M.A., B.C.L., Fellow of New Coll., Oxford, *late* Rector of Bubbenhall and Hunningham, co. Warwick (*Lushington Road, Eastbourne*), b. 28 Mar. 1830 ; m. 1st, 27 Ap. 1855, Sarah, da. of John Parsons, d.s.p. 28 July 1891 ; 2ndly, Charlotte, da. of [——] Hall.

6b. Rev. Henry Leighton Fanshawe, M.A., Fellow of New Coll., Oxford, *late* Rector of Adwell and South Weston, co. Oxon. (*Chilworth, Oxon.*), b. 7 July 1832 ; m. 9 Dec. 1856, Ellen, da. of Guy Thomson of Baldon House, co. Oxford, d. 4 May 1890 ; and has issue 1c to 5c.

1c. Edward Arthur Fanshawe, Lieut.-Col. R.A., b. 4 Ap. 1859 ; m. 5 July 1893, Frances Rose, da. of Sir James Macaulay Higginson, K.C.B., Governor of the Mauritius ; and has issue 1d to 3d.

1d. Edward Leighton Fanshawe, b. 14 Nov. 1891.

2d. Robert Macaulay Fanshawe, b. 22 Feb. 1904.

3d. Mary Fanshawe, b. 6 Mar. 1895.

2c. Hew Dalrymple Fanshawe, *late* 19th Hussars, Lieut.-Col. 2nd Dragoon Guards, b. 3 Ap. 1860 ; m. 25 July 1894, Anna Paulina Mary, da. of Field-Marshal Sir Henry Evelyn Wood, V.C., G.C.M.G., G.C.B., 1st Class K.M. ; and has issue 1d to 3d.

1d. Evelyn Dalrymple Fanshawe, b. 25 May 1895.

2d. George Hew Fanshawe, b. 17 June 1897.

3d. Jeannette Ellen Fanshawe, b. 7 Feb. 1904.

3c. Robert Fanshawe, D.S.O., Lieut.-Col. Oxfordshire L.I., *late* D.A.A.G. 4th Div. 2nd Army Corps, b. 5 Nov. 1863 ; m. 8 Oct. 1903, Evelyne Isabel, da. of the late Archbishop (Knox) of Armagh.

4c. Mary Fanshawe.

5c. Annie Fanshawe.

7b. *Frances Anne Fanshawe*, b. 8 *Aug.* 1813 ; d. (? s.p.) 14 *May* 1901 ; m. 10 *June* 1844, *Capt. John Windham Dalling, R.N., son of Sir John Dalling, 1st Bart.* [*G.B.*], d. 10 *Oct.* 1853.

8b. Susan Cordelia Fanshawe, m. 30 May 1849, William Fox of Adbury Park, Hants, J.P., b. 20 Nov. 1820 ; d. 25 Dec. 1883 ; and has issue.

9b. Margaret Arabella Fanshawe.

2a. *Christiana Fanshawe*, b. 21 *Jan.* 1771 ; d. Dec. 1810 ; m. 1796, *the Rev. Dr. Francis Haggitt, D.D., Rector of Newnham Courtney, co. Oxford, and Preb. of Durham ; and had issue 1b.*

1b. Catherine Haggitt, m. the Rev. [——] Baker.

3a. *Elizabeth Fanshawe*, b. 4 *Feb.* 1772 ; d. 1848 ; m. *as 2nd wife*, 18 *Jan.* 1796, *Francis Glanville of Catchfrench, M.P., High Sheriff co. Cornwall* 1793, d. 1846 ; *and had issue 1b to 6b.*

1b. *Francis Glanville of Catchfrench, J.P., D.L.,* b. 13 *Ap.* 1797 ; d. 1881 ; m. 1821, *Amabel, da. of the Right Hon. Reginald Pole Carew of East Antony, co. Cornwall ; and had issue 1c to 4c.*

1c. Francis Robert Glanville, Major-Gen. *late* R.A. (*Catchfrench, near Liskeard*), b. 1827 ; m. 1860, Dona Maria Concepcion Guadalope, da. of Don Francisco Carreras of Gibraltar ; and has issue 1d to 10d.

1d. Francis Glanville, D.S.O., Capt. R.E., b. 16 May 1862 ; m. 1888, Frances Guenevere, da. of E. H. J. Craufurd of Auchenames.

2d. Arthur George Glanville, Capt. R.A., b. 15 Ap. 1866.

3d. Henry Estcourt Glanville, b. 1869.

4d. Reginald Glanville, b. 1869.

5d. Ernest Wilfred Glanville, b. 1870.

6d. Gerald Walter Glanville (*Adela House, The Triangle, Teignmouth*), b. 1872.

7d. Amabel Glanville, b. 1868.

8d. Mary Frances Glanville, b. 1881.

9d. Mary Ethel Maud Glanville, b. 1875.

10d. Mary Florence Victoria Glanville, b. 1877.　　　　[Nos. 34092 to 34118.

408

2c. Reginald Carew Glanville, M.A. (Oxon.), Bar.-at-Law (*Truro*), b. 1836.

3c. *Jemima Amabel Glanville*, d. 1892; m. 1855, *the Rev. Arthur Tatham, M.A., Rector of Boconnoe and Braddoe; and had issue.*

4c. Mary Agneta Glanville (*Langham Hill, Ivybridge, Devon*).

2b. *William Fanshawe Glanville, Capt. R.N.*, b. 1808; d. *Aug.* 1861; m. 1841, *Mary Ann, da. of Rear-Admiral William Bedford, R.N.*, d. *Oct.* 1880; *and had issue* 1c *to* 3c.

1c. Rev. Owen Fanshawe Glanville, B.A. (T.C.D.), Headmaster of Hillsborough Prep. Sch. (*Hillsborough, Teignmouth, Devon*), b. 15 Sept. 1847.

2c. Ranulph Glanville (*The Crags, Lustleigh, S. Devon*), b. 14 Feb. 1851.

3c. Julia Glanville (7 *Ferndale, Teignmouth*).

3b. *Charles Fanshawe Glanville*, d. (–); m.; *and had issue* 1c.

1c. Alice Glanville, m. the Rev. H. Macnamara (*The Rectory, Queenhithe, E.*).

4b. Elizabeth Mary Glanville.

5b. Cordelia Fanshawe Glanville.

6b. Catherine Fanshawe Glanville.

4a. *Susan Fanshawe*, b. 17 *Jan.* 1774; d. 18 *Oct.* 1855; m. *Jan.* 1806, *Admiral William Bedford, R.N.*, d. *Oct.* 1827; *and had issue* 1b *to* 3b.

1b. *William Bedford, General in the Army*, d. (–); m. *Elizabeth, da. of* [——] *Skeman; and had issue* 1c *to* 2c.

1c. Rev. Arthur Bedford.

2c. Alice Bedford.

2b. *Christina Bedford*, d. (–); m. *the Rev.* [——] *Campbell; and had issue* 1c *to* 5c.

1c. Rev. James Campbell.

2c. Mary Campbell.

3c. Charlotte Campbell.

4c. Frances Campbell, ⎱
5c. Penelope Campbell, ⎰ (*Paignton, S. Devon*).

3b. *Mary Ann Bedford*, d. *Oct.* 1880; m. 1841, *Capt. William Fanshawe Glanville*, d. *Aug.* 1861; *and had issue.*

See p. 409, Nos. 34121–34123.

5a. *Catherine Fanshawe*, b. 2 *Jan.* 1778; d. 25 *Mar.* 1849; m. *Aug.* 1798, *Sir Thomas Byam Martin, G.C.B., K.S., Admiral of the Fleet, and Vice-Admiral of the United Kingdom*, d. 21 *Oct.* 1854; *and had issue* 1b *to* 2b.

1b. *Sir William Fanshawe Martin, 4th Bart.* [G.B.], *G.C.B., Admiral R.N., and Rear-Admiral of the United Kingdom*, b. 5 *Dec.* 1801; d. 24 *Mar.* 1895; m. 2ndly, 21 *May* 1838, *Sophia Elizabeth, da. of Richard Hurt of Wirksworth, co. Derby*, d. 12 *Nov.* 1874; *and had issue* 1c *to* 5c.

1c. Sir Richard Byam Martin, 5th Bart. [U.K.] (7 *Esplanade, Plymouth*), b. 28 Ap. 1841; m. 20 July 1869, Catherine, da. and h. of Capt. Knipe, 5th Dragoon Guards; and has issue 1d to 3d.

1d. Mary Catherine Martin, m. 17 July 1894, William Henry Knight.

2d. Margaret Louisa Martin, m. 1902, Alexander Finlay Smith.

3d. Georgiana Phyllis Maud Martin.

2c. Caroline Martin.

3c. Grace Martin.

4c. Harriette Fanshawe Martin.

5c. Georgiana Fanshawe Martin (5 *Oxford Square, Hyde Park, W.*).

2b. *Elizabeth Anne Martin*, d. 24 *Mar.* 1863; m. *as 2nd wife,* 17 *July* 1834, *Francis John Davies of Danehurst, co. Sussex, J.P., Gen. in the Army and Col. 67th Foot*, b. 1 *May* 1791; d. 4 *Dec.* 1874; *and had issue* 1c *to* 4c.

[Nos. 34119 to 34145.

The Plantagenet Roll

1c. Henry Fanshawe Davies, J.P., Lieut.-Gen., *formerly* Col. Grenadier Guards and (1889–1893) Comdg. Cork District (*Elmley Castle, Pershore, Worcester*), *b.* 17 Feb. 1837; *m.* 4 Aug. 1863, Ellen Christine, da. of John Alexander Hankey of Balcombe Place, co. Sussex; and has issue 1*d* to 7*d*.

    1*d*. Francis John Davies, J.P., Major and Col. Grenadier Guards, *b.* 3 July 1864; *m.* 1896, Magdalen, da. of Major Hugh Scott of Gala, co. Selkirk; and has issue 1*e* to 2*e*.

        1*e*. Henry Rodolph Hugh Davies, *b.* 18 July 1903.

        2*e*. Grisel Madalen Agnes Davies, *b.* 20 June 1897.

    2*d*. Henry Rodolph Davies, Major 52nd Oxfordshire L.I., *b.* 28 Sept. 1865.

    3*d*. Hugh Warburton Davies, *b.* 26 Dec. 1871.

    4*d*. Christine Isabel Davies.

    5*d*. Mary Elizabeth Davies.

    6*d*. Lucy Cecil Davies.

    7*d*. Margaret Anna Davies, *m.* 30 Sept. 1903, Rev. E. E. Lea, Rector of Eastham, Worcestershire.

    2c. Byam Martin Davies, Bar.-at-Law (*Waltham Place, Maidenhead; Corsley House, Warminster*), *b.* 1 Oct. 1840; *m.* 21 Sept. 1874, Frances Anne, da. of Edward Conant of Lyndon, co. Rutland; and has issue 1*d* to 3*d*.

    1*d*. Warburton Davies, Capt. Rifle Brigade.

    2*d*. Claud Davies, Lieut. Rifle Brigade.

    3*d*. Maud Davies.

    3c. Catherine Anne Davies.

    4c. Charlotte Elizabeth Davies.

    6a. *Mary Fanshawe*, b. 1 *Oct.* 1787; d. 4 *June* 1866; m. 29 *June* 1809, *Adm. the Hon. Sir Robert Stopford, G.C.B., G.C.M.G., Admiral of the Red, Governor of Greenwich Hospital*, b. 5 *Feb.* 1768; d. 25 *June* 1847; *and had issue.*
See the Tudor Roll of "The Blood Royal of Britain," pp. 183–184, Nos. 20871–20886.

    7a. *Penelope Fanshawe*, b. 4 *Ap.* 1789; d. 1855; m. *Lieut.-Col. George Henry Duckworth*, 48th *Foot*, b. 25 *June* 1782; d. (*being killed at the battle of Albuera*) 16 *May* 1811; *and had issue* 1*b*.

    1b. *Ann Duckworth*, d. 1855; m. *as* 1st *wife*, 1840, *Gen. Sir Robert Percy Douglas, 4th Bart.* [*G.B.*], b. 29 *Aug.* 1805; d. 30 *Sept.* 1891; *and had issue* 1c *to* 3c.

    1c. Sir Arthur Percy Douglas, 5th Bart. [G.B.], Under-Sec. for Defence, New Zealand, *late* R.N. (*Wellington, New Zealand*), *b.* 1845; *m.* 16 Nov. 1871, Mary Caroline, da. of the Rev. William Foster of Stubbington House; and has issue 1*d* to 3*d*.

    1*d*. Laura Beatrice Douglas.

    2*d*. Annie Margaret Douglas.

    3*d*. Claudine Josephine Rose Douglas.

    2c. Anne Penelope Harriet Douglas, *m.* as 2nd wife, 1 Aug. 1885, Sir Hugh Low, G.C.M.G. (23 *De Vere Gardens, Kensington, W.*).

    3c. Helen Mary Douglas.   [Nos. 34146 to 34183.

337. Descendants of Charles Fanshawe, Counsellor-at-Law, Recorder of Exeter, Treasurer of the Inner Temple (see Table XXX.), *b. c.* 1740; *d.* 22 Mar. 1814; *m.* 22 June 1778, Elizabeth, da. of John Seale of Mount Boone, co. Devon, Sheriff for Devonshire 1749, *bur.* 26 Aug. 1784; and had issue 1*a*.

    1a. *Rev. John Charles Fanshawe of Cole House and Franklin, co. Devon, Rector of Chardstock, co. Somerset*, b. *May* 1780; d. 15 *Feb.* 1830; m. 11 *Feb.* 1806, *Frances Delia, da. of the Rev. William Henry Carrington, Rector of Ide, co. Devon*, d. 20 *Dec.* 1854; *and had issue* 1*b* to 5*b*.

# of The Blood Royal

1b. *Richard William Henry Fanshawe, Major Bengal Invalid Establishment,* b. 17 *June* 1819 ; d. 26 *June* 1885 ; m. 4 *Oct.* 1841, *Frances Elizabeth, da. of Major Joseph Leeson,* b. 13 *Feb.* 1822 ; d. 10 *Ap.* 1903 ; *and had issue* 1c *to* 5c.

1c. Richard Arthur Leeson Fanshawe, *late* Dist. Sup. of Police, Burmah (*Heatheshoe, Prowledge, near Farnham, Surrey*), b. 16 Aug. 1852 ; m. 22 Dec. 1896, Eleanor, da. of Thomas Stark Sutherland, C.E.

2c. *John Charles Fanshawe, Political Officer with H.H. the ex-King Theebaw of Burmah, Dist. Supt. of Police, Burmah,* b. 13 *Ap.* 1860 ; d. 10 Dec. 1895 ; m. *Nov.* 1887, *Agnes Rosalie, da. of Surg.-Gen. Bowhill, C.B. ; and had issue* 1d.

1d. Harvey Vernon Fanshawe, b. 1 June 1891.

3c. Alicia Louisa Fanshawe (9 *Kenilworth Road, Ealing, W.*), b. 30 Ap. 1846 ; *m.* 13 Aug. 1868, James Matthew Algie, C.E., Executive Engineer P.W.D., Burma, d. 19 July 1877 ; *and has issue* 1d *to* 3d.

1d. Ivor Allan Algie, National Bank of India, b. 5 Jan. 1871.

2d. Arthur Fanshawe Algie, b. 29 Oct. 1875.

3d. Elsie Camilla Algie, b. 20 June 1877.

4c. Clara Ellen Fanshawe, b. 16 Sept. 1854 ; *unm.*

5c. *Catherine Eliza Fanshawe,* b. 19 *May* 1862 ; d. 14 Nov. 1882 ; m. 13 *Ap.* 1880, *Alexander Martin Lindsay, in the Bank of Bengal Agency ; and had issue* 1d.

1d. Harry Alexander Fanshawe Lindsay, I.C.S. (*Behar, India*), b. 11 Mar. 1881.

2b. *Anna Maria Harriet Rogers Fanshawe,* b. 21 Nov. 1810 ; d. 31 Dec. 1887 ; m. 28 *Nov.* 1838, *Charles Wootton, Superintendent of the Naval Dockyard, Deal, and afterwards a Clerk of the Admiralty ; and had issue* 1c *to* 5c.

1c. John Charles Fanshawe Wootton (13 *St. Philip's Road, Surbiton*), b. 11 Oct. 1839 ; *m.* Aug. 1876, Fanny Louisa, da. of [——] Solly ; *and has issue* 1d *to* 4d.

1d. Charles Arthur Wootton, b. June 1882.

2d. Ella Wootton, b. 18 Oct. 1877.

3d. Amy Wootton, b. 16 Sept. 1878.

4d. Mabel Grace Wootton, b. 25 Sept. 1879.

2c. *Arthur Fanshawe Wootton,* b. 3 *June* 1845 ; d. 15 *July* 1901 ; m. 5 *Oct.* 1876, *Mary Stephaine, da. of* [——] *Lloyd ; and had issue* 1d *to* 5d.

1d. Arthur Garnier Wootton, b. 13 July 1877.

2d. Herbert Lloyd Wootton, b. 23 Dec. 1878.

3d. John Charles Wootton, b. 2 Jan. 1881.

4d. Clement Fanshawe Wootton (*Canada*), b. 5 Oct. 1883.

5d. Ethel Mary Wootton, b. 14 June 1885.

3c. Henry Fanshawe Wootton (*Southfields*), b. 7 Aug. 1850 ; *m.* 9 Ap. 1885, Alice, da. of Charles Woolley ; *and has issue* 1d *to* 4d.

1d. Norah Fanshawe Wootton, ⎫ b. (twins) 3 Jan. 1886.
2d. Ruth Mary Wootton, ⎭

3d. Margaret Olga Wootton, b. 31 Mar. 1887.

4d. Alice Rachel Wootton, b. 6 May 1889.

4c. Harriette Mary Fanshawe Wootton, b. 10 June 1843 ; *unm.*

5c. Camilla Fanshawe Wootton, b. 7 Aug. 1847 ; *m.* 28 Aug. 1875, the Rev. Edward Hughes Thomas, d. (–) ; *and has issue* 1d *to* 5d.

1d. Edward William Charles Thomas, b. 10 Mar. 1884.

2d. Arthur Lewis Thomas, b. 12 Mar. 1887.

3d. Dora Camilla Thomas, b. 4 June 1876.

4d. Winifred Mary Fanshawe Thomas, b. 1 Oct. 1881.

5d. Elsie Fanshawe Thomas, b. 31 July 1885.

3b. *Catherine Ellen Fanshawe,* b. 29 *Feb.* 1812 ; d. 3 *Oct.* 1902 ; m. 28 *Dec.* 1835, *Henry Brothers Bingham,* b. 1 *Ap.* 1801 ; d. 30 *Nov.* 1875 ; *and had issue* 1c *to* 2c. [Nos. 34184 to 34213.

The Plantagenet Roll

1c. Rev. Fanshawe Bingham, M.A. (Trin. Coll., Camb.), Rector of Horfield, Bristol, 1878–1899 (*Melcombe, St. Andrew's Road, Southsea*), b. 27 May 1841; m. 28 Nov. 1871, Gertrude Frances, da. of Edmund Ford Radcliffe, B.C.S.; and has issue 1d to 5d.

1d. Herbert Berkeley Fanshawe Bingham, b. 31 Aug. 1875.

2d. Henry Carrington Fanshawe Bingham, b. 22 Oct. 1881.

3d. Kathleen Gertrude Fanshawe Bingham, b. 3 Aug. 1872.

4d. Alice Mary Fanshawe Bingham, b. 17 Nov. 1873.

5d. Cecilia Mildred Fanshawe Bingham, b. 7 Mar. 1877.

2c. Elizabeth Ellen Bingham (43 *Wimbledon Park Road, Southfields*), b. 18 Nov. 1836; m. 2 Oct. 1862, Frederick John Skoulding, *afterwards* Skoulding-Cann, d. 6 Dec. 1869; and has issue 1d to 3d.

1d. Emmeline Gertrude Skoulding-Cann, b. 28 June 1863; m. 19 Nov. 1889, William Gregory Eccles of the Transvaal Civil Service (*Pietermaritzburg*); and has issue 1e to 6e.

1e. Launcelot William Gregory Eccles, b. (at Pietermaritzburg) 19 Sept. 1890.

2e. Horton Frederick De Laume Eccles, b. (at Pietermaritzburg) 21 Jan. 1903.

3e. Bryan Rupert Dorset Eccles, b. (at Pietermaritzburg) 18 May 1904.

4e. Doris Alleurid Catharine Eccles, b. (near Pietermaritzburg) 4 Ap. 1892.

5e. Aileen Margerum Fanshawe Eccles, b. (near Pietermaritzburg) 25 Sept. 1894.

6e. Hilda Natalie Emmeline Eccles, b. (at Pietermaritzburg) 24 Oct. 1899.

2d. Henrietta Florence Lucy Skoulding-Cann, b. 25 Ap. 1865; *unm.*

3d. Beatrice Eva Fanshawe Skoulding-Cann, b. 8 Feb. 1867.

4b. *Louisa Sarah Georgiana Fanshawe*, b. 27 Ap. 1815; d. (*at Richmond, Quebec*) 1 Nov. 1900; m. 14 Feb. 1847, *Henry Aspinwall Howe of Montreal, M.A., LL.D., Lise Carroll; and had issue 1c to 3c.*

1c. Henry Howe, m., sp., M.P. (Canada), Lieut.-Col. Canadian Art. Mil., *formerly* R.M.A.

2c. Louisa Blanche Fanny Howe, b. Ap. 1848; m. 5 Oct. 1870, the Hon. Henry Aylmer (son of Matthew, 8th Baron Aylmer [I.]) (*Lennoxville, Quebec, Canada*), s.p.

3c. Amelia Egerton Aspinwall Howe; *unm.*

5b. *Mariana Fanshawe*, b. 18 *May* 1817; d. 10 *Jan.* 1892; m. 23 *Oct.* 1843, *Peter Royle, M.D., J.P.*, d. 12 *Nov.* 1891; *and had issue 1c to 5c.*

1c. Arthur Fanshawe Waterloo Royle, b. 18 June 1847; m. 18 Feb. 1882, Harriette, da. of John Clegg of Woodheys Hall, J.P.; and has issue (4 sons).

2c. *Henry Lucius Fanshawe Royle, Vice-Admiral R.N.*, d. *June* 1906; m.; *and had issue.*

3c. Rev. Vernon Fanshawe Royle (*Stanmore Park, Stanmore*), m.; and has issue (4 sons).

4c. Charles Fanshawe Royle, *unm.*

5c. Mariana Fanshawe Royle, m. Beaumont Fanshawe Swete, d. (–); and has issue (4 sons and 1 da.). [Nos. 34214 to 34236.

338. Descendants, if any, of ANNE LEWIN (see Table XXVII.), b. c. 1616; being aged three in 1619.

339. Descendants, if any, of ELIZABETH CORBET, wife of ROBERT HOUGHTON of Ranworth; and of ANNE CORBET, wife of FRANCIS COREY of Bramerton (see Table XXVII.).

# of The Blood Royal

340. Descendants, if any, of EDWARD CAPELL, JOHN CAPELL, GAMA-LIEL CAPELL, and ROBERT CAPELL (see Table XXVII.).

341. Descendants of FRANCES CAPELL (see Table XXVII.), wife of Sir JOHN SHIRLEY, Serjeant-at-Law.

342. Descendants, if any surviving, of Sir HUMPHREY MILDMAY of Danbury Place, co. Essex, J.P. 1634 (see Table XXXI.), *m.* JANE, da. of Sir John CROFTS of Saxham, co. Suffolk ; and had issue 1*a* to 5*a*.

> 1*a. John Mildmay, aged 8 in* 1634 ; d.s.p.
> 2*a. Humphrey Mildmay.*
> 3*a. Edward Mildmay.*
> 4*a. Anthony Mildmay.*
> 5*a. Cicely Mildmay, m.* 1st, [——] *Haines ;* 2ndly, *Robert Mildmay of Terling.*

343. Descendants of JANE MILDMAY of Moulsham Hall, and Marks, co. Essex ; Hazelgrove, co. Somerset ; Shawford House, co. Hants ; and Mildmay Park, Stoke Newington (see Table XXXI.), *d.* 6 May 1857 ; *m.* 22 June 1786, Sir HENRY PAULET ST. JOHN, *afterwards* (R.L. 8 Dec. 1790) ST. JOHN-MILDMAY, 3rd Bart. [G.B.], M.P., *b.* 30 Sept. 1764 ; *d.* 11 Nov. 1808 ; and had issue 1*a* to 9*a*.

> 1*a. Sir Henry St. John Carew St. John-Mildmay, 4th Bart. [G.B.], M.P., b.* 15 *Ap.* 1787 ; *d.* 17 *Jan.* 1848 ; *m.* 1st, 7 *Aug.* 1809, *Charlotte, da. of the Hon. Bartholomew Bouverie, M.P., d.* 5 *Aug.* 1810 ; 2ndly *(by special permission of the King of Wurtemburg),* 1815, *Harriet (sometime Countess of Rosebery* [S.]), *younger sister of the preceding, d.* 9 *Dec.* 1834 ; *and had issue.*
> See the Clarence Volume, pp. 465–468, Nos. 20728–20740 and 20780–20796.
>
> 2*a. Paulet St. John-Mildmay of Farley Chamberlayne, &c., M.P., b.* 8 *Ap.* 1791 ; *d.* 19 *May* 1845 ; *m.* 12 *Mar.* 1813, *Anna Maria Wyndham, da. of the Hon. Bartholomew Bouverie, M.P., d.* 11 *Dec.* 1864; *and had issue.*
> See the Clarence Volume, pp. 468–469, Nos. 20797–20811.
>
> 3*a. George William St. John-Mildmay, Capt. R.N., b.* 20 *Ap.* 1792 ; *d.* 14 *Feb.* 1851 ; *m.* 1832, *Mary, widow of John Morrilt of Rokely Park, younger da. of Peter Baillie, younger of Dochfour, M.P., d.* 17 *Jan.* 1892 ; *and had issue* 1*b to* 2*b.*
>
> > 1*b.* Herbert Alexander St. John-Mildmay, Lieut.-Col., *late* Rifle Brigade, one of H.M.'s Hon. Corps of Gentlemen-at-Arms *(Travellers'; Army and Navy), b.* 20 July 1836 ; *m.* 7 May 1884, Susan Margaret Stacpole, da. of the Hon. John Lothrop Motley, D.C.L., U.S. Minister to the Court of St. James'.
> >
> > 2*b.* Geraldine Mary St. John-Mildmay (31 *St. George's Square, S.W.*), *m.* 5 Jan. 1858, Alfred Buckley, J.P., D.L., *d.* 15 Dec. 1900 ; and has issue 1*c* to 4*c.*
> >
> > > 1*c.* Edward Duncombe Henry Buckley, Major R.A. *(New Hall, Bodenham, Salisbury), b.* 2 Aug. 1860 ; *m.* 16 Sept. 1892, Ellen Cecilia, da. of Col. Frederick Bridgeman ; and has issue 1*d* to 2*d.*
> > >
> > > > 1*d.* Edward Geoffrey Mildmay Buckley, *b.* 18 Nov. 1893.
> > > > 2*d.* Felix George Buckley, *b.* 6 Nov. 1894.
> > >
> > > 2*c.* Christine Mary Buckley.
> > > 3*c.* Winifred Rosa Isabel Buckley.
> > > 4*c.* Elizabeth Ursula Buckley.

[Nos. 34237 to 34290.

The Plantagenet Roll

4a. Humphrey St. John-Mildmay, M.P., b. 11 *July* 1794; d. 9 *Aug.* 1853; m. 1*st*, 28 *Sept.* 1823, *the Hon. Anne Eugenia, da. of Alexander (Baring), 1st Baron Ashburton [U.K.],* d. 8 *Mar.* 1839; 2*ndly,* 20 *Sept.* 1843, *Marianne Frances, da. of Granville Harcourt Vernon, M.P.,* d. 13 *Feb.* 1873; *and had issue 1b to 4b.*

1*b. Henry Bingham Mildmay, J.P., D.L., High Sheriff co. Devon* 1886, b. 19 *June* 1828; d. 1 *Nov.* 1905; m. 24 *July* 1860, *Georgiana Frances, da. of John Crocker Bulteel of Flete (by his wife Lady Elizabeth, née Grey),* d. 2 *July* 1899; *and had issue 1c to 4c.*

1*c.* Francis Bingham Mildmay, M.P., Major and Hon. Lieut.-Col. West Kent. Imp. Yeo. (*Shoreham Place, Sevenoaks;* 46 *Berkeley Square, W., &c.; Travellers'; Brooks'; Marlborough, &c.*), b. 26 Ap. 1861.

2*c.* John Mildmay (*Turf; Hurlingham*), b. 24 Ap. 1868.

3*c.* Alfred Mildmay, b. 10 Aug. 1871.

4*c.* Beatrice Mildmay, b. 11 Aug. 1876.

2*b.*[2] Lucy Frances Jane Mildmay, *m.* 15 Sept. 1868, Capt. James Richard Thomas Lane-Fox, J.P., D.L. (*Bramham Park, York;* 26 *Upper Grosvenor Street, S.W., &c.*); and has issue 1*c* to 3*c.*

1*c.* George Richard Lane-Fox (*Hope Hall, Boston Spa, Yorks*), b. 15 Dec. 1870; *m.* 17 Sept. 1903, the Hon. Mary Agnes Emily, da. of Charles Lindley (Wood), 2nd Viscount Halifax [U.K.]; and has issue 1*d.*

1*d.* See p. 109, Nos. 1231–1232.

2*c.* Edward Charles Lane-Fox, b. 31 Mar. 1874.

3*c.* Maria Mary Charles Lane-Fox.

3*b.*[2] Emily Mary Mildmay (*The Terrace, Boston Spa, Yorks*).

4*b.*[2] Alice Catherine Mildmay, *m.* 23 Oct. 1873, Capt. the Hon. Henry Hervey Molyneux, R.N. (4 *Hay Hill, Berkeley Square, W.*).

5*a. Edward St. John-Mildmay,* b. 7 *July* 1797; d. 16 *May* 1868; m. 1*st*, *Marianne Catherine, da. of R. Sherston; and had issue 1b to 3b.*

1*b. Arthur George St. John-Mildmay,* b. 3 *Feb.* 1824; d. 8 *Mar.* 1883; m. 1*st,* 6 *Nov.* 1848, *Louisa Latham, da. of Capt. Henry Gough Ord, R.A.,* d. 5 *May* 1855; 2*ndly, Aug.* 1856, *Charlotte Mary, widow of Major John Thomas Douglas Halkett, da. of Charles Beague of Hollam House; and had issue 1c to 5c.*

1*c.* Charles Beague St. John-Mildmay, J.P., *late* Capt. R.A. and Somersetshire L.I. (*Hollam House, Dulverton*), b. 13 Jan. 1861; *m.* 22 Aug. 1892, Evelyn Augusta, da. of Capt. Edmond St. John-Mildmay; and has issue 1*d* to 2*d.*

1*d.* Dorothy St. John-Mildmay, b. 11 July 1893.

2*d.* Letitia St. John-Mildmay, b. 1895.

2*c.* John Walter Paulet St. John-Mildmay (*Stout's Hill, Dursley, Gloucester*), b. 1 Nov. 1866; *m.* 22 Aug. 1894, Bertha Mabel, da. of Joachim Theodore Satow; and has issue 1*d* to 2*d.*

1*d.* Michael Paulet St. John-Mildmay, b. 6 May 1901.

2*d.* Lorna Winifred St. John-Mildmay, b. 10 June 1895.

3*c.* Alice Frances St. John-Mildmay.

4*c.* Edith Charlotte St. John-Mildmay, *m.* 20 Nov. 1889, James Archibald Gordon Hamilton, Bar.-at-Law (64A *High Street, St. John's Wood, N.W.; Withypool, Exford, Taunton*).

5*c.* Emma Magdalen St. John-Mildmay, *m.* 14 June 1894, Albert Edward Bles, Assist. Under-Sec. to (Dutch) Ministry of Justice (28 *Van Speyk Straat, The Hague*).

2*b. Marianne Jane St. John-Mildmay,* d. 1883; m 22 *Ap.* 1847, *Charles George Barnett of London and Sunningdale, J.P., Banker,* b. 1816; d. (-); *and had issue 1c to 4c.* [Nos. 34291 to 34311.

414

# of The Blood Royal

1c. Charles Edward Barnett (*Edge Grove, Watford*), b. 29 Jan. 1848; m. 24 July 1872, the Hon. Augusta Rosa, da. of John Benn (Walsh), 1st Baron Ormethwaite [U.K.]; and has issue.
See the Clarence Volume, p. 259, Nos. 6237–6244f.

2c. Frances Carew Charles Barnett, b. 20 Dec. 1850; m. 9 May 1877, Emily Ursula, da. of Edward Hamilton, M.P.; and has issue.

3c. Philip Barnett, b. 4 May 1852.

4c. Hugh Drummond Hay Barnett, b. 7 Feb. 1855.

3b. *Jane Catherine St. John-Mildmay*, d. 15 *May* 1891; m. 19 *Ap.* 1849, *the Rev. Evelyn Hardolph Harcourt-Vernon of Grove Hall, Preb. of Lincoln,* b. 30 *Aug.* 1821; d. 26 *Jan.* 1890; *and had issue* 1c *to* 7c.

1c. Edward Evelyn Harcourt-Vernon, J.P., D.L., C.C., High Sheriff co. Notts 1894 (*Grove Hall, East Retford*), b. 19 Jan. 1853; m. 1st, 9 Jan. 1879, Grace, da. of the Rev. Alleyne FitzHerbert, d. 9 Mar. 1881; 2ndly, 22 Aug. 1883, Frances Theresa, da. of Sir William FitzHerbert, 4th Bart. [G.B.]; and has issue 1d to 6d.

1d. Granville Charles FitzHerbert Harcourt-Vernon, b. 30 May 1891.

2d. Egerton Gervase Edward Harcourt-Vernon, b. 13 July 1899.

3d. Sybil Ida Harcourt-Vernon, b. 6 June 1884.

4d. Ida Beatrice Harcourt-Vernon, b. 26 Sept. 1885.

5d. Muriel Therese Harcourt-Vernon, b. 13 June 1887.

6d. Evelyn Hermione Harcourt-Vernon, b. 27 May 1889.

2c. Rev. Algernon Hardolph Harcourt-Vernon, Vicar of Clocolan (*Keble, Clocolan, Orange River Colony*), b. 7 July 1858; m. 1st, 1881, Kate, da. of J. Caudler, d. 5 Ap. 1883; 2ndly, 5 May 1886, Georgina Marguerite, da. of John Martin; and has issue 1d to 5d.

1d. Granville Arthur Harcourt-Vernon, b. 1888.

2d. Hardolph Evelyn Harcourt-Vernon, b. 1889.

3d. Janet Kate Harcourt-Vernon, b. 27 Mar. 1883.

4d. Dorothy Margaret Harcourt-Vernon, b. 1887.

5d. Marjorie Frances Harcourt-Vernon, b. 1891.

3c. Walter Granville Harcourt-Vernon, *late* Lieut. Derbyshire Regt., b. 31 Oct. 1860; m. 1884, Helen Rebecca, da. of J. W. Traer; and has issue 1d.

1d. Evelyn Maude Harcourt-Vernon, b. 1886.

4c. Herbert Evelyn Harcourt-Vernon (*Toronto, Canada*), b. 12 Jan. 1863; m. 14 Nov. 1885, Mary Adelaide, da. of the Hon. George W. Allen of Moss Park, Toronto, Senator; and has issue 1d to 2d.

1d. Humphrey Bingham Harcourt-Vernon, b. 24 Mar. 1889.

2d. Arthur Arundell Harcourt-Vernon, b. 1895.

5c. Mary Frances Harcourt-Vernon, m. 24 Ap. 1879, the Rev. Algernon Frederick Ebsworth, M.A., Vicar of East Retford (*East Retford Vicarage, Notts*).

6c. Frances Jessie Harcourt-Vernon.

7c. Selina Jane Harcourt-Vernon, m. 6 Sept. 1893, Paulet Bertram St. John-Mildmay (*Eden Lodge, Tilford, Surrey*).

6a. *Ven. Carew Antony St. John-Mildmay, Archdeacon of Essex,* b. 2 Feb. 1800; d. 13 *July* 1878; m. 16 *Dec.* 1830, *the Hon. Caroline, da. of William (Waldegrave), 1st Baron Radstock* [*I.*], d. 7 *Jan.* 1878; *and had issue.*
See p. 182, Nos. 6492–6494.

7a. *Jane Dorothea St. John-Mildmay,* b. 11 *Ap.* 1788; d. 15 *Mar.* 1846; m. 31 *July* 1810, *Paul (Methuen), 1st Baron Methuen* [*U.K.*], b. 21 *June* 1779; d. 11 *Sept.* 1849; *and had issue* 1b *to* 3b.

1b. *Frederick Henry Paul (Methuen), 2nd Baron Methuen* [*U.K.*], b. 23 *Feb.* 1818; d. 26 *Sept.* 1891; m. 14 *Oct.* 1844, *Anna Horatio Caroline, da. of the Rev. John Sanford of Nynehead,* d. 3 *Mar.* 1899; *and had issue* 1c *to* 5c.

[Nos. 34312 to 34353.

415

The Plantagenet Roll

1c. Paul Sanford (Methuen), 3rd Baron Methuen [U.K.], G.C.B., K.C.V.O., C.M.G., a General in the Army (*Corsham Court, Wilts*), *b.* 1 Sept. 1845; *m.* 1st, 18 June 1878, Evelyn, da. of Sir Frederick Hervey-Bathurst, 3rd Bart. [U.K.], *d.s.p.* 2 June 1879; 2ndly, 9 Jan. 1884, Mary Ethel, da. of William Ayshford Sanford of Nynehead Court; and has issue 1*d* to 5*d*.

1*d*. Hon. Paul Ayshford Methuen, *b.* 29 Sept. 1886.

2*d*. Hon. Anthony Paul Methuen, *b.* 26 June 1891.

3*d*. Hon. Laurence Paul Methuen, *b.* 18 Sept. 1898.

4*d*. Hon. Ethel Christian Methuen, *b.* 7 Mar. 1889.

5*d*. Hon. Ellen Seymour Methuen, *b.* 23 Nov. 1893.

2*c*. Hon. Frederick George Paul Methuen, *b.* 10 Dec. 1851.

3*c*. Hon. Georgiana Horatio Sanford Methuen.

4*c*. Hon. Jane Charlotte Methuen, *m.* 18 Oct. 1870, Col. the Hon. Richard Southwell Stapleton-Cotton (*Somerford Hall, Brewood, Staffordshire*); and has issue.

See the Clarence Volume, p. 357, Nos. 12198–12202.

5*c*. Hon. Florence Geraldine Marion Methuen.

2*b. Hon. St. John George Paul Methuen,* b. 23 *Nov.* 1819; *d.* 17 *June* 1899; *m.* 12 *Sept.* 1854, *Anne* (*Clevelands, Guildford*), *da. of the Rev. Preb. William Thomas Sergison, Rector of Slaugham; and had issue* 1*c to* 4*c*.

1*c*. St. John Frederick Charles Methuen, Rector of Vange (*Vange Rectory, Essex*), *b.* 27 July 1862; *m.* 19 Jan. 1892, Louisa Elizabeth, da. of Major-Gen. James Hyde Champion; and has issue 1*d* to 6*d*.

1*d*. St. John Arthur Paul Methuen, *b.* 19 Nov. 1892.

2*d*. Charles Leslie Methuen, *b.* 4 Mar. 1901.

3*d*. Margaret Dorothea Methuen, *b.* 17 May 1894.

4*d*. Kathleen Louisa Mildmay Methuen, *b.* 25 Aug. 1896.

5*d*. Frances Mary Hyde Methuen, *b.* 29 July 1899.

6*d*. Beatrice Ethel Gertrude Methuen, *b.* 28 Ap. 1905.

2*c*. Janette Catherine Kemeys Methuen.

3*c*. Annie Mildmay Methuen.

4*c*. Mary Georgiana Methuen, *m.* 10 Aug. 1893, the Rev. Leonard Hugh Evans, M.A., a House Master at King's School, Canterbury (*Holme House, Canterbury*); and has issue 1*d*.

1*d*. Bertha Mary Evans, *b.* 1 Nov. 1895.

3*b. Hon. Jane Matilda Methuen,* d. 9 *Aug.* 1881; *m.* 1 Dec. 1849, *David Lewis,* d. 23 *Jan.* 1895.

8*a. Maria St. John-Mildmay,* b. 2 *Ap.* 1790; *d.* 21 *Dec.* 1836; *m.* 3 *June* 1812, *Henry* (*St. John*), 4th *Viscount Bolingbroke and* 5th *Viscount St. John* [*E.*], *d.* 1 *Oct.* 1851; *and had issue.*

See the Clarence Volume, p. 489, No. 21254.

9*a. Judith Anne St. John-Mildmay,* b. 2 *Ap.* 1790; *d.* 27 *Ap.* 1851; *m. as* 2nd *wife*, 24 *May* 1814, *William* (*Pleydell-Bouverie*), 3rd *Earl of Radnor* [*G.B.*], *d.* 9 *Ap.* 1869; *and had issue.*

See the Clarence Volume, pp. 502–504, Nos. 21839–21892.

[Nos. 34354 to 34434.

344. Descendants, if any, of Anne Mildmay (see Table XXXI.), *d.* 1820; *m.* 15 Nov. 1794, John Clerke of Worthing, co. Hants; and of Letitia Mildmay, *d.* 27 Mar. 1839; *m.* 4 Nov. 1791, George William Ricketts of Lainstone, co. Hants.

SIR EDWARD CHESTER OF ROYSTON.

THE COMMON ANCESTOR OF NOS. 34435-34716.

From the original painting in possession of Harry Chester, Esq., J.P., at Stansted.

# of The Blood Royal

345. Descendants of CATHERINE CHESTER (see Table XXXII.), *d.* 1758 ; *m.* Col. WILLIAM VACHELL of Coley, co. Berks, and Great Abingdon, co. Camb., *bapt.* 21 Oct. 1686 ; *bur.* 23 Jan. 1762 ; and had issue 1*a* to 2*a*.[1]

1*a*. *William Vachell of Hinxton Hall, co. Cambridge, and Coptfold Hall, co. Essex*, b. 1735 ; d. 12 *Mar.* 1807 ; m. 27 *May* 1759, *Mary, da. of John Bramsode Jones of Llanarth, co. Monmouth*, b. 1743 ; d. 8 *June* 1795 ; *and had issue* 1*b* *to* 5*b*.

1*b*. *Richard Vachell of Coptfold Hall, co. Essex*, b. 1761 ; d. 1832 ; m. 12 *June* 1783, *Margaret, da. and h. of the Rev. Richard Long*, d. 1828 ; *and had issue* 1*c*.

1*c*. *Horatio Vachell of Coptfold Hall (godson of Admiral Lord Nelson)*, b. 1799 ; d. 1862 ; m. 1822, *Mary, da. of William Honywood of Marks Hall, co. Essex, M.P.*, d. 3 *Ap.* 1865 ; *and had issue* 1*d* *to* 2*d*.

1*d*. *Richard Tanfield Vachell of Coptfold Hall*, b. 25 *June* 1830 ; d. 12 *Mar.* 1868 ; m. 28 *June* 1859, *Georgina, da. of Col. Arthur Lyttelton Annesley of Arley Castle, co. Worcester ; and had issue* 1*e* *to* 4*e*.

1*e*. Horace Annesley Vachell, author and novelist (*Beechwood, Totton, Hants*), b. 30 Oct. 1861 ; *m.* (at Templeton, California) 28 Mar. 1889, Lydie, da. of C. H. Phillips, *d.* 16 Aug. 1895 ; and has issue 1*f* to 2*f*.

1*f*. Richard Tanfield Vachell, *b.* (at San Luis Obispo, California) 29 June 1890.

2*f*. Lydie Lyttleton Vachell, *b.* (at San Luis Obispo, California) 3 July 1895.

2*e*. Arthur Honywood Vachell, *b.* 8 Nov. 1864.

3*e*. Guy Courtenay Vachell, *b.* (at Spa, Belgium) 4 Oct. 1867 ; *m.* 23 Aug. 1893, Josephine, da. of C. H. Phillips, *d.* 5 Dec. 1904 ; and has issue 1*f*.

1*f*. Arthur Annesley Vachell, *b.* (at San Luis Obispo, California) 6 Dec. 1896.

4*e*. Lucy Lyttleton Vachell, *b.* 20 Dec. 1862 ; *m.* 15 May 1884, Charles George Heathcote, J.P., Lieut.-Col. and Hon. Col. 1st Vol. Batt. Hampshire Regt. (*Beechwood, Totton, Hants*) ; and has issue.

See the Clarence Volume, p. 108, Nos. 1088–1092.

2*d*. Lucy Vachell, *b.* 1823 ; *m.* 1st, Henry Pearson of Cumberland, Bar.-at-Law, *d.* ; 2ndly, W. H. Bradley (*Kingswinford, co. Stafford*); and has (with other issue by 2nd husband) 1*e* to 2*e*.

1*e*. *Florence Elizabeth Pearson*, b. 12 *Sept.* 1851 ; d. (–) ; m. *Capt. John Beckett of Ingoldthorpe, Norfolk*.

2*e*. Edith Lucy Bradley, *b.* 1861.

2*b*. *Samuel Jones Vachell*, bapt. 20 *Oct.* 1768 ; d. 7 *July* 1831 ; m. 1st, 1794, *Anne, da. of William Andrews*, d.s.p. 22 *Jan.* 1797 ; 2ndly, 7 Feb. 1799, *Sarah, da. of John Milward of Bramley ; and had issue* 1*c*.

1*c*. Mary Ann Vachell, *m.* 1833, Charles Jenyns of Bottisham Hall.

3*b*. *Rev. John Vachell, Vicar of Hinxton* 1789–1795, *and of Littleport, Ely*, 1795, bapt. 22 *Nov.* 1764 ; d. 17 *Ap.* 1830 ; m. 14 *Oct.* 1796, *Charlotte Elizabeth, da. of Col. Leonard Jenyns of Bottisham Hall*, d. 23 *Jan.* 1837 ; *and had issue* 1*c* *to* 4*c*.

1*c*. *George Harvey Vachell, Captain to the Canton Factory*, b. 22 *Jan.* 1798 ; d. 1839 ; m. 1834, *Cecilia Catherine, da. of the Rev. John Lambton of Elmswell, co. Suffolk*, d. 3 *July* 1877 ; *and had issue* 1*d* *to* 2*d*.

1*d*. Henry Tanfield Vachell, General R.A., *b.* (at Macao, China) 26 Mar. 1835 ; *m.* 1st, Grace, da. of William Barthorpe of Hollesley House, co. Suffolk ; 2ndly, [——], widow of [——] Ambrose, da. of [——] ; and has issue 1*e*.

1*e*. Grace Vachell, *b.* 1878.

2*d*. Mary Louisa Vachell, *b.* (at Macao, China) 29 Aug. 1836 ; *m.* Robert Barthorpe of Hollesley House, co. Suffolk. [Nos. 34435 to 34452.

---

[1] See " A Short Account or History of the Family of Vachell," by Ivor Vachell, B.A., and Arthur Cadogan Vachell, privately printed, Cardiff, 1900.

The Plantagenet Roll

2c. *Rev. Harvey Vachell, Vicar of Ampthill*, b. 8 *Mar.* 1805; d. 6 *July* 1874; m. *Eleanor Sophia, da. of the Rev. Dr. Christopher Pemberton, Vicar of Millbrook; and had issue* 1d *to* 3d.

    1d. Harvey George Vachell, *b.* 24 June 1840, ⎫
    2d. John Henry Pemberton Vachell, *b.* 1 Oct. 1842, ⎬ *unm.* 1900.
    3d. Eleanor Sophia Vachell, *b.* 22 Nov. 1848. ⎭

    3c. *Mary Anne Vachell*, b. 16 *Nov.* 1801; d. (–); m. 1838, *Col. Charles E. Boyd, 35th Regt.; and had issue* 1d *to* 2d.
    1d. George Vachell Boyd, *b.* 18 June 1839.
    2d. Alexander William Jenyns Boyd.

    4c. *Charlotte Vachell*, b. 19 *May* 1803; d. 16 *July* 1876; m. 4 *June* 1822, *the Ven. Archdeacon Benjamin Philpot of Walpole, co. Suffolk*, d. 28 *May* 1889; *and had issue* 1d *to* 10d.
    1d. *William Benjamin Philpot*, b. 16 *Ap.* 1823; d. 16 *Ap.* 1889; m. 1*st*, 21 *Dec.* 1852, *Henrietta Georgina, da. of Col. Hamlet Obins*, d. 9 *Feb.* 1858; 2*ndly*, *Mary Jane, da. of Professor Conington of Bosto; and had issue* 1e *to* 2e.
    1e. Hamlet Stanley Philpot (2600 *Maryland Avenue, Baltimore, U.S.A.*), *b.* 9 Dec. 1855; *m.* 1st, 27 Mar. 1886, Emily Florence, da. of General William Wallace Dunlop; 2ndly, 26 June 1901, Ada Theodora, da. of Alexander Hotson; and has issue 1*f* to 3*f*.
    1*f*. Hamlet Cunningham Vachell Philpot, *b.* 21 Oct. 1887.
    2*f*. Frank Wallace Obins Philpot, *b.* 18 Oct. 1891.
    3*f*. William Thomas Archibald Philpot, *b.* 15 July 1905.

    2e. Annie Wilhelmina Philpot, *b.* 23 Mar. 1854.

    2d. Harvey John Philpot (1656 *Georgia Street, Vancouver, B.C.*), *b.* 9 Mar. 1833; *m.* 1860, Caroline, da. of Allan Ritchie of Canada; and has issue 1e to 6e.
    1e. Charles Vachell Philpot, *b.* 3 July 1862.
    2e. Benjamin Lawrence Philpot, *b.* 16 Aug. 1874.
    3e. Lilian Mary Philpot, *b.* 12 Ap. 1866; *m.* Gilbert Finlay (*Canada*); and has issue (2 sons) 1*f* to 2*f*.
    1*f*. Telfair Allan Hunter Finlay, *b.* 29 Aug. 1897.
    2*f*. [——] Finlay.

    4e. Mabel Philpot (twin), *b.* 1876; *m.* 1900, Verchoyle Cronin (*Canada*); and has issue 1*f* to 2*f*.
    1*f*. [son], *b.* 25 Aug. 1902.
    2*f*. [son].

    5e. Madeline Philpot (twin), *b.* 23 Sept. 1876.
    6e. Hylton Warburton Philpot, *b.* 1879.

    3d. Frederic Samuel Philpot (20 *Plympton Road, Brondesbury, N.W.*), *b.* 21 July 1834.
    4d. Charlotte Elizabeth Philpot (45 *Pembroke Square, W.*), *b.* 12 Sept. 1826; *m.* 10 Aug. 1853, the Rev. Sigismund Wilhelm Koelle, Ph.D., P.H., *b.* 14 July 1823; *d.* 18 Feb. 1902; and has issue 1e to 5e.
    1e. Rev. Constantine Philpot Koelle (*Langley Vicarage, Slough*), *b.* 29 Nov. 1862; *m.* 12 May 1896, Hebe, da. of John George Rygate; and has issue 1*f* to 2*f*.
    1*f*. John George Eric Koelle, *b.* 18 Dec. 1897.
    2*f*. Harry Philpot Koelle, *b.* 16 Aug. 1901.

    2e. Hermann Harvey Vachell Koelle (15 *McGregor Street, Montreal, Canada*), *b.* 18 Feb. 1866; *m.* Lyla, da. of Joseph Tiffin, Jr.; and has issue 1*f* to 2*f*.
    1*f*. Leitrim Eric Lester Koelle, *b.* 14 Sept. 1896.
    2*f*. Desmond Vachell Philpot Tiffin Koelle, *b.* 25 Nov. 1904.

[Nos. 34453 to 34481.

# of The Blood Royal

3e. Frederic Theodore Koelle (*Hong Kong and Shanghai Bank, Hamburg*), b. 20 Aug. 1870.

4e. Letitia Louisa Carmela Koelle, b. 29 Nov. 1857; m. 23 Mar. 1887, Robert Lascelles Gambier Noel, Capt. R.N. (80 *Coleherne Court, S.W.*); and has issue 1f to 3f.

 1f. Gambier Baptist Edward Noel, b. 24 June 1888.

 2f. Norman Philpot Robert Noel, b. 15 July 1891.

 3f. John Andrew Vernatti Noel, b. 23 May 1893.

5e. Charlotte Rosina Sharona Koelle, b. 12 Mar. 1859; *unm.*

5d. Caroline Augusta Philpot, b. 27 May 1830; m. 25 June 1857, Henry Gawler of Adelaide, S. Australia, d. 1 Dec. 1894; and has issue 1e to 3e.

1e. Douglas George Gawler (*Cottesloe, Western Australia*), b. 9 Nov. 1860; m. 23 Oct. 1893, Eva May, da. of Robert Newton Waldeck; and has issue 1f to 4f.

 1f. Douglas Reginald Gawler, b. 30 Sept. 1894.

 2f. Geoffrey Noel Gawler, b. 6 Mar. 1896.

 3f. Joan May Kneist Gawler, b. 10 June 1899.

 4f. Isabel Marian Gawler, b. 16 Oct. 1901.

2e. Maud Marian Gawler, b. 8 Feb. 1859; m. 1 Sept. 1880, Arthur Boult (*A.M.P. Buildings, Auckland, New Zealand*); and has issue 1f to 2f.

 1f. Doris Tennant Boult, b. 13 July 1882.

 2f. Phyllis Vachell Boult, b. 26 Aug. 1885.

3e. Ethela Caroline Gawler, b. 6 Ap. 1867; m. 29 Mar. 1886, James Lewis (*Katana, Woking*); and has issue 1f to 2f.

 1f. Fitzpatrick Lewis, b. 20 Dec. 1886.

 2f. Douglas Lewis, b. 6 Ap. 1888.

6d. Marian Jane Philpot (*Glycene House, Hampton-on-Thames*), b. 26 Oct. 1831; m. 18 Dec. 1849, the Very Rev. George Granville Bradley, Dean of Westminster, b. 11 Dec. 1821; d. 13 Mar. 1903; and has issue 1e to 7e.

1e. Arthur Granville Bradley, Author (*Red Cottage, Rye*), b. 11 Nov. 1850; m. Aug. 1874, Florence, da. of William Abel Rackham, M.R.C.S.; and has issue 1f.

 1f. Marion Eleanor Granville Bradley, b. 30 Jan. 1876.

2e. Hugh Vachell Bradley, Major 9th Goorkhas (*India*), b. 23 Mar. 1865; m. 1 Ap. 1898, Norah Louisa Margaret, da. of Charles James Foster of Dehra House, Fleet; and has issue 1f to 3f.

 1f. John Bertram Granville Bradley, b. 12 Mar. 1899.

 2f. Charles Hugh Granville Bradley, b. 11 Ap. 1901.

 3f. Kenneth Granville Bradley, b. 4 Jan. 1904.

3e. Edith Marian Bradley, b. 6 Aug. 1852; m. 1st, 18 Dec. 1876, Frederick Iltyd Nicholl, *d.s.p.*; 2ndly, 1898, Dr. Bowyer, d. 1901; 3rdly, Dec. 1905, Olaf Ellison of Mexico, U.S.A., d. 1906.

4e. Margaret Louisa Bradley, b. 20 Nov. 1855; m. 29 Mar. 1879, the Rev. Henry George Woods, Master of the Temple (*Master's House, The Temple, E.C.*); and has issue 1f to 3f.

 1f. George Gilbert Bradley Woods, b. 3 Jan. 1880.

 2f. Maurice Henry Woods, b. 3 Nov. 1883.

 3f. Gabriel Stanley Woods, b. 14 May 1885.

5e. Mabel Charlotte Bradley, b. 5 Oct. 1859; m. 1 Dec. 1886, Henry Birch enough, J.P., C.M.G. (79 *Eccleston Square, S.W.*); and has issue 1f to 2f.

 1f. Sylvia Birchenough, b. 1890.

 2f. Elizabeth Birchenough, b. 1895.

6e. Emily Tennyson Bradley, b. 29 Oct. 1863; m. 22 Ap. 1893, Alexander Murray Smith (40 *Queen Anne's Gate, S.W.*), *s.p.*

7e. Rose Marian Bradley, b. 19 June 1867; *unm.* [Nos. 34482 to 34516.

419

The Plantagenet Roll

7d. Emily Margaret Philpot (*Lydney Lodge, Kingston-on-Thames*), *b.* 26 Ap. 1837 ; *unm.*

8d. Eleanor Sophia Philpot (26 *Kingdon Road, N.W.*), *b.* 21 Sept. 1838 ; *m.* 22 Dec. 1869, Robert West Taylor, *d.* 16 Aug. 1889 ; and has issue 1*e* to 2*e.*

    1e. Herbert Edward Taylor (26 *Kingdon Road, West Hampstead, N.W.*), *b.* 6 June 1874 ; *m.* 22 Oct. 1897, Clare, da. of George Belcher ; and has issue 1*f* to 2*f.*

      1f. Launcelot Robert Herbert Taylor, *b.* 29 Nov. 1898.

      2f. Daphne Ursula Taylor, *b.* 23 June 1903.

    2e. Arthur Percy Taylor (*Montreal, Canada*), *b.* 20 Sept. 1879 ; *m.* Sept. 1905, Bertha, da. of [——] Jack of Montreal.

9d. Letitia Frances Philpot, *b.* 10 *Oct.* 1841 ; *d.* 9 *Nov.* 1874 ; *m.* 1861, *the Rev. Joseph Foster, d.* 18 *Dec.* 1878 ; *and had issue* 1*e to* 4*e.*

    1e. Turville Douglas Foster (*The Molt, Salcombe, Devon*), *b.* 28 Nov. 1865 ; *m.* 17 July 1888, Madeline, da. of [——] Cameron ; and has issue 1*f.*

      1f. Douglas Cameron Foster, *b.* 13 Jan. 1891.

    2e. Percival Lloyd Foster, *b.* 23 Oct. 1871 ⎫
    3e. Bertram Noel Foster, *b.* 1 Jan. 1873 ⎬(*Woodcote, St. Andrews, Guernsey*).

    4e. Raymond Leslie Foster, *b.* 1874.

10d. Anna Cecilia Philpot (*Dehra House, Fleet*), *b.* 10 Ap. 1844 ; *m.* 10 Feb. 1871, Charles James Foster, *d.* 18 Dec. 1899 ; and has issue 1*e* to 3*e.*

    1e. Chrystobel Mary Foster, *b.* 18 Jan. 1873.

    2e. Norah Louisa Margaret Foster, *b.* 21 July 1874 ; *m.* 1 Ap. 1898, Major Hugh Vachell Bradley ; and has issue.

    See p. 419, Nos. 34504–34506.

    3e. Rachel Dorothy Foster, *b.* 1 Feb. 1877.

4b. Mary Anne Vachell, b. 1 Ap. (? 13 Mar.) 1760 ; d. 2 Ap. 1829 ; m. 15 May 1786, Capt. Carr Thomas Brackenbury of Scremby Hall, co. Lincoln, and Bromfield Lodge, co. Essex, 54th Regt., bapt. 1 July 1760 ; d. 15 Feb. 1816 ; and had issue 1c.

    1c. Charlotte Emily Brackenbury, b. 3 June 1792 ; d. 11 Nov. 1883 ; m. 14 Nov. 1826, George Mordaunt Dickins, Capt. 54th and 95th Regts., d. 6 Mar. 1859 ; and had issue 1d to 2d.

      1d. George Dickens, b. 23 Dec. 1839, ⎫
      2d. Melita Dickens. ⎬ living *unm.* 1885.[1]

5b. Lucy Vachell, bapt. 24 Oct. 1763 ; m. the Rev. John Heron of Grantham.

2a. Lucy Vachell, m. 1755, the Rev. Richard Long, M.A. (Camb.), Vicar of Cowerham, co. Suffolk ; and had issue 1b.

    1b. Margaret Long, b. 1758 ; d. 1828 ; m. 12 June 1783, Richard Vachell of Coptfold Hall, d. 1832 ; and had issue.

    See p. 417, Nos. 34435–34448.   [Nos. 34517 to 34550.

346. Descendants of ROBERT CHESTER of the Middle Temple, Secretary to Queen Anne's Bounty, and Receiver of the Tenths of the Clergy (see Table XXXII.), *b.* 20 July 1726 ; *d.* 14 Sept. 1790 ; *m.* 29 Mar. 1758, HARRIOT, da. and co-h. of Charles Adelmare CÆSAR of Bennington Place, co. Herts ; and had issue 1*a* to 3*a.*

    1a. Sir Robert Chester of Bush Hall, co. Herts, J.P., D.L., Master of the Ceremonies to George III., George IV., William IV., and Queen Victoria, Lieut.-Col. Herts Militia, b. 5 Jan. 1768 ; d. 12 Aug. 1848 ; m. 10 Oct. 1797, Eliza, da. of John Ford of Ipswich, d. 31 Mar. 1855 ; and had issue 1b to 4b.

---

[1] Foster's " Noble and Gentle Families," &c., p. 116.

# of The Blood Royal

1b. *Charles Chester, Major-General in Bengal Army,* b. 19 *Aug.* 1803 ; d. (*being killed in action near Delhi*) 8 *June* 1857 ; m. 3 *Mar.* 1832, *Margaret Mundy, da. of Col. William Conrad Faithfull, H.E.I.C.S.,* d. 24 *Jan.* 1885 ; *and had issue* 1c *to* 2c.

1c. *Charles William Robert Chester, Major-Gen. Bengal Army,* b. 9 *Jan.* 1833 ; d. 20 *Oct.* 1898 ; m. 1*st,* 16 *Dec.* 1856, *Ellen Sarah, da. of John Baker,* d. 19 *Aug.* 1860 ; 2*ndly,* 23 *Jan.* 1862, *Selena Caroline, da. of Col. Edward Lee Ussher,* d. 6 *Feb.* 1886 ; *and had issue* 1d *to* 3d.

1d. Florence Margaret Chester, *b.* 12 Oct. 1857 ; *m.* 17 Mar. 1881, William Bernard Wilson, Bengal Staff Corps ; and has issue 1e to 3e.

1e. Dorothy Margaret Wilson, *b.* 18 Dec. 1881.

2e. Gabrielle Violet Wilson, *b.* 30 Ap. 1883.

3e. Dulcibella Chester Wilson, *b.* 16 July 1884.

2d. Edith Mary Chester, *b.* 9 Jan. 1865 ; *m.* 13 Ap. 1887, George Frederick Horace Dillon, Bengal Staff Corps ; and has issue 1e to 3e.

1e. George Charles Tracey Dillon, *b.* 6 Feb. 1888.

2e. Harry Chester Wentworth Dillon, *b.* 20 July 1889.

3e. Bernard Thomas Bryant Dillon, *b.* 18 June 1891.

3d. Lilian Isabel Chester, *b.* 26 June 1868 ; *m.* 8 Feb. 1893, Major Ernest de Vaynes Wintle, Indian Army ; and has issue 1e.

1e. Esme Beryl Chester Wintle, *b.* 15 Oct. 1895.

2c. *Harry Dawkins Eardley-Wilmot Chester,* b. 25 *Jan.* 1836 ; d. (? *unm.*) 24 May 1888.

2b. *Harry Chester, in Privy Council Office. Education Dept.,* b. 1 *Oct.* 1806 ; d. 5 *Oct.* 1868 ; m. 1*st,* 2 *Sept.* 1837, *Anna Maria, da. of Robert Isherwood,* d. *Dec.* 1854 ; 2*ndly,* 22 *Mar.* 1856, *Henrietta Mary, da. of George Goff ; and had issue* 1c *to* 4c.

1c. Harry Chester (*Broome End, Stansted, Essex*), J.P., *b.* 17 July 1860 ; *m.* 21 Sept. 1893, Mildred Mary, da. of John Granville Beaumont Pulteney ; and has issue 1d to 4d.

1d. Harry Keppel Chester, *b.* 19 July 1894.

2d. Robert Charles Chester, *b.* 14 Ap. 1896.

3d. Adela Judith Chester, *b.* 19 July 1897.

4d. Mary Chester, *b.* 2 Ap. 1901.

2c. Caroline Mary Chester, *b.* 24 Oct. 1850 ; *m.* 21 Dec. 1881, the Rev. Arnold Whitaker Oxford, M.D. (8 *Henrietta Street, Cavendish Square, W.*) ; and has issue 1d to 2d.

1d. *Mervyn Arnold Chester Oxford,* b. 28 *Dec.* 1883 ; d. 9 *Jan.* 1886.

2d. Dulcibella Mary Chester Oxford, *b.* Ap. 1887.

3c. Ella Sophia Mary Chester, *b.* 8 Jan. 1857 ; *m.* 8 Feb. 1877, Robert Fuller Maitland, J.P. (131 *Sloane Street, S.W. ; Stansted, Essex*).

4c. Leonora Louisa Chester, *b.* 22 Feb. 1858 ; *m.* 14 Dec. 1882, Frederick Yorke Smith (11 *Eccleston Square, S.W.*).

3b. *Eliza Chester,* d. 15 *Dec.* 1869 ; m. *as* 2*nd wife,* 30 *Aug.* 1819, *Sir John Eardley Eardley-Wilmot,* 1*st Bart.* [*U.K.*], *M.P., Governor of Tasmania,* b. 21 *Feb.* 1783 ; d. 3 *Feb.* 1847 ; *and had issue* 1c *to* 2c.

1c. Robert Charles Chester Eardley-Wilmot, *formerly* Secretary to Board of Directors of Convict Prisons (32 *Tedworth Gardens, S.W.*), *b.* 4 June 1822 ; *m.* 4 Dec. 1849 Jeannie Louisa Stewart, da. of John Dunn of Heathfield, Tasmania ; and has issue 1d to 2d.

1d. Eliza Catherine Eardley-Wilmot, *m.* Mar. 1878, Holland John Cotton, M.D. (33 *Lowndes Street, S.W.*) ; and has issue 1e to 3e.

1e. Arthur Disbrowe Cotton, *b.* 15 Jan. 1879.

2e. Robert Hugh Cotton, *b.* 9 Jan. 1881.

3e. Charles Geoffrey Cotton, *b.* 25 Ap. 1884.

2d. Constance Eardley-Wilmot

[Nos. 34551 to 34575.

3 H

The Plantagenet Roll

2c. *Charles Octavius Eardley-Wilmot, Capt.* 96th *and* 31st *Regts., b.* 2 *Oct.* 1824; d. 26 *July* 1886; m. 1st, 3 *May* 1849, *Grace Sophia, da. of John Dunn of Heathfield, Tasmania, d.* 30 *Sept.* 1865; 2ndly, 2 *Oct.* 1866, *Elizabeth* (26 *Lee Terrace, Blackheath, S.E.*), *da. of Charles Brooke of London; and had issue* 1d *to* 3d.

1d. Cecil Francis De Lys Eardley-Wilmot, Inspector H.M.'s Prisons, *late* Capt. 2nd Batt. Cheshire Regt. (35 *Tedworth Square, S.W.*), *b.* 4 Aug. 1855; *m.* 25 Ap. 1888, Alice Maule, da. of Edmund Scott of San Francisco.

2d. Violet Agnes Eardley-Wilmot, *m.* 12 Jan. 1882, Henry Sydney Smith (10 *St. Leonard's Terrace, Chelsea, S.W.*); and has issue 1e.

1e. Nevile Vere Smith, *b.* 25 Feb. 1883.

3d. Edith Mary Eardley-Wilmot, *m.* 21 May 1885, Major Jeffery Charles Marston, R.A., *d.* 4 Oct. 1899; and has issue 1e to 3e.

1e. Jeffery Eardley Marston, *b.* 26 June 1887.
2e. Cecil Gifford Marston, *b.* 2 July 1890.
3e. Maurice Allen Marston, *b.* 12 Mar. 1897.

4b. *Dulcibella Chester, b.* 9 *Sept.* 1803; *d.* 17 *Oct.* 1865; *m. as* 1st *wife,* 4 *Jan.* 1834, *the Rev. Charles Childers, Vicar* (1833–1843), *of Cantley, York, and* (1843–1884) *H.B.M. Chaplain at Nice, b.* 17 *May* 1806; *d.* 15 *Feb.* 1896; *and had issue* 1c *to* 4c.

1c. *Robert Cæsar Childers, the distinguished Oriental Scholar, b.* 12 *Feb.* 1838; *d. July* 1876; *m.* 1 *Jan.* 1866, *Anna, da. of Thomas Barton of Glendalough, co. Wicklow; and had issue* 1d *to* 5d.

1d. Henry Cæsar Childers, *b.* 23 Nov. 1869.
2d. Robert Erskine Childers (13 *Embankment Gardens, S.W.*), *b.* 25 June 1870; *m.* 6 Jan. 1903, Mary, da. of Hamilton Osgood of Boston, U.S.A., M.D.
3d. Sybil Rose Culling Childers, *b.* 22 July 1871.
4d. Dulcibella Mary Childers, *b.* 14 Jan. 1873.
5d. Constance Isabel Barton Childers, *b.* 8 Aug. 1875.

2c. Dulcibella Selena Eliza Childers, *b.* 24 Jan. 1837.

3c. Agnes Alexandra Childers, *b.* 31 Aug. 1848; *m.* 25 Oct. 1876, Charles William Barton of Glendalough House, J.P., High Sheriff co. Wicklow 1882; *b.* 13 July 1846; *d.* 3 Oct. 1900; and had issue 1d to 5d.

1d. Robert Childers Barton (*Glendalough House, Greystone, Wicklow*), *b.* 14 Mar. 1881.
2d. Charles Erskine Barton, *b.* 8 Dec. 1882.
3d. Thomas Eyre Barton, *b.* 15 Aug. 1884.
4d. Frances Margaret Barton, *b.* 21 Dec. 1877.
5d. Dulcibella Barton, *b.* 25 Jan. 1879.

4c. Florence Isabella Childers (*Cranbourne Grange, Micheldever*), *b.* 25 Aug. 1851.

2a. *Harriet Chester, b.* 17 *June* 1764; *d.* (–); *m.* 27 *Mar.* 1791, *the Rev. Thomas Ellis Owen, Rector of Llandyfydog, Anglesey; and had issue a large family.*

3a. *Catherine Chester, b.* 27 *Nov.* 1766; *d.* 7 *Ap.* 1825; *m.* 11 *Oct.* 1792, *the Rev. John Strange Dandridge, Rector of Rowsham, Oxon, and Syreham, Northants.*
[Nos. 34576 to 34595.

347. Descendants of the Rev. John Pern, M.A., Vicar of Gillingham, co. Dorset, and Knapwell, co. Cambs., Canon of Salisbury (see Table XXXII.), *d.* 6 Ap. 1770; *m. c.* 1743, Catherine, da. of Humphrey Fyshe of Ickwell, Northill, co. Beds., *d.* 14 Jan. 1748; and had issue 1a to 3a.

1a. *Catharine Pern, co-h. in* 1771, *m.* [——] *Snook.*

2a. *Mary Pern, co-h. in* 1771; *living* 1801; *m. William Tinney of Salisbury, d.* 1801; *and had issue* 1b.

# of ℭ𝔥𝔢 𝔅𝔩𝔬𝔬𝔡 ℜ𝔬𝔶𝔞𝔩

1*b*. *Maria Tinney, in her issue sole h. in* 1871;[1] b. 1769; d. 12 *July* 1843; m. 1795, *the Rev. Henry Stevens, M.A., Rector of Bradfield, co. Berks,* d. 19 *Oct.* 1842; *and had issue* 1*c to* 4*c*.

1*c*. *Rev. Thomas Stevens, M.A., Rector of Bradfield and Founder of Bradfield College,* b. 16 *May* 1809; d. 15 *May* 1888; *m.* 16 *May* 1843, *Susanna, da. of Robert Marriott, M.A., Rector of Cotesbach, co. Leicester,* d. 8 *July* 1866; *and had issue* 1*d to* 11*d*.

1*d*. Henry Stevens, H.M.'s Poor Law Inspector (*The White House, Eynsham, Oxon.*), b. 4 July 1847; *m.* 28 Oct. 1878, Ellen Mary Powell, da. of Francis Halhed; and has issue 1*e* to 7*e*.

1*e*. Henry John Henley Stevens, b. 30 June 1883.

2*e*. Paul Richard Bradfield Stevens, b. 14 Jan. 1887.

3*e*. Ellen Henrietta Judith Stevens, b. 8 Aug. 1879.

4*e*. Mary Caroline Halhed Stevens, b. 22 Feb. 1881.

5*e*. Frances Edith Marriott Stevens, b. 23 Jan. 1885.

6*e*. Joan Margery Bradfield Stevens, b. 14 Jan. 1887.

7*e*. Anne Catherine Tinney Stevens, b. 1 Aug. 1890.

2*d*. Thomas Stevens (7 *Lincoln's Inn Fields, W.C.; Bradfield, Reading*), b. 24 Mar. 1851; *m.* 15 Dec. 1880, Euphemia, da. of Samuel Scott, M.D.; and has issue 1*e* to 7*e*.

1*e*. Richard Henry Easington Stevens, b. 13 Jan. 1883.

2*e*. Thomas Stevens, b. 2 Dec. 1892.

3*e*. William Tinney Stevens, ⎱ b. (twins) 7 June 1894.
4*e*. John Longbourne Stevens, ⎰

5*e*. Amy Stevens, b. 21 Jan. 1891.

6*e*. Mary Stevens, b. 11 Dec. 1895.

7*e*. Miriam Stevens, b. 31 Oct. 1897.

3*d*. Robert Stevens (*New Zealand*), b. 17 Sept. 1853; *m.* 27 Ap. 1877, Sophia, da. of [——] Matthews; and has issue 1*e* to 2*e*.

1*e*. Thomas Edgar Stevens, b. 21 Mar. 1878.

2*e*. Ruth Mabel Stevens, b. Oct. 1887.

4*d*. William Henry Pern Stevens (34 *Ashburn Place, South Kensington, S.W.*), b. 20 Mar. 1862; *m.* May 1888, Katharine, da. of [——] Philips.

5*d*. Mary Anne Stevens, b. 13 Oct. 1844; *m.* 28 Ap. 1868, John Oldrid Scott, Architect (*Oxted, Surrey*); and has issue 1*e* to 9*e*.

1*e*. John Stevens Scott, b. 24 May 1869; *m.* 27 Oct. 1898, Jessie, da. of W. J. Fortune of Muircambus, co. Fife; and has issue 1*f* to 2*f*.

1*f*. Humphrey Gilbert Scott, b. 31 Oct. 1901.

2*f*. Mary Helen Gibson Scott, b. 3 Sept. 1899.

2*e*. Thomas Gilbert Scott, b. 13 Mar. 1874; *m.* 6 Jan. 1903, Violet Anne, da. of Charles Marriott of Cotesbach, co. Leic.; and has issue 1*f*.

1*f*. Nancy Marion Scott, b. 28 Oct. 1904.

3*e*. Henry George Scott, b. 9 Nov. 1875.

4*e* Charles Marriott Oldrid Scott, b. 26 Mar. 1880.

5*e*. Susanna Caroline Scott, b. 17 Nov. 1870.

6*e*. Helen Mary Scott, b. 5 May 1872.

7*e*. Margaret Georgina Scott, b. 17 June 1877.

8*e*. Mary Catherine Scott, b. 31 Mar. 1883.

9*e*. Hilda Frances Scott, b. 17 Ap. 1887.   [Nos. 34596 to 34628.

---

[1] On the death *s.p.* of her last surviving brother, William Henry Tinney, Q.C., a Master in Chancery.

6*d*. *Caroline Stevens*, b. 26 *Mar.* 1846; d. 8 *July* 1877; m. 4 *Aug.* 1866, *Arthur Crofts Powell* (*Minmickfold, Holmwood, Surrey*); *and had issue* 1*e to* 4*e.*

1*e*. Arthur Marriott Powell (*Crofton, Orpington*), *b*. 31 May 1869; *m*. 2ndly, 19 Ap. 1898, Frances Emily, da. of Frederick Pocklington of Chelsworth, co. Suffolk, Col. 5th Fusiliers; and has issue 1*f* to 2*f*.

2*f*. Arthur Guy Pykarell Powell, *b*. 21 May 1899.

2*f*. Roger Frederick Powell, *b*. 22 Mar. 1902.

2*e*. Robert Markham Powell (26 *Rue de St. Petersburg, Paris*), *b*. 13 Aug. 1870; *m*. 15 Oct. 1904, Mary Louisa, da. of Thomas Cowee of Ongar, Essex.

3*e*. Reginald Crofts Powell (*Surrey Farm, Uitenhage, Cape Colony*), *b*. 30 Mar. 1876; *m*. (at Calcutta) 27 Nov. 1901, Madeleine Jeanne Louise, da. of Charles Couret of Clermont Ferrand, Auvergne; and has issue 1*f* to 3*f*.

1*f*. Reginald Sydney Stevens Powell, *b*. (at Uitenhage) 23 Sept. 1905.

2*f*. Gladys Fernande Madeline Powell, *b*. (at Marseilles) 5 Sept. 1902.

3*f*. Phyllis Emilie Powell, *b*. (at Uitenhage) 29 Jan. 1904.

4*e*. Lucy Caroline Powell, *b*. 5 Sept. 1871.

7*d*. Susanna Stevens, *b*. 6 May 1849 ; *unm.*

8*d*. Margaret Stevens, *b*. 13 Oct. 1856 ; *unm.*

9*d*. Frances Stevens, *b*. 19 Nov. 1859 ; *m*. Edward Vickers (*Inglewood, N.Z.*) ; and has issue 1*e* to 6*e*.

1*e*. James Vickers, *b*. 1899.

2*e*. Barbara Vickers, *b*. 18 Nov. 1891.

3*e*. Elizabeth Vickers, *b*. Nov., 1892.

4*e*. Nancy Vickers, *b*. 1893.

5*e*. Rhoda Vickers, *b*. 1896.

6*e*. Frances Vickers, *b*. 1897.

10*d*. Anne Marriott Stevens, *b*. Sept. 1863; *m*. 1900, Alexander McLaren Thomson (*Inglewood, N.Z.*); and has issue 1*e* to 3*e*.

1*e*. Donald William Thomson, *b*. 1 Dec. 1902.

2*e*. Anne Margaret Thomson, *b*. 7 Aug. 1903.

3*e*. Helen Catherine Thomson, *b*. 30 Aug. 1905.

11*d*. Catherine Octavia Stevens, *b*. 23 Jan. 1865 ; *unm.*

2*c*. *Mary Stevens*, b. *May* 1796 ; d. 14 *Oct.* 1823 ; m. 12 *June* 1821, *the Rev. John Frewen Moor of Bradfield House, M.A.*, b. *Nov.* 1798 ; d. 29 *Dec.* 1879 ; *and had issue* 1*d*.

1*d*. *Rev. John Frewen Moor, M.A., late Vicar of Ampfield*, b. 23 *Sept.* 1823 ; d. 5 *Jan.* 1906 ; m. 24 *Nov.* 1853, *Frances Dorothy, da. of Col. Charles Grimston of Grimston Garth, Yorks ; and had issue* 1*e to* 2*e*.

1*e*. Rev. Charles Moor, B.D., *late* Vicar of Gainsborough and Canon of Lincoln (14 *Lexham Gardens, W.*), *b*. 10 May 1857 ; *m*. 10 July 1889, Constance Mary, da. of Robert Moon, M.A., Bar.-at-Law ; and has issue 1*f* to 5*f*.

1*f*. Christopher Moor, *b*. 2 Feb. 1892.

2*f*. Frewen Moor, *b*. 28 Ap. 1893.

3*f*. Oswald Moor, *b*. 26 July 1901.

4*f*. Rosalie Moor, *b*. 28 May 1890.

5*f*. Veronica Moor, *b*. 31 May 1897.

2*e*. Selina Mary Moor, *b*. 21 Sept. 1860.

3*c*. *Elizabeth Stevens*, b. 4 *Feb.* 1803; d. 26 *July* 1880; m. 25 *Ap.* 1843, *the Rev. John Marriott, M.A., Vicar of Hythe, Hants*, b. 3 *Feb.* 1809; d. 13 *Feb.* 1881; *and had issue* 1*d*.

1*d*. Maria Marriott (*The Red House, Eastleigh, R.S.O., Hants*), *b*. 10 Feb. 1844.

4*c*. *Ann Stevens*, b. 14 *Nov.* 1805; d. 10 *Ap.* 1892; m. 25 *Nov.* 1828, *the Rev. Thomas Horatio Walker, M.A.*, d. 18 *Oct.* 1841; *and had issue* 1*d to* 4*d*.

[Nos. 34629 to 34659.

# of The Blood Royal

    1*d.* Rev. Charles Henry Walker, M.A., Vicar of Walkhampton (*Walkhampton Vicarage, Devon*), *b.* 28 Dec. 1833 ; *m.* 18 Sept. 1860, Emily Jane, da. of Gen. John Slessor ; and has issue 1*e* to 6*e*.

      1*e.* Harold Walker, *b.* 29 Jan. 1866.

      2*e.* Bernard Stevens Walker, *b.* 25 Mar. 1873.

      3*e.* Agnes Emma Walker, *b.* 21 June 1861.

      4*e.* Ellen Walker, *b.* 16 Nov. 1862.

      5*e.* Ethel Amy Walker, *b.* 28 July 1867.

      6*e.* Jessie Beatrice Walker, *b.* 28 Sept. 1868.

    2*d.* Mary Harriet Walker (26 *Albany Road, Southsea*), *b.* 14 Mar. 1830 ; *m.* 3 Oct. 1854, Major-Gen. William Hamilton Elliot, *d.* 9 Dec. 1899 ; and has issue 1*e* to 2*e*.

      1*e.* Gilbert Thomas Elliot, *b.* 3 Nov. 1858.

      2*e.* Annie Letitia Elliot, *b.* 3 Sept. 1856.

    3d. Anne Elizabeth Walker, b. 23 Dec. 1835 (*? 23 Jan.* 1836) ; d. 11 *Ap.* 1879 ; m. 13 *Dec.* 1860, *James Henry Patteson,* d. 4 *July* 1904 ; *and had issue* 1*e to* 4*e.*

      1*e.* John Henry Patteson, *b.* 16 Sept. 1862 ; *m.* Edith, da. of Canon Kent.

      2*e.* Francis James Patteson, *b.* 19 Jan. 1864.

      3*e.* Frances Mary Patteson (*Barnsfield, Buckfastleigh, S. Devon*), *b.* 9 Mar. 1866 ; *unm.*

      4*e.* Janet Coleridge Patteson, *b.* 26 June 1870 ; *unm.*

    4*d.* Ellen Julia Walker (*The Gables, Cirencester*), *b.* 4 Oct. 1837 ; *m.* as 2nd wife, 4 Aug. 1859, the Rev. George Munn, Rector of Madresfield, *d.* 16 Jan. 1906 ; and has issue 1*e* to 7*e*.

      1*e.* Reginald George Munn, Capt. 36th Sikhs, *b.* 20 Aug. 1869.

      2*e.* Leonora Munn, *b.* 31 May 1878.

      3*e.* Anny Munn, *b.* 15 July 1862.

      4*e.* Alice Georgina Munn, *b.* 2 June 1864.

      5*e.* Edith Mary Munn, *b.* 8 Sept. 1866.

      6*e.* Margaret Munn, *b.* 20 Nov. 1871.

      7*e.* Hilda Frances Munn, *b.* 24 Sept. 1873.

    3a. Dorothy Pern, co-h. in 1771 ; *m.* [——] *Trip.*   [Nos. 34660 to 34681.

348. Descendants, if any surviving, of the Rev. Andrew Pern, D.D., J.P., Rector of Abingdon, co. Camb., and Norton, co. Suffolk (see Table XXXII.), *d.* 23 Nov. 1772 ; *m.* Anne, da. of [——] Dickman of Cambridge ; and had issue 1*a* to 2*a*.

    1a. Rev. Andrew Pern, B.A., Rector of Isham, co. Northants, and Clay, co. Herts, b. 6 *Dec.* 1751 ; d. 5 *Dec.* 1807 ; m. [——], *da. of* [——] ; *and had issue* 1*b to* 2*b.*

      1b. Andrew Pern, B.A. (Camb.).

      2b. John Chester Pern, b. 1777 ; *living* 1806.

    2a. Margaret Pern, b. 1754.

349. Descendants of John Fountayne of Melton (see Table XXXII.), *b.* 1684 ; *d.* 30 Oct. 1736 ; *m.* Elizabeth, da. of Francis Carew of Beddington, *b. c.* 1689 ; *d.* 9 Jan. 1768 ; and had issue 1*a* to 6*a*.

    1a. Thomas Fountayne of Melton, b. 4 *Dec.* 1713 ; d.s.p. 18 *Jan.* 1739.

    2a. Very Rev. John Fountayne, D.D., Dean of York, b. 1715 ; d. 14 *Feb.* 1802 ; m. 3rdly, *Anne, da. and h. of Charles Montagu of Papplewick,* d. 12 *Sept.* 1786 ; *and had issue* 1*b.*

The Plantagenet Roll

1b. *Elizabeth Fountayne,* b. 1 *Ap.* 1762; d. 10 *Jan.* 1786; m. 5 *Feb.* 1781, *Richard Wilson of Rudding Hall, co. York,* b. 31 *Dec.* 1752; d. 7 *June* 1787 ; *and had issue* 1c.

1c. *Richard Fountayne-Wilson of Melton Park, M.P., High Sheriff co. York* 1807; b. 9 *June* 1783 ; d. 24 *July* 1847 ; m. 3 *Oct.* 1807, *Sophia, da. of George Osbaldeston of Hutton Bushell, M.P.,* d. 21 *May* 1861 ; *and had issue* 1d *to* 6d.

1d. *Andrew Fountayne-Wilson, afterwards* (R.L. 27 *Feb.* 1826) *Montagu of Ingmanthorpe Hall, and Papplewick,* d.s.p. 8 *Oct.* 1895.

2d. *James Wilson, afterwards Montagu, of Melton Park, &c., J.P., High Sheriff co. Cambs and Hunts* 1874 ; b. 1819; d. *Jan.* 1891; m. 20 *Aug.* 1874, *Laura Adeline, da. of Ernest Thelluson of Mount Auldyn, Isle of Man ; and had issue* 1e *to* 7e.

1e. Frederick James Osbaldeston Wilson, *now* Montagu, J.P., *late* Lieut. Coldstream Guards (*Ingmanthorpe Hall, near Wetherby ; Melton Park, Doncaster ; Ely, Isle of Ely*), b. 9 Feb. 1878.

2e. James Fountayne Wilson (*Papplewick Hall, Notts*), b. 8 Dec. 1887.

3e. Adeline Elizabeth Wilson.

4e. Evelyn Sophia Wilson.

5e. Laura Wilson.

6e. Mary Edith Wilson.

7e. Amy Violet Wilson.

3d. *Elizabeth Ann Fountayne-Wilson,* d. (-) ; m. 25 *May* 1841, *Henley George Greaves of Elmsall Lodge, co. York,* b. 9 *Oct.* 1818 ; d. 14 *Aug.* 1872 ; *and had issue* 1e *to* 2e.

1e. *George Richard Greaves, J.P.,* b. 8 *Mar.* 1845 ; d. 25 *Feb.* 1899 ; m. 23 *Aug.* 1883, *Ellen Mary* (*Western House, Winslow, Bucks*), *da. of Thomas Newham of Winslow.*

2e. Maria Elizabeth Greaves, *m.* 22 Feb. 1866, John Shawe Phillips of Culham House, co. Oxon., J.P., D.L., *b.* 20 Jan. 1843; *d.* 5 Ap. 1893; and had issue 1f to 2f.

1f. John Henley Shawe Phillips (*Culham House, Abingdon*), b. 16 Ap. 1867.

2f. Gerald Edwin Phillips (*Frilford Lodge, Abingdon*), b. 22 Feb. 1870; *m.* 24 Oct. 1900, Louise Ellen, da. of Frank Long ; and has issue 1g to 2g.

1g. John Gerald Phillips, *b.* 4 Aug. 1905.

2g. Muriel Mary Phillips.

4d. Mary Fountayne Wilson (*Bournemouth*), now aged 88; *m.* Dec. 1839, Lieut.-Col. James O'Brien England, 71st Highland L.I., *d.* 13 Dec. 1847; and has issue 1e to 2e.

1e. James Montagu FitzRoy England, Lieut.-Col. (ret.) 87th Royal Irish Fusiliers (*Sorrento Lodge, Ryde*), b. 20 July 1845 ; *m.* 1 Dec. 1885, Helen Charlotte, da. of Admiral Wigston of Bitterne Court, co. Hants.

2e. Sophia Elizabeth England, *m.* Jan. 1867, Thomas Albyn Saunders, Capt. 9th Lancers; and has issue 1f to 3f.

1f. Cecil Fountayne Saunders, m. Constance, da. of [——] Craddock.

2f. Mary Saunders, *m.* 1st, Charles Faber ; 2ndly, George Champney Palmes.

3f. Inez Saunders, *m.* Gerald Lindsay Palmes.

5d. *Theodosia Wilson,* d. 4 *July* 1880 ; m. *as 2nd wife,* 1844, *Lieut.-Gen. Sir Richard England of St. Margaret's, co. Hants, G.C.B.,* b. 1793 ; d. 19 *Jan.* 1883 ; *and had issue* 1e *to* 2e.

1e. *Andrew Montagu England,* b. 10 *Aug.* 1848 ; d. 1886 ; m. (*in Australia*) *Isabella, da. of* [——] *Woods ; and had issue* 1f.

1f. Richard Fountayne England, *b.* 2 May 1886, now at Trin. Coll., Melbourne.

2e. *Theodosia England,* b. 6 *Dec.* 1846 ; d. 1 *Oct.* 1890 ; m. 27 *Ap.* 1876, *the Rev. Orlando Spencer Smith* (*Swanwick Glen, Southampton*); *and had issue* 1f *to* 6f.   [Nos. 34682 to 34700.

426

# of The Blood Royal

1*f*. Gerald Montagu Smith, Lieut. R.H.A., *b.* 4 June 1881.

2*f*. Richard Osbaldeston Smith, *b.* 18 Feb. 1885.

3*f*. Katharine Winifred Smith, *b.* 16 Ap. 1877 ; *m.* June 1905, George Winn of Holly Hill, Hants.

4*f*. Theodosia Lettice Smith, *b.* 20 Jan. 1879 ; *m.* 1899, Lieut. Edward Thomas, R.N. ; and has issue 1*g*.

1*g*. Joyce Theodosia Thomas, *b.* 1900.

5*f*. Pamela Smith, *b.* 8 Ap. 1883.

6*f*. Olive Dorothea Smith, *b.* 27 Ap. 1886.

6*d*. Catherine Judith Fountayne Wilson (*Emral Park, Worthenbury, co. Flint*), *m.* 7 June 1853, Sir Richard Price Puleston, 3rd Bart. [U.K.], *b.* 27 Dec. 1813 ; *d.* 14 Aug. 1893 ; and has issue 1*e* to 2*e*.

1*e*. Mary Sophia Puleston, *m.* 3 Feb. 1880, Lieut.-Col. Llewellyn England Sidney Parry of Graffwyn, co. Carnarvon, D.S.O. (*Pengwern, Rhuddlan, R.S.O.*) ; and has issue 1*f* to 5*f*.

1*f*. Ruby Parry.

2*f*. Pearl Parry, *m.* 1902, Francis John Lloyd Priestley.

3*f*. Mary Parry.

4*f*. Olive Parry.

5*f*. Ivy Parry.

2*e*. Catherine Theodosia Fountayne Puleston, *m.* 19 Ap. 1899, the Rev. Reginald William Wilberforce, Rector of Little Bittering (*Bittering Hall, East Dereham*) ; and has issue 1*f*.

1*f*. Barbara Fountayne Wilberforce, *b.* 1900.

3*a*. ⎫
4*a*. ⎬ *two younger sons.*

5*a*. *Elizabeth Fountayne*, m. *Charles Eyre, M.D.*

6*a*. *Anne Fountayne*, m. *Edward Weston.*   [Nos. 34701 to 34716.

350. Descendants, if any, of Anne Fountayne, wife of Simon Patrick ; and of Judith Fountayne, wife of Thomas Sherlock, Master of the Temple (see Table XXXII.).

351. Descendants, if any, of Elizabeth Chester (see Table XXXII.), *m.* 1689, Francis Flyer of Brent Pelham, co. Herts.

352. Descendants, if any, of Anne Chester (see Table XXXII.), *d.* 29 Dec. 1678 ; *m.* 1st, Robert Eade of Cambridge, M.D. ; 2ndly, Henry Hoogan of Lyme Regis, M.D. ; and of Cecilia Chester, wife of Thomas Turner of Walden.

353. Descendants of the Rev. Robert Chester, D.D., Professor of Theology, Rector of Stevenage (see Table XXXII.), *b.* 1597 ; *bur.* 9 Ap. 1664 ; *m.* Anne, da. of Sir Arthur Capel of Raineshall, co. Essex, *bur.* 26 Dec. 1679 ; and had issue.

See pp. 400–401, Nos. 33581–33584.   [Nos. 34717 to 34720.

The Plantagenet Roll

354. Descendants of HENRY WHITE of Dedham, co. Essex, and of Westminster, an Officer in the Army (see Table XXXII.), *d.* (–); *m.* ANN, da. of [——] CARRINGTON, *d.* ; and had issue 1*a* to 3*a*.

1*a. Henry White, Major 74th Highlanders, previously Grenadier Guards, 4th son, but in 1841 heir, b. 28 Ap. 1781; d. 23 Mar. 1849; m. 16 June 1803, Jean, da. and h. of John Hanna of Paisley, co. Renfrew, d. 14 Jan. 1870; and had issue 1b to 3b.*

1*b. George Francis White of Old Elvet, co. Durham, D.D., Lieut.-Col. 16th Lancers and 31st Foot, b. 20 June 1808; d. 23 July 1898; m. 6 Feb. 1839, Anne, da. of Thomas Greenwell of Greenwell, co. Durham, J.P., D.L., d. ; and had issue 1c to 6c.*

1*c.* George Frederick White, Lieut.-Col. *lately* Comdg. 1st Batt. King's Own (*Old Elvet, Durham*), *b.* 30 June 1845.

2*c. Edward Arthur White, F.S.A., a learned genealogist, Capt. Durham L.I.,* d.s.p. 13 *Feb.* 1895.

3*c. Aubrey Francis White, Major late 2nd Batt. Welsh Regt., b. 22 Aug. 1856.*

4*c.* Alice Isabella White.

5*c.* Ella Jeanne White.

6*c.* Evelyn White.

2*b. Augusta Alexander White, of H.M.'s Treasury, b. 1 Dec. 1823; d. (in Queensland) 22 Aug. 1889; m. 1st, 24 Jan. 1846, Sarah, da. of George Nevile of Skelbrooke Park, d. 18 Aug. 1854; and had issue 1c to 3c.*

1*c.* Charles Nevile White, *late* R.N., *b.* 2 Dec. 1846.

2*c.* Henry George White, *b.* 28 Dec. 1848.

3*c.* Augustus Alexander White, *b.* 2 Oct. 1850.

3*b. Vittoria Hanna White, m. (at Simla) 26 Oct. 1843, Col. William Lydiard,* d. 28 Aug. 1896; *and has issue* 1*c* to 4*c.*

1*c.* Arthur Combe Gordon Lydiard, Lieut.-Col. Indian Staff Corps, *late* 38th Regt., *b.* (–); *m.* ; and has issue.

2*c.* Walter Charles Lydiard, *m.* ; and has issue.

3*c. Donna Eliza Lydiard, d. 30 Oct. 1898; m. 8 June 1868, Richard Heneage Taylor, d. 1 Sept. 1891.*

4*c. Blanche Harriet Lydiard, d. 23 Feb. 1898; m. 28 Aug. 1877, the Hon. Lane Horton of Washington, U.S.A., d. 23 Feb. 1895; and had issue.*

2*a. Harriet White, d. 18 Aug. 1807; m. [——] Proctor.*

3*a. Penelope Ann White, d. 1850; m. John Robinson of Westminster; and had issue (at least 2 das.) 1b to 2b.*

1*b.* [——] Robinson, *m.* Thomas Cresswell.

2*b.* [——] Robinson, *m.* George Grenville Wilson.　　　[Nos. 34721 to 24733.

355. Descendants of Lieut.-Col. Sir EDWARD NIGHTINGALE, 10th Bart. [E.] (see Table XXXIII.), *b.* 14 Oct. 1760; *d.* 4 Dec. 1804; *m.* (once at Gretna Green and again at Bassingbourne) ELEANOR, da. and h. of Robert NIGHTINGALE of Kneesworth Hall, co. Camb., *d.* 20 Jan. 1825; and had issue 1*a* to 7*a.*

1*a. Sir Charles Ethelston Nightingale, 11th Bart. [E.], b. 1 Nov. 1784; d. 5 July 1843; m. Dec. 1805, Maria, da. of Thomas Lacy Dickonson of West Retford, co. Notts, d. (at Boulogne-sur-Mer) 8 Dec. 1846; and had issue 1b to 5b.*

# of The Blood Royal

1b. *Sir Charles Nightingale, 12th Bart.* [E.], b. 30 Ap. 1809; d. 17 Sept. 1876; m. 2 Feb. 1829, *Harriet Maria, da. of Capt. Edward Broughton Foster of Ayleston Hall, co. Leicester,* b. c. 1800; d. 22 Dec. 1881; *and had issue* 1c *to* 2c.

1c. Sir Henry Dickonson Nightingale, 13th Bart. [E.], Hon. Lieut.-Col. Army Pay Dept. (33 *Boulevard Mariette, Boulogne-sur-Mer, France*), b. (at Bruges) 15 Nov. 1830; m. 14 Aug. 1855, Mary, da. of Capt. Thomas Spark, R.N.; and has issue 1d to 5d.

1d. Edward Henry Nightingale, M.A. (*Camb.*), Bar.-at-Law, b. 17 *June* 1856; d. 26 *Jan.* 1895; m. 9 *July* 1887, *Lily Maitland, da. of Capt. Maitland Addison, late* 59th *Regt. ; and had issue* 1e.

1e. Edward Manners Nightingale, b. 1888.

2d. Valentine Charles Nightingale (*Highview, Highfield Hill, Upper Norwood, S.E.*), b. 3 Feb. 1859; m. 16 May 1894, Alice Mary, widow of Evaux Huggett, da. of the Rev. Henry Eastfield Bayley, M.A.

3d. Harry Ethelston Nightingale (*Kneesworth, Victoria Road, Upper Norwood, S.E. ; Albemarle Mansions, Medina Terrace, West Brighton*), b. 15 Mar. 1860; m. 17 May 1881, Coralie Louise Pauline, da. of Charles Louis d'Harcourt-Mary, LL.D.; and has issue 1e.

1e. Naomi Coralie Nightingale, b. 15 Jan. 1893.

4d. Emily Frances Mary Nightingale, m. 1 Jan. 1886, Mansfeldt Henry Mills (*Sherwood Hall, Mansfield, Notts*); and has issue 1e to 5e.

1e. Mansfeldt Charles Nightingale Mills, b. 9 Feb. 1891.

2e. Francis Robert Fenwick Mills, b. 31 Aug. 1895.

3e. Irene Frances Mary Mills, b. 28 Oct. 1886.

4e. Violet Edith Hilda Mills, b. 9 Ap. 1888.

5e. Vera Florence Emmeline Mills, b. 13 May 1897.

5d. Violet Harriet Nightingale, m. 24 Nov. 1894, Major Charles Herbert Clay, 7th Gurkha Rifles, and D.A.Q.M.G. (*Simla*); and has issue 1e to 2e.

1e. Charles Nightingale Clay, b. 5 Mar. 1902.

2e. Violet Miriam Nightingale Clay, b. 15 Sept. 1895.

2c. *Rosalind Agnes Nightingale,* d. 10 Nov. 1896; m. 22 *Sept.* 1857, *Lieut.-Col. Edward Smyth Mercer, late* 85th *Regt.*

2b. *Thomas Henry Nightingale, R.N., Port Capt. at Simon's Bay, Cape of Good Hope,* b. 18 Ap. 1810; d. 12 Dec. 1865; m. 22 Nov. 1830, *Hannah Elizabeth, da. of John Humphreys Parry, Bar.-at-Law,* d. 8 Aug. 1879; *and had issue* 1c *to* 8c.

1c. Percy Nightingale, *Inspecting Commissioner, Cape of Good Hope,* b. 10 *Jan.* 1836; d. 24 *May* 1895; m. 3 *July* 1860, *Frances Emma, da. of Peter Brophy of Dublin,* d. 9 *May* 1905; *and had issue* 1d *to* 7d.

1d. Thomas Slingsby Nightingale, Secretary to the Dept., and Deputy Agent-General for Cape Colony (*Kneesworth, Limpsfield, Surrey*), b. 29 Jan. 1866; m. 21 Ap. 1900, Doris Elizabeth, da. of Charles Stoughton Collison of East Bilney, Norfolk; and has issue 1e.

1e. Geoffrey Slingsby Nightingale, b. 24 Nov. 1904.

2d. Percy Athelstan Nightingale, M.D. (Edin.), a Companion of the Orders of the Crown of Johore, and of the White Elephant of Siam, *formerly* Physician to the British Legation and to Royal Palace, Bangkok, &c. (9 *Campden Hill Road, Kensington, W. ; 5 Hertford Street, Mayfair, W.*), b. 7 Oct. 1867; m. 7 Jan. 1899, Muriel Stoughton, da. of Charles Stoughton Collison of East Bilney, co. Norfolk; and has issue 1e.

1e. Charles Athelstan Nightingale, b. 23 July 1902.

3d. Lacy Gamaliel Nightingale, B.C.L., Bar. I.T., an Advocate of the Supreme Court and Assist. Law Adviser to the Crown, Cape Town (*Cape Town*), b. 25 Mar. 1869.

4d. Manners Ralph Wilmot Nightingale, Capt. 5th Gurkha Rifles, Indian Army (*Junior Naval and Military*), b. 15 Ap. 1871.   [Nos. 34734 to 34753.

The Plantagenet Roll

5*d*. Blanche Esther Nightingale, *m*. 17 Dec. 1891, Petrus Cornelius Van der Poel Hiddingh.

6*d*. Beatrice Marian Nightingale, *m*. 14 June 1889, Edward Bromley, C.E., *d*. 1 Nov. 1900; and has issue 1*e* to 2*e*.

    1*e*. Colin Bromley, *b*. 20 Mar. 1890.

    2*e*. Madelene Bromley, *b*. 26 Ap. 1894.

7*d*. Ethel Lemprière Nightingale, *m*. 20 Ap. 1887, W. H. Ross, M.D.

2*c*. James Edward Nightingale, *formerly* District Officer of Crown Forests, Cape Colony (*Alexandria, Eastern Province, Cape Colony*), *b*. 23 Mar. 1838; *m*. 1st, Feb. 1861, Louisa, da. of [——] Short, *d*. 29 Dec. 1869; 2ndly, 1883, Adriana Josena, da. of [——] Van Niekirk; and has issue 1*d* to 10*d*.

1*d*. Geoffrey Edward Nightingale, *b*. 5 Feb. 1862; *m*. 1882, Emily Christina, da. of [——] Austen; and has issue 1*e*.

    1*e*. Winifred Florence Nightingale, *b*. 1887.

2*d*. Ernest Albert Nightingale (*Quthing, Basutoland, South Africa*), *b*. 30 Ap. 1867; *m*. 1893, Sarah Annette Thornton, da. of [——] Austen; and has issue 1*e* to 3*e*.

    1*e*. Alfred Nightingale, *b*. 16 May 1905.

    2*e*. Ida Frances Nightingale, *b*. 1897.

    3*e*. Irene Mary Nightingale, *b*. 1899.

3*d*. Frank Leopold Nightingale, *b*. 27 Dec. 1869.

4*d*. Thomas Cecil Parry Nightingale, *b*. 1885.

5*d*. James Percy Nightingale, *b*. 1889.

6*d*.[1] Ada Constance Nightingale.

7*d*.[2] Eleanor Adeline Nightingale.

8*d*.[2] Effie Edith Nightingale.

9*d*. Julia Venning Nightingale, *b*. Ap. 1890.

10*d*. Ida Nellie Nightingale, *b*. 20 Nov. 1892.

3*c*. Arthur Nightingale, *b*. 26 Nov. 1841.

4*c*. *Lionel Brydges Nightingale, M.D.*, *b*. 29 *June* 1843; *d*. 14 *Mar*. 1889; m. 30 *Aug*. 1876, *Julia Stuart* (242 *New York Avenue, Brooklyn, New York*), *da. of William Henry Grenelle of New York; and had issue* 1*d to* 6*d*.

1*d*. Lionel Grenelle Nightingale, *b*. (at Brooklyn) 28 Feb. 1881.

2*d*. Eleanor Maria Nightingale, *b*. (at Brooklyn) 19 June 1877.

3*d*. Julia Huntingdon Grenelle Nightingale, *b*. (at Brooklyn) 24 Mar. 1879; *m*. 28 Sept. 1903, Harrison Bennet Perkins; and has issue 1*e*.

    1*e*. Lionel Nightingale Perkins, *b*. 2 Aug. 1905.

4*d*. Lucie Magown Nightingale, *b*. (at Brooklyn) 7 Oct. 1882.

5*d*. Ida Ethelstone Nightingale, *b*. (at Brooklyn) 16 Sept. 1884.

6*d*. Marguerite Nightingale, *b*. (at Brooklyn) 18 Mar. 1888.

5*c*. Geoffrey Ethelstone Nightingale (*Moonyana, Ellishdale, Cape Colony*), *b*. 17 *Sept*. 1853; *unm*.

6*c*. Eleanor Maria Nightingale (*Fernleigh*, 4 *Broad Park Avenue, Ilfracombe*), *m*. 1 Aug. 1872, Robert Robinson of S. Ann, co. Jamaica, *d.s.p.* 16 June 1876.

7*c*. Mary Julia Nightingale, *b*. 13 May 1845; *m*. 17 Feb. 1866, John Tucker Ross, M.R.C.S., R.N., *d.s.p.* 31 Dec. 1866.

8*c*. Ida Sophia Nightingale, *unm*.

3*b*. *Manby Nightingale*, b. 1 *Ap*. 1813; *d*. 1850; *m*. 4 *May* 1844, *Frederica Helen, da. of George F. Hurst* (*who re-m. 9 Feb. 1856, Lieut.-Gen. Charles Lionel Shower of St. John's, Worthing*), d. 1895; *and had issue* 1*c to* 2*c*.

1*c*. George Ewan Nightingale (*Cawnpore, India*), *b*. 19 Nov. 1847; *m*. (at

[Nos. 34754 to 34786.

Cawnpore) 10 Aug. 1871, Blanche Cecile, da. of Louis Enouf, Advocate of the Imperial Court, Pondicherry, *d.* 20 Sept. 1899 ; and has issue 1*d* to 3*d.*

1*d.* Lilian Marie Nightingale, *b.* 4 Dec. 1873.

2*d.* Clarice Marie Nightingale, *b.* 2 Aug. 1875; *m.* 24 Feb. 1900, James Morrison, Civil Surgeon (*Berar, India*); and has issue 1*e* to 3*e.*

1*e.* Cécile Marie Nightingale Morrison, *b.* 14 Aug. 1901.

2*e.* Ethel Violet Nightingale Morrison, *b.* 25 Aug. 1904.

3*e.* Florence Blanche Nightingale Morrison, *b.* 27 Jan. 1906.

3*d.* Violet Marie Nightingale, *b.* 1880.

2*c.* Ethel Nightingale.

4*b. George Lacy Nightingale, b.* 8 *May* 1815 ; d. 31 *May* 1859 ; m. 29 *Jan.* 1842, *Martha Ann, da. of Sylvester Fellows of New York ; and had issue* 1*c to* 5*c.*

1*c.* Henry Dickonson Nightingale, *b.* 23 Sept. 1843.

2*c.* James Wilson Nightingale, *b.* 7 Aug. 1845; *m.* 26 Nov. 1869, Elizabeth, da. of Enoch R. Lumbert of Bangor, Maine; and has issue 1*d* to 3*d.*

1*d.* George Lacy Nightingale, *b.* 17 June 1877.

2*d.* Eleanor Alison Nightingale.

3*d.* Bessie Barclay Nightingale.

3*c.* Charles Ethelstone Nightingale, *b.* 26 Nov. 1858.

4*c.* Mary Mills Nightingale.

5*c.* Julia Bissul Nightingale.

5*b. Ernest Nightingale of the Revenue Dept., Montreal, b.* 5 *June* 1821 ; d. 24 *Sept.* 1868 ; m. 22 Oct. 1842, *Helen Louisa, da. of Francis Evans of Dublin ; and had issue* 1*c to* 2*c.*

1*c.* Louisa Maria Nightingale (291 *St. Christopher Street, Montreal*), *m.* 13 June 1866, François Duquet, *d.* 1878.

2*c.* Emily Ernesta Nightingale, *m.* 19 Nov. 1867, Benjamin George Ballard.

2*a. Alexander Malcolm Nightingale, b.* 30 *Nov.* 1892 ; d. 11 *Jan.* 1826 ; m. 1818, *Marianne, da. of Major Herbert Beaver, 19th Regt., d.* 17 *Feb.* 1847 ; *and had issue* 1*b to* 3*b.*

1*b. Edward Herbert Nightingale, Capt.* 23*rd Regt. Madras L.I., b.* 15 *Ap.* 1821 ; d. 5 *May* 1856 ; m. *Sophia, da. of Lieut.-Gen. Robert Blackall, Bengal Army* (*who re-m.* 18 *Oct.* 1865, *Lieut.-Col. J. W. Carter*) ; *and had issue* 1*c.*

1*c.* Emily Grace Nightingale.

2*b. Manners Randolph Nightingale, Lieut.-Col. Bengal Staff Corps, b.* 30 *Ap.* 1823 ; d. 25 *July* 1892 ; m. 15 *May* 1851, *Elizabeth Ann, da. of Bryan William Stevens of Weston, co. Northants, d.* 1889 ; *and had issue* 1*c.*

1*c. Charles Alexander Malcolm Nightingale, b.* 12 *May* 1853 ; d. *May* 1905 ; m. 1878, *Caroline, da. of W. Johnson of the Green, Richmond, Surrey ; and had issue* 1*d to* 2*d.*

1*d.* Grace Caroline Nightingale.

2*d.* Elizabeth Anne Nightingale.

3*b.* Charles William Nightingale, J.P., Lieut.-Col., late B.S.C. (*Landscore House, Teignmouth*), *b.* 15 May 1825 ; *m.* 4 Feb. 1858, Martha, da. of Major James Winfield, Bengal Army ; and has issue 1*c.*

1*c.* Marianne Florence Nightingale.

3*a. Leonard Nightingale, b.* 9 *Feb.* 1794; d. (-) ; m. [——], *da. of* [——] *Perry (who re-m.* [——] *and settled in America)* ; *and had issue* (*several children settled in the United States*).

4*a. Ernest Nightingale, an Officer in the Foot Guards, b.* 12 *Aug.* 1796.

5*a. Geoffrey Nightingale, b.* 2 *Mar.* 1799 ; d. 15 *Jan.* 1864; m. 29 *June* 1822,

[Nos. 34787 to 34808.

The Plantagenet Roll

Mary, da. of Thomas Knowlys of Stockwell, d. 15 *Ap.* 1873; *and had issue* 1b *to* 2b.

    1b. Geoffrey Nightingale, Lieut.-Col. Madras Army, b. 2 Sept. 1823; d. 5 Oct. 1868; m. 25 Feb. 1858, *Anna Maria Martha, da. of Thomas John Knowlys of Heysham Tower, co. Lanc.; and had issue* 1c *to* 2c.

        1c. Louisa Florence Nightingale.

        2c. Emmeline Sophia Nightingale.

    2b. Frederic Charles Nightingale, Solicitor (*The Lynch, Clifton Road, Wimbledon; 2 Crown Court, Old Broad Street, E.C.*), b. 29 Aug. 1835; m. 10 Sept. 1868, Katherine Jane, da. of Francis Hamilton of Friars Place, Midx.; and has issue 1c to 2c.

        1c. Claude Robert Nightingale, b. 18 June 1878.

        2c. Dudley Arthur Nightingale, b. 4 Dec. 1880.

    6a. Julia Nightingale, d. 11 Mar. 1815; m. 16 Ap. 1808, James Markland, 63rd Regt.; and had issue 1b.

    1b. Eleanor Markland, d. (-); m. 8 Oct. 1833, Archibald Wyndham Bishop, 7th Dragoon Guards.

    7a. Elizabeth Sophia Nightingale, d. 25 June 1884; m. 22 May 1811, the Hon. Charles Ewan Law, M.P., Q.C., Recorder of London, b. 14 June 1792; d. 13 Aug. 1850; and had issue 1b to 3b.

    1b. Charles Edmund Towry (Law, afterwards (R.L. 1885) Towry-Law), 3rd Baron Ellenborough [U.K.], b. 17 Nov. 1820; d. 9 Oct. 1890; m. 1st, Nov. 1840, Lady Eleanor Cecil, da. of William Forward (Howard), 4th Earl of Wicklow [I.], K.P., d.s.p. 15 June 1852; 2ndly, 28 June 1855, Anna Elizabeth, da. of the Rev. John FitzGerald Day of Beaufort House, Killarney, d. 29 Feb. 1860; 3rdly, 26 Aug. 1863, Isabella, da. and h. of Alexander Ogilby of Pellipar, co. Londonderry, d. 22 Ap. 1874; 4thly, 1 Dec. 1874, Beatrice Joanna (15 Rosary Gardens, South Kensington), da. of Sir Norton Joseph Knatchbull, 10th Bart. [E.]; and had issue 1c to 2c.

        1c. Charles Towry Hamilton (Towry-Law), 4th Baron Ellenborough [U.K.], b. 21 Ap. 1856; d.s.p. 26 June 1902.

        2c. Hon. Emily Julia Towry-Law (19 King's Gardens, Hove, Brighton).

    2b. Mary Law, b. 20 Jan. 1816; d. 23 Ap. 1888; m. as 2nd wife, 3 Sept. 1839, John Cavendish (Browne), 3rd Baron Kilmaine [I.], b. 11 June 1794; d. 13 Jan. 1873; and had issue 1c to 5c.

        1c. Francis William (Browne), 4th Baron Kilmaine and a Rep. Peer [I.], 10th Bart. [S.] (Gaulston Park, Killucan, co. Westmeath; The Neale, Ballinrobe, co. Mayo), b. 24 Mar. 1843; m. 6 June 1877, Alice Emily, da. of Col. Deane Shute; and has issue 1d.

            1d. Hon. John Edward Deane Browne (The Neale House, Ballinrobe), b. 18 Mar. 1878; m. 17 Dec. 1901, Lady Aline, da. of Archibald (Kennedy), 3rd Marquis of Ailsa [U.K.]; and has issue 1e.

                1e. John Francis Archibald Browne, b. 22 Sept. 1902.

        2c. Hon. Arthur Henry Browne (41 Ailesbury Road, Dublin), b. 29 Ap. 1850; m. 29 Jan. 1885, Clotilde Georgina, da. of Sir John Don-Wauchope, 8th Bart. [S.]; and has issue 1d to 3d.

            1d. Clotilde Mary Hamilton Browne, b. 9 May 1886.

            2d. Clementina Bethea Evelyne Browne, b. 21 Dec. 1889.

            3d. Gertrude Cicely Juliet Browne, b. 1896.

        3c. Hon. Mary Eleanor Frances Browne, b. 22 Mar. 1841; d. 28 Oct. 1869; m. 1st, 17 June 1861, Major George Bagot, b. 5 May 1818; d.s.p. 9 May 1867; 2ndly, 30 Ap. 1868, Thomas Astell St. Quintin of Hartley Park, co. Camb., late Col. Comdg. 8th Hussars; and had issue.

        4c. Hon. Julia Sophia Browne.

                              [Nos. 34809 to 34822.

432

# of The Blood Royal

5c. Hon. Evelyne Browne, b. 5 Jan. 1848; d. 22 Ap. 1878; m. as 1st wife, 20 Nov. 1867, Major-Gen. Sir Owen Tudor Burne, G.C.I.E., K.C.S.I., &c. (132 Sutherland Avenue, Maida Vale, W.; Church Hatch; Christchurch, Hants); and had issue 1d to 5d.

1d. Francis Henry Burne, Capt. R.E., b. 20 Nov. 1870.

2d. Charles Richard Newdigate Burne, Comm. R.N., b. 1 Ap. 1873.

3d. Edward Robert Burne, Capt. R.A., b. 14 Aug. 1876.

4d. Gertrude Mary Burne, b. 19 Mar. 1869; m. 20 Aug. 1891, Arthur Edward Ash.

5d. Evelyn Alice Eleanor Burne, b. 20 Feb. 1878.

3b. Frederica Law, b. 19 Sept. 1824; d. 15 Nov. 1889; m. 17 May 1848, Edmund Law, d. 26 Mar. 1867; 2ndly, 1870, Henry Grevé, an Officer in the (?) French Army; and had issue (at least by 1st husband) 1c to 4c.[1]

1c. Edmund Law, b. 21 Jan. 1850.

2c. Henry Towry-Law, b. 29 May 1856.

3c. Edwin Law, b. 1861.

4c. Gertrude Marguerite Law, d. (? unm.) 6 June 1862.

[Nos. 34823 to 34830.

356. Descendants of Maria Eleanor Nightingale (see Table XXXIII.), b. 3 Jan. 1765; d. (–); m. Thomas Lacy Dickonson of West Retford, co. Notts, d. (–); and had (with possibly sons, an only da.) 1a.

1a. Maria Dickonson, d. 8 Dec. 1846; m. Dec. 1805, Sir Charles Ethelstone Nightingale, 11th Bart. [E.], d. 5 July 1843; and had issue.

See pp. 429–431, Nos. 34734–34803.   [Nos. 34831 to 34900.

357. Descendants of Eleanor Nightingale (see Table XXXIII.), d. 20 Jan. 1825; m. Sir Edward Nightingale, 10th Bart. [E.], d. 4 Dec. 1804; and had issue.

See pp. 429–433, Nos. 34734–34830.   [Nos. 34901 to 34997.

358. Descendants, if any, of Eleanor Nightingale (see Table XXXIII.), wife of Ernest Barnard, Page to Augusta, Princess of Wales.

359. Descendants, if any, of Granado Nightingale, bapt. 16 Jan. 1701; and of his sisters, Mildred, bapt. 20 May 1690; Anne, Elizabeth, and Mary, wife of Thomas Evans, Recorder of Bury; of Katherine Nightingale, wife of Thomas Hitch of Melbourne, co. Camb.; of Anne Nightingale, wife of Edmund Draper of Wandsworth, co. Surrey; and of Phœbe Nightingale (see Table XXXIII.).

---

[1] Foster's "Peerage," 1880, p. 236.

433

The Plantagenet Roll

360. Descendants, if any surviving, of ANNE NIGHTINGALE (see Table
XXXII.), *m*. Sir FRANCIS THEOBALD of Barking, co. Suffolk,
High Sheriff for that co. 1664; and had issue[1] 1*a* to 4*a*.

1*a*. *Frances Theobald, b.* 1654, *being* 10 *years old in* 1664.

2*a*. *Robert Theobald.*

3*a*. *Theodosia Theobald.*

4*a*. *Anne Theobald, m. the Rev. Joseph Gascoyne, Vicar of Enfield; and had*
(*with other*) *issue* 1*b*.

1*b*. *Robert Gascoyne of Enfield, co. Midx.* (2nd *son*), *inherited the Nightingale
Estates on the death, s.p.* (1722) *of his cousin the* 4*th Bart.; and d. unm. a few
months later.*

361. Descendants, if any, of EDWARD HINTON, *m*. MARY, da. of [——]
GREGORY; of SAMUEL HINTON, *m*. SUSAN, da. of [——]
NEVILL;[2] and of GRANADA HINTON, wife of EDWARD FRITH[3]
(see Table XXXIV.).

362. Descendants of SARAH FOWLER (see Table XXXIV.), *d*. 20 Jan.
1784; *m*. 15 Oct. 1750 JOHN LANE of Bentley Hall, co. Stafford, *b*. 1723; *d*. 28 June 1782; and had issue 1*a* to 3*a*.

1*a*. *John Lane of King's Bromley Manor, co. Staff., b.* 20 *Dec.* 1752; *d.* 21 *Dec.*
1824; *m.* 20 *Jan.* 1800, *Sarah, widow of Thomas Amler of Ford Hall, co. Salop,
da. of Thomas Lloyd of Wyle Cop, co. Salop, d.* 1 *Ap.* 1855; *and had issue* 1*b*.

1*b*. *John Newton Lane of King's Bromley, b.* 4 *Dec.* 1800; *d.* 13 *Oct.* 1869; *m.*
8 *Jan.* 1828, *the Hon. Agnes, da. of William* (*Bagot*), 2*nd Baron Bagot* [*G.B.*], *b.*
10 *Aug.* 1809; *d.* 4 *Nov.* 1885; *and had issue* 1*c* to 7*c*.

1*c*. *John Henry Bagot Lane of King's Bromley, J.P., b.* 24 *Feb.* 1829; *d.* 22 *Mar.* 1886; *m.* 28 *Jan.* 1864, *Susan Anne, da. and
co-h. of William Henry Vincent of Lily Hill, co. Bucks, d.* 1 *Oct.* 1899; *and had
issue* 1*d* to 6*d*.

1*d*. John Henry Hervey Vincent Lane of King's Bromley, J.P., D.L., late
Capt. 1st King's Own Staffordshire Militia (*King's Bromley, near Lichfield; Lily
Hill, Bracknell*), *b.* 3 Oct. 1867; *m.* 12 Ap. 1902, the Hon. Grace Louisa, da. of
William (Edwardes), 4th Baron Kensington [I.]; and has issue 1*e* to 3*e*.

1*e*. Thomas John Henry Vincent Lane, *b.* 24 Jan. 1905.

2*e*. Jane Lane, *b.* 21 Jan. 1903.

3*e*. Grace Lilian Jane Lane, *b.* 29 Jan. 1904.

2*d*. Arthur Edward Cecil Lane, J.P., *b.* 28 Aug. 1871.

3*d*. George Alfred Osbourne Lane, Coldstream Guards, *b.* 10 July 1875.

4*d*. Florence Louisa Jane Lane, *b.* 17 Dec. 1865; *m.* 3 Aug. 1886, the Hon.
Frederic William Anson, J.P. (8 *Pall Mall, S.W.; Cell Barnes, near St. Albans*);
and has issue 1*e* to 6*e*.

1*e*. Ernald Henry Anson, *b.* 28 June 1893.

2*e*. Arthur Anson, ⎫ *b.* (twins) 3 Mar. 1896.
3*e*. Frederic Anson, ⎭

4*e*. Helen Frances Anson, *b.* 7 June 1892.

5*e*. Sibyl Florence Anson, *b.* 24 Sept. 1894.

6*e*. Beryl Susan Anson, *b.* 12 Nov. 1904.   [Nos. 34998 to 35010.

---

[1] " Le Neves Knights," Harleian Soc. Pub., viii. p. 222.
[2] By whom he had issue a da. Bridget.
[3] They had issue Thomas, Rowland, and Charles.

434

5*d*. Constance Edith Jane Lane, *b.* 27 Ap. 1869.

6*d*. Lilian Emily Isabel Jane Lane, *b.* 9 Dec. 1878 ; *m.* 13 May 1902, Walter Bromley Davenport, *b.* 8 June 1864 ; and has issue 1*e* to 2*e.*

  1*e*. Walter Henry Davenport, *b.* 1902.

  2*e*. Arthur Richard Davenport, *b.* 1904.

2*c*. Sidney Leveson Lane of Baldersby Park, &c., *late* Capt. 1st Stafford Militia, J.P., D.L. (*The Manor House, Great Addington, Thrapston*), *b.* 13 Ap. 1831 ; *m.* 6 Jan. 1863, Mary Isabel, Dowager Viscountess Downe [I.], da. of the Hon. Richard Bagot, Lord Bishop of Bath and Wells, *d.* 14 Ap. 1900 ; and has issue 1*d* to 2*d.*

1*d*. Sidney Ernald Ralph Lane, *late* Capt. 3rd Batt. Yorks Regt., *b.* 14 Nov. 1863 ; *m.* 5 Aug. 1905, Mabel Emilie, widow of Capt. Philip Green, da. of Sir Edward Scott, 5th Bart. [U.K.].

2*d*. Mary Beatrice Sydney Lane, *m.* 24 Oct. 1891, Capt. Walter Richard Shaw Stewart, J.P., D.L., 1st Wilts Vol., *late* 4th Batt. Argyll and Sutherland Highlanders (*Hays, Shaftesbury*) ; and has issue 1*e* to 5*e.*

  1*e*. Walter Guy Shaw Stewart, *b.* 10 Aug. 1892.

  2*e*. Niel Shaw Stewart, *b.* 7 July 1894.

  3*e*. Michael Sidney Shaw Stewart, *b.* 29 June 1905.

  4*e*. Mary Sibell Agnes Shaw Stewart, *b.* 3 Ap. 1896.

  5*e*. Irene Beatrice Shaw Stewart, *b.* 11 Oct. 1901.

3*c*. *Cecil Newton Lane of Whiston Hall, co. Salop, C.M.G., J.P., Col. 1st Staffordshire Militia,* b. 27 *May* 1833 ; d. 29 *Mar.* 1897 ; m. 12 *Dec.* 1876, *Adela Mary* (*Rycote House, Leamington*), *da. of Rev. the Hon. Frederic Bertie ; and had issue* 1*d* to 4*d.*

  1*d*. Newton Frederic Seymour Lane, *b.* 15 Ap. 1879.

  2*d*. Percy Ernald Lane, *b.* 15 Jan. 1881.

  3*d*. John Ronald Lane, *b.* 31 Dec. 1884.

  4*d*. Georgina Agnes Jane Lane, *b.* 13 Jan. 1882.

4*c*. Very Rev. Ernald Lane, Dean of Rochester, sometime Archdeacon of Stoke-upon-Trent, and Rector of Leigh (*Deanery, Rochester*), *b.* 3 Mar. 1836 ; *m.* 1 July 1879, Evelyn Adelaide, da. of J. W. Philips of Heybridge, J.P. ; and has issue 1*d* to 2*d.*

  1*d*. Geoffrey Ernald William Lane, *b.* 10 June 1881.

  2*d*. Marjorie Agnes Jane Lane.

5*c*. Sir Ronald Bertram Lane, K.C.V.O., C.B., Major-Gen. *late* Rifle Brigade and Military Sec. at Headquarters, Deputy Governor of Chelsea Hospital, Extra Equerry to H.R.H. the Duke of Connaught, &c. (*Chelsea Hospital, S.W.*), *b.* 19 Feb. 1847 ; *m.* 11 Ap. 1893, Augusta Sarah, da. of John A. Beaumont of Wimbledon Park ; and has issue 1*d.*

  1*d*. George Ronald Lane, *b.* 27 Feb. 1894.

6*c*. Edith Emmeline Mary Lane, *m.* 25 Aug. 1868, Walter Henry (James), 2nd Baron Northbourne [U.K.] (*Betteshanger, Eastry, S.O., Dover*) ; and has issue 1*d* to 5*d.*

1*d*. Hon. Walter John James (1 *Courtfield Road, S.W.*), *b.* 2 Sept. 1869 ; *m.* 4 Oct. 1894, Laura Gwenllian, da. of Rear-Adm. Ernest Rice of Sibertswold Place ; and has issue 1*e* to 3*e.*

  1*e*. Walter Ernest Christopher James, *b.* 18 Jan. 1896.

  2*e*. Dorothea Gwenllian James, *b.* 16 Aug. 1897.

  3*e*. Mary Beatrix James, *b.* 1902.

2*d*. Hon. Cuthbert James, Capt. E. Surrey Regt. (*Junior United Service*), *b.* 29 Feb. 1872 ; *m.* 10 Aug. 1903, Florence, da. of Hulsey Packe of Prestwold Hall, co. Leic.   [Nos. 35011 to 35037.

The Plantagenet Roll

3*d.* Hon. Robert James, J.P. (*St. Nicholas, Richmond, Yorks.*), *b.* 13 May 1873 ; *m.* 18 June 1900, Lady Evelyn Kathleen, da. of Arthur Charles (Wellesley), 4th Duke of Wellington [U.K.] ; and has issue 1*e.*

    1*e.* Arthur Walter James, *b.* 6 Jan. 1904.

4*d.* Hon. Wilfred James (*Woodlands, Adisham, near Dover*), *b.* 7 Dec. 1874 ; *m.* 27 Feb. 1900, Margaret, da. of John Stogdon, Assist. Master of Harrow ; and has issue 1*e* to 2*e.*

    1*e.* John Wilfred James, *b.* 30 Dec. 1900.

    2*e.* Henry Norman James, *b.* 12 Feb. 1903.

5*d.* Hon. Sarah Agnes James, *m.* 21 June 1900, the Rev. Adolphus Benjamin Parry Evans, Vicar of Uttoxeter (*Uttoxeter, Staffordshire*) ; and has issue 1*e.*

    1*e.* Edith Anne Sarah Evans, *b.* 1904.

7*c.* *Isabel Emma Beatrice Lane,* d. 1 May 1876 ; m. *as 1st wife,* 11 Ap. 1872, *Percy Brodrick Bernard, J.P., D.L. (Castle Hacket, near Tuam) ; and had issue* 1*d.*

    1*d.* Ronald Percy Hamilton Bernard, *b.* 18 Mar. 1875.

2*a.* *Thomas Lane of Leyton Grange, co. Essex, and King's Bromley, co. Staffordshire, Clerk of the Goldsmiths' Company,* b. 30 Sept. 1754 ; d. 10 Jan. 1824 ; m. 4 Sept. 1784, Barbara, da. of Thomas Fowler of Pendeford, d. 15 July 1823 ; and had issue 1*b* to 4*b.*

    1*b.* *John Lane of Leyton Grange and King's Bromley, Clerk of the Goldsmiths' Company,* b. 6 June 1788 ; d. 16 Jan. 1852 ; m. *as 1st wife,* 19 Aug. 1817, Jane, da. of the Rev. John Williams, Vicar of Marston Magna, co. Somerset, Prebendary of Wells, d. 7 July 1818 ; 2ndly, 17 Jan. 1825, Elizabeth, da. of William Carter, d. 17 June 1852 ; and had issue 1*c* to 6*c.*

    1*c.* *Newton John Lane of Elmhurst Hall and King's Bromley, co. Staffordshire,* b. 25 Nov. 1828 ; d. 5 Feb. 1869 ; m. 26 Oct. 1854, Marianne Emily, da. of Henry Martin Blair (re-m. 20 Aug. 1872, Alexander John Clarke), d. 9 Sept. 1872 ; and had issue 1*d.*

    1*d.* Minnie Florence Newton Lane, *m.* 1st, 12 July 1876, Cecil Mark Fulford, *b.* 1840 ; *d.* 8 May 1881 ; 2ndly, 15 June 1882, Henry De la Poer Beresford Heywood ; and has issue 1*e* to 5*e.*

    1*e.* Marcus Beresford Heywood, *b.* 26 Nov. 1886.

    2*e.* Vere Newton Beresford Heywood, *b.* 30 Mar. 1890.

    3*e.* Muriel Florence Fulford, *b.* 20 Ap. 1877.

    4*e.* Olive Frances Emily Heywood, *b.* 25 June 1891.

    5*e.* Margaret Joan Heywood, *b.* 20 Aug. 1892.

2*c.* *Charles Leveson Lane,* Lieut. Royal Fusiliers, b. 21 Mar. 1839 ; d. 15 Ap. 1905 ; m. 29 May 1860, Fanny Henrietta Katharine, da. of Henry Manning ; and had issue 1*d* to 4*d.*

    1*d.* Charles Chester Leveson Lane (*Thames View, East Molesey*), *b.* 22 Jan. 1862 ; *m.* 25 Ap. 1892, Blanche, da. of Sidney Glendinning ; and has issue 1*e* to 2*e.*

    1*e.* Blanche Evelyn Leveson Lane, *b.* 6 Aug. 1893.

    2*e.* Dorothy Mary Leveson Lane, *b.* 10 Sept. 1896.

    2*d.* Guy Rupert Leveson Lane (*County Club, Westcliff on Sea*), *b.* 23 Dec. 1866 ; *m.* 14 July 1894, Georgine Phyllis, da. of George Lorimore ; and has issue 1*e.*

    1*e.* Selby George Cassell Lane, *b.* 10 Oct. 1901.

    3*d.* Harry Thomas Fenton Leveson Lane, *b.* 16 Aug. 1871 ; *m.* 8 Oct. 1896, Lily Agnes Clara, da. of William Henry Vaughan ; and has issue 1*e.*

    1*e.* John Chandos Lane, *b.* 4 Ap. 1897.

    4*d.* Evelyn Lucy Leveson Lane, *m.* 13 Oct. 1879, Carl Frederick Westergaard (*Arendal, Norway*) ; and has issue 1*e.*

    1*e.* Evelyn Charles Christian Lane Kenelm Westergaard, *b.* 14 May 1883.

[Nos. 35038 to 35060,

436

# of The Blood Royal

3c. *Mary Jane Lane*, b. 10 *June* 1818; d. 9 *Jan.* 1902; m. 12 *June* 1839, *John Salt of Lombard Street and Gordon Square, co. Middlesex*, b. 5 *Mar.* 1806; d. 12 *Jan.* 1865; *and had issue* 1d *to* 4d.

1d. *John Charles Salt*, b. 2 *May* 1840; d. 11 *Feb.* 1901; m. 27 *Ap.* 1871, *Alice Helen Frances*, da. *of John Carlyon Hughes*, d. 11 *Aug.* 1897; *and had issue* 1e *to* 2e.

1e. Rev. Frederick John Salt, *b.* 25 June 1872.

2e. Evelyn Mary Salt, *b.* 4 Ap. 1874; *m.* 26 June 1901, Edward Aubrey Thomas; and has issue 1f *to* 2f.

1f. Edward Llewellyn Thomas, *b.* 15 Oct. 1904.

2f. Winifred Alice Thomas, *b.* 31 Dec. 1902.

2d. Henry Salt, *b.* 22 July 1843.

3d. Sarah Ann Salt, *b.* 28 Sept. 1848; *m.* 29 Nov. 1888, Lieut.-Col. John Mitford; and has issue 1e.

1e. Lena Redesdale Mitford.

4d. Katherine Salt, *b.* 22 Aug. 1854.

4c. *Ada Barbara Lane*, *b.* 7 July 1837; *m.* 10 June 1861, Arthur Vendigain Davies Berrington (*Panty Goitre, co. Monmouth*), *b.* 30 Mar. 1833; and has issue 1d *to* 5d.

1d. Evelyn Delahay Davies Berrington, *b.* 6 Mar. 1862; *m.* 2 June 1894, Eleanor Anne, da. of [——] Witterton; and has issue 1e *to* 3e.

1e. Arthur John Davies Berrington, *b.* 26 Nov. 1895.

2e. Cedric Lister Davies Berrington, *b.* 7 Mar. 1903.

3e. Minnie Alice Florence Davies Berrington, *b.* 9 Oct. 1897.

2d. John Spencer Davies Berrington, *b.* 21 Ap. 1878.

3d. Hilda Ada Vendigain Davies Berrington (*Cleminstone, co. Glamorgan*), *b.* 20 Sept. 1865; *m.* 16 June 1891, Col. Charles Richard Franklin of Cleminstone, *d.* 24 July 1903; and has issue 1e *to* 3e.

1e. Hilda Evelyn Gwendolen Franklin, *b.* 15 July 1892.

2e. Mary Isabella Franklin, *b.* 18 Aug. 1897.

3e. Syssylt Franklin, *b.* 18 Sept. 1900.

4d. Florence Gwynedd Davies Berrington, *b.* 6 Dec. 1867; *m.* 7 Oct. 1903, Hubert Christian Corlette; and had issue 1e.

1e. Gwynedd Christian Corlette, *b.* 14 Sept. 1904.

5d. Edith Mary Davies Berrington, *b.* 11 Oct. 1869.

5c. *Sarah Amelia Lucy Lane*, b. 8 *Mar.* 1840; d. 30 *Jan.* 1902; m. 1st, 4 *Ap.* 1861, *George Temple of Bishopstrow, co. Wilts, J.P.*, b. 4 *June* 1834; d. 16 *Dec.* 1868; *2ndly*, 4 *Jan.* 1872, *the Rev. Aylmer Anthony Astley, Rector of Everleigh* (*Everleigh Rectory, Marlborough*); *and had issue* 1d *to* 3d.

1d. Grenville Newton Temple of Bishopstrow, J.P. (*Boreham Manor, Warminster*), *b.* 17 Jan. 1865; *m.* 11 May 1897, Katherine Annabella, da. of Frederick Addington Goodenough; and has issue 1e *to* 3e.

1e. Peter Grenville Temple, *b.* 5 May 1901.

2e. John Bruce Goodenough Temple, *b.* 14 June 1905.

3e. Vere Lucy Temple, *b.* 8 Feb. 1898.

2d. Madeleine Temple, *b.* 3 Nov. 1867.

3d. Margaret Violet Dorothea Astley.

6c. *Alice Julia Lane*, b. 5 *July* 1843; d. 1 *Oct.* 1893; m. 3 *Sept.* 1864, *Capt.* George Nicholl James Bradford, *8th* (*King's*) *Regt.*, b. 27 *Dec.* 1839; d. 11 *Dec.* 1896; *and had issue* 1d *to* 3d.

1d. William Hamilton Bradford (*Holford, Caterham, Surrey*), *b.* 29 Oct. 1867; *m.* 30 June 1897, Georgina Edith, da. of Thomas Norton Longman; and has issue 1e *to* 2e. [Nos. 35061 to 35088.

437   3 K

The Plantagenet Roll

1e. George Francis Norton Bradford, *b.* 22 July 1900.

2e. Helen Mary Bradford, *b.* 17 May 1898.

2d. Harry Bradford, *b.* 7 Feb. 1869; *m.* 8 Oct. 1895, Susie Bailey, da. of [——] Lett; and has issue 1*e*.

    1*e.* Copeland Lett Bradford, *b.* 5 Aug. 1900.

3d. Eva Fanny Bradford, *b.* 16 June 1866; *m.* 14 Jan. 1890, Lewis Evans (son of Sir John Evans, K.C.B.) (*Russells, Watford, Herts*), *b.* 15 Feb. 1853; and has issue 1*e* to 5*e*.

    1*e.* John Dickinson Evans, *b.* 27 May 1901.

    2*e.* Alice Dorothy Evans, *b.* 16 Feb. 1892.

    3*e.* Flora Jane Evans, *b.* 29 May 1896.

    4*e.* Eva Mary Evans, *b.* 11 Oct. 1897.

    5*e.* Anne Barbara Evans, *b.* 3 Jan. 1899.

2b. Rev. Charles Lane, Rector of Wrotham and Rural Dean of Shoreham, co. Kent, Hon. Canon of Canterbury, b. *2 Feb.* 1793; d. *23 Mar.* 1879; m. 1 *July* 1816, *Frances Catherine, da. of the Right Rev. Daniel Sandford, D.D., Lord Bishop of Edinburgh,* d. *26 Oct.* 1875; *and had issue* 1c *to* 7c.

1c. Richard Douglas Hay Lane, sometime Capt. 17th Lancers (Light Dragoons), b. *8 Dec.* 1823; d. *3 Ap.* 1901; m. 1st, 30 *Ap.* 1851, *Elizabeth Middleton, only da. of Thomas Ward of Heath House, co. Middlesex,* b. *2 Oct.* 1831; d. *12 Feb.* 1874; 2ndly, 5 *May* 1875, *Genette Anne, widow of Robert Moon, da. of George Adshead, J.P.,* d. *30 Sept.* 1876; *and had issue* 1d *to* 3d.

1d. Charles Middleton Robert Douglas Lane (*Westleigh House, Bideford, Devon*), *b.* 2 Feb. 1864; *m.* 1st, 13 June 1888, Lelia Marion, da. of Thomas Theodore Brewer Hooke of Norton Hall, co. Worcester, *d.* 5 Dec. 1899; 2ndly, 11 Aug. 1900, Vera Georgina Pellew, da. of James Stark Skipper of Thorpe Hamlet, co. Norfolk; and has issue 1*e* to 6*e*.

    1*e.* Graham Lewis Hay Douglas Lane, *b.* 15 Dec. 1893.

    2*e.* Robert Henry Douglas Lane, *b.* 15 Feb. 1896.

    3*e.* George Edward Douglas Lane, *b.* 4 Mar. 1899.

    4*e.* Charles Ivor Campbell Douglas Lane, *b.* 7 Dec. 1902.

    5*e.* Gordon Middleton Douglas Lane, *b.* 12 Ap. 1905.

    6*e.* Gladys Mary Douglas Lane, *b.* 24 Mar. 1904.

2d. Blanche Elizabeth Lydston Douglas Lane, *b.* 21 Mar. 1861; *m.* 25 Ap. 1889, Capt. Eric Edmund Moffat Davidson Manson, 1st Batt. South Lancashire Regt. (*Northgate, Bury St. Edmunds*); and has issue 1*e* to 3*e*.

    1*e.* Eric Douglas Manson, *b.* 14 Ap. 1893.

    2*e.* Blanche Manson, *b.* 6 Aug. 1890.

    3*e.* Ethel Belasyse Manson, *b.* 6 July 1894.

3d. Frances Catherine Genette Douglas Lane, *b.* 9 Mar. 1876; *m.* 29 Ap. 1899, Richard Berwick Hope, sometime Queen's Own Royal West Kent Regt.; and has issue 1*e*.

    1*e.* Betty Genette Hope, *b.* 1 Sept. 1902.

2c. Thomas Bruce Lane, sometime H.E.I.C.C.S., b. *29 Ap.* 1831; m. 20 July 1853, *Adelaide Fanny Spring, da. of William Hallows Belli, H.E.I.C.C.S.,* b. *29 Ap.* 1831; *and has issue* 1d *to* 3d.

1d. Cecil Bruce Lane, *b.* 11 Dec. 1857; *m.* 21 Sept. 1885, Frances Mary, da. of Joseph Martin; and has issue 1*e* to 4*e*.

    1*e.* John Francis Bruce Lane, *b.* 26 May 1890.

    2*e.* Edward de Lona Lane, *b.* 19 Feb. 1894.

    3*e.* Adelaide Mary Bruce Lane, *b.* 12 Nov. 1888.

    4*e.* Mary Cecilia Bruce Lane, *b.* 27 Ap. 1892.

2d. Arthur Bruce Lane, *b.* 3 Dec. 1858.   [Nos. 35089 to 35118.

# of The Blood Royal

3*d*. Herbert Edward Bruce Lane, Major Royal Garrison Artillery, *b*. 29 Sept. 1862 ; *m*. 12 Jan. 1893, Lilian Evangeline, da. of Gen. A. Cadell, Royal Engineers ; and has issue 1*e*.

1*e*. Gladys Lilian Grace Bruce Lane, *b*. 13 Nov. 1893.

3*c*. Henry Murray Lane, Chester Herald of Arms, and sometime Registrar of His Majesty's College of Arms, London (*St. Anthony's, Weybridge*), *b*. 3 Mar. 1833 ; *m*. 1st, 9 Oct. 1862, Mary Isabella, da. of Richard Fiennes Wykeham Martin, *d*. 29 Mar. 1881 ; 2ndly, 16 Feb. 1885, Amelia Elizabeth, da. of the Rev. Augustus Asgill Colvile, *d*. 31 Oct. 1897 ; 3rdly, 18 Feb. 1901, Mary Grace, da. of Thomas Norman Wightwick of Dane John House, Canterbury ; and has issue 1*d*.

1*d*. Gerald Stratford Murray Lane, *b*. 6 Dec. 1863.

4*c*. Rev. Francis Charles de Lona Lane, Rector of Whissonsett cum Horning-toft ·(*Whissonsett Rectory, co. Norfolk*), *b*. 21 June 1834 ; *m*. 12 Nov. 1879, Mary Anne, widow of Thomas Bracewell, da. of Archibald Dewhurst of Clitheroe, co. Lancashire, *d*. 8 May 1902.

5*c*. *Jane Lane*, *b*. 29 *May* 1817 ; *d*. 20 *Ap*. 1895 ; *m*. 24 *Aug*. 1843, *General Sir Edward Charles Warde, K.C.B.*, *b*. 13 *Nov*. 1810 ; *d*. 11 *June* 1884 ; *and had issue* 1*d* *to* 7*d*.

1*d*. Charles Edward Warde, M.P., Lieut.-Col. *late* 4th Hussars (*Barham Court, Maidstone*), *b*. 20 Dec. 1845 ; *m*. 10 July 1890, Helen, sister of Sydney James, 1st Baron Wandsworth [U.K.], da. of [——] (Stern), 1st Viscount de Stern [Portugal].

2*d*. Henry Murray Ashley Warde, Lieut.-Col. *late* 19th Hussars, Chief Constable of Kent (*Gallants, East Farleigh, Kent*), *b*. 3 Sept. 1850 ; *m*. 31 Mar. 1880, Louisa Anne, da. of Wilmot Lane, H.E.I.C.C.S. ; and has issue 1*e* to 3*e*.

1*e*. Louisa Kathleen Alice Warde, *b*. 13 Nov. 1880.

2*e*. Dorothy Mary Warde, *b*. 23 Aug. 1885.

3*e*. Gladys Joan Warde, *b*. 2 July 1887.

3*d*. St. Andrew Bruce Warde, Major R.A., Chief Constable of Hampshire (*West Hill, Winchester*), *b*. 23 Nov. 1852 ; *m*. 18 Ap. 1882, Olivia Louisa, da. of Col. George McCall of Elibank Lodge, co. Berks ; and has issue 1*e* to 2*e*.

1*e*. Claire Frances Mary Warde, *b*. 24 Ap. 1889.

2*e*. Jeana Winifred Mary Warde, *b*. 9 Jan. 1895.

4*d*. Alexander John Walter Warde (*Dean Lodge, Sevenoaks, Kent*), *b*. 19 Mar. 1855 ; *m*. 30 Oct. 1882, Enriqueta Petronilla, da. of James Fair ; and has issue 1*e* to 6*e*.

1*e*. Richard Edward Warde, *b*. 21 Dec. 1884.

2*e*. Basil Charles Conroy Warde, *b*. 28 Feb. 1892.

3*e*. Enriqueta Jenny Rosita Warde, *b*. 14 July 1883.

4*e*. Edith Dora Helen Warde, *b*. 9 Feb. 1886.

5*e*. Frances Dorothy Warde, *b*. 18 Aug. 1890.

6*e*. Alice Enderica Warde, *b*. 25 Jan. 1896.

5*d*. *Frances Molina Warde*, b. 3 *Aug*. 1844 ; d. 27 *Aug*. 1902 ; m. 2 *Aug*. 1872, *Ralph Cromwell Gregg, sometime Lieut.* 19*th Hussars* (*Heather Lodge, Breaksome Park, Bournemouth*) ; *and had issue* 1*e to* 3*e*.

1*e*. Ralph Charles Edward Carr Gregg, *b*. 27 Nov. 1874 ; *m*. 17 Sept. 1903, Florence Mabel, da. of Evan Kinsey, J.P.

2*e*. Ivo Francis Henry Carr Gregg, *b*. 5 Aug. 1876.

3*e*. Robert Gordon Cromwell Carr Gregg, *b*. 22 June 1878.

6*d*. Edith Pierrepont Warde, *b*. 23 July 1847.

7*d*. Louisa Jane Warde, *b*. 9 Feb. 1849.

6*c*. Eleanor Sarah Lane (*Sloane Terrace Mansions, S.W.*), *m*. 22 June 1854, John Bourryau Broadley of Kirk Ella, co. York, *b*. 3 May 1817 ; *d.s.p.* 29 June 1867.

7*c*. *Frances Lennox Heneage Lane*, *b*. 6 *June* 1825 ; *d*. 27 *May* 1859 ; *m. as 1st wife*, 23 *Nov*. 1853, *Arthur Vendigaid Davies Berrington ; and had issue* 1*d to* 3*d*.

[Nos. 35119 to 35144.

The Plantagenet Roll

1d. Arthur Tewdyr Davies Berrington, b. 7 Sept. 1854; m. 21 July 1901, Beatrice Maud, da. of the Rev. James Ruthborne, Rector of West Tetherley, Hants; and has issue 1e.

1e. Mary Gwendolen Davies Berrington, b. 15 Dec. 1903.

2d. Trevor Douglas Davies Berrington, b. 5 Dec. 1856; m. Ap. 1884, Ellen, da. of [——] Faithful, d. 9 Nov. 1887; and has issue 1e.

1e. Caradoc Trevor Davies Berrington, b. 30 Jan. 1886.

3d. Alice Gwendolen Davies Berrington, b. 6 Aug. 1858; m. 24 Oct. 1882, John Burden Blandy (Madeira); and has issue 1e to 2e.

1e. Geoffrey Kelvin Blandy, b. 24 June 1896.

2e. Florence Alice Blandy, b. 22 Feb. 1884.

3b. Richard Lane of Brunswick Square, Brighton, co. Sussex, b. 2 Oct. 1794; d. 27 Jan. 1870; m. 24 Ap. 1827, Sarah Pink, da. of George Thomas Tracy of Liskeard, co. Cornwall, d. 14 Feb. 1879; and had issue 1c to 4c.

1c. Charles Stuart Lane, General Bengal Staff Corps (Cromwell House, Southsea), b. 9 Feb. 1831; m. 23 Sept. 1852, Anne Josephine, da. of the Rev. Richard Bethuel Boyes; and has issue 1d to 8d.

1d. Charles Stuart Lane, b. 28 Nov. 1863; m. 16 Ap. 1890, Alice, widow of Arthur Sandys, da. of Richard N. Thweate of Chesterfield, U.S.A.; and has issue 1e.

1e. Florence Stuart Lane, b. 16 Nov. 1895.

2d. Henry Arthur Lane, Capt. Indian Staff Corps, sometime 3rd Dragoon Guards, b. 6 Oct. 1868; m. 5 Mar. 1899, Mary Elizabeth, da. of Gen. Henry Smithe, C.B.; and has issue 1e to 2e.

1e. Eva Mary Lane, b. 20 Feb. 1901.

2e. Margaret Elizabeth Lane, b. 17 Aug. 1905.

3d. Frederick Cecil Lane, Capt. R.A., b. 30 Ap. 1871.

4d. Lily Alice Lane, b. 28 June 1853; m. 26 Mar. 1873, Major-Gen. George Robert James Shakespear, Bengal Staff Corps (Rockville, Tenby, S. Wales); and has issue 1e to 4e.

1e. Helen Shakespear, b. 22 Mar. 1874; m. 15 Nov. 1894, Capt. Henry Fleetwood Thuillier, R.E.; and has issue 1f to 2f.

1f. Henry Shakespear Thuillier, b. 10 Sept. 1895.

2f. George Fleetwood Thuillier, b. 16 Feb. 1897.

2e. Lily Shakespear, b. 12 Feb. 1876; m. 1 Oct. 1895, Major Edmund Merritt Morris, Devon. Regt.

3e. Constance Shakespear, b. 2 Nov. 1881; m. 24 Oct. 1905, Capt. Samuel Arthur Cooke, Indian Army.

4e. Violet Shakespear, b. 5 Feb. 1888.

5d. Annie Lane, b. 8 May 1856; m. 24 Nov. 1875, Capt. Robert Mitford, 3rd Batt. East Yorkshire Regt., sometime 73rd Regt. (Mitford Castle, Northumberland), b. 25 Nov. 1846; and has issue 1e to 8e.

1e. Bertram Lane Mitford, b. 2 Nov. 1876.

2e. Robert Eustace Mitford, b. 10 June 1878.

3e. Humphrey Mitford, b. 2 Feb. 1892.

4e. Sybil Marguerite Elizabeth Mitford.

5e. Beatrice de Lona Mitford.

6e. Gladys Marion Mitford.

7e. Violet Edith Mitford.

8e. Margery Mitford.

6d. Emily Marion Lane, b. 3 Ap. 1858; m. 6 Nov. 1877, Capt. Sholto E. Pemberton, b. 17 Ap. 1840; d. 25 Sept. 1889; and has issue 1e to 4e.

1e. Sholto Pemberton, b. 13 Nov. 1883.

2e. Eva Pemberton, b. 29 Nov. 1878.

3e. Marion Ethel Pemberton, b. 16 Nov. 1880.

4e. Violet Pemberton, b. 14 Sept. 1882.   [Nos. 35145 to 35179.

# of The Blood Royal

7d. Florence Lane, *b.* 17 June 1859; *m.* 27 Sept. 1878, Leonard William Christopher, C.B., Lieut.-Col. Bengal Staff Corps (*Simla, Calcutta*); and has issue 1*e* to 4*e.*

    1*e.* Leonard de Lona Christopher, *b.* 21 Oct. 1883.

    2*e.* Charles de Lona Christopher, *b.* 16 May 1885.

    3*e.* Muriel de Lona Christopher.

    4*e.* Hazel de Lona Christopher.

8d. Eva Mary Lane, *b.* 28 Aug. 1861; *m.* 29 Oct. 1883, Lieut.-Col. Wentworth Grenville Bowyer, *late* R.E. (*Weston Manor, Olney, Bucks*), *b.* 10 Nov. 1850; and has issue 1*e* to 5*e.*

    1*e.* George Edward Wentworth Bowyer, *b.* 16 Jan. 1886.

    2*e.* Richard Grenville Bowyer, *b.* 18 May 1890.

    3*e.* John Francis Bowyer, *b.* 11 Jan. 1893.

    4*e.* Hilda Mary Bowyer, *b.* 2 Ap. 1887.

    5*e.* Mildred Elizabeth Bowyer, *b.* 16 Ap. 1898.

2c. Wilmot Lane, sometime H.E.I.C.C.S. (3 *Eaton Gardens, Hove, Sussex*), *b.* 19 Sept. 1833; *m.* 1st, 17 Oct. 1854, Louisa Sarah Anne, da. of Charles Patten Vale, *d.* 26 Sept. 1855; 2ndly, 16 Dec. 1862, Martha, da. of Lieut.-Col. Hervey Roche Osborn, Bengal Army; and has issue 1*d* to 11*d.*

    1*d.* Robert Hugh Lane, *b.* 16 Feb. 1866.

    2*d.* Wilmot Ernest Lane, *b.* 20 Mar. 1869.

    3*d.* John Osborn Lane, *b.* 28 July 1872.

    4*d.* Alfred Blornefield Lane, *b.* 1 Dec. 1873.

    5*d.* Frank Bernard Lane, *b.* 16 Aug. 1879.

    6*d.* Septimus Arthur Lane, *b.* 13 Oct. 1880.

    7*d.* Louisa Anne Lane, *b.* 21 Sept. 1855; *m.* 31 Mar. 1880, Lieut.-Col. Henry Murray Ashley Warde; and has issue.

See p. 439, Nos. 35126–35128.

    8*d.* Amy Lane, *b.* 15 Nov. 1863.

    9*d.* Elsie Lane, *b.* 22 June 1867.

    10*d.* Mabel Lane, *b.* 1 Feb. 1875.

    11*d.* Hilda Lane, *b.* 22 Aug. 1876.

3c. Sarah Magdalene Lane, b. 22 *July* 1837; *d.* 8 *Mar.* 1874; *m.* 22 *July* 1857, *Capt. Frederick John Helbert Helbert, sometime 5th Madras Light Cavalry* (15 *Victoria Square, S.W.*); *and had issue* 1*d to* 5*d.*

    1*d.* Frederic de Courcy Helbert, *b.* 14 July 1860.

    2*d.* Geoffrey Gladstone Helbert, *b.* 24 May 1867; *m. c.* 1891–2, Mabel, da. of [——] Dale; and has issue 1*e* to 5*e.*

        1*e.* Lionel Alexander Campbell Helbert, *b.* 1893.

        2*e.* Alfred Basil Charles Helbert, *b.* 1895.

        3*e.* Reginald Helbert.

        4*e.* Rose Helbert.

        5*e.* Violet Helbert.

    3*d.* Lionel Helbert (*West Downs, Winchester, Hants*), *b.* 13 June 1870.

    4*d.* Herbert Basil de Montfort Helbert, *b.* 24 Feb. 1873; *m.* 1902, Ida, da. of [——] Sutherland.

    5*d.* Adeline Rose Helbert, *b.* 20 Nov. 1861; *m.* 27 Ap. 1897, Capt. James Edward Clifford Goodrich, R.N.

4c. Emily Lane, b. 17 *Jan.* 1839; *d.* 17 *Jan.* 1905; *m.* 17 *Jan.* 1862, *Edmund Bernhard Liebert of Swinton Hall, co. Lanc., sometime Capt. 18th Hussars; and had issue* 1*d to* 5*d.*   [Nos. 35180 to 35215.

The Plantagenet Roll

1d. Bernhard Robert Liebert, sometime Capt. 7th Hussars (*May Hill House*, *Droxford, Hants*), *b.* 9 Jan. 1865; *m.* 14 July 1899, Violet Mary, da. of Capt. Clarence Trelawny, Austrian Hussars; and has issue *1e* to *2e.*

1e. Robert Liebert, *b.* 9 July 1903.

2e. Irene Liebert, *b.* 12 June 1900.

2d. Richard Alexander Douglas Liebert, *b.* 31 Jan. 1870.

3d. Emily Ada Liebert, *b.* 24 July 1863; *m.* 15 Dec. 1886, Cumberland Bentley; and has issue *1e.*

1e. Violet Esme Bentley, *b.* 7 Aug. 1898.

4d. Christine Liebert, *b.* 2 Sept. 1867; *m.* 10 Ap. 1888, Thomas Stanley Chappell (*Quar Wood, Stow-on-the-Wold*); and has issue *1e* to *2e.*

1e. Peter Stanley Chappell, *b.* 3 Dec. 1901.

2e. Phyllis Muriel Chappell, *b.* 18 Jan. 1891.

5d. Mildred Beatrice Liebert, *b.* 15 July 1872; *m.* as 2nd wife, 21 Ap. 1897, Sir Henry Bayley Meredyth, 5th Bart. [I.] (*Carlton*), *b.* 14 Jan. 1863; and has issue *1e.*

1e. Valla Meredyth, *b.* 8 Mar. 1898.

4b. Sarah Lane, b. 31 May 1790; d. 22 Dec. 1872; m. 14 Feb. 1812, William Cotton of Walwood House, co. Essex, one of the Directors and sometime Governor of the Bank of England, b. 12 Sept. 1786; d. 1 Dec. 1866; and had issue 1c to 3c.

1c. Right Hon. Sir Henry Cotton, P.C., Lord Justice of Appeal, b. 20 May 1821; d. 22 Feb. 1892; m. 16 Aug. 1853, Clemence Elizabeth, da. of the Rev. Thomas Streatfeild of Charts Edge, co. Kent, d. 12 May 1891; and had issue 1d to 3d.

1d. Henry Streatfeild Cotton (*Oaklands, Isfield, Uckfield, Sussex*), *b.* 12 May 1858; *m.* 8 Sept. 1896, Gwendolen, da. of Edward Coode of Polapit Tamar, co. Cornwall; and has issue *1e* to *5e.*

1e. Henry Perceval Coode Cotton, *b.* 12 Dec. 1898.

2e. Benjamin Harold Coode Cotton, *b.* 27 July 1900.

3e. William Edward Coode Cotton, *b.* 14 Dec. 1901.

4e. Oliver John Coode Cotton, *b.* 15 Mar. 1904.

5e. Gwendolen Coode Cotton, *b.* 10 Sept. 1897.

2d. Alfred Ernest Cotton, *b.* 13 July 1864.

3d. Phœbe Cotton, *b.* 23 Jan. 1860.

2c. Rev. Arthur Benjamin Cotton, *b.* 22 Sept. 1832; *m.* 1 June 1892, Clare Elizabeth, da. of the Rev. Thomas Pelham Dale, Rector of Sausthorpe.

3c. Sarah Cotton, b. 21 July 1815; d. 25 Oct. 1878; m. 14 July 1846, Sir Henry Wentworth Dyke Acland, 1st Bart. [U.K.], Regius Professor of Medicine in the University of Oxford, b. 23 Aug. 1815; d. 16 Oct. 1900; and had issue 1d to 7d.

1d. Vice-Admiral Sir William Alison Dyke Acland, 2nd Bart. [U.K.], C.V.O. (*Rocklands, Chudleigh, Devon*), *b.* 18 Dec. 1847; *m.* 7 July 1887, the Hon. Emily Anna, da. of the Right Hon. William Henry Smith and Emily, 1st Viscountess Hambleden [U.K.]; and has issue *1e* to *2e.*

1e. William Henry Dyke Acland, *b.* 16 May 1888.

2e. Hubert Guy Dyke Acland, *b.* 8 June 1890.

2d. Henry Dyke Acland, F.G.I., F.G.S.I., sometime Manager of Worcester Old Bank, Great Malvern, *b.* 14 Oct. 1850; *m.* 16 Nov. 1878, Margaret Hichens, da. of John Jope Rogers.

3d. Theodore Dyke Acland, M.D. (19 *Bryanston Square, S.W.*), *b.* 14 Nov. 1851; *m.* 12 Ap. 1888, Caroline Cameron, da. of Sir William Withey Gull, 1st Bart. [U.K.], M.D.; and has issue *1e.*

1e. Theodore William Gull Acland, *b.* 7 Nov. 1890.

4d. Reginald Brodie Dyke Acland, J.P., K.C., Bar.-at-Law, Recorder of Oxford

[Nos. 35216 to 35242.

442

# of The Blood Royal

(*Cold Ash, Newbury, Berks*), *b.* 18 May 1856; *m.* 12 Aug. 1885, Helen Emma, da. of the Rev. Thomas Fox, Rector of Temple Combe, co. Somerset; and has issue 1*e* to 4*e*.

1*e*. Edward Fox Dyke Acland, *b.* 9 Nov. 1891.

2*e*. Wilfrid Reginald Dyke Acland, *b.* 26 July 1894.

3*e*. Hilda Mary Acland, *b.* 18 June 1890.

4*e*. Ruth Helen Acland, *b.* 10 Mar. 1899.

5*d*. Francis Edward Dyke Acland, M.I.C.E., M.I.M.E., sometime Capt. R.A. (*Walwood, Banstead, Surrey*), *b.* 12 May 1857; *m.* 8 Jan. 1885, Marion Sarah, da. of the Right Rev. William Kenneth Macrorie, D.D., Lord Bishop of Maritzburg; and has issue 1*e* to 4*e*.

1*e*. Herbert Arthur Dyke Acland, *b.* 9 Oct. 1886.

2*e*. Kenneth Francis Dyke Acland, *b.* 16 Oct. 1890.

3*e*. Charis Agnes Acland, *b.* 14 June 1888.

4*e*. Clemence Margaret Acland, *b.* 9 Oct. 1889.

6*d*. Alfred Dyke Acland, Major 1st Royal Devon Yeo. Cav. (3 *Cadogan Square, S.W.*), *b.* 19 Aug. 1858; *m.* 30 July 1885, the Hon. Beatrice Danvers, da. of the Right Hon. William Henry Smith, P.C., M.P., and Emily, 1st Viscountess Hambledon [U.K.]; and has issue 1*e* to 5*e*.

1*e*. Arthur William Acland, *b.* 20 Nov. 1897.

2*e*. Peter Bevil Edward Acland, *b.* 9 July 1902.

3*e*. Angela Cicely Mary Acland, *b.* 26 Aug. 1888.

4*e*. Katharine Acland, *b.* 28 Sept. 1892.

5*e*. Sarah Beatrice Acland, *b.* 11 Sept. 1896.

7*d*. Sarah Angelina Acland (*Clevedon House, Oxford*), *b.* 26 June 1849.

3*a*. *Maria Lane*, b. 29 *Jan.* 1757; *d.* 4 *Nov.* 1843; m. 28 *Ap.* 1788, *the Rev. John Lucy of Charlecote Park, Warwick, d.* 12 *Jan.* 1823; *and had issue* 1*b*.

1*b*. *George Lucy of Charlecote Park, b.* 8 *June* 1789; *d.* 30 *June* 1845; m. 2 *Dec.* 1823, *Mary Elizabeth, da. of Sir John Williams of Bodelwydelan, 1st Bart.* [*G.B.*], *d.* 15 *Mar.* 1890; *and had issue* 1*c* to 3*c*.

1*c*. *Henry Spencer Lucy of Charlecote Park, J.P., D.L.,* b. 28 *Nov.* 1830; *d.* 6 *Nov.* 1890; m. 5 *July* 1865, *Christina, da. of Alexander Campbell of Monzie, co. Perth; and had issue* 1*d* to 3*d*.

1*d*. Ada Christina Lucy of Charlecote Park, *b.* 23 Ap. 1866; *m.* 26 July 1892, Sir Henry William Ramsay-Fairfax, now (R.L. 26 Aug. 1892) Ramsay-Fairfax-Lucy, 3rd Bart. [U.K.], J.P., D.L. (*Maxton, St. Boswells, N.B.; Charlecote Park, Warwickshire*); and has issue 1*e* to 6*e*.

1*e*. William George Thomas Spencer Ramsay-Fairfax-Lucy, *b.* 7 Ap. 1895.

2*e*. Henry Montgomerie Ramsay-Fairfax-Lucy, *b.* 20 Oct. 1896.

3*e*. Brian Fulke Ramsay-Fairfax-Lucy, *b.* 18 Dec. 1898.

4*e*. Ewen Aymer Robert Ramsay-Fairfax-Lucy, *b.* 31 Dec. 1899.

5*e*. Alianore Mary Christina Ramsay-Fairfax-Lucy, *b.* 8 Jan. 1894.

6*e*. Sybil Radegunde Joyce Ramsay-Fairfax-Lucy (twin), *b.* 7 Ap. 1895.

2*d*. Constance Linda Lucy.

3*d*. Joyce Alianore Lucy.

2*c*. Edmund Berkeley Lucy, *b.* 1842; *m.* 1869, Laura Margaret Mulgrave, da. and co-h. of William Standish of Duxbury Park, co. Lancaster; and has (with other) issue 1*d*.

1*d*. Reginald Lucy, *b.* 10 May 1879.

3*c*. *Caroline Lucy, d.* 5 *May* 1864; m. as 1st *wife*, 12 *Sept.* 1857, *Major-Gen. Charles Powlett Lane, J.P., D.L., late 21st Lancers (Glanden, Wimborne); and had issue* 1*d*.

1*d*. Aymer Powlett Lane, *b.* 10 July 1860. [Nos. 35243 to 35270.

443

The Plantagenet Roll

363. Descendants of ELIZABETH FOWLER (see Table XXXIV.), *bapt.* 3 Dec. 1725 ; *bur.* 5 June 1784 ; *m.* 22 Ap. 1756, the Rev. WILLIAM INGE, Canon Residentiary of Lichfield, *b.* 1722 ; *d.* 23 Ap. 1807 ; and had issue 1*a*.

1*a*. Richard Inge of Benn Hill, co. Leicester, b. 23 Dec. 1758; d. 7 Jan. 1844 ; m. 12 Sept. 1785, Mary, da. of Thomas Fowler of Pendeford Hall, d. 1 Feb. 1837 ; and had issue 1b.

1*b*. Charles Inge of Benn Hill,[1] b. 15 Dec. 1796; d. 5 Sept. 1858; m. (shortly before 18 Sept.) 1824, Mary Anne, da. of the Rev. Charles Oldershaw, D.D., Rector of Tarvin, co. Chester, b. 30 Dec. 1802 ; d. 8 Ap. 1876 ; and had issue 1c to 7c.

1*c*. Rev. William Inge, D.D., Provost of Worcester College, Oxford, b. 4 July 1829 ; d. 23 May 1903 ; m. 30 June 1859, Susanna Mary, da. of the Ven. Edward Churton, Rector of Crayke, Yorks., and Archdeacon of Cleveland ; and had issue 1d to 3d.

1*d*. Rev. William Ralph Inge, D.D., Fellow of King's Coll., Camb., and Hertford Coll., Oxon., Vicar of All Saints, Ennismore Gardens (All Saints Vicarage, 34 Rutland Gate, S.W.), b. 6 June 1860 ; m. 3 May 1905, Mary Catharine, da. of the Ven. Henry Maxwell Spooner, Archdeacon of Maidstone.

2*d*. Rev. Charles Cuthbert Inge (The Elms, Cranleigh, Guildford), b. 2 May 1868 ; m. 18 Oct. 1904, Arabella Hamilton, da. of Col. Hamilton Sams; and has issue 1e.

1*e*. Caroline Mary Inge, b. 6 Dec. 1905.

3*d*. Agnes Sophia Inge, b. 1 May 1862.

2*c*. Charles Henry Inge (Broom Leasoe, Whittington, Lichfield), b. 5 Jan. 1833 ; m. 11 Aug. 1864, Henrietta Charlotte, da. of Walter Peter Giffard of Chillington Hall ; and has issue 1d.

1*d*. Charles William Giffard Inge (Norwood, Lichfield), b. 4 June 1872 ; m. 21 June 1901, Lyly, da. of John Andrew ; and has issue 1e to 2e.

1*e*. Charles Henry William Giffard Inge, b. 19 June 1902.

2*e*. John Walter Giffard Inge, b. 28 Feb. 1904.

3*c*. John Walter Inge, Lieut.-Col. R.H.A. (Cranleigh, Guildford), b. 31 Mar. 1839 ; m. 2 Ap. 1891, Caroline Jane, widow of Col. Charles Hamilton Sams, da. of Philip Vavasour Robin ; s.p.

4*c*. Rev. Francis George Inge, Vicar of Baswich and Walton (Walton Vicarage, Stafford), b. 1840 ; m. Catherine, da. of [———] Spooner of Walton Lodge, Stafford, s.p.

5*c*. Mary Louisa Inge, b. 21 Jan. 1827 ; d. 15 Feb. 1902 ; m. 5 Sept. 1855, Thomas Maynard How of Nearwell, Shrewsbury ; and had issue 1d to 5d.

1*d*. William Maynard How (Nearwell, Shrewsbury), b. 15 June 1856.

2*d*. Charles Walsham How (20 Montagu Road, Richmond), b. 27 Dec. 1857 ; m. 11 June 1896, Mabel Louisa, da. of Frederick Chapman ; and has issue 1e to 2e.

1*e*. John Christian How, b. 8 Nov. 1897.

2*e*. Frederick Robert Wybergh How, b. 19 Mar. 1900.

3*d*. Walter Wybergh How, Fellow and Tutor of Merton Coll., Oxford (21 Merton Street, Oxford), b. 28 May 1861 ; m. 1 Jan. 1902, Elizabeth Dorothy, da. of Major-Gen. William Noel Waller of Farmington Lodge, co. Gloucester (a descendant of the poet) ; and has issue 1e.

1*e*. Richard William Walsham How, b. 23 Oct. 1903.

4*d*. Louisa Christian How.

5*d*. Margaret Elizabeth How. [Nos. 35271 to 35288.

---

[1] The dates of his birth and death, and of those of his wife, are taken from the tombstone in St. Giles' Churchyard, Shrewsbury.

6c. Harriet Inge (*Westgate, Lichfield*), b. 19 Aug. 1828; *m.* 11 May 1865, Arthur Hinckley of Stowe Hill, Lichfield; and has issue 1d to 2d.

1d. Richard Arthur Hinckley, b. 25 Mar. 1867; *m.* 30 June 1904, Emma, da. of Matthew Sykes Scholefield.

2d. Harriet Mary Hinckley, b. 18 Sept. 1869.

7c. *Anna Maria Inge*, b. 16 *Dec.* 1830; d. (?.s.p.) 27 *Mar.* 1898; m. 18 *Sept.* 1866, *Frederick Hinckley (Nether Stowe, Lichfield).* [Nos. 35289 to 35291.

364. Descendants of THOMAS FOWLER of Pendeford Hall (see Table XXXIV.), *bapt.* 11 Jan. 1729; *bur.* 10 Ap. 1795; *m.* (sett. dated 26 Feb. 1756) MARY, da. and h. of Richard LEVERSAGE of Nantwich, co. Chester, *bapt.* 13 Aug. 1734; *bur.* 16 Jan. 1767; and had issue 1a to 4a.

1a. *Thomas Leversage Fowler of Pendeford Hall*, b. 8 *Nov.* 1759; d. 26 *Sept.* 1817; m. 16 *June* 1788, *Harriet, da. and h. of the Rev. Richard Fowler of Brewood,* d. 4 *July* 1835; *and had issue* 1b *to* 4b.

1b. *Richard Fowler, afterwards* (*R.L. 11 Feb.* 1824) *Butler of Pendeford Hall,* b. 5 *Mar.* 1794; d. 13 *Mar.* 1864; m. 1*st*, 2 Oct. 1819, *Elizabeth Anne, da. of William Wynne of La Mancha, co. Westmeath,* d. 2 *Mar.* 1834; 2*ndly*, 1 *June* 1837, *Eliza, da. of Robert Faux of Cliff House, co. Leicester,* d. 26 *May* 1838; *and had issue* 1c *to* 2c.

1c. Robert Henry Fowler-Butler, J.P., Major-Gen. Comdg. troops in Barbados, *late* Col. 7th Fusiliers (*Pendeford Hall, Wolverhampton ; Barton Hall, Burton-on-Trent*), b. 11 May 1838; *m.* 26 Oct. 1864, Agnes de Courey, da. of the Rev. John de Courey O'Grady of Knockany, co. Limerick, *d.* 29 Jan. 1900; and has issue 1d.

1d. Richard Fowler-Butler, b. 25 Sept. 1865.

2c. *Eleanor Harriet Fowler-Butler*, b. 9 *Nov.* 1821; d. 22 *Ap.* 1864; m. *Henry (son of Sir John) Head Burgoyne,* bur. 1 *Mar.* 1855; *and had issue.*

2b. *William Fowler of Birmingham, and afterwards of Maney, Sutton Coldfield*, b. 28 *June* 1801; d. (–); m. 12 *Aug.* 1826, *Elizabeth, da. of Thomas Wilkins of Sutton Coldfield*, d. 23 *Sept.* 1863; *and had issue* 1c *to* 4c.

1c. William Fowler, b. 2 June 1827; living *unm.* 1876.[1]

2c. Thomas Leversage Fowler, b. 13 Oct. 1828; living *unm.* 1876.[1]

3c. Rev. Robert Fowler of Barton, co. York, b. 31 Mar. 1831; *m.* 7 Ap. 1875, Mary Ann, widow of Ferdinand Frederick Randolph Maier of Newcastle-on-Tyne, da. of William Downie of North Shields.

4c. Harriet Fowler, *b.* 30 Aug. 1832; living *unm.* 1876.[1]

3b. *Elizabeth Fowler*, b. 10 *May* 1790; d. 20 *Jan.* 1829; m. 10 Dec. 1816, *Samuel Gerrard of Tallypo, co. Westmeath ; and had issue.*

4b. *Mary Fowler*, bapt. 8 Mar. 1800; d. 20 *Jan.* 1863; m. 19 *Sept.* 1833, *Robert Harry Owen Roche of St. Marylebone, and afterwards of Paddington,* d. (? s.p.) 7 *Aug.* 1864.

2a. *Barbara Fowler*, b. 27 *Jan.* 1757; d. 15 *July* 1823; m. 4 *Sept.* 1784, *Thomas Lane of Leyton Grange, co. Essex,* d. 10 *Jan.* 1824; *and had issue.*

See p. 436, Nos. 35046–35258.

3a. *Mary Fowler*, b. 25 *July* 1758; d. 1 *Feb.* 1837; m. 12 *Sept.* 1785, *Richard Inge of Benn Hill, co. Leic.*, d. 7 *Jan.* 1814; *and had issue.*

See p. 444, Nos. 35271–35291.

4a. *Diana Fowler*, b. 12 *Oct.* 1761; d. 2 *Aug.* 1834; m. *the Rev. Thomas Walker, Perpetual Curate of the Collegiate Church of St. Peter's, Wolverhampton,* d. 5 *Ap.* 1834; *and had issue.* [Nos. 35292 to 35531.

---

[1] Pedigree in the College of Arms, Norfolk, 13, 121.

The Plantagenet Roll

365. Descendants of the Rev. RICHARD FOWLER of Brewood, co. Stafford (see Table XXXIV.), *bapt.* 3 Feb. 1732; *d.* 23 Mar. 1762; *m.* 2 Ap. 1761, MARY, da. of Thomas ALLSOPP of Derby, *d.* 16 May 1796; and had issue 1*a.*

1*a.* Harriet Fowler, b. 21 Dec. 1761; d. 4 *July* 1835; m. 16 *June* 1788, *Thomas Leversage Fowler of Pendeford Hall,* d. 26 *Sept.* 1817; *and had issue.*
See p. 445, Nos. 35292–35297.   [Nos. 35532–35537.

366. Descendants of CHARLES FOWLER of Bellstones, Shrewsbury (see Table XXXIV.), *bapt.* 20 Aug. 1741; *d.* 31 Dec. 1797; *m.* 2ndly, FRANCES, da. of the Rev. Thomas AMLER of Ford Hall, co. Salop (re-m. Lieut.-Gen. Lethbridge), *d.* 17 Feb. 1825; and had issue 1*a.*

1*a.* Frances Fowler, d. 12 *June* 1862; m. 6 *Sept.* 1804, *Samuel Allsopp of Burton-on-Trent,* b. 12 *Aug.* 1780; d. 26 *Feb.* 1838; *and had issue* 1b *to* 2b.

1*b.* Henry (Allsopp), 1st Baron Hindlip and a Baronet (1880) [U.K.], b. 19 Feb. 1811; d. 3 Ap. 1887; m. 21 Aug. 1839, Elizabeth, da. and eventual co-h. of William Tongue of Comberford Hall, d. (–); and had issue 1c to 10c.

1*c.* Samuel Charles (Allsopp), 2nd Baron Hindlip and a Baronet [U.K.], b. 24 Mar. 1842; d. 12 July 1897; m. 28 Ap. 1868, Georgiana Millicent (33 Hill Street, W.), da. of Charles Rowland Palmer-Morewood of Alfreton Hall, J.P., D.L.; and had issue 1d.

1*d.* Charles (Allsopp), 3rd Baron Hindlip and a Baronet [U.K.], J.P., D.L. (*Hindlip Hall, Worcester; Alsop-en-le-Dale, Derbyshire*), b. 22 Sept. 1877; m. 1904, Agatha Lilian, da. of John Charles Thynne.

2*c.* Hon. William Henry Allsopp, Underwriter at Lloyd's, *late* Major and Hon. Lieut.-Col. 3rd Batt. Worcester Regt., b. 9 Nov. 1843; m. 1888 (m. annulled 1893), Isabel Margaret, da. of Thomas Owthwaite Hutton.

3*c.* Hon. George Higginson Allsopp, sometime (1885–1906) M.P., J.P., D.L. (*8 Hereford Gardens, W.*), b. 28 Mar. 1846; m. 16 July 1895, Lady Mildred Georgiana, da. of Anthony (Ashley), 8th Earl of Shaftesbury [E.]; and has issue 1d to 2d.

1*d.* Anthony Victor George Allsopp, b. 7 Sept. 1899.

2*d.* Winifred Violet Allsopp, b. 6 May 1896.

4*c.* Hon. Ranulph Allsopp, Lieut.-Col. Hon. Artillery Coy., *late* R.A. (*Naval and Military*), b. 27 July 1848; m. 5 Jan. 1898, Margaret, da. of William Whitbread; and has issue 1d to 2d.

1*d.* Samuel Ranulph Allsopp, b. 7 Mar. 1899.

2*d.* Sybil Maud Elizabeth Allsopp, b. 28 Jan. 1901.

5*c.* Hon. Herbert Tongue Allsopp, J.P., *late* Capt. 10th Hussars (*Walton Bury, near Stafford*), b. 5 Dec. 1855; m. 11 Aug. 1891, Edith Mary, da. of Haughton Charles Okeover of Okeover Hall, J.P., D.L.; and has issue 1d.

1*d.* Cynthia Bridget Allsopp, b. 18 Sept. 1895.

6*c.* Hon. Frederic Ernest Allsopp, *late* Capt. R.A. (*Naval and Military; White's*), b. 21 Sept. 1857.

7*c.* Hon. Alfred Percy Allsopp, J.P., D.L., sometime (1887–1895) M.P. (*Battenhall Mount, Worcester*), b. 26 Aug. 1861; m. 23 July 1890, Lilian Maud, da. of the Rev. Stanley Chesshire, M.A., sometime Rector of Hindlip; and has issue 1d.

1*d.* Dorothy Allsopp, b. 25 Ap. 1891.   [Nos. 35538 to 35550.

8c. Hon. Frances Elizabeth Allsopp, *m.* 23 Aug. 1877, the Rev. Melville Russell Moore (2 *Albemarle Villas, Stoke, Devonport*).

9c. Hon. Elizabeth Sydney Allsopp (*Linden House, Linden Gardens, Bayswater, W.*), *m.* 7 July 1874, Thomas Eades Walker of Studley Castle and Berkswell Hall, M.P., *b.* 24 Feb. 1843 ; *d.* 13 Jan. 1899 ; and has issue 1d to 7d.

1d. Thomas Henry Walker, *b.* 17 Aug. 1880.

2d. George Frederick Walker, *b.* 10 Jan. 1884.

3d. Charles Eades Walker, *b.* 26 Sept. 1886.

4d. Elizabeth Walker, *b.* 19 June 1876 ; *m.* 10 Sept. 1903, Capt. Charles Reginald Scott-Elliot, Indian Army.

5d. Ellen Walker, *b.* 2 Aug. 1878.

6d. Ethel Ruth Walker, *b.* 13 Jan. 1883 ; *m.* 17 Aug. 1905, Arthur Leonard Scott (*Dumfries*).

7d. Rose Walker, *b.* 5 Sept. 1893.

10c. Hon. *Ada Katharine Allsopp*, b. 19 *Dec.* 1853 ; d.s.p. 2 *Jan.* 1903 ; m. 10 *Feb.* 1881, *Edward Waldron Haywood, LL.D., J.P., D.L., High Sheriff co. Worcester* 1875, *late Capt. and Hon. Major Worcestershire Yeo. Cav.* (*Sillins, near Redditch*).

2b. *Frances Allsopp*, b. 22 *Oct.* 1807 ; d. 28 *July* 1848 ; m. *as 2nd wife*, 23 *Jan.* 1828, *William Wybergh How of Nearwell, Shrewsbury*, d. 26 *Nov.* 1862 ; *and had issue* 1c.

1c. *Frances Jane How*, b. 21 *Jan.* 1829 ; d. 11 *Dec.* 1899 ; m. 22 *Jan.* 1850, *the Rev. William Willoughby Douglas of Salwarpe, J.P., Patron and Rector of Salwarpe, Hon. Canon of Worcester*, b. 13 *July* 1824 ; d. 19 *Feb.* 1898 ; *and had issue* 1d *to* 13d.

1d. Archibald Douglas of Salwarpe, M.A. (*Kingsland, Newcastle-under-Lyme, Stafford*), b. 10 Ap. 1853 ; *m.* 23 Ap. 1885, Caroline Ada, da. of Major-Gen. Arthur Frances of Cheltenham ; and has issue 1e to 5e.

1e. Francis William Gresley Douglas, *b.* 15 Jan. 1886.

2e. Harold Archibald Douglas, *b.* 2 Sept. 1887.

3e. Ada Gladys Douglas, *b.* 5 Nov. 1889.

4e. Margaret Elspeth Douglas, *b.* 14 Jan. 1892.

5e. Kathleen Mary Douglas, *b.* 29 Dec. 1893.

2d. William Douglas (*The School, Malvern Links*), *b.* 4 Aug. 1854 ; *m.* 5 Sept. 1899, Martha Mauleverer, da. of G. E. M. Taylor of Malvern ; and has issue 1e to 3e.

1e. Eileen Mary Douglas, *b.* 1 Dec. 1900.

2e. Frances Joan Douglas, *b.* 28 May 1902.

3e. Barbara Eleanor Douglas, *b.* 11 Mar. 1904.

3d. Rev. Robert Gresley Douglas (*Rondebosch, Cape Colony*), *b.* 24 Mar. 1862 ; *m.* 27 Nov. 1895, Ethel Annie, da. of Thomas Blunt, M.D. ; and has issue 1e.

1e. Robert Claude Gresley Douglas, *b.* 18 Sept. 1898.

4d. Edward Herbert Douglas, *b.* 17 Jan. 1865.

5d. Rev. Arthur Jeffreys Douglas, *b.* 9 Oct. 1871.

6d. Rev. Gerald Wybergh Douglas, *b.* 17 June 1875.

7d. Frances Douglas, *b.* 8 Dec. 1850.

8d. Ellen Douglas, *b.* 7 Feb. 1856.

9d. Mary Alice Douglas, *b.* 29 Nov. 1860.

10d. Lucy Jane Douglas, *b.* 6 Sept. 1863.

11d. Edith Christian Douglas, *b.* 18 Aug. 1866.

12d. Katharine Margaret Douglas, *b.* 2 Feb. 1868.

13d. Janet Maude Douglas, *b.* 8 Aug. 1869.　　[Nos. 35551 to 35581.

The Plantagenet Roll

367. Descendants, if any surviving, of WILLIAM FOWLER (see Table XXXIV.), *bapt.* 14 Feb. 1671 ; living 1711 (when he is mentioned in father's will) ; *m.* and had issue.[1]

368. Descendants, if any, of LUCY WIGHTWICK (see Table XXXIV.), wife of SAMUEL HALL LORD of Pool Castle, Barbados ; *temp.* (?) 1825.

369. Descendants of ELIZABETH WIGHTWICK, *temp.* (1700), wife of THOMAS TURNPENNY of Wolverhampton ; and of her sister, GRANADA WIGHTWICK, wife of JOHN PARGITER (see Table XXXIV.).

370. Descendants, if any surviving, of M̄ARY FOWLER (see Table XXXIV.), *bapt.* 16 Jan. 1662 ; *m.* 21 Jan. 1684, JOHN WIGHTWICK of Fairwell, co. Stafford, *d.* 1703 ; and had issue 1*a*.

1*a*. *John Wightwick of Fairwell, near Lichfield,* m. *Mary, da. of John Floyer, and grandda. of Sir John Floyer, Physician to King Charles II. ; and had issue* 1*b*.
1*b*. *Mary Wightwick,* m. 1*st,* [——] *Floyer, an officer in the Army,* d.s.p. *(being killed in America in the action under General Braddock) ; 2ndly, Peter Calmell, who sold Fairwell in 1790 to the Ashmoles.*

371. Descendants, if any, of FRANCES CHESTER (see Table XXXII.), wife of GEORGE PIGOT of Abingdon, co. Camb.

372. Descendants, if any, of the Hon. PENELOPE PITT (see Table XXXV.), *b.* 23 Feb. 1749 ; *d.* 1827 ; *m.* 1st, as 1ṣt wife (div. 7 Nov. 1771), 16 Dec. 1766, EDWARD (LIGONIER), 1st EARL LIGONIER [I.], *d.s.p.* 14 June 1782 ; 2ndly, 1784, Capt. SMITH ; and had issue.

373. Descendants of the Hon. LOUISA PITT (see Table XXXV.), *d.* 4 May 1791 ; *m.* 22 Mar. 1773, PETER BECKFORD of Stapleton, co. Dorset, M.P., *d.* (-) ; and had issue 1*a* to 2*a*.

1*a*. *Horace William (Beckford, afterwards (R.L. 26 Nov. 1828) Pitt Rivers) 3rd Baron Rivers [U.K.],* b. 2 *Dec.* 1777 ; d. 23 *Jan.* 1831 ; m. 9 *Feb.* 1808, *Frances, da. of Col. Francis Hale Rigby of Mistley Hall, co. Essex,* d. 6 *Sept.* 1860 ; *and had issue* 1*b to* 3*b*.
1*b*. *George (Pitt-Rivers), 4th Baron Rivers [U.K.],* b. 16 *July* 1810 ; d. 28 *Ap.* 1866 ; m. 2 *Feb.* 1833, *Lady Susan Georgiana, da. of Granville (Leveson-Gower), 1st Earl Granville [U.K.],* d. 30 *Ap.* 1866 ; *and had issue.*
See the Tudor Roll of " The Blood Royal of Britain," pp. 234–235, Nos. 22374–22400. [Nos. 35582 to 35608.

---

[1] Pedigree in the College of Arms, Norfolk, 13, 121.

# of The Blood Royal

2*b.* Horace (*Pitt-Rivers*), 6*th and last Baron Rivers* [*U.K.*], b. 12 *Ap.* 1814 ; d.s.p. 31 *Mar.* 1880.

3*b.* Hon. *Fanny Pitt*, b. 19 *Mar.* 1809 ; d. 1 *Feb.* 1836 ; m. 24 *July* 1834, *Frederick William Cox*.

2*a.* Harriet Pitt, b. 2 *Jan.* 1779 ; d. (–) ; m. 27 *Jan.* 1807, *Henry Seymer, afterwards* (R.L. 1830) *Ker-Seymer of Hanford, co. Dorset, J.P., D.L., High Sheriff* 1810, b. 22 *Jan.* 1782 ; d. 1834 ; *and had issue* 1*b to* 4*b.*

1*b.* Henry *Ker-Seymer of Hanford, M.P., J.P., D.L., D.C.L., High Sheriff co. Dorset* 1842, b. 1807 ; d. 1864 ; m. 4 *July* 1839, *Isabella Helen, da. of William Webber of Binfield Lodge, co. Berks ; and had issue* 1*c.*

1*c.* Gertrude Ker-Seymer of Hanford (*Hanford, near Blandford, co. Dorset*), m. 11 *Ap.* 1864, Henry Ernest Clay, *afterwards* (R.L. 1864) Clay-Ker-Seymer, *J.P., D.L., High Sheriff co. Dorset* 1877, b. 1832 ; d. 18 June 1899 ; *and has issue* 1*d to* 4*d.*

1*d.* Evelyn Clay-Ker-Seymer, b. 26 Feb. 1865.

2*d.* Horace Vere Clay-Ker-Seymer, b. 19 Sept. 1866.

3*d.* Winifred Clay-Ker-Seymer, b. 29 Oct. 1868.

4*d.* Violet Clay-Ker-Seymer, b. 25 Jan. 1873.

2*b.* Harriet Marcia Ker-Seymer, d. *Jan.* 1864 ; m. 22 *Feb.* 1827, *the Rev. James Duff Ward*, d. *Jan.* 1831.

3*b.* Louisa Mary Ker-Seymer, d. 22 *Sept.* 1841 ; m. 27 *June* 1839, *the Right Rev. Edward Denison, D.D., Lord Bishop of Salisbury.*

4*b.* Grace Emma Ker-Seymer, d. (–) ; m. *William Webber.*

[Nos. 35609 to 35613.

374. **Descendants of the Hon.** Marcia Lucy Pitt (**see Table XXXV.**), *b.* 29 Mar. 1756 ; *d.* 5 Aug. 1822 ; *m.* 23 July 1789, James Lane-Fox **of Bramham Park, co. York, M.P.,** *b.* 1757 ; *d.* 7 Ap. 1821 ; **and had issue** 1*a* **to** 5*a.*

1*a.* George Lane-Fox of Bramham Park, M.P., D.L., b. 1793 ; d. Nov. 1848 ; m. 20 *Sept.* 1814, *Georgiana Henrietta, da. of Edward Pery Buckley of Menistead Lodge, co. Hants* (by his wife Lady Georgiana, née West) ; *and had issue* 1*b to* 3*b.*

1*b.* George Lane-Fox of Bramham Park, J.P., D.L., High Sheriff co. Leitrim 1846 and co. York 1873, b. 13 Nov. 1816 ; d. 2 Nov. 1896 ; m. 17 Nov. 1837, *Katherine Mary, da. of John Stein, M.P.,* d. 4 *July* 1873 ; *and had issue* 1*c to* 5*c.*

1*c.* George Sackville Frederick Lane-Fox, J.P. (81 *Cadogan Gardens, S.W.*), b. 9 Nov. 1838 ; m. 1st, 10 Sept. 1870, Fanny Maule, da. of Lieut.-Gen. Marcus John Slade, d. Ap. 1875 ; 2ndly, 22 Ap. 1879, Annette Mary, da. of Thomas Weld-Blundell of Ince-Blundell, co. Lanc. ; and has issue 1*d* to 9*d.*

1*d.* Rev. Philip Edward Joseph Lane-Fox, b. 27 July 1871.

2*d.* Francis Lane-Fox, b. 28 Nov. 1872.

3*d.* Joseph Lane-Fox, b. 1 Ap. 1874.

4*d.* Rev. Richard Lane-Fox, b. 16 Feb. 1880.

5*d.* Mary Lane-Fox, b. 23 Ap. 1875.

6*d.* Helen Lane-Fox, b. 5 Sept. 1881 ; m. 28 Jan. 1903, Major Cecil E. Pereira, Coldstream Guards.

7*d.* Dorothy Lane-Fox, b. 19 Feb. 1883.

8*d.* Gertrude Lane-Fox, b. 25 Aug. 1884.

9*d.* Grace Lane-Fox, b. 13 Dec. 1888.

2*c.* James Thomas Richard Lane-Fox, J.P., D.L., *late* Capt. Grenadier Guards (*Bramham Park, Yorks. ; 26 Upper Grosvenor Street, W.*), b. 28 Feb. 1841 ; m. 15 Sept. 1868, Lucy Frances Jane, da. of Humphrey St. John-Mildmay ; and has issue 1*d* to 3*d.*

[Nos. 35614 to 35624.

449

1*d*. George Richard Lane-Fox (*Hope Hall, Boston Spa*), *b*. 15 Dec. 1870; *m*. 17 Sept. 1903, the Hon. Mary Agnes Emily, da. of Charles Lindley (Wood), 2nd Viscount Halifax [U.K.]; and has issue 1*e* to 2*e* (2 das.).

    1*e*. [———].

    2*e*. [———].

2*d*. Edward Lane-Fox, *b*. 31 Mar. 1874.

3*d*. Marcia Mary Lane-Fox.

3*c*. Marcia Lane-Fox.

4*c*. Carolina Alexina Lane-Fox (*Lavant House, Chichester*), *m*. 20 Ap. 1876, Major John Cavendish Orred of Tranmere, co. Chester, J.P., *late* 12th Lancers, *d*. Oct. 1905; and has issue 1*d* to 4*d*.

    1*d*. Roland George Orred, *b*. 27 Dec. 1886.

    2*d*. Alexina Katherine Orred, *b*. 18 Feb. 1877.

    3*d*. Mary Selina Orred, *b*. 25 Feb. 1880.

    4*d*. Rachel Orred, *b*. 13 Sept. 1882.

5*c*. Kathleen Mary Lane-Fox, *m*. 22 Ap. 1884, Francis Charles Liddell (*The Firs, Inner Park Road, Wimbledon*).

2*b*. Georgiana Maria Lane-Fox.

3*b*. *Frederica Elizabeth Lane-Fox, d*. 29 *Nov*. 1867; *m*. 14 *Oct*. 1845, *the Hon. Sir Adolphus Frederick Octavius Liddell, K.C.B., O.C., d*. 27 *June* 1885; *and had issue*.

See the Clarence Volume, pp. 91–92, Nos. 616–630.

2*a*. *William Augustus Pitt Lane-Fox, Grenadier Guards, b*. 1796; *d*. 1832; *m*. 31 *Dec*. 1817, *Lady Caroline, sister to George Sholto*, 18*th Earl of Morton* [*S*.], *da. of the Hon. John Douglas, d*. 7 *Nov*. 1873; *and had issue* 1*b*.

    1*b*. *Augustus Henry Lane-Fox, afterwards* (R.L. 25 *May* 1880) *Lane-Fox-Pitt-Rivers of Rushmore, D.C.L., F.R.S., Lieut.-Gen. &c., b*. 14 *Ap*. 1827; *d*. 4 *May* 1900; *m*. 3 *Feb*. 1853, *the Hon. Alice Margaret, da. of Edward John* (*Stanley*), 2*nd Baron Stanley of Alderley* [*U.K.*]; *and had issue*.

    See the Clarence Volume, pp. 442–443, Nos. 18841–18865.

3*a*. *Sackville Walter Lane-Fox, M.P., b*. 24 *Mar*. 1797; *d*. 18 *Aug*. 1874; *m*. 22 *June* 1826, *Lady Charlotte Mary Anne Georgiana, da. and in heir issue* (1859) *co-h. of George* (*Osborne*), 6*th Duke of Leeds, and* 10*th Baron Conyers* [*E*.], *d*. 17 *Jan*. 1836; *and had issue*.

See the Clarence Volume, pp. 626–627, Nos. 28040–28053.

4*a*. *Rev. Thomas Henry Lane-Fox*.

5*a*. *Marcia Bridget Lane-Fox, d*. 10 *June* 1826; *m*. 5 *Aug*. 1813, *the Hon. Edward Marmaduke Stourton, afterwards* (R.L. 27 *Feb*. 1826) *Vavasour*, 1*st Bart*. [*U.K.*], *d*. 15 *Mar*. 1847; *and had issue*.

See the Clarence Volume, pp. 364–366, Nos. 12443–12513.

[Nos. 35625 to 35762.

375. Descendants, if any, of Lucy Pitt (see Table XXXV.), *m*. James Kerr of Morriston and Kessfield, co. Berwick.

376. Descendants of John Pitt of Encombe, M.P. (see Table XXXV.), *d*. 1787; *m*. Marcia, da. of Marcus Morgan; and had issue 1*a* to 2*a*.

1*a*. *William Morton Pitt of Kingston House, co. Dorset, M.P., d*. (–); *m*. 1782, *Margaret, sister to James*, 1*st Baron Gambier* [*U.K.*], *da. of James Gambier, Lieut.-Governor of the Bahamas ; and had issue* 1*b*.

1*b*. *Sophia Pitt, b*. 11 *Oct*. 1783; *d*. 9 *Sept*. 1812; *m. as* 1*st wife*, 9 *Sept*. 1806,

# of The Blood Royal

Charles (Marsham), 2nd Earl [U.K.], and 4th Baron [G.B.] Romney, d. 29 *Mar.* 1845; *and had issue.*

See the Tudor Roll of "The Blood Royal of Britain," pp. 271–274, Nos. 24610–24647, 24651–24746.

    2*a. Marcia Pitt,* d. *May* 1808; m. *as 1st wife,* 17 *Aug.* 1790, *George James Cholmondeley, Receiver-General of Excise,* d. 5 *Nov.* 1830; *and had issue.*

See the Clarence Volume, pp. 129–130, Nos. 1580–1603.

[Nos. 35763 to 35920.

377. Descendants, if any, of ELIZABETH PITT (see Table XXXV.), *d.* (−); *m.* 22 Ap. 1738, WILLIAM BURTON, M.P., co. Rutland; of LORA PITT, wife of FRANCIS GWYN (? GEORGE) of Ford Abbey, co. Dorset; of ANNE PITT, and of MARY PITT.

378. Descendants of MARY PITT (see Table XXXV.), *d.* Aug. 1739; *m. c.* 1694, Sir CHARLES BROWN of Kiddington, co. Oxon., 2nd Bart. [E.], *b. c.* 1663; *d.* 24 Dec. 1751; and had issue.

See the Clarence Volume, pp. 420–424, Nos. 16223–16380.

[Nos. 35921 to 36074.

379. Descendants of the Hon. MARY FITZWILLIAM (see Table XXXV.), *d.* 20 Sept. 1752; *m.* 11 Mar. 1719, GEORGE TALBOT, *d.* 12 Dec. 1733; and had issue.

See pp. 282–284, Nos. 11157–11446.   [Nos. 36075 to 36364.

380. Descendants, if any, of ANNE HILDYARD (see Table XXXV.), *b.* 19 Feb. 1697; *d.* 8 July 1732; *m.* as 1st wife, 8 Sept. 1715, ADRIAN BIRCH of Cockerington, co. Lincoln, *d.* 18 Sept. 1738.[1]

381. Descendants of JANE HILDYARD (see Table XXXV.), *b.* 23 Jan. 1699; *bur.* at Louth; *m.* 21 Dec. 1715, JOHN MARSHALL of Louth, co. Lincoln, Surgeon R.N., *b. c.* 1690; *d.* 17 Ap. 1759; and had issue 1*a* to 8*a*.[1]

    1*a. John Marshall,* b. 1716.

    2*a. Christopher Marshall, Surgeon R.N.,* b. 13 *July* 1720.

    3*a. Hildyard Marshall, Surgeon R.N., Admiral of Great Grimsby,* b. 29 *Feb.* 1723; bur. 13 *Mar.* 1797; m. *Mary, da. of* [——] *Bowis of Great Grimsby,* b. *c.* 1640; bur. 18 *June* 1812; *and had issue* 1*b to* 2*b.*

    1*b. Mary Anne Marshall, da. and co-h.,* b. 4 *July* 1769; d. 11 *Ap.* 1818; m. 10 *June* 1800, *the Rev. John Crosby Leppington of Louth,* b. *c.* 1767; d. 3 *Ap.* 1833; *and had issue* 1*c to* 3*c.*

    1*c. Rev. John Crosby Leppington of Haverstock Hill, Hampstead, co. Middx.,* b. 21 *Oct.* 1807; d. (−); m. 10 *Dec.* 1840, *Caroline, da. of Timothy Bentley of Lockwood, co. York,* b. 11 *July* 1812; d. (−); *and had issue* 1*d to* 4*d.*

    1*d.* Hildyard Leppington, *b.* 21 Sept. 1841.

    2*d.* Cyril Harry D'Eyncourt Leppington, *b.* 10 Sept. 1853.

    3*d.* Dora Leppington, *b.* 9 Nov. 1842.

    4*d.* Blanche Leppington, *b.* 22 Feb. 1845.   [Nos. 36365 to 36368.

---

[1] Burke's "Visitation of the Seats and Arms of the Noblemen and Gentlemen of Great Britain and Ireland," 1855, p. 56.

The Plantagenet Roll

2c. Hildyard Marshall Leppington of Great Grimsby, co. Lincoln, J.P., Surgeon, b. 27 Oct. 1808; d. (–); m. 3 July 1839, Jane, da. of Thomas Tomlinson of Great Grimsby; and had issue 1d to 3d.

    1d. Mary Jane Leppington, b. 13 July 1840.

    2d. Anne Elizabeth Leppington, b. 6 Nov. 1842.

    3d. Caroline Marshall Leppington, b. 21 Ap. 1845.

    3c. Jane Pitt Leppington, m. John Barley (both living 1854).

  2b. Mary Marshall, da. and co-h., m. Thomas Tomlinson of Humberstone, and afterwards of Great Grimsby; and had with other issue 1c.

    1c. Jane Tomlinson, 2nd da., d. (–); m. 3 July 1839, Hildyard Marshall Leppington of Great Grimsby, Surgeon; and had issue.

    See p. 452, Nos. 36369–36371.

    4a. Henry Marshall, R.N., b. 5 Mär. 1724; d. (at Gibraltar) 2 Aug. 1756.

    5a. George Marshall, b. 1 Dec. 1726.

    6a. Jane Marshall, b. 1716.

    7a. Anne Marshall, b. 1718.

    8a. Dorothy Marshall, b. 15 Dec. 1721.   [Nos. 36369 to 36374.

---

382. Descendants of DOROTHY HILDYARD (see Table XXXV.), b. 19 Ap. 1700;[1] bur. 5 Mar. 1781; m. 1st, 30 Jan. 1719, GEORGE CLAYTON of Great Grimsby, Alderman, a Baltic Merchant, bapt. 30 Jan. 1694; d. 2 Oct. 1734;[1] 2ndly, RALPH TENNYSON of Grimsby, Attorney, bapt. 14 June 1720; d. 20 Ap. 1767; and had issue 1a.

  1a. Elizabeth Clayton, fifth child and the only one to leave issue,[2] b. 30 Dec. 1725; d. 6 Jan. 1755; m. Michael Tennyson of Preston, co. York, and of Stainton, co. Linc., Apothecary; bapt. 20 Sept. 1721; d. 6 Oct. 1796; and had issue 1b to 2b.

    1b. George Tennyson of Bayons Manor and Usselby Hall, co. Linc., M.P., J.P., D.L., b. 7 Feb. 1750; d. 4 July 1835; m. 1775, Mary, da. and ev. h. of John Turner of Caistor, co. Linc., d. 20 Aug. 1825; and had issue 1c to 4c.

    1c. Rev. George Clayton Tennyson, LL.D., Vicar of Grimsby, bapt. 10 Dec. 1778; d. 16 Mar. 1831; m. 6 Aug. 1805, Elizabeth, da. of the Rev. Stephen Fytche of Louth, d. 21 Feb. 1865; and had issue 1d to 6d.

    1d. Frederick Tennyson of Great Grimsby, b. 5 June 1807; d. 26 Feb. 1898; m. (at Florence) Maria Caroline, da. of [——] Giuliotti, Chief Magistrate of Siena, d. 22 Jan. 1884; and had issue 1e to 5e.

    1e. Julius George Tennyson of Thorpe Hall, late Capt. 17th Regt., b. 30 June 1840; d. 15 Sept. 1904; m. 8 Jan. 1873, Sophia (Thorpe Hall, Louth, co. Linc.), da. of Henry Cooper of Aberdeen; and had issue 1f to 5f.

    1f. Frederick Henry Tennyson, late Lieut. 3rd Batt. Cheshire Regt., b. 3 Dec. 1873.

    2f. Sydney Harold Tennyson, R.N., b. 24 July 1877; m. 25 Oct. 1904, Mildred Broughton, da. of [——] Want of Sydney, N.S.W.

    3f. Charles Arthur Tennyson, Lieut. R.M.L.I., b. 27 Ap. 1884.

    4f. Julietta Marian Tennyson, m. 10 Oct. 1905, Richard Graham Hopwood.

    5f. Sylvia Mary Beatrice Tennyson.

    2e. Alfred Tennyson, b. 25 Dec. 1854.   [Nos. 36375 to 36380.

---

[1] Burke's "Visitation of the Seats and Arms," &c., p. 56.

[2] Her brother, Capt. David Clayton, perished in the Black Hole of Calcutta, 20 July 1756. See "Our Noble and Gentle Families of Royal Descent," by Joseph Foster, M.A., p. 23.

# of The Blood Royal

3e. Elizabeth Tennyson, m. 20 Ap. 1876, John Francis de Carteret of Oak-lands, Jersey, *late* Lieut. 21st Royal Scots Fusiliers ; and has issue 1f to 4f.

    1f. Hugh John Tennyson de Carteret, Lieut. King's Own, b. 15 Oct. 1878.

    2f. Frederick Lionel Oakland de Carteret, b. 29 Aug. 1884.

    3f. Robert Francis Edward de Carteret, b. 4 May 1886.

    4f. Leonore Mary Elizabeth de Carteret, b. 1 Feb. 1877.

4e. Emilia Tennyson, m. 4 Nov. 1875, Major Charles William Randle Ford, 84th Regt. (89 *Shooter's Hill Road, Blackheath ;* 11 *Lansdown Place, East Bath*); and has issue 1f to 4f.

    1f. Wilbraham Tennyson Randle Ford, Lieut. R.N., b. 19 Jan. 1880.

    2f. Vincent Tennyson Randle Ford, 2nd Lieut. Y. and L. Regts., b. 24 Nov. 1885.

    3f. Hallam Tennyson Randle Ford, b. 22 Jan. 1887.

    4f. Muriel Dulcibella Ford, b. 17 Aug. 1876 ; m. 23 Ap. 1904, Thomas Marchant, d. 23 May 1905.

5e. *Matilda Tennyson*, d. 19 Feb. 1892 ; m. 18 *Jan.* 1877, *Col. John Johnson Bradshaw, late 5th Fusiliers,* d. 9 *Sept.* 1896 ; *and had issue* 1f.

    1f. Mary Lilian Bradshaw, b. 4 May 1879 ; a nun in the Convent of the Sacred Heart at Roehampton.

2d. *Alfred (Tennyson), 1st Baron Tennyson* [*U.K.*], *D.C.L., F.R.S., Poet Laureate* 1850–1892, b. 6 *Aug.* 1809 ; d..6 *Oct.* 1892 ; m. 13 *June* 1850, *Emily, da. of Henry Sellwood aforesaid,* d. 10 *Aug.* 1896 ; *and had issue* 1e *to* 2e.

    1e. Hallam (Tennyson), 2nd Baron Tennyson [U.K.], G.C.M.G., sometime (1902–1904) Governor-Gen. of Australia, &c. (*Aldworth, near Haslemere ; Farring-ford, Freshwater, I.W.*), b. 11 Aug. 1852 ; m. 25 June 1884, Audrey Georgiana Florence, da. of Charles John Boyle ; and has issue 1f to 3f.

        1f. Hon. Lionel Hallam Tennyson, b. 7 Nov. 1889.

        2f. Hon. Alfred Aubrey Tennyson, b. 2 May 1891.

        3f. Hon. Harold Courtenay Tennyson, b. 27 Ap. 1896.

    2e. Hon. *Lionel Tennyson*, b. 16 *Mar.* 1854 ; d. 20 *Ap.* 1886 ; m. 25 *Feb.* 1878, *Eleanor Mary Bertha, da. of Frederick Locker, by his first wife, Lady Charlotte Christian Bruce (who re-m. 5 May 1888, the Right Hon. Augustine Birrell, P.C., M.P., K.C., LL.D.,* 70 *Elm Park Road, S.W.*) ; *and had issue* 1f *to* 3f.

        1f. Alfred Browning Stanley Tennyson, b. 20 Nov. 1878.

        2f. Charles Bruce Locker Tennyson, B.A., 1st Class Classics Camb., b. 8 Nov. 1879.

        3f. Michael Sellwood Tennyson, b. 10 Dec. 1883.

3d. *Horatio Tennyson,* b. 25 *Sept.* 1819 ; d. 2 *Oct.* 1899 ; m. 1*st,* 16 *Ap.* 1857, *Charlotte, da. of Capt. Dudley Christopher Cary-Elwes,* d. 31 *Oct.* 1868 ; *and had issue.*

See p. 341, Nos. 24726–24728.

4d. *Mary Tennyson,* b. 11 *Sept.* 1810 ; d. 4 *Ap.* 1884 ; m. 7 *July* 1851, *Alan Ker, Bar.-at-Law, M.T., Judge of the High Court, Jamaica,* d. 20 *Mar.* 1885 ; *and had issue* 1e.

    1e. Walter Charles Alan Ker, M.A. (Camb.), Bar.-at-Law, I.T. (5 *Vicarage Gardens, Kensington*), b. 10 May 1853 ; m. 13 Aug. 1885, Julia Susan Christiana, sister of Sir Robert Arbuthnot Holmes, da. of Robert Holmes of Moycashel, co. Westmeath ; and has issue 1f.

        1f. Dorothy Mary Ker, b. 9 July 1886.

5d. *Emily Tennyson,* b. 25 *Oct.* 1811 ; d. 24 *Jan.* 1887 ; m. 24 *Jan.* 1842, *Capt. Richard Jesse, R.N. ; and had issue* 1e *to* 2e.

    1e. *Arthur Henry Hallam Jesse, of the Exchequer,* b. 18 *Jan.* 1843 ; d. *unm.*

    2e. Rev. Richard Eustace Russell Jesse, *afterwards* Tennyson-D'Eyncourt, b. 19 Sept. 1853.   [Nos. 36381 to 36404.

The Plantagenet Roll

6d. Cecilia Tennyson, *b.* 10 Oct. 1817; *m.* 14 Oct. 1842, Edmund Law Lushington of Park House, Maidstone, *b.* 10 Jan. 1811; *d.* 1893; and has issue 1e.

1e. Cecilia Lushington (*Park House, Maidstone*), *unm.*

2c. *Right Hon.* **Charles Tennyson**, *afterwards* (R.L. 27 *July* 1835) *Tennyson-D'Eyncourt of Bayons Manor and Usselby House, co. Linc., P.C., M.P., Equerry to H.R.H. the Duke of Sussex,* bapt. 20 *July* 1784; *d.* 21 *July* 1864; *m.* 1 *Jan.* 1808, *Frances Mary, da. and h. of the Rev. John Hutton of Morton, co. Linc., d.* 26 *Jan.* 1878; *and had issue* 1d *to* 2d.

1d. *Edwin Clayton Tennyson - D'Eyncourt of Bayons Manor, &c., C.B., Admiral R.N., b.* 4 *July* 1813; *d.* 13 *Jan.* 1903; *m.* 1 *Mar.* 1859, *Lady Henrietta, da. of Henry (Pelham-Clinton), 4th Duke of Newcastle [G.B.], K.G., d.* 19 *Aug.* 1890; *and had issue* 1e.

1e. Henrietta Charlotte Tennyson-D'Eyncourt, *m.* 8 Feb. 1888, Alfred Henry Tarleton, M.V.O., J.P., D.L., *Lieut.* R.N. (*Breakspears, Uxbridge;* 58 *Warwick Square, S.W.*); and has issue 1f to 3f.

1f. Freda Henrietta Tarleton.

2f. Vera Constance Tarleton.

3f. Helen Maud Tarleton.

2d. *Louis Charles Tennyson-D'Eyncourt, Bayons Manor, Lincolnshire, J.P., sometime* (1851–1890) *a Metropolitan Police Magistrate, b.* 23 *July* 1814; *d.* 11 *Dec.* 1896; *m.* 31 *Aug.* 1852, *Sophia, da. and co-h. of John Ashton Yates of Dinglehead, M.P.; and had issue* 1e *to* 5e.

1e. Edmund Charles Tennyson-d'Eyncourt, a Metropolitan Police Magistrate and a J.P. for eleven counties (*Bayons Manor, Markets Rasen*), *b.* 11 Feb. 1855; *m.* 20 July 1892, Charlotte Ruth, da. and h. of Augustus Frederick Godson of Westwood Park, M.P.; and has issue 1f to 6f.

1f. Alfred Edmund Clayton Tennyson-d'Eyncourt, ⎫ *b.* (twins) 25 Ap. 1899.

2f. Walter Louis Frederick Tennyson-d'Eyncourt, ⎭

3f. Ralph Eustace Lovett Tennyson-d'Eyncourt, *b.* 21 Feb. 1904.

4f. Dorothy Ruth Tennyson-d'Eyncourt.

5f. Millicent Ellen Jane Tennyson-d'Eyncourt.

6f. Helena Catherine Sophia Tennyson-d'Eyncourt.

2e. Ashton Lovett Tennyson-d'Eyncourt, *late* Capt. Royal Berkshire Regt., *b.* 14 Dec. 1860.

3e. Eustace Henry William Tennyson-d'Eyncourt (*Callerton Hall, Northumberland*), *b.* 1 Ap. 1868; *m.* 20 July 1898, Janet, widow of John Burns, da. of Matthew Watson Finlay of Middlebank, Langside; and has issue 1f to 2f.

1f. Eustace Gervais Tennyson-d'Eyncourt, *b.* 19 Jan. 1902.

2f. Cecily Lovett Tennyson-d'Eyncourt, *b.* 21 Aug. 1899.

4e. Emma Frances Mary Tennyson-d'Eyncourt.

5e. Henrietta Clara Eliza Tennyson-d'Eyncourt (*Caversfield House, Bicester*), *m.* 28 July 1891, Herbert Edward Phillips, *d.* 9 Nov. 1904; and has issue 1f to 3f.

1f. Herbert Hildeyard Phillips, *b.* 25 June 1892.

2f. Eustace Edward Lovett Phillips, *b.* 27 Jan. 1894.

3f. Henrietta Sophia Maud Phillips, *b.* 8 Aug. 1902.

3c. *Elizabeth Tennyson,* bapt. 18 *Ap.* 1776; *d.* (–); *m.* 23 *Jan.* 1798, *Matthew Russell of Brancepeth, co. Durham, M.P., d.* 7 *May* 1822; *and had issue* 1d.

1d. *Emma Maria Russell; d.* 29 *Ap.* 1870; *m.* 9 *Sept.* 1828, *Gustavus Frederick (Hamilton), 7th Viscount Boyne [I.], d.* 27 *Oct.* 1872; *and had issue.*

See p. 492, Nos. 43146–43158.

4c. *Mary Tennyson,* bapt. 4 *May* 1777; *d.* 26 *Ap.* 1864; *m. Aug.* 1811, *John Bourne of Dalby, co. Linc., d.* 15 *D.c.* 1850.   [Nos. 36405 to 36439.

454

CATHERINE, *suo jure* COUNTESS OF DORCHESTER, *née* SIDLEY.

THE COMMON ANCESTRESS OF NOS. 36442–36702.

From the picture in possession of Lord Spencer.

# of The Blood Royal

2b. Anne Tennyson, bapt. 29 *Ap.* 1753; d. 1 *Jan.* 1814; m. *as 2nd wife, William Raines Wyton,* co. *York,* d. 30 *Nov.* 1798 ; *and had issue* 1c.

1c. *Elizabeth Clayton Raines,* m. *the Rev. George Inman, M.A., Rector of Skeffing, Easington, and Kilnsea ; and had issue* 1d.

   1d. Sarah Inman, *m.* 21 Feb. 1860, James Dunn ; and has issue 1e.

   1e. Maud Dunn. [Nos. 36440 to 36441.

383. Descendants, if any, of ANNE PITT (see Table XXXV.), *m.* FREDERICK TYLNEY.

384. Descendants, if any, of Lady CATHERINE CAROLINE COLYEAR (see Table XXXV.), *m.* 1810, JAMES BRECKNELL.

385. Descendants of Lady CAROLINE COLYEAR (see Table XXXV.), *b.* Dec. 1733 ; *d.* 7 Feb. 1812 ; *m.* 27 Oct. 1750, NATHANIEL (CURZON), 1st BARON SCARSDALE of Scarsdale [G.B.], *d.* 6 Dec. 1804 ; and had issue 1a.

1a. Nathaniel (Curzon), 2nd Baron Scarsdale [G.B.], b. 27 *Sept.* 1751; d. 26 *Jan.* 1837; m. 1*st,* 11 *Aug.* 1777, *the Hon. Sophia Susanna, da. and eventual co-h. of Edward (Noel), 1st Viscount Wentworth [G.B.],* d. 28 *June* 1782; 2*ndly,* 18 *Nov.* 1798, *Felicité Anne Josephe, da. of Francis Joseph des Wattines of Tournay,* d. 16 *Dec.* 1850; *and had issue* 1b *to* 5b.

   1b. Nathaniel (Curzon), 3rd Baron Scarsdale [G.B.], b. 3 *Jan.* 1781; d. *unm.* 12 *Nov.* 1856.

   2b. Rev. the Hon. Alfred Curzon, b. 17 *Ap.* 1801 ; d. 12 *Jan.* 1850 ; m. 14 *July* 1825, *Sophia, da. of Robert Holden of Nuttall Temple,* co. *Notts,* d. 9 *Feb.* 1890 ; *and had issue* 1c *to* 2c.

      1c. Alfred Nathaniel Holden (Curzon), 4th Baron Scarsdale [G.B.], 8th Bart. [E.], in Holy Orders, M.A. (Oxon.), Rector of Kedleston (*Kedleston, near Derby*), *b.* 12 July 1831; *m.* 3 July 1856, Blanche, da. of Joseph Pocklington Senhouse of Netherhall, W. Cumberland, *d.* 4 Ap. 1875; and has issue 1d to 10d.

         1d. George Nathaniel (Curzon), 1st Baron Curzon of Kedleston [I.], P.C., G.C.S.I., G.C.I.E., F.R.S., Viceroy of India 1898-1905 (1 *Carlton House Terrace, S.W.*), *b.* 11 Jan. 1859; *m.* 22 Ap. 1895, Mary Victoria, C.I., da. of Levi Zeigler Leiter of Dupont Circle, Washington, U.S.A., *d.* July 1906 ; and has issue 1e to 3e.

            1e. Hon. Mary Irene Curzon, *b.* 20 Jan. 1896.

            2e. Hon. Cynthia Blanche Curzon, *b.* 23 Aug. 1898.

            3e. Hon. Alexandra Naldera Curzon, *b.* 20 Mar. 1904.

         2d. Hon. Alfred Nathaniel Curzon, Lieut.-Col. Comdg. 3rd Batt. Sherwood Foresters (*Weston Underwood, near Derby*), *b.* 12 Mar. 1860; *m.* 29 Ap. 1891, Henrietta Mary, da. of the Hon. Spencer Dudley Robinson Montagu ; and has issue 1e to 3e.

            1e. Richard Nathaniel Curzon, *b.* 3 July 1898.

            2e. Magdalen Blanche Curzon, *b.* 10 Mar. 1892.

            3e. Rosamond Mary Curzon, *b.* 24 Dec. 1893.

         3d. Hon. Francis Nathaniel Curzon (11 *Mount Street, W.*), *b.* 15 Dec. 1865.

         4d. Hon. Assheton Nathaniel Curzon (34 *Stanhope Gardens, S.W.*), *b.* 10 May 1867 ; *m.* 20 July 1897, Mercy Lilian, da. of Haughton Charles Okeover ; and has issue 1e to 4e.

            1e. Ralph Okeover Nathaniel Curzon, *b.* 24 July 1904.

            2e. Joan Doreen Curzon, *b.* 13 June 1898.

            3e. Rhona Lilian Curzon, } *b.* (twins) 5 Nov. 1900.
            4e. Vera Lilian Curzon, }   [Nos. 36442 to 36456.

455

5d. Sophia Caroline Curzon (*Walpole St. Peter, Norfolk*), *b*. 20 Nov. 1857 ; *m*. 17 Jan. 1882, the Rev. Charles MacMichael, Rector of Walpole St. Peter, *b*. 8 Mar. 1854 ; *d*. 22 Dec. 1905 ; and has issue 1*e* to 5*e*.

    1*e*. Harold Alfred MacMichael, *b*. 15 Oct. 1882.

    2*e*. Arthur William MacMichael, *b*. 5 June 1885.

    3*e*. Ernest Charles Montagu MacMichael, *b*. 20 May 1889.

    4*e*. Humphrey Curzon MacMichael, *b*. 29 Aug. 1890.

    5*e*. Hilda Margaret MacMichael, *b*. 21 Feb. 1898.

6d. Hon. Blanche Felicia Curzon, *b*. 18 Ap. 1861.

7d. Hon. Eveline Mary Curzon (*Manderston, Duns ; Hamilton House, Newmarket ; 45 Grosvenor Square, W.*), *b*. 16 Feb. 1864 ; *m*. 19 Jan. 1893, Sir James Percy Miller, 2nd Bart. [U.K.], D.S.O., J.P., D.L., Hon. Major in the Army and Major Lothians and Berwickshire Imp. Yeo., *b*. 22 Oct. 1864 ; *d.s.p.* 22 Jan. 1906.

8d. Hon. Elinor Florence Curzon, *b*. 13 Feb. 1869.

9d. Hon. Geraline Emily Curzon, *b*. 8 May 1871 ; *m*. 28 Feb. 1901, William Tower Townshend (*Myross Wood, Leap, Cork ; Derry, Rosscarbery, Cork*) ; and has issue 1*e* to 2*e*.

    1*e*. Blanche Hermione Townshend, *b*. 15 Dec. 1901.

    2*e*. Marjorie Townshend, *b*. 5 Oct. 1905.

10d. Hon. Margaret Georgina Curzon, *b*. 23 Dec. 1873 ; *m*. 26 Jan. 1899, Hardress John Waller (45 *Stanhope Gardens, S.W.*) ; and has issue 1*e* to 2*e*.

    1*e*. Joyce Margaret Waller, *b*. July 1900.

    2*e*. Allison Dorothea Waller, *b*. 30 Nov. 1905.

2c. Hon. (R.W. 2 May 1857) Mary Catherine Curzon (25 *Belgrave Square, S.W.*), *b*. 14 Dec. 1837, *m*. as 2nd wife, 15 Ap. 1858, Arthur Edwin (Hill-Trevor), 1st Baron Trevor [U.K.], *b*. 4 Nov. 1819 ; *d*. 25 Dec. 1894 ; and has issue 1*d* to 7*d*. See pp. 321–322, Nos. 23961–23970.

3b. *Hon. Frances James Curzon*, b. 25 *Ap*. 1803 ; d. 24 *May* 1851 ; m. *Louisa, da. of* [——], d. 6 *Nov.* 1840.

4b. *Hon. Mary Elizabeth Curzon*, b. 28 *Mar*. 1806 ; d. 11 *Oct*. 1868 ; m. 29 *Aug*. 1825, *John Beaumont of Barrow*, co. *Derby*, d. 11 *Mar*. 1834 ; *and had issue* (4 *sons*).

5b. *Hon. Caroline Esther Curzon*, b. 17 *Mar*. 1808 ; d. 16 *Oct*. 1886 ; m. 13 *Feb*. 1827, *William Drury Holden, afterwards* (R.L. 19 *July* 1853) *Lowe of Denby and Locko Park*, J.P., D.L., *High Sheriff* co. *Derby* 1854, b. 5 *Oct*. 1802 ; d. 26 *Feb*. 1877 ; *and had issue* 1*c* to 8*c*.

    1*c*. William Drury Nathaniel Lowe, *now* (R.L. 16 Aug. 1884) Drury-Lowe, J.P., D.L., High Sheriff co. Derby 1893, *formerly* Lieut. 11th Hussars and 3rd Light Dragoons (*Locko Park, Derby ; Myria, Llanrwst, N. Wales*), *b*. 13 July 1828 ; *m*. 16 Dec. 1876, Lady Lucy Jane, sister to Francis Charles, 3rd Earl of Kilmorey [I.], K.P., da. of Francis Jack Needham, *styled* Viscount Newry ; and has issue 1*d* to 7*d*.

        1*d*. William Drury Drury-Lowe, Lieut. Grenadier Guards, *b*. 30 Sept. 1877 ; *m*. 16 Oct. 1902, the Hon. Hylda Harriet Marianne, da. of Edward Burtenshaw (Sugden), 2nd Baron St. Leonards [U.K.].

        2*d*. John Alfred Edwin Drury-Lowe, *late* Lieut. Scots Guards, *b*. 6 Dec. 1881 ; *m*. 12 Jan. 1905, Dorothy, da. of Casben Boteler ; and has issue 1*e*.

            1*e*. [son] Drury-Lowe, *b*. Oct. 1905.

        3*d*. Lawrence Robert Charles Drury-Lowe, *b*. 7 Aug. 1883.

        4*d*. Edward Nathaniel Drury-Lowe, *b*. 22 Oct. 1888.

        5*d*. Lucy Ann Drury-Lowe, *m*. 16 July 1904, Cecil Ord Durham.

        6*d*. Dorothy Margaret Drury-Lowe.

        7*d*. Grace Drury-Lowe.

[Nos. 36457 to 36491.

# of The Blood Royal

2c. Sir Drury Curzon Drury-Lowe, G.C.B., J.P., Lieut.-General and Col. Comdg. 17th Lancers, &c. &c. (*Keydell, Horndean, Hants*), *b.* 3 Jan. 1830; *m.* 1876, Elizabeth, da. of T. Smith.

3c. Robert Henry Drury-Lowe, J.P., Col. *late* Grenadier Guards, *b.* 7 Oct. 1831; *m.* 1st, 15 May 1862, Ellen, da. of Joseph Pocklington Senhouse of Netherhall, *d.* 13 Sept. 1890; 2ndly, 6 Oct. 1891, Ida, da. of [——] Beauchamp; and has issue 1*d* to 3*d*.

   1*d*. Ernest Henry Curzon Drury-Lowe, *b.* 3 June 1863.
   2*d*. Sidney Robert Drury-Lowe, Com. R.N., *b.* 19 Oct. 1871.
   3*d*. Florence Felicité Drury-Lowe, *b.* 23 Jan. 1869.

4c. *Vincent Francis Keppel Drury-Lowe, late 63rd Regt.*, b. 1 *July* 1847; d. 30 *Ap*. 1905; *m.* 28 *Ap*. 1877, *Elizabeth Mary, da. of Dr. Christmas; and had issue.*

5c. Richard Curzon Sherwin Drury-Lowe, *late* 10th Hussars, *b.* 23 July 1849; *m.* 21 Feb. 1900, Gertrude Elizabeth, da. of William Petch of Southcotes, *s.p.*

   6c. Felicia Drury-Lowe, *b.* 23 Jan. 1833; *unm.*

   7c. Caroline Mary Drury-Lowe, *b.* 4 Dec. 1834; *unm.*

8c. *Florence Catherine Drury-Lowe, d.* 31 *July* 1879; *m. as 1st wife,* 2 *Ap.* 1868, *Francis Nicholas Smith, J.P. (Wingfield Park, Derby); and had issue* 1*d* to 3*d*.

   1*d*. Violet Esther Drury Smith, *m.* 1892, Walter John Clutterbuck.
   2*d*. Florence Louisa Felicia Smith, *m.* 1899, Joseph Bourne Wheeler (*Netherlea, Holbrooke, Derby*); *s.p.*

   3*d*. Rachel Mary Elizabeth Smith.   [Nos. 36492 to 36502.

386. Descendants of Lady JULIANA COLYEAR (see Table XXXV.), *b.* 1735; *d.* 29 Ap. 1821; *m.* 24 Nov. 1759, HENRY DAWKINS of Over Norton, co. Oxon. and Standlynch Park, co. Wilts, M.P., *b.* 24 May 1728; *d.* 1814; and had issue 1*a* to 8*a*.

1*a*. *James Dawkins, afterwards Colyear of Over Norton, M.P., m. and had issue, who all* d.s.p., *the last in* 1857.

2*a*. *George Hay Dawkins, afterwards Pennant of Penrhyn Castle, N. Wales,* b. 1764; d. 17 Dec. 1840; m. 1*st*, 25 *June* 1807, *the Hon. Sophia Mary, da. of Cornwallis (Maude), 1st Viscount Hawarden* [*I.*], *b.* Oct. 1771; *d.* 23 *Jan.* 1812; *and had issue* 1*b* to 2*b*.

1*b*. *Juliana Isabella Mary Pennant, d.* 25 *Ap.* 1842;. *m. as 1st wife,* 6 *Aug.* 1833, *Col. the Hon. Edward Gordon Douglas, afterwards (R.L.* 25 *Jan.* 1841) *Douglas-Pennant, 1st Baron Penrhyn* (1866) [*U.K.*], *b.* 20 *June* 1800; *d.* 31 *Mar.* 1886; *and had issue* 1*c* to 5*c*.

1*c*. George Sholto Gordon (Douglas-Pennant), 2nd Baron Penrhyn [U.K.] (*Penrhyn Castle, Bangor ; Wicken Park, Stony Stratford ; Mortimer House, Halkin Street, S.W.*), *b.* 30 Sept. 1836; *m.* 1st, 23 Aug. 1860, Pamela Blanche, da. of Sir Charles Rushout, *previously* Cockerell, 2nd Bart. [U.K.], *d.* 5 Feb. 1869; 2ndly, 21 Oct. 1875, Gertrude, da. of the Rev. Henry Glynne of Hawarden; and has issue 1*d* to 15*d*.

1*d*. (Son by 1st wife.) See the Clarence Volume, p. 220, Nos. 4439–4444.

2*d*–3*d*. (Sons by 2nd wife.) See the Tudor Roll of "The Blood Royal of Britain," p. 224, Nos. 22088–22089.

4*d*–9*d*. (Das. by 1st wife.) See the Clarence Volume, p. 220, Nos. 4445–4457.

10*d*–15*d*. (Das. by 2nd wife.) See the Tudor Roll of "The Blood Royal of Britain," p. 224, Nos. 22090–22097.

2*c*. Hon. *Archibald Charles Henry Douglas-Pennant, Lieut.-Col. Grenadier Guards,* b. 22 *Nov.* 1837; *d.* 7 *Sept.* 1884; *m.* 5 *Jan.* 1865, *the Hon. Harriet Ella*
[Nos. 36503 to 36532.

The Plantagenet Roll

(*Lillingstone Dayrell, Buckingham*), *da. of Robert Francis (Gifford), 2nd Baron Gifford [U.K.]; and had issue.*

See the Tudor Roll of "The Blood Royal of Britain," p. 471, Nos. 33018–33031.

3*c*. Hon. Caroline Elizabeth Emma Douglas-Pennant (17 *Grosvenor Gardens, S.W.; The Lodge, Eastbourne*), *m.* 31 Aug. 1857, James Macnaghton (Hogg, *afterwards* (R.L. 8 Feb. 1877) McGarel-Hogg), 1st Baron Magheramorne [U.K.], K.C.B., *b.* 3 May 1823; *d.* 27 June 1890; and has issue 1*d* to 6*d*.

1*d*. James Douglas (*McGarel-Hogg*), 2nd Baron Magheramorne [U.K.], b. 16 *Jan.* 1861; *d.* 10 *Mar.* 1903; *m.* 23 *Oct.* 1889, *Lady Evelyn Harriet (62 Avenue Malakoff, Paris), da. of Anthony (Ashley-Cooper), 8th Earl of Shaftesbury [E.]; and had issue* 1*e*.

1*e*. Hon. Norah Evelyn McGarel-Hogg, *b.* 1 Sept. 1890.

2*d*. Dudley Stuart (McGarel Hogg), 3rd Baron Magheramorne [U.K.] (*Park House, Marden, Kent*), *b.* 3 Dec. 1863.

3*d*. Hon. Ronald Tracy McGarel-Hogg (*Park House, Marden*), *b.* 28 July 1865.

4*d*. Hon. Archibald Campbell M'Garel-Hogg, Architect (36 *Lincoln's Inn Fields, W.C.*), *b.* 21 Sept. 1866.

5*d*. Hon. Gerald Francis M'Garel-Hogg (*Carlton*), *b.* 6 Aug. 1868.

6*d*. Hon. Edith Mary M'Garel-Hogg, *m.* 3 Aug. 1881, the Hon. Arthur Saumarez (17 *Grosvenor Gardens, S.W.; The Lodge, Eastbourne*); and has issue 1*e* to 3*e*.

1*e*. Reginald Stafford Saumarez, *b.* 11 Jan. 1886.

2*e*. Muriel Antoinette Saumarez, *b.* 15 July 1882.

3*e*. Rosalind Edith Saumarez, *b.* 15 May 1899.

4*c*. Hon. Emma Julia Sophia Douglas-Pennant,
5*c*. Hon. Eleanor Frances Susan Douglas-Pennant, } 16 *South Eaton Place, S.W.*

2*b*. *Emma Pennant, d.* 14 *July* 1888; *m.* 25 *Aug.* 1831, *Thomas Charles (Hanbury-Tracy), 2nd Baron Sudeley [U.K.], d. (at Pau)* 19 *Feb.* 1863; *and had issue.*

See the Clarence Volume, pp. 603–604, Nos. 26540–26605.

3*a*. *Henry Dawkins, M.P., b.* 1765; *d.* 25 *Oct.* 1852; *m.* 1788, *Augusta, da. of Gen. Sir Henry Clinton, K.B.; and had issue.*

See the Clarence Volume, pp. 177–179, Nos. 2948–2989.

4*a*. *Richard Dawkins, a Commissioner of Excise, b.* 1768; *d.* 1848; *m.* 1791, *Jane Catherine, da. of Edward Long; and had issue* 1*b* to 3*b*.

1*b*. *Edward James Dawkins, H.B.M.'s Minister at the Court of Athens, b.* 1792; *d. Feb.* 1865; *m. Mary, da. of John Petre of Westwick, co. Norfolk; and had issue* 1*c*.

1*c*. Mary Dawkins, *m.* Major James Duff; and has issue.

2*b*. *Charles Colyear Dawkins, Capt. R.N., b.* 1804; *d. Nov.* 1863; *m.; and had issue.*

3*b*. *Amelia Elizabeth Dawkins, d.* 30 *Jan.* 1875; *m.* 8 *Nov.* 1821, *the Rev. Arthur Atherley of Heavitree, co. Devon, b.* 8 *Feb.* 1794; *d.* 14 *Feb.* 1857; *and had issue* 1*c* to 6*c*.

1*c*. *Francis Henry Atherley, of Landguard Manor, Isle of Wight, J.P., Col. I.W. Vol. Batt., b.* 30 *May* 1831; *d.* 31 *Mar.* 1897; *m.* 18 *June* 1863, *Lady Isabel Julia Elizabeth, da. of Charles John (Howard), 17th Earl of Suffolk [E.]; and had issue* 1*d*.

1*d*. Arthur Harry Howard Atherley, J.P., D.L. (*Landguard Manor, Shanklin, I.W.*), *b.* 25 May 1865; *m.* 25 Sept. 1902, Eleanor Gertrude, da. of James Forbes Lumsden of Viewfield House, Aberdeen; and has issue 1*e*.

1*e*. Isabel Eleanor Evelyn Atherley, *b.* 7 Mar. 1904.

2*c*. *Edward Gambier Atherley, Capt.* 60*th Rifles, d.* 10 *Oct.* 1898.

[Nos. 36533 to 36670.

3c. *Sydney Kerr Buller Atherley*, d. 27 Feb. 1878 ; m. 3 *Ap.* 1877, *Georgiana Louisa, da. of Grenville L. Berkeley.*

4c. Louisa Atherley, *m.* 2 Jan. 1845, Charles Davers Osborn, *b.* 17 Ap. 1819 ; *d.* (? *s.p.*) 8 Dec. 1846.

5c. Arabella Jane Catherine Atherley.

6c. Henrietta Frances Isabella Atherley.

5a. *Rev. Edward Dawkins*, b. 1769 ; d. 1816 ; m. 1803, *Hannah, da. of Thomas Littledale.*

6a. *Charles Dawkins, Grenadier Guards*, b. 1772 ; d. (*of wounds received in action in Holland*) 1799.

7a. *John Dawkins, Fellow of All Souls, Oxford*, b. 1773 ; d. 1844.

8a. *Elizabeth Dawkins*, d. 1831 ; m. *William Rookes Leedes Serjeantson of Hanlith Hall and Camphill, co. York, J.P., D.L., Lieut.-Col. 1st Dragoon Guards*, d. 1840 ; *and had issue* 1b *to* 2b.

1b. *Juliana Mary Serjeantson*, d. 1 Sept. 1859 ; m. *as 1st wife*, 27 *June* 1822, *the Rev. Henry Bowen Cooke, LL.D., Rector of Darfield*, b. 29 *Mar.* 1797 ; d. 27 *Feb.* 1879 ; *and had issue* 1c.

1c. *Edward Bowen Cooke of Swinton Hall, Yorks, Major* 83rd *Regt.*, b. 8 *Sept.* 1815 ; d. 11 *Ap.* 1877 ; m. 9 *Ap.* 1863, *Marianne Jane* (13 *Montpelier Square, S.W.*), *da. of George Lloyd of Cowsby Hall ; and had issue* 1d *to* 2d.

1d. Rosabelle Juliana Cooke.

2d. Evelyn Mary Cooke.

2b. *Elizabeth Henrietta Serjeantson*, d. *Mar.* 1881 ; m. *as 2nd wife*, 7 *June* 1825, *George Lloyd of Cowsby Hall*, b. 25 *May* 1786 ; d. 1844 ; *and had issue* 1c *to* 9c.

1c. *Thomas William Lloyd, J.P., D.L.*, b. 8 *Mar.* 1826 ; d. 31 *Oct.* 1904 ; m. 1849, *Elizabeth Anne, da. of Francis Benyon Hacket of Moor Hall*, d. 20 *Mar.* 1894.

2c. *George Walter Edward Lloyd, Capt. R.N.*, b. 10 *May* 1828 ; d. 9 *Nov.* 1889 ; m. 17 *Oct.* 1876, *Fannie, da. of W. H. Powell of New York ; and had issue* 1d.

1d. William Alexander Charles Lloyd (*Cowsby Hall, Northallerton ; Spotland, Rochdale*), b. 8 May 1885.

3c. *Alfred Hart Lloyd*, b. 28 *Aug.* 1837 ; d. *July* 1904 ; m. 28 *Mar.* 1883, *Maria, da. of* [——] *Walker of Dumbleton, co. Gloucester ; and has issue* 1d *to* 5d.

1d. Richard Serjeantson Lloyd, *b.* 27 Aug. 1887,

2d. Humphrey Charles Lloyd, *b.* 10 Oct. 1889.

3d. Mary Eleanor Susan Lloyd.

4d. Marjorie Elizabeth Anne Lloyd.

5d. Ruth Lloyd.

4c. Caroline Anne Lloyd.

5c. Marianne Jane Lloyd (13 *Montpelier Square, S.W.*), *m.* 9 Ap. 1863, Major Edward Bowen Cooke, 83rd Regt., *d.* 11 Ap. 1877 ; and has issue.

See p. 459, Nos. 36674–36675.

6c. Rosabelle Susan Lloyd, *m.* 21 Sept. 1854, Edward Lloyd of Lingcroft, near York, *b.* 1823 ; *d.* 4 Feb. 1869 ; and has issue 1d to 3d.

1d. Georgina Rosabelle Lloyd, *m.* 15 July 1879, Guy St. Maur Palmes, *late* 14th Hussars (*Lingcroft, near York*) ; and has issue 1e to 5e.

1e. Geoffrey St. Maur Palmes, *b.* 26 Dec. 1881.

2e. Edward William Eustace Palmes, *b.* 23 Aug. 1884.

3e. Bryan Wilfred Palmes, *b.* 3 June 1891.

4e. Cecil Muriel Palmes.

5e. Joan Mary Georgina Palmes.

[Nos. 36671 to 36692.]

The Plantagenet Roll

2d. Edith Marie Graeme Lloyd, m. 22 Ap. 1879, Frederick Reynard, J.P., D.L. (*Sunderlandwick, Driffield ; Hobgreen, Ripley*) ; and has issue 1e to 2e.
1e. Claude Edward Reynard, b. 9 Feb. 1880.
2e. Charles Frederick Peter Reynard, b. 14 Jan. 1889.

3d. Cecil Mary Lloyd, m. 9 Nov. 1887, Henry Charles Talbot Rice, Capt. *late* 4th Batt. Gloucestershire Regt. (*North Cerney House, Cirencester*) ; and has issue 1e to 3e.
1e. Henry Talbot Rice, b. 27 July 1889.
2e. John Arthur Talbot Rice, b. 3 Jan. 1892.
3e. David Talbot Rice, b. 11 July 1903.

7c. Cecilia Amy Lloyd.
8c. Lucy Emma Lloyd.
9c. Eleanor Lloyd.   [Nos. 36693 to 36702.

387. Descendants, if any, of Lady MARY SAVAGE (see Table XXXV.), m. HENRY KILLEGREW, Groom of the Bedchamber to King James II. and VII.

388. Descendants of Sir ROGER MOSTYN, 5th Bart. [E.], M.P. (see Table XXXVI.), b. c. 1735 ; d. 26 July 1796 ; m. 19 May 1776, MARGARET, da. and h. of the Rev. Hugh WYNNE, Preb. of Salisbury, d. 14 Oct. 1792 ; and had issue 1a to 3a.

1a. *Sir Thomas Mostyn, 6th Bart. [E.], b. c.* 1776 ; d. *unm.* 17 *Ap.* 1831.
2a. *Elizabeth Mostyn,* d. 8 *Nov.* 1742 ; m. 11 *Feb.* 1794, *Edward Pryce (Lloyd),* 1st *Baron Mostyn [U.K.], b.* 17 *Sept.* 1768 ; d. 3 *Ap.* 1854 ; *and had issue 1b.*
1b. *Edward (Lloyd), afterwards (R.L.* 9 *May* 1831) *Lloyd-Mostyn), 2nd Baron Mostyn [U.K.], b.* 13 *Jan.* 1805 ; d. 16 *Mar.* 1884 ; m. 20 *June* 1827, *Lady Harriet Margaret, da, of Thomas (Scott), 2nd Earl of Clonmell [I.],* d. 3 *June* 1891 ; *and had issue.*
See the Tudor Roll of "The Blood Royal of Britain," pp. 197–198, Nos. 21274–21294.

3a. *Anne Maria Mostyn,* d. (–) ; m. *Sir Robert Williams Vaughan ; and had issue (at least) 1b.*
1b. *Robert Williams Vaughan.*   [Nos. 36703 to 36723.

389. Descendants, if any, of ANNE MOSTYN (see Table XXXVI.), d. 1802 ; m. 1777, THOMAS PENNANT of Downing and Bychton, co. Flint, the celebrated Naturalist, b. 14 June 1726 ; d. 16 Dec. 1798.

390. Descendants of MARMADUKE (LANGDALE), 3rd BARON LANGDALE [E.] (see Table XXXVI.), d. 12 Dec. 1718 ; m. FRANCES, da. of Richard DRAYCOTT of Painesley, co. York ; and had issue 1a to 3a.

1a. *Marmaduke (Langdale), 4th Baron Langdale [E.],* d. 8 *Jan.* 1771 ; m. *the Hon. Elizabeth, da. of William (Widdrington), 3rd Baron Widdrington [E.],* d. 7 *Jan.* 1765 ; *and had issue 1b to 2b.*

# of The Blood Royal

1b. Marmaduke (Langdale), 5th Baron Langdale [E.], d. 5 Ap. 1778; m. Constantia, da. of Sir John Smythe of Acton Burnel, co. Salop, d. c. 1792; and had issue 1c.

1c. Hon. Mary Langdale (eventual sole heir), d. 12 Ap. 1841; m. 12 July 1775, Charles Philip (Stourton), 17th Baron Stourton [E.], d. 29 Ap. 1816; and had issue.

See the Clarence Volume, Table XXXIX., pp. 363–371, Nos. 12397–12711.

2b. Hon. Elizabeth Langdale.

2a. Hon. Elizabeth Langdale, d. (–); m. Peter Middleton of Stockeld; and had issue.

See pp. 333–336, Nos. 24284–24535.

3a. Hon. Frances Langdale, d. (–); m. Nicholas Blundell of Crosby, co. Lanc.; and had issue 1b.

1b. Frances Blundell of Crosby (eventual sole heir), d. 17 Ap. 1773; m. Henry Peppard, d. 1772; and had issue 1c to ?

1c. Nicholas Peppard, afterwards (1772) Blundell of Crosby, d. 1795; m. 1784, Clementina, da. of Stephen Walter Tempest of Broughton, d. 21 July 1821; and had issue.

See the Clarence Volume, pp. 326–327, Nos. 9450–9505.

2c.⎫
3c.⎬ ? other children.
4c.⎭
[Nos. 36724 to 37346.

391. Descendants of MARMADUKE ANNE of Frickley, co. York (see Table XXXVI.), *d.* 28 Aug. 1722; *m.* ELIZABETH, da. of Robert PLUMPTON of Plumpton, *b.* 26 May 1692; and had issue 1*a* to 2*a*.

1a. George Anne of Burghwallis, b. 1717; d. 5 June 1785; m. 2ndly, Mary, da. of Robert Needham of Hilston, co. Monmouth, d. 15 June 1816; and had issue 1b.

1b. Michael Anne, afterwards (R.L. 20 June 1810) Tasburgh of Burghwallis, b. 4 Oct. 1777; d. (at Calais) 10 July 1853; m. 23 Ap. 1810, Maria Augusta Rosalia Anne, widow of George Tasburgh of Rodney, co. Norfolk, da. and h. of George Crathorne, d. May 1844; and had issue.

See the Clarence Volume, pp. 384–385, Nos. 14618–14643.

2a. Anne Anne, d. (–); m. Arnold Knight of Busling Thrope, co. Lincoln, by whom she was grandmother of Sir Arnold Knight of Sheffield, M.D.

[Nos. 37347 to 37372.

392. Descendants of ANNE ANNE (see Table XXXVI.), wife of EDWARD KILLINGBECK.

393. Descendants of HUGH (SMITHSON, *afterwards* (1750 PERCY), 1st DUKE OF NORTHUMBERLAND [G.B.] (see Table XXXVI.), *b. c.* 1714; *d.* 6 June 1786; *m.* 16 July 1740, Lady ELIZABETH, da. and h. of Algernon (SEYMOUR), Duke of Somerset [E.], and 1st Earl of Northumberland [G.B.], *b.* 26 Nov. 1716; *d.* 5 Dec. 1776; and had issue.

See the Tudor Roll of "The Blood Royal of Britain," Table XXIV., pp. 186–195, Nos. 20946–21229.

[Nos. 37373 to 37655.

3 N

The Plantagenet Roll

394. Descendants of HENRY (POWLETT), 6th DUKE OF BOLTON [E.] (see Table XXXVII.), *b. c.* 1719; *d.* 25 Dec. 1794; *m.* 1st, 13 May 1752, HENRIETTA, da. of [——] NUNN of Eltham, co. Kent, *d.* 31 May 1764; 2ndly, 8 Ap. 1765, KATHARINE, sister to James, 1st Earl of Lonsdale [G.B.], da. of Robert LOWTHER, Governor of Barbados, *d.* 21 Mar. 1809; and had issue 1*a* to 2*a*.

1*a*. *Lady Mary Henrietta Powlett, b. Oct.* 1753; *d.* 30 *Mar.* 1779; *m. as 2nd wife, 25 Ap.* 1772, *John (Montagu), afterwards 5th Earl of Sandwich* [E.], *d. 6 June* 1814; *and had issue.*
See p. 363, Nos. 26221–26240.

2*a*. *Lady Katherine Margaret Powlett, d.* 17 *June* 1807; *m. as 1st wife,* 19 *Sept.* 1787, *William Henry (Vane), 1st Duke of Cleveland* [*U.K.*], *3rd Earl of Darlington* [G.B.], *5th Baron Barnard* [E.], *K.G., d.* 29 *Jan.* 1842; *and had issue.*
See the Clarence Volume, pp. 581–584, Nos. 24444–24510.

[Nos. 37656 to 37738.

395. Descendants, if any, of Lady CATHERINE POWLETT (see Table XXXVII.), *d.* 8 Oct. 1774; *m.* 1st, 4 Jan. 1749, WILLIAM ASHE, M.P. for Heytesbury, co. Wilts, *d.* 11 July 1750; 2ndly, Feb. 1755, ADAM DRUMMOND, 4th of Meggins and 11th of Lennoch, M.P., *d.s.p.*

396. Descendants, if any, of Lady MARY POWLETT (see Table XXXVII.), *m.* 1st, CHARLES O'NEIL, *d.* 1716; 2ndly, the Hon. ARTHUR MOORE, *d.s.p.*

397. Descendants, if any, of ANNE TOWNSHEND (see Table XXXVII.), wife of CHARLES HEDGES; and of DOROTHY TOWNSHEND, wife of MILES BUTTEN ALLEN.

398. Descendants of Lady JANE POWLETT (see Table XXXVII.), *b. c.* 1655; *d.* 23 May 1716; *m.* as 2nd wife, 2 Ap. 1673, JOHN (EGERTON), 3rd EARL OF BRIDGEWATER [E.], K.B., *b.* 9 Nov. 1646; *d.* 19 Mar. 1701; and had issue.

See the Tudor Roll of "The Blood Royal of Britain," pp. 358–388, Nos. 27543–29272.
[Nos. 37739 to 39463.

399. Descendants of MARY JENKINS (see Table XXXVII.), *d.* 14 Mar. 1767; *m.* 26 Ap. 1707, Sir HENRY GOODRICKE, 4th Bart. [E.], *b.* 8 Sept. 1677; *d.* 21 July 1738; and had issue 1*a* to 5*a*.

1*a*. *Sir John Goodricke of Ribston, 5th Bart.* [E.], *P.C., M.P.,, b.* 20 *May* 1708; *d.* 3 *Aug.* 1789; *m.* 28 *Sept.* 1731, *Mary Johnson, natural da. of Robert (Benson), 1st Baron Bingley* [G.B.],[1] *d.* (–); *and had issue* 1*b*.

---

[1] G. E. C.'s "Complete Baronetage," ii. p. 137.

# of The Blood Royal

1b. Henry Goodricke, b. 6 *Ap*. 1741; d.v.p. 9 *July* 1784; m. *c*. 1764 (*at Wold-huysen, East Friesland*), *Lavinia Benjamina, da. of Peter Sesster of Namur; and had issue* 1c *to* 3c.

1c. Sir Henry Goodricke, *6th Bart.* [*E.*], b. 12 *Oct.* 1765; d. 23 *Mar.* 1802; m. 30 *Nov.* 1796, *Charlotte, da. of the Right Hon. James Fortescue*, d. 10 *Aug.* 1842; *and had issue* 1d.

1d. Sir Henry Goodricke, *7th Bart.* [*E.*], b. 16 *Sept.* 1797; d. *unm.* 22 *Aug.* 1833.

2c. *Mary Goodricke*, m. *Charles Gregory Fairfax of Gilling Castle, co. York.*

3c. *Elizabeth Goodricke.*

2a. *Henry Goodricke*, d. (*apparently* s.p. *and certainly* s.p.m.).

3a. *Thomas Goodricke, Lieut.-Col. in the Army*, b. 12 *Mar.* 1712; d. *July* 1803; m. *Elizabeth, da. of James Bution of Rochester; and had issue* 1b *to* 2b.

1b. Sir Thomas Goodricke, *8th Bart.* [*E.*], b. 24 *Sept.* 1762; d.s.p. 9 *Mar.* 1839.

2b. *Harriott Goodricke*, d. (? *unm.*).

4a. *Sarah Goodricke*, d. *Jan.* 1787; m. 9 *Oct.* 1742, *Thomas Clough of Otley, co. York*, d. (–); *and had issue* (9 *children, of whom the* 5*th*) 1b.[1]

1b. *Thomas Clough of Bishops Stortford, co. Herts, J.P., D.L.*, b. 25 *Ap.* 1848; d. 1838; m. 1785, *Susanne, da. of John Tyler of Bishops Stortford; and had issue* 1c.

1c. *Edward Clough, afterwards* (*R.L.* 12 *Sept.* 1807) *Taylor of Kirkham Abbey, J.P., D.L.*, b. 28 *Jan.* 1786; d. 14 *May* 1851; m. 8 *Jan.* 1822, *Emma Georgiana Bentley, da. of William Badcock*, d. 28 *Feb.* 1885; *and had issue* 1d *to* 2d.

1d. *Edward Clough-Taylor of Kirkham Abbey and Firby Hall, J.P., D.L.*, b. 25 *Sept.* 1822; d. 13 *Dec.* 1892; m. 1 *Sept.* 1848, *Sophia Mary, da. and co-h. of the Rev. Thomas Harrison of Firby Hall; and had issue* 1e *to* 5e.

1e. Edward Harrison Clough-Taylor, Lieut.-Col. *late* Royal Welsh Fusiliers (*Firby Hall, Kirkham Abbey, Yorks*), b. 19 June 1849; *m.* 1st, 17 July 1880, Lady Elizabeth, da. of George (Campbell), 8th Duke of Argyll [S.], K.G., d. 24 Sept. 1896; 2ndly, 21 Dec. 1898, Lady Mary, da. of Henry James (Stuart), 5th Earl of Castlestuart [I.]; and has issue 1f to 4f.

1f. Edward Lorne Frederic Clough-Taylor, b. 26 Oct. 1881.

2f. Leonard Goodricke Stuart Clough-Taylor, b. 13 Aug. 1901.

3f. Walter Stuart Augustus Clough-Taylor, b. 12 Oct. 1905.

4f. Lesley Venetia Clough-Taylor, b. 14 Sept. 1886.

2e. Horatio George Clough-Taylor, Major Leicestershire Y.C., b. 12 Oct. 1856; *m.* 9 Jan. 1889, Ethel Maud, da. of Rev. the Hon. Augustus Byron.

3e. Sophia Leonora Clough-Taylor, *m.* 9 Nov. 1875, Henry Barrington Callander.

4e. Harriet Anna Georgina Clough-Taylor.

5e. Constance Caroline Clough-Taylor, *m.* 5 Aug. 1885, Capt. Augustus William Byron (*Junior Carlton*); and has issue 1f to 2f.

1f. Nora Hermione Wentworth Byron.

2f. Ada Constance Frederica Byron.

2d. *Emma Sarah Clough-Taylor*, d. 27 *Nov.* 1893; m. 6 *Feb.* 1855, *Major Henry Pratt Gore*, d. 4 *Sept.* 1863; *and had issue.*

5a. *Jane Goodricke*, m. *the Rev. Francis Wanley, D.D., Dean of Ripon.*

[Nos. 39464 to 39474.

400. Descendants, if any, of the Hon. ELIZABETH SAVAGE (see Table XXXV.), *m.* Sir JOHN THIMBLEBY of Irnham, co. Lincoln.

---

[1] Burke's "Landed Gentry," 1900, p. 1544.

The Plantagenet Roll

401. Descendants of GEORGE (BRUDENELL), 3rd EARL OF CARDIGAN [E.] (see Table XXXVIII.), *d.* 5 July 1732; *m.* 15 May 1707, Lady ELIZABETH, da. of Thomas (BRUCE), 3rd Earl of Elgin [S.], 2nd Earl of Ailsbury [E.], *d.* Dec. 1745; and had issue.

See the Tudor Roll of "The Blood Royal of Britain," Table XV., pp. 156–186, Nos. 19724–20945. [Nos. 39475 to 40689.

402. Descendants of the Hon. JAMES BRUDENELL, M.P. (see Table XXXVIII.), *d.* 9. Aug. 1746; *m.* SUSAN, da. of Bartholomew BURTON of North Luffenham, co. Rutland; and had issue 1*a* to 2*a*.

1*a*. *Caroline Brudenell,* d. 10 *Oct.* 1803; m. *as 2nd wife,* 1758, *Sir Samuel Fludyer,* 1st *Bart.* [G.B.], *M.P., Lord Mayor of London,* d. 18 *Jan.* 1768; *and had issue* 1*b to* 2*b.*

1*b*. *Sir Samuel Brudenell Fludyer, 2nd Bart.* [G.B.], b. 8 *Oct.* 1759; d. 17 *Feb.* 1833; m. 5 *Oct.* 1786, *Maria, da. of Robert Weston,* d. 23 *Nov.* 1818; *and had issue* 1*c to* 2*c.*

1*c*. *Sir Samuel Fludyer, 3rd Bart.* [G.B.], b. 31 *Jan.* 1800; d. *unm.* 12 *Mar.* 1876.

2*c*. *Caroline Louisa Fludyer* (*sole heir in* 1884), b. 1798; d. 12 *Dec.* 1888; m. *as 2nd wife,*[1] 13 *Nov.* 1828, *Cobbett Derby of Horton, Bucks,* d. 1883; *and had issue* 1*d to* 2*d.*

1*d*. Katharine Louisa Derby (18 *Hans Place, S.W.*), *m.* 10 July 1855, the Hon. Arthur Hay-Drummond, Capt. R.N., *d.s.p.* 28 Jan. 1900.

2*d*. Ellen Maria Derby (27 *Great Cumberland Place, W.*), *m.* 6 June 1861, Admiral Mark Robert Pechell, R.N., *d.* 9 July 1902; and had issue.
See the Clarence Volume, p. 634, Nos. 28396–28411.

2*b*. *George Fludyer of Ayston, co. Rutland, M.P.,* b. *Sept.* 1861; d. 15 *Ap.* 1837; m. 16 *Jan.* 1792, *Lady Mary, da. of John* (*Fane*), 9*th Earl of Westmorland* [E.], d. 27 *June* 1855; *and had issue.*
See the Tudor Roll of "The Blood Royal of Britain," p. 488, Nos. 33668–33677.

2*a*. *Louisa Bridges Brudenell,* m. 16 *Sept.* 1760, *Richard Weston; and had issue* (*at least*) 1*b.*

1*b*. *Maria Weston,* d. 23 *Nov.* 1818; m. 5 *Oct.* 1786, *Sir Samuel Brudenell Fludyer, 2nd Bart.* [G.B.], d. 17 *Feb.* 1833; *and had issue.*
See p. 464, Nos. 40690–40691. [Nos. 40690 to 40719.

403. Descendants of the Hon. MARY MOLYNEUX (see Table XXXVIII.), *d.* (–); *m.* 1st, THOMAS CLIFTON of Clifton and Lytham, *b.* 1696; *d.* 16 Dec. 1734; 2ndly, 8 Feb. 1752, WILLIAM ANDERTON of Euxton Hall, co. Lancaster, *d.* (–); and had issue 1*a* to 3*a*.

1*a*. *Thomas Clifton of Clifton and Lytham,* b. 1728; d. 11 *May* 1783; m. 3*rdly,* 29 *Sept.* 1760, *Lady Jane, da. of Willoughby* (*Bertie*), 3*rd Earl of Abingdon* [E.], d. 25 *Feb.* 1791; *and had issue.*
See pp. 81–84, Nos. 220–332. [Nos. 40720 to 40833.

---

[1] See the Clarence Volume, p. 351, for 1st wife and her issue.

# of The Blood Royal

2a. *William Anderton of Euxton*, d. 1811; m. *Frances, da. and h. of Christopher Ince of Ince Hall, co. Lancaster; and had issue* 1b *to* 4b.

1b. *William Ince Anderton of Euxton and Ince*, d. (-); m. 11 *Nov.* 1823, *Mary Frances, da. of Christopher Crook of London; and had issue* 1c.

1c. *William Michael Ince Anderton of Euxton*, J.P., D.L., b. 29 *Sept.* 1825; d. 1884; m. 1st, 12 *Sept.* 1850, *Lady Emma Frances, da. of Arthur James (Plunkett), 9th Earl of Fingall* [I.], d. 14 *Oct.* 1866; 2ndly, *Caselda, da. of* [——] *Hunloke; and had issue* 1d *to* 6d.

1d. William Arthur Alphonsus Joseph Ince Anderton, J.P., Major *late* Grenadier Guards (*Euxton Hall, near Chorley*), b. 22 Dec. 1855; m. 21 Jan. 1892, Ida Mary Winifred, da. of J. W. Johnstone of Barnard Castle.

2d. Francis Robert Anderton, b. 22 Feb. 1859.

3d. Henry Philip John Anderton, b. 7 June 1880.

4d. *Mary Louisa Anne Frances Josephine Martha Anderton*, d. 2 *Nov.* 1889; m. *as 2nd wife*, 19 *Mar.* 1873, *George Augustus Curzon*, J.P., Col. *late 2nd Life Guards and Rifle Brigade (Westwood, Windlesham, Surrey); and had issue* 1e.

1e. Mary Cecil Curzon, *m. as* 2nd wife, 12 Nov. 1901, Sir Frederick William Francis George Frankland, 10th Bart. [E.] (3 *Queen's Gardens, Windsor*); and has issue 1f.

1f. Thomas William Assheton Frankland, b. 18 Aug. 1902.

5d. *Emma Adelaide Mary Sobieski Anderton*, m. Capt. D. T. Hammond, *late* Connaught Rangers.

6d. Maud Margaret Dolores Anna Anderton, m. 19 July 1898, Edmund Arthur Le Gendre Starkie, J.P., Capt. 3rd Batt. East Lancashire Regiment.

2b. *Robert Anderton.*

3b. *Thomas Anderton.*

4b. *Francis Anderton.*

3a. *Catherine Anderton*, d. 13 *Jan.* 1821; m. *Sir Robert Cansfield Gerard, 9th Bart.* [E.], d. 6 *Mar.* 1784; *and had issue* 1b *to* 4b.

1b. *Sir Robert Gerard, 10th Bart.* [E.], d. unm. (*at Liege*) 26 *Aug.* 1791.

2b. *Sir William Gerard, 11th Bart.* [E.], b. 12 *July* 1773, d.s.p. 2 *Aug.* 1826.

3b. *John Gerard of Windle Hall, co. Lancaster*, d. 22 *May* 1822; m. 22 Feb. 1803, *Elizabeth, da. of Edward Ferrers of Baddesley Clinton; and had issue* 1c *to* 5c.

1c. *Sir John Gerard, 12th Bart.* [E.], b. 8 *Dec.* 1804; d.s.p. 21 *Feb.* 1854.

2c. *Robert Tolver (Gerard), 1st Baron Gerard* [U.K.], *13th Bart.* [E.], b. 12 *May* 1808; d. 15 *Mar.* 1887; m. 14 *Feb.* 1849, *Harriet, da. of Capt. Edward Clifton*, d. 20 *July* 1888; *and had issue.*

See the Clarence Volume, p. 431, Nos. 16900–16914.

3c. *Frederic Sewallis Gerard of Aspull House, co. Lancaster*, J.P., D.L., b. 23 *Dec.* 1811; d. 7 *May* 1884; m. 2 *Sept.* 1835, *Mary Ann, da. of the Rev. Thomas Wilkinson of Kirkhallam*, d. 28 *Mar.* 1883; *and had issue* 1d *to* 3d.

1d. Frederic Gerard, J.P., *late* Capt. 23rd Fusiliers (*Kinwarton, Alcester*), b. 6 Aug. 1839; m. 29 Ap. 1869, Catherine, da. of Charles Porter of the Mythe, Tewkesbury; and has issue 1e.

1e. Edith Gerard, *m.* 24 Sept. 1896, Edward Charles Riddell (*Hermeston Hall, Notts*); and has issue 1f to 2f.

1f. Arthur Frederick Riddell, b. 27 July 1897.

2f. Ralf Riddell, b. 13 Aug. 1899.

2d. *Mary Anne Gerard*, d. 5 *Nov.* 1868; m. *as* 1st *wife*, 15 *Oct.* 1856, *Sir John Lawson, 2nd Bart.* [U.K.], J.P., D.L. (*Brough Hall, Catterick, Yorks*); *and had issue.*

See the Clarence Volume, p. 319, Nos. 9229–9233.

[Nos. 40834 to 40864.

The Plantagenet Roll

3*d*. Emma Eliza Gerard, *m*. 1st, 13 Sept. 1859, Henry Valentine (Stafford-Jemingham), 9th Baron Stafford [E.], *d.s.p.* 30 Nov. 1884; 2ndly, 24 Aug. 1887, Basil Thomas Fitzherbert, J.P., D.L. (*Swynnerton Park, Stone, co. Stafford*).

4*c*. Thomas Alexander Gerard, *29th Regt.*, b. 11 *July* 1812; d. 3 *Ap*. 1850; m. *and had issue*.

5*c*. Eliza Gerard, d. 5 *June* 1872; m. *as 2nd wife*, 30 *Ap*. 1830, *Henry Raymond Arundell of Kenilworth*, d. *14th Mar.* 1886; *and had issue*.

See the Clarence Volume, p. 465, Nos. 20705–20727.

4*b*. Maria Gerard, d. 9 *Feb*. 1827; m. *Thomas Stapylton of The Grove, Richmond, Yorks*. [Nos. 40865 to 40888.

404. Descendants of Lord GEORGE HENRY LENNOX, M.P. (see Table XXXVIII.), *b*. 29 Nov. 1737; *d*. 22 Mar. 1805; *m*. 25 Dec. 1758, Lady LOUISA MARY, da. of William Henry (KERR), 4th Marquis of Lothian [S.], *d*. 25 Dec. 1830; and had issue.

See the Clarence Volume, pp. 636–637, Nos. 28451–28849.

[Nos. 40889 to 41286.

405. Descendants of GEORGINA CAROLINA, *suo jure* 1st BARONESS HOLLAND of Holland (1762) [G.B.], (see Table XXXVIII.), *b*. 27 Mar. 1723; *d*. 24 July 1774; *m*. 2 May 1744, HENRY (FOX), 1st BARON HOLLAND of Foxley (1763) [G.B.], *b*. 1705; *d*. 1 July 1774; and had issue 1*a* to 3*a*.

1*a*. Stephen (*Fox*), 2nd Baron Holland [G.B.], b. 20 *Feb*. 1745; d. 26 *Dec*. 1774; m. 20 *Ap*. 1766, *Lady Mary*, da. *of John* (*Fitzpatrick*), 1st Earl *of Upper Ossory* [I.], d. 6 Oct. 1778; *and had issue* 1*b*.

1*b*. Henry Richard (*Fox, afterwards Vassall*), 3rd Baron Holland [G.B.], F.R.S., b. 21 *Nov*. 1773; d. 22 Oct. 1840; m. 9 *July* 1797, *Elizabeth, sometime wife of Sir Godfrey Webster, 4th Bart.* [E.], da. and h. of Richard Vassall, d. 16 Nov. 1845; *and had issue*.

See p. 183, Nos. 6495–6511.

2*a*. Right Hon. Charles James Fox, P.C., M.P., b. 13 *Jan*. 1749; d.s.p. 8 *July* 1742.

3*a*. Hon. Henry Edward Fox, Gen. in the Army and Col. 16th Foot, b. 4 *Mar*. 1755; d. 18 *July* 1811; m. 14 *Nov*. 1786, *Marianne, da. of William Clayton of Harleyford, co. Bucks, by his wife Lady Louisa*, née *Fermor*, d.; *and had issue* 1*b* to 2*b*.

1*b*. Louisa Amelia Fox, d. (*at Genoa*) 1828; m. *as 1st wife*, 4 *Ap*. 1807, Sir Henry Edward Bunbury, 7th Bart. [E.], M.P., F.S.A., b. 4 *May* 1778; d. 13 *Ap*. 1860; *and had issue* 1*c* to 4*c*.

1*c*. Sir Charles James Fox Bunbury, 8th Bart. [E.], b. 4 *Feb*. 1809; d.s.p. 18 *June* 1886.

2*c*. Sir Edward Herbert Bunbury, 9th Bart. [E.], M.P., b. 8 *July* 1811; d. *unm*. 5 *Mar*. 1895.

3*c*. Henry William St. Pierre Bunbury, C.B., Col. in the Army, b. 2 Sept. 1812; d. 18 *Sept*. 1875; m. 30 *Nov*. 1852, *Cecilia, da. of Lieut.-Col. Sir George Napier, K.C.B.*; *and had issue* 1*d* to 4*d*.

1*d*. Sir Henry Charles James Bunbury, 10th Bart. [E.], D.L. (*Barton Hall, Bury St. Edmunds; Manor House, Mildenhall*), b. 9 Jan. 1855; *m*. 11 Mar. 1884, Laura, da. of Gen. Thomas Wood of Littleton, M.P.; *and has issue* 1*e* to 4*e*.

1*e*. Charles Henry Napier Bunbury, *b*. 19 Jan. 1886.

2*e*. Henry William Bunbury, *b*. 27 Jan. 1889.

3*e*. Cecilia Frances Laura Bunbury.

4*e*. Laura Constance Eleanor Bunbury. [Nos. 41287 to 41308.

# of The Blood Royal

2d. George Edward Bunbury, *late* Lieut. 1st Batt. Norfolk Regt. (*Hilden Manor, Tonbridge*), *b.* 17 Oct. 1856; *m.* 30 Oct. 1884, Beatrice Dora, da. of Thomas John Cottle of Altadore, Woodstock, Ontario; and has issue 1e.

1e. Noreen Winifred Bunbury.

3d. William St. Pierre Bunbury, *late* Major R.A. and sometime Instructor of Mil. Topography at Royal Mil. Acad., Woolwich (*Freiburg-in-Baden, Germany*); and has issue 1e to 4e.

1e. Gerald Bruce St. Pierre Bunbury, Lieut. Indian Army, *b.* 21 Mar. 1883.

2e. Noel Louis St. Pierre Bunbury, *b.* 25 Dec. 1890.

3e. Godfrey Hugh Bunbury, *b.* 6 Jan. 1895.

4e. Marjorie Ellinor Bunbury, *b.* 28 Jan. 1887.

4d. Emily Louisa Margaret Bunbury (*New Lodge, Totton, Southampton*).

4c. *Richard Hanmer Bunbury, Capt. R.N., b.* 18 *Dec.* 1813; *d.* 23 *Dec.* 1857; *m.* 19 *Dec.* 1838, Sarah Susanna, da. of Richard Clement Sconce, d.; *and had issue* 1d *to* 6d.

1d. *Henry Fox Bunbury, Capt.* 35th *N.I., b. Oct.* 1839; *d.* 16 *Oct.* 1870; m. 1863, *Elizabeth, da. of J. Kelsey,* d. 1875; *and had issue* 1e *to* 2e.

1e. Cecil Edward Francis Bunbury, I.C.S., *b.* 1 Dec. 1864; *m.*

2e. William Clement Hanmer Bunbury, Capt. Royal Scots (*East India ; United Service*), *b.* 17 Feb. 1868; *m.* 9 Dec. 1903, Lilian Maude, da. of William Fox Tomson of Effingham, Thanet.

2d. Cecil Hanmer Bunbury, *formerly* Col. Comdg. 2nd Batt. Connaught Rangers, *b.* 12 Feb. 1845; *m.* 1st, 12 Feb. 1873, Frances Susan, da. of Gen. William Craig Emilius Napier, *d.* 6 Nov. 1878; 2ndly, 9 Sept. 1897, May Lennox, da. of Thomas Atkins of Belle View House, Chepstow.

3d. Robert Clement Sconce Bunbury, Bar. I.T., *b.* Jan. 1847; *m.*

4d. Herbert Napier Bunbury, Col. in the Army and a Col. on the Staff and Director of Supplies and Transport, Irish Command, *b.* 15 Feb. 1851; *m.* 8 Aug. 1878, Mary Louisa, da. of Major Donald Patrick Campbell of Balliveolan; and has issue 1e to 3e.

1e. Rev. Patrick Stanney St. Pierre Bunbury, *b.* 1879.

2e. Richard Seymour Bunbury, Lieut. R.A., *b.* 19 Sept. 1880.

3e. Evan Campbell Bunbury, Lieut. R.N., *b.* 1881.

5d. Louisa Harriet Cometina Bunbury, *m.* 26 Mar. 1874, Dr. Max Marckwald of Heidelberg and Berlin; and has issue (a da.) 1e.

1e. [——] Marckwald, *b.* 27 Sept. 1879.

6d. Frances Susanna Bunbury, *m.* 27 Mar. 1873, John Frederic Symons-Jeune, son of the Lord Bishop of Peterborough) (*Watlington Park, Oxfordshire*); and has issue 1e to 2e.

1e. Bertram Hanmer Symons-Jeune, *b.* 1883.

2e. Dorothy Effield Cecil Symons-Jeune, *b.* 188–.

2b. *Caroline Amelia Fox, d.* 26 *Mar.* 1860; *m.* 14 *Mar.* 1812, *Gen. Sir William Francis Patrick Napier, K.C.B., Author of the " History of the Peninsular War," d.* 12 *Feb.* 1860; *and had issue* 1c *to* 5c.

1c. *John Moore Napier, b.* 4 *Nov.* 1816; *d.* 24 *Ap.* 1867; *m.* 22 *June* 1847, *Elizabeth Amelia Henrietta, da. of Col. Charles Alexander, R.E., d.* 19 *Oct.* 1888; *and had issue* 1d *to* 3d.

1d. William Charles Napier, *b.* 7 Ap. 1854.

2d. *Louisa Blanche Napier, b.* 30 *July* 1850; *d.* (*at Wynberg, Cape Colony*) 1878; *m. Arthur Gordon Schneider.*

3d. *Rose Leslie Napier, b.* 13 *Ap.* 1852; *d. Oct.* 1891; *m. as* 1st *wife,* 17 *Jan.* 1878, *Major Edward Robert Portal, M.A.* (*Oxon.*), *J.P.* (*Eddington House, Hungerford*); *and had issue.*

[Nos. 41309 to 41330.

The Plantagenet Roll

2c. *Elizabeth Marianne Napier*, d. 27 Ap. 1899; m. 1 *Mar.* 1838, *Philip Yorke (Gore), 4th Earl of Arran [I.], K.P.*, b. 23 Nov. 1801; d. 25 *June* 1884; *and had issue.*

See the Clarence Volume, pp. 500–502, Nos. 21757–21838.

3c. *Louisa Augusta Napier*, d. 8 Sept. 1856; m. *as 1st wife*, 15 *July* 1844, *Lieut.-Gen. Sir Patrick Leonard McDougall, K.C.M.G.*

4c. Pamela Adelaide Napier (*King's Weston House, Bristol*), m. 21 Dec. 1846, Philip William Skinner Miles of King's Weston, Jn. P., J.P., D.L., d. 1 Oct. 1881; and has issue 1d.

1d. Philip Napier Miles, J.P. (*King's Weston, Bristol*), b. 1865; m. 1 Feb. 1899, Sybil Marguerite Goune, da. of Arthur John (de Hochepied-Larpent), 8th Baron de Hochepied (1704) [Hungary].

5c. *Norah Creina Blanche Napier*, d. 27 Ap. 1897; m. *as 2nd wife*, 17 *Aug.* 1854, *Henry Austin (Bruce), 1st Baron Aberdare [U.K.], P.C., G.C.B.*, b. 16 Ap. 1815; d. 25 Feb. 1895; *and had issue 1d to 9d.*

1d. Hon. William Napier Bruce, C.B., Bar.-at-Law, Principal Assist. Secretary in Secondary Education Branch of Board of Education (34 *Leinster Gardens, W.*), b. 15 Jan. 1858; m. 5 Aug. 1882, Emily, da. of Gen. Sir William Montagu Scott MacMurdo, G.C.B.; and has issue 1e to 2e.

1e. William Fox Bruce, b. 7 Aug. 1883.

2e. Susan Norah Bruce, b. 7 Nov. 1884.

2d. Hon. Charles Granville Bruce, M.V.O., Capt. and Brevet-Major Indian Army, b. 7 Ap. 1866; m. 12 Sept. 1894, Finetta Madelina Julia, da. of Col. Sir Edward Fitzgerald Campbell, 2nd Bart. [U.K.].

3d. Hon. Caroline Louisa Bruce (*Pen Pole House, Shirehampton, Bristol*).

4d. Hon. Sarah Napier Bruce, m. 17 Aug. 1888, Montagu Johnstone Muir-Mackenzie, Recorder of Sandwich, &c. (21 *Hyde Park Gate, S.W.*); and has issue 1e.

1e. Enid Muir-Mackenzie.

5d. *Hon. Norah Creina Blanche Bruce*, b. 10 *July* 1859; d. 26 *May* 1886; m. 4 *Jan.* 1883, *Henry Arthur Whately* (*Laurel Lodge, Dancer's Hill, near Barnet*); and had issue 1e to 2e.

1e. Francis Bruce Whately, b. 1 May 1884.

2e. Nora Creina Bruce Whately.

6d. Hon. Isabel Ellen Bruce, m. 12 July 1887, Champion Branfill Russell, J.P. (*Stubbers, North Ockendon, Essex*); and has issue 1e to 6e.

1e. Champion Maxwell Russell, b. 5 Ap. 1890.

2e. Henry Branfill Russell, b. 10 Nov. 1894.

3e. John Napier Russell, b. 4 Oct. 1899.

4e. Rachel Augusta Russell.

5e. Isabel Marjorie Russell.

6e. Pamela Russell, b. 2 Ap. 1898.

7d. Hon. Elizabeth Fox Bruce, m. 9 Ap. 1896, Percy Ewing Matheson, Fellow and Tutor of New College, Oxford (1 *Savile Road, Oxford*).

8d. Hon. Pamela Georgina Bruce (222 *Banbury Road, Oxford*).

9d. Hon. Alice Moore Bruce, Vice-Principal, Somerville College, Oxford.

[Nos. 41331 to 41432.

406. Descendants of Lady EMILIA MARY LENNOX (see Table XXXVIII.), b. 6 Oct. 1731; d. 27 Mar. 1814; m. 1st, 7 Feb. 1747, JAMES (FITZGERALD), 1st DUKE OF LEINSTER [I.] and VISCOUNT LEINSTER [G.B.], b. 29 May 1722; d. 19 Nov. 1773; 2ndly, 1774, WILLIAM OGILVY, b. 1740; d. 18 Nov. 1832; and had issue 1a to 10a.

# of The Blood Royal

1a. William Robert (FitzGerald), 2nd Duke of [I.] and Viscount [G.B.] Leinster, K.P., b. 13 Mar. 1749; d. 20 Oct. 1804; m. 4 Nov. 1775, the Hon. Emilia Olivia, da. and h. of St. George (Usher, afterwards (1734) St. George), 1st Baron St. George [I.], d. 23 June 1798; and had issue 1b to 8b.

1b. Augustus Frederick (FitzGerald), 3rd Duke of [I.] and Viscount [G.B.] Leinster, P.C., b. 21 Aug. 1791; d. 10 Oct. 1874; m. 16 June 1818, Lady Charlotte Augusta, da. of Charles (Stanhope), 3rd Earl of Harrington [G.B.], d. 15 Feb. 1859; and had issue.

See the Clarence Volume, p. 350, Nos. 11426–11457.

2b. Lord William Charles O'Brien FitzGerald, b. 4 Jan. 1793; d. (? s.p.) 8 Dec. 1864.

3b. Lady Mary Rebecca FitzGerald, b. 6 May 1777; d. 28 Sept. 1842; m. as 2nd wife, 15 Ap. 1799, Lieut.-Gen. Sir Charles Lockhart Ross, 7th Bart. [S.], d. 8 Feb. 1814; and had issue 1c to 4c.

1c. Sir Charles William Augustus Lockhart-FitzGerald, 8th Bart. [S.], b. 19th Jan. 1812; d. 26 July 1883; m. 2ndly, 2 Mar. 1865, Rebecca Sophia, da. of Henry Barnes of Tufnell Park; and had issue 1d.

1d. Sir Charles Henry Augustus Frederick Lockhart-Ross, 9th Bart. [S.], D.L., Major Lovat's Scouts (Balnagowan Castle, Ross; Bonnington House, Lanark), b. 4 Ap. 1872; m. 1st, 26 Ap. 1893, Winifred, da. of Alexander Augustus Berens (marriage dissolved 1897); 2ndly, 19 Nov. 1901, Patricia, da. of Andrew Ellison of Louisville, Ky.

2c. Emilia Olivia Lockhart-Ross, d. 24 June 1866; m. 29 Feb. 1820, Sir Charles Macdonald-Lockhart, 2nd Bart. [U.K.], b. 8 Feb. 1799; d. 8 Dec. 1832; and had issue 1d.

1d. Mary Macdonald-Lockhart, d. 10 Dec. 1851; m. 15 Sept. 1837, the Hon. Augustus Henry Moreton, afterwards Moreton Macdonald of Largie, M.P., d. 14 Feb. 1862; and had issue.

See the Tudor Roll of "The Blood Royal of Britain," pp. 268–269, Nos. 24520–24544.

3c. Mary Lockhart-Ross, d. 11 June 1852; m. 11 May 1825, Sir William Foulis of Ingleby, 8th Bart. [E.], bapt. 29 May 1790; d. 7 Nov. 1845; and had issue 1d.

1d. Mary Foulis, b. 19 May 1826; d. 14 June 1891; m. as 1st wife, 23 Ap. 1850, Philip (Sydney), 2nd Baron de L'Isle and Dudley [U.K.], d. 17 Feb. 1898; and had issue.

4c. Geraldine Lockhart-Ross, unm.

4b. Lady Emily Elizabeth FitzGerald, b. 13 May 1778; d. 9 Feb. 1856; m. 13 Mar. 1801, John Joseph Henry of Straffan, co. Kildare (which he sold 1829), d. 28 June 1846; and had issue 1c to 6c.

1c. Charles John Henry, b. 4 Nov. 1806; d. 3 Oct. 1879; m. 25 June 1838, Lady Selina Constantia, da. of Francis (Rawdon-Hastings), 1st Marquis of Hastings [U.K.], K.G., d. 8 Nov. 1867; and had issue 1d to 3d.

1d. Mabel Elizabeth Henry (2 Northwick Villas, Douro Road, Cheltenham).

2d. Agnes Olivia Henry (Moira, Craneswater Avenue, Southsea).

3d. Eva Geraldine Henry (1 Argyll Villas, The Park, Cheltenham).

2c. Sir Hastings Reginald Henry, afterwards Yelverton, G.C.B., Admiral R.N., d. 23 July 1878; m. 9 Ap. 1845, Barbara (Yelverton), Dowager Marchioness of Hastings [U.K.] and suo jure 20th Baroness Grey de Ruthyn [E.], d. 18 Nov. 1858; and had issue 1d.

1d. Hon. Barbara Yelverton, m. 23 Sept. 1872, John (Yarde-Buller), 2nd Baron Churston [U.K.] (Lupton House, Churston Ferrers, Devon); and has issue 1e to 2e.

1e. Hon. John Reginald Lopes Yarde-Buller, M.V.O., Capt. Scots Guards (Guards; White's, &c.), b. 9 Nov. 1873.

2e. Hon. Barbara Lois Yarde-Buller. [Nos. 41433 to 41497.

The Plantagenet Roll

3c. *George Augustus Henry, Comm. R.N.*, b. 9 Oct. 1809; d. 27 Feb. 1853; m. 30 Oct. 1845, *Etheldreda Lucy Emily, da. of Samuel Bates Ferris, Lieut.-Col. in the Hanoverian Service, Treasurer of the Mauritius*, b. 4 Aug. 1820; d. 1 July 1887; *and had issue* 1d.

    1d. Etheldreda Olivia Henry (45B *Chester Square, S.W.*), b. 23 Nov. 1846.

4c. *Clifford Henry, Capt. 40th Regt.*, d. 27 Oct. 1874; m. 1st, 1845, *Mary, da. of* [——] *Mason*, d. 1846; *2ndly*, 1848, *Zoë, da. of H. H. St. Leger*, d. Nov. 1896; *and had issue* 1d to 3d.

    1d. Frederick Thomas Clifford Henry, a Clerk in the Charity Commission (*Fort Henry, Birdhill, Ireland*), b. 20 Oct. 1850; *m.* 20 Ap. 1881, Catherine Jeannie, da. of the Rev. William Blake Doveton, Vicar of Corston; and has issue 1e.

        1e. Joseph Wingfield Henry, b. 20 Feb. 1882.

    2d.[1] Emily Barbara Henry, b. 4 Oct. 1846.

    3d.[2] Geraldine Henry, *m.* 4 June 1872, Ellis Elias; and has issue 1e to 2e.

        1e. Clifford Elias, b. 1875.

        2e. Zoë Ellen Elias, b. 1873.

5c. *Emily Elizabeth Henry*, d. 21 Mar. 1859; m. *as 2nd wife*, 1830, *John Michael Henry Fock (de Robeck), 3rd Baron de Robeck* (1750) [*Sweden*], b. 14 July 1790; d. Oct. 1856; *and had issue* 1d to 3d.

    1d. *Hastings St. John de Robeck, Lieut. R.N.*, b. 24 June 1832; d. 17 Oct. 1880; m. 14 Mar. 1861, *Mary Catherine, da. of W. G. Atherstone of Grahamstown, South Africa, M.D.*, d. 18 Dec. 1887; *and had issue* 1e to 2e.

        1e. Geraldine Grace de Robeck.

        2e. Emily Olivia de Robeck, *m.* 29 Jan. 1898, Marlay Carolin (*Johannesburg, Transvaal*); and has issue 1f to 3f.

            1f. Hastings Marlay Carolin, b. 13 Aug. 1902.

            2f. Matilda Olivia Carolin, b. 25 Sept. 1898.

            3f. Phyllis Gertrude Carolin, b. 16 Aug. 1900.

    2d. George Henry de Robeck (*Windham*), b. 4 Dec. 1839.

    3d. Charles Louis Constantine de Robeck, Major *late* 60th Rifles (*Junior Constitutional*), b. 1 July 1841; *m.* 14 Dec. 1882, Elinor Maude, da. of William Parry-Okeden of Turnworth, Dorset; and has issue 1e.

        1e. Nesta Mary Emily de Robeck, b. 28 July 1886.

6c. *Olivia Henry*, d. 27 June 1859; m. *as 2nd wife*, 17 July 1850, *Sir Thomas Gage Saunders Sebright, 8th Bart.* [*E.*], b. 1802; d. 29 Aug. 1864; *and had issue* 1d to 3d.

    1d. Sir Edgar Reginald Saunders Sebright, 11th Bart. [E.], J.P., D.L., *formerly* Major and Hon. Lieut.-Col. 4th Batt. Bedfordshire Regt., Equerry to H.R.H. the Duchess of Teck (*Beechwood, Dunstable*), b. 8 Nov. 1854.

    2d. Guy Thomas Saunders Sebright, *late* Coldstream Guards (82 *Eaton Place, S.W.*), b. 19 Aug. 1856; *m.* 27 June 1882, Olive Emily, da. of Arthur Frederick; and has issue 1e.

        1e. Guy Ivo Sebright, b. 1883.

    3d. Arthur Edward Saunders Sebright, *late* Bedfordshire Regt., b. 30 Mar. 1859; *m.* 1889, Emily Eva, widow of W. Ingram of the U.S.A., da. of John Bowen of Ellesmere; and has issue.

5b. *Lady Elizabeth Mary Fitzgerald*, b. 30 Oct. 1780; d. 28 Feb. 1857; m. 22 July 1805, *Sir Edward Baker Littlehales, afterwards* (R.L. 6 Jan. 1817) *Baker, 1st Bart.* [*U.K.*], d. 4 Mar. 1825; *and had issue* 1c to 3c.

    1c. Sir Edward Baker, 2nd Bart. [U.K.], b. 4 Nov. 1806; d. *unm.* 29 Mar. 1877.

    2c. Rev. Sir Talbot Hastings Bendall Baker, 3rd Bart. [U.K.], *Preb. of Salisbury*, b. 9 Sept. 1820; d. 6 Ap. 1900; m. *2ndly*, 30 Dec. 1875, Amy Susan, da. of Lieut.-Col. George Marryat; *and had issue* 1d to 3d.   [Nos. 41498 to 41516.

# of The Blood Royal

1d. Sir Randolf Littlehales Baker, 4th Bart. [U.K.] (*Ranston, near Blandford*) b. 20 July 1879.

2d. Florence Letitia Baker, b. 16 Nov. 1876.

3d. Eunice Evelyn Baker, b. 22 Sept. 1888.

3c. *Emilia Maria Baker*, d. 31 *July* 1889; m. 22 *July* 1828, *Thomas Mills Goodlake of Wadley House, co. Berks*, d. 1877; *and had issue* 1d *to* 5d.

1d. *Thomas Leinster Goodlake, J.P.*, b. 13 *May* 1829; d. 1903; m. 22 *Nov.* 1855, *Mary Frederica* (18 *Charles Street, Berkeley Square, W.*), *sister to Sir Richard George Glyn, 3rd Bart.* [G.B.], *da. of Robert Glyn of Bath.*

2d. *Edward Wallace Goodlake, Bar.-at-Law*, b. 19 *Sept.* 1830; d. (–); m. 1st, 28 *Dec.* 1859, *the Hon. Caroline, da. of John* (*Wrottesley*), *2nd Baron Wrottesley* [U.K.], d.s.p. 1 *Sept.* 1860; 2ndly, *Cecilia, da. of* [——] *Ellis*, d. 1890.

3d. *Gerald Littlehales Goodlake, Col. Coldstream Guards, V.C., A.D.C. to Queen Victoria*, b. 14 *May* 1832; d. 1890; m. *Margaret* (*Denham, Fishery, Uxbridge;* 36 *Chester Square, S.W.*), *da. of* [——] *Curwen.*

4d. *Emilia Jane Goodlake*, d. *Dec.* 1889; m. 15 *July* 1857, *William Frederick Webb of Newstead Abbey, Notts, J.P., D.L., High Sheriff* 1865, b. *Mar.* 1829; d. 24 *Feb.* 1899; *and had issue* 1e *to* 4e.

1e. Roderick Beauclerk Webb, *late* of Newstead Abbey, Notts, and Cowton, Northallerton, York (*Queensland*), b. 8 Mar. 1867.

2e. Augusta Zelia Webb, *m.* 7 Aug. 1889, Philip Affleck Fraser of Reelig, J.P. (*Moniack, Beauly, Inverness*); and has issue 1f to 3f.

1f. Charles Ion Fraser, b. 1903.

2f. Phyllis Mary Fraser, b. 6 June 1890.

3f. Violet Mabel Fraser, b. 12 Mar. 1892.

3e. Geraldine Katherine Webb, *m.* 27 Dec. 1899, Lieut.-Gen. Sir Herbert Charles Chermside, G.C.M.G., C.B., sometime (1901–1904) Governor of Queensland, &c. (*Newstead Abbey, Nottingham*).

4e. Ethel Mary Webb.

5d. Olivia Elizabeth Goodlake, *m.* 10 Aug. 1878, Louis Peter Gilbert (de Lasteyrie du Saillant), 4th Marquis of Lasteyrie (1791) [F.] (*La Grange, Courpalay, Seine et Marne*); and has issue 1e to 2e.

1e. Guy Louis Jules de Lasteyrie du Saillant, b. 3 Oct. 1879.

2e. Louis Sidney Gilbert de Lasteyrie du Saillant, b. 20 Sept. 1881.

6b. *Lady Isabella Charlotte FitzGerald*, b. 16 *July* 1784; d. 9 *Ap.* 1868; m. 1 *June* 1809, *Major-Gen. Louis William de Rohan-Chabot, Viscount de Chabot, K.C.H.*, d. (–); *and had issue* 1c *to* 2c.

1c. *Philip Ferdinand Augustus de Rohan-Chabot, Count of Jarnac, French Ambassador to the Court of St. James*, d. 22 *Mar.* 1875; m. 10 *Dec.* 1844, *the Hon. Geraldine Augusta, da. of Thomas* (*Foley*), *3rd Baron Foley* [G.B.], d. 23 *Mar.* 1887.

2c. *Anne Rosalie Olivia de Rohan-Chabot*, b. 28 *June* 1813; d. 7 *July* 1899; m. 10 *Aug.* 1846, *Adrian Jules* (*de Lasteyrie du Saillant*), *3rd Marquis of Lasteyrie* (1791) [F.], b. 3 *Oct.* 1810; d. *Nov.* 1884; *and had issue* 1d.

1d. Louis Peter Gilbert (de Lasteyrie du Saillant), 4th Marquis of Lasteyrie (1791) [F.] (*La Grange, Courpalay, Seine et Marne*), b. 19 Aug. 1849; *m.* 10 Aug. 1878, Olivia Elizabeth, da. of Thomas Mills Goodlake of Wadley House; and has issue.

See p. 471, Nos. 41528–41529.

7b. *Lady Cecilia Olivia Geraldine FitzGerald*, b. 3 *Mar.* 1786; d. 27 *July* 1863; m. 18 *Aug.* 1806, *Thomas* (*Foley*), *3rd Baron Foley* [G.B.], b. 22 *Dec.* 1780; d. 16 *Ap.* 1833; *and had issue.*

See the Clarence Volume, pp. 353–354, Nos. 11520–11570.

8b. *Lady Olivia Letitia Catherine FitzGerald*, b. 9 *Sept.* 1787; d. 28 *Feb.* 1858; m. 8 *May* 1806, *Charles* (*Kinnaird*), *8th Baron Kinnaird* [S.], b. 8 *Ap.* 1780; d. 11 *Dec.* 1826; *and had issue* 1c *to* 2c. [Nos. 41517–41582.

The Plantagenet Roll

1c. George William Fox (Kinnaird), 9th Baron Kinnaird [*S.*], *1st Baron Rossie* (1831), *and Kinnaird of Rossie* (1860) [*U.K.*], *K.T.*, b. 14 *Ap.* 1807; d. 7 *Jan.* 1878; m. 14 *Dec.* 1837, *Hon. Frances Anne Georgiana, da. of William Francis Spencer (Ponsonby), 1st Baron de Manley* [*U.K.*]; *and had issue* 1d.

1d. *Hon. Olivia Barbara Kinnaird, d. 6 Aug.* 1861; m. 27 *July* 1859, *Sir Reginald Howard Alexander Ogilvy, 10th Bart.* [*S.*], *J.P., D.L., &c.* (*Baldovan House, Strathmartine, Forfar*); *and had issue.*

See the Clarence Volume, p. 435, Nos. 18161–18167.

2c. Arthur FitzGerald (Kinnaird), 10th Baron Kinnaird [*S.*], *M.P.*, b. 8 *July* 1814; d. 26 *Ap.* 1887; m. 28 *June* 1843, *Mary Jane, da. of William Henry Hoare of The Grove, Mitcham, d.* 1 *Dec.* 1888; *and had issue.*

See p. 199, Nos. 7147, and 7154–7164; p. 190, Nos. 6852–6857.

2a. Lord Henry FitzGerald, b. 30 *July* 1761; d. 8 *July* 1829; m. 4 *Aug.* 1791, *Charlotte, suo jure 21st Baroness de Ross* [*E.*], d. 9 *Jan.* 1831; *and had issue.*

See the Tudor Roll of "The Blood Royal of Britain," p. 254 *et seq.*, Nos. 23286–23323.

3a. Lord Edward FitzGerald, the Irish Patriot, b. 15 *Oct.* 1763; d. 4 *June* 1798; m. (*at Tournay*) 27 *Dec.* 1792, *Stephanie Caroline Anne Syms, known as Pamela, and said to have been a natural da. of the Duke of Orleans (who re-m.* [——] *Pitcairn, U.S. Consul at Hamburg*), d. *Nov.* 1831; *and had issue* to 3b.

1b. Edward Fox FitzGerald, Capt. 10th *Hussars and 3rd Dragoons, b.* 10 *Oct.* 1794; d. 25 *Jan.* 1863; m. 6 *Nov.* 1827, *Jane, da. of Sir John Dean Paul, 1st Bart.* [*U.K.*], d. 2 *Nov.* 1891; *and had issue.*

See the Clarence Volume, p. 101, Nos. 911–912.

2b. Pamela FitzGerald, b. 1795; d. 25 *Nov.* 1869; m. *as 2nd wife, Sir Guy Campbell, 1st Bart.* [*U.K.*], *C.B.*, b. 21 *Nov.* 1820; d. 26 *Jan. 1849*; *and had issue* 1c to 9c.

1c. Sir Edward FitzGerald Campbell, 2nd Bart. [*U.K.*], *Col. and Lieut.-Col.* 60th *Regt.*, b. 25 *Oct.* 1822; d. 23 *Nov.* 1882; m. 25 *Oct.* 1853, *Georgiana Charlotte Theophila, 2nd da. of Sir Theophilus Metcalfe, 4th Bart.* [*U.K.*], d. 17 *Oct.* 1872; *and had issue* 1d to 10d.

1d. Sir Guy Theophilus Campbell, 3rd Bart. [U.K.], Lieut.-Col. Reserve of Officers, *late* King's Royal Rifle Corps, &c. (*The Lodge, Thames Ditton*), b. 16 Oct. 1854; m. 30 Ap. 1884, Nina, da. of Frederick Lehmann of 15 Berkeley Square, W.; and has issue 1e to 5e.

1e. Guy Colin Campbell, b. 31 Jan. 1885.

2e. Ronald Ion Campbell, b. 7 June 1890.

3e. Edward FitzGerald Campbell, b. 7 Oct. 1893.

4e. John Archibald Campbell, b. 18 Feb. 1898.

5e. Sylvia Nina Campbell, b. 18 Mar. 1888.

2d. Charles James Napier Campbell (*Thames Ditton*), b. (twin) 5 Feb. 1856; m. 18 Feb. 1889, Geraldine Harriette, da. of the Rev. Charles Stuart Stanford, D.D.; and has issue 1e.

1e. Edward FitzGerald Campbell, b. Sept. 1890.

3d. Gerald Fitzgerald Campbell (*Sports*), b. 25 Ap. 1862.

4d. Rev. Colin Arthur FitzGerald Campbell, Rector of Street, *formerly* Senior Domestic Chaplain to the late Archbishop of Canterbury (*Street Rectory, Somerset*), b. (twin) 17 June 1863.

5d. Percy FitzGerald Campbell (*Holta Tea Estate, Kangra Valley, Punjab*), b. 12 June 1865; m. 1889, Isabel, da. of R. Ballard of Palumpar, Kangra Valley; and has issue 1e to 3e.

1e. Ion Percy Fitzgerald Campbell, b. Nov. 1890.

2e. Gerald Arthur FitzGerald Campbell, b. May 1893.

3e. Madeline Georgiana Annie Campbell. [Nos. 41583 to 41661.

# of The Blood Royal

6*d*. Ion Douglas FitzGerald Campbell, Supt. of Govt. Estates, Terai and Bhaber, U.P. and Oudh (*Richmond House, Naini Tal, N.W. Provinces, India*), *b.* 12 Mar. 1868; *m.* 8 May 1891, Mabel, da. of Col. Unsworth Quin of Shanganan, Bray, J.P.; and has issue 1*e* to 3*e*.

1*e*. Ion Edward Fitzgerald Campbell, *b.* 12 Mar. 1897.

2*e*. Nina Mabel Mary Campbell, *b.* 29 Dec. 1892.

3*e*. Pamela Georgiana Theophila Campbell, *b.* 25 Ap. 1899.

7*d*. George Theophilus Campbell (*Sports*), *b.* 17 Oct. 1862.

8*d*. Annie Charlotte Campbell, *m.* 3 Dec. 1896, Stratford Hely Hutchinson Keightley (17 *Church Street, Kensington, W.*).

9*d*. Finetta Madeline Julia Campbell, *m.* 12 Sept. 1894, Major the Hon. Charles Granville Bruce, M.V.O., Indian Staff Corps.

10*d*. Griselda Mary Theophila Campbell, *m.* 7 June 1894, Dudley Francis Amelius Hervey, C.M.G., M.R.A.S., F.R.G.S. (*Westfields, Aldeburgh, Suffolk*); and has issue 1*e* to 2*e*.

1*e*. Dudley Edward Francis Cyril Hervey, *b.* 12 May 1895.

2*e*. Griselda Harriet Violet Finetta Georgiana Hervey, *b.* 1 Oct. 1901.

2*c*. Frederic Augustus Campbell, Capt. *late* 60th Rifles, a Gentleman Usher to H.M. the Queen, *b.* 15 Mar. 1839; *m.* Aug. 1862, Emma Mary, da. of Major Hugh Higgins-Brabazon of Brabazon Park, co. Mayo; and has issue 1*d* to 4*d*.

1*d*. John St. Clair Campbell, *b.* 23 May 1865.

2*d*. Guy Edward Spencer Campbell, *b.* 1873.

3*d*. Florence Emma Augusta Campbell.

4*d*. Pamela Louisa Augusta Ambrosa Campbell, *m.* 2 June 1891, Lord Ernest William Hamilton (*Shantock Hall, Bovington, Herts*); and has issue 1*e* to 4*e*.

1*e*. Guy Ernest Frederic Hamilton, *b.* 11 Nov. 1894.

2*e*. John George Peter Hamilton, *b.* 15 Oct. 1900.

3*e*. Mary Brenda Hamilton, *b.* 28 Mar. 1897.

4*e*. Jean Barbara Hamilton, *b.* 6 Sept. 1898.

3*c*. *Pamela Louisa Campbell*, d. 1 *Feb.* 1859; m. 20 *July* 1841, *the Rev. Charles Stuart Stanford, D.D., Rector of St. Thomas', and Preb. of Christchurch, Dublin*, d. (–); *and had issue* 1*d to* 5*d*.

1*d*. Guy Howard Stanford (*Riverside, Upton Borrine, Quebec*), *b.* Nov. 1842; *m.* Julia, da. of Charles Warne of Upper Borrine.

2*d*. Charles Edward FitzGerald Stanford, Head Master of St. Aubyn School, Rottingdean (*St. Aubyn's School, Rottingdean*), *b.* July 1854; *m.* 1892, Ellen Mary, da. of Henry Lucius Dampier, C.I.E.; and has issue 1*e*.

1*e*. Mary Agnes Geraldine Stanford, *b.* 1895.

3*d*. Harriet Geraldine Stanford, *b.* 1848; *m.* 1889, Charles James Napier Campbell (*Weston Grange, Thames Ditton*); and has issue 1*e*.

1*e*. Edward FitzGerald Campbell, *b.* 1890.

4*d*. Lucy Frances Felicité Stanford, *b.* 1852; *m.* 1891, Reginald Bean Anderson (*Windsor House, Bodmin, Cornwall*).

5*d*. Helen Emily Stanford (*Weston Grange, Thames Ditton*), *b.* 1856; *m.* Edward Frederick FitzGerald Campbell, *d.* 1904.

4*c*. *Georgina Geneviève Louisa Campbell*, d. 6 *Ap.* 1899; m. 29 *Ap.* 1847, *Thomas Henry Preston of Moreby Hall, near York, J.P., D.L., formerly Capt.* 7*th Hussars*, d. 3 *Feb.* 1906; *and had issue* 1*d to* 3*d*.

1*d*. Henry Edward Preston, J.P. (*Middlethorpe Manor, York*), *b.* 13 July 1857; *m.* 1886, Beatrice, da. of the Most Rev. William Thomson, D.D., Archbishop of York; and has issue 1*e* to 2*e*.

1*e*. Thomas Preston, *b.* 1886.

2*e*. Beatrice Zoë Preston.

[Nos. 41662 to 41690.

473

The Plantagenet Roll

2*d*. Maria Emma Georgiana Preston, *m*. 1st, 1 June 1871, William Ulick O'Connor (Cuffe), 4th Earl of Desart [I.] (marriage dissolved 11 May 1878); 2ndly, Charles Sugden; and has issue 1*e*.

1*e*. Lady Kathleen Mary Alexina Cuffe, *m*. 23 July 1895, Col. Sir Thomas Edward Milborne-Swinnerton-Pilkington, 12th Bart. [S.] (2 *Upper Berkeley Street, S.W.; Chevet Park, Wakefield*); and has issue 1*f* to 4*f*.

1*f*. Arthur William Milborne-Swinnerton-Pilkington, *b*. 7 Ap. 1898.

2*f*. Ulick O'Connor Milborne-Swinnerton-Pilkington, *b*. 1903.

3*f*. Phyllis Milborne-Swinnerton-Pilkington.

4*f*. Pamela Irene Milborne-Swinnerton-Pilkington.

3*d*. Pamela Mary Preston.

5*c*. *Lucy Sophia Julia Campbell, d*. 13 *Nov*. 1897; *m*. 20 *Nov*. 1848, *Gen. Sir Edward Selby-Smyth, K.C.M.G., d*. 26 *Sept*. 1896; *and had issue* 1*d to* 2*d*.

1*d*. *Edward Guy Selby-Smyth, Lieut.-Col. Royal Irish Rifles, b*. 14 *May* 1851; *d*. 30 *July* 1904; *m*. 24 *June* 1879, *Georgiana Florence* (*Darby House, Sunbury-on-Thames;* 42 *Cromwell Gardens, S.W.*), *da. of Capt. the Hon. John James Bury, R.E.; and had issue* 1*e to* 3*e*.

1*e*. Miles Bury Selby-Smyth, Lieut. 7th Batt. Rifle Brigade, *b*. 17 Nov. 1884.

2*e*. Lucy Theresa Selby-Smyth.

3*e*. Eva Beaujolois Selby-Smyth.

2*d*. Geraldine Lucy Isabella Selby-Smyth, *m*. 1 June 1882, Col. Charles Haggard, 2nd Batt. Royal Irish Rifles (*Berkeley Towers, Western Road, Bournemouth*); and has issue 1*e* to 6*e*.

1*e*. Christopher Amyard Haggard, *b*. 21 Sept. 1885.

2*e*. Bevis Charles Haggard, *b*. 4 Sept. 1895.

3*e*. Denis James Haggard, *b*. 28 Oct. 1901.

4*e*. Pamela Patricia Haggard.

5*e*. Mab Geraldine Haggard.

6*e*. Georgiana Dulic Caroline Haggard.

6*c*. *Mary Louisa Campbell, d*. (–); *m*. 8 *July* 1867, *Major William Frederick Carleton*, 60*th Rifles; and had* (*with other*) *issue* 1*d to* 2*d*.

1*d*. Guy Frederic Carleton, *b*. 8 Oct. 1871.

2*d*. Margaret Theodora Carleton.

7*c*. Emily Campbell, *m*. 17 Nov. 1859, Major Charles David Cunynghame Ellis (*La Luquette, Hyères, Var, France; Branksome Chine House, near Bournemouth*); and has issue 1*d* to 4*d*.

1*d*. Augustus Frederick Guy Ellis (*Fort George Pen, Jamaica*), *b*. 10 Dec. 1868; *m*. 10 Jan. 1899, Mary Agnes, widow of the Hon. E. G. Levy of Jamaica, and da. of the Hon. Henry Westmorland of Jamaica.

2*d*. Mary Pamela Ellis (11 *Dick Place, Edinburgh*), *m*. as 2nd wife, 2 July 1889, Col. David Milne-Home of Wedderburn, J.P., D.L., *d*. 19 Nov. 1901; and has issue 1*e*.

1*e*. Charles Alexander Milne-Home, *b*. 25 Ap. 1891.

3*d*. Helen Louisa Georgina Ellis, *m*. 16 Ap. 1885, James Grahame Stewart (13 *Rue du Lycée, Pau*); and has issue 1*e* to 2*e*.

1*e*. John Cecil Stewart, *b*. 1897.

2*e*. Felicia Louise Marie Stewart, *b*. 1899.

4*d*. Lucy Emily Madeline Ellis.

8*c*. Madeline Caroline Frances Eden Campbell, *m*. 16 Oct. 1860, Capt. the Hon. Percy Scawen Wyndham, J.P., D.L., *formerly* M.P. (44 *Belgrave Square, S.W.; Clouds, Salisbury*); and has issue 1*d* to 5*d*.

1*d*. Right Hon. George Wyndham, P.C., M.P., sometime (1900–1905) Chief Secretary for Ireland, &c. (*Saighton Grange, Chester;* 35 *Park Lane, W.*), *b*.

[Nos. 41691 to 41719.

# of The Blood Royal

29 Aug. 1863; *m.* 7 Feb. 1887, Sibell Mary, Dowager Countess Grosvenor, da. of Richard George (Lumley), 9th Earl of Scarbrough [E.]; and has issue 1*e*.

   1*e*. Percy Lyulph Wyndham, *b.* 5 Dec. 1887.

   2*d*. Guy Percy Wyndham, Lieut.-Col. Comdg. 16th Lancers, *b.* 19 Jan. 1865; *m.* 14 May 1892, Edwina Virginia Joanna, widow of John Monck Brooke, da. of the Rev. Frederick Fitzpatrick of Cloone; and has issue 1*e* to 3*e*.

   1*e*. George Heremon Wyndham, *b.* 25 Oct. 1893.

   2*e*. Guy Richard Charles Wyndham, *b.* 29 Aug. 1896.

   3*e*. Olivia Madeline Grace Mary Wyndham, *b.* 30 Nov. 1897.

   3*d*. Mary Constance Wyndham, *m.* 9 Aug. 1883, Hugo Richard Wemyss-Charteris-Douglas, Lord Elcho (*Stanway, Winchcombe*); and has issue.
See the Clarence Volume, p. 253, Nos. 6096–6101.

   4*d*. Madeline Pamela Constance Blanche Wyndham, *m.* 23 July 1888, Charles Robert Whorwood Adeane, J.P., D.L. (*Babraham, near Cambridge*); and has issue.
See the Clarence Volume, p. 98, Nos. 819–823.

   5*d*. Pamela Geneviève Adelaide Wyndham, *m.* 11 July 1895, Sir Edward Priaulx Tennant, 2nd Bart. [U.K.] (*Wilsford House, Salisbury; 31 Lennox Gardens, S.W.*); and has issue 1*e* to 4*e*.

   1*e*. Edward Wyndham Tennant, *b.* 1 July 1897.

   2*e*. Christopher Grey Tennant, *b.* 14 June 1899.

   3*e*. David Francis Tennant, *b.* 22 May 1902.

   4*e*. Clarissa Madeline Georgiana Felicite Tennant, *b.* 13 July 1896.

   9*c*. Julia Elizabeth Henrietta Campbell (*Chuffs, Maidenhead*), *m.* 25 Sept. 1862, Major-Gen. Fitzroy William Fremantle, C.B., *d.* 12 Feb. 1894; and has issue 1*d* to 4*d*.

   1*d*. Guy Fremantle, *late* Capt. and Brevet-Major Coldstream Guards (13 *Hans Place, S.W.*), *b.* 26 May 1867; *m.* 7 June 1899, Alice Florence, widow of Col. Dickson of Chatto, da. of J. W. Seaburne.

   2*d*. Agnes Fremantle, *m.* 9 Jan. 1890, Capt. Charles Henry Sheffield Pretyman, *late* R.N.

   3*d*. Pamela Fremantle.

   4*d*. Frances Fremantle, *m.* 9 Jan. 1902, Lieut.-Col. George Handcock Thesiger, Rifle Brigade, D.A.A.G.

   3*b*. *Lucy Louisa FitzGerald, b.* 1798; *d. Sept.* 1826; m. 5 *Sept.* 1825, *Capt. George Francis Lyon, R.N.,* d. 8 *Oct.* 1832; *and had issue* 1*c*.

   1*c*. *Lucy Pamela Sophia Lyon, b. Sept.* 1826; *d.* 10 *Ap.* 1904; m. 1849, *the Rev. T. Ovens of Highwood, Essex; and had issue* 1*d* to 3*d*.

   1*d*. Gerald Hedley Ovens, C.B., Col. Border Regt. (*Kildare, Hartley, Plymouth*), *b.* 22 May 1856; *m.* 1893, Julia, da. of Col. T. T. Carter Campbell, R.E.; and has issue 1*e* to 3*e*.

   1*e*. Sheila Lucy Pamela Ovens, *b.* 24 Jan. 1894.

   2*e*. Lucy Emily Ovens, *b.* 28 Aug. 1898.

   3*e*. Pamela Noel Geraldine Ovens, *b.* 15 Dec. 1903.

   2*d*. Geraldine Lucy Ovens, *m.* 1890, A. Thompson.

   3*d*. Lucy Elizabeth Sophia Ovens (11 *Richmond Terrace, Clifton*).

   4*a*. *Lord Robert Stephen FitzGerald, M.P., b.* 15 *Jan.* 1765; *d.* 2 *Jan.* 1833; m. 22 *July* 1792, *Sophia, da. of Charles Fielding, R.N.,* d. 19 *Sept.* 1834; *and had issue* 1*b* to 2*b*.

   1*b*. *Matilda FitzGerald, b.* 31 *May* 1793; *d.* 11 *Mar.* 1850; m. 24 *Dec.* 1817, *General the Chevalier Victor de Marion Gaja of Languedoc, d.* 31 *Jan.* 1875; *and had issue* 1*c* to 2*c*.

   1*c*. *Emilie de Gaja, d.* (–); m. *Mary Anne, da. of* [——] *Hammond; and had issue* 1*d*.

   1*d*. Emilie de Gaja, *m.* Henry Hoare (*Dunton Buck's Green, Rudgwick, Sussex*), *s.p.* [Nos. 41720 to 41754.

475

The Plantagenet Roll

2c. *Emilie de Gaja*, d. 1883; m. *Jan.* 1846, *Sir Edmund Bradstreet, 6th Bart.* [*I.*], b. 24 *Aug.* 1820; d. 30 *Mar.* 1905; *and had issue* 1*d to* 4*d.*

1*d.* Sir Edward Simon Victor Bradstreet, 7th Bart. [I.] (*Castilla, Clontarf, Dublin*), b. 27 May 1856; *m.* 1888, Fortuna Mary, da. of Fiori de Lerichi of Bougie, Algeria; and has issue 1*e.*

1*e.* Gerald Edmund Bradstreet, b. 14 Feb. 1891.

2*d.* Anna Matilda Clara Bradstreet; *unm.*

3*d.* Geraldine Mary Emily Bradstreet; *unm.*

4*d.* Sophia Alicia Bradstreet; *unm.*

2*b. Sophia Charlotte FitzGerald*, b. (*twin*) 14 *Mar.* 1799; d. 19 *Mar.* 1875; m. *Nov.* 1831, *the Rev. Henry Dalton*, d. (–); *and had issue.*

5*a.* [——] Ogilvie (son by 2nd husband).[1]

6*a. Lady Emelia Maria Margaret FitzGerald*, b. 15 *Mar.* 1751; d. 8 *Ap.* 1818; m. 20 *Aug.* 1774, *Charles (Coote), 1st Earl of Bellomont* [*I.*], *&c., K.B.*, bapt. 12 *Ap.* 1738; d. 20 *Oct.* 1800; *and had issue* 4 *das. who all* d. *unm.*

7*a. Charlotte Mary Gertrude* (née *FitzGerald*), *suo jure* 1*st Baroness Rayleigh* (1821) [*U.K.*], b. 29 *May* 1758; d. 12 *Sept.* 1836; m. 23 *Feb.* 1789, *Col. Joseph Holden Strutt of Terling Place, M.P.*, d. 18 *Feb.* 1845; *and had issue* 1*b.*

1*b. John James (Strutt), 2nd Baron Rayleigh* [*U.K.*], b. 30 *Jan.* 1796; d. 14 *June* 1873; m. 3 *Feb.* 1842, *Clara Elizabeth La Touche, da. of Capt. Richard Vicars, R.E.*, d. 4 *Mar.* 1900; *and had issue* 1*c* to 6*c.*

1*c.* John William (Strutt), 3rd Baron Rayleigh [U.K.], O.M., D.C.L., LL.D., F.R.S., &c. &c. (*Terling Place, Witham, Essex*), b. 12 Nov. 1843; *m.* 19 July 1871, Evelyn Georgiana Mary, da. of James Maitland Balfour of Whittinghame; and has issue.

See p. 218, Nos. 7724–7726.

2*c.* Hon. Richard Strutt, Member of the London Stock Exchange (*Rayleigh House, Chelsea Embankment, S.W.*), b. 29 Feb. 1848; *m.* 24 Ap. 1879, Augusta, da. of Charles (Neville), 5th Baron Braybrooke [G.B.], d. 22 Jan. 1903; and has issue 1*d* to 3*d.*

1*d.* Richard Neville Strutt, b. 22 July 1886.

2*d.* Geoffrey St. John Strutt, b. 28 Mar. 1888.

3*d.* Olivia Maude Strutt, b. 11 Sept. 1890.

3*c.* Hon. Charles Hedley Strutt, J.P., N.P. (*Blunts Hall, Witham, Essex; 90 Onslow Gardens, S.W.*), b. 18 Ap. 1849.

4*c.* Hon. Edward Gerald Strutt, a Surveyor and Member of Council of Surveyors' Institution (*Whitelands, Hatfield Peverel, Witham*), b. 10 Ap. 1854; *m.* 29 Oct. 1878, Maria Louisa, da. of John Jolliffe Tufnell of Langleys; and has issue 1*d* to 6*d.*

1*d.* Gerald Murray Strutt, *formerly* Lieut. Suffolk Imp. Yeo. (*Ampton, Bury St. Edmunds*), b. 9 Oct. 1880.

2*d.* John James Strutt, Professional Associate of Surveyors' Institution, b. 26 Oct. 1881.

3*d.* Edward Jolliffe Strutt, b. 4 Jan. 1884.

4*d.* Emily Norah Strutt, b. 10 Sept. 1879.

5*d.* Evelyn Mary Strutt, b. 6 Feb. 1883.

6*d.* Clara Helena Strutt, b. 24 Mar. 1888.

5*c.* Hon. *Hedley Vicars Strutt*, b. 17 *July* 1864; d. 22 *Jan.* 1891; m. *Sept.* 1885, *Elizabeth, da. of J. Knight*, d. 1888; *and had issue* 1*d.*

1*d.* Hilda Elizabeth Strutt, b. 28 Oct. 1886.   [Nos. 41755 to 41776.

---

[1] Brydges' "Collins," vi. p. 197.

# of The Blood Royal

6c. Hon. Clara Emily Charlotte Strutt (*St. Catherine's Court, Bath ; 90 Onslow Gardens, S.W.*), *m.* 12 Sept. 1871, John Paley, *d.* 4 Oct. 1894 ; and has issue 1*d.*

1*d.* George Arthur Paley (*Ampton Hall, Bury St. Edmunds*), *b.* 14 Nov. 1874 ; *m.* 22 Feb. 1900, Frances Mary, da. of Percy Brodrick Bernard ; and has issue 1*e* to 2*e.*

1*e.* Percy John Paley, *b.* 26 June 1904.

2*e.* Gerald George Paley, *b.* 23 Nov. 1905.

8*a. Lady Lucy Anne FitzGerald*, *b.* 5 *Feb.* 1771 ; *d.* 1851 ; *m.* 31 *July* 1802, *Thomas Foley of Abermarles, co. Carmarthen, G.C.B., Admiral R.N.*, *d.* 1833.

9*a. Cecilia Margaret Ogilvie*, *b.* 9 *July* 1775 ; *d.* 1824 ; *m.* 12 *July* 1795, *Charles Lock of Norbury Park, Surrey*, *d.* 1804 ; *and had issue* 1*b to* 2*b.*

1*b. Emily Frederica Lock*, *b.* 1796 ; *d.* 1822 ; *m. c.* 1815, *Count George de Very ; and had issue* 1*c to* 3*c.*

1*c.* Count Eugene de Very, in Italian Navy.

2*c.* Count George de Very, in Italian R.A.

3*c.* Emily de Very.

2*b. Lucy Frances Lock*, *b.* 28 *June* 1801 ; *d.* 1892 ; *m.* 1826, *Capt. Alexander Ellice, R.N.*, *d.* 1853 ; *and had issue* 1*c to* 4*c.*

1*c. Augustus Edward Ellice*, *b.* 1827 ; *d.* 1866 ; *m.* [——], *da. of* [——] *Tour-field*, *d.* 1903.

2*c. Cecilia Elizabeth Ellice*, *d.* 1890 ; *m.* 1874, *Edward Wallace Goolake of Wadley*, *d.* (? s.p.) 1881.

3*c. Katharine Frederica Ellis*, *d.* 13 *Ap.* 1884 ; *m.* 16 *June* 1855, *Francis Fortescue, D.L., Capt. Scots Guards*, *b.* 19 *Aug.* 1826 ; *d.* 1897 ; *and had issue* 1*d* to 3*d.*

1*d.* Henry Fortescue, Col. 17th Lancers (*Falmouth House, Newmarket*), *b.* 15 May 1856 ; *m.* 26 May 1885, Maud Elizabeth, da. of William Holden.

2*d.* Francis Alexander Fortescue, Col. 60th Rifles (*Colonel's House, New Barracks, Gosport*), *b.* 10 Ap. 1858 ; *m.* 25 June 1885, Mary Theresa, da. of Henry T. J. Jenkinson ; and has issue 1*e.*

1*e.* Katerine Fortescue, *b.* 1886.

3*d.* Hugh Charles Fortescue, Major and Hon. Lieut.-Col. 4th Batt. Oxford L.I. (*Brooks'*), *b.* 7 July 1860.

4*c.* Helen Anne Ellice, *b.* 1840 ; *m.* 28 Mar. 1881, Col. Percy Francis Lambart, *late* 5th Northumberland Fusiliers (*The Elms, Wisborough Green, Bellingshurst ; Arthur's*).

10*a. Emily Charlotte Ogilvie*, *b.* 12 *May* 1778 ; *d.* 22 *Jan.* 1832 ; *m.* 29 *Ap.* 1799, *Charles George Beauclerk*, *b.* 20 *Jan.* 1774 ; *d.* 25 Dec. 1846 ; *and had issue* 1*b to* 8*b.*

1*b. Aubrey William Beauclerk of Ardglass, co. Down, M.P.*, *b.* 20 Feb. 1802 ; *d.* 1 Feb. 1854 ; *m.* 1*st*, 13 Feb. 1834, Ida, *da. of Sir Charles Forster Goring, 7th Bart.* [*E.*], *d.* 23 *Ap.* 1838 ; 2*ndly*, 7 Dec. 1840, Rose Matilda, *da. of Joshua Robinson*, *d.* 20 *July* 1878 ; *and had issue* 1*c to* 4*c.*

1*c.* Aubrey De Vere Beauclerk, J.P., High Sheriff co. Down (*Ardglass, Down*), *b.* 5 Oct. 1837 ; *m.* 1st, 1 Dec. 1858, Evelyn Matilda, da. of Henry FitzRoy of Salcey (who obtained a divorce Nov. 1895) ; 2ndly, 16 Nov. 1895, Catherine Lucy, widow of Com. J. Collier Tuckner, R.N., da. of [——] ; *s.p.s.*

2*c.* Augusta Beauclerk, *m.* 4 Jan. 1866, Thomas Edward Howe, Bar.-at-Law ; and has issue 1*d* to 6*d.*

1*d.* Henry Beauclerk Howe, in Bank of England (*Burlington Gardens, W.*), *b.* 27 Sept. 1869.

2*d.* Francis Cecil Howe, *b.* 11 June 1873.

3*d.* Reginald Lake Howe, *b.* 4 Sept. 1874.

4*d.* Charles Maitland Howe, *b.* 1883.

5*d.* Ida Louisa Howe.

6*d.* Evelyn Howe.

[Nos. 41777 to 41796.

3 P

Ꮯꜧe Ᵽlantagenet Ꭱoll

3c.[2] Louisa Katherine Beauclerk (*Millbeck Cottage, Keswick, Cumberland*).

4c. Isabella Julia Beauclerk, *m.* 19 Oct. 1867, Surgeon-Major George Palatiano, M.D. (*Corfu, Ionian Islands*) ; and has issue 1d to 3d.

1d. Constantine Beauclerk Palatiano, *b.* 11 Oct. 1868 ; *m.* 1901, Euphrosine, da. of [——] Rhally of Athens ; and has issue 1e.

1e. Anthony Palatiano, *b.* 1902.

2d. Louisa Katharine Aspasia Palatiano, *m.* 1897, Antonio Roditi of Corfu.

3d. Veronika Rosa Palatiano.

2b. *Charles Robert Beauclerk, Fellow of Caius Coll., Camb.,* b. 6 *Jan.* 1802 ; d. 22 *Feb.* 1872 ; m. *Mar.* 1842, *Joaquina, da. of H. E. Don Jose M. de Zamora, Chief Magistrate of Cuba,* d. 16 *Nov.* 1881 ; *and had issue* 1c *to* 6c.

1c. Ferdinand Beauclerk, Capt. (ret.) R.E. (*Naval and Military*), *b.* 15 Jan. 1851 ; *m.* 9 Feb. 1872, Emily, da. of Col. Robert Clifford Lloyd.

2c. Charles Sidney Beauclerk, *b.* 1 Jan. 1855.

3c. Henry Sidney Beauclerk, *b.* 25 Nov. 1857.

4c. Robert Sidney Beauclerk (*Port Oratava, Teneriffe*), *b.* 14 Dec. 1858 ; *m.* 30 Oct. 1894, Beatrice Annie Elliott, da. of Alfred Richard Hollebone ; and has issue 1d.

1d. Nevil Alfred de Vere Beauclerk, *b.* 13 Oct. 1895.

5c. William Topham Beauclerk, *b.* 1864.

6c. Mary Beauclerk, *b.* 17 Ap. 1861.

3b. *George Robert Beauclerk of King's Castle, co. Down, Capt. Royal Welsh Fusiliers,* b. 28 *Feb.* 1803 ; d. 5 *Dec.* 1803 ; m. 2 *June* 1861, *Maria Sarah* (22 *Eaton Place, Brighton*)*, da. of Ralph Lonsdale ; and had issue* 1c *to* 5c.

1c. Amelius George Beauclerk, *late* Lieut. 1st Vol. Batt. Suffolk Regt., *b.* 1 Oct. 1871.

2c. Georgiana Beauclerk.

3c. Caroline Elizabeth Beauclerk, *m.* 24 Ap. 1895, the Rev. Alfred Norris Cope, Vicar of Dormington with Bartestree (*Dormington Vicarage, Hereford*).

4c. Emily Kathleen Beauclerk.

5c. Ida Beauclerk, *m.* 30 July 1891, George Francis Berney (*Furze Bank, Wimbledon*) ; and has issue 1d to 3d.

1d. George Norman Berney, *b.* 14 June 1892.

2d. Diana Brenda Berney, *b.* 13 May 1894.

3d. Ida Rosemary Berney, *b.* 16 Sept. 1900.

4b. *Caroline Anne Beauclerk,* b. 12 *Jan.* 1804 ; d. 11 *Sept.* 1869 ; m. 20 *Oct.* 1829, *Robert Aldridge of St. Leonard's Forest, J.P., D.L., High Sheriff co. Sussex* 1815, b. 24 *June* 1801 ; d. 26 *May* 1871 ; *and had issue* 1c *to* 4c.

1c. *John Aldridge of St. Leonard's Forest, J.P., D.L., Col. Comdg. 3rd and* 4th *Batts. Royal Sussex Regt.,* b. 4 *Jan.* 1832 ; d. 23 *Feb.* 1888 ; m. 18 *July* 1863, *Mary Alethea, widow of Thomas Broadwood of Holmbush, da. of Samuel Matthews ; and had issue* 1d *to* 4d.

1d. Charles Powlett Aldridge, Capt. Royal Sussex Regt. (*St. Leonard's Forest, Horsham*), *b.* 27 Sept. 1866 ; *m.* 27 Ap. 1898, Gwladys Edith Henrietta, da. of Lieut.-Col. Thomas Faulconer Wisden of Broadwater ; and has issue 1e to 2e.

1e. Hilda Aldridge, *b.* 27 Ap. 1904.

2e. Diana Aldridge, *b.* 19 Mar. 1905.

2d. Herbert Henry Aldridge, *b.* 25 Feb. 1869.

3d. John Barttelot Aldridge, Capt. R.A., *b.* 8 Feb. 1871 ; *m.* 1 Aug. 1899, Margaret Jessie, da. of J. Goddard of the Manor House, Newton Harcourt.

4d. *Emily Marian Aldridge,* d. 16 *Mar.* 1897 ; m. 18 *June* 1891, *the Rev. Richard Aubrey Chichester Bevan ; and had issue* 1e *to* 2e.

1e. Robert Hesketh Bevan, *b.* Jan. 1892.

2e. Humphrey Charles Bevan, *b.* 28 Feb. 1895.   [Nos. 41797 to 41824.

478

# of The Blood Royal

2c. *Emily Louisa Aldridge,* d. 20 *Aug.* 1893; m. 1 *June* 1852, *Rev. the Hon. Robert Henley, M.A., Vicar of Putney (Eden Lodge, Putney); and had issue* 1d *to* 7d.

1d. Rev. Robert Eden Henley, M.A. (Oxon.), Vicar of Wharton (*Wharton Vicarage, near Winsford*), b. 10 Sept. 1861.

2d. Charles Beauclerk Henley, b. 7 Feb. 1869.

3d. Constance Laura Henley, m. 16 Ap. 1890, the Rev. Robert Stewart Gregory, Rector of Much Hadham (*Much Hadham Rectory, Herts*); and has issue 1e to 5e.

1e. Robert Henley Gregory, b. 1891.

2e. Francis Stewart Gregory, b. 1893.

3e. John Stephen Gregory, b. 1898.

4e. Violet Emily Gregory.

5e. Mary Noel Gregory.

4d. Beatrice Mary Henley.

5d. Ethel Maud Henley.

6d. Mildred Caroline Henley.

7d. Mabel Augusta Henley.

3c. Anne Maria Aldridge, *m.* 2 June 1855, Charles Spencer Scrase-Dickins of Coolhurst, J.P., D.L., d. 1 May 1884; and has issue.

See the Clarence Volume, p. 200, Nos. 3945–3952.

4c. *Caroline Diana Aldridge (Hampton Court Palace), m.* 24 Jan. 1857, Major the Hon. Charles James Keith-Falconer, b. 1 July 1832; d. 7 Jan. 1889; and has issue 1d to 6d.

1d. Charles Adrian Keith-Falconer (*The Garth, Bicester*), b. 12 Dec. 1861; *m.* 11 June 1887, Williamine Emily, da. of the Right Hon. William Wentworth FitzWilliam Hume Dick, P.C.; and has issue 1e.

1e. Adrian Wentworth Keith-Falconer, b. 17 June 1888.

2d. Diana Mary Keith-Falconer.

3d. Florence Keith-Falconer, *m.* 5 Aug. 1893, the Rev. Hesketh France-Hayhurst, *late* Vicar of Middlewich (*Middlewich, Cheshire*); and has issue 1e to 3e.

1e. Reginald Geoffrey France-Hayhurst, b. 7 May 1896.

2e. Marion France-Hayhurst, b. 2 June 1898.

3e. Cecily France-Hayhurst, b. 2 June 1901.

4d. Ida Madaleine Keith-Falconer.

5d. Evelyn Millicent Keith-Falconer.

6d. Sybil Blanche Keith-Falconer.

5b. *Diana Olivia Beauclerk,* b. 21 *June* 1806; d. 9 *Feb.* 1875; m. 10 *Ap.* 1823, *Sir Francis Fletcher-Vane, 3rd Bart.* [G.B.], b. 29 *Mar.* 1797; d. 15 *Feb.* 1842; *and had issue* 1c *to* 2c.

1c. Sir Henry Ralph Fletcher-Vane, 3rd Bart. [G.B.], J.P., D.L., Hon. Col. Westmorland and Cumberland Yeo. Cav. (*Hutton-in-the-Forest, Penrith; Scarness Cottage, Bassenthwaite, Keswick*), b. 13 Jan. 1830; *m.* 12 Ap. 1871, Margaret, da. of Thomas Steuart Gladstone of Capenoch.

2c. *Gertrude Elizabeth Fletcher-Vane,* d. 21 *Aug.* 1893; m. 29 *Ap.* 1857, *Major Vincent Wing,* d. 30 *Sept.* 1874; *and had issue* 1d *to* 2d.

1d. Frederick Drummond Vincent Wing, C.B., Lieut.-Col. R.A., b. 29 Nov. 1860.

2d. Evelyn Diana Wing.

6b. *Jane Elizabeth Beauclerk,* b. 1807; d. 15 *July* 1892; m. 24 *July* 1830, *Henry FitzRoy of Salcey Lawn, co. Northants,* d. 5 *Dec.* 1877; *and had issue.*

See the Tudor Roll of "The Blood Royal of Britain," pp. 334–336, Nos. 26588–26615. [Nos. 41825 to 41887.

The Plantagenet Roll

7b. Isabella Elizabeth Beauclerk, b. 10 *Oct.* 1808; d. 21 *July* 1864; m. 12 *Mar.* 1840, *Adm. John William Montagu, R.N.*, b. 18 *Jan.* 1790; d. 12 *Dec.* 1882; *and had issue* 1c *to* 3c.

1c. *George Edward Montagu, J.P., Capt.* 84th *Foot*, b. 19 *Feb.* 1841; d.v.p. 23 *Nov.* 1878; m. *Annie Mary Augusta, da. of Edward Devlin of Enniskillen (who re-m.* 19 *Aug.* 1881 [——] *Curry*); *and had issue* 1d *to* 2d.

1d. John William Montagu of Stowell, b. 1876.

2d. James Drogo Montagu (38 *Lexham Gardens, S.W.*), b. 10 July 1878.

2c. Annie Diana Montagu, m. 19 May 1881, the Rev. William Francis Dashwood Lang (*Lisburne, Torquay*).

3c. Emily Stuart Montagu, m. 15 Jan. 1884, Col. Arthur Corbet Maurice, *late* Royal Munster Fusiliers.

8b. Katherine Katinka Beauclerk, b. *May* 1812; d. 1 *June* 1882; m. 5 *Ap.* 1845, *Col. Sir George Ashley Maude, K.C.B.*, b. 11 *Nov.* 1817; d. 31 *May* 1894; *and had issue* 1c *to* 7c.

1c. Charles John Maude, Assist. Paymaster-Gen. (*Royal Mews, Hampton Court; Arranmore House, co. Donegal*), b. 17 Mar. 1847; m. 14 June 1871, Sarah Maria, da. of Admiral Sir Watkin Owen Pell; and has issue 1d to 2d.

1d. Hubert William Maude, b. 27 June 1877.

2d. Constance Margaret Maude.

2c. Eustace Downman Maude, Com. R.N. (ret.), b. 31 Aug. 1848; m. 1885, Amy, da. of Oliver Williams; and has issue 1d to 4d.

1d. George Maude, b. 1889.

2d. Ruth Katinka Maude.

3d. Cyrene Marie Maude.

4d. Valerie Beauclerc Maude.

3c. Ashley Henry Maude, Bar.-at-Law, J.P., C.C., *late* Clerk in Board of Trade (*Ivy Mount, Eastbourne*), b. 14 Mar. 1850; m. 29 Ap. 1876, Emma Constance, da. and co-h. of John Snowdon Henry of Eastdene, I.W., D.L., d. 1 Sept. 1889; and has issue 1d to 5d.

1d. Edith Frances Maude, b. 19 Mar. 1877.

2d. Sybil Margaret Maude, b. 26 Feb. 1878.

3d. Dorothea Clara Maude, b. 26 Feb. 1879.

4d. Frances Blanche Maude, b. 26 Ap. 1880.

5d. Alice Muriel Maude, b. 5 Ap. 1881.

4c. Aubrey Maurice Maud, *late* Lieut.-Col. the Cameronians (50 *Seymour Street, W.*), b. 1 Aug. 1852; m. 23 July 1883, Amy Florence, da. of Sir Thomas Lucas, 1st Bart. [U.K.]; and has issue 1d to 2d.

1d. Christian George Maude.

2d. Nancy Maude.

5c. Alwyne Edward Maude (*Drottningholm, Sweden*), b. 23 July 1854; m. 1st, June 1880, Katherine Lucy, da. of John Campbell, d. 1892; 2ndly, 2 Aug. 1895, Louise, widow of [——] Laurin of Stockholm and Breidablik; and has issue 1d to 2d.

1d. Kathleen Cecil Maude, b. 1881.

2d. Charmian Maude, b. 1886.

6c. Frederick William Maude, C.C. (*The Elms, New Romney, Kent;* 9 *Cadogan Gardens, S.W.*), b. 28 Feb. 1857; m. 8 Oct. 1878, Ellen Maude, da. of Sir John Kelk, 1st Bart. [U.K.], and has issue 1d to 3d.

1d. John William Ashley Maude, b. 12 Oct. 1885.

2d. Norah Diana Maude, b. 21 Ap. 1889.

3d. Catherine Elizabeth Maude, b. 23 Mar. 1892.

7c. Emily Diana Maude, m. 7 Nov. 1867, Jonathan Peel Baird, J.P. (*Castlemains, Douglas, Lanarkshire*); and has issue 1d to 8d.　　　[Nos. 41888 to 41916.

# of The Blood Royal

1*d*. Randolph Eustace Wemyss Baird, Capt. 3rd Batt. H.L.I., *b.* 1879.

2*d*. Helena Emily Baird.

3*d*. Alice Anne Baird, ⎫
4*d*. Katrine Maclean Baird, ⎬ twins.
⎭

5*d*. Mary Isabel Baird.

6*d*. Diana Margaret Baird.

7*d*. Georgina Marian Baird.

8*d*. Constance Kennedy Baird.   [Nos. 41917 to 41924.

---

407. Descendants of Lady SARAH LENNOX (see Table XXXVIII.), *b.* 14 Feb. 1745 ; *d.* Aug. 1826 ; *m.* 2ndly, as 2nd wife, 27 Aug. 1781, Col. the Hon. GEORGE NAPIER, *b.* 11 Mar. 1751 ; *d.* 13 Oct. 1804 ; and had issue 1*a* to 3*a*.

1*a. Sir George Thomas Napier, K.C.B., Gen. in the Army,* b. 30 *June* 1784 ; d. 8 *Sept.* 1855 ; m. 1*st*, 28 *Oct.* 1812, *Margaret, da. of John Craig of Glasgow,* d. 31 *Aug.* 1819 ; *and had issue* 1*b to* 4*b.*

1*b. George Thomas Conolly Napier, C.B., Major-Gen. in the Army,* b. 1816 ; d. (? s.p.l.) 5 *May* 1873.

2*b. John Moore Napier, Capt. 62nd Foot,* b. 1817 ; d. (*in Scinde*) 7 *July* 1846 ; m. *July* 1843, *Maria, da. of Capt. Richard Alcock, R.N., and had issue* 1*c.*

1*c. Sarah Napier,* b. (*posthumous*) 11 *July* 1846 ; d. 30 *Ap.* 1901 ; m. 23 *June* 1872, *Col. Lord Albert Charles Seymour,* d. 21 *Mar.* 1891 ; *and had issue.*

See the Clarence Volume, p. 133, Nos. 1698-1700.

3*b. William Craig Emilius Napier, K.M., Gen. in the Army, and Governor of the Royal Military College, Sandhurst,* b. 18 *Mar.* 1818 ; d. 1903 ; m. 21 *Ap.* 1845, *Emily Cephalonia* (*Oaklands, Waterlooville, Hants*), *nat. da. of Gen. Sir Charles James Napier, G.C.B. ; and had issue* 1*c to* 7*c.*

1*c.* Charles James Napier, *late* Capt. E. Surrey Regt., *b.* 2 Aug. 1858 ; *m.* 1887, Ellen Frederica, da. of Frederick Thompson, C.E. ; and has issue 1*d.*

1*d.* Cecil Napier.

2*c.* Georgiana Anne Emily Napier.

3*c.* Hester Johnson Napier.

4*c.* Emily Caroline Napier.

5*c.* Margaret Cephalonia Napier.

6*c.* Sarah Lennox Napier.

7*c.* Violet Bunbury Napier.

4*b. Sarah Napier,* d. 29 *Ap.* 1850 ; m. *Thomas Clarke.*

2*a. Sir William Francis Patrick Napier, K.C.B., Gen. in the Army, Author of the* " *History of the Peninsular War,*" b. 17 *Dec.* 1785 ; d. 12 *Feb.* 1860 ; m. 14 *Mar.* 1812, *Caroline Amelia, da. of Gen. the Hon. Henry Edward Fox,* d. 1860 ; *and had issue.*

See p. 467, Nos. 41330–41432.

3*a. Henry Edward Napier, Capt. R.N.,* b. 5 *Mar.* 1789 ; d. 13 *Oct.* 1853 ; m. *Caroline, da. of* [——] *Bennett,* d. 5 *Sept.* 1836 ; *and had issue* 1*b to* 2*b.*

1*b. Charles George Napier, F.G.S., C.E.,* b. 20 *July* 1829 ; d. 2 *Sept.* 1882 ; m. 13 *Dec.* 1860, *Susanna, da. of Samuel John Caroline; and had issue* 1*c to* 3*c.*

1*c.* Henry Edward Napier, Major 1st Batt. Cheshire Regt., *b.* 21 Sept. 1861 ; *m.* 11 Oct. 1887, Mary Ada, da. of Capt. W. F. Stewart, B.S.C. ; and has issue 1*d* to 3*d.*   [Nos. 41925 to 42039.

The Plantagenet Roll

1*d.* Charles Lee Napier, *b.* 19 Feb. 1895.
2*d.* Lilias Mary Napier, *b.* 25 July 1892.
3*d.* Hester Caroline Napier, *b.* 22 Oct. 1896.
2*c.* Lilias Juliana Napier, *m.* 4 June 1902, Ernest Stork, M.B.
3*c.* Mabel Christiana Napier, *m.* 16 Nov. 1897, John Peere Williams-Freeman, M.D. (*Weyhill, Andover*) ; and has issue 1*d* to 3*d.*
1*d.* Flora Elizabeth Williams-Freeman, *b.* 31 Jan. 1900.
2*d.* Grizelda Mary Olga Williams-Freeman, *b.* 23 July 1901.
3*d.* Vivian Rosalind Williams-Freeman, *b.* 7 Oct. 1905.
2*b.* *Augusta Sarah Napier, d. 4 May* 1897 ; *m. 6 Oct.* 1853, *Frederick Peere Williams-Freeman of Greatham, Sussex, b. 2 Jan.* 1814 ; *d.* 17 *Jan.* 1870 ; *and had issue* 1*c to* 3*c.*
1*c.* Frederick Henry Peere Williams-Freeman, Capt. R.N. (*United Service*), *b.* 1 May 1855.
2*c.* *George Charles Peere Williams-Freeman, Chief Constable of Shropshire, formerly Capt.* 1*st Batt. Royal Sussex Regt., b.* 11 *Aug.* 1856 ; *d.* 27 *Dec.* 1905 ; *m.* 17 *Aug.* 1883, *Lavinia Augusta Charlotte, da. of Gen. Sir Arthur A. Cunynghame, G.C.B. ; and has issue* 1*d to* 5*d.*
1*d.* Anthony Peere Williams-Freeman, *b.* 5 Jan. 1888.
2*d.* Frederick Arthur Peere Williams-Freeman, *b.* 23 July 1889.
3*d.* George Napier Peere Williams-Freeman, *b.* 21 Jan. 1891.
4*d.* Rose Emily Williams-Freeman.
5*d.* Eleanor Augusta Williams-Freeman.
3*c.* John Peere Williams-Freeman, M.D. (*Weyhill, Andover*), *b.* 13 Ap. 1858 ; *m.* 16 Nov. 1897, Mabel Christiana, da. of Charles George Napier, F.G.S. ; and has issue.

See p. 482, Nos. 42045–42047. [Nos. 42040 to 42057.

408. Descendants of AUGUSTUS (BERKELEY), 4th EARL OF BERKELEY [E.], K.T. (see Table XXXVIII.), *b.* 18 Feb. 1716 ; *d.* 9 Jan. 1755 ; *m.* 7 May 1744, ELIZABETH, da. of Henry DRAX of Charborough (who re-m. as 3rd wife, 2 Jan. 1757, ROBERT (NUGENT), 1st Earl Nugent [I.], and) *d.* 29 June 1792 ; and had issue 1*a* to 4*a.*

1*a.* *Frederick Augustus* (*Berkeley*), 5*th Earl of Berkeley* [E.], *b.* 24 *May* 1745 ; *d.* 8 *Aug.* 1810 ; *m.* 16 *May* 1796, *Mary, da. of William Cole, d.* 30 *Oct.* 1844 ; *and had issue* 1*b to* 4*b.*
1*b.* *Thomas Moreton FitzHardinge* (*Berkeley*), *de jure* 6*th Earl of Berkeley, b.* 19 *Oct.* 1796 ; *d. unm.* 27 *Aug.* 1882.
2*b.* *Hon. Craven FitzHardinge Berkeley, b. May* 1805 ; *d.* 1 *July* 1855 ; *m.* 1*st,* 10 *Sept.* 1839, *Augusta, widow of the Hon. George Henry Talbot, nat. da. of Sir Horace St. Paul, 1st Bart.* [*U.K.*]*, d.* 25 *Ap.* 1841 ; *and had issue* 1*c.*
1*c.* *Louisa Mary* (*Berkeley*), *suo jure* 15*th Baroness Berkeley* [E.], *b.* 28 *May* 1840 ; *d.* 10 *Dec.* 1899 ; *m.* 3 *Ap.* 1872, *Major-Gen. Gustavus Hamilton Lockwood Milman, R.A. ; and had issue* 1*d.*
1*d.* Eva Mary FitzHardinge (Milman), *suo jure* 16th Baroness Berkeley [E.] (*Martins Heron, Bracknell, Berks*)*,* *b.* 4 Nov. 1875 ; *m.* 5 Aug. 1903, Capt. Frank Wigram Foley, D.S.O. ; and has issue 1*e.*
1*e.* Hon. Mary Lalle Foley, *b.* 9 Oct. 1905.
3*b.* *Lady Caroline FitzHardinge Berkeley, d.* 20 *Jan.* 1886 ; *m.* 24 *Dec.* 1829, *James Maxse, d.* 3 *Mar.* 1864 ; *and had issue* 1*c to* 4*c.*
1*c.* *Sir Henry FitzHardinge Berkeley Maxse, K.C.M.G., Lieut.-Col. in the Army, b.* 1832 ; *d.* 1883 ; *m.* 1859, *Augusta* (1 *Richmond Gardens, Bournemouth*)*, da. of* [——] *von Rudloff of Austria ; and had issue* 1*d to* 3*d.* [Nos. 42058 to 42059.

482

1*d*. Ernest George Berkeley Maxse, C.M.G., F.R.G.S., H.B.M.'s Consul for Réunion (1 *Whitehall Gardens, S.W.*), *b.* 18 Nov. 1863 ; *m.* 5 May 1888, Sarah Alice, da. of Thomas Nottage Miller of Bishops Stortford ; and has issue 1*e* to 2*e*.

1*e*. Henry FitzHardinge Berkeley Maxse, *b.* 3 Dec. 1889.

2*e*. Sarah Algeria Marjorie Maxse.

2*d*. Craven FitzHardinge Maxse, *b.* 1865 ; *m.* 1886, Clara, da. of E. Basch of Hanover.

3*d*. Reginald Edgar Maxse, *b.* 1869.

2*c*. *Frederick Augustus Maxse, Admiral R.N.*, *b.* 13 *Ap.* 1833 ; *d.* 25 *June* 1900 ; *m.* 1862, *Cecilia, da. of Gen. Steel ; and had issue* 1*d* to 4*d*.

1*d*. Frederick Ivor Maxse, C.B., D.S.O., Lieut.-Col. Coldstream Guards (2 *Gloucester Street, Portman Square, S.W.*), *b.* 22 Dec. 1862 ; *m.* 18 Dec. 1899, the Hon. Mary Caroline, da. of Henry (Wyndham), 2nd Baron Leconfield [U.K.] ; and has issue 1*e* to 2*e*.

1*e*. John Herbert Maxse, *b.* 18 Nov. 1901.

2*e*. Frederick Henry Joseph Maxse, *b.* 20 Jan. 1904.

2*d*. Leopold James Maxse, Editor of *The National Review* (25 *Montpelier Square, S.W.*), *b.* 11 Dec. 1864 ; *m.* 23 Dec. 1890, Katharine, da. of His Honour Judge Vernon Lushington.

3*d*. Olive Hermione Maxse.

4*d*. Violet Georgina Maxse, Lady of Grace of St. John of Jerusalem, *m.* 18 June 1894, Lord Edward Herbert Gascoigne-Cecil (*Cairo, Egypt*) ; and has issue.

3*c*. Ella Henrietta Maxse (29 *Clifton Crescent, Folkestone ; 19 Westbourne Gardens, Folkestone*), *m.* as 2nd wife, 18 Nov. 1862, Lieut.-Gen. the Hon. Edward Thomas Gage, C.B., K.M., *b.* 28 Dec. 1825 ; *d.* 21 May 1889 ; and has issue 1*d* to 4*d*.

1*d*. Ælla Molyneux Berkeley Gage, Major and Hon. Lieut.-Col. 3rd County of London Imp. Yeo., *formerly* 14th Hussars (*Sludge Hall, Billesdon, Leicester*), *b.* 29 Sept. 1863 ; *m.* 30 Oct. 1888, Ethel Marion, da. of John Lysaght ; and has issue 1*e*.

1*e*. John Fitzhardinge Berkeley Gage, *b.* 3 June 1901.

2*d*. James Seton Drummond Gage, Lieut. 5th Dragoon Guards, *b.* 28 June 1870.

3*d*. Moreton Foley Gage, Capt. 7th Dragoon Guards and Adj. Dorset Imp. Yeo. (*Army and Navy*), *b.* 12 Jan. 1873 ; *m.* 8 Oct. 1902, Anne Massie, da. of William Everard Strong of New York City ; and has issue 1*e*.

1*e*. Berkeley Everard Foley Gage, *b.* 27 Feb. 1904.

4*d*. *Mabel Maria Gage*, *b.* 10 *June* 1866 ; *d.* 12 *May* 1901 ; *m. as* 1*st wife,* 27 *Ap.* 1899, *Lieut.-Col. William Eliot Peyton, D.S.O., 15th Hussars ; and had issue.*

4*c*. Beatrice Maxse, *m.* 9 Jan. 1866, Major-Gen. Robert William Duff, *late* R.E. (*Firbank, Ascot*) ; and has issue 1*d*.

1*d*. Beatrice Caroline Duff, *m.* 1899, Frederick J. Sharpe.

4*b*. *Lady Emily Elizabeth Berkeley*, *d.* 30 *Mar.* 1895 ; *m.* 10 *Aug.* 1839, *Col. Sydney Augustus Capel of Boss Hall, co. Suffolk ; and had issue* 1*c* to 2*c*.

1*c*. Sydney Augustus Berkeley Capel, *formerly* Capt. New Zealand Colonial Forces, *b.* 1842 ; *m.* ; and has issue (five das.).

2*c*. Berkeley FitzHardinge Capel, *b.* 1845.

2*a*. *Hon. Sir George Cranfield Berkeley, G.C.B., Admiral R.N., and Lord High Admiral of Portugal,* b. 10 *Aug.* 1753 ; *d.* 25 *Feb.* 1818 ; *m. Emilia Charlotte, da. of Lord George Lennox, d.* 19 *Oct.* 1832 ; *and had issue.*

See the Clarence Volume, p. 636, Nos. 28692–28836.

3*a*. *Lady Georgiana Augusta Berkeley*, *b.* 18 *Sept.* 1749 ; *d.* 24 *Jan.* 1820 ; m.
[Nos. 42060 to 42225.

The Plantagenet Roll

1st, as 2nd wife, 20 Ap. 1766, George (Forbes), 5th Earl of Granard [I.], b. 2 Ap. 1740; d. 16 Ap. 1780; 2ndly, Jan. 1781, the Rev. Samuel Little, D.D.; and had issue 1b to 6b.

1b. Hon. Henry Forbes, b. 6 Sept. 1767; d. (–); m. 29 Dec. 1794, Elizabeth, sister of John, 1st Baron Tara [I.], da. of John Preston.

2b. Hon. Frederick Forbes, b. 7 Nov. 1776; d. 2 Feb. 1817; m. 1796, Enary, da. of William Butler.

3b. George Little, b. 1782.

4b. Lady Anne Georgina Forbes, b. 7 July 1772; d. (–); m. 1796, Col. Archibald M'Neil of Colonsay, N.B.

5b. Lady Augusta Forbes, b. 4 Oct. 1773; m. 14 Feb. 1798, Lieut.-Gen. Sir James Leith, G.C.B.

6b. Lady Louisa Georgiana Forbes, b. Dec. 1779; d. 25 Jan. 1830; m. Sir William Pratt Call, 2nd Bart. [G.B.], b. Nov. 1781; d. 3 Dec. 1851; and had issue 1c to 3c.

1c. Sir William Berkeley Call, 3rd Bart. [G.B.], b. 10 May 1815; d. 22 Dec. 1864; m. 14 Ap. 1841, Laura Emma, da. of Charles Wright Gardiner of Coombe Lodge, Oxford, d. 25 Dec. 1889; and had issue 1d to 2d.

1d. Sir William George Montagu Call, 4th Bart. [G.B.], J.P., b. 6 Feb. 1849; d. 21 Oct. 1903; m. 1884, Marie Valentine, da. of Capt. Mauléon of Anjou.

2d. Blanche Call, d. 14 May 1896; m. 21 Nov. 1865, Sir Samuel Edmund Falkiner, 6th Bart. [I.], b. 2 Feb. 1841; d. 12 May 1893; and had issue 1e to 2e.

1e. Sir Leslie Edmund Percy Riggs Falkiner, 7th Bart. [I.] (Annemount, Cork; 85 Sloane Street, S.W.), b. 2 Oct. 1866; m. 1st, 16 Oct. 1894, Elaine Maynard, da. of William Mortimer Maynard Farner of Bina Gardens, S.W., d.s.p. 28 Dec. 1900; 2ndly, 16 Ap. 1902, Kathleen Mary, da. of the Hon. Henry Robert Orde-Powlett; and has issue 1f.

1f. Terence Edmund Patrick Falkiner, b. 17 Mar. 1903.

2e. Mabel Rose Falkiner, b. 14 Mar. 1868; m. 21 Jan. 1902, Com. Pennant Athelwold Iremonger Lloyd, R.N. (Pentiebyn Mold, N. Wales).

2c. Phillida Elizabeth Call, d. 16 Aug. 1889; m. Sept. 1835, the Rev. George Henry Somerset of St. Mabyn, d. 12 Oct. 1882; and had issue.

See the Clarence Volume, p. 332, Nos. 9861–9866.

3c. Augusta Call, d. 4 Nov. 1893; m. 1st, 21 June 1838, Capt. George Dacres Paterson, 98th Regt., b. 11 Jan. 1813; d. 3 Ap. 1847; 2ndly, as 1st wife, 17 Jan. 1849, Admiral Sir Windham Hornby, K.C.B.; and had issue 1d to 4d.

1d. Charles Edward Paterson, 23rd Regt., b. 28 Jan. 1844.

2d. Eleanor Philippa Paterson.

3d. Augusta Matilda Paterson.

4d. Georgina Lucy Paterson.

4a. Lady Elizabeth Berkeley, b. 17 Dec. 1750; d. 13 Jan. 1828; m. 1st, 30 May 1867, William (Craven), 6th Baron Craven [E.], b. 11 Sept. 1738; d. 26 Sept. 1791; 2ndly, 13 Oct. 1791, Christian Frederick, Margrave of Brandenburg, Anspach, and Bayreuth, b. 24 Feb. 1736; d. 5 Jan. 1806; and had issue 1b to 5b.

1b. William (Craven), 7th Baron [E.] and 1st Earl of [U.K.] Craven, b. 1 Sept. 1770; d. 30 July 1825; m. 12 Dec. 1807, Louisa, the celebrated actress, da. of John Brunton of Norwich, d. 27 Aug. 1860; and had issue 1c to 3c.

1c. William (Craven), 2nd Earl of [U.K.] and 8th Baron [E.] Craven, b. 18 July 1809; d. 25 Aug. 1866; m. 5 Sept. 1835, Lady Emily Mary, da. of James Walter (Grimston), 1st Earl of Verulam [U.K.], b. 4 Feb. 1815; d. 21 May 1901; and had issue 1d to 7d.

1d. George Grimston (Craven), 3rd Earl of [U.K.] and 9th Baron [E.] Craven, b. 16 Mar. 1841; d. 7 Dec. 1883; m. 17 Jan. 1867, the Hon. Evelyn Laura, da. and co-h. of George William (Barrington), 7th Viscount Barrington of Ardglass [I.]; and had issue.

See the Clarence Volume, p. 94, Nos. 683–691.   [Nos. 42226 to 42217.

# of The Blood Royal

2*d.* Hon. Osbert William Craven, J.P., Lieut.-Col. and Hon. Col. Berks Yeo. Cav. (110 *Mount Street, W.; Ashdown Park, Shrivenham, Berks*), *b.* 6 Feb. 1848.

3*d.* Lady Elizabeth Charlotte Louisa Craven, *m.* 1st, 11 Aug. 1858, Arthur Edward (Egerton), 3rd Earl of Wilton [U.K.], *d.s.p.* 18 Jan. 1885; 2ndly, 14 Sept. 1886, Arthur Vickris Pryor (*Egerton Lodge, Melton Mowbray*).

4*d.* Lady Evelyn Mary Craven, *m.* 1st, 7 Aug. 1862, George John Brudenell-Bruce (eldest son of Ernest, 3rd Marquis of Ailesbury [U.K.]), *b.* 15 May 1839; *d.v.p.* (at Ajaccio) 28 May 1868; 2ndly, 4 Dec. 1869, Capt. Henry Amelius Coventry (marriage dissolved 1877); and 3rdly, 30 Aug. 1877, Capt. George William Hutton-Riddell, *late* 16th Lancers (*Miselee, Hawick; Bragborough Hall, Rugby*); and has issue 1*e* to 5*e.*

1*e.* *George William Thomas* (*Brudenell Bruce*), *4th Marquis of Ailesbury* [*U.K.*], *10th Earl of Cardigan* [*E.*], *and 5th Earl of Ailesbury* [*G.B.*], *b.* 8 June 1863; *d.s.p.* 10 *Ap.* 1894.

2*e.* Henry Robert Beauclerk Coventry (*Monkton Park, Chippenham*), *b.* 20 Sept. 1871; *m.* 18 July 1893, Lady Mary Muriel Sophie, da. of Henry (Howard), 18th Earl of Suffolk [E.]; and has issue 1*f* to 3*f.*

1*f.* Henry Dan Beauclerk Coventry, *b.* 28 Nov. 1899.

2*f.* Arthur Beauclerk Coventry, *b.* 6 Dec. 1900.

3*f.* Muriel Joan Vi Vi Eleanor Coventry, *b.* 6 Nov. 1897.

3*e.* George Hutton-Riddell, M.V.O., Capt. 16th Lancers (*Cavalry*), *b.* 1878.

4*e.* William Hutton-Riddell, *b.* 1880.

5*e.* Lady (R.W. 1887) Mabel Emily Louisa Brudenell-Bruce, *m.* 1 Oct. 1892, Robert Standish Sievier; and has issue.

See the Tudor Roll of "The Blood Royal of Britain," p. 178, Nos. 20449–20451.

5*d.* Lady Blanche Craven, *m.* 25 Jan. 1865, George William (Coventry), 9th Earl of Coventry [E.], P.C. (*Croome Court, Severn Stoke, Worcester, &c.*); and has issue.

See the Clarence Volume, pp. 220–221, Nos. 4459–4475.

6*d.* Lady Beatrix Jane Craven, V.A., *m.* 16 May 1865, George Henry (Cadogan), 5th Earl Cadogan [G.B.] and 3rd Baron Oakley [U.K.], K.G., P.C., LL.D., sometime (1895–1902) Lord-Lieut. of Ireland (*Culford Hall, Bury St. Edmunds; Chelsea House, Cadogan Place, S.W.*); and has issue 1*e* to 8*e.*

1*e.* Henry Arthur Cadogan, Viscount Chelsea, D.L., sometime (1890–1900) M.P. (48 *Bryanston Square, W.*), *b.* 13 June 1868; *m.* 30 Ap. 1892, the Hon. Mildred Cecilia Harriet, da. of Henry Gerard (Sturt), 1st Baron Allington [U.K.]; and has issue.

See the Tudor Roll of "The Blood Royal of Britain," p. 175, Nos. 20325–20329.

2*e.* Hon. Gerald Oakley Cadogan, Capt. 3rd Batt. Suffolk Regt., *b.* 30 May 1869.

3*e.* Hon. Lewin Edward Cadogan, *b.* 9 Oct. 1872.

4*e.* Hon. William George Sydney Cadogan, Capt. 10th Hussars, *b.* 31 Jan. 1879.

5*e.* Hon. Edward Cecil George Cadogan, *b.* 15 Nov. 1880.

6*e.* Hon. Alexander George Montagu Cadogan, *b.* 25 Nov. 1884.

7*e.* Lady Emily Julia Cadogan, *m.* 7 Feb. 1893, William (Brownlow), 3rd Baron Lurgan [U.K.], K.C.V.O., State Steward to the Lord-Lieut. of Ireland (*Brownlow House, Lurgan; 21 Lowndes Square, S.W.*); and has issue 1*f.*

1*f.* Hon. William George Edward Brownlow, *b.* 22 Feb. 1902.

8*e.* Lady Sophie Beatrix Mary Cadogan, *m.* 29 June 1896, Sir Samuel Edward Scott, 6th Bart. [U.K.], M.P. (*Westbury Manor, near Brackley, Northants; 38 South Street, Mayfair, W.*). [Nos. 42248 to 42293.

The Plantagenet Roll

7*d*. Lady Emily Georgiana Craven, *m.* 6 Aug. 1868, Victor Bates Van de Weyer, Lieut.-Col. Royal Berks Militia (*New Lodge, Windsor ;* 21 *Arlington Street, W.*); and has issue 1*e* to 8*e*.

    1*e*. William John Bates Van de Weyer, Capt. 3rd Batt. Royal Berkshire Regt., M.V.O., *b.* 29 Dec. 1870.

    2*e*. Edward Bates Van de Weyer, *b.* 29 Mar. 1874.

    3*e*. Bates Grimston Van de Weyer, Capt. 1st Scots Guards, *b.* 22 Feb. 1876.

    4*e*. John Bates Van de Weyer, *late* Lieut. Scots Guards, *b.* 9 Aug. 1881.

    5*e*. Brenda Van de Weyer, *b.* 14 Ap. 1872.

    6*e*. Margery Van de Weyer, *b.* 13 Feb. 1877.

    7*e*. Joan Van de Weyer, *b.* 26 Nov. 1879.

    8*e*. Elizabeth Bates Van de Weyer, *b.* (twin) 9 Aug. 1881.

    2*c*. Hon. *George Augustus Craven*, b. 15 Dec. 1810; *d.* 26 *July* 1836; m. 23 Dec. 1833, *Georgiana, da. of Walter Smythe of Bambridge House, Hants (who re-m.* 19 *Oct.* 1844 *Edmond, Duke of La-Force* [F.] *and*) d. 11 Dec. 1867 *; and had issue* 1*d to* 2*d*.

    1*d*. *William George Craven, Capt. Gloucester Yeo. Cav., formerly* 1st *Life Guards,* b. 12 *May* 1835; d. 2 *Jan.* 1906; m. 20 *July* 1857, *Lady Mary Catherine, da. of Charles Philip* (*Yorke*), 4th *Earl of Hardwicke* [G.B.], d. 14 Dec. 1890; *and has issue.*

    See the Clarence Volume, p. 99, Nos. 830–838.

    2*d*. *Walter Arthur Keppel Craven, late Lieut. R.N.*, b. 16 *Mar.* 1836; d. 21 Dec. 1894; m. 22 *Sept.* 1864, *the Countess Elizabeth Maria Louisa Taddea, da. of Count Ercole Oldofredi Tadini,* d. 1881; *and had issue* 1*e to* 4*e*.

    1*e*. Arthur Julius Craven, Capt. and Brevet-Major R.E., *b.* 11 Dec. 1867.

    2*e*. Louis Bertrand Craven, *b.* 19 Aug. 1869.

    3*e*. Mary Julia Craven.

    4*e*. Julia Mary Elizabeth Craven.

    3*c*. *Lady Louisa Elizabeth Frederica Craven,* d. 20 *Oct.* 1858; m. 1st, 24 *Oct.* 1840, *Sir George Frederic Johnstone,* 7th *Bart.* [S.], *M.P.,* b. Dec. 1810; d. 7 *May* 1841; 2ndly, 15 *Aug.* 1844, *Alexander Haldane Oswald of Auchincruive, M.P.,* d. 6 *Sept.* 1868; *and had issue* 1*d to* 4*d*.

    1*d*. Sir Frederic John William Johnstone, 8th Bart. [S.] (*Westerhall, Dumfries*), *b.* (posthumous and a twin) 5 Aug. 1841; *m.* 7 June 1899, Laura Caroline, Dowager Countess of Wilton, da. of William Russell.

    2*d*. George Charles Keppel Johnstone, *formerly* Lieut.-Col. Grenadier Guards (*Rothsay, Cowes, Isle of Wight*), *b.* (posthumous and a twin) 5 Aug. 1841; *m.* 29 June 1875, Agnes Caroline, da. of Thomas Chamberlayne of Cranbury Park, J.P., D.L.; and has issue 1*e* to 4*e*.

    1*e*. George Frederic Thomas Tankerville Johnstone (*Medina House, East Cowes, I.W.*), *b.* 1 Aug. 1876; *m.* 23 July 1901, Ernestine, da. of Lieut.-Col. Alan Roger Charles Porcelli-Cust; and has issue 1*f* to 3*f*.

    1*f*. Laura Adeline Johnstone, *b.* 27 May 1902.

    2*f*. Violet Florence Ernestine Johnstone, *b.* 19 Ap. 1903.

    3*f*. Dorothy Catherine Frances Johnstone, *b.* 4 Oct. 1904.

    2*e*. Charles John Johnstone, *late* Lieut. 4th Batt. Rifle Brigade, *b.* 20 Dec. 1877.

    3*e*. Agnes Louisa Barbara Snowflake Johnstone.

    4*e*. Rose Mary Adeline Dagmar Amelia Johnstone.

    3*d*. *Louisa Elizabeth Oswald,* d. 8 *Aug.* 1870; m. 19 Nov. 1864, *Lieut.-Col. James Ross Farquharson of Invercauld, J.P., D.L.,* b. 9 *Jan.* 1834; d. 19 *Mar.* 1888; *and had issue* 1*e to* 3*e*.

    1*e*. Alexander Haldane Farquharson of Invercauld, *late* 10th Hussars (*Inver-*

[Nos. 42294 to 42325.

486

# of The Blood Royal

cauld, Ballater, Aberdeen ; 40 Park Street, Grosvenor Square, W.), b. 12 Mar. 1867 ; m. 16 Jan. 1893, Zoë Caroline, da. of Sir Richard Musgrave, 11th Bart. [E.] ; and has issue 1f to 2f.

　　1f. Myrtle Farquharson, b. 30 Jan. 1897.

　　2f. Sylvia Farquharson, b. 24 Dec. 1899.

　　2e. Louisa Elizabeth Farquharson.

　　3e. Elo Janet Catherine Farquharson.

　　4d. Edith Mary Oswald, m. 9 Jan. 1869, John Manners (Yorke), 7th Earl of Hardwicke [G.B.] (52 Rutland Gate, S.W.) ; and has issue.

　　See the Clarence Volume, p. 98, Nos. 811–815.

　　2b. Hon. Henry Augustus Berkeley Craven, a Major-Gen. in the Army, b. 21 Dec. 1776 ; d. 1836 ; m. 1829, Marie Clarisse, da. of [——] Trebhault, d. 4 Ap. 1865.

　　3b. Hon. Elizabeth Craven, b. 20 Ap. 1868 ; d. 3 Jan. 1799 ; m. 17 Ap. 1792, John Edward Maddocks of Glanywern and Vale Mascall, co. Kent; and had issue.[1]

　　4b. Hon. Margaretta Craven, b. 26 Ap. 1769 ; d. 9 Mar. 1851 ; m. 1 Jan. 1792, William Philip (Molyneux), 2nd Earl [I.] and 1st Baron [U.K.] Sefton, d. 20 Nov. 1838 ; and had issue.

　　See the Clarence Volume, pp. 351–353, Nos. 11472–11519.

　　5b. Hon. Arabella Craven, d. 9 June 1819 ; m. as 2nd wife, 6 Ap. 1793, Gen. the Hon. Frederick St. John, d. 19 Nov. 1844 ; and had issue.

　　See the Clarence Volume, pp. 490–492, Nos. 21280–21327.

[Nos. 42326 to 42430.

409. Descendants of GEORGE (KEPPEL), 3rd EARL OF ALBEMARLE [E.], K.G. (see Table XXXVIII.), b. 5 Ap. 1724 ; d. 13 Oct. 1772 ; m. 20 Ap. 1770, ANNE, da. of Sir John MILLER, 4th Bart. [E.], d. 3 July 1824 ; and had issue.

See the Clarence Volume, pp. 512–515, Nos. 22136–22365.

[Nos. 42431 to 42659.

410. Descendants of Right Rev. the Hon. FREDERICK KEPPEL, D.D., Lord Bishop of Exeter (see Table XXXVIII.), b. 19 Jan. 1728 ; d. 27 Dec. 1777 ; m. 13 Sept. 1758, LOUISA, natural da. of Sir Edward WALPOLE, K.B., d. 27 July 1813 ; and had issue 1a to 4a.

　　1a. Frederick Keppel of Lexham Hall, co. Norfolk, b. 12 Nov. 1762 ; d. 12 Ap. 1830 ; m. 5 Ap. 1796, Louisa, da. of George Clive, d. 16 Mar. 1832 ; and had issue 1b to 2b.

　　1b. Frederick Walpole Keppel of Lexham Hall, b. 23 May 1797 ; d. 24 Dec. 1858 ; m. 22 July 1848, Mary Anne, widow of Robert R. Wilson, da. of E. Hodgkinson, d. 12 Jan. 1880 ; and had issue 1c.

　　1c. Fanny Cunigunda Clive Keppel, b. 2 May 1851 ; d. 17 Jan. 1891 ; m. as 1st wife, 4 Oct. 1882, Charles William Neville-Rolfe of Queensland; and had issue 1d to 4d.

　　　　1d. Clive Neville-Rolfe.

　　　　2d. Randolph Neville-Rolfe.

　　　　3d. Louisa Ethel Neville-Rolfe.

　　　　4d. Kunegunda Neville-Rolfe.　　　　　　　　　　　[Nos. 42660 to 42663.

---

[1] Brydges' " Collins," vi. p. 459.

The Plantagenet Roll

2b. Rev. William Arnold Walpole Keppel of Lexham Hall, Rector of Haynford, &c., b. 7 Oct. 1804; d. 26 Nov. 1888; m. 7 Sept. 1830, *Frances Georgiana Sophia, da. of Robert Marsham of Stratton Strawless,* d. 7 June 1883; *and had issue 1c to 3c.*

    1c. Frederick Charles Keppel, Col. Gren. Guards, b. 25 Aug. 1831; d. (? unm.) 2 Mar. 1876.

    2c. William Henry Augustus Keppel of Lexham Hall, Lieut.-Col. 2nd Brigade, E. Div. R.A., b. 6 Aug. 1845; d. 31 Oct. 1889; m. 10 July 1873, the Hon. Charlotte Elizabeth Eleanor, da. of Alexander (Fraser), 17th Lord Saltoun [S.]; and had issue 1d to 3d.

        1d. Bertram William Arnold Keppel, Capt. Norfolk Imp. Yeo. (Lexham Hall, Swaffham), b. 12 Jan. 1876; m. 4 Oct. 1898, the Hon. Alice Evelyn Agatha, da. of Charles Douglas Richard (Hanbury-Tracy), 4th Baron Sudeley [U.K.]; and has issue 1e to 2e.

            1e. Marguerite Keppel, b. 8 Sept. 1899.

            2e. Judith Iris Keppel, b. 5 Nov. 1900.

        2d. Frances Isabel Eleanor Keppel, m. 14 May 1902, the Hon. Harold Edward FitzClarence (Pretoria); and has issue (a son and da.).

        3d. Violet Eleanor Keppel.

    3c. Edward George Keppel, J.P., one of H.M.'s Hon. Corps of Gentlemen-at-Arms, Hon. Col., formerly Highland L.I. (Stratton Strawless Hall, Norwich), b. 28 June 1847; m. 14 Dec. 1875, Mary Cecilia Georgiana, da. of Major George King; and has issue 1d to 3d.

        1d. Frederick George Keppel, b. 5 May 1878.

        2d. Arnold Ramsay Keppel, Lieut. The King's Own Yorkshire L.I., b. 14 Sept. 1879.

        3d. Evelyn Maud Keppel, b. 15 Ap. 1887.

2a. Anna Maria Keppel, b. 17 June 1759; d. 1836; m. 1790, *Lieut.-Gen. William Stapleton,* b. 6 June 1770; d. 1826; *and had issue.*

See p. 350.

3a. Laura Keppel, b. 14 Mar. 1765; d. 20 June 1798; m. *as 1st wife,* 21 Ap. 1784, *George Ferdinand (FitzRoy), 2nd Baron Southampton [G.B.],* d. 14 June 1810; *and had issue.*

See the Clarence Volume, p. 344.

4a. Charlotte Augusta Keppel, b. 6 June 1771; d. (–); m. 24 Dec. 1802, *Robert Foote of Charlton Place, co. Kent.*   [Nos. 42664 to 42672.

411. Descendants of Lady CAROLINE KEPPEL (see Table XXXVIII.), b. 20 Aug. 1737; d. 11 Sept. 1769; m. 1759, ROBERT ADAIR of Stratford Place, Marylebone, co. Midx., d. (–); and had issue 1a to 2a.

1a. Robert Adair, H.B.M.'s Envoy Extraordinary to the Court of Vienna in 1806.[1]

2a. Elizabeth Adair, d. 2 Mar. 1841; m. 12 Feb. 1788, *George (Barrington), 5th Viscount Barrington [I.], D.D., Preb. of Durham,* b. 16 July 1761; d. 4 Mar. 1829; *and had issue 1b to 7b.*

    1b. William Keppel (Barrington), 6th Viscount Barrington [I.], b. 1 Oct. 1793; d. 9 Feb. 1867; m. 21 Ap. 1823, the Hon. Jane Elizabeth, da. of Thomas (Liddell), 1st Baron Ravensworth [U.K.], d. 22 Mar. 1883; and had issue.

See the Clarence Volume, pp. 93–96, Nos. 676–762.

    2b. Hon. George Barrington, Capt. R.N., b. 20 Nov. 1794; d. 2 June 1835; m. 15 Jan. 1827, Lady Caroline, V.A., da. of Charles (Grey), 2nd Earl Grey [U.K.], K.G., d. 28 Ap. 1875; and had issue 1c to 2c.   [Nos. 42673 to 42759.

---

[1] Brydges' "Collins," iii. pp. 7, 11.

# of The Blood Royal

1*c*. Charles George Grey Barrington, C.B., *formerly* a Principal Clerk in the Treasury and sometime Auditor of Civil List and Assist. Sec. (13 *Morpeth Mansions, Victoria Street, S.W.*), *b*. 27 Oct. 1827; *m*. 15 May 1897, Mary Caroline, da. of Capt. Gore Sellon, 21st B.N.I.

2*c*. *Mary Barrington*, b. 27 *May* 1833; d. 20 *June* 1894; m. 12 *Aug*. 1858, *the Right Hon. Sir Algernon Edward West, P.C., G.C.B., J.P., &c*. (1 *Mount Street, W.; Wanborough Manor, Guildford*); *and had issue* 1*d* to 5*d*.

1*d*. Horace Charles George West, Gentleman Usher of Privy Chamber in Ordinary to H.M. (*Brooks'*), *b*. 6 Nov. 1859; *m*. Dec. 1893, Alice, da. of the Rev. Canon Leighton, Warden of All Souls.

2*d*. Reginald Jervoise West, *formerly* of the Bank of England, Leeds, *b*. 11 July 1861; *m*. 1885, Ida Agnes Vane, da. of the Hon. Charles Rowley Hay-Drummond, *previously* Hay; *and has issue* 1*e* to 2*e*.

1*e*. Algernon Henry Pascoe West, *b*..1886.

2*e*. Lionel Reginald Everard West, *b*. 1888.

3*d*. Gilbert Richard West, *b*. 11 Nov. 1863.

4*d*. Augustus William West (18 *Lowndes Square, S.W.*), *b*. 6 Aug. 1865; *m*. 31 July 1890, the Hon. Edith Maria, da. of Arthur Edwin (Hill-Trevor, *previously* Hill), 1st Baron Trevor [U.K.].

5*d*. Constance Mary West.

3*b*. *Rev. the Hon. Lowther John Barrington*, b. 17 *July* 1805 ; d. 17 *Mar*. 1897 ; m. 26 *Oct*. 1837, *Lady Caroline Georgiana, da. of Thomas (Pelham), 2nd Earl of Chichester* [U.K.], d. 18 *Jan*. 1885 ; *and had issue*.

See the Clarence Volume, p. 629, Nos. 28180–28185.

4*b*. *Hon. Henry Frederick Francis Adair Barrington*, b. 28 *July* 1808 ; d. 25 *Mar*. 1882 ; m. 25 *July* 1848, *Mary Georgiana, da. of Col. Wright Knox*, d. (–) ; *and had issue* 1*c* to 5*c*.

1*c*. William Gordon Samuel Shute Barrington (*Thain Farm, Port Haney, Fraser River, British Columbia*), *b*. 24 Nov. 1855 ; *m*. 29 Ap. 1896, Emily Mary, da. of John Montagu, Col. Sec. at Cape of Good Hope.

2*c*. Florina Elizabeth Jane Barrington.

3*c*. Katharine Caroline Barrington, *m*. 1st, 1890, Francis Newdegate, *d*. 1900 ; 2ndly, 1903, Lieut.-Col. James M. Maurice, *formerly* Royal Lancaster Regt. (*Portland, Knysna, Cape Colony*) ; *and has issue* 1*d* to 5*d*.

1*d*. Francis William Newdegate, *b*. 1893.

2*d*. Henry Arthur Newdegate, *b*. 1897.

3*d*. John Wilfrid Newdegate, *b*. 1899.

4*d*. Eleanor Imar Newdegate, *b*. 1891.

5*d*. Dorothy Katharine Newdegate, *b*. 1892.

4*c*. Idonea Maria Barrington, *m*. 8 Ap. 1896, Lieut. Edward Lindsay Ashley Foakes, R.N.

5*c*. Gabrielle Carlotta Barrington.

5*b*. *Hon. Frances Barrington*, b. 20 *Oct*. 1802 ; d. 11 *Aug*. 1849 ; m. *as 2nd wife*, 25 *Oct*. 1828, *William (Legge), 4th Earl of* [G.B.] *and 5th Baron* [E.], *Dart-mouth*, b. 29 *Nov*. 1784 ; d. 22 *Nov*. 1853 ; *and had issue*.

See the Tudor Roll of "The Blood Royal of Britain," pp. 306–307, Nos. 25779–25840.

6*b*. *Hon. Georgiana Christiana Barrington*, b. 9 *May* 1810 ; d. 11 *July* 1881 ; m. *as 2nd wife*, 1 *Nov*. 1847, *James Hamilton Lloyd Anstruther of Hintlesham Hall, Suffolk*, b. 31 *Dec*. 1806 ; d. 23 *Dec*. 1882 ; *and had issue*.

See p. 370, Nos. 26654–26661.

7*b*. *Hon. Elizabeth Frances Barrington*, b. 18 *Oct*. 1811 ; d. 26 *July* 1886 ; m. *as 2nd wife*, 13 *Dec*. 1836, *the Rev. Thomas Mills, Rector of Sutton, Great Saxham, and Little Henny, Hon. Canon of Norwich ' and Chaplain-in-Ordinary to Kings George III., George IV., and William IV., and Queen Victoria*, b. 17 *Nov*. 1791 ; d. 29 *Sept*. 1879.   [Nos. 42760 to 42853.

The Plantagenet Roll

412. Descendants of Lady ELIZABETH KEPPEL (see Table XXXVIII.), *b.* 15 Nov. 1739; *d.* 2 Nov. 1768; *m.* 9 June 1764, FRANCIS RUSSELL, styled MARQUIS OF TAVISTOCK, *b.* 27 Sept. 1739; *d.v.p.* 22 Mar. 1767; and had issue 1*a* to 3*a*.

1*a*. Francis (*Russell*), 5th Duke of Bedford [*E.*], *b.* 23 *July* 1765; *d. unm.* 2 *Mar.* 1802.

2*a*. John (*Russell*), 6th Duke of Bedford [*E.*], *K.G.*, *b.* 6 *July* 1766; *d.* 20 *Oct.* 1839; *m.* 1*st*, 21 *Mar.* 1786, *the Hon. Georgiana Elizabeth, da. of George* (*Byng*), 4th Viscount Torrington [*G.B.*], *d.* 11 *Oct.* 1801; 2*ndly*, 23 *June* 1803, *Lady Georgiana, da. of Alexander* (*Gordon*), 4th Duke of Gordon [*S.*], *d.* (*at Nice*) 24 *Feb.* 1853; *and had issue.*

See the Tudor Roll of "The Blood Royal of Britain," pp. 426–428, Nos. 30609–30661, and pp. 480–484, Nos. 33383–33561.

3*a*. Lord William Russell, *b.* (*posthumous*) 20 *Aug.* 1767; *d.* 6 *May* 1840; *m.* 11 *July* 1789, *Lady Charlotte Anne, da. of George* (*Villiers*), 4th Earl of Jersey [*E.*], *d.* 31 *Aug.* 1808; *and had issue.*

See the Tudor Roll of "The Blood Royal of Britain," pp. 359–360, Nos. 27569–27604. [Nos. 42854 to 43121.

413. Descendants, if any, of the Hon. ANNE BELLEW (see Table XXXIX.), *m.* [——] BUTLER.

414. Descendants of VINCENT (GIUSTINIANI), 6th PRINCE GIUSTINIANI (22 Nov. 1644) [P.S.] and *de jure* 6th EARL OF NEWBURGH [S.] (see Table XXXIX.), *b.* 1759; *d.* 13 Nov. 1826; *m.* (at St. George's, Naples) 21 May 1789, NICOLETTA, da. and h. of Domenico (GRILLO), Duke of Mondragone [Naples], *d.* (-); and had issue 1*a*.

1*a*. Maria Cecilia Agatha Anna Josepha Laurentia Donata Melchiora Balthasara Gaspara (*Giustiniani*), *suo jure* 7th Countess of Newburgh [*S.*], *Duchess of Mondragone* [*Naples*], *b.* (*in Rome*) 5 Feb. 1796; *d.* 2 *Jan.* 1847; *m.* 21 *Sept.* 1815, *Charles* (*Bandini*), 4th Marquis (*Bandini*) of Lanciano and Rustano (30 *May* 1753) [*P.S.*], *b.* 3 *Sept.* 1779; *d.* 4 *July* 1850; *and had issue* 1*b* to 5*b*.

1*b*. Sigismund Nicholas Venantius Gaetano Francis (Bandini, now (1850) Giustiniani-Bandini), 8th Earl of Newburgh (21 Dec. 1660), Viscount Kynnaird (13 Sept. 1647) and Lord Levingstone of Flacraig (21 Dec. 1660) [S.], 1st Prince Giustiniani-Bandini (17 Jan. 1863), 5th Marquis (Bandini) of Lanciano and Rustano (30 May 1753) [P.S.], Duke of Mondragone and Count of Carinola [Naples], Patrician of Rome, &c. (*Palazzo Altieri, Rome*); and has issue 1*c* to 7*c*.

1*c*. Charles Giustiniani-Bandini, styled Duke of Mondragone in Italy and Viscount Kynnaird in Scotland (*Rome*), *b.* (at Rome) 1 Jan. 1862; *m.* (at Florence) 8 Aug. 1885, Maria Lanza, da. of [——], Prince of Trabia and Butera; and has issue 1*d* to 4*d*.

1*d*. Hon. Sigismund Maria Bandini Joseph (Giuseppe) Giustiniani-Bandini, *b.* 20 June 1886.

2*d*. Hon. Lawrence (Lorenzo) Maria Giustiniani-Bandini, *b.* 14 Ap. 1898.

3*d*. Hon. Maria Sofia Josephine (Giuseppina) Giustiniani-Bandini, *b.* 4 May 1889.

4*d*. Hon. Josepha (Giuseppe) Maria Giustiniani-Bandini, *b.* 3 Sept. 1896.

2*c*. Lady Caroline Maria Elena Gioachina Giustiniani-Bandini, *b.* (at Rome) 11 June 1851; *m.* (there) 8 Ap. 1872, Guardino, Count of Colleoni Porto and Sobza (*Vicenza, Italy*). [Nos. 43122 to 43128.

490

# of The Blood Royal

3c. Lady Elena Maria Concetta Isabella Gioachina Josepha Giustiniani-Bandini, *b.* (at Rome) 8 June 1853; *m.* (there) 25 June 1876, Prince Camillo Rospigliosi, Comm. of the Noble Guard of H.H. the Pope (*Rome, Palazzo Rospigliosi; Quirinal*); and has issue 1*d* to 10*d*.

    1*d.* Prince Giambattista Rospigliosi, *b.* (at Rome) 5 May 1877.

    2*d.* Prince Thomas (Tommaso) Rospigliosi, *b.* (at Rome) 28 June 1879.

    3*d.* Prince Francis (Francesco) Rospigliosi, *b.* (at Rome) 8 July 1880.

    4*d.* Prince Louis (Ludovico) Rospigliosi, *b.* (at Rome) 16 Oct. 1881.

    5*d.* Prince Ferdinand Rospigliosi, *b.* (at Rome) 24 July 1883.

    6*d.* Prince Clement Rospigliosi, *b.* (at Rome) 23 Nov. 1895.

    7*d.* Princess Octavia (Oltavia) Rospigliosi, *b.* (at Rome) 27 May 1878; *m.* (there) 2 Oct. 1898, Robert, Count San Severino-Vimercati.

    8*d.* Princess Maria Rospigliosi, *b.* (at Rome) 23 Feb. 1886.

    9*d.* Princess Madeline (Maddalena) Rospigliosi, *b.* (at Rome) 8 May 1889.

    10*d.* Princess Carolina Rospigliosi, *b.* (at Rome) 14 Oct. 1891.

    4c. Lady Nicoletta Maria Giustiniani-Bandini, *m.* (at Rome) 20 Feb. 1881 Mario, Duke Grazioli (*Rome, 102 Via Plebescito*).

    5c. Lady Maria Christina Giustiniani-Bandini.

    6c. Lady Isabella Giustiniani-Bandini, *m.* (at Rome) 17 Nov. 1898, Esmé William Howard, M.V.O., Consul-General for Crete (*British Consulate-General, Canea, Crete; 21 Egerton Gardens, S.W.*); and has issue 1*d* to 2*d*.

    1*d.* Esmé Joseph Henry Sigismund Howard, *b.* 17 Oct. 1903.

    2*d.* Francis P. R. Howard, *b.* 5 Oct. 1905.

    7c. Lady Maria Cecilia Giustiniani-Bandini.

    2*b. Lady Nicoletta Bandini*, b. 1817; d. 1836; m. 1835, *Charles, Marquis Santa Croce of Villahermosa.*

    3*b. Lady Elizabeth Bandini*, b. 1820; d. (–); m. 1841, *Marquis Augustin Trionfi of Ancona.*

    4*b. Lady Christina Bandini*, b. 1822; d. 4 *July* 1865; m. 1845, *Count Marcello Marcelli-Flori.*

    5*b. Lady Maria Bandini*, b. 1825; d. (–); m. 1851, *Count Frederic Pucci Boncambi of Perugia.*   [Nos. 43129 to 43145.

415. Descendants, if any, of the PRINCESS MARIA ISABELLA GIUS-TINIANI (see Table XXXIX.), *d.* 1783; *m.* (? as 1st wife) 1781, FRANCIS (RUSPOLI), PRINCE RUSPOLI [Rome], *b.* 19 Feb. 1752; *d.* 8 Mar. 1829.

416. Descendants of the PRINCESS CATHERINE GIUSTINIANI (see Table XXXIX.), *d.* 1813; *m.* 1777, BALTHAZAR (ERBA) II., PRINCE ODESCALCHI, *d.* 1810; and had issue.

417. Descendants of GUSTAVUS (HAMILTON), 5th VISCOUNT BOYNE [I.] (see Table XXXIX.), *b.* 20 Dec. 1749; *d.* 29 Feb. 1816; *m.* 1 Ap. 1773, MARTHA MATILDA, da. of Sir Quaile SOMERVILLE, 2nd Bart. [I.] (who re-m. 11 July 1821, Sir THOMAS WEBB, 6th Bart. [E.], and) *d.* 16 Aug. 1826; and had issue 1*a* to 4*a*.

    1*a. Gustavus (Hamilton), 6th Viscount Boyne [I.]*, b. 12 *Ap.* 1777; d. 30 *Mar.* 1855; m. 4 *Aug.* 1796, *Harriet, da. of Benjamin Baugh of Burwarton House, co. Salop,* d. 1 Nov. 1854; *and had issue* 1*b*.

The Plantagenet Roll

1b. Gustavus Frederick (Hamilton, afterwards (R.L. 26 Feb. 1850, Hamilton-Russell), 7th Viscount Boyne [I.], 1st Baron Brancepeth [U.K.], b. 11 May 1797; d. 27 Oct. 1872; m. 9 Sept. 1828, Emma Maria, da. and eventual h. of Matthew Russell of Brancepeth Castle, d. 29 Ap. 1870; and had issue 1c.

1c. Gustavus Russell (Hamilton-Russell), 8th Viscount Boyne [I.], 2nd Baron Brancepeth [U.K.] (Brancepeth Castle, Durham; 16 Grosvenor Gardens, S.W.), b. 28 May 1830; m. 2 Sept. 1858, Lady Katharine, da. of John (Scott), 2nd Earl of Eldon [U.K.], d. 19 May 1903; and has issue 1d to 9d.

1d. Hon. Gustavus William Hamilton-Russell, J.P., D.L., late Capt. 3rd Batt. Northumberland Fusiliers (Hardwick, Sedgefield, co. Durham), b. 11 Jan. 1864.

2d. Hon. Frederick Gustavus Hamilton-Russell, J.P., D.L. (45 Gloucester Place, W.), b. 12 June 1867; m. 27 Ap. 1897, Lady Margaret, da. of John (Scott), 3rd Earl of Eldon [U.K.].

3d. Hon. Claud Eustace Hamilton-Russell, J.P., D.L., late Cheshire Regt. (Cleobury Court, Bridgnorth), b. 4 Mar. 1871; m. 11 Ap. 1899, Maria Lindsay, da. of Sir Lindsay Wood, 1st Bart. [U.K.]; and has issue 1e.

1e. Arthur Gustavus Lindsay Hamilton-Russell, b. 30 Ap. 1900.

4d. Hon. Arthur Hamilton-Russell, Capt. 1st Dragoons, b. 8 Sept. 1872.

5d. Hon. Eustace Scott Hamilton-Russell, late Lieut. 3rd Batt. Northumberland Fusiliers.

6d. Hon. Alice Katharine Hamilton-Russell, m. 27 July 1889, Capt. Wyndham Paulet St. John Mildmay, J.P. (Hazlegrove, Spackford).

7d. Hon. Maud Harriet Hamilton-Russell.

8d. Hon. Constance Elizabeth Hamilton-Russell, m. 9 Aug. 1898, the Rev. Albert Victor Baillie, Rector of Rugby (The Rectory, Rugby); and has issue 1e to 2e.

1e. Alexander Gustavus Baillie, b. 1901.

2e. Ian Claud Baillie, b. 1904.

9d. Hon. Florence Rachel Hamilton-Russell.

2a. Hon. Richard Somerville Hamilton, R.N., b. 1 June 1778; d. (? s.p.).

3a. Hon. Sarah Hamilton, b. 23 Feb. 1775; d. 1849; m. 1809, the Rev. George Monk.

4a. Hon. Georgiana Hamilton, b. 14 Feb. 1776; d. (-); m. as 1st wife, Henry Woodgate.   [Nos. 43146 to 43158.

418. Descendants, if any, of the Hon. CHARLES HAMILTON (see Table XXXIX.), Capt. 12th Dragoons, b. 6 Oct. 1750; d. 1794; m. Sept. 1785, [——], da. of Christopher KIRWAN LISTER; and of the Hon. RICHARD HAMILTON, b. 21 July 1774.

419. Descendants of the Hon. CATHERINE HAMILTON (see Table XXXIX.), b. 28 Aug. 1754; d. (-); m. 3 Feb. 1773, HUGH LYONS, afterwards LYONS-MONTGOMERY, d. 1792; and had issue 1a to 4a.

1a. Hugh Lyons-Montgomery of Belhavel, co. Leitrim, d. 26 Ap. 1826; m. 27 Jan. 1812, Elizabeth, da. of the Very Rev. Stewart Blacker of Carrick, Dean of Leighlin (who re-m. [——] de Champre); and had issue 1b to 7b.

1b. Hugh Lyons-Montgomery of Belhavel, M.P., J.P., D.L., b. 1816; d. 16 July 1882; m. 26 June 1840, Elizabeth, da. of Henry Smith of Annesbrook, co. Meath, d. 30 Sept. 1899; and had issue 1c to 12c.

# of The Blood Royal

1c. Henry Willoughby Stewart Lyons-Montgomery, *late* Lieut. Leitrim Militia (*Belhavel, Killurque, Leitrim*), *b.* 16 Sept. 1850; *m.* 6 Ap. 1876, Jane Singer, da. and h. of Capt. Travers Crofton of Lakefield.

2c. De Winton Lyons-Montgomery.

3c. Foster Kynaston Walter Lyons-Montgomery.

4c. Elizabeth Lyons-Montgomery, *m.* 3 Oct. 1865, Richard Ruxton Fitzherbert, J.P., D.L., High Sheriff co. Monaghan 1880 (*Black Castle, Navan ; Shantonagh, Castle Blayney*) ; and has issue 1d to 3d.

1d. Richard Ruxton Walter Fitzherbert, J.P., Major 4th Batt. King's Own, *b.* 9 Sept. 1866 ; *m.* 9 Dec. 1897, Violet Caroline, da. of James Moffatt of Windsor, D.L.

2d. Bertram Richard Edward Fitzherbert, *b.* 12 Jan. 1871.

3d. Gladys Lilian Ruxton Fitzherbert.

5c. Caroline Lyons-Montgomery.

6c. Ada Lyons-Montgomery, *m.* May 1858, G. C. Smyth of Newtown, Drogheda.

7c. Eveleen Clemina Lyons-Montgomery, *m.* 19 Mar. 1873, Arthur Vesey Fitzherbert (*Estancia, Media Aqua, S. America*) ; and has issue.
See the Clarence Volume, p. 307, Nos. 8555–8560.

8c. Henrietta Emily Anna Lyons-Montgomery, *m.* 17 Ap. 1890, Lieut.-Col. J. K. Kesterman, *late* 100th Regt.

9c. Florence Lyons-Montgomery, *m.* 19 Mar. 1873, F. Barton.

10c. Norma Lyons-Montgomery, *m.* Oct. 1873, W. A. Beyton.

11c. *Ethel Constance Lyons-Montgomery*, d. 28 Oct. 1891 ; m. *as 1st wife, John Molony ; and had issue 1d to 2d.*

1d. Otho Hugh Chartres Molony.

2d. John Barré de Winton Molony.

12c. Beatrice Lyons-Montgomery.

2b. *Lambert Stewart Lyons-Montgomery, Lieut.-Col. Scots Fusiliers,* d. (–) ; m. [——], *da. of Gen. Young, H.E.I.C.S. ; and had issue 1c.*

1c. Constance Mary Lyons-Montgomery, *m.* 30 Dec. 1882, Lieut.-Col. H. W. Appelby, *late* 9th Lancers.

3b. *Charles Lyons-Montgomery, Lieut.-Gen. Bengal Staff Corps, b. 6 Feb.* 1824 ; d. (–) ; m. [——], *da. of* [——] *Masters of Calcutta.*

4b. *Elizabeth Lyons-Montgomery,* d. (–) ; m. 1st, *Joseph May of Hale, co. Southampton ; 2ndly, Robert Maxwell of Islanmore, co. Limerick.*

5b. *Caroline Lyons-Montgomery, b.* 1815 ; d. (–) ; m. 1839, *Count Adolphus Cavagnari, Major in the French Army,* d. 1899 ; *and had issue 1c to 4c.*

1c. *Sir Peter Louis Napoleon Cavagnari, K.C.B., C.S.I., H.B.M.'s Envoy to the Court of Kabul, b.* 4 *July* 1841 ; d.s.p. (*being massacred by Afghans*) 3 *Sept.* 1879 ; m. 23 *Nov.* 1871, *Mercy Emma* (*Ravensnest, Lyndhurst*), *da. of Henry Graves of Cookstown, co. Tyrone, Surgeon.*

2c. Montgomery Cavagnari, *b.* 1845, went to Australia, and has not since been heard of.

3c. *Elizabeth Louise Cavagnari,* b. 1840 ; d. 1906 ; m. 1870, *William Wiggett* (2 *Auriol Mansions, West Kensington*) ; *and had issue.*

4c. *Lambertine Cavagnari,* b. 1843 ; d. (–) ; m. 1865, *Robert Wallace, 23rd Welsh Fusiliers,* d. 1893 ; *and had issue.*

6b. *Sophia Lyons-Montgomery,* d. 21 *Mar.* 1850 ; m. *as 1st wife,* 23 *Ap.* 1840, *John Barré Beresford of Learmount, &c., J.P., D.L., Vice-Lieut. co. Derry, b.* 19 *Ap.* 1815 ; d. 30 *Aug.* 1895 ; *and had issue 1c.*

1c. *John Claudius Montgomery Beresford, Major R.E., A.D.C., and Assistant*
[Nos. 43159 to 43182.

The Plantagenet Roll

Private Sec. to the Duke of Marlborough, Lord-Lieut. of Ireland, b. 3 Feb. 1850; d. 19 *Sept.* 1894; m. 16 *Jan.* 1884, *Rose, da. of Ralph Smith of Greenhills; and had issue* 1d.

1d. Ralph Henry Barré de La Poer Beresford (*Learmount, Londonderry*), *b.* 26 Nov. 1886.

7b. *Louisa Lyons-Montgomery, d.* (–); m. *Ralph Smith of Greenhills, co. Louth, d.* (–); *and had issue (at least)* 1c.

1c. Rose Smith, *m.* 16 Jan. 1884, Major John Claudius Montgomery Beresford, *d.* 19 Sept. 1894; and has issue.

See p. 494, No. 43183.

2a. *Rev. Charles Lyons-Montgomery, Rector of Innismagrath, d.* 3 *Sept.* 1859; m. 26 *June* 1815, *Emily, da. of Humphrey Nixon of Nixon Lodge, co. Cavan; and had issue* 1b *to* 4b.

1b. *Hugh Lyons-Montgomery, d.* (–); m. 11 *June* 1856, *Henrietta Constance, da. of the Rev. Henry Lucas St. George of Kilrush; and had issue* 1c *to* 2c.

1c. *Henry Lucas St. George Lyons-Montgomery, b.* 2 *Nov.* 1859; *d.* (? *unm.*) 2 *Jan.* 1887.

2c. Emily Laura Lyons-Montgomery, *m.* 17 Sept. 1898, William Stewart Archdale.

2b. *Charles Nixon Lyons-Montgomery, d.* (? *unm.*) 10 *May* 1843.

3b. *Emily Lyons-Montgomery, d.* (–); m. 19 *Feb.* 1844, *John O'Donnell of Larkfield, co. Leitrim.*

4b. *Elizabeth Lyons-Montgomery, d.* (–); m. 27 *Dec.* 1858, *the Rev. Julius S. Hearn.*

3a. *Dorothea Elizabeth Lyons-Montgomery, b.* 25 *Oct.* 1775; *d.* (–); m. 1795, *Captain Nathaniel Cooper of Cooper Hill, co. Meath, 68th Regt., d.* 1818; *and had (with other) issue* 1b.

1b. *Nathaniel Cooper of Cooper Hill, d.* 1852; m. *Anne, da. of Henry Irwin of Streamtown, co. Sligo, d.* (–); *and had (with other) issue* 1c.

1c. Henry Alexander Cooper (*Cooper Hill, co. Meath*).

4a. *Catherine Lyons-Montgomery, d.* 8 *Aug.* 1825; m. *Mar.* 1799, *Thomas Norman of Dublin, d.* 23 *Dec.* 1838; *and had issue* 1b *to* 4b.

1b. *Charles Norman, J.P., co. Londonderry, d. Aug.* 1843; m. 27 *Ap.* 1829, *Anna Eliza, da. of Edward Kough of New Ross; and had issue* 1c.

1c. *Thomas Norman of Glengollan, J.P., D.L., High Sheriff co. Donegal* 1864, b. 5 *Mar.* 1835; *d.* 13 *May* 1895; m. 3 *Oct.* 1878, *Annie, da. of Conolly Norman of Fahan House, co. Donegal, d.* 8 *Ap.* 1881; *and had issue* 1d *to* 2d.

1d. Charles Norman, J.P. (*Glengollan, Fahan, Londonderry*), *b.* 16 May 1879.

2d. Annie Norman, *b.* 23 Mar. 1881.

2b. *Rev. Hugh Norman, Rector of Aughanunshin, b.* 1808; *d.* 30 *Nov.* 1875; m. *Anne, da. of William Ball of Buncrana, d.* 20 *Sept.* 1883; *and had issue* 1c *to* 3c.

1c. Thomas Norman, *late* I.C.S. (*Strode Manor, Beaminster, Dorset*), *b.* 15 Oct. 1841; m. 10 Jan. 1872, Annie, da. of John Carpenter; and has issue 1d to 3d.

1d. Harold Hugh Norman, Capt. R.A.M.C., *b.* 8 Aug. 1875.

2d. Maud Norman, *b.* Oct. 1872.

3d. Ida Norman, *b.* May 1874.

2c. Rev. John Gage Norman (15 *Effingham Crescent, Dover*), *b.* 14 June 1851; m. 3 Oct. 1895, Triphosa, da. of Francis John Lace of Stone Gappe, Yorks.

3c. Conolly Norman, F.R.C.P.I. (*St. Dymphna's, North Circular Road, Dublin*), *b.* 12 Mar. 1853; *m.* 6 June 1882, Mary Emily, da. of Randal Y. Kenny, M.D.   [Nos. 43183 to 43195.

3b. Catherine Norman, b. 20 *Jan.* 1816; d. 19 *Oct.* 1885; m. 21 *Feb.* 1837, *Thomas Kough of Enniscorthy, co. Wexford,* b. 11 *Feb.* 1810; d. 12 *Nov.* 1873; *and had issue* 1c *to* 6c.

1c. *Edward Kough,* M.B., T.C.D., b. 13 Dec. 1837; d. 11 *Nov.* 1895; m. 1st, *Elizabeth, da. of the Rev. Robert William Burton, M.A., Rector of Raheny, Dublin; 2ndly,* 12 *Aug.* 1873, *Mary Elizabeth, da. of Adam Millar of Queen's Park, Monkstown, Dublin; and had issue* 1d *to* 4d.

1d. Thomas Macgregor Kough, now (by Deed Poll 7 Ap. 1905) Keogh, Capt. R.A., *b.* 20 May 1874.

2d. Edward Fitzadam Kough, B.A., M.B., T.C.D., *b.* 22 July 1878.

3d. Kathleen Beulah Kough, *b.* 19 Oct. 1869.

4d. Isabel Mary Kough, *b.* 7 July 1875.

2c. *Thomas Kough,* b. 31 *Dec.* 1838; d. 23 *Jan.* 1903; m. 7 *June* 1866, *Harriet Elizabeth, da. of Major-Gen. T. C. Hanyngton, Bengal Army; and had issue* 1d *to* 6d.

1d. Thomas Norman Kough, Burmese C.S., *b.* 21 Nov. 1878.

2d. Harriet Constance Kough, *b.* 7 July 1867; *m.* 8 Jan. 1903, Howard Carr, R.A.M.C.; and has issue 1e.

1e. Terence Carr, *b.* 14 May 1905.

3d. Kathleen Kough, *b.* 6 Oct. 1869; *m.* 10 Ap. 1899, James Poe, Solicitor (*Kilkenny*); and has issue 1e to 2e.

1e. Patricia Poe, *b.* 13 Ap. 1901.

2e. Dorothy Poe, *b.* 28 Nov. 1902.

4d. Fanny Norman Kough, *b.* 11 Mar. 1871; *m.* 4 Sept. 1895, William Hewat, Egyptian P.W.D.; and has issue 1e to 2e.

1e. Eileen Hewat, *b.* 9 July 1893.

2e. Constance Hewat, *b.* 25 Dec. 1897.

5d. Patience Caroline Kough, *b.* 27 Oct. 1875.

6d. Eileen Mary Kough, *b.* 18 Mar. 1881.

3c. Charles Kough, B.A., I.C.S. (*ret.*) (7 *Alma Road, Monkstown, co. Dublin*), b. 17 May 1843; *m.* 13 Aug. 1867, Jane Mary Elizabeth, da. of William Newport White of Downpatrick, M.D., F.R.C.S.I.; and has issue 1d to 3d.

1d. Charles Norman Kough, B.A., B.L., *b.* 25 July 1879.

2d. Edith Jane Kough, *b.* 5 Nov. 1872; *m.* 7 Oct. 1903, Thomas Lloyd Rooke of Monkstown, Dublin.

3d. Mabel Charlotte Kough, *b.* 20 Dec. 1877.

4c. James Thomas Kough, C.E., *b.* 30 Mar. 1851; *m.* 26 Feb. 1889, Clara, da. of Major F. Lacy of St. Katherine's, Parkstone, Dorset.

5c. Kathleen Norman Kough, *b.* 8 June 1847.

6c. Sophia Kough, *b.* 16 Dec. 1854; *m.* William Robinson Lee of Kingstown, Dublin, d. 2 Ap. 1889, and has issue 1d to 2d.

1d. Norman R. Lee, *b.* 26 Dec. 1889.

2d. Amy Liss Lee, *b.* 2 Aug. 1881.

4b. Florinda Norman, d. 26 *Mar.* 1896; m. 14 *Feb.* 1843, *Livingstone Thompson of co. Armagh,* d. 19 *Sept.* 1874; *and had issue* 1c.

1c. Robert Norman Thompson, M.D. (*Kindelstown, Delgany, co. Wicklow*), b. 20 Feb. 1853; *m.* 8 Jan. 1878, Helen Constance, da. of William Basil Orpin of Kindelstown; and has issue 1d to 4d.

1d. Livingstone William Norman Thompson, *b.* 5 Oct. 1878.

2d. William Orpin Thompson, *b.* 11 Mar. 1881.

3d. Cicely May Norman Thompson, *b.* 6 Aug. 1891.

4d. Florinda Norman Thompson, *b.* 11 Ap. 1896. [Nos. 43196 to 43224.

The Plantagenet Roll

420. Descendants, if any, of the Hon. MARY HAMILTON, *b.* 24 Jan. 1762; Hon. BARBARA HAMILTON, *b.* 9 Dec. 1766; Hon. SOPHIA HAMILTON, *b.* 3 Dec. 1769, wife 1st of WILLIAM JOHN LOWE, and 2ndly of HENRY HENZELL; and of the Hon. ANNE HAMILTON, *b.* 2 Mar. 1777; *d.* 1828, wife of THOMAS CRAVEN (see Table XXXIX.).

421. Descendants, if any, of GEORGE BRIDGES of Keynsham and Abington, co. Hants, M.P. 1714–1751, *d.* 1751, or of his brothers and sisters, if any (see Table XXXVIII.).

422. Descendants of LUCY (ROTHE), *suo jure* 3rd COUNTESS DE ROTHE [F.] (see Table XXXVIII.), *d.* Sept. 1782; *m.* as 1st wife, 1769, Lieut.-Gen. the Hon. (COUNT) ARTHUR DILLON, Knight of St. Louis, *d.* (being guillotined during the Reign of Terror) 13 Ap. 1794; and had issue.

See the Clarence Volume, pp. 445–446, Nos. 18975–18988.

[Nos. 43225 to 43238.

423. Descendants, if any, of JOHN SAVAGE, RICHARD SAVAGE, and WILLIAM SAVAGE (see Table XXXV.).

424. Descendants, if any surviving, of ELIZABETH SAVAGE (see Table XXXV.), *bur.* 24 Dec. 1614; *m.* as 2nd wife, 1st, THOMAS MAINWARING; 2ndly, Sir RAUFE DONE of Duddon, co. Chester, *bur.* 14 Jan. 1660; and had issue (at least by 2nd husband) 1*a* to 3*a*.

1*a*. *Ralph Done*, d.s.p.
2*a*. *John Done*, d.s.p.
3*a*. *Thomas Done of London, Auditor to Kings Charles II. and James II. and VII.*, m. *Jane, da. and h. of Sir Thomas Griffith; and had issue.*[1]

425. Descendants of GRACE WILBRAHAM (see Table XL.), *bur.* 2 May 1740; *m.* 1680, LIONEL (TOLLEMACHE), 3rd EARL OF DYSART [S.], *b.* 30 Jan. 1648; *d.* 23 Feb. 1727; and had issue 1*a* to 2*a*.

1*a*. *Lionel Tollemache, styled Lord Huntingtower, b. 6 June* 1682; d.v.p. 26 *July* 1712; m. *c.* 1708, *Henrietta Heneage, nat. da. of William (Cavendish), Duke of Devonshire* [E.], d. 11 *Jan.* 1718; *and had issue* 1b *to* 2b.

1*b*. *Lionel (Tollemache), 4th Earl of Dysart* [S.], *K.T., b. June* 1707; d. 10 *Mar.* 1770; m. 22 *July* 1729, *Lady Grace, da. of John (Carteret), 1st Earl Granville* [G.B.], d. 23 *July* 1755; *and had issue.*
See the Tudor Roll of "The Blood Royal of Britain," Table XXXII., pp. 201–211, Nos. 21378–21653.

[Nos. 43239 to 43513.

---

[1] Ormerod's "Cheshire," ii. p. 249.

# of The Blood Royal

2b. Hon. *Henrietta Tollemache*, m. *John Clutterbuck of Mill Green, co. Essex.*

2a. Lady *Catherine Tollemache*, d. 17 *Jan.* 1754 ; m. 1 *Sept.* 1724, *John Brydges, styled Marquis of Carnarvon, M.P.*, d.v.p. 8 *Ap.* 1729 ; *and had issue* 1b.

1b. Lady *Catherine Brydges, da. and h.*, b. 17 *Dec.* 1725 ; m. 1st, *William Berkeley Lyon of the Horse Guards,* d. app. s.p. ; 2ndly, 9 *Aug.* 1753, *Edwyn Francis Stanhope,* d. 15 *May* 1807 ; *and had issue (by 2nd husband).*

See the Clarence Volume, pp. 109–114, Nos. 1104–1239.

[Nos. 43514 to 43649.

426. Descendants of HENRY (BRIDGEMAN), 1st BARON BRADFORD [G.B.] and 5th Bart. [E.] (see Table XL.), *b.* 7 Sept. 1725 ; *d.* 5 June 1800 ; *m.* 12 July 1755, ELIZABETH, da. and h. of the Rev. John SIMPSON of Stoke Hall, co. Derby, *d.* 6 Mar. 1806 ; and had issue 1*a* to 4*a*.

1a. *Orlando* (*Bridgeman*), *2nd Baron* [*G.B.*] *and 1st Earl of* [*U.K.*] *Bradford,* b. 19 *Mar.* 1762 ; d. 7 *Sept.* 1825 ; m. 29 *May* 1788, *the Hon. Lucy Elizabeth, da. and co-h. of George* (*Byng*), *4th Viscount Torrington* [*G.B.*], b. 17 *Oct.* 1766 ; d. 20 *Sept.* 1844 ; *and had issue.*

See the Tudor Roll of "The Blood Royal of Britain," pp. 422–426, Nos. 30459–30608.

2a. Hon. *John Bridgeman, afterwards* (*Act of Parl. May* 1785) *Simpson,* b. 13 *May* 1763 ; d. 5 *June* 1850 ; m. 1st, 3 *June* 1784, *Henrietta Francis, da. of Sir Thomas Worsley of Appuldercombe, 6th Bart.* [*E.*], d. 25 *July* 1791 ; 2ndly, 27 *Nov.* 1793, *Grace, da. of Samuel Estwicke,* d. 1 *Jan.* 1839 ; *and had issue* 1b *to* 4b.

1b. Rev. *William Bridgeman Simpson,* b. 9 *Sept.* 1813 ; d. 1 *Ap.* 1895 ; m. 23 *June* 1837, *Lady Frances Laura, da. of Charles William Wentworth-FitzWilliam, 5th Earl FitzWilliam* [*I.*], d. 25 *Mar.* 1887 ; *and had issue.*

See p. 255, Nos. 9674–9688.

2b. *Henrietta Anna Maria Charlotte Bridgeman Simpson,* b. *Ap.* 1788 ; d. 30 *July* 1813 ; m. 11 *Aug.* 1806, *Charles* (*Anderson-Pelham*), *1st Earl of* [*U.K.*] *and 2nd Baron* [*G.B.*] *Yarborough,* d. 5 *Sept.* 1846 ; *and had issue.*

See the Tudor Roll of "The Blood Royal of Britain," pp. 421–422, Nos. 30415–30458.

3b. *Louisa Elizabeth Bridgeman Simpson,* b. *Sept.* 1801 ; d. 23 *Mar.* 1880 ; m. 25 *Aug.* 1820, *Rev. the Hon. Henry Edmund Bridgeman,* d. 15 *Nov.* 1872 ; *and had issue.*

See the Tudor Roll of "The Blood Royal of Britain," pp. 425–426, Nos. 30597–30608.

4b. *Georgiana Lucy Bridgeman Simpson,* b. 3 *Oct.* 1808 ; d. 6 *Ap.* 1898 ; m. 16 *Feb.* 1841, *Lieut.-Gen. Sir William Eyre, K.C.B.,* b. 21 *Oct.* 1805 ; d. 8 *Sept.* 1859 ; *and had issue* 1c.

1c. Arthur Hardolph Eyre, *b.* 1851.

3a. Hon. *Charlotte Bridgeman,* b. 28 *Jan.* 1761 ; d. 6 *July* 1802 ; m. 15 *May* 1784, *Henry Greswolde Lewis of Malvern Hall, co. Warwick.*

4a. Hon. *Elizabeth Diana Bridgeman,* b. 5 *June* 1764 ; d. 5 *May* 1810 ; m. 10 *Feb.* 1794, *Sir George William Gunning, 2nd Bart.* [*G.B.*], *M.P.*, b. 15 *Feb.* 1763 ; d. 7 *Ap.* 1823 ; *and had issue* 1b *to* 5b.

1b. *Sir Robert Henry Gunning, 3rd Bart.* [*G.B.*], b. 26 *Dec.* 1795 ; d. 22 *Sept.* 1862.

2b. Rev. *Sir Henry John Gunning, 4th Bart.* [*G.B.*], b. 17 *Dec.* 1797 ; d. 30 *June* 1885 ; m. 1st, 27 *Feb.* 1827, *Mary Catherine, da. of William Ralph Cartwright of Aynho, M.P.*, d. 25 *May* 1877 ; *and had issue* 1c.

[Nos. 43650 to 43870.

The Plantagenet Roll

1c. Sir George William Gunning, 5th Bart. [G.B.], b. 10 Aug. 1828; d. 21 Oct. 1903; m. 15 May 1851, Isabella Mary Frances Charlotte, da. of Col. William Chester-Master of Knole Park; and had issue 1d to 5d.

1d. Sir Frederick Digby Gunning, 6th Bart. [G.B.] (Little Horton, near Northampton), b. 13 Nov. 1853.

2d. Charles Vere Gunning, Major Reserve of Officers, late Durham L.I. (Junior United Service), b. 31 Oct. 1859; m. 17 Oct. 1888, Ethel Beatrice, da. of the Rev. William Robert Finch-Hatton; and has issue 1e.

1e. Essex Vere Gunning.

3d. Rev. Henry William Maude Gunning, M.A. (Oxon.), Rector of Abington (Abington Rectory, Northants), b. 21 Ap. 1865; m. 9 May 1905, Gertrude Alga, da. of the Rev. Canon James Tufton Bartlet.

4d. Emma Louisa Gunning, m. 2 Oct. 1890, Christopher Smyth (Little Houghton, Northampton); and has issue 1e to 2e.

1e. Barbara Mary Smyth.

2e. Ursula Catherine Smyth.

5d. Georgiana Mary Gunning.

3b. Orlando George Gunning, afterwards (R.L. 26 Mar. 1850) Gunning-Sutton of Blendworth, Hants, Capt. R.N., b. 12 May 1799; d. 5 May 1852; m. 22 June 1830, Mary Dorothea, da. of Admiral Sir Michael Seymour, 1st Bart. [G.B.], d. 31 Mar. 1900; and had issue 1c.

1c. Mary Diana Gunning, d. 8 Dec. 1890; m. as 1st wife, 8 Dec. 1852, Henry George (Liddell), 2nd Earl of Ravensworth [U.K.], d. 22 July 1903; and had issue 1d to 2d.

1d. Lady Mary Maud Diana Liddell, m. 17 Nov. 1892, Lieut.-Col. George Townshend Forestier-Walker, R.A., D.A.A.G. at Headquarters (Stanleys, Lymington, Hants); and has issue 1e to 2e.

1e. Lilian Diana Forestier-Walker, b. 12 Jan. 1894.

2e. Helen Mary Cecilia Forestier-Walker, b. 17 Ap. 1895.

2d. Lady Lilian Mary Harriet Diana Liddell.

4b. Rev. Spencer Greswolde Gunning, J.P., b. 27 Oct. 1800; d.[1] 29 May 1867; m. 20 Mar. 1839, Anne Janette, da. of James Connell of Conheath, co. Dumfries.

5b. John Gunning, Major H.E.I.C.S., b. 21 Dec. 1801; d. 13 Oct. 1845; m. 8 Sept. 1827, Jessie, da. of the Rev. Charles Maitland Babington; and had issue 1c to 4c.

1c. Charles George Gunning, Major Madras C.S., b. 27 Feb. 1834; d. 13 June 1878; m. 12 Jan. 1859, Emma Cameron, da. of Lieut.-Gen. Archibald Spiers Logan; and had issue 1d to 2d.

1d. Charles Archibald John Gunning (Zanzibar), b. 15 Oct. 1859; m. 16 Oct. 1900, Beatrice Constance, da. of Robert Raaf Purvis; and has issue 1e to 2e.

1e. Robert Charles Gunning, b. 2 Dec. 1901.

2e. Josephine Gunning, b. 30 June 1904.

2d. George Hamilton Gunning, Capt. 21st Indian Cav. (Junior Naval and Military), b. 3 Nov. 1876.

2c. John Campbell Gunning, Col. Indian Army, formerly Comy. Gen., Madras (32 Prince's Square, W.), b. 19 June 1835; m. 1865, Mary Anne, da. of J. R. Boyson; and has issue 1d to 4d.

1d. Charles John Gunning, Capt. I.S.C., b. 3 Dec. 1865.

2d. Orlando George Gunning, Capt. Indian Army (East India United Service), b. 31 July 1867; m. 1 Nov. 1902, Margaret Cecilia, da. of Clinton George Dawkins.

[Nos. 43871 to 43889.]

---

[1] Forster's "Baronetage," 1880, p. 259, says he had a son, b. Nov. 1839; other authorities, however, say that he had no issue.

# of The Blood Royal

3d. Henry Ross Gunning, Capt. 1st Batt. Devonshire Regt. (*Junior Naval and Military*), b. 30 Ap. 1879.

4d. Jessie Helen Gunning, m. 24 Sept. 1891, Capt. Leonard Wilkinson Cleveland Kerrich, 3rd Madras Lancers.

3c. *Lily Anne Gunning*, d. 16 *Ap*. 1869; m. 9 *Dec*. 1852, *the Rev. Granville Sykes Howard Vyse of Boughton Hall, Northants*, b. 30 *Sept*. 1818; d. (–); *and had issue* 1d.

1d. Mabel Diana Howard-Vyse, da. and (on death of last surv. brother 1892) h., m. 6 July 1882, Howard Henry Howard-Vyse, J.P., D.L., High Sheriff co. Northants 1887; and has issue 1e to 2e.

1e. Richard Glanville Hylton Howard-Vyse, b. 27 June 1883.

2e. George Cecil Howard-Vyse, b. 20 Nov. 1884.

4c. Lucy Bridgeman Gunning (*Hendon, Middlesex*). [Nos. 43890 to 43895.

427. Descendants of Sackville (Tufton), 7th Earl of Thanet [E.] (see Table XL.), b. 11 May 1688; d. 4 Dec. 1753; m. 11 June 1722, Lady Mary, da. and co-h. of William (Savile), 2nd Marquis of Halifax [E.], d. 30 July 1750; and had issue.

See p. 321, Sec. 242.

428. Descendants of Frances Puleston, Heiress of Gwysaney, &c. (see Table XLI.), b. 30 Oct. 1765; d. 1 Jan. 1818; m. as 1st wife, 18 Dec. 1786, Bryan Cooke of Owston, M.P., Col. 3rd West York Militia, and High Sheriff co. Denbigh 1794, b. 8 June 1756; d. 8 Nov. 1821; and had issue 1a to 3a.

1a. *Philip Davies Cooke, afterwards Davies-Cooke of Owston, Hafod-y-wern and Gwysaney, J.P., D.L., F.L.S., F.G.S., F.Z.S., High Sheriff co. Flint* 1824, *&c.*, b. 11 *Aug*. 1793; d. 20 *Nov*. 1853; m. 8 *Dec*. 1829, *Lady Helena Caroline, da. of George (King), 3rd Earl of Kingston* [I.], d. 9 *May* 1871; *and had issue* 1b *to* 4b.

1b. *Philip Bryan Davies-Cooke of Owston, Gwysaney, and Hafod-y-wern, J.P., D.L., F.S.A., High Sheriff co. Flint* 1858, *&c.*, b. 2 *Mar*. 1832; d. 29 *Sept*. 1903; m. 17 *July* 1862, *Emma Julia, da. of Sir Tatton Sykes, 4th Bart.* [G.B.]; *and had issue* 1c *to* 5c.

1c. Philip Tatton Davies-Cooke of Owston, &c., J.P., D.L., Major Denbigh Imp. Yeo. (*Gwysaney, Mold*), b. 15 May 1863; m. 14 Aug. 1894, Doris, da. of Charles Donaldson-Hudson of Cheswardine, M.P.; and has issue 1d.

1d. Philip Ralph Davies-Cooke, b. 27 Nov. 1896.

2c. Mary Helena Davies-Cooke.

3c. Emma Catherine Davies-Cooke.

4c. Mildred Emily Davies-Cooke.

5c. Helena Frances Anna Davies-Cooke.

2b. Bryan George Davies-Cooke, J.P., D.L., Col. *formerly* Comdg. 2nd Vol. Batt. Royal Welsh Fusiliers, *previously* Capt. 73rd Regt., A.D.C. to His Majesty, &c. (*Colomendy, Mold*), b. 3 Jan. 1835; m. 14 June 1860, Judith Caroline Halsted, da. of Capt. William Halsted Poole of Terrick Hall; and has issue 1c to 4c.

1c. Bryan Davies-Cooke, *formerly* Capt. 3rd Batt. Royal Welsh Fusiliers (*Arthur's*), b. 9 Sept. 1861; m. 8 Sept. 1890, Georgiana Mary, da. of Charles Fenwick of Harpenden; and has issue 1d to 3d.

1d. Bryan Cudworth Halsted Davies-Cooke, b. 9 Nov. 1892.

2d. Richard Domville Davies-Cooke, b. 26 Jan. 1900.

3d. Judith Mimi Davies-Cooke. [Nos. 43896 to 43906.

The Plantagenet Roll

2c. William Hugh Davies-Cooke (*Tyn Twll, Nannerch, Mold ; Travellers'*), b. 13 Oct. 1862 ; m. 27 June 1900, Mabel Louisa, da. of Capt. Philips of Rhûal ; and has issue (with 2 younger children) 1d to 2d.

    1d. Sybil Gwenydd Davies-Cooke, b. 1901.

    2d. Kathleen Mabel Davies-Cooke, b. 1903.

3c. Helena Adelaide Sara Davies-Cooke, m. 12 Feb. 1896, Basil Edwin Philips (*Rhual, Mold, co. Flint*) ; and has issue 1d.

    1d. Gwenllian Margaret Philips, b. 12 Mar. 1897.

4c. Gwendolen Mary Davies-Cooke.

3b. Rev. George Robert Davies-Cooke, *formerly* Vicar of Hythe (*Streethorpe, Southampton*), b. 29 May 1836 ; m. 10 Feb. 1863, Diana, da. of Henry Yarborough Parker of Streethorpe.

4b. James Robert Davies-Cooke, Major R.A., b. 4 *July* 1837 ; d. 1 *Sept.* 1883 ; m. 2 *July* 1868, *Clara Louisa* (25 *Charles Street, Berkeley Square, W.*), *da. of John Webb ; and had issue* 1c *to* 2c.

    1c. Aubrey George King Davies-Cooke, Lieut. 10th Hussars (*White's*), b. 18 June 1873.

    2c. Beatrice Helena Mary Davies-Cooke.

2a. Rev. *Robert Bryan Cooke, Preb. of York Minster,* b. 26 *Aug.* 1800 ; d. 17 *Oct.* 1887 ; m. 15 *Jan.* 1824, *Emily Carteret, da. of Philip Smith Webb of Milford House, co. Surrey, d.* 16 *Aug.* 1880 ; *and had issue* 1b.

    1b. *Emily Charlotte Hannah Cooke,* b. 25 *Feb.* 1825 ; d. 24 *Mar.* 1902 ; m. 9 *Aug.* 1848, *Oliver William Farrer of Binnegar Hall, Bar.-at-Law,* b. 18 *Mar.* 1819 ; d. 6 *Nov.* 1876 ; *and had issue* 1c *to* 3c.

        1c. Philip Farrer, Col. 2nd Dorset Regt. (*Binnegar Hall, Dorset*), b. 17 Nov. 1853 ; m. 3 Jan. 1893, Eleanor Clare, da. of Major-Gen. Hewett, R.E., C.M.G.

        2c. Bryan Farrer, Bar.-at-Law (*77 Onslow Square, S.W.*), b. 25 Nov. 1858 ; m. 15 Dec. 1892, Mabel Gertrude, da. of J. Smith of Mickleham Hall, co. Surrey ; and has issue 1d to 2d.

            1d. John Oliver Farrer, b. 31 Jan. 1894.

            2d. Walter Leslie Farrer, b. 30 Jan. 1900.

        3c. Rev. Walter Farrer, Rector of Wincanton (*Wincanton Rectory, Somerset*), b. 20 May 1862.

3a. *Mary Frances Cooke,* b. 22 *Aug.* 1788 ; d. 3 *Ap.* 1865 ; m. 8 *June* 1818, the Rev. *William Margesson of Van, co. Surrey and Woldringfold, co. Sussex,* b. 7 *Feb.* 1792 ; d. 20 *May* 1871 ; *and had issue* 1b *to* 3b.

    1b. William George Margesson, K.L.H., Lieut.-Col. (ret.) *formerly* 56th and 80th Regts. (*Findon Place, Findon, Sussex*), b. 6 June 1821 ; m. 14 Oct. 1863, Lucy Matilda, da. of Edward Blackett Beaumont of Woodhall ; and has issue 1c to 8c.

        1c. Evelyn William Margesson, Capt. and Brevet Major Norfolk Regt., b. 16 May 1865.

        2c. Wentworth Henry Davies Margesson, Comm. R.N., b. 22 July 1869.

        3c. Edward Cuninghame Margesson, Capt. South Wales Borderers, b. 13 Dec. 187.

        4c. Hugh Somerset Margesson, b. 11 Oct. 1875.

        5c. Anthony Robert Margesson, b. 19 Nov. 1878.

        6c. Maud Eleanor Margesson.

        7c. Rosamond Mary Frances Margesson.

        8c. Ierne Lucy Margesson.

    2b. Rev. *Reginald Whitehall Margesson, Rector of Blendworth Horndean,* b. 5 *Dec.* 1827 ; d. 3 *Oct.* 1901 ; m. 3 *May* 1860, *Louisa Sophia, da. of the Rev. David Rodney Murray, d.* 12 *Sept.* 1895 ; *and had issue* 1c *to* 6c.   [Nos. 43907 to 43929.

500

1c. Mortimer Reginald Margesson (*Foxlydiate House, Redditch*), *b.* 16 Mar. 1861; *m.* 10 Nov. 1886, Lady Isabella Augusta, sister of Sydney (Carr), 7th Earl of Buckinghamshire [G.B.], da. of Frederick John Hobart, Lord Hobart; and has issue 1*d* to 4*d.*

    1*d.* Henry David Reginald Margesson, *b.* 1890.

    2*d.* Thomas Vere Hobart Margesson, *b.* 1902.

    3*d.* Catherine Sydney Louisa Margesson, *b.* 29 Sept. 1887.

    4*d.* Albinia Helena Margesson, *b.* 1889.

2c. Rev. Henry Philip Montolieu Margesson, Vicar of Ebbesbourne Wake (*Ebbesbourne Wake Vicarage, near Salisbury*), *b.* 26 Aug. 1862; *m.*; and has issue (a da.).

3c. Reginald Elibank Murray Margesson (*Canada*), *b.* 22 Sept. 1863; *m.*

4c. Philip Alexander Margesson (*New Zealand*), *b.* 20 May 1865; *unm.*

5c. Mary Louisa Margesson, *unm.*

6c. Amy Helena Margesson, *unm.*

3b. Emily Charlotte Margesson, *b.* 8 Feb. 1823; *unm.* [Nos. 43930 to 43940.

429. Descendants of ANNE ELIZABETH DAVIES of Llanerch and Broughton, co. Flint (see Table XLI.), *d.* (−); *m.* 10 Nov. 1794, the Rev. GEORGE ALLANSON of Middleton Quernbow, co. York, *b.* 1759; *d.* 1 Dec. 1826; and had issue 1*a* to 3*a.*[1]

    1*a. George Allanson of Quernbow,* b. *6 Sept.* 1796; *d.s.p.*

    2*a. Elizabeth Allanson,* d. *22 Ap.* 1837; m. *as 1st wife,* 18 *Nov.* 1822, *John Whitehall Dodd of Cloverley Hall, co. Salop, M.P.,* b. 17 *Sept.* 1797; *and had issue a son, Whitehall Dodd of Cloverley,* b. 2 *Feb.* 1823; *d.s.p.* 22 *Feb.* 1878.

    3*a. Dorothy Allanson,* 2nd da. *and eventual* (1878) *sole h.,* d. *Ap.* 1881; m. 8 *July* 1830, *Sir Digby Cayley of Brompton,* 7th *Bart.* [E.], b. 13 *Mar.* 1807; d. 21 *Dec.* 1883; *and had issue* 1*b to* 4*b.*

    1*b. Sir George Allanson Cayley,* 8th *Bart.* [E.], b. 31 *Dec.* 1831; d. 10 *Oct.* 1895; m. 5 *July* 1859, *Catherine Louisa, da. of Sir William Worsley,* 1st *Bart.* [U.K.]; *and had issue* 1*c to* 3*c.*

    1c. Sir George Everard Arthur Cayley, 9th Bart. [E.], J.P., D.L., &c. (*The Green, Brompton, R.S.O., High Hall, Brompton, R.S.O.; Llannerch Park, St. Asaph*), *b.* 8 July 1861; *m.* 17 Sept. 1884, Lady Mary Susan, sister of James John, 2nd Earl of Wharncliffe [U.K.], da. of the Hon. Francis Dudley-Montagu-Stuart-Wortley; and has issue 1*d* to 5*d.*

    1*d.* Francis Digby Edward Cayley, *b.* 4 Feb. 1894.

    2*d.* Kenelm Henry Ernest Cayley, *b.* 24 Sept. 1896.

    3*d.* Dorothy Francis Cayley.

    4*d.* Margaret Renée Cayley.

    5*d.* Ann Letitia Mary Cayley.

    2c. Digby William Cayley, *b.* 16 Sept. 1862.

    3c. Ethel Barbara Cayley.

    2b. Digby Cayley, J.P., C.C. (*Norton Grove, Malton*), *b.* 7 June 1834; *m.* 15 Nov. 1859, Charlotte Philadelphia, da. of Robert Bower of Welham; and has issue 1*c* to 13*c.* [Nos. 43941 to 43949.

---

[1] See "Genealogical History of the House of Gwysaney," by Sir Bernard Burke, 1847.

3 S

The Plantagenet Roll

1c. Digby Leonard Arthur Cayley, J.P., D.L. (*Lovely Hall, Salesbury, Blackburn*), *b.* 25 Sept. 1864; *m.* 18 Ap. 1894, Beatrice, da. of Sir William Coddington, 1st Bart. [U.K.]; and has issue 1*d* to 2*d*.

    1d. Digby Coddington Cayley, *b.* 17 July 1895.

    2d. William Arthur Seton Cayley, *b.* 11 Sept. 1896.

2c. George Cuthbert Cayley, Capt. R.N., *b.* 30 Aug. 1866; *m.* 1897, Cecil Mildred May, da. of Col. Price Jones.

3c. Valentine Charles Hugh Cayley, *b.* 11 Jan. 1868.

4c. Harry Francis Cayley, *late* Lieut. R.N., *b.* 4 July 1873; *m.* 19 Ap. 1900, Margery, da. of Sir Thomas George Freake, 2nd Bart. [U.K.], *d.* 4 Mar. 1901; and has issue 1*d*.

    1d. Alexandra Margery Eileen Cayley, *b.* 21 Feb. 1901.

5c. Herbert Cayley, *late* Lieut. R.N., *b.* 24 Oct. 1874.

6c. Lewis Richard Cayley, *b.* 19 Aug. 1877.

7c. Helen Dora Cayley, *m.* as 2nd wife, 1 Mar. 1892, Christopher John Leyland (*Haggerston Castle, Beal, Northumberland*); and has issue 1*d* to 6*d*.

    1d. Christopher Digby Leyland, *b.* 24 Dec. 1892.

    2d. Stanley Cuthbert Leyland, *b.* 9 Aug. 1901.

    3d. Robert Clive Leyland, *b.* 10 Ap. 1903.

    4d. Dorothy Leyland.

    5d. Joan Leyland.

    6d. Angela Leyland.

8c. Julia Philadelphia Cayley, *m.* 3 Feb. 1891, Ernest Richard Bradley Hall-Watt, *previously* Hall, J.P., D.L., High Sheriff co. York 1896 (*Bishop Burton, Beverley ; Carr Head, Keighley, Yorks*); and has issue 1*d* to 2*d*.

    1d. Richard Hall-Watt, *b.* 30 Ap. 1898.

    2d. Alverey Digby Hall-Watt, *b.* 6 June 1901.

9c. Beatrice Mary Eugenia Cayley, *m.* 26 Oct. 1898, John William Coulthurst, J.P. (*Gargrave House, Yorkshire*).

10c. Alice Erica Cayley.

11c. Catherine Eleanor Millicent Cayley, *m.* 13 Feb. 1901, Comm. Walter Henry Cowan, M.V.O., D.S.O., R.N.

12c. Lucy Violet Cayley.

13c. Octavia Cayley.

3b. Rev. Reginald Arthur Cayley, M.A., Rector of Stowell (*Stowell Rectory, Sherborne*), *b.* 15 Aug. 1837; *m.* 3 May 1864, Mary Louisa, da. of the Rev. Edmund Hiley Bucknall-Estcourt; and has issue 1*c* to 6*c*.

1c. Cecil Reginald Cayley, *b.* 5 Feb. 1865; *m.* 7 Sept. 1893, Ida Rutherford, da. of George Rutherford Gibbs of Madeira ; and has issue 1*d*.

    1d. Philip Estcourt Cayley, *b.* 17 Dec. 1894.

2c. Lionel Richard Cayley, *b.* 15 Mar. 1867.

3c. Edmund Henry George Cayley, *b.* 4 Aug. 1870; *m.* 3 Aug. 1898, Maria Olga, da. of Olto Martin of Valparaiso ; and has issue 1*d* to 2*d*.

    1d. Digby Edgar Cayley, *b.* 7 Aug. 1904.

    2d. Evelyn Olga Vivienne Cayley.

4c. Dora Cayley.

5c. Isabel Mary Cayley.

6c. Hester Charlotte Cayley.

4b. Dora Cayley, *m.* 22 Sept. 1870, George Arthur Thompson, Registrar of Deeds for the East Riding, *late* 12th Lancers (*Register House, Beverley ; Terrington Hall, York*); and has issue 1*c* to 7*c*.

    1c. George Leonard Thompson.

    2c. Francis Edward Thompson.

[Nos. 43950 to 43986.

# of The Blood Royal

3c. Everilda Mary Thompson, *m.* 18 July 1900, Arthur Cowie Stamer (*Kirk Hammerton Lodge, York*).

4c. Alice Dora Thompson.

5c. Helena Constance Thompson.

6c. Bertha Mildred Thompson.

7c. Lilian Agnes Thompson.　　　　　　　　　　　　　　　[Nos. 43987 to 43991.

430. Descendants of the Rev. JOHN ROBERT LLOYD of Aston, co. Salop (see Table XLI.), *d.* 1803; *m.* MARTHA, da. of John SHAKESPEARE of London, *d.* (–); and had issue 1*a* to 5*a*.

1*a. William Lloyd of Aston, J.P., D.L., High Sheriff co. Salop* 1810, *b.* 21 Dec. 1779; *d.* 29 *Ap.* 1843; *m.* 1805, *Louisa, da. and co-h. of Admiral Sir Eliab Harvey of Rolls Park, co. Essex, G.C.B., d.* 7 *Mar.* 1866; *and had issue* 1*b to* 2*b*.

1*b. Richard Thomas Lloyd of Aston Hall and Rolls Park, J.P., D.L., High Sheriff co. Salop* 1874, *and Col. Shropshire Yeo. Cav., &c., b.* 9 *Sept.* 1820; *d.* 4 *Nov.* 1898; *m.* 19 *Aug.* 1852, *Lady Frances, da. of Thomas Robert (Hay),* 10*th Earl of Kinnoull* [S.], *d.* 31 *Jan.* 1886; *and had issue* 1*c to* 9*c*.

1*c.* Francis Lloyd, C.B., D.S.O., J.P., Brig.-Gen. Comdg. Guards Brigade, Aldershot (*Aston Hall, Oswestry; Rolls Park, Chigwell*), *b.* 12 Aug. 1853; *m.* 6 Aug. 1881, Mary, da. of George Gunnis of Leckie.

2*c.* Fitzwarren Lloyd, *b.* 16 Aug. 1859; *m.* 29 Ap. 1891, Agnes Elizabeth, da. of William Robert Hunter of Wellfield, co. Berwick.

3*c.* Rev. Rossendale Lloyd, Rector of Selattyn (*Selattyn Rectory, Oswestry*), *b.* 14 Sept. 1863; *m.* 26 Sept. 1899, Katherine Frances, da. of the Rev. Walter Hook, Preb. of Wells; and has issue 1*d*.

1*d.* Andrew Francis Lloyd, *b.* 31 Oct. 1903.

4*c.* Richard Harvey Lloyd, *b.* 17 Ap. 1868; *m.* 12 July 1890, Kathleen Agnes, da. of J. Day.

5*c.* Eva Lloyd, *m.* 21 Ap. 1881, the Rev. E. J. Rees, Vicar of Letchworth, *d.* 19 Jan. 1886.

6*c.* Louisa Selina Lloyd.

7*c.* Edith Lloyd, *m.* 1 Nov. 1886, Admiral William Harvey Pigott, R.N., J.P. (*Doddershall Park, Aylesbury*); and has issue 1*d* to 2*d*.

1*d.* Editha Ivy Pigott.

2*d.* Lettice Harvey Pigott.

8*c.* Ada Lloyd, *m.* 25 Sept. 1884, the Rev. Hugh Holbech, M.A. (Oxon.), Vicar of Farnborough (*Farnborough Vicarage, Warwickshire*); and has issue 1*d* to 6*d*.

1*d.* Charles Hugh Holbech, *b.* 18 July 1885.

2*d.* Laurence Holbech, *b.* 6 Mar. 1888.

3*d.* David Holbech, *b.* 9 Sept. 1897.

4*d.* Gertrude Frances Holbech, *b.* 31 Aug. 1886.

5*d.* Mary Helen Holbech, *b.* 10 Oct. 1889.

6*d.* Anne Holbech, *b.* 16 Mar. 1902.

9*c.* Maud Lloyd, *m.* 18 Jan. 1893, Reginald Beech, Capt. 4th Batt. Staffordshire Regt., *d.* 1905.

2*b. Charlotte Lloyd, d.* 9 *Sept.* 1883; *m. as 2nd wife,* 30 *Oct.* 1838, *Col. George Grenville Wandesford Pigott of Doddershall Park, M.P., d.* 4 *Jan.* 1865; *and had issue* 1*c.*

1*c.* William Harvey Pigott, J.P., Admiral R.N. (*Doddershall Park, Aylesbury*), *b.* 8 Mar. 1848; *m.* 1 Nov. 1886, Edith, da. of Col. Richard Thomas Lloyd of Aston, J.P., D.L.; and has issue.

See p. 503, Nos. 44000–44001.　　　　　[Nos. 43992 to 44012.

The Plantagenet Roll

2a. Rev. Charles Arthur Albany Lloyd, Rector of Whittington, co. Salop, b. 1785; d. 1851; m. Hannah Simpson, widow of [——] Cowan, da. of [——]; and had issue (3 children).

3a. Rev. George Newton Kynaston Lloyd, Rector of Selattyn, co. Salop, b. 1786; d. 1848; m. [——], da. of [——] Corrie; and had issue (3 children).

4a. Elizabeth Lloyd, d. (-); m. Robert Curtis; and had issue.

5a. Louisa Charlotte Lloyd, d. 11 Ap. 1869; m. 21 Ap. 1803, the Hon. Thomas Kenyon of Pradoe, co. Salop, b. 27 Sept. 1780; d. 4 Nov. 1851; and had issue 1b to 6b.

1b. John Robert Kenyon of Pradoe, D.C.L., Q.C., Fellow of All Souls, Oxford, Vinerian Professor and Judge of the Vice-Chancellor's Court, Recorder of Oswestry, &c., b. 13 Jan. 1807; d. 17 Ap. 1880; m. 11 Aug. 1846, Mary Eliza, da. of Edward Hawkins, F.R.S., d. 28 Jan. 1903; and had issue 1c to 10c.

1c. Robert Lloyd Kenyon, M.A. (Oxon.), J.P., D.L., Bar. M.T., Deputy Chairman of Quarter Sessions, Recorder of Oswestry, and Deputy Chancellor of Lichfield Diocese, &c. &c. (*Pradoe, Oswestry*), b. 18 Jan. 1848; m. 9 June 1886, Ellen Frances, da. of the Right Rev. William Walsham How, Lord Bishop of Wakefield.

2c. Edward Ranulph Kenyon, Lieut.-Col. and Brevet-Col. R.E., in Command of R.E. Salisbury Plain Dist. (*Salisbury*), b. 3 Nov. 1854; m. 14 Sept. 1880, Katharine Mary McCrea, da. of Major-Gen. John Cromie Blackwood De Butts, R.E.; and has issue 1d to 5d.

1d. Herbert Edward Kenyon, Lieut. R.G.A., b. 2 Dec. 1881.

2d. Katherine Mary Rose Kenyon, b. 17 July 1887.

3d. Ellen Blackwood Kenyon, b. 7 May 1889.

4d. Winifred Lilian Kenyon, b. 27 Jan. 1892.

5d. Frances Margaret Kenyon, b. 18 July 1894.

3c. Eustace Alban Kenyon, Indian Telegraph Dept. (*Bombay*), b. 24 Sept. 1859; m. 10 Mar. 1896, Caroline Ethel Jane, da. of the Rev. William Cornish Hunt; and has issue 1d to 5d.

1d. William Patrick Kenyon, b. 17 Mar. 1898.

2d. Rowland Lloyd Kenyon, b. 16 Jan. 1901.

3d. Dorothy Ethel Kenyon, b. 4 Mar. 1897.

4d. Violet Mary Kenyon, b. 11 June 1899.

5d. Irene Helen Kenyon, b. 11 June 1902.

4c. Frederic George Kenyon, M.A. (Oxon.), Assist. Keeper of MSS. at British Museum, Fellow British Academy, a Corresponding Member of Berlin Academy, &c. &c. (*Harrow-on-the-Hill*), b. 15 Jan. 1863; m. 6 Aug. 1891, Amy, da. of Rowland Hunt of Boreatton Park, co. Salop; and has issue 1d.

1d. Kathleen Mary Kenyon, b. 5 Jan. 1906.

5c. Rev. Gerald Kenyon, M.A. (Oxon.), Rector of Hordley (*Hordley Rectory, Ellesmere*), b. 7 Aug. 1864.

6c. Evelyn Oswald Kenyon (*Melincue, Argentina*), b. 5 Oct. 1865.

7c. Lionel Richard Kenyon, Capt. R.A. (*United Service*), b. 26 July 1867; m. 9 Sept. 1896, Elizabeth Jane, da. of Peter Cormack Sutherland of Pietermaritzburg, M.D.; and has issue 1d to 2d.

1d. Harold Anthony Kenyon, b. 11 June 1897.

2d. Lionel Frederick Robert Kenyon, b. 6 Aug. 1900.

8c. Mary Kenyon,
9c. Eliza Charlotte Kenyon, } (*Hordley Rectory, Ellesmere*).
10c. Emma Kenyon,

2b. George Kenyon, Com. R.N., b. 10 Mar. 1811; d. 18 Mar. 1866; m. 24 Ap. 1856, Mary, da. of Robert Usherwood of Whitby; and had issue 1c to 3c.

[Nos. 44013 to 44035.

# of The Blood Royal

1c. Rev. Alfred Ernest Lloyd Kenyon, M.A. (Oxon.), Vicar of Clun (*Clun Vicarage, Salop*), b. 30 Jan. 1859.

2c. Edgar Thomas Kenyon, a Sup. Travelling Inspector in Board of Agriculture (*Grafton Lodge, Baschurch, Shrewsbury*), b. 13 Oct. 1860.

3c. Georgina Mary Kenyon, m. 1 June 1892, the Rev. James Mackay, M.A., Vicar of Holy Trinity, Shrewsbury (*Holy Trinity Vicarage, Shrewsbury*).

3b. *William Kenyon, afterwards (R.L. 23 July 1862) Kenyon-Slaney of Hatton Grange, J.P., D.L., Lieut.-Col. Shropshire R.V.,* b. 20 Feb. 1815; d. 10 Dec. 1884; m. 9 Oct. 1845, Frances Catherine, da. and co-h. of Robert Aglionby Slaney of Hatton Grange; d. 18 Oct. 1896; *and had issue.*

See p. 280, Nos. 11144–11156.

4b. *Rev. Charles Orlando Kenyon, M.A., Vicar of Moreton,* b. 28 *Sept.* 1816; d. 6 *Nov.* 1890; m. 15 *Aug.* 1844, *Matilda Eloisa, da. of the Rev. Henry Calveley Colton,* d. 23 Mar. 1892; *and had issue* 1c *to* 3c.

1c. Charles Robert Kenyon (91 *Burnt Ash Road, Lee, S.E.*), b. 22 Sept. 1845; m. 1885, Jessie, da. of Charles Willett of Liverpool; and has issue 1d to 2d.

1d. Charles Orlando Kenyon, b. 30 Ap. 1886.

2d. Elena Georgiana Matilda Kenyon.

2c. Henry Thomas Kenyon (*El Prado, Gualegnaychu, Buenos Ayres*), b. 18 Ap. 1852; m. 8 July 1897, Hilda Beatrice, da. of William Pettit Dewes of Ashby-de-la-Zouch.

3c. Alice Matilda Kenyon (*Breidden Cottage, Oswestry*).

5b. *Arthur Richard Kenyon,* b. 18 *June* 1818; d. 3 *June* 1888; m. 18 *Jan.* 1859, *Augusta Mary Johnstone, widow of Capt. George Wilder, R.H.A., da. of Samuel Clogstoun; and had issue* 1c *to* 6c.

1c. Arthur Augustus Kenyon (*Spring Hill, Douglas, Wyoming, U.S.A.*), b. 23 Nov. 1868; m. 1900, Agnes, da. of W. A. Oliver-Rutherfurd of Edgerston, Jedburgh.

2c. John Hubert Kenyon, Indian Revenue Dept. (*Madras*), b. 4 Aug. 1870; m. 8 Feb. 1898, Caroline, da. of S. P. Bussell of Sydney, N.S. Wales; and has issue 1d.

1d. Eileen Sibyl Kenyon, b. 18 Sept. 1899.

3c. Caroline Walcott Kenyon, m. 30 Ap. 1894, Cuthbert G. W. Clogstoun, Madras Police (*Madras*); and has issue 1d.

1d. Muriel Augusta Clogstoun, b. 14 Aug. 1897.

4c. Peregrina Dora Kenyon.

5c. *Leonora Constance Kenyon,* b. 6 *July* 1864; d. *June* 1893; m. 21 *Dec.* 1886, *Capt. Francis Douglas Lumley, Middlesex Regt.; and had issue (a da.).*

6c. Sibyl Mary Kenyon.

6b. *Charlotte Kenyon,* b. 4 *May* 1813; d. 14 *Jan.* 1884; m. 17 *Dec* 1833, *the Rev. John Hill, M.A., younger brother to Rowland, 2nd Viscount Hill [U.K.],* b. 11 *Mar.* 1803; d. 15 *June* 1891; *and had issue* 1c *to* 4c.

1c. John Hill, J.P. (*Marsh Brook House, Church Stretton, Salop*), b. 23 July 1840; m. 12 July 1865, Mary, da. of James Gothorp of Mowbray Hill, Bedale, J.P.; and has issue 1d to 4d.

1d. John Kenyon Hill, Hon. Lieut. in Army, *previously* 5th Batt. Imp. Yeo., and Assist.-Director of Agriculture at Govt. Experimental Farms, Naivasha, British East Africa, b. 13 Jan. 1869.

2d. Frederick Rowland Hill, b. 23 Jan. 1870.

3d. Bessie Georgina Jane Hill.

4d. Charlotte Helen Hill, m. 22 Dec. 1903, William Gilchrist (*Felhampton Court, Shropshire*).

2c. *George William Hill, Vice-Admiral R.N.,* b. 20 *July* 1843; d. 25 *Sept.*
[Nos. 44036 to 44068.

The Plantagenet Roll

1905; m. 1st, 9 Nov. 1882, Mary Caroline, da. of Admiral Morgan Singer, R.N., d. 21 Oct. 1896; 2ndly, 15 Nov. 1898, Helen Maude (Stoney Stretton Hall, Yockleton, Shrewsbury), da. of Frederick Woodman; and had issue 1d to 7d.

    1d. Cyril John Percy Hill, b. 14 Feb. 1884.

    2d. Hubert George Morgan Hill, b. 11 Feb. 1888.

    3d. Guy Charles Dunlop Hill, b. 12 Nov. 1890.

    4d. Geoffrey Frank Kenyon Hill, b. 12 Jan. 1900.

    5d.[1] Gladys Frances Charlotte Hill.

    6d.[1] Gwendoline Mary Kenyon Hill.

    7d. Eileen Edith Singer Hill.

    3c. Sir Clement Lloyd Hill, K.C.M.G., K.C.B., M.P., Head of the African Dept. of the Foreign Office, and Sup. of African Protectorates (2 Whitehall Court, S.W.), b. 5 May 1845; m. 15 May 1889, Charlotte Eliza Mary, widow of Charles Waring, da. of Sir George William Denys, 2nd Bart. [U.K.], d. 11 Jan. 1900.

    4c. Brian Hubert Hill, b. 4 June 1847; d. 18 Dec. 1893; m. 8 Ap. 1891, Alice Mary (Drayton, Penkridge, Stafford), da. of Charles Langton of Barkhill, Liverpool; and had issue 1d.

    1d. Nina Hill, b. 28 July 1892.   [Nos. 44069 to 44077.

431. Descendants, if any surviving, of THOMAS DAVIES of Trefynant, co. Denbigh (see Table XLI.), b. 8 Nov. 1757; d. (–); m. MARGARET, da. of John PEPLOE of Peploe, co. Salop, d. 24 June 1809; and had issue 1a to 2a.[1]

    1a. Owen Davies of Chilwell Hall, co. Notts and Eton House, co. Kent, b. 4 Nov. 1796; d. (–); m. 4 Nov. 1826, Frederica Wilhelmina, da. of Samuel Cutler Hooley of Woodthorpe, co. Notts; and had issue 1b to 4b.

    1b. Owen Davies, Lieut. 11th Foot, b. 1 Mar. 1831; m. 10 Jan. 1854, Jane, da. of Thomas Maclaine of the Isle of Mull; and has issue.

    1c. Owen Mytton Davies, b. 10 Nov. 1854.

    2c. Mary Constance Davies, b. 1 Nov. 1856.

    2b. Thomas Davies, Ensign 11th Foot, b. 2 Feb. 1833.

    3b. Margaret Davies, b. 4 Sept. 1827; m. 11 July 1850, Michael Joseph Charles Rippert of Paris, Advocate, Cour de Cassation; and has issue.

    1c. Charles Frederic Amadeus Rippert, b. 12 July 1854.

    4b. Mary Hooley Davies, b. 12 May 1829; m. 16 Aug. 1853, Viscount John Baptist Amable de Montaignac de Chauvance, [3rd son of Viscount Raymond Aimé de Montaignac de Chauvance, a younger son of Amable (de Montaignac), Count of Montaignac of Chauvance and of the Rochebriant [F.], K.S.L.]; and has issue 1c.

    1c. Chevalier Louis de Montaignac de Chauvance, b. 3 Dec. 1855.

    2a. Elizabeth Davies, b. 6 Sept. 1782; d. 4 Ap. 1844; m. 27 Mar. 1800, William Hughes of Pen-y-Clawdd, co. Denbigh, d. 18 Jan. 1836; and had issue 1b to 3b.

    1b. William Hughes of Gayton Mansion, co. Northants, b. 18 Ap. 1801; d. (–); m. 11 July 1835, Eliza Anne, da. of William Henry Worthington of Sandiway Bank, co. Chester; and had issue 1c to 2c.

    1c. William O'Farrel Hughes of Emmanuel Coll., Camb. 1857, b. (at Nancy, Lorraine) 18 Feb. 1838.

    2c. Frances Eliza Margaretta Hughes, b. 27 June 1836.

                                 [Nos. 44078 to 44087.

---

[1] See "A Genealogical History of the House of Gwysaney," by Sir Bernard Burke, 1847.

506

# of The Blood Royal

2b. Thomas Hughes, M.D., F.R.C.S., b. 22 Aug. 1803 ; d. (? *unm.*).

3b. John Hughes of Cleveland Row, St. James', Westminster, and the Inner Temple, Bar.-at-Law, b. 6 Oct. 1805 ; d. (–) ; m. 5 *July* 1832, *Dorothea, da. of Richard Hughes Lloyd of Plymoy, co. Denbigh ; Bashall, co. York, &c.*, d. 27 *Jan.* 1848 ; *and had issue* 1c.

1c. Talbot de Bashall Hughes, Ensign Cape Mounted Rifles, b. 15 Dec. 1836.

[No. 44088.

432. Descendants, if any, of MARY DAVIES (see Table XLI.), living *unm.* 24 Oct. (36 Char. II.) 1685 ; and 16 Dec. 1716, when she was wife of the Rev. THOMAS HOLLAND of Berow, co. Anglesey.

433. Descendants of FRANCES BROOKE (see Table XL.), d. (–) ; *m.* GEORGE SALUSBURY TOWNSHEND OF CHESTER, b. 19 Ap. 1742 ; d. 21 Sept. 1801 ; and had (with possibly other) issue 1a.

1a. George Brooke Brigges Townshend, afterwards (R.L. 1797) Brooke of Haughton, High Sheriff co. Salop 1811, d. 25 *May* 1845 ; m. 1799, *Henrietta, da. and h. of Richard Massey of Walton-on-the-Hill, co. Lancaster*, d. 9 *Ap.* 1843 ; *and had issue* 1b.

1b. Rev. John Brooke of Haughton, Vicar of Shifnal, b. 1 *Mar.* 1803 ; d. 27 *Jan.* 1881 ; m. 27 *July* 1843, *Georgiana Frances, da. of John Cotes of Woodcote*, d. *Sept.* 1846 ; *and had issue* 1c *to* 2c.

1c. John Townshend Brooke of Haughton Hall, J.P., b. 6 *Oct.* 1844 ; d. 31 *Jan.* 1899 ; m. 30 *June* 1874, *Lady Wilhelmina, da. of William (Legge), 4th Earl of Dartmouth* [*G.B.*] ; *and had issue* 1d *to* 6d.

1d. William John Brooke (*Haughton Hall, Shifnal*), b. 6 May 1876 ; m. 1901, Gwendolen Margaret, da. of James Dalgleish Kellie MacCallum of Quinton Rising, Chief Constable of Northants ; and has issue 1e to 2e.

1e. Richard Townshend Brooke, b. 1903.

2e. Margaret Eleanor Brooke, b. 1902.

2d. George Townshend Brooke, b. 9 May 1878.

3d. Basil Richard Brooke, Lieut. R.N., b. 28 Nov. 1882.

4d. Madeline Harriet Brooke, b. 4 Nov. 1879.

5d. Evelyn Georgiana Brooke, b. 17 May 1881.

6d. Bertha Mary Brooke, b. 3 Dec. 1884.

2c. Rev. Charles Brooke, M.A. (Oxon.), *Vicar of Grendon* (*Grendon Vicarage, Northampton*), b. 17 Aug. 1846 ; *m.* 31 Jan. 1884, Bertha Ann, da. of the Rev. William Thornton of Kingsthorpe. [Nos. 44089 to 44097.

434. Descendants, if any, of the Hon. MARY BRERETON (see Table XLII.), wife of Sir MICHAEL HUTCHINSON.

435. Descendants of CHARLES (COKAYNE), 3rd VISCOUNT CULLEN [I.] (see Table XLII.), b. 15 Nov. 1658 ; d. 30 Dec. 1688 ; m. 26 Dec. 1678, the Hon. KATHARINE, da. of William, 6th Baron WILLOUGHBY of Parham [E.], b. 14 May 1655 ; d. 11 Feb. 1689 ; and had issue.

See pp. 93–97, Nos. 603–748.   [Nos. 44098 to 44243.

The Plantagenet Roll

436. Descendants of the Hon. ELIZABETH COKAYNE (see Table XLII.), *b.* 20 Oct. 1666; *bur.* 19 Nov. 1739; *m.* THOMAS CRATHORNE of Crathorne and Ness, co. York, *b. c.* 1658; *d.* 5 Ap. 1714; and had issue 1*a* to 3*a*.[1]

1*a.* *Ralph Crathorne of Crathorne and Ness,* d. 19 *Ap.* 1755, *having had issue, who all* d. unm.

2*a.* *George Crathorne of Ness, a nonjuror* 1715, d. *a.* 1755; m. *Margaret, da. and co-h. of Francis Trapps of Mild; and had issue* 1*b.*

1*b.* *Thomas Crathorne of Crathorne,* bur. (*there*) 2 *Feb.* 1764; m. 1755, *Isabel, da. of Sir John Swinburne, 3rd Bart.* [*E.*]; *and had issue* 1*c.*

1*c.* *George Crathorne, afterwards Tasburgh, of Crathorne* (*3rd, but in 1815, only surv. s. and h.*), *b. c.* 1761; bur. 9 *Sept.* 1825; m. *Barbara, widow of George Tasburgh of Bodney, da. of Thomas Fitzherbert of Norbury and Swynnerton,* d. *July* 1808; *and had issue.*
See the Clarence Volume, pp. 384–385, Nos. 14618–14683.

3*a.* *Catherine Crathorne,* m. *Major Wansborough.*   [Nos. 44244 to 44309.

437. Descendants of MARGARET PIERSON of Bishop Middleham, co. Durham (see Table XLII.), *bapt.* 26 June 1679; *bur.* 12 May 1731; *m.* as 2nd wife, 1 Sept. 1701, GILBERT SPEARMAN, Barrister, *bapt.* 17 Aug. 1675; *bur.* 12 May 1738; and had issue 1*a* to 2*a*.

1*a.* *George Spearman of Bishop Middleham,* bapt. 23 *Ap.* 1714; bur. 23 *Ap.* 1761; m. *Anne, da. of Ralph Sneyd,* bur. 8 *July* 1752; *and had issue* 1*b.*

1*b.* *Elizabeth Honoria Spearman of Bishop Middleham* (*sold* 1769), *da. and in her issue sole h.,* d. 28 *July* 1824; m. *Aug.* 1758, *Lieut.-Col. William George Spearman Wasey of St. Anne's, Soho,* d. 12 *Mar.* 1817; *and had issue* 1*c* to 2*c.*

1*c.* *William George Wasey,* d. (*at Palamcote in the East Indies*) *May* 1785; m. *Hannah, da. of William Butterworth* (*who re-m. 2ndly, N. Kindersley*); *and had issue* 1*d.*

1*d.* *Eliza Honoria Margaret Wasey, living* unm. 1813.

2*c.* *Rev. George Wasey, B.D.* (*Oxon.*), *Rector of Ulcombe, Kent,* 1811–1838; *b.* 1773; d. 24 *Mar.* 1838; m. *c.* 1811, *Anne Sophia, da. of Capt. John Frodsham, R.N.; and had issue* 1*d* to 3*d.*

1*d.* *Rev. William George Leigh Wasey, M.A.* (*Oxon.*), *Vicar of Morville, Salop* 1840–1877, b. 1811; d. (? unm.) 9 *June* 1877.

2*d.* *Willoughby Clement Wasey,* b. 1812; d. ?

3*d.* *Rev. John Spearman Wasey, M.A.* (*Oxon.*), *Vicar of Compton Parva, Berks, in* 1853, d. (–); m. 24 *Nov.* 1853, *Harriet Jemima, da. of Edward Cockburn Kindersley of Harley Street; and had issue.*[2]

2*a.* *Margaret Spearman,* bapt. 10 *Feb.* 1706; m. *c.* 1734, *William Wasey of Gerard Street, Soho, M.D.,* b. *c.* 1695; d. 1 *Ap.* 1757; *and had issue* 1*b.*

1*b.* *William George Spearman Wasey of St. Anne's, Soho, Lieut.-Col. in the Army,* b. *c.* 1733; d. 12 *Mar.* 1817; m. *Elizabeth Honoria, da. and h. of George Spearman, Bishop Middleham,* d. 28 *July* 1824; *and had issue.*
See p. 508.

See p. 508.

1 Information kindly supplied by G. E. Cokayne, Esq., Clarenceux King of Arms.
2 A son was *b.* 15 Mar. 1859, and Cyril Leigh Wasey, R.A., 5th son, *d.* at Malta, 16 Mar. 1892, aged 26. See also p. 318.

# of The Blood Royal

438. Descendants of EDWARD (STANLEY), 12th EARL OF DERBY [E.] (see Table XLIII.), *b.* 12 Sept. 1752 ; *d.* 21 Oct. 1834 ; *m.* 1st, Lady ELIZABETH, da. of James (HAMILTON), 6th Duke of Hamilton [S.] and 3rd Duke of Brandon [E.], K.T., *b.* 26 Jan. 1753 ; *d.* 14 Mar. 1797 ; 2ndly, 1 May 1797, ELIZA,[1] da. of George FARREN of Cork, *d.* 23 Ap. 1829 ; and had issue 1*a* to 4*a*.

1*a*–3*a*. (Children by 1st wife.) See pp. 364–368, Nos. 26241–26558.

4*a*. *Lady Mary Margaret Stanley, b.* 23 *Mar.* 1801 ; *d.* 16 *Dec.* 1858 ; *m. as 1st wife,* 29 *Nov.* 1821, *Thomas* (*Grosvenor, afterwards* (*R.L.* 27 *Nov.* 1821) *Egerton*), 2nd *Earl of Wilton* [*U.K.*], *G.C.H., P.C., b.* 30 *Dec.* 1799 ; *d.* 7 *Mar.* 1882 ; *and had issue* 1*b* *to* 5*b*.

1*b*. Arthur Edward Holland Grey (Egerton), 3rd Earl of Wilton [U.K.], *b.* 25 Nov. 1833 ; d.s.p. 18 *Jan.* 1885.

2*b*. *Seymour John Grey* (*Egerton*), 4th *Earl of Wilton* [*U.K.*], *b.* 20 *Jan.* 1839 ; *d.* 3 *Jan.* 1898 ; *m.* 9 *Aug.* 1862, *Laura Caroline, da. of William Russell* (*who* re-m. 7 *June* 1899 *Sir Frederick Johnstone,* 8th *Bart.* [*S.*]) ; *and had issue* 1*c* *to* 2*c*.

1*c*. Arthur George (Egerton), 5th Earl of Wilton [U.K.] (*Houghton Hall, Swaffham*), *b.* 17 May 1863 ; *m.* 28 Aug. 1895, the Hon. Mariota, da. of Frederick (Thellusson), 5th Baron Rendlesham [I.] ; and has issue 1*d* to 3*d*.

1*d*. Seymour Edward Frederic Egerton, Viscount Grey de Wilton, *b.* 1 Aug. 1896.

2*d*. Hon. George Arthur Egerton, *b.* 25 Jan. 1898.

3*d*. Lady Mary Cecilia Egerton, *b.* 1901.

2*c*. Lady Elizabeth Emma Geraldine Egerton, *m.* 17 Nov. 1887, George William Taylor, *late* Coldstream Guards (*Pickenham Hall, Swaffham*) ; and has issue 1*d* to 4*d*.

1*d*. Seymour George Frederick Taylor, *b.* 1892.

2*d*. Sylvia Olive Frances Taylor, *b.* 1890.

3*d*. Miriam Katharine Taylor, *b.* 1894.

4*d*. Phyllis Evelyn Taylor, *b.* 1896.

3*b*. *Lady Elizabeth Grey Egerton, b.* 5 *July* 1832 ; *d.* 14 *Mar.* 1892 ; *m.* 12 *Oct.* 1853, *Dudley Charles* (*FitzGerald de Ros*), 24th *Baron de Ros* [*E.*], *K.C.V.O., &c.* (*Old Court, Strangford, co. Down*) ; *and had issue.*
See the Clarence Volume, p. 241, Nos. 5163–5166.

4*b*. Lady Katherine Grey Egerton, an Extra Woman of the Bedchamber to H.R.H. the Princess of Wales, *m.* 22 July 1861, the Hon. Henry John Coke (*Longford Hall, near Brailsford ;* 124 *Sloane Street, S.W.*) ; and has issue.
See the Clarence Volume, p. 515, Nos. 22306–22309.

5*b*. Lady Alice Magdalene Grey Egerton (18 *Stafford Place, Buckingham Gate, S.W.*), *m.* 13 Aug. 1863, Sir Henry Dalrymple Des Vœux, 5th Bart. [I.], *b.* 1824 ; *d.* 20 Jan. 1894 ; and has issue 1*c* to 2*c*.

1*c*. Constance Margaret Des Vœux.

2*c*. Mary Victoria Des Vœux, *m.* 9 Nov. 1897, Richard Sydney Sabine Pasley (*Holbrook, Shooter's Hill, Kent*) ; and has issue 1*d* to 4*d*.

1*d*. Arthur Dalrymple Sabine Pasley, *b.* 14 July 1903.

2*d*. Catherine Constance Sabine Pasley, *b.* 3 Aug. 1900.

3*d*. Sybil Mary Sabine Pasley, *b.* 21 Oct. 1901.

4*d*. Audrey Christina Sabine Pasley, *b.* 5 May 1905. [Nos. 44310 to 44516.

---

[1] The celebrated actress.

The Plantagenet Roll

439. Descendants, if any, of HARRIET SUSANNA ANNE HORTON (see Table XLIII.), *d.* (−); *m.* 1805, GEORGE POLLARD of Exeter.

440. Descendants of EDMUND HORNBY of Dalton Hall, co. Westmorland, M.P. (see Table XLIII.), *b.* 11 June 1773; *d.* 18 Nov. 1857; *m.* 22 Aug. 1796, Lady CHARLOTTE,[1] da. of Edward (STANLEY), 12th Earl of Derby [E.], *b.* 17 Oct. 1776; *d.* 25 Nov. 1805; and had issue 1*a.*

See pp. 366–367, Nos. 26337–26357.   [Nos. 44517 to 44537.

441. Descendants of the Rev. GEOFFREY HORNBY, Rector of Bury (see Table XLIII.), *b.* 4 Ap. 1780; *d.* 4 Mar. 1850; *m.* the Hon. GEORGINA, da. of John (BYNG), 5th Viscount Torrington [G.B.], *b.* 1788; *d.* 23 July 1856; and had issue 1*a* to 2*a.*

1*a.* Stanley Byng Hornby, Lieut. R.N., b. 15 Nov. 1814; d. 21 Nov. 1843; m. 8 *July* 1836, Caroline Sarah, da. of Joseph Thompson; and had issue 1*b.*
  1*b.* Stanley Henry Edward Hornby, b. 31 *July* 1842; d. 1904 *or* 1905; m. [——], da. of [——]; and had issue 1*c* to 3*c.*
    1*c.* Windham Hornby.
    2*c.* Frederick Hornby.
    3*c.* George Hornby.

2*a.* Edward James Geoffrey Hornby, M.A., Rector of Bury, Canon of Manchester, and Rural Dean, b. 9 Nov. 1816; d. 19 *June* 1888; m. 19 *Aug.* 1841, Elizabeth, da. of Hornby Roughsedge, b. 25 Dec. 1819; and had issue 1*b.*
  1*b.* Cecil Roughsedge Hornby, Major in the Army, b. 29 Dec. 1842; *m.* Marion, da. of [——] Lane; and has issue 1*c.*
    1*c.* Cecil Geoffrey Hornby, b. 23 Aug. 1883.   [Nos. 44538 to 44542.

442. Descendants of Admiral Sir PHIPPS HORNBY, R.N., K.C.B. (see Table XLIII.), *b.* 27 Ap. 1785; *d.* Mar. 1867; *m.* 22 Dec. 1814, MARIA, sister of Field-Marshal Sir John Fox Burgoyne, 1st Bart. [U.K.], G.C.B., *d.* 25 Dec. 1860; and had issue 1*a* to 7*a.*

1*a.* Phipps John Hornby, b. 20 *Ap.* 1820; d. 8 *Ap.* 1848; m. 7 *Mar.* 1844, Frederica, da. of Capt. Breton; and had issue 1*b* to 2*b.*
  1*b.* Frederica Lucy Phipps Hornby, b. 22 Dec. 1844; *m.* 30 July 1874, Charles Edward Henry Stanley, *late* Lieut.-Col. Grenadier Guards; and has issue 1*c* to 5*c.*
    1*c.* Charles Douglas Stanley, b. 9 Ap. 1878.
    2*c.* Phipps Edward Stanley, b. 21 Ap. 1881.
    3*c.* John William Stanley, b. 10 Mar. 1886.
    4*c.* Frances Ellinor Stanley, b. 1 May 1882.
    5*c.* Alice Margaret Stanley, b. 6 June 1884.
  2*b.* Lina Mary Phipps Hornby, b. 4 Oct. 1846; *m.* Oct. 1869, John Lambert Ovans, b. 15 Dec. 1836; *d.* 1883; and has issue 1*c* to 8*c.*   [Nos. 44543 to 44549.

---

1 For her descent from Kings Henry VII. and Edward IV. see the Tudor Roll of "The Blood Royal of Britain," Table CXIV., &c.

1c. Charles Phipps John Ovans, b. 18 Dec. 1874 ; m. 1901, Cecily Katharine, da. of [——] Wilson ; and has issue 1d.

1d. Joyce Rosemary Ovans, b. 14 Oct. 1904.

2c. Hugh Lambert Ovans, b. 12 Mar. 1881.

3c. Edward Hornby Ovans, b. 22 Dec. 1882.

4c. Lina Janet Ovans, b. 24 July 1870 ; m. 24 July 1901, the Right Rev. Hugh James Foss, Lord Bishop of Osake (*The Firs, Kobe, Japan*) ; and has issue 1d to 3d.

1d. Hugh Rose Foss, b. 13 May 1902.

2d. Emily Hornby Foss, b. 19 Oct. 1904.

3d. Margaret Evelyn Foss, b. 16 Mar. 1906.

5c. Evelyn Mary Ovans, b. 12 Oct. 1873 ; m. 1903, Hugh Thomas Dyke Acland, F.R.C.S. (*Christchurch, New Zealand*) ; and has issue 1d to 2d.

1d. Hugh John Dyke Acland, b. 19 Jan. 1904.

2d. Geoffrey Dyke Acland, b. 27 Ap. 1905.

6c. Vere Katharine Ovans, b. 8 Dec. 1873 ; m. 1900, John M. M. Collard, d. 1904.

7c. Winifred Margaret Ovans, b. 4 Mar. 1876 ; m. 10 Oct. 1905, James Adams.

8c. Christobel Frederica Ovans, b. 7 Sept. 1877 ; m. 1903, Francis Fowke ; and has issue 1d to 2d.

1d. Christobel Evelyn Isore Fowke, b. 5 Jan. 1904.

2d. Francis John Fowke, b. 15 June 1905.

2a. *Sir Geoffrey Thomas Phipps Hornby, G.C.B., Admiral of the Fleet,* b. 20 Feb. 1825 ; d. 3 Mar. 1895 ; m. 27 Ap. 1853, *Emily Frances Cowper, da. of the Rev. John Coles, d.* 1892 ; *and had issue* 1b *to* 6b.

1b. Geoffrey Stanley Phipps Hornby, J.P., Capt. Rifle Brigade (*Little Green, near Petersfield ; Lordington, Emsworth ; Sandley House, Gillingham, co. Dorset*), b. 15 Dec. 1856 ; m. 1884, Jessie Wilson, da. of T. B. Gunston of 38 Princes Gardens, S.W., J.P. ; and has issue 1c to 3c.

1c. Geoffrey Hardinge Phipps Hornby, b. 1889.

2c. Violet Jessie Phipps Hornby, b. 1885.

3c. Marion Ethel Phipps Hornby, b. 1886.

2b. Edmund John Phipps Hornby, V.C., Col. *late* R.A., b. 31 Dec. 1857 ; m. 31 Jan. 1895, Anna, da. of Carl Jay of Blendon Hall, Bexley ; and has issue 1c to 2c.

1c. Irene Hornby, b. 1895.

2c. Betty Hornby, b. 1902.

3b. Robert Stewart Hornby, Capt. R.N., b. 9 July 1866 ; m. 31 Oct. 1895, Rose, da. of Henry O'Malley ; and has issue 1c to 2c.

1c. Windham Hornby, b. 1896.

2c. Rosemary Hornby, b. 1904.

4b. Emily Frances Phipps Hornby, b. 1854 ; m. 30 June 1886, Col. Arthur Spencer Pratt, R.A., C.B. (*Broom Hall, Shooter's Hill, co. Kent*) ; and has issue 1c.

1c. Geoffrey Pratt, b. 1893.

5b. Mary Augusta Phipps Hornby, b. 1855 ; m. 5 Nov. 1879, Admiral Frederick Wilbraham Egerton, R.N.

6b. Ethel Mary Phipps Hornby, b. 1861 ; m. 30 Ap. 1895, Henry Edmund Christy ; and has issue 1c to 2c.

1c. Stephen Christy, b. 1896.

2c. Basil Christy, b. 1897.

3a. Rev. James John Hornby, D.D., D.C.L., C.V.O., Provost of Eton College, and Hon. Chaplain to H.M. the King (*The Lodge, Eton College ; Gale Cottage, Underskiddaw, Keswick*), b. 18 Dec. 1826 ; m. 5 Aug. 1869, Augusta Eliza, da. of the Rev. J. C. Evans ; and has issue 1b to 4b.   [Nos. 44550 to 44582.

The Plantagenet Roll

1*b*. Robert Phipps Hornby, *b.* 9 June 1876; *m.* 20 Dec. 1902, Mary, da. of Edward Taylor; and has issue 1*c*.

1*c*. John Phipps Hornby, *b.* 16 Oct. 1903.

2*b*. Rev. William Hornby, *b.* 4 Aug. 1878.

3*b*. Mary Sophia Hornby, *b.* 13 Feb. 1873.

4*b*. Eveline Augusta Hornby, *b.* 6 July 1879.

4*a*. Mary Elizabeth Hornby, *b.* 28 Oct. 1817.

5*a*. *Caroline Lucy Hornby*, b. 30 *Nov.* 1818; *d.* 24 *July* 1899; m. 29 *Nov.* 1838, *Major-Gen. Sir William Denison, K.C.B., R.E., successively Governor of Tasmania, Australia, and Madras, b. 3 May* 1804; *d.* 19 *Jan.* 1871; *and had issue* 1*b* to 8*b*.

1*b*. William Evelyn Denison, J.P., D.L., *late* Capt. R.H.A. and (1874–1880) M.P., High Sheriff co. Notts 1895 (*Ossington Hall, near Newark*), *b.* 25 Feb. 1843; *m.* 25 Nov. 1877, Lady Elinor, da. of William Pitt (Amherst), 2nd Earl Amherst [U.K.]; and has issue 1*c*.

1*c*. William Frank Evelyn Denison, *b.* 22 Dec. 1878.

2*b*. Rev. Henry Denison, Prebendary of Wells (*Wells*), *b.* 3 June 1848.

3*b*. Alfred Denison, *b.* 8 Ap. 1857; *m.* 30 July 1903, Kathleen, da. of Z. H. Kelly; and has issue 1*c*.

1*c*. William Maxwell Evelyn Denison, *b.* 31 Dec. 1904.

4*b*. George Denison, *b.* 5 Jan. 1861.

5*b*. Susan Denison, *b.* 16 Ap. 1841; *m.* 19 Feb. 1863, James Breeks, *d.* 6 June 1872; and has issue 1*c* to 3*c*.

1*c*. Richard Breeks, Major R.H.A., *b.* 30 Nov. 1863; *m.* Ap. 1893, Olive, da. of H. A. Blyth; and has issue 1*d*.

1*d*. Audrey Breeks, *b.* 4 Nov. 1894.

2*c*. Charles Breeks, *b.* 11 Aug. 1870.

3*c*. William Breeks, *b.* 4 Nov. 1871.

6*b*. Lucy Denison, *b.* 19 Aug. 1846.

7*b*. Caroline Denison, *b.* 1 Feb. 1850.

8*b*. Katharine Denison, *b.* 6 Sept. 1865.

6*a*. *Susan Charlotte Margaret Hornby*, b. *Nov.* 1821; *d. Sept.* 1903; *m.* 18 *Ap.* 1844, *the Ven. William Hornby of St. Michael's, co. Lancaster,* d.; *and had issue* 1*b* to 5*b*.

1*b*. Hugh Hornby, *b.* Mar. 1849.

2*b*. Phipps Hornby, *b.* 10 Jan. 1853; *m.* 1888, Agnes, da. of E. Leycester Penrhyn; and has issue 1*c* to 6*c*.

1*c*. Hugh Leycester Hornby, *b.* 20 Nov. 1888.

2*c*. Geoffrey Phipps Hornby, *b.* 1 Sept. 1890.

3*c*. William Hornby, *b.* 18 Aug. 1893.

4*c*. Edward Windham Hornby, *b.* 15 Ap. 1895.

5*c*. Cecil Vere Hornby, *b.* 15 May 1892.

6*c*. Kathleen Hornby, *b.* 19 Mar. 1897.

3*b*. James J. Hornby, *b.* 18 Dec. 1854.

4*b*. William Starkie Hornby, *b.* 2 Sept. 1861; *m.* Vida, da. of [——] Jones; and has issue 1*c*.

1*c*. Sybil Hornby.

5*b*. Annie Hornby, *b.* 22 Oct. 1850; *m.* 9 Ap. 1385, Richard Heywood Thompson.

7*a*. Elizabeth Hornby, *b.* 1 Feb. 1828; *m.* 22 June 1854, the Rev. John Cross, *d.* 18 Feb. 1897.   [Nos. 44583 to 44615.

512

443. Descendants of Lucy Hornby (see Table XLIII.), *b.* 11 Jan. 1775; *d.* 25 Nov. 1849; *m.* the Rev. Henry William Champneys, *formerly* Burt, of Ostenhanger, co. Kent, Rector of Badsworth; and had issue 1*a* to 6*a*.

1*a. Phipps Champneys.*
2*a. Edward Champneys.*
3*a. Hugh Champneys.*
4*a. Lucy Champneys, m. the Rev. William Kelk; and had issue 1b.*
1*b. William Kelk.*
5*a. Louisa Champneys, m.*
6*a. Emily Champneys, m. Adam Hodson; and had issue.*

444. Descendants of Charlotte Margaret Hornby (see Table XLIII.), *b.* 20 Oct. 1778; *d.* 16 June 1817; *m.* 30 June 1798, Edward (Stanley), 13th Earl of Derby [E.], *b.* 21 Ap. 1775; *d.* 30 June 1851; and had issue 1*a* to 5*a*.

See pp. 364–366, Nos. 26241–26336.   [Nos. 44616 to 44711.

445. Descendants, if any, of Harriet Susanna Horton (see Table XLIII.), *m.* 1813, Capt. Charles Rhys of Bath.

446. Descendants of Lady Elizabeth Stanley (see Table XLIII.), *b.* 1715; *d.* 25 Aug. 1780; *m.* 2 Feb. 1746, Sir Peter Warburton of Arley, 4th Bart. [E.], *d.* 18 Mar. 1774; and had issue 1*a* to 3*a*.

1*a. Sir Peter Warburton, 5th Bart.* [E.], b. 27 *Oct.* 1754; d.s.p. 14 *May* 1813.
2*a. Harriot Warburton, elder da. and co-h.,* d. (–); *m. John Rowlls-Legh of Prestbury and Adlington Hall, co. Chester; and had issue 1b.*
1*b. Elizabeth Hester Rowlls-Legh,* d. 15 *Nov.* 1821; *m.* 28 *Mar.* 1800, *Thomas Delves Broughton,* d. 24 *Jan.* 1846; *and had issue.*
See p. 223, Nos. 7970–8057.

3*a. Emma Warburton, younger da. and co-h.,* d. (–); *m.* 1st, *James Croxton of Norley Bank, co. Chester,* d. 27 *Aug.* 1792; 2*ndly, John Hunt; and had issue (a da. by each marriage) 1b to 2b.*
1*b. Emma Croxton, b.* 1782; *d.* 16 *Sept.* 1881; *m.* 13 *Oct.* 1803, *the Rev. Rowland Egerton, afterwards (R.L.* 9 *Aug.* 1813) *Warburton, b.* 9 *Mar.* 1778; *d.* 20 *May* 1846; *and had issue 1c to 9c.*
1*c. Rowland Eyles Egerton-Warburton, of Warburton and Arley, J.P., D.L., High Sheriff co. Chester* 1833, *b.* 14 *Sept.* 1804; *d.* 6 *Dec.* 1891; *m.* 7 *May* 1831, *Mary, da. of Sir Richard Brooke, 6th Bart.* [E.], *d.* 21 *Ap.* 1881; *and had issue 1d to 3d.*
1*d.* Piers Egerton-Warburton, J.P., D.L., *formerly* Lieut.-Col. Comdg. Cheshire Yeo. Cav., and sometime (1876–1885) M.P. (*Arley Hall, Northwich, Cheshire*), *b.* 22 May 1839; *m.* 30 Sept. 1880, the Hon. Antoinette Elizabeth, da. of John St. Vincent (Saumarez), 3rd Baron de Saumarez [U.K.]; and has issue 1*e* to 6*e*.
1*e.* John Egerton-Warburton, Lieut. Scots Guards, *b.* 13 Dec. 1883.
2*e.* Geoffrey Egerton-Warburton, *b.* 18 Feb. 1888.
3*e.* Dorothy Egerton-Warburton.
4*e.* Eveline Egerton-Warburton.
5*e.* Margery Egerton-Warburton.
6*e.* Lettice Egerton-Warburton.   [Nos. 44712 to 44820.

The Plantagenet Roll

2d. Mary Alice Egerton-Warburton, d. 27 *Jan.* 1901 ; m. 13 *Sept.* 1859, *William Edward Brinckman, R.N.*, d. 10 *Jan.* 1872 ; *and had issue.*
See the Clarence Volume, p. 628, Nos. 28094–28105.

3*d.* Mary Egerton-Warburton, *m.* 1st, 6 Sept. 1860, Robert Newcomen Gore-Booth, *d.s.p., v.p.* 29 Oct. 1861 ; 2ndly, 4 Nov. 1865, John Ussher (*The Dene, Northwich, Cheshire*) ; and has issue 1*e* to 2*e.*

1*e. Edward Ussher, Capt. Scots Guards, D.S.O.*, d. (*being killed in action during the Boer War*) 20 *Feb.* 1902 ; m. 21 *July* 1897, *Selina, da. of John G. Bowen of Burt House, co. Donegal ; and had issue* 1*f.*

1*f.* Richard Ussher, *b.* 26 Dec. 1899.

2*e.* Mary Ussher, *b.* 20 Oct. 1874 ; *m.* 29 July 1896, J. Kenneth Foster, and has issue 1*f* to 3*f.*

1*f.* Barbara Mary Foster, *b.* 27 May 1897.

2*f.* Joan Mary Foster, *b.* 7 June 1899.

3*f.* Mary Patience Winifred Foster, *b.* 20 July 1903.

2*c. Rev. James Francis Egerton-Warburton*, b. 15 *Ap.* 1807 ; d. 12 *Sept.* 1849 ; m. 19 *Feb.* 1839, *Anne, da. of George Stone of Blisworth*, d. 13 *Mar.* 1886 ; *and had issue* 1*d to* 5*d.*

1*d.* George Egerton-Warburton (*Sandicroft, Northwich*), *b.* 24 Feb. 1844 ; *m.* 14 Oct. 1886, Ruth, da. of the Hon. Arthur Lascelles.

2*d.* Rev. Geoffrey Egerton-Warburton, Rector of Warburton (*Warburton Rectory, Warrington*), *b.* 7 Ap. 1846 ; *m.* 4 July 1878, Adela Georgina Victorine, widow of H. T. Kelsey, da. of B. G. Goode, Bar.-at-Law.

3*d.* Arthur Egerton-Warburton (143 *Burngreave Road, Sheffield*), *b.* 3 Jan. 1848 ; *m.* 8 July 1874, Edna, da. of James Stowe, *d.* 7 May 1901 ; and has issue 1*e* to 2*e.*

1*e.* Arthur Francis Egerton-Warburton, *b.* 11 Nov. 1879.

2*e.* Ruth Egerton-Warburton.

4*d.* Katharine Anne Egerton-Warburton, Mother Superior of St. Saviour's Priory, Great Cambridge Street, E.

5*d.* Eleanor Werburghe Egerton-Warburton (*St. Saviour's Priory*).

3*c. Henry William Egerton-Warburton, Major 47th Foot*, b. 16 *Aug.* 1808 ; d. 27 *Feb.* 1868 ; m. 27 *May* 1835, *Harriette Elizabeth, da. of Major-Gen. Thomas Evans, C.B.*, d. 14 *Mar.* 1895 ; *and had issue* 1*d to* 3*d.*

1*d. Harriette Sophia Egerton-Warburton*, d. (–) ; m. 21 *July* 1860, *Thomas Bennett, Staff Surgeon-Major, Indian Army ; and had issue* 1*e to* 2*e.*

1*e.* Rowland Egerton-Bennett, *b.* 5 Jan. 1868.

2*e.* Thomas Evans Bennett, *b.* 3 Dec. 1868.

2*d.* Charlotte Edith Egerton-Warburton, *m.* 1872, Capt. David Ogden, 55th Regt. ; and has issue 1*e.*

1*e.* Mary Isabel Edith Ogden.

3*d.* Emma Isabel Egerton-Warburton, *m.* 12 Sept. 1877, the Very Rev. Charles Saul Bruce, Dean of Cork (*The Deanery, Cork*).

4*c. Peter Egerton-Warburton, C.M.G., Col. E.I.C.S., formerly R.N., Col. Comdg. Vol. Forces South Australia 1869–1871, &c.*, b. 15 *Aug.* 1813 ; d. 5 *Nov.* 1889 ; m. 8 *Oct.* 1838, *Alicia, da. of Henry Mant of Bath*, d. *Feb.* 1892 ; *and had issue* 1*d to* 5*d.*

1*d.* Richard Egerton-Warburton, *b.* 31 May 1840.

2*d.* Rowland James Egerton-Warburton (*Tarporley, Malvern, Melbourne, Victoria*), *b.* 4 Feb. 1846 ; *m.* 14 May 1872, Annie, da. of George Hart, C.M.G. ; and has issue 1*e* to 6*e.*

1*e.* John Egerton-Warburton, *b.* 11 Feb. 1873.

2*e.* Peter Egerton-Warburton, *b.* 28 Sept. 1877. [Nos. 44821 to 44854.

514

# of The Blood Royal

3e. Wilbraham Egerton-Warburton, b. 1882.

4e. Rowland Egerton-Warburton, b. 1885.

5e. Margaret Gilmour Egerton-Warburton, b. 1875.

6e. Katherine Egerton-Warburton, b. 1879.

3d. William Egerton-Warburton (North Adelaide, S. Australia), b. 5 Sept. 1847; m. 1877, Edith, da. of W. M. Sandford; and has issue 1e to 3e.

1e. Richard Egerton-Warburton, b. 30 Jan. 1880.

2e. Philip Egerton-Warburton, b. 1882.

3e. Ethel Egerton-Warburton, b. 1877.

4d. Ethel Catherine Egerton-Warburton (Bickham Grange, S. Australia), m. 28 Oct. 1871, Henry Augustus Short of Buttamuc (son of the Lord Bishop of Adelaide); and has issue 1e to 7e.

1e. Augustus Egerton Short, b. 1880.

2e. Henry Mayow Short, b. 1883.

3e. Frank Piers Short, b. 1886.

4e. Alicia Millicent Short, b. 1872.

5e. Ethel Augusta Short, b. 1874.

6e. Albinia Frances Short, b. 1876; m. Ap. 1903, Herbert Tolmer; and has issue 1f.

1f. Ethel Mary Tolmer.

7e. Eva Winifred Short, b. 1879.

5d. Mary Egerton-Warburton (Burnside, South Australia), m. 1893, the Rev. Philip Pymar Dodd, Rector of St. David's, Burnside, Canon of St. Peter's Cathedral, and Chaplain to the Lord Bishop of Adelaide, d. 23 Feb. 1906.

5c. George Edward Egerton-Warburton, 51st Regt., b. 25 Mar. 1819; d. 1889; m. 1st, 23 Nov. 1842, Augusta, da. of Sir Richard Spencer, R.N., d. 14 Nov. 1871; 2ndly, 14 Ap. 1873, Emily, da. of the Rev. James Coghlan of Markfield, d. 1896; and had issue 1d to 14d.

1d. George Grey Egerton-Warburton, J.P. (Yeriminup, West Australia), b. 9 Oct. 1843; m. 23 May 1872, Amy, da. of Edward Hester; and has issue 1e to 4e.

1e. Philip Grey Egerton-Warburton, b. 1877.

2e. Georgia Egerton-Warburton, m. 20 Dec. 1900, Leslie Peel Hall of the Audit Office, Perth (Perth, West Australia).

3e. Mary Augusta Egerton-Warburton.

4e. Winifred Amy Egerton-Warburton.

2d. Rowland Egerton-Warburton, b. 14 Nov. 1845; d. (–); m. 1881, Mary (Stonyhurst, Williams River, W. Australia), da. of John M'Kail; and has issue 1e to 9e.

1e. Rowland Egerton-Warburton, b. 1883.

2e. Reginald John Egerton-Warburton, b. 1885.

3e. Cecil Edward Egerton-Warburton, Lieut. 1st City of London R.G.A (Vol.), b. 1887.

4e. Piers Egerton-Warburton, b. 1892.

5e. Philip Augustus Egerton-Warburton, b. 1894.

6e. Farquhar Grey Egerton-Warburton, b. 1896.

7e.
8e. } 3 das.
9e.

3d. Horace Egerton-Warburton (St. Werburgh's, West Australia), b. 9 Nov. 1848; m. 19 Aug. 1875, Selina, da. of John M'Kail; and has issue 1e to 6e.

[Nos. 44855 to 44884.

515

The Plantagenet Roll

1e. John Le Belward Egerton-Warburton, *b.* 20 Aug. 1882.

2e. Horace Grey Egerton-Warburton, *b.* 1891.

3e. Maud Mary Egerton-Warburton, *m.* 1897, George Edward Mullens.

4e. Augusta Henrietta Egerton-Warburton, *m.* 1903, W. M. Graham.

5e. Sibilla Florence Egerton-Warburton, *m.* 1905, the Rev. F. C. Carr.

6e. Helen Egerton-Warburton.

4d. Augustus Egerton-Warburton (*Balgarrup, W. Australia*), *b.* 26 Mar. 1850 ; *m.* 1880, Fanny, da. of Edward Hester ; and has issue 1e to 7e.

1e. George Edward Egerton-Warburton, *b.* 1882.

2e. Angus Egerton-Warburton, *b.* 1889.

3e. Reginald Hubert Egerton-Warburton, *b.* 1894.

4e. Blanche Egerton-Warburton.

5e. Mabel Augusta Egerton-Warburton.

6e. Isabel Frances Egerton-Warburton.

7e. Jessie Egerton-Warburton.

5d. Reginald Egerton-Warburton, *b.* 27 June 1855.

6d. Philip Egerton-Warburton, *b.* 28 Aug. 1856.

7d. Randle Egerton-Warburton (*Blackwood Park, Bridgetown, W. Australia*), *b.* 17 Sept. 1860 ; *m.* 1890, Eva, da. of Edward Hester ; and has issue (with 3 das.) 1e.

1e. Piers Edward Egerton-Warburton.

8d. Edward Egerton-Warburton (*Ongerup, West Australia*), *b.* 25 May 1867.

9d. Francis Joseph Egerton-Warburton, M.A. (Oxon.), *b.* 3 Mar. 1876.

10d. Cecil William Egerton-Warburton, M.A. (Oxon.), *b.* 20 Nov. 1878.

11d.¹ Alice Egerton-Warburton, *m.* 13 Mar. 1870, the Rev. Waldyve Willington Tarleton (*Sydney, New South Wales*).

12d.¹ Mary Egerton-Warburton, *m.* 25 July 1870, Cecil Rogers, Surgeon.

13d.¹ Emma Egerton-Warburton.

14d.¹ Ann Egerton-Warburton.

6c. *Emma Elizabeth Egerton-Warburton, d. (–); m. 28 Nov. 1843, the Ven. James Saurin, Archdeacon of Dromore, d.* 1879.

7c. *Frances Mary Egerton-Warburton, d. 11 Jan. 1898 ; m. 21 Ap.* 1829, *Robert Eden, b. 13 May* 1800 ; *d. 23 Ap.* 1879; *and had issue 1d to 2d.*

1d. *Morton Robert Eden, Col. 56th Regt., b. 9 May* 1830 ; *d. 30 Aug.* 1900 ; *m.* 31 *Mar.* 1864, *Frances Maria, da. of Nathaniel Clarke Barnardiston of The Ryes, Suffolk, d.* 11 Feb. 1900 ; *and had issue 1e.*

1e. Ethel Eden, *m.* 1903, Capt. Herbert Charles Selwyn Heath, 2nd Batt. Essex Regt.

2d. *Charles Henry Eden, late R.N., b. 20 Mar.* 1839 ; *d.* 16 Feb. 1900 ; *m.* 11 *May* 1863, *Georgiana (The Haven, Sheringham), da. of Capt. Frederick William Hill, 10th Foot ; and had issue 1e to 2e.*

1e. Guy Ernest Morton Eden, Bar. I.T. (70 *Belgrave Road, S.W.*), *b.* 6 May 1864 ; *m.* 4 Dec. 1897, Ethel, da. of William Holman of 30 Gledhow Gardens, S.W. ; and has issue 1f to 2f.

1f. Rodney Guy Morton Eden, *b.* 4 May 1899.

2f. Kathleen Ethel Eden, *b.* 4 Feb. 1902.

2e. Victoria Beatrice Edith Eden.

8c. *Maria Sybella Egerton-Warburton, d. 4 May* 1895 ; *m.* 24 *Ap.* 1838, *James Bateman of Biddulph Grange and Knypersley Hall, co. Stafford, F.R.S., F.L.S., F.G.S., J.P., D.L., b.* 18 *July* 1811 ; *d.* 1897 ; *and had issue 1d to 4d.*

1d. John Bateman, J.P., D.L. (*Moveron's Manor, Essex ; Brightlingsea Hall,*
[Nos. 44885 to 44915.

Colchester), *b.* 19 Mar. 1839; *m.* 4 Oct. 1865, the Hon. Jessy Caroline, da. of the Hon. Richard Bootle Wilbraham, M.P.; and has issue 1*e.*

    1*e.* Agnes Mary Bateman, *m.* 1889, Capt. Robert Maxwell D'Arcy Thornton D'Arcy-Hildyard, 68th Durham L.I. (*Colborn Hall, near Richmond, Yorks*).

    2*d.* Rev. Rowland Bateman, M.A., *b.* 1 Nov. 1840; *m.* 25 Nov. 1879, Helen, da. of Philip Melvill, C.S.I., H.B.M.'s Resident at the Court of Baroda; and has issue 1*e.*

    1*e.* John Melvill Bateman.

    3*d.* Robert Bateman (*Biddulph Hall, co. Stafford*), *b.* 12 Aug. 1842; *m.* 18 Oct. 1883, Caroline Octavia, widow of the Rev. C. P. Wilbraham, da. of Very Rev. the Hon. Henry Howard.

    4*d.* Katherine Bateman (*Hill House, Long Melford, Suffolk*), *m.* 9 July 1868, Ulrick Ralph Burke, M.A., *d.* 18 July 1895; and has issue.

    See the Clarence Volume, p. 499, Nos. 21737–21740.

    9*c. Charlotte Egerton-Warburton*, *d.* 27 *Feb.* 1906; *m.* 10 *Sept.* 1859, *the Rev. Henry Leslie, Rector of Kilclief, co. Down, d.* 19 *Nov.* 1870.

    2*b.* [——] *Hunt* (*da. by 2nd husband*).   [Nos. 44916 to 44924.

447. Descendants of CATHERINE (O'BRIEN), *suo jure* 8th BARONESS CLIFTON of Leighton Bromswold [E.] (see Table XLII.), *bapt.* 29 Jan. 1673; *d.* (at New York) 11 Aug. 1706; *m.* 10 July 1688, EDWARD (HYDE), then styled VISCOUNT CORNBURY, *afterwards* (1709) 3rd EARL OF CLARENDON [E.], *b.* Dec. 1661; *d.* 31 Mar. 1723; and had issue.

    See pp. 387–396, Nos. 32552–33533.   [Nos. 44925 to 45906.

448. Descendants, if any, of ELIZABETH SAVAGE, wife of THOMAS LANGTON, Baron of Newton [I.]; of ELEANOR SAVAGE, wife 1st of Sir HENRY BAGNELL, and 2ndly of Sir SACKVILLE TREVOR; of MARY SAVAGE, wife of Sir RICHARD MILLES of co. Hants; and of FRANCES SAVAGE, wife of THOMAS WILKES of co. Hants (see Table XXXV.).

449. Descendants, if any, of the Hon. Sir RICHARD MANNERS (see Table II.), who *m.* 1st, MARGARET, widow of RICHARD VERNON of Haddon, da. of Sir Robert DYMOKE of Scrivelsby, *d.s.p.* 1550; 2ndly, [——], widow of Sir WILLIAM COFFYN, by whom he had issue 1*a.*

    1*a. John Manners.*

450. Descendants, if any surviving, of THOMAS WARD of Bexley, co. Norfolk (see Table XLIV.), *d.* 1632; *m.* ELEANOR, da. of Thomas GODSALVE of Buckenham, co. Norfolk, *d.* 1602; and had issue; and of his immediate younger brothers.

The Plantagenet Roll

451. Descendants of HUMBLE (WARD), 1st BARON WARD [E.] (see Table XLIV.), *d*. 14 Oct. 1670; *m*. 1628, FRANCES (SUTTON), *suo jure* 10th Baroness Dudley [E.], *d*. Aug. 1697; and had issue.

See the Tudor Roll of " The Blood Royal of Britain," pp.[213–357, Nos. 26028–27542. [Nos. 45907 to 47421.

452. Other descendants, if any surviving, of MARGARET CAPEL and her husband ROBERT WARD of Kirby Bedon, co. Norfolk, High Sheriff co. Herts and Essex to Henry VIII. (see Table XLIV.).

453. Descendants of VALENTINE KNIGHTLEY of Fawsley, M.P. (see Table XLV.), *b*. 1 May 1718; *d*. 6 May 1754; *m*. 21 Dec. 1740, ELIZABETH, da. of Edward DUMMER of Swathling, *d*. 11 Aug. 1760; and had issue 1*a* to 3*a*.

1*a. Sir John Knightley of Fawsley, 1st Bart. [G.B.], b.* 17 *Feb.* 1746; *d.s.p.* 29 *Jan.* 1812.

2*a. Rev. Charles Knightley, LL.B., b.* 29 *Oct.* 1753; *d. before* 6 *Aug.* 1787; *m.* 13 *June* 1779, *Elizabeth, da. of Henry Boulton of Moulton, d.* 18 *Feb.* 1835; *and had issue* 1*b to* 4*b.*

1*b. Sir Charles Knightley, 2nd Bart. [G.B.], b.* 30 *June* 1781; *d.* 30 *Aug.* 1864; *m.* 24 *Aug.* 1813, *Selina Mary, da. of Felton Lionel Hervey of Englefield Green, d.* 27 *July* 1856; *and had issue* 1*c to* 2*c.*

1*c. Rainald (Knightley), 1st Baron Knightley [U.K.], 3rd Bart. [G.B.], b.* 22 *Oct.* 1819; *d.s.p.* 19 *Dec.* 1895.

2*c. Sophia Selina Knightley, d.* 4 *May* 1886; *m.* 31 *Aug.* 1840, *the Hon. Henry Edward Hall Gage, b.* 9 *Jan.* 1814; *d.v.p.* 8 *Sept.* 1875; *and had issue.*

See p. 269, Nos. 10335–10343.

2*b. Rev. Henry Knightley, b.* 23 *Jan.* 1786; *d.* 9 *Sept.* 1813; *m.* 1810, *Jane Diana, da. of the Rev. Philip Story of Lockington Hall, d.* 4 *Mar.* 1875; *and had issue* 1*c to* 3*c.*

1*c. Rev. Sir Valentine Knightley, 4th Bart. [G.B.], b.* 30 *Sept.* 1812; *d. unm.* 28 *Ap.* 1898.

2*c. Rev. Henry Charles Knightley, b.* 22 *Dec.* 1813; *d.* 12 *Aug.* 1884; *m.* 22 *Ap.* 1851, *Mary Maria, da. of Capt. Sylvester Richmond; and had issue* 1*d to* 5*d.*

1*d*. Sir Charles Valentine Knightley, 6th Bart. [G.B.], J.P., D.L. (*Fawsley, Daventry*), *b*. 22 July 1853; *m*. 26 Ap. 1883, Juliet Clandine, da. of T. W. Watson of Lubenham.

2*d*. Rev. Henry Francis Knightley (*Houndshill, Stratford-on-Avon*), *b*. 30 July 1854; *m*. 14 Feb. 1884, Florence Mary, da. and h. of Capt. Thomas Garratt of Braunston House, Northants.

3*d*. Selina Mary Knightley, *m*. 27 Dec. 1877, Francis Mills (*The Manor House, Pillerton, near Warwick*); and has issue 1*e* to 4*e*.

1*e*. Henry Valentine Mills, *b*. 23 Nov. 1881.

2*e*. Mabel Frances Mills.

3*e*. Phœbe Mills.

4*e*. Esther Mary Mills.

4*d*. Jane Edith Knightley, *m*. 1896, Jestyn Hume Nicholl, *late* of St. Mark's, Clondalken, co. Dublin.

5*d*. Mary Knightley, *m*. 10 Sept. 1885, Major Stopford Crosby Hickman, *d*. (in India) 1897; and has issue 1*e*.

1*e*. Beryl Hickman. [Nos. 47422 to 47440.

518

3c. *Mary Anne Knightley*, d. 21 *Sept.* 1875 ; m. 18 *Aug.* 1838, *Edward Hawks ; and had issue* 1d.

1d. Jane Diana Hawks, *m.* 28 Sept. 1865, William Boyd (*Prestwick Lodge, Ponteland, Newcastle-upon-Tyne*).

3b. *Elizabeth Knightley*, m. *William Lee.*

4b. *Sophia Knightley*, b. 1 *June* 1787 ; d. 22 *May* 1881 ; m. 19 *June* 1807, *John Bainbrigge Story of Lockington, co. Leicester*, b. 30 *Sept.* 1779 ; d. 26 *May* 1827 ; *and had issue* 1c *to* 5c.

1c. *John Bainbrigge Story of Lockington, J.P., D.L.*, b. 29 *July* 1812 ; d. 7 *Jan.* 1872 ; m. 20 *Aug.* 1833, *Frances Maria, da. of Robert Holden of Nuttall Temple, co. Notts*, b. 19 *Ap.* 1812 ; d. 14 *June* 1885 ; *and had issue* 1d *to* 4d.

1d. Charles William Story of Ruddington, co. Notts, *b.* 8 Sept. 1839 ; *m.* Clara Jane, da. of [——] Reed, *b.* 1841 ; *d.* 1 Feb. 1875.

2d. Rev. Robert Lacock Story, Vicar of Lockington 1873, *b.* 23 Dec. 1841 ; *m.* 1874, Charlotte, da. of the Rev. Miles Galloway Booty, M.A., Rector of Middleham ; and has issue 1e *to* 3e.

1e. John Bainbrigge Story, *bapt.* 2 Sept. 1875.

2e. Robert Nathaniel Walter Story.

3e. Violet Story.

3d. Henry Valentine Story of Ruddington, *b.* 6 Nov. 1843 ; *m.* 15 June 1880, Emily Isabel, da. of Frederick Bright of Woodcote, Liverpool.

4d. Emily Mary Story (*Ruddington, co. Notts*).

2c. Rev. Philip William Story, B.A. (Oxon.), Vicar of Fawsley 1843, *b.* 22 Dec. 1816.

3c. *Valentine Frederick Story, Gen. in the Army*, b. 21 Feb. 1818 ; d. 23 *Ap.* 1906 ; m. 30 *Dec.* 1847, *Williamina, da. of William Moody of Roe House, Newtown Limavady, co. Derry*, b. 20 *Mar.* 1825 ; *and had issue* 1d *to* 6d.

1d. William Frederick Story, Lieut.-Col. 3rd Highland Light Inf. Militia (*The Forest, Nottingham*) b. 3 Ap. 1852.

2d. Valentine Charles Story, C.E. (*Australia*), b. 14 Oct. 1853 ; *m.* 7 Jan. 1886, Lena Josephine, da. of Ernest Kruth of Sydney, N.S.W., *b.* 1 Jan. 1864 ; and has issue 1e.

1e. Olive Wilhelmina Schreier Story, *b.* (at Carlton, Melbourne, Victoria) 15 Oct. 1886.

3d. Edwin Henry Story of Manchester, *b.* 6 Ap. 1857.

4d. Richard Hawksworth Story, Lieut. R.N., *b.* 7 July 1859.

5d. Mary Sophia Story.

6d. Jane Blanche Story.

4c. *Sophia Elizabeth Story*, b. 19 *June* 1808 ; d. 17 *Mar.* 1874 ; m. 4 *Nov.* 1846, *Henry Charles Whalley*, d. 15 *Feb.* 1877 ; *and had issue* (2 sons and 1 da.).

5c. *Ellen Martha Story*, b. 5 *Jan.* 1810 ; d. 28 *July* 1901 ; m. 4 *Sept.* 1830, *the Rev. Ayscough Fawkes, Rector of Leathley, co. York, and of Farnley Hall, co. York*, d. 21 *July* 1871 ; *and had issue* 1d *to* 5d.

1d. *Rev. Frederick Fawkes of Farnley Hall, Rector of Escrick*, b. 16 *Mar.* 1833 ; d. 3 *Feb.* 1900 ; m. 29 *July* 1868, *Ellen Mary, da. of Frederick Arkwright of Willersley, co. Derby ; and had issue* 1e *to* 8e.

1e. Frederick Hawksworth Fawkes, J.P., D.L. (*Farnley Hall, Otley ; Hawksworth Hall, Guiseley*), b. 4 Oct. 1870.

2e. Richard Ayscough Hawksworth Fawkes, b. 26 Oct. 1872.

3e. Walter Hawksworth Fawkes, b. 27 May 1876.

4e. Stephen Hawksworth Fawkes, b. 25 Sept. 1878.

5e. Mabel Augusta Fawkes, *m.* 3 Sept. 1891, the Rev. Le Gendre George Horton, Vicar of Wellow (*Wellow Vicarage, Bath*) ; and has issue 1f *to* 3f.

[Nos. 47441 to 47461

The Plantagenet Roll

1f. Le Gendre George William Horton, b. 1892.
2f. Frederick Henry Le Gendre Horton, b. 1894.
3f. Dorothy Mary Horton, b. 1893.

6e. Dorothy Fawkes.
7e. Ellen Beatrice Hawksworth Fawkes.
8e. Susan Rachel Hawksworth Fawkes.

2d. Francis Fawkes, J.P., Major *late* 71st Highlanders (*Elmfield, Bayshill, Cheltenham*), b. 3 Sept. 1837 ; m. 20 Feb. 1873, Constance, da. and co.-h. of Edward Arkwright of Hatton, co. Warwick ; and has issue 1e to 8e.

1e. Rupert Edward Francis Fawkes, b. 26 Ap. 1879.
2e. Valentine Hawksworth Fawkes, b. 17 Feb. 1884.
3e. Harriet Constance Fawkes.
4e. Margaret Ayscough Fawkes.
5e. Violet Lucy Fawkes.
6e. Madeline Charlotte Fawkes.
7e. Olive Mary Fawkes.
8e. Everilda Ellen Fawkes.

3d. *Ellen Fawkes*, d. 4 *July* 1890 ; m. *as 1st wife*, 11 *May* 1871, *George John Armytage, now Sir George John Armytage, 6th Bart.* [G.B.], *D.L., F.S.A.* (*Kirklees Park, Brighouse, York ; 27 Cambridge Square, W.*) ; *and had issue* 1e to 3e.

1e. George Ayscough Armytage, Capt. King's Royal Rifle Corps (*Carlton*), b. 2 Mar. 1882 ; m. 12 July 1899, Aimee, da. of Sir Lionel Milborne-Swinnerton-Pilkington, 11th Bart. [S.] ; and has issue 1f to 3f.

1f. John Lionel Armytage, b. 23 Nov. 1901.
2f. Reginald William Armytage, b. 18 May 1903.
3f. Barbara Ellen Armytage, b. 24 Mar. 1906.

2e. John Hawksworth Armytage (*Isthmian*), b. 19 May 1873.
3e. Edith Beatrice Armytage, m. 19 July 1905, Marjoribanks Keppel North ; and has issue 1f.

1f. George Montagu North, b. 4 June 1906.

4d. Mary Sophia Fawkes.
5d. Lena Maria Fawkes.

3a. *Jane Knightley*, b. 3 *Nov.* 1749 ; d. (–) ; m. *John Kingston of Oakhill, co. Herts, and Belmont, M.P. for Lymington,* d. (–) ; *and had* (*with possibly other*) *issue* [1] 1b to 2b.

1b. *James Kingston, a Commr. at Somerset House,* d. Sept. 1839 ; m. *Harriet Ann, da. of the Hon. Sir Giles Rooke, a Judge of the Common Pleas ; and had issue* 1c to 5c.

1c. Arthur Burrard Kingston, Lieut. R.N.
2c. *Eleanor Kingston,* d. (–) ; m. 31 *Mar.* 1838, *the Rev. Cuthbert Orlebar,* b. 1807 ; d. 1 *Aug.* 1861 ; *and had issue* 1d to 5d.

1d. *Cuthbert Knightley Orlebar,* b. 1844 ; d. (? unm.) 23 *Jan.* 1882.
2d. *Vere Bernard Orlebar, late* Comm. H.M.S. *Revenge,* b. 1846 ; m. 31 Dec. 1885, Agnes Dorothea, da. of [——] Fergusson.
3d. Eleanor Edith Orlebar.
4d. Mary Louisa Orlebar.
5d. Florence Orlebar, m. 2 Dec. 1874, George William Boase of Dundee.

3c. *Emily Kingston.*
4c. *Louisa Kingston.*
5c. *Laura Kingston,* m. *Capt. James Costobadie.*

2b. *Lucy Henry Kingston,* d. *July* 1851 ; m. 1812, *Frances Sophia, da. of the Hon. Sir Giles Rooke, a Judge of the Common Pleas ; and had issue* 1c to 9c.

[Nos. 47462 to 47489.

---

[1] Burke's " Royal Descents and Pedigrees of Founders' Kin," Pedigree XVIII., and " Landed Gentry," Orlebar Pedigree.

# of The Blood Royal

1c. *William Henry Giles Kingston, Knight of the Military Order of Christ (by Letters Patent of the Queen of Portugal, 1846), d. (–); m. Agnes, da. of Capt. Charles Kinloch of Gourdie.*

2c. George Templeman Kingston, M.A. (Camb.), Principal of the Nautical College of Canada, *m.* 1851, Harriet, da. of Edmund Malone; and has issue 1*d*.

  1d. Alice Laura Marion Kingston.

3c. Charles Kingston, *m.* Mar. 1852, Catherine, da. of Reid Edward Woodham.

4c. Frederic Kingston, Bar.-at-Law.

5c. Edward Kingston of Caius College, Cambridge, and King's College, London.

6c. Francis Knightley Kingston.

7c. Laura Kingston.

8c. Harriet Kingston.

9c. Caroline Kingston.   [Nos. 47490 to 47498.

454. Descendants of JANE KNIGHTLEY **(see Table XLV.), b. 25 Aug. 1726;**[1] **d. Feb. 1781; m. 29 Ap. 1744,** RICHARD WILLIAMSON **of Eydon, co. Northants, Capt. Coldstream Guards 1740–1745, d. Feb. 1768; and had (with 12 other children, who all appear to have died in infancy) 1a to 6a.**

1a. *Thomas Williamson, b. 25 Aug. 1750.*

2a. *Lucy Williamson (son), b. 5 Jan. 1757.*

3a. *Valentine Williamson, b. 20 Nov. 1759.*

4a. *Barbara Williamson, b. 26 Dec. 1746.*

5a. *Jane Grey Williamson, b. 3 Dec. 1754; d. (–); m. as 1st wife, 7 May 1779, the Rev. Newdigate Poyntz, Rector of Tormarton, co. Gloucester, d. 19 Dec. 1825; and had issue 1b to 2b.*

  1b. *Rev. Nathaniel Poyntz of Alvescot House, Oxon., b. 12 Aug. 1782; d. Mar. 1873; m. Ann, da. and event. h. of Richard Jenkins of Llanharan House, co. Glamorgan; and had issue 1c.*

    1c. *Caroline Anne Poyntz (assumed the name of Blandy-Jenkins 1856), d. 1888; m. 15 Aug. 1837, John Blandy of Kingston Bagpuize, co. Berks, b. 1815; d. 17 Jan. 1844; and had issue 1d to 4d.*

      1d. John Blandy-Jenkins, J.P., D.L., High Sheriff co. Berks 1866 (*Kingston Bagpuize, near Abingdon; Llanharan, Pontyclown, Glamorgan*), *b.* 28 June 1839; *m.* 1st, 17 Oct. 1861, Alice Martha, da. of Charles Wilson Faber of Northaw House, co. Hertford, *d.* 23 Dec. 1895; 2ndly, 13 Feb. 1897, Elizabeth Nora, da. of Major-Gen. George Drury; and has issue 1*e* to 5*e*.

        1e. *John Blandy Blandy-Jenkins, J.P., Capt. West Africa Frontier Force, b. 9 July 1865; d. (at Las Palmas) 20 Mar. 1901; m. 26 Aug. 1891, Helen Mary, da. and h. of Thomas Duffield of New House, Abingdon; and had issue 1f to 2f.*

          1f. John Blandy-Jenkins, *b.* 4 Dec. 1893.

          2f. Helen Blandy-Jenkins, *b.* 9 July 1892.

        2e. Alice Blandy-Jenkins, *b.* 12 Feb. 1867; *m.* 26 June 1894, Leolin Charles Forestier-Walker, J.P. (son of Sir George Forestier-Walker, 2nd Bart. [G.B.], J.P., D.L.) (*Park House, Rhiwdevin, Newport*); and has issue 1*f* to 2*f*.

          1f. Rosemary Forestier-Walker, *b.* 27 Aug. 1898.

          2f. Daphne Forestier-Walker, *b.* 3 Dec. 1902.

        3e.[1] *Eva Blandy-Jenkins, d. 13 Dec. 1902; m. 25 Oct. 1899, Capt. Walter Ernest Lawrence, 2nd Dragoons, late 2nd Batt. South Wales Borderers.*

        4e. Ethel Blandy-Jenkins, *b.* 27 Sept. 1873; *m.* July 1898, William Morgan Cobbett; and has issue 1*f*.

          1f. Nancy Cobbett, *b.* 16 Nov. 1899.   [Nos. 47499 to 47506.

---

[1] Foster's "Noble and Gentle Families," p. 354.

521

The Plantagenet Roll

5e. Janet Blandy-Jenkins, *b.* 29 Oct. 1904.

2d. Adam Fettiplace Blandy-Jenkins (*The Warren, Radley, Berks*), *b.* 3 Dec. 1842; *m.* 6 Feb. 1868, Elizabeth Mary, da. of John Whitlock Nicholl Stradting-Carne of St. Donat's Castle, co. Glamorgan; and has issue (with one other) 1*e* to 10*e*.

1e. John Carne Blandy-Jenkins, *b.* 11 July 1872.

2e. Lyster Fettiplace Blandy-Jenkins, Capt. R.E., *b.* 21 Sept. 1874; *m.* 10 Jan. 1905, Violet Mary, da. of Charles A. Vernon of Troy Hill, Victoria, B.C.

3e. Sydenham Harvey Brancker Blandy-Jenkins, *b.* 11 June 1879.

4e. Blanche Gwendolyn Blandy-Jenkins, *b.* 29 Dec. 1868; *m.* 16 Ap. 1903, James Lees Norton; and has issue 1*f*.

1f. Josephine Elizabeth Margaret Norton, *b.* 1 Sept. 1904.

5e. Constance Mary Blandy-Jenkins, *b.* 14 May 1871; *m.* 1905 [——] Sapila.

6e. Caroline Winifred Blandy-Jenkins, *b.* 15 Feb. 1877; *m.* 28 Ap. 1897, the Rev. Seys Whitlock Nicholl, F.L.S., F.G.S. (*Usk, co. Monmouth*); and has issue 1*f* to 2*f*.

1f. Robert George Iltyd Nicholl, *b.* 14 Nov. 1898.

2f. Edward Poyntz Whitlock Nicholl, *b.* 8 Mar. 1902.

7e. Mabel Beatrix Blandy-Jenkins, *b.* 4 Mar. 1878.

8e. Mary Nicholl Blandy-Jenkins, *b.* 22 Oct. 1880; *m.* 8 Ap. 1902, the Rev. John Arthur Constantine Lysaght, Vicar of Carham (son of Rev. the Hon. Henry Lysaght) (*Carham Vicarage, Coldstream*); and has issue 1*f* to 2*f*.

1f. Winifred Joyce Lysaght, *b.* 4 May 1903.

2f. Kathleen Mary Lalage Lysaght, *b.* 28 Jan. 1905.

9e. Margaret Jane Blandy-Jenkins, *b.* 29 May 1882.

10e. Elizabeth Sydney Reueiva Blandy-Jenkins, *b.* 5 Mar. 1884.

3d. Anne Blandy-Jenkins, *b.* 6 May 1838.

4d. Mary Blandy-Jenkins, b. 24 *July* 1840 ; *d.* 5 *Nov.* 1870 ; m. 3 *Aug.* 1864, *the Rev. Sainsbury Langford Sainsbury, M.A. (Oxon.), Rector of Beckington (Beckington Rectory, near Bath); and had issue* 1*e to* 4*e*.

1e. Rev. Thomas Langford Sainsbury, B.A., *b.* 23 Sept. 1868; *m.* 2 Dec. 1896, Emma, da. of Arthur Harvey Thursby; and has issue 1*f* to 2*f*.

1f. Thomas Audley Sainsbury, *b.* 6 Dec. 1897.

2f. Hugh Waller Sainsbury, *b.* Jan. 1903.

2e. Grace Mary Langford Sainsbury, *b.* 16 July 1865; *m.* 1895, the Rev. Walter Errington (*Hunsdon Rectory, Ware, Herts*); and has issue 1*f* to 3*f*.

1f. John Errington, *b.* Feb. 1899.

2f. [son] Errington, *b.* 1902.

3f. [da.] Errington, *b.* 29 Ap. 1903.

3e. Katherine Langford Sainsbury, *b.* 13 Sept. 1867.

4e. Mary Langford Sainsbury, *b.* 4 Nov. 1870.

2b. Newdigate Poyntz, Capt. R.N., b. 14 *Ap.* 1785; *d.* 15 *Nov.* 1853; m. 30 *Sept.* 1827, *Alice, da. of John Bryan, d.* 21 *Ap.* 1875 ; *and had issue* 1*c to* 4*c*.

1c. Rev. Newdigate Poyntz, M.A. (Oxon.), Vicar of St. Mary's, Shrewsbury (*St. Mary's Vicarage, Shrewsbury*), *b.* 23 Nov. 1842; *m.* 18 July 1874, Margaret Julia, da. of Henry Sweeting of Godmanchester ; and has issue 1*d* to 7*d*.

1d. Newdigate Poyntz, *b.* 2 June 1875.

2d. Nathaniel John Poyntz, *b.* 4 July 1882.

3d. Robert Hugh Poyntz, *b.* 10 Oct. 1883.

4d. Margaret Alice Poyntz.

5d. Mary Dorothy Poyntz.

6d. Caroline Ursula Poyntz.

7d. Eleanor Jane Poyntz.   [Nos. 47507 to 47541.

# of The Blood Royal

2c. Rev. Nathaniel Cartleton Stephen Poyntz, B.A. (Oxon.), Vicar of Dorchester (*Dorchester Vicarage, near Oxford*), *b.* 19 Oct. 1846 ; *m.* 28 Dec. 1882, Helen Willis, da. of James Munro Minor of New York, M.D. ; and has issue 1*d.*

1*d.* Richard Stephen Pierrepont Poyntz, *b.* 25 Nov. 1883.'

3c. Jane Poyntz, *m.* 29 Sept. 1859, the Rev. Arthur Cardinal Saunders, M.A. (Oxon.), *late* Rector of Lydiard Millicent ; and has issue 1*d* to 5*d.*

1*d.* Frederick Stephen Poyntz Saunders.

2*d.* Nathaniel Argent Saunders.

3*d.* Caroline Alicia Saunders.

4*d.* Catharine Saunders.

5*d.* Mary Elizabeth Poyntz Saunders.

4c. Mary Poyntz, *m.* 16 July 1863, Spencer Phipps Brett, Capt. R.N.

6a. *Charlotte Williamson*, d. 1833 ; m. 25 *Jan.* 1785, *Thomas Mariott, 2nd Dragoon Guards*, d. *May* 1840 ; *and had issue* 1*b* *to* 4*b*.

1*b. Thomas Mariott, b.* 28 *July* 1790 ; *d.* 1825 ; m. 1823, *Harriet, da. of* [——] *Goodman (re-m. John East); and had issue* 1*c.*

1*c.* Charlotte Elizabeth Mariott.

2*b. Katherine Mariott, b.* 31 *Oct.* 1786 ; *d.* (–) ; m. *James Hill ; and had issue* 1*c to* 3*c.*

1*c.* [son] Hill.

2*c.* Caroline Hill.

3*c.* Eleanor Hill.

3*b. Lucy Mariott, b.* 16 *June* 1789 ; m. [——] *Thorniwark.*

4*b. Knightley Goodman Mariott, b.* 23 *Sept.* 1785 ; *d.* 14 *Ap.* 1878 ; m. 10 *Feb.* 1824, *the Rev. Henry Thomas Burne of Grittleton, M.A., b.* 7 *Ap.* 1799 ; *d.* 14 *Aug.* 1865 ; *and had issue* 1*c to* 14*c.*

1*c. Henry Knightley Burne, C.B., Lieut.-Gen. Bengal Staff Corps, sometime* (1870–1871) *Mil. Secretary to the Indian Government, b.* 26 *Nov.* 1825 ; *d.* (–) ; m. 22 *Sept.* 1853, *Fanny* (13 *Montpelier Terrace, Brighton), da. of T. Spens ; and had issue* 1*d to* 4*d.*

1*d. Henry Thomas George Burne, Lieut. Bengal Staff Corps, b.* 23 *July* 1854 ; *d.* 14 *May* 1883 ; m. 21 *Aug.* 1880, *Alice, da. of Edward Baker ; and had issue* 1*e to* 2*e.*

1*e.* Guy Edward Knightley Burne, *b.* 6 Nov. 1882.

2*e.* Fanny Caroline Knightley Burne.

2*d.* Knightley Owen Burne, Major Indian Army, *b.* 6 Aug. 1863.

3*d.* Caroline Eleanor Mary Burne, *m.* 11 Nov. 1878, Major William Loch, Bengal Cavalry ; and has issue 1*e* to 2*e.*

1*e.* Granville Oliver Coutts Loch, *b.* 22 Aug. 1880.

2*e.* Ruby Loch.

4*d.* Laura Frances Burne, *m.* 27 Mar. 1879, Edward Laurie, Bengal Medical Service ; and has issue 1*e.*

1*e.* Edith Burne Laurie, *m.* Capt. Ross Hayter, Cheshire Regt.

2*c. George Charles Burne, an elder Brother of the Trinity House, b.* 31 *Jan.* 1827 : d. 11 *Dec.* 1903 ; m. 6 *May* 1857, *Mary Anne* (17 *Randolph Road, W.), da. of Col. Sir George Henry Hewitt, 2nd Bart.* [*U.K.*]*; and had issue* 1*d.*

1*d.* George Henry Poyntz Burne, Lieut.-Col. Leicestershire Regt., *b.* 1 Mar. 1858.

3*c. Newdigate Hooper Kearney Burne, Bar.-at-Law, b.* 14 *Nov.* 1830 ; *d.* 3 *May* 1898 ; m. 15 *Sept.* 1853, *the Hon. Caroline Penelope* (*Lea Cottage, Albury, Guildford), da. of William Leonard* (*Addington), 2nd Viscount Sidmouth* [*U.K.*]*; and had issue* 1*d to* 9*d.* [Nos. 47542 to 47563.

The Plantagenet Roll

1*d*. Newdigate Addington Knightley Burne, Lieut.-Col. 40th Pathans, *b.* 23 Nov. 1855; *m.* 1886, Gertrude Abigail,⸸da. of C. Cox of Newcastle-on-Tyne; and has issue 1*e*.

2*e*. Frank Owen Newdigate Burne, *b.* 20 Oct. 1887.

2*d*. Knightley Poyntz Burne, Lieut.-Col. Comdt. 38th Dogras, *b.* 10 Nov. 1858; *m.* 1887, Emmie Marian, da. of J. B. Summers of Rose Moor, co. Pembroke, J.P.

3*d*. Herbert William Leonard Burne, sometime of the Central and S. American Telegraph Co., *b.* 27 Mar. 1865.

4*d*. Rainald Owen Burne, Major Army Service Corps, *b.* 3 Jan. 1871; *m.* 1897, Sybil Mary, da. of D. H. Owen, Principal Registrar, Probate Court; and has issue 1*e*.

1*e*. Newdigate Owen Burne, *b.* 1898.

5*d*. Ethel Caroline Burne.

6*d*. Dora Mary Louisa Burne, *m.* 1887, Capt. Edward Hugh Franklyn Finch, *late* E. Lancashire Regt.; and has issue 1*e*.

1*e*. Lionel Hugh Knightley Finch, *b.* 1888.

7*d*. Lilian Ursula Burne, *m.* 1884, Arthur Brooks Larkins of the Indian Telegraph Dept.; and has issue 1*e* to 3*e*.

1*e*. Edward Arthur Malcolm Larkins, *b.* 1894.

2*e*. Lilian Eveline Mabel Larkins, *b.* 1885.

3*e*. Viola Maud Larkins, *b.* 1886.

8*d*. Eveline Clara Burne, *m.* 14 Mar. 1900, Henry Gray (*Bank of Bengal, Rangoon*); and has issue 1*e* to 4*e*.

1*e*. Henry Newdigate Gray, *b.* 18 Aug. 1903.

2*e*. Eveline Hilary Gray, *b.* 13 Jan. 1901.

3*e*. Sylvia Charity Gray, *b.* 28 Ap. 1902.

4*e*. Rosetta Joyce Gray, *b.* 10 Feb. 1905.

9*d*. Christabel Lucy Burne.

4*c*. *Arthur Stephen Burne, Solicitor, formerly Private Sec. to the Right Hon. Edward Horsman, b.* 26 *Ap.* 1832; d. (? *unm.*) 1893.

5*c*. *Felix Neeld Burne, J.P., Queensland, b.* 17 *July* 1833; d. 17 *May* 1882; *m.* 25 *Aug.* 1859, *Laura Mary, da. of Capt. Robert Adair McNaghten; and had issue* 1*d to* 4*d*.

1*d*. Felix Malcolm Poyntz Burne, *b.* 12 May 1871.

2*d*. Newdigate Halford Marriott Burne, Capt. Cape Mounted Rifles, *b.* 21 July 1872.

3*d*. Beata Mabel Burne.

4*d*. Ellen Gertrude Burne.

6*c*. Alfred Bodicote Burne, Clerk of Petty Sessions (*Hill End, New South Wales*), *b.* 23 Nov. 1835.

7*c*. Sir Owen Tudor Burne, G.C.I.E., K.C.S.I., Major-Gen. (ret.), *late* Member of the Council of India, &c. &c. (132 *Sutherland Avenue, Maida Vale, W.; Church Hatch, Christchurch, Hants*), *b.* 12 Ap. 1837; *m.* 1st, 20 Nov. 1867, the Hon. Evelyne, da. of John (Browne), 3rd Baron Kilmaine [I.], *d.* 22 Ap. 1878; 2ndly, 9 Aug. 1883, Lady Agnes Charlotte, da. of George Sholto (Douglas), 17th Earl of Morton [S.]; and has issue.

See p. 433, Nos. 34823–34827.

8*c*. Frederick Burne, Clerk of Petty Sessions (*Tumut, New South Wales*), *b.* 14 Ap. 1839; *m.* 16 May 1872, Bessie, da. of Frederick R. Ferrier of Ferrier's Vale, New South Wales; and has issue 1*d* to 6*d*.

1*d*. Frederick Charles Meredith Burne.

2*d*. Edward Owen Poyntz Burne.

3*d*. Claude Hector Burne.

4*d*. Knightly Ferrier Burne.

5*d*. Vera Newdigate Burne.

6*d*. Maud Burne.

[Nos. 47564 to 47600.

524

# of The Blood Royal

9c. Jasper Burne, Col. Bengal Staff Corps, b. 25 Jan. 1841; m. 3 Dec. 1878, Annie, da. of Thomas Hendley of Charlton, Kent.

10c. Alan de Leyburn Burne (*Hereford Lodge, Cambridge Road, Aldershot*), b. 19 Sept. 1845; m. Alice Edith, da. of [——] Bidewill-Edwards of St. Germans, co. Norfolk; and has issue 1d to 2d.

    1d. Cyril Grey Burne, b. 27 Aug. 1886.

    2d. Helen May Burne, b. 11 Ap. 1896.

11c. Knightley Grey Burne, *late* Commr. of Arakan, and previously Additional Session Judge, Burmah (*St. Margaret's, South Norwood Hill, S.E.*) b. 14 May 1847; m. 16 Ap. 1872, Mary Eliott, da. of Major-Gen. William Carmichael Russell, R.A.; and has issue 1d to 9d.

    1d. Knightley Arthur Lloyd Burne, b. 26 Oct. 1873.

    2d. Lindsay Elliott Lumley Burne, b. 1 July 1877.

    3d. Roy Douglas Burne, *late* 4th Batt. Leicestershire Regt., b. 9 Sept. 1884.

    4d. Rainald Hugo Burne, R.N., Midshipman H.M.S. *Powerful*, b. 27 Sept. 1888.

    5d. Evelyne Mary Burne, b. 18 Sept. 1875; m. 1900, Robert Charles Elphinstone Underwood, Dist. Sup. of Police, Burmah.

    6d. Beatrice Maude Burne.

    7d. Mary Adela Burne, b. 26 Feb. 1881; m. 1902, Samuel William Cocks, Indian Educational Department.

    8d. Sybil Marion Burne, b. 15 Ap. 1886.

    9d. Vera Muriel Burne, b. 15 Mar. 1894.

12c. *Douglas Edward Burne*, b. 10 Dec. 1852; d. 1899; m. *Helen, da. of* [——] *Hinckley; and had issue 1d.*

    1d. Henry Wallace Burne.

13c. Caroline Mary Burne, b. 31 Aug. 1842.

14c. Eleanor Elizabeth Lumley Burne (*2 Buckingham Place, Clifton, Bristol*), b. 9 Feb. 1850; m. as 5th wife, 16 Oct. 1873, Gen. Sir James Brind, G.C.B., R.A., d. 1888; and has issue 1d to 5d.

    1d. *Percy Edwin Owen Brind*, b. 17 *Jan.* 1877; d. 4 *Mar.* 1900.

    2d. Ralph Montacute Brind, Lieut. 37th Dogras, Indian Army, b. 2 Dec. 1881.

    3d. Paul Hughenden Brind, b. 19 Ap. 1886.

    4d. Eleanor Jane Marriott Brind.

    5d. Joan Knightley Brind.   [Nos. 47601 to 47621.

455. Descendants, if any, of LUCY KNIGHTLEY (see Table XLV.), b. 10 Oct. 1727; d. 1800; m. 1749, JOSEPH SMYTH of Shelbrooke Lawn, Whittlebury Forest, co. Northants, Sergeant-at-Arms to George II. and George III., d. 1799 (aged 88); and had issue.

456. Descendants of the Hon. ANNE GREY (see Table XLV.), wife of JAMES GROVE of Pool Hall, Alveley, co. Salop, Sergeant-at-Law; and had issue 1a to 2a.

1a. *James Grey Grove, M.P. in 1714, whose issue became extinct shortly after 1820.*

2a. *Penelope Anna Grove, in her issue heir, m. Ralph Browne of Chaughley, co. Salop; and had issue 1b.*

The Plantagenet Roll

1b. Elizabeth Browne, co-heir, m. *Thomas Wylde of Glazeley, co. Worcester;* and had issue *1c.*

1c. Ralph Browne Wylde, afterwards *Wylde-Browne,* d. Dec. 1810; m. 1793, *Mary, da. of Thomas Whitmore;* and had issue *1d.*

1d. Thomas Whitmore Wylde-Browne *of Woodlands, co. Salop,* b. 19 Sept. 1800; d. 8 Nov. 1877; m. *Catherine, da. of Lewis William Brouncker,* d. 1836; and had issue *1e* to *3e.*

1e. William Wylde-Browne, *9th Bombay Native Infantry,* b. 11 Mar. 1823; d. Sept. 1890; m. *1st,* 16 Dec. 1857 (*his cousin-german*), Geraldine Fanny Winifred, *da. of Richard Brouncker of Bouveridge, co. Dorset, J.P.,* d. 30 Nov. 1874; *2ndly,* 4 Oct. 1877, Emily Dysart (*30 Stanford Road, Kensington, W.*), *da. of the Rev. George Warwick Bampfylde Daniel;* and had issue *1f* to *7f.*

1f. Francis Frederick Wylde-Browne (*Friend, Saline co., Nebraska, U.S.A.*), b. 5 Oct. 1862.

2f. William Ralph Wylde-Browne (*Cadwell House, Paignton, Devon*), b. 27 Aug. 1866.

3f. Gerald Hopton Wylde-Browne, *late* Capt. Loyal North Lancashire Regt. (*Sanger, Fresno, co. California, United States*), b. 6 May 1869; m. (at Ceylon) 3 Nov. 1896, Helen, da. of Major Raven; and has issue *1g* to *3g.*

1g. Geraldine Margaret Wylde-Browne, b. (in Ceylon) 17 Oct. 1897.

2g. May Audley Hope Wylde-Browne, b. 16 Mar. 1900.

3g. Norah Lilian Wylde-Brown, b. 25 July 1903.

4f. John Harry Wylde-Browne, of the Colonial Rubber Co. (*Rushcutter's Bay, Sydney, N.S.W.*), b. 26 June 1872.

5f. Mariana Wylde-Browne (*Craven Hotel, Eastbourne Terrace, W.*), b. 17 Aug. 1860.

6f. Grace Winifred Wylde-Browne, b. 27 Mar. 1868; m. Edmund Leicester, M.D. (*Lerryan, Lostwithiel, Cornwall*).

7f. Katharine Eva Wylde-Browne, b. 21 Nov. 1874.

2e. Ralph Wylde-Browne, *of New Zealand,* b. 21 Mar. 1831; d. (*in New Zealand*) 1899; m. *Grace J.* (*New Zealand*), *da. of* [——] *Wilson of Ireland;* and had issue *1f* to *5f.*

1f. Francis William Wylde-Browne (*Glenalva, Eneggera, Brisbane*), b. (in New Zealand), m. 1902, Wynifred Anne, da. of Walter Jones of Carmarthen; and has issue (a son).

2f. Charles H. A. Wylde-Browne, in Bank of New South Wales (*Greymouth, New Zealand*), b. (in New Zealand).

3f. Mary Wylde-Browne, m. A. G. Clarke (*Leafield View Road, Auckland, New Zealand*).

4f. Alice Wylde-Browne, m. Redge Masefield (*Ellerton, Ponsonby, Auckland, New Zealand*).

5f. C. J. Wylde-Browne, *unm.*

3e. Harry Wylde-Browne (*Redhill, Bridgetown, Totnes*), b. 28 Nov. 1833; m. (at Maritzburg) 29 Dec. 1864, Caroline Maria Mackenzie, da. of Capt. Donald Moodie, R.N., cadet of Melsetter, sometime (1845–1849) Colonial Secretary of Natal, and (1857) Speaker of the Legislative Assembly; and has issue *1f* to *6f.*

1f. Edward Ernest Wylde-Browne, b. (at Umzinto, Natal) 20 Sept. 1867.

2f. Harry Cecil Bickersteth Wylde-Browne, b. (at Umzinto) 14 June 1886.

3f. Katherine Edith Wylde-Browne, b. (at Umzinto) 24 Nov. 1865; m. (at Maritzburg) 12 Aug. 1896, Arthur Seymour Woodgate (*Callcott, Estcourt, Natal*); and has issue *1g* to *2g.*

1g. Dorothy Mary Woodgate, b. 20 Sept. 1897.

2g. Enid Alice Woodgate, b. 8 July 1903.

4f. Geraldine Mary Wylde-Browne, b. (at Maritzburg) 11 Jan. 1873; m. (there) 25 July 1898, Capt. John Nugent Murray MacGregor, Royal Dublin Fusiliers.   [Nos. 47622 to 47643.

526

5f. Monica Wylde-Browne, *b.* (at Maritzburg) 16 June 1874.

6f. Leonard Agnes Wylde-Browne, *b.* (at Maritzburg) 5 May 1876; *m.* 1st (there), 4 May 1898, Capt. Charles Albert Hensley, Royal Dublin Fusiliers, *d.* (being killed at Venterspruit) Jan. 1900; 2ndly, 18 Feb. 1901, Harry Whitworth; and has issue 1g to 2g.

    1g. Leonora Angela Whitworth, *b.* 28 Sept. 1901.

    2g. Joan Marguerite Whitworth, *b.* 8 Dec. 1902.   [Nos. 47644 to 47647.

457. Descendants, if any, of MARY MACKWORTH (see Table XLV.).

458. Descendants of Lady ANNE BOURCHIER (see Table XLV.), *b.* 1628; *bur.* 9 Sept. 1662; *m.* 1st, 3 Mar. 1646, JAMES (CRANFIELD), 2nd EARL of MIDDLESEX [E.], *bapt.* 27 Dec. 1621; *bur.* 13 Sept. 1651; 2ndly, *c.* 1653, Sir CHICHESTER WREY, 3rd Bart. [E.], *bur.* 17 May 1668; and had issue.

See Table VI., &c., pp. 128–158, Nos. 1646–2470.   [Nos. 47648 to 48466.

459. Descendants, if any, of the Hon. HENRY BOURCHIER, the Hon. FULKE BOURCHIER, Lady MARY BOURCHIER, wife of Hugh WYOT of Exeter; and of Lady CECILIA BOURCHIER, wife of THOMAS PEYTON of Plymouth, Customer (see Table XLV.).

460. Descendants, if any, of HESTER NOYE (see Table XLVI.), *m.* (at Oakehampton) 22 July 1695, HENRY DAVIES of St. Buryan, co. Cornwall; and had issue 1a to 6a.

    1a. *William Davies, whose issue became extinct.*

    2a. *Henry Davies, bapt. (at St. Buryan) 12 Aug. 1701.*

    3a. *Humphrey Davies,[1] bapt. (at St. Buryan) 22 Ap. 1705.*

    4a. *John Davies, bapt. 5 Feb. 1712.*

    5a. *Hester Davies,[1] bapt. 1707.*

    6a. *Anne Davies, bapt. (at St. Buryan) 5 Oct. 17—.*

461. Descendants of CATHERINE DAVIES (see Table XLVI.), *b.* 6 Jan. 1728; *d.* 3 Feb. 1803; *m.* the Rev. EDWARD GIDDY, M.A.; and had issue (with possibly das.) 1a.

    1a. *Davies Giddy, afterwards (1808, Gilbert of Tredrea, co. Cornwall, M.P.) President of the Royal Society, b. 1767; d. 24 Dec. 1839; m. 18 Ap. 1808, Mary*

---

[1] A Humphrey Davies of the diocese of Cork and Ross, *m.* 1742, Elizabeth Wade, and a Hester Davies and Richard Heacock, both of Great Island, Cork, were *m.* 19 Nov. 1728; and had, with other issue (1) George Heacock, *m.* 1750, Elizabeth Trewen; (2) Hester Haycock or Heacock, *m.* 1st, in Dublin, 3 Feb. 1749, John Grosse, and 2ndly, (?) 1757, John Pigott (not Paget); (3) Anne, *m.* 1758 (as one of his four wives), Alexander Durdin of Shanagarry Castle, co. Cork, and Huntington Castle, co. Carlow, and was mother of Richard Durdin of Shanagarry, who founded the town of Huntington, in Pennsylvania. He *m.* (Mar. lic. Bond dated Dublin 1785) Frances (who re-m. [——] Lewis), da. of Sir James Esmonde, 7th Bart. [I.], and had issue Alexander, *b.* 1786, living 29 Ap. 1819, *d.* in the United States probably *s.p.*; Richard Haycock, *b.* 1790, *bur.* in Philadelphia 22 July 1809, and Frances Maria Esmonde, *b.* 1788, *d.* in Philadelphia 17 Dec. 1812. *Ex inform.* William Jackson Pigott of Dundrum Manor House, Esq.

Anne, da. and h. of Thomas Gilbert of Eastbourne, co. Sussex; and had issue 1b to 3b.

1b. *John Davies Gilbert of Trelissick, Tredrea, and Eastbourne,* b. 1811; d. 16 *Ap.* 1854; m. 7 *Oct.* 1851, *the Hon. Anna Dorothea, da. of Robert Shapland* (*Carew*), *1st Baron Carew* [*I. and U.K.*], *K.P.,* b. *Dec.* 1822; d. (-), *and had issue* 1c.

1c. Carew Davies Gilbert, J.P., D.L., a co-h. to the Barony of Sandys [E.] (*Trelissick, Truro, Cornwall; The Manor House, Eastbourne*), b. 1 Aug. 1852; m. 26 Ap. 1881, Grace Katherine Rosa, da. of George Staunton King Massy Dawson of Ballinacourté, co. Tipperary; and has issue 1d to 5d.

1d. Minnie Davies Gilbert, b. 1882.

2d. Patience Davies Gilbert, b. 1883; m. 1904, Capt. C. H. Harding, Gloucestershire Militia; and had issue 1e.

1e. Charles Gilbert Harding.

3d. Grace Dorothy Davies Gilbert, b. 1891.

4d. Hester Louisa Edith Davies Gilbert, b. 1892.

5d. Honor Davies Gilbert, b. 1893.

2b. *Catherine Gilbert,* d. 1893; m. 17 *Ap.* 1834, *John Samuel Hunt, afterwards* (*R.L.* 27 *Dec.* 1813) *Enys of Enys, J.P., High Sheriff co. Cornwall* 1824, b. 21 *Sept.* 1796; d. 29 *May* 1872; *and had issue* 1c to 4c.

1c. Francis Gilbert Enys, J.P., D.L., High Sheriff co. Cornwall 1876, Deputy Warden of the Stannaries (*Enys, Penryn, Cornwall*), b. 30 July 1836.

2c. John Davies Enys, F.R.G.S., b. 11 Oct. 1837.

3c. *Jane Mary Enys,* d. 18 *Oct.* 1874; m. *as 1st wife,* 28 *Aug.* 1860, *Henry Rogers, Capt. R.N.* (*Hartley, Plymouth*); *and had issue* 1d to 8d.

1d. Rev. Enys Henry Rogers, M.A. (*Starr's Green House, Battle*), b. 23 May 1861; m. 13 Jan. 1896, Sarah Louisa, da. of George Duffus of Charlestown, South Carolina; and has issue 1e.

1e. Charles Reginald Saltren Rogers, b. 13 Feb. 1897.

2d. Charles Gilbert Rogers, b. 17 Oct. 1864.

3d. Ernest Rogers, B.A. (Oxon.), Indian C.S., b. 10 Nov. 1865; m. 1895, [——], da. of [——]; and has issue (2 children).

4d. Claude Somerset Rogers, b. 6 Jan. 1867.

5d. Leonard Rogers, b. 18 Jan. 1868.

6d. Rev. Kenneth St. Aubyn Rogers, B.A. (Oxon.), a Missionary in East Africa, b. 7 Mar. 1869.

7d. John Davies Rogers, Lieut. R.N., b. 7 Aug. 1872.

8d. Catherine Mary Rogers, b. 9 Aug. 1870.

4c. Mary Ann Enys.

3b. *Hester Elizabeth Gilbert,* d. 25 *June* 1885; m. 1840, *William Sancroft Holmes of Gawdy Hall, J.P., D.L.,* d. 1849; *and had issue* 1c to 2c.

1c. John Sancroft Holmes, J.P., D.L., *late* Lieut.-Col. Prince of Wales' Own Norfolk Artillery (*Gawdy Hall, Harleston*), b. 1847; m. 1877, Edith, da. of Henry Kingscote.

2c. Mary Ann Holmes, m. 1886, W. H. Pemberton of Denton House, Norfolk, d.s.p. 1894. [Nos. 48467 to 48487.

462. Descendants, if any, of the Hon. ALETHEA SANDYS, wife of FRANCIS GOSTON of Alderidge, co. Hants; of the Hon. MARY SANDYS, wife of Dr. HENRY SAVAGE, Principal of Balliol College, Oxford; and of the Hon. JANE SANDYS, wife of JOHN HARRIS of Old Woodstock, co. Oxford (see Table XLVI.).

# of The Blood Royal

463. Descendants, if any, of SOPHIA MILL (see Table XLVI.), wife of the Chevalier DE LA CAINCA of Naples, *temp.* (?) 1770.

464. Descendants, if any, of MARGARET, PHILADELPHIA, ELIZABETH, MARY, and MARTHA MILL, das. of Sir Richard MILL, 5th Bart. [E.], *d.* 1760; and of (their aunt) MARGARET MILL, wife of ROBERT KNOLLYS, son of Robert KNOLLYS of Grove Place, co. Herts (see Table XLVI.).

465. Descendants, if any, of JANE FORTESCUE (see Table XLVI.), wife of WILLIAM COLEMAN.

466. Descendants, if any, of the Hon. JANE SANDYS (see Table XLVI.), *d.* 8 Aug. 1643; *m.* the Rev. JOHN ENGLISH, D.D.[1]

467. Descendants, if any, of THOMAS SANDYS and MARGERY SANDYS, wife of HENRY CAREY of Hamworthy, co. Dorset, brother and sister to William, 3rd BARON SANDYS [E.]; and of the Hon. Sir WALTER SANDYS and his two younger brothers and six sisters, children of Thomas, 2nd BARON SANDYS [E.] (see Table XLVI.).

468. Descendants of ANNE CONSTABLE (see Table XLVII.), *d.* (–); *m.* WILLIAM HAGGERSTON (2nd son of Sir Thomas HAGGERSTON, 2nd Bart. [E.], *d.v.p.*; and had issue 1*a* to 2*a*.

1*a*. *Sir Carnaby Haggerston, 3rd Bart. [E.], d. 1756; m. 30 Nov. 1721, Elizabeth, da. and eventual h. of Peter Middelton of Stockeld, co. York, d. Dec. 1769; and had issue.*
See pp. 333–336, Nos. 24284–24535.

2*a*. *Anne Haggerston,* m. 1716, *Bryan Salvin of Croxdale,* d. 1 *Mar.* 1751; *and had issue* 1*b* to 2*b*.

1*b*. *William Salvin of Croxdale,* b. 28 *Nov.* 1723; d. 21 *Jan.* 1800; m. 2*ndly,* 1758, *Catherine, da. and h. of Thomas Thornton of Nether Witton, co. Northumberland; and had issue* 1*c* to 5*c*.

1*c*. *William Thomas Salvin of Croxdale,* b. 4 *July* 1768; d. 8 *June* 1842; m. 22 *July* 1800, *Anne Maria, da. of John Webbe Weston, previously Webbe of Sutton Place, co. Surrey; and had issue* 1*d* to 2*d*.

1*d*. *Gerard Salvin of Croxdale, J.P.,* b. 24 *Sept.* 1804; d. 22 *Oct.* 1870; m. 23 *Sept.* 1834, *Winifred, da. of Henry Thomas Maire Witham, previously Silvertop, of Lartington; and had issue.*
See the Clarence Volume, p. 320, Nos. 9258–9266.

2*d*. *Marmaduke Charles Salvin of Burn Hall, J.P., D.L.,* b. 11 *Feb.* 1812; d. 27 *Dec.* 1885; m. *Sept.* 1845, *Caroline, da. of Sir Charles Wolseley, 7th Bart. [E.]; and had issue.*
See p. 280, Nos. 11105–11110.

2*c*. *Catherine Salvin,* d. 1798; m. *Sir Thomas Stanley-Massey-Stanley, 7th Bart. [E.]; and had issue* 1*d* to 6*d*.

1*d*. *Sir William Stanley-Massey-Stanley, 8th Bart. [E.], d. unm.* 1803.
[Nos. 48488 to 48756.

---

[1] M.I. at Cheltenham, "Mis. Gen. et Her.," N.S. ii. 412.

The Plantagenet Roll

2d. *Sir Thomas Stanley-Massey-Stanley, 9th Bart.* [E.], d. Aug. 1841; m. *Jan. 1805, Mary, da. of Sir Carnaby Haggerston, 5th Bart.* [E.], d. 20 Aug. 1857; *and had issue.*

See p. 333, Nos. 24284–24290.

3d. *Charles Stanley-Massey-Stanley*, m. 22 Oct. 1829, *Barbara, da. of Sir Edward Montagu, Bart.*

4d. *James Stanley-Massey-Stanley.*

5d. *Henry Stanley-Massey-Stanley.*

6d. *Catherine Stanley-Massey-Stanley*, d. 12 *Jan.* 1862; m. *William Blundell of Crosby Hall, co. Lancaster, J.P., D.L.,* d. 11 *July* 1854 (aged 45); *and had issue.*

See the Clarence Volume, p. 326, Nos. 9450–9505.

3c. *Mary Salvin*, d. (? *unm.*).

4c. *Isabella Salvin*, d. 1 *Mar.* 1853; m. 2*ndly*, 9 *May* 1803, *Ralph Riddell of Cheeseburn Grange, co. Northumberland,* d. 24 *Sept.* 1831; *and had issue* 1d.

1d. *Francis Henry Riddell of Cheeseburn Grange, J.P.*, b. 30 *May* 1813; d. 30 *Jan.* 1892; m. 30 *Sept.* 1862, *Ellen, da. of Michael Henry Blount of Mapledurham; and had issue.*

See the Clarence Volume, pp. 375–376, Nos. 12927–12942.

5c. *Eliza Salvin*, d. (? *unm.*).

2b. *Mary Salvin*, d. (–); m. *George Markham of Claxby.*

[Nos. 48757 to 48835.

469. Descendants of WILLIAM SHELDON of Weston and Beoly (see Table XLVII.), *d.* (–); *m.* MARGARET FRANCES DISNEY, da. of James ROOKE of Bigsware, co. Gloucester, *d.* 1766; and had issue 1*a* to 5*a*.

1a. *Ralph Sheldon of Weston, M.P., Col. of the Oxford Loyal Vol.,* d. 1822; m. *Jane, da. of Admiral Francis Holburne of Menstrie, N.B.; and had issue* 1b *to* 3b.

1b. *Edward Ralph Charles Sheldon of Brailes House, J.P., D.L., M.P., Major Warwickshire Militia,* b. 2 *Mar.* 1782; d. 11 *June* 1836; m. 14 *Aug.* 1817, *Marcella, da. of Thomas Meredith Winstanley of Lisson Hall, co. Dublin,* d. 23 *July* 1849; *and had issue* 1c *to* 2c.

1c. Henry James Sheldon, J.P., High Sheriff co. Worcester 1860 (*Brailes House, Banbury, co. Warwick*), b. 12 Sept. 1823; *m.* 3 Ap. 1852, Alicia Mary, widow of William Oakeley, da. of Gen. Sir Evan Lloyd.

2c. Isabel Sheldon, *m.* 1st, 17 June 1854, Col. Frederic Granville of Wellesburne Hall, Warwick, J.P., D.L., *b.* 3 Feb. 1810; *d.* Oct. 1885; 2ndly, 22 Sept. 1887, Vincent Pollexfen Calmady of Langdon Court, co. Devon, J.P., *d.s.p.* 5 Mar. 1896.

2b. *Jane Louisa Sheldon,* d. 10 *Dec.* 1871; m. *as* 2nd *wife,* 26 *Dec.* 1815, *Robert Fellowes of Shotesham Park, co. Norfolk, J.P., D.L.,* d. 14 *Ap.* 1869; *and had issue* 1c *to* 5c.

1c. Robert Fellowes, J.P., D.L., High Sheriff co. Norfolk 1874 (*Shotesham Park, near Norwich*), b. 13 Oct. 1817; *m.* 19 Aug. 1845, Frances Ann, da. of John Clutterbuck of Warkworth, J.P., d. 16 Jan. 1898; and has issue.

See the Clarence Volume, pp. 88–89, Nos. 377–409.

2c. *Edward Fellowes, Major-Gen. in the Army,* d. (? s.p.) 10 *July* 1879; m. *Margaret Augusta, da. of Col. (and grand-da. of Sir John) Kirkland.*

3c. *Louisa Fellowes,* d. 3 *May* 1901; m. 27 *Aug.* 1835, *Sir Thomas Gladstone, 2nd Bart.* [U.K.], *M.P.,* b. 25 *July* 1804; d. 20 *Mar.* 1889; *and had issue* 1d *to* 2d.

1d. Sir John Robert Gladstone, 3rd Bart. [U.K.], J.P., D.L. (*Fasque, Laurencekirk, Kincardineshire*), b. 26 Ap. 1852.

2d. Mary Selina Gladstone.

4c. *Fanny Fellowes,* d. 2 *Ap.* 1884; m. 4 *Sept.* 1851, *Edward Howes of Morningthorpe, M.P.,* d. 26 *Mar.* 1871; *and had issue* 1d. [Nos. 48836 to 48873.

# of The Blood Royal

1*d. Henrietta Louisa Howes*, b. 1 *Jan.* 1856; d. 13 *Dec.* 1887; m. 13 *Feb.* 1883, *Thomas Holmes, Comm. R.N.; and had issue* 1*e.*

1*e. Susan Holmes, b.* 4 Dec. 1885.

5*c. Margaret Fellowes*, d. 7 *Jan.* 1892; m. 2 *Nov.* 1854, *William Rose (Mansfield), 1st Baron Sandhurst* [*U.K.*], *G.C.B., G.C.S.I.,* b. 21 *June* 1819; d. 23 *June* 1876; *and had issue* 1*d* to 5*d.*

1*d.* William (Mansfield), 2nd Baron Sandhurst [U.K.], G.C.S.I., G.C.I.E., sometime (1895–1900) Governor of Bombay, &c. (60 *Eaton Square, S.W.*), b. 21 Aug. 1855; m. 20 July 1881, Lady Victoria Alexandrina, C.I., da. of Frederick (Spencer), 4th Earl Spencer [G.B.], K.G.

2*d.* Hon. John William Mansfield, Bar. I.T. (37*a Duke Street, St. James',* S.W.; *Edgebrook, Sheringham*), b. 10 July 1857; m. 11 Sept. 1888, Edith Mary, da. of John Higson of Oakmere Hall, Cheshire; and has issue 1*e* to 2*e.*

1*e.* Ralph Sheldon Mansfield, b. 19 July 1892.

2*e.* Edith Margery Mansfield, b. 10 July 1889.

3*d.* Hon. Henry William Mansfield, Major 2nd County of London Imp. Yeo., *late* 1st Dragoons (*Cavalry*), b. 2 Dec. 1860; m. 9 June 1885, Katharine Rachel, da. of James Charles of Kennet House, Harrow, J.P.; and has issue 1*e* to 4*e.*

1*e.* William Henry Charles Mansfield, b. 3 Oct. 1887.

2*e.* James Cleland Mansfield, b. 20 Feb. 1890.

3*e.* John Hamilton Mansfield, b. 12 Sept. 1893.

4*e.* Katharine Rose Mansfield, b. 2 May 1886.

4*d.* Hon. James William Mansfield, *late* Lieut. Duke of Cambridge's Own (10 *Cadogan Gardens, S.W.*), b. 12 Feb. 1862.

5*d.* Hon. Margaret Louisa Mansfield.

3*b. Fanny Anne Sheldon*, d.s.p.; m. *the Count d'Orfeuille.*

2*a. James Sheldon*, m. [——], *da. and h. of the Rev.* [——] *Mostyn.*

3*a. Charles Henry Sheldon of Haute Fontaine, France,* m. 1784, *Elizabeth, widow of Charles Graham of Netherby, da. of Richard Gorges of Eye, co. Hereford.*

4*a. George Sheldon of Ems, Upper Austria,* m. *the Princess Frances of Auersberg.*

5*a. Margaret Frances Sheldon*, d. (–); m. *as* 2nd *wife,* 18 *May* 1772, *Francis Talbot of Witham Place, co. Essex,* d. 1813; *and had issue.*

See p. 284, Nos. 11252–11287. [Nos. 48874 to 48921.

470. OTHER SHELDON, CONSTABLE, METHAM, and LANGDALE, descendants, if any surviving (see Table XLVII.).

471. Descendants of RUDSTON CALVERLEY, *afterwards* RUDSTON of Hayton, co. York (see Table XLVIII.), d. 15 June 1806; m. 1 Oct. 1761, ANNE, da. of William STOCKDALE of Scarborough; and had issue 1*a* to 4*a.*

1*a. Rev. Thomas Cutler Rudston, afterwards Rudston-Read of Hayton and Sand Hutton,* b. 19 *Nov.* 1762; d. 17 *Sept.* 1838; m. 26 *May* 1803, *Louisa, da. of Henry Hopkins Cholmley, previously Fane, of Whitby Abbey and Howsham, co. York; and had issue* 1*b* to 7*b.*

1*b. William Henry Rudston-Read of Hayton, J.P., F.L.S., F.H.S.,* b. 14 *May* 1808; d. unm. 15 *Aug.* 1826.

2*b. Rev. George Rudston-Read, Rector of Sulton-on-Derwent,* b. 24 *Feb.* 1810; d. 31 *Dec.* 1864; m. 3 *Nov.* 1836, *Teresa, da. of the Rev. William Wheler (son of Sir Charles Wheler, 7th Bart.* [*E.*], d. 31 *Mar.* 1897; *and had issue* 1*c* to 4*c.*

531

The Plantagenet Roll

1c. Trevor Wheler Rudston-Read, now Calverley-Rudston, Lord of the Manor of Hayton, J.P., D.L., F.R.S., F.R.H.S. (*Hayton, E. R., co. York; Allerthorpe Hall, Pocklington*), b. 30 Dec. 1851; m. 1873, Annie, da. of Gilbert Wilkes of Chadwick Manor, co. Warwick, d. 28 Dec. 1899; and has issue 1d to 3d.

1d. William George Trevor Calverley-Rudston, b. 14 Feb. 1874.

2d. Annie Teresa Calverley-Rudston, b. 5 Feb. 1875; m. 1904, Capt. Webber, R.E.

3d. Evelyn Maud Calverley-Rudston, b. 19 Jan. 1880.

2c. Louisa Rudston-Read (*Champion Lodge, Leamington*), m. 11 Aug. 1863, William Feilding Harding of Baraset, co. Warwick, J.P., b. 22 Sept. 1829; d. 22 Jan. 1887; and has issue 1d to 6d.

1d. Henry George Harding of Baraset, *late* Royal Naval Reserve (19 *Lower Belgrave Street, S.W.*), b. 18 Dec. 1865; m. 17 Ap. 1890, Edith Georgina, da. of Frederic William Steward of Cornwall Gardens; and has issue 1e to 4e.

1e. William Oliver Feilding Harding, b. 17 May 1892.

2e. Basil Frederic Hamilton Harding, b. 14 July 1897.

3e. Lionel Henry Powys Harding, b. 12 Aug. 1898.

4e. Gwendolen Harding.

2d. Arthur Hamilton Harding, b. (-); m. Ebba, da. of [——] Braunerjhelm, Col. (King's Dragoon Guards) in the Swedish Service; and has issue 1e to 2e.

1e. Trevor Harding.

2e. Lilian Harding.

3d. Cecil Cholmley Harding.

4d. Edward Powys Harding.

5d. Helen Louisa Harding, m. Ap. 1898, Edward Powys Cobb, Royal Welsh Fusiliers.

6d. Katherine Emily Harding.

3c. Georgiana Rudston-Read, m. 11 Aug. 1863, Frederic William Steward of Cornwall Gardens, South Kensington, d. 9 Oct. 1896; and had (with other) issue 1d.

1d. Edith Georgina Steward (2nd da.), m. 17 Ap. 1890, Henry George Harding of Baraset (19 *Lower Belgrave Street, S.W.*); and has issue.

See p. 532, Nos. 48928–48931.

4c. Teresa Charlotte Rudston-Read (*Alveston Hall, Warwick*), m. 26 Nov. 1872, Charles John Townsend, J.P., d. 12 Sept. 1902.

3b. *Rev. Thomas Frederick Rudston-Read, M.A., Rural Dean and Rector of Withyham, co. Kent,* b. 4 *June* 1811; d. 20 *Jan.* 1892; m. 2ndly, 23 *May* 1867, *Barbara Louisa Fell, da. of William Thompson of Priorletham, co. Fife, M.D.; and had issue* 1c.

1c. Frederica Louisa Rudston-Read.

4b. *Edward Rudston-Read, Major in the Army,* b. 13 *Oct.* 1812; d. 1884; m. 29 *Ap.* 1847, *Isabella, da. of E. S. Strangways of Alne,* d. 9 *May* 1897; *and had issue* 1c to 5c.

1c. D'Arcy Wellesley Edward Rudston-Read.

2c. Harry Rudston-Read, m. 6 Mar. 1888, Lilian, da. of Frederick Cox, of 10 Belgrave Square.

3c. *Noel Rudston-Read,* d. (-).

4c. Constance Rudston-Read.

5c. Ada Rudston-Read.

5b. *Ama Rudston-Read,* d. (? s.p.) 5 *May* 1889; m. 20 *Feb.* 1839, *the Rev. John Harding, Rector of Walkerne,* d. 7 *Feb.* 1873.

6b. *Katherine Rudston-Read,* d. 23 *Feb.* 1873; m. 21 *May* 1845, *the Rev. Joseph*
[Nos. 48922 to 48950.

William Atkinson, Vicar of Brodsworth, co. York, d. 25 *May* 1867 ; *and had issue* 1c *to* 4c.

    1c. William Atkinson.

    2c. *Arthur Atkinson,* d. (–).

    3c. *Emily Atkinson,* d. (–).

    4c. Katherine Atkinson.

    7b. *Elizabeth Amelia Rudston-Read,* d. (–) ; m. 7 *July* 1840, *Thomas Faulconer, Capt. in the Army, and afterwards Sharebroker of the Stock Exchange,* d. (–) ; *and had issue* 1c *to* 6c.

        1c. Robert Faulconer.

        2c. Rudston Faulconer.

        3c. Catherine Faulconer.

        4c. Louisa Faulconer, *m.* Alfred Chatfield, Admiral R.N.

        5c. *Amy Faulconer,* d. (–) ; m. *F. Norgan.*

        6c. *Carrie Faulconer,* d. (–) ; m. *Howden Hamilton.*

    2a. *George Rudston of Hull, Linen Draper,* m. ; *and had (with possibly other) issue* 1b.

        1b. *Henry Rudston, lost at sea, presumably, unm.*

    3a. *Charles Rudston of Hull, Merchant,* b. 2 *Sept.* 1773 ; d. (? s.p.) 30 *July* 1855.

    4a. *Charlotte Rudston, m. Richard Vawser ; and had issue.*

[Nos. 48951 to 48956.

472. Descendants of ESTHER CALVERLEY (see Table XLVIII.), *b.* 1754 ; *d.* 30 July 1829 ; *m.* July 1771, MATTHEW ETTY of Hayton, and *afterwards* of Feasegate, York, Miller, *b.* 1743 ; *d.* 24 Dec. 1818 ; and had issue (10 sons, of whom 5 died young) 1*a* to 5*a*.

    1a. *Walter Etty,* b. 26 *Feb.* 1774 ; d. 23 *Feb.* 1850 ; m. 28 *Aug.* 1810, *Jane, da. of Benjamin Hamilton ; and had issue* 1b *to* 3b.

        1b. Thomas Bodley Etty, *b.* 8 *Mar.* 1820 ; *m.* 21 July 1853, Sarah, da. of R. M. Craven of Hull.

        2b. *Jane Elizabeth Etty,* b. 15 *Sept.* 1813 ; d. 4 *July* 1891 ; m. 15 *June* 1842, *Robert Edward Smithson of York,* d. 14 *Mar.* 1898 ; *and had issue* 1c *to* 3c.

            1c. *Edward Walter Smithson, late of York (Hitchin),* b. 2 *Ap.* 1843 ; *m.* 4 Aug. 1869, Sarah, da. and h. of the Rev. William Kay, Fellow of Lincoln College, Oxford.

            2c. *William Hugh Smithson,* b. 23 *July* 1847 ; d. 22 *Sept.* 1896 ; m. *and had issue.*

            3c. Eleanor Susan Smithson, *b.* 10 Jan. 1852 ; *m.* 21 Feb. 1878, George Ellis of Acomb, near York, *d.* 14 Feb. 1893 ; and had issue 1*d.*

                1d. Mabel Ellis, *b.* 29 May 1883 ; *m.* 11 Oct. 1905, Henry Raley (*Clayton, near Scarborough*).

        3b. *Martha Etty,* b. 6 *Dec.* 1817 ; d. [——] ; m. 1847, *William Piercy Dimes of Oldstone, Devon,* d. 18 *Ap.* 1885 ; *and had issue* 1c *to* 3c.

            1c. *William Stephen Dimes, b.* 3 June 1848 ; *m.* 6 May 1876, Lucy Mary, da. of Charles Narracott; 2ndly, 8 Nov. 1891, Emily Kate, sister of the preceding ; 3rdly, 2 June 1900, Catherine Martin, widow of James Sims, da. of Samuel Henry Pearce ; and has issue 1*d* to 8*d.*

                1d. Charles William Dimes, *b.* 21 Mar. 1877 ; *m.* 2 June 1900, Louisa Ann, da. of [——] Evans ; and has issue 1*e.*

                    1e. William Eric Dimes, *b.* 22 Dec. 1904.

[Nos. 48957 to 48963.

2d. Percy Etty Dimes, b. 22 Oct. 1878 ; m. 5 Mar. 1904, Grace, da. of Henry Cleater ; and has issue 1e.

    1e. Una Etty Dimes, b. 10 Dec. 1905.

3d. Cyril Dimes, b. 10 Oct. 1880.

4d. Louis Thomas Dimes, b. 12 Oct. 1884.

5d. Douglas Dimes, b. 16 May 1886.

6d. Dorothy Dimes, b. 17 Nov. 1882.

7d. Pauline Dimes, b. 3 Mar. 1888.

8d. Ruby Dimes, b. 8 Ap. 1893.

2c. Matilda Jane Dimes, b. 24 Aug. 1855 ; m. 1881, John Shapley ; and has issue 1d to 2d.

    1d. John Shapley, b. 1882.

    2d. Walter Shapley, b. 1885.

3c. Ellen Martha Dimes (4 *Crown Terrace, Scarborough*), b. 15 Jan. 1859 ; m. 15 May 1879, John Ferris, F.R.C.V.S., L.R.C.S., L.R.C.P. (Ed.), Hon. Lieut.-Col. A.V.D., *d.s.p.*

    2a. *John Etty.*[1]

    3a. *Thomas Etty.*[1]

    4a. *William Etty* (7th son), *the well-known R.A.*, b. *Mar.* 1787 ; d. *13 Nov.* 1849.

    5a. *Charles Etty,*[1] b. 1791 *or* 1792 ; d. (*in Java*) *4 Dec.* 1856.

[Nos. 48964 to 48975.

473. Other CALVERLEY, RUDSTON, and SALTONSTALL descendants, if any surviving (see Table XLVIII.).

474. Descendants, if any, of JANE CONSTABLE (see Table XLVII.), bapt. 29 Ap. 1589 ; bur. 18 July 1630 ; m. ROBERT SOTHEBY of Pocklington, York, bapt. 30 Mar. 1583 ; d. 27 Nov. 1652 ; and had issue 1a to 11a.[2]

    1a. *Robert Sotheby of Pocklington, eldest son and heir*, 1652.

    2a. *Henry Sotheby*, d.s.p.

    [3a. *Marmaduke Sotheby of Long Riston*, bur. 29 *Sept.* 1681 ; *and had issue* 1b.

    1b. *Robert Sotheby*, bapt. 30 *Aug.* 1657.]

    4a. *Roger Sotheby.*

    5a. *John Sotheby.*

    6a. *Philip Sotheby.*

    7a. *Frances Sotheby*, bur. 16 *Jan.* 1655.

    8a. *Mary Sotheby*, ? m. 13 *Oct.* 1640, *Thomas Rawson, Clerk.*

    9a. *Marjory Sotheby.*

    10a. *Anne Sotheby.*

    11a. *Averill Sotheby*, bur. 4 *Mar.* 1630.

475. Descendants, if any, of EVERILDA CONSTABLE (see Table XLVII.), wife of WILLIAM CONSTABLE of Drax.

---

[1] A niece of William Etty's, Mrs. Binnington, apparently a daughter of one of these, is mentioned in the Preface to Gilchrist's Life of him, but the Editor has been unable to ascertain anything further of her or her possible descendants.

[2] Foster's "Yorkshire Pedigrees."

# of The Blood Royal

476. Descendants of THOMAS FAIRFAX of Steeton and Newton Kyme, co. York (see Table XLIX.), *b.* 1698; *d.* 2 Ap. 1774; *m.* 27 May 1730, ELIZABETH, da. of John SIMPSON of Babworth Hall, Notts, *b.* 1699; *d.* 9 Feb. 1780; and had issue 1*a* to 3*a*.

1*a. John Fairfax of Steeton, &c.,* b. 9 *Mar.* 1734; d. 28 *Feb.* 1811; m. *Jane, da. and co-h. of George Lodington of Bracebridge Hall, co. Lincoln,* d. 15 *Aug.* 1809; *and had issue* 1*b.*

1*b. Thomas Lodington Fairfax of Steeton,* b. 30 *May* 1770; d. 1 *July* 1840; m. 12 *Aug.* 1799, *Theophania, da. of Edward Chaloner of Lincoln,* b. 23 *Jan.* 1779; d. 9 *June* 1857; *and had issue* 1*c* to 3*c.*

1*c. Thomas Fairfax of Steeton, Bilbrough, &c., J.P., D.L.,* b. 2 *Nov.* 1804; d. *Nov.* 1882; m. 29 *July* 1839, *Louisa Constantia, da. of George Ravenscroft, H.E.I.C.S.; and had issue* 1*d* to 7*d.*

1*d. Thomas Ferdinand Fairfax of Steeton, Bilbrough, &c., Lieut.-Col. Grenadier Guards,* b. 6 *Oct.* 1839; d. 6 *Feb.* 1885; m. 14 *Ap.* 1868, *Evelyn Selina, da. of Sir William Milner, 5th Bart.* [G.B.], d. 11 *Feb.* 1900; *and had issue* 1*e* to 3*e.*

1*e.* Guy Thomas Fairfax, J.P. (*Bilbrough Hall, York; Steeton Hall, Tadcaster*), *b.* 13 Ap. 1870; *m.* 6 July 1899, the Hon. Joan, da. of Charles Henry (Wilson), 1st Baron [——] [U.K.].

2*e.* Bryan Charles Fairfax, Lieut. Durham L.I., *b.* 12 Sept. 1873.

3*e.* Evelyn Constance Fairfax, *b.* 10 Oct. 1872.

2*d.* Reginald Guy Fairfax, R.N. (*Queensland, Australia*), *b.* 5 Nov. 1845.

3*d.* Rev. Charles Henry Fairfax, M.A. (Oxon.), Rector of Dumbleton (*Dumbleton Rectory, Gloucester*), *b.* 2 Jan. 1849; *m.* 9 Oct. 1873, Emmeline Marian, da. of James Cookson of Neasham Hall, Durham, *d.* 10 May 1898; and has issue 1*e* to 5*e.*

1*e.* Gabriel Fairfax, *b.* 1878.

2*e.* Sybelle Fairfax.

3*e.* Mary Fairfax.

4*e.* Theophania Fairfax.

5*e.* Josephine Fairfax.

4*d.* Constance Frances Fairfax, *m.* 30 Mar. 1864, David Craigie Halkett Inglis (*Cramond House, near Edinburgh*).

5*d. Emma Louisa Fairfax,* b. 27 *June* 1838; d. 30 *Jan.* 1870; m. 22 *June* 1859, *the Hon. Charles Pierrepoint D'Arcy Lane-Fox,* d. 13 *Sept.* 1874; *and had issue.*

See the Clarence Volume, p. 627, Nos. 28047–28053.

6*d. Katherine Henrietta Fairfax,* b. 10 *Oct.* 1842; d. 4 *July* 1892; m. 27 *Oct.* 1868, *William Wickham, J.P.* (*Chestnut Grove, near Boston Spa, York*); *and had issue* 1*e* to 7*e.*

1*e.* Thomas Lamplugh Wickham, now Wickham-Boynton (*Burton Agnes Hall, Driffield*), *b.* 24 Oct. 1869; *m.* 8 Nov. 1899, Cycely Mabel, da. and h. of Sir Henry Somerville Boynton, 11th Bart. [E.]; and has issue 1*f* to 2*f.*

1*f.* Henry Fairfax Wickham-Boynton, *b.* 29 Sept. 1900.

2*f.* Marcus William Wickham-Boynton, *b.* 6 Ap. 1904.

2*e.* Reginald William Wickham, *b.* 4 Mar. 1871.

3*e.* Henry Francis Wickham, *b.* 1 Jan. 1873.

4*e.* Charles George Wickham, *b.* 14 Sept. 1879.

5*e.* Alice Wickham, *m.* 1897, Capt. C. Warner, 17th Lancers.

6*e.* Florence Wickham.

7*e.* Katharine Louisa Wickham, *m.* 27 Sept. 1899, the Hon. George Herbert Jackson (*Walton House, Boston Spa, Yorks*); and has issue 1*f* to 2*f.*

1*f.* George William Lawies Jackson, *b.* 1903.

2*f.* Dorothy Grace Jackson.

[Nos. 48976 to 49004.

The Plantagenet Roll

7d. Isabel Augusta Fairfax, b. 17 Nov. 1843; d. 1875; m. *as 1st wife*, 27 *Jan.* 1870, *Edward Christopher York of Hutton Hall, J.P.*, b. 14 Oct. 1842; d. 14 Dec. 1885; *and had issue 1e to 2e.*

    1e. Edward York, Capt. 1st Royal Dragoons (*Hutton Hall, Yorks*), b. 16 Jan. 1872.

    2e. Beatrix Penelope Lucy York, *b.* Ap. 1874.

  2c. Elizabeth Fairfax, b. 20 Mar. 1802; d. 6 Oct. 1893; m. 4 Feb. 1833, *the Rev. Thomas Hart Dyke, Rector of Long Newton*, b. 11 Dec. 1801; d. 25 *June* 1866; *and had issue 1d to 2d.*

    1d. Thomas Dyke, M.I.C.E. (*Long Ashton, Somerset*), b. 1 Ap. 1834; *m.* 26 Feb. 1863, Georgina Isabella Russell, da. of Robert Edward Fullerton of Sheethonger Manor, Tewkesbury; and has issue 1e to 4e.

      1e. Percyvall Hart Dyke, Capt. Indian Army (*Junior Army and Navy*), b. 24 Aug. 1872; *m.* 10 Oct. 1900, Louisa Catherine, da. of Admiral John Halliday Cave, C.B.

      2e. Ethel Frances Dyke.

      3e. Winifred Evelyn Dyke.

      4e. Theophania Louisa Dyke.

    2d. Rev. Percival Hart Dyke, Preb. of Salisbury (*Lullingstone, Wimborne*), b. 1 June 1835; *m.* 12 Jan. 1864, Margaret Isabella, da. of Robert John Peel of Burton-on-Trent; and has issue 1e to 3e.

      1e. Robert Percyvall Hart Dyke (19 *Victoria Square, S.W.*), b. 3 Nov. 1864.

      2e. Mabel Louisa Dyke, *m.* 11 Feb. 1892, Harold Gordon (*Meddecombra, Watagoda, Ceylon*).

      3e. Maud Cecilia Dyke, *m.* 16 Ap. 1891, the Rev. Walter Basil Broughton, M.A., Vicar of Brackley (*East Hill, Brackley*).

  3c. Theophania Fairfax, b. 4 *May* 1803; d. (–); m. 24 *Nov.* 1846, *Henry Collingwood Blackett of Sockburn Hall, Durham.*

  2a. William Fairfax.

  3a. Elizabeth Fairfax.   [Nos. 49005 to 49015.

477. Descendants, if any, of CATHERINE FAIRFAX (see Table XLIX.), b. 1701; d. 20 Mar. 1767; m. 23 Aug. 1720, HENRY PAWSON, Lord Mayor of York.

478. Descendants, if any, of MARY STAPYLTON (see Table XLIX.), m. (publication of banns at St. Giles' in the Fields 20 Feb.) 1654, WALTER MOYLE of Twyford Abbey, Midx.

479. Descendants of Sir JOSEPH PENNINGTON, 2nd Bart. [E.], M.P. (see Table XLIX.), b. 4 Oct. 1677; d. 3 Dec. 1744; m. 20 Mar. 1706, the Hon. MARGARET, da. and in her issue co-h. of John (LOWTHER), 1st Viscount Lonsdale [E.], P.C., d. 15 Sept. 1738; and had issue 1a to 3a.

  1a. Sir John Pennington, 3rd Bart. [E.], *M.P.*, d. unm. 24 Mar. 1768.

  2a. Sir Joseph Pennington, 4th Bart. [E.], bapt. 20 *Jan.* 1718; d. 3 Feb. 1793; m. *Sarah, da. and h. of John Moore of co. Somerset*, bur. 12 *Sept.* 1783; *and had issue 1b to 4b.*

# of The Blood Royal

1b. John *(Pennington), 1st Baron Muncaster* [I.], *5th Bart.* [E.], *d. 8 Oct.* 1813; *m. 26 Sept.* 1778, *Penelope, da. of James Compton, d. 13 Nov.* 1806; *and had issue.*

See the Clarence Volume, p. 17 and pp. 227–230, Nos. 4614–4706.

2b. Lowther *(Pennington), 2nd Baron Muncaster* [I.], *6th Bart.* [E.], *d. 29 July* 1818; *m. 13 Jan.* 1802, *Esther, widow of Capt. James Morrison, 58th Regt., da. of Thomas Barry of Clapham, d. 7 Oct.* 1827; *and had issue 1c.*

1c. Lowther Augustus John *(Pennington), 3rd Baron Muncaster* [I.], *7th Bart.* [E.], *b. 14 Dec.* 1802; *d. 30 Ap.* 1838; *m. 15 Dec.* 1828, *Frances Catherine, da. of Sir John Ramsden, 4th Bart.* [E.], *d. 30 Jan.* 1853; *and had issue 1d to 4d.*

1d. Gamel Augustus *(Pennington), 4th Baron Muncaster* [I.], *&c., b. 3 Dec.* 1831; *d.s.p. 13 June* 1862.

2d. Josslyn Francis (Pennington), *5th* [I.] *and 1st* [U.K.] *Baron Muncaster, 9th Bart.* [E.] *(Muncaster Castle, Ravenglass, Cumberland; 5 Carlton Gardens, S.W.), b. 25 Dec.* 1834; *m. 9 Ap.* 1863, *Constance Ann, da. of Edmund L'Estrange of Tynte Lodge, co. Leitrim.*

3d. Hon. Alan Joseph Pennington, *formerly R.N. and Lieut. Rifle Brigade (Burleigh Hall, Loughborough; 14 Lowndes Square, S.W.), b. 5 Ap.* 1837; *m. 9 Dec.* 1880, *Anna Eleanora, da. of Edward Bourchier Hartopp of Dalby Hall.*

4d. Hon. Louisa Theodosia Pennington, *b. 30 May* 1838; *d. 17 June* 1886; *m. 25 Nov.* 1858, *Edgar Atheling Drummond, d. 10 May* 1893; *and had issue.*

See the Clarence Volume, p. 210, Nos. 4168–4181.

3b. Jane Pennington.

4b. Margaret Pennington.

3a. Catherine Pennington, *d. 7 Dec.* 1764; *m. 22 June* 1731, *Robert Lowther of Mouldesmeaburn, Governor of Barbados, b. 13 Dec.* 1681; *d. Sept.* 1745; *and had issue 1b to 3b.*

1b. James *(Lowther), 1st Earl of Lonsdale* [G.B.], *&c., d.s.p. 24 May* 1802.

2b. Margaret Lowther, *d. 10 Sept.* 1800; *m. 10 Mar.* 1757, *Henry (Vane), 2nd Earl of Darlington* [G.B.], *d. 8 Sept.* 1792; *and had issue.*

See the Clarence Volume, p. 62 and pp. 581–584, Nos. 24444–24510.

3b. Catherine Lowther, *d. 21 Mar.* 1809; *m. as 2nd wife, 8 Ap.* 1765, *Henry (Powlett), 6th Duke of Bolton* [E.], *b. 6 Nov.* 1720; *d. 24 Dec.* 1794; *and had issue 1c.*

1c. Lady Katherine Margaret Powlett, *d. 16 June* 1807; *m. as 1st wife, 19 Sept.* 1787, *William Henry (Vane), 1st Duke of Cleveland* [U.K.], *&c., d. 29 Jan.* 1842; *and had issue.*

See the Clarence Volume, pp. 581–584, Nos. 24444–24510.

[Nos. 49016 to 49258.

480. Descendants, if any surviving, of ELIZABETH PENNINGTON (see Table XLIX.), wife, 1st, of JOHN ARCHER of Oxenholme, co. Westmorland; 2ndly, of THOMAS STRICKLAND of Sizergh.

481. Descendants, if any, of JANE STAPYLTON (see Table XLIX.), *d.* 1694; *m.* 1693, ROWLAND MOSLEY of York; of ELIZABETH STAPYLTON, *b.* 1656; and of ESTHER STAPYLTON, *b.* 1659; *m.* JOHN SAUNDERS of Grosmont Abbey, near Whitby.

The Plantagenet Roll

482. Descendants of HENRY STAPYLTON of Wighill (see Table XLIX.), *b.* 1721; *d.* 15 Sept. 1746; *m.* ELIZABETH, da. of George HEALEY of Gainsborough (who re-m., 1752, BERNARD WEBB of Beverley); and had issue 1*a.*

1*a.* Henry Stapylton of Wighill, *b.* 26 *Mar.* 1741; *d.* 4 *Ap.* 1779; *m.* 1765, *Harriet, da. and co-h. of Sir Warton Pennyman-Warton of Beverley, Bart., bapt.* 15 *Aug.* 1737, *d.* 5 *Oct.* 1791; *and had issue* 1*b.*

1*b.* Martha Stapylton of Wighill, *b.* 1766; *d.* 20 Nov. 1822; *m.* 29 *July* 1783, *Major-Gen. the Hon. Granville Anson Chetwynd, afterwards (R.L. 2 Aug.* 1783) *Chetwynd-Stapylton (son of the 4th Viscount Chetwynd [I.]), b.* 25 *Sept.* 1758; *d.* 2 *Dec.* 1834; *and had issue* 1*c to* 2*c.*

1*c.* Henry Richard Chetwynd-Stapylton of Wighill, Major 10*th Hussars, b.* Jan. 1789; *d.* 4 *Ap.* 1859; *m.* 13 *Dec.* 1820, *Margaret, da. of George Hammond of Portland Place, d.* 24 *July* 1882; *and had issue* 1*d to* 4*d.*

1*d.* Henry Edward Chetwynd-Stapylton of Shenley Lodge, co. Herts, J.P., *b.* 12 *Mar.* 1822; *d.* 21 *Jan.* 1900; *m.* 1*st.,* 29 *Ap.* 1851, *Esther Charlotte, da. and h. of Edward Goulburn, Sergeant-at-Law, d.* 3 *July* 1853; 2*ndly,* 23 *Oct.* 1856, *Ellen, widow of the Rev. James Lewis Venables of Shenley Lodge, da. of Henry Hoyle Oddie of Colney House, Herts, d.* 27 *Feb.* 1870; *and had issue* 1*e to* 4*e.*

1*e.* Henry Goulburn Chetwynd-Stapylton, M.A., J.P., Bar.-at-Law (*Hilliers, Petworth, Sussex*), *b.* 20 May 1852; *m.* 1 June 1886, Mary, da. of Charles Watkin Williams-Wynn of Coed-y-maen, J.P., D.L. (by his wife the Lady Annora Charlotte, *née* Pierrepont); and has issue 1*f* to 2*f.*

1*f.* Henry Miles Chetwynd-Stapylton, *b.* 21 Aug. 1887.

2*f.* Annora Esther Chetwynd-Stapylton, *b.* 16 Sept. 1889.

2*e.* Miles Chetwynd-Stapylton, *formerly* Capt. 7th Batt. King's Royal Rifle Corps (*Great Berkhampstead*), *b.* 22 June 1860; *m.* 7 Feb. 1888, Helen, da. of Arthur Preston of Norwich; and has issue 1*f* to 3*f.*

1*f.* Philip Miles Chetwynd-Stapylton, *b.* 11 Feb. 1889.

2*f.* Geoffrey Chetwynd-Stapylton, *b.* 27 Dec. 1892.

3*f.* Joan Helen Chetwynd-Stapylton.

3*e.* Beatrice Chetwynd-Stapylton,   } (*72 Warwick Square, S.W.*).
4*e.* Evelyn Mary Chetwynd Stapylton, }

2*d.* Granville George Chetwynd-Stapylton, Lieut.-Gen. *late* 32nd Regt. (*7 West Eaton Place, S.W.*), *b.* 22 Mar. 1823; *m.* 8 Dec. 1864, Lady Barbara Emily, da. of Joseph (Leeson), 4th Earl of Milltown [I.], K.P.; and has issue 1*e* to 3*e.*

1*e.* Granville Joseph Chetwynd-Stapylton, Capt. R.F.A., *b.* 11 Sept. 1871; *m.* 17 Feb. 1906, Elizabeth, da. of Christopher Lethbridge.

2*e.* Bryan Henry Chetwynd-Stapylton, Capt. Cheshire Regt., *b.* 10 June 1873; *m.* 5 Dec. 1905, Dorothy Constance, da. of Chambré Ponsonby.

3*e.* Barbara Margaret Chetwynd-Stapylton.

3*d.* Rev. William Chetwynd-Stapylton, Hon. Canon of Rochester and Rector of Hallaton (*Hallaton Rectory, Leicestershire*), *b.* 15 May 1825; *m.* 1st, 26 Oct. 1852, Elizabeth Biscoe, da. of the Rev. Robert Tritton, Rector of Morden, *d.* 18 Sept. 1893; 2ndly, 21 Ap. 1898, Mary Elizabeth, da. of Fred Johnson; and has issue 1*e* to 4*e.*

1*e.* Edward Chetwynd-Stapylton (*Larchwood, Weybridge, Surrey*), *b.* 20 July 1855; *m.* 27 Sept. 1879, Beatrice Mary, da. of Henry Cowie of Calcutta; and has issue 1*f* to 6*f.*

1*f.* Richard Chetwynd-Stapylton, *b.* 28 June 1880.

2*f.* William Eric Chetwynd-Stapylton, *b.* 10 Nov. 1895.

3*f.* Lilian Beatrice Chetwynd-Stapylton, *b.* 14 Aug. 1881; *m.* 28 Sept. 1901, Harold Hollocombe Gordon.

4*f.* Dorothy Chetwynd-Stapylton, *b.* 23 Dec. 1883.   [Nos. 49259 to 49277.

5f. Grace Mary Chetwynd-Stapylton, *b.* 24 Aug. 1887.

6f. Vera Chetwynd-Stapylton, *b.* 22 Jan. 1890.

2e. Frederick Chetwynd-Stapylton (*Englefield Lodge, Englefield Green, Surrey*), *b.* 15 Oct. 1857 ; *m.* 27 June 1891, Maud, da. of William Hiram Morrison of New York ; and has issue 1*f.*

1f. Helen Maud Chetwynd-Stapylton, *b.* 13 Mar. 1895.

3e. Granville Chetwynd-Stapylton, b. 11 *Dec.* 1858; *d.* 1902; *m.* 15 *Dec.* 1885, *Elizabeth* (*Leesburg, Florida, U.S.A.*), *da. of James Routledge; and had issue* 1*f to* 2*f.*

1f. Granville Brian Chetwynd-Stapylton, *b.* 19 Sept. 1887.

2f. Ella Mabel Chetwynd-Stapylton, *b.* 22 Nov. 1889.

4e. Ella Chetwynd-Stapylton, *m.* 5 June 1886, Henry Cockburn of Kensington Gate ; and has issue 1*f* to 3*f.*

1f. Archibald William Cockburn, *b.* 1887.

2f. Ernest Henry Cockburn, *b.* 1888.

3f. Reginald Stapylton Cockburn, *b.* 1889.

4d. Margaret Diana Chetwynd-Stapylton (5 *Park Terrace, Cambridge*), *m.* 25 Sept. 1856, George Carnac Barnes, C.B., Commissioner of the Cis-Sutlej States, *d.* 13 May 1861 ; and has issue 1*e* to 3*e.*

1e. George Stapylton Barnes, Comptroller of Companies' Department, Board of Trade (*Fox Holm, Cobham, Surrey*), *b.* 8 Feb. 1858 ; *m.* 16 Aug. 1887, Sybil de Gournay, da. of Charles Buxton, M.P. ; and has issue 1*f* to 3*f.*

1f. Ralph George Barnes, *b.* 7 Aug. 1888.

2f. Anthony Charles Barnes, *b.* 13 Oct. 1891.

3f. Lucy Eleanor Barnes, *b.* 25 Dec. 1897.

2e. Very Rev. Monsignor Arthur Stapylton Barnes (*Llandaff House, Cambridge*), *b.* 31 May 1861.

3e. Margaret Louisa Stapylton Barnes, *m.* 3 Ap. 1883, the Rev. William Neville Usher, Vicar of Wellingore (*Wellingore Vicarage, Lincoln*) ; and has issue 1*f* to 4*f.*

1f. Hugh Neville Usher, *b.* 27 Dec. 1884.

2f. Reginald Neville Usher, *b.* 11 Mar. 1886.

3f. William Arthur Usher, *b.* 12 Sept. 1887.

4f. Margaret Dorothy Usher, *b.* 28 Jan. 1884.

2c. Diana Clarissa Chetwynd-Stapylton, d.s.p. 28 *Sept.* 1825 ; *m. as* 1*st wife, Sept.* 1824, *Peter Mere Latham, M.D.,* b. 1 *July* 1789.   [Nos. 49278 to 49298.

483. Descendants, if any, of CATHERINE STAPYLTON (see Table XLIX.), wife of GEORGE LESSON of Dublin ; and of ISABEL STAPYLTON, wife of [——] BIGGS of Rye.

484. Descendants of HENRY (HERBERT), 10th EARL OF PEMBROKE and 7th EARL OF MONTGOMERY [E.] (see Table L.), *b.* 3 July 1734 ; *d.* 26 Jan. 1794 ; *m.* 13 Mar. 1756, Lady ELIZABETH, da. of Charles (SPENCER), 3rd Duke of Marlborough [E.], *b.* 29 Dec. 1737 ; *d.* 30 Ap. 1831 ; and had issue 1*a.*

1a. George Augustus (Herbert), 11*th Earl of Pembroke and* 8*th Earl of Montgomery* [*E.*]*, K.G.,* b. 11 *Sept.* 1759; *d.* 26 *Oct.* 1827; *m.* 1st, 8 *Ap.* 1787, *Elizabeth, da. of Topham Beauclerk,* d. 25 *Mar.* 1793; 2*ndly,* 25 *Jan.* 1808, *the Countess Catherine, da. of Simon, Count Woronzow of Russia, G.C.B.,* d. 27 *Mar.* 1856; *and had issue* 1*b to* 6*b.*

The Plantagenet Roll

1b. Robert Henry (*Herbert*), 12*th Earl of Pembroke and 9th Earl of Montgomery* [*E.*], b. 19 *Sept.* 1791; d.s.p. 25 *Ap.* 1862.

2b. Sidney (*Herbert*), 1*st Baron Herbert of Lea* [*U.K.*], b. 16 *Sept.* 1810; d. 2 *Aug.* 1861; m. 12 *Aug.* 1846, *Elizabeth, da. of Lieut.-Gen. Charles Ashe A'Court ; and had issue* 1c *to* 6c.

1c. George Robert Charles (*Herbert*), 13*th Earl of Pembroke and* 10*th Earl of Montgomery* [*E.*], 2*nd Baron Herbert of Lea* [*U.K.*], b. 6 *July* 1850; d.s.p. 3 *May* 1895.

2c. Sidney (Herbert), 14th Earl of Pembroke and 11th Earl of Montgomery [E.], 3rd Baron Herbert of Lea [U.K.], P.C., G.C.V.O., Lord Steward of the Royal Household 1895–1905, &c. (*Wilton House, Salisbury*), b. 20 Feb. 1853; m. 29 Aug. 1877, Lady Beatrix Louisa, da. of George (Lambton), 2nd Earl of Durham [U.K.]; and has issue 1d to 4d.

1d. Reginald Herbert, Lord Herbert, M.V.O., b. 8 Sept. 1880; m. 21 Jan. 1904, Beatrice Eleanor, da. of Lord Alexander Victor Paget; and has issue 1e to 2e.

1e. Hon. Sidney Charles Herbert, b. 9 Jan. 1906.

2e. Hon. Patricia Herbert, b. 12 Nov. 1904.

2d. Hon. George Sidney Herbert, b. 8 Oct. 1886.

3d. Lady Beatrix Frances Gertrude Herbert, m. 29 Ap. 1903, Capt. Nevile Rodwell Wilkinson, 3rd Batt. Coldstream Guards (*Southampton Lodge, Highgate*); and has issue 1e.

1e. Gwendolen Eleanor May Wilkinson, b. 15 May 1904.

4d. Lady Muriel Katherine Herbert.

3c. Right Hon. and Hon.[1] Sir Michael Henry Herbert, P.C., G.C.M.G., C.B., *H.B.M.'s Ambassador at Washington*, b. 25 *June* 1857; d. 30 *Sept.* 1903; m. 27 *Nov.* 1888, *Lelia, da. of Richard Wilson ; and had issue* 1d *to* 2d.

1d. Sidney Herbert, b. 1890.

2d. Michael George Herbert, b. 1893.

4c. Lady[1] Mary Catherine Herbert, m. 27 Nov. 1873, Frederick (von Hügel), 3rd Baron of Hügel (Freiherr von Hügel) (1790), [H.R.E.] (13 *Vicarage Gate, Kensington, W.*); and has issue 1d to 3d.

1d. Baroness Gertrud von Hügel, b. 27 Mar. 1877.

2d. Baroness Hildegard von Hügel, b. 13 Nov. 1879.

3d. Baroness Thekla Marie von Hügel, b. 11 Mar. 1886.

5c. Lady[1] Elizabeth Maude Herbert, m. 25 June 1872, Sir Charles Hubert Hastings Parry, 1st Bart. [U.K.], D.C.L., Mus.D. (*Knight's Croft, Rustington, Worthing ;* 17 *Kensington Square, W.*); and has issue 1d to 2d.

1d. Dorothea Parry, m. 12 Ap. 1898, Arthur Augustus William Harry Ponsonby (*Shulbrede Priory, Linchmere, Haslemere*); and has issue 1e to 2e.

1e. Matthew Henry Hubert Ponsonby, b. 28 July 1904.

2e. Elizabeth Ponsonby, b. 28 Dec. 1900.

2d. Gwendolen Parry, m. 20 July 1899, Harry Plunket Greene, the well-known singer (*Hurstbourne Priors, Whitchurch, Hants*); and has issue 1e to 2e.

1e. Richard George Hubert Greene, b. 1 July 1901.

2e. David Plunket Greene, b. 19 Nov. 1904.

6c. Lady[1] Constance Gladys Herbert, m. 1st, 6 July 1878, St. George Henry (Lowther), 4th Earl of Lonsdale [U.K.], d. 8 Feb. 1882; 2ndly, 7 May 1885, Frederick Oliver Robinson, Earl de Grey, K.C.V.O. (*Combe Court, Kingston Hill, Surrey*); and has issue 1d.

1d. Lady Gladys Mary Juliet Lowther, b. 9 Ap. 1881; m. 9 June 1903, Robert

[Nos. 49299 to 49321.

---

[1] R. W. 30 May 1862.

George Vivian Duff, Lieut. 2nd Life Guards (*Essex Lodge, Osborne Road, Windsor*); and has issue 1*e*.

    1*e*. Victoria Maud Veronica Duff, *b*. 17 Sept. 1904.

    3*b*. Lady Diana Herbert, b. 6 *Feb*. 1790; d. 2 *Dec*. 1841; m. 17 *May* 1816, *Welbore Ellis* (*Agar*), *2nd Earl of Normanton* [*I.*], *b*. 12 *Nov*. 1778; d. 26 *Aug*. 1868; *and had issue* 1*c to* 3*c*.

    1*c*. *James Charles Herbert Welbore Ellis* (*Agar*), *3rd Earl of Normanton* [*I.*], *1st Baron Somerton* [*U.K.*], *b*. 17 *Sept*. 1818; d. 19 *Dec*. 1896; m. 9 *Ap*. 185–, *the Hon. Caroline Susan Augusta, da. of William Keppel* (*Barrington*), *6th Viscount Barrington* [*I.*]; *and had issue*.

    See the Clarence Volume, pp. 95–96, Nos. 739–754.

    2*c*. Hon. *Herbert Welbore Ellis Agar*, b. 19 *Sept*. 1823; d. 9 *Aug*. 1901; m. 10 *Aug*. 1871, *Helen Millicent* (*Stanton House, Stanton Fitzwarren, Highworth*); *and had issue* 1*d to* 3*d*.

    1*d*. Charles Herbert Agar, M.A. (Camb.), *b*. 25 Sept. 1872.

    2*d*. Constance Diana Agar, *b*. 14 Feb. 1874.

    3*d*. Laura Mary O'Neill Agar, *b*. 13 Sept. 1875.

    3*c*. Lady Mary Jane Diana Agar, *m*. 28 July 1845, Horatio (Nelson), 3rd Earl Nelson [U.K.] (*Trafalgar, Salisbury*); and has issue 1*d to* 7*d*.

    1*d*. Herbert Horatio Nelson, Viscount Trafalgar, J.P., D.L. (*Braydon House, Minety, Malmesbury*), *b*. 19 July 1854; *m*. 5 Aug. 1879, Eliza Blanche, da. of Frederick Gonnerman Dalgety of Lockerley Hall, Hants.

    2*d*. Hon. Thomas Horatio Nelson, *b*. 21 Dec. 1857.

    3*d*. Hon. Edward Agar Horatio Nelson, Lieut. 3rd Batt. Wiltshire Regt. (3 *Wheeleys Road, Edgbaston*), *b*. 10 Aug. 1860; *m*. 7 Aug. 1889, Geraldine, da. of Henry H. Cave of Rugby; and has issue 1*e* to 6*e*.

    1*e*. Albert Francis Joseph Horatio Nelson, *b*. 2 Sept. 1890.

    2*e*. Henry Edward Joseph Horatio Nelson, *b*. 22 Ap. 1894.

    3*e*. Charles Sebastian Joseph Horatio Nelson, *b*. 26 Ap. 1896.

    4*e*. Edith Mary Josephine Nelson.

    5*e*. Mary Winefride Nelson.

    6*e*. Geraldine Mary Diana Nelson.

    4*d*. Lady Alice Mary Diana Nelson (*St. Laurence's, Worcester*).

    5*d*. Lady Constance Jane Nelson, *m*. 21 Ap. 1870, Rev. the Hon. Bertrand Pleydell-Bouverie, Preb. of Salisbury (*Pewsey Rectory, Wilts*).

    6*d*. Lady Edith Nelson, b. 7 *Jan*. 1850; d. 24 *Aug*. 1877; m. *as 1st wife*, 5 *July* 1870, *Charles Clement Tudway, J.P., D.L.* (*The Cedars, Wells, Somerset*); *and had issue* 1*e*.

    1*e*. Madeline Constance Tudway, *b*. 18 Ap. 1873.

    7*d*. Lady Mary Catherine Nelson, b. 5 *Oct*. 1850; d. 17 *Nov*. 1901; m. 21 *Oct*. 1890, *Richard Shaw of Audlem, Cheshire*.

    4*b*. Lady Elizabeth Herbert, b. 31 *Mar*. 1809; d. 20 *Sept*. 1858; m. 3 *July* 1830, *Richard* (*Meade*), *3rd Earl of Clanwilliam* [*I.*], *and 1st Baron Clanwilliam* [*U.K.*], d. 7 *Oct*. 1879; *and had issue*.

    See p. 391, Nos. 33054 to 33073.

    5*b*. Lady Catherine Herbert, b. 31 *Oct*. 1814; d. 12 *Feb*. 1886; m. 27 *Sept*. 1836, *Alexander Edward* (*Murray*), *6th Earl of* [*S.*] *and 2nd Baron* [*U.K.*] *Dunmore, b. 1 June* 1804; d. 15 *July* 1845; *and had issue*.

    See the Tudor Roll of "The Blood Royal of Britain," pp. 489–490, Nos. 33678–33705.

    6*b*. Lady Emma Herbert, b. 23 *Aug*. 1819; d. 10 *Oct*. 1884; m. 19 *Sept*. 1839, *Thomas* (*Vesey*), *3rd Viscount De Vesci* [*I.*], d. 23 *Dec*. 1875; *and had issue*.

    See the Clarence Volume, pp. 305–306, Nos. 8507–8523.

[Nos. 49322–49419.

The Plantagenet Roll

**485. Descendants of the Hon. FRANCES FITZWILLIAM (see Table
L.), d. 30 July 1789 ; m. 23 May 1732, GEORGE (EVANS),
2nd Baron CARBERY [I.], d. 2 Feb. 1759 ; and had issue
1a to 3a.**

1a. *George (Evans), 3rd Baron Carbery [I.], d. 26 May 1783 ; m. 1st, 7 Feb.
1760, Lady Juliana, da. of Baptist (Noel), 3rd Earl of Gainsborough [G.B.], d.
18 Dec. 1760; 2ndly, 13 Dec. 1862, Elizabeth, da. of Christopher Horton of Catton,
co. Derby, d. 1809 ; and had issue 1b to 2b.*

1b. *George (Evans), 4th Baron Carbery [I.], b. 18 Feb. 1766; d.s.p. 31 Dec.
1804.*

2b. *Hon. Juliana Evans, b. Dec. 1760; d. 20 May 1807; m. 16 Ap. 1782,
Edward Hartopp-Wigley of Dalby House, co. Leicester ; and had issue.*

See p. 201, Nos. 7236–7252.

2a. *John (Evans), 5th Baron Carbery [I.], b. 1738; d. 4 Mar. 1807; m. 15 Ap.
1759, Emma, da. of the Very Rev. William Grove, Dean of Clonfert, d. 6 Jan.
1806 ; and had issue 1b to 2b.[1]*

1b. *Hon. Frances Dorothea Evans, da. and co-h., d. (–) ; m. 1789, William
Preston ; and had issue 1c to 6c.*

1c. *Eyre William Preston of Clontarf.*

2c. *Algernon Thomas Preston.*

3c. *Sir George Preston, one of the Sheriffs for the City of Dublin 1833, d. Ap.
1870 ; m. 1832, [——], da. of Alexander Montgomery of Dublin.[2]*

4c. *Rev. Decimus William Preston.*

5c. ⎱
6c. ⎰ *2 daughters.*

2b. *Hon. Maria Juliana Evans, da. and co-h., d. June 1847 ; m. 1796, Col.
Thomas Barry of Leigh's Brook, co. Meath, d. (–) ; and had issue 1c to 2c.*

1c. *Emily Barry, da. and co-h., d. (–) ; m. the Rev. Arthur Smith Adamson.*

2c. *Maria Anna Barry, da. and co-h., d. (–) ; m. 21 July 1825, the Rev.
John Delmege, Rector of Bannagher, and Preb. of Droughta and Island Eddy,
d. 19 Ap. 1874 ; and had issue 1d to 8d.*

1d. *John Evans Delmege of Mountgraigue, co. Limerick, M.A., J.P., b. 1830 ;
d. 1892 ; m. Dec. 1865, Constance, da. of Richard Studdert of Fort House, co. Clare ;
and had issue 1e to 2e.*

1e. John Richard Delmege (*Mountgraigue, near Croom*), b. 12 Aug. 1870.

2e. Frances Maria Constance Delmege.

2d. Adam William Stafford Delmege, Bar.-at-Law (*Ballywise, Tipperary*),
b. (–) ; m. 1st, 15 June 1871, Jane, da. of the Rev. Barry Denny, *d.s.p.* 1884 ;
2ndly, Frances Catherine, da. of James William Butler Scott of Annesgrove Abbey,
Queen's co. ; and has issue 1e to 2e.

1e. Eyre Bolton Massey Delmege.

2e. Hugh Barry Evans Delmege.

3d. Julius James John Delmege.

4d. Maria Juliana Evans Delmege.

5d. Emily Jane Barry Delmege, *m.* 17 July 1861, Col. Francis Hugh Massey
Wheeler.

6d. Margaret Isabella Johanna Delmege.

7d. Henrietta Octavia Delmege, *m.* 4 May 1861, Thomas Bourchier.

8d. Eveline Ida Anna Johanna Delmege. [Nos. 49420 to 49447.

---

[1] See Burke's " Peerage," 1900, p. 264.

[2] *Ex inform.* G. D. Burtchaell, Esq. The name of the Rev. Eyre Loftus
Preston, B.A. (T.C.D.), Dublin Univ. Miss., Ranchi, Bengal, appears in Crockford's
" Clerical Directory." He is probably a descendant of this family.

# of The Blood Royal

3a. Hon. Frances Anne Evans, d. 12 *July* 1802; *m.* 1*st*,[1] 1756, *Edward Warter-Wilson of Bilboa, High Sheriff co. Limerick* 1757; *and had issue* 1*b.*

1*b.* Frances Juliana Warter-Wilson, *da. and h.*, *d.* 20 *June* 1790; *m. as* 1*st wife, Jan.* 1788, *Sir John Rous, 6th Bart.* [*E.*], *afterwards* (1821) 1*st Earl of Stradbroke* [*U.K.*], *b.* 30 *May* 1750; *d.* 27 *Aug.* 1827; *and had issue* 1*c.*

1*c.* Lady Frances Anne Juliana Rous, *b.* 10 *May* 1790; *d.* 31 *Jan.* 1859; *m.* 6 *July* 1816, *Vice-Admiral the Hon. Sir Henry Hotham, K.C.B., G.C.M.G., b.* 19 *Feb.* 1777; *d.* 19 *Ap.* 1833; *and had issue* 1*d to* 2*d.*

1*d.* Rev. Frederick Harry Hotham, *Rector of Rushbury, b.* 3 *Aug.* 1824; *d.* 11 *Ap.* 1887; *m.* 17 *Dec.* 1851, *Eleanor, da. of Robert Gosling of Botleys Park, Chertsey; and had issue.*

See the Clarence Volume, pp. 598–599, Nos. 26261–26274.

2*d.* Beaumont Williams Hotham, *late* Capt. Gren. Guards, and sometime (1859–1882) H.B.M.'s Consul at Calais (4 *Eaton Gardens, Hove, Brighton*), *b.* 22 *Aug.* 1825; *m.* 13 Mar. 1855, Charlotte Amelia, da. of Admiral George Frederic Rich; and has issue 1*e* to 6*e.*

1*e.* Rev. Charles George Beaumont Hotham (*Theydon Priory, Essex*), *b.* 19 Sept. 1858; *m.* 22 Jan. 1891, Laura, da. of Sir Charles Cunliffe Smith, 3rd Bart. [U.K.].

2*e.* John Henry Beaumont Hotham, *b.* 2 May 1866.

3*e.* Frances Charlotte Agnes Hotham, *m.* as 2nd wife, 22 Aug. 1882, Collingwood Lindsay Wood, J.P., D.L. (*Freeland, Forgandenny, Perth*); and has issue 1*f* to 2*f.*

1*f.* Frances Charlotte Lindsay Wood, *b.* 20 May 1883.

2*f.* Evelyn Alice Lindsay Wood, *b.* 16 Dec. 1884.

4*e.* Alice Caroline Hotham, *m.* 20 Feb. 1879, Col. Eustace Beaumont Burnaby, *late* 10th Regt.; and has issue 1*f* to 4*f.*

1*f.* Eustace Hotham Burnaby, Lieut. 2nd Batt. Gloucestershire Regt., *b.* 9 Mar. 1880.

2*f.* Alice Muriel Burnaby, *b.* 20 Mar. 1881.

3*f.* Olive Burnaby, *b.* 22 Mar. 1884.

4*f.* Winifred Emily Burnaby, *b.* 14 June 1886.

5*e.* Mary Eleanor Hotham, *m.* 21 Mar. 1882, the Hon. William Charles Wordsworth Rollo, Master of Rollo (*Marshall's Manor, Maresfield, Sussex*); and has issue 1*f.*

1*f.* Rosalind Mary Agnes Rollo, *b.* 18 June 1896.

6*e.* Margaret Hotham, *m.* 8 May 1890, Capt. Richard Dacre Vincent, *late* R.D.F.; and has issue 1*f.*

1*f.* Richard Beaumont Vincent, *b.* 2 Mar. 1891.　　[Nos. 49448 to 49476.

486. Descendants, if any, of the Hon. MARY FITZWILLIAM (see Table L.), wife of STEPHEN FITZWILLIAM BROWNE of Castle Browne, co. Kildare.[2]

---

[1] In Burke's "Peerage" she is said to have *m.* 2ndly, Eleazer Davey of Ubbeston Hall, co. Suffolk, but this must have been a third marriage, as in 1764 a licence was issued in the Dublin Diocesan Courts for the marriage of Sir Thomas Adams, Bart., and the Hon. Frances Anne Warter Wilson. This Sir Thomas Adams, 6th Bart. [E.], *d.s.p.* (in Virginia) 2 Ap. 1770. See G. E. C.'s "Complete Baronetage," iii. p. 39.

[2] "Lodge is responsible for the statement that Hon. [——] Fitzwilliam *m.* her first cousin Stephen Fitzwilliam Browne. There is no record of this marriage in the Ulster Office. Burke's pedigree of Browne of Castle Browne is certainly incorrect in some respects. Lodge states John Browne *m.* Hon. Mary Fitzwilliam in 1685, but if so, their son Christopher could not have been 53 at the time of his death in 1736, and Stephen could not have *m.* Judith Wogan in 1697, as stated by Burke. Both the Fitzwilliam and Wogan pedigrees are deficient in dates and other particulars much to be desired." *Ex. inform.* G. D. Burtchaell, Esq.

The Plantagenet Roll

487. Descendants, if any surviving, of LEONARD POWELL (see Table XLIX.), *d.* (–); *m.* MARGARET, da. of Sir Francis LAWLEY, 2nd Bart. [E.] (who re-m. Sir NATHAN WRIGHT, 3rd Bart. [E.] and) *d.* Jan. 1748; and had issue (two sons and a da.), of whom the sons must have been dead, certainly *s.p.m.* before 5 July 1742, when the Powell baronetcy (1661) [E.] became extinct.

488. Descendants of HENRIETTA CATHERINE CHOLMLEY (see Table XLIX.), *b.* 24 May 1645; *d.* 25 June 1680; *m.* 1657, Sir JOHN TEMPEST of Tong, 1st Bart. [E.], *d.* 23 June 1693; and had issue 1*a* to 2*a*.

1*a.* *Sir George Tempest of Tong, 2nd Bart.* [E.], bapt. 22 *May* 1672; bur. 11 *Oct.* 1745; *m.* 16 *Oct.* 1694, *Anne, da. and h. of Edward Frank, otherwise Ashton, of Campsal,* bapt. 2 *Dec.* 1676; bur. 13 *Jan.* 1746; *and had issue* 1*b* to 2*b*.

1*b.* *Sir Henry Tempest of Tong, 3rd Bart.* [E.], bapt. 1 *Sept.* 1696; *d.* 9 *Nov.* 1753; *m.* 31 *Aug.* 1749, *Maria, da. of Francis Holmes of Wigston, co. Leicester,* d. 5 *Feb.* 1795; *and had issue* 1*c* to 3*c*.

1*c.* *Sir Henry Tempest of Tong, 4th Bart.* [E.], b. 13 *Jan.* 1753; d.s.p. 29 *Jan.* 1819.

2*c,* 3*c. Two daughters.*[1]

2*b.* *John Tempest of Nottingham, Capt. in Churchill's Dragoons,* d. 1753; m., *Elizabeth, da. of William Scrimshire of Cotgrave, co. Notts; and had issue* 1*c*.

1*c.* *Elizabeth Tempest of Tong Hall (in* 1819), *d. Sept.* 1823; *m. William Plumbe of Wavertree Hall, and Aughton, co. Lancaster,* d. 7 *June* 1806; *and had issue* 1*d* to 2*d*.

1*d.* *John Plumbe, afterwards (R.L.* 1824) *Tempest of Tong and Aughton, J.P., D.L., Col. 1st Royal Lancashire Militia,* d. 6 *Ap.* 1859; *m. Sarah, da. of the Rev. William Plumbe, Rector of Aughton,* d. 31 *Dec.* 1856; *and had issue* 1*e* to 3*e*.

1*e.* *Thomas Richard Plumbe Tempest of Tong, &c., J.P., D.L.,* d.s.p. 1881.

2*e.* *Frances Penelope Tempest,* d. 4 *May* 1825; *m.* 26 *July* 1824, *Thomas Rawson of Nidd Hall, co. York; and had issue* 1*f*.

1*f.* *Frances Penelope Rawson,* d. 19 *Oct.* 1886; *m.* 11 *Mar.* 1844, *Henry Edmund (Butler), 13th Viscount Mountgarret* [I.], b. 20 *Feb.* 1816; d. 26 *Aug.* 1900; *and had issue* 1*g* to 2*g*.

1*g.* Henry Edmund (Butler, *sometime* (1891–1902) Butler-Rawson), 14th Viscount Mountgarret [I.], &c. (*Ballyconra, Kilkenny; Nidd Hill, Ripley; Eaglehall, Pateley Bridge*), b. 18 Dec. 1844; *m.* 1st, 1 Oct. 1868, Mary Eleanor, da. of St. John Chiverton Charlton of Apley Castle, co. Salop, *d.* 12 May 1900; 2ndly, 1902, Robinia Marion, da. of Col. Edward Hanning Hanning-Lee, J.P.; and has issue 1*h* to 4*h*.

1*h.* Hon. Edmund Somerset Butler (111 *Park Street, Grosvenor Square, W.*), *b.* 1 Feb. 1875; *m.* 1 June 1897, Cecily, da. of Arthur Duncombe of Sutton Hall, co. York.

2*h.* Hon. Piers Henry Augustine Butler, *b.* 28 Aug. 1903.

3*h.* Hon. Elinor Frances Butler, *m.* 28 Feb. 1889, Andrew S. Lawson (*Aldborough Manor, Boroughbridge*); and has issue 1*i* to 2*i*.

1*i.* Margery Elinor Lawson, *b.* 1889.

2*i.* Mary Doreen Lawson, *b.* 1892. 　　　　　　[Nos. 49477 to 49482.

---

[1] Foster's "Yorkshire Pedigrees."

4*h.* Hon. Ethel Mary Butler, *m.* 2 Mar. 1897, Henry Rimington Wilson (*Blyborough Hall, Kirton-in-Lindsay*); and has issue 1*i* to 3*i*.

1*i.* Henry Edmund Rimington Wilson, *b.* 1899.

2*i.* Pamela Rimington Wilson, } *b.* (twins) 1900.
3*i.* Lettice Rimington Wilson,

2*g.* Hon. Frances Sarah Butler, *m.* 29 Sept. 1892, Edward Arthur Whittuck of Oriel College, Oxford (*Claverton Manor, near Bath; 77 South Audley Street, W.*).

3*e. Henrietta Tempest, d. (at Florence) 13 Nov. 1838; m. as 1st wife, 31 May 1834, Admiral Sir Cornwallis Ricketts, 2nd Bart. [U.K.], d. 30 Jan. 1885; and had issue 1f.*

1*f. Sir Robert Tempest Ricketts, afterwards (R.L. 23 Ap. 1884) Tempest of Tong, 3rd Bart. [U.K.], b. (at Rome) 7 Dec. 1836; d. 4 Feb. 1901; m. 26 July 1861, Amelia Helen, da. and in her issue h. of John Steuart of Dalguise, d. 26 Dec. 1869; and had issue 1g to 2g.*

1*g.* Sir Tristram Tempest Tempest of Tong, 4th Bart. [U.K.] (*Tong Hall, Bradford; Aughton, Ormskirk; Dalguise, Perth*), *b.* 10 Jan. 1865; *m.* 1902, Mabel Ethel, da. of Major-Gen. Sir George Hall MacGregor, K.C.B., *d.* 16 Ap. 1906.

2*g.* Henrietta Frances May Tempest, *m.* 12 Jan. 1886, John Hicks Graves (*Bradenham House, West Wycombe*).

2*d. Catherine Townley Plumbe, d. 11 Sept. 1819; m. Henry Dixon of Brook Farm, near Liverpool; and had issue 1e to 11e.*[1]

1*e. Henry Dixon, Col. late 81st Regt., b. 22 Jan. 1796; d. (–); m. 28 July 1826, Harriet Amelia, da. of the Hon. James Fraser, Member of Council, Halifax, N.S.; and had issue 1f to 10f.*

1*f.* Thomas Fraser Dixon, Major 39th Regt., *b.* 15 Mar. 1832; *m.* 15 Oct. 1856, Clara Georgiana Cecilia, da. of Col. Edmund Antrobus; and has issue 1*g* to 4*g*.

1*g.* Henry Antrobus Dixon.

2*g.* George Fraser Dixon.

3*g.* Thomas Bradford Dixon.

4*g.* Henriana Ethelda Dixon.

2*f.* Henry Dixon, Capt. R.M.L.I., *b.* 28 July 1842; *m.* 15 Aug. 1872, Alicia Kate, da. of James Adam Chandler of Portsmouth; and has issue 1*g*.

1*g.* Virginia Kate Dixon.

3*f.* Charles Tempest Dixon.

4*f.* Francis Edmund Maclean Dixon.

5*f.* Arthur Noel Harris Dixon.

6*f.* Catherina Townley Dixon, *m.* 1845, Lewis George Jones of Woodhill, co. Sligo.

7*f.* Emily Georgiana Dixon, *m.* 13 Sept. 1853, the Rev. Gilbert Henderson Philips, M.A., Vicar of Brodsworth, co. York and Rural Dean, *d.*

8*f.* Harriet Rachel Gore Dixon, *m.* 28 Ap. 1853, Richard Hamilton of Oakfield, co. Fermanagh.

9*f.* Charlotte Ann Dixon.

10*f.* Henrietta Maria Dixon, *m.* 8 Nov. 1870, the Rev. Ernest Celestine Tollemache of Weem, Aberfeldy.

2*e.* John Dixon, living 1873.

3*e.* George Dixon, C.B., Gen. *late* 77th Regt., living 1873.

4*e.* Charles Dixon, living 1873.

5*e.* Catherina Townley Dixon.

6*e.* Caroline Dixon.

7*e.* Mary Dixon.

8*e.* Elizabeth Townley Dixon.   [Nos. 49483 to 49511.

---

[1] Foster's "Yorkshire Pedigrees."

The Plantagenet Roll

9e. Frances Elizabeth Dixon, m. George Swann of Ashfield, co. York.

10e. Georgiana Charlotte Dixon, m. John Swann of Askham Hall, co. York.

11e. Henriana Anabella Dixon, m. 11 Nov. 1851, the Rev. Robert Hale, Vicar of Thorpe Bassett, co. York, d. 17 June 1869.

2a. *Henrietta Tempest*, bapt. 15 *Ap*. 1675; m. 10 *Oct*. 1699, *Ferdinando Latus of Cumberland ; and had issue 1b to 2b.*

    1b. [——] *Latus*, m. *Ferdinando Huddleston of Millum Castle.*

    2b. [——] *Latus*, m. *William Blencowe of Lowick Hall, near Ulverstone.*

[Nos. 49512 to 49514.

489. Descendants of MARY ST. QUINTIN (see Table LI.), *b.* 14 June 1735; *d.* 27 Mar. 1772 ; *m.* GEORGE DARBY of Newtown, co. Hants, Vice-Admiral of England ; and had issue 1a to 2a.

    1a. *William Thomas Darby, afterwards St. Quintin of Scampston, co. York*, b. 26 *May* 1769; d. 18 *Jan*. 1805; m. *Arabella Bridget, da. of Gen. Thomas Calcraft*, d. 26 *Jan*. 1841; *and had issue 1b to 3b.*

    1b. *Matthew Chitty Downes St. Quintin of Scampston and Lowthorpe, Col. 17th Lancers*, b. 19 *Dec*. 1800 ; d. 19 *Ap*. 1876 ; m. 23 *Ap*. 1850, *Amy Elizabeth, da. of George Henry Cherry of Denford, Berks ; and had issue 1c to 3c.*

    1c. William Herbert St. Quintin, J.P., D.L., High Sheriff co. York 1899 (*Scampston Hall, York ; Lowthorpe Lodge, Hull*), b. 24 Ap. 1851 ; *m.* 22 July 1885, Violet Helen, da. of the Hon. Cecil Duncombe of Nawton Grange ; and has issue 1d.

    1d. Margery Violet St. Quintin, b. 29 Ap. 1886.

    2c. Geoffrey Apsley St. Quintin (*Cromarty House, Cromarty*), b. 15 June 1861 ; *m.* 2 June 1892, Muriel Frances Charlotte, da. of Col. the Hon. George Henry Essex Grant of Easter Elchies ; and has issue 1d.

    1d. Geoffrey Hugh Willoughby St. Quintin, *b.* 17 Nov. 1899.

    3c. Cecil Amy St. Quintin.

    2b. *Arabella Cecil St. Quintin*, d. 25 *Feb*. 1860; m. 12 *June* 1824, *the Hon. Thomas William Gage of Westbury*, d. 26 *Jan*. 1855 ; *and had issue 1c.*

    1c. *Arabella Gage*, d. 8 *Nov*. 1860; m. *as* 1*st wife*, 17 *Jan*. 1856, *Gen. the Hon. Edward Gage, C.B.*, b. 28 *Dec*. 1825 ; d. 21 *May* 1889; *and had issue.*

    See p. 269, Nos. 10344–10345 and 10351–10354.

    3b. *Catherine St. Quintin*, d. *Aug*. 1871 ; m. 1 *June* 1824, *David Ricardo of Gatcombe Park, co. Gloucester, J.P.*, b. 18 *May* 1803 ; d. 17 *May* 1864; *and had issue 1c to 2c.*

    1c. *Henry David Ricardo of Gatcombe, J.P.*, b. 8 *Mar*. 1833 ; d. 18 *Feb*. 1873 ; m. 24 *June* 1858, *Ellen, da. of the Ven. William Crawley, Archdeacon of Monmouth ; and had issue 1d to 10d.*

    1d. Henry George Ricardo, Major *late* R.A., *b.* 23 June 1860 ; *m.* 1885, Adela, da. of John Patteson Cobbold, M.P. ; and has issue 1e.

    1e. Marjorie Adela Ricardo, b. 18 Jan. 1887.

    2d. Arthur David Ricardo, Lieut. R.N., b. 14 Sept. 1861.

    3d. William Crawley Ricardo, b. 6 Ap. 1864.

    4d. Ambrose St. Quintin Ricardo, Capt. Royal Inniskilling Fusiliers, b. 21 Nov. 1866.

    5d. Ellen Gertrude Ricardo.

    6d. Katherine Cecil Ricardo.

    7d. Arabel Mary Ricardo.

    8d. Rachel Bertha Ricardo.

    9d. Magdalen Harriett Ricardo.

    10d. Ellen Amy Ricardo.

    2c. Catherine Ricardo.

[Nos. 49515 to 49537.

# of The Blood Royal

2a. Matthew Chitty Darby, afterwards (R.L. 1801) *Darby-Griffith of Padworth, Gen. in the Army,* d. 1821; m. 1803, *Louisa, da. of Thomas Hankey of Fetcham Park, co. Surrey; and had issue* 1b *to* 3b.

1b. Christopher Darby-Griffith of Padworth, J.P., D.L., M.P., d. *Mar.* 1886; m. *May* 1855, *Arabella Sarah, da. of Edward Francis Colston of Filkins Hall, co. Oxford, and Roundway Park, co. Wilts,* d. *Mar.* 1891; *and had issue* 1c.

1c. Christopher William Darby-Griffith, J.P., Capt. *late* Grenadier Guards (*Padworth House, Reading*), *b.* 17 June 1858.

2b. George Darby-Griffith, Major in the Army, d. (–); m. [——], *da. of* [——] *Dimsdale; and had issue* 1c.

1c. Agnes Darby-Griffith (*Ashton Hayes, Chester*), *m.* 22 Nov. 1866, Capt. Thomas Parr of Ashton Hayes, &c., J.P., *b.* 25 Feb. 1834; *d.s.p.* 29 Oct. 1891.

3b. Louisa Darby-Griffith, d. *Mar.* 1892; m. *Capt. Thomas Knox, R.N.; and had issue* 1c.

1c. Brownlow Darby Knox. [Nos. 49538 to 49540.

490. Descendants, if any, of FRANCES ST. QUINTIN (see Table LI.), *bapt.* 30 Dec. 1655; *m.* THOMAS ROUNDELL of Hutton.[1]

491. Descendants of JAMES HEBLETHWAITE, who bought the Rectory of Bridlington (see Table LI.), *b.* 10 Aug. 1727; *d.* 2 Nov. 1773; *m.* 28 Dec. 1747, MARY, da. of Thomas JOHNSON, *b.* 25 Dec. 1731; *d.* 12 July 1815; and had issue (with other who died *unm.* or *s.p.*) 1a to 4a.

1a. Charles Heblethwaite, one of the six Clerks, b. 23 Ap. 1751; *d.* 28 Nov. 1811; m. [——], *da. of* [——] *Conyers of Driffield; and had issue* 1b.
1b. Mary Heblethwaite.

2a. Mary Heblethwaite, b. 5 *Jan.* 1749; *d.* 13 *May* 1815; m. 1st, *as 2nd wife,* 1 *Aug.* 1768, *Sir Griffith Boynton, 6th Bart.* [E.], d. 6 *Jan.* 1778; *2ndly,* 24 *July* 1798, *George John Parkhurst of Catesby Abbey, co. Northants; and had issue* 1b *to* 3b.

1b. Sir Griffith Boynton, 7th Bart. [E.], d.s.p. 10 *July* 1801.

2b. Sir Francis Boynton, 8th Bart. [E.], b. 28 *Mar.* 1777; d.s.p. 19 Nov. 1832.

3b. Sir Henry Boynton, 9th Bart. [E.], b. 22 *Mar.* 1778; *d.* 28 Aug. 1854; m. 1 *Jan.* 1810, *Mary, da. of Capt. Gray,* d. 26 *June* 1877; *and had issue* 1c to 6c.

1c. Sir Henry Boynton, 10th Bart. [E.], b. 2 *Mar.* 1811; *d.* 25 *June* 1869; m. *2ndly,* 7 Feb. 1843, *Harriet, da. of Thomas Lightfoot of Sevenoaks,* d. 13 Sept. 1889; *and had issue* 1d to 2d.

1d. Sir Henry Somerville Boynton, 11th Bart. [E.], b. 23 *June* 1844; *d.* 11 Ap. 1899; m. 27 *July* 1876, *Mildred Augusta (Cherry Burton, Beverley), da. of the Rev. Canon Thomas Bradley Paget; and had issue* 1e.

1e. Cycely Mabel Boynton, *m.* 8 Nov. 1899, Thomas Lamplugh Wickham, *now* Wickham-Boynton of Chestnut Grove (*Burton Agnes Hall, Driffield*); *and has issue.* See p. 535, Nos. 48995–48996.

2d. Katherine Maude Boynton, *m.* 31 July 1866, Major-Gen. William Mussenden, Col. 8th Hussars (25 *Eaton Square, S.W.*); and has issue 1e to 2e.

1e. Henry Clement Mussenden, *b.* 1868.

2e. Francis William Mussenden, Major 8th Hussars, *b.* 1869.

[Nos. 49541 to 49546.

---

[1] Foster's "Yorkshire Pedigrees," St. Quintin Pedigree. No Thomas Roundell of Hutton, however, appears in the Roundell Pedigree in the same work.

The Plantagenet Roll

2c. Rev. Griffith Boynton, M.A., Rector of Barmston, b. 4 *Nov.* 1815; d. 19 *May* 1898; m. 1 *Oct.* 1840, *Selina, da. of William Watkins of Badby House, co. Northants, d.* 2 *Jan.* 1898; *and had issue* 1*d to* 6*d.*

    1*d.* Sir Griffith Henry Boynton, 12th Bart. [E.], *b.* 31 May 1849; *m.* 14 Ap. 1885, Euphemia Violet, da. of John Inglis Chalmers of Aldbar Castle; and has issue 1*e* to 3*e.*

        1*e.* Griffith Wilfred Norman Boynton, *b.* 1889.

        2*e.* Gladys Mary Boynton.

        3*e.* Constance Mary Boynton.

    2*d.* Rev. Charles Ingram William Boynton, M.A. (T.C.D.), Rector of Barmston (*Barmston Rectory, Driffield*), *b.* 7 Ap. 1853; *m.* Feb. 1886 the Hon. Mary, da. of Samuel (Cunliffe-Lister), 1st Baron Masham [U.K.], *d.* 31 Dec. 1896; and has issue 1*e.*

        1*e.* Mary Constance Boynton.

    3*d.* Selina Charlotte Boynton, *m.* 15 Nov. 1860, Alfred Newdigate, M.A., *formerly* Vicar of Kirk-Hallam (27 *Clarendon Square, Leamington*); and has issue 1*e* to 8*e.*

        1*e.* Rev. Charles Alfred Newdigate, *b.* 31 Mar. 1863.

        2*e.* Bernard Henry Newdigate, *b.* 12 Ap. 1869.

        3*e.* Sebastian Francis Newdigate, *b.* 13 Oct. 1880.

        4*e.* Mary Newdigate.

        5*e.* Agnes Newdigate.

        6*e.* Edith Margaret Newdigate.

        7*e.* Katherine Margaret Mary Newdigate.

        8*e.* Barbara Maria Newdigate.

    4*d. Constance Mary Boynton, d.* 24 *Aug.* 1895; m. 20 *Ap.* 1870, *Col. James Swinburne of Marcus, co. Forfar, D.L.,* d. 1881; *and had issue* 1*e.*

        1*e.* Ethel Maude Swinburne, *m.* 18 Feb. 1903, Everard Joseph Stourton, Hon. Lieut. Imp. Yeo. (32 *Ovington Square, S.W.; Marcus, Forfar, N.B.*); and has issue 1*f* to 2*f.*

            1*f.* Everard Botolph Stourton, *b.* 20 July 1905.

            2*f.* Enid Mary Stourton.

    5*d.* Eliza Boynton, *m.* 10 Ap. 1883, Arthur Edward Pedder, *late* of Brandiston Hall, Norfolk (25 *Westbourne Square, W.; Barmston, Mundesley-on-Sea, Norfolk*); and has issue 1*e* to 5*e.*

        1*e.* Francis Alban Newsham Pedder, *b.* 17 Ap. 1884.

        2*e.* Edward Boynton Pedder, *b.* 6 Feb. 1889.

        3*e.* Guy Richard Pedder, *b.* 7 July 1892.

        4*e.* Evelyn Mary Pedder.

        5*e.* Madeleine Mary Pedder.

    6*d. Dora Louisa Henrietta Boynton, d.* 25 *Feb.* 1894; m. 7 *Ap.* 1891, *the Rev. Gwyn Lloyd Moore Rees, Vicar of Howden* (*Howden Vicarage, York*).

    3*c.* Charles Boynton (*Somerville House, Nottingham Road, Croydon*), *b.* 16 Jan. 1825; *m.* 13 Mar. 1856, Mary, da. of Fewster Wilkinson of Kirkella, near Hull; and has issue 1*d* to 6*d.*

    1*d.* Harry Somerville Boynton (*Junior Constitutional*), *b.* 27 Nov. 1856.

    2*d.* Francis Boynton, Major in the Army, and Hon. Lieut.-Col. Royal Anglesey R.E., *late* Division Officer, R.E., Warwick (*The Butts, Warwick*), *b.* 16 June 1859; *m.* 3 May 1887, Elsie, da. of Major-Gen. Thomas Phillips of Ashenhurst, co. Stafford, Col. 18th P.W.O. Hussars; and has issue 1*e* to 2*e.*

        1*e.* Thomas Bruis Boynton, *b.* 7 May 1888.

        2*e.* Elsie Evelyn Boynton.

    3*d.* Charles Boynton (3 *Nottingham Road, Croydon*), *b.* 16 May 1862.

[Nos. 49547 to 49576.

# of The Blood Royal

4*d*. Walter Boynton, *late* Capt. and Hon. Major East Surrey Regt. (*Junior United Service*), *b*. 5 Dec. 1864.

5*d*. Mary Boynton.

6*d*. Adriana Boynton, *m*. 2 Ap. 1890, Arthur Henry Wyborn, M.D. (181 *Camden Road, N.W.*); and has issue 1*e*.

1*e*. Cecil Fewster Boynton Wyborn.

4*c*. George Hebblethwaite Lutton Boynton, *Capt*. 17*th Lancers*, b. 10 *May* 1828; d. 18 *May* 1888; m. 1*st*, 25 *July* 1849, *Elizabeth Laura, da. of Thomas Henry Keeling*; 2*ndly*, 1 Oct. 1865, *Elizabeth Anne, da. of Lieut.-Col. Thomas Prickett, d. 15 Ap*. 1877; *and had issue* 1*d* to 2*d*.

1*d*. George Henry Keeling Boynton, *b*. 23 Aug. 1851; *m*. 1st, 5 July 1873, Charlotte Isabella, da. of A. C. Barrett, *d*. 1885; 2ndly, 1886, Frances, da. of G. W. Smyth of Dover Street, W.; and has issue 1*e*.

1*e*. Lilian Constance Boynton.

2*d*. Eva Mary Julia Boynton (48B *South Street, Mayfair, W.*).

5*c*. *Eliza Boynton, d.* 26 *Dec.* 1833; *m*. 16 *July* 1832, *Charles Swaby of Gristhorpe, co. York, and Jamaica.*

6*c*. Louisa Boynton (6 *The Crescent, Scarborough*), *m*. 1st, 19 Oct. 1843, John Rickaby of Bridlington Quay, *d*. 1860; 2ndly, 3 Dec. 1861, Richard Sterne Carroll of Tolston Lodge, Tadcaster, *d.s.p*. 1879; and has issue 1*d* to 3*d*.

1*d*. John Rickaby, J.P., *late* Major and Hon. Lieut.-Col. West Yorkshire Regt. (*Manor House, Bridlington Quay; Yorkshire Club, York*), *b*. 1845; *m*. 1st, 1877, Catherine, da. of W. Fowler, *d*. 1893; 2ndly, 1897, Henrietta, da. of Capt. James A. Somerville.

2*d*. Louisa Rickaby.

3*d*. Margaret Rickaby, *m*. 1873, Major Edward Henry de Freville, *d*. 1901.

3*a*. *Margaret Hebblethwaite, b.* 3 *June* 1772; *d*. 23 *Dec.* 1847; *m.* [——] *Harland of Bridlington.*

4*a*. *Frances Hebblethwaite, b.* 3 *Mar.* 1768; m. *John Pitt of Newcastle-on-Tyne, Lieut.-Col. of the Bridlington Volunteers.*[1]   [Nos. 49577 to 49587.

492. Descendants, if any, of MARY ST. QUINTIN, *m*. 4 Feb. 1707, JAMES HUSTLER; and of MARGARET ST. QUINTIN, *bapt*. 18 Mar. 1657; of MARY ST. QUINTIN, *bur*. 11 May 1671, *m*. MATTHEW ALURED of Beverley, *bur*. 28 Aug. 1694; and of DEBORAH ST. QUINTIN, *m*. 11 July 1687, Major ANDREW BIRCH of London (see Table LI.).

493. Descendants, if any, of JANE STAPYLTON (see Table XLIX.), wife of WILLIAM FENWICK, 2nd son of Sir John Fenwick of Wallington, co. Northumberland.

494. Descendants of Sir WILLIAM WYVILL of Constable Burton, 4th Bart. [E.] (see Table LII.), *b*. 1645; *d. c*. 1684; *m*. ANNE, da. of James BROOKE of Ellingthorpe, co. York; and had issue 1*a* to 3*a*.

1*a*. *Sir Marmaduke Wyvill, 5th Bart. [E.], M.P., d.* 2 *Nov.* 1722; m. 29 *Mar.* 1688, *Henrietta Maria, da. of Sir Thomas Yarburgh of Bane Hall and Snaith, bapt.* 8 *Oct.* 1667; *d*. 15 *Aug.* 1738; *and had issue* 1*b* to 3*b*.

---

[1] "The Genealogist," XIV. p. 50.

The Plantagenet Roll

1b. Sir *Marmaduke Wyvill, 6th Bart.* [*E.*], b. 1692; d.s.p. 27 *Dec.* 1754.

2b. *Christopher Wyvill, Commr. of Excise,* d. 26 *Ap.* 1752; m. 2*ndly,* 1783, *Henrietta, da. and co-h. of Francis Asty of Black Notley, co. Essex,* d. 1742; *and had issue* 1e.

1e. *Sir Marmaduke Asty Wyvill, 7th Bart.* [*E.*], d. *unm.* 23 *Feb.* 1744.

3b. *Ursula Wyvill,* d. 1733; m. *Landon Jones of Furnival's Court, London; and had issue.*

2a. *D'Arcy Wyvill,* d. 4 *Jan.* 1735; m. [——], *da. of* [——]; *and had issue* 1b *to* 2b.

1b. *William Wyvill of America,* b. 1706 (*being aged 13, 14 June* 1719); d. (*on his passage from America*) 1750; m. [——], *da. of* [——]; *and had issue* 1c.

1c. *Sir Marmaduke Wyvill, 8th Bart.* [*E.*], d. 7 *Sept.* 1784; m. 1*st* (*at St. James' Church, Anne Arundel, co. Maryland*), 15 *Mar.* 1764, *Harriet, da. of* [——] *Rateby;* 2*ndly* (*at the same place*), 15 *Oct.* 1775, *Susanna, da. of* [——] *Burgers; and had issue* (2 *sons and* 3 *das. by* 1*st wife, and* 2 *sons and* 6 *das. by* 2*nd*) 1d *to* 3d.

1d. *Sir Dary Wyvill of Anne Arundel co., 9th Bart.* [*E.*], bapt. 1766; *d.* (-); m. [——], *da. of* [——]; *and had issue* 1e.

1e. *Sir Robert Wyvill, 10th Bart.* [*E.*], d.s.p.

2d. *Sir Marmaduke Wyvill, 11th Bart.* [*E.*], b. 5 *Feb.* 1771; d. 1808; m. *a.* 1807 [——], *da. of* [——]; *and had issue* 1e.

1e. *Harriet Rateby Wyvill,* b. 7 *Mar.* 1807; d. 1 *Dec.* 1886; m. *c.* 1827, *Robert Garraway Pendill; and had issue.*

3d. *Sir Walter Wyvill of Calvert, co. Maryland, 12th Bart.* [*E.*], b. 4 *Feb.* 1780; d. (-); m. [——] (*at St. James' Church aforesaid*), 3 *June* 1811, *Anna, da. of* [——] *Wood; and had* (*with possibly other*) *issue* 1e.

1e. Sir Edward Hale Wyvill of Cavart co., *b.* 14 Sept. 1812; living 1890; *m.* 29 Nov. 1832, Mary, da. of [——] Davis; and had (with possibly other) issue 1f.

1f. Walter Davis Wyvill of Washington, U.S.A., Merchant, son and heir in 1890,[1] *b.* 8 May 1834.

2b. *Edward Wyvill, Gen. Supervisor of Excise at Edinburgh,* d. 12 *Mar.* 1791; m. 18 *Dec.* 1737, *Christian Catherine, da. of William Clifton of Edinburgh; and had issue*[2] 1c.

1c. *Rev. Christopher Wyvill, Rector of Black Notley, co. Essex,* d. *Mar.* 1822; m. 1*st,* Oct. 1773, *Elizabeth, sister and co-h. of Sir Marmaduke Wyvill, 5th Bart.* [*E.*], d.s.p. 23 *July* 1783; 2*ndly,* 9 *Aug.* 1787, *Sarah, da. of J. Codling; and had issue* 1d *to* 2d.

1d. *Marmaduke Wyvill of Constable Burton, M.P., J.P., D.L.,* b. 14 *Feb.* 1791; d. 1872; m. 13 *Dec.* 1813, *Rachel, da. of Richard Slater Milnes of Fryston, M.P.,* d. 16 *Sept.* 1856; *and had issue* 1e *to* 3e.

1e. *Marmaduke Wyvill of Constable Burton, M.P., J.P., D.L.,* b. 1815; d. 25 *June* 1896; m. 8 *Ap.* 1845, *Laura, da. of Sir Charles Ibbetson, previously Selwin, 4th Bart.* [*G.B.*]; *and had issue* 1f *to* 5f.

1f. Marmaduke D'Arcy Wyvill, M.P., J.P., D.L. (*Constable Burton, Bedale, co. Yorks; Denton Park, Ben Rydding, Leeds*), b. 5 Mar. 1849; *m.* 1st, 12 June 1871, Isabella, da. of John Banner Price, d. 8 Mar. 1895; 2ndly, 19 Mar. 1898, Elizabeth, da. of Sir William Henry Wilson-Todd of Tranby Park, 1st Bart. [U.K.], J.P., D.L.; and has issue 1g to 4g.

1g. Marmaduke Ibbetson Wyvill, *b.* 8 June 1882.

2g. Laura Louisa Wyvill.

3g. Ethel Wyvill.

4g. Edith Wyvill.

2f. Frederic Christopher Wyvill, *b.* 26 May 1852.   [Nos. 49588 to 49595.

---

[1] G. E. C.'s " Complete Baronetage," i. p. 104, from which the particulars regarding the American line are taken.

[2] See, however, Foster's " Yorkshire Pedigrees."

# of The Blood Royal

3f. Laura Charlotte Rachel Wyvill, *m.* 28 Nov. 1877, Robert Barclay, Chief of the Barclays of Malthers and Urie, J.P., D.L., High Sheriff co. Surrey 1878 (*Bury Hill, Dorking*); and has issue 1*g* to 5*g*.

1*g.* Robert Wyvill Barclay, *b.* 23 Nov. 1880.
2*g.* Thomas Hubert Barclay, *b.* 13 Ap. 1884.
3*g.* Arthur Victor Barclay, *b.* 11 Aug. 1887.
4*g.* George Eric Barclay, *b.* 25 July 1889.
5*g.* Ellen Rachel Barclay, *b.* 16 Dec. 1881.

4f. Alice Henrietta Wyvill, d. 12 Dec. 1892 ; m. *as 1st wife,* 10 *Aug.* 1886, *the Rev. Godfrey Armytage Littledale, M.A., Vicar and Rural Dean of Chipping Norton ; and had issue* 1*g to* 2*g.*

1*g.* Anthony Godfrey Littledale, *b.* 13 May 1888.
2*g.* Dorothy Laura Littledale.

5*f.* Maud Wyvill.

2e. Henrietta Catherine Wyvill, d. 25 *Jan.* 1900; m. 21 *Sept.* 1840, *Robert Gurney Barclay.*

3e. Elizabeth Jane Wyvill, d. 31 *Mar.* 1906; m. 19 *Feb.* 1846, *Rev. the Hon. Thomas Orde-Powlett of Wensley, b.* 24 *Jan.* 1822 ; *d.* 12 *Sept.* 1894; *and has issue* 1*f to* 5*f.*

1*f.* Thomas Charles Orde-Powlett, Col. *late* Comdg. Regt. Dist. No. 48 (*Naval and Military*), *b.* 3 Feb. 1849 ; *m.* 15 Sept. 1886, Harriet Georgiana, da. of the Rev. Plumer Pott Rooper ; and has issue 1*g* to 2*g*.

1*g.* Gladys Harriet Orde-Powlett.
2*g.* Beryl Georgina Louisa Orde-Powlett.

2*f.* Rev. Ernest Orde-Powlett, Rector of Wensley (*Wensley Rectory, Leyburn R.S.O.*), *b.* 27 July 1850; *m.* 19 June 1879, Anne Gertrude, ¹da. of the Rev. Alexander Hunter.

3*f.* Elizabeth Letitia Orde-Powlett, *m.* 28 Nov. 1877, Capt. James Edward Hunter, R.N. (*United Service*) ; and has issue 1*g* to 2*g*.

1*g.* Edward Thomas Gurney Hunter, *b.* 1880.
2*g.* Ronald Muir Hunter, *b.* 1883.

4*f.* Louisa Rachel Orde-Powlett, *m.* 18 Jan. 1883, Capt. Charles¹Michell, J.P. ; *d.s.p.* 25 Jan. 1900 (*Glassel, Kincardineshire*).

5*f.* Henrietta Maria Orde-Powlett, *m.* 1st, 29 Aug. 1888, the Rev. Robert Blair Maconochie, Chancellor of Otley, *d.s.p.* 3 Jan. 1890 ; 2ndly, 3 Oct. 1893, the Rev. Henry Milner Sharples (*Finghall Rectory, Yorks*); and has issue 1*g* to 3*g*.

1*g.* Thomas Henry Wilfred Sharples, *b.* 5 Feb. 1895.
2*g.* Evelyn Horace Guy Sharples, *b.* 6 Sept. 1898.
3*g.* Muriel Elizabeth Hilda Sharples, *b.* 3 Mar. 1897.

2d. Rev. Edward Wyvill, Rector of Finghall and Spennithorne, d. (–) ; m. *Frances Pulleine, widow of the Rev. Frederick Dodsworth, D.D., da. of* [——], *d.* 1831 ; *and had issue* 1*e.*

1*e.* Rev. Edward Christopher Wyvill of New Zealand, *b.* 1826.

3a. Priscella Wyvill, m. *Major Kempe ; and had issue.* [Nos. 49596 to 49617.

495. Descendants of DOROTHY WYVILL (see Table LII.), *bur.* 21 Dec. 1664 ; *m.* 22 May, 1655, CHARLES TANCRED (TANKARD) of Whixley, co. York, *b. c.* 1637 ; *bur.* 12 Jan. 1669; and had issue 1*a* to 4*a*.[1]

1*a. Christopher Tancred of Whixley, High Sheriff co. York* 1685–86, *M.P.,* b. 1660; *d.* 21 *Nov.* 1705; m. 1st, 19 *Nov.* 1679, *Catherine, da. of Sir John Armytage of Kirklees,* 2nd *Bart.* [G.B.], bapt. 7 *Ap.* 1654 ; *d.* (–) ; *and had issue* 1*b to* 4*b.*

---

[1] Foster's " Yorkshire Pedigrees."

551

The Plantagenet Roll

1b. Christopher Tancred of Whixley, b. 16 Nov. 1689; d. *unm.* 30 Aug. 1754.

2b. Dorothy Tancred, b. 11 Feb. 1683 [? *wife of Major Lambart*].[1]

3b. Elizabeth Tancred, a co-h. to the Barony of Scrope of Masham [E.], b. 20 *Jan.* 1687; d. 11 *June* 1768; m. 11 *Aug.* 1716, *William Dobson, Alderman and Lord Mayor* (1729) *of York,* d. 31 *July* 1749; *and had issue 1c.*

1c. Ann Tancred Dobson, m. *William Burrell Massingberd of Ormsby, High Sheriff co. Linc.* 1745; d. 18 *Aug.* 1802; *and had issue 1d to 3d.*

1d. Charles Burrell Massingberd of Ormsby and Braziers, High Sheriff co. Oxford, b. 1749; d. *Nov.* 1835; m. 1st, 29 *Dec.* 1774, *Anne, da. and h. of William Blackall of Braziers, co. Oxford,* d. *Nov.* 1835; *and had issue 1e.*

1e. Harriet Massingberd of Ormsby, senior co-h. to the Barony of Scrope of Masham [E.], d. 22 *Ap.* 1864; m. 26 *June* 1806, *Charles Godfrey Mundy of Buxton Hall, High Sheriff co. Leic.,* d. 23 *Ap.* 1838; *and had issue 1f.*

1f. Charles John Henry Mundy, afterwards (R.L. 29 *Ap.* 1863) *Massingberd-Mundy of Ormsby, J.P., D.L.,* b. 21 *June* 1808; d. 19 *Feb.* 1882; m. 13 *Sept.* 1838, *Elizabeth Susan, da. of John Young of Westridge, I.W.,* d. 19 *Jan.* 1892; *and had issue 1g to 2g.*

1g. Charles Francis Massingberd-Mundy, J.P., D.L. (*Ormsby Hall, Alford, Lincoln*), b. 30 June 1839; *m.* 8 Aug. 1865, *Louisa Charlotte, da. of Charles John Bigge of Linden; and has issue 1h to 4h.*

1h. Godfrey Bertram Massingberd-Mundy, J.P., D.L., *b.* 25 Mar. 1872.

2h. Oswald Francis Massingberd-Mundy, *b.* 30 Aug. 1874; *m.* 6 Ap. 1904, Eleanor Hyacinthe, da. of the Rev. William Mondeford Bramston; and has issue 1*i.*

1i. Francis Massingberd-Mundy, *b.* 1 Sept. 1905.

3h. Henry Louis Massingberd-Mundy, *b.* 9 Aug. 1879; *m.* Emily Elizabeth, da. of William Arthur Merriden.

4h. Philippa Alice Massingberd-Mundy.

2g. Sophy Jane Massingberd-Mundy.

2d. Anne Massingberd, d. (–); m. 6 *Dec.* 1777, *the Rev. William Maxwell of Falkland, co. Monaghan, D.D.,* d. 3 *Sept.* 1818; *and had issue 1e.*

1e. Anne Maxwell, b. 1796; d. 7 *Jan.* 1856; m. 21 *Jan.* 1818, *the Rev. Henry Francis Lyte of Berry Head, Brixham, co. Devon, M.A.,* d. 20 *Nov.* 1847; *and had issue 1f to 4f.*

1f. Henry William Maxwell Lyte, b. 29 *Sept.* 1818; d. 3 *June* 1856; m. 10 *June* 1843, *Emily, da. of Edward Pretyjohn; and had issue 1g to 2g.*

1g. Philippa Massingberd Maxwell Lyte, *m.* 15 Sept. 1864, the Rev. Arthur Cyril Pearson (1 *Portman Mansions, York Place, W.*); and has issue 1*h* to 4*h.*

1h. Cyril Arthur Pearson (*Frensham Place, Farnham, Surrey*), *b.* 24 Feb. 1866; *m.* 1st, 18—, [——], da. of the Rev. John Bennet; 2ndly, Ethel, da. of J. W. Fraser; and has issue 1*i* to 4*i.*

1i. Neville Arthur Pearson.

2i. Isla Marion Pearson.

3i. Muriel Pearson.

4i. Nora Pearson.

2h. Mabel Pearson, *m.* the Rev. Alfred Sydney Menzies, Vicar of Burley on the Hill, co. Rutland.

3h. Marion Pearson.

4h. Olive Pearson, *m.* H. Arnold.

2g. Ellen Maxwell Lyte, *m.* 4 June 1869, Clement James Hoey; and has issue 1*h.*

1h. Maud Hoey.   [Nos. 49618 to 49635.

---

[1] Dugdale's "Visitation of Yorkshire," edited by G. W. Clay, F.S.A. "The Genealogist," x. p. 167.

# of The Blood Royal

2f. John Walker Maxwell Lyte, b. 2 Dec. 1823; d. 28 *July* 1848; m. 22 *June* 1847, *Emily Jeannette, da. of Col. John Craigie, H.E.I.C.S.; and had issue* 1g.

1g. Sir Henry Churchill Maxwell Lyte, K.C.B., M.A., F.S.A., Deputy Keeper of the Records (3 *Portman Square, London*), b. 29 May 1848; m. 3 Jan. 1871, Frances Fownes, da. of James Curtis Somerville of Dinder House, co. Somerset, J.P., D.L.; and has issue 1h to 6h.

1h. John Maxwell Lyte, *late* Lieut. Northumberland Fusiliers, b. 11 May 1875.

2h. Walter Maxwell Lyte, b. 4 Mar. 1877.

3h. Arthur Maxwell Lyte, B.A., b. 10 Ap. 1881.

4h. Agnes Maxwell Lyte.

5h. Edith Maxwell Lyte.

6h. Margaret Maxwell Lyte, m. 9 Aug. 1904, Edward Richard Massie (*Coddington, co. Chester*); and has issue 1i.

1i. Barbara Massie, b. 29 Ap. 1906.

3f. Farnham Maxwell Lyte, M.A., F.C.S., b. 10 *Jan.* 1828; d. 4 *Mar.* 1906; m. 6 *Feb.* 1851, *Eleanora Julia, da. of Cornelius Henry Bolton of Faithlegg, co. Waterford; and had issue* 1g *to* 4g.

1g. Cecil Henry Maxwell Lyte (1 *Portman Mansions, York Place, London, W.*), b. 26 Aug. 1855; m. 4 Oct. 1894, the Hon. Mary Lucy Agnes, da. of Alfred Joseph (Stourton), 23rd Baron Mowbray, &c. [E.].

2g. Alice Anne Maxwell Lyte, m. 20 June 1900, Francis Nevile Hulton.

3g. Ida Mary Maxwell Lyte, a nun.

4g. Beatrice Katharine Maxwell Lyte, m. 20 Mar. 1890, Charles Laird James Albert Lewall; and has issue 1h to 2h.

1h. James Farnham Lewall, b. 17 Jan. 1891.

2h. Bernard Cecil Lewall, b. 30 Nov. 1894.

4f. Anna Maria Maxwell Lyte, d. 30 *July* 1889; m. 24 *June* 1846, *the Rev. John Roughton Hogg, Vicar of St. Mark's, Torquay,* d. 1 *Dec.* 1867; *and had issue* 1g *to* 3g.

1g. Anna Maria Maxwell Hogg (*Berry Head, Brixham, Devon*).

2g. Margaret Louisa Maxwell Hogg, a Sister of Mercy.

3g. Alice Massingberd Maxwell Hogg, m. 22 June 1881, the Rev. Arthur Lindsay Palmes, Rector of Saltwood (*Saltwood Rectory, Kent*); and has issue 1h to 2h.

1h. John Lindsay Palmes, b. 10 Mar. 1886.

2h. James Arthur Palmes, b. 20 Jan. 1901.

3d. Elizabeth Massingberd, d. (–); m. 14 *Ap.* 1795, *the Rev. Francis Massingberd of Washingborough,* d. 11 *Ap.* 1817; *and had issue.*

See p. 406, Nos. 34054–34055.

4b. Ursula Tancred.

2a. Ursula Tancred, b. 16 *Ap.* 1656; bapt. 15 *Oct.* 1661;[1] m.[1] (*lic.* 1 *Oct.*) 1678, *Richard Wood of St. Gregory's, London, Laceman.*

3a. Mary Tancred, m. *Francis Molineux (younger son of Francis Molineux of Mansfield, co. Notts, High Sheriff for that co.* 1662, *and grandson of Sir Francis Molineux of Taversal, Bart.* [E.]); *and had issue* (4 *das.*).

4a. Anne Tancred, b. 1664.   [Nos. 49636 to 49656.

496. Descendants, if any, of Barbara Wyvill (see Table LII.), wife of Sir John Thompson of Crawley, co. Beds.

---

[1] Dugdale's "Visitation of Yorkshire," edited by G. W. Clay, F.S.A. "The Genealogist," **x.** p. 167.

The Plantagenet Roll

497. Descendants, if any surviving, of Sir MARMADUKE BECKWITH, 3rd Bart. [E.], a Merchant in Virginia (see Table LII.), *b.* June 1687 ; *d.* (–) ; *m.* and had issue.[1]

498. Descendants, if any, of JANE WYVILL (see Table LII.), wife of ROBERT WYLDE of Hunton, co. York.

499. Descendants of the Hon. MARY D'ARCY (see Table LII.), *b. c.* 1671 ; *d.* 17 June 1737 ; *m.* WILLIAM JESSOP of Broom Hall, Sheffield, M.P., *b. c.* 1664 ; *d.* 15 Nov. 1734 ; and had issue 1*a* to 3*a*.

1*a.* James (*Jessop, afterwards D'Arcy*), 2nd Baron D'Arcy Navan [*I.*], d.s.p. 1733.

2*a.* Barbara Jessop, d. (–) ; *m. Andrew Wilkinson of Boroughbridge, co. York, M.P.; and had issue* 1*b.*

1*b.* John Wilkinson of the Middle Temple (7th son, but the only one to have issue), d. (–) ; *m. and had issue* 1*c.*

1*c.* Barbara Isabella Wilkinson, hss. of Boroughbridge Hall, d. 18 June 1838 ; *m.* 14 *Ap.* 1791, *the Rev. Marmaduke Lawson, M.A., Rector of Sproatley, Preb. of Lincoln,* d. 1814; *and had issue* 1*d to* 5*d.*

1*d.* Andrew Lawson of Boroughbridge, heir to his brother 1823, b. 1800; d. 28 Feb. 1853; m. 1 Feb. 1823, *Marianne Anna Maria, da. of Sir Thomas Sherlock Gooch, 5th Bart.* [*G.B.*], d. 5 Nov. 1855 ; *and had issue* 1*e to* 6*e.*

1*e.* Andrew Sherlock Lawson of Boroughbridge and Aldborough, J.P., D.L., b. 1 Nov. 1824; d. 22 May 1872 ; m. 1 July 1852, *Isabella, da. of John Grant of Nuttall Hall, co. Lancaster; and had issue* 1*f to* 7*f.*

1*f.* Andrew Sherlock Lawson, J.P., D.L., *late* Capt. and Hon. Major Yorkshire Hussars Y. C. (*Aldborough Manor, near Boroughbridge; Boroughbridge Hall, York*), *b.* 22 Feb. 1855 ; *m.* 28 Feb. 1889, the Hon. Elinor Frances, da. of Henry Edmund (Butler), 14th Viscount Mountgarrett [I.]; and has issue 1*g* to 2*g.*

1*g.* Margery Elinor Lawson, *b.* 29 Nov. 1889.

2*g.* Mary Doreen Lawson, *b.* 13 Aug. 1892.

2*f.* Sir John Grant Lawson, 1st Bart. [U.K.], J.P., M.P. (*Knavesmire Lodge, York; Carlton*), *b.* 28 July 1856 ; *m.* 31 July 1902, Sylvia, da. of Charles Edward Hunter ; and has issue 1*g* to 2*g.*

1*g.* Peter Grant Lawson, *b.* 28 July 1903.

2*g.* Griselda Grant Lawson, *b.* 22 May 1905.

3*f.* Richard Lawson, *b.* 9 Mar. 1864; *m.* Aug. 1893, Lilian, da. of William Henry Fife of Lee Hall, co. Northants ; and has issue 1*g* to 2*g.*

1*g.* Digby Richard Lawson, *b.* 9 Sept. 1894.

2*g.* Frances Cynthia Rosaby Lawson.

4*f.* Jane Grant Lawson, *m.* 1 Oct. 1874, John C. Wilmot Smith (*Ballynanty, Limerick*); and has issue 1*f* to 6*g.*   [Nos. 49657 to 49666.

---

[1] Tarply, son of Sir Marmaduke Beckwith of Virginia, *d.* in England 27 Dec. 1748 (*Gentleman's Magazine*). Another son, Marmaduke, is given as living in Virginia 1777, in Kimber's "Baronetage." Sir Jonathan Beckwith is stated to have been the then Baronet by Betham (1803) and Playfair (1811). See also G. E. C.'s "Complete Baronetage," iv. p. 115. Foster ("Yorkshire Pedigrees") says of Sir Marmaduke, 3rd Bart., "whose descendants are now in the United States, 1866."

1*g*. Charles Wilmot Smith, *b*. 4 Sept. 1880.

2*g*. Andrew Wilmot Smith, Sub.-Lieut. R.N., *b*. 21 May 1885.

3*g*. Charlotte Isabella Wilmot Smith.

4*g*. Kathleen Jane Wilmot Smith.

5*g*. Florence Wilmot Smith.

6*g*. Barbara Wilmot Smith.

5*f*. Isabella Grace Lawson.

6*f*. Mary Florence Lawson.

7*f*. Roberta Grant Lawson.

2*e*. Edward John Lawson, Lieut. R.N., *b*. 8 Ap. 1826.

3*e*. Marmaduke Charles Lawson, Lieut.-Col. Madras Horse Art., *b*. 16 Oct. 1827; *m*. 6 Jan. 1870, Mary Eliza, da. of W. M. Caddell, M.C.S.; and has issue (a son).

4*e*. *Thomas William Lawson, Capt. 74th Highlanders, b.* 1 *Mar.* 1833; *d.* (−); *m.* 22 *Dec.* 1863, *Harriet Frances, da. of the Rev. Barry O'Meara Deane; and had issue* 1*f to* 4*f*.

1*f*. Thomas Edward Marmaduke Lawson, *b*. 14 Oct. 1868.

2*f*. Mary Isabella Lawson.

3*f*. Harriet Rose Lawson.

4*f*. Marianne Louisa Lawson.

5*e*. *Mary Lawson, d.* 13 *Ap.* 1851; *m.* 9 *Dec.* 1847, *John Dunn Gardner of Charteris and Cambridge,* 1859, *J.P., D.L., High Sheriff, and sometime* (1841–47) *M.P.* (37 *Grosvenor Place, S.W.*); *and had issue* 1*f to* 2*f*.

1*f*. Arthur Andrew Cecil Dunn-Gardner, J.P., *b*. 3 Jan. 1851; *m*. 1890, Rose, da. of Andrew Lawrie.

2*f*. Mary Marianne Mariana Dunn-Gardner, *m*. 17 Feb. 1870, William Robinson of Dullingham House, co. Camb., and Denston Hall, co. Suffolk, *d*. 23 June 1889.

6*e*. *Anne Matilda Lawson, d.* (−); *m.* 3 *Feb.* 1858, *the Rev. William Henry Thompson, Incumbent of Roecliffe, near Boroughbridge; and had issue* (2 *das.*).

2*d*. Rev. James Lawson, Vicar of Buckminster, d. (? unm.).

3*d*. Rev. John Lawson, Incumbent of Seaton Carew, co. Durham, d. (? unm.).

4*d*. Barbara Lawson.

5*d*. Dorothy Lawson, d. (−); m. 1833, the Rev. Edward Bird, Rector of Tattenhall, co. Chester.

3*a*. Isabella Jessop, m. before 17 May 1735, John Eyre, afterwards Gill, of Hopton, co. Derby; and had issue. [Nos. 49667 to 49683.]

500. Descendants of the Hon. ELIZABETH D'ARCY (see Table LII.), *bur.* 10 June 1739; *m.* as 2nd wife, 5 Mar. 1726, JOHN HUTTON of Marske, co. York, *b.* 1691; *d.* 16 Jan. 1768; and had issue 1*a* to 3*a*.

1*a*. *James Hutton of Aldburgh* (3*rd son, but in his issue h.*), bapt. 11 *June* 1739; d. 2 *Mar.* 1798; m. *Mary, da. of John Hoyle of Ashgill, co. York; and had issue* 1*b*.

1*b*. *James Henry D'Arcy Hutton of Aldburgh,* bapt. 24 *Mar.* 1796; d. (−); m. 1821, *Harriet, da. of* [——] *Aggas of Bungay; and had issue* 1*c to* 3*c*.

1*c*. *John Timothy D'Arcy Hutton of Marske and Aldburgh, J.P., b.* 29 *Mar.* 1822; d. 24 *Oct.* 1874; m. 1845, *Emma Rebecca, da. of Thomas Marsh Lamb of Middleham, d.* 6 *Feb.* 1896; *and had issue* 1*d to* 3*d*.

1*d*. John Timothy D'Arcy Hutton, J.P., *formerly* 1st Royal Dragoons (*Marske*, [No. 49684.

The Plantagenet Roll

Richmond; Aldborough Hall, Masham), b. 5 June 1847; *m.* 1868, Edith Constance, da. of Thomas Barroll Phipson of Heathfield, Kent; and has issue 1*e* to 5*e*.

1*e*. John Timothy D'Arcy Hutton, *b.* 22 Feb. 1869.

2*e*. Harold Edward D'Arcy Hutton, *b.* 26 Dec. 1872; *m.* 1 Mar. 1898, Lilian Marion Louisa, da. of Gen. Mackenzie of Gruinard; and has issue 1*f*.

1*f*. Harold Colville D'Arcy Hutton, *b.* 7 Ap. 1900.

3*e*. Edith Flora Hutton.

4*e*. Hilda Winifred D'Arcy Hutton, *m.* 14 Oct. 1897, Capt. E. H. Hamilton Gordon, *late* Gordon Highlanders; and has issue 1*f*.

1*f*. Harriet Hermione Gordon.

5*e*. Aldyth Lorna Hutton.

2*d*. Emily Harriet Hutton, *m.* 7 Dec. 1869, Ernest Birch, Judge of the High Court, Calcutta.

3*d*. Elizabeth Jane Hutton.

2*c*. *James Henry Hutton, Lieut. 15th Lancers, b.* 1823; *d.* (? s.p.) 24 *Nov.* 1874; *m.* 1868, *Amy Caroline, da. of the Rev. Thomas W. Robson.*

3*c*. *Harriet Emma Hutton, d.* 1 *Dec.* 1854; *m.* 1848, *the Rev. Canon Richard Cattley of Worcester; and had issue* 1*d*.

1*d*. *Richard D'Arcy Cattley, d.* (? *unm.*) 21 *Aug.* 1894.

2*a*. *Anne Hutton, bapt.* 1 *June* 1732; *d.* 1 *Sept.* 1781; *m.* (*her cousin*) *George Wanley Bowes of Eyford, co. Gloucester and Thornton, co. Durham, b. c.* 1700; *d.* 1752.

3*a*. *Elizabeth Hutton, bapt.* 24 *Feb.* 1736; *d. June* 1816; *m.* 11 *Feb.* (? *Sept. or Oct.*) 1764, *Henry Pulleine of Carleton, co. York, d.* (–); *and had issue* 1*b* to 2*b*.

1*b*. *Henry Percy Pulleine of Carleton, and afterwards of Crake Hall, J.P., b.* 30 *Nov.* 1770; *d.* 1 *May* 1833; *m. Elizabeth, da. of Anthony Askew of London, M.D., d.* 24 *Ap.* 1839; *and had issue* 1*c* to 7*c*.

1*c*. *James Pulleine of Crake Hall and Clifton Castle, J.P., D.L., High Sheriff co. York* 1870, *b.* 31 *Oct.* 1804; *d.* 23 *Mar.* 1879; *m.* 7 *Aug.* 1841, *Anne Caroline, da. of Edward Marjoribanks of Wimpole Street, W., d.* 28 *Mar.* 1889; *and had issue* 1*d*.

1*d*. *Georgina Elizabeth Pulleine of Crake and Clifton* (*Crake Hall, and Clifton Castle, near Bedale*), *b.* 5 *Feb.* 1846; *m.* 5 *Feb.* 1868, Major-Gen. the Right Hon. Sir John Clayton-Cowell, R.E., P.C., K.C.B., Master of the Household to H.M. Queen Victoria, *d.* 29 Aug. 1894; and has issue 1*e* to 4*e*.

1*e*. Albert Victor John Cowell, Capt. Rifle Brigade, *b.* (H.M. Queen Victoria sponsor) 12 June 1869.

2*e*. Henry Pulleine John Cowell, Lieut. R.H.A., *b.* 20 Mar. 1879.

3*e*. Alice Anne Cowell, *b.* 6 Dec. 1873; *m.* 25 Feb. 1892, Capt. the Hon. Assheton Gore Curzon-Howe, R.N., C.V.O., C.B., C.M.G.; and has issue 1*f* to 3*f*.

1*f*. Leicester Charles Assheton St. John Curzon-Howe, *b.* 1894.

2*f*. Assheton Penn Curzon-Howe, *b.* 1898.

3*f*. Victoria Alexandrina Alice Curzon-Howe, *b.* 1896.

4*e*. Marie Cowell, *b.* 20 Mar. 1876.

2*c*. *Rev. Robert Pulleine of Kirby Wiske, b.* 18 *Sept.* 1806; *d.* 23 Oct. 1868; *m.* 7 *Oct.* 1835, *Susan, da. of H. Burmester of Burntwood Lodge, Surrey; and had issue* 1*d* to 3*d*.

1*d*. *Henry Burmester Pulleine, Lieut.-Col. in the Army, b.* 12 *Dec.* 1838; *d.* (*being killed at the Battle of Isandula*) 27 *Jan.* 1879; *m.* 1866, *Frances Katharine, da. of Frederick Bell of Fermoy; and had issue* 1*e* to 3*e*. [Nos. 49685 to 49701.

556

1e. Henry Percy Pulleine of Linton (*Sandford House, Richmond, Yorks*), *b.* 4 Sept. 1867; *m.* 27 Aug. 1895, Alice, da. of A. Foucart; and has issue 1*f* to 2*f*.

1*f*. Robert Percy Pulleine, *b.* 1897.

2*f*. Violet Pulleine.

2e. Amy Pulleine.

3e. Mabel Glyn Pulleine.

2*d*. Right Rev. John James Pulleine, D.D., Lord Bishop Suffragan of Richmond (*Stanhope Rectory, co. Durham*), *b.* 10 Sept. 1841; *m.* 1st, 4 Feb. 1869, Elizabeth Esther, da. of Thomas Cowper Hincks of Breckenbrough, *d.* 10 May 1882; 2ndly, 23 Ap. 1889, Louisa, da. of the Rev. Pennyman Warton Worsley, Canon. Resid. of Ripon; and has issue 1*e* to 10*e*.

1e. Rev. Robert Pulleine, Vicar of Queensbury, Yorks, *b.* 28 June 1871; *m.* 31 Aug. 1898, Kate, da. of the Rev. John Thomas Waller of Castletown, co. Limerick; and has issue 1*f*.

1*f*. Elizabeth Irene Pulleine, *b.* 2 Oct. 1899.

2e. John James Pulleine, *b.* 15 Feb. 1873; *m.* 29 Oct. 1902, Evangeline Anna, da. of Edward Tew; and has issue (a da.).

3e. Hubert Henry Worsley Pulleine, *b.* 29 Ap. 1890.

4e. Humphrey Pulleine, *b.* (twin) 13 May 1894.

5e. Richard Pulleine, *b.* (twin) 13 May 1894.

6e.[1] Elizabeth Susan Pulleine.

7e.[1] Sarah Winifred Pulleine, *m.* 3 Sept. 1902, the Rev. Ernest William Tew of Crakehall; and has issue (2 sons).

8e.[1] Frances Annie Pulleine, *m.* 27 July 1904, the Rev. Philip Edmond Kynaston of Kynnersley.

9e.[1] Marianne Pulleine.

10e.[2] Dorothy Helena Pulleine.

3*d*. Frederick Arthur Pulleine, *b.* 20 Dec. 1843; *m.* 1868, Lucy, da. of Archdeacon Butt of New Zealand; and has issue (6 sons and 1 da.).

3*c*. *Eliza Dorothy Pulleine, d. 26 July 1870; m. as 2nd wife, 22 May 1831, Arthur Lysaght, Adm. R.N., b. 22 Nov. 1782; d. 19 Mar. 1859; and had issue 1d.*

1*d*. Percy Pulleine Lysaght, *b.* 30 Nov. 1833; *m.* 30 Dec. 1875, Charlotte Amy, da. of Major Chalmer of Larbert, N.B.

4*c*. *Anne Pulleine, d. Mar. 1875; m. the Rev. Thomas Richard Ryder, M.A., Vicar of Ecclesfield, co. York; d. 24 July 1839; and had issue (2 sons and 4 das.).*

5*c*. *Frances Pulleine, d. 9 Jan. 1835; m. as 1st wife, 25 Feb. 1834, the Rev. Robert William Bosanquet, M.A., of Rock, Northumberland, J.P., sometime Rector of Bolingbroke, co. Lincoln, b. 26 Jan. 1800; d. 25 Dec. 1880; and had issue 1d.*

1*d*. *Charles Bertie Pulleine Bosanquet of Rock Hall, J.P., b. 27 Dec. 1834; d. 18 June 1905; m. 31 July 1862, Eliza Isabella, da. of Ralph Carr, afterwards Carr-Ellison of Dunston Hill, co. Durham; and had issue 1e to 8e.*

1e. Robert Carr Bosanquet, M.A. (Camb.) (*Rock Hall, near Alnwick, co. Northumberland*), *b.* 7 June 1871; *m.* 8 July 1902, Sophia, da. of Thomas Hodgkin, D.C.L.; and has issue 1*f*.

1*f*. Charles Ion Carr Bosanquet, *b.* (at Athens) 17 Ap. 1903.

2e. George Pulleine Bosanquet, *b.* 16 Feb. 1873.

3e. Frances Elizabeth Bosanquet.

4e. Amy Caroline Bosanquet.

5e. Ellen Pulleine Bosanquet.

6e. Elizabeth Feilde Bosanquet.

7e. Caroline Henrietta Bosanquet.

8e. Rosalie Ellison Bosanquet.

[Nos. 49702 to 49730.

The Plantagenet Roll

6c. Marianne Pulleine, *m.* 17 Sept. 1835, Thomas Cowper Hincks of Brecken-brough, J.P., M.A., *b.* 17 Jan. 1788; *d.* 2 Sept. 1865; and has issue 1*d* to 4*d*.

1*d.* *Thomas Cowper Hincks of Breckenbrough, J.P., late Capt.* 49*th Regt., b.* 20 *Aug.* 1840; d. 13 *Mar.* 1902; m. 4 *June* 1872, *Mary E. C., da. of Col. H. Stobart of Etherley House, co. Durham; and had issue* 1*e to* 7*e.*

1*e.* Thomas Cowper Hincks (*Barons Down, Dulverton*), Capt. Royal Berks Regt., *b.* 31 Jan. 1875.

2*e.* Henry Hincks, *b.* 10 June 1879.

3*e.* John Stobart Hincks, *b.* 18 Mar. 1884.

4*e.* Mary Hincks, *b.* 27 Mar. 1873; *m.* 7 Sept. 1905, Henry Cuthbert Barnard of Bury Orchard, Wells, Somerset.

5*e.* Frances Elizabeth Hincks, *b.* 22 Sept. 1876; *m.* 5 Dec. 1900, John Charles Rivis of Newstead, Malton, Yorks.

6*e.* Alice Katharine Hincks, *b.* 22 May 1881.

7*e.* Eleanor Marjorie Hincks, *b.* 13 Oct. 1886.

2*d.* *Mary Joanna Hincks, m.* 17 June 1868, William Robert Craster, R.A.; and has issue (3 sons and 2 das.).

3*d.* *Elizabeth Esther Hincks,* d. 10 *May* 1882; m. *as* 1*st wife,* 4 *Feb.* 1869, *the Right Rev. John James Pulleine, D.D., Lord Bishop Suffragan of Richmond* (*Stanhope Rectory, co. Durham*); *and had issue.*

See p. 557, Nos. 49708 and 49714–49717.

4*d.* Maria Hincks.

7*c.* *Charlotte Pulleine,* d. *July* 1837; m. 7 *Sept.* 1835, *William Roddam of Roddam; and had issue (an only da.).*

2*b.* *Ann Babington Pulleine,* d. (–); m. *Thomas Pulleyn Mosley of Burley Hall.* [Nos. 49731 to 49747.

501. Descendants of GRACE WYVILL (see Table LII.), *m.* GEORGE WITHAM of Cliffe, co. York, *b. c.* 1629 (being aged 36, 21 Aug. 1665); *d.* 1748; and had issue 1*a* to 8*a.*

1*a.* *John Witham of Cliffe,* b. *c.* 1652 (*being aged* 13, 21 *Aug.* 1665); d. (–); m. 1*st* (*settl. dated* 18 *Jan.*) 1678, *Elizabeth, da. of Edward Standish of Standish; and had issue* 1*b to* 4*b.*

1*b.* *William Witham of Cliffe, will dated* 8 *July* 1723; m. 20 *Sept.* 1707, *Anne, da. of Sir Henry Lawson of Brough,* 3*rd Bart.* [E.]; *and had issue* 1*c to* 2*c.*

1*c.* *Henry Witham of Cliffe,* d. 21 *Sept.* 1771; m. *Catherine, da. and co-h. of Anthony Meaburne of Pontop,* d. 12 *Ap.* 1803; *and had issue* 1*d to* 4*d.*

1*d.* *William Witham of Cliffe,* d.s.p. 2 *Aug.* 1802.

2*d.* *Thomas Witham of Headlam, co. Durham,* d. (–); m. *Mary, da. of James Thornton of Nether Witton,* d. *May* 1793; *and had issue* 1*e.*

1*e.* *Eliza Witham, sole h.* 1831; d. 15 *Nov.* 1847; m. *Henry Thomas Maire Silvertop, afterwards Witham of Lartington, co. York,* b. 28 *May* 1779; d. 28 *Nov.* 1844; *and had issue.*

See the Clarence Volume, pp. 319–320, Nos. 9241–9266.

3*d.* *Anne Witham,* d. 6 *May* 1794; m. 11 *Nov.* 1754, *Philip Howard of Corby Castle,* b. 1730; d. 8 *Jan.* 1810; *and had issue* 1*e to* 3*e.*

1*e.* *Henry Howard of Corby Castle, High Sheriff co. Cumberland* 1832, b. 2 *July* 1757; d. 1 *Mar.* 1842; m. 2*ndly,* 18 *Mar.* 1793, *Catherine Mary, da. of Sir Richard Neave,* 1*st Bart.* [G.B.], d. 16 *Jan.* 1849; *and had issue* 1*f to* 5*f.*

1*f.* *Philip Henry Howard of Corby Castle, M.P., J.P., D.L., F.S.A., High Sheriff co. Cumberland* 1860, b. 22 *Ap.* 1801; d. 1 *Jan.* 1883; m. 16 *Nov.* 1843, *Eliza Minto, da. of Major John Canning, E.I.C. Service,* d. 11 *Feb.* 1865; *and had issue* 1*g to* 2*g.* [Nos. 49748 to 49773.

558

# of The Blood Royal

1g. Philip John Canning Howard, J.P. (*Corby Castle, Carlisle; Foxcote, Shipston-on-Stour*), b. 14 Mar. 1853; m. 4 Feb. 1875, Alice Clare, da. of Peter Constable Maxwell; and has issue 1h.

1h. Ursula Mary Howard, b. 11 Sept. 1879; m. 22 Nov. 1899, Henry Joseph Lawson (*Brough, Yorkshire*).

2g. Margaret Jane Howard, b. 17 Nov. 1849.

2f. *Sir Henry Francis Howard, G.C.B., late H.B.M.'s Plen. to Brazil, Portugal, and Hanover*, b. 3 Nov. 1809; d. 28 Jan. 1898; m. 1st, 23 Dec. 1830, Sevilla, da. of David Montagu (Erskine), 2nd Lord Erskine [U.K.], d. 12 Mar. 1835; 2ndly, 30 Aug. 1841, Marie Ernestine, da. of William Leopold von der Schulenburg of Priemern, Prussia, d. 25 Dec. 1897; and had issue 1g to 5g.

1g. Sir Henry Howard, K.C.M.G., C.B., Envoy Extrao. and Min. Plen. at The Hague (*St. James'; Travellers'*), b. 11 Aug. 1843; m. 2 Oct. 1867, Cecilia, da. of George W. Riggs of Washington, U.S.A.; and has issue 1h to 5h.

1h. George Howard, b. 26 Nov. 1869; m. 5 Nov. 1902, Mary Allen, da. of [——] Clagett.

2h. Henry Mowbray Howard, b. 1 June 1873.

3h. Maria Ernestine Howard, m. 5 Sept. 1894, Rudolph H. Baron von Recum, Brunswick Hussars; and has issue.

4h. Janet Madeleine Cecilia Howard.

5h. Alice Lawrason Howard.

2g. Sir Francis Howard, K.C.H., C.M.G., Major-Gen. on the Staff and Commander-in-Chief Western Dist., *formerly* Comdg. 2nd Batt. Rifle Brig. (*Castle Godwyn, Painswick, Gloucester; Chester*), b. 26 Mar. 1848; m. 23 Ap. 1895, Gertrude, da. of Hugh Conyngham Boyd of Woodside, Torquay; and has issue 1h.

1h. Marjorie Howard, b. 9 Aug. 1903.

3g.[1] Adela Howard, a Benedictine nun (*St. Scholastica's Priory, Atherstone*).

4g. Catherine Mary Howard, m. 17 July 1873, Count Ernest von Rechberg and Rothenloewen; and has issue.

5g. Mary Louisa Howard, m. 27 June 1872, Ludwig, Baron von Aretin, of Haidenburg, Bavaria, d. 5 Feb. 1884.

3f. *Catherine Howard*, d. 27 Jan. 1874; m. 28 July 1829, *the Hon. Philip Henry Joseph Stourton*, b. 14 Jan. 1793; d. 3 Aug. 1860; *and had issue.*
See the Clarence Volume, p. 367, Nos. 12546–12552.

4f. *Emma Agnes Howard*, d. 10 Feb. 1861; m. *as 2nd wife*, 14 Ap. 1823, *William Henry Francis (Petre), 11th Lord Petre* [E.], b. 22 Jan. 1793; d. 3 July 1850; *and had issue.*
See the Clarence Volume, pp. 372–374, Nos. 12824–12888.

5f. *Adeliza Maria Howard*, d. 9 Sept. 1833; m. *as 2nd wife*, 20 Ap. 1830, *Henry William Petre of Dunkenhalgh*, b. 23 Ap. 1791; d. 26 Nov. 1852; *and had issue.*
See the Clarence Volume, p. 376, Nos. 12955–12960.

2e. *Catherine Howard*, b. 6 Aug. 1755; d.s.p. 11 Jan. 1836; m. 18 Mar. 1776, John Gartside of Crumpsall, co. Lancaster.

3e. *Maria Howard*, d. 11 June 1837; m. 1st, 6 Aug. 1786, *the Hon. George William Petre*, b. 10 Jan. 1766; d. 22 Oct. 1797; 2ndly (? as 2nd wife), 1802, Col. Henry Espinasse.
See the Clarence Volume, pp. 376–377, Nos. 12944–12969.

4d. *Mary Witham*, d. (–); m. *Gustavus de Strom*.

2c. *Thomas Witham of Durham, M.D.*, d. 28 Jan. 1786; m. 19 May 1748, *Elizabeth, da. of George Meynell of Aldborough*, d. 20 Sept. 1806; *and had issue* 1d.

1d. *William Witham*, b. 27 Oct. 1754; d. 22 Mar. 1825; m. 27 Nov. 1783, Dorothy, da. of Thomas Langdale, d. 13 Ap. 1838; *and had issue* 1e to 3e.

[Nos. 49774 to 49891.]

The Plantagenet Roll

1*e*. *William Witham of Gray's Inn and Eaton Square, London,* d. 13 Dec. 1848; m. 23 *July* 1812, *Frances Elizabeth, da. of James Brooks of Fair Mile House, co. Oxon,* d. 31 *Jan.* 1861; *and had issue* 1*f to* 6*f*.

    1*f*. *Robert Shawe James Witham, afterwards Maxwell-Witham, J.P., D.L.,* b. 4 *Sept.* 1819; d. 21 *May* 1893; m. 8 *Nov.* 1843 (*or* 17 *Ap.* 1844), *Dorothy Mary, da. and h. of James Maxwell of Kirkconnell (Kirkconnell House, New Abbey, Kirkcudbright); and had issue* 1*g to* 4*g*.

    1*g*. James Kirkconnell Maxwell-Witham, J.P., D.L., Col. *late* 3rd Batt. King's Own Scottish Borderers, *b*. 4 Oct. 1848.

    2*g*. Robert Bernard Maxwell-Witham, *b*. 8 Aug. 1856.

    3*g*. Frances Mary Maxwell-Witham.

    4*g*. Dorothy Maud Maxwell-Witham.

    2*f*. *James Witham,* b. 27 *Dec.* 1820; d. (–); m. 2*ndly, Oct.* 1860, *Harriet Selina, da. of Richard Wells; and had issue* 1*g to* 7*g*.

    1*g*. James Wells Witham, *b*. 4 Jan. 1863.

    2*g*. William Witham, *b*. 23 Dec. 1863.

    3*g*. Ernest Witham, *b*. 15 Mar. 1865.

    4*g*. Charles Richard Witham, *b*. 18 Sept. 1867.

    5*g*. Henry Witham, *b*. 1 May 1870.

    6*g*. Frances Elizabeth Witham.

    7*g*. Agnes Monica Witham.

    3*f*. Mary Theresa Witham, *m*. James Roderick O'Flanagan of Avondhu Grange, Fermoy, co. Cork; and has issue (3 sons).

    4*f*. Winifred Monica Witham.

    5*f*. Frances Agnes Witham.

    6*f*. *Ellen Josephine Witham,* d. 18 *Mar.* 1889; m. 1864, *William Francis Eyre of Paris; and had issue* (2 *sons*).

    2*e*. *Sir Charles Witham, R.N.,* b. 15 *Aug.* 1791; d. 30 *Nov.* 1853; m. 18 *Nov.* 1829, *Jane, da. of John Hoy of Stoke-by-Nayland; and had issue* 1*f to* 4*f*.

    1*f*. *Thomas Maxwell Witham, Bar.-at-Law, M.T.,* b. 8 *Jan.* 1837.

    2*f*. *John Davey Witham,* b. 13 Dec. 1839; *m*. 1877, Harriet, da. of T. Dutton of Queensland.

    3*f*. *Philip Witham* (*Sutton Place, Guildford*), *b*. 4 Aug. 1842; *m*. 20 Aug. 1878, Louisa, da. of Marmaduke Charles Salvin of Burn Hall, J.P.; and has issue. See p. 280.

    4*f*. *Constantia Witham, m.* George Herbert, Bar.-at-Law; and has issue.

    3*e*. *Dorothy Witham,* d. 6 *Mar.* 1835; m. *as* 2*nd wife, James Maxwell of Kirkconnell,* d. 5 *Feb.* 1827; *and had issue* 1*f*.

    1*f*. *Dorothy Mary Maxwell of Kirkconnell* (*Kirkconnell House, New Abbey, Kirkcudbright*), *m*. 8 Nov. 1843, Robert Shawe James Witham, *afterwards* Maxwell, Witham, J.P., D.L., *d*. 21 May 1893; and had issue. See p. 560, Nos. 49892–49895.

    2*b*. *Elizabeth Witham,* d. (–); m. *Thomas Salkeld.*

    3*b*. *Grace Witham,* d. (? *unm.*).

    4*b*. *Dorothy Witham,* d. (? *unm.*).

    2*a*. *Rev. George Witham, D.D., Vicar Apostolic of the Northern District.*

    3*a*. *William Witham, aged* 11 *in* 1665; d. (? *unm.*).

    4*a*. *Rev. Christopher Witham,* d. *unm.*

    5*a*. *Rev. Robert Witham, President of the English College at Douai.*

    6*a*. *Marmaduke Witham, aged* 8 *in* 1665; d. (? s.p.); m. 1*st*, [——], *da. of T. Leyburne of Cunswick and Witherslack;* 2*ndly*, [——], *da. of Sir Thomas Tancred.*

    7*a*. *Lawrence Witham, aged* 6 *in* 1665; d. (? s.p.); m. *Margaret, da. of Sir Henry Swale,* 2*nd Bart.* [*E.*].   [Nos. 49892 to 49913.

8a. *Ann Witham*, bur. 3 *May* 1704; m. *George Palmes of Naburn, co. York*, b. 3 *Nov.* 1666; d. (–); *and had issue 1b.*

1b. *George Palmes of Naburn, co. York*, d. (–); *m. Frances, da. and co-h. of Robert Plumpton of Plumpton; and had issue 1c.*

1c. *John Palmes of Naburn*, d. 1783; m. 16 *Nov.* 1775, *Susannah, da. of Thomas Wharrie of Hull; and had issue 1d to 2d.*

1d. *George Palmes of Naburn, J.P., D.L.*, b. 18 *Oct.* 1776; d. *Mar.* 1851; m. 15 *Jan.* 1810, *Margaret Isabella, da. of William Lindsay of Oaklands, co. Lanark*, d. 8 *Ap.* 1869; *and had issue 1e to 8e.*

1e. *Rev. William Lindsay Palmes, M.A., of Naburn Hall, co. York, J.P., Vicar of Honnsea with Long Riston, and Rural Dean*, b. 29 *June* 1813; d. 1 *Ap.* 1888; m. 27 *June* 1849, *Marianne, da. of Amaziah Empson of Spellow Hill, Boroughbridge; and had issue 1f to 7f.*

1f. Rev. George Palmes, M.A. (Oxon.), of Naburn Hall, co. York, *late* Vicar of Hillfarrance, Taunton, and late Rector of Elston, Newark (*Naburn Hall, near York; United University*), b. 17 Mar. 1851; m. 1882, Eva Blanche, da. of Henry Dalbiac Harrison of Holbrook Park, Sussex; and has issue 1g to 7g.

1g. George Bryan Palmes, b. 29 July 1884.

2g. William Tevery Palmes, b. 17 Aug. 1888.

3g. Guy Nicholas Palmes, b. 14 July 1894.

4g. Stephen Saltmarshe Palmes, b. 4 Sept. 1895.

5g. Maud Cecil Palmes, m. 14 June 1904, Lieut. E. C. Poret, West Yorks Regt.

6g. Blanche Marjorie Palmes.

7g. Mary Evelyn Palmes.

2f. Rev. Arthur Lindsay Palmes, Rector of Saltwood and Preb. of Endellion (*Saltwood Rectory, Hythe*), b. 18 Ap. 1853; m. 22 June 1881, Alice, da. of M. M. Hogg of Berry Head; and has issue 1g to 2g.

1g. John Palmes.

2g. James Palmes, b. 22 Jan. 1900.

3f. Guy St. Maur Palmes, *late* 14th Hussars (*Lingcroft, York*), b. 13 Ap. 1854; m. 15 July 1879, Georgina Rosabelle, da. and co-h. of Edward Lloyd of Lingcroft; and has issue 1g to 5g.

1g. Geoffrey St. Maur Palmes, b. 26 Dec. 1881.

2g. Edward William Eustace Palmes, Lieut. 10th Royal Hussars, b. 23 Aug. 1884.

3g. Bryan Wilfrid Palmes, b. 3 June 1891.

4g. Cecil Muriel Palmes.

5g. Joan Mary Georgina Palmes.

4f. Bryan William Palmes of Queensland, b. 31 Mar. 1858; m. Ellen, da. of [——] Lawless; and has issue.

5f. *John Edmund Palmes*, b. 1861; d. (*in Australia*) 6 *Ap.* 1894.

6f. Ellen Isabella Palmes.

7f. Marian Edith Palmes.

2e. *John Philip Palmes, Capt. R.N.*, d. 21 *Feb.* 1869; m. 12 *July* 1849, *Mary, da. of* [——] *Head of Halifax, Nova Scotia; and had issue 1f to 3f.*

1f. Francis Jerome Palmes, b. 13 Jan. 1855; m. Mary Theresa, da. of H. Broadbent.

2f. Philip Palmes, Major North Lancashire Regt., b. 7 Oct. 1856; m. Hylda, da. of [——] Gervoise.

3f. Maud Sophia Palmes.

3e. *Manfred Leslie Palmes*, d. (*at Trinidad*) 1839.

4e. *Ven. Rev. James Palmes, D.D., M.A., Rector of Burton Agnes, co. York, and Archdeacon of the East Riding*, b. 11 *Aug.* 1825; d. 3 *June* 1898; m. 1849,

[Nos. 49914 to 49936.

The Plantagenet Roll

Annie Augusta, da. of George Champney of Fangfoss Hall and Middlethorpe Manor, York; and had issue 1f to 10f.

1f. Bryan Palmes, Major *late* Somerset L.I., *b.* 2 July 1851.

2f. Percy Edward Palmes, *b.* 29 Sept. 1853.

3f. George Champney Palmes, Major South Wales Borderers, *b.* 9 Feb. 1857; *m.*

4f. Gerald Lindsay Palmes, Capt. Royal Lancashire Regt., *b.* 2 Mar. 1864; m. 15 June 1897, Inez Charlotte, da. of Albin Saunders, 9th Lancers.

5f. Louisa Dundas Palmes, *m.* 1881, Arthur Walker (*Rose Bank House, Oban*); and has issue (3 sons).

6f. Edith Mary Evelyn Palmes, *m.* 1879, Reginald Pearce Browne.

7f. Alice Elizabeth Palmes.

8f. Mary Palmes, *m.* 1893, the Rev. Herbert E. Worthington, Rector of Netherscale (*Netherscale Rectory, Ashby-de-la-Zouch*).

9f. Helen Palmes, *m.* 1903, Capt. Bertram Waterfield (*Kohat, India*).

10f. Constance Palmes, *m.* 1904, Horace Twiss.

5e. Isabella Palmes, *m.* 1834, James Bruce Jardine of Hallside, co. Lanark; and has issue.

6e. Georgiana Palmes (*Newton Bushey, Waterford*), *m.* John Brotherton of Esher, *d.* 1 Sept. 1878; and has issue.

See the Clarence Volume, p. 305, Nos. 8495–8506.

7e. Eliza Palmes, *m.* Capt. Willoughby Carter, 7th Fusiliers; and has issue.

8e. Frances Edith Palmes, *m.* the Rev. George Carpenter of Chadlington; and has issue.

2d. Elizabeth Palmes, b. c. 1778; *d.* 4 *Ap.* 1867; *m.* 29 *Ap.* 1801, *Samuel Walker of Masborough, near Rotherham, N.P.,* b. 4 *Sept.* 1779; *d.* 30 *Jan.* 1851; *and had issue 1e to 8e.*[1]

1e. Samuel Walker of Hemmingham Hall, co. Warwick, Lieut.-Col. in the Army, b. 13 *Ap.* 1803; *d.* (–); *m.* 12 *Jan.* 1833, *Arabella, da. of James Braddell of New Ross; and had issue 1f to 4f.*

1f. Edward James Walker, R.A., *b.* 4 Mar. 1837.

2f. Arabella Elizabeth Mary Walker, *b.* 3 Ap. 1842; *m.* 5 July 1860, the Rev. Lewis Stanhope Kenny, Rector of Kirby Knowle, co. York, *b.* 3 Jan. 1827; *d.* (–); and has issue.

3f. Emma Louise Walker.

4f. [——] Walker.

2e. John Walker of Mount St. John, Thirsk, b. 12 *Jan.* 1812; *d.* (–); *m.* (*at Madeira*) 24 *Jan.* 1867, *Frances Emma, da. and co-h. of Major James Hobson Serjeantson.*

3e. Edmund Walker, b. 12 *Jan.* 1812; *d.* 17 *May* 1873; *m.* 8 *Feb.* 1866, *Charlotte Frances, da. of the Rev. C. Johnstone, Canon of York; and had issue 1f to 2f.*

1f. Frederick John Walker, *b.* 23 Dec. 1869; *m.*

2f. Arthur Edmund Walker, *b.* 27 Mar. 1871.

4e. Elizabeth Walker, b. 2 *May* 1802; *d.* (–); *m.* 24 *May* 1827, *Major Francis Holcombe, R.H.A.*

5e. Emma Walker, b. 29 *Mar.* 1808; *d.* (–); *m.* 2 *Aug.* 1838, *the Rev. Edward Serjeantson, Rector of Kirby Knowle, d.s.p.* 1857.[2]

6e. Mary Walker, b. 26 *Feb.* 1813; *d.* (–); *m.* 15 *Nov.* 1866, *Richard Rowed of Dinan.*

7e. Agnes Walker, *unm.* in 1873.

8e. Harriet Emily Walker, *unm.* in 1873.　　　　　[Nos. 49937 to 49970.

---

[1] Foster's " Yorkshire Pedigrees."
[2] Burke's " Landed Gentry," 1900.

# of The Blood Royal

502. Descendants of OLIVIA WYVILL (see Table LII.), *m.* GEORGE MENNELL or MEYNELL of Aldborough, co. York, *b.* 1630; *d.* (–); and had issue 1*a* to 4*a*.

1*a*. *George Meynell of Aldborough, b. 1659; d. (–); m. Ellen, da. of* [——] *Massey of Lancaster; and had issue 1b to 2b.*

1*b*. *George Meynell of Aldborough and Dalton, d. (–); m. Elizabeth, da. and h. of George Cockson of Cold Pighill, co. Durham; and had issue 1c to 3c.*

1*c*. *Elizabeth Meynell, eldest da. and co-h., b. c. 1725; d. 20 Sept. 1806; m. 19 May 1748, Thomas Witham of Durham, M.D., d. 28 Jan. 1786; and had issue.*
See p. 560, Nos. 49892–49913.

2*c*. *Anne Clementina Meynell, 2nd da. and co-h., d. (–); m. Simon Scrope of Danby, de jure 18th Earl of Wilts [E.], d. 3 Jan. 1788; and had issue 1d.*

1*d*. *Simon Thomas Scrope of Danby, de jure 19th Earl of Wilts [E.], b. 29 Dec. 1858; d. 14 Aug. 1838; m. 3 Mar. 1789, Catherine Dorothy, da. of Edward Meynell of Kilvington, d. 19 Ap. 1839; and had issue.*
See p. 337, Nos. 24547–24569.

3*c*. *Frances Olive Meynell, 3rd da. and co-h., d. 4 Sept. 1795; m. 21 Dec. 1748, Stephen Walter Tempest of Broughton, d. 9 Sept. 1784; and had issue.*
See the Clarence Volume, pp. 320–327, Nos. 9267–9505.

2*b*. *Olive Meynell, d. (? unm.).*

2*a*. *Elizabeth Meynell,*
3*a*. *Mary Meynell,* } *d. (? unm.).*
4*a*. *Olive Meynell,*   [Nos. 49971 to 50254.

503. Descendants of ELIZABETH WYVILL (see Table LII.), *m.* Sir WILLIAM DALTON of Hauxwell, *b. c.* 1629; *d.* 23 Mar. 1675; and had issue 1*a* to 5*a*.

1*a*. *Rev. Darcy Dalton, Rector of Aston, Preb. of York (3rd son), b. 1670; d. 27 Mar. 1734; m. 2ndly, Jane, da. of* [——], *d. 5 Mar. 1719; and had issue 1b to 4b.*

1*b*. *Francis Dalton, one of the six Clerks in Chancery, b. c. 1720; d. 21 Nov. 1792; m. Mary, da. of John Tasker of Wimbledon, Att.-at-Law; and had issue 1c.*

1*c*. *Mary Dalton, da. and h., living 1792; m. 3 Ap. 1779, Henry Gale of Scruton and of Hauxwell, p.u., b. 1744; d. 1821; and had issue 1d.*

1*d*. *Harriet Gale of Scruton, eldest da. and h., d. 15 Dec. 1839; m. 1816, Lieut.-Col. Foster Lechmere Coore of Firby, b. 1780; d. 1837; and had issue 1e to 4e.*

1*e*. *Henry Coore of Scruton Hall, J.P., D.L., b. 18 Jan. 1820; d. 4 May 1890; m. 3 July 1841, Augusta Caroline, da. of Mark Milbank of Thorpe Perrow, by his wife Lady Augusta, née Vane, d. Aug. 1889; and had issue 1f to 4f.*

1*f*. *Henry Mark Coore, afterwards (1890) Gale of Scruton Hall, J.P., D.L., b. 6 June 1842; d. 24 Sept. 1890; m. 21 Aug. 1872, the Hon. Mary Emily, da. of Edward (Strutt), 1st Baron Belper [U.K.] (who re-m. 8 Ap. 1893, Henry Handford, M.D., F.R.C.P.); and had issue 1g to 7g.*

1*g*. Alice Mary Gale,	
2*g*. Sybil Augusta Gale,	
3*g*. Dorothy Gale,	*(Hardwicke House, Cavendish Crescent North,*
4*g*. Hilda Frances Gale,	*The Park, Nottingham; Elm Field,*
5*g*. Winifred Emily Gale,	*Southwell).*
6*g*. Margaret Gale,	
7*g*. Gertrude Veronica Gale,	[Nos. 50255 to 50261.

The Plantagenet Roll

2*f*. Rev. Alfred Thomas Coore, M.A. (Camb.) (*Scruton Hall, Bedale*), *b*. 3 Sept. 1845; *m*. 4 July 1871, Louisa, da. of the Rev. Charles Gray of Godmanchester; and has issue 1*g* to 6*g*.

1*g*. Alban Coore, *b*. 21 May 1872.

2*g*. Alfred Coore, *b*. 11 May 1873.

3*g*. Basil Coore, *b*. 30 June 1877.

4*g*. Cyril Coore, *b*. 4 Mar. 1881.

5*g*. Edith Coore, } *b*. (twins) 20 Feb. 1883.
6*g*. Gladys Coore, }

3*f*. George Barnard Milbank Coore (*Board of Education, Whitehall*), *b*. 28 Dec. 1865; *m*. 1891, Augusta, da. of Gen. von Schmeling; and has issue 1*g* to 4*g*.

1*g*. Edmund Burchardt Coore, *b*. 1894.

2*g*. Constance Araminta Coore.

3*g*. Monica Coore.

4*g*. Gertrude Coore.

4*f*. Caroline Augusta Coore (2 *Cavendish Place, Bath*), *m*. as 3rd wife, 1896 Capt. Robert Peel Floyd, *d*. (*s.p*. by her) 3 May 1899.

2*e*. *Mary Coore, d*. (–); *m*. *Col. Hamlet Coote Wade.*

3*e*. *Augusta Coore, d*. (–); *m*. *Major Frederick Gordon Christie.*

4*e*. *Charlotte Coore, d*. (–); *m*. *Capt. Samuel Stovin Hood Inglefield.*

2*b*. *Barbara Dalton*, b. 1709; d. (–); m. *before* 28 *June* 1739, *Charles Tancred of Arden.*

3*b*. *Mary Dalton, m. after* 28 *June* 1739, *the Rev. Gilbert Knowler, D.D., and was living a widow in* 1788 *with* 4 *das., one of whom was m. to Henry Kitchinman.*[1]

4*b*. *Elizabeth Dalton, b. c.* 1704; *d.* 2 *Nov.* 1792; *m. the Rev. Samuel Drake, D.D., Rector of Treeton and Holme-on-Spaldingmoor, and was living a widow, aged* 84, *in* 1788, *with* 1 *son and* 2 *das.*[1]

2*a*. *Isabella Dalton, b.* 1657 (*being aged* 8 *in* 1665); *d.* 25 *Feb.* 1684; m. *Roger Croft of East Appleton, co. York; and had issue.*

3*a*. *Dorothy Dalton, bur.* 17 *Mar.* 1707; *m. as 2nd wife,* 1 *Mar.* 1690, *the Rev. William Stainforth, D.D., Canon Residentiary of York.*

4*a*. *Elizabeth Dalton.*

5*a*. *Ursula Dalton, m. Sir Barrington Bourchier of Beningbrough, co. York; and had issue.* [Nos. 50262 to 50274.

504. Descendants of ANNE WYVILL (see Table LII.), *b. c.* 1633; *d.* 28 Nov. 1675; *m.* (lic. 16 Mar.) 1665, THOMAS DALTON of York and Bedale, *d. c.* 1710 (admon. 10 July 1710); and had issue 1*a* to 2*a*.

1*a*. *John Dalton of Bedale, b.* 25 *Nov.* 1675; *bur.* 29 *Feb.* 1701; *m. June* 1698, *Jane, da. of* [——] *Thornton; and had issue* 1*b*.

1*b*. *James Dalton, Capt.* 6*th Regt.,* bapt. 22 *May* 1699; *d.* (*on service in the West Indies*) 1742; *m. Elizabeth, da. of William Smith of Penrith* (*see below*), *d.* 11 *July* 1769; *and had issue* 1*c*.

1*c*. *John Dalton, Capt. H.E.I.C.S., Governor of Trichinopoly* 1752–1774, *d. July* 1811; *m.* 1756, *Isabella, da. and in her issue* (1805) *h. of Sir John Wray of Glentworth,* 12*th Bart.* [E.], *d.* 29 *May* 1780; *and had issue.*

See the Clarence Volume, pp. 574–581, Nos. 24241–24443.
[Nos. 50275 to 50477.

---

[1] Foster's " Yorkshire Pedigrees."

2a. Dorothy Dalton, d. (–); m. 16 *Ap.* 1696, *William Smith of Penrith ; and had issue 1b.*

1b. Elizabeth Smith, d. 11 *July* 1769 ; m. *Capt. James Dalton,* d. 1742 ; *and had issue.*

See p. 564, Nos. 50275–50477.   [Nos. 50478 to 50680.

505. Descendants, if any, of ELIZABETH WYVILL, wife of [——] BELLINGHAM of co. Linc., of OLIVE WYVILL, wife of CUTHBERT COLLINGWOOD of Eslington, co. Northumberland; and of MARY WYVILL, *bapt.* 1 Ap. 1599, wife 1st of JOHN WYLDE of Hunton, co. York; and 2ndly, of ANTHONY BULMER (see Table LII.).

506. Descendants, if any surviving, of KATHERINE WYVILL (see Table LII.), *m.* JOHN WHARTON of Kirkby Thore, co. Westmorland, *d.* Nov. 1648 ; and had issue 1*a* to 10*a*.[1]

1a. John Wharton of Kirkby Thore, b. *c.* 1627 *(aged 37, 22 Mar.* 1664*)*; d. (–) ; m. *Anne, da. of Richard Crakenthorpe of Little Strickland ; and had issue (in* 1664*)* 1b *to* 3b.

1b. Bridget Wharton, b. *c.* 1650 *(being aged* 13, 22 *Mar.* 1664*).*

2b. Jane Wharton.

3b. Ann Wharton.

2a. Stephen Wharton.

3a. Henry Wharton.

4a. Charles Wharton, d. *unm.*

5a. Philip Wharton.

6a. Thomas Wharton.

7a. Mary Wharton, m. *George Emerson of Wardell, co. Durham.*

8a. Isabella Wharton, d. *unm.*

9a. Jane Wharton.

10a. Petronilla Wharton, d. *unm.*

507. Descendants, if any, of PHILIPPA WYVILL (see Table LII. wife of RICHARD SALE of Hopcare, co. Lancaster.

508. Descendants, if any surviving, of JOHN CONSTABLE of Kitesby (Kexby) (see Table XLVII.), *m.* DOROTHY, da. and h. of St. Robert OUGHTRED ; and had issue 1*a* to 3*a*.[2]

1a. Thomas Constable of Kitesby, bur. 13 *Jan.* 1604.

2a. Marmaduke Constable of Kitesby, m. *Audrey, da. of Robert Hungate of Saxton ; and had issue* 1b *to* 5b.

1b. Marmaduke Constable of Kitesby, living 1612 ; m. 2 *Aug.* 1599, *Catherine, da. of Anthony Teale of Kitesby,* bur. 5 *Mar.* 1624 ; *and had issue* 1c *to* 8c.

---

[1] " Pedigrees recorded at the Herald's Visitations [1615 and 1664] of Cumberland and Westmorland," edited by Joseph Foster, M.A.

[2] Glover's "Visitation of Yorkshire," edited by Joseph Foster, M.A., p. 507.

1c. *Marmaduke Constable of Kitesby*, b. 1600; m. 1st, *Dorothy, da. of* [——];
2ndly, *Matilda, da. of Everingham Cressy of Birkin ; and had issue* 1d *to* 7d.

1d.¹ *William Constable*, b. 1611 ; d. 1611.

2d.² *William Constable*, bapt. 11 *Oct.* 1630.

3d. *Everingham Constable of Leeds*, d. 6 *Jan.* 1691.

4d. *Jane Constable*.

5d. *Dorothy Constable*.

6d. *Grace Constable*.

7d. *Mary Constable*, b. 1631 ; d. 1633.

2c. *John Constable*, m. ; *and had issue* 1d.

1d. *John Constable*, bapt. 27 *Aug.* 1637.

3c. *Philip Constable*, bur. 4 *Oct.* 1617.

4c. *Christian Constable*.

5c. *Anthony Constable*.

6c. *Faith Constable*.

7c. *Catherine Constable*.

8c. *Barbara Constable*, m. 19 *Feb.* 1622, *Tristram Olbye*.

2b. *Ralph Constable*.

3b. *Francis Constable*.

4b. *John Constable of Kitesby*, bur. 6 *May* 1637.

5b. *Catherine Constable*, m. 6 *Ap.* 1604, *Anthony Teale*, bur. *May* 1621.

3a. *Anne Constable*.

509. Descendants of PHILIP SALTMARSHE of Saltmarshe (see Table LIII.), *b.* 1753; *d.* 19 Ap. 1791; *m.* 10 May 1779, ELIZA-BETH, da. of Christopher RAWSON of Stony Royd, *d.* 1834 ; and had issue 1*a* to 2*a*.

1a. *Philip Saltmarshe of Saltmarshe, J.P., D.L.,* b. 15 *Mar.* 1780; d. 28 *Nov.* 1846; m. 10 *May* 1824, *Harriet, da. of Robert Denison of Kilnwick Percy, co. York,* d. 1863 ; *and had issue* 1b *to* 4b.

1b. Philip Saltmarshe of Saltmarshe, J.P., D.L., Lieut. Col. East Yorkshire R.V., *late* 8th Hussars (*Saltmarshe, near Howden, York*), b. 9 *Mar.* 1825 ; *m.* 1st, 12 May 1852, Blanche, da. of Robert Denison of Waplington Manor, *d.* 21 Ap. 1880 ; 2ndly, 4 Ap. 1889, Harriet, da. of Capt. George Hotham, R.E., *d.* July 1897 ; and has issue 1c to 5c.

1c. Philip Saltmarshe, J.P., Col. *late* R.A. (*Daresbury, York*), b. 9 June 1853 ; *m.* 5 Sept. 1883, Ethel Murray, da. of C. Murray Adamson of North Jesmond ; and has issue 1d to 4d.

1d. Philip Saltmarshe, b. 18 Ap. 1894.

2d. Blanche Violet Saltmarshe, b. 2 July 1884.

3d. Ivy Oswald Saltmarshe, b. 15 June 1885.

4d. Myrtle Elnard Saltmarshe, b. 22 Jan. 1891.

2c. Ernest Saltmarshe, b. 22 Nov. 1859.

3c. Lionel Saltmarshe, b. 19 Ap. 1863.

4c. Harold Saltmarshe, b. 28 Sept. 1866 ; *m.* (at Brisbane) 1901, Lilian, da. of E. Drury, Manager of the Bank of Queensland ; and has issue 1d.

1d. Evelyn Saltmarshe.

5c. Humphrey Arthur Saltmarshe, b. 16 Sept. 1868.

2b. Arthur Saltmarshe, Lieut.-Col. 70th Regt., b. 8 Sept. 1832.

[Nos. 50681 to 50692.

3*b*. *Henrietta Maria Saltmarshe*, d. 25 *Oct*. 1898; m. 4 *July* 1850, *Rev. the Hon. Frank Sugden*, b. 17 *May* 1817; d. 17 *Jan*. 1886; *and had issue* 1*c to* 3*c*.

1*c*. Frank Sugden (*Oaklands, Kingsdown, Sevenoaks*), b. 28 Oct. 1852; *m.* 18 Dec. 1894, Edyth Mary, da. of Gen. Sir Arthur Becher, K.C.B., d. 27 Jan. 1904.

2*c*. Rev. Henry Richard Sugden, M.A. (*Benhall Vicarage, Saxmundham*), b. 13 July 1862; *m.* 9 May 1899, Honoria Lawrence, da. of William Hulbert Wathen of Westerham.

3*c*. Ethel Sugden (16 *Calverley Park, Tunbridge Wells*).

4*b*. Catherine Elizabeth Saltmarshe, *m.* as 2nd wife, 1859, Henry Allfrey of Hemingford House, Stratford-on-Avon, d. 1887; and has issue 1*c* to 2*c*.

1*c*. Alice Allfrey, *m.* Charles Busby of Chesterfield, *s.p.*

2*c*. Mabel Allfrey.

2*a*. *Christopher Saltmarshe of London, Merchant*, d. 16 *Oct*. 1862; m. 1*st*, 3 *June* 1817, *Emma, da. of John Rawson of Stony Royd*, d. 15 *July* 1834; *and had issue* 1*b* to 3*b*.

1*b*. Emma Saltmarshe, *m.* Feb. 1858, Henry Dalbiac Harrison (*The Brow, Malton, Yorks*); and has issue.

See the Clarence Volume, p. 578, Nos. 24360–24369.

2*b*. Delia Saltmarshe, *m.* Dec. 1851, Robert Pattison of Edinburgh, *s.p.*

3*b*. Catherine Elizabeth Saltmarshe, *m.* Dec. 1852, Gabriel Lang; and has issue 1*c* to 2*c*.

1*c*. Alexander Dennistoun Lang.

2*c*. Mary Louisa Lang. [Nos. 50693 to 50713.

510. Descendants of WILLIAM SALTMARSHE of York and Newby Wiske (see Table LIII.), *bapt*. 20 Mar. 1707; *d*. (at Nancy, Lorraine); *m*. Lady ANNE, da. of Robert (PLUNKETT), 6th Earl of Fingall [I.], living 1794; and had issue (9 sons, of whom 8 died in infancy, and 7 das.) 1*a* to 8*a*.

1*a*. *Philip Saltmarshe of York and Newby Wiske*, b. 6 *Jan*. 1754; d.s.p.l. 29 *Mar*. 1797.

2*a*. *Anne Catherine Saltmarshe*, m. (*at Nancy*) [——] *Gartaldy; and had issue* (1 son and 2 das.).

3*a*. *Henrietta Maria Saltmarshe*.

4*a*. *Mary Anne Saltmarshe*.

5*a*. *Anastasia Saltmarshe*.

6*a*. *Elizabeth Saltmarshe*.

7*a*. *Theresa Saltmarshe*.

8*a*. *Catherine Saltmarshe, youngest da.*, b. 1766; bur. 4 *Nov*. 1777.

511. Other Descendants, if any, of the SALTMARSHES (see Table LIII.).

512. Descendants, if any, of WILLIAM BABTHORPE; of his brothers FRANCIS, JOHN, and ALBERT; and his uncles ROBERT, RICHARD, and THOMAS BABTHORPE (see Table LIV.).

The Plantagenet Roll

513. Descendants of THOMAS YORKE of Halton Place, co. Yorks, Barrister-at-Law (see Table LIV.), *b.* 5 June 1738; *d.* 3 July 1811; *m.* 8 Feb. 1774, JANE, da. of Joseph REAY of Killingworth, Northumberland, *b.* 6 May 1749; *d.* 17 Ap. 1840; and had issue 1*a* to 3*a*.

1*a*. *John Yorke of Halton Place and Bewerley, J.P., D.L., High Sheriff co. York* 1818, b. 20 Feb. 1776; d. 5 Feb. 1857; m. 9 Aug. 1821, Mary, da. of Ichabod *Wright of Maperley, d. 24 June 1883; and had issue 1b to 4b.*

1*b*. *John Yorke of Bewerley, &c., J.P., D.L.,* b. 28 Mar. 1827; d.s.p. 3 Oct. 1883.

2*b*. Thomas Edward Yorke, J.P., High Sheriff co. York 1889 (*Bewerley Hall, Pateley Bridge, Yorks ; Halton Place, Hellifield-in-Craven, Yorks*), b. 4 Aug. 1832; m. 1st, 17 Feb. 1863, Augusta Margaret, da. of Rev. the Hon. John Baillie, d. 13 Ap. 1879; 2ndly, 20 Oct. 1883, Fanny, da. of Sir John Walsham of Knill Court, 1st Bart. [U.K.]; and has issue 1c to 7c.

1*c*. John Cecil Yorke, J.P., Capt. Yorkshire Militia Art., b. 10 Nov. 1867.

2*c*. Henry Reay Yorke, Lieut. Royal Munster Fusiliers, b. 26 Jan. 1875.

3*c*. Mary Augusta Yorke.

4*c*. Helen Margaret Yorke, *m.* 23 Ap. 1896, Arthur Bailey (*Wramplingham Hall, Wymondham, Norfolk*); and has issue.

5*c*. Louisa Caroline Yorke, *m.* 7 Feb. 1900, the Rev. Arthur Herbert Watson, Vicar of Long Preston (*Long Preston Vicarage, Leeds*); and has issue 1*d* to 3*d*.

1*d*. Edward Shepley Watson, b. 1901.

2*d*. Arthur Oliver Watson, b. 1902.

3*d*. Martin Yorke Watson, b. 1905.

6*c*. Katherine Elizabeth Yorke.

7*c*. Ethel Lilian Yorke.

3*b*. Frances Mary Yorke.

4*b*. *Caroline Yorke, d.* 6 *Dec.* 1883; *m. as 2nd wife, 2 Jan.* 1861, *the Rev. Richard St. John Tyrwhitt, Vicar of St. Mary Magdalen, Oxford, d.* 6 *Dec.* 1895; *and had issue.*

See the Clarence Volume, p. 191, Nos. 3239–3248.

2*a*. *Rev. Thomas Henry Yorke, Vicar of Bishop Middleham,* b. 29 *Jan.* 1785; d. (? s.p.) *Feb.* 1868; m. 1 *July* 1823, *Maria, da. of Major-Gen. the Hon. Mark Napier,* d. 1 Feb. 1868.

3*a*. *Edmund Yorke, M.A.,* b. 8 Feb. 1787; d. 1871.   [Nos. 50714 to 50735.

514. Descendants of CATHERINE YORKE (see Table LIV.), *bapt.* 6 Sept. 165–; *d.* 29 Nov. 1723; *m.* as 1st wife, 28 Jan. 1703, Sir JAMES CLAVERING, 6th Bart. [E.], *bapt.* 19 Aug. 1680; *d.* 12 May 1748; and had issue 1*a* to 3*a*.

1*a*. *Sir Thomas Clavering, 7th Bart. [E.], LL.D.,* b. 19 *June* 1719; d.s.p. 14 Oct. 1794.

2*a*. *George Clavering of Greencroft,* b. 1720; d. 23 *May* 1794; m. 2*ndly, Anna Maria, widow of Sir John Pole, 5th Bart. [E.], da. of the Rev. [——] Palmer of Comb Raleigh ; and had issue 1b.*

1*b*. *Sir Thomas John Clavering, 8th Bart. [E.],* b. 6 *Ap.* 1771; d. 1853; m. 21 *Aug.* 1791, *Clara, da. of John (de Callais de la Bernadine), Count de la Sable of Anjou [F.], d. (abroad)* 1854; *and had issue 1c to 3c.*

1*c*. *Sir William Aloysius Clavering, 9th Bart. [E.],* b. 21 *Jan.* 1800; d. unm. 8 Oct. 1872.

2c. *Clara Anne Martha Clavering*, d. 28 *July* 1879; m: 8 *Feb.* 1826, *General the Baron de Knyffe of Brussels.*

3c. *Agatha Catherine Clavering*, m. 12 *Feb.* 1821, [——], *Baron de Montfaucon of Avignon.*

3a. *Sir John James Clavering, K.B., Lieut.-Gen. in the Army, Second in the Council and Commander-in-Chief in Bengal*, d. (*in Calcutta*) 30 *Aug.* 1777 ; m. 1*st*, 9 *Nov.* 1756, *Lady Diana, da. of John (West), 1st Earl de la Warr* [*G.B.*], d. *Mar.* 1766 ; *and had issue* 1b *to* 4b.

1b. *Henry Mordaunt Clavering, Brig.-Gen. in the Army*, m. *Lady Augusta, da. of John (Campbell), 5th Duke of Argyll* [*S.*], b. 31 *Mar.* 1760 ; d. 22 *June* 1831 ; *and had issue* 1c *to* 2c.

1c. *Rawdon Forbes Clavering, Lieut. R.E.*, d. 1831 ; m. 11 *July* 1822, *Jean, da. of Sir Archibald Dunbar of Northfield, 5th Bart.* [*S.*], d. *Feb.* 1825 ; *and had issue* 1d.

1d. *Sir Henry Augustus Clavering, 10th and last Bart.* [*E.*], *Capt. R.N.*, b. 30 *Aug.* 1824 ; d. 9 *Nov.* 1893 ; m. 12 *Jan.* 1853, *Christina, da. of Andrew Alexander, LL.D.*, d. 17 *Nov.* 1898 ; *and had issue* 1e *to* 3e.

1e. Augusta Maria Valentine Clavering.

2e. *Ivy Valerie Clavering*, d. 29 *June* 1898 ; m. 5 *July* 1876, *Henry Alexander Campbell, J.P., Capt. Royal E. Kent. Yeo. Cav., formerly R.H.A.* (*Lynford Hall, Mundford, Norfolk*) ; *and had issue* 1f *to* 6f.

1f. Rawdon Clavering Campbell, Lieut. 1st Batt. Highland L.I., b. 13 Ap. 1877.

2f. Claude Henry Campbell, Lieut. Queen's Own Cameron Highlanders, b. 4 Dec. 1878.

3f. Gerald Victor Campbell, b. 29 Ap. 1884.

4f. Eric William Campbell, b. 8 Ap. 1886.

5f. Harold George Campbell, b. 6 Ap. 1888.

6f. Ivy Geraldine Campbell.

3e. *Geraldine Bertrade Clavering*, d. (? *unm.*).

2c. *Charlotte Catherine Clavering*, m. 27 *Dec.* 1817, *Miles Fletcher.*

2b. *Maria Margaret Clavering*, d. 29 *Dec.* 1821 ; m. 13 *Ap.* 1784, *Francis (Napier), 8th Lord Napier* [*S.*], b. 23 *Feb.* 1758 ; d. 1 *Aug.* 1823 ; *and had issue* 1c *to* 5c.

1c. *William John (Napier), 9th Lord Napier* [*S.*], b. 13 *Oct.* 1786 ; d. 11 *Oct.* 1834 ; m. 28 *Mar.* 1816, *Elizabeth, da. of the Hon. Andrew James Cochrane Johnstone*, d. 6 *June* 1883 ; *and had issue* 1d *to* 5d.

1d. *Francis (Napier), 10th Lord Napier* [*S.*], *1st Baron Ettrick* [*U.K.*], *K.T., P.C., Acting Viceroy of India* 1872, *&c. &c.*, b. 15 *Sept.* 1819 ; d. 19 *Dec.* 1898 ; m. 2 *Sept.* 1845, *Anne Jane Charlotte* (*Ettrick Cottage, Farnborough*), *C.I., da. of Robert Manners Lockwood of Dan-y-Greig ; and had issue* 1e *to* 3e.

1e. William John George (Napier), 11th Lord Napier [S.], 2nd Baron Ettrick [U.K.] (*Marlborough*), b. 22 Sept. 1846 ; m. 1st, 5 Jan. 1876, Harriet Blake Armstrong, da. of Edward Lamb of Wellington Lodge, co. Surrey, d. 5 June 1897 ; 2ndly, 19 July 1898, Grace, da. of James Cleland Burns ; and has issue 1f to 3f.

1f. Francis Edward Basil Napier, Master of Napier, b. 19 Nov. 1876 ; m. 12 Dec. 1899, the Hon. Clarice Jessie Evelyn, da. of James (Hamilton), 9th Lord Belhaven and Stenton [S.] ; and has issue 1g to 3g.

1g. William Francis Cyril James Napier, b. 9 Sept. 1900.

2g. (son), Napier, b. 25 Jan. 1904.

3g. Augusta Caroline Harriet Georgina Napier, b. 28 Nov. 1901.

2f. Hon. Frederick William Scott Napier, *late* Lieut. King's Own Scottish Borderers, b. 9 May 1878.

3f. Hon. Archibald Lennox Colquhoun William John George Napier, b. 11 Dec. 1899. [Nos. 50736 to 50749.]

569

The Plantagenet Roll

2e. Hon. John Scott Napier, C.M.G., Lieut.-Col. and Brevet-Col. and Inspector of Army Gymnasia, sometime Comdg. Gordon Highlanders (*Victoria House, Farnborough*), *b.* 13 Nov. 1848; *m.* 6 Ap. 1876, Isabella, widow of Major James Leith, V.C., da. of Thomas Shaw of Ditton, co. Lancaster; and has issue 1*f.*

1*f.* Lilias Dorothea Scott Napier, *b.* 13 Ap. 1884.

3e. Hon. Mark Francis Napier, Barrister I.T., sometime (1892–1895) M.P. (*Puttenden Manor, Lingfield, Surrey*), *b.* 21 Jan. 1852; *m.* 30 May 1878, Emily Jones, nat. da. of Thomas Heron (Jones), 7th Viscount Ranelagh [I.]; and has issue 1*f* to 2*f.*

1*f.* Claude Inverness Napier, *b.* 1 Ap. 1880.

2*f.* Philip Henry Napier, *b.* 16 Ap. 1884.

2*d. Hon. W,illiam Napier, Clerk of the Works, Hong Kong, b. 27 July 1821; d. 21 Jan. 1876; m. 3 May 1854, Louisa Mary (55 Cottesmore Gardens, Kensington, W.), da. of John Horatio Lloyd, Q.C.; and had issue 1e to 7e.*

1e. Francis Horatio Napier, M.B., F.R.C.S., *b.* 7 Feb. 1861; *m.* 26 Ap. 1893, Margaret Elizabeth, da. of Lieut.-Col. William Hope, V.C.; and has issue 1*f* to 2*f.*

1*f.* Archibald John Robert Napier, *b.* 19 Mar. 1894.

2*f.* Lawrence Scott Napier, *b.* 1896.

2e. Charles Frederick Napier, Barrister M.T. (*The Devonshire*), *b.* 24 Feb. 1862.

3e. William John Napier, Major R.A., *b.* 10 Nov. 1863; *m.* 4 Sept. 1889, Maude Denison Gooch, da. of Col. Edward Nicol William Holbrook, R.M.L.I.; and has issue 1*f.*

1*f.* Arthur Francis Scott Napier, *b.* 20 Sept. 1890.

4e. Archibald Scott Napier (*Mangalore, Madras*), *b.* 9 June 1865; *m.* 16 Mar. 1889, Katharine Edith, da. of Robert Liveing of 11 Manchester Square, W., M.D.; and has issue 1*f* to 2*f.*

1*f.* Charles Scott Napier, *b.* 3 Feb. 1899.

2*f.* Alexander Napier.

5e. Mary Eliza Napier.

6e. Beatrice Napier.

7e. Lilias Napier, *m.* 1st, 27 July 1881, William Rose Robinson, *d.* 1885; 2ndly, 18 Oct. 1893, Henry Alfred Constant Bonar, H.B.M.'s Consul at Yokohama (*Yokohama, Japan*).

3*d. Hon. Maria Margaret Napier, b. 18 Mar. 1817; d. 18 Ap. 1896; m. 19 Ap. 1837, John Gellibrand (Hubbard), 1st Baron Addington [U.K.], P.C., b. 21 Mar. 1805; d. 28 Aug. 1889; and had issue 1e to 7e.*

1e. Egerton (Hubbard), 2nd Baron Addington [U.K.] (*Addington Manor, Winslow, Bucks; 24 Prince's Gate, S.W.*), *b.* 19 Dec. 1842; *m.* 3 June 1880, Mary Adelaide, da. of Sir Wyndham Spencer Portal, 1st Bart. [U.K.]; and has issue 1*f* to 5*f.*

1*f.* Hon. John Gellibrand Hubbard, Lieut. 1st Bucks Rifle Vol., *b.* 7 June 1883.

2*f.* Hon. Raymond Egerton Hubbard, *b.* 11 Nov. 1884.

3*f.* Hon. Francis Spencer Hubbard, *b.* 1 July 1888.

4*f.* Hon. Winifred Mary Hubbard, *b.* 6 Sept. 1881.

5*f.* Hon. Ruth Mary Hubbard, *b.* 30 Oct. 1896.

2e. Hon. Cecil John Hubbard, J.P., *late* Major and Lieut.-Col. Grenadier Guards (3 *South Place, Knightsbridge, S.W.; Kingsbridge, Steeple Claydon, Bucks*), *b.* 6 Sept. 1846; *m.* 15 Ap. 1872, Helen Jane, da. of Arthur Macdonald-Ritchie; and has issue 1*f* to 4*f.*

1*f.* John Francis Hubbard, Capt. 5th Batt. Lancashire Fusiliers, *b.* 5 June 1880.

2*f.* Muriel Hubbard.

3*f.* Hilda Mary Hubbard.

4*f.* Irene Margaret Hubbard.　　　　　　　　　　　　　　　[Nos. 50750 to 50777.

# of The Blood Royal

3e. Hon. *Arthur Gellibrand Hubbard, Secretary for Native Officers, Cape Colony,* b. 6 *Feb.* 1848 ; d. 7 *Mar.* 1896 ; m. 29 *June* 1881, *Amy d'Esterre (Selwyn Lodge, Westgate-on-Sea), da. of Charles Hugh Huntley, C.M.G., Civil Comr. and Resident Mag. of Albany, Cape Colony ; and had issue 1f to 4f.*

1f. Gerald Napier Hubbard, Lieut. 1st Batt. Rifle Brig., b. 27 Aug. 1882.

2f. Kathleen d'Esterre Hubbard.

3f. Dorothy Isabel Hubbard.

4f. Noel Agnes Hubbard.

4e. Hon. Evelyn Hubbard, of Messrs. John Hubbard & Co. of London, and of Egerton Hubbard & Co. of St. Petersburg, a Commr. of Public Works Loans, and a Director of the Bank of England, &c. (*The Rookery, Down, Kent*), b. 18 Mar. 1852 ; m. 25 Aug. 1881, Eveline Maude, da. of Sir Wyndham Spencer Portal, 1st Bart. [U.K.] ; and has issue 1f to 3f.

1f. Harold Evelyn Hubbard, b. 12 Feb. 1883.

2f. Eric Wyndham Hubbard, b. 28 Oct. 1885.

3f. Bertram John Hubbard, b. 27 Aug. 1895.

5e. Hon. Alice Eliza Hubbard (24 *Prince's Gate, S.W.*), b. 2 Dec. 1841.

6e. Hon. Rose Ellen Hubbard (*Seven Gables, Winslow*), b. 18 Mar. 1851.

7e. Hon. Clemency Hubbard, b. 26 Aug. 1856 ; m. 4 Sept. 1888, Col. George Barker, C.B., Inspector of R.E. (*Cardfields, Hatfield Peverel ; Queen Anne's Mansions, S.W.*) ; and has issue 1f to 3f.

1f. Francis Worsley Barker, b. 1889.

2f· Evelyn Hugh Barker, b. 1894.

3f. Dorothea Margaret Barker, b. 1890.

4d. Hon. *Eliza Napier*, b. 26 *Sept.* 1822 ; d. 2 *Ap.* 1901 ; m. 18 *Aug.* 1847, *Admiral the Right Hon. Sir John Charles Dalrymple-Hay, 3rd Bart. [G.B.], P.C., G.C.B., F.R.S., D.C.L., LL.D., J.P., D.L., sometime (1862–1885) M.P., and (1866–1868) a Lord of the Admiralty, &c. (Park Place, Glenluce, N.B. ; 108 St. George's Square, S.W.) ; and had issue 1e to 8e.*

1e. James Francis Dalrymple-Hay, J.P., D.L., *late* Major 3rd Batt. Royal Scots Fusiliers (*Dunlop House, Dunlop, Ayrshire*), b. 31 May 1848 ; m. 15 Ap. 1873, Ellen Douglas, da. of Robert Hathorn-Johnston-Stewart of Physgill and Glasserton, d. 2 Ap. 1901 ; and has issue 1f.

1f. Eleanor Louisa Dalrymple-Hay, m. 27 Aug. 1903, Major John Archibald Houison Craufurd, 7th Bombay Pioneers ; and has issue 1g.

1g. John Douglas Craufurd, b. 2 June 1904.

2e. William Archibald Dalrymple-Hay, *sometime* a Clerk in the Treasury (*Junior Carlton*), b. 30 Jan. 1851 ; m. 2 June 1906, Mary, da. of William M'Chlery, B.C.S.

3e. Charles John Dalrymple-Hay, a Clerk in the Privy Council Office (*Carlton*), b. 21 Mar. 1865 ; m. 17 Ap. 1906, Rose, da. of Capt. W. T. Hickman, 50th Regt.

4e. Evelyn Eliza Dalrymple-Hay, b. 12 May 1852.

5e. Clara Georgiana Dalrymple-Hay, b. 8 July 1855.

6e. Mary Elizabeth Dalrymple-Hay, b. 24 Nov. 1856.

7e. Ellinor Alice Dalrymple-Hay, b. 12 Jan. 1862.

8e. Violet Susan Dalrymple-Hay, b. 3 Ap. 1868 ; m. 18 July 1899, Professor Edward Howard Marsh, M.A., M.C. (10 *Scroope Terrace, Cambridge*).

5d. Hon. *Ellinor Alice Napier*, b. 11 *May* 1829 ; d. 11 *May* 1903 ; m. 10 *Nov.* 1853, *the Hon. George Grey Dalrymple, b. 22 May 1832 ; d. 30 Nov. 1900 ; and had issue 1e to 3e.*

1e. George North Dalrymple, b. 14 Feb. 1856.

2e. *Walter Francis Dalrymple*, b. 27 *July* 1857 ; d. 11 *Jan.* 1892 ; m. 9 *Jan.* 1886, *Agnes Raney, da. of William Charles Owen of Penrhos, co. Pembroke ; and had issue 1f to 3f.*   [Nos. 50778 to 50802,

The Plantagenet Roll

1*f*. Donald Francis Napier Dalrymple, *b*. 20 Nov. 1888.

2*f*. Basil Walter Dalrymple, *b*. 26 Jan. 1891.

3*f*. Zeila Raney Dalrymple, *b*. 18 Oct. 1886.

3*e*. Mary Adelaide Wilhelmina Elizabeth Dalrymple (*Elliston, St. Boswells, N.B.*).

2*c*. Hon. Charles Napier, Major in the Army, *b*. 24 Oct. 1794; d. 15 Dec. 1874; m. 1*st*, 1824, Alice Emma, *da. of* Roger Barnston, d. 16 *May* 1834; 2*ndly*, 2 *July* 1840, Annabella Jane, *da. of* Edward Gatacre *of* Gatacre, D.L., d. 6 *Mar.* 1885; *and had issue* 1d to 8d.

1*d*. Rev. John Warren Napier, now (*R.L.* 8 *Feb.* 1894) *Napier-Clavering of* Axwell, sometime Vicar *of* Stretton, *b*. 16 *Sept.* 1832; d. 9 *June* 1906; m. 30 *Sept.* 1857, Anna Maria Margaret Helen, *da. of* Col. Francis Hunter, H.E.I.C.S., d. 2 *Feb.* 1900; *and had issue* 1e to 6e.

1*e*. Charles Warren Napier-Clavering, Lieut.-Col. and Brevet-Col. Somerset L.I. (*Army and Navy*), *b*. 19 Aug. 1858; *m*. 24 Oct. 1899, Margaret Nevile, da. of Nevile Reid of Oaks, Hanworth; and has issue 1*f*.

1*f*. Hélène Margaret Napier-Clavering, *b*. 6 Oct. 1900.

2*e*. Francis Napier-Clavering, M.A. (Camb.), Principal of the Tower School, Dovercourt (*The Tower, Dovercourt, Essex*), *b*. 22 Nov. 1859; *m*. 11 Jan. 1888, Elizabeth, da. of Thomas Cowan; and has issue 1*f* to 3*f*.

1*f*. Noel Warren Napier-Clavering, *b*. 24 Dec. 1888.

2*f*. Francis Donald Napier-Clavering, *b*. 28 Ap. 1892.

3*f*. Edith Margaret Napier-Clavering, *b*. 8 Sept. 1890.

3*e*. Rev. Henry Percy Napier-Clavering, M.A. (Camb.), Rector of Stella, *late* Principal of Trin. Coll., Kandy (*Stella Rectory, Blaydon-on-Tyne*), *b*. 7 July 1861.

4*e*. Arthur Lenox Napier, *late* Capt. 2nd Batt. Yorkshire Regt. (*Army and Navy*), *b*. 3 Dec. 1863; *m*. 15 Oct. 1890, Marian, da. of Louis Valentine; and has issue 1*f* to 3*f*.

1*f*. John Lenox Clavering Napier, *b*. 9 Dec. 1898.

2*f*. Lilias Edith Napier, *b*. 3 Jan. 1892.

3*f*. Marian Ellen Napier, *b*. 9 Oct. 1893.

5*e*. Alan Bertram Napier, Kaiser-i-Hind Medal, Dep. Commr. Central Provinces, India, *b*. 1 Oct. 1867.

6*e*. Claude Gerald Napier-Clavering (*The Manor House, Harborne*), *b*. 3 Feb. 1869; *m*. 31 July 1897, Millicent Mary, da. of the Right Hon. William Kenrick; and has issue 1*f* to 3*f*.

1*f*. Mark Napier-Clavering, *b*. 5 May 1898.

2*f*. Alan William Napier-Clavering, *b*. Jan. 1903.

3*f*. Mary Helen Napier-Clavering, *b*. 14 May 1900.

2*d*. Edward Napier, Col., sometime Comdg. 6th Dragoon Guards, and Comdt. Cav. Depôt, Canterbury (39 *Queen Anne's Gate Gardens, S.W.*), *b*. 12 June 1841; *m*. 12 June 1866, Martha Louise, da. of William Barber Buddicom of Penbedw Hall, co. Flints.; and has issue 1e to 6e.

1*e*. Egbert Napier, Capt. 3rd Batt. Gordon Highlanders, *b*. 12 Aug. 1867; *m*. 20 Sept. 1901, Evangeline Senekal, da. of [——] Dreyer of Valschrivierdrift, O.R.C.

2*e*. Owen Lloyd Hownam Napier, Indian Forest Service, *b*. 1 Aug. 1869; *m*. 21 Oct. 1898, Eliza Davidson, da. of Gen. David Pott, C.B.

3*e*. George Charles Napier, *b*. 20 Aug. 1873.

4*e*. Phyllis Louise Napier, *m*. 23 Jan. 1899, Henry Staveley Lawrence, Director of Land Records and Agriculture, Bombay; and has issue 1*f* to 3*f*.

1*f*. George Napier Lawrence, *b*. 1899.

2*f*. Henry Michael Lawrence, *b*. 1902.

3*f*. Margaret Louise Lawrence, *b*. 1904.

[Nos. 50803 to 50830.

# of The Blood Royal

5e. Diana Caroline Marie Napier, *m.* 17 June 1899, the Rev. Arthur Nesham Bax, Rector of Duloe, *formerly* Domestic Chap. and Sec. to the Bishop of Southwell (*Duloe Rectory, R.S.O., Cornwall*); and has issue 1*f* to 3*f*.

1*f*. Stephen Napier Bax (twin), *b.* 21 June 1900.

2*f*. Oliver Napier Thomas Nesham Bax, *b.* 13 July 1902.

3*f*. Amice Clemency Bax (twin), *b.* 21 June 1900.

6e. Jane Rosamond Napier.

3d. *William Archibald Napier*, b. 24 *Ap.* 1845; d. 13 *Aug.* 1901; m. 30 *Ap.* 1879, *Mabel* (*Braeside, Wimbledon*), da. *of William Edward Royds of Greenhill, Rochdale; and had issue* 1e to 4e.

1e. Clarence Napier, *b.* 14 Feb. 1880.

2e. Alan Napier, *b.* 9 July 1881.

3e. Esmè Napier, *b.* 9 July 1884; *m.* 25 July 1905, Frank Douglas Montgomerie of Upperfold, Roehampton.

4e. Lenox Napier, *b.* 26 Aug. 1887.

4d. *Lenox Napier, Comm. R.N.*, b. 17 *Sept.* 1846; d. 21 *Jan.* 1886; m. 21 *June* 1873, *Ellin* (*Catisfield Cottage, Fareham, Hants*), da. *of William Barber Buddicom of Penbedw Hall; and had issue* 1e to 4e.

1e. Henry Lenox Napier, Lieut. Derbyshire Regt., *b.* 18 June 1876.

2e. William Rawdon Napier, Lieut. R.N., *b.* 13 June 1877; *m.* 22 July 1902, Florence Marie, da. of James O'Reilly Nugent.

3e. Patrick Ronald Napier, Lieut. Army Service Corps, *b.* 3 Ap. 1879; *m.* 6 Oct. 1903, Kathleen Hilda Mary, da. of James O'Reilly Nugent; and has issue 1*f*.

1*f*. Patricia Marion Barbara Napier, *b.* 27 July 1904.

4e. Ellin Winifred Napier, *b.* 12 Mar. 1881.

5d. Alfred Napier (4 *Marlborough Terrace, Taunton*), *b.* 13 May 1848; *m.* 20 July 1886, Mary Louisa, da. of Gen. Charles Vanbrugh Jenkins of Cruckton Hall; and has issue 1e to 2e.

1e-2e. See p. 234, Nos. 8285–8286.

6d. Annabella Jane Napier, *d.s.p.* 6 Jan. 1902; *m.* 5 Aug. 1869, Thomas William Gill (*Trewerne, Oswestry*).

7d. Lilias Napier, *m.* 5 Aug. 1874, Sir Thomas Wilmot Peregrine Blomefield, C.B., 4th Bart. [U.K.] (6 *The Grange, Wimbledon Common, S.W.*); and has issue 1e to 5e.

1e. Thomas Charles Alfred Blomefield, Lieut. R.N., *b.* 27 June 1875; *m.* 27 June 1904, Margaret Josephine, da. of Edward Palmer Landon of Shenfield, The Drive, Wimbledon; and has issue 1*f*.

1*f*. Angela Blomefield.

2e. Nigel Napier Blomefield, *b.* 15 Mar. 1877.

3e. Wilmot Blomefield, *b.* 26 Nov. 1879.

4e. Lilias Marow Blomefield, *b.* 30 Sept. 1880; *m.* 8 Oct. 1903, Cedric Llewellyn Longstaff (*The Close, Lichfield*); and has issue 1*f*.

1*f*. Andrew Llewellyn Longstaff, *b.* 29 Jan. 1906.

5e. Nancy Blomefield, *b.* 16 May 1883; *m.* 1 June 1904, Francis Palmer Landon (*Roden Cottage, Oxshott, Surrey*); and has issue 1*f*.

1*f*. Richard Francis Palmer Landon, *b.* 15 Mar. 1905.

8d. Louisa Augusta Napier.

3c. Hon. *Maria Margaret Napier*, b. 9 *Sept.* 1785; d. ¶19 *July* 1861; m. 29 *Aug.* 1816, *the Rev. Arthur William Kilvington, Vicar of Brignall, Yorks*, d. 17 *Oct.* 1854; *and had issue* 1d.

1d. *Maria Kilvington*, d. (–); m. *Henry Yarborough Parker of Streethorpe, nr. Doncaster*, d. (–); *and had issue* 1e to 6e.   [Nos. 50831 to 50858.

573   4 D

The Plantagenet Roll

1e. Yarborough Francis Harry Parker, *b.* 2 Mar. 1844.

2e. Orfeur George Parker, *b.* 15 May 1845.

3e. Charles Donald Kilvington Parker.

4e. Francis Kilvington Parker, *b. c.* 1858.

5e. Diana Parker, *b.* 17 Jan. 1843; *m.* 10 Feb. 1863, the Rev. George Robert Cooke (*Southampton*).

6e. Mary Elizabeth Parker, *b.* 9 Ap. 1848; *m.* 14 Feb. 1871, George Bryan Cooke-Yarborough, J.P., D.L. (*Campsmount, Doncaster*); and has issue 1*f* to 8*f*.

    1*f*. George Eustace Cooke-Yarborough, Bar.-at-Law, *b.* 12 Jan. 1876.

    2*f*. Henry Alfred Cooke-Yarborough, *b.* 27 Mar. 1877.

    3*f*. Orfeur Frederic Cooke-Yarborough, *b.* 26 Nov. 1878.

    4*f*. Humfrey Charles Cooke-Yarborough, *b.* 24 Dec. 1880.

    5*f*. Edmund Selwyn Cooke-Yarborough, *b.* 5 Feb. 1882.

    6*f*. Geoffrey Arthur Cooke-Yarborough, *b.* 10 June 1883.

    7*f*. Mary Alice Cooke-Yarborough.

    8*f*. Mary Violet Cooke-Yarborough.

4c. *Hon. Anne Napier, b. 11 Dec. 1789; d. 7 Dec. 1862; m. as 2nd wife, 8 June 1816, Sir Thomas Gibson-Carmichael, 7th Bart. [S.], b. 21 Dec. 1774; d. 13 Dec. 1849; and had issue 1d to 4d.*

    1d. *Sir Thomas Gibson-Carmichael, 9th Bart. [S.], b. 27 Oct. 1817; d.s.p. 30 Dec. 1855.*

    2d. *Rev. Sir William Henry Gibson-Carmichael, 10th Bart. [S.], b. 9 Oct. 1827; d. 19 Dec. 1891; m. 12 May 1858, Eleanora Anne, da. of David Anderson of St. Germains, d. 6 Jan. 1861; and had issue 1e to 2e.*

        1e. Sir Thomas David Gibson-Carmichael, 11th Bart. [S.], J.P., D.L., a Trustee and Commr. of Board of Manufactures in Scotland, sometime (1895–1900) an M.P. (*Castle Craig, Dolphinton, Peebles*), *b.* 18 Mar. 1859; *m.* 1 July 1886, Mary Helen Elizabeth, da. of Albert Nugent of 143 Sloane Street, S.W.

        2e. John Murray Gibson-Carmichael, *b.* 27 Dec. 1860; *m.* 27 Ap. 1892, Amy Katherine, da. of Frederick Archdale of Baldock, Herts, *d.* 9 Mar. 1899; and has issue 1*f* to 3*f*.

            1*f*. Alexander David Gibson-Carmichael, *b.* 10 Feb. 1895.

            2*f*. Eleanora FitzRoy Gibson-Carmichael, *b.* 13 Feb. 1893.

            3*f*. Penelope FitzRoy Gibson-Carmichael, *b.* 2 Mar. 1899.

    3d. *Maria Clavering Gibson-Carmichael, d. 20 Ap. 1853; m. 1852, Sir James Philip Lacaita, K.C.M.G., K.R. (Brazil), sometime (1861–1865) a member of the Italian Parliament, and subsequently a Senator of the kingdom of Italy; d. 4 Jan. 1895; and had issue 1e.*

        1e. Charles Carmichael Lacaita, sometime M.P. (*Selham House, Petworth; 65 Eaton Square, S.W.*), *b.* 5 Ap. 1853; *m.* 2 June 1885, Mary Anabel, da. of Sir Francis Hastings Charles Doyle, 2nd Bart. [U.K.]; and has issue 1*f* to 2*f*.

            1*f*. Francis Charles Lacaita, *b.* 19 Oct. 1887.

            2*f*. Sidney Guendolen Lacaita.

    4d. Sophia Caroline Gibson-Carmichael, *m.* 2 May 1859, Francis Nevile Reid of Palazzo de Rufoli, Ravello, *d.s.p.* July 1892.

5c. *Hon. Caroline Napier, b. 18 Dec. 1798; d. 9 Nov. 1844; m. as 2nd wife, 9 Ap. 1825, Nevile Reid of Runnymede, co. Berks, b. 1789; d. 28 Sept. 1839; and had issue 1d to 7d.*

    1d. *Francis Nevile Reid of Palazzo de Rufoli, Ravello, Italy, d.s.p. July 1892; m. 2 May 1859, Sophia Caroline, da. of Sir Thomas Gibson-Carmichael, 7th Bart. [S.].*

    2d. Nevile Reid of The Oaks, co. Middlx., and Shandwick, co. Ross (*The Oaks,*
[Nos. 50859 to 50882.

574

# of The Blood Royal

Hanworth), *b.* 11 Jan. 1839; *m.* 16 Aug. 1866, Caroline, da. of the Rev. Henry Vigne, Vicar of Sunbury-on-Thames; and has issue 1*e* to 6*e*.

1*e.* Nevile Reid, *b.* June 1873; *m.* 2 May 1905, Mary, da. of Henry Beaumont of Grantham; and has issue 1*f.*

1*f.* Nevile Reid, *b.* 1 Mar. 1906.

2*e.* Mary Caroline Reid, *b.* June 1867; *m.* 8 Feb. 1898, Charles Pretyman Hayes of Ceylon; and has issue 1*f* to 2*f.*

1*f.* Charles Eric Pretyman Hayes, *b.* 1 Jan. 1903.

2*f.* Aileen Mary Hayes, *b.* 18 Jan. 1899.

3*e.* Violet Reid, *m.* 2 June 1896, Harold Muir Evans, M.D. (*Lowestoft*); and has issue 1*f* to 3*f.*

1*f.* Harold George Muir Evans, *b.* 24 Oct. 1898.

2*f.* Alan Henry Evans, *b.* 18 Dec. 1901.

3*f.* Margaret Muir Evans, *b.* 17 Mar. 1897.

4*e.* Caroline Nevile Reid, *unm.*

5*e.* Margaret Nevile Reid, *m.* 24 Oct. 1899, Lieut.-Col. Charles Warren Napier Clavering (*Oxwell Park, Blaydon-on-Tyne*); and has issue 1*f.*

1*f.* Helene Margaret Reid, *b.* 6 Oct. 1900.

6*e.* Elsie Lilias Reid, *unm.*

3*d. Anna Maria Churchill Reid, d.* 18 *June* 1880; m. 13 *Dec.* 1852, *James Warburton Begbie of Edinburgh, M.D., d.* 25 *Feb.* 1876; *and had issue* 1*e to* 6*e.*

1*e.* Francis Warburton Begbie, Major R.A.M.C. (*Military Hospital, Millbank, S.W.*), *b.* 13 June 1864; *m.* 6 Feb. 1895, Catherine Mary, da. of Walter Reynolds of Hawkswick, St. Albans, J.P., *s.p.*

2*e.* George Edward Begbie, D.S.O., Brevet-Major 71st Highland L.I., *b.* 9 Sept. 1868.

3*e.* Caroline Elizabeth Begbie (*Knolebury, Knole Road, Bournemouth*), *b.* 17 Nov. 1865; *unm.*

4*e.* Emily Hope Begbie, *b.* 25 June 1867; *unm.*

5*e.* Florence Annie Begbie, *b.* 23 Aug. 1870; *m.* as 2nd wife, 31 Oct. 1901, Alan Walter Lennox Boyd, Bar.-at-Law (*Loddington, Bournemouth*); and has issue 1*f* to 2*f.*

1*f.* George Edward Lennox Boyd, *b.* 20 Aug. 1902.

2*f.* Alan Tindal Lennox Boyd, *b.* 18 Nov. 1904.

6*e.* Mary Augusta Begbie, *b.* 29 Oct. 1872; *unm.*

4*d.* Caroline Sophia Kenneth Reid (*Salisbury Lodge, 36 Canevnge Square, Clifton, Bristol; La Storietta, Bordighera, Italy*), *m.* 13 July 1852, Joseph Story of Bingfield, J.P., High Sheriff co. Cavan and Leitrim 1872, *b.* 17 Mar. 1817; *d.* 27 Nov. 1875; and has issue 1*e* to 7*e.*

1*e.* Robert Story, Lieut.-Col. *late* King's Royal Rifle Corps (*Bingfield, Crossdoney, Cavan*), *b.* 11 July 1854; *m.* 1st, 15 May 1879, Florence Mansfield, da. of Harrington Bush of Clifton, *d.* Aug. 1888; 2ndly, 1896, Mary, da. of Edward Jollie of Waireka, Taranaki, N.Z., M.H.R.; and has issue (with 3 younger sons and 1 younger da. all by 2nd wife) 1*f* to 2*f.*

1*f.* Arthur Patrick Story, *b.* 19 Nov. 1896.

2*f.* Vida Hope Carmichael Story, *b.* 8 Feb. 1881; *m.*

2*e.* William Oswald Story, Capt. R.N., *b.* 18 Ap. 1859; *m.* 1892, Olave, da. of [——] Baldwin of New Zealand; and has issue.

3*e.* Evelyn James Story (*Errington, co. Tyrone*), *b.* 28 Feb. 1866; *m.* 1897, Hilda Greenside, da. of Richard Brinsley Hooper of Clifton; and has issue 1*f* to 4*f.*

1*f.* George Frederick Story.

2*f.* Richard Story (twin).

3*f.* Mary Josephine Story.

4*f.* Lilian Story (twin).

[Nos. 50883 to 50913.

575

4e. Francis Napier Story, *b,* 11 Mar. 1867; *m.*; and has issue.

5e. Louisa Fanny Story, *b.* 26 [——] 1856; *m.* 23 May 1882, Edward M. Field, one of H.M.'s Inspectors of Schools; and has issue.

6e. Charlotte Eliza Story, *b.* 7 Jan. 1869; *unm.*

7e. Florence Emily Story, *b.* 6 Sept. 1871; *unm.*

5d. Charlotte Anna Reid, d. 11 Nov. 1868; m. 13 *July* 1854, *Major-Gen. Ferdinand Whittingham, C.B.,* d. 28 *Ap.* 1878; *and had issue* 1e *to* 5e.

1e. Samford Hart Frere Whittingham, *b.* 24 Nov. 1863.

2e. Rev. George Gustavus Napier Whittingham, *b.* 18 Nov. 1866; *m.* 6 Ap. 1891, Emma Maud Marion, da. of Arcedeckne Duncan; and has issue 1*f.*

1f. Duncan Napier Whittingham, *b.* 7 June 1894.

3e. Clementina Louisa Whittingham, b. 29 *Aug.* 1855; *d.* 23 *Jan.* 1896; *m. as* 1st *wife,* 6 *Mar.* 1886, *Alan Walter Lennox Boyd, Bar.-at-Law (Loddington, Bournemouth); and had issue* 1*f.*

1f. Phyllis Georgie Lennox Boyd, *b.* 30 July 1890.

4e. Georgiana Sophia Whittingham, *unm.* ⎱ (9 *York Terrace, Millbrook,*
5e. Clara Monttessoy Whittingham, *unm.* ⎰ *Southampton).*

6d. Louisa Reid, b. 31 *Jan.* 1832; *d.* 20 Dec. 1905; *m.* 15 Nov. 1860, *Woodward Stanford of Dublin,* d. (–); *and had issue* 1e *to* 6e.

1e. Henry Bedel Stanford, Major in the Army, b. 9 *Oct.* 1861; *d.* 14 *July* 1904; *m.* 10 *Oct.* 1887, *Florence Contart, da. of Major Carter; and had issue* 1*f to* 3*f.*

1f. Jack Stanford, *b.* 27 July 1888.

2f. Norah Stanford, *b.* 21 Aug. 1889.

3f. Aileen Stanford, *b.* 9 Nov. 1890.

2e. Rev. Charles Woodward Stanford, Vicar of Elkington (*Elkington Vicarage, Lincoln*), *b.* 13 Jan. 1863; *m.* 1 Nov. 1893, Emily Mary, da. of the Rev. Canon Smyth; and has issue 1*f.*

1f. Mary Dorothy Stanford, *b.* 24 Aug. 1898.

3e. Walter John Stanford, Civil and Mining Engineer (*Johannesburg*), *b.* 10 May 1864; *m.* 28 Aug. 1895, Robina, da. of [——] Bellancy; and has issue 1*f.*

1f. Doreen Napier Stanford, *b.* 6 Aug. 1896.

4e. Archibald Ambrose Stanford, *b.* 10 May 1880.

5e. Elizabeth Mary Stanford (20 *Bath Road, Reading*), *b.* 10 Sept. 1865.

6e. Charlotte Barbara Stanford, *b.* 22 Aug. 1869.

7d. Clara Vernon Reid (11 *Observatory Gardens, Kensington, W.*), *unm.*

3b. Charlotte Clavering, d. 23 *Oct.* 1841; *m.* 28 *Ap.* 1783, *Major-Gen. Sir Thomas Pechell, afterwards* (1801) *Brooke-Pechell, 2nd Bart.* [G.B.], b. 23 *Jan.* 1753; *d.* 18 *June* 1826; *and had issue* 1c *to* 3c.

1c. Sir Samuel John Brooke-Pechell, 3rd Bart. [G.B.], *F.R.S., C.B., K.C.H., Rear-Admiral R.N., b.* 1 Sept. 1785; *d.s.p.* 3 *Nov.* 1849.

2c. Sir George Richard Brooke-Pechell, 4th Bart. [G.B.], *M.P., Vice-Admiral R.N., b.* 30 *June* 1789; *d.* 29 *June* 1860; *m.* 1 *Aug.* 1826, *the Hon. Katharine Annabella, da. and co-h. of Cecil (Bisshopp), 12th Baron Zouche* [E.], *d.* 29 *July* 1871; *and had issue* 1d.

1d. Adelaide Harriet Brooke-Pechell, *m.* 24 Sept. 1857, Col. Sir Alfred Plantagenet Frederick Charles Somerset, K.C.B. (*Enfield Court, Middlesex*); and has issue.

See the Clarence Volume, p. 334, Nos. 9934–9937.

3c. Frances Katherine Brooke-Pechell, d. 30 *Sept.* 1864; *m.* 3 *Aug.* 1824, *the*

[Nos. 50914 to 50939.

# of The Blood Royal

Rev. Robert Tredcroft, M.A., Preb. *of Chichester and Rural Dean*, &c., b. 3 Dec. 1791; d. 19 Dec. 1846; *and had issue* 1d *to* 4d.

1d. Charles Lennox Tredcroft, J.P., C.A., Lieut.-Col., *late* Capt. R.H.A. and Adj. 2nd Royal Surrey Militia *(Glen Ancrum, near Guildford)*, b. 24 Oct. 1832; *m.* 1st, 19 Nov. 1863, Harriette Sophia Louisa, da. of J. H. Woodward, d. 8 Dec. 1869; 2ndly, 27 Ap. 1871, Elizabeth, da. of Sir William Scott of Ancrum, 6th Bart. [S.], M.P., d. 10 Ap. 1886; 3rdly, 4 Mar. 1889, the Hon. Constance Mary, da. of Edward (Fitzalan-Howard), 1st Baron Howard of Glossop [U.K.]; and has issue 1e to 6e.

1e. Cyril Arthur Lennox Tredcroft, b. 5 Jan. 1878.

2e. John Lennox Tredcroft, b. 13 Dec. 1889.

3e.[1] Mary Olivia Georgina Tredcroft, *m.* 18 Ap. 1892, Major Ralph Pudsey Littledale, R.E.; and has issue 1f to 2f.

1f. Robert Littledale, b. 27 Jan. 1895.

2f. Olivia Littledale.

4e.[2] Edith Veronica Sholta de Mont d'Aurensan Tredcroft.

5e.[2] Hilda Mary Clavering Tredcroft, *m.* as 2nd wife, 20 Sept. 1904, Gilbert George Reginald (Sackville), 8th Earl de la Warr [G.B.] *(Marina Court, Bexhill)*.

6e.[3] Augusta Mary Gwendolen Tredcroft.

2d. *Frances Tredcroft*, d. 4 *Jan*. 1899; m. 24 *Jan*. 1865, *Sir Henry Edward Leigh Dryden, 7th Bart. of Ambrosden* (1733) *and 4th Bart. of Canons Ashby* (1795) [G.B.], b. 17 Aug. 1818; d. 24 July 1899; *and had issue* 1e.

1e. Alice Dryden *(Bradford-on-Avon)*.

3d. *Georgina Tredcroft*, d. 27 *Jan*. 1892; m. 12 *May* 1854, *Sir Charles Watson afterwards* (R.L. 12 *Mar*. 1887) *Watson-Copley, 3rd Bart.* [G.B.], b. 6 Ap. 1828; d. 6 Ap. 1888; *and had issue* 1e to 3e.

1e. Selina Frances Watson-Copley of Sprotborough, *m.* 2 Feb. 1886, Lieut.-Col. Robert Calverley Alington Bewicke Bewicke, *now* (R.L. 1892) Bewicke-Copley, J.P., D.L. *(Sprotborough Hall, Doncaster; Coulby Manor, Middlesborough)*; and has issue 1f to 4f.

1f. Redvers Lionel Calverley Bewicke-Copley, b. 17 Sept. 1890.

2f. Robert Godfrey Wolseley Bewicke-Copley, b. 23 May 1893.

3f. Gladys Bewicke-Copley.

4f. Dorothy Albreda Bewicke-Copley.

2e. Caroline Selina Watson-Copley, *m.* 13 Ap. 1893, John Home A. Peebles-Chaplin *(Colliston, Forfarshire)*.

3e. Amabel Jemima Watson-Copley, *m.* 19 Ap. 1887, Capt. Edward Lygon Somers Cocks, *late* 52nd Regt. (47 *Wilton Crescent, S.W.*); and has issue 1f to 2f.

1f. James Charles Somers Cocks, b. 18 Mar. 1888.

2f. Amabel Caroline Somers Cocks, b. 12 Aug. 1890.

4d. Emily Susan Tredcroft, *m.* 29 Jan. 1861, William Fermor Ramsay (59 *Chester Square, S.W.*); and has issue 1e to 3e.

1e. Norman Robert Ramsay, *m.* Ap. 1896, Frances, da. of Aubrey Cartwright of Edgcote.

2e. Emily Frances Ramsay, *m.* 1st as 2nd wife, 25 Jan. 1893, Philip (Sidney), 2nd Baron De L'Isle and Dudley [U.K.], d. 17 Feb. 1898; 2ndly, as 2nd wife, 21 Feb. 1903, Sir Walter George Stirling, 3rd Bart. [G.B.] (50 *Lennox Gardens, S.W.; Boothwood, I.W.*).

3e. Gertrude Ramsay.

4b. *Caroline Clavering*, d. 1839; m. 12 Dec. 1780, *Admiral Sir John Borlase Warren, 1st Bart.* [G.B.], K.C.B., M.P., b. 2 *Sept.* 1753; d 1822; *and had issue*.

See pp. 90–92, Nos. 509–574.   50940 to 51028.

The Plantagenet Roll

515. Descendants of DIANA BLACKETT (see Table LIV.), *b. c.* 1703; *d.* 2 May 1737; *m.* 1st, HENRY MAINWARING of Over Peover, co. Chester, *d.* 1726; 2ndly, the Rev. THOMAS WETENHALL, Rector of Walthamstow, co. Essex, and afterwards of Nantwich, *bapt.* 26 Sept. 1708; *bur.* 20 Oct. 1776; and had issue 1*a* to 2*a*.

1*a*. *Sir Henry Mainwaring, 3rd Bart.* [*E.*], b. (*posthumous*) 7 Nov. 1726; d. *unm.* 6 *Ap.* 1797.

2*a*. *Thomas Wetenhall, afterwards Mainwaring of Over Peover*, b. 26 Nov. 1736; d. 4 *July* 1798; m. 21 *June* 1781, *Catherine, da. of William Walkins of Nantwich*, d. 5 *July* 1804; *and had issue* 1*b* to 2*b*.

1*b*. *Sir Henry Mainwaring Mainwaring, 1st Bart.* [*U.K.*], b. 25 *Ap.* 1782; d. 11 *Jan.* 1860; m. 28 *Dec.* 1803, *Sophia, sister of Stapleton, 1st Viscount Combermere* [*U.K.*], *da. of Sir Robert Salisbury Cotton, 5th Bart.* [*E.*], d. 24 *Mar.* 1838; *and had issue* 1*c* to 6*c*.

1*c*. *Sir Henry Mainwaring, 2nd Bart.* [*U.K.*], b. 3 *Nov.* 1804; d. 23 *Sept.* 1875; m. 24 *Jan.* 1832, *Emma, da. of Thomas William Tatton of Withenshaw*, d. 10 *Sept.* 1886; *and had issue* 1*d* to 8*d*.

1*d*. *Sir Stapleton Thomas Mainwaring, 3rd Bart.* [*U.K.*], b. 6 *Jan.* 1837; d.s.p. 4 *Aug.* 1878.

2*d*. *Sir Philip Tatton Mainwaring, 4th Bart.* [*U.K.*], b. 11 *Sept.* 1838; d. 21 *Feb.* 1906; m. 7 *Oct.* 1875, *Louisa Emily, da. of the Rev. George Pitt of Cricket Court, Somerset; and had issue* 1*e* to 3*e*.

1*e*. Sir Harry Stapleton Mainwaring, 5th Bart. [U.K.] (*Peover Hall, Knutsford*), b. 25 Aug. 1878.

2*e*. Hester Marjorie Mainwaring.

3*e*. Violet Mainwaring.

3*d*. *Randle Cotton Mainwaring*, b. 27 *Aug.* 1840; d. 6 *Sept.* 1875; m. 1872, [——], *da. of* [——] *Goode of Auckland, N.Z.; and had issue* (*a da.*).

4*d*. Rowland Leycester Mainwaring (*New Zealand*), b. 3 June 1845; m. 1879, Elizabeth, da. of [——] Sextie; and has issue (3 das.).

5*d*. Emma Sophia Mainwaring.

6*d*. Henrietta Elizabeth Mainwaring (73 *Eccleston Square, S.W.*), m. as 2nd wife, 21 Dec. 1871, Sir Richard Brooke, 7th Bart. [E.], b. 13 Dec. 1814; d. 3 Mar. 1888; and has issue 1*e* to 2*e*.

1*e*. Constance Ida Brooke.

2*e*. Rosalind Hester Brooke.

7*d*. Susan Maude Mainwaring.

8*d*. Ellinor Caroline Louisa Mainwaring, m. 11 May 1869, Henry Gaskell Close (101 *Eaton Square, S.W.*); and has issue 1*e* to 4*e*.

1*e*. Thomas Close, *late* Rifle Brigade, b. 1873; m. 1899, Angela Frances Mary, da. of Guy Paget of Humberstone Hall, co. Leicester.

2*e*. Frederick Close.

3*e*. Henrietta Close.

4*e*. [——] Close.

2*c*. *Arthur Mainwaring, Capt. 66th Regt.*, b. 15 *July* 1815; d. 25 *Aug.* 1876; m. 13 *July* 1843, *Emma Eliza, da. of Pelham Warren, M.D.*, d. 1899.

3*c*. *Charlotte Augusta Mainwaring*, d. 7 *June* 1903; m. 21 *Feb.* 1832, *the Rev. George Pitt, M.A., Vicar of Audlem*, d. 28 *Ap.* 1865; *and had issue* 1*d* to 8*d*.

1*d*. Thomas Henry Pitt, J.P., Hon. Col. (ret.) R.A. (*Hayle Place, Maidstone*), b. 6 Feb. 1833; m. 9 Oct. 1862, Fanny, da. of William Palmer of Portland Place, W.; and has issue 1*e* to 8*e*. [Nos. 51029 to 51043.

# of The Blood Royal

1e. Thomas Morton Stanhope Pitt, Capt. 1st Royal Dragoons, b. 10 Oct. 1871 ; m. 15 Oct. 1903, Inez Mary, da. of N. Mitchell Innes of Ayton Castle.

2e. Fanny Charlotte Elizabeth Pitt, b. 12 Aug. 1863.

3e. Ada Augusta Georgina Mainwaring Pitt, m. July 1889, Capt. Horace Mann, Queen's Own, d. (being killed in South Africa) June 1900 ; and has issue 1f to 3f.

    1f. Horace Galfriders Trevelyan Mann, b. 1894.

    2f. Frances Gladys Trevelyan Mann, b. 1891.

    3f. Audrey Eleanor Agnes Mann, b. 1893.

4e. Pearl Evelyn Mainwaring Pitt, m. 22 Oct. 1890, Capt. Hugh Cecil Westall Beeching, Queen's Own (*Turkey Court, Maidstone*) ; and has issue 1f to 2f.

    1f. Cecil Pearl Beeching, b. 16 Sept. 1891.

    2f. Thomas Hugh Pitt Beeching, b. 20 Mar. 1900.

5e. Agnes May Mainwaring Pitt.

6e. Cecil Catherine Mainwaring Pitt, m. 1 Dec. 1900, Sam Mendel ; and has issue 1f.

    1f. Sam Mendel, b. 3 Dec. 1901.

7e. Ina Agnes Mainwaring Pitt.

8e. Stella Mary Mainwaring Pitt.

2d. William Pitt, b. 2 Ap. 1834.

3d. John George Pitt, b. 25 Oct. 1836.

4d. Robert Francis Salusbury Pitt, b. 6 Oct. 1857 ; m. 29 May 1890, Lydia, da. of Col. Raban ; and has issue 1e.

    1e. [da.] b. May 1896.

5d. Georgina Augusta Pitt (*Eaton Villa, Clifton*), m. 5 Aug. 1863, Capt. Francis Philip Egerton, R.N., d.s.p. 2 Mar. 1893.

6d. Mary Charlotte Pitt, m. 1871, Henry Lamond (7 *North Park Terrace, Hillhead, Glasgow*) ; and has issue 1e.

    1e. Claude Henry Pitt Lamond, M.A. (Oxon.), Barrister, M.T., b. 1878.

7d. Louisa Emily Pitt, m. 7 Oct. 1875, Sir Philip Tatton Mainwaring, 4th Bart. [U.K.] (*Peover Hall, Knutsford*) ; and has issue.

See p. 578, Nos. 51029–51031.

8d. Anna Maria Pitt, m. Dec. 1875, James Moray Brown, 75th Highlanders, d. 1894 ; and has issue.

4c. *Katharine Mainwaring*, d. 13 *Ap.* 1901 ; m. 12 *Aug.* 1846, *Thomas Wynne Eyton of Leeswood*, d. 16 *Sept.* 1870 ; *and had issue* 1d *to* 3d.

1d. John Hope Wynne Eyton, J.P., Major, *late* Shropshire L.I. (*Leeswood, and The Tower, Mold, co. Flint*), b. 19 Ap. 1852 ; m. 25 Aug. 1881, Cecily Mary, da. of the Rev. James Yorke ; and has issue 1e.

    1e. Violet Hope Wynne Eyton.

2d. Robert William Wynne Eyton, b. 24 June 1854 ; m. 1882, Margaret Wynne, da. of John Scott Banks of Soughton Hall, Northop, co. Flint.

3d. Charles Edward Wynne Eyton, b. 17 Aug. 1857 ; m. 17 Oct. 1882, Aline Mary, da. of Godfrey Wills of The Elms, co. Bucks, d. 7 Mar. 1897 ; and has issue 1e to 5e.

    1e. Robert Mainwaring Wynne Eyton, b. 1886.

    2e. Charles Sandford Wynne Eyton, b. 1888.

    3e. Dorothy Elizabeth Wynne Eyton.

    4e. Joan Katherine Wynne Eyton.

    5e. Aline Margaret Wynne Eyton.

5c. *Mary Mainwaring*, d. 28 *Mar.* 1906 ; m. 12 *Oct.* 1847, *Henry Eardley Aylmer Dalbiac of Durrington*, J.P., d. 17 *June* 1889 ; *and had issue* 1d *to* 3d.

1d. Charles William Dalbiac, Solicitor (*Burton House, Twickenham*), b. 13 May 1852 ; m. 5 Aug. 1884, Rhoda Mary, da. of the Rev. Archibald Paris ; and has issue.

See p. 222, Nos. 7945-7948.

[Nos. 51044 to 51083.

The Plantagenet Roll

2d. Philip Hugh Dalbiac, Lieut.-Col. Comdg. and Hon. Col. 4th Vol. Batt. Rifle Brigade, *late* Sherwood Foresters, a partner in Swan Sonnenschein & Co., sometime (1895–1900) M.P. (*Harperbury, Radlett, Herts*), *b.* 20 Sept. 1856; *m.* 7 June 1888, Lilian, da. of Sir Charles Seely, 1st Bart. [U.K.]; and has issue 1*e* to 6*e*.

1*e*. Richard Henry Dalbiac, *b.* 10 Nov. 1890.

2*e*. Charles James Shelley Dalbiac, *b.* 15 Feb. 1896.

3*e*. Elizabeth Mary Dalbiac, *b.* 5 May 1889.

4*e*. Emily Hester Dalbiac, *b.* 17 Nov. 1891.

5*e*. Cicely Florence Dalbiac, *b.* 6 Mar. 1894.

6*e*. Lilian Philippa Dalbiac, *b.* 9 Aug. 1897.

3*d*. Mary Eleanor Dalbiac.

6*c*. *Caroline Mainwaring*, d. 21 *Ap.* 1902; *m.* 11 *Sept.* 1850, *the Rev. James Yorke, M.A., Vicar of Marbury, Cheshire*, d. 9 *Mar.* 1875; *and had issue* 1*d* to 4*d*.

1*d*. Sophia Lucy Caroline Yorke, *m.* 8 June 1880, the Rev. Henry Glanville Barnacle, M.A., F.R.A.S., Principal of The Hermitage School, Grimsargh (*Grimsargh, near Preston, Lancashire*); and has issue 1*e* to 7*e*.

1*e*. Glanville Alban Stepney Barnacle, *b.* 24 May 1885.

2*e*. Henry Alfred Yorke Barnacle, *b.* 29 Dec. 1888.

3*e*. Robert Cotton Barnacle, *b.* 4 Nov. 1895.

4*e*. Glwadys Caroline Barnacle, *b.* 5 Ap. 1881.

5*e*. Vere Hester Yorke Barnacle, *b.* 10 Sept. 1882.

6*e*. Ida Elizabeth Mary Barnacle, *b.* 17 Jan. 1887.

7*e*. Norah Ruthven Barnacle, *b.* 24 May 1891.

2*d*. Cicely Mary Yorke, *m.* 25 Aug. 1881, Major John Hope Wynne Eyton (*The Tower, Mold*); and has issue.

See p. 579, No. 51071.

3*d*. Alice Maud Yorke (*Melton Park, Malvern*), *m.* 20 Jan. 1886, Llewellyn Lloyd of Hafod, Mold, *d.* 1889; and has issue 1*e*.

1*e*. Llewellyn Sydney Lloyd, *b.* 7 Dec. 1886.

4*d*. Hester Maria Julia Yorke, *m.* 24 June 1894, John Randal Orred, Bar.-at-Law (*Borras Head, Gresford, Denbigh*); and has issue 1*e*.

1*e*. Hester Frances Orred, *b.* 24 Feb. 1899.

2*b*. *Rev. Edward Mainwaring, Vicar of Calverhall, co. Salop*, b. 22 *Nov.* 1792; d. 6 *July* 1869; *m.* 1*st*, 1 *Feb.* 1820, *Elizabeth, da. of James Fenton of Loversall, co. York*, d. 1844; *and had issue* 1*c*.

1*c*. William George Mainwaring, Col. Bombay S.C., *b.* 24 Ap. 1823.

[Nos. 51084 to 51106.

516. Descendants of Sir EDWARD BLACKETT, 4th Bart. [E.], M.P. (see Table LIV.), *b.* 9 Ap. 1719; *d.* (at Thorpe, Chertsey) 3 Feb. 1804; *m.* Sept. 1751, ANNE, da. and h. of Oley DOUGLAS of Matfen, co. Northumberland, *b. c.* 1725; *d.* 30 Dec. 1805; and had issue 1*a* to 2*a*.

1*a*. *Sir William Blackett, 5th Bart. [E.],* b. 16 *Feb.* 1759; d. 27 *Oct.* 1816; m. 8 *Aug.* 1801, *Mary Anne, da. of Benjamin Keene of Westoe Lodge, co. Camb.*, d. 7 *Aug.* 1859; *and had issue* 1*b* to 2*b*.

1*b*. Sir Edward Blackett, 6th Bart. [E.], J.P., D.L., b. 23 *Feb.* 1805; d. 23 *Nov.* 1885; m. 1*st*, 1 *May* 1830, *Julia, da. of Sir Charles Monck of Belsay Castle, 6th Bart. [E.]*, d. 25 *June* 1846; *and had issue* 1*c* to 8*c*.

1*c*. Sir Edward William Blackett, 7th Bart. [E.], C.B., K.L.H., Major-Gen. (ret.) in the Army, &c. (*Matfen Hall, Corbridge*), *b.* 22 Mar. 1831; *m.* 23 Nov. 1871, the Hon. Julia Frances, da. of Kenelm (Somerville), 17th Lord Somerville [S.]; and has issue 1*d* to 3*d*.   [No. 51107.

580

# of The Blood Royal

1*d*. Hugh Douglas Blackett, Capt. Northumberland Imp. Yeo., *b.* 24 Mar. 1873 ; *m.* 5 Feb. 1903, Helen Katharine, da. of George William Lowther ; and has issue 1*e*.

1*e*. Charles Douglas Blackett, *b.* 15 Aug. 1904.

2*d*. Arthur Edward Blackett, *b.* 14 May 1874.

3*d*. Ralph Blackett, Capt. Inniskilling Fusiliers, *b.* 19 Sept. 1877.

2*c*. Charles Francis Blackett, Hon. Major *late* Capt. Rifle Brigade (*Naval and Military ; Burlington*), *b.* 6 Jan. 1841 ; *m.* 27 Nov. 1886, Henrietta Louise Johanna Martha, da. of Carl Friedrich Schmidt of Dresden ; and has issue 1*d*.

1*d*. Vera Katharine Blackett, *b.* 19 Dec. 1888.

3*c*. Henry Wise Ridley Blackett, Lieut.-Col., *late* Major 19th Hussars (*Army and Navy*), *b.* 24 June 1842.

4*c*. Louisa Blackett, d. 17 *July* 1870 ; m. *as 1st wife*, 8 Dec. 1863, *the Hon. Sir Charles Gilbert John Brydone Elliot, K.C.B., Admiral of the Fleet (ret.),* b. 12 Dec. 1818 ; d. 21 *May* 1895 ; *and had issue* 1*d*.

1*d*. Bertram Charles Elliot (*The Old Manor Cottage, Haslemere*), *b.* 5 Dec. 1867 ; *m.* 29 Oct. 1901, Norah Kathleen, da. of Walter Raleigh Trevelyan.

5*c*. Frances Julia Blackett.

6*c*. Anna Maria Blackett (1 *Percy Villas, Campden Hill, Kensington, W.*). *m.* 10 Mar. 1863, Lieut.-Col. Godfrey Wentworth Beaumont, Scots Guards, *d.* 23 Aug. 1876 ; and has issue 1*d* to 8*d*.

1*d*. Ronald Wentworth Beaumont, *b.* 25 Feb. 1864.

2*d*. Hugh Dylais Beaumont, *b.* 20 Jan. 1873.

3*d*. Ernest Godfrey Beaumont, *b.* 22 Dec. 1874.

4*d*. Evelyn Julia Beaumont.

5*d*. Marion Edith Beaumont, *m.* 2 Sept. 1897, Major Robert Bell Turton, 4th Batt. Yorkshire Regt. (*Kildale Hall, Grosmont, York*) ; and has issue 1*e* to 3*e*.

1*e*. Godfrey Edmund Turton, *b.* 4 Jan. 1901.

2*e*. Robert Hugh Turton, *b.* 8 Aug. 1903.

3*e*. Cecilia Marion Turton, *b.* 11 Nov. 1898.

6*d*. Ethel Alice Beaumont.

7*d*. Sybil Helen Beaumont.

8*d*. Lilian Laura Beaumont.

7*c*. Georgiana Emma Blackett (*Shelley Court, Tite Street, S.W.*), *m.* 2 Aug. 1871, Rear-Admiral John Crawford Wilson, R.N., *d.* 1885 ; and has issue 1*d*.

1*d*. Julia Margaret Wilson, *m.* 1898, Major Robert Henry Isacke.

8*c*. Mary Elizabeth Blackett (*The Mount, York*), *m.* 5 Aug. 1865, George Mark Leicester Egerton of The Mount, *d.* 2 Sept. 1898 ; and has issue.

See the Clarence Volume, pp. 271–272, Nos. 7250–7257.

2*b*. *John Charles Blackett of Thorpe Lea, Chertsey,* b. 3 *Ap.* 1813 ; d. 8 *Aug.* 1896 ; m. 1*st*, 2*?* *June* 1845, *Maria, da. of Benjamin Berthon of Woodlands, Tasmania,* d. 23 *Aug.* 1847 ; 2*ndly*, 18 *Mar.* 1852, *Emily Jane, da. of Col. William Wild Cockcraft, 58th Regt.,* d. 2*?* *Dec.* 1899 ; *and had issue* 1*c* to 10*c*.

1*c*. Harold Blackett (*Pine Wood, Sunninghill, near Ascot*), *b.* 27 Jan. 1854 ; *m.* 15 Sept. 1881, Marion, da. of Richard Gosling of Ecclesfield, Ashford ; and has issue 1*d* to 2*d*.

1*d*. Henry Beaumont Blackett, *b.* 20 June 1886.

2*d*. Kathleen Marion Blackett, *b.* 3 Sept. 1882.

2*c*. Rev. John Charles Blackett (*Newbury, Gillingham, Dorset*), *b.* 23 Feb. 1865.

3*c*. Henry Blackett, Comm. R.N. (*Army and Navy*), *b.* 28 Nov. 1867.

4*c*. Maria Patience Blackett, *m.* 14 June 1866, Col. Charles William Hood, *formerly* Comdg. Royal West Surrey Regt. ; and has issue 1*d* to 2*d*.

[Nos. 51108 to 51145.

1*d.* William Edward Hood, Capt. Bedfordshire Regt.

2*d.* Ethel Maria Berthon Hood.

5*c.* Frances Ida Blackett.

6*c. Louisa Blackett,* d. 28 *Mar.* 1900; m. 22 *June* 1882, *James Blenkinsop,* d. (*at Chertsey*) *Feb.* 1906; *and had issue* 1*d to* 3*d.*

    1*d.* Bertram James Douglas Blenkinsop, *b.* 2 Mar. 1883, ⎫

    2*d.* William Hope Blenkinsop, *b.* 26 Sept. 1884, ⎬ (*Weir Lodge,*

    3*d.* Henry Colin Blenkinsop, *b.* 18 Jan. 1888, ⎭   *Chertsey*).

7*c.* Emily Blackett.

8*c.* Edith Blackett.

9*c.* Nesta Mary Blackett, *m.* 15 Dec. 1898, Lionel Charles Lane Fox-Pitt, J.P., F.R.G.S. (*Cliff House, Shaftesbury*).

10*c.* Evelyn Blackett, *m.* 24 Feb. 1902, Major Christopher Montagu Blackett.

2*a. Anne Blackett,* d. (–); m. 15 *Nov.* 1785, *Lieut.-Gen. William Scott; and had* (*with possibly other*) *issue* 1*b.*

1*b. William Henry Scott, a Gen. in the Army,* d. 1868; m. 20 *Aug.* 1835, *the Hon. Harriet Alethea, da. of John Thomas* (*Stanley*), 1*st Baron Stanley of Alderley* [*U.K.*], d. 24 *Ap.* 1888; *and had issue* 1*c to* 4*c.*

1*c.* William Charles Scott, J.P. (*Thorpe, Chertsey*), *b.* June 1842; *m.* 14 Jan. 1880, Ursula Katherine, da. of Gen. Augustus Henry Lane Fox-Pitt-Rivers of Rushmore; and has issue.

See the Clarence Volume, p. 442, Nos. 18852–18854.

2*c.* Marian Scott, *m.* as 2nd wife, 3 Aug. 1871, William Williams of Parcieu; *d.* 18 Aug. 1892; and has issue 1*d* to 3*d.*

    1*d.* Lawrence Williams, Capt. Duke of Cornwall's L.I., J.P. (*Plas Llanddyfnan, Llangefni*), *b.* 5 Ap. 1876; *m.* 1897, Catherine Elizabeth Anne, da. of Col. Phibbs; and has issue 1*e* to 3*e.*

        1*e.* Reginald Lawrence William Williams, *b.* 1900.

        2*e.* Mona Rosamond Alice Williams, *b.* 1898.

        3*e.* Violet Kathleen Mary Williams, *b.* 1902.

    2*d.* Margaret Williams, *m.* 24 Oct. 1894, William Edward Southwell Sotherby (*Sussex Lodge, Slough*); and has issue 1*e* to 2*e.*

        1*e.* Lionel Frederick Southwell Sotherby, *b.* 1895.

        2*e.* Nigel Walter Adeane Sotherby.

    3*d.* Rosamond Williams.

3*c.* Alethea Rianette Anne Scott, *m.* 1st as 4th wife, 5 Aug. 1880, Sir Edward Blackett, 4th Bart. [E.]; *d.* 23 Nov. 1885; 2ndly, 5 Nov. 1888, Henry Gisborne Holt (*The Grove, Ropley, Hants*).

4*c.* Adela Jane Scott.   [Nos. 51146 to 51170.

517. Descendants, if any, of WILLIAM, HENRY, JOHN ERASMUS, and MATTHEW BLACKETT; of CHRISTOPHER BLACKETT; of ELIZABETH BLACKETT, *d.* 1811, having *m.* JOHN WISE of Ripon, York; of HENRIETTA MARIA BLACKETT, wife of Major JOHN SAVILLE of Westminster; of ISABELLA NORTON, wife of WILLIAM THORNTON of East Newton, co. York; of ANNE BLACKETT, wife of [——] RISDALE; and of CHRISTIAN BLACKETT, wife of [——] CURTIS (see Table LIV.).

518. Descendants, if any, of FRANCES YORKE (see Table LIV.), wife of THOMAS BARNEY of Dole Bank, co. York.

# of The Blood Royal

519. Descendants of the Hon. DAVID LESLIE, otherwise ANSTRUTHER, of Huntsmore Park, co. Berks (see Table LV.), m. [——], da. of [——] DONALDSON of Allachie, co. Aberdeen; and had issue 1a to 2a.

1a. *Robert Leslie Anstruther, Col. 6th Bengal Light Cavalry, b. 10 June 1787 ; d. (–) ; m. 2ndly, 14 Dec. 1814, Elizabeth, da. of the Rev. E. Gardner, Rector of Stoke Hammond, co. Bucks, d. 8 Jan. 1843 ; and had issue 1b to 5b.*

    1b. *George Peel John Leslie Anstruther, b. 1 Ap. 1829 ; d. before 1880 (? s.p.).*

    2b. *Mary Henrietta Leslie Anstruther, m. 16 Aug. 1835, [——] Yule.*

    3b. *Caroline Louisa Leslie Anstruther, d. Aug. or Sept. 1848 ; m. 14 July 1835, F. Cardew.*

    4b. *Emily Leslie Anstruther, d. (on her passage home from India) 25 May 1844 ; m. as 1st wife, July 1839, William Vansittart, H.E.I.C.S., M.P. for Windsor, b. 2 May 1813 ; d. 15 Jan. 1878 ; and had issue 1c to 2c.*

        1c. William Henry Vansittart.

        2c. Emily Eden Vansittart, *m.* 1 Oct. 1861, George Palmer (son of Gen. Palmer of Nazing Park, Essex).

    5b. *Sophia Catherine Leslie Anstruther, d. (in India) 8 Oct. 1845 ; m. as 2nd wife, 29 Feb. 1840, Capt. Robert Price, 67th Bengal N.I., b. 13 July 1813 ; d. (being killed in action) 4 Feb. 1853 ; and had issue 1c.*

        1c. *Ralph Anstruther Price, Lieut.-Col. late B.S.C. (Gila Lodge, 61 Bassett Road, North Kensington, W.), b. 11 Aug. 1842 ; m. 2 July 1867, Fanny Hughes, da. of James Lamb of Calcutta ; and has issue 1d to 2d.*

            1d. *Robert James Stafford Price (Junior Constitutional), b. 18 Feb. 1870.*

            2d. Mary Sophia Price.

2a. *Mary Leslie, otherwise Anstruther, d. Ap. 1860 ; m. 1st as 2nd wife, Capt. Henry Mitford, R.N., b. 12 Sept. 1769 ; d. (being lost at sea in the " York ") 24 Dec. 1803 ; 2ndly, 13 Ap. 1809, Farrer Grove Spurgeon, afterwards (R.L. 1799) Farrer of Cold Brayford, co. Bucks, b. 12 July 1783 ; d. 12 Oct. 1826 ; and had issue 1b to 7b.*

    1b. *Henry Reverley Mitford of Exbury, co. Hants, and Newton Park, co. Northumberland, J.P., D.L., b. 21 June 1804 ; d. Dec. 1883 ; m. 28 Feb. 1828, Lady Georgiana Jemima, da. of George (Ashburnham), 3rd Earl of Ashburnham [G.B.] ; and had issue.*

See the Tudor Roll of " The Blood Royal of Britain," pp. 192–193, Nos. 21153–21164.

    2b. *William Frederick Farrer of Cold Brayford, J.P., D.L., d. 1872 ; leaving issue an only son, who d. unm. 2 Feb. 1879.*

    3b. *George Denis Farrer of Cold Brayford, Brayford House, Newport Pagnell, b. 2 Feb. 1815 ; d. (? unm.).*

    4b. *Francis Morgan Farrer, d. (? unm.)*

    5b. Rev. *Frederick Farrer, M.A. (Oxon.), Rector of Bourton on the Hill, Moreton-in-Marsh, b. 29 Sept. 1826 ; m. 1st, June 1852, Georgina Ann, da. of the Rev. W. J. E. Bennett of Frome, d. 4 Oct. 1856 ; 2ndly, Aug. 1869, Maria Elizabeth, da. of the Rev. J. A. Barron of Great Stanmore ; and has issue 1c to 6c.*

        1c. Denis Hubert Farrer, *b.* 9 May 1874.

        2c.[1] Mary Farrer, *b.* 10 Sept. 1853.

        3c. *Georgina Ann Farrer, b. 20 Sept. 1856 ; d. 9 Mar. 1883 ; m. Ap. 1882, Henry Appleby Wollaston ; and had issue (a da.).*

        4c.[2]. Clarence Annie Mary Farrer, *m.* 19 Sept. 1899, John Henry Dods, and has issue (a son and da.).   [Nos. 51171 to 51191.

The Plantagenet Roll

5c. Betty Marie Noel Farrer, *m.* 20 Jan. 1897, Alexander Forbes Douglas.

6c. Dorothy Acton Farrer.

6b. Mary Farrer (20 *Chapel Street, Grosvenor Place, S.W.*), *m.* 20 Jan. 1855, Col. Sir Matthew Edward Tierney, 3rd and last Bart. [U.K.], *b.* 18 Jan. 1818; *d.* Dec. 1860.

7b. Annie Louisa Farrer. [Nos. 51192 to 51195.

520. Descendants, if any, of the Hon. WILLIAM LESLIE (see Table LV.), *b.* June 1759; *m.* 2 Nov. 1801, [——], da. of [——] SENIOR, and niece of Sir Robert Smith, a Gen. in the Danish Service; and of the Hon. ELIZABETH LESLIE, *d.* (at Boulogne) 20 June 1787; *m.* [——] MAGNUS of London, Merchant; and had issue.

521. Descendants of the Hon. JANE LESLIE (see Table LV.), *d.* 8 Jan. 1790; *m.* JOHN SANFORD of Nynehead, co. Somerset, *d.* 1779; and had issue 1*a* to 2*a*.

1*a. William Ayshford Sanford of Nynehead, d. 30 Ap. 1833; m. Aug. 1793, Mary, da. of the Rev. Edward Marshall of Breage, co. Cornwall, d. 20 Jan. 1855; and had issue 1b.*

1*b. Edward Ayshford Sanford of Nynehead, F.R.S., M.P., J.P., D.L., &c., b. 23 May 1794; d. 1 Dec. 1871; m. 1st, 4 Nov. 1817, Henrietta, da. of Sir William Langham, 8th Bart. [E.], d. 24 Aug. 1836; and had issue.*
See the Clarence Volume, pp. 585–586, Nos. 24544–24573.

2*a. Rev. John Sanford, Vicar of Nynehead, b. 20 Feb. 1778; d. 27 Sept. 1855; m. Eliza, da. of Major-Gen. George Morgan, d. 12 June 1857; and had issue 1b.*

1*b. Anna Horatia Caroline Sanford, d. 3 Mar. 1899; m. 14 Oct. 1844, Frederick Henry Paul (Methuen), 2nd Baron Methuen [U.K.], b. 23 Feb. 1818; d. 26 Sept. 1891; and had issue 1c to 5c.*

1*c.* Paul Sanford (Methuen), 3rd Baron Methuen [U.K.], G.C.B., K.C.V.O., C.M.G., Gen., late Col. Scots Guards, &c. (*Corsham Court, Corsham, Wilts*), *b.* 1 Sept. 1845; *m.* 9 Jan. 1884, Mary Ethel, da. of William Ayshford Sanford of Nynehead; and has issue.
See p. 416, Nos. 34355–34359.

2*c.* Hon. Frederick Paul George Methuen, *b.* 10 Dec. 1851.

3*c.* Hon. Georgiana Horatia Methuen.

4*c.* Hon. Jane Charlotte Methuen, *m.* 18 Oct. 1870, Col. the Hon. Richard Southwell Stapleton-Cotton (*Somerford Hall, Brewood, Staffordshire*); and has issue.
See the Clarence Volume, p. 357, Nos. 12198–12202.

5*c.* Hon. Florence Geraldine Marion Methuen. [Nos. 51196 to 51240.

522. Descendants of the Hon. HELEN ANSTRUTHER (see Table LV.), *d.* 21 Feb. 1787; *m.* 6 June 1743, the Rev. JOHN CHALMERS, of Raderney, D.D., Minister of Kilconquhar, *b. c.* 1711; *d.* 7 Ap. 1791; and had issue 1*a* to 2*a*.[1]

1*a. William Béthune Chalmers of Edinburgh, W.S.*

2*a. Jean Chalmers, m. David Walker of Fafield.*

---

[1] Hew Scott's *Fasti Ecclesiæ Scoticanæ*, vol. ii. pt. 2, p. 438.

of The Blood Royal

523. Descendants, if any, of the Hon. GRIZEL LESLIE (see Table LV.), wife of THOMAS DRUMMOND of Logiealmond.

524. Descendants of HUGH CATHCART, Capt. Indian Navy (see Table LV.), *d.* 25 Dec. 1770; *m.* [——], da. of [——] WATSON; and had issue 1*a.*

1*a.* *Hugh Cathcart,* m. *Ap.* 1809, *Caroline, da. of Conway Montgomery; and had issue* 1*b.*

1*b.* *Sir John Andrew Cathcart, 5th Bart.* [*S.*], *b.* 18 *Feb.* 1810; *d.* 25 *Mar.* 1878; *m.* 5 *July* 1836, *Lady Eleanor, da. of Archibald Kennedy, Earl of Cassilis, d.* 8 *May* 1877; *and had issue* 1*c to* 2*c.*

1*c.* Sir Reginald Archibald Edward Cathcart, 6th Bart. [S.], Capt. *late* Coldstream Guards (*Killochan Castle, Ayrshire; Titness Park, Sunninghill, Berks*), *b.* 1838; *m.* 5 Dec. 1880, Emily Eliza Steele, widow of John Gordon of Cluny, da. of John Robert Pringle.

2*c.* *Florence Margaret Isabella Cathcart, d.* 1902; m. 15 *Nov.* 1864, *Lieut.-Col. Michael Walker Heneage, Coldstream Guards; and had issue (a son and 3 das.).*

[No. 51241.

525. Descendants, if any, of JANE KENNEDY, wife of JOHN BLAIR of Dunskey; of CLEMENTINA KENNEDY, wife of GEORGE WATSON of Belton Park; and of JEAN KENNEDY, wife of Sir GILBERT KENNEDY of Girvanmains (see Table LV.).

526. Descendants of ARCHIBALD (MONTGOMERIE), 11th EARL OF EGLINTON [S.] (see Table LV.), *b.* 18 May 1726; *d.* 30 Oct. 1796; *m.* 2ndly, 9 Aug. 1783, FRANCES, da. of Sir William TWYSDEN of Raydon Hall, 6th Bart. [E.], *d.* (-); and had issue 1*a.*

1*a.* *Lady Mary Montgomerie, d.* 12 *June* 1848; m. 1*st,* 29 *Mar.* 1803, *Archibald Montgomerie, Lord Montgomerie, b.* 30 *July* 1773; *d.v.p.* (*at Alicante*) 4 *Jan.* 1814; 2*ndly, as* 1*st wife,* 30 *Jan.* 1815, *Sir Charles Montolieu Lamb, 2nd Bart.* [*G.B.*], *b.* 8 *July* 1785; *d.* 21 *Mar.* 1860; *and had issue* 1*b to* 2*b.*

1*b.* *Archibald (Montgomerie),* 13*th Earl of Eglinton* [*S.*], 1*st Earl of Winton* [*U.K.*], *K.T., b.* 29 *Sept.* 1812; *d.* 4 *Oct.* 1861; *m.* 1*st,* 17 *Feb.* 1841, *Theresa, widow of Richard Howe Cockerell, Comm. R.N., da. of Charles Newcomen, d.* 16 *Dec.* 1853; 2*ndly,* 3 *Nov.* 1858, *Lady Adela, da. of Arthur Algernon (Capell),* 6*th Earl of Essex* [*E.*], *d.* 31 *Dec.* 1860; *and had issue* 1*c to* 6*c.*

1*c.* *Archibald William (Montgomerie),* 14*th Earl of Eglinton* [*S.*], *b.* 3 *Dec.* 1841; *d.* 30 *Aug.* 1892; *m.* 6 *Dec.* 1862, *Lady Sophia Adelaide Theodosia, da. of Charles (Anderson-Pelham),* 2*nd Earl of Yarborough* [*U.K.*], *d.* 21 *Sept.* 1886; *and had issue.*

See p. 339, Nos. 24636–24648.

2*c.* *Hon. Seton Montolieu Montgomerie, b.* 15 *May* 1846; *d.* 26 *Nov.* 1883; *m.* 11 *June* 1870, *Nina Janet Bronwen* (*Downs House, Eling, Totton*), *da. of Col. Peers Williams, M.P.; and had issue* 1*d to* 2*d.*

1*d.* Alowen Dorothy Rose Montgomerie.

2*d.* Viva Seton Montgomerie.

3*c.* George Arnulph (Montgomerie), 15th Earl of Eglinton [S.], 2nd Earl of Winton [U.K.], Hereditary Sheriff of Renfrew, &c. (*Eglinton Castle, Irvine; The*

[Nos. 51242 to 51257.

The Plantagenet Roll

Pavilion, Ardrossan), b. 23 Feb. 1848 ; *m.* 13 Nov. 1873, Janet Lucretia, da. of Boyd Alexander Cuninghame of Craig Ends, co. Renfrew ; and has issue 1*d.* to 4*d.*

   1*d.* Archibald Seton Montgomerie, Lord Montgomerie, Lieut. 2nd Life Guards, and A.D.C. to Lieut.-Gen. Comdg. Bombay Forces (*Bachelors'; Boodle's*), *b.* 23 June 1880.

   2*d.* Hon. Francis Cuninghame Montgomerie, *b.* 25 Jan. 1887.

   3*d.* Lady Georgiana Theresa Montgomerie, *m.* 25 Ap. 1895, William Mure of Caldwell, D.L. (*Caldwell, by Glasgow*) ; and has issue 1*e.* to 2*e.*

      1*e.* William Mure, *b.* 9 Aug. 1898.

      2*e.* Marjorie Janet Mure, *b.* 4 Feb. 1896.

   4*d.* Lady Edith Mary Montgomerie, *m.* 22 July 1901, Capt. Algernon Richard Trotter, M.V.O., D.S.O., 2nd Life Guards (24 *Gloucester Place, W.; Merton Hall, Edinburgh*) ; and has issue 1*e.* to 3*e.*

      1*e.* Henry Redvers Trotter, *b.* 29 June 1902.

      2*e.* George Richard Trotter, *b.* 26 Feb. 1906.

      3*e.* Joan Catherine Trotter, *b.* 28 June 1903.

   4*c. Lady Egidia Montgomerie,* b. 17 *Dec.* 1843 ; d. 13 *Jan.* 1880 ; m. 4 *July* 1861, *Frederick William Brook* (*Thellusson*), *5th Baron Rendlesham* [*U.K.*] (*Rendlesham Hall, Woodbridge, Suffolk*) ; *and had issue* 1*d to* 8*d.*

   1*d.* Hon. Frederick Archibald Charles Thellusson (*White's ; Bachelors'*), *b.* 8 June 1868.

   2*d.* Hon. Percy Edward Thellusson, *b.* 30 Oct. 1874.

   3*d.* Hon. Hugh Edmund Thellusson, Lieut. R.A., *b.* 7 June 1876.

   4*d.* Hon. Adeline Egidia Thellusson, *m.* 22 Ap. 1891, Lewis Kerrison Jarvis (51 *South Street, Park Lane, W.*) ; and has issue 1*e.*

      1*e.* Louis Archibald Jarvis, *b.* 1892.

   5*d.* Hon. Miriam Isabel Thellusson, *m.* 26 Feb. 1901, Godfrey Williams (*Aberpergwn, Meath, Glamorganshire*).

   6*d.* Hon. Cecilia Blanche Thellusson.

   7*d.* Hon. Ruby Alexandrina Elizabeth Thellusson.

   8*d.* Hon. Mariota Thellusson, *m.* 28 Aug. 1895, Arthur George (Egerton), 5th Earl of Wilton [U.K.] (*Houghton Hall, Swaffham*) ; and has issue 1*e.* to 3*e.*

      1*e.* Seymour Edward Frederic Egerton, Viscount Grey de Wilton, *b.* 1 Aug. 1896.

      2*e.* Hon. George Arthur Egerton, *b.* 25 Jan. 1898.

      3*e.* Lady Mary Cecilia Egerton, *b.* 10 May 1901.

   5*c*². Lady Sybil Amelia Adela Montgomerie.

   6*c*². Lady Hilda Rose Montgomerie, *m.* 22 Feb. 1881, Tonman Mosley (2nd son of Sir Tonman Mosley, 3rd Bart. [G.B.]), J.P., D.L., C.A., Chairman Bucks County Council, and *late* Chairman Derby Quarter Sessions (*Bangors Park, Iver, Bucks*) ; and has issue 1*d.* to 4*d.*

   1*d.* Nicholas Mosley, Lieut. N. Stafford Regt., *b.* 28 July 1882.

   2*d.* Edward Hugh Mosley, *b.* 16 July 1884.

   3*d.* Hildred Mosley, *b.* 9 June 1887.

   4*d.* Hildegarde Sybil Mosley, *b.* 14 Jan. 1896.

   2*b. Charles James Savile Montgomerie Lamb,* b. 7 *Oct.* 1816 ; d. 11 *Dec.* 1856 ; m. 1841, *Anna Charlotte, da. of Arthur Grey of Bersted, co. Sussex* (*who re-m.* 4 *July* 1871, *Count H. A. de Chasse-Loap-Lanbat*), *and* d. 29 *Oct.* 1880 ; *and had issue* 1*c to* 4*c.*

   1*c.* Sir Archibald Lamb, 3rd Bart. [G.B.], *late* Major 2nd Life Guards, &c. (*Beauport, Battle, Sussex*), *b.* 5 Nov. 1845 ; *m.* 20 Mar. 1875, Louisa Mary Caroline, widow of John Richard Fenwick, da. of Sir Henry Estridge Durrant, 3rd Bart. [G.B.].   [Nos. 51258 to 51285.

# of The Blood Royal

2c. Charles Anthony Lamb, M.V.O., Lieut.-Col. and Brevet-Col. (ret.) Rifle Brigade, Mil. Attaché at Rome (*British Embassy, Rome; Naval and Military*), *b.* (posthumous) 21 Mar. 1857 ; *m.* 30 Dec. 1886, Lelia Frances, da. of William Rushton Adamson of Rushton Park, D.L.

3c. Mary Montgomerie Lamb, *m.* 1st, 27 Feb. 1864, Henry Sydenham Singleton of Mell, co. Louth, *d.* 16 Mar. 1893 ; 2ndly, 24 Jan. 1894, Philip Henry Wodehouse (Currie), 1st Baron Currie [U.K.], P.C., G.C.B., *late* H.B.M.'s Ambassador to the Court of Italy (*Hawley, Blackwater, Hants ; 8 Prince's Gate, S.W.*) ; and has issue 1*d* to 3*d*.

1*d.* John Rolland Singleton of Mell and of Hazely Heath, co. Hants (*Piers Court, Shercock, co. Cavan*), *b.* 31 July 1869 ; *m.* 1893, Frederica Julia, da. of the Rev. Julius Henry Rowley ; and has issue 1*e* to 2*e*.

1*e.* John Henry Philip Archibald Singleton, *b.* 1894.

2*e.* Mark Rodney Singleton, *b.* 1896.

2*d.* Clara Patience Sarah Singleton, *m.* 1895, [———], Baron de Groote, Belgian Minister to the Court of Athens.

3*d.* Sophy Mary Theresa Singleton, *m.* 1893, Lionel Anthony Harbord, of the Egyptian Police, *late* Bedfordshire Regt. ; and has issue 1*e* to 2*e*.

1*e.* Phyllis Mary Harbord, *b.* 1895.

2*e.* Patience Harbord, *b.* 1900.

4c. Flora Caroline Lamb, *m.* 12 Ap. 1871, Lieut.-Gen. George Hay Moncrieff, *late* Scots Guards (38 *Thurloe Square, S.W.*). [Nos. 51286 to 51295.

527. Descendants, if any, of Lady SUSANNAH MONTGOMERIE (see Table LV.), *d.* 27 July 1754 ; *m.* JOHN RENTON of Lamberton.

528. Descendants of Lady MARGARET MONTGOMERIE (see Table LV.), *d.* 30 Mar. 1799 ; *m.* as 2nd wife, 24 Ap. 1739, Sir ALEXANDER MACDONALD of Slate, 7th Bart. [S.], *d.* 23 Nov. 1746 ; and had issue 1*a* to 3*a*.

1*a. Sir James Macdonald, 8th Bart.* [S.], d. unm. (at Rome) 26 July 1766.

2*a. Alexander (Macdonald), 1st Baron Macdonald* [I.], d. 12 Sept. 1795 ; m. 3 May 1768, Elizabeth Diana, da. of Godfrey Bosville of Gunthwaite, co. York, d. 18 Oct. 1789 ; and had issue 1b to 9b.

1*b. Sir Alexander Wentworth (Macdonald), 2nd Baron Macdonald* [I.], d. unm. 9 June 1824.

2*b. Godfrey (Macdonald, sometime (1814–1824) Macdonald-Bosville), 3rd Baron Macdonald* [I.], b. 14 Oct. 1775 ; d. 13 Oct. 1832 ; m. 15 Dec. 1803, Louisa Maria, da. of Farley Edsir, d. 10 Feb. 1835 ; and had issue 1c to 8c.

1*c. Godfrey William Wentworth (Macdonald), 4th Baron Macdonald* [I.], b. 16 Mar. 1809 ; d. 25 July 1863 ; m. 21 Aug. 1845, Maria Anne, da. of George Thomas Wyndham of Cromer Hall, d. 21 Ap. 1892 ; and had issue 1d to 5d.

1*d. Somerled James Brudenell (Macdonald), 5th Baron Macdonald* [I.] b. 2 Oct. 1849 ; d. unm. 25 Dec. 1874.

2*d.* Ronald Archibald (Macdonald), 6th Baron Macdonald of Slate [I.], 14th Bart. [S.] *Armadale Castle, Isle of Skye ; 20 Chesham Place, S.W.*), *b.* 9 June 1853 ; *m.* 1 Oct. 1875, Louisa Jane Hamilton, da. of Col. George William Holmes Ross of Cromarty ; and has issue 1*e* to 4*e*.

1*e.* Hon. Somerled Geoffrey James Macdonald, *b.* 21 July 1876.

2*e.* Hon. Godfrey Evan Hugh Macdonald, *late* Lieut. Scots Guards, *b.* 5 Mar. 1879.

3*e.* Hon. Ronald Ian Macdonald, Lieut. 3rd Batt. Cameron Highlanders, *b.* 1 Oct. 1884.

4*e.* Hon. Iona Mary Adelaide Hope Macdonald. [Nos. 51296 to 51300.

The Plantagenet Roll

3d. Hon. **Eva Maria Louisa Macdonald**, *m.* 17 June 1873, Capt. Algernon Langham, Gren. Guards, *d.* 20 Dec. 1874; 2ndly, 27 Jan. 1885, Robert William (Napier), 2nd Baron Napier of Magdala [U.K.] (*66 Portland Place, W.; Lyndale, Portree, Isle of Skye*); and has issue 1*e.*

    1e. Hon. Eva Lilian Cecilia Napier.

4d. Hon. **Lilian Janet Macdonald**, *m.* 1st, 2 Aug. 1876, Francis (Mackenzie, *previously* Leveson-Gower), 2nd Earl of Cromartie [U.K.], *d.* 24 Nov. 1893; 2ndly, 7 Oct. 1895, Reginald F. Cazenove, *late* 6th Dragoon Guards (*North Lodge, Ascot*); and has issue 1*e* to 2*e.*

    1e. Sibell Lilian (Mackenzie), 3rd Countess of Cromartie [U.K.], *b.* 14 Aug. 1878; *m.* 16 Dec. 1899, Major Edward Walter Blunt (*Tarbat House, Ross-shire*); and has issue 1*f.*

        1f. Roderick Grant Blunt, Viscount Tarbat, *b.* 24 Oct. 1904.

    2e. Lady Constance Mackenzie, *b.* 1882; *m.* 19 Ap. 1904, Capt. Sir Edwin Austin Stewart-Richardson, 15th Bart. [S.] (*Pitfour Castle, Perthshire*); and has issue 1*f.*

        1f. Ian Rory Hay Stewart-Richardson, *b.* 25 Sept. 1904.

5d. Hon. **Alexandrina Victoria Macdonald** (H.M. Queen Victoria sponsor), *m.* 11 Nov. 1886, Capt. Anthony Charles Sykes Abdy (*18 Lowndes Square, S.W.*); and has issue 1*e* to 3*e.*

    1e. Grace Lilian Abdy, *b.* 22 Sept. 1887.

    2e. Violet Abdy, *b.* 4 Jan. 1892.

    3e. Constance Abdy, *b.* 4 June 1895.

2c. Hon. James William Bosville-Macdonald, Lieut.-Gen. and Col. 21st Lancers, C.B., K.L.H., K.M., b. 31 *Oct.* 1810; d. 4 *Jan.* 1882; m. 26 *Sept.* 1859, *the Hon. Elizabeth Nina, da. of Joseph Henry (Blake), 3rd Baron Wallscourt [I.],* d. 21 *July* 1890 ; *and had issue* 1d *to* 2d.

    1d. George ǀ Geoffrey Bosville-Macdonald, Capt. *late* Grenadier Guards, *b.* 17 May 1861.

    2d. Maria Selina Honoria Bosville-Macdonald, *m.* 14 Aug. 1889, the Hon. Alexander Hugh Willoughby (*Huntingdon, York*); and has issue 1*e* to 2*e.*

        1e. James Alexander Willoughby, *b.* 31 July 1890.

        2e. Joe Henry Claude Willoughby, *b.* 25 Jan. 1892.

3c. Hon. Elizabeth Diana Macdonald, b. 27 *Feb.* 1804 ; d. 9 *June* 1839 ; m. *as* 1st *wife,* 20 *June* 1825, *Duncan Davidson of Tulloch, Lord-Lieut. co. Ross, M.P.,* d. 20 *Sept.* 1882; *and had issue* 1d *to* 6d.

    1d. Duncan Henry Caithness Reay Davidson of Tulloch, J.P., D.L., Lieut.-Col. Ross Vol., b. 30 *June* 1836 ; d. 29 *Mar.* 1889 ; m. 26 *Jan.* 1860, *Georgiana Elizabeth, da. of John Mackenzie of Eileanach ; and had issue* 1e *to* 7e.

        1e. Duncan Davidson, 6th of Tulloch, J.P., D.L. (*Tulloch Castle, Dingwall, N.B.; 109 Belgrave Road, S.W.*), *b.* 3 Oct. 1865; *m.* 15 Nov. 1887, Gwendoline, da. of William D. Mackenzie, of Fawley Court.

        2e. Godfrey Bayne Davidson, *b.* 28 Mar. 1882.

        3e. Mary Davidson, *m.* 1879, Thomas George Dundas of Fingask (*Carron Hall, Larbert, N.B.*); and has issue 1*f* to 2*f.*

            1f. Thomas Archibald Dundas.

            2f. Ronald Dundas.

        4e. Elizabeth Diana Davidson, *m.* 1888, Capt. MacNicol; and has issue 1*f* to 4*f.*

            1f. Bayne MacNicol.

            2f. Valentine MacNicol.

            3f. Drusilla MacNicol.

            4f. Iris MacNicol.

        5e. Adelaide Lucy Davidson, *m.* 26 Jan. 1889, Capt. Harold Edwin Boulton,

[Nos. 51301 to 51326.

588

# of The Blood Royal

M.V.O., J.P., *late* 3rd Batt. Cameron Highlanders (*Copped Hall, Totteridge, co. Herts*); and has issue 1*f* to 3*f*.

1*f*. Denis Duncan Harold Owen Boulton.

2*f*. Christian Harold Ernest Boulton.

3*f*. Louise Kythe Veronica Boulton.

6*e*. Georgiana Veronica Davidson, *m.* 2 Jan. 1890, Rowland Hunt, M.P., J.P. (*Boratton Park, Shrewsbury; Kibworth Hall, Leicester*); and has issue 1*f* to 3*f*.

1*f*. Rowland Edward Brian Hunt.

2*f*. Benedict Philip Gerald Hunt.

3*f*. Marigold Veronica Hunt, *b.* 10 Nov. 1905.

7*e*. Christine Isabel Davidson, *m.* 8 Feb. 1896, Capt. the Hon. George Cecil Beaumont Weld Forester (*Barrow, Broseley, Salop*); and has issue 1*f*.

1*f*. Cecil George Wilfrid Weld Forester, *b.* 12 July 1899.

2*d*. *Caroline Louisa Davidson*, d. 1860; m. *Capt. George Wade; and had issue* 1*e* to 2*e*.

1*e*. Elizabeth Wade.

2*e*. Mary Wade.

3*d*. *Julia Bosville Davidson*, d. 17 *Oct.* 1901; m. 8 *Feb.* 1858, *the Hon. Henry Weyland Chetwynd, Capt. R.N.*, b. 8 *Oct.* 1829; d. 27 *Nov.* 1893; *and had issue* 1*e to* 7*e*.

1*e*. Henry Goulburn Willoughby Chetwynd, *b.* 12 Dec. 1858; *m.* 7 Nov. 1893, Eva Constance Elizabeth Fanny, da. of Augustus Berney of Sydney; and has issue 1*f* to 2*f*.

1*f*. Dorothy Constance Chetwynd.

2*f*. Sylvia Chetwynd.

2*e*. Godfrey Chetwynd (*Park Lane Hall, Doncaster*), b. 3 Oct. 1863; *m.* 1st, 12 Ap. 1893, Baroness Hilda, da. of Baron George von Alvensleben-Rusteberg (*mar. dissolved*); 2ndly, 10 Feb. 1904, the Hon. Mary, da. of William George (Eden), 4th Baron Auckland [G.B.].

3*e*. Walter James Bosville-Chetwynd, *b.* 30 Ap. 1865; *m.* 5 Mar. 1890, Ashton Yate, da. of Ashton Benyon of Stelchworth Park.

4*e*. Louis Wentworth Pakington Chetwynd, Comm. R.N., *b.* 16 Dec. 1866; *m.* 17 Jan. 1903, Augusta, da. of E. R. Robinson of 23 Washington Square, New York; and has issue 1*f*.

1*f*. Wentworth Randolph Chetwynd, *b.* 16 Dec. 1903.

5*e*. Ida Helen Lizzie Chetwynd, *m.* 14 Nov. 1899, Archibald William Merry of Belladrum, Beauly (14 *Upper Grosvenor Street, S.W.*); and has issue 1*f*.

1*f*. Eion James Henry Merry, *b.* 3 Jan. 1904.

6*e*. Katherine Adelaide Chetwynd, *m.* 8 Nov. 1893, Douglas Vickers (*Old Chapel House, Charles Street, Berkeley Square, W.*); and has issue 1*f* to 3*f*.

1*f*. Oliver Henry Douglas Vickers, *b.* 13 Sept. 1898.

2*f*. Sholto Douglas Vickers, *b.* 14 July 1902.

3*f*. Angus Douglas Vickers, *b.* 15 Feb. 1904.

7*e*. Margaret Diana Hopetoun Chetwynd, *m.* 2 June 1894, Sir Thomas Stanley Birkin, 2nd Bart. [U.K.] (*Aspley Hall, Nottingham*); and has issue 1*f* to 4*f*.

1*f*. Thomas Richard Chetwynd Birkin, *b.* 5 Mar. 1895.

2*f*. Henry Ralph Stanley Birkin, *b.* 26 July 1896.

3*f*. Charles Archibald Cecil Birkin, *b.* 30 Mar. 1905.

4*f*. Margaret Ida Maud Birkin, *b.* 8 Feb. 1900.

4*d*. *Adelaide Lucy Davidson*, d. 3 *Mar.* 1860; m. 20 *Ap.* 1849, *George William Holmes Ross of Cromarty, Lieut.-Col. and Hon. Col. Highland Rifle Militia, J.P., D.L., &c.*, b. 29 *Aug.* 1875; d. *Nov.* 1883; *and had issue* 1*e to* 5*e*.

[Nos. 51327 to 51355.

The Plantagenet Roll

1e. Duncan Munro Ross of Cromarty, J.P., D.L., d.s.p. 14 Jan. 1887.

2e. Walter Charteris Ross of Cromarty, C.B., J.P., Brevet-Col. Durham L.I. (*Cromarty House, Cromarty*), *b.* 5 Aug. 1857; *m.* 1st, 8 June 1887, May, da. of Field-Marshal Sir Donald Martin Stewart, 1st Bart. [U.K.], G.C.B., *d.* 2 June 1891; 2ndly, 5 Aug. 1897, Gertrude May Gathorne, da. of Charles Hill of Clevedon Hall, J.P.; and has issue 1*f* to 5*f*.

    1f. George Duncan Noël Ross, *b.* 25 Dec. 1903.

    2f¹. Pamela May Ross.

    3f². Jean Marina True Ross.

    4f². Meriel Diana Violet Ida Ross.

    5f. Sheila Mary Adelaide Ross.

3e. Katharine Elizabeth Julia Ross, *m.* 12 Feb. 1874, Major Francis Maude Reid, 71st Highland L.I.

4e. Louisa Jane Hamilton Ross, *m.* 1 Oct. 1875, Ronald Archibald (Macdonald), 6th Baron Macdonald [I.] (*Armadale Castle, Isle of Skye, &c.*); and has issue.

    See p. 587, Nos. 51297–51300.

5e. Ida Eleanora Constance Ross, *m.* 15 June 1881, Capt. the Hon. Godfrey Ernest Percival Willoughby, heir presumptive to Baron of Middleton [G.B.] (*The Green, Brompton R.S.O., Yorks*); and has issue 1*f* to 8*f*.

    1f. Henry Ernest Digby Hugh Willoughby, Sub-Lieut. R.N., *b.* 1 July 1882.

    2f. Michael Guy Percival Willoughby, *b.* 21 Oct. 1887.

    3f. Francis George Godfrey Willoughby, *b.* 29 Aug. 1890.

    4f. Rothwell Charles Wentworth Willoughby, *b.* 13 Feb. 1896.

    5f. Adelaide Daphne Hermione Willoughby, *b.* 20 Nov. 1883.

    6f. Leila Myrtle Dorothea Willoughby, *b.* 21 June 1886.

    7f. Ida Mary Hazel Willoughby, *b.* 30 Ap. 1889.

    8f. Julia Violet Monica Louise Willoughby, *b.* 8 Dec. 1893.

5d. Matilda Justina Davidson, *m.* June 1854, Lieut.-Col. John Cornelius Craigie-Halkett of Cramond, J.P., *late* 45th Regt. (*New Eltham, Kent*); and has issue 1*e* to 7*e*.

1e. Alice Louisa Craigie-Halkett, *m.* 20 Jan. 1876, George Frederick William Callander, J.P., D.L. (*Craigforth House, Stirling, &c.*).

2e. Elizabeth Diana Craigie-Halkett, *m.* 1884, Major George Samuel Abercromby Harvey; and has issue (a son).

3e. Susan Sinclair Craigie-Halkett.

4e. Ida Craigie-Halkett, *m.* 26 Jan. 1888, Cecil Colvin (*Felix Hall, Essex*).

5e. Maude Alexandrina Craigie-Halkett.

6e. Constance Mary Craigie-Halkett.

7e. Mabel Craigie-Halkett.

6d. Elizabeth Diana Davidson, *m.* 5 Jan. 1865, Patrick Alexander Watson Carnigy of Lour and Turin, J.P., D.L., *late* Capt. 15th Hussars (*Lour, Forfar*).

4c. Hon. Julia Macdonald, *b.* 30 Oct. 1805; *d.* 11 July 1884; *m.* 11 Oct. 1838, the Rev. Charles Walter Hudson, Rector of Trowell, Notts.

5c. Hon. Susan Hussey Macdonald, *b.* 24 Aug. 1807; *d.* 5 Nov. 1879; *m.* 9 Feb. 1832, Capt. Richard Beaumont, R.N., *d.* 2 Nov. 1877; and had issue.

6c. Hon. Diana Macdonald, *b.* 12 Ap. 1812; *d.* 8 Dec. 1880; *m.* 25 Ap. 1837, Col. John George Smyth of Heath Hall, co. York, M.P., *d.* 10 June 1869; and had issue.

    See the Clarence Volume, p. 340, Nos. 10891–10911.

7c. Hon. Marianne Macdonald, *b.* 27 July 1816; *d.* 12 July 1876; *m.* 28 July 1840, Capt. Henry Martin Turnor, King's Dragoon Guards; and had (with other) issue 1*d* to 2*d*.   [Nos. 51356 to 51406.

# of The Blood Royal

1d. *Archibald Henry Turnor*, d. (*? unm. in Japan*) *Dec.* 1867.

2d. Harriet Mina Turnor, *m.* 1 July 1869, John (Scott), 3rd Earl of Eldon [U.K.] (*Stowell Park, Northleach, Gloucester ; 43 Portman Square, W.*) ; and has issue 1e to 7e.

1e. *John Scott, Viscount Encombe*, b. 8 *May* 1870 ; d, 18 *Aug*. 1900 ; m. 25 *May* 1898, *the Hon. Mary Laura, da. of Simon (Fraser), 15th Lord Lovat* [S.] ; *and had issue 1f to 2f.*

1f. John Scott, Viscount Encombe, *b.* 29 Mar. 1899.

2f. Hon. Michael Simon Scott, *b.* 1 Ap. 1900.

2e. Hon. Ernest Stowell Scott, 2nd Sec. Diplo. Ser., *b.* 1 Nov. 1872.

3e. Hon. Osmund Scott, *b.* 24 Mar. 1876.

4e. Hon. Denys Scott, Lieut. R.N., Devon Imp. Yeo., *formerly* Royal Welsh Fusiliers, *b.* 1 June 1877.

5e. Hon. Michael Scott, *b.* 31 Aug. 1878.

6e. Lady Louisa Katharine Scott, *m.* 26 May 1898, John Longley, sometime Private Secretary to the Lord Privy Seal (Marquis of Salisbury) (41 *Draycott Place, S.W.*).

7e. Lady Margaret Rachel Scott, *m.* 27 Ap. 1897, the Hon. Frederick Gustavus Hamilton-Russell, J.P., D.L. (45 *Gloucester Place, W.*).

8c. *Hon. Octavia Sophia Macdonald*, d. 27 *Jan.* 1897 ; m. 7 *Dec.* 1841, *William James Hope-Johnstone, Younger of Annandale*, d.v.p. 17 *Mar.* 1850 ; *and had issue.* See the Clarence Volume, p. 251, Nos. 6048–6052.

3b. *Hon. Archibald Macdonald*, b. 21 *May* 1777 ; d. 5 *Feb.* 1861 ; m. 29 *Oct.* 1802, *Jane, da. and co-h. of Duncan Campbell of Ardneave,* d. *Oct.* 1860 ; *and had (with other, who all apparently* d.s.p.) *issue 1c to 2c.*

1c. Alexander George Macdonald, *b.* 5 Feb. 1813.

2c. Mary Macdonald, *b.* 18 Sept. 1806.

4b. *Hon. Dudley Stewart Erskine Macdonald*, b. 14 *Feb.* 1786 ; d. (*? unm.*) 26 *Aug.* 1840.

5b. *Hon. John Sinclair Macdonald*, b. 11 *Mar.* 1788.

6b. *Hon. William Macdonald.*

7b. *Hon. Diana Macdonald*, d. 22 *Ap.* 1845 ; m. *as 2nd wife,* 5 *Mar.* 1788, *the Right Hon. Sir John St. Clair of Ulbster, 1st Bart.* [G.B.], *P.C., M.P., D.C.L., F.R.S., &c.,* b. 1754 ; d. 21 *Dec.* 1835 ; *and had issue 1c to 5c.*

1c. *Sir George Sinclair, 2nd Bart.* [G.B.], b. 23 *Aug.* 1790 ; d. 9 *Oct.* 1868 ; m. 1 *May* 1816, *Lady Catherine Camilla, sister of Lionel (Tollemache), 6th Earl of Dysart* [S.], d. 17 *Mar.* 1863 ; *and had issue.* See the Tudor Roll of "The Blood Royal of Britain," pp. 205–206, Nos. 21482–21506.

2c. *Rev. William Sinclair, Rector of Pulborough and Preb. of Chichester,* b. 4 *Sept.* 1804 ; d. 8 *July* 1878 ; m. 1st, 28 *Dec.* 1837, *Helen, da. of William Ellice,* d. *Oct.* 1842 ; 2ndly, 15 *Ap.* 1846, *Sophia Mary Georgiana, da. of the Rev. James Tripp of Spofforth ; and had issue 1d to 6d.*

1d. *Walter Sinclair, Lieut.-Col. South Stafford Regt.,* b. 15 *Ap.* 1841 ; d. 1887 ; m. 4 *Feb.* 1874, *Kathleen, da. of Henry Dickinson of Ashton Keynes (who re-m.* 8 *Nov.* 1893, *Major-Gen. George Upton Prior, Comdg. at the Curragh*) ; *and had issue 1e.*

1e. Gladys Muriel Sinclair.

2d. Ven. William Macdonald Sinclair, D.D., Archdeacon of London and Canon of St. Paul's, &c. (*The Chapter House, St. Paul's Cathedral*).

3d. Rev. John Stewart Sinclair, M.A. (Oxon.), Vicar of Cirencester, Proctor in Convocation, Rural Dean and Hon. Canon of Gloucester (*The Vicarage, Cirencester*), *b.* 15 May 1853 ; *m.* 9 Aug. 1893, Clara Sophia, da. of John Dearman Birchall of Bowden Hall ; and has issue 1e to 4e. [Nos. 51407 to 51450.

The Plantagenet Roll

1e. Ronald Sutherland Brook Sinclair, *b.* 5 Sept. 1894.

2e. John Alexander Sinclair, *b.* 29 May 1897.

3e. Diana Clara Sinclair, *b.* 19 Oct. 1899.

4e. Margaret Sinclair, *b.* 5 Feb. 1903.

4d. Hugh Montgomerie Sinclair, Col. and A.Q.M.G. Southern Command (*Salisbury*), *b.* 23 Feb. 1855; *m.* 4 July 1905, Rosalie Sybil, da. of Sir John Jackson; and has issue 1e.

    1e. John Montgomerie Sinclair, *b.* 7 May 1906.

5d. Helen Sinclair, *m.* 27 Oct. 1880, the Rev. George Edmund Hasell, Rector of Aikton, Rural Dean of Wigton, and Hon. Canon of Carlisle (*Aikton Hall, Wigton*); and has issue 1e to 2e.

    1e. Edward William Hasell, *b.* 16 Jan. 1888.

    2e. Godfrey Sinclair Hasell, *b.* 2 Nov. 1889.

6d. Janet Mary Sinclair (*The Chapter House, St. Paul's Cathedral*).

3c. *Julia Sinclair, d. 19 Feb. 1868; m. as 2nd wife, 13 Nov. 1824, George (Boyle), 4th Earl of Glasgow [S.], 1st Baron Ross of Hawkhead [U.K.], b. 26 Mar. 1766; d. 6 July 1843; and had issue 1d.*

    1d. *George Frederick (Boyle), 6th Earl of Glasgow [S.], 3rd Baron Ross [U.K.], b. 9 Oct. 1825; d. 23 Ap. 1890; m. 29 Ap. 1856, the Hon. Montagu, da. of George Ralph (Abercromby), 3rd Baron Abercromby [U.K.]; and had issue 1e to 2e.*

    1e. Lady Gertrude Julia Georgina Boyle, *m.* 2 Dec. 1880, the Hon. Thomas Horatio Arthur Ernest Cochrane, M.P. (*Crawford Priory, Springfield, Fife*); and has issue 1f to 7f.

        1f. Thomas George Frederick Cochrane, *b.* 19 Mar. 1883.

        2f. Archibald Douglas Cochrane, R.N., *b.* 8 Jan. 1885.

        3f. Ralph Alexander Cochrane, *b.* 24 Feb. 1895.

        4f. Roger Cochrane, *b.* 2 June 1898.

        5f. Louisa Gertrude Montagu Cochrane, *b.* 8 Jan. 1882.

        6f. Katherine Elizabeth Cochrane, *b.* 16 Mar. 1890.

        7f. Dorothy Agnes Cochrane, *b.* 30 Aug. 1891.

    2e. Lady Muriel Louisa Diana Boyle, *b.* 18 Nov. 1873.

4c. *Catherine Sinclair, a distinguished Authoress, d. unm. 6 Aug. 1864.*

5c. *Helen Sinclair, d. 25 Ap. 1845; m. 10 Aug. 1826, Stair Hathorn-Stewart of Glasserton and Physgill, J.P., D.L., b. 29 Sept. 1796; and had issue 1d to 4d.*

    1d. Stair Agnew Stewart, *b.* 20 Aug. 1830.

    2d. John Sinclair Stewart, *b.* 26 Dec. 1836.

    3d. Diana Wentworth Stewart, *d.* 14 *July* 1897; *m.* 12 *May* 1847, *Brooke Cunliffe of Bathafarn, co. Denbigh, d. 27 Feb. 1897; and had issue 1e to 4e.*

        1e. Brooke Stewart Cunliffe, Chief Constable of Wigton, *formerly* 93rd Highlanders (*Wigton*), *b.* 12 June 1848; *m.* 3 July 1883, Grace Amey, da. of Thomas Gordon; and has issue 1f to 3f.

            1f. Brooke Foster Gordon Cunliffe, *b.* 2 Mar. 1889.

            2f. Mary Grace Hamilton Cunliffe.

            3f. Gladys Egerton Cunliffe.

        2e. Helen Edith Cunliffe,

        3e. Gwenwdd Cunliffe,   } (*Tyddyn, St. Asaph*).

        4e. Lettice Frederica Cunliffe,

    4d. Isabella Agnew Stewart (*Wallhouse, Bathgate, Linlithgow*), *m.* as 3rd wife, 22 Jan. 1874, Col. Andrew Gillon of Wallhouse, J.P., D.L., *b.* 22 Ap. 1823; *d.* June 1888; and had issue 1e to 3e.

        1e. Andrew Gillon, Capt. 4th Batt. Highland L.I., *b.* Dec. 1874.

        2e. Stair Agnew Gillon, *b.* Sept. 1877.

        3e. Helen Mary Gillon, *b.* Nov. 1879.

8b. *Hon. Elizabeth Macdonald, d. (? unm.).*

9b. *Hon. Annabella Macdonald, d. (? unm.).*   [Nos. 51451 to 51482.

# of The Blood Royal

3a. *Sir Archibald Macdonald, 1st Bart.* [*U.K.*]*, Chief Baron of the Court of Exchequer,* d. 18 *May* 1826; m. 27 *Nov.* 1777, *Lady Louisa, da. of Granville* (*Leveson-Gower*), 1st *Marquis of Stafford* [*G.B.*]*, K.G.,* d. 29 *Jan.* 1827; *and had issue.*

See the Tudor Roll of "The Blood Royal of Britain," p. 376, Nos. 28393–28394. [Nos. 51483 to 51484.

529. Descendants of Lady Christian Montgomerie (see Table LV.), d. (–); m. 1737, James Moray, 14th of Abercairny, d. (–); and had issue 1a to 3a.

1a. *Alexander Moray, 15th of Abercairny,* d.s.p.

2a. *Charles Moray, 16th of Abercairny,* d. 1810; m. [———]*, da. and h. of Sir William Stirling of Ardoch, 4th Bart.* [*S.*]; *and had issue 1b to 3b.*

1b. *James Moray, 17th of Abercairny, J.P., D.L., Lieut.-Col. Perth Militia, formerly 15th Hussars,* d.s.p. *Dec.* 1840.

2b. *William Moray, afterwards Moray-Stirling, 18th of Abercairny and of Ardoch,* d.s.p. 9 *Feb.* 1850.

3b. *Christian Stirling Moray, 19th of Abercairny, &c.,* b. 1779; d. 29 *Nov.* 1864; m. 14 *Ap.* 1812, *Henry Home-Drummond of Blair Drummond, M.P.,* b. 28 *July* 1783; d. 12 *Sept.* 1867; *and had issue 1c to 2c.*

1c. *George Stirling-Home-Drummond of Blair Drummond, Ardoch, &c.,* d.s.p. 3 *June* 1876.

2c. *Charles Stirling-Home-Drummond-Moray of Blair-Drummond, Abercairny, &c., J.P., D.L.,* b. 17 *Ap.* 1816; d. 24 *Sept.* 1891; m. 11 *Dec.* 1845, *Lady Anne Georgina, da. of Charles* (*Douglas*), 5th *Marquis of Queensberry* [*S.*]*, K.T.; and had issue 1d to 3d.*

1d. Henry Edward Stirling-Home-Drummond of Blair Drummond and Ardoch, J.P., D.L., Vice-Lieut. co. Perth, Capt. and Lieut.-Col., *late* Scots Guards, and sometime (1878–1880) M.P. (*Blair Drummond, Stirling; Ardoch, Braco*), b. 15 Sept. 1846; m. 23 Jan. 1877, Lady Georgina Emily Lucy, da. of Francis Hugh George (Seymour), 5th Marquis of Hertford [G.B.].

2d. William Augustus Home-Drummond-Moray, 21st of Abercairny, J.P., D.L., Capt. *late* Scots Guards (*Abercairny, Crieff, co. Perth*), b. 12 Ap. 1852; m. 27 Ap. 1899, the Hon. Gwendolen, da. of William (Edwardes), 4th Baron Kensington [I.].

3d. Caroline Frances Drummond, now Drummond Forbes of Millearne (*Millearne, Perth*), m. 25 Oct. 1881, Arthur Edward Whitmore Forbes, *afterwards* Drummond-Forbes; d. 12 Ap. 1904; *and has issue 1e to 2e.*

1e. Charles William Arthur Drummond, b. 16 Jan. 1885.

2e. Mary Christian Drummond, b. 12 Oct. 1882.

3a. *Susanna Moray,* m. *Col. John Seaton* (*said by Burke to have been heir and representative of the Earls of Dunfermline* [*S.*])*; and had issue.*

[Nos. 51485 to 51489.

530. Descendants of Sir James Kinloch, 4th Bart. [S.] (see Table LVI.), *bapt.* 8 Aug. 1705; d. (at Giez, Switzerland) 25 Mar. 1778; m. (at Pormy, near Berne) 9 Oct. 1731, Anne Marguerite, da. of Jean Rodolphe Wild of Berne; and had issue 1a to 5a.[1]

1a. [*Sir*] *James Kinloch* [de jure 5th Bart. [*S.*]], *Burgess of Cronay and Giez,* bapt. (*at Yverdon*) 29 *Jan.* 1749; d.s.p. (*there*) 22 *Oct.* 1802.

---

[1] See the descendants of Sir James Kinloch, Bart., by Henry Wagner, F.S.A., in "The Genealogist," N.S. 1898, xiv. pp. 200–261.

The Plantagenet Roll

2a. Louise (or Lisette) Kinloch, b. (at Yverdon) 8 Oct. 1733; d. 15 Mar. 1814; m. (at Champvent) 12 Mar. 1757, Frederic Casimir (de Brackel), Baron de Brackel in Courland, Seigneur de Chamblon, near Yverdon, d. (there) 1 Nov. 1779; and had issue 1b to 4b.

1b. Henri Frederic (de Brackel), Baron de Brackel, Seigneur de Chamblon, bapt. (at Yverdon) 11 July 1764; d. (there) 5 June 1857; m. 26 Feb. 1878, Henrietta, da. of John Rodolph Marcuard of Berne, d. (at Yverdon) 29 Nov. 1842; and had issue 1c to 2c.

1c. Rodolph Henry (de Brackel), Baron de Brackel, Lieut.-Col. in the service of the Duke of Zwei-Brücken, b. (at Yverdon) 27 Oct. 1790; d.s.p. 1853.

2c. Anne Marie de Brackel, b. 17 Jan. 1793; d. (at Yverdon) 3 Mar. 1878; m. (there) 14 May 1821, Francis Frederic Rusillon, Burgess of Yverdon, Belmont, Berne, and Neuchâtel b. (at Yverdon) 11 July 1781; d. (there) 28 Dec. 1853; and had issue 1d.

1d. Anne Antoinette Rusillon, b. 15 Nov. 1827; d. (–); m. as 1st wife, Dr. Lardy of Neuchâtel; and had issue 1e.

1e. Ernest Lardy, living s.p. 1898.

2b. Marie Margaret de Brackel, b. (at Yverdon) 5 Mar. 1766; d. (at Geneva) 9 Feb. 1838; m. (at Mathod) 12 Nov. 1791, Francis Augustus Maurice (de Vasserot), Baron de Vasserot, Seigneur de Vinci, Gilly and les Vaux, Burgess of Rolle, Gilly and Geneva, Col. in the French Service, b. (at Geneva) 29 May 1754; d. 12 Dec. 1841; and had issue 1c to 2c.

1c. Albert Francis James (de Vasserot), Baron de Vasserot, &c., b. 26 Jan. 1795; d.s.p. (at Geneva) 8 Mar. 1872.

2c. John Albert Arthur William de Vasserot, served in the Swiss Regt. in the Neapolitan Service, b. 18 Jan. 1802; d. (? s.p.).

3b. Anne de Brackel, b. (at Yverdon) 26 Ap. 1767; d. 8 Dec. 1823; m. (lic. Berne, 10 July) 1794, the Rev. William Douglas, Canon of Salisbury and Westminster and Vicar of Gillingham (son of the Bishop of Salisbury), b. 25 Dec. 1768; d. 19 Mar. 1819; and had issue 1c to 2c.[1]

1c. William Douglas of Lansdowne House, Bath, M.C.S., b. 29 June 1806; d. (–); m. 2ndly (at Madras), 5 July 1834, Caroline, da. of Capt. Joseph Hare, 22nd Dragoons. d. (–); and had issue 1d to 7d.

1d. John Charles Douglas, Major 29th Regt., b. (at Madras) 13 June 1842; m. 10 Dec. 1874, Agnes, da. of George Bird, M.C.S.; and has issue 1e to 2e.

1e. William Sholto Douglas, b. (at Jersey) 18 Sept. 1875.

2e. Lilian Vanda Douglas, b. (at Mhow, Bombay) 24 July 1879.

2d. Charles Whittingham Horsley Douglas, Capt. 92nd Highlanders, b. (at Cape of Good Hope) 17 July 1850.

3d. William Douglas, Lieut. 1st Royal Scots, b. 13 Aug. 1858.

4d. Selina Mary Douglas, b. (at Madras) 23 Nov. 1838; m. 13 July 1858, Robert Cotton Money, B.Sc.; and has issue 1e to 5e.

1e. Robert Cotton Money, b. 10 Jan. 1861.

2e. Ernest Douglas Money, b. (at Calcutta) 11 Mar. 1866.

3e. Harold Dalton Watson Moore Money, b. 30 June 1872.

4e. Audley Herbert Kyrle Money, b. 10 Sept. 1879.

5e. Sophia Ernle Money, b. 7 Dec. 1867.

5d. Caroline Annie Douglas, b. 27 Aug. 1840; m. 5 Mar. 1863, Charles Hinton Moore, sometime Royal Canadian Rifles; and has issue 1e to 3e.

1e. Laura Grace Moore, b. (at London, Canada) 6 Dec. 1863.

2e. Madeline Annie Moore, b. 30 May 1865.

3e. Caroline Ethel Moore, b. 20 July 1874.　　　　　　　　　[Nos. 51490 to 51505.

---

[1] "The Genealogist," 1881, O.S., v. p. 197.

# of The Blood Royal

6*d. Annie Elizabeth Douglas,* b. (*at Constallum, Madras*) 28 *Aug.* 1843; d. 22 *Ap.* 1876; m. (*at Kingston, Canada*) 16 *Sept.* 1867, *Frederick Bassett Doveton, sometime Royal Canadian Rifles; and had issue* 1*e.*

1*e.* Douglas Frederick Doveton, *b.* 28 July 1872.

7*d. Louisa Douglas,* b. (at Cape of Good Hope); *m.* 12 Sept. 1876, George Hobart, R.M.L.I.; and has issue 1*e* to 2*e.*

1*e.* Mary Hobart, *b.* 3 June 1877.

2*e.* Irene Hobart, *b.* 6 Aug. 1878.

4*b. Catherine Rose de Brackel,* b. 29 *Mar.* 1771; d. 4 *Nov.* 1857; m. (*a Bümplitz, Berne*) 23 *Aug.* 1797, *and again* (*at St. Osyth's, Essex*) 14 *July* 1798, *Frederick Nassau of St. Osyth's Priory,* d. 31 *July* 1845; *and had issue* 1*c to* 3*c.*

1*c. William Frederick Nassau of St. Osyth's Priory,* b. 6 *Dec.* 1798; d. 24 *Nov.* 1857; m. *Elizabeth, da. of Henry Garnet,* b. 10 *Sept.* 1809; d. 9 *Aug.* 1857; *and had issue* 1*d to* 2*d.*

1*d.* Elizabeth Nassau, *b.* 3 Nov. 1827; *m.* 7 Ap. 1845; John Roberts Kirby, *b.* 23 July 1819; *d.* (–); and has issue 1*e* to 4*e.*

1*e. D'Arcy Nassau Kirby, afterwards Nassau,* b. 9 *Oct.* 1859; *d.* 1 *Feb.* 1892; m. 3 *June* 1884, *Ada Georgina Alice, da. of Thomas Braddell,* C.M.G., *Attorney-Gen. of the Straits Settlements,* b. 1 *Ap.* 1854; *d.* 1887; *and had issue* 1*f.*

1*f.* Thomas D'Arcy Nassau, *b.* 2 Aug. 1886.

2*e.* Elizabeth Catherine Nassau Kirby, *b.* 3 Oct. 1846; *m.* 1880, Cecil Lamotte.

3*e.* Violet Nassau Kirby, *b.* 14 Feb. 1862; *m.* 16 Sept. 1879, Thomas de Multon Lee Braddell, Barrister-at-Law I.T.; and has issue.

4*e.* Maud Ethel Nassau Kirby, *b.* 12 Dec. 1867; *m.* 3 Jan. 1891, Henry Guy Harper of Oxford.

2*d.* Eliza Nassau, *b.* 10 July 1833; *m.* 15 May 1851, Charles Brandreth, 4th Light Dragoons, *b.* 20 Mar. 1827; *d.* 10 Aug. 1892; and has issue 1*e.*

1*e.* Margaret Brandreth, *b.* 14 Nov. 1866.

2*c. John Augustus Nassau,* b. 16 *Jan.* 1800; d. (–); m. *Mary, da. of* [——], d. 30 *Oct.* 1851; *and had issue.*

3*c. Anne Catherine Rose Nassau,* b. 15 *May* 1806; d. (–); m. 15 *Aug.* 1825, *Thomas Manning of Barbados.*

3*a. Rose Marguerite Kinloch,* b. (*at Giez*) 11 *May* 1735; bur. (*at Yverdon*) 21 *June* 1789; m. (*at Giez*) 6 *June* 1755, *Charles Louis de Coppet,* bapt. (*at Yverdon*) 15 *Ap.* 1730; d. 7 *Sept.* 1795; *and had issue* 1*b.*

1*b. Francis Casimir de Coppet, Burgess of Yverdon,* bapt. (*there*) 3 *July* 1758; bur. (*there*) 12 *July* 1831; m. 1785, *Anne Frances, da. of John James Perceret of Yverdon,* b. (*there*) 8 *Sept.* 1767; bur. (*there*) 5 *Dec.* 1832; *and had issue* 1*c to* 2*c.*

1*c. Louis de Coppet,* b. 8 *Oct.* 1788; d. (*at Yverdon*) 10 *Aug.* 1833; m. *Phillippine Frances, da. of John Daniel Herf of Kreutznach,* d. (*at Yverdon*) 24 *Feb.* 1824; *and had issue* 1*d to* 2*d.*

1*d. John Edward de Coppet of New York,* b. (*at Yverdon*) 11 *Sept.* 1810; d. (*at Lausanne*) 9 *Nov.* 1873; m. (*at Brooklyn, N.Y.*) 11 *Mar.* 1848, *Jane Maria, da. of Valentine Wightman Weston of New York,* b. (*in New York*) 11 *Aug.* 1785; d. (*there*) 15 *Oct.* 1863; *and had issue* 1*e.*

1*e. Constance Elsie de Coppet,* b. 29 *Sept.* 1850; d. (*at Lausanne*) 15 *Nov.* 1900; m. (*there*) 8 *May* 1871, *Edward Bernard Charles de Cérenville,* M.D. (*Lausanne*); *and had issue* 1*f to* 4*f.*

1*f.* Rene Charles de Cérenville, *b.* 27 Ap. 1875.

2*f.* Bernard Armand de Cérenville, *b.* 28 Ap. 1878.

3*f.* Ferdinand Roger de Cérenville, *b.* 4 Ap. 1880.

4*f.* Jane Emma de Cérenville, *b.* 26 Mar. 1873; *m.* 13 Ap. 1896, the Rev. Gonzalve Albert de Haller, Pastor of Montrewe (*Vevey*). [Nos. 51506 to 51520.

The Plantagenet Roll

2d. *Casimir Louis de Coppet of New York*, b. (*at Bingen on the Rhine*) 19 *May* 1813; d. (*at Bex*) 9 *Aug.* 1884; m. (*at New York*) 16 *Mar.* 1839, *Juliet Minerva, da. of Valentine Wightman Weston of New York*, b. (*at Balston Springs, U.S.A.*) 30 *Mar.* 1813; d. (*at Nice*) 14 *Ap.* 1898; *and had issue* 1e *to* 5e.

1e. Louis Casimir de Coppet, Ph.D. (Heidelberg), Burgess of Yverdon (*Nice*), b. (in New York) 21 July 1841; m. 1st (at Vienna), 13 Nov. 1869, Marie, da. of George de Carouso (by his wife, *née* the Princess Anne Dolgorouky), divorced 23 June 1886; 2ndly (at Lausanne), 25 July 1887, Julia Hortense Emma, da. of Thomas Joseph Adolphus Bouis of Moscow; and has issue 1f to 4f.

1f. Charles Alexander de Coppet, b. (at Lausanne) 4 Dec. 1888.

2f. Gerald Henry Frederic de Coppet, b. (at Lausanne) 26 Sept. 1892.

3f. Irene de Coppet, b. (at Lausanne) 24 Oct. 1870.

4f. Edith Valesca Julia de Coppet, b. (at Nice) 15 Mar. 1894.

2e. Henry de Coppet of New York (754 *Park Avenue, New York*), b. (at New York) 7 Feb. 1843; m. (there) 25 Feb. 1873, Laura, da. of Frederick Fawcett; and has issue 1f to 3f.

1f. Theakston de Coppet, Broker (754 *Park Avenue, New York*), b. (at New York) 31 Oct. 1876.

2f. Beatrice de Coppet, b. (at New York) 4 Oct. 1878.

3f. Gertrude de Coppet, b. (at New York) 30 Oct. 1880.

3e. Frederick de Coppet of New York (44 *Broadway, New York*), b. (at Brooklyn, U.S.A.) 10 Mar. 1845; m. 17 Sept. 1869, Jane A., da. of Martin Armstrong Howell of New Brunswick, N.J.; and has issue 1f to 2f.

1f. Louis Casimir de Coppet, Broker (24 *East* 10*th Street, New York*), b. (in New Brunswick, N.J.) 10 Dec. 1871.

2f. Ernest Howell de Coppet, Banker (14 *Central Park, W. New York*), b. (in New Brunswick N.J.) 24 Nov. 1873; m. (at Lausanne) Wilhelmina Henriette, da. of Capt. Henry Zegers Veeckens of the Dutch Service.

4e. Jules Edward de Coppet of New York, Broker (314 *West* 85*th Street, New York*), b. (in New York) 28 May 1855; m. (at Nice) 18 Jan. 1883, Claire Julia Pauline, da. of Thomas Joseph Adolphus Bouis of Moscow; and has issue 1f to 2f.

1f. Andrew Maurice de Coppet, b. (at New York) 10 Nov. 1891.

2f. Juliet de Coppet, b. (at New York) 25 Feb. 1883.

5e. Anne Laura de Coppet, b. (at New York) 27 July 1850; m. (at Nice) 27 Ap. 1881, Ernest Henry George Bellivet of Paris.

2c. *Rev. John Francis de Coppet*, b. 19 *Nov.* 1791; d. (*at Yverdon*) 12 *Oct.* 1870; m. (*at Correvon*) 10 *Ap.* 1823, *Adele, da. of Louis Lambert, Counsellor of State*, d. (*at Yverdon*) 6 *May* 1866; *and had issue* 1d *to* 3d.

1d. Paul Charles de Coppet, Burgess of Yverdon (*Paris*), b. 19 *May* 1827; m. (at New York) 21 Sept. 1853, Mary, da. of Peter Burtsell of New York, d. (near Paris) 4 Jan. 1889; and has issue 1e.

1e. Elsie Adele de Coppet, b. (in New York) 1856; m. (at Paris) 2 June 1892, Armand Domenech Diego of Perpignan (*Paris*).

2d. *Anne Louisa Frances de Coppet*, b. 18 *Mar.* 1824; d. (*at Mentone*) 31 *Dec.* 1862; m. *Louis Edward Piguet; and had issue.*

3d. Adele Emilie Jenny de Coppet, b. 1 July 1832.

4a. *Catherine Kinloch*, b. 2 *June* 1736; d. (–); m. (*at Giez*) 24 *June* 1763, *the Rev. Robert Brown, D.D., Minister of the English Church* (1751) *and British Agent at Utrecht* (1763), d. (*there*) 6 *Jan.* 1777; *and had issue* 1b *to* 2b.

1b. Lawrence James Brown, bapt. (*at Utrecht*) 11 *June* 1769.

2b. *Anne Elizabeth Brown*, b. (*at Utrecht*) 11 *June* 1764; d. (–); m. (*there*) 29 *May* 1786 (*her cousin-german*), *Dr. William Lawrence Brown, Prof. of Moral Philosophy and* Rector Magnificus *of the Univ. of Utrecht* (1788–1790), *and Principal of the Univ. of Aberdeen* (1796), b. (*at Utrecht*) 7 *Jan.* 1755; d. 11 *May* 1830; *and had issue.*   [Nos. 51521 to 51539.

596

# of The Blood Royal

5a. *Margaret Susanna Kinloch*, b. (*at Giez*) 14 *Oct.* 1742 ; bur. (*there*) 16 *Nov.* 1813 ; m. (*at Utrecht*) 10 *July* 1774, *John Christopher William de Rham*, b. (*at Lichtenberg, Brunswick*) 1733 ; bur. (*at Giez*) 18 *July* 1812 ; *and had issue* (4 *sons and 2 das. of whom*) 1b.

1b. *Rev. William Lewis de Rham, Vicar of Winkfield, Berks*, 1808–1843, b. *c.* 1781 ; d. *Oct.* 1843.

531. Descendants of Sir ALEXANDER KINLOCH, 8th Bart. [S.] (see Table LVI.), *d.* 12 Feb. 1813 ; *m.* 20 June 1801, ISABELLA, da. and co-h. of John STOWE of Newton, co. Lincoln, *d.* (at Nice) 10 Mar. 1861 ; and had issue 1*a*.

1a. *Sir David Kinloch, 9th Bart.* [S.], b. 1 *Sept.* 1805 ; d. 23 *Feb.* 1879 ; m. 5 *June* 1829, *Eleanor Hyndford, da. of Sir Thomas Gibson Carmichael, 7th Bart.* [S.], d. 15 *Oct.* 1849 ; *and had issue* 1b *to* 3b.

1b. Sir Alexander Kinloch, 10th Bart. [S.], J.P., D.L. (*Gilmerton, Haddington, N.B.*), b. 1 Feb. 1830 ; *m.* 12 Aug. 1852, Lucy Charlotte, da. of Sir Ralph Abercrombie Anstruther, 4th Bart. [S.], *d.* 14 Nov. 1903 ; and has issue.
See p. 369, Nos. 26632–26641.

2b. Isabella Anne Kinloch, *m.* 2 July 1863, Harington Balfour, *late* B.C.S. ; and has issue 1c.

1c. Nigel Harington Balfour, Major Motor Vol. Corps. (*Arthur's*), b. 12 June 1871 ; *m.* 1894, Grace Annette Marie, da. of Henry Madocks ; and has issue 1d to 3d.

1d. Sydney Harington Balfour.

2d. Harold Harington Balfour.

3d. Islay Monica Marie Balfour.

3b. Harriet Kinloch (5 *Cranley Place, S.W.*), *m.* 25 Ap. 1872, Admiral Sir Henry Fairfax, K.C.B., R.N., *d.s.p.* 20 Mar. 1900.   [Nos. 51540 to 51556.

532. Descendants of MARY KINLOCH (see Table LVI.), *d.* (–) ; *m.* 1775, Sir THOMAS ASHE of Ashefield in Meath, M.P. ; and had issue 1*a* to 3*a*.

1a. *Joseph Ashe.*

2a.
3a. } (2 das.).

533. Descendants of HARRIET KINLOCH (see Table LVI.), *d.* 9 Sept. 1830 ; *m.* 1 Oct. 1781, Sir FOSTER CUNLIFFE, 3rd Bart. [G.B.], *b.* 8 Feb. 1755 ; *d.* 15 June 1834 ; and had issue 1*a* to 5*a*.

1a. *Sir Robert Henry Cunliffe, 4th Bart.* [G.B.], C.B., b. 22 *Ap.* 1785 ; d. 10 *Sept.* 1859 ; m. 1st, 15 Dec. 1805, *Louisa, widow of Major Arthur Forest, da. of* [——], *d.* 4 *May* 1822 ; 2ndly, 2 *Ap.* 1825, *Susan Emily, da. of Col. John Paton, Commissary-Gen. of the Bengal Army, d.* 11 Nov. 1856 ; *and had issue* 1b *to* 9b.

1b. Robert Ellis Cunliffe, H.E.I.C.S., b. 27 *Mar.* 1808 ; d.v.p. 31 *Mar.* 1855 ; m. 2 *May* 1837, Charlotte, da. of Ilted Howel, d. 1856 ; and had issue 1c to 6c.

1c. Sir Robert Alfred Cunliffe, 5th Bart. [G.B.], J.P., D.L., Hon. Col. 3rd Batt. Royal Welsh Fusiliers, &c. (*Acton Park, Wrexham*), b. 17 Jan. 1839 ; *m.* 1st, 5 Aug. 1869, Eleanor Sophia Egerton, da. of Col. Egerton Leigh of West Hall and Godrell Hall, co. Chester, M.P., *d.* 13 Mar. 1898 ; 2ndly, 5 Jan. 1901, Cecilie
[No. 51557.

Victoria, da. of Lieut.-Col. the Hon. William Edward Sackville West; and has issue 1*d* to 4*d*.

1*d*. Foster Hugh Egerton Cunliffe, M.A. (Oxon.), *b.* 17 Aug. 1875.

2*d*. Robert Neville Henry Cunliffe, *b.* 8 Feb. 1884.

3*d*. Mary Evelyn Cunliffe.

4*d*. Hythe Cunliffe.

2*c*. Walter Howell Cunliffe, J.P., Lieut.-Col. *late* Oxfordshire L.I. (*The Shrubbery, Newbury, Berks; Naval and Military*), *b.* 8 Sept. 1850; *m.* 14 Sept. 1875, Gertrude, da. of William Fry Foster; and has issue 1*d*.

1*d*. Gwynedd Sybilla Cunliffe.

3*c*. Rhoda Helen Cunliffe.

4*c*. Charlotte Caroline Cunliffe, *m.* 7 Jan. 1874, the Rev. Henry Samuel Priestly, Vicar of Talyllyn, d. 190–; and has issue 1*d*.

1*d*. Francis John Lloyd Priestly, *b.* 1874; *m.* 1902, Pearl, da. of Lieut.-Col. Llewellyn England Sidney Parry, D.S.O.

5*c*. Lucy Mary Cunliffe, *m.* 19 Ap. 1865, the Rev. Francis Furse Vidal, M.A., Rector of Creeting SS. Mary, Olave and All Saints (*Creeting St. Mary Rectory, Needham Market*); and has issue 1*d* to 9*d*.

1*d*. Owen Cunliffe Vidal, *b.* Mar. 1869; *m.*

2*d*. Iltyd Cunliffe Vidal, *b.* 11 July 1874; *m.* Mary, da. of [——] M'Laughlin.

3*d*. Alan Cunliffe Vidal, *b.* May 1880.

4*d*. Norman Cunliffe Vidal, *b.* June 1882.

5*d*. Gwynedd Lilian Cunliffe Vidal, *b.* 9 Feb. 1867.

6*d*. Maude Cunliffe Vidal, *b.* 8 Feb. 1868; *m.* 1892, Frederic Scrutton.

7*d*. Helen Cunliffe Vidal, *b.* July 1871.

8*d*. Violet Cunliffe Vidal, *b.* Feb. 1873.

9*d*. Gladys Cunliffe Vidal, *b.* July 1884.

6*c*. Rose Geraldine Cunliffe, *m.* 23 Aug. 1877, the Rev. Reginald Edwards, Vicar of Speen (*Speen Vicarage, near Newbury*).

2*b*. *David Cunliffe, B.C.S.*, *b.* 14 *Feb.* 1815; *d.* 19 *Sept.* 1873; *m.* 24 *Oct.* 1837, *Fanny Priscilla, da. of Samuel Davies, M.D.*, d. 6 *Nov.* 1896; *and had issue* 1*c* to 7*c*.

1*c*. David Arthur Cunliffe, *b.* 5 May 1850.

2*c*. Foster Kinloch Cunliffe, *b.* 28 June 1851; *m.* 1st, 1881, Henrietta, da. of J. H. Worthington of Oxton, J.P., *d.* 3 Mar. 1889; 2ndly, Adele, da. of Capt. Horatio Gillmore; and has issue 1*d* to 4*d*.

1*d*. Helen Brooke Cunliffe, *b.* 21 Nov. 1882.

2*d*. Nora Dorothy Cunliffe, *b.* 22 Nov. 1885.

3*d*. Phyllis Rowena Cunliffe, *b.* 12 Dec. 1886.

4*d*. Cecily Agnes Cunliffe, *b.* 10 Aug. 1888.

3*c*. Alfred Edward Cunliffe (3 *Old Ballyganj, Calcutta*), *b.* 5 July 1853; *m.* 28 Ap. 1886, Agnes, da. of J. M. Comley of Calcutta, M.D.; and has issue 1*d* to 3*d*.

1*d*. Robert Ellis Cunliffe, *b.* 17 Oct. 1893.

2*d*. Cyril Henley Cunliffe, *b.* 3 Mar. 1901.

3*d*. Muriel Hyde Cunliffe, *b.* 1 July 1890.

4*c*. Ernest William Cunliffe, Lieut.-Col. Indian Army, *b.* 24 Feb. 1857; *m.* 1st, 1885, Mary Adeline, da. of Major-Gen. David Limond, C.B., *d.* 1899; 2ndly, 1900, Isabella Fergusson, da. of John Bradford; and has issue 1*d* to 4*d*.

1*d*. Robert David Cunliffe, *b.* 1887.

2*d*. William Lockhart Cunliffe, *b.* 1902.

3*d*. Ethel Laura Cunliffe, *b.* 1886.

4*d*. Thelma Cunliffe, *b.* 1890.

[Nos. 51558 to 51592.

# of The Blood Royal

5c. Ada Frances Cunliffe, *m.* 2 Ap. 1865, Charles Tweedie; and has issue 1d to 4d.

1d. James Walter Tweedie, *b.* 21 Nov. 1869.

2d. Mina Frances Tweedie.

3d. Ada Mabel Tweedie.

4d. Mary Dorothea Tweedie.

6c. Emma Charlotte Cunliffe, *m.* as 2nd wife, 30 Sept. 1863, James Tweedie, *late* of Rachan, Quarter, &c., co. Peebles, J.P., D.L. (*Conservative*); and has issue 1d to 6d.

1d. Thomas Cunliffe Tweedie, *b.* 14 Aug. 1864; *m.* 1893, Emily Sophia, da. of Major-Gen. Jackson Muspratt Muspratt-Williams; and has issue 1e.

1e. Douglas Oswald Tweedie, *b.* 20 Oct. 1895.

2d. Percy Charles Tweedie, *b.* 23 Mar. 1868.

3d. Lawrence William Tweedie, *b.* 17 Aug. 1870.

4d. Francis James Tweedie, *late* E. Lancashire Regt., *b.* 21 Feb. 1872.

5d. Gerald Scott Tweedie, Capt. 1st Royal Scots, *b.* 24 Nov. 1874.

6d. Amy Charlotte Tweedie.

7c. Laura Cunliffe.

3b. *Louisa Harriot Cunliffe, d. 10 Feb. 1899; m. 21 Oct. 1835, Lieut.-Col. Hippisley Marsh; and had issue 1c to 3c.*

1c. Hippisley Cunliffe Marsh, Col. *late* B.S.C., *b.* 14 Aug. 1864; *m.* 1877, Emma, da. of Col. Hebbert, R.E.; and has issue 1d to 2d.

1d. Cunliffe Ellis Marsh.

2d. Alexander Marsh, *b.* 1888.

2c. Frank Hall Berwick Marsh, Col. B.S.C., *b.* 23 Mar. 1869; *m.* 1878, Sophia, da. of Col. C. E. Taylor, M.C.S.; and has issue 1d to 4d.

1d. Bruce Marsh.

2d. Clara Marsh.

3d. Gertrude May Marsh.

4d. Ethel Emily Marsh.

3c. Amy Charlotte Marsh.

4b. Mary Cunliffe.

5b. Harriot Cunliffe.

6b. Emily Cunliffe.

7b. *Janet Victoria Cunliffe, d. 3 July 1900; m. 19 Feb. 1867, Major-Gen. Andrew Aldcorn Munro, B.S.C., d. 2 Feb. 1898; and had issue 1c to 2c.*

1c. Ronald Martin Cunliffe Munro, *b.* 1874.

2c. Annabel Emily Munro.

8b. *Clare Cunliffe, d. (–); m. 6 Oct. 1875, Thomas William Hopper Tollbort, B.C.S., Deputy Commissioner at Ambala.*

9b. Alicia Cunliffe.

2a. *Ellis Watkin Cunliffe, b. 5 Sept. 1787; d. 20 Dec. 1866; m. 13 June 1822, Caroline, da. of John Kingston, d. 1856; and had issue 1b to 3b.*

1b. Ellis Brooke Cunliffe, J.P., Capt. 6th Dragoons (*Petton Park, Shrewsbury*), *b.* 6 July 1832; *m.* 17 July 1867, Emma Florence, da. and h. of the Rev. John Sparling of Petton Park; and has issue.

See the Clarence Volume, p. 325, Nos. 9424–9440.

2b. *Caroline Cunliffe, d. (–); m. 23 Dec. 1850, William Fry Foster of Lee Court, co. Hants; and had issue 1c to 7c.*

1c. Reginald Cunliffe Foster, *b.* 5 Oct. 1860.

2c. Ellis Cunliffe Foster, *b.* 22 Ap. 1863.   [Nos. 51593 to 51638.

3c. Gertrude Foster, *m.* 14 Sept. 1895, Col. Walter Howell Cunliffe, J.P.; and has issue.

See p. 598, No. 51563.

4c. Sybella Caroline Foster.

5c. Florence Annabel Foster.

6c. Helen Mary Foster.

7c. Lucy Edith Foster.

3b. *Gertrude Cunliffe,* d. 24 *June* 1876; m. *as 2nd wife,* 4 *June* 1868, *Edmund Swetenham of Cam-yr-Alyn, co. Denbigh, Bar.-at-Law, Q.C., J.P.,* b. 15 *Nov.* 1822; d. 19 *Mar.* 1890; *and had issue* 1c *to* 2c.

1c. Foster Swetenham, Lieut. Royal Scots Greys, *b.* 21 June 1876.

2c. Florence Swetenham.

3a. *Brooke Cunliffe of Erbistock Hall, co. Denbigh, H.E.I.C.S.,* b. 23 *July* 1790; d. 11 *Dec.* 1857; m. 1*st,* 1814, *Mary, da. of John Pirie of Aberdeen,* d. 11 *Sept.* 1825; 2*ndly,* 1827, *Elizabeth, da. of John Rayson,* d. 4 *Aug.* 1833; 3*rdly,* 12 *Sept.* 1850, *Frances, da. of the Rev. James Radcliffe Lyon,* d. 16 *Jan.* 1865; *and had issue* 1b *to* 5b.

1b. *Brooke Cunliffe of Bathafarn,* b. 6 *Sept.* 1815; d. 1897; m. 12 *May* 1847, *Diana Wentworth, da. of Stair Hathorn-Stewart of Physgill, J.P., D.L.,* d. 1897; *and had issue.*

See p. 592, Nos. 51472–51478.

2b. *George Gordon Cunliffe, Major-Gen. in the Army,* b. 24 *Sept.* 1824; d. 29 *Jan.* 1900; m. 22 *May* 1858, *Pauline, da. of Capt. J. Lumsdaine; and had issue* 1c *to* 5c.

1c. Frederick Hugh Gordon Cunliffe, Capt. Royal Inniskilling Fusiliers, now serving as Major N. Nigeria Regt., *b.* 6 Sept. 1861; *m.* 1895, Ellie Sophia, da. of David Gaussen; and has issue 1*d.*

1d. Cecilie Gertrude Cunliffe.

2c. Gertrude Mary Blanche Cunliffe, *m.* 1881, Lewis Gordon Mortimer.

3c. Mary Dora Cunliffe.

4c. Ethel Brooke Cunliffe.

5c. Louisa Egerton Cunliffe, *m.* 1895, John Williams Rogerson; and has issue 1*d.*

1d. Violet Cunliffe Rogerson.

3b. Foster Lionel Cunliffe, Lieut.-Col. and Brevet-Col. R.H.A., *b.* 26 Ap. 1855; *m.* 10 Ap. 1894, Alice Mary, da. of Edward Lyon of Windlesham Hall, Bagshot; and has issue 1*c* to 2*c.*

1c. Robert Lionel Brooke Cunliffe, *b.* 15 Mar. 1895.

2c. [da.] Cunliffe, *b.* 1 July 1900.

4b. *Louisa Cunliffe,* d. *June* 1902; m. 11 *Mar.* 1840, *Rev. William Henry Egerton, Preb. of Lichfield and Rector of Whitchurch (Whitchurch Rectory, Salop); and had issue* 1c *to* 4c.

1c. Rev. Brooke de Malpas Egerton, M.A. (Oxon.), Rector of Stoke-on-Terne and Vicar of Child's Ercall, Market Drayton, *b.* 19 Aug. 1845; *m.* 26 June 1878, Alice Catherine, da. of the Rev. Edward Rose Breton.

2c. Frederick Philip Egerton, *b.* 8 Aug. 1853.

3c. Mary Egerton.

4c. Mabel Egerton, *m.* 13 Nov. 1893, Robert Peel, Ethelston (*Hinton, Salop*).

5b. *Frances Brooke Cunliffe,* d. (–); m. 29 *Ap.* 1876, *George Le Mesurier Gretton, Bar.-at-Law* (49 *Drayton Gardens, South Kensington*); *and had issue* 1c *to* 4c.

1c. [son] Gretton, *b.* 11 Ap. 1878.

2c. [son] Gretton, *b.* 7 May 1880.

3c. [da.] Gretton, *b.* 11 Feb. 1877.

4c. [da.] Gretton, *b.* 11 Jan. 1882.

[Nos. 51639 to 51670.

# of The Blood Royal

4a. *Mary Cunliffe*, d. 14 *June* 1838; m. 9 *Ap.* 1806, *the Right Hon. Charles Watkin Williams Wynn, P.C., M.P.,* d. 2 *Sept.* 1850; *and had issue.*

See the Tudor Roll of "The Blood Royal of Britain," pp. 276–277, Nos. 24824–24860.

5a. *Harriet Cunliffe*, d. 13 *Ap.* 1825; m. 4 *Dec.* 1809, *Sir Richard Brooke of Norton, 6th Bart.* [*E.*], b. 18 *Aug.* 1785; d. 11 *Nov.* 1865; *and had issue* 1b *to* 8b.

1b. *Sir Richard Brooke, 7th Bart.* [*E.*], b. 13 *Dec.* 1814; d. 3 *Mar.* 1888; m. 1st, 12 *Dec.* 1848, *Lady Louisa, sister of James (Duff), 5th Earl of Fife* [*I.*], d. 23 *Sept.* 1864; 2ndly, 21 *Dec.* 1871, *Henrietta Elizabeth, da. of Sir Harry Mainwaring, 2nd Bart.* [*U.K.*]; *and had issue* 1c *to* 12c.

1c. Sir Richard Marcus Brooke, 8th Bart. [E.], J.P., D.L. (*Norton Priory Halton, Runcorn*), b. 26 *Nov.* 1850; m. 16 Jan. 1883, Alice, da. of John Sambrooke Crawley of Stockwood, Luton; and has issue 1d.

1d. Richard Christopher Brooke, b. 8 Aug. 1888.

2c. Basil Poynings Brooke, b. 28 Sept. 1853.

3c. Jocelyn James Pusey Brooke, b. 21 Jan. 1855.

4c. Victor Alexander Brooke, b. 20 Ap. 1857.

5c. Octavius George Brooke (*Junior Carlton*), b. 19 June 1858.

6c. Lionel Brooke, b. 17 Nov. 1859.

7c. Reginald Cecil Brooke, b. 6 July 1861.

8c. Mabel Dorothy Brooke.

9c. Winifred Agnes Emily Brooke.

10c. Lilian Louisa Lettice Brooke.

11c. Constance Ida Brooke.

12c. Rosalind Hester Brooke.

2b. *Thomas Brooke, Gen. and Col. 28th Regt.,* b. 2 *Ap.* 1817; d. 4 *Nov.* 1880; m. 8 *Dec.* 1840, *Catherine Marie Diana, da. of Col. Draper, Scots Guards; and had issue* 1c *to* 2c.

1c. Alured de Vere Brooke, Col. R.E., b. 10 Nov. 1841; m. 14 July 1873, Mary Augusta, da. of Bonamy Dobree of 4 Queen's Gate Place; and has issue 1d.

1d. Maye Amelie Lucile Brooke, m. 20 Ap. 1904, Lieut. Archibald Cochrane, R.N.

2c. Lucile Diana Mauritia Brooke, m. 22 Dec. 1874, Robert Edward Tomkinson (6 *Buckingham Palace Gardens, S.W.*).

3b. *Arthur Brooke*, b. 24 *Ap.* 1819; d. 7 *June* 1903; m. 19 *Feb.* 1852, *Susan, da. of the Rev. Alexander Buchanan of Hales,* d. 25 *Nov.* 1852; *and had issue* 1c.

1c. Helen Maude Brooke (twin), m. 26 June 1878, the Rev. William Wentworth Wodehouse, d. 26 Mar. 1888; and has issue 1d to 2d.

1d. Arthur Hugh Wodehouse, Lieut. R. Dublin Fusiliers, b. 26 Ap. 1879.

2d. Alice Mary Wodehouse.

4b. *Mary Brooke*, d. 21 *Ap.* 1881; m. 7 *May* 1831, *Rowland Eyles Egerton-Warburton of Arley,* d. 6 *Dec.* 1891; *and had issue.*

See p. 513, Nos. 44814–44838.

5b. *Harriet Brooke*, d. 16 *July* 1898; m. 23 *Nov.* 1837, *William (Brabazon), 11th Earl of Meath* [*I.*], *2nd Baron Chaworth* [*U.K.*], d. 26 *May* 1887; *and had issue.*

See p. 204, Nos. 7310–7317.

6b. *Jessy Brooke*, d. 18 *July* 1892; m. 22 *May* 1832, *the Hon. Richard Bootle-Wilbraham, M.P.,* b. 27 *Oct.* 1801; d.v.p. 5 *May* 1844; *and had issue* 1c *to* 4c.

1c. *Edward (Bootle-Wilbraham), 2nd Baron Skelmersdale and 1st Earl of Latham* [*U.K.*], *G.C.B., Lord Chamberlain of the Household to Queen Victoria,* b. 12 *Dec.* 1837; d. 19 *Nov.* 1898; m. 16 *Aug.* 1860, *Lady Alice, da. of George William Frederick (Villiers), 4th Earl of Clarendon* [*G.B.*], d. 23 *Nov.* 1897; *and had issue* 1d *to* 6d.
[Nos. 51671 to 51759.

601

The Plantagenet Roll

1*d*. Edward George (Bootle-Wilbraham), 2nd Earl of Lathom [U.K.], &c. (*Lathom House, Ormskirk; Bryanston Square, W.*), *b*. 26 Oct. 1864; *m*. 15 Aug. 1889, Lady Wilma, da. of William (Pleydell-Bouverie), 5th Earl of Radnor [G.B.]; and has issue 1*e* to 4*e*.

    1*e*. Edward William Bootle-Wilbraham, Lord Skelmersdale, *b*. 16 May 1895.

    2*e*. Lady Helen Alice Bootle-Wilbraham, *b*. 12 Aug. 1890.

    3*e*. Lady Barbara Ann Bootle-Wilbraham, *b*. 2 May 1893.

    4*e*. Lady Rosemary Wilma Bootle-Wilbraham, *b*. 2 Oct. 1903.'

    2*d*. Hon. Villiers Richard Bootle Wilbraham, *b*. 17 Ap. 1867; *m*. 1900, Violet Inez, da. of [——] de Romeiro.

    3*d*. Hon. Reginald Francis Bootle Wilbraham (*The Bath*), *b*. 26 July 1875; *m*. 1903, Lilian Mary, da. of Major William Lister Holt.

    4*d*. Lady Alice Maud Bootle Wilbraham (Princess Alice sponsor) (26 *Lower Sloane Street, S.W.*).

    5*d*. Lady Florence Mary Bootle Wilbraham, *m*. 16 Aug. 1887, the Rev. Lord Rupert Ernest William Gascoyne-Cecil; and has issue.

See p. 216, Nos. 7658–7663.

    6*d*. Lady Bertha Mabel Bootle Wilbraham, *m*. 9 May 1903, Major Arthur Frederick Dawkins, *d*. (*in Mauritius*) 1905; and has issue.

See p. 458, No. 36655.

    2*c*. Hon. Jessy Caroline Bootle Wilbraham, *m*. 4 Oct. 1865, John Bateman (*Moverons Manor, co. Essex; The Hall, Brightlingsea*); and has issue 1*d*.

    1*d*. Agnes Mary Bateman, *m*. 1889, Capt. Robert D'Arcy Hildyard, 1st Batt. Durham L.I.

    3*c*. *Hon. Edith Bootle-Wilbraham*, *b*. 16 *Jan*. 1840; *d*. 2 *Feb*. 1894; *m*. 7 *Feb*. 1859, *Ynyr Henry Burges, J.P., D.L., High Sheriff co. Tyrone* (*Parkanaur, Castle Caulfield, Tyrone*); *and had issue* 1*d* to 5*d*.

    1*d*. *Ynyr Richard Patrick Burges*, *b*. 15 *Mar*. 1866; *d*. 20 *Dec*. 1905; *m*. 23 *Oct*. 1895, *Frederica, da. of Alfred Gillett; and had issue*.

    2*d*. Edith Alice Burges, *m*. 17 Oct. 1895, Arthur Howard Frere (19 *Eccleston Square, S.W.*); and has issue.

    3*d*. Ethel Margaret Burges, *m*. 7 Oct. 1885, Major James Henry Stronge, 5th Bart. [U.K.] (*Tynan Abbey, co. Armagh*); and has issue 1*e* to 6*e*

    1*e*. James Matthew Stronge, *b*. 10 Jan. 1891.

    2*e*. Zoë Edith Stronge.

    3*e*. Daphne Helen Stronge.

    4*e*. Rose Ethel Stronge.

    5*e*. Jessy Stronge.

    6*e*. Joy Winifred Stronge.

    4*d*. Myrtle Constance Burges, *m*. John Poer O'Shea; and has issue.

    5*d*. Irene Caroline Burges, *m*. 9 Feb. 1898, Ernald Edward Richardson, J.P., Capt. Royal Carmarthen Artillery Militia (*Glanbrydan, Manordils, R.S.O., Carmarthenshire; Junior Carlton*); and has issue (with 3 others) 1*e*.

    1*e*. Rose Eirene Ynyr Stella Richardson, *b*. 6 Jan. 1899.

    4*c*. Hon. Rose Bootle-Wilbraham (*Blythe Hall, Ormskirk*).

    7*b*. *Caroline Frances Brooke, d*. 8 *Jan*. 1895; *m*. 18 *Nov*. 1834, *the Hon. Arthur Lascelles of Norley*, *b*. 25 *Jan*. 1807; *d*. 19 *July* 1880; *and had issue* 1*c* to 8*c*.

    1*c*. *Walter Richard Lascelles of Norley, J.P., D.L., Col. late Rifle Brigade, sometime* (1885–1886) *Assist. Mil. Sec. and* (1886–1891) *A.A.G. at Headquarters, &c.; b*. 30 *Oct*. 1837; *d. May* 1906; *m*. 6 *June* 1861, *Ellen* (55 *Hans Road, S.W.*), *da. of Charles Kane Sivewright; and had issue* 1*d* to 5*d*.   [Nos. 51760 to 51790.

# of The Blood Royal

1*d*. *Walter Edward Lascelles, Capt. Rifle Brigade,* b. 21 *Mar.* 1862; d. 23 *Jan.* 1897; m. 2 *Sept.* 1891, *Mabel Gwendoline, da. of Lieut.-Col. Richard Hasell Thursby; and had issue* 1*e to* 2*e.*

    1*e*. Violet Rachel Lascelles, *b.* 9 June 1892.

    2*e*. Constance Gertrude Lascelles, *b.* 6 Oct. 1894.

2*d*. George Reginald Lascelles, Major *late* Royal Fusiliers, *b.* 14 Ap. 1864; *m.* 25 June 1895, Beatrice, da. of R. T. Pulteney, Rector of Ashley; and has issue 1*e* to 3*e.*

    1*e*. John Norman Pulteney Lascelles, *b.* 16 May 1898.

    2*e*. Joan Lascelles, *b.* 13 Ap. 1896.

    3*e*. Barbara Judith Lascelles, *b.* 28 Mar. 1903.

3*d*. Ernest Lascelles, *formerly* Lieut. 4th Batt. Rifle Brig. (*Winkfield Lodge, Windsor Forest*), *b.* 19 May 1870; *m.* 18 Jan. 1898, Flora Evelyn, da. of John Bulteel of Pamflete, Ivybridge, Devon; and has issue 1*e* to 2*e.*

    1*e*. Guy Ernest Lascelles, *b.* 27 Nov. 1898.

    2*e*. Faith Evelyn Lascelles, *b.* 27 Jan. 1903.

4*d*. Richard Lascelles, *b.* 9 Mar. 1883.

5*d*. Gertrude Lascelles, *m.* 28 July 1897, William Gerald Dease (*The Cottage, Celbridge, co. Kildare*); and has issue 1*e* to 2*e.*

    1*e*. Ernest Joseph Dease, *b.* Jan. 1899.

    2*e*. Cynthia Mary Dease, *b.* Sept. 1902.

2*c*. Arthur George Lascelles, *b.* 31 July 1855.

3*c*. Brian Piers Lascelles, *b.* 30 Aug. 1859.

4*c*. Clare Henrietta Lascelles (*Top o' Town, Dorchester*), *m.* 6 Dec. 1860, Arthur Edmund Mansel, J.P., *late* Capt. 3rd Light Dragoons, *d.* 20 July 1905; and has issue 1*d* to 7*d.*

    1*d*. Algernon Lascelles Mansel, *b.* 6 Sept. 1868.

    2*d*. Hugh Arthur Mansel, *late* Capt. 2nd Batt. Dorsetshire Regt., *b.* 7 Nov. 1869.

    3*d*. Evelyn Louisa Mansel.

    4*d*. Margaret Blanche Mansel.

    5*d*. Susan Emma Mansel.

    6*d*. Clare Frances Mansel, *m.* 16 Aug. 1905, Francis de Sausmarez Shortt, *late* Capt. Royal Fusiliers.

    7*d*. Eleanor Maud Mansel.

5*c*. *Selina Lascelles,* d. 16 *Dec.* 1889; m. 4 *Feb.* 1869, *Arthur de Cardonnel* (*Rice*), *6th Baron Dynevor* [G.B.] (*Dynevor Castle, Llandilo, co. Carmarthen; Carlton*); *and had issue.*

See the Clarence Volume, p. 619, Nos. 27148–27156.

6*c*. *Catherine Lascelles,* d. 22 *July* 1890; m. 30 *Dec.* 1868, *Granville Edwin Lloyd Baker of Hardwicke Court, J.P.* (*Hardwicke Court, near Gloucester; Carlton*); *and had issue* 1*d to* 7*d.*

    1*d*. Michael Granville Lloyd Baker (*The Cottage, Hardwicke, Gloucester*), *b.* 16 Jan. 1873; *m.* 13 Ap. 1898, Hon. Blanche, da. of Henry (Verney), 18th Baron Willoughby De Broke [E.]; and has issue 1*e* to 2*e.*

        1*e*. Hylda Blanche Lloyd Baker, *b.* 2 June 1900.

        2*e*. Olive Katharine Lloyd Baker, *b.* 15 Aug. 1902.

    2*d*. Arthur Barwick Lloyd Baker, *b.* 3 Ap. 1883.

    3*d*. Mary Ruth Lloyd Baker.

    4*d*. Catherine Lascelles Lloyd Baker.

    5*d*. Clare Lloyd Baker.

    6*d*. Eleanor Lloyd Baker.

    7*d*. Grace Lloyd Baker.

[Nos. 51791 to 51831.

The Plantagenet Roll

7c. Eleanor Frances Lascelles (*Garboldisham, East Harling*), *m.* 29 Sept. 1868, Cecil Thomas Molineux-Montgomerie of Garboldisham, Norfolk, *d.* 17 Ap. 1901; and has issue.

See the Clarence Volume, p. 354, Nos. 11563–11570.

8c. Ruth Lascelles, *m.* 14 Oct. 1886, George Egerton Warburton (*Sandicroft, Northwich*).

8b. *Clare Emily Brooke*, *d.* 24 *Jan.* 1867; *m. as 2nd wife*, 23 *Sept.* 1845, *Sir Frederick Hutchinson Hervey-Bathurst, 3rd Bart.* [*U.K.*], *b.* 6 *June* 1807; *d.* 29 *Oct.* 1881; *and had issue* 1c *to* 6c.

1c. Lionel Hervey-Bathurst (ret.), Lieut.-Col. *formerly* Major Rifle Brig. (*Worsham House, Bexhill, Sussex*), *b.* 7 July 1849; *m.* 29 Jan. 1885, Mary Ethel Paston, da. of Sir Astley Paston Paston-Cooper, 3rd Bart. [U.K.]; and has issue 1d to 2d.

1d. Sidney Lionel Hervey-Bathurst, *b.* 15 Dec. 1887.

2d. Arthur Reginald Hervey-Bathurst, *b.* 19 Nov. 1890.

2c. Arthur Cecil Hervey-Bathurst, *formerly* Capt. 1st Batt. Royal Sussex Regt. (*Naval and Military*), *b.* (twin) 2 July 1851.

3c. Ernest Frederick Hervey-Bathurst, *formerly* in R.N., *b.* 18 Feb. 1853.

4c. Claud Hervey-Bathurst, *formerly* Capt. 1st Batt. Essex Regt., *b.* 23 Nov. 1855.

5c. Clare Emily Hervey-Bathurst, *m.* 13 Oct. 1874, Charles Nicholas Paul Phipps, J.P., D.L. (*Chalcot, Westbury, Wilts*); and has issue 1d to 7d.

1d. Charles Bathurst Hele Phipps, *b.* 8 Feb. 1889.

2d. Evelyn Cecilia Phipps, *m.* 10 Aug. 1901, Capt. William Pery Standish, J.P. (*Marwell Hall, Winchester; Scaleby Castle, Cumberland*); and has issue 1e to 2e.

1e. Edward William Standish, *b.* 8 Ap. 1903.

2e. Etheldreda Mary Standish, *b.* 1905

3d. Norah Jacintha Phipps, *m.* 1898, John Michael Fleetwood Fuller, M.P. (*Jaggard's House, Corsham*); and has issue 1e to 4e.

1e. John Gerard Henry Fleetwood Fuller, *b.* 8 July 1906.

2e. Bridget Fleetwood Fuller, *b.* 12 Jan. 1901.

3e. Patience Irene Fleetwood Fuller, *b.* 31 May 1902.

4e. Maude Fleetwood Fuller, *b.* 15 Oct. 1903.

4d. Alice Mary Phipps.

5d. Clare Dorothy Phipps.

6d. Gladys Rose Phipps.

7d. Violet Victoria Phipps.

6c. Alice Constance Hervey-Bathurst, *m.* as 2nd wife, 15 Jan. 1884, Charles Clement Tudway, J.P., D.L. (*The Cedars, Wells; Stoberry Park, Wells, Somerset; 15 Savile Row, W.*); and has issue 1d to 4d.

1d. Hervey Robert Charles Tudway, *b.* 23 Sept. 1888.

2d. Lionel Charles Paul Tudway, *b.* 5 Aug. 1893.

3d. Gladys Clare Alice Tudway, *b.* 3 Sept. 1887.

4d. Pamela Violet Tudway, *b.* 13 Mar. 1896. [Nos. 51832 to 51866.

534. Descendants of ALEXANDER KINLOCH, *afterwards* ROCHEID of Inverleith (see Table LVI.), *d.* 11 May 1755; *m.* 4 Ap. 1750, JANET, da. of John WATSON of Muirhouse, co. Edinburgh (by the Hon. ANNE MACKAY), *d.* 1813 ; and had issue (at least) 1a.

1a. *James Rocheid, d.* (–); *m. Susan* [*da. of* ——] *Wood; and had issue* (*at least*) 1b.

1*b*. *James Rocheid*, b. 1809; d. (*at Mannheim*) 3 *Mar.* 1840; m. 1*st*, 1830, *Baroness Mary Anne, da. of the Baron Dankelman of Mayenne, Saxony,* d. 1831; 2*ndly,* 31 *Jan.* 1837, *Sarah Catherine, da. of Capt. William Patterson, R.N.; and had issue* 1*c* to 2*c.*

1*c*. *Charles Frederick James Everard William George Rocheid,* b. 25 *Jan.* 1831; d. 19 *Jan.* 1864; m. 21 *May* 1852, *Baroness Matilda, da. of Peter Heinrick de Salviati* (*who re-m.* 14 *Dec.* 1865, *Julius, Baron von Busshe, Vice-Master of the Horse to the King of Hanover*), d. 1892; *and had issue* 1*d.*

1*d*. Charles Henry Alexander Frederick Camillo Everard John James Rocheid, B.A. (Oxon.) (*Marin, Mecklenburg Strelitz*), b. 3 Oct. 1853; *m*. 7 Mar. 1878, Baroness Marie, da. of Feodor von Grote; and has issue 1*e* to 3*e.*

1*e*. Charles Alexander Julius William David Rocheid, b. 22 Dec. 1878.

2*e*. Colin William Hilmar Otto Rocheid, b. 1881.

3*e*. Elizabeth Emma Natalie Anna Rocheid, *m*. 1898, Baron George Behr von Torgelow.

2*c*². Constance Isabella Rocheid, *m*. as 2nd wife, 3 July 1860, Major-Gen. David Briggs (*Strathairly House, Largo, Fife*), s.*p.*   [Nos. 51867 to 51871.

535. Descendants, if any, of MARY KINLOCH (see Table LVI.), *d.* (–); *m*. ALEXANDER HAMILTON of Beil.

536. Descendants of MAGDALEN KINLOCH (see Table LVI.), *d.* (–); *m*. (contract dated 5 Ap.) 1745, JOHN WILKIE of Foulden, *b.* 1705; *d*. Sept. 1780; and had (with possibly other) issue 1*a.*

1*a*. *James Wilkie of Foulden, Capt. in the Army,* d. 8 *Sept.* 1817; m. *Sarah, da. of* [——] *Price; and had* (*with other*) *issue* 1*b.*

1*b*. *James Wilkie,* d. 1814; m. 1804, *Harriet, da. of Sir Robert Dalyell of Binns, 4th Bart.* [S.]; *and had issue* (*an only son*) 1*c.*

1*c*. *John Wilkie of Foulden, D.L.,* d. 21 *June* 1884; m. 1864, *Henrietta Eleanor, da. of Thomas Bruce of Arnot, co. Kinross; and had issue* 1*d* to 4*d.*

1*d*. James Bruce Wilkie of Foulden, J.P., Capt. 3rd Batt. K.O. Scottish Borderers (*Foulden House, co. Berwick*), b. 1 May 1867; *m*. 6 Feb. 1894, Mary Marjoribanks, da. of Watson Askew Robertson of Pallinsburn and Ladykirk; and has issue 1*e.*

1*e*. See p. 334, No. 24297.

2*d*. John Dalyell Wilkie, b. 20 Sept. 1870.

3*d*. Harriet Charlotte Wilkie.

4*d*. Eleanor Bruce Wilkie.   [Nos. 51872 to 51876.

537. Descendants, if any, of JANET KINLOCH (see Table LVI.), *d.* (–); *m*. CHARLES BROUN of Coulstoun, a Senator of the College of Justice.

538. Descendants of JOHN FLETCHER CAMPBELL of Saltoun, co. Haddington, and Boquhan, co. Stirling, Gen. in the Army (see Table LVI.), *d.* (–); *m*. 1795, ANN, da. of [——] THRIEPLAND; and had issue 1*a* to 2*a.*

1*a*. *Andrew Fletcher of Saltoun Hall, J.P., D.L.,* b. 20 *Aug.* 1796; d. 9 *Ap.* 1879; m. 7 *Sept.* 1825, *Lady Charlotte, da. of Francis* (*Charteris*), 8*th Earl of Wemyss and March* [S.], b. 1804; d. 3 *Mar.* 1886; *and had issue.*

See the Clarence Volume, p. 256, Nos. 6148–6166.   [Nos. 51877 to 51896.

The Plantagenet Roll

2a. Henry Fletcher-Campbell of Boquhan, co. Stirling, J.P., D.L., d. 1877; m. Ann, da. of John Hathorn of Castle Wigg, co. Wigton, d. 8 Ap. 1869; and had issue 1b to 5b.

1b. Henry John Fletcher-Campbell of Boquhan, C.B., J.P., D.L., late Rear-Adm. R.N. (Boquhan, Stirling, N.B.; Beach Lodge, Wimbledon), b. 1837.

2b. John Fletcher-Campbell, afterwards Hathorn of Castle Wigg, J.P., D.L., Lieut.-Col. Coldstream Guards, b. 29 Aug. 1839; d. 16 Nov. 1888; m. 1 Mar. 1875, Charlotte Anne (Kentchurch Court, Hereford), da. of Sir John Dick-Lauder, 8th Bart. [S.]; and had issue 1c to 2c.

1c. Hugh Fletcher Hathorn of Castle Wigg, co. Wigton (Kentchurch Court, Hereford), b. 19 July 1877.

2c. Anne Catherine Hathorn.

3b. Hugh Fletcher-Campbell, b. 1842; m. 1877, Harriet Nina, da. of J. E. Douglas Stewart.

4b. Mary Fletcher-Campbell, m. 20 Jan. 1869, the Right Hon. Sir Herbert Eustace Maxwell of Monreith, 7th Bart. [S.], P.C., M.P., LL.D., F.R.S. (Monreith, Whauphill, Wigtonshire; 49 Lennox Gardens, S.W.; Carlton; Scottish Conservative); and has issue 1c to 4c.

1c. Aymer Edward Maxwell, Capt. Grenadier Guards, b. 26 Oct. 1877.

2c. Ann Christian Maxwell, m. 12 Nov. 1901, Sir John Maxwell Stirling-Maxwell, 10th Bart. [S. and G.B.], M.P. (Pollok House, Renfrewshire; 48 Belgrave Square, S.W.).

3c. Winifred Edith Maxwell, m. 11 Nov. 1897, Alistair Erskine Graham Moir (Leckie, Stirlingshire); and has issue 1d to 2d.

1d. Charles William Moir, b. 1898.

2d. Beatrice Moir, b. 1900.

4c. Beatrice Mary Maxwell, m. 10 Oct. 1901, Ernest Robert Walker (Shenleybury House, Shenley, Herts); and has issue 1d to 2d.

1d. James Herbert Walker, b. 17 Feb. 1905.

2d. Sylvia Mary Walker, b. 12 Ap. 1903.

5b. Ann Catherine Christina Fletcher-Campbell. [Nos. 51897 to 51910.

539. Descendants, if any, of [——] KINLOCH (see Table LVI.), m. JAMES HOME of Earles, Advocate.

540. Descendants of GEORGE PALMES of Naburn, co. York (see Table LVII.), b. 3 Nov. 1666; d. (–); m. ANNE, da. of George WITHAM of Cliffe, bur. 3 May 1704; and had issue.

See pp. 561–562, Nos. 49914–49970. [Nos. 51911 to 51967.

541. Descendants, if any, of MARY PALMES, wife of THOMAS SMITH of Bidlesden, Northumberland; of WILLIAM PALMES; of CATHERINE PALMES; of BRIDGET PALMES, wife of MICHAEL METCALFE of Otterington, near Northallerton; and of ELLEN PALMES, bur. 8 Nov. 1661; m. 1st, ALEXANDER VADCOC of York, M.D., bur. 5 Sept. 1644; 2ndly, WILLIAM CONSTABLE (see Table LVII.).

542. Descendants, if any, of ELIZABETH BABTHORPE (see Table LIV.), wife of GEORGE CONSTABLE of Caythorpe; and had issue.

# of The Blood Royal

543. Descendants, if any surviving, of ANN INGLEBY (see Table LIV.), *m.* THOMAS DALTON of Myton and Swyne, co. York, *b.* 1583; *d.* 1639; and had issue 1*a* to 5*a*.[1]

1*a. John Dalton of Swyne, b. 1623 (being aged 42, 2 Sept. 1665).*

2*a. James Dalton, m. Catherine, da. of James Clarke, Citizen and Chirurgeon of London.*

3*a. Thomas Dalton, named on list of recusants 6 July 1669.*

4*a. Elizabeth Dalton, m. Samuel Snawsdale.*

5*a. Catherine Dalton, m. Robert Dickenson of Canwick juxta Lincoln.*

544. Descendants of Sir EDWARD DERING, 5th Bart. [E.] (see Table LVIII.), *b. c.* 1706; *d.* 15 Ap. 1762; *m.* 1st, 24 Feb. 1728, ELIZABETH, da. and co-h. of Edward HENSHAW of Well Hall in Eltham, *d.* Mar. 1735; 2ndly, 11 Sept. 1735, MARY, widow of HENRY MOMPESSON, and da. of Capt. Charles FOTHERBY of Barham Court, R.N.; and had issue 1*a* to 2*a*.

1*a. Sir Edward Dering, 6th Bart. [E.], M.P., b. 28 Sept. 1732; d. 8 Dec.* 1798; *m.* 1st, 8 Ap. 1755, *Selina, da. and co-h. of Sir Robert Furnesse, 2nd Bart.* [E.], *of Waldershare, Kent,* d. 29 *Mar.* 1757; 2ndly, 1 *Jan.* 1765, *Deborah, da. of John Winchester of Nethersole,* d. 20 *Mar.* 1818; *and had issue* 1*b to* 6*b.*

1*b. Sir Edward Dering, 7th Bart. [E.], b. 16 Feb. 1757; d. 30 June 1811; m.* 25 *Ap.* 1782, *Anne, da. of William Hale of King's Walden, Herts,* d. 17 *July* 1830; *and had issue* 1*c to* 3*c.*

1*c. Edward Dering, b. 1783; d.v.p. 19 Sept. 1808; m. as 1st husband,* 25 *Jan.* 1805, *Henrietta, da. and co-h. of Richard Nevill of Furness, co. Kildare,* d. 18 *Jan.* 1870; *and had issue* 1*d to* 2*d.*

1*d. Sir Edward Cholmeley Dering, 8th Bart. [E.], D.L., M.P. for East Kent* 1852–1857 *and* 1863–1868, *b.* 19 *Nov.* 1807; *d.* 1 *Ap.* 1896; *m.* 10 *Ap.* 1832, *the Hon. Jane, da. of William (Edwardes), 2nd Lord Kensington [I.],* d. 1 *Sept.* 1897; *and had issue* 1*e to* 4*e.*

1*e.* Sir Henry Nevill Dering, 9th Bart. [E.], K.C.M.G., C.B. (*Travellers'; St. James'; Surrenden, Dering, Ashford, Kent; British Legation, Rio de Janeiro*), *b.* 21 Sept. 1839; *m.* 20 Oct. 1863, Rosa, da. of Joseph Underwood of 5 Hyde Park Gardens, W.; and has issue 1*f* to 3*f*.

1*f.* Henry Edward Dering, J.P., D.L., Major 1st Batt. Scots Guards (*Sheerland House, Ashford, Kent; Guards; Wellington*), *b.* 9 May 1866; *m.* 15 Nov. 1890, May Astel Rosina, da. of William Jameson of Montrose, co. Dublin; and has issue 1*g* to 4*g*.

1*g.* Anthony Miles Cholmeley Dering, *b.* 29 July 1901.

2*g.* Ivy Maud Dering, *b.* 3 Feb. 1893.

3*g.* Myrtle Dering, *b.* 7 June 1898.

4*g.* Clare Dering, *b.* 5 May 1900.

2*f.* Herbert Guy Nevill Dering, 2nd Sec. in Diplo. Ser. *b.* (at Florence) 13 Nov. 1867.

3*f.* Arthur Cholmeley Odo Fitzhardinge Dering, *b.* 18 Nov. 1877.

2*e. George Edwardes Dering, Barrister, Recorder of Faversham, b.* 12 *Jan.* 1841; *d.* 15 *Ap.* 1902; *m.* 1st, 1868, *Jane Alice, da. of Thomas Taylor,* d. 13 *June* 1874; 2ndly, 12 *Jan.* 1882, *Pauline, da. of the Rev. William Lewis Mason, Chaplain at Compiègne, France; and had issue* 1*f.*

1*f.* Violet Alice Jane Dering. [Nos. 51968 to 51976.

---

[1] Foster's " Yorkshire Pedigrees."

The Plantagenet Roll

3e. Arthur Robert Dering, *formerly* Lieut. East Kent Militia (*Windham*), *b.* 7 Oct. 1847; *m.* 7 Sept. 1880, Beatrice, da. of Eyre Legard of The Château Hydra, Algiers.

4e. Adela Dorothy Jane Dering.

2d. Henrietta Charlotte Dering, bapt. 25 *May* 1806; d. 1 *Dec.* 1904; m. 14 *May* 1829, *Rev. Julius Deedes, Rector of Wittersham, Kent, d.* 24 *Oct.* 1879, *and had issue* (2 sons and 4 das.).

2c. Cholmeley Charles William Dering of Avot St. Lawrence, Herts, b. 1 May 1785; d. 6 Feb. 1858; m. 1st, 27 July 1809, Charlotte Bucknall, da. of Willam Hale of King's Walden, d. 18 Sept. 1843; 2ndly, 30 July 1846, Charlotte Mary, da. of Sir William Walter Yea, 2nd Bart. [G.B.], d. 5 Ap. 1882; and had issue 1d to 3d.

1d. Heneage William Dering, b. 14 Nov. 1819; d. 21 May 1902; m. 21 Jan. 1847, Ann Caroline, da. of Capt. Clotworthy Upton, R.N., d. 10 Dec. 1901; and had issue 1e to 3e.

1e. Evelyn John Heneage Dering, *b.* 13 Feb. 1850; *m.* 4 Oct. 1879, Emma Cordelia, da. of Henry Stephen Gates of Brighton; and has issue 1f.

1f. Evelyn Henry Heneage Dering, *b.* 26 Mar. 1881.

2e. Emily Constance Mary Dering.

3e. Alice Lucy St. John Dering, *m.* 27 Oct. 1874, Arthur Cotton Beare, *d.* 5 July 1876.

2d. Edgar William Wallace Dering, Lieut.-Col. 2nd Batt. King's Own Borderers, b. 15 Aug. 1848; d. 2 Dec. 1894; m. 22 Ap. 1879, Marianna Emily (Instow, North Devon), da. of Thomas Goldie Harding of Hallsannery, Devon; and had issue 1e to 4e.

1e. Rupert Cholmeley Yea Dering, Lieut. 2nd Batt. King's Own Scottish Borderers, *b.* 7 Ap. 1883.

2e. Claud Lacy Dering, Sub.-Lieut. R.N., *b.* 13 Oct. 1885.

3e. Anthony Yea Lionel Dering, *b.* 18 May 1890.

4e. Beatrice Adela Frances Dering, *b.* 1 Ap. 1880.

3d. Lionel Ashton Dering, b. 17 Sept. 1850; d. 15 May 1890; m. 20 Sept. 1876, Katherine Edith, da. of Burton Archer-Burton; and had issue 1e.

1e. Dorothy Dering.

3c. Charlotte Dering, d. 14 Feb. 1839; m. 20 Feb. 1808, Henry Richard Hoare, only son of Sir Richard Colt Hoare, 2nd Bart. [G.B.], d.v.p. 19 Sept. 1836; and had issue 1d.

1d. Anne Hoare, d. 17 Jan. 1872; m. 26 Mar. 1835, Capt. Sir George Benvenuto Buckley Mathew, K.C.M.G., H.M.'s Envoy Extraordinary and Min. Plen. to Brazil (she divorced him 9 Dec. 1847), d. 22 Oct. 1879; and had issue (5 sons and a da.).[1]

2b. Cholmeley Dering, Col. Light Dragoons, b. 25 Oct. 1766; d. 7 Nov. 1836; m. 9 June 1789, Charlotte Elizabeth, da. of Sir Joseph Yates, Knt., d. 22 Oct. 1845; and had issue 1c.

1c. Rev. Cholmeley Edward John Dering, Preb. of St. Paul's, Rector of Pluckley, Kent, and Chaplain to Queen Victoria, b. 18 Mar. 1790; d. 12 Aug. 1848; m. 27 May 1817, Maria, da. of Barrington Price, d. 6 Dec. 1884; and had issue.

See the Clarence Volume, pp. 84–85, Nos. 301–315.

3b. George Dering, b. 13 Feb. 1776; d. 19 May 1820; m. 28 June 1798, Elizabeth, da. of Charles Dering of Barham Court, bur. 11 Oct. 1810; and had issue 1c to 4c.

1c. Robert Dering of Lockleys, J.P., b. 7 May 1802; d. 12 Ap. 1859; m. 4 June 1829, Letitia, da. of Sir George Shee, 1st Bart. [I.], d. 19 June 1852; and had issue 1d. [Nos. 51977 to 52002.

---

[1] See Foster's "Peerage," 1880, p. 295.

# of The Blood Royal

1*d*. George Edward Dering (*Lockleys, Welwyn, Herts ; Dunmore House, Galway ; Barham Court, Canterbury*).

2*c*. *Charlotte Elizabeth Dering*, d. 12 *June* 1867 ; m. 12 *June* 1834, *the Rev. Frederick Fitzherbert Haslewood, Rector of Smarden*, d. 25 *Nov*. 1876 ; *and had issue* 1*d to* 6*d*.

1*d*. Rev. Frederick George Haslewood, LL.D. (Camb.), Vicar of Chislet (*Chislet Vicarage, Canterbury*), *b*. 19 Mar. 1835 ; *m*. 27 May 1869, Louisa, da. of Andrew John William Lyon, *d*. 2 Ap. 1901 ; and has issue 1*e* to 6*e*.

1*e*. Charles George Dering Haslewood, Capt. Gold Coast Regt., *b*. 1 May 1870.

2*e*. Rev. Christopher Francis Beevor Haslewood, Vicar of Pelton (*Pelton Vicarage, Durham*), *b*. 9 Feb. 1873 ; *m*. 12 Nov. 1903, Sybil Beatrice, da. of Dr. R. Clark Newton of Eldon Tower, Harrogate.

3*e*. Noel Alfred Fitzherbert Haslewood, *b*. 26 Dec. 1881.

4*e*. Arthur Ethelbert Lyon Haslewood, *b*. 21 June 1883.

5*e*. Laura Elizabeth Haslewood, *m*. 10 Aug. 1904, the Rev. Thomas Haworth Jervis, Vicar of Rowde (*Rowde Vicarage, Wilts*).

6*e*. Mary Charlotte Haslewood.

2*d*. *Rev. Francis Haslewood, Rector of St. Matthew's, Ipswich*, *b*. 2 May 1840 ; *d*. 7 *Ap*. 1900 ; m. 1*st*, 31 *May* 1866, *Frances Ellen, da. of Daniel Henderson of Woodleigh, Chertsey*, d. 24 *Ap*. 1890 ; 2*ndly*, 4 *Sept*. 1894, *Ellen, widow of Samuel Edward Rope, da. of Thomas Cooper of Ardleigh, Essex ; and had issue* 1*e to* 7*e*.

1*e*. Francis Frederick Haslewood, *b*. 23 Ap. 1869.

2*e*. Herbert Haslewood, *b*. 20 Ap. 1870.

3*e*. Vivian Charles Haslewood, *b*. 1 June 1879.

4*e*. George Robert Haslewood, *b*. 3 Mar. 1881.

5*e*. Alice Cordelia Haslewood.

6*e*. Charlotte Elizabeth Haslewood.

7*e*. Eveline Fanny Haslewood.

3*d*. Charlotte Cordelia Haslewood (*The Shrubbery, Norwich*), *m*. 21 Jan. 1879 Elijah Crosier Bailey, Clerk of the Peace for Norwich, *d*. 7 Aug. 1883.

4*d*. Caroline Haslewood.

5*d*. Emily Elizabeth Haslewood, *m*. 23 Oct. 1866, the Rev. Seaman Curteis Tress Beale, Vicar of St. Michael's, Tenterden, *d*. 23 Dec. 1885.

6*d*. *Louisa Fanny Haslewood*, d. 8 *Mar*. 1895 ; m. 3 *Ap*. 1866, *the Rev. John Frederick Blake, M.A.* (*Camb.*) (*35 Harlesden Gardens, N.W.*).

3*c*. *Harriet Mary Dering*, d. 30 *Sept*. 1893 ; m. 5 *Aug*. 1828, *John Routledge Majendie, Capt. 92nd Highlanders* (*son of the Lord Bishop of Bangor*), d. 12 *July* 1850.

4*c*. *Caroline Dering*, d. 28 *July* 1880 ; m. 20 *Jan*. 1857, *Baron Charles von Buseck of Alten Buseck, Chamberlain and Master of the Horse to the Landgrave of Hesse Homburg*, d. 14 *Oct*. 1873.

4*b*. *Selina Dering*, b. 9 *Feb*. 1756 ; d. 19 *Ap*. 1836 ; m. *the Rev. Dr. Dealtry*.

5*b*. *Elizabeth Dering*, d. (–) ; m. *Daniel Byam Mathew of Felix Hall, Essex*.

6*b*. *Charlotte Dering*, d. 1836 ; m. 1803, *the Rev. P. Moneypenny, Vicar of Hadlow*.

2*a*. *Charles Dering*, d. 1815 ; m. 1770, *Elizabeth, da. and h. of Sir Thomas Farnaby, 2nd Bart.* [*G.B.*]. [Nos. 52003 to 52020.

545. Descendants, if any, of CECILIA DERING (see Table LVIII.), *m*. GEORGE SCOTT of Scott's Hall.

The Plantagenet Roll

546. Descendants of MARGARET CHOLMELEY of Chipsted (see Table LVIII.), *d.* 13 Oct. 1744 ; *m.* 1676, CHARLES TURNER of Kirkleatham, co. York, *d.* 2 Aug. 1719 ; and had issue[1] 1*a* to 7*a*.

1*a. Cholmley Turner of Kirkleatham, M.P.,* bapt. 20 *July* 1685 ; bur. 18 *May* 1757 ; m. 1709, *Jane, da. of George Marwood of Little Busby,* bapt. 10 *May* 1688 ; bur. 26 *Ap.* 1764 ; *and had issue* 1*b.*

    1*b. Jane Turner,* m. 1745, *Philip William Casimir van Straubenzee, Capt. in Dutch Guards* (*nat. by Act of Parliament*), d. 1765 ; *and had issue.*

2*a. William Turner of Kirkleatham,* bapt. 15 *Nov.* 1697 ; *d.* 12 *Aug.* 1774 ; m. 9 *Feb.* 1725, *Jane, da. of Charles Bathurst of Clints,* bapt. 28 *July* 1706 ; bur. 13 *Ap.* 1759 ; *and had issue* 1*b.*

    1*b. Sir Charles Turner, 1st Bart.* [*G.B.*]*, M.P.,* bur. 3 *Nov.* 1783 ; m. 2*ndly,* 30 *Sept.* 1771, *Mary, da. of James Shuttleworth of Gawthorp* (*who re-m.* 4 *Nov.* 1784, *Sir Thomas Gascoigne of Partington*), d. 1 *Feb.* 1786 ; *and had issue* 1*c to* 3*c.*

        1*c. Charles Turner, 2nd Bart.* [*G.B.*]*, b.* 28 *Jan.* 1773 ; bur. s.p. 19 *Feb.* 1810.

        2*c. Mary Turner, b.* 3 *Aug.* 1782 ; *m. Richard Oliver Gascoigne of Parlington.*

        3*c. Elizabeth Turner,* m. *Col. Campbell.*

3*a. Jane Turner,* bapt. 3 *Oct.* 1683 ; *d.* (–) ; m. 8 *Sept.* 1701, *Sir Thomas Standish of Duxbury, 2nd Bart.* (1677) [*E.*] ; *d.* 13 *or* 21 *Dec.* 1756 ; *and had issue* 1*b.*

    1*b. Margaret Standish, da. and in her issue* (1812) *sole heir, d.* 1776 ; m. 1*st, William Wombwell,* d.s.p. ; 2*ndly, Anthony Hall of Flass ; and had issue* 1*c.*

        1*c. Anne Hall, da. and in her issue* (1841) *sole h., d.* 1774 ; m. *as* 1*st wife, the Rev. Ralph Carr, M.A. ; and had issue* 1*d to* 3*d.*

        1*d. Ralph Carr of Cocken Hall, co. Durham,* d. (–) ; *m. Mary, da. of Samuel Andrews ; and had issue* 1*e.*

        1*e. William Standish Carr, afterwards Standish of Duxbury, J.P., D.L., High Sheriff co. Lancaster* 1845–1846, *b.* 1807 ; *d.* 9 *July* 1857 ; m. 27 *Aug.* 1829, *Susan, da. of Richard Jenkins of Beachley Lodge, co. Glouc., J.P., D.L.,* d. (–) ; *and had issue* 1*f to* 4*f.*

        1*f. William Standish Standish of Duxbury, J.P., D.L., b.* 28 *Feb.* 1835 ; *d. unm.* 21 *Feb.* 1878.

        2*f. Emma Isabella Harriet Carr-Standish, co-h., d.* 1889 ; m. 22 *Nov.* 1853, *Sir John George Tollemache Sinclair of Ulbster, 3rd Bart.* [*G.B.*] (*Thurso Castle, Caithness*) ; *and had issue.*

See the Tudor Roll of " The Blood Royal of Britain," p. 205, Nos. 21482–21489.

        3*f. Susan Amelia Georgina Standish, co-h., d.* 18 *Oct.* 1888 ; m. *as* 1*st wife,* 3 *Dec.* 1863, *Col. Charles William Paulet of Wellesbourne Hall, b.* 27 *Sept.* 1832 ; *d.* 8 *Ap.* 1897 ; *and had issue* 1*g to* 2*g.*

        1*g.* Charles Standish Paulet, Capt. Warwickshire Imp. Yeo., Heir presumptive to the Marquisate of Winchester [*E.*] (*Staple Hill, Wellesbourne*), *b.* Oct. 1873 ; *m.* 24 Oct. 1901, Lilian, da. of Major W. T. E. Foserbery of Warwick.

        2*g.* Cecil Henry Paulet, *b.* Mar. 1875 ; *m.* 6 Sept. 1898, Ethel Frances, da. of Major Cowan of Alveston Lodge.

        4*f.* Margaret Laura Mulgrave Standish, *m.* 19 May 1869, Edmund Berkeley Lucy (*Cocken Hall, Durham*) ; and has (with other) issue 1*g.*

        1*g.* Reginald Lucy, *b.* 10 May 1879.   [Nos. 52021 to 52032.

---

[1] " The Seize Quartiers of the Family of Bryan Cooke, Esq., of Owston, and of Frances his wife." Privately printed, London, 1857 ; and Dugdale's " Visitation of Yorkshire," with additions by J. W. Clay, F.S.A. " The Genealogist," x. 103.

# of The Blood Royal

2d. Elizabeth Anne Carr, bapt. 12 *Mar.* 1769; d. 31 *Mar.* 1831; m. *as 2nd wife*, 31 *Aug.* 1790, *Chidley Coote of Ash Hill, co. Limerick*, d. 6 *June* 1799; *and had issue* 1e *to* 4e.

    1e. Sir Charles Henry Coote, 9th Bart. [*I.*], b. 2 *Jan.* 1794; d. 8 *Oct.* 1864; m. 1814, *Caroline, da. of John Whaley of Whaley Abbey*, d. 11 *Mar.* 1871; *and had issue.*

    See p. 393, Nos. 33104–33140.

    2e. Robert Carr Coote, Capt. 18th *Hussars*, d. 5 *Nov.* 1834; m. *Margaret, da. of* [——] *Greer; and had issue* 1f *to* 3f.

    1f. Charles Coote, afterwards Purdon-Coote of Ballyclough Castle, d. 3 *Sept.* 1848; m. 1846, *Lydia Lucy, da. of the Rev. John Digby Wingfield-Digby of Coleshill* (*who re-m. as 2nd wife*, 9 *Dec.* 1857, *James* (*Hewitt*), 5th *Viscount Lifford* [*I.*]); *and had issue* 1g.

    1g Charles Purdon Coote of Ballyclough Castle, J.P., D.L., b. 8 *Aug.* 1847; d. 20 *Sept.* 1893; m. 22 *June* 1871, *Harriet Louisa, da. of Robert Perceval Maxwell of Groomsport House, co. Down; and had issue* 1h *to* 3h.

    1h. Charles Robert Purdon-Coote of Ballyclough Castle and Bearforest, co. Cork (98 *St James' Street, Dublin*), b. 23 Jan. 1875.

    2h. Lydia Coote, b. 5 July 1872.

    3h. Aileen Selina Coote, b. 16 Oct. 1878; m. 8 Oct. 1903, Arthur Kenlis (Maxwell), 11th Baron Farnham [I.] (*Farnham, co. Cavan*); and has issue 1i.

    1i. Hon. Somerset Arthur Maxwell, b. 20 Jan. 1905.

    2f. Chidley Coote, supposed living *unm.* abroad in 1880.[1]

    3f. Maria Coote, d. (*being murdered at Barbavilla*) 2 *Ap.* 1882; m. 3 *Dec.* 1855, *Henry Matthew Smythe of Barbavilla and of New Park, co. Roscommon, J.P.*, b. 1810; d. 6 *Sept.* 1893; *and had issue* 1g *to* 6g.

    1g. William Lyster Smythe, J.P., D.L., Col. Comdg. Dublin City Art. Mil., A.D.C. to the Lord-Lieut. (Lord Aberdeen), and High Sheriff co. Westmeath 1888 (*Barbavilla, Collinstoun, Westmeath*), b. 29 Sept. 1859; m. 6 Oct. 1885, Agnes Mary Henrietta, da. and h. of Capt. Richard Weld Litton; and has issue 1h to 5h.

    1h. Henry Ingoldsby Lyster Smythe, b. 4 June 1890.

    2h. Cecil St. George Lyster Smythe, b. 17 Mar. 1895.

    3h. Richard Litton Lyster Smythe, b. 3 July 1897.

    4h. Gladys Mary Lyster Smythe.

    5h. Elizabeth Oliver Lyster Smythe.

    2g. Margaret Altha Maria Smythe (*Glananea, Drumcree, Killucan*), m. 3 Dec. 1880, William Edward Smyth of Glananea, J.P., High Sheriff co. Westmeath 1878, d. 15 June 1890; and has issue 1h to 3h.

    1h. Ralph Alfred Edward Smyth of Glananea, b. 11 Dec. 1881.

    2h. Abel Edward Smyth, b. 9 Jan. 1885.

    3h. Lucy Jane Loftus Smyth.

    3g. Elizabeth Ada Mary Smythe, m. 1st, 1878, Christopher W. Bailey of Moorock House, co. Clare; 2ndly, 21 Dec. 1885, James Hume Dodgson.

    4g. Louisa Ellen Lyster Smythe.

    5g. Lydia Lucy Lyster Smythe, m. 30 July 1887, Robert Darley Guinness, B.A. (Camb.), Bar.-at-Law (*Shanganagh Grove, Ballybrack, Dublin; Carlton*); and has issue 1h to 2h.

    1h. Richard Smythe Guinness, b. 13 June 1888.

    2h. Elizabeth Muriel Smythe Guinness.

    6g. Maud Frances Lyster Smythe, m. 20 Aug. 1891, Henry G. Richards, K.C.

    3e. Chidley Coote of Huntington, Queen's Co., Lieut.-Col 31st *Regt.*, b. 10 *Jan.*
[Nos. 52033 to 52090.

---

[1] Foster's "Baronetage," 1880, p. 130.

The Plantagenet Roll

1798; d. 21 *July* 1876; m. 1st, 8 *May* 1827, *Jane Deborah, da. of the Rev. Samuel Close of Elm Park*, d. 2 *Dec*. 1857; 2ndly, 3 *Feb*. 1859, *Catherine Maria* (*The Cedars, Portarlington*), *da. of William Philip Brabazon of Mornington; and had issue* 1f *to* 2f.

    1f. Ralph Brabazon Coote, *b*. 2 Feb. 1860.

    2f. *Jane Elizabeth Anna Coote*, d. 26 *Dec*. 1873; m. *as* 1st *wife*, 2 *Jan*. 1855, *the Rev. Charles Lyndhurst Vaughan*, b. 6 *Feb*. 1828; d. (–); *and had* (*with other*) *issue* [1] 1g *to* 10g.

        1g. John Maxwell Vaughan, *b*. Oct. 1856.

        2g. Henry Bathurst Vaughan, *b*. 18 Feb. 1858.

        3g. Francis Philip Vaughan, *b*. 1870.

        4g. Emily Jane Vaughan.

        5g. Louisa Vaughan.

        6g. Eleanor St. John Vaughan.

        7g. Mary Caroline Vaughan.

        8g. Edith Augusta Vaughan.

        9g. Kathleen Olga Vaughan.

        10g. Janet Arthur Vaughan.

    4e. *Mary Coote*, d. 6 *Feb*. 1852; m. 15 *Jan*. 1815, *Charles Launcelot Sandes of Indiaville, Queen's Co.*, d. *May* 1855; *and had issue*.

    3d. Mary Carr, b. 1771.

    4a. [*da*.] *Turner*, m. [——] *Stapylton*.

    5a. *Catherine Turner*, bapt. 21 *Nov*. 1678; bur. 28 *July* 1730; m. 25 *July* 1697, *William Wentworth of Woolley, co. York*, d.s.p. 3 *June* 1729.

    6a. *Theophila Turner*, bapt. 31 *Mar*. 1684; d. 12 *June* 1745; m. *Thomas Davison of Blackiston, co. Durham*.

    7a. *Margaret Turner*, bapt. 31 *Dec*. 1686; d. (–); m. 23 *Dec*. 1717, *Anthony Eyre of Rampton, High Sheriff co. Notts* 1729, d. 1748; *and had issue* 1b *to* 2b.

    1b. *Anthony Eyre of Grove and Adwick-le-Street, M.P.*, b. 9 *Jan*. 1727; d. 14 *Feb*. 1788; m. 1755, *Julia Letitia, da. and h. of John Bury of Nottingham*, d. 1800; *and had issue* 1c *to* 3c.

    1c. *Anthony Hardolph Eyre of Grove, M.P., Lieut.-Col. in the Army*, b. 8 *Mar*. 1757; d. 1836; m. 20 *Dec*. 1783, *Francisca Alicia, sister to Edward, 1st Baron Skelmersdale* [*U.K.*], *da. of Richard Wilbraham-Bootle of Rode, M.P.*, d. 3 *Sept*. 1810; *and had issue* 1d *to* 3d.

    1d. *Mary Letitia Eyre*, d. 7 *Sept*. 1860; m. 23 *Aug*. 1804, *Charles Herbert* (*Pierrepont*), 2nd *Earl Manvers* [*U.K.*] *and Viscount Newark* [*G.B.*], d. 27 *Oct*. 1860; *and had issue*.

    See p. 292, Nos. 14582–14627.

    2d. *Frances Eyre*, d. 5 *Feb*. 1844; m. *as* 1st *wife*, 22 *Feb*. 1814, *Granville Harcourt-Vernon of Grove Hall, co. Notts*, d. 8 *Dec*. 1879; *and had issue*.

    See the Tudor Roll of "The Blood Royal of Britain," p. 381, Nos. 29052–29078.

    3d. *Henrietta Eyre*, d. (–); m. 1st, *her cousin-german, John Hardolph Eyre*, d.s.p. 1817; 2ndly, *Henry Galley Knight of Firbeck Hall, co. York*.

    2c. *Ven. John Eyre, Archdeacon of Nottingham*, b. 19 *Feb*. 1758; d. *Mar*. 1830; m. 12 *Ap*. 1720, *Charlotte, da. of Sir George Armytage, 3rd Bart.* [*G.B.*]; *and had issue* 1d *to* 3d.

    1d. *Rev. Charles Wasteneys Eyre of Rampton*, b. 7 *Mar*. 1802; d. 30 *Oct*. 1862; m. 26 *Ap*. 1821, *Lucy Dorothea, da. of John Robinson Foulis of Hesterton*, d. 1886; *and had issue* 1e *to* 3e.   [Nos. 52091 to 52174.

---

[1] See Foster's " Baronetage," 1880, p. 262.

# of The Blood Royal

1e. Henry Eyre of *Rampton, C.B., M.P., J.P., D.L., Lieut.-Col. N. Notts Rifle Vol.,* b. 4 Feb. 1834; d. (–); m. 7 Mar. 1861, *Kathleen, da. of the Rev. Robert Machell of Crackenthorpe,* d. 20 Dec. 1899; *and had issue 1f to 3f.*

1f. Gervas Malcolm Eyre, b. 17 May 1862.

2f. Morland Stanhope Eyre, Capt. R.A., b. 16 May 1863.

3f. Charles Roland Babington Eyre, b. 7 Ap. 1880.

2e. Arthur Stanhope Eyre, b. 3 Aug. 1840.

3e. Lucy Harriet Eyre, m. Ap. 1865, Capt. Robert Scott Machell, 62nd Regt.; and has issue 1f.

1f. Walter Leonard Machell, b. 6 Feb. 1866.

2d. *Anthony Gervase Eyre,* b. *Aug.* 1812; d. (–).

3d. *Charlotte Eyre,* d. 20 *Sept.* 1845; m. 20 *June* 1815, *Henry Willoughby of Birdsall, co. York,* d. 20 Nov. 1849; *and had issue 1e to 6e.*

1e. *Henry (Willoughby), 8th Baron Middleton* [G.B.], b. 28 *Aug.* 1817; d. 19 *Dec.* 1877; m. 3 *Aug.* 1843, *Julia Louisa, da. of Alexander William Bosville of Thorpe and Gunthwaite, co. York, and Armadale Castle, Skye,* d. 11 Oct. 1901; *and had issue 1f to 11f.*

1f. Digby Wentworth Bayard (Willoughby), 9th Baron Middleton [G.B.] (*Wollaton Hall, Notts; Birdsall House, Yorks; Middleton Hall, near Tamworth, &c.*), b. 24 Aug. 1844; m. 5 Aug. 1869, Eliza Maria, da. of Sir Alexander Penrose Gordon-Cumming, 3rd Bart. [U.K.].

2f. Hon. Godfrey Ernest Percival Willoughby, *late* Capt. 9th Lancers, *privately* R.N. (*The Green, Brompton, R.S.O., Yorks*), b. 18 June 1847; m. 15 June 1881, Ida Eleanora Constance, da. of George William Holmes Ross of Cromarty; and has issue.

See p. 590, Nos. 51369–51376.

3f. Hon. Leopold Vincent Harold Willoughby, M.A. (Oxon.) (*The Wood House, Epping*), b. 19 Nov. 1851.

4f. Hon. Tatton Lane Fox Willoughby (*Hildenley Home Farm, Malton, Yorks*), b. 29 Dec. 1860; m. 18 June 1898, Esther Ann, da. of Sir Charles William Strickland, 8th Bart. [E.].

5f. Hon. Claud Henry Comaraich Willoughby, Lieut.-Col. 9th Lancers, and Mil. Sec. to Gov.-Gen. of Australia (*Bachelors'*), b. 7 July 1862; m. 24 Oct. 1904, Sybil Louise, da. of Charles James Murray of Loch Carron, M.P.

6f. Hon. Alexander Hugh Willoughby, *late* Capt. Yorkshire Regt. (*Barton Hill House, Yorks*), b. 18 Sept. 1863; m. 14 Aug. 1889, Mary Selina Honora, da. of Gen. the Hon. James Bosville-Macdonald, C.B.; and has issue.

See p. 588, Nos. 51314–51315.

7f. Hon. Alexandrina Henrietta Matilda Willoughby, m. 3 Feb. 1869, Sir John Henry Thorold, 12th Bart. [E.], LL.D., J.P., D.L. (*Syston Park, near Grantham*); and has issue 1g to 4g.

1g. John George Thorold, Capt. and Hon. Major 4th Batt. Lincolnshire Regt.

2g. James Ernest Thorold (*Sandon Lodge, Stone*), b. 27 Jan. 1877; m. 16 Dec. 1902, Katharine, da. of the Rev. William Rolfe Tindal Atkinson; and has issue 1h to 2h.

1h. Anthony Henry Thorold, b. 7 Sept. 1903.

2h. Montague Thorold, b. 27 Mar. 1906.

3g. Aline Thorold, m. 8 Aug. 1894, Ernest James Wythes (*Copped Hall, Epping*).

4g. Dorothy Marion Thorold.

8f. *Hon. Leila Louisa Millicent Willoughby,* b. 21 *Sept.* 1853; d. 24 *Feb.* 1886; m. 10 *Feb.* 1876, *the Rev. Henry Charles (son of Lord Charles) Russell (Wollaton Rectory, Notts); and had issue.*

See the Tudor Roll of " The Blood Royal of Britain," p. 481, Nos. 33386–33394.

[Nos. 52175 to 52212.

4 I

The Plantagenet Roll

9f. Hon. Hylda Maria Madeline Willoughby, *m*. 20 Ap. 1882, William Henry Garforth of Wiganthorpe and Dalby (*Swinton Grange, Malton*); and has issue 1g to 3g.

1g. William Godfrey Willoughby Garforth, *b*. 1883.

2g. Lavinia Marion Garforth, *b*. 1884.

3g. Harmione Mary Christian Garforth, *b*. 1887.

10f. Hon. Lettice Hermione Violet Willoughby, *m*. as 2nd wife, 18 Ap. 1895, Col. William Gordon Gordon-Cumming, *late* Indian Staff Corps (*Forres House, Forres*).

11f. *Hon. Marri Myrtle Willoughby*, b. 27 *Sept.* 1859; d. 13 *Nov.* 1900; m. 1 *Jan.* 1880, *William Bethell, J.P., D.L.* (*Rise Park, near Hull; Watton Abbey, near Beverley*); *and had issue* 1g *to* 2g.

1g. William Adrian Vincent Bethell, *b*. 11 Sept. 1890.

2g. Phyllis Mary Hermione Bethell, *b*. 26 Ap. 1889.

2e. *Rev. the Hon.*[1] *Charles James Willoughby*, b. 5 *Feb.* 1822; d. 6 *Nov.* 1875; m. 7 *Aug.* 1845, *Charlotte Payne, da. of Henry John Hyde Seymour of Wells*, d. 13 *Jan.* 1892; *and had issue* 1f *to* 10f.

1f. *Rev. Hugh St. Maur Willoughby, Vicar of Fawley*, b. 13 *June* 1847; d. 3 *Sept.* 1904; m. 22 *Sept.* 1874, *Anne Blanche, da. of George Thomas Davy; and had issue* 1g *to* 2g.

1g. Magdalen Willoughby, *m*. 14 Nov. 1901, Hugh Ker Colville (*Ballaport Hall, Salop*).

2g. Bridget Willoughby.

2f. Charles Stuart Percival Willoughby, *late* Paymaster and Hon. Major Army Pay Dept., *b*. 13 Aug. 1848; *m*. 2 Dec. 1880, Elizabeth, da. of Frederick A. Wiggins of 9 Porchester Terrace, W.; and has issue 1g.

1g. Geoffrey St. Maur Willoughby, Lieut. 1st Vol. Batt. Hants Regt., *b*. 11 Nov. 1881.

3f. Cecil Edward Willoughby, *late* Lieut. R.N. (*Wilford, Notts*); *b*. 2 Feb. 1851; *m*. 26 July 1883, Harriet Maud, da. of Sir Thomas Isaac Birkin of Ruddington Grange, 1st Bart. [U.K.], J.P., D.L.; and has issue 1g to 2g.

1g. Gladys Maud Willoughby, *b*. 24 Ap. 1884.

2g. Hilda St. Maud Willoughby, *b*. 16 Sept. 1885.

4f. Gerald Francis Willoughby, *b*. 28 June 1853.

5f. Henry Somerset Willoughby, *b*. 1 July 1854.

6f. James Frederick Digby Willoughby, M.R.C.S. (Eng.), L.R.C.P. (Lond.) (*Southwell, Notts*), *b*. 19 May 1856; *m*. 26 Oct. 1881, Mary Elizabeth, da. of the Rev. Edward John Randolph, Canon of York; and has issue 1g to 4g.

1g. Ronald James Edward Willoughby, Mid. R.N., *b*. 7 May 1884.

2g. Archibald Macdonald Willoughby, Mid. R.N., *b*. 20 May 1887.

3g. Bernard Digby Willoughby, *b*. 8 Ap. 1896.

4g. Katherine Mary Seymour Willoughby.

7f. Leonard Broke Willoughby, Capt. 3rd and 4th Batt. Lancashire Fusiliers, *b*. 24 Nov. 1860; *m*. 18 July 1888, Ada Mary, da. of Charles Baxter Cousens of 2 Clanricarde Gardens, W.; and has issue 1g to 2g.

1g. Charles d'Eresby Willoughby, *b*. 12 Sept. 1889.

2g. Gilbert de Bee Willoughby, *b*. 15 May 1894.

8f. Julia Mary Willoughby, *m*. 1st, 9 July 1878, the Rev. Gordon Heslop, Rector of Levisham, *d*. 1894; 2ndly, 29 Sept. 1898, Benjamin Day (*Shafton, Barnsley*).

9f. *Mildred Cassandra Willoughby*, b. 25 *July* 1857; d. 28 *Sept.* 1903; m. 5 *June* 1881, *Granville Walter Randolph; and had issue* 1g *to* 4g.

[Nos. 52213 to 52237.

---

[1] R W. 13 Mar. 1857.

614

1g. Charles Edward Randolph, *b.* 1883.

2g. Thomas Granville Randolph, *b.* 1886.

3g. George Algernon Randolph, *b.* 1890.

4g. Hylda Mary Randolph, *b.* 1884.

10f. Evelyn Willoughby, *m.* 20 Nov. 1884, the Rev. Robert John Thorp (*Royston Vicarage, Barnsley*); and has issue 1g to 6g.

1g. Robert Gordon Thorp, *b.* 19 Sept. 1885.

2g. Charles William Thorp, *b.* 2 Feb. 1890.

3g. John Bernard Thorp, *b.* 15 Jan. 1906.

4g. Marion Frances Thorp, *b.* 9 Ap. 1887.

5g. Elsie Thorp, *b.* 5 June 1888.

6g. Evelyn Mary Thorp, *b.* 12 May 1892.

3e. Rev. the Hon.[1] Percival George Willoughby, M.A. (Camb.), *late* Rector of Durweston-cum-Bryanstone (6 *Egerton Gardens, S.W.*), *b.* 1 Mar. 1827; *m.* 20 Ap. 1852, Sophia, da. of Edward Blackett Beaumont of Wood Hall, Yorks; and has issue 1f to 6f.

1f. Herbert Perceval Willoughby, Lieut.-Col. and Brevet-Col. R.A., *b.* 19 Jan. 1853; *m.* 20 Aug. 1875, Mary Louisa, da. of T. Allen Brown of Allahabad; and has issue 1g to 5g.

1g. Nesbit Edward Willoughby, Lieut. 1st Batt. E. Surrey Regt., *b.* 4 July 1878.

2g. Percival Francis Willoughby, Mid. R.N., *b.* 16 Oct. 1882.

3g. John Herbert Willoughby, *b.* 13 Ap. 1896.

4g Eva Mary Willoughby.

5g. Mabel Isabel Willoughby.

2f. Rev. Nesbit Edward Willoughby, Vicar of Cruwys Morehard (*Cruwys Morehard Vicarage, Tiverton*), *b.* 5 Ap. 1854; *m.* 1st, 18 June 1889, Florence Mary Tottenham, da. of the Rev. E. Lowe, *d.s.p.* 15 Sept. 1897; 2ndly, 29 Oct. 1901, Marjorie Helen, da. of J. E. Kaye of Bretton; and has issue 1g to 3g.

1g. Guy Willoughby, *b.* 7 Nov. 1902.

2g. Veronica Willoughby, *b.* 4 Dec. 1903.

3g. Gwendolen Mary Willoughby, *b.* 11 Sept. 1905.

3f. Aubrey Frederick Willoughby, Solicitor (6 *Egerton Gardens, S.W.*), *b.* 1 July 1857.

4f. Sydney Beaumont Willoughby (*Rockmount, Bedford*), *b.* 29 June 1859; *m.* 7 June 1887, the Hon. Mary Katherine, da. of John (Erskine), 4th Baron Erskine [U.K.], *previously* wife of the Rev. Evelyn Henry Villebois Barnaby; and has issue 1g.

1g. Christopher John Willoughby, *b.* 1889.

5f. Mabel Eleanor Willoughby, *b.* 4 Oct. 1860.

6f. Ethel Mary Willoughby, *b.* 29 June 1862.

4e. Charlotte Henrietta Willoughby, b. 7 Ap. 1816; d. 25 Jan. 1844; m. 26 Oct. 1839, *Henry Willoughby Legard, 9th Lancers,* b. 1805; d. 21 Nov. 1845; *and had issue 1f to 2f.*

1f. Sir Algernon Willoughby Legard, 12th Bart. [E.] (*Ganton Hall, Yorks*), *b.* 14 Oct. 1842; *m.* 27 July 1872, Alicia Egerton, da. of the Rev. George Brooks, M.A.

2f. Rev. Cecil Henry Legard, M.A. (Camb.), LL.M., Rector of Cottesbrooke (*Cottesbrooke Rectory, Northampton*), *b.* 28 Nov. 1843; *m.* 29 Ap. 1873, Emily Mary, da. of James Hall of Scorboro Hall; and has issue 1g to 2g.

1g. Digby Algernon Hall Legard, *b.* 7 Dec. 1876; *m.* 2 June 1904, Georgina Blanche Elaine, da. of William Joseph Starkey Barber-Starkey.

2g. Gertrude Cassandra Legard, *b.* 8 Nov. 1879. [Nos. 52238 to 52268.

The Plantagenet Roll

5e. Hon.[1] Emma Willoughby (13 *St. Mary's, York;* m. 11 Ap. 1850, the Rev. Richard Beverley Machell, M.A., J.P., Canon of York, Lord of the Manor and Patron of the Living of Asby, *b.* 8 Jan. 1823; *d.* 18 Aug. 1898; and has issue 1*f* to 6*f*.

1*f*. Hugh Lancelot Machell, B.A. (Camb.), Solicitor, *b.* 14 Aug. 1851; *m.* 22 July 1876, Helena Margaret, da. of Abel Chapman of Woodford; and has issue 1*g* to 4*g*.

1*g*. Lancelot Machell, *b.* 25 Feb. 1877.
2*g*. Julian Machell, *b.* 23 Mar. 1878.
3*g*. Humphrey Gilbert Machell, *b.* 12 Oct. 1887.
4*g*. Hope Duleis Machell, *b.* 14 Nov. 1886.

2*f*. Reginald Willoughby Machell, *b.* 20 June 1854; *m.* 2 Aug. 1876, Ada Mary, da. of the Rev. Charles Sympson of Kirkby Misperton; and has issue 1*g* to 2*g*.

1*g*. Henry Reginald Machell, *b.* 17 Sept. 1880.
2*g*. Montagu Arthur Machell, *b.* 29 July 1888.

3*f*. Percy Wilfrid Machell, Adviser to the Egyptian Ministry of the Interior (Cairo), *late* Capt. Essex Regt., &c. (*Army and Navy*), *b.* 5 Dec. 1862; *m.* 5 Dec. 1905, the Countess Victoria (Valda), da. of Prince Victor of Hohenlohe-Langenburg, 1st Count Gleichen, G.C.B.

4*f*. Lancelot Wentworth Machell (*Surbiton Station, Queensland*), *b.* 11 June 1865.

5*f*. Eva Magdalen Machell, *m.* 15 Dec. 1886, Charles Henry Holme (*Rathbourne, Duns, N.B.*).

6*f*. Beatrice Cassandra Machell, *m.* 22 Aug. 1888, William George Dickinson (*Roos Hall, Hull*); and has issue 1*g* to 2*g*.

1*g*. Michael William Dickinson, *b.* 21 Dec. 1890.
2*g*. John Cuthbert George Dickinson, *b.* 25 Aug. 1893.

6e. *Hon.[1] Harriet Cassandra Willoughby*, b. 21 *Feb.* 1825; *d.* 28 *Sept.* 1903; m. 5 *July* 1864, *Godfrey Wentworth Bayard Bosville of Thorpe and Gunthwaite*, b. 6 *Jan.* 1826; *d.* 11 *Oct.* 1865; *and had issue* 1*f*.

1*f*. Alexander Wentworth Macdonald Bosville, J.P., D.L., C.C. (*Thorpe Hall, Bridlington*), *b.* 26 Sept. 1865; *m.* 20 Oct. 1886, Alice Edith, da. of John Middleton of Kinfauns; and has issue 1*g* to 2*g*.

1*g*. Godfrey Middleton Bosville, *b.* 25 Sept. 1887.
2*g*. Celia Violet Bosville, *b.* 28 Jan. 1889.

3c. *Sir George Eyre, K.C.B., K.C.M.G., Vice-Adm. of the Red*, b. 23 *Ap.* 1769; d. 15 *Feb.* 1839; m. 1 *Nov.* 1800, *Georgina, da. of Sir George Cooke, 7th Bart.* [*E.*], d. (–); *and had issue* 1*d to* 6*d*.

1*d*. *Rev. George Hardolph Eyre, Vicar of Beighton*, b. 20 *Sept.* 1801; d. (? *unm.*) *Feb.* 1865.

2*d*. *Sir William Eyre, K.C.B., Lieut.-Gen. Comdg. Forces in Canada*, b. 21 *Oct.* 1805; d. 8 *Sept.* 1859; m. 16 *Feb.* 1841, *Georgiana Lucy, da. of the Hon. John Bridgman Simpson*, d. 6 *Ap.* 1898; *and had issue*.

3*d*. *Mary Charlotte Eyre*, d. *Aug.* 1889; m. *as 2nd wife*, 9 *June* 1846, *the Rev. Charles Bradshaw Bowles of Bradshaw and Abney, Vicar of Woking*, b. 3 *Oct.* 1806; d. 26 *Aug.* 1885; *and had issue* 1*e to* 4*e*.

1*e*. Charles Eyre Bradshaw Bowles of Abney and Bradshaw, M.A. (Oxon.), J.P. (*Abney Manor, Hathensage, Derby; The Nether House, Wirksworth*), *b.* 17 Aug. 1848; *m.* 8 Aug. 1878, Jane Charlotte, da. of John Charles Burton Borough of Chetwynd Park, co. Salop, J.P., D.L.; and has issue 1*f* to 3*f*.

1*f*. Humphrey Charles Bradshaw Bowles, *b.* 15 Sept. 1879.
2*f*. Dorothy Mary Bowles.
3*f*. Cecily Frances Bowles.

2*e*. Arthur Humphrey Bowles (*Temple Court, near Guildford*), *b.* 1 Dec. 1849; *m.* 14 Aug. 1873, Gertrude, da. of Spencer Mackay; and has issue 1*f* to 6*f*.

[Nos. 52269 to 52292.

---

[1] R. W. 13 Mar. 1857.

# of The Blood Royal

1f. Arthur Frederick Vansittart Bowles, *b.* 10 Nov. 1875.

2f. Charles Edward Bowles, *b.* 27 Nov. 1876.

3f. Rosa Eleanor Gertrude Bowles, *m.* 18 Aug. 1903, Henry Clutton-Brock; and has issue 1*g.*

    1g. Hugh Alan Clutton-Brock, *b.* 7 June 1904.

4f. Mary Edith Bowles, *m.* 16 May 1905, Guy Fleming.

5f. Lilian Maude Bowles.

6f. Margaret Irene Bowles.

3e. Frederick Augustus Bowles, Col. R.A., *b.* 18 May 1851; *m.* 10 May 1882, Isabella, da. of Robert Scotland; and has issue 1*f.*

    1f. James Arthur Bowles, Lieut. R.A., *b.* 9 Mar. 1883.

4e. William Henry Bowles, Bar.-at-Law, Lincoln's Inn (*Hillside, Timsbury, near Bath*), *b.* 16 July 1853; *m.* 1st, Jan. 1887, Edith, da. of the Rev. S. M. Barkworth, D.D., *d.* 14 Mar. 1896; 2ndly, 14 Feb. 1901, Constance, da. of Sir Alfred Hughes, 9th Bart. [G.B.]; and has issue 1*f* to 5*f.*

    1f. Ranulph Francis Bowles, *b.* 13 Nov. 1887.

    2f. John Godfrey Bowles, *b.* 14 Jan. 1890.

    3f. Anthony Walter Bowles, *b.* 19 Aug. 1891.

    4f. Henry William Bowles, *b.* July 1902.

    5f. Janet Catherine Bowles.

4d. Caroline Julia Eyre.

5d. Charlotte Maria Eyre.

6d. Julia Letitia Eyre.

2b. Mary Eyre, b. 21 Oct. 1726; d. 13 *Aug.* 1785; m. 26 *Oct.* 1752, *Anthony Cooke of Owston,* b. 1710; d. 30 *Ap.* 1763; *and had issue* 1c *to* 2c.

    1c. Bryan Cooke of Owston, M.P., b. 8 *June* 1756; d. 8 Nov. 1821; m. 1*st,* 18 Dec. 1786, *Frances, da. and h. of Philip Puleston of Gwysaney, &c.;* d. 1 *Jan.* 1818; *and had issue.*

    See p. 499, Nos. 43896–43940.

    2c. Anne Cooke, d. (–); m. *St. Andrew Warde of Hooton Pagnell;* bapt. 27 *May* 1745; bur. 22 *Mar.* 1822; *and had issue.*

    See the Clarence Volume, p. 609, Nos. 26783–26790.   [Nos. 52293 to 52362.

547. Descendants of Sir HUGH CHOLMLEY, 4th Bart. [E.] (see Table LVIII.), *b.* 21 July 1632; *d.* 9 Jan. 1689; *m.* 19 Feb. 1666, Lady ANNE, da. of Spencer (COMPTON), 2nd Earl of Northampton [E.], *b. c.* 1637; *d.* 26 May 1705; and had issue.

See the Clarence Volume, Table XXVI., and pp. 230–237, Nos. 4707–4920.

[Nos. 52363 to 52577.

548. Descendants of ANN CHOLMLEY (see Table LVIII.), *bapt.* 7 Dec. 1634; *d.* (–); *m.* at St. Giles in the Fields, co. Midx. (Cert. of Publication 29 June), 1654, RICHARD STEPHENS of Eastlington, co. Gloucester, named as a Knight of the Royal Oak in 1660, *b.* 1620; *d.* 1678; and had issue 1*a* to 3*a*.[1]

1a. Nathaniel Stephens of Eastlington, High Sheriff co. Gloucester 1698, b. 1655; d. 1742; m. *Eliza, da. of Sir Francis Pemberton, Lord Chief-Justice of the King's Bench and Common Pleas; and had issue* 1b.

    1b. Anne Stephens, da., and in her issue, if any, sole h., m. *John Jacob of Hullavington.*

2a. Robert Stephens of the Middle Temple, Solicitor to the Customs to Anne and George I., b. 1664; d. (–); m. *Mary, widow of Nathaniel Cholmley, da. of Sir Hugh Cholmley, 4th Bart.* [E.].

---

[1] Fosbrooke's "Gloucestershire," 1803–7, i. pp. 318–319.

617

The Plantagenet Roll

3a. *Elizabeth Stephens*, d. (–); m. *John Packer of Shellingford, co. Berks ; and had issue* 1b *to* 3b.

1b. *Robert Packer of Shellingford*, d. (–); m. *Mary, da. and co-h. of Sir Henry Winchcombe, 2nd Bart.* [E.]; *and had issue.*

See the Clarence Volume, Table LXXVII., and pp. 624–625, Nos. 27991–27995.

2b. [——] *Packer*, m. *as 1st wife, Sir Edward Hannes ; and had issue* 1c.

1c. [——] *Packer*, m. *John Willis of Redingfield Hall, co. Suffolk ; and had issue* 1d *to* 5d.

1d. *John Willis*, d.s.p.

2d. *Rev. Henry Willis*, m. *Jane, da. of Richard Lubbock of North Walsham, co. Norfolk ; and had (with other das.) issue* 1e *to* 5e.

1e. *Richard Willis.*

2e. *Lubbock Willis.*

3e. *Henry Willis, afterwards Stephens of Eastlington, Horsley, and Fretherne.*

4e. *Winchcombe Hartley Willis, an Officer in the Army.*

5e. *(Temperance) Jane Willis.*

3d. *Mary Willis.*

4d. *Lucy Willis*, d.s.p.

5d. *Elizabeth Willis*, m. *the Rev. George* [*son of Archdeacon*] *Basset of co. Lincoln.*

3b. [——] *Packer*, m. *Thomas Gisborne ; and had issue* 1c.

1c. [——] *Gisborne*, m. [——], *da. of* [——] *Bateman ; and had issue (2 sons and 2 or 3 das.).* [Nos. 52578 to 52582.

549. Descendants of Sir HENRY CHOLMLEY of West Newton Grange, co. York, Lawyer (see Table LVIII.), *b. c.* 1609; *d.* 1666; *m.* KATHERINE, widow of Sir GEORGE TWISLETON of Barley, 1st Bart., da. of Henry STAPYLTON of Wighill, *bur.* 14 June 1672; and had issue.

See pp. 544–546, Nos. 49477–49514. [Nos. 52583 to 52620.

550. Descendants of MARGARET CHOLMLEY (see Table LVIII.), *d.* Jan. 1704; *m.* (Lic. Fac. 11 July) 1666, Sir JOHN D'OYLEY of Chiselhampton, 1st Bart. [E.], M.P., *b.* Nov. 1640; *d.* 13 Ap. 1709; and had issue 1a to 6a.

1a. *Sir John D'Oyley, 2nd Bart.* [E.], b. c. 1670; d. 1746; m. 1st (Lic. Vic. Gen. Jan.) 1695, Susan, da. of Sir Thomas Putt, 1st Bart. [E.], d. Aug. 1722; and had issue 1b to 7b.

1b. *Sir Thomas D'Oyley, 3rd Bart.* [E.], b. c. 1701; bur. 14 Feb. 1759; m. c. 1737, Margaret, da. of Samuel Wotton of Ingleborne (or Englebourn), co. Devon, d. (between 7 June and Aug.) 1780; and had issue 1c.

1c. *Susan D'Oyley, da. and h.*, b. 1737; d. c. 1768; m. as 1st wife, 1767, the Right Rev. William Newcome, D.D., Lord Bishop of Dromore 1766–1775, and afterwards (1775–1779) of Ossory, and (1779–1795) Waterford and Lismore, and finally (1795) Archbishop of Armagh and Lord Primate of all Ireland, b. 9 Ap. 1829; d. 11 June 1800; and had issue 1d.

1d. *Maria Newcome, da. and h. of her mother*, b. 1768; d. 12 Ap. 1858; m. 21 Jan. 1794, the Rev. Mungo Henry Noble, afterwards (R.L. 1809) Waller of Glassdrummond, co. Fermanagh, and Allenstown, co. Meath, b. 1759; d. 16 June 1831; and had issue 1e to 2e.

1e. *Rev. Robert Noble of Glassdrummond*, b. 29 *Aug.* 1796; d. *Oct.* 1870; m. 25 *Oct.* 1833, *Catherine, da. of the Rev. John Annesley Burrowes of Castleconnor; and had issue 1f to 7f.*

1f. *William Henry Noble of Glassdrummond, Major-Gen. R.A.*, b. 14 *Oct.* 1834; d. 17 *May* 1892; m. 11 *July* 1861, *Emily, da. of Frederick Marriott of Taunton; and had issue 1g to 6g.*

1g. Shirley Newcome Noble (*Glassdrummond, Fermanagh*), b. 7 June 1865.

2g. Vere D'Oyly Noble, b. 7 Feb. 1867; *m.* 24 Jan. 1895, Dora Mary Robinson, da. of James Robinson Pease of Hesslewood; and has issue 1h.

1h. Henry Francis D'Oyly Noble, b. 23 June 1896.

3g. Mawde Lettice Noble.

4g. Violet Alice Agnes Noble, *m.* 24 Nov. 1894, James Montagu Oldham (*Ormidale, Ascot*); and has issue 1h to 2h.

1h. Reginald D'Oyly Oldham, b. 15 Oct. 1895.

2h. Gerald Wolseley Oldham, b. 27 Sept. 1896.

5g. Phyllis D'Oyly Noble, *m.* 29 Aug. 1895, Edward Byas Sheppard (*Leggatts, Herts*); and has issue.

6g. Sybil Cholmley Waller Noble.

2f. John D'Oyly Noble, b. 17 Nov. 1835; *m.* 26 Aug. 1869, Helen, da. of Stafford Frederick Kirkpatrick of Kingston, Canada; and has issue 1g to 4g.

1g. Robert Kirkpatrick Noble, b. 9 June 1870.

2g. Stafford D'Oyly Noble, b. 25 Oct. 1871.

3g. James Burrowes Noble, b. 17 Feb. 1873.

4g. Ernest Annesley Noble, b. 20 Nov. 1876.

3f. Edwin St. George Noble, b. 19 Oct. 1842.

4f. Robert D'Oyly Noble, b. 6 July 1846.

5f. Helen Catherine Noble, *m.* 18 Aug. 1863, the Rev. Graham Craig, Rector of Tullamore; and has issue 1g to 6g.

1g. Robert Stewart Craig, b. 5 Sept. 1864.

2g. Henry Graham Craig, b. 28 Oct. 1865.

3g. Herbert Newcome Craig, b. 17 Sept. 1868.

4g. Arthur William Craig, b. 18 June 1872.

5g. Allan Noble Craig, b. 22 Dec. 1874.

6g. Helen Mary Stewart Craig.

6f. Emily Mary Noble, *m.* 25 Aug. 1864, Robert Stewart Craig; and has issue 1g to 2g.

1g. Edwin Stewart Craig, b. 2 June 1865.

2g. Robert Annesley Craig, b. 17 July 1869.

7f. Maria Louisa Noble, *m.* 7 Ap. 1877, Edmund Noble Waller.

2e. *James Noble Waller of Allenstown, J.P., D.L., High Sheriff co. Meath* 1845–1846, b. 28 *July* 1800; d. 18 *Dec.* 1874; m. 1st, 22 *Mar.* 1838, *Julia, da. of Charles Arthur Tisdall of Charlesfort*, d. 17 *Ap.* 1848; 2ndly, 15 *May* 1858, *Anna Marie, da. of the Rev. James Annesley Burrowes*, d. 17 *Sept.* 1891; *and had issue 1f to 4f.*

1f. William Newcome Waller, J.P., D.L., High Sheriff co. Meath (*Allenstown Kells, Meath*), b. 13 Aug. 1839.

2f. James Henry Waller, b. 25 Mar. 1845; d. (? unm.) 13 Mar. 1884.

3f. Edmund Noble Waller (*Uruguay*), b. 11 June 1846; *m.* 7 Ap. 1877, Maria Louisa, da. of the Rev. Robert Noble of Glassdrummond.

4f². Catherine Maria Waller.

2b. *Sir John D'Oyly, 4th Bart.* [E.], b. c. 1702; d. *unm.* 24 Nov. 1773.

3b. *Shirley D'Oyly*, d.s.p.; m. *and app.* s.p.

4b. *William D'Oyly, sometimes erroneously called 5th Bart.* [E.], d.s.p.s., *a.* 1771.

5b. *Margaret D'Oyly.*   [Nos. 52621 to 52650.

6*b*. *Ursula D'Oyly*, m. *Thomas Young of Newington, co. Oxon. ; and had issue* (*a son and da.*).

7*b*. *Cholmley D'Oyly*, m. *William Jones of Naas, co. Gloucester ; and had issue* (2 sons and 1 da.).

2*a*. *Thomas D'Oyly, in the Customs*, m. [——], *widow of Hugh Fortescue, da. of* [——].

3*a*. *Robert D'Oyly, Lieut.-Col. in the Army and Governor of the Tower*, m. *the sister of Ralph Freeman of Hamels, co. Herts, M.P.*

4*a*. *Hugh D'Oyly, in the Customs.*

5*a*. *Mary D'Oyly*, m. *Samuel Wotton of Englebourne, co. Devon; and had issue* (at least) 1*b*.

1*b*. *Mary Wotton*, d. *between 7 June and Aug.* 1780; m. *c.* 1737, *Sir Thomas D'Oyly, 3rd Bart.* [E.]; *and had issue.*

See p. 619, Nos. 52621–52650.

6*a*. *Elizabeth D'Oyly*, d. 1720; m. *as 2nd wife, after 26 May* 1714, *Rev. the Hon. George Mordaunt*, d. 28 *July* 1728; *and had issue.*

See the Clarence Volume, Table **XXXI.**, and pp. 264–269, Nos. 7028–7202.

[Nos. 52651 to 52855.

551. Descendants of Ursula Cholmley (see Table LVIII.), *d.* 1674 ; *m. c.* 1675, Sir Thomas Putt of Combe Gillisham, co. Devon, 1st Bart. [E.], M.P., *d.* 1686 ; and had issue 1*a* to 4*a*.

1*a*. *Sir Thomas Putt, 2nd Bart.* [E.], b. *c.* 1675 ; d.s.p. 5 *May* 1721.

2*a*. *Margaret Putt*, d. (–) ; m. *Robert (Dillon), 6th Earl of Roscommon* [I.], d. 14 *May* 1715; *and had issue* 1*b* to 2*b*.

1*b*. *Robert (Dillon), 7th Earl of Roscommon* [I.], d.s.p. 9 *Jan.* 1721.

2*b*. *James (Dillon), 8th Earl of Roscommon* [I.], d. *unm.* 20 *Aug.* 1746.

3*a*. [——] *Putt*, m. *Charles Gorsuch.*

4*a*. *Susan Putt*, d. *Aug.* 1722 ; m. *as 1st wife* (*Lic. Vic. Gen. Jan.*), 1695, *Sir John D'Oyley, 2nd Bart.* [E.], d. 1746; *and had issue.*

See p. 619, Nos. 52621–52650. [Nos. 52856 to 52885.

552. Descendants of Margaret Sibthorp (see Table LIX.), *d.* 1823 ; *m.* Mar. 1773, Thomas O'Reilly of Baltrasna, co. Meath, J.P., *b.* 22 Ap. 1741 ; *d.* Dec. 1805 ; and had issue 1*a* to 2*a*.

1*a*. *James O'Reilly of Baltrasna, J.P.*, b. 22 *June* 1775 ; d. 19 *Mar.* 1853 ; m. 1 Oct. 1799, *Henrietta Catherine Blanche, da. of Oliver Nugent of Farren Connell, co. Cavan ; and had issue* 1*b* to 3*b*.

1*b*. *Anthony O'Reilly of Baltrasna, J.P., D.L., High Sheriff co. Cavan* 1845, b. 23 *June* 1812; d. 1874; m. 14 *May* 1836, *Alicia Maria, da. of Capt. John Fortescue*, d. 20 *Feb.* 1858; *and had issue* 1*c* to 6*c*.

1*c*. *Alicia Margaret O'Reilly*, da. and co-h., d. (–) ; m. 28 *Dec.* 1867, *Edward Watts-Russell*, d. (–) ; *and had* (*with other*) *issue* 1*d*.

1*d*. James Watts-Russell, *now* O'Reilly, J.P. (*Baltrasna, Oldcastle, Meath*), b. 1869.

2*c*. Harriet Georgina O'Reilly, da. and co-h., *m.* 24 June 1865, Matthew R. Weld O'Conor (*Viewmount, Longford*) ; and has issue.

3*c*. Florence Henrietta O'Reilly, da. and co-h., *m.* 6 Dec. 1871, Capt. John Archibald Murray, 97th Regt. (*Hornby Hall, Lancaster*) ; and has issue.

4*c*. Edith Sophia O'Reilly, da. and co-h., *m.* 3 Oct. 1878, Capt. Philip Julius Honywood Ayscoghe Barne, *late* 60th Rifles (*East Walton, King's Lynn*).

[Nos. 52886 to 52889.

5c. Olivia Blanche O'Reilly, da. and co-h., *m.* 12 Jan. 1869, William George Clayton Wade of Clonbraney, Jr., *b.* 1842; *d.* 1882; and has issue 1*d* to 3*d*.

1*d. Olive Frances Wade, d. 27 Mar. 1900; m. 1 Aug. 1894, Graham Wood, of The Glebe, Champion Hill, London; d. 3 Mar. 1905; and had issue 1e.*

1*e.* Christopher William Graham Wood, *b.* 18 Feb. 1900.

2*d.* Mabel Alice Wade.

3*d.* Norah Edith Annie Wade.

6c. Eva Cornelia O'Reilly, da. and co-h., *m.* 16 Ap. 1879, Capt. Albert Beauchamp Astley Cooper, J.P., *late* R.A. (9th son of Sir Astley Paston Cooper, 2nd Bart. [U.K.]) (*Temple Hill, East Budleigh, Devon*); and has issue 1*d* to 3*d*.

1*d.* Geoffrey Beauchamp Astley Cooper, Lieut. Middlesex Regt., *b.* 5 Mar. 1884.

2*d.* Olive Sylvia Beauchamp Cooper, *b.* 26 Mar. 1882.

3*d.* Rosalind Beauchamp Cooper, *b.* 21 Sept. 1885.

2*b. Robert John O'Reilly of Millcastle, co. Meath, Bar.-at-Law, b. 9 July 1813; d. 18 Dec. 1879; m. 2ndly, 29 Aug. 1857, Eleanor Grace, da. of Sir Norton Joseph Knatchbull, 10th Bart. [E.]; and had issue 1c.*

1*c.* Kathleen Mary O'Reilly.

3*b. Henrietta Catharine O'Reilly, d. (–); m. Richard Bolger of Ballard, co. Westmeath; and had issue.*

2*a. Anthony Alexander O'Reilly, Col. in the Army, b. 23 Sept. 1781; d. (–); m. 5 Aug. 1799, Anne, da. of Edward Graves of Maryborough; and had issue 1b to 7b.*

1*b. Thomas O'Reilly.*

2*b. James O'Reilly, d. (–); m. [——], da. of [——] Henricke of Somerset, Cape Colony; and had issue.*

3*b. John Robert O'Reilly, Cape Mounted Rifles.*

4*b. George O'Reilly.*

5*b. Anthony O'Reilly.*

6*b. Anne O'Reilly, d. (–); m. 25 Nov. 1817, Joseph Leeson, Major 42nd Bengal N.I. (son of the Hon. John, 2nd son of Brice, 3rd Earl of Milltown, [I.]), b. 25 Mar. 1796; d. 15 Feb. 1847; and had issue 1c to 5c.*

1*c. Joseph Lowther Leeson, b. 22 Aug. 1820; d.s.p. 7 Feb. 1883.*

2*c. Cecil John Leeson, d. unm.*

3*c. John Leeson, the senior Claimant to the Earldom of Milltown [I.], b. 19 Aug. 1827; d. 25 Jan. 1905; m. 1st, 9 Ap. 1850, Winifred Rose, da. of T. W. Collins of Delhi, Dep. Collector to joint Magistrate and Sup. of Abkari and Opium, &c., d. 14 Feb. 1898; 2ndly (in Umballa), 1900, Mary Jane Howgill, da. of William Lowther; and had issue 1d to 2d.*

1*d.* Olivia Caroline Collins Leeson, *m.* 5 Jan. 1887, James Arthur Magry (*Umballa, Punjab*); and has issue 1*e* to 5*e*.

1*e.* Joseph Leeson Collins Alcide Magry, *b.* 2 May 1887.

2*e.* Kathleen Annie Maria Collins Leeson Magry, *b.* 23 Ap. 1890.

3*e.* Ruby Eileen Bethel Collins Leeson Magry, *b.* 11 Ap. 1892.

4*e.* Winifred Rose Pearl Collins Leeson Magry, *b.* 29 Mar. 1899.

5*e.* Olivia Frances Shelah Collins Leeson Magry, *b.* 17 Sept. 1903.

2*d.* Eleanor Lavinia Leeson, *b.* 30 May 1862; *m.* 29 Jan. 1883, Charles Edward Richard Earle, Punjab Police; and has issue 1*e*.

1*e.* Roderic Collins Leeson Earle, U.P. and Oudh Police (*Charbagh, Lucknow*), *b.* 7 Dec. 1883.

4*c. Henry Corbett Leeson, d. 29 Sept. 1887; m. [——], da. of [——] Robinson; and had issue 1d.*

1*d.* Henry Saunders Leeson (? *dead*).

5*c. Frances Elizabeth Leeson, b. Feb. 1822; d. 1903; m. 4 Oct. 1841, Major Richard William Henry Fanshawe, d. 26 June 1885; and had issue.*

See p. 411, Nos. 34184–34191.

7*b. Catherine O'Reilly, d. (–); m. Col. M'Clean, 27th Regt.*

[Nos. 52890 to 52914.

4 K

The Plantagenet Roll

553. Descendants, if any, of BETTY COCHRANE (see Table LIX.), *m.* 1st, HENRY CAREY HAMILTON of Holycross; 2ndly, 3 June 1759, Lieut.-Col. NATHANIEL GOULD.

554. Descendants of THOMAS (COCHRANE), 10th EARL OF DUNDONALD [S.], and 1st MARQUIS OF MARANHAM (1824) [Brazil], Rear-Admiral of the United Kingdom, G.C.B., &c. (see Table LIX.), *b.* 14 Dec. 1775; *d.* 31 Oct. 1860; *m.* (secretly at Annan, co. Dumfries) 8 Aug. 1812, and again publicly 22 June 1818, KATHERINE FRANCES CORBET, da. of Thomas BARNES of Romford, co. Essex, *d.* (at Boulogne) 25 Jan. 1865; and had issue 1*a* to 3*a*.

1*a*. Thomas (*Cochrane*), 11*th Earl of Dundonald* [S.], 2nd Marquis of Maranham [Brazil], b. 18 Ap. 1814; d. 15 Jan. 1885; m. 1 Dec. 1847, Louisa Harriet, da. of William Alexander Mackinnon of Mackinnon, d. 24 Feb. 1902; and had issue 1*b* to 6*b*.

1*b*. Douglas Mackinnon Baillie Hamilton (*Cochrane*), 12th Earl of Dundonald and a Rep. Peer [S.], 3rd Marquis of Maranham [Brazil], C.V.O., C.B. (*Gwrych Castle, Abergele, N. Wales; 34 Portman Square, W.*), b. 29 Oct. 1852; m. 18 Sept. 1878, Winifred, da. of Robert Bamford-Hesketh of Gwrych Castle, Denbigh; and has issue 1*c* to 5*c*.

1*c*. Thomas Hesketh Douglas Blair Cochrane, Lord Cochrane, *b.* 21 Feb. 1886.

2*c*. Hon. Douglas Robert Hesketh Roger Cochrane, *b.* 24 June 1893.

3*c*. Lady Grizil Winifred Louisa Cochrane, *b.* 14 May 1880; *m.* 2 Mar. 1904, the Hon. Ralph Gerard Alexander Hamilton, Master of Belhaven.

4*c*. Lady Jean Alice Elaine Cochrane, *b.* 27 Nov. 1887.

5*c*. Lady Marjorie Gwendolen Elsie Cochrane, *b.* 18 Dec. 1889.

2*b*. Hon. Thomas Horatio Arthur Ernest Cochrane, M.P., Major and Hon. Lieut.-Col. Argyll and Sutherland Highlanders (*Crawford Priory, Springfield, Fife*), b. 2 Ap. 1857; m. 2 Dec. 1880, Lady Gertrude, da. of George Frederick (Boyle), 6th Earl of Glasgow [S.]; and has issue.

See p. 592, Nos. 51462–51468.

3*b*. Lady Louisa Katherine Emma Cochrane, *m.* 30 June 1873, Edward (O'Neill), 2nd Baron O'Neill [U.K.] (*Shane's Castle, Antrim*); and has issue 1*c* to 5*c*.

1*c*. Hon. Arthur Edward Bruce O'Neill, Capt. 2nd Life Guards (22 *Montagu Square, W.*), b. 19 Sept. 1876; m. 21 Jan. 1902, Lady Annabel Hungerford, da. of Robert Offley Ashburton (Crewe-Milnes), 1st Earl of Crewe [U.K.]; and has issue 1*d* to 2*d*.

1*d*. Sibyl O'Neill, *b.* 15 Dec. 1902.

2*d*. Mary Louisa Hermione O'Neil, *b.* 19 Aug. 1905.

2*c*. Hon. Robert William Hugh O'Neill, *b.* 8 June 1883.

3*c*. Hon. Louisa Henrietta Valdivia O'Neill.

4*c*. Hon. Rose Anne Mary O'Neill.

5*c*. Hon. Alice Esmeralda O'Neill.

4*b*. Lady Alice Laura Sophia Cochrane (*Croxton Park, St. Neots*), *m.* as 3rd wife, 27 July 1878, George Onslow Newton of Croxton Park, *d.* 7 Dec. 1900; and has issue 1*c* to 5*c*.

1*c*. George Douglas Cochrane Newton, J.P. (*Croxton Park, St. Neots*), *b.* 14 July 1879.

2*c*. Denzil Onslow Cochrane Newton, *b.* 27 Oct. 1880.   [Nos. 52915 to 52939.

622

3c. Thomas Cochrane Newton, b. 1885.

4c. William Alexander Cochrane Newton, b. 1886.

5c. Basil Cochrane Newton, b. 1889.

5b. Lady Elizabeth Mary Harriet Cochrane.

6b. Lady Esther Rose Georgina Cochrane.

2a. Hon. Sir Arthur Auckland Leopold Pedro Cochrane, K.C.B., Admiral (ret.) R.N. (*United Service*), b. 24 Sept. 1824.

3a. Hon. Ernest Grey Lambton Cochrane, J.P., D.L. (*Red Castle, Minteagh's Lodge, Donegal*), b. 4 June 1834; m. 1st (at Freetown, Sierra Leone), 15 Sept. 1864, Adelaide, da. of Col. Samuel W. Blackwall, Governor of Sierra Leone, d. 3 Oct. 1864; 2ndly, 16 Oct. 1866, Elizabeth Frances Maria, da. and h. of Richard Doherty of Red Castle, J.P.; and has issue 1b to 8b.

1b. Richard Francis Ernest Cochrane, Capt. 5th Batt. Royal Inniskilling Fusiliers, b. 18 Sept. 1873.

2b. Ernest Algernon Cochrane, b. 11 May 1877.

3b. Horace Cochrane Egerton Cochrane, b. 1883.

4b. Elizabeth Rosetta Stewart Cochrane, b. 19 Oct. 1867.

5b. Adelaide Maria Cochrane, b. 19 Aug. 1874.

6b. Frances Katherine Cochrane, b. 8 Nov. 1875.

7b. Blanche Edith Cochrane, b. 4 Oct. 1879.

8b. Mabel Alice Maria Cochrane, b. 6 Mar. 1884.   [Nos. 52940 to 52954.

555. Descendants of Major the Hon. WILLIAM ERSKINE COCHRANE (see Table LIX.), b. 1781; d. 16 Mar. 1869; m. MARY ANNE, da. of Alexander MANSON, d. 22 Oct. 1860; and had issue 1a.

1a. *William Marshall Cochrane, Lieut.-Col. 1st Royal Lanark Militia,* b. 22 Dec. 1817; d. 31 *July* 1898; m. *1st,* 14 *Oct.* 1846, *Mary, widow of Philip Bennett Marshall, da. of William Hussey,* d. 24 *Aug.* 1871; *and had issue* 1b *to* 6b.

1b. William Francis Dundonald Cochrane, C.B., Col. (ret.) in the Army (*Naval and Military*), b. 7 Aug. 1847; m. 30 Dec. 1893, Carola, da. of Enrique Teodoro Möller of Hamburg; and has issue 1c.

1c. Mary Rosita Carola Isabel Cochrane.

2b. Thomas Erskine Cochrane, Comm. (ret.) R.N. (*Cairntoigh, Banchory, Kincardine*), b. 12 Oct. 1849; m. 24 Mar. 1886, Mary, da. of John Bell-Irving of Whitehill, Lockerbie; and has issue 1c to 3c.

1c. Mary Cochrane, b. 18 Nov. 1889.

2c. Jessie Edith Cochrane, b. 22 July 1891.

3c. Daisey Bell-Irving Cochrane, b. 30 July 1894.

3b. John Palmer Cochrane, *late* Capt. Cape Mounted Rifles (*Stutterheim, Cape Colony*), b. 28 Mar. 1852; m. 19 June 1882, Frances, da. of William Gilbert of Canterbury; and has issue 1c to 7c.

1c. Basil William Dundonald Cochrane, b. 17 May 1891.

2c. John Erichsen Blair Cochrane, b. 20 Mar. 1894.

3c. Douglas Thomas Archibald Nelthorpe Cochrane, b. 24 Feb. 1900.

4c. Marion Mary Erskine Cochrane, b. 10 Sept. 1883.

5c. Cecily Somerville Cochrane, b. 7 Oct. 1886.

6c. Una Fairfax Cochrane, b. 19 Nov. 1888.

7c. Carola Urquhart Cochrane, b. 4 Oct. 1896.

4b. Arthur Henry Douglas Cochrane (*Blairfield Wyke, Chichester*), b. 19 Aug. 1856; m. 20 July 1882, Maria Josephine Clegg, da. of George Killick of Kirby Hall; and has issue 1c to 4c.   [Nos. 52955 to 52969.

1*c.* Douglas Erskine Cochrane, *b.* 3 Feb. 1883.

2*c.* Arthur Blair Dundonald Cochrane, *b.* 28 Ap. 1888.

3*c.* Gladys Cochrane, *b.* 14 Ap. 1891.

4*c.* Ruby Stella Cochrane, *b.* 2 June 1897.

5*b.* Caroline Katherine Laura Mary Cochrane, *m.* 7 Aug. 1878, Arthur Octavius Bayly, *d.* Sept. 1892; 2ndly, Aug. 1896, Henry Herbert Lyde (3 *Cadogan Court Gardens, Cadogan Place, S.W.*); and has issue 1*c* to 3*c.*

1*c.* Hugh Alexander Cochrane Bayly, *b.* Aug. 1881.

2*c.* William Erskine Cochrane Bayly, *b.* Feb. 1886.

3*c.* Isobel Edith Cochrane Bayly, *b.* 1883.

6*b.* Edith Hamilton Cochrane, *m.* 13 Ap. 1893, John Matheson Fraser (84 *Lange Voorhout, The Hague*). [Nos. 52970 to 52978.

556. Descendants of the Hon. ARCHIBALD COCHRANE of Hetton Hall, co. Durham, Capt. R.N. (see Table LIX.), *b.* 1783; *d.* 6 Aug. 1829; *m.* 11 Jan. 1812, HANNAH JANE, da. of Arthur Mowbray of Sherburn Hall, co. Durham, *d.* 8 Oct. 1864; and had issue 1*a* to 5*a.*

1*a.* Robert Alexander Cochrane (*The Downs. St. Neots*), *b.* 18 Mar. 1816; *m.* 27 Oct. 1847, Julia, da. of Gen. Denzil Onslow, *d.* 23 Mar. 1895; and has issue 1*b* to 3*b.*

1*b.* Blair Onslow Cochrane, J.P., *late* Capt. R.A. (*Oakleigh, St. John's Park, Ryde, I.W.*), *b.* 11 Sept. 1853; *m.* 9 May 1881, Mary Evelyn, da. of Sir Richard Sutton, 4th Bart. [G.B.]; and has issue 1*c* to 3*c.*

1*c.* Mary Evelyn Cochrane, *b.* 11 Feb. 1883.

2*c.* Joan Cochrane, *b.* 4.June 1884.

3*c.* Jeanie Harriet Dorothy Cochrane, *b.* 30 Sept. 1891.

2*b.* Constance Amelia Cochrane, *b.* 3 June 1850.

3*b.* Florence Amy Cochrane, *b.* 15 Jan. 1852.

2*a. Basil Edward Arthur Cochrane, D.L. b.* 21 *Dec.* 1817; *d.* 24 *Mar.* 1895; *m.* 2 Oct. 1839, *Salby Caroline, da. of Lieut.-Col. Edward Fitzgerald of Carrigoran, co. Clare, d. 3 Jan.* 1892; *and had issue* 1*b to* 9*b.*

1*b.* Basil Edward Cochrane, Vice-Admiral R.N. (*Windlesham House, Windlesham, Surrey*), *b.* 24 Aug. 1841; *m.* 11 June 1873, Cornelia Ramsay, da. of Capt. John Robinson Owen of Windlesham House, R.N.; and has issue 1*c* to 3*c.*

1*c.* Archibald Cochrane, Lieut. R.N., *b.* 20 June 1874; *m.* 20 Ap. 1904, Maye Amelia Lucile, da. of Col. Alured de Vere Brooke, R.E.; and has issue 1*d.*

1*d.* Marie Cecilia Cochrane, *b.* 3 Aug. 1905.

2*c.* Edward Owen Cochrane, Lieut. R.N., *b.* 17 Aug. 1881.

3*c.* Grizil Martha Lily Cochrane, *b.* 11 Mar. 1876.

2*b.* Blair Hamilton Cochrane (*The Bungalow, Harting, Sussex*), *b.* 22 Ap. 1853; *m.* 18 Sept. 1899, Beatrice Elizabeth Laura, da. of John Henry Grant; and has issue 1*c.*

1*c.* Alwyne Archibald Hamilton Cochrane, *b.* 3 Aug. 1902.

3*b.* William Edward Cochrane, *b.* 8 Sept. 1858; *m.* 19 Feb. 1887, Evelyn, da. of Charles Lamb of Ryton, co. Durham; and has issue 1*c.*

1*c.* Arthur Fitzgerald Cochrane, *b.* 9 Jan. 1888.

4*b.* Charles Thomas Fitzgerald Cochrane, *late* Capt. Leinster Regt. (*Castle Hill, Thurso, N.B.*), *b.* 14 Ap. 1863; *m.* 11 Ap. 1896, Maude Mary, da. of Robert de Ros Rose of Ardhu and Ahabeg, co. Limerick; and has issue 1*c* to 3*c.*

[Nos. 52979 to 52995.

# of The Blood Royal

1c. Baset Robert Cochrane, b. 16 Feb. 1898.

2c. Thomas Fitzgerald Cochrane, b. 2 Sept. 1899.

3c. Alexander Francis Cochrane, b. 29 Mar. 1903.

5b. Katherine Elizabeth Cochrane (*Bill Hill, Wokingham*), m. 1 May 1879, John Edward Leveson Gower of Bill Hill; and has issue.

See p. 172, Nos. 5450–5451.

6b. Anna Louisa Cochrane.

7b. Caroline Mary Cochrane (*Alcombe, Dunster*), m. as 2nd wife, 25 Oct. 1871, the Rev. Lionel Corbett, d. June 1905; and has issue 1c to 5c.

1c. Rev. Lionel Edward Corbett, Vicar of Hawkley (*Hawkley Vicarage, Hants*) b. 14 Nov. 1873.

2c. Cyril Corbett, b. 20 Feb. 1875.

3c. Edmund Henry Corbett, b. 20 Feb. 1876.

4c. Frances Hayes Corbett, b. 28 July 1878.

5c. (da.) Corbett, b. 2 Ap. 1880.

8b. Helen Frances Cochrane (*Craigside, Torquay*).

9b. Margaret Grizil Cochrane, m. 13 Feb. 1884, Hugh Henry Powel of Castle Madoc, co. Brecknock, J.P. (26 *First Avenue, Brighton*); and has issue 1c to 4c.

1c. Hugh Evan Price Powel, b. 14 Dec. 1887.

2c. Charles Vaughan Powel, b. 30 Aug. 1894.

3c. Eleanor Mary Powel, b. 11 June 1890.

4c. Dorothy Grizil Powel, b. 8 May 1897.

3a. Archibald Hamilton Cochrane, J.P. (*Dalnabreek, Blairgowrie; Brookfield Weston, Bath*), b. 2 June 1819; m. 22 May 1856, Rose, da. of G. P. Hutchinson of Egglestone Hall, Durham.

4a. Arthur Mowbray Cochrane, J.P. (*Astwell, Torquay*), b. 2 Oct. 1826; m. 10 June 1850, Mary, da. of John Michael Maloney.

5a. *Caroline Elizabeth Cochrane*, b. 15 *June* 1814; d. 25 *Oct.* 1861; m. 18 *Nov.* 1835, *Benjamin Holme Wiggin, afterwards* (R.L. 5 *Nov.* 1835) *Mowbray*, b. 17 *May* 1808; d. (–); *and had issue 1b to 4b.*

1b. Arthur Holme Mowbray, b. 8 Ap. 1842; m. (at Calcutta) 30 Mar. 1871, Katie, da. of Surgeon-Major Charles Palmer.

2b. Charles Cochrane Mowbray, b. Oct. 1843; m. Louisa, da. of Capt. John Brotherton of Esher, d. 1887; and has issue 1c.

1c. John Leslie Mowbray, R.H.A.

3b. Anna Jane Mowbray, m. Gen. Henry Thomas Arbuthnot.

4b. Louisa Mowbray.   [Nos. 52996 to 53021.

557. Descendants of the Hon. Sir ALEXANDER FORRESTER INGLIS COCHRANE, G.C.B., Admiral of the Blue (see Table LIX.), b. 22 Ap. 1758; d. 29 June 1832; m. Ap. 1788, MARIA, widow of Capt. Sir Jacob Wheate, R.N., d. 18 Mar. 1856; and had issue 1a to 4a.

1a. *Sir Thomas John Cochrane, G.C.B., Admiral of the Fleet*, b. 5 *Feb.* 1789; d. 19 *Oct.* 1872; m. 1st, 6 *Jan.* 1812, *Matilda Rose Wishart, da. of Gen. Sir Charles Lockhart Ross, 7th Bart.* [S.], d. 4 *Sept.* 1819; 2ndly, 8 *Jan.* 1853, *Rosetta, da. of Sir Jonah Denny Wheeler-Cuffe, 1st Bart.* [I.], d. 27 *May* 1901; *and had issue 1b to 6b.*

1b. *Alexander Dundas* (*Ross-Wishart-Cochrane-Baillie*), *1st Baron Lamington* [U.K.], b. 24 *Nov.* 1816; d. 15 *Feb.* 1890; m. 4 *Dec.* 1844, *Annabella Mary Elizabeth, da. of Andrew Robert Drummond of Cadland; and had issue.*

See the Clarence Volume, p. 210, Nos. 4195–4213.   [Nos. 53022 to 53040.

Ʈhe Plantagenet Roll

2b. *Charles Stuart Cochrane* (? *of Brooklyn, New York*), *Capt. 7th Foot,* d. (–) ; m. 4 *Aug.* 1878, *Letitia Agnes, da. of William Naylor Frushard.*

3b. Thomas Belhaven Henry Cochrane, M.V.O., J.P., D.L., Dep. Gov. Steward and Sheriff of the Isle of Wight, and Capt. of Carisbrooke Castle, *formerly* Lieut. R.N. (*Quarr Abbey House, Ryde ; Carisbrooke Castle, I.W.*), b. 24 Nov. 1856 ; m. 19 Feb. 1887, Lady Adela, da. of John Edward Cornwallis (Rous), 2nd Earl of Stradbroke [U.K.].

4b. *Maria Theresa Cochrane,* b. 1814 ; d. 16 *Sept.* 1897 ; m. 1*st,* 24 *Mar.* 1851, *Alexander Robert Sutherland of Silver Hill, Torquay, M.D.,* b. 1781 ; d. 24 *May* 1861 ; 2*ndly, Sept.* 1864, *Thomas Charles Waye Scott of Beechwood, co. Forfar.*

5b. Rosetta Susan Louisa Cochrane (2 *Montagu Square, W.*).

6b. Annette Minna Cochrane, a Lady in Waiting to H.R.H. the Princess Henry of Battenberg, and a Lady of Grace of St. John of Jerusalem (2 *Montagu Square, W.*).

2a. *Andrew Coutts Cochrane,* b. 5 *Ap.* 1799 ; d. 22 *June* 1870 ; m. 1835, [——], *da. of the Baron von Strack, a Col. in the Austrian Service,* d. (–) ; *and had issue* 1b *to* 3b.

1b. Victoria Alexandrina Cochrane.

2b. Florence Bruce Katherine Cochrane.

3b. Maria Louisa Frederica Cochrane.

3a. *Anna Maria Cochrane,* d. 14 *May* 1873 ; m. 19 *Oct.* 1810, *Sir Edward Thomas Troubridge, 2nd Bart.* [*G.B.*], *C.B., Rear-Adm. of the Red,* d. 7 *Oct.* 1852 ; *and had issue* 1b *to* 2b.

1b. *Sir Thomas St. Vincent Hope Cochrane Troubridge, 3rd Bart.* [*G.B.*], *C.R., K.L.H., K.M., &c., Dept. Adj.-Gen. to the Forces,* b. 25 *May* 1815 ; d. 26 *Oct.* 1867 ; m. 1 *Nov.* 1855, *Louisa Jane, da. of Daniel Gurney of North Runcton* (*by his wife Lady Harriet,* née *Hay*), d. 29 *Aug.* 1867 ; *and had issue* 1c *to* 6c.

1c. Sir Thomas Herbert Cochrane Troubridge, 4th Bart. [G.B.], *late* Capt. King's Royal Rifle Corps (66 *Gloucester Gardens, Hyde Park, W.*), b. 13 Sept. 1860 ; m. 13 July 1893, Laura, da. of Charles Gurney ; and has issue 1d to 3d.

1d. Thomas St. Vincent Wallace Troubridge, b. 15 Nov. 1895.

2d. Louise Rachel Troubridge, b. 30 May 1894.

3d. Rosemary Blanche Troubridge, b. 6 Ap. 1905.

2c. Ernest Charles Thomas Troubridge, C.M.G., M.V.O., O.L.H., Capt. R.N. (1 *Durham Place, Chelsea, S.W.*), b. 15 July 1862 ; m. 29 Dec. 1891, Edith Mary, da. of William Duffus of Halifax, Nova Scotia, d. 10 Jan. 1900 ; and has issue 1d to 3d.

1d. Thomas Hope Troubridge, b. 1 Feb. 1895.

2d. Mary Laura Troubridge, b. 13 Feb. 1894.

3d. Edith Charlotte Troubridge, b. 28 Aug. 1896.

3c. Amy Louisa Harriet Troubridge.

4c. Laura Elizabeth Rachel Troubridge (*The Tower House, Tite Street, S.W.*), m. 2 Aug. 1888, Adrian Charles Francis Hope, b. 8 Mar. 1858 ; d. 11 May 1904 ; and has issue 1d.

1d. Jaqueline Louise Rachel Hope.

5c. Violet Elizabeth Emily Troubridge, m. 22 Nov. 1893, Walter Somerville Gurney (*Mangreen Hall, Norwich*) ; and has issue 1d to 3d.

1d. Daniel Walter Thomas Gurney, b. 29 Ap. 1878.

2d. Diana Katharine Gurney.

3d. Philippa Gurney.

6c. Helen Cecil Margaret Troubridge.

2b. *Maria Louisa Troubridge,* d. 1867 ; m. 1856, *the Rev. Theodore Augustus Walrond,* d. Oct. 1873.

4a. *Jane Cochrane,* d. 22 *June* 1830 ; m. *as* 1*st wife,* 6 *Feb.* 1822, *Vice-Adm. Sir Henry William Bruce, K.C.B.,* b. 2 *Feb.* 1792 ; d. 14 *Dec.* 1863.

[Nos. 53041 to 53062.

626

# of The Blood Royal

558. Descendants of Col. the Hon. ANDREW JAMES COCHRANE, *afterwards* (1793) COCHRANE-JOHNSTONE, M.P., Governor of Dominica (see Table LIX.), *b.* 24 May 1767 ; *d.* (–) ; *m.* 1st, 20 Nov. 1793, Lady GEORGIANA, da. and co-h. of James (HOPE), 3rd Earl of Hopetoun [S.], *d.* 17 Sept. 1797 ; and had issue 1*a*.

1*a. Elizabeth Cochrane-Johnstone, da. and h.*, b. 26 Dec. 1794 ; d. 6 *June* 1883 ; m. 28 *Mar.* 1816, *William John (Napier), 9th Baron Napier* [S.], d. 11 *Oct.* 1834 ; *and had issue.*
See p. 569, Nos. 50743–50806. [Nos. 53063 to 53126.

559. Descendants of Lady ELIZABETH COCHRANE (see Table LIX.), *b.* 27 Aug. 1745 ; *d.* 19 Feb. 1811 ; *m.* 18 Dec. 1775, PATRICK HERON of Heron, M.P., *d.* 1803 ; and had issue 1*a*.

1*a. Mary Heron of Heron, da. and h.*, d. 18 *June* 1856 ; m. 4 *Jan.* 1802, *Lieut.-Gen. Sir John Shaw-Maxwell, afterwards* (1803) *Heron-Maxwell, 4th Bart.* [S.], M.P., b. 29 *June* 1772 ; d. 29 *Jan.* 1830 ; *and had issue* 1*b* to 8*b*.

1*b. Sir Patrick Heron-Maxwell, 5th Bart.* [S.], b. 1 *Jan.* 1805 ; d. *unm.* 27 *Aug.* 1844.

2*b. Sir John Heron-Maxwell, 6th Bart.* [S.], *Capt. R.N.*, b. 7 *Mar.* 1808 ; d. 22 *Aug.* 1885 ; m. 7 *Nov.* 1833, *Caroline, da. of the Hon. Montgomery Granville John Stewart*, d. 22 Oct. 1896 ; *and had issue.*
See the Tudor Roll of "The Blood Royal of Britain," pp. 503–504, Nos. 34156–34197.

3*b. Rev. Michael Heron-Maxwell, afterwards* (1856) *Maxwell-Heron of Heron*, b. 8 *Nov.* 1809 ; d. 4 *Ap.* 1873 ; m. 24 *Feb.* 1834, *Charlotte Frances, da. of Capt. Frederick William Burgoyne*, d. 26 Dec. 1886 ; *and had issue.*
See the Clarence Volume, p. 615, Nos. 26917–26925.

4*b. Edward Heron-Maxwell, afterwards Heron-Maxwell-Blair of Teviot Bank, co. Roxburgh, and Penningham, co. Wigtown, D.L.*, b. 2 *Mar.* 1821 ; d. 4 *Sept.* 1890 ; m. 20 *Oct.* 1847, *Elizabeth Ellen, da. and* (in 1875) *h. of William Henry Stopford-Blair of Penningham*, d. 28 *June* 1901 ; *and had issue* 1*c* to 9*c*.

1*c*. William Henry Stopford Heron-Maxwell, J.P., Major and Hon. Lieut.-Col. S.E. Scotland R.G.A., *formerly* Royal Fusiliers (*Teviot Bank, Hawick, N.B.*), *b.* 14 June 1582 ; *m.* 26 Feb. 1884, Adeline Helen, da. of Osgood Hanbury of Holfield Grange ; and has issue 1*d* to 4*d*.

1*d*. Helen Alice Heron-Maxwell.

2*d*. Elizabeth Marion Heron-Maxwell.

3*d*. Nora Heron-Maxwell.

4*d*. Mary Adeline Heron-Maxwell.

2*c*. Patrick Heron-Maxwell, J.P. (*Arthur's*), *b.* 26 Mar. 1856 ; *m.* 27 Feb. 1886, Frances Jane, da. of Admiral James Cockburn.

3*c*. Edward James Heron-Maxwell (*Greensted House, Ongar*), *b.* 8 Mar. 1866 ; *m.* 26 Nov. 1898, Constance Violet, da. of Sir John Ralph Blois, 8th Bart. [E.] ; and has issue 1*d* to 3*d*.

1*d*. John Edward Blois Heron-Maxwell, *b.* 19 Sept. 1899.

2*d*. Patrick Archibald Heron-Maxwell, *b.* 14 Sept. 1903.

3*d*. Margaret Violet Heron-Maxwell.

4*c*. Mira Heron-Maxwell.

5*c. Stuart Mary Heron-Maxwell*, d. Aug. 1891 ; m. 16 *Dec.* 1880, *John Clarence Hay Pierson of Havre.*

6*c*. Jane Elizabeth Heron-Maxwell. [Nos. 53127 to 53189.

The Plantagenet Roll

7c. Helenora Catherine Heron-Maxwell, *m.* 30 Ap. 1892, George Stehn (54 *Manchester Street, W.*); and has issue 1d to 3d.

    1d. Arthur Edward Stehn, *b.* 8 Oct. 1894.

    2d. Helenora Margaret Stehn.

    3d. Elizabeth Kathleen Stehn.

8c. Margaret Emily Heron-Maxwell, *m.* 10 Jan. 1901, Harold William Kemble (*The Homestead, Quenington, Fairford, Gloucester*); and has issue 1d to 2d.

    1d. Marjorie Kemble, *b.* 1901.

    2d. Elizabeth Laura Kemble, *b.* 1904.

9c. Georgina Florence Heron-Maxwell, *m.* 15 Nov. 1904, Ralph Brunton Umfreville, *late* Lieut. 4th Batt. Worcestershire Regt.

5b. *Elizabeth Heron-Maxwell, d.* 14 *Feb.* 1821; m. *as* 1st *wife,* 27 *Sept.* 1819, *Sir James Dalrymple-Hay, 2nd Bart.* [*G.B.*], b. 8 *July* 1788; d. 19 *Mar.* 1861; *and had issue* 1c.

    1c. Right Hon. Sir John Charles Dalrymple-Hay of Park, 3rd Bart. [G.B.], P.C., G.C.B., F.R.S., D.C.L., LL.D., Admiral R.N., sometime (1862–1885) M.P., and (1866–1868) a Lord of the Admiralty, &c. &c. (*Park Place, Glenluce;* 108 *St. George's Square, S.W.*), b. 11 Feb. 1821; *m.* 18 Aug. 1847, the Hon. Eliza, da. of William John (Napier), 9th Baron Napier [S.].

    See p. 571, Nos. 50792–50801.

6b. *Jane Stuart Heron-Maxwell, d.* 27 *Dec.* 1886; m. 15 *Aug.* 1827, *John Shaw Stewart, Advocate, Sheriff co. Stirling* (*son of Sir Michael Shaw-Stewart, 5th Bart.* [*S.*]), b. 24 *July* 1793; d. *June* 1840; *and had issue* 1c *to* 6c.

    1c. *Michael John Maxwell Shaw-Stewart, b.* 24 *Nov.* 1828; d. 3 *Ap.* 1894; m. 11 *Ap.* 1867, *Julia, da. of Augustus Hermann Kindermann, d.* 10 *June* 1899; *and had issue* 1d *to* 2d.

        1d. Michael John Shaw-Stewart, *b.* 22 Sept. 1870.

        2d. Margaret Veronica Shaw-Stewart, *b.* 20 Mar. 1869.

    2c. John Heron-Maxwell Shaw-Stewart, Major-Gen., *late* R.E. (7 *Inverness Terrace, W.*), *b.* 9 Sept. 1831; *m.* 7 Sept. 1871, Mary Catherine Bedingfeld, da. of Col. George Chancellor Collyer, R.E.; and has issue 1d to 4d.

        1d. Basil Heron Shaw-Stewart, Capt. R.A., *b.* 8 Dec. 1877.

        2d. Patrick Houston Shaw-Stewart, *b.* 17 Aug. 1888.

        3d. Mary Winifred Shaw-Stewart.

        4d. Katharine Bedingfeld Shaw-Stewart.

    3c. Mary Elizabeth Shaw-Stewart, *m.* 5 Mar. 1856, James Howden (25 *Melville Street, Edinburgh*); and has issue 1d to 7d.

        1d. John Michael Howden (11 *Eton Terrace, Edinburgh*), *b.* 22 Mar. 1857; *m.* 1885, Florence Annie, da. of the Hon. Lord Fraser; and has issue 1e to 2e.

            1e. Patrick Howden, *b.* 1888.

            2e. Margaret Mary Ruth Howden, *b.* 1889.

        2d. Charles Robert Andrew Howden, Advocate, *b.* 18 Jan. 1862.

        3d. Ian Dalrymple Clark Howden, J.P. (6 *Cambridge Terrace, Dover*); *b.* 12 May 1870; *m.* 30 June 1897, Violet, da. of Col. Campbell, Seaforth Highlanders.

        4d. Helen Louisa Howden, *m.* Aug. 1889, George Kerr of Chapeldonan.

        5d. Jane Stuart Mary Howden.

        6d. Mary Elizabeth Howden, *m.* 27 Ap. 1899, the Rev. A. B. Macaulay, M.A. (23 *Windsor Street, Dundee*); and has issue 1e to 2e.

            1e. Mary Helen Macaulay.

            2e. Margaret Euphemia Macaulay.

        7d. Isobel Nora Howden, *m.* 15 Ap. 1904, James Campbell White Barrett; and has issue 1e.

            1e. John Campbell Maitland Barrett, *b.* 6 Ap. 1905.   [Nos. 53190 to 53228.

628

# of The Blood Royal

4c. *Jane Charlotte Shaw-Stewart*, d. 19 *Feb.* 1900; m. 19 *Feb.* 1885, *the Rev. William Duncan Thomson, M.A.*

5c. Margaret St. Maur Shaw-Stewart.

6c. Helenora Grace Shaw-Stewart, *m.* 18 May 1870, Capt. Ian Dalrymple Clark, 8th Madras L.I., *d.* 14 June 1870.

7b. *Mary Heron-Maxwell*, d. 16 *Nov.* 1876; m. 27 *Ap.* 1836, *Sir James Dalrymple-Horn-Elphinstone, 2nd Bart.* [*U.K.*], *M.P.*, b. 20 *Nov.* 1805; d. 26 *Dec.* 1886; *and had issue* 1c *to* 3c.

1c. *Sir Robert Elphinstone Dalrymple-Horn-Elphinstone, 3rd Bart.* [*U.K.*] (*twin*), b. 12 *Sept.* 1841; d.s.p. 11 *Feb.* 1887.

2c. *Sir Græme Hepburn Dalrymple-Horn-Elphinstone, 4th Bart.* [*U.K.*] (*twin*), b. 12 *Sept.* 1841; d. (*in the Straits Settlements*) *May* 1900; m. 5 *Jan.* 1875, *Margaret Anne Alice, da. of James Ogilvie Fairlie of Coodham; and had issue* 1d *to* 2d.

1d. Mary Constance Dalrymple-Horn-Elphinstone.

2d. Esther Winifred Dalrymple-Horn-Elphinstone.

3c. Margaret Burnet Dalrymple-Horn-Elphinstone (*Sandhurst, Burnham, Somerset*), *m.* 11 Sept. 1873, the Rev. John Maturin Warren of Uplands, Bawdrip, *d.* 24 Ap. 1901; and has issue 1d to 4d.

1d. John Maxwell-Dalrymple-Elphinstone Warren, Lieut. R.N., *b.* 23 June 1874.

2d. James Græme Hepburn Warren, *b.* 30 Aug. 1875.

3d. William Henry Farrington Warren, Sub-Lieut. R.N.R., *b.* 19 Oct. 1877.

4d. Frederick Drummond Warren, Natal Mounted Police, *b.* 23 Aug. 1881.

8b. *Helenora Catherine Heron-Maxwell*, d. 2 *Nov.* 1889; m. 6 *Nov.* 1838, *Hew Drummond Elphinstone-Dalrymple*, b. 29 *July* 1807; d. 28 *Ap.* 1893; *and had issue* 1c.

1c. Sir Robert Græme Elphinstone-Dalrymple of Horn and Logie Elphinstone, 5th Bart. [U.K.], Col. I.S.C. (*Homington House, Coombe Bisset, Salisbury*), b. 17 Jan. 1844; *m.* 27 Ap. 1871, Flora Loudoun, da. of James Macleod; and has issue 1d to 3d.

1d. Edward Arthur Elphinstone-Dalrymple, Lieut. Indian Army, *b.* 3 Oct. 1877.

2d. Francis Napier Elphinstone-Dalrymple, Lieut. R.A., *b.* 17 July 1882.

3d. Helenora Catherine Elphinstone-Dalrymple.   [Nos. 53229 to 53241.

560. Descendants, if any, of Euphemie Cochrane (see Table LIX.), wife of Col. John Erskine, cadet of Alva; and had issue 1a.[1]

1a. *Mary Erskine, bapt. at Edinburgh, 8 June* 1715; d. 28 *Nov.* 1766; m. 1737, *the Rev. Alexander Webster, D.D., Minister of the Tolbooth Church, Edinburgh, one of H.M.'s Chaplains in Ordinary* [S.] *and Dean of the Chapel Royal, Founder of the Widows of Clergy of the Church of Scotland Fund, b.* 1707; d. 25 *Jan.* 1784; *and had issue* (6 *sons and* 1 *da. of whom*) 1b *to* 5b.

1b. [——] *Webster, Major in the Army, eldest surv. son in* 1802.

2b. [——] *Webster, Col. in the Army, killed in America.*

3b. *George Webster, Civil Paymaster H.E.I.C.S., d.* (*in Bengal*) *July* 1794.

4b. *Alexander Webster, Mate of the Dalton East Indiaman, d. on passage* 1782.

5b. *Anne Webster, d.* 16 *May* 1786; m. *Capt. Eyre Robert Mingay, 66th Foot.*

---

[1] Hew Scott's " Fasti," i. p. 51; " Dic. Nat. Bio."; *Scots Magazine*, 1802, lxiv. p. 284; *Gentleman's Magazine.*

Ⱖⱒⰵ ⱀⰾⰰⱀⱅⰰⰳⰵⱀⰵⱅ Ⱃⱁⰾⰾ

The Plantagenet Roll

561. Descendants of MARY PRESTON (see Table LIX.), *d.* 21 Aug. 1813; *m.* 16 Aug. 1774, ROBERT WELWOOD of Garvock; and had issue 1*a* to 3*a*.

1*a*. *Robert Welwood of Garvock, d.* (–); *m.; and had issue 1b to 2b.*

1*b*. *Isabella Welwood, d.* 1826; *m.* 1800, *Robert Clarke of Comrie Castle, co. Perth, J.P., D.L., d.* 1843; *and had issue 1c to 3c.*

1*c*. *Rev. William Colin Clarke, afterwards Preston of Valleyfield House, J.P., b.* 10 *July* 1810; *d. Dec.* 1870; *m.* 15 *May* 1856, *Anne Charity, da. of William Dowdall Pigott of Dysart, Queen's co.; and had issue 1d to 7d.*

1*d*. Robert William Pigott Clarke Preston, now (1878) Campbell-Preston of Ardchattan and Valleyfield, J.P., Major 3rd Batt. Royal Highlanders (*Valleyfield House, Culross, N.B.; Ardchattan Priory, Taynuilt, Argyll*), *b.* 17 June 1865; *m.* 1 June 1905, Mary Augusta, da. of Augustus Thorne; and has issue 1*e*.

1*e*. Mary Charity Campbell Preston, *b.* 2 Mar. 1906.

2*d*. Arthur Colley Preston, *b.* 6 Nov. 1869.

3*d*. Eliza Isabella Welwood Preston, *m.* 1877, Henry Edward-Murray Anderdon (*Henlade House, Taunton*).

4*d*. Isabella Mary Anne Preston.

5*d*. Mary Anne Fergusson Preston, *m.* Arthur Hassall, M.A., Fellow of Christ Church, Oxford.

6*d*. Jane Preston, *m.* Capt. Norman Steuart Ogilvie, R.A.; and has issue.

7*d*. Lily Campbell Preston, *m.* 16 July 1891, Philip Heathcote Rawson, M.A. (Oxon.), Bar.-at-Law, I.T.; and has issue 1*e* to 2*e*.

1*e*. Colin Rawson, *b.* July 1896.

2*e*. Barbara Helen Rawson, *b.* 2 Mar. 1893.

2*c*. *Eliza Clarke, d.* (–); *m. William Kerr.*

3*c*. *Susan Clarke, d.* (–); *m. the Rev.* [——] *McGowan.*

2*b*. *Mary Welwood, d.* (–); *m. Laurence Johnson of Sands; and had issue (a son).*

2*a*. *Andrew Welwood.*

3*a*. *Elizabeth Welwood, b.* 1752; *d. Aug.* 1822; *m. Allan Maconochie of Meadowbank, a Senator of the College of Justice as Lord Meadowbank, d.* 14 *June* 1816; *and had issue 1b to 2b.*

1*b*. *Alexander Maconochie, afterwards Maconochie-Welwood of Meadowbank and Garvock, M.P., J.P., a Senator of the College of Justice as 2nd Lord Meadowbank, sometime Solicitor-General [S.] and Lord Advocate, b. Mar.* 1777; *d.* 1861; *m.* 1805, *Anne, da. of the Right Hon. Robert Blair of Avontoun, Lord President, d.* 28 *Jan.* 1866; *and had issue 1c to 3c.*

1*c*. *Robert Blair Maconochie-Welwood of Gattonside, co. Roxburgh, J.P.* (*2nd son*), *b.* 21 *May* 1814; *d.* 4 *Oct.* 1883; *m.* 6 *Jan.* 1846, *Charlotte Joanna, da. of John Tod of Kirkhill, d.* 23 *June* 1901; *and had issue 1d to 3d.*

1*d*. John Allan Maconochie-Welwood of Kirknewton and Garvock, J.P., &c. (*Kirknewton House, Kirknewton, Midlothian; Pitliver House, co. Fife*), *b.* 23 Feb. 1848; *m.* 28 Ap. 1892, Winifred Louisa, da. of Edgar Atheling Drummond of Cadland (by his wife the Hon. Louisa Theodosia, *née* Pennington); and has issue 1*e* to 2*e*.

1*e*. Laurence Robert Maconochie-Welwood, Younger of Kirknewton, *b.* 13 Aug. 1902.

2*e*. Cynthia Louisa Winifred Maconochie-Welwood, *b.* 9 Ap. 1900.

2*d*. Charles Cornelius Maconochie, K.C., Sheriff-Substitute of the Lothians

[Nos. 53242 to 53255.

and co. Peebles, *b.* 2 Jan. 1852; *m.* 20 July 1882, Alice Mary, da. of Robert Robertson of Auchleeks, co. Perth; and has issue 1*e* to 4*e*.

1*e*. Robert Henry Maconochie, *b.* 11 May 1883.

2*e*. Charles Ernest Maconochie, *b.* 27 Jan. 1886.

3*e*. Veronica Charlotte Maconochie, *b.* 10 Dec. 1884.

4*e*. Emily Bridget Maconochie, *b.* 29 Aug. 1889.

3*d*. Helen Anne Maconochie, *m.* 1885, the Rev. Francis Conder, M.A.; and has issue 1*e* to 2*e*.

1*e*. Joan Conder.

2*e*. Dorothy Conder.

2*c*. *William Maximilian George Maconochie-Welwood, Lieut.-Col. Edinburgh Artillery, formerly Bengal Light Cavalry, d. 1882; m. Maria, da. of Gen. Sir Abraham Roberts, G.C.B., d. 25 Dec. 1886; and had issue 1d.*

1*d*. Alexander Maconochie-Welwood, *m.*; and has issue.

3*c*. *Mary Anne Welwood, d. 1854; m. as 1st wife, 1834, Steuart Bayley Hare of Calder Hall, J.P., D.L., d. 1878; and had issue 1d to 4d.*

1*d*. James Hare, J.P., Lieut.-Col., *late* 60th Rifles and 22nd Regt. (*Calder Hall, Midlothian; Blairlogie, Stirling*), *b.* 16 Aug. 1836; *m.* 1862, Alice Charlotte, da. of John Tait, Sheriff, co. Perth, and niece of the late Archbishop of Canterbury; and has issue 1*e* to 3*e*.

1*e*. Steuart Welwood Hare, Capt. King's Royal Rifle Corps, *b.* 9 Sept. 1867; *m.* 1896, Mary, da. of F. Ruttledge.

2*e*. Mary Sitwell Hare.

3*e*. Lucy Edith Hare.

2*d*. *Anne Isabella Hare*, d. 1871; *m. as 2nd wife*, 1870, *John George Chancellor of Shieldhill, co. Lanark, J.P., D.L.*, *b.* 27 *Sept.* 1821; *d.* 1894; *and had issue* 1*e*.

1*e*. John Steuart Hare Chancellor, *b.* 5 Sept. 1871.

3*d*. Harriet Hare, *m.* 28 June 1859, Thomas Alexander Hog of Newliston, J.P., D.L. (*Newliston, Kirkliston, Linlithgow*); and has issue 1*e* to 5*e*.

1*e*. Steuart Bayley Hog, Younger of Newliston, *b.* 11 Sept. 1864; *m.* 1892, Jemima Christian, da. of Ralph Dundas; and has issue 1*f* to 4*f*.

1*f*. Roger Thomas Alexander Hog, *b.* 19 June 1893.

2*f*. Ralph Dundas Hog, *b.* 30 Ap. 1897.

3*f*. Evelyn Emily Hog, *b.* 4 Feb. 1900.

4*f*. Harriet Christian Hog, *b.* 14 June 1905.

2*e*. Thomas Alexander Frederick Hog, *b.* 6 July 1866.

3*e*. Alan Welwood Hog, *b.* 28 July 1868; *m.* 17 Ap. 1900, Winifred Alice, da. of Ralph Dundas of Edinburgh, W.S.; and has issue 1*f*.

1*f*. Penelope Emily Hog, *b.* 15 June 1903.

4*e*. Mary Welwood Hog.

5*e*. Helen Hog.

4*d*. Mary Elizabeth Steuart Hare.

2*b*. *Robert Maconochie of Devonshire Place, W., sometime Master of the Mint at Madras.*   [Nos. 53256 to 53280.

562. Descendants, if any surviving, of JOHN COCHRANE of Waterside (see Table LIX.), *b. c.* 1663; *d.* (–); *m.* HANNAH, da. of [——] de Worth of London; and had issue (eight sons and seven das.).[1]

---

[1] One of his sons, James Cochrane, was a member of the Faculty of Advocates, 1724, and Judge-Advocate, which office he resigned in favour of his eldest son William, 1757. Wood's "Douglas' Peerage," i. p. 474.

The Plantagenet Roll

563. Descendants, if any, of GRIZIL COCHRANE (see Table LIX.), wife of JOHN KER of Morristoun, co. Berwick.

564. Descendants, if any, of MILCHA STRICKLAND (see Table LIX.), wife of WILLIAM LAWSON.

565. Descendants of ELIZABETH STRICKLAND (see Table LIX.), *bur.* 3 Oct. 1700; *m.* 18 Dec. 1653, WILLIAM ST. QUINTIN of Muston, *b.* 1632; *bur. v.p.* 6 Nov. 1695; and had issue.

See pp. 546–549, Nos. 49515–49587. [Nos. 53281 to 53353.

566. Descendants of Sir ROWLAND BELASYSE, K.B. (see Table LX.), *b. c.* 1632; *d.* 16 Aug. 1699; *m.* ANNE, da. and h. of Humphrey DAVENPORT of Sutton, co. Chester; and had issue 1*a* to 2*a*.

1*a. Thomas (Belasyse), 3rd Viscount Fauconburg [E.], d. (at Brussels) 26 Nov. 1718; m. a. July 1698, Bridget, da. and eventual h. of Sir John Gage of Firle, 4th Bart. [E.], d. 18 Nov. 1732; and had issue 1b to 3b.*

1*b. Thomas (Belasyse), 4th Viscount Fauconburg [E.] and (1756) 1st Earl of Fauconburg [G.B.], b. 27 Ap. 1699; d. 4 Feb. 1774; m. 5 Aug. 1726, Catherine, da. and h. of John Betham, alias Fowler, of Rowington, co. Warwick, d. 30 May 1760; and had issue 1c.*

1*c. Henry (Belasyse), 3rd Earl of [G.B.] and 5th Viscount [E.] Fauconburg, b. 13 Ap. 1743; d. 23 Mar. 1802; m. 1st, 29 May 1766, Charlotte, da. of Sir Matthew Lamb of Brocket Hall, 1st Bart. [G.B.], d. 1 Ap. 1790; and had issue.*

See p. 402, Nos. 33782–33990.

2*b. Hon. Henry Belasyse, d. (? unm.).*

3*b. Hon. Mary Belasyse, d. (–); m. 4 Ap. 1721, John Pitt, 3rd son of Thomas Pitt, Governor of Fort St. George.*

2*a. Rowland Belasyse, m. the Hon. Frances, da. of Christopher (Roper), 5th Baron Teynham [E.]; and had issue.*
See the Clarence Volume, Table XLV. and p. 420. [Nos. 53354 to 53562.

567. Descendants of RICHARD (LUMLEY-SAUNDERSON), 4th EARL OF SCARBROUGH [E.] and 5th VISCOUNT LUMLEY [I.] (see Table LX.), *b.* May 1725; *d.* 12 May 1782; *m.* 26 Dec. 1752, BARBARA, sister and h. of Sir George SAVILE of Rufford, 7th Bart. [E.], *d.* 22 July 1797; and had issue 1*a* to 5*a*.

1*a. George Augusta (Lumley), 5th Earl of Scarbrough [E.], &c., b. 22 Sept. 1753; d. unm. 5 Sept. 1807.*

2*a. Richard (Lumley, afterwards (Act of Parl. 1783) Savile, and finally (1807) Lumley-Saunderson), 6th Earl of Scarbrough [E.], b. 16 Ap. 1757; d.s.p. 17 June 1832.*

3*a. John (Lumley, afterwards (R.L. 8 Sept. 1807) Savile), 7th Earl of Scarbrough [E.], 8th Viscount Lumley [I.], Preb. of York, &c., b. 15 June 1760; d. 24 Feb. 1835; m. 5 Nov. 1785, Anna Maria, da. of Julius Herring of Heybridge, co. Essex, d. 17 Mar. 1850; and had issue 1b to 3b.*

632

1b. John (Savile, afterwards (R.L. 14 Oct. 1836) Lumley-Savile), 8th Earl of Scarbrough [E.], 9th Viscount Lumley [I.], b. 18 July 1788; d. unm. 29 Oct. 1856.

2b. Lady Louisa Frances Savile, otherwise Lumley, b. 1794; d. 7 Jan. 1885; m. 25 Sept. 1825, the Rev. Thomas Cator of Skelbrook Park, Yorks, M.A., b. 19 Feb. 1790; d. 24 Aug. 1864; and had issue 1c to 4c.

1c. Thomas William Cator of Ollerton House, co. Notts, Lieut.-Col. 76th Foot, b. 20 Aug. 1829, d. (? s.p.) 14 Jan. 1900; m. 18 Nov. 1873, Jane Louisa, da. of Rear-Admiral Sotheby.

2c. Rev. William Lumley Bertie Cator, M.A. (Camb.), Rector of Eakring, Notts, and Hon. Canon of Southwell Cathedral, b. 22 June 1834.

3c. Charles Oliver Frederick Cator of The Hall, Beckenham, Kent, M.A. (Camb.), Barrister, b. 21 Ap. 1836; d. 10 Dec. 1876; m. 14 Dec. 1865, Isabella Maria (44 Green Street, W.), da. of Sir George Baker, 3rd Bart. [G.B.]; and had issue 1d.

1d. Charles George Lumley Cator, M.A. (Camb.) (64 Upper Berkeley Street, W.), b. 26 Jan. 1872; m. 1 June 1905, Adelaide Louisa, da. of Sir John Ralph Blois, 8th Bart. [E.].

4c. Frederick Henry Cator of Leominster, co. Hereford (44 Belgrave Road, S.W.; Junior Carlton), b. 21 Aug. 1838; m. 1st, 1 Dec. 1863, Frances Sophia Vaughan (divorced 19 Jan. 1881), da. and h. of Sir Edward Harry Vaughan Colt, 6th Bart. [E.]; 2ndly, 14 July 1892, Letitia Elizabeth, widow of Charles Campbell Prinsep, da. of Gordon Willoughby James Gyll of Remenham; and has issue 1d to 4d.

1d. Frederick Edward Thomas Lumley Cator (22 Dorset Square, N.W.; Junior Carlton), b. 24 Sept. 1864; m. 8 Aug. 1891, Agnes Sophia, da. of Capt. Edward Nares, R.N.; and has issue 1e.

1e. Vera Muriel Cator.

2d. Arthur Charles Albemarle Cator, b. 28 Jan. 1873; m. 21 June 1905, Helène, da. of R. D. Lee of Harrow-on-the-Hill.

3d. Geraldine Frances Louisa Cator.

4d. Algitha Malet Vaughan Cator.

3b. Lady Henrietta Barbara Savile, otherwise Lumley, b. 1796; d. 27 July 1864; m. 1st, 2 Sept. 1821, the Rev. Frederick Manners-Sutton, d. 30 Aug. 1826; 2ndly, 24 Aug. 1837, John Lodge Ellerton of Bodsilin, co. Carnarvon; and had issue (at least by 1st husband).

See p. 160, Nos. 2825–2830.

4a. Hon. Frederick Lumley of Tickhill Castle, b. 17 Oct. 1761; d. 20 Sept. 1831; m. 1st, 20 Feb. 1786, Harriet, da. of John Boddington, d. 20 July 1810; and had issue 1b.

1b. Frederick Lumley, afterwards (Act of Parl. 1834) Lumley-Savile of Tickhill Castle, b. 14 Jan. 1788; d. 27 Feb. 1837; m. 2 May 1812, Charlotte Mary, da. of the Right Rev. George de la Poer Beresford, Lord Bishop of Kilmore (she re-m., 20 July 1839, Robert Henry Southwell, and) d. Feb. or Oct. 1851; and had issue 1c to 4c.

1c. Richard George (Lumley), 9th Earl of Scarbrough [E.], 10th Viscount Lumley [I.], b. 7 May 1813; d. 5 Dec. 1884; m. 8 Oct. 1846, Frederica Mary Adeliza, da. of Andrew Robert Drummond; and had issue.

See the Clarence Volume, pp. 211–213, Nos. 4215–4268.

2c. Lady[1] Frances Charlotte Arabella Lumley, d. 3 Aug. 1879; m. 8 Mar. 1836, Col. Charles John Hill of Cotgrave, co. Notts, d. 22 May 1867; and had issue 1d to 3d.

1d. Frederick John George Hill, Lieut.-Col. R.A. (9 Great Marlborough Street, Regent Street, London, W.), b. 17 Sept. 1837; m. 1 Ap. 1870, Helen Mary Alera Ann, da. of Gen. Colin Troup; and has issue 1e to 3e.   [Nos. 53563 to 53631.

---

[1] R.W. 7 Mar. 1857.

The Plantagenet Roll

1e. Frederick Charles Lumley Hill, b. 11 Mar. 1871.

2e. Colin Thomas Hill, b. 19 Oct. 1873.

3e. Ivor Hill, b. 24 Feb. 1876.

2d. Charles Lumley Hill (*Bellevue Station, Brisbane, Queensland*), b. 13 Aug. 1840; m. 24 July 1901, Ethel Maud, widow of G. C. Taylor, da. of G. Harris, s.p.

3d. Georgina Mary Hill (*Lissadell, co. Sligo*), m. 29 Ap. 1867, Sir Henry William Gore-Booth, 5th Bart. [I.], b. 1 July 1843; d. 13 Jan. 1900; and has issue 1e to 5e.

1e. Sir Josslyn Augustus Richard Gore-Booth, 6th Bart. [I.] (*Lissadell, co. Sligo*), b. 26 Feb. 1869.

2e. Mordaunt Gore-Booth, b. 5 Dec. 1878; m. 30 Jan. 1906, Evelyn, da. of [——] Scholfield.

3e. Constance Georgina Gore-Booth, m. 29 Sept. 1900, Casimir Dunin de Markieviez, a Noble of Russia (*Zyvotovka, Staro Zyvotov, Poland*); and has issue 1f.

1f. Maeve de Markieviez, b. 1901.

4e. Eve Selina Gore-Booth.

5e. Mabel Olive Gore-Booth, m. 1 Dec. 1900, Charles Percival Foster, Lieut. 2nd Dragoons; and has issue 1f.

1f. Moira Foster.

3c. Lady[1] *Henrietta Susan Beresford Lumley*, d. (–); m. 5 Nov. 1835, *Edmund L'Estrange of Tynte Lodge, co. Leitrim*, d. Aug. 1866; and had (*with other*[2]) *issue* 1d to 5d.

1d. Rev. Savile Richard William L'Estrange-Malone, Minor Canon of Worcester, Rector of Dalton Holme (*Pallas Park, King's co.; Dalton Holme Rectory, Yorks*), b. 22 Mar. 1838; m. 10 Oct. 1876, Frances Mary, da. of George Savile Foljambe of Osberton, &c.; and has issue.

See the Clarence Volume, p. 608, Nos. 26745–26749.

2d. Henry Frederick L'Estrange-Malone.

3d. Harriet *Georgina L'Estrange-Malone*, d. 1864; m. *as 1st wife*, 12 *Sept.* 1861, *John Henry Cole Wynne of Ardaghowen, co. Sligo.*

4d. Constance L'Estrange-Malone, m. 9 Ap. 1863, Josslyn Francis (Pennington) 5th [I.] and 1st [U.K.] Baron Muncaster (*Muncaster Castle, Ravenglass, Cumberland; 5 Carlton Gardens, S.W.*).

5d. Mary Caroline L'Estrange-Malone, m. 11 Aug. 1875, Charles Gore (Hay), 20th Earl of Erroll and 23rd Hereditary Lord High Constable of Scotland, K.T., C.B., &c. (*Slains Castle, Port Erroll, R.S.O., Aberdeen; Walls, Cumberland; 20 Buckingham Gate, S.W.*); and has issue 1e to 3e.

1e. Victor Alexander Sereld Hay, Lord Kilmarnock (*White's; St. James'*), b. 17 Oct. 1876; m. 22 May 1900, Mary Lucy Victoria, da. of Sir Allan Russell Mackenzie, 2nd Bart. [U.K.]; and has issue 1f to 3f.

1f. Hon. Josslyn Victor Hay, b. 11 May 1901.

2f. Hon. Gilbert Allan Rowland Hay, b. 15 Jan. 1903.

3f. Hon. Rosemary Constance Ferelith Hay, b. 15 May 1904.

2e. Hon. Sereld Mordaunt Allan Josslyn Hay, Lieut. R.N., b. 25 Nov. 1877.

3e. Hon. Ivan Josslyn Lumley Hay, sometime a Page of Honour to Queen Victoria and King Edward VII., b. 31 Oct. 1884.

4c. Lady[3] *Anne Georgina Lumley*, b. 21 *Aug.* 1820; .d. 2 *Feb.* 1877; m. 16 *Ap.* 1844, *Sir William Mordaunt Edward Milner, 5th Bart.* [G.B.], *M.P.,* d. 12 *Feb.* 1867; *and had issue.*

See the Clarence Volume, p. 270, Nos. 7203–7211.   [Nos. 53632 to 53667.

---

[1] R.W. 7 Mar. 1857.   [2] Foster's "Peerage," 1880, p. 572.   [3] R.W. 7 Mar. 1857

# of The Blood Royal

5a. *Lady Louisa Lumley*, b. 1773; d. 1811; m. 26 *Feb.* 1798, *Winchcombe Henry Hartley ; and had issue* [1] *1b to 3b.*

1b. *Winchcombe Henry Savile Hartley*, b. 2 *Aug.* 1800.

2b. [*son*] *Hartley*, b. *before* 1812.

3b. *Barbara Hartley*, b. *Nov.* 1798.

568. Descendants of Lady MARY LUMLEY (see Table LX.), *d.* 10 Dec. 1726 ; *m.* as 2nd wife, GEORGE (MONTAGU), 1st EARL OF [G.B.] and 2nd BARON HALIFAX, K.B., *b. a.* 1685 ; *d.* 9 May 1739 ; and had issue.

See the Clarence Volume, pp. 615–619, Nos. 26908–27008.

[Nos. 53668 to 53768.

569. Descendants of Sir THOMAS FRANKLAND of Thirkleby, 5th Bart. [E.], M.P., Admiral of the White (see Table LX.), *d.* 20 Mar. or Nov. 1784 ; *m.* (in South Carolina) May 1743, SARAH, da. or grandda. of [——] RHETT, Chief-Justice of South Carolina, *b. c.* 1724 ; *d.* 20 Ap. 1808 ; and had issue 1*a* to 7*a*.

1a. *Sir Thomas Frankland, 6th Bart.* [E.], b. *Sept.* 1750 ; d. 4 *Jan.* 1831 ; m. *Mar.* 1773, *Dorothy, da. of William Smelt*, d. 19 *May* 1820 ; *and had issue* 1b.

1b. *Sir Robert Frankland, afterwards (R.L. Feb.* 1837) *Frankland-Russell, 7th Bart.* [E.], b. 16 *July* 1784 ; d. 11 *Mar.* 1849 ; m. 30 *Nov.* 1815, *Louisa Anne, da. of the Right Rev. Lord George Murray, Lord Bishop of St. David's*, d. 21 *Feb.* 1871 ; *and had issue.*

See the Tudor Roll of "The Blood Royal of Britain," pp. 454–455, Nos. 31836–31878.

2a. *Rev. Roger Frankland, Canon of Wells*, d. 25 *Mar.* 1826 ; m. 19 *June* 1792, *the Hon. Catherine, da. of John (Colville), 8th Lord Colville* [S.], d. 19 *Sept.* 1843 ; *and had issue* 1b *to* 10b.

1b. *Sir Frederick William Frankland, 8th Bart.* [E.], b. 11 *May* 1793 ; d. 11 *Mar.* 1878 ; m. 21 *Aug.* 1821, *Katherine Margaret, da. of Isaac Scarth of Stakesby*, d. 1 *Nov.* 1851 ; *and had issue* 1c *to* 3c.

1c. *Sir William Adolphus Frankland of Thirkleby, 9th Bart.* [E.], b. 12 *Aug.* 1837 ; d. 29 *Nov.* 1883 ; m. 25 *Feb.* 1864, *Lucy Ducarel, da. of Francis Adams of Clifton and Cotswold Grange, co. Gloucester ; and had issue* 1d *to* 5d.

1d. Sir Frederick William Francis George Frankland, 10th Bart. [E.], *late* Bedfordshire Regt. and Royal Dublin Fusiliers (*Westwood, Windlesham*), *b.* 2 Sept. 1868 ; *m.* 1st, 10 Dec. 1890, Charlotte, da. of John Augustus de Zerega of Island Hall, West Chester, New York, *d.s.p.* 24 Mar. 1892 ; 2ndly, 12 Nov. 1901, Mary Cecil, da. of Col. George Augustus Curzon ; and has issue 1*e*.

1e. Thomas William Assheton Frankland, *b.* 18 Aug. 1902.

2d. Arthur Pelham Frankland, D.S.O., Capt. Lancashire Fusiliers (*White's*), *b.* 24 Dec. 1874 ; *m.* Oct. 1898, Margaret Annie Phœbe, da. of Charles Compton Seton of Heath House, Hopton Heath ; and has issue 1*e*.

1e. Marion Annie Margaret Frankland.

3d. Ethel Maud Frankland.

4d. Frances Cromwell Frankland, *m.* 12 June 1897, Claud Neville.

5d. Evelyn Rose Frankland. [Nos. 53769 to 53818.

---

[1] Brydge's "Collins," iii. p. 719.

635

The Plantagenet Roll

2c. Colville Frankland, *late* Col. 2nd Batt. Royal Dublin Fusiliers, and some-time (1884–1889) in command 102nd Regt. Dist. (*Junior United Service*), *b.* 26 Nov. 1839 ; *m.* 22 Sept. 1870, Mary Jay, da. of William Dawson of New York ; and has issue 1*d* to 6*d*.

1*d*. Robert Cecil Colville Frankland, *late* Lieut. S. Staffordshire Regt., *b.* 7 July 1877.

2*d*. Thomas Hugh Colville Frankland, Lieut. 2nd Batt. Royal Dublin Fusiliers, *b.* 17 Oct. 1879.

3*d*. Katherine Marian Colville Frankland.

4*d*. Eleanor Frankland.

5*d*. Beatrice Frankland.

6*d*. Mary Olive Elsie Frankland.

3c. Eliza Henrietta Augusta Frankland (*Muntham, St. Ronan's Road, South-sea*), *m.* 12 Jan. 1861, Major-Gen. Frederick Smith Vacher, *d.* 17 Mar. 1893 ; and has issue 1*d* to 5*d*.

1*d*. Charlotte Frankland Vacher.

2*d*. Fanny Edith Vacher.

3*d*. Helen Katherine Vacher.

4*d*. Eliza Georgina Vacher.

5*d*. Maud Mary Frankland Vacher.

2*b*. *Edward Augustus Frankland, Rear-Adm. R.N., d. (? s.p.).*

3*b*. *Charles Colville Frankland, Admiral R.N., d. (? s.p.) Ap. 1876.*

4*b*. *George Frankland, Lieut. 65th Regt., b. Jan. 1800 ; d. 30 Dec. 1838 ; m. 18 July 1822, Anne, da. of Thomas Mason of London, Solicitor ; and had issue 1c to 2c.*

1*c*. Sophia Catherine Frankland, *b.* 22 June 1823 ; *m.* 1st, 28 Sept. 1846, Gore Boland Munbee, Capt. Bombay Engineers, *d.* (–) ; 2ndly, 2 July 1862, Col. Charles Payne Barras, *late* Indian Army.

2*c*. *Georgina Anne Frankland, b.* 22 *June* 1824 ; *d.* 1887 ; *m.* 12 *Sept.* 1847, *Major-Gen. John Thomas Francis, H.E.I.C.S., d.* 1896.

5*b*. *Arthur Frankland, d. (? unm.).*

6*b*. *Emma Frankland,*

7*b*. *Matilda Frankland,*

8*b*. *Catherine Henrietta Frankland,* } *d. (? unm.).*

9*b*. *Octavia Frankland,*

10*b*. *Louisa Frankland,*

3*a*. *Anne Frankland, d.* (–) ; *m. 1st, John Lewis of Harpton Court, co. Radnor ; 2ndly, as 3rd wife, the Rev. Robert Hare, Rector of Hurstmonceaux, d.* (s.p. *by her*) 24 *Feb.* 1832.

4*a*. *Dinah Frankland, d.* (–) ; *m. William Bowles ; and had issue.*

5*a*. *Catharine Frankland, d.* (–) ; *m. Thomas Whinyates.*

6*a*. *Charlotte Frankland, d.* (–) ; *m. Robert Nicholas of Ashton Keynes, co. Wilts, M.P.*

7*a*. *Grace Frankland,* d. (–) ; m. [——] *Gossett of* [——] *in France ; and had* issue. [Nos. 53819 to 53832.

570. Descendants of ANNE FRANKLAND (see Table LX.), *d.* 5 Mar. 1813 ; *m.* 15 June 1754, THOMAS (PELHAM), 1st EARL OF CHICHESTER [U.K.] and 2nd BARON PELHAM OF STANMER [G.B.], *b.* 28 Feb. 1828 ; *d.* 8 Jan. 1805 ; and had issue 1*a* to 4*a*.

1*a*. *Thomas (Pelham), 2nd Earl of Chichester [U.K.] and 3rd Baron Pelham [G.B.], b.* 28 *Ap.* 1756 ; *d.* 4 *July* 1826 ; *m.* 16! *July* 1801, *Lady Mary Henrietta*

# of The Blood Royal

Juliana, da. of Francis Godolphin (Osborne), 5th Duke of Leeds [E.], d. 21 Oct. 1862; and had issue.

See the Clarence Volume, p. 629, Nos. 28118–28185.

2*a*. Hon. *Henry Pelham, M.P.*, b. 10 *July* 1759; d. 16 *Jan.* 1797; m. 2 *Nov.* 1788, *Catherine, da. of Charles*[1] (*or Thomas*)[2] *Cobbe by his wife Lady Elizabeth, née Beresford*, d. 22 *Dec.* 1838; *and had issue* 1*b*.

1*b*. *Fanny Pelham*, d. 22 *Feb.* 1860; m. 1834, *Capt. James Hamilton Murray, R.N.*, d. 1841.

3*a*. Lady *Henrietta Anne Pelham*, b. 1 *Sept.* 1757; d. 5 *Dec.* 1797; m. *as 1st wife*, 24 *May* 1789, *George William (Glanville, otherwise Leslie), 13th Earl of Rothes* [*S.*], b. 28 *Mar.* 1768; d. 11 *Feb.* 1817; *and had issue* 1*b*.

1*b*. *Henrietta Anne (Glanville, otherwise Leslie), suo jure 14th Countess of Rothes* [*S.*], b. 26 *Mar.* 1790; d. 30 *Jan.* 1819; m. 1806, *George Gwyther, afterwards Leslie*, d. 24 *Mar.* 1829; *and had issue* 1*c to* 3*c*.

1*c*. *George William Evelyn (Leslie), 15th Earl of Rothes* [*S.*], b. 8 *Nov.* 1809; d. 10 *Mar.* 1841; m. 7 *May* 1831, *Louisa, da. of Col. Anderson Morshead, R.E.*, d. 21 *Jan.* 1886; *and had issue* 1*d to* 2*d*.

1*d*. *George William Evelyn (Leslie), 16th Earl of Rothes* [*S.*], b. 4 *Feb.* 1835; d. *unm.* 2 *Jan.* 1859.

2*d*. *Henrietta Anderson Morshead (Leslie), suo jure 17th Countess of Rothes* [*S.*], b. 1832; d.s.p. 10 *Feb.* 1886.

2*c*. *Mary Elizabeth (Leslie), suo jure 18th Countess of Rothes* [*S.*], b. 9 *July* 1811; d. 19 *Sept.* 1893; m. 11 *Aug.* 1835, *Martin Edward Haworth, afterwards* (*R.L. Mar.* 1886) *Haworth-Leslie of Barham Wood, co. Herts*, d. 2 *Nov.* 1886; *and had issue* 1*d to* 6*d*.

1*d*. *Martin Leslie Haworth, afterwards* (*R.L.* 13 *Jan.* 1865) *Leslie of Shrub Hill, co. Surrey*, b. 12 *Mar.* 1839; d.v.p. 22 *Dec.* 1882; m. 10 *June* 1873, *Georgina Frances (Brandon, Paignton, Devon), da. of Henry Studdy of Waddeton Court, co. Devon; and had issue* 1*e to* 4*e*.

1*e*. Norman Evelyn (Leslie), 19th Earl of Rothes [S.] (*Leslie House, Leslie, Fife*), *b.* 13 July 1877; *m.* 19 Ap. 1900, Lucy Noëlle Martha, da. and h. of Thomas Dyer-Edwardes of Prinknash Park, co. Gloucester; and had issue 1*f*.

1*f*. Malcolm George Dyer-Edwardes Leslie, Lord Leslie, *b.* 8 Feb. 1902.

2*e*. Lady[1] Mary Eleanor Leslie, *b.* 18 Oct. 1875.

3*e*. Lady[1] Mildred Emily Leslie, *b.* 22 Dec. 1878.

4*e*. Lady[1] Georgina Leslie, *b.* 1 Dec. 1879.

2*d*. Hon. Edward Courtenay Haworth-Leslie (*Earee, Burria, Shoalhaven, N.S. Wales*), *b.* 2 July 1840; *m.* 1 Oct. 1890, Caroline Edith, da. of Thomas Tregenna Biddulph of The Earee, Shoalhaven; and has issue 1*e to* 5*e*.

1*e*. Edward Biddulph Haworth-Leslie, *b.* 31 Jan. 1895.

2*e*. Martin Tregenna Haworth-Leslie, *b.* 2 May 1896.

3*e*. Norman Evelyn Haworth-Leslie, *b.* 26 Jan. 1898.

4*e*. Mary Henrietta Haworth-Leslie, *b.* 26 Sept. 1892.

5*e*. Alice Veronica Haworth-Leslie, *b.* 14 Aug. 1901.

3*d*. Lady Mary Euphrasia Haworth-Leslie (26 *Wetherby Mansions, S. Kensington, S.W.*).

4*d*. Lady Emily Louisa Haworth-Leslie (44 *Wetherby Mansions, S. Kensington, S.W.*), *m.* 25 Ap. 1871, James Frederick Cherry, Clerk and Librarian, R.N. Coll., Greenwich, *d.* June 1884; and has issue 1*e to* 3*e*.

1*e*. Charles Cameron Leslie Cherry, *b.* 19 Nov. 1873; *m.* 1898, Grace, da. of Walter Dudley of Melbourne.

2*e*. Miriam Emily Cherry, *m.* 1901, Herbert Taylor.

3*e*. Gladys Cherry. [Nos. 53833 to 53909.

---

[1] Foster's "Peerage," 1880, p. 134.   [2] Burke's "Peerage," 1900, p. 308.

637   4 M

The Plantagenet Roll

5d. Lady Alice Julia Haworth-Leslie (26 *Wetherby Mansions, S. Kensington, S.W.*).

6d. Lady Grace Haworth-Leslie, *m.* 10 Feb. 1876, John Bazley White, *afterwards* (R.L. 1887) Bazley-White, J.P., D.L., sometime (1885–1892) M.P. for Gravesend (*Wierton Grange, Maidstone*); and has issue 1*e* to 8*e*.

1e. John Bazley-White, *b.* 9 Sept. 1878.

2e. Richard Booth Leslie Bazley-White, Lieut. 2nd Batt. Queen's Own, *b.* 25 May 1886.

3e. Mary Evelyn Bazley-White, *m.* 30 July 1903, Cholmeley Edward Carl Branfill Harrison, Col. Comdg. 1st Batt. Queen's Own.

4e. Henrietta Maud Bazley-White.

5e. Grace Winifred Bazley-White, *m.* 15 Feb. 1905, Robert Henry Style, Lieut. 6th Dragoon Guards.

6e. Margaret Iris Bazley-White.

7e. Victoria Constance Bazley-White.

8e. Joan Alice Bazley-White.|

3c. Lady Anna Maria Leslie, b. 19 *July* 1815; *d.* 18 *Feb.* 1897; *m.* 6 *Jan.* 1835, *Henry (Courtenay), 13th Earl of Devon* [*E.*], *d.* 29 *Jan.* 1904; *and had issue.*

See p. 109, Nos. 1233–1239.

4a. Lady Frances Pelham, b. 4 *Dec.* 1760; *d.* 23 *June* 1783; *m. as 1st wife,* 5 *Dec.* 1778, *George (Brodrick), 4th Viscount Midleton* [*I.*] *and 1st Baron Brodrick* [*U.K.*], *d.* 12 *Aug.* 1836; *and had issue.*

See the Clarence Volume, pp. 587–588, Nos. 24801–24851.

[Nos. 53910 to 53977.

---

571. Descendants of MARY FRANKLAND (see Table LX.), *bur.* 4 Sept. 1722; *m.* as 1st wife, 1710, THOMAS WORSLEY of Hovingham, co. York, *b.* 16 Nov. 1686; *bur.* 2 Mar. 1750; and had issue 1*a* to 5*a*.

1a. Thomas Worsley of Hovingham, M.P., b. 22 *Nov.* 1710; *d.* 13 *Dec.* 1778; *m.* 5 *July* 1757, *Elizabeth, da. of the Rev. J. Lister, d.* 19 *Nov.* 1809; *and had issue* 1*b*.

1b. Rev. George Worsley, Rector of Stonegrave and Scawton, b. 15 *Nov.* 1761; *d.* 4 *Feb.* 1815; *m. Anne, da. of Sir Thomas Cayley, 5th Bart.* [*E.*], *d.* 31 *Aug.* 1854; *and had issue* 1*c* to 9*c*.

1c. Sir William Worsley of Hovingham, 1st Bart. [*U.K.*], bapt. 26 *Aug.* 1792; *d.* 5 *Mar.* 1879; *m.* 18 *Jan.* 1827, *Sarah Philadelphia, da. of Sir George Cayley, 6th Bart.* [*E.*], *d.* 23 *Ap.* 1885; *and had issue* 1*d* to 5*d*.

1d. Sir William Cayley Worsley, 2nd Bart. [*U.K.*], *b.* 6 *Dec.* 1828; *d.s.p.* 10 *Sept.* 1897.

2d. Arthington Worsley, b. 22 *Dec.* 1830; *d.* 3 *June* 1861; *m.* 13 *Mar.* 1860, *Marianne Christina Isabella, da. of Col. the Hon. Henry Hely-Hutchinson of Weston Hall, d.* 11 *Aug.* 1893; *and had issue* 1*e* to 2*e*.

1e. Sir William Henry Arthington Worsley, 3rd Bart. [*U.K.*], &c. (*Hovingham Hall, York*), *b.* 12 Jan. 1861; *m.* 6 Oct. 1887, Augusta Mary Chivers, da. of Edward Chivers Bower of Broxholme, Scarborough; and has issue 1*f* to 5*f*.

1f. William Arthington Worsley, *b.* 5 Ap. 1890.

2f. Edward Marcus Worsley, *b.* 13 June 1891.

3f. Winifred Mary Worsley, *b.* 9 Dec. 1888.

4f. Ethel Isabel Worsley, *b.* 19 Oct. 1892.

5f. Victoria Worsley, *b.* 23 Feb. 1900. [Nos. 53978 to 53983.

# of The Blood Royal

2e. Arthington Worsley, C.E. (*Mandeville House, Isleworth*), *b.* (posthumous) 9 Dec. 1861; *m.* 5 Jan. 1900, Helen, widow of Thomas Bartlett Thomas Griffiths of Stourbridge, da. of S. H. Harding; and has issue 1*f.*

1f. Marcus Rurik Worsley, *b.* 28 May 1901.

3d. Catherine Louisa Worsley (*Ebberston House, Scarborough*), *m.* 5 July 1859, Sir George Allanson Cayley, 8th Bart. [E.], *b.* 31 Dec. 1831; *d.* 10 Oct. 1895; and has issue.

See p. 501, Nos. 43941–43948.

4d. Anne Barbara Worsley, *unm.*

5d. Emma Frances Worsley, d. 15 May 1893; m. 20 Aug. 1861, *the Right Hon. Edward Robert King-Harman, P.C., M.P., Lord-Lieut. co. Roscommon &c., b.* 3 *Ap.* 1838; *d.* 10 *June* 1888; *and had issue* 1*e.*

1e. Frances Agnes King-Harman, *m.* 22 May 1890, Thomas Joseph Stafford, F.R.C.S.I., Commr. of Local Govt. Board [I.] (*Taney House, Dundrum, co. Dublin*); and has issue 1*f* to 2*f.*

1f. Edward Charles Stafford, now (R.L. 1900) Stafford-King-Harman, *b.* 13 Ap. 1891 (*Rockingham, Boyle, Roscommon*).

2f. Cecil William Francis Stafford, *b* 6 Jan. 1895.

2c. Frederick Cayley Worsley, b. 1803; *d.* (–); *m.* 29 *Jan.* 1840, *Juliana, da. of John Wright; and had issue* 1*d* to 11*d.*

1d. Frederick Marcus Worsley, *b.* 1849 (? 1848); *m.* 8 Sept. 1880, Mary Louise Jodrell, da. of [——] Bishop.

2d. Edward Cayley Worsley, *b.* 28 Sept. 1851 (? 1850); *m.* 21 Oct. 1886, Agnes Mary, da. of Marmaduke Charles Salvin of Burn Hall, J.P., D.L.

3d. Arthur Arthington Worsley, *b.* 1852 (? 1851).

4d. Digby Thomas Worsley, b. 1858; *d.* (? *unm.*) 9 *Dec.* 1884.

5d. Julia Worsley, d. 12 *Mar.* 1882.

6d. Laura Worsley.

7d. Hilda Mary Agnes Worsley, *m.* 25 July 1867, Henry Carnsew of Somers, co. Sussex, *d.* 22 May 1884.

8d. Edith Worsley.

9d. Clara Frances Worsley, d. 12 *Sept.* 1869; *m.* 20 *Sept.* 1866, *Charles Henry Plowden, Major Madras S.C.; and had issue.*

10d. Alice Emily Worsley, *m.* 8 Feb. 1882, Thomas Manby Colegrave.

11d. Florence Kathleen Worsley, *m.* 17 Aug. 1886, William J. Speed.

3c. Septimus Lancelot Worsley, M.A., b. 1804; *d.* 29 *Sept.* 1889; m. *and had issue* 1*d.*

1d. Arthur Worsley.

4c. Henry Francis Worsley of New Zealand, b. 1806; *d.* 24 *July* 1876; m. 1st, *Catherine, da. of B. Blackden; 2ndly, Caroline Hankinson, previously Cust; and had issue (with other sons by 1st marriage)* 1*d* to 5*d.*

1d.[1] Henry Worsley.

2d.[1] Charles Worsley.

3d.[1] Arthur Worsley.

4d.[2] Frederic Worsley, *b.* 18 Jan. 1849.

5d.[1] Catherine Worsley.

5c. Charles Valentine Worsley, Bar.-at-Law, b. 1808; *d.* (–); *m.* 4 *May* 1848, *Sophia, widow of* [——] *Kent, da. of John Kimble,* d.s.p. 14 *Jan.* 1880.

6c. Arthur Worsley, late 51st *N.I., b.* 10 *May* 1810; *d.* (–); *m.* 11 *Nov.* 1858, *Winifred Sherring, da. of the Rev. J. W. Evans of Basingthorpe; and had issue* 1*d* to 3*d.*

1d. Daniel Arthur Worsley, *b.* 15 July 1862.

2d. Emma Frances Worsley.

3d. Alice Marion Worsley.   [Nos. 53984 to 54015.

639

The Plantagenet Roll

7c. *Isabella Worsley*, d. 27 *Jan.* 1865; m. 1824, *John C. Blackden; and had issue.*

8c. *Philadelphia Worsley*, d. (–); m. 6 *June* 1826, *William Joseph Coltman, Naburn Hall, co. York,* d. 17 *Aug.* 1869; *and had issue* 1d *to* 2d.

1d. Laura Coltman, elder da. and co-h., m. 1851, the Rev. Albert Sydney Wilde, M.A. (Camb.), Rector of Louth (*Louth Rectory, Lincoln*).

2d. *Mary Mackenzie Coltman,* d. (–); m. 19 *Sept.* 1855, *James Stovin Pennyman of Ormesby, J.P.,* d. 2 *June* 1896; *and had issue* 1e *to* 4e.

1e. James Worsley Pennyman, J.P., D.L., Bar.-at-Law (*Ormesby Hall, York-shire*), b. 10 Aug. 1856; m. 6 Oct. 1882, Dora Maria, da. of H. F. Beaumont of Whitley Beaumont; and has issue 1f to 3f.

1f. James Beaumont Worsley Pennyman, Lieut. 25th King's Own Scottish Borderers, b. 17 Dec. 1883.

2f. Thomas Henry Pennyman, b. 16 May 1892.

3f. Mary Dorothy Pennyman, b. 22 Feb. 1889.

2e. Alfred Worsley Pennyman, *late* Lieut.-Col. 25th King's Own Scottish Borderers, b. 7 Oct. 1858.

3e. Rev. William Geoffrey Pennyman, Vicar of Bishopsthorpe, Chaplain to the Archbishop of York, b. 3 May 1870; *m.* 8 Feb. 1901, Beatrice Jane Frances, da. of Sir James Walker of Sand Hutton, 3rd Bart. [U.K.]; and has issue 1f to 2f.

1f. Joan Mary Pennyman.

2f. Angela Beatrix Pennyman.

4e. Edith Mary Pennyman, *m.* 26 June 1890, Major George Henry Fraser Phillips, 14th Regt., and has issue 1f.

1f. George Wyndham Phillips.

9c. *Frances Worsley*, d. (–); m. 19 *May* 1835, *the Rev. George Henry Webber, Canon of Ripon.*

2a. *Robert Worsley*, d. (–); m. *and had issue* 1b.

1b. *Elizabeth Worsley*, m. *James Hobson of Kirby Moorside.*

3a. *Rev. James Worsley, Rector of Stonegrave,* bapt. 28 *Aug.* 1722; *d.* 19 *Aug.* 1777; *m.* 17 *Dec.* 1761, *Dorothy, sister of Sir James Pennyman of Ormesby, 6th Bart.* [E.], *d.* 14 *Nov.* 1811; *and had issue* 1b *to* 2b.

1b. *James Worsley of Worksop, Col. in the Army,* b. 14 *Ap.* 1764; *d.* 26 *Nov.* 1807; *m.* 5 *Nov.* 1789, *Lydia, sister to Sir Thomas Wollaston White, 1st Bart.* [U.K.], *da. of Taylor White,* d. 19 *Ap.* 1832; *and had issue* 1c *to* 3c.

1c. *James White Worsley, afterwards* (R.L. 18 *Ap.* 1853) *Pennyman of Ormesby, J.P., Capt. R.E.,* b. 5 *Nov.* 1792; *d:* 1 *Feb.* 1870; *m.* 24 *Mar.* 1828, *Frances, da. of the Rev. James Stovin, D.D.,* d. 6 *June* 1869; *and had issue* 1d *to* 2d.

1d. *James Stovin Pennyman of Ormesby,* b. 15 *Oct.* 1830; *d.* 2 *June* 1896; *m.* 19 *Sept.* 1855, *Mary Mackenzie, da. and co-h. of William Joseph Coltman of Naburn Hall; and had issue.*

See p. 640, Nos. 54017–54026.

2d. Frances Maria Pennyman (92 *Ashley Gardens, S.W.*), *m.* 17 July 1855, Forbes Macbean, *late* Lieut.-Col. 92nd Highlanders, *d.* 1900; and has issue 1e to 5e.

1e. Forbes Macbean, C.V.O., C.B., Brig.-Gen. Comdg. Highland Regimental Dist., *late* 92nd Highlanders (*Perth*), b. 3 Jan. 1857; *m.* 27 July 1889, Mary K. F., da. of Capt. Jackson, R.N., and has issue 1f.

1f. Duncan Gillies Forbes Macbean, b. 19 July 1893.

2e. William Alleyne Macbean, Major R.A., b. 13 Oct. 1863, *m.*; and has issue.

3e. Frances Katherine Macbean, *m.* Lieut.-Col. Alexander Gordon Duff.

4e. Ethel Macbean, *m.* Lieut. Ingram Conway Gordon; and has issue.

5e. Marion Lily Macbean. [Nos. 54016 to 54044.

640

2c. Rev. *Charles Pennyman Worsley, Vicar of Thurlby*, b. 5 *Mar.* 1798; d. 17 *Dec.* 1863; m. 10 *May* 1826, *Caroline, da. of Peter Acklom of Beverley; and had issue* 1d *to* 3d.

1d. Pennyman White Worsley, *late* Capt. 60th Rifles, b. 14 Aug. 1838, m.; and has issue.

2d. Mary Caroline Worsley, m. 11 June 1857, the Rev. Edward Martin Chapman, Rector of Low Toynton, Linc. ; and has issue 1e to 5e.

1e. Charles Edward Chapman, b. 26 Aug. 1860.

2e. Frank Emerson Chapman, b. 9 Oct. 1864.

3e. George Herbert Chapman, b. 5 Feb. 1867.

4e. Florence Mary Chapman.

5e. Ellen Chapman.

3d. Harriet Maria Worsley.

3c. Rev. *William Worsley, Rector of Bratoft*, b. 27 *June* 1800; d. 26 *Aug.* 1881; m. 7 *July* 1825, *Louisa, da. of the Rev. William Benson Ramsden; and had issue* 1d *to* 6d.

1d. *William Ramsden Worsley*, b. 10 *Ap.* 1832; d. 11 *Mar.* 1871; m. 1862, *Mary, da. of Æneas Macdonald of Kingston, Canada ; and had issue* 1e *to* 2e.

1e. Weston Macdonald Worsley, b. 1863.

2e. Lydia Worsley.

2d. Francis Worsley, Capt. Mercantile Marine (187 *Queen's Gate*, S.W.), b. 18 Feb. 1836; m. 22 Oct. 1863, Katherine Elizabeth Edith, da. of the Rev. Francis Pickford; d. 14 Mar. 1885; 2ndly, Emma, da. of the Rev. John Chancourt Girardot of Car Colston Hall, Notts ; and has issue.

See p. 263, Nos. 9918–9923.

3d. *Richard Worsley, Major-Gen. 36th Bengal N.I.*, b. *Jan.* 1838; d. (–); m. 30 *Aug.* 1877, *Edith Meaburn, da. of Meaburn Staniland of Harrington Hall, co. Linc. ; and had issue* 1e *to* 5e.

1e. Richard Stanley Worsley, b. 7 Sept. 1879.

2e. Geoffrey Worsley, b. 17 Feb. 1881.

3e. Ralph Marcus Meaburn Worsley, b. 11 June 1887.

4e. Edith Dorothy Worsley, b. 12 June 1882.

5e. Marjory Louisa Worsley, b. 9 June 1884.

4d. Louisa Augusta Worsley, m. 6 Oct. 1863, George Boden, Q.C., Recorder of Derby, d.s.p. 16 Feb. 1880.

5d. *Emily Worsley*, d. 21 Oct. 1870 ; m. *as* 1st *wife*, 4 *Aug.* 1852, *Major George Charles Uppleby of Barrow Hall, J.P., D.L., High Sheriff co. Linc.* 1863, b. 23 *Ap.* 1819 ; d. 1891 ; *and had issue* 1e *to* 4e.

1e. Rev. George Crowle Uppleby of Barrow, M.A. (Camb.), *late* Vicar of Bonby (*Barrow Hall, Hull*), b. 13 Feb. 1858; m. 15 Jan. 1891, Margaret Augusta, da. of Lieut.-Col. Charles Brown Constable of Wallaie Craigie, co. Forfar, J.P., D.L. ; and has issue 1f.

1f. Emily Margaret Cecilia Uppleby, b. 23 Nov. 1899.

2e. Emily May Uppleby.

3e. Leila Frances Uppleby, m. 17 June 1885, the Rev. Charles John Boden, M.A., Rector of N. Wingfield (*North Wingfield Rectory, Chesterfield*).

4e. Laura Violet Uppleby, m. 7 Nov. 1894, David George Hogarth, Fellow of Magdalen College.

6d. *Constance Worsley*, d. 1883 ; m. 6 *May* 1863, *Henry Winteringham, C.E.*, d. *Aug.* 1877 ; *and had issue.*

2b. Rev. *Ralph Worsley, Rector of Finchley, co. Middlesex*, b. 1766 ; d. 23 *Mar.* 1848 ; m. *Elizabeth, da. of Thomas Gildart*, d. (–) ; *and had issue* 1c *to* 2c.

[Nos. 54045 to 54072.

The Plantagenet Roll

1c. Rev. Pennyman Warton Worsley, Canon Resid. of Ripon, b. 20 July 1800;
d. 1885; m. 1st, 12 Sept. 1839, Helen, da. of the Rev. William Potchett, Vicar of
Grantham, d. 14 Oct. 1854; and had issue 1d to 5d.

1d. Rev. Pennyman Ralph Worsley, Rector of Little Ponton, Lincs., b. 3 July
1842; m. 1st, 29 Sept. 1868, Sophie Matilda, da. of Capt. Herbert Mackworth,
R.N., d. 30 Aug. 1875; 2ndly, 12 Sept. 1877, Jessie Rosa, da. of Robert Wilson of
Thorndale; and has issue 1e to 3e.

1e. Ralph Wilson Worsley, b. 7 Dec. 1879.

2e. Henry Meyer Worsley, b. 22 Aug. 1887.

3e. Jessy Helen Worsley.

2d. Henry Gildart Worsley, J.P., Lieut.-Col. King's Own Scottish Borderers
(Belleisle, Richmond, Yorks), b. 12 Feb. 1848; m. Georgina, da. of J. G. Hyde;
and has issue 1e to 3e.

1e. Hugh Gildart Worsley, b. 1885.

2e. Ronald Henry Warton Worsley, Lieut. King's Own Scottish Borderers,
b. 1886.

3e. Violet Georgina Worsley.

3d. Helena Sophia Worsley, m. 1883, the Rev. Henry Cust-Nunn, Vicar of
Sharow, Ripon, and has issue.

4d. Emily Isabella Worsley, m. 1890, the Rev. S. Reed, Precentor of Ripon
Cathedral.

5d. Louisa Worsley, m. as 2nd wife, 23 Ap. 1889, the Right Rev. John James
Pulleine, D.D., Lord Bishop Suffragan of Richmond; and has issue.

See p. 557, Nos. 49711–49713, and 49718.

2c. Harriet Worsley, d. 1869; m. 1828, William Gillison Bell of Melling, co.
Lanc.

4a. Mary Worsley, b. 1712; d. 24 June 1752; m. 1735, Marmaduke Constable
of Wassand, bapt. 20 Jan. 1708; d. 16 Ap. 1762; and had issue 1b to 3b.

1b. Marmaduke Constable of Wassand, d.s.p. 1812.

2b. Ven. Thomas Constable of Beverley, Archdeacon of the West Riding, d.
(–); m. 1769, Sarah, da. and in her issue (1826) h. of Christopher Goulton of
Walcot, co. Lincoln, d. (–); and had issue 1c.

1c. Rev. Charles Constable of Wassand, b. 24 Ap. 1773; d. 1852; m. June
1796, Lucy, da. of Jonathan Acklon of Wiselon; and had issue 1d.

1d. Mary Constable of Wassand, co. York, and Walcot, co. Lincoln, d. 10 Jan.
1865; m. as 1st wife, 30 Mar. 1818, Sir George Strickland, afterwards (R.L. 17 Mar.
1865) Cholmeley of Boynton, 7th Bart. [E.], M.P., 23 Dec. 1874; and had issue.

See the Clarence Volume, pp. 232–233, Nos. 4763–4801.

3b. Mary Constable, d. (–); m. Jonathan Acklon of Wiselon; and was probably mother of 1c.

1c. Lucy Acklon, d. (–); m. June 1796, the Rev. Charles Constable of Wassand;
and had issue.

See p. 642, Nos. 54088–54126.

5a. Frances Worsley, b. 1716; bur. 6 Nov. 1750; m. 13 July 1737, Thomas
(Robinson), 1st Baron Grantham [G.B.], P.C., d. 30 Sept. 1770; and had issue 1b
to 2b.

1b. Thomas (Robinson), 2nd Baron Grantham [G.B.], b. 30 Nov. 1738; d.
20 July 1786; m. 17 Aug. 1780, Lady Mary Jemima, da. and co-h. of Philip
(Yorke), 2nd Earl of Hardwicke [G.B.] (by Jemima, suo jure Marchioness Grey), d.
Jan. 1830; and had issue 1c to 2c.

1c. Thomas Philip (Robinson, sometime (R.L. 7 May 1803) Weddell, and
finally (R.L. 24 June 1833) De Grey), 3rd Baron Grantham [U.K.] and (in 1833)
2nd Earl de Grey [U.K.] and 5th Baron Lucas [E.], K.G., &c., b. 8 Dec. 1781; d.
14 Nov. 1859; m. 20 July 1805, Lady Henrietta Frances, da. of William (Cole), 1st
Earl of Enniskillen, d. 2 July 1848; and had issue.

See pp. 64–65, Nos. 2017–2056.   [Nos. 54073 to 54205.

# of The Blood Royal

2c. *Frederick John (Robinson), 1st Earl of Ripon* [*U.K.*], b. 1 Nov. 1782; d. 28 *Jan.* 1859; m. 1 *Sept.* 1814, *Lady Sarah Albinia Louisa, da. and h. of Robert (Hobart), 4th Earl of Buckinghamshire* [*G.B.*], d. 9 *Ap.* 1867; *and had issue.*
See the Clarence Volume, pp. 590–591, Nos. 25396–25397.

2b. *Hon. Theresa Robinson*, b. 1 *Jan.* 1744; d. 21 *Dec.* 1775; m. *as 2nd wife,* 18 *May* 1769, *John (Parker), 1st Baron Boringdon* [*G.B.*], d. 27 *Ap.* 1788; *and had issue* 1c *to* 2c.

1c. *John (Parker), 2nd Baron Boringdon* [*G.B.*] *and* (1815) 1*st Earl of Morley* [*U.K.*], *F.R.S.,* b. 3 *May* 1772; d. 14 *Mar.* 1840; m. 2*ndly,* 23 *Aug.* 1809, *Frances, da. of Thomas Talbot of Gonville, co. Norfolk,* d. 7 *Dec.* 1857; *and had issue* 1d.

1d. *Edmund (Parker), 2nd Earl of Morley* [*U.K.*], 3*rd Baron Boringdon* [*G.B.*], b. 10 *June* 1810; d. 28 *Aug.* 1864; m. 1 *Mar.* 1842, *Harriet Sophia, widow of William Coryton of Pentillie Castle, da. of Montagu Edmund Parker of Whiteway, co. Devon,* d. 15 *Feb.* 1897; *and had issue* 1e *to* 2e.

1e. *Albert Edmund (Parker), 3rd Earl of Morley* [*U.K.*], 4*th Baron Boringdon* [*G.B.*], *P.C.,* b. 11 *June* 1843; d. 26 *Feb.* 1905; m. 17 *June* 1876, *Margaret, da. of Robert Stayner Holford of Westonbirt, co. Glouc., and Dorchester House, Park Lane, M.P.; and had issue* 1f *to* 4f.

1f. Edmund Robert (Parker), 4th Earl of Morley [U.K.], 5th Baron Boringdon [G.B.] (*Saltram, near Plympton, Devon; 31 Princes Gardens, S.W.*), b. 19 Ap. 1877.

2f. Hon. Montagu Brownlow Parker, Lieut. Grenadier Guards, and A.D.C. to Major-Gen. Comdg. Home Dist., b. 13 Oct. 1878.

3f. Hon. John Holford Parker, b. 22 June 1886.

4f. Lady Mary Theresa Parker, b. 13 Dec. 1881.

2e. Lady Emily Katherine Parker (*Whiteway, Chudleigh, Devon*).

2c. *Hon. Theresa Parker*, b. 22 *Sept.* 1775; d. 12 *Jan.* 1856; m. 17 *Ap.* 1798, the Hon. George Villiers, d. 21 *Mar.* 1827; *and had issue.*
See pp. 379–384, Nos. 26875–27057.   [Nos. 54206 to 54395.

572. Descendants of FRANCES FRANKLAND (see Table LX.), wife of ROGER TALBOT.

573. Descendants, if any surviving, of GRACE FRANKLAND (see Table LX.), *m.* LEONARD SMELT of Kirkby Fletham; and had issue.[1]

574. Descendants, if any surviving, of BARBARA MABELLA WEBB (see Table LXI.), *d.* 1770; *m.* as 1st wife, *a.* 1758, Sir EDWARD HALES, 5th Bart. (and[2] 3rd EARL OF TENTERDEN) [E.], *d.* Aug. 1802; and had issue 1*a* to 3*a*.

1a. *Sir Edward Hales, 6th Bart.* [*E.*], b. 1758; d.s.p. 15 *Mar.* 1829.
2a. *Barbara Hales*, m. [——] *Jouchere, a French Officer.*
3a. *Mary Hales*, m. [——] *Demorlaincourt, a French Officer.*

575. Descendants of BARBARA WEBB (see Table LXI.), *d.* (at Florence) 5 Oct. 1819; *m.* 17 July 1786, ANTHONY (ASHLEY-COOPER), 5th EARL OF SHAFTESBURY [E.], *b.* 17 Sept. 1671; *d.* 14 May 1811; and had issue.

See the Tudor Roll of "The Blood Royal of Britain," Table XCVIII. and p. 428, Nos. 30995–31028.   [Nos. 54396 to 54429.

---

[1] Burke's "Peerage," 1902; p. 621.
[2] By creation of King James II. and VII., 3 May 1692.

576. Descendants of Lady MARY RADCLIFFE (see Table LXI.), *d.* 31 Jan. 1760; *m.* 2 May 1732, ROBERT JOHN (PETRE), 8th BARON PETRE [E.], *b.* 3 June 1713; *d.* 2 July 1742; and had issue.

See the Clarence Volume, pp. 424–427, Nos. 16381–16735.

[Nos. 54430 to 54783.

577. Descendants of MARY WEBB (see Table LXI.), *d.* 22 Jan. 1719; *m.* 1714, JAMES (WALDEGRAVE), 1st EARL [G.B.] and 2nd BARON [E.] WALDEGRAVE, K.G., *b.* 1684; *d.* 11 Ap. 1741; and had issue 1*a* to 3*a*.

1*a. James (Waldegrave), 2nd Earl [G.B.] and 3rd Baron [E.] Waldegrave, K.G., P.C.,* b. *4 Mar.* 1715; d. *13 Ap.* 1763; m. *15 May* 1759, *Maria, illegitimate da. of the Hon. Sir Edward Walpole, K.B. (who re-m. 6 Sept.* 1766, *H.R.H. Prince William Henry (Guelph), 1st Duke of Gloucester and Edinburgh [G.B.], by whom she had issue, and)* d. *22 Aug.* 1807; *and had issue* 1*b to* 3*b.*

1*b. Lady Elizabeth Laura Waldegrave,* b. *24 Mar.* 1760; d. *29 Jan.* 1816; m. *5 May* 1782, *George (Waldegrave). 4th Earl of [G.B.] and 4th Baron [E.] Waldegrave,* d. *22 Oct.* 1789; *and had issue.*

See pp. 178–180, Nos. 6402–6449.

2*b. Lady Charlotte Maria Waldegrave,* b. *11 Oct.* 1761; d. *1 Feb.* 1808; m. *16 Nov.* 1784, *George Henry (FitzRoy), 4th Duke of Grafton [E.], K.G.,* d. *28 Sept.* 1844; *and had issue.*

See the Clarence Volume, Table XXXVI. and pp. 338–342, Nos. 10843–10938.

3*b. Lady Anna Horatia Waldegrave,* b. *8 Nov.* 1762; d. *12 July* 1801; m. *2 Ap.* 1786, *Admiral Lord Hugh Seymour,* d. *11 Sept.* 1801; *and had issue.*

See the Clarence Volume, Table XII. and pp. 132–141, Nos. 1683–1905.

2*a. John (Waldegrave), 3rd Earl [G.B.] and 5th Baron [E.] Waldegrave,* b. *28 Ap.* 1718; d. *22 Oct.* 1784; m. *7 July* 1751, *Lady Elizabeth, da. of John (Leveson-Gower), 1st Earl Gower [G.B.],* d. *28 Ap.* 1784; *and had issue.*

See pp. 178–182, Nos. 6402–6494.

3*a. Lady Henrietta Waldegrave,* b. *2 Jan.* 1717; d. *31 May* 1753; m. *7 July* 1734, *Lord Edward Herbert,* d. *Nov.* 1734; *and had issue* 1*b.*

1*b. Barbara Herbert,* b. *(posthumous) 24 June* 1735; d. c. 1786; m. *30 Mar.* 1751, *Henry Arthur (Herbert), 1st Earl of Powis [G.B.],* b. c. 1703; d. *10 Sept.* 1772; *and had issue.*

See the Tudor Roll of " The Blood Royal of Britain," Table XCI. and pp. 431–433, Nos. 31124–31221.

[Nos. 54784 to 55342.

578. Descendants of BARBARA WEBB (see Table LXI.), *b. c.* 1699; *d.* 7 Ap. 1779; *m.* 28 July 1720, ANTHONY (BROWNE), 6th VISCOUNT MONTAGU [E.], *b.* 1686; *d.* 23 Ap. 1767; and had issue.

See the Clarence Volume, Table XLV. and p. 394, Nos. 15001–15076.

[Nos. 55343 to 55516.

# of The Blood Royal

579. Descendants of MARY (? SARAH) SLINGSBY, Maid of Honour to Queen Anne (see Table LXII.), *d.* (–); *m.* 18 Aug. 1714, THOMAS DUNCOMBE of Duncombe and Helmsley, High Sheriff co. York 1728, *d.* 23 Mar. 1746 ; and had issue 1*a* to 4*a*.

1*a*. *Thomas Duncombe of Duncombe and Helmsley,* d. 25 Nov. 1779 ; m. 1st, 9 Feb. 1740, *Lady Diana, da. of Henry (Howard), 4th Earl of Carlisle* [E.], bapt. 24 Mar. 1724 ; d. 6 Mar. 1770 ; 2ndly, [——], *da. of Sir Philip Jennings Clarke, 1st Bart.* [G.B.] ; *and had issue* 1*b to* 2*b.*

1*b.* (*da. by 1st wife*). See p. 308, Nos. 19416–19495.

2*b. Frances Duncombe,* d. 12 Oct. 1861 ; m. 6 *June* 1796, *the Right Hon. Sir George Henry Rose, G.C.H., P.C., M.P. ; d.* 18 *June* 1855 ; *and had issue* (*with* 3 *other das.*) 1*c* to 5*c.*

1*c. Charles Philip Rose.*

2*c. Hugh Henry* (*Rose*), *1st Baron Strathnairn* [U.K.], *P.C., G.C.B., G.E.S.T., K.L.H., Field-Marshal,* b. 6 *Ap.* 1803 ; d.s.p. 16 *Oct.* 1885.

3*c. Arthur Robert Rose.*

4*c.* Frederick Edward Rose.

5*c. Frances Theodora Rose,* d. 12 *July* 1879 ; m. 3 *July* 1817, *George Sholto* (*Douglas*), *19th Earl of Morton* [S.], b. 23 *Dec.* 1789 ; d. 31 *Mar.* 1858 ; *and had issue* 1*d to* 10*d.*

1*d. Sholto John* (*Douglas*), *20th Earl of Morton* [S.], b. 13 *Ap.* 1818 ; d. 24 Dec. 1884 ; m. 1st, 24 *Jan.* 1844, *Helen, da. of James Watson of Saughton ;* d. 23 Dec. 1850 ; *and had issue* 1*e.*

1*e.* Sholto George Watson (Douglas), 21st Earl of Morton [S.], a Rep. Peer (*Dalmahoy, Midlothian ; Aberdour, Fife ; Loddington Hall, Leic., &c.*), *b.* 5 Nov. 1844 ; *m.* 25 July 1877, the Hon. Ellen Geraldine, da. of Charles Frederick (Ponsonby), 20th Baron De Mauley [U.K.] ; and has issue 1*f* to 5*f.*

1*f.* Sholto Charles Watson Douglas, Lord Aberdour (*Strouchreggan, Fort William*), *b.* 4 Dec. 1878 ; *m.* 7 June 1905, Minnie Christina Brenda, da. of Admiral of the Fleet, Lord John Hay, G.C.B.

2*f.* Hon. Charles William Sholto Douglas, *b.* 19 July 1881.

3*f.* Hon. Archibald Roderick Douglas, *b.* 11 Sept. 1883.

4*f.* Hon. William Sholto Douglas, *b.* 11 June 1886.

5*f.* Hon. Ronald John Sholto Douglas, *b.* 22 Ap. 1890.

2*d. Hon. George Henry Douglas, Admiral R.N.,* b. 5 Oct. 1821 ; d. 19 *June* 1905 ; m. 15 *July* 1850, *Charlotte Martha* (10 *Park Crescent, Portland Place*), *da. of Admiral Sir William Parker, 1st Bart.* [U.K], *G.C.B. ; and had issue* 1*e to* 2*e.*

1*e.* George Sholto Douglas, *late* Capt. 1st Batt. Cameronians (*Newtonairds, Dumfries*), *b.* 27 Ap. 1858 ; *m.* 30 Ap. 1889, Lady Laura Mary, da. of William Wentworth Fitzwilliam, Viscount Milton ; and has issue.

See p. 254, Nos. 9637–9640.

2*e.* Blanche Douglas, *m.* 29 Sept. 1887, George Ponsonby Talbot (*Cortworth House, Wentworth, Rotherham*) ; and has issue 1*f* to 2*f.*

See the Clarence Volume, p. 336, Nos. 9974–9975.

3*d.* Rev. the Hon. Henry Douglas, M.A., D.C.L. (U.S.) (*Uplands, Worcester*), *b.* 17 Dec. 1822 ; *m.* 7 June 1855, Lady Mary, da. of George (Baillie-Hamilton), 10th Earl of Haddington [S.] ; *d.* 29 Mar. 1904 ; and has issue 1*e.*

1*e.* Mary Douglas.

4*d.* Hon. Edward William Douglas, J.P., D.L. (*Heatherlea, Christchurch*), *b.* 19 Oct. 1825 ; *m.* 1st, 16 July 1857, Augusta Ann, da. of the Right Hon. George Bankes, *d.s.p.* 6 May 1880 ; 2ndly, 27 Sept. 1881, the Hon. Evelyn Anne, da. of Charles Rudolph (Trefusis), 19th Baron Clinton [E.] ; and has issue 1*e.*

1*e.* Gertrude Evelyn Augusta Douglas, *b.* 19 Jan. 1883.

[Nos. 55517 to 55615.

The Plantagenet Roll

5d. Right Rev. the Hon. Arthur Gascoigne Douglas, Lord Bishop of Aberdeen and Orkney, D.D., D.C.L., b. 5 *Jan.* 1827; d. 19 *July* 1905; m. 17 *April* 1855, *Anna Maria Harriet* (57 *Queen's Road, Aberdeen*), *da. of Richard Richards of Caerynwch; and had issue* 1e to 9e.

1e. Sholto James Douglas, b. 21 Aug. 1866.

2e. Arthur Hugh Douglas, b. 14 Sept. 1867.

3e. Rev. Archibald William Douglas, Rector of Hatherop and Gloucester (*Hatherop Rectory, Gloucester*), m. 1902, Ursula Helen, da. of Capt. Robert Watts Davies of Bloxham, R.N.; and has issue 1f.

1f. Helen St. Bride Douglas, b. 14 July 1904.

4e. Helen Douglas.

5e. Margaret St. Bride Douglas.

6e. Ela Douglas, m. 10 Feb. 1892, the Rev. Charles Rowland Fawke, M.A., (*Newland Cottage, Malvern Links*); and has issue 1f.

1f. Charles Arthur Freer Fawke, b. 9 Jan. 1893.

7e. Cecil Douglas.

8e. Annie Lilla Douglas, m. 19 Oct. 1887, Major Henry Bayly, Gordon Highlanders; d. 1892; and has issue.

9e. Beatrice Mary Douglas.

6d. Lady Frances Harriet Douglas, b. 29 *Sept.* 1819; d. 15 *June* 1895; m. 10 *Sept.* 1838, *William Thomas Spencer* (*Wentworth-Fitzwilliam*), 6th [I.] *and* 4th [G.B.] *Earl Fitzwilliam, K.G.;* d. 20 *Feb.* 1902; *and had issue.*

See pp. 254–255, Nos. 9632–9661.

7d. Lady Ellen Susan Anne Douglas, V.A. (*The Close, Salisbury*), b. 25 Sept. 1824; m. 15 July 1851, Rev. the Hon. Douglas Hamilton-Gordon; d. 6 Sept. 1901; and has issue.

See the Tudor Roll of "The Blood Royal of Britain," pp. 464–465, Nos. 32785–32794.

8d. Lady Alice Louisa Douglas (*Clovelly, Budleigh Salterton, Devon*), b. 18 Sept. 1830; m. 26 June 1862, the Right Rev. Alexander Ewing, Lord Bishop of Argyll and the Isles, D.C.L., *d.s.p.* 22 May 1873.

9d. Lady Gertrude Jane Douglas, b. 7 Sept. 1836; m. 6 Oct. 1860, the Hon. Mark George Kerr Rolle (R.L. 30 Jan. 1852), previously Trefusis (*Stevenstone, Torrington, N. Devon, &c.*); and has issue.

See the Tudor Roll of "The Blood Royal of Britain," p. 170, Nos. 20203–20204.

10d. Lady Agnes Charlotte Douglas, b. 6 Dec. 1842; m. as 2nd wife, 9 Aug. 1883, Gen. Sir Owen Tudor Burne, G.C.I.E., K.C.S.I. (132 *Sutherland Avenue, Maida Vale, &c.*).

2a. Charles Slingsby Duncombe of Duncombe and Helmsley, d. 11 *Sept.* 1803; m. *Isabel, da. of Robert Soleby of Helmsley,* d. 18 *Ap.* 1800; *and had issue (with several das.)* 1b. *to* 3b.

1b. *Charles* (*Duncombe*), 1st *Baron Feversham* [U.K.], b. 5 *Dec.* 1764; d. 16 *July* 1841; m. 24 *Sept.* 1795, *Lady Charlotte, da. of William* (*Legge*), 2nd *Earl of Dartmouth* [G.B.], d. 5 *Nov.* 1848; *and had issue* 1c *to* 6c.

1c. *William* (*Duncombe*), 2nd *Baron Feversham* [U.K.], b. 14 *Jan.* 1798; d. 11 *Feb.* 1867; m. 18 *Dec.* 1823, *Lady Louisa, da. of James* (*Stewart*), 8th *Earl of Galloway* [S.], K.T., d. 5 *Mar.* 1889; *and had issue.*

See the Tudor Roll of "The Blood Royal of Britain," pp. 500–502, Nos. 34067–34121.

2c. Hon. Arthur Duncombe of Kilnwick Percy, Admiral R.N., M.P., &c., b. 24 *Mar.* 1806; d. 6 *Feb.* 1889; m. 1st, 14 *July* 1836, *Delia, da. and co-h. of John Wilmer Field of Heaton Hall, co. Yorks,* d. 5 *May* 1873; *and had issue* 1d *to* 7d.

[Nos. 55616 to 55728.

646

# of The Blood Royal

1*d*. Charles Wilmer Duncombe, J.P., Major-Gen. *formerly* Lieut.-Col. Comdg. 1st Life Guards (*Kilnwick-Percy, Pocklington, Yorks*), *b.* 19 Sept. 1838.

2*d*. Arthur Duncombe, now (R.L. 9 Oct. 1905) Grey, J.P., D.L., M.A. (Oxon.), Chairman E. Riding Quarter Sessions, *formerly* (1885–1892) M.P. (*Sutton Hall, Easingwold; Bradgate House, Leicester*), *b.* 11 Feb. 1840 ; *m.* 12 June 1869, Katharine Henrietta Venezia, da. of Henry John Newsham Milbank ; and has issue. See the Clarence Volume, p. 255, Nos. 6145–6146.

3*d*. *Frederic William Duncombe, Capt. Grenadier Guards,* b. 28 *Jan.* 1842 ; d. 6 *Feb.* 1878 ; *m.* 28 *July* 1868, *Lady Katherine, da. of Archibald (Acheson), 3rd Earl of Gosford [I.], K.P.,* d. 5 *Mar.* 1898 ; *and had issue* 1e *to* 3e.

1*e*. Basil Archibald Charles Duncombe (*Ampthill, St. John's, Ryde, I.W.*), *b.* 12 Jan. 1870 ; *m.* 12 Jan. 1896, Ida, da. of Alfred Hope Doeg ; and has issue 1*f* to 3*f*.

1*f*. Hubert Basil Elliot Duncombe, *b.* 21 May 1901.

2*f*. Phyllis Gertrude Duncombe.

3*f*. Katharine Duncombe.

2*e*. Wilfred Duncombe, now (R.L. 6 June 1905) Duncombe-Anderson, Lieut. Reserve of Officers (*Lea Hall, Gainsborough*), *b.* 30 Sept. 1871 ; *m.* 7 June 1905, Margaret Louisa, da. and co-h. of Francis Anderson (eldest surv. son of Sir Charles Henry John Anderson of Broughton, 9th and last Bart. [E.]).

3*e*. Ethel Coralie Duncombe, *m.* 11 July 1900, John Quayle (*New Valley, Norwood, Ceylon*).

4*d*. George Augustus Duncombe, J.P., D.L., Hon. Col. 3rd Batt. E. Yorkshire Regt. (*St. Mary's, Beverley, Yorks*), *b.* 25 May 1848 ; *m.* 15 July 1890, Hester, da. of Col. Allardice of Scarborough ; and has issue 1*e*.

1*e*. Archibald Charles Duncombe, *b.* 16 June 1894.

5*d*. *Charlotte Duncombe,* b. 21 *Aug.* 1837 ; d. 30 *Nov.* 1904 ; m. 1*st*, 12 *May* 1859, *Capt. Joseph Alfred Sykes of Raywell, co. York, 94th Regt.,* d. 1 *Sept.* 1865 ; 2*ndly,* 29 *Ap.* 1889, *the Rev. William Rowe Jolley, M.A., Dep. Clerk of the Closet* (*Tranby House, Westwood, Scarborough*); *and had issue* 1e *to* 2e.

1*e*. Henry Arthur Sykes, *b.* 1864.

2*e*. Mary Augusta Sykes.

6*d*. Mary Louisa Duncombe (*The Firs, Clifton, Bristol*), *m.* 1st, 21 Feb. 1871, the Hon. Ashley Carr Glyn, *d.* 11 Sept. 1875 ; 2ndly, 22 June 1886, the Right Rev. Isaac Hellmuth, D.D., D.C.L., sometime (1871–1883) Bishop of Huron, *d.* 28 May 1901 ; and has issue 1*e* to 2*e*.

1*e*. Delia Mary Glyn, *m.* 7 Jan. 1897, Paul Winsloe Phillipps.

2*e*. Mildred Glyn, *m.* 4 Oct. 1899, the Rev. Raymond Alured Bond, Vicar of Woodbastwick (*Woodbastwick Vicarage, Norwich*); and has issue 1*f*.

1*f*. Ashley Raymond Bond, *b.* 18 Aug. 1902.

7*d*. Edith Frances Duncombe, *m.* 22 Ap. 1873, Rear-Admiral Charles Francis Walker, R.N. (*The Hall, Beverley*) ; and has issue 1*e* to 2*e*.

1*e*. Edgar Wilmer Walker, *b.* 3 Aug. 1875.

2*e*. Philip Charles Walker, *b.* 1 Sept. 1878.

3*c*. *Very Rev. the Hon. Augustus Duncombe, D.D., Dean of York,* b. 2 *Nov.* 1814 ; d. 26 *Jan.* 1880 ; *m.* 13 *May* 1841, *Lady Harriet Christian, da. of Charles* (*Douglas*), *5th Marquis of Queensberry* [S.], d. 26 *July* 1902 ; *and had issue* 1d *to* 3d.

1*d*. Alfred Charles Duncombe, J.P., *late* Capt. 1st Life Guards, &c., High Sheriff co. Stafford 1883 (*Calwich Abbey, Stafford*), *b.* 5 June 1843 ; *m.* 5 Dec. 1876, Lady Anne Florence Adelaide, da. of William (Montagu), 7th Earl of Sandwich [E.].

2*d*. Augustus Gerald Duncombe (*Arthur's*), *b.* 9 Aug. 1849.

3*d*. Eleanor Harriet Duncombe. [Nos. 55729 to 55752.

The Plantagenet Roll

4c. Hon. Octavius Duncombe of Waresley Park, co. Beds, M.P., b. 8 *Ap.* 1817; d. 3 Dec. 1879; m. 31 *Mar.* 1842, *Lady Emily Caroline, da. of John Frederick (Campbell), 1st Earl Cawdor* [*U.K.*]; *and had issue.*

See the Tudor Roll of "The Blood Royal of Britain," p. 216, Nos. 21780–21789.

5c. Hon. Frances Duncombe, b. *June* 1802; d. 15 *June* 1881; m. 31 *May* 1832, *Sir Thomas Digby Legard of Ganton, 8th Bart.* [*E.*], b. 30 *May* 1803; d. 10 *Dec.* 1860; *and had issue* 1d *to* 4d.

1d. Sir Francis Digby Legard, 9th Bart. [*E.*], b. 8 *May* 1833; d. *unm.* (*at Madeira*) 5 *Jan.* 1865.

2d. Sir D'Arcy Widdrington Legard, 10th Bart. [*E.*], b. 10 *Dec.* 1843; d. *unm.* (*at Rome*) 12 *Ap.* 1866.

3d. Sir Charles Legard, 11th Bart. [*E.*], b. 12 *Ap.* 1846; d.s.p. 6 *Dec.* 1901.

4d. Caroline Jane Legard, m. as 2nd wife, 18 Ap. 1865, William Henry (son of Sir John) Fife, d. 24 Feb. 1874; and has issue 1e to 4e.

1e. Herbert Legard Fife, J.P. (*Staindrop House, Staindrop, Darlington*), b. 6 Mar. 1866; m. 11 Feb. 1897, Florence Josephine, da. of Henry Toulmin of the Pré, St. Albans.

2e. Ronald D'Arcy Fife, Capt. Yorkshire Regt. and an A.D.C. to the Gov. of Madras, b. 19 Mar. 1868; m. 29 July 1898, Alice Louisa, da. of Arthur Duncombe, d. 1 Aug 1898.

3e. Lucy Caroline Fife, d. 26 Oct. 1901; m. 15 *July* 1897, *Robert Wilford* (*de Yarburgh-Bateson*), 3rd *Baron Deramore* [*U.K.*], (*Hislington Hall, York*); *and had issue* 1f.

1f. Hon. Moira Faith Lilian de Yarburgh-Bateson.

4e. Frances Lilian Fife, m. 9 Aug. 1893, Richard Lawson (*Ousecliffe, York*); and has issue 1f to 2f.

1f. Digby Richard Lawson, b. 9 Sept. 1894.

2f. Frances Cynthia Rosalys Lawson, b. 19 July 1897.

6c. Hon. Louisa Duncombe, b. 16 *Nov.* 1807; d. 18 *Nov.* 1852; m. 1 *Oct.* 1831, *John (Scott), 2nd Earl of* [*U.K.*] *and Baron* [*G.B.*] *Eldon, D.C.L.,* b. 10 *Dec.* 1805; d. 18 *Sept.* 1854; *and had issue* 1d *to* 6d.

1d. John (Scott), 3rd Earl of [U.K.] and Baron [G.B.] Eldon (*Stowell Park, Northleach, Gloucester;* 43 *Portman Square, W.*), b. 8 Nov. 1845; m. 1 July 1869, Henrietta Mina, da. of Capt. Henry Martin Turnor; and has issue.

See p. 591, Nos. 51408–51415.

2d. Lady Charlotte Elizabeth Scott, b. 26 *Aug.* 1834; d. 22 *Feb.* 1864; m. 9 *Oct.* 1856, *the Rev. Eldon Surtees Bankes, Rector of Corfe Castle; and had issue* 1e *to* 4e.

1e. Arthur Eldon Bankes, b. 28 Nov. 1857.

2e. Eustace Ralph Bankes (*Norden, Corfe Castle*), b. 9 Feb. 1861; m. 17 Jan. 1900, Grace, da. of Sir St. Vincent Alexander Hammick, 3rd Bart. [U.K.].

3e. Louisa Bankes.

4e. Charlotte Helen Bankes.

3d. Lady Augusta Henrietta Scott, m. 8 Sept. 1859, Thomas Francis (Fremantle), 2nd Baron Cottesloe [U.K.] and 3rd Baron Fremantle (1816) [Austria] (*Swanbourne, Winslow, Bucks;* 43 *Eaton Square, S.W.*); and has issue 1e to 5e.

1e. Hon. Thomas Francis Fremantle, J.P., D.L., Major 1st Bucks Rifle Vol. (V.D.), sometime (1900–1903) Assist.-Sec. to Sec. of State for War (*Wistow House, Chelsea Embankment, S.W.; The Old House, Swanbourne, &c.*), b. 5 Feb. 1862; m. 16 Ap. 1896, Florence, da. of Thomas Tapping; and has issue 1f to 5f.

1f. Thomas Francis Halford Fremantle, b. 20 Jan. 1897.

2f. John Walgrave Halford Fremantle, b. 2 Mar. 1900.

3f. Edward St. John Fremantle, b. 23 Aug. 1901.

4f. Florence Mary Fremantle, b. 11 Mar. 1898.

5f. Margaret Augusta Fremantle, b. 2 Dec. 1904.   [Nos. 55753 to 55789.

# of The Blood Royal

2e. Hon. Reginald Scott Fremantle (5 *Sloane Gardens, S.W.*), *b.* 11 Feb. 1863; *m.* 26 July 1900, Hilda Lucy, da. of E. M. Barry, R.A.; and has issue 1*f* to 3*f*.

1*f.* Gerald Barry Fremantle, *b.* 8 Jan. 1906.

2*f.* Rosamund Beatrice Fremantle, *b.* 17 Nov. 1902.

3*f.* Joan Lucy Fremantle, *b.* 16 June 1904.

3e. Hon. Cecil Fremantle (*Wellington*), *b.* 12 Dec. 1865.

4e. Hon. Walter Fremantle, now (Deed Poll 1901) Fremantle-Gaunt (*Savile*), *b.* 13 Mar. 1869.

5e. Hon. Mary Louisa Fremantle.

4d. *Lady Katharine Frances Scott,* b. 15 *Dec.* 1837; d. 19 *May* 1903; m. 2 *Sept.* 1858, *Gustavus Russell* (*Hamilton-Russell*), 8th *Viscount Boyne* [*I.*], 2nd *Baron Brancepeth* [*U.K.*]; *and had issue.*
See p. 492, Nos. 43147–43158.

5d. Lady Gertrude Louisa Scott, *m.* 18 Sept. 1860, Lord Eustace Brownlow Gascoyne-Cecil (*Lytchett Heath, Poole;* 111 *Eaton Square, S.W.*); and has issue.
See p. 217, Nos. 7676–7681.

6d. *Lady Selina Jane Scott,* b. 22 *Mar.* 1843; d. 17 *Dec.* 1891; m. 10 *Nov.* 1864, *Nathaniel Bond, J.P., D.L.* (*Creech Grange, near Wareham, Dorset*); *and had issue* 1e *to* 11e.

1e. John Wentworth Garneys Bond, J.P., D.L., Bar.-at-Law, a Clerk to the House of Commons (*Travellers'; Wellington*), *b.* 12 Sept. 1865.

2e. Gerald Denis Bond, J.P., Capt. 1st Vol. Batt. Dorset Regt. (*Holme Priory, Dorset*), *b.* 12 Sept. 1869.

3e. Rev. Raymond Alured Bond, Vicar of Woodbastwick (*Woodbastwick Vicarage, Norwich*), *b.* 16 Sept. 1873; *m.* 4 Oct. 1899, Mildred, da. of the Hon. Ashley Carr Glyn; and has issue 1*f*.

1*f.* Ashley Raymond Bond, *b.* 18 Aug. 1902.

4e. Claud Nathaniel Bond, *b.* 13 Oct. 1874.

5e. Kenneth Duncombe Bond, *b.* 5 Dec. 1875.

6e. Nigel de Mundeville Bond, *b.* 29 Aug. 1877.

7e. Herbert Ivo de Kenton Bond, *b.* 27 July 1879.

8e. Walter de Grey Bond, *b.* 13 Oct. 1882.

9e. Louisa Charlotte Bond.

10e. Leonora Sophia Bond.

11e. Rachel Adela Bond, *m.* 18 Sept. 1900, Capt. Paul Warner Bush, R.N.; and has issue 1*f* to 3*f*.

1*f.* George Victor Denis Cromwell Bush, *b.* 22 June 1901.

2*f.* Ronald Paul Bush, *b.* 22 Aug. 1902.

3*f.* Geoffrey Russell Bush, *b.* 8 Ap. 1904.

2b. *Thomas Duncombe of Copgrove, co. York,* b. 1769; d. 7 *or* 17 *Dec.* 1847; m. 24 *Sept.* 1795, *Emma, da. of the Right Rev. John Hinchliffe, D.D., Lord Bishop of Peterborough,* d. 23 *Jan.* 1840; *and had issue* 1c *to* 4c.

1c. *Rev. Henry John Duncombe, Rector of Kirby Sigston,* d. (–); m. 11 *Oct.* 1831, *Georgiana, da. of John Dowthwaite Nesham; and had issue* 1d *to* 2d.[1]

1d. Julia Duncombe.

2d. Elizabeth Duncombe, *m.* 12 Feb. 1861, Henry Bramwell, J.P., Capt. North Durham Militia (*Crown East Court, St. John's, Worcester*); and has issue 1e.

1e. Henry Duncombe Bramwell, Capt. 15th Hussars, *b.* 1869; *m.* 3 Nov. 1898, the Hon. Mary Emily, da. of Thomas Kane (M'Clintock-Bunbury), 2nd Baron Rathdonnel [I.].

2c. *Rev. Edward Duncombe, Rector of Barthomley,* b. 4 *May* 1802; d. 25 *Mar.*
[Nos. 55790 to 55834.

---

[1] Foster's "Peerage," 1880, p. 259.

1888; m. 22 *Nov.* 1825, *Susan, da. of the Rev. Charles Mainwaring of Oteley*, d. 1854; *and had issue* 1d *to* 2d.

    1d. Fanny Duncombe, *m.* 25 Oct. 1855, Charles Mostyn-Owen of Walton House, co. Oxon., *d.* 2 Sept. 1894; and has issue 1e to 5e.

        1e. Henry Mostyn-Owen, *b.* 26 Ap. 1858.

        2e. Charles Mostyn-Owen, *b.* 4 May 1859.

        3e. Hugh Mostyn-Owen, *b.* 3 Sept. 1860.

        4e. Florence Mostyn-Owen.

        5e. Diana Susan Mostyn-Owen, *m.* 20 Oct. 1898, Richard Henry Ramsden (*Boston House, Boston Spa*).

    2d. Emma Susan Duncombe, d. 25 *May* 1897; m. 1*st*, 28 *Jan.* 1858, *Ellis Gosling of Busbridge Hall, co. Surrey*, d. 26 *Jan.* 1861; 2*ndly*, 14 *Ap.* 1863, *Capt. John Charles Francis Ramsden, R.A., J.P., D.L.* (*Willinghurst, Guildford*); *and had issue* 1e *to* 6e.

        1e. Frederick William Ramsden, Capt. Reserve of Officers, *late* Coldstream Guards (5 *Upper Brook Street, W.*), *b.* 17 Feb. 1864; *m.* 30 July 1887, Lady Elizabeth Maud, da. of George Henry (Conyngham), 3rd Marquis Conyngham [I.]; and has issue 1f to 4f.

            1f. Charles Frederick Ingram Ramsden, *b.* 4 May 1888.

            2f. Cynthia Maud Ramsden.

            3f. Moyra Gwendolen Ramsden.

            4f. Enid Florence Beatrice Ramsden.

        2e. Richard Henry Ramsden (*Boston House, Boston Spa, Yorks*), *b.* 10 Nov. 1866; *m.* 20 Oct. 1898, Diana, da. of Charles Mostyn-Owen.

        3e. Caryl John Ramsden, *late* Capt. and Brevet-Major 1st Batt. Seaforth Highlanders (*White's*), *b.* 18 Dec. 1868.

        4e. Henry Ramsden, Capt. R.H.A. (*White's; Bachelors'*), *b.* 14 Mar. 1871; *m.* 3 June 1902, Dorothy Lynch, da. of Col. Edward Thomas Davenant Cotton-Jodrell, C.B.; and has issue 1f to 2f.

            1f. Susan Dorothy Ramsden, *b.* 28 Ap. 1903.

            2f. Barbara Ramsden, *b.* 6 Ap. 1905.

        5e. Josslyn Vere Ramsden, M.A. (Oxon.), Lieut. R.H.A. (*White's*), *b.* 1 Dec. 1876.

        6e. Vere Gosling, Lady of Justice of St. John of Jerusalem [E.], *m.* 24 July 1879, George Edmund Milnes (Monckton-Arundell), 7th Viscount Galway [I.], 1st Baron Monckton [U.K.] (*Serlby Hall, Bawtry, &c.*); and has issue.

See p. 168, Nos. 3628–3630.

    3c. Emma Duncombe, d. Dec. 1864; m. 15 *Sept.* 1821, *Col. Henry Dawkins of Over Norton, M.P.*, d. 13 *Nov.* 1864; *and had issue.*

See the Clarence Volume, p. 177, Nos. 2948–2960.

    4c. Harriet Duncombe, d. 1882; m. 20 Feb. 1834, *Richard Henry Vade, afterwards* (*R.L.* 31 *Oct.* 1844) *Vade-Walpole of Freethorpe, co. Norfolk*, d. (? s.p.).

    3b. Slingsby Duncombe of Winthorpe Hall, Capt. 1st Foot Guards, *b.* 21 Nov. 1779; d. 12 *Oct.* 1851; m. 23 *June* 1812, *Martha, da. of Henry Elvy*, d. 24 *Mar.* 1871; *and had issue* (*with several das.*) 1c.

        1c. George Thomas Duncombe, now (*R.L.* 1887) Peirse-Duncombe, *late* Capt. 11th Hussars (*Winthorpe Hall, Newark; 25 Queen's Gate, S.W.*), *b.* 14 June 1825; *m.* 27 July 1853, Arabella Georgina, da. and h. of Capt. Richard William Peirse of Northallerton, 3rd Dragoon Guards; and has issue 1d to 8d.

        1d. Charles Slingsby Peirse-Duncombe, *b.* 18 May 1870.

        2d. Richard Slingsby Peirse-Duncombe, *b.* 25 Aug. 1872; *m.* 1898, Josephine Foster.

        3d. Elizabeth Slingsby Peirse-Duncombe.

        4d. Georgiana Slingsby Peirse-Duncombe.

        5d. Edith Slingsby Peirse-Duncombe.   [Nos. 55835 to 55874.

6*d*. Ruth Slingsby Peirse-Duncombe, *m*. 5 May 1892, Comm. Richard Nigel Gresley, R.N. (*Rotherley Weeke, Winchester*) ; and has issue 1*e* to 2*e*.

1*e*. Roger Gresley, *b*. 26 Feb. 1895.

2*e*. Dorothy Gresley, *b*. 6 May 1893.

7*d*. Mildred Slingsby Peirse-Duncombe, *m*. 30 July 1888, Thomas Herbert Bindley ; and has issue 1*e* to 2*e*.

1*e*. Herbert Duncombe Bindley, *b*. 8 Feb. 1891.

2*e*. Mildred Duncombe Bindley, *b*. 12 Sept. 1889.

8*d*. Winifred Slingsby Peirse-Duncombe.

3*a*. *Henry Duncombe of Copgrove, co. Yorks, M.P.*, 1791 ; d. (*? unm*.).

4*a*. *Barbara Duncombe*, m. *Christopher Crow of Kiplin, co. York*.

[Nos. 55875 to 55881.

580. Descendants of ANNE TALBOT (see Table LXII.), *b. c.* 1665 ; *bur.* 19 Mar. 1720 ; *m.* (lic. Vic. Gen. Office, 15 May) 1683, Sir JOHN IVORY of New Ross, co. Wexford, M.P., *b. c.* 1656 ; *d.* 24 Feb. 1694 ; and had issue 1*α* to 3*α*.[1]

1*a*. *John Ivory, afterwards Talbot of Lacock, co. Wilts, and Selwarp, co. Worcester, LL.D., M.P., b. between* 1687–1692; *bur.* 16 *Nov.* 1772; *m. (lic. Vic. Gen. Office,* 30 *June*) 1716, *the Hon. Mary, da. and in her issue* (1786) *h. of Thomas* (*Mansel*), *1st Baron Mansel of Margam* [*G.B.*], *b.* 1 *Feb.* 1697 ; *bur.* 21 *Oct.* 1735 ; *and had issue* 1*b to* 3*b*.

1*b*. *John Talbot of Lacock, b.* 23 *Nov.* 1717 ; *bur. s.p.* 2 *May* 1778.

2*b*. *Rev. Thomas Talbot of Margam, co. Glamorgan, b.* 25 *Mar.* 1719 ; *d. Mar.* 1758 ; *m.* 1746, *Jane, da. of Thomas Beach of Keevil, co. Wilts, LL.D. ; and had issue* 1*c*.

1*c*. *Thomas Mansel Talbot of Margam,* d. 10 *May* 1813 ; *m. Feb.* 1794, *Lady Mary Lucy, da. of Henry Thomas* (*Fox-Strangways*), *2nd Earl of Ilchester* [*G.B.*], d. 3 *Feb.* 1855 ; *and had issue* 1*d to* 4*d*.

1*d*. *Christopher Rice Mansel Talbot of Margam and Penrice Castle, co. Glamorgan, M.P., b.* 10 *May* 1803 ; *d.* 17 *Jan.* 1890 ; m. 28 *Dec.* 1835, *Lady Charlotte, da. of Richard* (*Butler*), *1st Earl of Glengall* [*I.*], d. 22 *Mar.* 1846 ; *and had issue* 1*e to* 2*e*.

1*e*. Emily Charlotte Talbot of Margam and Penrice Castle (*Margam Park, Port Talbot ; Penrice Castle, Swansea ; 3 Cavendish Square, W.*).

2*e*. Bertha Isabella Talbot (*Saltoun Hall, co. Haddington*), *m.* 25 Oct. 1866, John Fletcher Fletcher of Saltoun, J.P., D.L., *d.* Jan. 1903 ; and has issue.

See the Clarence Volume, p. 256, Nos. 6148–6164.

2*d*. *Jane Harriot Talbot*, d. 11 *Jan.* 1874; *m.* 14 *Dec.* 1821, *the Right Hon. John Nicholl of Merthyr Mawr, co. Glamorgan, M.P., D.C.L., b.* 21 *Aug.* 1797 ; *d.* (*at Rome*) 27 *Jan.* 1853 ; *and had issue* 1*e to* 6*e*.

1*e*. *John Cole Nicholl of Merthyr Mawr, J.P., D.L., High Sheriff co. Glamorgan* 1884 ; *b.* 30 *Aug.* 1823 ; *d.* 20 *Mar.* 1894 ; *m.* 30 *May* 1860 *Mary de la Beche, da. of Lewis Llewelyn Dillwyn of Hendrefoilan, M.P. ; and had issue* 1*f to* 6*f*.

1*f*. John Iltyd Dillwyn Nicholl, J.P., D.L., High Sheriff co. Glamorgan, 1899 (*Merthyr Mawr, Bridgend, Glamorgan*), *b.* 1 May 1861 ; *m.* 23 Ap. 1889, Eleanor

[Nos. 55882 to 55900*a*.

---

[1] For the great majority of dates, most of which are now for the first time printed, and other particulars in this section, the author is indebted to C. H. Talbot of Lacock, Esq., and to Malcolm Low of Clatto, Esq., the latter gentleman having most courteously given him free access to his valuable MS. collection of notes on this and other allied families.

Dorothy, da. of John Battersby Harford of Blaine Castle, co. Gloucester, &c.; and has issue 1g to 5g.

    1g. John William Harford Nicholl, b. 24 Oct. 1892.

    2g. Robert Iltyd Nicholl, b. 29 Dec. 1896.

    3g. Gladys Mary Nicholl.

    4g. Olive Eleanor Nicholl.

    5g. Rachel Charlotte Nicholl.

    2f. Lewis Dillwyn Nicholl, b. 25 Sept. 1864; m. 10 Aug. 1898, Beatrice Lucy, da. of Major-Gen. Rice Nicholl; and has issue 1g.

    1g. David William Dillwyn Nicholl.

    3f. Rice Mansel Dillwyn Nicholl, now Dillwyn, b. 14 June 1875; m. Harriet, da. of Arthur Gilbertson of Glanrhyd, co. Glamorgan; and has issue 1g.

    1g. Theresa Harriet Dillwyn.

    4f. Mary Theresa Nicholl, m. 1885, John Fitzherbert Campbell (*Woodseat, Stafford*); and has issue 1g to 3g.

    1g. Colin Campbell.

    2g. Henry Campbell.

    3g. Gwenllian Mary Campbell.

    5f. Gwenllian Jane Nicholl, m. 1894, Henry Fleetwood Fuller (*Neaton Park, Wilts*); and has issue 1g to 3g.

    1g. Dillwyn Henry Fleetwood Fuller, b. 5 July 1896.

    2g. Mary Gwenllian Fuller, b. 5 Nov. 1894.

    3g. Joyce Fuller.

    6f. Dorothy Caroline Nicholl, m. 12 Ap. 1898, Charles Gresford Irving Edmondes (only son of the late Archdeacon Edmondes of Old Hall, Cowbridge); and has issue.

    2e. *Iltyd Thomas Mansel Nicholl, Capt. R.N., b. 19 May 1828; d. 17 Dec. 1885; m. 1st, 30 Sept. 1862, Cecilia Mary Josephine, da. and co-h. of Admiral Arthur William Jerningham, d. 15 Feb. 1879; 2ndly, Isabel, da. of [——] Strickland; and had issue 1f to 7f.*

    1f.–6f. (Children by 1st wife.) See the Clarence Volume, p. 106, Nos. 1027–1035.

    7f. Carmela Nicholl.

    3e. Rev. Edward Powell Nicholl, M.A., Vicar of Ascot, b. 14 Aug. 1831; m. Ap. 1866, Sarah, da. of John Jenkins of Llanblethian; and has issue 1f to 6f.

    1f. Theodore Nicholl, b. Jan. 1867; m.; and has issue.

    2f. Gilbert Henry Nicholl, b. June 1871.

    3f. Hubert Mansel Nicholl, b. July 1872.

    4f. Denys Edward Nicholl, b. Oct. 1876.

    5f. Ernestine Mersa Nicholl, m.; and has issue.

    6f. Gwendoline Nicholl.

    3e. Rev. Stephen Fox Nicholl, M.A., Rector of Llandough (*Llandough Rectory, Glamorgan*), b. 28 July 1835; m. 21 Ap. 1868, Sarah Frances, da. of the Ven. T. King, Archdeacon of Rochester; and has issue 1f to 3f.

    1f. Henry Nicholl, m. Ethel, da. of [——] Bell; and has issue 1g.

    1g. Irene Nicholl.

    2f. Christopher Nicholl.

    3f. Archibald Nicholl, m. Ethel, da. of the Rev. [——] Heberden.

    4e. Christopher Rice Havard Nicholl, *late* Major-Gen. Rifle Brigade (*St. Hilary, near Cowbridge, Glamorgan*), b. 15 Dec. 1836; m. 23 Ap. 1868, Florence Emma, da. of the Rev. Charles Rumsey Knight of Tythegston Court; and has issue 1f to 9f.

    1f. Basil Rice Nicholl, Capt. 2nd Gurkhas.

    2f. Cecil Rice Nicholl, Lieut. R.N.

    3f. Edward Aubrey Rice Nicholl.

[Nos. 55901 to 55944.

4*f*. Beatrice Lucy Nicholl, *m*. 10 Aug. 1898, Lewis Dillwyn Nicholl; and has issue.

See p. 652, No. 55907.

5*f*. Mary Margaret Nicholl.
6*f*. Sylvia Jane Nicholl.
7*f*. Monica Nicholl.
8*f*. Olive Theresa Nicholl.
9*f*. Florence Mary Christina Nicholl.

5*e*. Spencer Perceval Talbot Nicholl, Major in the Army, *b*. 10 July 1841; *m*. Keziah, da. of [——] Sellar; and has issue 1*f* to 2*f*.

1*f*. Charles Nicholl.
2*f*. Ruth Nicholl.

6*e*. Katherine Maria Nicholl, *unm*.

3*d*. *Isabella Catherine Talbot*, d. (−); *m*. *Richard Franklin of Clemenstone, co. Glamorgan*, d. (−); *and had issue* 1*e* to 2*e*.

1*e*. Charles Franklin, Lieut.-Col. in the Army, *m*. Hilda, da. of A. D. Berrington of Panlygoitre; and has issue 1*f* to 3*f*.

1*f*. Eveline Franklin.
2*f*. Mary Franklin.
3*f*. Sysselt Franklin.

2*e*. Thomas Mansel Franklin, M.A. (Oxon.), *m*. Florence, da. of Thomas Allen of Freestone, co. Pembroke.

4*d*. *Emma Thomasina Talbot*, d. (−); *m*. 10 *June* 1833, *John Dillwyn-Llewelyn of Penllergare*, F.R.S., J.P., D.L., d. 24 *Aug*. 1882; *and had issue* 1*e* *to* 5*e*.

1*e*. Sir John Talbot Dillwyn-Llewelyn, 1st Bart. [U.K.], J.P., D.L. (*Penllergare, near Swansea; 39 Cornwall Gardens, S.W.*), *b*. 26 May 1836; *m*. 7 May 1861, Caroline Julia, da. of Sir Michael Hicks-Beach, 8th Bart. [E.]; and has issue 1*f* to 3*f*.

1*f*. Charles Leyshon Dillwyn-Llewelyn, now (R.L. 27 June 1893) Dillwyn-Venables-Llewelyn, J.P., D.L. (*Llysdinam, Newbridge-on-Wye, Radnor*), *b*. 29 June 1870; *m*. 23 Aug. 1893, Katherine Mina, da. of the Rev. Richard Lister Venables of Llysdinam; and has issue 1*g* to 3*g*.

1*g*. John Lister Dillwyn-Venables-Llewelyn.
2*g*. Charles Michael Dillwyn-Venables-Llewelyn.
3*g*. Agnes Barbara Dillwyn-Venables-Llewelyn.

2*f*. Gwendoline Harriet Dillwyn-Llewelyn.
3*f*. Gladys Mary Dillwyn-Llewelyn.

2*e*. Theresa Mary Dillwyn-Llewelyn, *m*. 29 June 1858, Mervin Herbert Nevil Story-Maskelyne, F.R.S., J.P., D.L., sometime (1880–1892) M.P., late Professor of Mineralogy at Oxford, and for twenty years Keeper of the Mineral Department at the British Museum, &c. (*Basset Down House, Swindon; Salthrop Lodge, Wroughton, Wilts*); and has issue 1*f* to 3*f*.

1*f*. Margaret Emma Story-Maskelyne.
2*f*. Mary Lucy Story-Maskelyne, *m*. 29 July 1885, Oakeley Arnold Forster, M.P.; and has issue 1*g* to 4*g*.

1*g*. William Edward Arnold-Forster, *b*. 8 May 1886.
2*g*. Mervyn Nevil Arnold-Forster, *b*. 21 Mar. 1886.
3*g*. John Anthony Arnold-Forster, *b*. 20 Sept. 1889.
4*g*. Hugh Christopher Arnold-Forster, *b*. 1890.

3*f*. Thereza Charlotte Story-Maskelyne, *m*. 7 Sept. 1892, Arthur Rücker, F.R.S.; and has issue 1*g*.

1*g*. Arthur Nevill Rücker, *b*. 26 June 1895.

3*e*. Emma Charlotte Dillwyn-Llewelyn, *m*. Henry Benyon Crichton, d. 1889; and has issue.

4*e*. Ellinor Amy Dillwyn-Llewelyn.
5*e*. Lucy Catharine Dillwyn-Llewelyn.

[Nos. 55945 to 55979.

The Plantagenet Roll

3b. Martha Talbot, bapt. 15 Nov. 1720, bur. 6 *May* 1790; m. 22 *July* 1751, *the Rev. William Davenport, LL.D., Rector of Bredon and Salwarpe;* bur. 7 *May* 1781; *and had issue* 1c *to* 2c.

1c. William Davenport, afterwards Talbot of Lacock Abbey, b. 1 *Aug.* 1763; d. 30 *July* 1800; m. 17 *Ap.* 1796, *Lady Elizabeth Theresa, da. of Henry Thomas (Fox-Strangways), 2nd Earl of Ilchester* [G.B.] *(who re-m.* 24 *Ap.* 1804, *Rear-Adm. Charles Feilding, R.N., and)* d. 12 *Mar.* 1846; *and had issue* 1d.

1d. William Henry Fox Talbot of Lacock Abbey, LL.D., F.R.S., M.P., High Sheriff co. Wilts, b. 11 *Feb.* 1800; d. 17 *Sept.* 1877; m. 20 *Dec.* 1832, *Constance, da. of Francis Mundy of Markeaton,* d. 9 *Sept.* 1880; *and had issue* 1e *to* 2e.

1e. Charles Henry Talbot, J.P. (*Lacock Abbey, Chippenham*), b. 2 Feb. 1842.

2e. Matilda Caroline Talbot, m. 16 June 1859, John Clark, *afterwards* Gilchrist-Clark of Speddoch, J.P., d. 18 Aug. 1881; and has issue 1f to 6f.

1f. John Henry Gilchrist-Clark, J.P., b. 25 *Aug.* 1861; d. unm. 17 *Oct.* 1902.

2f. Rev. William Gilchrist-Clark, now Clark-Maxwell of Carruchan, co. Kirkcudbright, Vicar of Clunbury (*Clunbury, Aston-on-Clun, co. Salop*), b. 28 May 1865; m. 25 June 1896, Harriet Alice, da. of the Rev. William Selwyn of Bromfield; and has issue 1g to 3g.

1g. George Selwyn Clark-Maxwell, b. 5 May 1900.

2g. John Noel Clark-Maxwell, b. 31 Mar. 1903.

3g. Katherine Mary Clark-Maxwell.

3f. Constance Gilchrist-Clark, m. 9 Jan. 1896, the Rev. Edward Hamilton Stewart, Rector of Croxdale (*Croxdale Rectory, Durham*); and has issue.

4f. Mary Emily Gilchrist-Clark (*Speddoch, Dumfries*).

5f. Matilda Theresa Gilchrist-Clark.

6f. Grace Elinor Horatia Gilchrist-Clark.

2c. Mary Davenport, b. 17 *Oct.* 1757; bur. 28 *Dec.* 1793; m. *as first wife,* 8 *May* 1782, *John Shakespear, sometime of Brookwood Park, and afterwards of Twyford Lodge, co. Hants, B.C.S.;* bapt. 23 *Mar.* 1749; d. 10 *Jan.* 1825; *and had issue* 1d *to* 5d.

1d. John Talbot Shakespear, B.C.S., Chief of Police, Upper and Lower Provinces, Presidency of Bengal at Calcutta, 1823; b. 15 *Ap.* 1783; d. *(at sea on board the ship "Rose")* 12 *Ap.* 1825; m. *(at Calcutta)* 28 *Mar.* 1803, *Amelia ("Emily"), da. of William Makepeace Thackeray of Hadley, co. Middlesex, B.C.S.,* bapt. 9 *Sept.* 1780; bur. *(at Calcutta)* 30 *Sept.* 1824; *and had issue* 1e *to* 6e.

1e. Sir Richard Campbell Shakespear, C.B., Col. Bengal Art., Resident and Agent to the Govt. in Central India, b. 11 *May* 1812; d. *(at Indore, India)* 28 Oct. 1861; m. *(at Agra)* 5 *Mar.* 1844, *Maria Sophia, da. of George Powney Thomson, B.C.S.; and had issue.*

2e. Emily Anne Shakespear, b. 8 *Ap.* 1804; d. 5 *May* 1887; m. 1821, *William Fleming Dick, B.C.S.; and had issue.*

3e. Augusta Ludlow Shakespear, b. *(in India)* 4 *Mar.* 1809; d. 16 *Aug.* 1892; m. *(at Mussoorie, India)* 10 *Ap.* 1829, *Gen. Sir John Low of Clatto, G.C.S.I., K.C.B., Mil. Member of Supreme Govt. of India, &c.;* b. 13 *Dec.* 1788; d. 10 *Jan.* 1880; *and had issue* 1f *to* 7f.

1f. William Malcolm Low of Clatto, J.P., D.L., B.C.S., sometime Commr. of the Nerbudda Division, and (1886–1892) M.P. Grantham, (*Clatto, Cupar, Fife;* 22 *Roland Gardens, S.W.*), b. (at Lucknow) 6 Nov. 1835; *m.* 30 July 1872, Lady Ida Matilda Alice, da. of William Basil Percy (Feilding), 7th Earl of Denbigh [E.] and 6th Earl of Desmond [I.]; and has issue 1g to 2g.

1g. Ida Mary Ursula Low, b. (at Pachmarhi, India) 8 May 1874.

2g. Hilda Lucy Adelaide Low, b. 23 May 1875; *m.* 9 Nov. 1899, William Arthur Mount of Wasing Place, Berks, sometime (1900–1905) M.P. (*Wasing Place, Berks*); and has issue 1h.

1h. William Malcolm Mount, b. 28 Dec. 1904.

[Nos. 55980 to 55993.

654

# of The Blood Royal

2*f*. Sir Robert Cunliffe Low, G.C.B., Gen. (ret.) (*Shalburne, Camberley*), b. (at Lucknow) 27 Jan. 1838; *m.* 23 Ap. 1862, Constance, da. of Capt. Robert Taylor, Bengal Army; *d.* (at Poona, India) 20 June 1900; and has issue 1*g* to 5*g*.

1*g*. Robert Balmain Low, D.S.O., Major Indian Staff Corps, *b.* 7 Oct. 1864; *m.* 7 Sept. 1899, Mabel Violet, da. of Major-Gen. O'Grady Haly, C.B.

2*g*. John Metcalfe Bruere Low, *b.* 3 Aug. 1882.

3*g*. Helen Graham Low, *b.* 12 Nov. 1872.

4*g*. Olive Talbot Low, *b.* 11 Mar. 1876; *m.* 13 Oct. 1899, Lieut.-Col. Henry Ernest Stanton, R.A., D.S.O.; and has issue 1*h* to 2*h*.

1*h*. Joseph Edward Low Stanton, *b.* 3 May 1905.

2*h*. Doris Constance Stanton, *b.* 22 June 1900.

5*g*. Emily Shakespear Low, *b.* 22 Nov. 1879; *m.* 17 Oct. 1903, Capt. James Leslie Alexander, 3rd Bombay Cavalry.

3*f*. John Alves Low, Capt. (ret.) R.A., *b.* (at Cape of Good Hope) 11 Jan. 1840; *m.* Jane, da. of William Hooper, Lieut. R.N.; and has issue 1*h*.

1*h*. Charlotte Low, *m.* 30 Aug. 1894, Frank Tate Ellis.

4*f*. *Irvine Low, Major Bengal Cav. and Dep. Commr. in Oude, b. (at Calcutta)* 27 *Dec.* 1841; d. (*at Simla*) 26 *June* 1881; m. 29 *Nov.* 1865, *Janet Agnes Harriet, da. of Sir William Liston-Foulis, 8th Bart.* [S.]; *and had issue* 1*g to* 3*g*.

1*g*. *Henry Robert Low,* b. (*at Lucknow*) 5 *Sept.* 1865; d. (*at Cape of Good Hope*) 3 *Feb.* 1902; m. (*at Cape of Good Hope*) 28 *Oct.* 1897, *Maria, da. of the Rev. N. I. Hofmeyer; and had issue* 1*h to* 2*h*.

1*h*. Irvine Low, *b.* 21 Oct. 1898.

2*h*. Mimi Low, *b.* 6 Nov. 1899.

2*g*. Nora Florence Charlotte Low, *b.* 20 Mar. 1874.

3*g*. Harriet Edith Low, *b.* (at Oonao, India) 26 Jan. 1876.

5*f*. *Charlotte Herbert Low,* b. (*at Lucknow*) 4 *May* 1833; d. (*at Simla*) 26 *Sept.* 1853; m., *as* 1*st wife*, 14 *Oct.* 1851, *Theophilus John, afterwards* (1853) *Sir Theophilus John Metcalfe, 5th Bart.* [*U.K.*], *C.B.,* b. 28 *Nov.* 1828; d. 8 *Nov.* 1883; *and had issue* 1*g*.

1*g*. Sir Charles Herbert Theophilus Metcalfe, 6th Bart. [U.K.] (2 *Victoria Mansions, S.W.*), *b.* 8 Sept. 1853.

6*f*. Augusta Georgina Low, *b.* 6 Ap. 1844; *unm.*

7*f*. Selina Morison Low, *b.* 23 Sept. 1845; *unm.*

4*e*. *Charlotte Mary Anne Shakespear,* b. 19 *Dec.* 1813; d. (*at Akyab, East Indies*) 26 *May* 1849; m. (*at Calcutta*) 25 *Ap.* 1833, *James Henry Crawford, B.C.S.; and had issue.*

5*e*. *Marianne Eliza Sparks Shakespear,* b. 16 *May* 1816; d. 23 *July* 1891; m. (*at Allahabad, India*) 1835, *Lieut.-Col. Archibald Irvine, C.B.*

6*e*. Sarah Eliza Donnithorne Shakespear, *b.* 14 Aug. 1820; *unm.*

2*d*. *William Oliver Shakespear, M.C.S., First Judge of Prov. Court (Western Div.),* b. 14 *July* 1784; d. (*at Telicherry*) 10 *Aug.* 1838; m.; *and had issue.*

3*d*. *Henry Davenport Shakespear, B.C.S., Member Supreme Govt. of India, at Calcutta,* b. 9 *Feb.* 1786; d. (*at Calcutta*) 20 *Mar.* 1838; m.; *and had issue.*

4*d*. *Arthur Shakespear, Capt.* 10*th Hussars,* b. 13 *July* 1789; d. 2 *July* 1845; m.; *and had issue.*

5*d*. *Mary Ann Shakespear,* b. 20 *Nov.* 1793; d. 18 *Nov.* 1850; m. 15 *May* 1829, *the Rev. Francis Thackeray;* d. 18 *Feb.* 1842; *and had issue.*

2*a*. *Talbot Ivory, went to Ireland; fate unknown.*

3*a*. *Barbara Ivory,* d. 1748; m. *as* 2*nd wife,* 18 *Aug.* 1715, *Henry Davenport of Worfield, co. Salop,* b. 10 *Feb.* 1678; d. 6 *Ap.* 1731; *and had issue* 1*b*.

1*b*. *Rev. William Davenport, LL.D., Rector of Bredon, co. Worcester,* b. 29 *May* 1725; bur. 7 *May* 1781; m. 22 *July* 1751, *Martha, da. of John Ivory, afterwards Talbot of Lacock; and had issue.*

See p. 654, Nos. 55980–56011.   [Nos. 55994 to 56043

The Plantagenet Roll

581. Descendants of HENRY (YELVERTON), 3rd EARL OF SUSSEX [G.B.], 3rd VISCOUNT DE LONGUEVILLE and 18th BARON GREY DE RUTHYN [E.] (see Table LXII.), *b.* 7 July 1728; *d.* 22 Ap. 1799; *m.* 1st, 17 Jan. 1757, HESTER, da. of John HALL of Mansfield Woodhouse, co. Notts, *d.* 11 Jan. 1777; and had issue 1*a.*

1*a.* Lady Barbara *Yelverton, b.* 19 *June* 1760; *d.v.p.* 8 *Ap.* 1781; *m. as 1st wife, Oct.* 1775, *Edward Thoroton Gould of Woodham Mansfield, co. Notts,* *d.* (–); *and had issue* 1*b to* 2*b.*

1*b.* Henry Edward *(Gould, afterwards (R.L.* 21 *Feb.* 1800) *Yelverton*), 19*th Baron Grey de Ruthyn* [E.], *b.* 8 *Sept.* 1780; *d.* 29 *Oct.* 1810; *m.* 21 *June* 1809, *Maria, da. of William Kelham of Ryton (who re-m.* 18 *Jan.* 1820, *Rev. the Hon. William Eden*), *b.* 10 *Aug.* 1792; *d.* 23 *Oct.* 1875; *and had issue* 1*c.*

1*c.* Barbara *(Yelverton),* suo jure 20*th Baroness Grey de Ruthyn* [E.], *b.* 29 *May* 1810; *d.* 18 *Nov.* 1858; *m.* 1st, 1 *Aug.* 1831, *George Augustus Francis (Rawdon-Hastings), 2nd Marquis of Hastings* [U.K.], *7th Earl of Loudoun* [S.], *3rd Earl of Moira* [I.], *Baron Botreaux, Hungerford, De Moleyns, and Hastings* [E.], *and 2nd Baron Rawdon* [G.B.], *d.* 13 *Jan.* 1844; *2ndly,* 9 *Ap.* 1845, *Admiral Sir Reginald Hastings Henry, afterwards Yelverton, R.N., D.C.B., d.* 23 *July* 1878; *and had issue* 1*d to* 7*d.*

1*d*–6*d.* (Children by 1st husband.) See the Clarence Volume, pp. 71–72, Nos. 1–31.

7*d.* (Daughter by 2nd husband.) See p. 469, Nos. 41495–41497.

2*b.* Mary Gould, *b.* 6 *May* 1778; *d.* 19 *Jan.* 1837; *m.* 15 *Oct.* 1807, *Rev. the Hon. Frederick Powys, b.* 13 *Mar.* 1782; *d.* 31 *Dec.* 1850; *and had issue* 1*c to* 2*c.*

1*c.* Barbara Yelverton Powys, *co-h. to her brothers, b. c.* 1807; *d.* 9 *Nov.* 1887; *m.* 17 *Sept.* 1844, *Roger Dawson of Tyddynroe, St. Asaph ; and had issue* 1*d.*

1*d.* Roger Yelverton Dawson, *afterwards* (under the will of his grandfather, the Earl of Sussex) Dawson-Yelverton, Bar.-at-Law, *b.* 15 June 1845; *m.* 30 May 1872, Ellen, da. of James Lawrence of Park Hill, Liverpool, J.P.; and has issue 1*e.*[1]

1*e.* Edith Longueville Dawson-Yelverton.

2*c.* Mary Powys, *co-h. to her brothers, d.* 9 *Ap.* 1872; *m.* 18 *Aug.* 1836, *Frederick Brooksbank Bicknell, d.* 17 *Ap.* 1851; *and had issue* 1*d to* 4*d.*[1]

1*d.* Marion Bicknell.

2*d.* Edith Bicknell.

3*d.* Frederica Bicknell.

4*d.* Henrietta Bicknell. [Nos. 56044 to 56083.

582. Descendants of BARBARA CALTHORPE (see Table LXII.), *b.* 1716; *d.* 13 Ap. 1782; *m.* as 2nd wife, 2 July 1741, Sir HENRY GOUGH, 1st Bart. [G.B.], M.P., *b.* 9 Mar. 1708; *d.* 8 June 1774; and had issue 1*a* to 5*a.*

1*a.* Henry *(Gough, afterwards (R.L.* 7 *May* 1783) *Gough-Calthorpe), 1st Baron Calthorpe* [G.B.], *b. c.* 1748; *d.* 16 *Mar.* 1798; *m.* 1 *May* 1785, *Frances, da. and co-h. of Gen. Benjamin Carpenter, b.* 10 *June* 1761; *d.* 1 *May* 1827; *and had issue* 1*b to* 3*b.*

1*b.* Charles *(Gough-Calthorpe), 2nd Baron Calthorpe* [G.B.], *b.* 22 *Mar.* 1786; *d. unm.* 5 *June* 1807.

---

[1] Foster's "Peerage," 1880, p. 389.

# of The Blood Royal

2b. George (Gough-Calthorpe), 3rd Baron Calthorpe [G.B.], b. 22 June 1787 ; d. unm. (at Lyons) Sept. 1851.

3b. Frederick (Gough-Calthorpe, afterwards (R.L. for self only 14 May 1845) Gough), 4th Baron Calthorpe [G.B.], b. 14 June 1790 ; d. 2 May 1868 ; m. 12 Aug. 1823, Lady Charlotte Sophia, da. of Henry Charles (Somerset), 6th Duke of Beaufort [E.], d. 12 Nov. 1865 ; and had issue.
See " The Tudor Roll of the Blood Royal of Britain," p. 520, Nos. 34874–34916.

2a. Rev. Richard Thomas Gough, M.A. (Oxon.), Rector of Ampton, co. Suffolk (1796), b. 13 Feb. 1752 ; d. (? unm.).

3a. John Calthorpe Gough, Bar.-at-Law, Commissioner of Bankrupts (1783), b. 18 Ap. 1754 ; d. (? unm.).

4a. Barbara Gough, b. 21 Mar. 1746 ; d. (–) ; m. 9 Jan. 1770, Isaac Spooner of Elmdon, co. Warwick.

5a. Charlotte Gough, b. 9 Dec. 1747 ; d. 8 Aug. 1783 ; m. 25 Jan. 1768, Sir John Palmer, 5th Bart. [E.], M.P., d. 11 Feb. 1817 ; and had issue.
See pp. 87–92, Nos. 423–574. [Nos. 56084 to 56278.

583. Descendants of MARY INGRAM and of DOROTHY CHOLMLEY, bapt. 15 Ap. 1587 ; m. 5 Nov. 1611, NICHOLAS BUSHELL of Whitby ; of HILDA CHOLMLEY, m. HUGH WRIGHT ; and of MARGARET CHOLMLEY, bapt. 26 July 1584 ; m. 1st, THOMAS MENILL of Hawnby ; 2ndly, TIMOTHY CUMYN of Durham (see Table LVIII.).

584. Descendants of BRIAN (FAIRFAX), 8th LORD FAIRFAX [S.] (see Table LXIII.), b. 1737 ; d. (at Mount Eagle, Va.) Aug. 1802 ; m. 1st, 1757, ELIZABETH, da. of Col. Jefferson CARY of Ceelys, Virginia, d. c. 1788 ; 2ndly, JENNY, da. of [——] DENISON ; and had issue 1a to 3a.

1a. Thomas (Fairfax), 9th Lord Fairfax [S.], b. 1762 ; d. (at Vaucluse, Va.) 21 Ap. 1846 ; m. 3rdly, c. 1800, Margaret, da. of William Herbert, d. 1860 ; and had issue 1b to 6b.

1b. Hon. Albert Fairfax of Vaucluse, Fairfax, co. Virginia, b. 15 Ap. 1802 ; d.v.p. 9 May 1835 ; m. 8 Ap. 1828, Caroline Eliza, da. of Richard Snowden of Oakland, Maryland (re-m. William Saunders and) d. 28 Dec. 1899 ; and had issue 1c to 2c.

1c. Charles Snowden (Fairfax), 10th Lord Fairfax [S.], Speaker of the Californian House of Delegates, b. (at Vaucluse, Virginia) 8 Mar. 1829 ; d.s.p. (at Baltimore) 7 Ap. 1869.

2c. John Contée (Fairfax), 11th Lord Fairfax [S.], M.D., b. 13 Sept. 1830 ; d. 28 Sept. 1900 ; m. 8 Oct. 1857, Mary (Northampton (Largo P.O.), Prince George's, co. Maryland), da. of Col. Edward Kirby, U.S. Army ; and had issue 1d to 6d.

1d. Albert Kirby (Fairfax), 12th Lord Fairfax [S.] (22 Upper George Street, Bryanston Square, W.), b. 23 June 1870.

2d. Hon. Charles Edmund Fairfax (162 East 46th Street, New York), b. 29 Ap. 1876.

3d. Hon. Caroline Snowden Fairfax.

4d. Hon. Josephine Fairfax, m. Mar. 1892, Tunstall Smith (520 Park Avenue, Baltimore, Maryland) ; and has issue 1e to 2e.

1e. Josephine Tunstall Smith, b. 29 May 1894.

2e. Louise Tunstall Smith, b. 19 July 1895.

5d. Hon. Mary Cecilia Fairfax. [Nos. 56279 to 56285.

The Plantagenet Roll

6d. Hon. Frances Marvin Fairfax, *m.* 28 Oct. 1903, Edward Lowndes Rhett (*Brooklyn, U.S.A.*).

2b. Hon. Henry Fairfax *of Ashgrove*, b. 4 *May* 1804; d. 14 *Aug.* 1847; m. 1827, *Anna Caroline, da. of the Hon. John Carlyle Herbert of Maryland, and had issue* 1c *to* 3c.

1c. Raymond Fairfax, C.E., *formerly* Major Confederate States Army, *b.* 19 July 1829; *m.* 7 Jan. 1865, Anna, da. of Sylvester L. Burford of Amherst, co. Virginia; and has issue 1*d* to 5*d*.

1d. Ronald Randolph Fairfax (*Roanoke, Virginia*), b. 22 Aug. 1870; *m.* 1901, Annie Ridge, da. of Charles Early of Washington.

2d. Guy Percy Fairfax, b. 21 Feb. 1872; *m.* 1900, Elsie Ida, da. of [——] Crook.

3d. Henry Raymond Fairfax, b. 2 Aug. 1875.

4d. Isabella Christian Fairfax.

5d. Ada Raymond Fairfax.

2c. Herbert Carlyle Fairfax, *formerly* Capt. Confederate States Army, *b.* 29 Ap. 1838; *m.* 3 June 1861, Jane Davies, da. of Dr. Frederick Baker; and has issue 1*d* to 2*d*.

1d. Eugenia Chalmers Fairfax.

2d. Caroline Herbert Fairfax.

3c. Henry Malcolm Fairfax, b. 9 Oct. 1849.

3b. Hon. Orlando Fairfax, M.D., *b.* 1806; d. 1882; m. 21 *May* 1829, *Mary Randolph, da. of Wilson Jefferson Cary of Carysbrooke, Virginia; and had issue* 1c *to* 5c.

1c. Ethelbert Fairfax, *formerly* Lieut. Confederate States Army (*Washington, U.S.A.*), *b.* 23 Jan. 1845.

2c. Thomas Fairfax (*Washington, U.S.A.*), *b.* 1849.

3c. Monimia Fairfax, d. (–); m. 1866, *the Hon. George Davis of Wilmington, North Carolina, Attorney-General Confederate States.*

4c. Jane Cary Fairfax.

5c. Mary Edith Fairfax, *m.* 1877, Dr. John Jaqueline Moncure.

4b. Hon. Eugenia Fairfax, *d.* (–); m. 1st, *Edgar Mason of Charles co., Maryland;* 2ndly, *Charles Keith-Hyde of New York.*

5b. Hon. Aurelia Fairfax, d. (–); m. 1852, *Col. James W. Irwin of Washington.*

6b. Hon. Monimia Fairfax, d. (–); m. 15 Nov. 1838, *Archibald Cary, d.* 1854.

2a. Hon. Ferdinand Fairfax of Shannon Hill, Jefferson co., Virginia, b. 1766; d. 24 *Sept.* 1820; m. *Elizabeth Blair, da. of Col. Wilson Miles Cary of Ceelys, Virginia, d.* 19 *Jan.* 1822; *and had issue* 1b *to* 4b.

1b. George William Fairfax, b. 5 *Nov.* 1797; d. (–); m. Nov. 1815, *Isabella, da. of Major W. Gibbs MacNeill of New York; and had issue* 1c.

1c. Donald MacNeill Fairfax, Rear-Admiral U.S. Navy, the only Fairfax who fought on the side of the North, b. 1821; d. 1894; m. 1st, 1854, *Virginia Cary, da. of Thomas Ragland of Virginia, d.* 1878; 2ndly, 1879, *Josephine, da. of Rear-Admiral A. H. Foote; and had issue* 1d.

1d. William MacNeill Fairfax (*Washington, Hagerstoun, Maryland*).

2b. Wilson Miles Cary Fairfax of Washington, b. 1 *Dec.* 1878; d. 8 *Aug.* 1860; m. 2 *Mar.* 1824, *Lucy Anna, da. of David Griffith of New York, d. Jan.* 1861; *and had issue* 1c *to* 3c.

1c. Frederick Fairfax, U.S. Coast Survey, b. 26 *Sept.* 1835; d. 3 *Mar.* 1904; m. 14 *Jan.* 1868, *Mary Allen* (235 *Second Street South, Capitol Hill, Washington*), *da. of Lieut.-Com. John Aquila Cooke, U.S.A.; and had issue* 1d *to* 2d.

1d. Lilian Vere Fairfax.

2d. Gwendolind Owner Fairfax.   [Nos. 56286 to 56303.

658

# of The Blood Royal

2c. *Emily Cary Fairfax*, b. 15 Dec. 1824; d. 19 *Mar*. 1894; m. 15 *May* 1848, *the Right Rev. Francis McNeece Whittle, D.D., LL.D., Bishop of Virginia*, d.; *and had issue* 1d *to* 5d.

  1d. Fortescue Whittle, b. 20 May 1852.

  2d. Francis McNeece Whittle, b. 20 May 1856.

  3d. *Llewelyn Fairfax Whittle*, b. 22 Nov. 1858; d. (? s.p.) *before* 1901.

  4d. *Lucy Tucker Whittle*, d. 2 *Aug*. 1876; m. 19 *Nov*. 1873, *John N. Upsher, M.D.; and had issue* 1e.

    1e. Francis Whittle Upsher, b. 4 Dec. 1874.

  5d. Emily Cary Whittle.

  3c. Anne Fairfax (*Richmond, Va.*).

3b. *Ferdinando Fairfax of King George co., Virginia, M.D.*, b. 9 *Jan*. 1803 d. 30 *Dec*. 1873; m. 1st, 11 *Jan*. 1831, *Mary Anne, da. of Baily Jett of Westmoreland co., Va.*, d. 6 *May* 1848; 2ndly, 28 *Nov*. 1855, *Mary Jane, cousin german of the preceding, da. of James Jett*, d. 15 *July* 1864; *and had issue* 1c *to* 7c.

  1c. William Henry Fairfax, M.D., Treasurer of Westmoreland, *formerly* Surgeon Confederate States Army (*Montross, Westmoreland co., Va.*), b. 10 Dec. 1834; *m.* 26 Feb. 1866, Eleanor, da. of Edward Colville Griffith of Westmoreland co.; and has issue 1d.

    1d. Frederick Griffith Fairfax, b. 25 Oct. 1867, *m.* 29 Ap. 1903, Mary Fernando Fairfax, da. of Capt. Edmund Wharton; and has issue 1e to 2e.

      1e. William Henry Fairfax, b. 27 Oct. 1904.

      2e. Edith Wharton, b. 1 Dec. 1905.

  2c.[1] Emma Fairfax, *m.* 23 Dec. 1870, James Chandler; and has issue 1d.

    1d. Juliette Critcher Chandler, b. (at Bannockburn, Tipton co., Tennessee) 23 Ap. 1873; *m.* John A. Wharton.

  3c.[1] Ella Louisa Fairfax, *m.* Capt. Edmund Wharton, C.S.A.; and has issue (at least) 1d.

    1d. Mary Fernando Wharton, *m.* 29 Ap. 1903, Frederick Griffith Fairfax; and has issue.

    See p. 659, Nos. 56311–56312.

  4c.[2] Evangeline May Fairfax (*Arkansas*), *m.* White Boyd; d. (–).

  5c.[2] Mary Jett Fairfax, *m.* William Musser (*Washington, D.C.*).

  6c.[2] Ethel Blair Fairfax, *m.* William Hook (*Concana, Texas*).

  7c. Ada Susan Fairfax, *m.* 1892, Allen Monroe Chandler (*Montross, Westmoreland co., Va.*).

4b. *Archibald Blair Fairfax, Capt. U.S. Navy, formerly Com. Confederate States Navy*, b. 22 *May* 1809; d. 3 *Jan*. 1867; m. 1st, Nov. 1832, *Sarah Carlyle, da. of the Hon. John Carlyle Herbert of Maryland*, d. 23 *Jan*. 1850; 2ndly, 2 *Mar*. 1852, *Eliza Mary, da. of the Rev. Oliver Norris of Alexandra, Va.; and had issue* 1c *to* 3c.

  1c. *Archibald Carlyle Fairfax, Confederate States Army*, b. 24 *Aug*. 1843; d. 4 *Aug*. 1879; m. 30 *Ap*. 1873, *Virginia Caroline (re-m.* 1892, *Henry Byrd Lewis of Clive Manor and Fawkes, Port Conway, King George co., Va.), da. of William H. Redwood of Baltimore; and had issue* 1d *to* 2d.

    1d. John Carlyle Fairfax, Lieut. 21st U.S. Infantry, b. 22 Dec. 1874.

    2d. William Redwood Fairfax (*Fredericksburg, Va.*), b. 3 Dec. 1876.

  2c. Llewellyn Cary Fairfax, b. 28 Aug. 1855; *m.* 1880, Priscilla Hall, da. of Reginald Wright of Baltimore, M.D.

  3c. Arthur Percy Fairfax (*Baltimore, Maryland*), b. 2 Feb. 1857; *m.* 2 Feb. 1882, Nancy Hunter, da. of the Hon. John Blair Hoge of Virginia.

[Nos. 56304 to 56326.

3a. Hon. Elizabeth Fairfax, d. (–) ; m. *David Griffith of New York ; and had (with other) issue 1b.*

   1b. Lucy Anne Griffith, 2nd da., d. *Jan.* 1861; m. 2 *Mar.* 1824, *Wilson Miles Cary Fairfax,* d. 8 *Aug.* 1860; *and had issue.*

   See p. 658, Nos. 56302–56308.   [Nos. 56327 to 56333.

585. Descendants, if any surviving, of ANNE FAIRFAX (see Table LXIII.), *b.* (at Salem, Mass.) 1728 ; *m.* 1st, 1743, LAWRENCE (brother to Gen. George) WASHINGTON, *d.s.p.* 1752; 2ndly, GEORGE LEE of Virginia, and had issue 3 sons; of SARAH FAIRFAX, wife of Major JOHN CARLYLE of Alexandra, Va. ; and of HANNAH FAIRFAX, wife of WARNER (cousin of Gen. George) WASHINGTON.

586. Descendants, if any surviving, of BRYAN FAIRFAX of Wetherby (see Table LXXII.), *m.* 1730 ; and had issue (at least a son, *b.* 1731); of DOROTHY FAIRFAX, *b.* 16 May 1689; *m.* 1731, HENRY CLAPHAM of Thirsk, an Officer in the Customs at Hull ; and had issue (a son William); and of ANNE FAIRFAX, *b.* 11 July 1693.

587. Descendants of the Hon. DOROTHY FAIRFAX (see Table LXIII.), *b.* 1655; *d.* 14 Jan. 1745; *m.* 1st, ROBERT STAPLETON of Wighill, *d.s.p.* ; 2ndly, BENNET SHERARD of Whissendine, co. Rutland, M.P., *d.* 1701 ; and had issue 1*a* to 2*a*.

   1a. Philip (Sherard), 4th Baron Sherard [I.], 2nd Earl of Harborough [G.B.], d. 20 *July* 1750; m. *Anne, da. and h. of Nicholas Pedley,* d. 16 *Feb.* 1750; *and had issue 1b to 3b.*

   1b. Bennet (Sherard), 5th Baron Sherard [I.], 3rd Earl of Harborough [G.B.], d. 24 *Feb.* 1770; m. *2ndly,* 2 *July* 1757, *Frances, da. of the Hon. William Noel, one of the Judges of the Court of Common Pleas,* d. 15 *Sept.* 1860; *and had issue 1c.*

   1c. Lady Frances Sherard, b. 12 *Ap.* 1759; m. 18 *Ap.* 1776, *Major-Gen. George Morgan, Foot Guards.*

   2b. Robert (Sherard), 6th Baron Sherard [I.], 4th Earl of Harborough [G.B.], Preb. of Salisbury, b. 21 *Oct.* 1719 ; d. 21 *Ap.* 1799 ; m. *2ndly,* 10 *Jan.* 1767, *Jane, da. of William Reeve of Melton Mowbray,* d. 9 *Nov.* 1770; *and had issue 1c to 2c.*

   1c. Philip (Sherard), 7th Baron Sherard [I.], 5th Earl of Harborough [G.B.], b. 10 *Oct.* 1767 ; d. 10 *Dec.* 1807; m. 4 *July* 1791, *Eleanor, da. of the Hon. John Monckton of Fineshade,* d. 9 *Oct.* 1809 ; *and had issue 1d to 5d.*

   1d. Robert (Sherard), 8th Baron Sherard [I.], 6th Earl of Harborough [G.B.], b. 26 *Aug.* 1797 ; d.s.p. 28 *July* 1859.

   2d. Lady Lucy Eleanor Sherard, b. 20 *May* 1792; d. 8 *June* 1848; m. *the Hon. Henry Cecil Lowther, M.P.,* d. 6 *Dec.* 1867; *and had issue.*

   See the Clarence Volume, p. 602, Nos. 26480–26519.

   3d. Lady Anna Maria Sherard, b. 3 *Oct.* 1794; d. 21 *Nov.* 1848; m. 7 *Mar.* 1816, *William Cuffe of St. Albans, co. Kilkenny,* d. 28 *July* 1848.

   4d. Lady Sophia Sherard, b. 16 *Nov.* 1795; d. 22 *Sept.* 1751; m. *1st,* 9 *Ap.* 1812, *Sir Thomas Whichcote, 6th Bart. [E.],* b. 10 *Aug.* 1781; d. 23 *Aug.* 1829; *and had issue 1e to 3e.*   [Nos. 56334 to 56373

# of The Blood Royal

1e. *Sir Thomas Whichcote, 7th Bart.* [E.], b. 23 *May* 1813; d. 17 *Jan.* 1892; m. *2ndly*, 25 *Mar.* 1856, *Isabella Elizabeth, da. of Sir Henry Conyngham Mont-gomery, 1st Bart.* [U.K.], M.P., d. 29 *Aug.* 1892; *and had issue 1f.*

1f. Isabella Whichcote (*Deeping St. James Manor, Market Deeping;* 114 *Ashley Gardens, S.W.*), m. 7 Sept. 1875, Brownlow (Cecil), 4th Marquis [U.K.] and 13th Earl [E.] of Exeter, d. 9 Ap. 1898; and has issue.

See the Clarence Volume, p. 261, Nos. 6295–6296.

2e. *Sir George Whichcote, 8th Bart.* [E.], b. 31 *May* 1817; d. 14 *Ap.* 1893; m. 10 *Ap.* 1866, *Louisa Day, da. of Thomas William Clagett of Fetcham; and had issue 1f to 3f.*

1f. Sir George Whichcote, 9th Bart. [E.], J.P., D.L. (*Aswarby Park, Folking-ham, Lincoln*), b. 3 Sept. 1870.

2f. Hugh Christopher Whichcote.

3f. Louisa Mary Whichcote.

3e. *Sophia Whichcote*, d. 1 *Aug.* 1868; m. 9 *Jan.* 1840, *the Rev. Algernon Turnor*, d. *Aug.* 1842.

5d. *Lady Susan Sherard*, b. 1 *July* 1802; d. 3 *Sept.* 1864; m. 11 *July* 1821, *Gen. John Reeve of Leadenham House, co. Linc., J.P., D.L.*, d. 3 *Oct.* 1864; *and had issue 1e to 3e.*

1e. *John Reeve of Leadenham House, J.P., D.L., High Sheriff co. Linc.* 1871, *Lieut.-Col. Grenadier Guards*, b. 1 *June* 1822; d. 2 *Jan.* 1897; m. *2ndly*, 3 *Feb.* 1863, *the Hon. Edith Anne, da. of Rev. the Hon. Charles Dundas*, d. 12 *Aug.* 1902; *and had issue 1f.*

1f. John Sherard Reeve, J.P., Lieut. Grenadier Guards (*Leadenham House, Lincoln*), b. 3 Ap. 1872.

2e. *William Henry Reeve, Lieut.-Col. Coldstream Guards*, b. 1827; d. 1868.

3e. *Susan Millicent Reeve*, d. 12 *Dec.* 1877; m. 7 *Aug.* 1861, *William Dash-wood Fane of Fulbeck Hall; and had issue.*

See p. 353, Nos. 25781–25795.

2c. *Lady Lucy Sherard*, b. *Oct.* 1769; d. 27 *Mar.* 1858; m. *1st*, 2 *June* 1791, *Sir Thomas Cave, 7th Bart.* [E.], *M.P.*, d.s.p. 15 *Jan.* 1792; *2ndly*, 20 *Aug.* 1798, *the Hon. Philip Bouverie, afterwards Bouverie-Pusey of Pusey, co. Berks*, b. 8 *Oct.* 1746; d. 14 *Ap.* 1828; *and had issue 1d to 4d.*

1d. *Philip Bouverie-Pusey, M.P.*, b. 25 *June* 1799; d. 9 *July* 1855; m. 4 *Oct.* 1822, *Lady Emily Frances Theresa, da. of Henry George (Herbert), 2nd Earl of Carnarvon* [G.B.], d. 16 *Nov.* 1854; *and had issue 1e to 3e.*

1e. Sidney Edward Bouverie Bouverie-Pusey, J.P. (*Pusey House, near Faring-don, Berks;* 35A *South Audley Street, W.*), b. 15 Sept. 1839; m. 1st, 29 Ap. 1871, Wilhelmina Maria, da. of Lord William Hervey, d. 16 Nov. 1885; 2ndly, 5 July 1890, Helen Henrietta, widow of the Right. Hon. William Massey, M.P., da. of Patrick Grant.

2e. Edith Lucy Bouverie Bouverie-Pusey.

3e. Clara Bouverie-Pusey, *m.* 30 Oct. 1862, Capt. Francis Charteris Fletcher, *d.* 25 Jan. 1891; and has issue 1f to 2f.

1f. Philip Francis Fletcher.

2f. Constance Fletcher.

2d. *Rev. Edward Bouverie-Pusey, D.D., Canon of Christ Church and Regius Professor of Hebrew at Oxford Univ.*, b. 22 *Aug.* 1800; d. 16 *Sept.* 1882; m. 12 *June* 1828, *Maria Catherine, da. of John Raymond Barker of Fairford Park, co. Glouc.*, d. 26 *May* 1839; *and had issue 1e.*

1e. Mary Amelia Bouverie-Pusey (*Old Manor House, Willesborough, Kent*), m. 13 July 1854, the Rev. James Gram Brine, B.D., Rector of Lower Hardres, d. 12 Mar. 1901; and has issue 1f to 8f.   [Nos. 56374 to 56401.

661   4 P

The Plantagenet Roll

1*f*. Rev. James Edward Bouverie Brine, M.A. (Oxon.), Vicar of Cadmore End (*Cadmore End Vicarage, near High Wycombe*), *b*. 18 Ap. 1855; *m*. 1st, 1888, Margaret, da. of Thomas Ekin, *d*. 20 Feb. 1892; 2ndly, 18 Jan. 1896, Louisa Florence, da. of Col. James George; and has issue 1*g* to 2*g*.

1*g*. Norah Bouverie Brine, *b*. 6 Feb. 1900.

2*g*. Mary Gramina Bouverie Brine, *b*. 11 Feb. 1904.

2*f*. Perceval Forbes Brine, Major Reserve of Officers, *late* The Buffs (*Lardstock, Herne Bay*), *b*. 25 Oct. 1857 ; *m*. 6 Dec. 1888, Annie Mary, da. of John Quain of Dublin, *d*. 6 Sept. 1891 ; and has issue 1*g*.

1*g*. Percival John Frederic Brine, *b*. 30 June 1890.

3*f*. Philip Arthur Sherard Brine, British Vice-Consul at Richmond (*British Consulate, Richmond, Virginia*), *b*. 12 July 1861; *m*. 1st, 14 Jan. 1886, Elvira Patrick, da. of Capt. Claiborne of Claremont, Va., *d*. 16 Feb. 1890; 2ndly, 1903, Anne Gordon, da. of Henry S. Coleman of Halifax co., Va. ; and has issue 1*g*.

1*g*. Philip Edward Pusey Brine, *b*. 4 Feb. 1887.

4*f*. Rev. Algernon Lindsay Brine, M.A. (Oxon.), Rector of Willesborough (*Willesborough Rectory, Kent*), *b*. 22 Aug. 1864; *m*. 29 Dec. 1897, Marian Fanny, da. of Brig.-Surg. John Adcock of Purbeck House, Weymouth, M.D.

5*f*. Frederick George Brine, Lieut. R.N., *b*. 8 Aug. 1873; *m*. 23 Aug. 1899, Irene Mary, da. of J. B. Bettington of Brindley Park, Merriwa, N.S.W ; and has issue 1*g*.

1*g*. Mary Sophia Bouverie Brine, *b*. 1 Nov. 1903.

6*f*. Lucy Maria Bouverie Brine.

7*f*. Edith Mary Adelaide Brine, *m*. 4 Jan. 1893, Col. William Henry M'Causland, 79th Cameron Highlanders, *d*. 30 Dec. 1905 ; and has issue 1*g* to 2*g*.

1*g*. Eileen Maud M'Causland, *b*. 27 Dec. 1893.

2*g*. Mary Caress M'Causland, *b*. 21 July 1895.

8*f*. Eleanor Maud Brine, *m*. 1893, George Leycester Borradaile.

3*d*. *Rev. William Bouverie-Pusey, M.A., Rector of Langley*, *b*. 14 *May* 1810 ; *d*. 19 *Ap*. 1888 ; m. 7 *June* 1836, *Catherine, da. of Thomas Freeman*, *d. Nov.* 1873 ; *and had issue 1e to 2e.*

1*e*. Edward Bouverie-Pusey, Capt. (ret.) R.N. (*United Service*), *b*. 12 June 1838; *m*. 25 June 1870, Esther Elliot Cox, da. of the Rev. Richard Cox Hales; and has issue 1*f* to 4*f*.

1*f*. Edward Bouverie Bouverie-Pusey, Lieut. 2nd Batt. Yorkshire Regt., *b*. 19 Mar. 1873.

2*f*. Catherine Louisa Bouverie-Pusey, *m*. 4 Aug. 1892, John Bowyer Buchanan Nichols (7 *Bryanston Street, W.*).

3*f*. Ethel Mary Bouverie-Pusey, *m*. 18 Aug. 1900, the Hon. Adrian Verney Verney-Cave (*Stanford-on-Avon, Rugby*) ; and has issue 1*g* to 2*g*.

1*g*. Thomas Adrian Verney-Cave, *b*. 26 July 1902.

2*g*. Lucy Agnes Vera Verney-Cave, *b*. 1 Jan. 1905.

4*f*. Lucy Bouverie-Pusey.

2*e*. Frances Mary Bouverie-Pusey.

4*d*. *Elizabeth Bouverie-Pusey*, b. 25 *May* 1803 ; d. 1883 ; m. 14 Oct. 1827, *the Rev. James H. Montagu Luxmore, Preb. of St. Asaph* (*son of the Lord Bishop of St. Asaph*), d. *Mar.* 1860.

3*b*. *Lady Dorothy Sherard*, d. (–) ; m. *the Rev. James Torkington of Great Stukeley, co. Hants ; and had issue 1c to 8c.*[1]

1*c*. *James Torkington of Great Stukeley*, d. (–) ; m. *Maria, da. of Edward Bourchier of co. Herts ; and had issue 1d to 2d.*   [Nos. 56402 to 56424.

---

[1] Burke's " Landed Gentry," 7th edition, 1886, ii. p. 128.

# of The Blood Royal

1*d*. *James Torkington of Great Stukeley*, d. 1828; m. 22 *Oct*. 1799, *Elizabeth, da. of Charles Bourchier of Sandridge Lodge, co. Herts, B.C.S.; and had issue* 1*e to* 5*e*.

1*e*. *Laurence John Torkington of Great Stukeley, co. Hants, J.P.*, b. 27 *Sept.* 1809; d. 1874; m. 26 *Sept*. 1839, *Mary Anne, da. of Lieut.-Col. Walker, R.A.; and had issue* 1*f to* 5*f*.

1*f*. Charles Torkington of Great Stukeley, Capt. 41st Regt. (22 *Langham Mansions, Earl's Court, S.W.*), b. 1847; *m*. 3 Aug. 1875, Florence Elizabeth Caroline,[1] da. of Richard George Coke; and has issue 1*g* to 4*g*.

1*g*. Gerard Stukeley Torkington, I.S.C., 69th Punjabis, b. 23 Sept. 1878.

2*g*. Charles Coke Torkington, Welsh Regt., b. 7 Mar. 1881.

3*g*. John Elmsley Bourchier Torkington, Manchester Regt., b. 19 Nov. 1884.

4*g*. Dorothy Mary Torkington.

2*f*. Mary Dorothy Torkington.

3*f*. Alice Torkington.

4*f*. Isabella Torkington.

5*f*. Gertrude Torkington, *m*. 1868, the Rev. Canon Allen, Vicar of Lancaster.

2*e*. James Torkington.

3*e*. Henry Theodore Torkington.

4*e*. *Rev. Charles Torkington*, d. (–); m. 1*st*, 1842, *Anna, da. of James Powell of Clapton; 2ndly, 1849, Ellen Eliza, da. of the Rev.* [——] *Cookson; and had issue* (1 *son and* 3 *das. by* 1*st marriage, and* 3 *sons and* 2 *das. by second*).

5*e*. *Barbara Emily Torkington*.

2*d*. *Mary Dorothy Torkington*.

2*c*. *Philip Torkington*.

3*c*. *John Torkington*.

4*c*. *Anna Torkington*.

5*c*. *Dorothea Torkington*.

6*c*. *Maria Torkington*.

7*c*. *Elizabeth Torkington*.

8*c*. *Sarah Torkington*.

2*a*. *Margaret Sherard*, d. *a*. 1761; m. *the Rev. John Gilbert, D.D., Archbishop of York and Lord High Almoner* 1757; d. 19 *Aug.* 1761; *and had issue* 1*b*.

1*b*. *Emma Gilbert, da. and h.*, b. 28 *July* 1729; d. 26 *Dec.* 1807; m. 16 *Aug.* 1761, *George* (*Edgcumbe*), 3*rd Baron and* 1*st Earl of Mount Edgcumbe* [*G.B.*], b. 3 *Mar.* 1720; d. 4 *Feb.* 1795; *and had issue* 1*c*.

1*c*. *Richard* (*Edgcumbe*), 2*nd Earl of Mount Edgcumbe* [*G.B.*], b. 13 *Sept.* 1764; d. 26 *Sept.* 1739; m. 21 *Feb.* 1789, *Lady Sophia, da. and co-h. of John* (*Hobart*), 2*nd Earl of Buckinghamshire* [*G.B.*]*; and had issue* 1*d to* 3*d*.

1*d*. *Ernest Augustus* (*Edgcumbe*), 3*rd Earl of Mount Edgcumbe* [*G.B.*], *F.R.S., F.S.A.*, b. 23 *Mar.* 1797; d. 3 *Sept.* 1861; m. 6 *Dec.* 1831, *Caroline Augusta, V.A., da. of Rear-Admiral Charles Feilding, R.N.*, d. 2 *Nov.* 1881; *and had issue* 1*e to* 3*e*.

1*e*. William Henry (Edgcumbe), 4th Earl of Mount Edgcumbe [G.B.], P.C., G.C.V.O., Lord-Lieut. and Vice-Admiral of Cornwall, &c., *formerly* (1879–1880) Lord Chamberlain and (1885–1886) Lord High Steward of the Household to Queen Victoria (*Mount Edgcumbe, Plymouth; Cotchele House, St. Dominick, R.S.O.*), b. 5 Nov. 1832; *m*. 26 Oct. 1858, Lady Katherine Elizabeth, da. of James (Hamilton), 1st Duke of Abercorn [I.], *d*. 3 Sept. 1874; 2ndly, 1906, Caroline, Countess Dowager of Ravensworth [U.K.], da. of the Hon. George Edgcumbe; and has issue 1*f* to 4*f*. [Nos. 56425 to 56436.]

---

[1] See the Clarence Volume, p. 185, for her descent from George, Duke of Clarence.

The Plantagenet Roll

1*f*. Piers Alexander Hamilton Edgcumbe, Viscount Valletort, Lieut.-Col. Duke of Cornwall's L.I. (*Marlborough*), *b.* 2 July 1865.

2*f*. Lady Victoria Frederica Caroline Edgcumbe, *m.* 3 Aug. 1880, Lord Algernon Malcolm Arthur Percy, J.P., D.L. (*Guy's Cliff, Warwick*); and has issue 1*g* to 2*g*.

1*g*. Algernon William Percy, *b.* 29 Nov. 1884.

2*g*. Katherine Louisa Victoria Percy, *b.* 22 Mar. 1882.

3*f*. Lady Albertha Louisa Florence Edgcumbe, *m.* 10 Oct. 1891, Henry Yarde Buller Lopes, J.P., D.L. (s. and h. of the Right Hon. Sir Lopes Massey-Lopes, 3rd Bart. [U.K.], P.C.) (*Roborough House, Roborough, Devon*); and has issue 1*g* to 5*g*.

1*g*. Massey Henry Edgcumbe Lopes, *b.* 4 Oct. 1903.

2*g*. Katherine Frederica Albertha Lopes, *b.* 25 Sept. 1892.

3*g*. Bertha Louisa Victoria Lopes, *b.* 1895.

4*g*. Margaret Beatrice Lopes, *b.* 12 Feb. 1898.

5*g*. Constance Elizabeth Lopes, *b.* 24 Aug. 1901.

4*f*. Lady Edith Hilaria Edgcumbe, *m.* 23 June 1892, the Hon. John Townshend St. Aubyn, Lieut.-Col. Comdg. 3rd Batt. Grenadier Guards (53 *Cadogan Place, S.W.*); and has issue 1*g* to 2*g*.

1*g*. Marjory Katharine Elizabeth Alexandra St. Aubyn.

2*g*. Hilaria Lily St. Aubyn.

2*e*. Hon. Charles Ernest Edgcumbe, J.P., Hon. Col. City of London Regt., *late* Grenadier Guards (23 *Down Street, W.*).

3*e*. Lady Ernestine Emma Horatia Edgcumbe (*Mount Edgcumbe, Plymouth*).

2*d. Hon. George Edgcumbe, b.* 23 *June* 1800; *d.* 18 *Feb.* 1882; *m.* 19 *May* 1834, *Fanny Lucy, da. of Sir John Shelley, 6th Bart.* [*E.*], *d.* 11 *May* 1899; *and had issue.*

See pp. 312–315, Nos. 23309–23322.

3*d. Lady Caroline Edgcumbe, b.* 22 *Oct.* 1792; *d.* 10 *Ap.* 1824; *m. as 1st wife,* 13 *Feb.* 1812, *Reginald George Macdonald of Clanranald, 25th Chief of his Clan, M.P., J.P., D.L., b.* 29 *Aug.* 1788; *d.* 11 *Mar.* 1873; *and had issue* 1*e to* 5*e.*

1*e. Sir Reginald John Macdonald of Clanranald, 26th Chief of his Clan, K.C.B., K.C.S.I., Vice-Adm. R.N., b.* 7 *Oct.* 1819; *d.* 15 *Dec.* 1899; *m.* 12 *June* 1855, *the Hon. Adelaide Louisa, da. of George John (Vernon), 5th Baron Vernon* [*G.B.*]; *and had issue.*

See p. 92, Nos. 567–570.

2*e. Caroline Sophia Macdonald, d.* 16 *Oct.* 1887; *m.* 8 *Sept.* 1842, *the Hon. Charles Henry Cust, M.P., b.* 27 *Sept.* 1813; *d.* 23 *May* 1875; *and had issue* 1*f to* 2*f.*

1*f*. Emma Augusta Charlotte Cust (*Castle Rock, West Cowes, I.W.*; 13 *Great Stanhope Street, W.*).

2*f*. Alice Marian Cust (*Arthingworth, Northants; Cliff Side, West Cowes;* 13 *Great Stanhope Street, W.*), *m.* 9 Sept. 1876, Lieut.-Col. Allan Roger Charles Porcelli, *afterwards* (R.L. 2 Dec. 1893) Porcelli-Cust, J.P., *d.* 15 Mar. 1897; and has issue 1*g* to 3*g*.

1*g*. Margaret Mary Ernestine-Dorothy Porcelli-Cust, *m.* 1900, Capt. William Coldingham Masters Nicholson, R.N.; and has issue 1*h* to 3*h*.

1*h*. Adelbert William Cust John Nicholson, *b.* 1901.

2*h*. Reginald Wodehouse James Nicholson, *b.* 1902.

3*h*. Dorothy Vernon Alice Nicholson, *b.* 1905.

2*g*. Adelaide Florence Caroline Porcelli-Cust.

3*g*. Ernestine Annie Porcelli-Cust, *m.* 23 July 1901, George Frederick Thomas Tankerville Johnstone (*Hardwicke Cottage, West Cowes*); and has issue 1*h* to 4*h*.

1*h*. Frederic Allan George Johnstone, *b.* 23 Feb. 1906.

2*h*. Laura Adeline Johnstone, *b.* 27 May 1902.

3*h*. Violet Florence Ernestine Johnstone, *b.* 17 June 1903.

4*h*. Dorothy Catherine Frances Johnstone, *b.* 4 Oct. 1904.

[Nos. 56437 to 56481.

3e. *Emma Hamilla Macdonald*, d. 5 *Ap.* 1852; m. 4 *Ap.* 1840, *Rev. the Hon. Alfred Wodehouse*, b. 10 *June* 1814; d. 6 *Sept.* 1848; *and had issue* 1f *to* 5f.

1f. Hobart Wodehouse, b. 23 Ap. 1842.

2f. Henry Wodehouse, b. 2 Jan. 1849.

3f. *Hamilla Caroline Wodehouse*, b. *Jan.* 1841; d. (? s.p.) 1879; m. 8 *Nov.* 1876, *Edward Taylor, H.B.M.'s Vice-Consul at Dunkirk.*

4f. Ernest Emma Wodehouse (*The Island, Derwentwater, Keswick*), m. 17 May 1866, John Marshall, d. 1894.

5f. *Laura Sophia Wodehouse*, b. 1846; d. (? s.p.); m. 23 *Nov.* 1882, *Lieut.-Col. Charles Wyndham, Royal Irish Rifles.*

4e. *Louisa Emily Macdonald*, d. 13 *Feb.* 1897; m. 1st, 13 *Ap.* 1841, *Charles William Marsham of Stratton Strawless, d.v.p.* 13 *Dec.* 1852; 2ndly, *as* 2nd *wife*, 4 *Dec.* 1858, *Col. Hugh* [*son of Lord Henry*] *FitzRoy*, d. 27 *Feb.* 1879; *and had issue* 1f *to* 2f.

1f. Adela Louisa FitzRoy.

2f. *Augusta Caroline FitzRoy*, b. 9 *Feb.* 1859; d. (−); m. 25 *Sept.* 1884, *Robert William Rankine Wilson, Bar.-at-Law.*

5e. *Annie Sarah Macdonald*, d. 18 *Aug.* 1897; m. 1st, 2 *Ap.* 1848, *Alfredo Salvatore Ruggiero Andrea (Porcelli), Baron Porcelli di Sant' Andrea in Calabria* [*Two Sicilies*], d. 18 *Jan.* 1884; 2nd, *Major Woolhouse; and had issue* 1f *to* 4f.

1f. Alfred (Porcelli), Baron Porcelli di Sant' Andrea [Two Sicilies], Lieut.-Col. and Brevet-Col. R.E. (ret.) (*The Cottage, Heatherley Road, Camberley*), b. 16 Jan. 1849; m. 1st, Aug. 1885, Effie Constance, widow of Col. F. Brownlow, da. of Col. Robert Christopher Tytler, d. 26 June 1886; and has issue 1g.

1g. Ernest George Macdonald Porcelli, Lieut. 2nd Batt. Duke of Cornwall's L.I., b. 27 May 1886.

2f. Ernest Frederic Joseph (Giuseppe) Porcelli, b. 7 Ap. 1850; m. 1877, Constance, da. of Herbert Mayo, s.p.

3f. *Allan Roger Charles Porcelli, afterwards* (*R.L.* 2 *Dec.* 1893) *Porcelli-Cust, J.P., Lieut.-Col. 4th Batt. Lancashire Regt.*, b. 21 *Sept.* 1851; d. 15 *Mar.* 1897; m. 9 *Sept.* 1876, *Alice Marian, da. and co-h. of the Hon. Charles Henry Cust; and had issue.*

See p. 664, Nos. 56472–56481.

4f. Flora Katharine Emma Porcelli (*The Gate House, West Malling*), m. 24 May 1870, the Rev. Herbert Schomberg St. George, d. 8 Dec. 1899; and has issue 1g to 2g.

1g. James Hamilton Pakenham St. George, b. 17 June 1877.

2g. Bertha Caroline Annie St. George, b. 17 May 1874. [Nos. 56482 to 56501.

588. Descendants, if any, of the Hon. FRANCES FAIRFAX (see Table LXIII.), b. 1663; d. 1723; m. 1686, the Rev. NICHOLAS RYMER, Rector of Newton Kyme.

589. Descendants of ISABELLA CARR (see Table LXIII.), b. 1722; d. 2 June 1767; m. 6 Oct. 1741, Sir HENRY IBBETSON, 1st Bart. [G.B.], b. 1703; d. 22 June 1761; and had issue 1a to 4a.

1a. *Sir James Ibbetson, 2nd Bart.* [*G.B.*], d. 4 *Sept.* 1795; m. 7 *Feb.* 1768, *Jane, da. of John Caygill of Shaw, co. Yorks*, d. 21 *Aug.* 1816; *and had issue* 1b *to* 3b.

1b. Sir Henry Carr Ibbetson, 3rd Bart. [G.B.], d.s.p. 5 June 1825.

2b. *Sir Charles Ibbetson, sometime* (*R.L.* 18 *Feb.* 1817—5 *Aug.* 1825) *Selwin, 4th Bart.* [*G.B.*], b. 26 *Sept.* 1779; d. 9 *Ap.* 1839; m. 4 *Feb.* 1812, *Charlotte*

The Plantagenet Roll

Elizabeth, da. of Thomas Stoughton of Ballyhorgan, co. Kerry, d. 15 Jan. 1827 ; and had issue 1c to 2c.

1c. Sir Charles Henry Ibbetson, 5th Bart. [G.B.], b. 24 July 1814 ; d.s.p. 6 July 1861.

2c. Laura Ibbetson (*Constable Burton, Finghall, R.S.O., Yorks ; Denton Park, Ben Rhydding, Leeds*), m. 8 Ap. 1845, Marmaduke Wyvill of Constable Burton, d. 25 June 1896 ; and has issue.

See p. 550, Nos. 49590–49604.

3b. *Sir John Thomas Ibbetson, afterwards* (1825) *Selwin, 6th Bart.* [G.B.], b. 1789 ; d. 20 Mar. 1869 ; m. 8 Sept. 1825, Isabella, da. of Gen. John Leveson Gower of Bill Hill, co. Berks, d. 24 Sept. 1858 ; and had issue.

See pp. 172–173, Nos. 5461–5482.

2a. *Henry Ibbetson of St. Anthonys, co. Northumberland, d. (–) ; m. Grace Ord, da. and h. of Andrew Morton of Newcastle-on-Tyne ; and had issue 1b.*

1b. *Isabella Grace Ibbetson, da. and (in 29 May 1811) h., d. (–) ; m. 21 July 1804, Cuthbert Ellison of Hebburn Hall, co. Durham, M.P., J.P., D.L., b. 12 July 1783 ; d. June 1860 ; and had issue 1c to 5c.*

1c. *Isabella Caroline Ellison, d. 14 Oct. 1853 ; m. as 1st wife, 30 Oct. 1824, George John (Venables-Vernon), 5th Baron Vernon* [G.B.], d. 31 May 1866 ; and had issue.

See pp. 90–92, Nos. 509–570.

2c. *Henrietta Ellison, d. (–) ; m. 28 June 1824, William Henry Lambton, b. 27 Mar. 1796 ; d. 3 Ap. 1866 ; and had issue.*

See the Tudor Roll of "The Blood Royal of Britain," pp. 362–363, Nos. 27679–27694.

3c. *Louisa Ellison, d. 24 Nov. 1837 ; m. 8 Ap. 1829, William David (Murray), 3rd Earl of Mansfield (1776) and 4th Earl of Mansfield (1792)* [G.B.], *9th Viscount Stormont, K.T.,* b. 21 Feb. 1806 ; d. 2 Aug. 1898 ; and had issue 1d to 2d.

1d. *William David Murray, Viscount Stormont,* b. 22 July 1835 ; d.v.p. 12 Oct. 1893 ; m. 6 Aug. 1857, Emily Louisa, da. of Sir John Atholl Macgregor of Macgregor, 3rd Bart. [G.B.] ; and had issue 1e to 5e.

1e. *William David (Murray), 4th (1776) and 5th (1792) Earl of Mansfield* [G.B.], *10th Viscount Stormont* [S.], b. 20 July 1860 ; d. unm. Ap. 1906.

2e. Alan David (Murray), 5th (1776) and 6th (1792) Earl of Mansfield [G.B.], 11th Viscount Stormont [S.] (*Scone Palace, Perth ; Comlongon Castle, Dumfries ; 6 St. James' Place, S.W.*), b. 25 Oct. 1864 ; m. 20 Ap. 1899, Margaret Helen Mary, da. of Rear-Adm. Sir Malcolm Macgregor, 4th Bart. [G.B.] ; and has issue 1f.

1f. Mungo David Malcolm Murray, Viscount Stormont, b. 9 Aug. 1900.

3e. Hon.[1] Alexander David Murray, Capt. 3rd Batt. Black Watch (*Scones, Lethenby, Perth*), b. 3 May 1871.

4e. Lady[1] Marjory Louisa Murray, m. 8 Ap. 1891, Sir Kenneth John Mackenzie, 7th Bart [S.] (*Gairloch, Ross ; 10 Moray Place, Edinburgh, &c.*) ; and has issue 1f to 3f.

1f. Hector David Mackenzie, b. 6 June 1893.

2f. Roderick Ian Mackenzie, b. 27 May 1895.

3f. Marjory Kythé Mackenzie, b. 25 Jan. 1892.

5e. Lady[1] Mabel Emily Murray, m. 30 Mar. 1905, Capt. Herbert Goodenough King Hall, D.S.O., R.N.

2d. Lady Louisa Nina Murray, m. 21 July 1851, the Hon. George Edwin Lascelles (*Sion Hill, Thirsk*) ; and has issue.

See the Tudor Roll of "The Blood Royal of Britain," p. 219, Nos. 21873–21886.   [Nos. 56502 to 56644.

---

[1] R.W. 13 Mar. 1899.

# of The Blood Royal

4c. *Laura Jane Ellison*, d. 26 Feb. 1846 ; m. 12 Oct. 1833, *William* (*Edwardes*), 3rd Baron Kensington [I.], b. 3 Feb. 1801 ; d. 1 Jan. 1872 ; *and had issue* 1d *to* 7d.

1d. *William* (*Edwardes*), 4th [I.] *and* 1st [U.K.] *Baron Kensington*, b. 11 May 1835 ; d. 7 Oct. 1896 ; m. 19 Sept. 1867, *Grace Elizabeth*, da. of Robert Johnstone-Douglas of Lockerbie ; *and had issue.*

See the Tudor Roll of "The Blood Royal of Britain," p. 168, Nos. 20124–20133.

2d. Hon. Cuthbert Ellison Edwardes, *late* Lieut.-Col. Rifle Brigade (39 *Lancaster Gate, W.*), b. 16 Jan. 1838 ; *m.* 14 June 1882, Lady Blanche Henrietta Maria, da. of John (Butler), 2nd Marquis of Ormonde [I.], K.P. ; *and has issue* 1e *to* 5e.

1e. Hubert William John Edwardes, b. 21 June 1883.

2e. Arthur Henry Francis Edwardes, b. 8 Feb. 1885.

3e. Cuthbert Theobald Edwardes, b. 9 Ap. 1887.

4e. Richard Edwardes, ⎫
5c. Owen Edwardes, ⎬ *b.* (twins) 6 May 1894.

3d. Hon. *Henry George Edwardes*, b. 15 Dec. 1844 ; d. 30 Dec. 1896 ; m. 4 July 1878, *Cecilia Elenthera Douglas* (7 *Herbert Crescent, S.W.*), da. of Charles J. Bayley, C.B. ; *and had issue* 1e.

1e. Hon. Sylvia Gay Edwardes, a Maid of Honour to H.M. Queen Alexandra, and previously to Queen Victoria.

4d. Hon. *Laura Jane Edwardes* (3 *West Eaton Place, S.W.*), *m.* 24 Sept. 1885, Major-Gen. Raymond Herbert White, *d.s.p.* 13 July 1894.

5d. Hon. *Louisa Jane Edwardes* (40 *Belgrave Road, S.W.*), *m.* as 2nd wife, 23 Sept. 1880, Capt. William Henry Newenham of Tory Hill, W. Limerick, d. 21 July 1898.

6d. Hon. *Elizabeth Edwardes* (14 *Carlisle Mansions, Victoria Street, S.W.*).

7d. Hon. *Caroline Edwardes*, *m.* 10 Nov. 1897, the Rev. Joseph Robertson Vincent (*Shenley Rectory, Bletchley, Bucks*).

5c. *Sarah Caroline Ellison*, d. 21 Jan. 1890 ; m. 17 Ap. 1841, *Walter Charles* (*James*), 1st Baron Northbourne [U.K.], b. 3 June 1816 ; d. 4 Feb. 1893 ; *and had issue* 1d *to* 2d.

1d. *Walter Henry* (*James*), 2nd Baron Northbourne [U.K.] (*Betteshanger, near Dover*), b. 25 Mar. 1846 ; *m.* 25 Aug. 1868, Edith Emeline Mary, da. of John Newton Lane of Kings Bromley Manor ; *and has issue.*

See pp. 435–436, Nos. 35033–35044.

2d. Hon. *Sarah James*, *m.* 26 Sept. 1871, Sir John Arthur Godley of Killegar, *formerly* Private Secretary to the Right Hon. William Ewart Gladstone, P.C., M.P., K.C.B. (29 *Sloane Gardens, S.W. ; Minley Lodge, Farnborough*) ; *and has issue* 1e *to* 4e.

1e. Hugh John Godley, b. 12 June 1877.

2e. Helen Sarah Godley, *m.* 1895, Henry Rice (*Dane Court, Dover*) ; *and has issue* 1f *to* 2f.

1f. Edward Denis Rice, b. 30 Oct. 1899.

2f. Patrick Arthur Rice, b. 7 Ap. 1902.

3e. Eveline Charlotte Godley.

4e. Katharine Euphemia Godley.

3a. *Isabella Ibbetson*, d. (–) ; *m.* 1764, *Thomas Rea Cole*, Major 98th Regt., d. 1807 ; *and had issue* 1b *to* 3b.

1b. *Stephen Thomas Cole of Stoke Lyne, co. Oxford, and Twickenham, co. Middlesex*, b. 26 Ap. 1765 ; d. 6 Sept. 1835 ; m. 15 Jan. 1795, *Lady Elizabeth Henrietta*, da. of Edward (*Stanley*), 12th Earl of Derby [E.], d. 1857 ; *and had issue.*

See the Tudor Roll of "The Blood Royal of Britain," pp. 495–497, Nos. 33851–33915.

[Nos. 56645 to 56750.

The Plantagenet Roll

2b. Henry Cole, d. 1815; m. *Jane Elizabeth, da. and co-h. of John Owen of Ratconnell, co. Monaghan ; and had issue 1c to 3c.*

1c. Owen Blayney Cole of Brandrum, D.L., High Sheriff co. Monaghan 1835, b. 4 Oct. 1808; d. 26 Nov. 1886; m. 25 Aug. 1834, *Lady Frances Isabella, da. and co-h. of Henry Stanley (Monck), 1st Earl of Rathdonne [I.], b. 20 July* 1809; d. 9 *June* 1871; *and had issue 1d to 4d.*

1d. Francis Burton Owen Cole, J.P., D.L., Capt. 7th Fusiliers (*Llys Merichion, Denbigh*), b. 1 May 1838; *m.* 1st, 25 Sept. 1872, Mary Georgiana, da. of George Fosbery Lyster of Gisburne, d. 1881; 2ndly, 1883, Maria Susan, widow of the Rev. Robert le Poer McClintock, da. of F. C. Heyland; and has issue 1e to 2e.

1e. Mowbray Lyster Owen Cole, b. 22 Feb. 1875.

2e. Violet Owen Cole, b. 7. Dec. 1873.

2d. Blayney Owen Cole, b. 1846; *m.* 1872, [——], da. of [——] Benyon.

3d. Frances Elizabeth Owen Cole (84 *Chester Square, S.W.*), *m.* 13 Aug. 1861, Col. the Hon. Richard Monck, b. 23 Oct. 1829; d. 7 Oct. 1904; and has issue 1e.

1e. Cecil Stanley Owen Monck, Major Coldstream Guards, b. 24 July 1863.

4d. Emily Cole.

2c. *Eliza Ibbetson Cole*, d. 1896; m. *John Charles Metge of Sion House, co. Meath, M.P., J.P.*, d. 1870; *and had issue 1d to 6d.*

1d. Francis Burton Metge (*Ladywell, Athlone, Dardistown, Killiecan, West-meath*), b. 18—; *m.* Anne, da of Henry Cole Bowen, d. 1897; and has issue 1e to 6e.

1e. John Metge.

2e. Charles Metge, b. 1871.

3e. Harry Metge.

4e. Frances Burton Metge.

5e. Anne Metge.

6e. Henrietta Cole Metge.

2d. Peter Ponsonby Metge (*Rathkea, Tipperary*), b. 18—; *m.* 18—, Julia, da. of W. Westropp Brereton, Q.C. ; and has issue 1e to 4e.

1e. Peter Ponsonby Metge.

2e. Geraldine Metge.

3e. Janet Ibbetson Metge.

4e. Ella Cole Metge.

3d. Robert Henry Metge, J.P., LL.B., Bar.-at-Law, sometime (1880–1884) M.P. (*Athlumney, Kilcairne, Meath*), b. 1850; *m.* 1874, Frances Thomasina Virginia, da. of the Rev. Charles Lambart, Rector of Navan, d. 1891; 2ndly, 1894, Lilian Margaret, da. of Richard Cambridge Grubb of Cahir Abbey; and has issue 1e to 14e.

1e. Robert Henry Metge, Lieut. 1st Batt. Welsh Regt., b. 1875.

2e. Pierre Ponsonby Metge, b. 1878.

3e. Radulph Cole Metge, b. 1881.

4e. Selwyn Ibbetson Cole Metge, b. 1886.

5e. Francis Charles Cole Metge, b. 1889.

6e.[1] Virginia Maria Frances Cole Metge.

7e.[1] Louisa Charlotte Cole Metge.

8e.[1] Eileen Mary Cole Metge.

9e.[1] Ethel Cole Metge.

10e.[1] May Cole Metge.

11e.[1] Edith Cole Metge.

12e.[1] Gladys Ibbetson Cole Metge.

13e.[2] Lilian Gwendaline Cole Metge.

14e.[2] Dorothy Elsie Cole Metge.

4d. Elizabeth Ibbetson Cole Metge.   [Nos. 56751 to 56785.

5*d*. Henrietta Cole Metge, *m*. 31 Mar. 1874, George Charles Mulock (*Kilna-garna, King's Co.*); and has issue 1*e* to 4*e*.

    1*e*. John Charles Metge Mulock.

    2*e*. Henrietta Georgina Ethel Mulock.

    3*e*. Sophia Eliza Ethel Mulock.

    4*e*. Emily Cole Mulock.

6*d*. Louisa Charlotte Metge, *m*. Thomas Preston Walsh, 38th Regt.

3*c*. *Henrietta Isabella Cole*, d. 1847; m. *as 1st wife*, 1837, *the Rev. John William Finlay of Corkagh, co. Dublin, M.A.*, b. 1805; d. 1879; *and had issue* 1*d* to 4*d*.

1*d*. Henry Thomas Finlay, J.P., Lieut.-Col. 5th Batt. Royal Dublin Fusiliers (*Corkagh House, Clondalkin*), *b*. 15 Feb. 1847; *m*. 1st., 4 Dec. 1877, Helen Lucy, da. of the Rev. Robert Hedges Dunne; 2ndly, 18 July 1906, Emily Octavia, widow of James Acheson Lyle of Glundon, da. of Rev. the Hon. Henry Ward; and has issue 1*e* to 4*e*.

    1*e*. George Guy Finlay, *b*. 26 Dec. 1889.

    2*e*. Robert Alexander Finlay, *b*. 2 Feb. 1893.

    3*e*. Edith Maud Olivia Finlay.

    4*e*. Alice Caroline Finlay.

2*d*. Elizabeth Owen Finlay, *m*. 20 Jan. 1866, Richard John Ussher, J.P., D.L. (*Cappagh House, Lismore*); and has issue 1*e* to 4*e*.

    1*e*. Beverley Grant Ussher, *b*. 19 Feb. 1867.

    2*e*. Percy John Ussher, *b*. 28 Aug. 1868.

    3*e*. Arthur Hamilton Ussher, *b*. 14 Sept. 1869.

    4*e*. Isabella Mary Grant Ussher, *b*. 20 May 1871; *m*. 23 Mar. 1901, Capt. William Odell, Inniskilling Fusiliers; and has issue.

3*d*. Henrietta Ellen Finlay.

4*d*. Olivia Anna Finlay, *m*. 30 Nov. 1879, Capt. Ernest Edward Foley, Midx. Regt.; and has issue.

3*b*. *Harriet Cole*, d. (–); m. *Capt. William Tudor.*

4*a*. *Thomasina Ibbetson*, d. (–); m. *James Tenton of co. York.*

[Nos. 56786 to 56803.

590. Descendants of the Rev. RALPH CARR, M.A., Rector of Alder-ley, co. Chester (see Table LXIII.), *b*. Nov. 1737; *d*. 1810; *m*. 1st, ANNE, da. and h. of Anthony HALL of Flass, co. Durham, *d*. 1774; 3rdly, MARY, widow of Joseph Gubbins of Kilfnish, co. Limerick, da. of George STAMES of Cahirnelly, co. Clare, *d*. 1812; and had issue 1*a* to 4*a*.

1*a*–3*a*. (Children by 1st wife). See p. 610, Nos. 52021–52101.

4*a*.³ *Georgina Margaret Carr*, b. 1791; d. (–).   [Nos. 56804 to 56884.

591. Descendants of FRANCES CARR (see Table LXIII.), *d*. 1735; *m*. as 2nd wife, WINGATE PULLEINE of Carleton Hall, co. York; *d*. Aug. 1763; and had issue 1*a* to 3*a*.

1*a*. *Thomas Babington Pulleine of Carleton Hall*, b. 21 *June* 1731; d. (–); m. *Winifred, da. of Edward Collingwood of Dissington Hall; and had issue* 1*b*.

1*b*. *Mary Winifred Pulleine*, d. *Dec.* 1850; m. 1783, *John Stanhope, afterwards Spencer-Stanhope, of Hosforth and Cannon Hall, M.P.*, d. 10 *Ap*. 1821; *and had issue* (7 sons and 1 da. who married).

669

4 Q

The Plantagenet Roll

2a. Henry Pulleine of Carleton Hall, b. 1734; d. (–); m. 11 Sept. 1764 *Elizabeth, da. of George Hutton of Marske;* d. *June* 1816; *and had issue.* See p. 556, Nos. 49694–49747.

3a. Isabella Pulleine, d. 25 *Aug.* 1812; m. *Charles Wilkinson of Thorp, co. York.* [Nos. 56885 to 56938.

592. Descendants, if any, of Susanna Cholmley (see Table LVIII.), *m.* 19 Nov. 1615, Robert Theakston of Trousdale.

593. Descendants of the Rev. Henry Wickham, D.D., Rector of Guiseley, co. York, Chaplain to the Prince of Wales (see Table LXIV.), *b. c.* 1699; *d.* 2 June 1772; *m.* 1st, Anne, da. of William Calverley, *b. c.* 1709; *d.* 11 Ap. 1736; and had issue 1*a* to 2*a*.

1*a. Henry Wickham of Cottingley, co. York, J.P., Lieut.-Col. Foot Guards,* bapt. 7 *Sept.* 1731; d. 9 *Oct.* 1804; m. 16 *Feb.* 1761, *Elizabeth, da. and h. of the Rev. William Lamplugh, Vicar of Dewsbury,* b. *c.* 1738; d. 23 *Ap.* 1815; *and had issue* 1*b* to 2*b*.

1*b. Right Hon. William Wickham of Cottingley, co. York, and Binsted-Wyck, co. Hants, M.A.* (*Oxon.*), *D.C.L., P.C., M.P., Secretary of State for Ireland* 1802 *and Lord of the Treasury* 1806; bapt. 11 *Dec.* 1761; d. 22 *Oct.* 1840; m. 10 *Aug.* 1788, *Eleonore Madeleine, da. of Louis Bertrand of Geneva,* b. (*at Geneva*) 16 *July* 1763; d. (*there*) 15 *Ap.* 1836; *and had issue* 1*c*.

1*c. Henry Louis Wickham of Binsted-Wyck, Receiver-Gen. of Gibraltar and* (1838–1848) *Chairman of the United Boards of Stamps and Taxes,* b. 19 *May* 1789; d. 27 *Oct.* 1864; m. 19 *June* 1830, *Lucy, da. of William Markham of Becca Hall, co. York* (*and grandda. of William Markham, Archbishop of York*), d. 11 *July* 1885; *and had issue* 1*d* to 3*d*.

1*d. William Wickham of Binsted-Wyck, M.P., J.P., D.L., F.L.S., F.R.G.S., High Sheriff co. Hants* 1888, *&c.,* b. 10 *July* 1831; d. 16 *May* 1897; m. 9 *May* 1860, *Sophia Emma* (*Binsted-Wyck, Alton*), *da. and co-h. of Henry Francis Shaw Lefevre;* and had issue 1*e* to 2*e*.

1*e. Lucy Wickham* (48 *Park Street, W.*), m. 22 Oct. 1889, Col. William Lewis Kinloch Ogilvy, C.B., Col. King's Royal Rifle Corps, b. 30 Ap. 1840; d. 3 Feb. 1900; *and has issue* 1*f* to 2*f*.

    1*f.* William Wickham Ogilvy, b. 31 Jan. 1896.

    2*f.* Charlotte Helen Ogilvy.

2*e. Eleonore Wickham, m.* 31 Oct. 1893, Henry John Beresford Clements, J.P., D.L., High Sheriff co. Cavan 1891, and of co. Leitrim 1893 (*Lough Rynn, Leitrim; Killadoon, Cellbridge*); *and has issue* 1*f* to 5*f*.

    1*f.* Henry Theophilus Wickham Clements, b. 12 Nov. 1898.

    2*f.* Charles Marcus Lefevre Clements, b. 4 Nov. 1904.

    3*f.* Eleanore Mary Sophia Clements.

    4*f.* Cecily Catharine Clements.

    5*f.* Violet Gertrude Clements.

2*d.* Henry Lamplugh Wickham, J.P., *late* Capt. Rifle Brigade (*Army and Navy; Boodle's*), b. 19 Feb. 1838; *m.* 24 Feb. 1873, the Hon. Theresa Mary Josephine,[1] widow of Sir Alfred Joseph Doughty Tichborne, 11th Bart. [E.], da. of [Nos. 56939 to 56948.

---

[1] See the Clarence Volume, p. 364, for her descent from George, Duke of Clarence.

# of The Blood Royal

Henry Benedict (Arundell), 11th Baron Arundell of Wardour [E.]; and has issue 1e to 3e.

1e. William Joseph Wickham, Capt. Scots Guards (*Guards'; Boodle's; Bachelors'*), b. 5 Nov. 1874.

2e. Cyril Henry Wickham, Lieut. Royal Fusiliers (*Bachelors'*), b. 25 May 1878.

3e. Cecily Mary Wickham, m. 14 Sept. 1897, Frederick William Alfred Herbert Gillett; and has issue.

See p. 115, Nos. 1359-1360.

3d. Leonora Emma Wickham (*Frimley Park, Farnborough; 53 Warwick Square, S.W.*), m. 5 Jan. 1858, Herbert Crompton Herries of Frimley Park, d. 19 Mar. 1870: and has issue 1e to 4e.

1e. William Herbert Herries, Member of the New Zealand House of Representatives (*Shaftesbury, Te Aroha, New Zealand*), b. 19 Ap. 1859; m. (at Ohineroa) 4 Dec. 1889, Catherine, da. of Edward Francis Roche of Ohineroa.

2e. Robert Stansfield Herries, b. 19 Nov. 1860; m. 18 Ap. 1900, Mabel, da. of George Andrew Spottiswoode of Chattan, co. Devon.

3e. David Charles Herries, b. 7 Feb. 1863.

4e. Edward Francis Herries, b. 8 Dec. 1866.

2b. *Rev. Lamplugh Wickham, afterwards (2 Feb. 1795) Hird of Low Moor House, near Bradford, Preb. of York*, b. 14 *May* 1768; d. 1842; m. 1st, 2 Feb. 1795, Sarah Elizabeth, da. of Richard Hird of Rawdon, d. 24 Ap. 1812; 2ndly, 1813, Hannah Frances, da. of the Rev. Lascelles Sturdy Lascelles of Hunton, d. 1835; and had issue 1c to 7c.

1c. Henry Wickham Hird, afterwards (1843) *Wickham of Bradford, M.P., J.P., D.L.*, b. 23 Nov. 1800; d.s.p. 23 Sept. 1867.

2c. *Lamplugh Wickham Hird, afterwards Wickham of Chestnut Grove, near Tadcaster, J.P., D.L.*, b. 27 June 1807; d. 2 Jan. 1883; m. 1st, 1834, Frances, da. of Col. William Hale of Acomb, d. 14 Dec. 1842; 2ndly, 24 Aug. 1848, Mary, da. of George Stone of Blissworth Hall, d. 1877; and had issue 1d to 4d.

1d. William Wickham Wickham, J.P. (*Chestnut Grove, near Boston Spa*), b. 16 Sept. 1835; m. 27 Oct. 1868, Katherine Henrietta, da. of Thomas Fairfax of Newton-Kyme; and has issue.

See p. 535, Nos. 48994-49004.

2d. George Lamplugh Wickham, Major *late* Royal Horse Guards (*The Oaks, Thornhaugh, Wansford, R.S.O.*), b. 9 Mar. 1852; m. 28 Feb. 1885, Lady Elena Mary, da. of Charles (Gordon), 10th Marquis of Huntly [S.]; and has issue 1e.

1e. John Lamplugh Wickham, Lieut. Scots Guards, b. 6 June 1886.

3d. Henry Wickham Wickham, Lieut.-Col. Northants Imp. Yeo., *formerly* Scots Guards (*Barnwall Castle, Oundle*), b. 5 Oct. 1855; m. 16 Sept. 1884, Lady Ethelreda Caroline, da. of Charles (Gordon), 10th Marquis of Huntly [S.]; and has issue 1e to 2e.

1e. Mary Ethel Wickham.

2e. Alice Joan Wickham.

4d.[2] Frances Mary Wickham (*5 Upper George Street, Bryanston Square, W.*).

3c. *Charles Wickham Hird, Lieut. 74th Regt.*, b. 7 Oct. 1808; d. 1841; m. and had issue (with a son and da. who d. unm.) 2 das. now living.

4c. *Christiana Wickham*, b. 1801; d. 22 Feb. 1844; m. 18—, George Brooke Nelson of Leeds.

5c. *Sarah Elizabeth Wickham*, b. 1805; d. (–); m. the Rev. Joshua Fawcett of Wibsey.

6c. *Annabella Wickham*, b. 7 July 1810; d. (–); m. the Rev. George Hodgson.

7c. Jane Wickham, b. 19 Mar. 1818.   [Nos. 56949 to 56977.

The Plantagenet Roll

2*a. Mary Wickham*, bapt. 7 *Feb.* 1734; d. 7 (*or* 11) *Ap.* 1807; m. 9 *Ap.* 1752, *Jeremiah Dixon of Gledhow Hall, co. York, F.S.A., D.L.*, b. 1726; d. 7 *June* 1782; *and had issue* 1*b to* 4*b*.

1*b. John Dixon of Gledhow, Col. 1st West York Militia, J.P., D.L.*, b. 27 *June* 1753; d. 18 *Ap.* 1824; m. 13 *July* 1784, *Lydia, da. and eventual co-h. of the Rev. John Parket of Astle Hall, co. Chester*, b. 10 *Dec.* 1763; d. 1844; *and had issue* 1*c to* 2*c*.

1*c. John Dixon of Gledhow and Astle, Lieut.-Col. 1st Royals, J.P., D.L., 2nd son and eventual* (1838) *h.*, b. 19 *Feb.* 1799; d. 10 *Mar.* 1873; m. 14 *May* 1840, *Sophia, da. of Thomas William Tatton, previously Egerton of Wythenshaw,* d. 1885; *and had issue.*

See the Tudor Roll of " The Blood Royal of Britain," pp. 330–331, Nos. 26477–26498.

2*c. Mary Dixon,* d. (–); m. *George Stone of Blissworth Hall; and had* (*with possibly other*) *issue* 1*d*.

1*d. Mary Stone,* d. 1877; m. *as* 2*nd wife,* 24 *Aug.* 1848, *Lamplugh Wickham Hird, afterwards Wickham of Chestnut Grove; and had issue.*

2*b. Henry Dixon of Brooke Farm, near Liverpool,* d. 1819; m. *Catherine Townley, da. of Thomas Plumbe of Tong Hall, co. York; and had issue.*

3*b. Frances Dixon,* d. (–); m. *the Rev. William Shepley, M.A., P.C. of Horsforth,* b. 5 *Jan.* 1753.

4*b. Annabella Dixon,* d. (–); m. *Ellis Leckonby Hodgson of Stapleton Hall.*

[Nos. 56978 to 57031.

594. Descendants of ANNABELLA WICKHAM (see Table LXIV.), wife of the Rev. JAMES SCOTT, M.A., Fellow of Univ. Coll., Oxford, Vicar of Holy Trinity Church, Leeds, and of Bardsey; *b. c.* 1700; *d.* 11 Feb. 1782; *and had issue* 1*a to* 3*a*.[1]

1*a. Rev. James Scott, D.D., Rector of Simonburn, political writer,* b. 1733; d. s.p.s. 10 *Dec.* 1814; m. *Anne, da. of Henry Scott.*

2*a. John Scott of Charter House Square, London,* d. (–); m. *Margaret, da. of* [——] *Cunningham; and had issue* 1*b*.

1*b. Margaret Scott,* b. c. 1774; d. 7 *Dec.* 1853; m. 1*st, as* 2*nd wife,* 26 *Feb.* 1795, *Sir Richard Nauden-Bempde-Johnstone, 1st Bart.* [G.B.], *M.P.*, b. 21 *Sept.* 1732; d. 12/14 *July* 1807; 2*ndly, William Gleadowe; and had issue* (*by* 1*st husband*) 2 *sons and* 2 *das*.

3*a.* [*da.*] *Scott.*

595. Descendants of HENRY (WILLOUGHBY), 5th BARON MIDDLETON [G.B.] (see Table LXIV.), *b.* 19 Dec. 1726; *d.* 14 June 1800; *m.* 25 Dec. 1756, DOROTHY, da. and co-h. of George CARTWRIGHT of Ossington, *d.* 18 Sept. 1808; and had issue 1*a* to 2*a*.

1*a. Henry* (*Willoughby*), 6*th Baron Middleton* [G.B.], b. 24 *Ap.* 1761; d.s.p. 19 *June* 1835.

2*a. Hon. Dorothy Willoughby,* b. 13 *July* 1758; d.s.p. 13 *Ap.* 1824; m. 24 *Nov.* 1784, *Richard Langley of Wykeham Abbey.*

---

[1] Whitaker's *Thoresby's Ducatus Leodensis*, 1816, p. 13.

# of The Blood Royal

596. Descendants of the Rev. JAMES WILLOUGHBY, LL.B., Rector of Guiseley (see Table LXIV.), *bapt.* 23 Jan. 1732; *d.* 16 Feb. 1816; *m.* 4 Nov. 1772, ELEANOR, da. and co-h. of James HOBSON of Kirkby Moorside, *d.* 22 June 1830; and had issue 1*a* to 2*a*.

1*a. Henry Willoughby of Birdsall and Settrington, co. York,* b. 15 Dec. 1780; d. 20 Nov. 1849; m. 20 June 1815, Charlotte, da. of the Ven. John Eyre, d. 20 Sept. 1845; and had issue.
See p. 613, Nos. 52181–52286.

2*a. Elizabeth Willoughby,* b. 24 Feb. 1774; d. 25 Sept. 1858; m. 30 Oct. 1798, John Savile Foljambe of Aldwarke,[1] d.v.p. 14 Jan. 1805; and had issue 1b to 3b.

1*b. George Savile Foljambe of Osberton and Aldwarke,* b. 14 June 1800; d. 18 Dec. 1869; m. 1st, 9 Dec. 1828, Harriet Emily Mary, da. of Sir William Mordaunt Sturt Milner, 4th Bart. [G.B.], d. 28 Dec. 1830; 2ndly, 28 Aug. 1845, Selina Charlotte, Dowager Viscountess Milton, 2nd (but eldest to leave issue) da. and co-h. of Charles Cecil Cope (Jenkinson), 3rd (and last) Earl of Liverpool [G.B.]; and had issue 1c to 6c.

1*c.* Right Hon. Francis John Savile Foljambe, P.C., J.P., D.L., &c. (*Osberton, Worksop*), *b.* 9 Ap. 1830; *m.* 20 Feb. 1856, Lady Gertrude Emily, da. of Archibald (Acheson), 4th Earl of Gosford [I.], K.P.; and has issue 1c to 3c.
See the Clarence Volume, p. 271, Nos. 7241–7249.

2*c.* Cecil George Savile (Foljambe), 1st Earl of Liverpool [of the new (1905) creation, and 4th Earl in direct descent from the grantee of 1796] and Baron Hawkesbury [U.K.], F.S.A., F.R.G.S., J.P., D.L., Lord-Steward of the Household to H.M. the King, *formerly* (1894–1895) Lord-in-Waiting to Queen Victoria, &c. (*Kirkham Abbey, York; Ollerton House, Notts; Haselbech Hall, Northants; 2 Carlton House Terrace, S.W.*), *b.* 7 Nov. 1846; *m.* 1st, 22 July 1869, Louisa Blanche, da. of Frederick John Howard of Compton Place, Sussex, by his wife, Lady Fanny Cavendish, *d.* 7 Oct. 1871; 2ndly, 21 July 1877, Susan Louisa, da. of Lieut.-Col. William Henry Frederick Cavendish of West Stoke, Sussex, by his wife, Lady Emily Augusta Lambton; and has issue 1d to 11d.

1*d.* Arthur William de Brito Savile Foljambe, Viscount Hawkesbury, M.V.O., Capt. Rifle Brigade, State Steward and Chamberlain of the Household to the Lord-Lieutenant of Ireland (Lord Aberdeen), *b.* 27 May 1870; *m.* 27 July 1897, the Hon. Annette Louisa, da. of Henry (Monck), 5th Viscount Monck [I.].

2*d.* Hon. Gerald William Frederick Savile Foljambe, Capt. Oxfordshire L.I., *b.* 12 May 1878.

3*d.* Hon. Josceline Charles William Savile Foljambe, Lieut. Northumberland Fusiliers, *b.* 16 Oct. 1882.

4*d.* Hon. Robert Anthony Edward St. Andrew Savile Foljambe, *b.* 3 Ap. 1887.

5*d.* Hon. Bertram Marmaduke Osbert Savile Foljambe, *b.* 6 Jan. 1891.

6*d.* Hon. Victor Alexander Cecil Savile Foljambe (Queen Victoria sponsor), *b.* 19 Jan. 1895.

7*d.* Lady Edith Margaret Emily Mary Foljambe.

8*d.* Lady Alice Etheldreda Georgiana Mary Foljambe.

9*d.* Lady Mabel Evelyn Selina Mary Foljambe.

10*d.* Lady Constance Blanche Alethea Mary Foljambe.

11*d.* Lady Rosamond Sylvia Diana Mary Foljambe.

3*c.* Henry Savile Foljambe, *b.* 14 Oct. 1849.   [Nos. 57032 to 57160.

---

[1] See the Clarence Volume, p. 607, for his descent from George, Duke of Clarence.

The Plantagenet Roll

4c. Elizabeth Anne Foljambe, *b.* 17 Oct. 1847; *m.* 31 Jan. 1888, the Rev. William Bury, Canon of Peterborough (*Harleston Rectory, Northants*); and has issue 1*d*.

    1*d.* Violet Mary Bury, *b.* 3 Feb. 1893.

5c. Frances Mary Foljambe, *b.* 17 Oct. 1848; *m.* 10 Oct. 1876, the Rev. Savile Richard William L'Estrange-Malone, Minor Canon of Worcester, Rector of Dalton Holme (*Pallas Park, King's co.; Dalton Holme Rectory, Yorks*); and has issue 1*d* to 5*d*.

    1*d.* Edmund George Savile L'Estrange-Malone, Lieut. Royal City of London Fusiliers, *b.* 19 June 1878.

    2*d.* Cecil John L'Estrange-Malone, Naval Cadet R.N., *b.* 7 Sept. 1890.

    3*d.* Dorothy Elizabeth L'Estrange-Malone.

    4*d.* Selina Constance L'Estrange-Malone.

    5*d.* Mary Sibell L'Estrange-Malone.

6c. Caroline Frederica Foljambe, b. 16 Oct. 1850; d. 20 Oct. 1895; m. 4 Aug. 1881, Arthur Francis Gresham Leveson Gower, F.S.A., H.M.'s Diplomatic Service (British Legation, The Hague); and had issue 1d to 4d.

    1*d.* William George Gresham Leveson Gower, *b.* 12 Mar. 1883.

    2*d.* Osbert Charles Gresham Leveson Gower, Mid. R.N., *b.* 3 Nov. 1888.

    3*d.* Emily Selina Augusta Gresham Leveson Gower.

    4*d.* Victoria Sibell Ermyntrude Gresham Leveson Gower (Empress Frederick sponsor).

2b. Mary Arabella Foljambe, b. 27 Nov. 1801; d. 2 May 1859; m. 30 Dec. 1824, Rev. the Hon. Leland Noel Noel, b. 21 Aug. 1797; d. 10 Nov. 1870; and had issue.

    See the Clarence Volume, p. 608, Nos. 26754–26757.

3b. Emma Foljambe, b. 7 May 1803; d. 8 Aug. 1870; m. 11 Sept. 1832, Sir Charles Henry John Anderson of Broughton and Lea, 9th and last Bart. [E.], b. 24 Nov. 1804; d. 8 Oct. 1891; and had issue 1c to 3c.

    See the Clarence Volume, p. 608, Nos. 26758–26762.   [Nos. 57161 to 57181.

597. Descendants of Lucy Grimston (see Table LXIV.), *d.* May 1812; *m.* as 1st wife, 29 Mar. 1796, Sir Robert Wilmot, 3rd Bart. [G.B.], *b.* 5 July 1765; *d.* 13 July 1842; and had issue 1*a* to 6*a*.

1a. Sir Henry Sacheverel Wilmot, 4th Bart. [G.B.], b. 11 Feb. 1801; d. 11 Ap. 1872; m. 13 Dec. 1826, Maria, da. of Edward Miller Mundy of Shipley Hall, co. Derby, d. 24 Dec. 1865; and had issue 1b to 4b.

    1*b.* Sir Henry Wilmot, 5th Bart. [G.B.], K.C.B., V.C., M.P., *b.* 3 Feb. 1831; d.s.p. 7 *Ap.* 1901.

    2*b.* Rev. Arthur Alfred Wilmot, Rector of Morley with Smalley, *b.* 14 Feb. 1845; *d.* 11 *May* 1876; *m.* 16 *Jan.* 1872, *Harriet Cecilia, da. of the Rev. Alleyne Fitzherbert of Warsop;* and had issue 1*c*.

        1*c.* Sir Ralph Henry Sacheverel Wilmot, 6th Bart. [G.B.], Capt. Coldstream Guards (*Chaddesden Hall, Derby*), *b.* 8 June 1875.

    3*b. Maria Wilmot,* d. 1 Nov. 1897; m. 15 June 1854, James William Mitchell.

    4*b.* Constance Harriet Wilmot.

2a. John Wilmot, afterwards (R.L. 21 July 1860) Grimston of Neswick, b. 10 May 1807; d. 3 May 1879; m. 23 Sept. 1835, Jane, da. of Thomas Bewes, M.P., d. 18 Dec. 1889; and had issue 1b.

    1*b.* Fanny Wilmot (*Neswick Hall, Bainton, Driffield*) (sole h. in 1895), *m.*
                                [Nos. 57182 to 57184.

# of The Blood Royal

9 July 1868, Walter Francis Wrangham of Hotham House, Brough, *d.* 12 Dec. 1893; and has issue 1c to 5c.

1c. Digby Francis Wrangham, J.P., Capt. 3rd Batt. East Yorks Regt. (*Tickton Hall, Beverley*), *b.* 27 Ap. 1869; *m.* 18 Ap. 1899, Anna Maria, da. of Col. Arthur Brooksbank, J.P.; and has issue 1d to 2d.

1d. John Digby Wrangham, *b.* 1900.

2d. Hugh Heywood Wrangham, *b.* 1902.

2c. Walter George Wrangham, Bar. I.T. (*The Manor House, St. Margaret's, Ware*), *b.* 6 Mar. 1872; *m.* 7 Feb. 1899, Evelyn Agnes Fannie, da. of Edward Wilberforce, Master of the Supreme Court of Judicature; and has issue 1d to 2d.

1d. Geoffrey Walter Wrangham, *b.* 16 June 1900.

2d. Audrey Evelyn Fanny Wrangham.

3c. Wilmot John Wrangham, *b.* 1 Sept. 1874.

4c. Darcy George Wrangham, Lieut. 2nd Batt. East Yorks Regt., *b.* 29 Oct. 1878.

5c. Fanny Margaret Wrangham.

3a. *Edward Woollett Wilmot*, b. 3 *Aug.* 1808; d. 25 *June* 1864; m. *2ndly*, 13 *Jan.* 1841, *Emma Elizabeth, da. of Sir Francis Sacheverell Darwin*, d. 22 *Dec.* 1898; *and had issue 1b to 4b.*

1b. Rev. Darwin Wilmot, Heir presumptive to the Baronetcy (1759) [G.B.], Head-Master Macclesfield Grammar School, &c. (*Westbrook, Macclesfield*), *b.* 14 Oct. 1845; *m.* 3 Oct. 1876, Louisa Lilla, da. of the Rev. Charles Bickmore, D.D.; and has issue 1c to 4c.

1c. Edward Darwin Wilmot, *b.* 16 Mar. 1882.

2c. Sacheverell Darwin Wilmot, Lieut. R.A., *b.* 22 Feb. 1885.

3c. Dorothy Wilmot.

4c. Cicely Wilmot.

2b. Reginald Mead Wilmot (*Gobles Corner, Ontario, Canada*), *b.* 15 May 1852; *m.* 14 Mar. 1893, Melinda, da. of [——] Daniells; and has issue 1c to 2c.

1c. Garton Woollett Wilmot, *b.* 3 Dec. 1900.

2c. Frances Ellen Wilmot.

3b. Emma Maria Wilmot, *m.* 11 Oct. 1866, Godfrey Franceys Meynell, J.P., High Sheriff co. Derby 1874 (*Meynell Langley, Derby*); and has issue 1c to 6c.

1c. Godfrey Meynell, Capt. Shropshire L.I., *b.* 19 Aug. 1870; *m.* 1903, Violet, da. of George Earnwell of Brookfield Manor; and has issue 1d to 2d.

1d. Godfrey Meynell, *b.* 1904.

2d. [da.] Meynell, *b.* 1905.

2c. Hugo Meynell, Capt. Suffolk Regt. and A.D.C. to Governor of Bombay, *b.* 1 July 1875.

3c. Eleanor Meynell, *m.* 1st, 18 Oct. 1894, Capt. Alick Thornber England, *d.* (on active service in South Africa) 24 Feb. 1900; 2ndly, 1906, Charles Walker; and has issue 1d.

1d. Barbara Eleanor England.

4c. Mary Meynell.

5c. Emma Meynell.

6c. Margaret Meynell.

4b. Frances Jane Wilmot.

4a. *Edmund Wilmot Wilmot*, J.P., D.L., b. 15 *Oct.* 1809; d. 29 *June* 1869; m. 1 *June* 1848, *Ann, da. of Francis Edward Hurt of Adderwasley*, d. 1 *Nov.* 1893; *and had issue 1b to 7b.*

1b. Rev. Francis Edmund William Wilmot, M.A. (Oxon.), Rector of Monnington-on-Wye (*Monnington-on-Wye, Hereford*), *b.* 21 May 1849; *m.* 25 July 1878,

[Nos. 57185 to 57213.

The Plantagenet Roll

Katharine, da. of Col. Thomas Coningsby Norbury Norbury, C.B.; and has issue 1c to 11c.

  1c. Robert Wilmot, b. 14 July 1886.

  2c. Henry Cecil Wilmot, b. 13 June 1891.

  3c. Edward Wilmot, b. 24 Ap. 1893.

  4c. Thomas Norbury Wilmot, b. 18 Mar. 1896.

  5c. Laurence Mead Wilmot, b. 10 Aug. 1898.

  6c. Winifred Anne Wilmot.

  7c. Mary Sacheverel Wilmot, m. 1904, George Robins Joyce, House Master of Darlington Court, Bath College (Bath); and has issue 1d.

    1d. Audrey Marion Joyce, b. 1905.

  8c. Gertrude Wilmot.

  9c. Audrey Wilmot.

  10c. Katharine Joyce Wilmot.

  11c. Meriel Wilmot.

  2b. Edmund Mead Wilmot, Capt. late Sherwood Foresters (Sports), b. 17 Oct 1860; m. 1885, Agatha Georgiana, da. of Francis J. Jessopp; and has issue 1c to 2c.

    1c. Edmund Sacheverell Wilmot, b. 6 Feb. 1892.

    2c. Francis Hurt Wilmot, b. 8 Aug. 1894.

  3b. Rev. Richard Hurt Wilmot, M.A. (Oxon.), Vicar of Poulton (Poulton Vicarage, Fairford, Gloucester), b. 1 Mar. 1864; m. 19 Ap. 1893, the Hon. Charlotte Frances, da. of the Hon. Henry Sugden.

  4b. Rose Wilmot, m. 19 Feb. 1873, John Henry Fox; and has issue 1c to 3c.

    1c. Edmund John Fox, b. 1874; m. 1900, Lilian Maude, da. of Surgeon Major-Gen. Sir John Bycole Reade, K.C.B.

    2c. Esther Caroline Fox.

    3c. Celia Fox, m. 1897, Cuthbert Biddell.

  5b. Selina Maria Wilmot, m. 10 June 1872, Gerrard Andrewes Wigram (Jersey Lodge, Maidenhead); and has issue 1c.

    1c. Gerrard Edmund Wigram, M.A. (Camb.) (Cherry Orchard, Lichfield), b. 6 Oct. 1877; m. 11 Oct. 1902, Maria Isména, da. of William Townson-Mayne; and has issue 1d to 2d.

      1d. Francis Gerrard Mayne Wigram, b. 13 May 1905.

      2d. Margaret Isména Wilmot Wigram, b. 12 Oct. 1903.

  6b. Esther Ellen Wilmot.

  7b. Dora May Wilmot, m. 1880, Arthur Popham Hyde Parker; and has issue 1c to 2c.

    1c. Arthur Charles Hyde Parker, b. 1880.

    2c. Dulcibella Ruby Hyde Parker.

  5a. Lucy Maria Wilmot, d. (–); m. 1819, the Rev. Samuel Rickards, M.A., Rector of Stowlangtoff, co. Suffolk.

  6a. Harriet Wilmot, d. 19 Nov. 1866; m. 1821, the Rev. George J. Cornish of Salcombe, Preb. of Exeter.   [Nos. 57214 to 57241.

598. Descendants of MARIA GRIMSTON (see Table LXIV.), d. 10 Dec. 1813; m. as 1st wife, 28 Aug. 1794, WALTER RAMSDEN HAWKSWORTH FAWKES of Farnley, M.P., High Sheriff co. York 1823; b. 2 Mar. 1769; d. 1825; and had issue 1a to 10a.

  1a. Francis Hawksworth Fawkes of Farnley, J.P., D.L., b. 31 Jan. 1797; d. s.p. 13 Mar. 1871.

# of The Blood Royal

2a. Rev. Ayscough Fawkes of Farnley, d. 21 *July* 1871 ; m. *4 Sept.* 1830, *Ellen Martha, da. of John Bainbrigge Story of Lockington,* d. 28 *July* 1901 ; *and had issue.*

See p. 519, Nos. 47457–47484.

3a. Richard Fawkes, Major in the Army, b. 26 *July* 1809 ; d. 6 *Dec.* 1896 ; m. *4 Dec.* 1839, *Fanny, da. of Archibald Paris,* d. 17 *Jan.* 1893 ; *and had issue* 1b *to* 7b.

1b. Montagu Fawkes, Lieut.-Col. *late* Royal Irish Fusiliers (*White Lodge, Parkstone*), *b.* 1 June 1843 ; *m.* 4 Oct. 1884, Florence Geraldine, da. of the Rev. C. J. Dickenson, Vicar of Bodmin ; and has issue 1c to 3c.

1c. Charles Hawksworth Fawkes, *b.* 25 Aug. 1885.

2c. Lionel Richard Fawkes, *b.* 3 Feb. 1889.

3c. Cecil Wentworth Fawkes, *b.* 25 Ap. 1896.

2b. Wilmot Hawksworth Fawkes, Capt. R.N., *b.* 22 Dec. 1846 ; *m.* 18 Aug. 1875, Juliana, da. of Major John William Gooch Spicer of Spye Park, *s.p.s.*

3b. Rev. Richard Wentworth Fawkes, Vicar of Woodbury-Salterton, *formerly* Lieut. R.N. (*Woodbury-Salterton Vicarage, Exeter*), *b.* 7 Ap. 1848 ; *m.* 8 Ap. 1873, Isabel, da. of the Rev. Atkinson Holden of Nuttall, co. Notts ; and has issue 1c to 3c.

1c. Walter Hawksworth Fawkes, *b.* 26 Dec. 1875.

2c. Averil Mary Fawkes.

3c. Sibyll Fawkes.

4b. Lionel Grimston Fawkes, Col. *late* R.A. (*The Elms, Bedhampton, Havant*), *b.* 2 May 1849 : *m.* 28 Ap. 1891, Lady Constance Eleanor, da. of Archibald (Kennedy), 2nd Marquis of Ailsa [U.K.] ; and has issue 1c to 2c.

1c. Monica Fawkes.

2c. Lois Fawkes.

5b. Rev. Reginald Fawkes, Vicar of Poole, *b.* 2 Aug. 1850 ; *m.* 1st, 23 Feb. 1886, Elizabeth Janet, da. of Right Rev. the Hon. Samuel Waldegrave, D.D., *d.* 14 June 1890 ; 2ndly, 1 Dec. 1891, Elizabeth Mary, da. of Henry Abel Smith of Wilford House, Notts ; *s.p.s.*

6b. Algernon Fawkes, *b.* 23 Dec. 1851 ; *m.* Bertha, da. of Col. Dalgety.

7b. Archibald Walter Fawkes, Q.C., Attorney-Gen. of Gibraltar (*Gibraltar*), *b.* 3 Ap. 1855 ; *m.* 1884, Evelyn Fanny, da. of George John Johnson of Castlesteads, co. Cumberland.

4a. Maria Fawkes, d. (–) ; m. *Gen. Sir Edward Barnes, G.C.B.*

5a. Amelia Fawkes, d. (–) ; m. *Digby Cayley Wrangham, Serjeant-at-Law.*

6a. Fanny Fawkes, d. (–).

7a. Anne Fawkes, d. 9 *June* 1842 ; m. 20 *June* 1822, *Godfrey Wentworth of Woolley Park, J.P., D.L., High Sheriff co. York* 1862, b. 14 *Sept.* 1797 ; d. 22 *Sept.* 1865 ; *and had issue* 1b *to* 4b.

1b. Godfrey Hawksworth Wentworth, D.L. (*Woolley Park, near Wakefield*), *b.* 29 Jan. 1828.

2b. William Digby Wentworth, Capt. *late* 3rd Dragoon Guards, *b.* 4 Nov. 1839 ; *m.* 1885, Gertrude, da. of [——] Lancaster.

3b. Anne Wentworth.

4b. Katherine Mary Wentworth, *m.* 19 June 1860, Peter Withington, Lieut.-Col. 7th Dragoon Guards, *d.* 19 June 1875 ; and has issue 1c to 3c.

1c. Guy Edward Wentworth Wentworth, *b.* 15 July 1861 ; *m.* 19 Dec. 1892, Eleanor Maria, da. of Gen. Ewart, C.B.

2c. Everilda Wentworth, *m.* 19 Sept. 1895, Capt. Nichalls, 17th Lancers.

3c. Rosamond Wentworth, *m.* 11 Nov. 1896, Bertram Davenant Corbet, *late* Lieut. 1st Life Guards ; and has issue 1d.

1d. Hersey Muriel Corbet, *b.* 1897.

8a. Harriet Fawkes, d. (–).

[Nos. 57242 to 57292.

4 R

The Plantagenet Roll

9a. *Charlotte Fawkes*, d. (–) ; m. *Thomas Paris.*

10a. *Lucy Susan Fawkes*, d. (–) ; m. 1836, *Sir Anthony Cleasby of Penoyre, a Baron of the Exchequer* 1868–1878, d. 1879 ; *and had issue* 1b *to* 3b.

1b. Richard Digby Cleasby of Penoyre, J.P., D.L., High Sheriff co. Brecon 1890 (*Cecil Lodge, Abbots Langley, Herts*), b. 1838 ; m. 19 Ap. 1870, Edith Anne, da. of Edward Arkwright of Hatton, co. Warwick.

2b. Edith Mary Cleasby, m. 7 Dec. 1865, Ayscough Fawkes of Farnley, J.P., D.L., *d.s.p.* 21 June 1899.

3b. Lucy Antonia Cleasby, m. Frederick McClintock.   [Nos. 57293 to 57295.

599. Descendants of ELIZA ANN MARY GRIMSTON (see Table LXIV.), *bapt.* 12 May 1780 ; d. (–) ; *m.* FRANCIS RAMSDEN HAWKS-WORTH, *otherwise* FAWKES, of Brambro Grange, Doncaster, *b.* 12 Oct. 1774 ; d. (–) ; and had issue 1a to 2a.

1a. *Anne Elizabeth Hawksworth*, d. 1887 ; m. 23 *June* 1828, *George Legard of Westhorpe House, Scarborough*, b. 10 *June* 1802 ; d. 31 *Oct.* 1882 ; *and had issue* 1b *to* 6b.

1b. *Rev. Francis Digby Legard, Rector of Stokesley*, b. 13 *Mar.* 1829 ; d. 20 *Nov.* 1883 ; m. 18 *Ap.* 1872, *Jane, da. of Admiral Frederick Vernon Harcourt*, d. 22 *Mar.* 1875 ; *and had issue* 1c *to* 2c.

1c. D'Arcy Legard, Major 17th Hussars, *b.* 5 June 1873.

2c. Marcia Legard, *m.* 1902, the Rev. Arthur Crosbie Blunt, Vicar of Ganton (*Ganton Vicarage, Yorks*); and has issue 1d to 2d.

1d. Dorothy Marcia Blunt.

2d. Violet Alice Blunt.

2b. *John Hawksworth Legard*, b. 30 *Ap.* 1838 ; d. 28 *Feb.* 1906 ; m. 26 *Ap.* 1873, *Frances, widow of Major Coates, da. of the Rev. Slingsby Duncombe Shafto ; and has issue* 1c *to* 2c.

1c. George Shafto Legard, *b.* 29 July 1874.

2c. Ralph Hawksworth Legard, *b.* 1875.

3b. Albert George Legard, H.M.'s Chief Inspector of Schools for Wales (123 *Cathedral Road, Cardiff*), b. 31 May 1845 ; *m.* 7 Jan. 1875, Anna Mildreda, da. of Matthew R. Bigge of Stamford.

4b. Constance Legard.

5b. Anne Everilda Legard (108 *Bootham, York*), m. as 2nd wife, 9 Feb. 1871, Charles Granby Burke, Master of the Common Pleas [I.], d. 15 May 1898.

6b. Agnes Lucy Legard (*Appleton-le-Street House, Malton, Yorks*), m. 19 Jan. 1860, the Rev. Charles Pierrepont Peach, Vicar of Appleton-le-Street, d. 6 Oct. 1886 ; and has issue 1c to 6c.

1c. Rev. James Legard Peach, sometime Rector of St. James', Calcutta, *b.* 3 July 1861.

2c. Charles Edmond Cleaver Peach, *b.* 11 Oct. 1875 ; *m.* 24 June 1903, Georgina, da. of Admiral Hulton.

3c. Mary Emily Peach, *m.* as 2nd wife, 21 Ap. 1891, Charles Marriott, J.P. (*Cotesbach House, near Lutterworth*) ; and has issue.

See the Clarence Volume, p. 232, Nos. 4781–4787 and 4790.

4c. Agnes Ellin Peach.

5c. Clara Rose Peach.

6c. Georgina Peach.

2a. *Amelia Hawksworth*, d. 10 *Nov.* 1885 ; m. *as 2nd wife* 11 *July* 1844, *Capt. George Hotham, R.E.*, b. 11 *Sept.* 1796 ; d. 14 *Ap.* 1860 ; *and had issue* 1b *to* 2b.
                                                        [Nos. 57296 to 57319.

# of The Blood Royal

1*b*. *Alice Hotham*, d. 31 *Jan.* 1898; *m.* 2 *July* 1868, *Capt. John Loftus Bland of Blandsfort, J.P., D.L., late 6th Dragoons (Blandsfort Abbey, Leix); and had issue* 1*c*.

1*c*. Humphrey Loftus Bland, *late* Lieut. 5th Northumberland Fusiliers, *b*. Ap. 1869.

2*b*. *Lora Hotham,* d. 1 *Aug.* 1882; *m. as 1st wife, 14 Nov.* 1872, *Montagu Lubbock, M.D., F.R.C.P., M.R.C.S.* (19 *Grosvenor Street, W.); and had issue* 1*c*.

1*c*. Montagu Hotham Lubbock, Lieut. (ret.) R.N., *b*. 11 May 1876.

[Nos. 57320 to 57321.

600. Descendants, if any, of EMMA WILLOUGHBY (see Table LXIV.), *d.* 11 Nov. 1781; *m.* the Rev. NATHANIEL HODGSON of Appleton-le-Street, co. Yorks; and of ANTHONINA WILLOUGHBY, *d.* (-); *m.* 1765, the Rev. HENRY HEWGILL of Smeaton, co. Yorks.

601. Descendants of ANTHONINA WICKHAM (see Table LXIV.), *bapt.* 29 Sept. 1623; *bur.* 7 Aug. 1701; *m.* 25 Feb. 1639, TOBY (or TOBIAS) JENKINS of Grimston, co. York, *b. c.* 1614, being aged 52 in 1666; *bur.* 12 Feb. 1697; and had issue 1*a* to 3*a*.

1*a*. *Toby (or Tobias) Jenkins of Grimston, M.P., Lord Mayor of York* 1701 *and* 1720, bapt. 16 *June* 1660; d. 1730; m. *1st, Lady Mary, da. of Charles (Paulet), 1st Duke of Bolton* [E.], bur. 16 *Mar.* 1689; *and had issue* 1*b*.[1]

1*b*. *Mary Jenkins,* d. (-); m. 26 *Ap.* 1707, *Sir Henry Goodricke, 4th Bart.* [E.], b. 8 *Sept.* 1677; d. 21 *July* 1738; *and had issue.*

See p. 462, Nos. 39464–39474.

2*a*. *Anthonina Jenkins* [? m.[2] (*mar. lic. dated* 20 *June* 1670, *she being aged about* 20) *Justinian Pagitt of Gray's Inn*].

3*a*. *Dorothy Jenkins,* bur. 20 *July* 1896; *m.* 1*st, Robert Benson of Wrenthorpe; 2ndly* (*mar. lic.* 3 *Mar.*), 1680, *Sir Henry Bellasis of Pottoe, co. York, and Brancepeth, co. Durham.*   [Nos. 57322 to 57332.

602. Descendants of ELIZABETH CONSTABLE (see Table XLVII.), *m.* EDWARD ELLERKER; and had issue 1*a* to 8*a*.

1*a*. *Sir Ralph Ellerker of Risby,* d. 1641; m. *Anne, da. of* [——] *Dalton; and had issue* 1*b to* 9*b*.

1*b*. *Ralph Ellerker of Risby,* b. 1582 (*being aged* 2 *in* 1584); d. 1654; m. *Eleanor, da. of Thomas Metham of Metham.*

2*b*. *James Ellerker of Stillingfleet,* m. *Frances, da. of Allan Percy; and had issue* 1*c to* 2*c*.

1*c*. *John Ellerker of Risby,* d. 1655; m. *Dorothy, da. of John Roper; and had issue* 1*d*.

1*d*. *Dorothy Ellerker,* m. *Sir James Bradshaw of Broomborough, co. Chester; and had issue* 1*e to* 6*e*.

---

[1] He is said to have *m.* 2ndly and had issue William, *bapt.* at Dunnington 3 Oct. 1708; *m.* 1742, Mary, da. and h. of Daniel Munro of the Crescent Estates, St. Mary's, Jamaica; Tobias, Com. as Ensign dated 1741; and Anthonina, *bapt.* at Dunnington 12 June 1710. See "The Genealogist," N.S., xi. p. 224.

[2] See "The Genealogist," N.S., xi. p. 224.

1e. *Ellerker Bradshaw,* d. 1742; m. *Rebecca, da. of Sir Edward Northy, Attorney-General; and had issue 1f to 2f.*

1f. *Lucy Bradshaw.*

2f. *Rebecca Bradshaw.*

2e. *Isabella Bradshaw.*

3e. *Dorothy Bradshaw.*

4e. *Frances Bradshaw.*

5e. *Elizabeth Bradshaw.*

6e. *Susannah Bradshaw.*

2c. *Ralph Ellerker of North Frothingham, living* 1676.

3b. *Edward Ellerker.*

4b. *Robert Ellerker.*

5b. *Henry Ellerker.*

6b. *John Ellerker.*

7b. *Thomas Ellerker of Risby.*

8b. *Barbara Ellerker.*

9b. *Katharine Ellerker.*

2a. *Robert Ellerker.*[1]

3a. *William Ellerker.*[1]

4a. *Francis Ellerker.*[1]

5a. *John Ellerker.*[1]

6a. *Anne Ellerker.*

7a. *Eleanor Ellerker.*

8a. *Margaret Ellerker.*

603. Descendants, if any, of DOROTHY CREYKE (see Table LXVI.) wife of [——] CURRER.

604. Descendants of JAMES (BOYD, *afterwards* (1758) HAY) [*de jure* 5th EARL OF KILMARNOCK [S.] and (1758)] 15th EARL OF ERROLL and Hereditary Lord High Constable [S.] (see Table LXVI.), *b.* 20 Dec. 1726; *d.* 3 July 1778; *m.* 1st, 15 Sept. 1749, REBECCA, da. of Alexander LOCKHART, Lord Covington of Session, *d.* 2 May 1761; 2ndly, 10 Aug. 1762, ISABELLA, da. and in her issue (1795) h. of [Sir] William CARR of Etal [claiming to be 8th Bart. [S.]], *d.* 3 Nov. 1808; and had issue 1a to 6a.

1a. *George* (Hay), *16th Earl of Erroll* [S.], *&c., b.* 13 *May* 1767; *d.s.p.* 14 *June* 1798.

2a. *William* (Hay, *sometime* (R.L. 28 *Mar.* 1795–1798) *Carr),* 17th Earl of *Erroll* [S.], *&c., b.* 12 *Mar.* 1772; *d.* 26 *Jan.* 1819; *m.* 1st, 7 *Jan.* 1792, *Jane, da. of Matthew Bell of Woolsingham,* d. 14 *Ap.* 1793; 2ndly, 3 *Aug.* 1796, *Alicia, da. of Samuel Elliot of Antigua,* d. 24 *Ap.* 1812; 3rdly, 14 *Oct.* 1816, *the Hon. Harriet, sister to Mark* (Somerville), *6th Baron Somerville* [S.], *b.* 23 *May* 1786; *d.* 28 *Jan.* 1864; *and had issue 1b to 9b.*

---

[1] Other accounts give the sons as James, Edward. Henry, and Marmaduke. See George Oliver's "History of Beverley," p. 508; Poulson's "History of Holderness," i. p. 394; and Foster's "Visitations of Yorkshire," p. 136.

ALEXANDER WILLIAM GEORGE, DUKE OF FIFE, K.T., P.C.

A DESCENDANT OF ANNE (PLANTAGENET), DUCHESS OF EXETER.

Photo, W. & D. Downey, London.

# of The Blood Royal

1b. *William George (Hay), 18th Earl of Erroll [S.], 1st Baron Kilmarnock [U.K.], &c., K.T., G.C.H.,* b. 21 Feb. 1821 ; d. 19 *Ap.* 1846 ; m. 4 *Dec.* 1820, *Lady Elizabeth Fitzclarence, illegitimate da. of King William IV.,* d. 16 *Jan.* 1856 ; *and had issue* 1c *to* 4c.

1c. *William Henry (Hay), 19th Earl of Erroll [S.], 2nd Baron Kilmarnock [U.K.], &c.,* b. 3 *May* 1823 ; d. 3 *Dec.* 1891 ; m. 20 *Sept.* 1848 *Eliza Amelia V. A., da. of the Hon. Sir Charles Gore, G.C.B., K.H.; and had issue* 1d *to* 4d.

1d. Charles Gore (Hay), 20th Earl of Erroll [S.] [and but for the attainder of 1746], 10th Earl of Kilmarnock [S.], 3rd Baron of Kilmarnock [U.K.], Hereditary 23rd Lord High Constable of Scotland, &c., &c. (*Slains Castle, Port Erroll, R.S.O.; Walls, Cumberland ; 20 Buckingham Gate, S.W.*), b. 7 Feb. 1852 ; *m.* 11 Aug. 1875, Mary Caroline, da. of Edmund L'Estrange (by his wife Lady Harriet, *née* Lumley) ; and has issue 1e to 3e.

1e. Victor Alexander Sereld Hay, Lord Kilmarnock (*White's ; St. James'*), b. (H.M. Queen Victoria sponsor) 17 Oct. 1876 ; *m.* 22 May 1900, Mary Lucy Victoria, da. of Sir Allan Russell Mackenzie, 2nd Bart. [U.K.] ; and has issue 1f to 3f.

1f. Hon. Josslyn Victor Hay, b. 11 May 1901.

2f. Hon. Gilbert Allan Rowland Hay, b. 15 Jan. 1903.

3f. Hon. Rosemary Constance Ferelith Hay, b. 15 May 1904.

2e. Hon. Sereld Mordaunt Alan Joseph Hay, Lieut. R.N., b. 25 Nov. 1877.

3e. Hon. Ivan Josslyn Lumley Hay, sometime (1896–1901) a Page of Honour to T.M.'s Queen Victoria and King Edward VII.

2d. Hon. Arthur Hay, Capt. Reserve of Officers and a Gentleman Usher to H.M. the King, *formerly* Cameron Highlanders (*Guards'*), b. 16 Sept. 1855.

3d. Lady Cecilia Leila Hay, *m.* 31 Oct. 1883, Capt. George Allan Webbe, *late* 15th Hussars (31 *Hans Place, S.W.*).

4d. Lady Florence Agnes Adelaide Hay, *m.* 9 May 1895, Capt. Harry Wolsige-Gordon, 79th Cameron Highlanders (*Howey Hall, Llandrindod Wells, R.S.O., Radnor*).

2c. *Lady Ida Harriet Augusta Hay,* b. 18 *Oct.* 1821 ; d. 22 *Oct.* 1867 ; m. 1 *Nov.* 1841, *Charles George (Noel), 2nd Earl of Gainsborough [U.K.],* d. 13 *Aug.* 1881 ; *and had issue.*

See p. 188, Nos. 6777–6791.

3c. *Lady Agnes Georgina Elizabeth Hay,* b. 12 *May* 1829 ; d. 18 *Dec.* 1869 ; m. 16 *Mar.* 1846, *James (Duff), 5th Earl Fife [I.], 1st Baron Skene [U.K.], K.T.,* b. 6 *July* 1814 ; d. 7 *Aug.* 1879 ; *and had issue* 1d *to* 4d.

1d. Alexander William George (Duff), 6th Earl Fife [I.] and 1st Duke of Fife (1889–1900) [U.K.], &c., P.C., K.T., G.C.V.O. (*Duff House, Banff ; Mar Lodge, Braemar, N.B.; 15 Portman Square, W., &c.*), b. 10 Nov. 1849 ; *m.* 27 July 1889, H.R.H. Louise Victoria Alexandra Dagmar, Princess Royal of Great Britain and Ireland, da. of H.M. King Edward VII. ; and has issue 1e to 2e.

1e. H.H. Princess Alexandra Victoria Alberta Edwina Louise of Great Britain and Ireland, Heir Presumptive to the Dukedom of Fife (1900), b. 17 May 1891.

2e. H.H. Princess Maud Alexandra Victoria Georgina Bertha of Great Britain and Ireland, b. 3 Ap. 1893.

2d. Lady Anne Elizabeth Clementina Duff, *m.* 17 Oct. 1865, John Villiers Stuart (Townshend), 5th Marquis [G.B.] and 8th Viscount [E.] Townshend, d. 26 Oct. 1899 ; and has issue 1e to 2e.

1e. John James Dudley Stuart (Townshend), 6th Marquis [G.B.] and 9th Viscount [E.] Townshend (*Raynham Hall, Norfolk ; Brook Street, W.*), b. 17 Oct. 1866 ; *m.* 9 Aug. 1905, Gladys Ethel Gwendolen Eugenie, da. of Thomas Sutherst of Fountain Court, Temple, Bar.-at-Law.

2e. Lady Agnes Elizabeth Audrey Townshend, b. 12 Dec. 1870 ; *m.* 2 Sept. 1903, James Andrew Durham (8 *Norfolk Square, W.*) ; and has issue 1f.

1f. Nicholas James Redvers John Townshend Durham, b. 13 Jan. 1905.

[Nos. 57333 to 57364.

681

The Plantagenet Roll

3d. Lady Ida Louisa Alice Duff (72 *Gloucester Place, W.*), *m.* 1st, 3 June 1867, Adrian Elias Hope of 55 Prince's Gate (who obtained a div. 1873); 2ndly, 20 Sept. 1880, William Wilson of Hill Street, Berkeley Square, *d.* 16 Feb. 1905; and has issue 1*e* to 3*e*.

1*e.* Agnes Henriette Ida Mary Hope, *m.* 28 Aug. 1889, Edwin Joseph Lisle March-Phillipps de Lisle, J.P., D.L., F.S.A., *late* M.P. (*Charnwood Lodge, co. Leicester*); and has issue.

See the Clarence Volume, p. 452, Nos. 19585–19592.

2*e.* Mildred Hope.

3*e.* Ethel Hope, *m.* 21 Ap. 1903, John Percy Lockhart Mummery, F.R.C.S. (10 *Cavendish Place, W.*).

4d. Lady Agnes Cecil Emmeline Duff, *m.* 1st, 4 Oct. 1871, George Robert Hay, Viscount Dupplin (who obtained a div. July 1876), *b.* 27 May 1849; *d.v.p.* 10 Mar. 1886; 2ndly, 5 Aug. 1876, Herbert Flower, *d.* 30 Dec. 1880; 3rdly, 4 July 1882, Sir Alfred Cooper, F.R.C.S. (*Cooper Angus Lodge, Whiting Bay, Isle of Arran; 9 Henrietta Street, Cavendish Square, W.*); and has issue 1*e* to 5*e*.

1*e.* Alfred Duff Cooper, *b.* 22 Feb. 1890.

2*e.* Hon. Agnes Blanche Marie Hay, *m.* 3 Feb. 1903, Baron Herbert von Beneckendorff und von Hindenburg, Secretary of the Imperial German Legation (*Stockholm*).

3*e.* Stephanie Agnes Cooper, *m.* 19 Dec. 1903, Arthur Francis Levita (15 *Queen Street, Mayfair, W.*); and has issue 1*f*.

1*f.* Violet Levita, *b.* 10 Sept. 1904.

4*e.* Hermione May Louise Cooper, *m.* 1904, Neil Arnott (5 *and* 6 *Marina Bungalows, Bexhill-on-Sea*); and has issue 1*f*.

1*f.* Ian Duff Neil Arnott, *b.* 1905.

5*e.* Sybil Mary Cooper, *m.* 16 Jan. 1904, Richard Hart Davis (79 *Victoria Road, Kensington, W.*); and has issue 1*f*.

1*f.* [son] Davis, *b.* 23 Aug. 1905.

4c. Lady Alice Mary Emily Hay, b. 7 *July* 1835; d. 7 *June* 1881; m. 16 *May* 1874, Col. *Charles Edward Louis Philip Casimir* (*Stuart otherwise Hay-Allan, styled*) 4*th Count of Albany* [*Comte d'Albanie*],[1] d.s.p. 8 *May* 1882.

2b. Rev. the Hon. Somerville Hay, b. 20 *July* 1817; d. 25 Sept. 1853; m. 6 *June* 1843, Lady Alicia Diana, da. of Henry David (*Erskine*), 12*th Earl of Buchan* [S.] (*who re-m.* 5 *July* 1858, *Capt. James Young, and*) d. 3 *Oct.* 1891; *and had issue* 1*c*.

1*c.* Somerville Hay, *b.* (posthumous) 19 Nov. 1853.

3b. Lady Dulcibella Jane Hay, b. 1793; d. 10 *Jan.* 1885; m. 19 *Dec.* 1821, the Ven. Charles Nourse Wodehouse, Preb. of Norwich, b. 8 *Sept.* 1790; d. 17 *Mar.* 1870; *and had issue* 1*c to* 6*c*.

1*c.* Charles Wodehouse, b. 31 Dec. 1822; d. 29 *Ap.* 1902; m. 8 *Nov.* 1856, Maria, da. of Matthew Potts of Corrhill, d. 1895; *and had issue* 1*d to* 5*d*.

1*d.* Rev. Armine Wodehouse, Rector of Trimley (*St. Mary's Rectory, Trimley, Suffolk*), *b.* 7 May 1860.

2*d.* Jane Wodehouse.

3*d.* Alice Mary Wodehouse.

4*d.* Isabel Wodehouse.

5*d.* Lucy Wodehouse.   [Nos. 57365 to 57391.

---

[1] He was the only son of Charles Edward, 3rd Count (*b.* at Versailles 1799; *d.* 25 Dec. 1880), who with his elder brother John Sobieski Stolberg, 2nd Count (*d.s.p.* 1872), claimed that their father James Stuart, 1st Count, *otherwise* Thomas Hay-Allan, Lieut. R.N., was a legitimate son of Prince Charles Edward (King Charles III.) (who after 1 Jan. 1766, being then in exile, was generally known as Earl of Albany [Comte d'Albanie]), by his consort Louisa of Stolberg.

H.R.H. LOUISE, PRINCESS ROYAL, DUCHESS OF FIFE, AND THE
PRINCESSES ALEXANDRA AND MAUD.

THE ONLY TWO MEMBERS OF THE ROYAL HOUSE IN WHOM IS UNITED THE BLOOD
OF KING EDWARD IV. AND OF HIS SISTER THE DUCHESS OF EXETER.

By permission of Messrs. W. & D. Downey, London.

# of The Blood Royal

2c. James Hay Wodehouse, *late* Major Norfolk Art. Mil., sometime (1892–1894) Min. Resident and Consul Gen. for the Hawaiian Islands, *b.* 23 Ap. 1824; *m.* 19 Jan. 1861, Annette Fanny, da. of William Massey of Watton; and has issue 1*d* to 8*d*.

1*d*. James Hay Wodehouse, *b.* 30 Dec. 1861; *m.* 1900, Annie Pauhi, da. of the Hon. A. S. Cleghorn of Waikiki, Honolulu.

2*d*. Guy Armine Wodehouse, *b.* 8 June 1863.

3*d*. Ernest Hay Wodehouse, *b.* 1868.

4*d*. Kenneth Charles Wodehouse, *b.* 1873.

5*d*. Annette Maud Wodehouse, *m.* 1887, Robert Lambert.

6*d*. Amy Dulcibella Wodehouse, *m.* 1891, Louis von Tunpsky.

7*d*. Ethel Jane Wodehouse.

8*d*. Lela Bernice Wodehouse, *m.* [——]; and has issue.

3*c*. *Herbert Wodehouse*, b. 29 *July* 1827; d. 1889; m. 1856, *Mary, da. of George Wood*, d. 17 *Nov.* 1866; *and had issue (several children, of whom)* 1*d* to 2*d*.

1*d*. Edith Neville Wodehouse (2nd da.), *m.* 8 Oct. 1885, Philip Henry Clifford, Fellow of Christ's College, Oxon., Bar.-at-Law, *d.s.p.* 1895.

2*d*. Constance Wodehouse (4th da.), *m.* 25 Ap. 1903, Walter Barrington Beare.

4*c*. *Isabella Jane Wodehouse*, d. (–); m. 7 *Oct.* 1845, *the Rev. Arthur Wilson Upcher, Rector of Ashwellthorpe and Wriningham*; *and had issue* 1*d to* 4*d*.

1*d*. Rev. Arthur Charles Wodehouse Upcher, Rector of Hingham and Rural Dean (*Hingham Rectory, Attleborough*), *b.* 29 Aug. 1847; *m.* 9 July 1881, Margaret Ada Barham, da. of Rev. John Barham Johnson of Welborne; and has issue 1*e* to 6*e*.

1*e*. Cecil Upcher, *b.* 2 Feb. 1884.

2*e*. Sidney Wodehouse Upcher, R.N., *b.* 13 Nov. 1889.

3*e*. Alice Margaret Upcher.

4*e*. Sybil Upcher.

5*e*. Ruth Upcher.

6*e*. Christine Mary Upcher.

2*d*. Ven. James Hay Upcher, Archdeacon of Mashonaland (*Rusape Mission, Enkeldoorn, Mashonaland*), *b.* 21 Jan. 1854.

3*d*. Jane Upcher.

4*d*. Mary Upcher.

5*c*. *Emily Jane Wodehouse*, d. 17 *Ap.* 1901; m. 29 *May* 1856, *William John* (Legh), 1st Baron Newton [*U.K.*], b. 19 *Dec.* 1828; d. 15 *Dec.* 1898; *and had issue* 1*d to* 4*d*.

1*d*. Thomas Wodehouse (Legh), 2nd Baron Newton [U.K.] (*Lyme Park, Disley; Golborne Park, Warrington; 6 Belgrave Square, S.W.*), *b.* 18 Mar. 1857; *m.* 24 July 1880, Evelyn Caroline, da. of William Bromley Davenport, M.P.; and has issue 1*e* to 5*e*.

1*e*. Hon. Richard William Davenport Legh, *b.* 18 Nov. 1888.

2*e*. Hon. Piers Walter Legh, *b.* 12 Dec. 1890.

3*e*. Hon. Lettice Legh.

4*e*. Hon. Hilda Margaret Legh.

5*e*. Hon. Phyllis Eleanor Legh.

2*d*. Hon. Gilbert Legh, *late* Major Grenadier Guards (*The Drove House, Thornham, King's Lynn*), *b.* 21 Ap. 1858; *m.* 28 June 1894, Louisa, widow of Col. the Hon. George Villiers, C.B., C.M.G., da. of George Disney Maquay; and has issue 1*e*.

1*e*. Peter Legh, *b.* 4 Sept. 1896.

3*d*. Hon. Dulcibella Jane Legh.

4*d*. Hon. Mabel Maud Legh, *m.* 25 July 1889, Major the Hon. William Chambre Rowley (10 *Cliveden Place, S.W.*).

[Nos. 57392 to 57422.

The Plantagenet Roll

6c. Alice Maria Wodehouse (*Sandecotes Cottage, Parkstone, Dorset*), *m.* 20 Ap. 1854, the Rev. Robert Wilson Pearse, *d.* (–); and has issue 1*d* to 4*d*.

1*d*. Hugh Wodehouse Pearse, D.S.O., Col. *late* East Surrey Regt., *b.* 13 Aug. 1855; *m.* 3 Jan. 1889, Ada Gordon, da. of Walter Scott of 4 Adelaide Mansions, Brighton; and has issue 1*e* to 2*e*.

2*e*. Hugh Armine Wodehouse Pearse, *b.* 27 Jan. 1892.

2*e*. Dulcibella Wodehouse Pearse, *b.* 10 June 1890.

2*d*. *Charles Wodehouse Pearse*, b. 20 Feb. 1857; d. (? unm.).

3*d*. Armine Wodehouse Pearse, *b.* 23 Jan. 1862; *m.*

4*d*. Dulcibella Jane Pearse.

4*b*. *Lady Isabella Hay*, b. 24 Feb. 1800; d. 28 July 1868; m. 14 Ap. 1820, Lieut.-Gen. William Wemyss, b. 5 Sept. 1790; d. 30 Nov. 1852; and had issue (with two sons, who both apparently d.s.p.) 1c.

1*c*. Isabella Harriet Jane Wemyss, *m.* Count Reventlow-Criminil.

5*b*. *Lady Harriet Jemima Hay*, b. 9 Jan. 1803; d. 8 Feb. 1837; m. 12 Dec. 1822, Daniel Gurney of North Runcton, High Sheriff co. Norfolk 1853, d. 14 June 1880; and had issue 1c to 6c.

1*c*. *Francis Hay Gurney*, J.P., D.L., Lieut.-Col. West Suffolk Yeo. Cav., b. 1826; d. 1 Dec. 1891; m. 8 July 1847, Margaret Charlotte, da. of Sir William Browne ffolkes, 2nd Bart. [G.B.], d. 23 May 1899; and had issue 1d to 11d.

1*d*. Reginald Gurney, *b.* 1849; *m.* 1889, Maud, da. of William Robertson.

2*d*. Lewis Edmund Gurney, Capt. *late* 20th Hussars, *b.* 6 Jan. 1852.

3*d*. Cecil Francis Gurney, *b.* 1862.

4*d*. Lovel Wodehouse Gurney, Capt. 3rd Batt. Norfolk Regt., *b.* 1865.

5*d*. Edward Hay Gurney, *b.* 1866; *m.* 28 Aug. 1894, Isabel Louisa, da. of Samuel Gurney Buxton of Catton Hall; and has issue 1*e* to 2*e*.

1*e*. Sylvia Margaret Hay Gurney.

2*e*. Catherine Isabel Gurney.

6*d*. Hudson Gurney, *b.* 1868.

7*d*. Harriet Charlotte Gurney.

8*d*. Rachel Louisa Gurney.

9*d*. Helen Mary Gurney.

10*d*. Millicent Gurney.

11*d*. Beatrice Gurney.

2*c*. *Rev. William Hay Gurney*, Rector of North Runcton, d. 29 May 1898; m. 8 Sept. 1852, Anna Maria, da. of Sir John Peter Boileau, 1st Bart. [U.K.], d. 21 Nov. 1891; and had issue 1d to 7d.

1*d*. Mortimer Hay Gurney, *b.* 12 Jan. 1855; *m.* 1882, Isabella Symington, da. of Wemyss Simpson of Sault St. Marie, Ontario.

2*d*. Gerald Boileau Gurney, *b.* 12 Mar. 1856.

3*d*. Anselm Gurney, *b.* 24 Aug. 1864.

4*d*. Harriet Eva Louisa Gurney, *m.* 1882, Major George Cresswell of King's Lynn.

5*d*. Winifred Henrietta Catherine Gurney.

6*d*. Kathleen Laura Alicia Gurney, *m.* 2 June 1893, Cresswell Cresswell.

7*d*. Richenda Agnes Paulina Gurney.

3*c*. *Charles Henry Gurney*, b. 1833; d. (–); m. 8 Oct. 1861, Alice, da. of the Hon. Toby Henry Princep, Member of the Council, East Indies (who re-m. 1897, Major John Bourchier Stracey); and had issue.

4*c*. Somerville Arthur Gurney, J.P., D.L., Mayor of King's Lynn 1896–1897 (*North Runcton Hall, King's Lynn*); and has issue 1*d* to 10*d*.

[Nos. 57423 to 57450.

1*d*. Walter Somerville Gurney, *b.* June 1858; *m*, 22 Nov. 1893, Violet Elizabeth Emily, da. of Sir Thomas Vincent Hope Cochrane Troubridge, 4th Bart. [G.B.]; and has issue.

See p. 626, Nos. 53059–53061.

2*d*. Anthony Francis Gurney, *b.* Aug. 1864.

3*d*. Hugh Gurney, *b.* Nov. 1867.

4*d*. Philip Hamond Gurney, *b.* Dec. 1876.

5*d*. Rose Katherine Gurney, *m.* W. John Birkbeck.

6*d*. Lily Cecilia Gurney, *m.* Adair Craigie.

7*d*. Ruth Gurney.

8*d*. *Mabel Gurney*, d. 26 *Ap.* 1888; m. *as 1st wife*, 14 *Ap.* 1887, *Sir William Michael Curtis, 4th Bart.* [*U.K.*] (*Caynham Court, Ludlow*); *and had issue* 1*e*.

1*e*. Constance Mabel Curtis.

9*d*. Audrey Florence Gurney.

10*d*. Muriel Constance Amy Gurney, *m.* 12 Ap. 1899, the Rev. Edmund Seymour Daubeney, Rector of Brancaster (*Brancaster Rectory, Lynn*).

5*c*. *Louisa Jane Gurney*, d. 29 *Aug.* 1867; m. 1 *Nov.* 1855, *Sir Thomas St. Vincent Hope Cochrane Troubridge, 3rd Bart.* [*G.B.*], d. 2 Oct. 1867; *and had issue*. See p. 626, Nos. 53047–53062.

6*c*. *Margaret Barclay Gurney*, d. (–); m. 5 *June* 1856, *James Henry Orde of Hopton, co. Suffolk, J.P.*, b. 30 *Sept.* 1830; d. 21 *Feb.* 1880; *and had issue*. See the Tudor Roll of "The Blood Royal of Britain," p. 521, Nos. 34917–34932.

6*b*. *Lady Caroline Augusta Hay*, b. *May* 1805; d. 19 *Aug.* 1877; m. 18 *Sept.* 1823, *John Morant of Brokenhurst, J.P., D.L.,* High Sheriff co. Hants 1820; b. 27 *Jan.* 1878; d. 5 *May* 1857; *and had issue* 1*c* to 3*c*.

1*c*. *John Morant of Brokenhurst, J.P., D.L.,* High Sheriff co. Hants, b. 11 *Feb.* 1825; d. 30 *May* 1899; m. *2ndly*, 2 *Ap.* 1866, *Flora Jane, da. of Rev. the Hon. William Eden ; and had issue* 1*d* to 3*d*.

1*d*. Edward John Harry Eden Morant, J.P., Hon. Attaché Diplo. Ser. (*Brokenhurst Park, near Lymington, Hants*), *b.* 1868.

2*d*. Francis George Morant, *b.* 1869.

3*d*. Mabel Caroline Flora Morant, *m.* 1889, Herbert George Alexander; and has issue.

2*c*. *Hay Richardo Morant of Ringwood*, d. 1895; m. 2 *Nov.* 1861, *Elizabeth, da. of Charles Fluder of Lymington ; and had (with other) issue* 1*d*.

1*d*. Hay George Samuel Morant, *b.* 26 Dec. 1862.

3*c*. *William Samuel Morant, Capt. Grenadier Guards*, d. (? s.p.) 12 *Feb.* 1879 ; m. *Isabella, da. of F. B. Long.*

7*b*. *Lady Emma Hay*, b. 29 *Jan.* 1809; d. 17 *July* 1841; m. 8 *Aug.* 1826, *James Erskine-Wemyss of Wemyss Castle and Torrie, Rear-Adm. R.N.*, b. 9 *July* 1789; d. 3 *Ap.* 1854; *and had issue* 1*c* to 2*c*.

1*c*. *James Hay Erskine-Wemyss of Wemyss Castle and Torrie, M.P.,* High Sheriff co. Fife 1864; b. 29 *Aug.* 1829; d. 29 *Mar.* 1864; m. 17 *Ap.* 1855, *Millicent Anne Mary, da. of the Hon. John Kennedy Erskine*, d. 11 *Feb.* 1895; *and had issue* 1*d* to 5*d*.

1*d*. Randulph Gordon Erskine-Wemyss, D.L., late A.D.C. to Inspector-Gen. Imp. Yeo. (*Wemyss Castle, Kirkcaldy*), *b.* 11 July 1858; *m.* 1st, 28 July 1884, Lady Lilian Mary, da. of John (Paulet), 14th Marquis of Winchester [E.] (who obtained a div. 1898); 2ndly, 23 Nov. 1898, Lady Eva Cecilia, da. of William Henry (Wellesley), 2nd Earl Cowley [U.K.]; and has issue 1*e* to 2*e*.

1*e*. Michael John Erskine-Wemyss, *b.* 8 Mar. 1888.

2*e*. Mary Millicent Erskine-Wemyss, *b.* 15 May 1885.

2*d*. Hugo Erskine-Wemyss, *b.* 31 May 1861.

The Plantagenet Roll

3d. Rosslyn Erskine Erskine-Wemyss, M.V.O., Capt. R.N., Comdt. Royal Naval Coll., Osborne, Commander of the *Ophir* during the Colonial Tour of T.R.H. the Prince and Princess of Wales, &c. (*Governor's House, Royal Naval College, Osborne*), b. (posthumous) 12 Ap. 1864; m. 1903, Victoria, da. of the Right Hon. Sir Barnet David Morier, P.C., G.C.B., G.C.M.G.

4d. *Dora Mona Kittina Erskine-Wemyss*, d. 24 Dec. 1894; m. 21 *Ap.* 1887, *Lord Henry George Grosvenor* (*Tittensor, Stoke-upon-Trent*); *and had issue* 1e *to* 3e.

1e. William Grosvenor, b. 23 Dec. 1894.

2e. Millicent Constance Grosvenor.

3e. Dorothy Alice Margaret Augusta Grosvenor.

5d. Mary Frances Erskine-Wemyss, m. 22 Feb. 1882, Capt. Cecil Stratford Paget; and has issue 1e to 2e.

1e. Louis George Paget, b. 26 Feb. 1891.

2e. Agnes Millicent Augusta Dorothy Canning Paget.

2c. *Frances Harriet Erskine-Wemyss*, b. 27 *Ap.* 1827; d. 14 *Dec.* 1877; m. 16 *May* 1850, *Capt. Charles Balfour, R.N., Cadet of Balbirnie*, d. 3 *Feb.* 1878; *and had issue* 1d.

1d. Alicia Hay Balfour, m. 16 Oct. 1886, the Rev. Edward Seymour Awdry (*Manor Cottage, Seend, Melksham*).

8b. *Lady Fanny Hay*, b. 18 *Aug.* 1818; d. 28 *Aug.* 1853; m. 2 *Aug.* 1848, *the Rev. Stephen Ralph Cartwright, Rector of Aynhoe*, d. 9 *Aug.* 1862; *and had issue* 1c.

1c. Augusta Emma Cartwright.

9b. *Lady Margaret Julia Hay*, b. (*posthumous*) 31 *Aug.* 1819; d. 31 *Oct.* 1891; m. 23 *Sept.* 1846, *Frederick Astell Lushington of Rosiere, Hants, J.P.*, b. 1 *Nov.* 1815; d. 18 *Sept.* 1892; *and had issue* 1c *to* 5c.

1c. Algernon Hay Lushington, Heir-presumptive to Baronetcy (1791) [G.B.] (*Lansdowne, Shanklin, I.W.*), b. 29 Sept. 1847; m. 1st, 2 Ap. 1872, Emma Jane, da. of Charles Castleman of Glasshayes, d. 4 Oct. 1879; 2ndly, 6 Jan. 1881, Effie Lilian, da. of Capt. W. E. Newall, 92nd Highlanders; and has issue 1d to 3d.

1d. Herbert Castleman Lushington, b. 15 Sept. 1879.

2d. Montagu Hay Lushington, b. 24 Nov. 1881.

3d. Muriel Evelyn Lushington.

2c. Rev. Somerville Henry Lushington, Rector of Boothby Pagnell (*Boothby Pagnell Rectory, Lincolnshire*), b. 24 May 1856.

3c. Beatrice Harriet Lushington (*Lyndhurst, Hants*).

4c. Constance Fanny Lushington (*Shrubbs Hill, Lyndhurst*), m. 13 May 1889, Rear-Admiral Henry Compton Aitchison, R.N., d. 6 Sept. 1901; and has issue 1d to 2d.

1d. Constance Margaret Aitchison.

2d. Stella Catharine Aitchison.

5c. Violet Margaret Lushington, m. 3 May 1899, Henry A'Court Pigott, M.A. (Oxon.) (*Junior Conservative*).

3a. *Lady Mary Hay*, b. 24 *July* 1754; d. (–); m. 5 *Nov.* 1770, *Gen. John Scot of Balcomie, M.P.* (*who obtained a div. and*) d. 7 *Dec.* 1775; *and had issue.*

4a. *Lady Margaret Hay*, b. 12 *Dec.* 1769; d. 1832; m. 6 *Aug.* 1789, *Charles Cameron of Messrs. Harley, Cameron & Co. of London, Bankers ; and had issue* 1b *to* 4b.

1b. *Charles Hay Cameron.*

2b. *Isabella Hay Cameron.*

3b. *Mary Hay Cameron.*

4b. *Margaret Hay Cameron.*

[Nos. 57504 to 57522.

# of The Blood Royal

5a. *Lady Maria Elizabeth Hay*, b. 30 *Ap*. 1771; d. 3 *June* 1804; m. 19 *June* 1795, *the Rev. George Moore, Rector of Wrotham (son of the Archbishop of Canterbury)*; and had issue 1b.

    1b. *Caroline Mary Moore.*

6a. *Lady Flaminia Hay*, b. 24 *Sept.* 1774; d. 1821; m. 6 *May* 1809, *George James, Capt. Royal Scots.*

605. Descendants of the Hon. CHARLES BOYD of Slains Castle, an officer in the service of Prince Charles (see Table LXV.), d. 3 Aug. 1782; *m.* 1st (in France) a French lady; and had issue 1*a* to 2*a*.

1a. *Charles Boyd, Major in the Army*, d. (–); m. 24 *Dec.* 1784, [——], *da. of John Haliburton of Princes Street, Edinburgh*, d. 3 *Sept.* 1785; and had issue 1b.

    1b. *[son] Boyd*, b. *Sept.* 1785.

2a. *Charlotte Boyd*, d. (–); m. 22 *Ap.* 1773, *Charles Edward Gordon, 4th of Wardhouse and Kildrummy*, b. 14 *Feb.* 1750; d. 23 *Dec.* 1832; and had issue 1b.

1b. *John David Gordon, 5th of Wardhouse and Kildrummy*, d. 4 *Aug.* 1850; m. 1805, *Maria del Carmen, da. of* [——] *Beigbeder of Jeroz de La Frontera in Spain*; and had issue 1c to 5c.

1c. *Pedro Carlos Gordon, 6th of Wardhouse and Kildrummy*, b. 23 *Dec.* 1806; d. *Feb.* 1857; m. *Rosa Elena, da. of Joseph Prendergast of Cadiz*; and had issue 1d to 3d.

    1d. *Jean Jose Gordon, 7th of Wardhouse*, b. 22 *Dec.* 1837; d.s.p. 26 *May* 1866.

2d. Maria de las Mersedes Gordon, *m.* 12 *May* 1862, the Count of Carlet (Conde de Carlet).

    3d. Maria de la Concepcion Gordon.

2c. *Carlos Pedro Gordon, 8th of Wardhouse, Knt. of St. John of Jerusalem, J.P., D.L., H.B.M.'s Consul at Jeroz de La Frontera*, b. 6 *Dec.* 1814; d. (–); m. 28 *Nov.* 1838, *Elena Maria, da. of Joseph Prendergast of Cadiz*, d. 1894; and had issue 1d to 10d.

1d. *Carlos Pedro Gordon, Younger of Wardhouse*, b. 27 *July* 1844; d.v.p. 31 *Mar.* 1876; m. 18 *Sept.* 1871, *Rosa, da. of* [——], *Count of Mirasol (Conde de Mirasol)*; and had issue 1e to 2e.

1e. Rafael Gordon, 9th of Wardhouse (*Wardhouse, Insch, Aberdeen; The Lodge, Kildrummy, Mossat*), b. 28 May 1873.

    2e. Pedro Gordon, b. 30 Aug. 1875.

    2d. Arturo Leon Gordon, b. 28 June 1850.

    3d. Rev. Pedro Carlos Gordon, S.J., b. 17 Feb. 1853.

    4d. Joseph Maria Gordon, b. 18 Mar. 1856.

    5d. Maria del Carmen Gordon, *m.* Capt. Rivero, Spanish Navy.

    6d. Christina Gordon, *m.* Juan Oronez of Jerez de La Frontera.

    7d. Elena Maria Gordon, *m.* Miguel La Fuente of Jerez de La Frontera.

    8d. Rosa Edwarda Gordon.

9d. Marie Magdalena Gordon, *m.* 15 Jan. 1874, Hugh Gordon Lumsden of Auchindoir, J.P., D.L. (*Auchindoir, co. Aberdeen*); and has issue 1e to 2e.

    1e. Hugh Patrick Lumsden, b. 17 Mar. 1876.

    2e. Carlos Barron Lumsden, b. 19 July 1878.

10d. Ursula Maria Gordon, *m.* 2 Ap. 1894, Francis Archibald Fairlie, Cadet of Holmes; and has issue 1e to 3e.

    1e. Francis Gerald Luis Fairlie, b. 1 Nov. 1899.

    2e. Consuelo Fairlic.

    3e. Clare Fairlie.

[Nos. 57523 to 57540.

3c. Alexander Gordon, b. 17 Aug. 1828; m. Doña Maria Josefa, da. of Don Fermin Doz; and has issue.

4c. Luis Gordon, b. Sept. 1829; m. Doña Petra Davila, da. of [———], Marquis of Villamarta (Marqués de Villamarta); and has issue.

5c. *Josefa Gordon*, d. 31 *Aug.* 1870; m. *Don Francisco (Ponce de Leon), Marquis of the Castillo del Valle de Signena (Marqués del Castillo del Valle de Signena); and had issue.* [Nos. 57541 to 57542.

606. Descendants, if any, of Capt. the Hon. JAMES BOYD; Capt. the Hon. CHARLES BOYD, d. 1737; the Hon. ROBERT BOYD; the Lady MARY BOYD, wife of Sir ALEXANDER MACLEAN; the Lady CATHERINE BOYD, wife of ALEXANDER PORTERFIELD of Porterfield; and of the Hon. EVA BOYD, wife of Sir DAVID CUNNINGHAM of Robertland (see Table LXVI.).

607. Descendants, if any, of EVERILDA CREYKE (see Table LXVI.), wife of RICHARD MUSGRAVE.

608. Descendants of the Rev. JOHN CREYKE, Rector of Leven (see Table LXVI.), b. 29 Ap. 1713; d. (–); m. CATHERINE, da. of John AUSTEN of Adisham, co. Kent; and had issue 1a to 3a.

1a. *Ralph Creyke of Marton, Col. East Riding Militia*, b. 6 *July* 1745; d. 24 May 1826; m. 6 *Feb.* 1772, *Jane, da. of Richard Langley of Wykeham Abbey*, d. 31 Dec. 1794; *and had issue (with 5 das., Everilda, Catherine, Jane, Elizabeth, and Anne, who apparently d. unm.) 1b to 3b.*

1b. *Ralph Creyke of Marton and Rawcliffe*, b. 11 *Ap.* 1776; d. 7 *June* 1828; m. 14 Nov. 1807, *Frances, da. of Robert Denison of Kilnwick Percy*, d. 1840; *and had issue 1c to 6c.*

1c. *Ralph Creyke of Rawcliffe and Marton, J.P., D.L.*, b. 13 *Sept.* 1813; d. 7 *Feb.* 1858; m. 27 *Aug.* 1846, *Louisa Frances, da. of Col. Croft of Stillington Hall*, d. 20 *July* 1890; *and had issue 1d to 5d.*

1d. Ralph Creyke, J.P., D.L., High Sheriff co. York 1894, sometime (1880–1885) M.P. for York City (*Rawcliffe Hall, Goole; Marton, Bridlington*), b. 5 Sept. 1849; m. 28 Dec. 1882, Frances Elizabeth, da. of Sir Henry Hickman Bacon, Premier Baronet [E.]; and has issue 1e to 3e.

1e. Ralph Creyke, b. 17 Oct. 1883.

2e. Edmund Ralph Creyke, b. 26 Oct. 1886.

3e. Everilda Frances Creyke, b. 9 Nov. 1889.

2d. *Everilda Elizabeth Creyke*, d. 1 *Aug.* 1890; m. 26 *Oct.* 1874, *Christopher John Naylor, now (since* 1891) *Leyland, J.P. (Haggerston Castle, Beal, Northumberland, &c.); and had issue 1e.*

1e. Hilda Georgina Naylor, m. 21 Ap. 1900, Richard Vernon Cholmondeley; and has issue 1f to 2f.

1f. Hilda Cholmondeley.

2f. Victoria Millicent Cholmondeley.

3d. Katherine Harriet Creyke, m. 29 June 1879, Col. Arthur Henry Armytage, R.A. (*The White House, Clifton, Yorks*); and has issue.

See the Clarence Volume, p. 124, Nos. 1434–1436.

4d. Blanche Priscilla Creyke. [Nos. 57543 to 57554.

# of The Blood Royal

5d. Louisa Creyke, m. Nov. 1888, Clement William Swetenham, J.P., *late* R.N. (*Somerford Booths, Congleton, Chester*) ; and has issue 1e.

  1e. Edmund Swetenham, b. 30 Ap. 1890.

2c. *Richard Boynton Creyke,*
3c. *Robert Gregory Creyke,*
4c. *Frances Creyke,*
5c. *Mary Anne Elizabeth Creyke,*
} d. (? *unm.*).

6c. *Emma Jane Creyke,* d. 8 Ap. 1869 ; m. *as 1st wife,* 20 *June* 1843, *Charles Granby Burke, Master of the Court of Common Pleas* [*I.*], d. 15 *May* 1898 ; *and had issue.*

See the Clarence Volume, p. 499, Nos. 21737–21746.

2b. *Frances Creyke,* d. (–) ; m. 11 Dec. 1797, *Digby Legard of Watton Abbey,* co. Yorks, b. 1766 ; d. (–) ; *and had issue* 1c *to* 3c.

  1c. *George Legard of Westhorpe House, Scarborough,* b. 10 *June* 1802 ; d. 31 *Oct.* 1882 ; m. 23 *June* 1828, *Anne Elizabeth, da. and co-h. of Francis Ramsden Hawksworth of Bambro Grange ; and had issue.*

  See p. 678, Nos. 57296–57319.

  2c. *Rev. Digby Charles Legard,* b. 29 *May* 1815 ; d. 3 *July* 1851 ; m. 6 *Oct.* 1846, *Henrietta Isabella, da. of the Rev. Francis Simpson,* d. 3 *July* 1851 ; *and had issue.*

  See the Clarence Volume, p. 236, Nos. 4874–4883.

  3c. *Agnes Legard,* d. 3 *Jan.* 1868 ; m. 14 *Ap.* 1832, *Thomas Marshall of Hartford Beach, co. Cheshire,* d. 20 *Mar.* 1838.

3b. Agnes Creyke, m. the Ven. Francis Wrangham, Archdeacon of the East Riding, and Vicar of Hunmanby, co. York ; and has issue (at least) 1c.

  1c. *Agnes Everilda Frances Wrangham,* d. 17 *Nov.* 1834 ; m. *as 1st wife,* 16 *June* 1832, *the Ven. Robert Isaac Wilberforce, Archdeacon of the East Riding* (*brother of the Bishop of Oxford*), b. 19 *Dec.* 1802 ; d. 3 *Feb.* 1857 ; *and had issue* 1d *to* 2d.

    1d. *Rev. William Francis Wilberforce, M.A.* (*Oxon.*), b. 27 *June* 1833 ; d. (? s.p.) 25 *Dec.* 1905 ; m. 20 *Oct.* 1870, *Elizabeth, da. of Charles Hope Maclean ;* d. 15 *Mar.* 1904.

    2d. Edward Wilberforce, Barrister and Master of Supreme Court of Judicature (*The Manor House, St. Margaret's, Ware, Herts*), b. 9 Nov. 1834 ; m. 3 May 1860, Fannie, da. of Alexander Flash of New Orleans, d. 31 Oct. 1895 ; and has issue 1e to 4e.

      1e. Lionel Robert Wilberforce, b. 18 Ap. 1861 ; m. 13 Aug. 1891, Margaret, da. of the Rev. W. Raynes.

      2e. Herbert William Wrangham Wilberforce (*Drayton Hall, West Drayton*), b. 8 Feb. 1864 ; m. 5 Nov. 1892, Florence, da. of C. J. Monk of Bedwell Park, Hatfield ; and has issue 1f to 2f.

        1f. Irene Florence Wilberforce, b. 9 Jan. 1900.

        2f. Judith Monica Wilberforce, b. 4 Feb. 1903.

      3e. *Alexander Basil Edward Wilberforce,* b. 9 *June* 1867 ; d. 17 *Feb.* 1902.

      4e. Evelyn Agnes Fannie Wilberforce, m. 7 Feb. 1899, Walter George Wrangham ; and has issue 1f to 2f.

        1f. Geoffrey Walter Wrangham, b. 16 June 1900.

        2f. Audrey Evelyn Fanny Wrangham, b. 25 Mar. 1904.

2a. Richard Creyke, Capt. R.N., and Governor Royal Naval College, b. 7 Aug. 1746 ; d. 3 Dec. 1826 ; m. Anne Leming, da. of George Adney of London ; and had issue 1b to 2b.

  1b. Ven. Stephen Creyke, Archdeacon of York, d. (–) ; m. 6 Sept. 1823, Sarah, da. of Col. George Hotham, d. (–) ; and had issue 1c to 7c. [Nos. 57555 to 57609.

The Plantagenet Roll

1c. Walter Pennington Creyke (*Seamore Place, Hyde Park, W.*), *b*. 17 Oct. 1828; *m*. 1870, Caroline, da. of Sir John Bennet Lawes of Rothamstead Park, 1st Bart. [U.K.].

2c. Alexander Stephen Creyke, Capt. R.E., *b*. 2 Feb. 1830; *m*. 28 Ap. 1859, Mayda Henrietta Edwardes, da. of John Edwardes Lyall, Advocate-General of Bengal; and has issue.

3c. *Alfred Richard Creyke*, b. 1 Sept. 1831; d. (? s.p.) *Dec*. 1894; m. *June* 1877, [——], *widow of Scott Russell, da. of* [——].

4c. Charles William Creyke, 67th Regt., *b*. 17 Sept. 1839.

5c. Caroline Julia Creyke, *m*. 1846, the Rev. Philip Salisbury Bagge.

6c. *Diana Jane Creyke, d*. 4 *Oct*. 1866; *m. as 1st wife*, 7 *Aug*. 1855, *Sir Robert Bateson Harvey, 1st Bart.* (1868) [*U.K.*], *M.P.*, b. 17 *Nov*. 1825; d. 23 *Mar*. 1887; *and had issue 1d to 5d*.

1d. Sir Robert Grenville Harvey, 2nd Bart. [U.K.] (*Langley Park, Slough*), *b*. 1 July 1856; *m*. 29 Ap. 1893, the Hon. Emily Blanche, da. of Montolieu Fox Oliphant (Murray), 10th Lord Elibank [S.]; and has issue 1e to 3e.

1e. Irene Alice Gertrude Harvey, *b*. 8 Mar. 1894.

2e. Diana Blanche Harvey, *b*. 2 Ap. 1897.

3e. Caroline Magdalen Harvey, *b*. 3 Nov. 1899.

2d. *Charles Bateson Harvey, Major 10th Hussars*, b. 13 *Jan*. 1859; d. (*being killed in action at Colesberg*) 4 *Jan*. 1900; m. 30 *July* 1891, *Catherine Maria (East Burnham Lodge, Slough), da. of Rev. the Hon. James Walter Lascelles; and had issue 1e*.

1e. Sylvia Harvey, *b*. 3 July 1899.

3d. Caroline Georgina Harvey.

4d. Diana Geneviève Harvey.

5d. Florence Anna Harvey, *m*. 19 Dec. 1891, Richard Henry Tillyer.

7c. Gertrude Creyke.

2b. *Anna Creyke*, d. (? unm.).

3a. *Priscilla Creyke*, d. (–); m. *William Lynes of London*.

[Nos. 57610 to 57622.

609. Other CREYKE descendants, if any (see Table LXVI.).

610. Descendants of GEORGE THORNHILL of Fixby, co. Yorks, and Diddington, co. Hunts (see Table LXVII.), *b*. 29 Aug. 1681; *d*. 30 Dec. 1754; *m*. 1733, SARAH, da. of George BARNE of London; and had issue 1*a* to 4*a*.

1a. *Thomas Thornhill of Fixby, d*. 22 *Mar*. 1800; *m*. 1779, *Eleanor, da. of* [——] *Lynne of Horsley, co. Essex*, d. 5 *May* 1785 (?); *and had issue 1b*.

1b. *Thomas Thornhill of Fixby, co. York, and Riddlesworth, co. Norfolk*, b. 15 *Dec*. 1780; d. (–); m. 1815, *Sarah, da. of* [——] *Sober of Southampton; and had issue*.

2a. *George Thornhill of Diddington, High Sheriff cos. Cambs and Hunts*, b. 1758; d. 22 *Sept*. 1827; m. 29 *Aug*. 1780, *Mary Anne, da. of Sir Cæsar Hawkins of Kelston, 1st Bart.* [*G.B.*], d. 12 *Feb*. 1830; *and had issue 1b to 3b*.

1b. *George Thornhill of Diddington, M.P., High Sheriff cos. Cambs and Hunts* 1836, b. 12 *June* 1783; d. 19 *May* 1852; m. 22 *June* 1809, *Charlotte Matilda, da. and h. of the Rev. Charles Greene of Offord d'Arcy; and had issue 1c to 10c*.

1c. *George Thornhill of Diddington, J.P., D.L., High Sheriff cos. Cambs and*

Hunts 1869, b. 10 *Aug.* 1811; d. *4 Feb.* 1875; m. *27 Sept.* 1845, *Elizabeth Mary,* da. *of Robert H. Wilkinson,* d. 18 *Mar.* 1899; *and had issue* 1*d* to 5*d.*

1*d.* Arthur John Thornhill, J.P., D.L., sometime M.P., High Sheriff cos. Cambs and Hunts 1893 (*Diddington, Buckden, Hunts*), b. 3 Ap. 1850.

2*d.* Francis Herbert William Thornhill, b. 8 Nov. 1851; *m.* 27 Nov. 1880, Helen Georgina, da. of the Rev. Charles Thornhill of Milesdown, co. Louth; and has issue 1*e* to 2*e.*

    1*e.* Noel Thornhill, b. 18 Dec. 1881.

    2*e.* Leslie Thornhill, b. 30 Jan. 1885.

3*d.* Edmund Henry Thornhill (*Boxworth, Cambs*), b. 9 Mar. 1856; *m.* 10 June 1896, Violet Mina, da. of Col. C. H. Campbell, R.A.; and has issue 1*e* to 3*e.*

    1*e.* Edmund Basil Thornhill, b. 27 Feb. 1898.

    2*e.* Arthur Henry Thornhill, b. 16 Mar. 1900.

    3*e.* Walter David Thornhill, b. 23 Feb. 1904.

4*d.* Charlotte Sarah Thornhill.

5*d.* Catherine Georgina Thornhill, *m.* 3 July 1879, Maunsell Bowers, Capt. 5th Dragoon Guards (*Beeston Grange, Sandy, Beds.*); and has issue 1*e* to 2*e.*

    1*e.* Arthur Hugh Maunsell Bowers, Lieut. 68th Regt.; b. 15 July 1880.

    2*e.* Herbert Maunsell Bowers, Lieut. 37th Regt., b. 3 Mar. 1883.

2*c. Rev. Charles Thornhill, in H.O., previously Capt.* 14*th Light Dragoons,* b. 1812; d. 31 *Aug.* 1881; m. *Margaret, da. of John Woolsey of Priorland, co. Louth, J.P.,* b. 12 *July* 1816; d. 6 *July* 1877; *and had issue* 1*d* to 7*d.*

1*d. Charles Thornhill, Col. R.A.,* b. 2 *July* 1839; d. (–); m. 20 *Dec.* 1866, *Anna Maria (The Crescent, Castle Bellingham), da. of Stephen Charles Moore of Barne, Clonmel, D.L.; and had issue* 1*e.*

    1*e. Charles John Thornhill,* b. 13 Aug. 1868.

2*d. George Robert Thornhill, Comm. R.N.,* d. (? s.p.).

3*d.* Frederic William Thornhill.

4*d.* John Henry Thornhill (*Plumpton House, Bury St. Edmunds*), b. 25 Oct. 1850; *m.* 20 June 1888, Rose, da. of E. Fowler; and has issue 1*e* to 2*e.*

    1*e.* Cecily Thornhill, b. 11 July 1889.

    2*e.* Muriel Thornhill, b. 23 Nov. 1891.

5*d.* Francis Evelyn Thornhill, J.P., co. Kildare, b. 1852; *m.* 1879, Marjory Anne, da. of John Jameson; and has issue 1*e* to 6*e.*

    1*e.* John Evelyn Thornhill, Seaforth Highlanders, b. 1880.

    2*e.* George Robert Thornhill, b. 1891.

    3*e.* Diones Margaret Thornhill.

    4*e.* Anne Marjory Thornhill.

    5*e.* Magdalene Thornhill.

    6*e.* Janet Isabella Thornhill.

6*d.* Hester Frances Thornhill, *m.* Major-Gen. N. Russell.

7*d.* Helen Georgina Thornhill, *m.* 27 Nov. 1880, Francis Herbert William Thornhill, and has issue.

See p. 691, Nos. 57625–57626.

3*c.* John Thornhill, *m.* Catherine, da. of Robert Wilkinson.

4*c. Rev. William Thornhill, Rector of Offord d'Arcy, co. Hunts,* b. 1822; d. 17 *Sept.* 1872; m. *Helen Jameson, da. of John Woolsey of Priorland, co. Louth, J.P.,* b. 10 *Nov.* 1820; d. (–); *and had issue* 1*d* to 4*d.*

1*d.* William Blundell Thornhill (*Castle Cosey, Castle Bellingham*), b. 13 Aug. 1857; *m.* 3 Oct. 1882, Florence Beatrice, da. of Joseph William Warburton (by his wife Lady Frances Anna, *née* King; and has issue 1*e* to 2*e.*

    1*e.* Henry Elliott Blundell Thornhill, b. 11 June 1887.

    2*e.* Helen Frances Beatrice Thornhill, b. 5 Aug. 1880.

[Nos. 57623 to 57654.

The Plantagenet Roll

2d. John Cecil Thornhill, Major (ret.) 6th Royal Irish Rifles (*Castle Belling-ham*), *b*. 28 Jan. 1862; *m*. 7 Sept. 1892, Florence Augusta, da. of the Rev. Francis Walsham; and has issue 1e to 3e.

1e. Humphrey O'Brien Thornhill, *b*. 18 Feb. 1895.

2e. Kathleen Alice Thornhill, *b*. 18 July 1893.

3e. Phyllis Irene Cecil Thornhill, *b*. 17 July 1902.

3d. Janet Alice Thornhill, *m*. 1886, Major J. Inglis, Wilts Regt.; *d*. (? s.p.) Jan. 1903.

4d. Evelyn Maud Thornhill, *b*. 8 Aug. 1860.

5c. Bryan Thornhill (*Bowerham, Cranford Rise, Maidenhead*), *m*. Sophia, da. of [——] Tuck; and has issue.

6c. Henry Jordan Thornhill, *m*. Elizabeth Julia, da. of Major Goldie, *d*. 4 Mar. 1895; and has (with other) issue 1d.

1d. Reginald Thornhill, *m*. Kathleen, da. of [——] Lawrence, I.C.S.

7c. Charlotte Matilda Thornhill.

8c. *Frances Thornhill, d. 8 Nov. 1878; m. 24 Ap. 1838, the Rev. John Pardoe, Lord of the Manor of Leyton, co. Essex, b. 31 Aug. 1813; d. 7 Jan. 1879; and had issue 1d to 7d.*

1d. *Rev. John Pardoe, Lord of the Manor of Leyton, and Rector and Patron of Graveley, b. 1 Ap. 1839; d. 23 Ap. 1892; m. 16 Aug. 1876, Isabella Charlotte, da. of Thomas Robert Wilson of Newlands, J.P.; and had issue 1e to 6e.*

2e. Edward Percy Hamilton Pardoe, *b*. 28 Ap. 1881.

3e. John Hubert Pardoe, *b*. 2 May 1883.

4e. Eric Wilson Pardoe, *b*. 1 May 1885.

5e. Lisa Gladys Pardoe, *b*. 6 May 1887.

6e. Ella Maud Cecil Pardoe, *b*. 14 June 1889.

2d. Charles William Pardoe, *late* Steward of Leyton Manor and a Freeman of the City of London, *b*. 5 Oct. 1848.

3d. Oliver Thornhill Pardoe, *b*. 5 Sept. 1863.

4d. Frances Matilda Pardoe.

5d. Juliana Elizabeth Pardoe.

6d. Harriet Anna Pardoe.

7d. Everilda Henrietta Pardoe.

9c. Lydia Anne Thornhill.

10c. *Georgiana Thornhill, d. (–); m. 1851, the Rev. Plummer Pott Rooper, Patron and Rector of Abbotts Ripton, J.P., d. 1881; and had (with other) issue 1d to 2d.*

1d. Rev. John George Rooper, Patron and Rector of Abbotts Ripton (*Abbotts Ripton, Hunts*), *b*. 7 Aug. 1852.

2d. Millicent Rooper, *m*. 1 Feb. 1883, Lieut.-Gen. Sir Roger William Henry Palmer, 5th Bart. [I.], J.P., D.L., *late* 2nd Life Guards (*Kenure Park, Rush, Dublin; Keenagh, Crossmolina, co. Mayo; Cefn Park, Wrexham*).

2b. *Mary Anne Thornhill,* m. *John Heathcote.*

3b. *Frances Thornhill,* m. 1st, *William Herbert Russell;* 2ndly, *John Harding.*

3a. *Mary Thornhill, d. (–); m. as 2nd wife, Miles Barne of Sotterley, co. Suffolk, M.P., d. 20 Dec. 1780; and had issue 1b to 5b.*

1b. *Michael Barne of Sotterley, M.P., Lieut.-Col. 7th Hussars, b. 1759; d. 20 June 1837; m. 20 Oct. 1798, Mary, da. of Ayscoghe Boucherett of Willingham, d. 11 Dec. 1858; and had issue.*

See the Clarence Volume, pp. 610–611, Nos. 26804–26810.

[Nos. 57655 to 57686.

# of The Blood Royal

2*b*. *Rev. Thomas Barne, M.A., Rector of Sotterley.*

3*b*. *Sarah Barne*, m. *John Harding.*

4*b*. *Elizabeth Barne.*

5*b*. *Anne Barne*, d. (–) ; m. *Charles Drake, afterwards* (1767) *Garrard of Lamer, co. Herts*, d. *July* 1817 ; *and had issue* 1c *to* 3c.

1*c*. *Charlotte Garrard, eldest da., and in her issue* (1884) *co-h.*, d. 1880 ; m. 9 *Sept.* 1819, *George Henry Cherry of Denford, J.P., D.L., High Sheriff co. Berks* 1829, b. *Aug.* 1793 ; d. 1848 ; *and had issue* 1d *to* 4d.

1*d*. Apsley Cherry, now (R.L. 1892) Cherry-Garrard, J.P., Major-Gen. in the Army (*Denford, Hungerford, Berks ; Lamer Park, Wheathampstall*), b. 1 Sept. 1832 ; m. 29 Jan. 1885, Evelyn Edith, da. of Henry Wilson Sharpin of Bedford ; and has issue 1*e* to 5*e*.

1*e*. Apsley George Benet Cherry-Garrard, b. 2 Jan. 1886.

2*e*. Ida Evelyn Cherry-Garrard, b. 21 Mar. 1887.

3*e*. Elsie Charlotte Cherry-Garrard.

4*e*. Mildred Cherry-Garrard.

5*e*. Margaret Ursula Cherry-Garrard.

2*d*. *Maria Anne Cherry*, d. 1895 ; m. 1850, *the Rev. John Butler, Vicar of Inkpen ; and had issue.*

3*d*. Emily Jane Cherry, m. 1853, John Smith of Hollyfild, co. Warwick ; d. 1888.

4*d*. Amy Elizabeth Cherry, m. 1850, Col. Matthew Chitty Downes St. Quintin of Scampston Hall, d. 1876 ; and has issue.

See p. 546, Nos. 49515–49519.

2*c*. Caroline Garrard, m. William Dawson of St. Leonards.

3*c*. *Emily Garrard*, d. 1879 ; m. *as 2nd wife*, 2 *Mar.* 1830, *the Rev. John Tyrwhitt-Drake*, d. 26 *June* 1860 ; *and had issue* 1d *to* 8d.

1*d*. John Charles Tyrwhitt-Drake, Capt. 2nd Queen's Regt., Chief Constable of Bucks, b. 1834 ; m. 1st, 29 Aug. 1851, Emily Harriet, da. of Major-Gen. D'Urban, d. (–) ; 2ndly, 1871, Lydia Mary, da. of A. H. Hamilton of Hullerhirst ; and has issue (by 1st marriage 5 children).

2*d*. Thomas Henry Tyrwhitt-Drake of Little Shardeloes, co. Bucks, J.P., Capt. Indian Army, b. 11 Nov. 1840.

3*d*. Arthur Frederick Tyrwhitt-Drake, m. Jane, da. of [——] Stewart ; and has issue (a da.).

4*d*. Hugh William Tyrwhitt-Drake, m. 14 Nov. 1878, Annie Margaret, widow of Frederick Graham Lacon, da. of the Ven. Augustus Macdonald Happer, Archdeacon of Norwich ; and has issue (a son).

5*d*. Emily Anne Tyrwhitt-Drake.

6*d*. Mary Caroline Tyrwhitt-Drake.

7*d*. Louisa Isabella Tyrwhitt-Drake, m. the Rev. F. Floyd ; and has issue.

8*d*. Frances Charlotte Tyrwhitt-Drake.

4*a*. *Sarah Thornhill*, d. 11 *July* 1808 ; m. *as 1st wife*, 3 *Feb.* 1762, *Sir John Blois, 5th Bart.* [*E.*], d. 17 *Jan.* 1810 ; *and had issue* 1b.

1*b*. *Sir Charles Blois, 6th Bart.* [*E.*], d. 20 *Aug.* 1850 ; m. 19 *Jan.* 1789, *Clara, da. of Jocelyn Price of Camblesforth Hall, co. York*, d. 22 *Feb.* 1847 ; *and had issue* 1c *to* 7c.

1*c*. *Sir Charles Blois, 7th Bart.* [*E.*], d. *unm.* 12 *June* 1855.

2*c*. *John Ralph Blois, Comm. R.N.*, b. 1795 ; d. 19 *June* 1853 ; m. 15 *Feb.* 1827, *Eliza Knox, da. of the Rev. John Barrett, Rector of Iniskeel*, d. 10 *Sept.* 1886 ; *and had issue* 1d *to* 3d.

1*d*. *Sir John Ralph Blois, 8th Bart.* [*E.*], b. 13 *Aug.* 1830 ; d. 31 *Dec.* 1888 ; m. 25 *Aug.* 1865, *Eliza Ellen, da. of Capt. Alfred Chapman, R.N. ; and had issue* 1e *to* 11e.　　　　　　　　　　　　　　　　　　　　　[Nos. 57687 to 57708.

The Plantagenet Roll

1e. Sir Ralph Barrett Macnaghten Blois, 9th Bart. [E.], D.L., Capt. Reserve of Officers (*Cockfield Hall, Yoxford, Suffolk*), b. 21 Nov. 1866; m. 30 Ap. 1898, Winifred Grace Hegan, da. of Col. Edmund Hegan Kennard of 25 Bruton Street, W. ; and has issue 1f to 3f.

    1f. Gervase Ralph Edmund Blois, b. 6 June 1901.

    2f. Iris Freda Blois.

    3f. Christiani Frances Blois.

2e. Eardley Steuart Blois, Lieut. Middlesex Imp. Yeo., b. 3 July 1869.

3e. Stephen Russell Blois, *late* Lieut. E. Surrey Regt., b. 6 Oct. 1870.

4e. Dudley George Blois, Capt. R.A., b. 12 Feb. 1875.

5e. Gervase Vanneck Blois, b. 25 May 1881.

6e. Alice Clara Blois.

7e. Maude Beatrice Blois, m. 18 Jan. 1902, the Rev. John Cossham Vawdrey, Rector of Kessingland, and Diocesan Inspector of Schools, &c. (*Kessingland Rectory, Suffolk*).

8e. Adeline Louisa Blois, m. 1 June 1905, Charles George Lumley Cator.

9e. Constance Violet Blois, m. 26 Nov. 1898, Edward James Heron-Maxwell, (*Greensted House, Ongar*) ; and has issue.

    See p. 627, Nos. 53185–53187.

10e. Cecily Mabel Blois.

11e. Hylda Letitia Grace Blois.

2d. *William Thornhill Blois, J.P., Lieut.-Col. 6th Royal Warwick Regt.,* b. 1 *Aug.* 1842; d. 5 *Ap.* 1889; m. 4 *June* 1874, Fanny Elizabeth (*Glencairn, Bournemouth*), da. of William Arkwright of Sutton Scarsdale ; and had issue 1e to 4e.

    1e. Eustace William Blois, *late* Lieut. Rifle Brigade, b. 4 Dec. 1877.

    2e. Ernest Peirepont Blois, b. 10 Mar. 1880.

    3e. Basil Frederick Blois, b. 1881.

    4e. Geoffrey Stephen Blois, b. 1884.

3d. Clara Palmer Blois.

3c. *William Blois, Col. in the Army,* d. (? s.p.) 14 *Nov.* 1866.

4c. *Thomas Blois, Lieut.-Col. in the Army,* d. (? s.p.) 16 *June* 1871.

5c. *Frances Mary Blois,* d. 12 *May* 1872 ; m. 14 *Dec.* 1815, the Rev. Eardley Norton, Vicar of Arncliff.

6c. *Clara Blois,* d. 10 *Sept.* 1865 ; m. 14 *Dec.* 1815, *William Palmer, afterwards* (*R.L. 19 July 1825*) *Palmer-Morewood of Alfreton and Ladbroke,* d. 23 *Feb.* 1863 ; *and had issue* 1d *to* 4d.

    1d. *Charles Rowland Palmer-Morewood of Alfreton and Ladbroke, J.P., D.L.,* b. 5 *Aug.* 1819 ; d. 21 *Feb.* 1873 ; m. 9 *June* 1842, the Hon. Georgina, da. of George Anson (*Byron*), 7th *Baron Byron* [*E.*], d. 23 *Jan.* 1893 ; *and had issue* 1e *to* 8e.

        1e. Charles Rowland Palmer-Morewood, J.P., D.L., High Sheriff co. Warwick 1880 (*Alfreton Park, Derby ; Ladbroke Hall, Southam, Warwick ; 66 Queen's Gate, S.W.*), b. 7 June 1843 ; m. 17 July 1873, Patience Mary, da. of the Right Rev. Lord Arthur Hervey, Bishop of Bath and Wells ; and has issue 1f to 2f.

            1f. Rowland Charles Arthur Palmer-Morewood, b. 9 Jan. 1879.

            2f. Clara Winifred Sarah Palmer-Morewood, b. 21 Dec. 1881.

        2e. George Herbert Palmer-Morewood, b. 1857.

        3e. Alfred Palmer-Morewood, b. 1859 ; m. 1883, Alice Beatrice, da. of the Rev. Francis John Hurt ; and has issue (2 das.).

        4e. Ernest Augustus Palmer-Morewood, b. 1860.

        5e. Georgina Millicent Palmer-Morewood (*33 Hill Street, Mayfair, W.*), m. 28 Ap. 1868, Samuel Charles (Allsopp), 2nd Baron Hindlip [U.K.], d. 12 July 1897 ; and has issue.

        See p. 446, No. 35538.

Nos. 57709 to 57738.

6e. Adela Palmer-Morewood, *m.* 12 Dec. 1867, George Algernon Beynon Disney Hacket, J.P. (*Moor Hall, Sutton Coldfield, Warwick*) ; and has issue.

See the Tudor Roll of "The Blood Royal of Britain," p. 466, Nos. 32813–32819.

7e. Frances Maude Palmer-Morewood, *m.* 30 Ap. 1872, Capt. Cecil Lyon, *late* 77th Regt.

8e. Ellen Mary Palmer-Morewood (*Alton Towers, Stoke-upon-Trent*), *m.* 1st, as 1st wife, 25 Sept. 1873, Alfred Edward Miller Mundy of Shipley Hall, J.P., D.L. (div.) ; 2ndly, 18 June 1882, Charles Henry John (Talbot), 20th Earl of Shrewsbury [E.] and Waterford [I.], 5th Earl Talbot [G.B.] ; and has issue 1*f* to 3*f.*

1f. Charles John Alton Chetwynd Chetwynd-Talbot, Viscount Ingestre (20 *Manchester Square, W.*), *b.* 8 Sept. 1882 ; *m.* 23 Ap. 1904, Winifred Constance, da. of Lord Alexander Paget.

2f. Evelyn Hester Mundy, *m.* 1899, Hugh Robert Edward Harrison of Caer-howel, Lieut. Grenadier Guards.

3f. Lady Nellie Viola Castalia Florence Chetwynd-Talbot, *b.* 3 July 1885.

2d. William Frederick Palmer-Morewood, d. (–) ; m. *Lucy, da. of the Rev. C. Johnson ; and had issue (a son).*

3d. Ellen Palmer-Morewood, d. Feb. 1892 ; m. 6 Feb. 1844, Capt. George Henry Elliott of Binfield Park, co. Berks, and Farnborough Park, co. Hants, 2nd Dragoon Guards ; and had (with other) issue 1e.

1e. George Henry Blois Elliott, *b.* 6 Feb. 1854.

4d. Lucy Anne Palmer-Morewood, d. (? unm.).

7c. Lucy Anne Blois, b. 1799 ; d. 3 Sept. 1889 ; m. as 2nd wife, 6 Jan. 1817, Joshua (Vanneck), 2nd Baron Huntingfield [G.B.], b. 12 Aug. 1778 ; d. 10 Aug. 1844 ; and had issue 1d.

1d. Charles Andrew (Vanneck), 3rd Baron Huntingfield [G.B.], b. 12 Jan. 1818 ; d. 21 Sept. 1897 ; m. 6 July 1839, Louisa, da. of Andrew Arcedeckne, d. 4 Feb. 1898 ; and had issue 1e to 7e.

1e. Joshua Charles (Vanneck), 4th Baron Huntingfield [G.B.] (*Heveningham Hall, Yoxford, Suffolk*), *b.* 27 Aug. 1842.

2e. Hon. William Arcedeckne Vanneck (*The Cupola, Leiston, Suffolk*), *b.* 30 Oct. 1845 ; *m.* 21 Mar. 1882, Mary, da. of William Armstrong of Toowoomba, Queensland, M.R.C.S. ; and has issue 1*f* to 4*f.*

1f. William Charles Arcedeckne Vanneck, Lieut. 13th Hussars, *b.* 3 Jan. 1883.

2f. Andrew Nicholas Armstrong Vanneck, *b.* 21 July 1890.

3f. Louisa Medora Hermione Vanneck, *b.* 11 Feb. 1885.

4f. Anne Mary Chaloner Vanneck, *b.* 30 Aug. 1892.

3e. Hon. Walter Vanneck (*Darsham Cottage, Saxmundham*), *b.* 9 Mar. 1849 ; *m.* 24 Sept. 1877, Catherine Medora, da. of William Armstrong of Toowoomba, Queensland, M.R.C.S. ; and has issue 1*f* to 5*f.*

1f. Joshua Walter Huntingfield Vanneck, *b.* 1 Nov. 1886.

2f. Ralph Wyndham Vanneck, *b.* 20 Sept. 1891.

3f. Nesta Frances Vanneck, *b.* 8 Sept. 1878.

4f. Hilda Arcedeckne Vanneck, *b.* 23 Oct. 1879.

5f. Catherine Gladys Vanneck, *b.* 15 Dec. 1881.

4e. Hon. Gerard Vanneck, b. 19 Ap. 1851 ; d. 11 Aug. 1904 ; m. 29 Ap. 1878, Harriette Oakley Beatson (Southport, near Warwick, Queensland) ; and had issue 1f.

1f. Harriet Louisa Cora Vanneck.

5e. Hon. Anne Vanneck.

6e. Hon. Frances Vanneck.

7e. Hon. Harriet Lucy Vanneck. [Nos. 57739 to 57768.

The Plantagenet Roll

611. Descendants of EVERILDA THORNHILL (see Table LXVII.), *bapt.* 22 June 1680; *d.* 12 Sept. 1753; *m.* 28 May 1699, Sir ARTHUR CAYLEY, 3rd Bart. [E.], *b. c.* 1654; *d.* 19 May 1727; and had (with possibly das.) 1*a.*

1*a.* Sir George Cayley, 4th Bart. [E.], b. c. 1707; d. Sept. 1791; m. 31 May 1730, Philadelphia, da. and eventual co.-h. of John Digby of Mansfield, Woodhouse, co. Notts, d. 14 Jan. 1765; and had issue 1b to 5b.

1*b.* Sir Thomas Cayley, 5th Bart. [E.], b. Aug. 1732; d. 15 Mar. 1792; m. 1763, Isabella, da. of John Seton of Parbroath, d. 30 July 1828; and had issue 1c to 5c.

1*c.* Sir George Cayley, 6th Bart. [E.], b. 27 Dec. 1773; d. 15 Dec. 1857; m. 9 July 1795, Sarah, da. of the Rev. George Walker of Nottingham, F.R.S., d. 8 Dec. 1854; and had issue 1d to 5d.

1*d.* Sir Digby Cayley, 7th Bart. [E.], b. 13 Mar. 1807; d. 21 Dec. 1883; m. 8 July 1830, Dorothy, da. and co-h. of the Ven. George Allanson, Preb. of Ripon, d. Ap. 1881; and had issue.

See p. 501, Nos. 43941–43991.

2*d.* Emma Cayley, d. 2 Aug. 1848; m. 30 Aug. 1823, Edward Stillingfleet Cayley of Wydale House, co. York, M.P., d. 25 Feb. 1862; and had issue 1e to 2e.

1*e.* Edward Stillingfleet Cayley of Wydale, J.P., D.L., Author of "European Revolutions of 1848," &c., b. 30 July 1824; d.s.p. 10 Sept. 1884.

2*e.* George John Cayley, Bar.-at-Law, author of several works, b. 26 Jan. 1826; d. 11 Oct. 1878; m. 11 Sept. 1860, Mary Anne Frances, da. of Montagu Wilmot of Osmaston (who re-m. 4 Dec. 1888, Baron Emile de Roger); and had issue 1f to 2f.

1*f.* Hugh Cayley (*Wydale, Yorks*), b. 6 Sept. 1861.

2*f.* Violet Cayley.

3*d.* Sarah Philadelphia Cayley, b. 1803; d. 23 Ap. 1885; m. 18 Jan. 1827, Sir William Worsley, 1st Bart. [U.K.], d. 5 Mar. 1879; and had issue.

See p. 638, Nos. 53978–53998.

4*d.* Catherine Cayley, b. 1812; d. 11 Mar. 1887; m. 1st, 19 May 1831, Henry Ralph Beaumont, d. 21 June 1838; 2ndly, 6 May 1845, Capt. James Anlaby Legard, R.N., K.T.S., b. 13 Oct. 1805; d. 25 June 1869; and had issue 1e to 9e.

1*e.* Henry Frederick Beaumont, J.P., D.L., sometime (1865–1892) M.P., &c. (*Whitley Beaumont, Huddersfield*), b. 10 Mar. 1833; m. 1 Sept. 1857, Maria Johanna, da. of William Garforth of Wiganthorpe; and has issue 1f to 10f.

1*f.* Henry Ralph Beaumont, Capt. late 4th Batt. Argyll and Sutherland Highlanders, J.P., D.L. (*Aldburgh Hall, Masham*), b. 17 Dec. 1865; m. 1904, Mary Helen, da. of Sir James Gibson-Craig, 3rd Bart. [U.K.].

2*f.* Richard Henry Beaumont, Capt. 60th Rifles, b. 2 Jan. 1868.

3*f.* Maria Catherine Beaumont, m. G. E. Darroch (70 *Stanhope Gardens, S.W.*).

4*f.* Emily Diana Maria Beanmont, m. 14 Jan. 1887, William Graham Lloyd.

5*f.* Dora Maria Beaumont, m. 6 Oct. 1882, James Worsley Pennyman, Bar.-at-Law, J.P., D.L. (*Ormesley Hall, Middlesbro'*); and has issue.

See p. 640, Nos. 54018–54020.

6*f.* Mary Frederica Maria Beaumont, m. 26 Sept. 1899, Capt. Maturin, R.N.

7*f.* Everilda Maria Beaumont, m. 16 July 1891, Arthur Gorell Barnes, J.P., late Capt. and Hon. Major 3rd Batt. Derbyshire Regt. (*Glapwell Hall, Chesterfield*); and has issue 1g to 5g.

1*g.* Theodore Arthur Richard Barnes, b. 14 Sept. 1892.

2*g.* Robin Arthur Barnes, b. 10 Nov. 1899.

3*g.* Muriel Emily Barnes.

4*g.* Joan Everilda Barnes.

5*g.* Violet Evelyn Barnes.

[Nos. 57769 to 57858.

8*f*. Margaret Louisa Maria Beaumont, *m*. 18 Aug. 1898, George Hector Grant.

9*f*. Octavia Maria Beaumont.

10*f*. Haidée Maria Beaumont, *m*. 12 June 1906, the Rev. William Outram, Vicar of St. George's, Barnsley.

2*e*. Thomas Richard Beaumont.

3*e*. James Digby Legard, C.B., J.P., D.L., Lieut.-Col. and Hon. Col. Yorkshire R.G.A., *late* R.A. (*Welham, Malton, Yorks*), *b*. 12 July 1846 ; *m*. 30 Aug. 1877, Julia Helen, da. of Alfred Arkwright of Wirksworth ; and has issue 1*f* to 9*f*.

1*f*. Alfred Digby Legard, Capt. King's Royal Rifle Corps, *b*. 19 June 1878 ; *m*. 1902, Winifred, da. of Col. William George Morris, C.B., C.M.G. ; and has issue 1*g*.

1*g*. Katherine Emily Winifred Legard, *b*. 6 June 1903.

2*f*. George Percy Legard, Lieut. R.N., *b*. 15 Aug. 1879.

3*f*. Richard Anlaby Legard, *b*. 10 Nov. 1880.

4*f*. Thomas Francis Legard, *b*. (twin) 1885.

5*f*. Reginald John Legard, *b*. 1893.

6*f*. Helen Mary Alice Legard.

7*f*. Evelyn Elizabeth Catherine Legard.

8*f*. Edith Victoria Legard.

9*f*. Pauline Octavia Legard.

4*e*. Allayne Legard, *late* Lieut. 60th Rifles, *b*. 14 Ap. 1847 ; *m*. 1881, Mary Adelaide, da. of T. Buckley of Detroit, U.S.A. ; and has issue 1*f* to 2*f*.

1*f*. Adrienne Catherine Legard.

2*f*. Mary Olive Legard.

5*e*. *Emily Beaumont*, d. 11 *Ap*. 1895 ; m. 19 *June* 1855, *the Rev. Richard Hugh Cholmondeley, late of Condover* (62 *Albert Gate Mansions, S.W.*); *and had issue*.

See the Clarence Volume, p. 494, Nos. 21554–21570.

6*e*. Mary Catherine Legard.

7*e*. Diana Legard.

8*e*. Marianne Legard.

9*e*. Sophia Legard.

5*d*. *Mary Agnes Cayley*, d. (‑) ; m. 7 *Aug*. 1846, *James Alexander, M.D.*

2*c*. *Elizabeth Cayley*, m. *Benjamin Blackden of High Wycombe*.

3*c*. *Philadelphia Sarah Cayley*, d. 1829 ; m. *Barry Slater, M.D.*

4*c*. *Isabella Cayley*, m. *Lancelot Shadwell*.

5*c*. *Anne Cayley*, b. 1767 ; d. 31 *Aug*. 1854 ; m. *the Rev. George Worsley of Stonegrave*, d. 4 *Feb*. 1815 ; *and had issue*.

See p. 638, Nos. 53978–54026.

2*b*. *Arthur Cayley*, d. (s.p.) ; m. *Anne Eleanor, da. of* [——] *Shultz*.

3*b*. Rev. Digby Cayley, Rector of Thormanby, *m*. Elizabeth, da. of Thomas Robinson of Welburn ; and has issue 1*c* to 3*c*.

1*c*. Lucy Cayley, *m*. the Rev. Arthur Cayley, Rector of Normanby, *d*. 22 Ap. 1848.

2*c*. Dorothy Cayley, *m*. the Ven. Archdeacon Wrangham.

3*c*. Frances Elizabeth Cayley, *m*. Thomas Smith, M.D.

4*b*. *John Cayley*, d. 1818 ; m. *Catherine, da. of Richard Langley of Wykeham Abbey ; and had issue* 1*c* to 3*c*.

1*c*. George St. Luke Cayley.

2*c*. Catharine Cayley.

3*c*. Harriette Cayley.

[Nos. 57859 to 57953.

The Plantagenet Roll

5b. Frances Cayley, d. (–); m. *the Rev. John Cayley of Low Hall, Brompton ; and had issue 1c.*

1c. *John Cayley of Low Hall*, d. 16 *June* 1846; m. 30 *May* 1798, *Elizabeth Sarah, da. and h. of the Rev. Edward Stillingfleet*, d. 1807; *and had issue 1d.*

1d. *Edward Stillingfleet Cayley of Wydale and Low Hall, J.P., D.L.*, b. 13 *Aug.* 1802; d. 25 *Feb.* 1862; m. 30 *Aug.* 1823, *Emma, da. of Sir George Cayley, 6th Bart.* [E.]; *and had issue.*

See p. 696, Nos. 57820–57821.　　　　　　　　　　　[Nos. 57954 to 57955.

612. Descendants, if any, of ANNE THORNHILL (see Table LXVII.), wife of PETER SUNDERLAND of Aikton ; of THOMAS THORNHILL, aged 7, 1666 ; and of EVERILDA THORNHILL, *b.* 1651 ; *m.* 1680, THOMAS HORTON of Barkisland.

613. Descendants, if any, of FRANCES WENTWORTH (see Table LXVII.), *m.* 12 Jan. 1657, THOMAS GRANTHAM of Meaux Abbey, co. York; will dated 29 Mar. 1668, proved 5 May following.[1]

614. Descendants of MARY BROOKE (see Table LXVII.), *d.* (–); *m.* (settl. dated 1 Aug.) 1777, THOMAS PIERSON FIRMAN of Firmount, co. Tipperary; will dated 20 Mar. 1824, proved 10 Nov. 1831;[2] and had issue 1*a* to 3*a*.

1a. *Thomas Pierson Firman of Firmount, co. Tipperary ; will dated 4 June 1830, proved 5 Jan. 1835 ;*[2] m. *Penelope, da. of [——] Chetwynd ; and had issue 1b to 6b.*

1b. *Thomas Pierson Firman of Firmount*, d. (–); m. *Ellen, da. of Ralph Smith of Milford, co. Tipperary ; and had issue 1c to 2c.*

　　1c. Thomas Pierson Firman.

　　2c. Ellen Firman.

2b. William Firman.

3b. Brooke Firman.

4b. Mary Firman.

5b. Emily Firman.

6b. Penelope Firman.

2a. *Brooke Firman, Lieut.-Col. 82nd Regt.*, d. (–); m. *Tryphena, da. of William Biggs of Castle Biggs, co. Tipperary ; and had issue 1b to 2b.*

1b. *Humphrey Brooke Firman of Brayton, co. York*, d. 28 *Jan.* 1868; m. *Anne Louisa, da. of Thomas FitzGibbon of Ballysuda, co. Limerick*, d. (–); *and had issue 1c to 8c.*

1c. Humphrey Brooke Firman, J.P., *late 16th Lancers* (*Gateforth, Selby, York ; Hans House, Hans Street, S.W.*), *b.* 18 June 1858; *m.* 15 Jan. 1880, Florence Adelaide, *da.* of Vice-Adm. Sir Arthur Cumming of Foston Hall, K.C.B. ; and has issue 1*d* to 3*d*.

　　1d. Humphrey Osbaldeston Brooke Firman, *b.* 1886.

　　2d. Ivy Firman, *b.* 13 Jan. 1881.

　　3d. Gladys Firman, *b.* 12 Dec. 1882.　　　　[Nos. 57956 to 57966.

---

[1] Foster's " Yorkshire Pedigrees."

[2] Burke's " Landed Gentry," 1900, p. 551.

# of The Blood Royal

2c. Robert Bertram Firman, Capt. Royal Welsh Fusiliers, *b.* 13 Sept. 1859.
3c. Charles Osbaldeston Firman, *b.* 30 Dec. 1867.
4c–8c. 5 das.

2b. Theodosia Firman.

3a. *Flood Firman, living* 22 *June* 1792.   [Nos. 57967 to 57969.

615. Descendants, if any, of ELIZABETH OSBALDESTON (see Table LXVII.), *bapt.* 9 Feb. 1691 ; *m.* 12 Sept. 1743, JOHN HEALY of Fordingham, co. Lincoln.

616. Descendants of Major ROBERT MITFORD of Mitford Castle (see Table LXVII.), *b.* 24 July 1717 ; *d.* 15 Jan. 1781 ; *m.* ANNA, da. of John LEWIS of Jamaica ; and had issue (with 18 children who *d.* in infancy) 1*a* to 5*a*.

1*a. Bertram Mitford of Mitford Castle,* b. 14 *June* 1748 ; d. *May* 1800 ; m. *Tabitha, da. of Francis Johnson of Newcastle ; and had issue* 1b *to* 7b.
1*b. Bertram Mitford, afterwards* (1835) *Osbaldeston-Mitford of Mitford and Hunmanby,* b. 17 *Dec.* 1777 ; d.s.p. 27 *Feb.* 1842.
2*b. Robert Mitford of Mitford Castle and Hunmanby, Adm. R.N.,* b. 26 *Jan.* 1781 ; d. 18 *June* 1870 ; m. 7 *Dec.* 1830, *Margaret, da. of James Dunsmore of Edinburgh ; and had issue* 1c.
1*c.* Margaret Susan Mitford, *m.* 4 June 1856, William Amhurst (Tyssen-Amherst), 1st Baron Amherst of Hackney [U.K.] (*Didlington Hall, near Brandon ;* 8 *Grosvenor Square, W.*) ; and has issue 1*d* to 6*d*.
1*d.* Hon. Mary Rothes Margaret Tyssen-Amherst, Lady of Justice of St. John of Jerusalem [E.], Heir presumptive (*Hunmanby Hall, Yorks*), b. 25 Ap. 1857 ; *m.* 2 Sept. 1885, Lord William Cecil, M.V.O. ; and has issue.
See the Clarence Volume, p. 262, Nos. 6306–6309.
2*d.* Hon. Sybil Margaret Tyssen-Amherst, Lady of Justice of St. John of Jerusalem [E.].
3*d.* Hon. Florence Tyssen-Amherst, Lady of Justice of St. John of Jerusalem, [E.].
4*d.* Hon. Margaret Mitford Tyssen-Amherst, Lady of Justice of St. John of Jerusalem [E.].
5*d.* Hon. Alice Margaret Tyssen-Amherst, Lady of Justice of St. John of Jerusalem [E.], *m.* 16 Feb. 1898, Evelyn Gascoyne-Cecil, M.P. (10 *Eaton Place, S.W.*) ; and has issue.
See p. 217, Nos. 7677–7679.
6*d.* Hon. Geraldine Margaret Tyssen-Amherst, *m.* 30 Ap. 1890, Capt. Malcolm Drummond, *late* Grenadier Guards (*Megginch Castle, Errol, N.B.*) ; and has issue 1*e* to 4*e*.
1*e.* John Drummond, *b.* 6 May 1900.
2*e.* Jean Drummond.
3*e.* Victoria Alexandrina Drummond.
4*e.* Frances Ada Drummond.

3*b. George Joseph Mitford, Capt. H.E.I.C.S.,* b. 1 *May* 1791 ; d. 2 *Sept.* 1875 ; m. *Anne, da. of* [——] *May ; and had issue* (2 *sons and* 2 *das.*).
4*b. Marianne Mitford,* b. 4 *Sept.* 1776 ; d. (–) ; m. 1796, *Col. J. Atherton.*
5*b. Tabitha Lewis Mitford,* d. 24 *Mar.* 1859 ; m. 17 *Dec.* 1810, *Prideaux John Selby of Twizell House and The Mote, J.P., D.L., High Sheriff co. Kent* 1821, b. 1789 ; d. 1867 ; *and had issue* 1c *to* 3c.   [Nos. 57970 to 57987.

699

The Plantagenet Roll

1c. Lewis Marianne Selby (*The Mote, Tunbridge, Kent*), *m.* 1st, 23 May 1833, Charles John Bigge, *b.* 11 Ap. 1803; *d.* 16 Mar. 1846; 2ndly, Oct. 1850, Major Robert Luard, *afterwards* (1876) Luard-Selby, J.P., R.A.; and has issue *1d* to *7d.*

1d. Charles Selby Bigge *of Long Horsley, co. Northumberland, J.P., b. 21 July 1834; d. 16 Jan.* 1889; *m.* 24 *July* 1856, *Katharina, da. of John W. Ogle of Oakwood ; and had issue 1e to 3e.*

1e. Charles Prideaux Ogle Bigge (*Long Horsley, Morpeth*), *b.* 25 July 1857.

2e. Lewis Amherst Bigge (*The Mote, Lytham, Kent*), *b.* 3 Ap. 1860; *m.* Edith Lindsay, *da.* of the Right Hon. John Robert Davison of Carlton and Under-river, Q.C.

3e. Denys Leighton Bigge, *b.* 11 Sept. 1864.

2d. Bertram Selby Luard-Selby, *b.* 1853.

3d. Mary Lewis Bigge, *m.* the Rev. G. C. S. Darby of Markly, Sussex.

4d. Fanny Alice Bigge, *m.* 6 June 1867, Thomas St. Leger Blaaow of Beechland, co. Sussex, J.P., *b.* 1 July 1839; *d.* 11 Sept. 1893; and has issue *1e* to *5e.*

1e. Henry Thomas Gillman Blaaow (*Beechland, Newick, Lewes*), *b.* 4 July 1874.

2e. Bertram William St. Leger Blaaow, *b.* 16 May 1876.

3e. Alice Agneta Emily Mitford Blaaow.

4e. Frances Catherine Blaaow.

5e. Margaret Louisa Blaaow.

5d. Louisa Charlotte Bigge, *m.* 8 Aug. 1865, Charles Francis Massingberd-Mundy, J.P., D.L. (*Ormsby Hall, Alford*); and has issue.

See p. 552, Nos. 49619–49623.

6d. Sybil Constance Bigge, *b.* posthumous.

7d. Beatrice Luard-Selby, *m.* A. Willink.

2c. Frances Margaret Selby of Twizell House, *m.* 1833, the Rev. Edmund Antrobus; and has issue (with possibly sons) *1d.*

1d. Fanny Lewis Antrobus, *m.* 5 Jan. 1859, William Henry Johnston of Malhenny, co. Dublin.

3c. Jane Selby, d. (–); *m.* 16 *Ap.* 1839, *Sir Thomas Tancred, 7th Bart.* [E.], *b.* 16 *Aug.* 1808; *d. Oct.* 1880; *and had issue 1d to 8d.*

1d. Sir Thomas Selby Tancred, 8th Bart. [E.], C.E. (29 *Westbourne Gardens, Bayswater*), *b.* 1 Oct. 1840; *m.* 19 May 1866, Mary Harriet, *da.* of Col. George Willoughby Hemans; and has issue *1e* to *6e.*

1e. Thomas Selby Tancred, Capt. I.S.C., *b.* 14 May 1870.

2e. Francis Willoughby Tancred, *b.* 21 Feb. 1874.

3e. Felicia Harriet Tancred, *m.* 3 Aug. 1905, Francis Murray.

4e. Gwendoline Sybel Tancred.

5e. Edith Mary Tancred.

6e. Constance Anne Tancred.

2d. Prideaux Francis Tancred, *b.* 2 Feb. 1850.

3d. Clement William Tancred, b. 16 *Sept.* 1853; *d.* 4 *Oct.* 1888; *m.* 16 *July* 1878, *Alice Maude* (*Frithwold Cottage, Chertsey*), *da. of Oswald Bloxsome of The Rangers, Sydney, N.S.W.; and had issue 1e to 3e.*

1e. Christopher Humphrey Tancred, *b.* 21 May 1888.

2e. Irene Maude Tancred.

3e. Esmé Isabelle Tancred.

4d. Seymer Mitford Tancred (62 *Vanburgh Park, Blackheath, S.E.*), *b.* 21 Ap. 1856; *m.* 4 June 1896, Charlotte Dorothea, *da.* of William Gillespie Dickson, LL.D., Sheriff Principal, co. Lanark; and has issue *1e* to *2e.*

1e. Mary Tytler Tancred, *b.* 21 Mar. 1897.

2e. Margaret Selby Tancred, *b.* 13 Feb. 1900.　　　　[Nos. 57988 to 58023.

5*d*. Harry George Tancred (*Arden, Park Road, Carterton, N.Z.*), *b.* 27 Dec. 1858; *m.* 19 Ap. 1881, Emily Alicia de Courcy, da. of Major Slingsby Bell of Burneah, India, and Napier, N.Z.; and has issue 1*e* to 5*e*.

> 1*e*. Cecil Mount-Stewart Tancred, *b.* 1884.
> 2*e*. Bertram Selby Tancred, *b.* 19 Ap. 1895.
> 3*e*. Vera Elphinstone Tancred.
> 4*e*. Valerie Waldegrave Mitford Tancred.
> 5*e*. Zillah Selby Tancred.

6*d*. Lucy Sybil Tancred, *m.* 28 Feb. 1867, Robert Samuel Hawkins (*Dunedin, New Zealand*); and has issue 1*e* to 6*e*.

> 1*e*. *John Robert Vernon Tancred Hawkins*, b. 1 *Mar.* 1870; d. (*? unm.*).
> 2*e*. Seymer Corrie Hanbury Selby Hawkins, *b.* 1874.
> 3*e*. Harry Bradford Tancred Hawkins, *b.* 1876.
> 4*e*. Lucy Sarah Crewe Hawkins.
> 5*e*. Ida Dorothy Hawkins.
> 6*e*. Margaret Sybil Hawkins.

7*d*. Edith Jane Tancred, *m.* 13 Jan. 1875, George Phipps Williams, M.I.C.E.

8*d*. Bertha Eveline Tancred, *m.* 23 Oct. 1878, William Fownes Somerville (*Gisborne, New Zealand*); and has (with other) issue 1*e* to 3*e*.

> 1*e*. William Tancred Somerville, *b.* 18 July 1879.
> 2*e*. Ernest Selby Somerville, *b.* 1882.
> 3*e*. Enid Bertha Somerville.

6*b*. Frances Mitford, *m.* George Hutton of Carlton-on-Trent.

7*b*. *Jane Honoria Alicia Mitford*, d. (–); *m.* 1807, *Philip Meadows Taylor of Liverpool*; and had issue 1*c* to 2*c*.

> 1*c*. Meadows Taylor, Col. C.S.I., the Author.
> 2*c*. Rev. Robert Mitford Taylor, Vicar of Hunmanby and Rural Dean.

2*a*. *John Mitford*, b. *Aug.* 1749; d. 1832; m. *Dorothy, da. of* [——] *Young of Northumberland; and had issue* 1*b* to 4*b*.

1*b*. *Robert Mitford of the Audit Office*, b. 9 *May* 1778; d. 25 Dec. 1818; m. 24 *Aug.* 1805, *Letitia, widow of William Lawrenson of Rosebrook, Queen's co., da. of the Rev. Edward Ledwich of Dublin, LL.D., the Antiquarian and Author*, d. 17 *Aug.* 1844; *and had issue* 1*c* to 4*c*.

1*c*. Edward Ledwich Mitford, *afterwards* (1895) Osbaldeston-Mitford, F.R.G.S., Lord of the Manors of Mitford and Hunmanby, &c. (*Mitford Castle, Morpeth; Hunmanby Hall, York*), b. 31 Oct. 1811; *m.* 1st, 11 Ap. 1844, Janet, da. of the Ven. Benjamin Bailey, Archdeacon of Ceylon, *d.* 13 July 1896; 2ndly, 27 Oct. 1896, Ella Elizabeth, da. of Cloudesley Shovell F. Mason, C.C.S.; and has issue 1*d* to 8*d*.

1*d*. Robert Mitford, J.P., F.R.G.S., *late* Capt. 3rd Batt. East Yorkshire Regt., and 73rd Regt. (*Carlton; Naval and Military*), *b.* 25 Nov. 1846; *m.* 24 Nov. 1875, Annie, da. of Major-Gen. Charles Stuart Lane; and has issue.

See p. 440, Nos. 35167–35174.

2*d*. Rev. Edward Mitford, M.A., Vicar of Hunmanby (*Hunmanby, York*), *b.* 4 Oct. 1853; *m.* 14 Aug. 1878, Annie Maria Louisa, da. of the Rev. E. H. Price, Vicar of Kimbolton; and has issue 1*e* to 6*e*.

> 1*e*. John Philip Mitford, Lieut. and Adj. 98th Infantry, Indian Army, *b.* 12 June 1880.
> 2*e*. Cuthbert William Mitford, *b.* 6 Nov. 1884.
> 3*e*. Maud Edith Mitford, *b.* 21 May 1879.
> 4*e*. Dorothy Frances Mitford, *b.* 19 May 1882.
> 5*e*. Ethel Margaret Gertrude Mitford, *b.* 20 Sept. 1886.
> 6*e*. Cecily Mitford, *b.* 8 Mar. 1890.

[Nos. 58024 to 58060.

The Plantagenet Roll

3d. Bertram Mitford, *b.* 13 June 1855; *m.* Zima Helen, da. of Alfred Johnson Ebden of Belmont, Cape Colony; and has issue.

4d. Rev. William Ledwich Mitford, Rector of Ickburgh (*Ickburgh, Norfolk*), *b.* 2 Ap. 1858; *m.* 8 Aug. 1889, Katharine, da. of James McArthur Moir; and has issue 1*e.*

1*e.* Margaret Constance Forrester Mitford, *b.* 9 Mar. 1893.

5d. Frances Letitia Mitford, *m.* 1875, Birnie Browne, I.C.S. (*d.s.p.*).

6d. Edith Hamilton Mitford, d. 19 Oct. 1891; m. *William Rigby, I.C.S.; and had issue* (2 *das.*).

7d. Mary Margaret Mitford, *m.* 28 July 1887, Walter Raymond; and has issue.

8d. Sybil Emma Mitford, b. 9 Ap. 1863; d. 2 June 1895; m. 4 Aug. 1886, *Arthur Montefiore Brice, Barrister, Middle Temple; and had issue* 1*e.*

1*e.* Arthur Cowell Mitford Brice, *b.* 22 Aug. 1888.

3c. Frances Mitford, d. 30 June 1831; m. *the Rev. Rowland Bateman, Rector of Silton, Dorset.*

4c. Marianne Mitford, d. June 1869; m. 26 Ap. 1855, Col. *Charles Teush-Hecker, 15th Hussars,* d. 1873.

2b. Bertram Mitford of Horsley, m. *and had issue* (4 *sons*).

3b. Anne Mitford, m. *Miles Bowker, afterwards of Cape Colony; and had issue.*

4b. Mary Mitford, m. *James Renshaw; and had issue* (1 *son and* 2 *das.*).

3a. William Henry Mitford, b. 1752; d. (? *unm.*).

4a. Anna Mitford, b. 1745; d. (–); m. *Richard Hesketh Shuttleworth.*

5a. Mary Mitford, b. 1751; d. (–); m. *William Bullock of Spital Hall, Mitford.* [Nos. 58061 to 58066.

---

617. Descendants of PHILADELPHIA MITFORD (see Table LXVII.), *m.* the Rev. JOHN WICKENS, D.D., Rector of Petworth, co. Sussex; and had issue 1*a.*

1*a. George Wickens, afterwards Osbaldeston of Hutton Bushel.*

---

618. Descendants of ANNE HUSTLER (see Table LXVII.), *d.* (–); *m.* 1700, THOMAS PEIRSE of Hutton Bonvile; and had (with possibly other) issue 1*a.*

1*a. Thomas Peirse, afterwards (R.L.) Hustler of Acklam Hall, co. York (to which he succeeded* 11 Jan. 1784), d. (–); m. 3rdly, Constance, da. of Ralph Hutton of Knapton; and had issue 1b to 3b.

1*b. Thomas Hustler of Acklam,* d. unm. 1819.

2*b. William Hustler,* d. 1818; m. 1st, 1800, Charlotte, da. of William Meade of Philadelphia; 2ndly, Sarah, da. of the Rev. John Bostock, Rector of East Grinstead; 3rdly, Mary, widow of [——] Wylam, da. of [——]; and had issue 1c to 3c.

1*c.*[1] *Thomas Hustler of Acklam, J.P.,* b. 1 Aug. 1801; d. 30 June 1874; m. 12 Aug. 1822, Charlotte Frances Eliza, da. of Richard Wells of Demerara, W.I., d. 25 July 1873; and had issue 1d to 3d.

1*d.* William Thomas Hustler, J.P., D.L. (*Acklam Hall, in Cleveland, Middlesbro'; Newsham Park, Durham; Sladnor Park, Devon*), *b.* 29 May 1823; *m.* 1st, 12 Nov. 1851, Anna Maria Watkyn, da. of the Rev. Thomas Watkyn Richards of Puttenham, *d.* 11 Dec. 1892; 2ndly, 28 Sept. 1893, Harriet, da. of Henry Badley of Glandwr, N. Wales; and has issue 1*e.* [No. 58067.

1e. *Marian Hustler*, d. 28 *Ap.* 1893; m. 26 *Nov.* 1878, *the Rev. Reginald E. Beaumont*, d. 22 *Sept.* 1890; *and had issue 1f to 3f.*

1f. R. H. Beaumont, *b.* 9 Sept. 1879.

2f. M. E. H. Beaumont, *b.* 12 Ap. 1881.

3f. W. H. Beaumont, *b.* 25 Jan. 1885.

2d. Rev. George Hustler, Rector of English Bicknor (*English Bicknor Rectory, Coleford, Gloucester*), *b.* 12 June 1826; *m.* 17 July 1849, Louisa, da. of Capt. Robert Toovey-Hawley, King's Dragoon Guards; and has issue 1e to 2e.

1e. Evereld Ellen Hustler, *m.* 5 Sept. 1872, Richard Hill, J.P., D.L., Hon. Major *late* Yorkshire Militia Artillery (*Thornton Hall, Pickering*); and has issue 1f to 4f.

1f. Richard Hill, J.P., *b.* 14 Nov. 1877.

2f. George Francis Gordon Hill, *b.* 26 Mar. 1885.

3f. Evereld Constance Hill.

4f. Kathleen Charlotte Hill.

2e. Constance Charlotte Hustler, *m.* 23 Nov. 1875, Col. Arthur Francis Bingham Wright; and has issue 1f.

1f. Arthur George Bingham Wright, *b.* 24 Mar. 1880.

3d. *Evereld Catherine Eliza Hustler*, d. 24 *Ap.* 1887; m. 21 *July* 1864, *William Randolph Innes Hopkins of Grey Towers, Nunthorpe.*

2c.² *William Hustler, Bar.-at-Law*, d. (*abroad*) 1 *June* 1845.

3c.² *Everild Catherine Hustler*, d. (*? s.p.*); m. *as 2nd wife*, 17 *Nov.* 1835, *the Rev. Thomas Watkyn Richards, Rector of Puttenham, co. Surrey, b.* 10 *Ap.* 1793; d. 2 *Nov.* 1859.

3b. *Evereld Hustler*, d. 1811; m. *Thomas Hopper of Shincliffe Grange, co. Durham.* [Nos. 58068 to 58078.

---

619. Descendants of Elizabeth Osbaldeston (see Table LXVII.), *b.* 13 Ap. 1658; *bur.* 22 Jan. 1694; *m.* 22 May 1677, Sir Matthew Wentworth, 3rd Bart. [E.], *bur.* 1 Mar. 1706; and had issue 1*a* to 4*a*.

1a. *Sir William Wentworth, 4th Bart.* [E.], bapt. 29 *Oct.* 1686; d. 1 *Mar.* 1763; m. 23 *June* 1720, *Diana, da. of Sir William Blackett, 1st Bart.* [E.], bur. 14 *Ap.* 1742; *and had issue 1b to 4b.*

1b. *Sir Thomas Wentworth, 5th Bart.* [E.], b. 12 *Ap.* 1726; d.s.p. 10 *July* 1792.

2b. *Diana Wentworth*, m. *Godfrey Bosvile of Gunthwaite, co. York; and had issue 1c.*

1c. *Elizabeth Diana Bosvile*, bapt. 25 *July* 1748; d. 18 *Oct.* 1789; m. 3 *May* 1768, *Alexander (Macdonald), 1st Baron Macdonald* [I.], d. 12 *Sept.* 1795; *and had issue.*

See p. 587, Nos. 51296–51482.

3b. *Elizabeth Wentworth*, m. *James Watson of Springhead, M.D.*

4b. *Julia Wentworth*, m. 1760, *the Rev. John de Chaire, Rector of Rissington.*

2a. *Grace Wentworth*, m. *Thomas Staines of Sowerby and Newby.*[1]

3a. *Ann Wentworth*, m. *Thomas Hassell of Thorp, co. York.*

4a. *Elizabeth Wentworth.* [Nos. 58079 to 58264.

---

[1] Thomas Hustler, previously Peirse, of Acklam (see p. 702) *m.* 1st, 1737, Jane, da. and co-h. of Staines of Sowerby, but does not appear to have had surviving issue by her, who, if a da. of this couple, will have been his second cousin. Burke's "Landed Gentry," 1900, p. 833.

The Plantagenet Roll

620. Descendants of Sir THOMAS TANCRED, 4th Bart. [E.] (see Table LXVIII.), *d.* 30 May 1759; *m. c.* 1740, JUDETH, da. of Peter DALTON of Greenanstown, co. Tipperary, *d.* 1781; and had issue 1*a* to 4*a*.

1*a*. Sir *Thomas Tancred, 5th Bart.* [*E.*], *d.* 3 *Aug.* 1784; m. 7 *Oct.* 1776, *Penelope, da. of Thomas Assheton Smith, d.* 21 *Ap.* 1837; *and had issue* 1*b*.

1*b*. Sir *Thomas Tancred, 6th Bart.* [*E.*], *b.* 24 *July* 1780; *d.* 29 *Aug.* 1844; m. 25 *Ap.* 1805, *Harriet Lucy, da. of the Rev. Offley-Crewe of Muxton, co. Staff., d.* 16 *June* 1864; *and had issue* 1*c* to 3*c*.

1*c*. Sir *Thomas Tancred, 7th Bart.* [*E.*], *b.* 16 *Aug.* 1808; *d. Oct.* 1880; m. 16 *Ap.* 1839, *Jane, da. of Prideaux John Selby of Twizel House, d. Dec.* 1901; *and had issue.*

See p. 700, Nos. 58010–58040.

2*c*. *Henry John Tancred, Chancellor New Zealand University, and sometime M.L.C., b.* 8 *Ap.* 1816; *d.* (? s.p.) 27 *Ap.* 1884; m. 3 *July* 1857, *Georgiana, da. of Lieut.-Col. Matthew Richmond of Nelson, N.Z., C.B.*

3*c*. Susan Tancred (*Milton House, Woolston, Hants*), m. 2 Jan. 1849, the Rev. Thomas Clarke Whitehead, M.A., *d.* 28 Ap. 1873; and has issue 1*d* to 7*d*.

1*d*. Thomas Tancred Whitehead, Solicitor (*Ramsgate*), *b.* 26 Sept. 1853.

2*d*. Hayward Reader Whitehead, L.R.C.P. (Edin.), F.R.C.S. (Eng.), R.A.M.C., Col. and Principal Medical Officer, Sialkote and Abbotabad Brigades, India (*Junior United Service*), *b.* 14 July 1855; *m.* 13 Feb. 1893, Evelyn Wynne, da. of Dep.-Surg.-Gen. Henry Cayley.

3*d*. Henry Hammond Whitehead (*Holland House, Isleworth*), *b.* 1860; *m.* 1886, Edith Miriam, da. of J. Cove of Northampton; and has issue 1*e* to 4*e*.

1*e*. Noel Tancred Whitehead, *b.* 1888.

2*e*. Henry Montague Whitehead, *b.* 1890.

3*e*. George Offley Whitehead, $\left.\begin{array}{c} \\ \end{array}\right\}$ *b.* (twins) 1894.
4*e*. Annette Whitehead,

4*d*. Susan Harriet Whitehead.

5*d*. Mary Elizabeth Hutton Whitehead.

6*d*. Annette Augusta Whitehead.

7*d*. Henrietta Mary Whitehead.

2*a*. *William Tancred.*

3*a*. *Charles Tancred.*

4*a*. *Barbara Tancred, d.* 21 *Mar.* 1817; m. *Thomas Taylor of Cornay, co. Durham.*　　　　　　　　　　　　　　　　　　　　[Nos. 58265 to 58307.

621. Descendants of THOMAS TANCRED of St. Paul's, Covent Garden (see Table LXVIII.), *m.* and had (with 3 other sons and younger das.) issue 1*a* to 2*a*.[1]

1*a*. *Charles Tancred.*

2*a*. *Anne Tancred, d.* 13 *Sept.* 1780; m. *Thomas Webbe of Brooke Green, Fulham*; *and had issue* 1*b* to 3*b*.

1*b*. *John Webbe, afterwards* (1782) *Webbe-Weston of Sutton Place, co. Surrey, b.* 1753; *d.* (–); m. 1st, *Elizabeth, da. of John Lawson of Bath, d.* 6 *Aug.* 1791; *2ndly, Mary, da. of William Constable of Everingham*; *and had issue* 1*c* to 7*c*.[2]

---

[1] Foster's "Yorkshire Pedigrees."

[2] See Burke's "Landed Gentry," 1900, p. 1389, where the five das. are said to have been by the 2nd wife. According to the earlier editions, however (1850, p. 1562, &c.), all the children were by the 1st wife, and this is confirmed by the present representative of this family, who says he had no issue by Miss Constable (for whose descent see p. 336 and Clarence Volume, p 394). I have, however, been unable to obtain satisfactory details.

1c. *John Webbe-Weston of Sutton Place*, b. 1784; d. (–); m. *Caroline, da. of Charles Graham, Younger of Netherby*, b. (*posthumous*) 1782; d. (–); *and had issue* 1d to 4d.

1d. *John Joseph Webbe-Weston of Sutton Place, Capt. 3rd Dragoons in the Austrian Service*, d.s.p. 24 Sept. 1849.

2d. Mary Webbe-Weston, *m.* in France.

3d. Matilda Webbe-Weston, *m.* in France.

4d. Caroline Webbe-Weston, *m.* F. Hicks of Henrietta Street, Cavendish Square.

2c. *Thomas Webbe-Weston, afterwards Monington, of Sarnesfield and of Sutton Place, High Sheriff co. Surrey*, b. 2 *July* 1790; d.s.p. 12 *Sept.* 1857.

3c. *Katherine Mary Webbe-Weston* (? d. 8 Feb. 1793).

4c. *Anna Maria Webbe-Weston*, d. (–); m. 22 *July* 1800, *William Thomas Salvin of Croxdale*, d. 8 *June* 1842; *and had issue.*

See p. 529, Nos. 48740–48756.

5c. *Melior Mary Webbe-Weston*, b. 30 *Mar.* 1786.

6c. *Elizabeth Mary Webbe-Weston*, b. 1 Oct. 1788.

7c. *Bridget Mary Webbe-Weston*, d.s.p. 1827; m. *as* 1st *wife Oct.* 1812, *Thomas Charles Hornyold of Blackmore Park, J.P., D.L.*; d.s.p. 17 *Jan.* 1859.

2b. *Anne Webbe*, m. *Christopher Chapman Bird of Reigate, co. Surrey.*

3b. *Teresa Webbe*, m. *John Wright of Kelvedon Hall, co. Essex.*

[Nos. 58308 to 58327.]

---

622. Descendants of HENRY THOMAS (FOX-STRANGWAYS), 2nd EARL OF ILCHESTER [G.B.] (see Table LXIX.), *b.* 9 Aug. 1747; *d.* 5 Sept. 1802; *m.* 1st, 20 Aug. 1772, MARY THERESA, da. of Standish O'GRADY of Cappercullen, co. Limerick, *d.* 14 June 1790; 2ndly, 28 Aug. 1794, MARIA, da. of Very Rev. the Hon. William DIGBY, Dean of Durham, *d.* (–); and had issue 1*a* to 7*a*.

1a. *Henry Stephen (Fox-Strangways), 3rd Earl of Ilchester [G.B.]*, b. 21 Feb. 1787; d. 3 *Jan.* 1858; m. *Feb.* 1812, *Caroline Leonora, da. of Lord George Murray, Bishop of St. David's*, d. 8 *Jan.* 1819; *and had issue.*

See the Tudor Roll of "The Blood Royal of Britain," pp. 453–454, Nos. 31809–31835.

2a. *William Thomas Horner (Fox-Strangways), 4th Earl of Ilchester [G.B.]*, b. 7 *May* 1795; d.s.p. 10 *Jan.* 1765.

3a. *Hon. John George Charles Fox-Strangways of Brickworth House, co. Wilts, M.P.*, b. 6 *Feb.* 1803; d. 8 *Sept.* 1859; m. 19 *Feb.* 1844, *Amelia, da. of Edward Marjoribanks*, d. 9 *Sept.* 1886; *and had issue* 1b to 2b.

1b. *Henry Edward (Fox-Strangways), 5th Earl of Ilchester [G.B.], P.C.*, b. 13 *Sept.* 1847; d. 6 *Dec.* 1905; m. 8 *Feb.* 1872, *Lady Mary Eleanor Anne, da. of Richard (Dawson), 1st Earl of Dartrey [U.K.]*; *and had issue* 1c to 2c.

1c. *Giles Stephen Holland Fox-Strangways, 6th Earl of Ilchester [G.B.]* (*Melbury House, near Dorchester; Abbotsbury Castle, Dorchester; Holland House, Kensington, W., &c.*), b. 31 May 1874; *m.* 25 Jan. 1902, Lady Helen Mary Theresa, da. of Charles Stewart (Vane-Tempest-Stewart), 6th Marquis of Londonderry [I.], K.G.; *and has issue* 1d to 2d.

1d. Edward Henry Charles James Fox-Strangways, Lord Stavordale, *b.* 1 Oct. 1905.

2d. Hon. Mary Theresa Fox-Strangways.

2c. Lady Muriel Augusta Fox-Strangways, *m.* 5 Aug. 1903, George Hugh Digby, J.P. (*Chalmington, Dorchester*).   [Nos. 58328 to 58363.

The Plantagenet Roll

2b. Lady Maria Georgiana Julia Fox-Strangways, *m.* 4 Ap. 1872, Arthur Wellington Alexander Nelson (Hood), 2nd Viscount Bridport [U.K.] and 4th Baron [I.] Bridport and 4th Duke of Bronté [Sicily], C.B. (*Sudley Lodge, Bognor*); and has issue.

See p. 323, Nos. 23986–23990.

4a. *Lady Elizabeth Theresa Fox-Strangways, b.* 16 *Nov.* 1773; *d.* 12 *Mar.* 1846; *m.* 1*st,* 17 *Ap.* 1796, *William Davenport Talbot of Lacock Abbey, co. Wilts, d.* 30 *July* 1800; 2*ndly,* 24 *Ap.* 1804, *Rear-Admiral Charles Feilding, R.N., d.* 2 *Sept.* 1837: *and had issue* 1*b to* 2*b.*

1b. *William Henry Fox Talbot of Lacock Abbey, LL.D., F.R.S., M.P., High Sheriff co. Wilts, b.* 11 *Feb.* 1800; *d.* 17 *Sept.* 1877; *m.* 20 *Dec.* 1832, *Constance, da. of Francis Mundy of Markeaton, d. Sept.* 1880; *and had issue.*

See p. 654, Nos. 55980–55989.

2b. *Caroline Augusta Feilding, V.A., b. Jan.* 1808; *d.* 2 *Nov.* 1881; *m.* 6 *Dec.* 1831, *Ernest Augustus* (*Edgcumbe*), 3*rd Earl of Mount Edgcumbe* [*G.B.*]*, b.* 23 *Mar.* 1797; *d.* 3 *Sept.* 1861; *and had issue* 1*c to* 3*c.*

1c. William Henry (Edgcumbe), 4th Earl of Mount Edgcumbe [G.B.], P.C., G.C.V.O., Lord-Lieut. and Vice-Admiral of Cornwall, &c., *formerly* (1879–1880) Lord Chamberlain and (1885–1886) Lord High Steward of the Household to Queen Victoria (*Mount Edgcumbe, Plymouth; Cotehele House, St. Dominick, R.S.O.*), *b.* 5 Nov. 1832; *m.* 26 Oct. 1858, Lady Katherine Elizabeth, da. of James (Hamilton), 1st Duke of Abercorn [I.], *d.* 3 Sept. 1874; and has issue 1*d* to 4*d.*

1d. Piers Alexander Hamilton Edgcumbe, Viscount Valletort, Major Duke of Cornwall's L.I. (*Marlborough*), *b.* 2 July 1865.

2d. Lady Victoria Frederica Caroline Edgcumbe, *m.* 3 Aug. 1880, Lord Algernon Malcolm Arthur Percy, J.P., D.L. (*Guy's Cliffe, Warwick*), and has issue 1*e* to 2*e.*

1e. Algernon William Percy, *b.* 29 Nov. 1884.

2e. Katherine Louisa Victoria Percy, *b.* 22 Mar. 1882.

3d. Lady Albertha Louisa Florence Edgcumbe, *m.* 10 Oct. 1891, Henry Yarde Buller Massey-Lopes, J.P., D.L. (son and heir of the Right Hon. Sir Lopes Massey-Lopes, 3rd Bart. [U.K.], P.C.) (*Roborough House, Roborough, Devon*); and has issue 1*e* to 5*e.*

1e. Massey Henry Edgcumbe Lopes, *b.* 4 Oct. 1903.

2e. Katherine Frederica Albertha Lopes, *b.* 25 Sept. 1892.

3e. Bertha Louisa Victoria Lopes, *b.* 30 Oct. 1895.

4e. Margaret Beatrice Lopes, *b.* 12 Feb. 1898.

5e. Constance Elizabeth Lopes, *b.* 24 Aug. 1901.

4d. Lady Edith Hilaria Edgcumbe, *m.* 23 June 1892, the Hon. John Townshend St. Aubyn, Lieut.-Col. Comdg. 3rd Batt. Grenadier Guards (53 *Cadogan Place, S.W.*); and has issue 1*e* to 2*e.*

1e. Marjory Katharine Elizabeth Alexandra St. Aubyn.

2e. Hilaria Lily St. Aubyn.

2c. Hon. Charles Ernest Edgcumbe, J.P., Hon. Col. City of London Regt., *late* Grenadier Guards (23 *Down Street, W.*).

3c. Lady Ernestine Emma Horatia Edgcumbe (*Mount Edgcumbe, Plymouth*).

5a. *Lady Mary Lucy Fox-Strangways, b.* 11 *Feb.* 1776; *d.* 3 *Feb.* 1855; *m.* 1*st, Feb.* 1794, *Thomas Mansel Talbot of Margram, d.* 10 *May* 1813; 2*ndly,* 28 *Ap.* 1815, *Capt. Sir Christopher Cole, K.C.B., R.N., d.* 24 *Aug.* 1836; *and had issue* (*with possible others by second husband*) 1*b.*

1b. See p. 651, Nos. 55882–55979.

6a. *Lady Harriot Fox-Strangways, b.* 17 *June* 1778; *d.* 6 *Aug.* 1844; *m.* 9 *Sept.* 1799, *James Frampton of Moreton, High Sheriff co. Dorset* 1793, *Lieut.-Col. Dorset Yeo. Cav., b.* 4 *Sept.* 1769; *d.* 8 *Feb.* 1855; *and had issue* 1*b to* 2*b.*

1b. *Henry Frampton of Moreton, b.* 7 *May* 1804; *d.* (–); *m.* 13 *May* 1833, *Charlotte Louisa, da. of Robert Willis Blencowe of Hayes, co. Midx., d.* (–); *and had issue* 1*c.* [Nos. 58364 to 58489.

706

# of The Blood Royal

1*c*. Louisa Mary Frampton of Moreton, *b.* 8 Ap. 1834; *m.* 22 Nov. 1855, Rupert Pennefather Fetherstonhaugh, now (1887) Fetherstonhaugh-Frampton of Balrath, co. Westmeath, J.P., D.L. (*Moreton, Dorchester*); and has issue 1*d* to 6*d*.

1*d*. Harry Rupert Fetherstonhaugh-Frampton J.P., *late* Lieut. Dorset Imp. Yeo., *b.* 7 Nov. 1861; *m.* 8 June 1893, Violet, da. of Col. Fox Reeve, Coldstream Guards; and has issue 1*e*.

1*e*. Philip Tregonwell Fetherstonhaugh-Frampton, *b.* 1896.

2*d*. Cuthbert Lionel Fetherstonhaugh (*Fort Qu'Appelle, N.W. Territories*), *b.* 29 July 1865; *m.* July 1893, Vera, da. of Charles Digby of Meriden Hall, co. Warwick; and has issue 1*e* to 2*e*.

1*e*. Mark Rupert Fetherstonhaugh, *b.* 1894.

2*e*. Anthea Fetherstonhaugh, *b.* 1905.

3*d*. Theresa Charlotte Fetherstonhaugh, *b.* 17 Nov. 1856.

4*d*. Ethel Maud Fetherstonhaugh, *b.* 14 Mar. 1858; *m.* 3 Jan. 1882, George Murray Farquharson of the War Office, a Cadet of Invercauld, *b.* 16 Aug. 1835; *d.* 7 May 1899; and has issue 1*e*.

1*e*. Janet Margaret Farquharson.

5*d*. *Dora Adelaide Fetherstonhaugh*, b. 5 *Ap.* 1859; d. 20 *Nov.* 1898; m 15 *Feb.* 1881, *Charles Wriothesley Digby, J.P.* (*Meriden Hall, Coventry*); *and had issue* 1*e* *to* 2*e*.

1*e*. Lettice Adelaide Digby, *b.* 17 June 1882.

2*e*. Margery Frances Digby, *b.* 14 Oct. 1883.

6*d*. Mary Blanche Fetherstonhaugh, *m.* June 1895, Frederick Bathurst.

2*b*. *Harriet Georgina Frampton*, d. 1886; m. 28 *Oct.* 1830, *William Mundy of Markeaton, M.P., J.P., D.L., High Sheriff co. Derby,* 1843'; b. 14 *Sept.* 1801; d. 10 *Ap.* 1877; *and had issue* 1*c*.

1*c*. *Frances Noel Mundy of Markeaton Hall, J.P., D.L., High Sheriff co. Derby,* b. 29 *Nov.* 1833; d. 1903; m. 12 *July* 1864, *Emily Maria Georgiana* (*Moreaton Hall, near Derby*), da. of the Hon. Richard Cavendish of Thornton Hall.

7*a*. *Lady Louisa Emma Fox-Strangways,* b. 27 *June* 1785; d. 3 *Ap.* 1851; m. 30 *Mar.* 1808, *Henry (Fitzmaurice), 3rd Marquis of Lansdowne* [G.B.], *4th Earl of Kerry* [I.], *K.G.,* d. 31 *Jan.* 1863; *and had issue.*

See p. 184, Nos. 6512–6542. [Nos. 58490 to 58532.

623. Descendants of Rev. the Hon. CHARLES REDLYNCH FOX-STRANGWAYS, Rector of Rewe, co. Devon (see Table LXIX.), *b.* 27 Ap. 1761; *d.* 4 Nov. 1836; *m.* 2 Aug. 1787, JANE, da. of the Rev. Dr. Nathan HAINES, D.D., *d.* 8 June 1830; and had issue 1*a* to 2*a*.

1*a*. Rev. Henry Fox-Strangways, Rector of Rewe, co. Devon, b. 25 Feb. 1793; d. 25 Feb. 1860; m. 26 June 1827, Hester Eleanora, da. of James Buller of Downes, d. 31 Jan. 1865; and had issue 1b to 3b.

1*b*. Rev. Henry Fox-Strangways, Rector of Silverton, co. Devon, b. 3 Mar. 1828; d. 23 Sept. 1894; m. 15 Ap. 1857, Charlotte Chester (44 St. David's Hill, Exeter), da. of Francis Copleston, I.S.C.; and had issue 1c to 8c.

1*c*. Theodore Stephen Fox-Strangways, *late* Major Royal Irish Rifles, and D.A.Q.M.G., Dublin (*Bloemfontein*), *b.* 4 Oct. 1862; *m.* 21 Ap. 1898, Rosamond Cleere, da. of Charles Edmund Newton of Mickleover Manor.

2*c*. Francis Copleston Fox-Strangways, B.A. (Oxon.), Assist. Master at Alton Burn, Nairn, *b.* 14 May 1870.

3*c*. Henry Wentworth Fox-Strangways, Assist. Master of the Old Riche School, Bournemouth, *b.* 1 Oct. 1871. [Nos. 58533 to 58535.

The Plantagenet Roll

4c. Rev. Henry George Fox-Strangways, Curate of Woodhall Spa, b. 13 June 1873; m. 15 Sept. 1903, Isabella Mary, da. of William Macartney Read of Stockwell, co. Devon.

5c. Alice Laura Fox-Strangways, m. 1890, Albert W. Searley (*Northernhay, Kingskerswell, Newton Abbott*); and has issue 1d to 4d.

1d. Henry Charles James Searley, b. 27 Jan. 1896.

2d. Muriel Alice Searley, b. 13 May 1892.

3d. Theodora Beatrice Searley, b. 2 Ap. 1894.

4d. Eveline Isabel Searley, b. 29 Jan. 1897.

6c. Eveline Charlotte Fox-Strangways, m. 2 Jan. 1890, the Right Rev. Ernest Arthur Copleston, Lord Bishop of Colombo.

7c. Margaret Christina Fox-Strangways, b. 3 June 1865.

8c. Henrietta Frances Fox-Strangways, b. 12 June 1867.

2b. *Walter Aston Fox-Strangways, K.L.H., Col. R.A.*, b. 14 Dec. 1832; d. 26 Feb. 1885; m. 19 Aug. 1858, *Harriet Elizabeth, da. of John Edward Buller of Chase Lodge, Enfield, d. 13 Ap. 1903; and had issue 1c to 4c.*

1c. Arthur Henry Fox-Strangways, M.A. (Oxon.), Assist. Master at Wellington College, Berks, b. 14 Sept. 1859.

2c. Maurice Walter Fox-Strangways, I.C.S., b. 23 Mar. 1862; m. 29 Dec. 1886, Louisa Blanche, da. of Major-Gen. George R. Phillips, I.S.C.; and has issue 1d to 4d.

1d. Walter Angelo Fox-Strangways, b. 24 Sept. 1887.

2d. Vivian Fox-Strangways, b. 1898.

3d. Sylvia Fox-Strangways, b. 11 July 1890.

4d. Elinor Fox-Strangways, b. 1 Ap. 1893.

3c. Harold Stephen Fox-Strangways, Major Indian Army and a Dep. Commr., Punjab, b. 24 Nov. 1864; m. 1891, Beatrice Talbot, da. of Major-Gen. William Howey, Bengal Inf.; and has issue 1d to 2d.

1d. Dorothy Kate Fox-Strangways, b. 27 Aug. 1893.

2d. Marjorie Fox-Strangways.

4c. Mary Beatrice Fox-Strangways, m. 3 Sept. 1895, Owen Gould (*Knowle, Lustleigh, S. Devon*); and has issue 1d to 2d.

1d. Arthur Nutcombe Gould, b. 7 May 1896.

2d. John Rashleigh Gould, b. 30 Oct. 1899.

3b. Charles Edward Fox-Strangways, Member of the Geological Survey of England (*Kylemore, Hollycroft Avenue, West Hampstead, N.W.*), b. 13 Feb. 1844; m. 2 Sept. 1868, Annie Maria, da. of George Flory of Ipswich, d. 27 June 1898.

2a. *Susanna Fox-Strangways*, b. 13 *Sept.* 1795; d. 11 *Jan.* 1854; m. 9 *Oct.* 1830, *Lieut.-Gen. Alexander Macdonald, R.A.*, d. 31 *May* 1856.

[Nos. 58536 to 58557.

624. Descendants, if any, of Lady Susannah Sarah Louisa Fox-Strangways (see Table LXIX.), b. 12 Feb. 1743; d. 1827; m. 7 Ap. 1773 (or 1764), William O'Brien of Stinsford, co. Dorset.

625. Descendants of Lady Lucy Fox-Strangways (see Table LXIX.), b. 15 Dec. 1748; d. 16 Aug. 1787; m. as 1st wife, 1 Oct. 1771, Col. the Hon. Stephen Digby, b. 10 May 1742; d. 30 May 1800; and had issue 1a.

1a. *Rev. Charles Digby, Canon of Windsor*, b. 31 *May* 1775; d. 23 *June* 1841; m. 8 June 1801, *Mary, da. of the Hon. Hugh Somerville*, d. 28 *Ap.* 1834; *and had issue 1b to 2b.*

# of The Blood Royal

1b. *Charles Wriothesly Digby of Studland, Manor House, Wareham*, b. 2 *May* 1802; d. 29 *Dec.* 1873; m. 1*st*, 21 *July* 1831, *Elizabeth, da. of the Rev. William Floyer*, d. 18 *July* 1834; 2*ndly*, 9 *July* 1840, *Frances Anna Margaret, widow of the Rev. G. Bingham, da. of Anthony Blagrave*, d. 22 *Aug.* 1849; 3*rdly*, 17 *June* 1856, *Adelaide, da. of the Right Hon. George Bankes*, d. 19 *May* 1878; *and had issue* 1*c to* 7*c.*

1c. Charles Wriothesly Digby, J.P. (*Meriden Hall, Coventry*), b. 31 Jan. 1859; m. 15 Feb. 1881, Dora Adelaide, da. of Rupert Pennefather Fetherstonhaugh-Frampton of Moreton, d. 20 Nov. 1898; 2ndly, 26 Oct. 1904, Evelyn Frances Adams, da. of Ralph Coker Adams Beck of Bookham Lodge, Cobham; and has issue 1*d* to 2*d.*

1d. Lettice Adelaide Digby, b. 17 June 1882.

2d. Margery Frances Digby, b. 14 Oct. 1883.

2c. *Elizabeth Mary Digby*, b. 26 *July* 1833; d. 12 *July* 1856; m. 2 *Aug.* 1854, *Henry Maitland Wilson; and had issue* 1*d.*

1d. Mary Digby Wilson, b. 1855.

3c. Frances Rachel Digby, b. 8 May 1841; *m.* 1st, 14 Feb. 1865, the Rev. Richard Henry Wingfield-Digby, *d.* 31 Oct. 1876; 2ndly, 21 Feb. 1882, Charles Thomas Palmer, J.P. (*Newland House, Coleford*); and has issue 1*d* to 3*d.*

1d. John Walter Somerville Wingfield-Digby, b. 9 Jan. 1870.

2d. Muriel Frances Wingfield-Digby, b. 3 Jan. 1866; m. 17 Ap. 1888, Jerome Nugent Bankes (68 *Avonmore Road, W.*); and has issue 1*e* to 7*e.*

1e. Henry Vivian Nugent Bankes, b. 25 June 1894.

2e. Michael Jerome Richard Bankes, b. 2 Dec. 1905.

3e. Cicely Muriel Bankes, b. 9 Oct. 1890.

4e. Rachel Mary Bankes, b. 14 May 1893.

5e. Mary Beatrice Margaret Bankes, b. 2 Feb. 1896.

6e. Joan Bankes, b. 27 Feb. 1898.

7e. Audrey Bankes, b. 1899.

3d. Beatrix Lucy Geraldine Wingfield-Digby.

4c. Adelaide Mabel Digby, *m.* 27 Ap. 1892, the Rev. Claude Samuel Homan, B.A. (*Tyneham Rectory, Wareham*); and has issue 1*d* to 2*d.*

1d. Digby Arden Homan, b. 30 July 1894.

2d. Claude Knox Homan, b. 12 July 1896.

5c. Augusta Henrietta Sophia Digby, *m.* 7 June 1892, Harry William Buddicom (*Penbedw, Mold, Flint*); and has issue 1*d* to 3*d.*

1d. Walter Digby Buddicom, b. 14 Jan. 1894.

2d. Venetia Digby Buddicom, b. 30 Dec. 1895.

3d. Marcia Sophia Buddicom, b. 26 Ap. 1900.

6c. Ethel Octavia Digby, b. 24 May 1867.

7c. Katherine Vera Digby, *m.* July 1893, Cuthbert Lionel Fetherstonhaugh (*Summerland, British Columbia*); and has issue.

See p. 707, Nos. 58494–58495.

2b. *George Somerville Digby, Capt. Grenadier Guards*, b. 27 *Sept.* 1805; d. 16 *Nov.* 1864; m. 6 *Sept.* 1836, *Lady Emily Jane, sister to George, 5th Earl of Lanesborough* [*I.*], *da. of the Hon. Augustus Richard Butler-Danvers*, d. 28 *Mar.* 1895; *and had issue* 1*c to* 5*c.*

1c. Noel Stephen Fox Digby, Vice-Admiral (ret.) R.N. (*Street Farm, Bramley, Basingstoke*), b. 2 Oct. 1839; *m.* 1st, 9 July 1879, Ethel Dorothea, da. of the Rev. William Webb-Spicer of Itchen Abbas, *d.s.p.* 3 Feb. 1881; 2ndly, 28 Nov. 1893, Sibella Frances, da. of Henry Drake of Reading; and has issue 1*d* to 2*d.*

1d. Noel Somerville Digby, b. 20 Feb. 1899.

2d. Emily Frances Digby, b. 12 Oct. 1894.   [Nos. 58558 to 58586.

The Plantagenet Roll

2c. Rev. Robert Charles Digby, M.A. (Camb.), Vicar of Meriden (*Meriden Vicarage, Coventry*).

3c. Elizabeth Jane Digby.

4c. Emily Lucy Neville Digby.

5c. Mary Frederica Cecilia Digby, *m.* as 2nd wife, 2 Jan. 1894, the Rev. John Trelawny Trelawny-Ross, D.D., Vicar of Paignton (*Paignton Vicarage, Devon ; Ham, Devon*); and has issue 1*d* to 3*d*.

1*d.* Stephen Matthew Trelawny Trelawny-Ross, *b.* 1894.

2*d.* Addis Emily Trelawny Trelawny-Ross, *b.* 1895.

3*d.* Katharine Lucy Trelawny Trelawny-Ross, *b.* 1898.

[Nos. 58587 to 58593.

626. Descendants of Lady CHRISTIAN HARRIOT CAROLINE FOX-STRANGWAYS (see Table LXIX.), *b.* 3 June 1750; *d.* 21 July 1815; *m.* 1771, Col. JOHN DYKE ACLAND of Pixton, *d.v.p.* 31 Oct. 1778; and had issue 1*a* to 2*a*.

1*a. Sir John Acland, 4th Bart. [E.], b. 1778; d.s.p. 23 Ap. 1785.*

2*a. Elizabeth Kitty Acland, b. 13 Dec. 1772; d. 5 Mar. 1813; m. 26 Ap. 1796, Henry George (Herbert), 2nd Earl of Carnarvon [G.B.], d. 16 Ap. 1833; and had issue 1b to 3b.*

1*b. Henry John George (Herbert), 3rd Earl of Carnarvon [G.B.], b. 8 June 1800; d. 10 Dec. 1849; m. 4 Aug. 1830, Henrietta Anne, da. of Lord Henry Thomas Howard-Molyneux-Howard, d. 26 May 1876; and had issue.*

See the Clarence Volume, p. 433, Nos. 18096–18132.

2*b. Lady Harriet Elizabeth Herbert, b. 23 June 1797; d. 22 Nov. 1836; m. 21 Ap. 1829, the Rev. John C. Stapleton, Rector of Teversale, co. Notts ; and had issue.*

3*b. Lady Emily Frances Theresa Herbert, d. 16 Nov. 1854; m. 4 Oct. 1822, Philip Pusey of Pusey, M.P., b. 25 June 1799; d. 9 July 1855; and had issue 1c to 3c.*

1*c.* Sydney Edward Bouverie Pusey, now Pusey-Bouverie, J.P. (*Pusey House, near Farington, co. Berks*), *b.* 15 Sept. 1839; *m.* 1st, 29 Ap. 1871, Wilhelmina Maria, *da.* of Lord William Hervey, *d.* 16 Nov. 1885; 2ndly, 5 July 1890, Helen Henrietta, widow of the Right Hon. William Massey, M.P., *da.* of Patrick Grant.

2*c.* Edith Lucy Bouverie Pusey.

3*c.* Clara Pusey, *m.* 30 Oct. 1862, Capt. Francis Charteris Fletcher, *d.* 25 Jan. 1891; and has issue 1*d* to 2*d*.

1*d.* Philip Francis Fletcher.

2*d.* Constance Fletcher.

[Nos. 58594 to 58635.

627. Descendants of Lady FRANCES MURIEL FOX-STRANGWAYS (see Table LXIX.), *b.* Aug. 1775; *d.* May 1814; *m.* as 1st wife, 24 Aug. 1777, VALENTINE RICHARD (QUIN), 1st EARL OF DUNRAVEN and MOUNT EARL (1822) [I.], *b.* 30 July 1752; *d.* 24 Aug. 1824; and had issue 1*a* to 2*a*.

1*a. Windham Henry (Quin, afterwards (1815) Wyndham-Quin), 2nd Earl of Dunraven and Mount Earl [I.], b. 24 Sept. 1782; d. 6 Aug. 1850; m. 27 Dec. 1810, Caroline, da. and h. of Thomas Wyndham of Dunraven Castle, co. Glamorgan, d. 26 May 1870; and had issue 1b to 2b.*

1*b. Edwin Richard Windham (Wyndham-Quin), 3rd Earl of Dunraven and Mount Earl [I.], 1st Baron Kenry [U.K.], K.P., b. 19 May 1812; d. 6 Oct. 1871;*

710

# of The Blood Royal

m. 1st, 18 *Aug.* 1836, *Augusta, da. of Thomas Goold, Master in Chancery,* d. 22 *Nov.* 1866 ; *and had issue* 1c *to* 4c.

1c. Windham Thomas (Wyndham-Quin), 4th Earl of Dunraven and Mount Earl [I.], 2nd Baron Kenry [U.K.], and 4th Baronet [G.B.], K.P., C.M.G., P.C. (*Dunraven Castle, Southerdown, Glamorgan ; Adare Manor, Limerick ; Kenry House, Putney Vale, S.W., &c.*), b. 12 Feb. 1841 ; m. 20 Ap. 1869, Florence Elizabeth, da. of Lord Charles Lennox Kerr ; and has issue 1d to 2d.

    1d. Lady Rachel Charlotte Wyndham-Quin, b. 20 Feb. 1872 ; d. 30 *Jan.* 1901 ; m. 28 *Oct.* 1897, *Desmond Fitzjohn Lloyd FitzGerald, Knight of Glin, J.P., D.L.* (*Glin Castle, co. Limerick*) ; *and had issue* 1e.

        1e. Desmond Windham Otho FitzGerald, b. 20 Jan. 1901.

    2d. Lady Aileen Mary Wyndham-Quin, b. 9 Ap. 1873.

2c. *Lady Augusta Emily Wyndham-Quin,* b. 10 *Aug.* 1839 ; d. 11 *Feb.* 1877 ; m. *as* 1st *wife,* 4 *Mar.* 1867, *Sir Arthur Pendarves Vivian, K.C.B., J.P., D.L., High Sheriff co. Cornwall* 1889, *Hon. Col.* 2nd *Vol. Batt. Welsh Regt., sometime* (1868–1895) *M.P., &c.* (*Bosahan, St. Martin, R.S.O., Cornwall ;* 23 *Buckingham Gate, S.W.*); *and had issue* 1d *to* 4d.

    1d. *Henry Windham Vivian, J.P., Major* 2nd *Vol. Batt. Welsh Regt.,* b. 3 *Feb.* 1868 ; d. 17 *Nov.* 1901 ; m. 19 *Jan.* 1899, *Lady Maude* (48 *Seymour Street, W.*), *da. of Robert Bermingham* (*Clements*), 4th *Earl of Leitrim* [I.] ; *and had issue* 1e.

        1e. Audrey Emily Vivian, b. 24 Sept. 1899.

    2d. Gerald William Vivian, Lieut. R.N., b. 10 June 1869.

    3d. Caroline Mabel Vivian, b. 26 June 1873 ; m. 21 June 1904, Capt. the Hon. James Ulysses Graham Raymond Colborne (*Venn, Ivybridge, Devon ;* 30 *Lowndes Square, S.W.*).

    4d. Clarice Gertrude Vivian, b. 3 Mar. 1875.

3c. *Lady Mary Frances Wyndham-Quin,* b. 25 *Nov.* 1844 ; d. 21 *Sept.* 1884 ; m. *as* 1st *wife,* 17 *Aug.* 1868, *the Right Hon. Arthur Hugh* (*Smith-Barry*), 1st *Baron Barrymore* (1902) [*U.K.*] (*Fota Island, co. Cork ; Marbury Hall, co. Chester ;* 20 *Hill Street, W.*); *and had issue* 1d.

    1d. Hon. Geraldine Smith-Barry, m. 18 July 1893, Henry Burleigh Lethem Overend, d. 1904.

4c. Lady Emily Anna Wyndham-Quin (12 *William Street, Lowndes Square, S.W.*).

2b. *Hon. Windham Henry Wyndham-Quin,* b. 2 *Nov.* 1829 ; d. 24 *Oct.* 1865 ; m. 24 *Jan.* 1856, *Caroline, da. of Vice-Admiral Sir George Tyler ; and had issue.*
See the Clarence Volume, p. 416, Nos. 15736–15741.

2a. *Lady Harriet Quin,* d. 13 Dec. 1845 ; m. 19 *Nov.* 1804, *Lieut.-Gen. Sir William Payne, afterwards* (*R.L.* 7 *Mar.* 1814) *Payne-Gallwey,* 1st *Bart.* [*U.K.*], d. 16 *Ap.* 1831 ; *and had issue* 1b *to* 4b.

    1b. *Sir William Payne-Gallwey,* 2nd *Bart.* [*U.K.*], *M.P.,* b. 1807 ; d. 19 *Dec.* 1881 ; m. 10 *Nov.* 1847, *Emily Anne, afterwards* (*R.L.* 2 *Oct.* 1882) *Payne-Frankland, da. and co-h. of Sir Robert Frankland-Russell,* 7th *Bart.* [*E.*] ; *and had issue.*
See the Tudor Roll of " The Blood Royal of Britain," pp. 454–455, Nos. 31838–31854.

    2b. *Henry John William Payne-Gallwey, Capt. R.N.,* d. (? *unm.*) 25 *May* 1875.

    3b. *Philip Payne-Gallwey, Capt.* 90th *Foot,* b. 1812 ; d. 23 *Feb.* 1894 ; m. 26 *May* 1854, *Fanny, da. of the Ven.* [——] *Warburton, Archdeacon of Rathkeal ; and had issue* 1c *to* 9c.

        1c. Stephen Philip Payne-Gallwey (*Junior Carlton*), b. 4 Aug. 1857.

        2c. Arthur Wyndham Payne-Gallwey (13 *Evelyn Mansions, Carlisle Place,*
                                 [Nos. 58636 to 58669.

The Plantagenet Roll

S.W.), b. 8 Oct. 1858; *m.* 1880, Grace Stanley, da. of William Pardy of San Francisco; and has issue 1*d.*

1*d.* Francis Pardy Payne-Gallwey.

3*c.* Rev. Francis Henry Payne-Gallwey, Vicar of Chirk (*Chirk Vicarage, North Wales*), *b.* 31 Dec. 1859; *m.* 17 Ap. 1888, Florence Kate Lowry, da. of Col. Arthur Lowry Cole; and has issue.

See the Clarence Volume, p. 148, Nos. 2127–2131.

4*c.* Alick Sackville Payne-Gallwey (*Kataboola, Kolmalie, Ceylon*), *b.* 16 Oct. 1861; *m.* 15 Oct. 1898, Norma Anne, da. of John Edward Arthur Dick-Lauder; and has issue 1*d.*

1*d.* Violet Payne-Gallwey.

5*c.* Herbert Philip Payne-Gallwey (*Singapore*), *b.* 24 Ap. 1864.

6*c.* Frederick Payne-Gallwey, Lieut. R.N., *b.* 24 June 1867.

7*c.* Albert Philip Payne-Gallwey (*Castle Hill, Bakewell*), *b.* 13 Dec. 1871; *m.* 17 Oct. 1900, Katherine Mary, da. of Major Vaughan Henning Vaughan-Lee of Dillington Park, M.P.; and has issue 1*d.*

1*d.* Janet Payne-Gallwey.

8*c.* Lilian Fanny Payne-Gallwey.

9*c.* Edith Caroline Payne-Gallwey.

4*b. Caroline Payne-Gallwey,* d. 12 Aug. 1858; m. *Count Lionel de Bonneval.*

[Nos. 58670 to 58684.

628. Descendants, if any, of JUDITH STRANGWAYS (see Table LXIX.), *m.* 1665, GEORGE AYLIFFE of Grittenham, co. Wilts; and of SUSANNA STRANGWAYS, *b.* 1651; *m.* 1672, JAMES (son of Sir Robert) LONG.

629. Descendants of HOWARDA STRANGWAYS (see Table LXIX.), *m.* 1st, 1612, EDWARD ROGERS of Bryanston, *d.* 1622; 2ndly, Sir LEWIS DYVE, Governor of Sherborne Castle in 1624, *b.* 3 Nov. 1599; *d.* 17 Ap. 1669; and had issue (at least by 2nd husband) 1*a* to 4*a.*[1]

1*a. Francis Dyve, b.* 1632; d.s.p. *or* s.p.m.[2] 1685; m. 1*st, Grace, da. of Giles Strangways of Melbury; 2ndly,* 14 Dec. 1665, *Theophila, da. of the Right Rev. John Hacket, D.D., Lord Bishop of Lichfield.*

2*a. Lewis Dyve, a Capt. in Army, b.* 1633; d. 1 Jan. 1686; m.; *and had issue (with 2 das.)* 1*b.*

1*b. Lewis Dyve, b.* 2 Jan. 1677; liv. 1708; m.; *and had issue* (4 das.).

3*a. John Dyve, Clerk to the Privy Council,* d. 1692; m. 29 Ap. 1673, Frances, *da. of Sir Robert Wolseley, 1st Bart.* [E.], d. 1702; *and had issue* 1*b to* 3*b.*

1*b. John Dyve,* d. 25 Jan. 1769; m. Dorothy, *da. and h. of Walter Ashton of Millwich, co. Stafford; and had issue* 1*c to* 4*c.*

1*c. John Dyve of Ranton Hall, co. Stafford, a Capt. in the Guards,* m. 1737, *Anne Dorothy, da. of Hugh Montgomery; and had issue* 1*d.*

1*d. Charlotte Dyve,* m. 1759, *John Edmondes; and had issue* 1*e.*

---

[1] See *The Gentleman's Magazine,* 1829, vol. 99, p. 327 *et seq.;* also the "Dict. Nat. Bio."

[2] Authorities differ.

# of The Blood Royal

1e. *Charlotte Edmondes*, d. 1798; m. *as* 1st *wife,* 20 *Aug.* 1787, *Llewellyn Traherne of Coedriglan and St. Hilary, High Sheriff co. Glamorgan* 1801; d. 1841; *and had issue (with 3 das. who all d.s.p.)* 1f.

1f. *Rev. John Montgomery Traherne of Coedriglan, J.P., D.L., F.R.S., F.S.A.,* b. 5 *Oct.* 1788; d.s.p. 7 *Feb.* 1860.

2c. *Charlotte Dyve, a Maid of Honour to the Princess of Wales,* b. c. 1712; d.s.p. 21 *May* 1773; m. *as* 2nd *wife, Samuel (Masham), 2nd Baron Masham [G.B.],* d.s.p. 14 *June* 1776.

3c. *Frances Dyve.*

4c. *Dorothy Dyve.*

2b. *Lewis Dyve.*

3b. *Charlotte Dyve, the favourite of Sarah, Duchess of Marlborough, and afterwards Mistress of the Robes to Caroline, Queen Consort of George II.,* d. 1 *Jan.* 1742; m. *William (Clayton), 1st Baron Sundon [I.],* d.s.p. 29 *Ap.* 1752.

4a. *Grace Dyve,* m. *George Hussey of Mamhull, co. Dorset,* b. 1622; d.; *and had issue* [1] 1b *to* 5b.

1b. *John Hussey of Mamhull,* b. 1666; d. 4 *May* 1736; m. *Mary, da. of Thomas Burdett of Smithfield; and had issue* 1c *to* 5c.

1c. *Giles Hussey of Mamhull, the celebrated Painter,* b. 10 *Feb.* 1710; d.s.p. *June* 1788.

2c. *Grace Hussey,* m. *Augustine Rowe of Beaston, co. Devon; and had issue* 1d.

1d. *John Rowe, afterwards (R.L.* 1788) *Hussey of Broadhelmstone, co. Devon,* d. 22 *Jan.* 1811; m. *Anne, da. of George Rowe of Cranborne; and had issue* 1e *to* 5e.

1e. *John Hussey of Mamhull,* b. 23 *Oct.* 1794; *liv.* 1871; m. 1820, *Christina, da. of* [——] *Arundell; and had issue* 1f *to* 4f.

1f. *Edward Giles Hussey of Mamhull,* b. 1827; d. (–); m. *Mary, da. of* [——] *Nichols; and had issue* 1g *to* 4g.

1g. *John Hussey.*

2g. *Edward Hussey.*

3g. *Donald Hussey,*

4g. *Grace Hussey.*

2f. *Herbert Edward Hussey,* b. 1835.

3f. *Mary Agnes Margaret Hussey,* b. 1822; d. (–); m. 10 *Oct.* 1855, *Robert Sadler of Freame, Gillingham; and had issue* 1g *to* 2g.

1g. *Bertram Edward Sadler,* b. 1856.

2g. *Ethel Mary Sadler,* b. 1860.

4f. *Maria Louisa Hussey,* b. 1824; d. (–); m. 1854, *Theodore Arundell,* d. 21 *Oct.* 1868; *and had issue* 1g *to* 6g.

1g. *Raymond Robert Arundell,* b. 11 Nov. 1856.

2g. *Edgar Clifford Arundell,* b. 20 Dec. 1859.

3g. *Gerald Arthur Arundell,* b. 11 Dec. 1861.

4g. *Agnes Mary Arundell,* b. 21 Aug. 1855.

5g. *Blanch Mary Arundell,* b. 8 Dec. 1857.

6g. *Maud Mary Arundell,* b. 18 July 1864.

2e. *Mary Ann Hussey,* b. 5 *May* 1796; d. (–); m. *Herman Scruers; and had issue.*

3e. *Teresa Hussey,* d. *June* 1868; m. 1st, *Spry Bartlett;* 2ndly, [——] *Mastraca; and had issue.*

4e. *Frances Hussey,* b. 1802; d. 1839; m. [——] *Cornett.*

5e. *Victoria Grace Hussey,* m. *George Shaw; and had issue.*

[Nos. 58685 to 58697.

---

[1] Hutchins' "Dorset," iii. p. 313.

The Plantagenet Roll

3c. Mary Hussey, m. *George Maire of Shaftesbury*, d. 1766; *and had issue.*

4c. Fanny Hussey.

5c. Anne Hussey.

2b. Susan Hussey.

3b. Cicely Hussey.

4b. Martha Hussey, m. *Barnard Addis.*

5b. Ann Hussey.

630. Other descendants of the STRANGWAYS, if any (see Table LXIX.).

631. Descendants of ELIZABETH MEUX (see Table LXIX.), *bapt.* 10 July 1677; *d.* 22 Ap. 1756; *m.* as 3rd wife, 2 May 1710, Sir JOHN MILLER, 2nd Bart. [E.], *b. c.* 1665; *d.* 29 Nov. 1721; and had issue (at least [1]) 1*a* to 7*a*.

1a. Sir Thomas Miller, 3rd Bart. [E.], *M.P.*, d. 1733; m. *Jane, da. of Alderman Gother of Chichester; and had issue.*

See the Clarence Volume, pp. 506–515, Nos. 21953–22365.

2a. John Miller, d. 1735; m. *Mary, da. and h. of Richard Challen of Oving, co. Sussex; and had issue.*

See the Clarence Volume, p. 515.

3a. Elizabeth Miller, d. 1774; m. 1737, *Sir Edward Worsley of Gatcombe, I.W.*, d. 1762; *and had issue* 1*b* to 6*b*.

1b. Edward Meux Worsley of Gatcombe, M.P., b. 1747; d. 1782; m. 1*st*, *Elizabeth, da. of* [——] *Crow;* 2*ndly*, 1772, *the Hon. Elizabeth, da. and co-h. of Leonard* (*Holmes, previously Troughear*), 1*st Baron Holmes* [I.] (*who re-m. Sir Henry Worsley, afterwards* (1804) *Worsley-Holmes, 8th Bart.* [E.] *and*) *d.* 20 *Jan.* 1832; *and had issue.*

See the Clarence Volume, pp. 515–517, Nos. 22366–22413.

2b. Rev. James Worsley, M.A., Rector of Gatcombe, b. *Mar.* 1749; d. 3 *Oct.* 1798; m. 11 *July* 1771, *Ann, da. of* [——] *Hayles*, d. 27 *Oct.* 1824; *and had issue* 1*c* to 2*c*.

1c. Edward Vaughan Worsley, Lieut.-Gen. R.A., b. 1772; d. 14 *Aug.* 1850; m. 1800, *Mary, da. of John Arthur of Plymouth*, d. 24 *Feb.* 1848; *and had issue* 1*d* to 2*d*.

1d. St. Helena Worsley, d. (–); m. *Capt. Froster.*

2d. Jessie Worsley, d. 3 *Nov.* 1876; m. 7 *Aug.* 1823, *John Montagu, Colonial Sec. of Cape Colony*, b. 21 *Aug.* 1797; d. 4 *Nov.* 1853; *and had issue* 1*e* to 3*e*.

1e. John Edward Montagu, Registrar-General, Cape of Good Hope, *b.* 27 June 1824; *m.* 1st, 6 Jan. 1848, Anna Maria, da. of Major H. Piers, *d.* 11 Nov. 1867; 2ndly, Elizabeth Adams, da. of Capt. S. Bush Brodribb, 14th Dragoons; and has issue 1*f* to 10*f*.

    1f. John Charles Worsley Montagu, *b.* 31 May 1849.

    2f. Edward Vaughan Montagu, *b.* 23 Jan. 1851.

    3f. Henry Southey Maclear Montagu, *b.* 7 June 1854.

    4f. Frederick George Montagu, *b.* 30 Jan. 1856.

    5f. Arthur Boyle Montagu, *b.* 8 Oct. 1859.   [Nos. 58698 to 59165.

---

[1] See the Clarence Volume, Table LXII.

# of The Blood Royal

6f. Ernest William Saunders Montagu, b. 10 Dec. 1862.

7f. Jessy Worsley Montagu, m. 4 Aug. 1874, Samuel John Brodribb

8f. Anne Montagu.

9f. Elizabeth Montagu.

10f. Georgina Montagu.

2e. *Alfred Worsley Montagu, Lieut.-Gen. Bengal S.C.*, b. 25 *Sept.* 1829: d. 9 *Mar.* 1897; m. 19 *Aug.* 1854, *Emily, da. of George Augustus Ward of Wisbech: and had (with other) issue 1f to 3f.*

1f. Alfred Worsley Montagu, b. 27 Sept. 1860.

2f. Arthur Henry Montagu, b. 4 June 1862.

3f. Francis Ward Montagu, b. 6 Mar. 1864.

3e. Emily Mary Montagu.

2c. *Anne Worsley,* b. *June* 1777; d. 23 *Sept.* 1800; m. 29 *Mar.* 1798, *Rear-Adm. Henry Hill.*

3b. *Rev. Henry Worsley, D.D., Rector of Gatcombe Woolverton and St. Lawrence, Isle of Wight,* b. 1755; d. 11 *Ap.* 1844; m. *Mary, da. of Thomas Dickonson of Newport, I.W.,* b. 19 Dec. 1761; d. 18 *June* 1843; *and had issue* 1c to 4c.

1c. *Rev. Henry Worsley, LL.D., Rector of Hayes, Middlesex,* b. 8 *May* 1772; d. 25 *Aug.* 1860; m. *Susan, da. of James Charles Still of Knoyle, co. Wilts.* d. 6 *Ap.* 1878; *and had issue* 1d to 3d.

1d. *Rev. Henry Worsley, M.A., Vicar of Ashford Bowdler, co. Salop,* b. 12 *Aug.* 1820; d. 12 *Ap.* 1893; m. 18 *Dec.* 1851, *Clara Magdalene (29 Westbourne Street, Hove, Brighton), da. and co-h. of Vice-Adm. Sir William George Parker, 2nd Bart.* [*G.B.*]; *and had issue* 1e to 7e.

1e. Henry Edward Worsley (*Broken Hill Mine, New South Wales*), b. 2 Dec. 1854; *m.* 2 Aug. 1897, Winifred Eva, da. of Joseph Darwent of Penola, S. Australia; and has issue 1f.

1f. Robert Henry Worsley, b. 15 June 1898.

2e. John Nevil Worsley (*Beechboro', Poultry Farm, near Perth, Western Australia*), b. 22 Ap. 1857.

3e. Robert Wake Worsley (*Yorkton, Saskatchewan, Canada*), b. 16 Feb. 1870; *m.* 11 Jan. 1905, Margaret Elizabeth, da. of Thomas Paul of Calcutta, I.C.S.; and has issue 1f.

1f. Robert Parker Worsley, b. 8 Nov. 1905.

4e. Clara Elizabeth Worsley (*Durban House, Albert Park Road, Malvern Link*), b. 26 Sept. 1853; *m.* 9 Jan. 1884, Edward John Baxter, a Missionary in German East Africa; and has issue 1f to 2f.

1f. Edward Worsley Baxter, b. 4 Aug. 1890.

2f. Beatrice May Baxter, b. 2 May 1888.

5e. Mary Catharine Worsley (*Marshwood Vicarage, Charmouth, Dorset*), b. 17 Feb. 1856.

6e. Susan Euphemia Charlotte Worsley, b. 20 Ap. 1865; *m.* 13 Feb. 1888, Worsley Grey Hambrough (*Santa Cruz, California, U.S.A.*); and has issue.

See p. 330, No. 24201.

7e. Louisa Margaret Worsley, b. 26 June 1872.

2d. *Susan Worsley,* b. 12 *Feb.* 1822; d. 15 *May* 1900; m. 26 *Ap.* 1848, *the Rev. James Roydon Hughes, Rector of Newton Longueville, co. Bucks,* d. 7 *Jan.* 1894; *and had issue* 1e to 5e.

1e. Rev. Charles Roydon Worsley Hughes (*Ditton Hill Rectory, Surrey*), b. 6 Ap. 1850; *m.* 9 Jan. 1889, Emily Frances, da. of Henry Masterman, d. 3 Jan. 1900; and has issue 1f to 4f.   [Nos. 59166 to 59187.

715

The Plantagenet Roll

1*f*. Herbert Masterman Hughes, Mid. R.N., *b*. 25 Oct. 1889.

2*f*. Edward Charles Hughes, *b*. 27 Jan. 1891.

3*f*. Lionel Worsley Hughes, *b*. 29 June 1892.

4*f*. Godfrey Roydon Hughes, *b*. 17 Ap. 1895.

2*e*. Thomas Bridges Hughes (*Bickington, Lelant, Cornwall*), *b*. 17 Sept. 1851.

3*e*. James Roydon Hughes (*Beechhurst, Maybury*), *b*. 9 June 1855; *m*. 9 Aug. 1887, Alice Stronach, da. of Andrew Nicol; and has issue 1*f*.

1*f*. Sybil Worsley Hughes, *b*. 27 May 1888.

4*e*. Rev. Cecil Hughes (*Chorleywood Vicarage, Herts*), *b*. 14 Jan. 1858; *m*. 20 Ap. 1887, Marion, da. of Stephen Goodhart; and has issue 1*f* to 4*f*.

1*f*. Cecil Roydon Hughes, *b*. 17 Mar. 1888.

2*f*. Aubrey Everard Hughes, *b*. 18 Sept. 1890.

3*f*. Vivian Grey Hughes, *b*. 28 Feb. 1893.

4*f*. Marjorie Grace Hughes, *b*. 4 Jan. 1896.

5*e*. Edith Margaret Hughes (*Heathcroft, Yateley, Hants*), *b*. 27 July 1860; *m*. 18 Sept. 1888, Lieut. John Masterman, R.N.; and has issue 1*f* to 2*f*.

1*f*. Christopher Hughes Masterman, *b*. 7 Oct. 1889.

2*f*. John Cecil Masterman, Cadet R.N.C., Dartmouth, *b*. 12 Jan. 1891.

3*d*. *Mary Worsley*, *b*. 17 *Sept*. 1823; *d*. *Ap*. 1895; *m*. 16 *Aug*. 1853, *the Rev. Windsor Edmund Hambrough, M.A., Rector of Evenlode, Gloucester*, d. 3 *Nov.* 1899; *and had issue.*

See p. 330, Nos. 24199–24208.

2*c*. *Rev. Charles Worsley, M.A., Rector of Lesnewth, co. Cornwall, and of Finchley, Middlesex*, b. 11 *Sept*. 1783; d. 8 *Aug*. 1854; m. 25 *June* 1833, *Madeline Maria Ann, da. of Philip Carteret Le Geyt of Greenwich Hospital*, d. 11 *Aug.* 1855; *and had issue* 1*d* to 4*d*.

1*d*. *Charles Fortescue Worsley, Bengal C.S.*, b. 23 *May* 1838; d. 7 *June* 1892; m. 7 *Jan*. 1863, *Caroline Jane* (80 *Hereford Road, W.*), *da. of Lieut.-Gen. Frederic Dyott Atkinson; and had issue* 1*e* to 3*e*.

1*e*. Frederic Stanhope Worsley (*Windermere, Erdington, Birmingham*), *b*. 15 Dec. 1863; *m*. 1st, 6 Sept. 1886, Jane, da. of John Urwin; 2ndly, 28 July 1904, Florence Rosalie, da. of Alphonsus Richard Thornber; and has issue 1*f*.

1*f*. Caroline Mercy Worsley, *b*. 24 June 1888.

2*e*. Richard Le Geyt Worsley, M.R.C.S., H.M. Prison Service (17 *Walton Park, Liverpool*), *b*. 30 Nov. 1874; *m*. 10 Nov. 1897, Eleanor, da. of Robert Dempster of Liverpool; and has issue 1*f* to 2*f*.

1*f*. Richard Robert Le Geyt Worsley, *b*. 10 Sept. 1899.

2*f*. Godfrey Patrick Dempster Worsley, *b*. 30 Oct. 1902.

3*e*. Caroline Margaret Worsley, *b*. 8 Sept. 1866; *m*. 11 Ap. 1893, John Paul Roughton, M.R.C.S. (*Kettering, Northants*); and has issue 1*f* to 2*f*.

1*f*. Francis John Worsley Roughton, *b*. 6 June 1899.

2*f*. Dorothy Worsley Roughton, *b*. 9 Jan. 1894.

2*d*. Godfrey Thomas Worsley (*Evelyns, Hillingdon, Middlesex*), *b*. 7 Sept. 1841; *m*. 12 Ap. 1882, Frances, da. of the Rev. Melsup Hill, Rector of Skelsky Beauchamp; and has issue 1*e* to 6*e*.

1*e*. Hugh Barrington Worsley, Lieut. R.N., *b*. 17 Feb. 1883.

2*e*. Evelyn Godfrey Worsley, *b*. 13 Mar. 1885.

3*e*. Francis Le Geyt Worsley, R.N., *b*. 27 Oct. 1886.

4*e*. John Fortescue Worsley, *b*. 8 Dec. 1888.

5*e*. Ralph Edward Worsley, *b*. 20 Feb. 1896.

6*e*. Madeline Rose Worsley, *b*. 3 Mar. 1884. [Nos. 59188 to 59227.

# of The Blood Royal

3*d*. Rev. Edward Worsley, M.A., Vicar of Evenley (*Evenley Vicarage, Brackley*), *b*. 4 Jan. 1844; *m*. 8 July 1880, Ethel Adela, da. of Edward Knight of Chawton, J.P., D.L.; and has issue 1*e* to 8*e*.

1*e*. Harold Montagu Worsley, *b*. 1 Ap. 1881.

2*e*. Arthur Edward Worsley, *b*. 10 Oct. 1882.

3*e*. Herbert Henry Knight Worsley, *b*. 27 Nov. 1885.

4*e*. Robert Lewkenor Worsley, *b*. 8 Dec. 1893.

5*e*. Charles Edward Austen Worsley, *b*. 30 May 1902.

6*e*. Madeline Ethel Worsley, *b*. 29 Oct. 1887.

7*e*. Helen Margaret Joan Worsley, *b*. 24 June 1889.

8*e*. Katharine Mary Worsley, *b*. 25 Nov. 1891.

4*d*. Harriette Eleanor Worsley (11 *St. James' Road, Surbiton*), *b*. 25 Jan. 1837; *m*. 7 July 1863, Capt. Miller Barrington Worsley, *d*. 7 Aug. 1886; and has issue 1*e* to 2*e*.

1*e*. Charles Barrington Worsley (11 *St. James' Road, Surbiton*), *b*. 24 July 1866.

2*e*. Edith Madeline Worsley, *b*. 19 May 1864.

3*c*. *Miller Worsley, R.N.*, b. 8 *July* 1791; d. (–); m. *Johanna Evered, da. of E. J. Harris of Llantrissant; and had issue* 1*d* to 2*d*.

1*d*. *Miller Barrington Worsley, Indian Navy*, b. 12 *Feb*. 1823; d. 7 *Aug*. 1886; m. 7 *July* 1863, *Harriette Eleanor, da. of the Rev. Charles Worsley; and had issue.*

See p. 717, Nos. 59238–59239.

2*d*. *Isabella Naysmith Worsley*, b. 4 *Nov*. 1821; d. 11 *Oct*. 1898; m. *the Rev. George Branson Dodwell, M.A., Rector of Wilmot, Nova Scotia*, d. *Nov*. 1891; *and had issue (with others)* 1*e*.

1*e*. Philip Rashleigh Dodwell, M.D. (57 *Albert Bridge Road, Battersea*).

4*c*. *Maria Worsley*, d. *Nov*. 1853; m. 2 *Nov*. 1813, *the Rev. George Rashleigh, M.A., Vicar and Patron of Horton Kirby, and Rector of Little Hardres, Kent*, b. 8 *June* 1784; d. 18 *Feb*. 1874; *and had issue* 1*d* to 6*d*.

1*d*. R. W. Henry Burville Rashleigh, Vicar and Patron of Horton Kirby (*Horton Kirby Vicarage, Dartford, Kent*), *b*. 14 Feb. 1820; *m*. 14 Sept. 1847, Susan Maria, da. of the Rev. James King, Rector of Henley-on-Thames; and has issue 1*e* to 4*e*.

1*e*. George Burvill Rashleigh, B.A. (Oxon.), Bar.-at-Law, Principal Sec. to the Master of the Rolls 1878 (*Riseley, Horton-Kirby, Dartford, Kent*), *b*. 31 Aug. 1848.

2*e*. Rev. Carleton Rashleigh.

3*e*. Mary Georgiana Rashleigh, *m*. 21 Sept. 1871, the Rev. James Charles Hale (son of the Archdeacon of London).

4*e*. Edith Maria Rashleigh.

2*d*. *Charles Edward Rashleigh of Farningham Hill, Kent*, b. 1 *Aug*. 1825; d. (–); m. 14 *June* 1849, *Charlotte Hinxman, da. of William Rashleigh of Menabilly; and had (with other) issue* 1*e* to 4*e*.

1*e*. William Worsley Rashleigh, *b*. 14 Dec. 1852.

2*e*. Henry George Rashleigh, *b*. 23 Nov. 1853.

3*e*. John Clayton Rashleigh, *b*. 16 May 1865.

4*e*. *Charlotte Jane Rashleigh*, d. 25 *Dec*. 1872; m. *as* 1*st wife* 11 *July* 187–, *the Rev. John Rendall Rashleigh, M.A. (Camb.), Rector of St. Ewe (St. Ewe Rectory, Cornwall); and had issue* 1*f*.

1*f*. John Kendall Rashleigh, *formerly* Lieut. Royal Irish Fusiliers and (1902–1904) S. African Constabulary (*La Nevada, Cana du Verde, F.C. al Pacific, Argentina*), *b*. Dec. 1872; *m*. 1903, Evelyn Anne, da. of William Henry Phillips Jenkins.

[Nos. 59228 to 59251.

3d. William Boys Rashleigh of Farningham Manor House, d. (–) ; m. 2 *July* 1863, *Frances Portia, da. of the Rev. James King; and had issue* 1e *to* 7e.

1e. William Rashleigh.

2e. Hugh Rashleigh, *b.* 8 June 1876.

3e. Portia Mary Rashleigh.

4e. Eva Mary Rashleigh.

5e. Clara Rashleigh.

6e. Agnes Lilian Rashleigh.

7e. Blanche Rashleigh.

4d. ⎫
5d. ⎬ 3 daughters.
6d. ⎭

4b. Jane Worsley, b. 1740; d. (–) ; m. *the Rev. Arthur Hodgkinson.*

5b. Elizabeth Worsley, b. 1743; d. (–) ; m. *Sir Samuel Marshall, K.B.; and had issue.*

See the Clarence Volume, p. 517, Nos. 22414–22476.

6b. Anne Worsley, b. 1743; d. (–) ; m. *Adm. Richard Rodney Bligh; and had issue.*

4a. Jane Miller, m. *Capt. Bockland.*

5a. Hannah Miller, d. *Mar.* 1746; m. *as 2nd wife, the Right Rev. Sir Thomas Gooch, 2nd Bart.* [G.B.], *successively Lord Bishop of Bristol, Norwich and Ely,* d. 13 *Feb.* 1754; *and had issue.*

See the Clarence Volume, p. 518.

6a. Mary Miller, d. 1738; m. *the Rev. John Buckshall of Blackall, LL.D., Rector of Chichester.*

7a. Margaret Miller, m. *Thomas Yates, M.P.*   [Nos. 59252 to 59320.

632. Descendants, if any, of JANE MEUX (see Table LXIX.), wife of [——] MEAD of Loft, co. Essex.

633. Descendants of BARTHOLOMEW MEUX of Lesland and Buxton, I.W. (see Table LXIX.), *d.* Dec. 1650; *m.* RADCLIFF, *da.* of [——] GERARD ; and had issue 1*a* to 3*a*.[1]

1a. Lewis Meux, liv. 1650.

2a. Henry Meux of Norton Bury, co. Herts, and afterwards of Clerkenwell, co. Middlesex, d. *Dec.* 1692; m. *2ndly, Anne, widow of* [——] *Clever, da. of* [——] *Brightwell, living* 1714; *and had issue* 1b *to* 4b.

1b. Thomas Meux of London, Citizen and Mercer, d. *Jan.* 1720; m. *Elizabeth, da. and eventual co-h. of Sir William Massingberd of Gunby, 2nd Bart.* [E.], *M.P.,* d. 1738; *and had issue* 1c *to* 2c.

1c. William Meux, afterwards (Act of Parl. 11 *Geo. II.) Massingberd of Gunby,* d. 1780–1; m. *1st,* [——], *da. of* [——] *Thornborough; 2ndly,* [——], *da. of* [——] *Drake; and had issue* 1d *to* 7d.

1d. Thomas Massingberd, d.v.p. 1777; m. *Elizabeth, da. of Alexander Emerson of Caistor, co. Linc.; and had issue* 1e *to* 3e.

1e. Henry Massingberd of Gunby, d. *c.* 1787; m. *Elizabeth, da. of* [——] *Hoare; and had issue* 1f.

1f. Elizabeth Mary Anne Massingberd of Gunby, d. 29 *Nov.* 1835; m. 18 *Aug.*

---

[1] Berry's " Hants Genealogies," pp. 56–57.

# of The Blood Royal

1802, *Peregrine Langton, afterwards Massingberd,* d. 23 *Sept.* 1856; *and had issue.*

See the Clarence Volume, pp. 546–547, Nos. 23387–23400.

2*e. Thomas Massingberd of Candlesby, co. Linc., Capt. R.N.,* b. 1763; d. (–); m. 12 *Feb.* 1794, *Elizabeth Hawksmore, da. of* [——] *Waterhouse; and had issue* 1*f to* 6*f.*

1*f.* Thomas Massingberd.

2*f.* Rev. Humphrey (? Henry) Massingberd, *m.* [——], da. of Fretwell; and had issue.

3*f.* Christina Massingberd.

4*f.* Louisa Massingberd.

5*f.* Ellen Massingberd.

6*f.* Mary Jane Massingberd.

3*e. Rev. Charles Massingberd, Rector of Kettlethorpe, co. Linc.,* b. 11 *Nov.* 1770; d. 27 *Mar.* 1836; m. 1805, *Mary, da. of John Smith of Gainsborough; and had issue* 1*f to* 4*f.*

1*f. Charles Massingberd,* b. 1806; d. 27 *Dec.* 1886; m. *Lucy, da. of the Rev. W. Keary, Rector of Nunnington; and had issue* 1*g to* 3*g.*

1*g.* Henry Alfred Massingberd.

2*g.* Arthur Keary Massingberd.

3*g.* Anne Alice Massingberd.

2*f.* Mary Mildred Massingberd, *m.* 1st, 1837, Capt. Frederick James Blair, R.N.; 2ndly, the Rev. William Fraine Fortescue, Vicar of Chesterton.

3*f.* Anna Maria Massingberd, *m.* 1836, the Rev. E. J. Atkinson.

4*f. Caroline Bosvile Massingberd,* d. (? *unm.*).

2*d.*[2] *William Massingberd,* m. [——], *da. of* [——] *Pastern.*

3*d.*[2] *George Massingberd, settled in America.*

4*d.*[2] *Ann Massingberd,* m. *John Pike.*

5*d.*[2] *Katherine Massingberd,* m. *the Rev. Francis Wilson.*

6*d.*[2] *Mary Joyce Massingberd,* d. 2 *Jan.* 1839; m. *the Rev. Edward Brackenbury of Skindleby Hall, co. Linc., J.P.,* b. 6 *Aug.* 1756; d.s.p. 3 *Jan.* 1828.

7*d.*[2] *Sarah Elizabeth Massingberd,* m. *Radcliffe Pearl Todd.*

2*c. Rev. Richard Meux, Rector of Wedington, co. Essex,* d. *Ap.* 1751; m. 12 *July* 1732, *Hannah, da. of* [——] *Bradshaw,* d. *Dec.* 1855; *and had issue* 1*d to* 2*d.*

1*d. Richard Meux of Ealing and Holborn, Brewer,* b. 4 *Oct.* 1734; d. 2 *July* 1813; m. 31 *July* 1767, *Mary, da. of Henry Brougham of Brougham Hall, co. Westmorland,* d. 1812; *and had issue* 1*e to* 5*e.*

1*e. Richard Meux of Liquorpona Street, Holborn,* b. 11 *Sept.* 1768; d. 1824; m. 28 *June* 1792, *Eliza, da. of Henry Roxby of Clapham Rise; and had issue* 1*f.*

1*f. Elizabeth Meux,* b. 15 *Sept.* 1793; d. (–); m. 1 *Oct.* 1816, *Thomas Starling Benson of Champion Lodge, Camberwell.*

2*e. Sir Henry Meux of Theobalds' Park, co. Herts, 1st Bart.* [U.K.], *Brewer,* bapt. 8 *May* 1770; d. 7 *Ap.* 1841; m. *Nov.* 1814, *Elizabeth Mary, da. of Thomas Smith of Castlebar House, co. Middlesex,* d. 18 *Sept.* 1851; *and had issue* 1*f to* 4*f.*

1*f. Sir Henry Meux, 2nd Bart.* [U.K.], M.P., b. 28 *Dec.* 1817; d. 1 *Jan.* 1883; m. 19 *Jan.* 1856, *Lady Louisa Caroline, da. of Ernest* (Brudenell-Bruce), *3rd Marquis of Ailesbury* [U.K.]; *and had issue* 1*g.*

1*g. Sir Henry Bruce Meux, 3rd Bart.* [U.K.], b. 21 *Nov.* 1856; d.s.p. 12 *Jan.* 1900.

2*f. Elizabeth Mary Meux,* b. 7 *July* 1819; d. (–); m. 10 *Oct.* 1839, *Richard Arabin of High Beech, co. Essex,* d. 6 *Sept.* 1865. [Nos. 59321 to 59345.

3*f.* Marianne Frances Meux, b. 20 *May* 1821; d. 11 *Mar.* 1875; m. *as* 1*st wife*, 2 *Ap.* 1839, *Sir William Bowyer-Smijth*, 11*th Bart.* [E.], M.P., b. 22 *Ap.* 1814; d. 20 *Nov.* 1883; *and had issue* 1g *to* 2g.

1*g.* Sir William Bowyer-Smijth, 12th Bart. [E.] (*Hill Hall, Theydon Mount, Epping; 4 Nevill Park, Tunbridge Wells*), b. 1 Sept. 1840.

2*g.* Cicely Bowyer-Smijth (4 *Nevill Park, Tunbridge Wells*).

4*f.* Emma Martha Meux (39 *Lowndes Street, S.W.*), b. 20 Dec. 1822; m. 23 Jan. 1853, Arthur de Vere Capell, Viscount Malden, *d.v.p.* 10 Mar. 1879; and has issue.

See p. 375, Nos. 26747–26758.

3*e.* Thomas Meux, b. 2 *Ap.* 1772; d. (*? unm.*).

4*e.* Mary Meux, m. *William St. Julian Arabin of High Beech, co. Essex, Serjeant-at-Law; and had issue* (*with possibly das.*) 1*f.*

1*f.* Richard Arabin *of High Beech*, d. 6 *Sept.* 1865; m. 10 *Oct.* 1839, *Elizabeth Mary, da. of Sir Henry Meux, 1st Bart.* [U.K.].

5*e.* Fanny Meux, m. *Vicisimus Knox, Bar.-at-Law.*

2*d.* Anne Meux, *living* 1739; m. *William West of Brentwood, co. Essex, Attorney-at-Law*, d. 17 *Aug.* 1812.

2*b.* John Meux, *living* 1714.

3*b.* Samuel Meux, *Merchant, living* 1709.

4*b.* Anne Meux, m. *William Higford of Gloucester*, d. *between* 8 *Dec.* 1709 *and Feb.* 1710.

3*a.* William Meux, m. *Elizabeth, da. of Sir Edward Vernon; and had issue* 1*b.*

1*b.* Anne Meux, *living* 1669.   [Nos. 59346 to 59360.

634. Descendants, if any, of ELEANOR MEUX, wife of WILLIAM COMPTON of Hartbury, co. Gloucester; of MARY MEUX, wife of WILLIAM HIGFORD of Dixon, co. Gloucester; of ANNE MEUX, wife of EDWARD WHITE of Winchelsea; and of ELEANOR MEUX, wife of WILLIAM OKEDON of Ellingham, co. Hants (see Table LXIX.).

CORRIGENDA AND ADDENDA

TABLE XX.—Since these pages were printed the Editor has had reason to doubt the correctness of the descent through Mary Pierrepont, and it seems open to question whether Robert Pierrepont had a daughter of this name. She is not mentioned in Brydges. It was first published by Mr. F. P. Barnard, F.S.A., in *The Genealogical Magazine* under the title of " Royal Descent of Barnard," and according to the particulars there given—supplemented by additional details courteously supplied to the Editor of the present work by Mr. Barnard from a pedigree drawn out by his grandfather—Mary Pierrepont, daughter of Robert Pierrepont, and co-heir of her brother William Pierrepont, who *d.s.p.* 1705, was *b.* at Nottingham 1682; *d.* 22 Mar. 1709; *bur.* at St. Mary's, Nottingham, beside her father; *m.* at St. Mary's, Nottingham, 6 June 1704, Nathaniel Kinderley of Nottingham and Setch (*b.* at Lynn 15 May 1673; *d.* 16 Jan. 1742; *bur.* at St. Mary's, Nottingham, having *m.* 2ndly, at Sutton, 13 Dec. 1710, Mary, da. of the Rev. William Steevens of Sutton, who *d.* 15 July 1714, and was *bur.* there); and had with other issue 2 sons—(1) the Rev. John Kinderley, father of an only child, Frances, wife of James Smith of Norwich, and (2) Nathaniel Kinderley, *afterwards* Kindersley, who *d.* 6 Sept. 1781, leaving an only son, Nathaniel Kindersley, Lieut.-Col. H.E.I.C.S., *b.* 18 Oct. 1734, and " *bapt.* ten days after birth at his uncle John's church of St. Helen's, Norwich, his uncle baptizing him," and adopting him after his father's death. A search among the registers of St. Helen's, Norwich, however, shows that they contain no entry of any such baptism between 1726 and 1740, and one of the registers of Nottingham and Sutton *has proved equally futile.* Indeed the registers of Moulton, co. Lincoln, show that Nathaniel Kinderley and Maria Stevens were *m.* there 2 Dec. 1697, and those of Wormgay show that Nathaniel, son of the Rev. John Kinderley, was *b.* there 18 Oct. 1732. But though the descent as set out on the authority of the pedigree in Mr. Barnard's possession is quite unreliable, there would·appear some grounds for supposing that the Kinderleys are in some way at present unknown descended from the Pierreponts, and so from the Lady Anne of Exeter. The names Francis, Frances, and Pierrepont have been used as Christian names for many generations, many Pierrepont pictures and relics are in their possession, and a tradition of their descent from Anne of Exeter exists in the various branches; and in the Memoir of Sir J. R. Smith by his widow, Lady Smith (London : Longman, 1832, i. p. 5), it is stated that " Nathaniel Kinderley, Sir James' great-grandfather, lived at Saltmarsh, between Stockton and Durham, and inherited a considerable fortune from his father Geoffrey, before mentioned. He married Mary, granddaughter of the Hon. Francis Pierrepont, uncle to Evelyn, Earl of Kingston, by whom he had issue John, Nathaniel, Audrey, and Mary."

TABLE XXIII.—The exact place of Sarah Pelham, wife of George Winn of South Ferraby, in the pedigree seems very doubtful. In the various Winn pedigrees she is called " da. of Charles Pelham of Brocklesby." This the dates render impossible. She may have been his sister; but since the Editor has had an opportunity of consulting Canon Maddison's valuable collection of Lincolnshire Pedigrees (iii. p. 765), he inclines to the belief that she was probably a da. of Charles Pelham, youngest son of Peregrine Pelham, and grandson of Sir William Pelham of Brocklesby.

Corrigenda and Addenda

TABLE XXXV.—The Hon. Charles Savage, *m.* and had issue a da. Mary, who *m.* Jeremy Thoresby of Leeds, and had issue (1) Elizabeth, and (2) Mary. Burke's " Extinct Peerage," p. 474.

TABLE XXXV.—Eleanor Savage and Sir Henry Bagnal of Newry Castle (slain 14 Aug. 1598) had issue (1) Arthur of Newry, whose issue became extinct 1712; (2) Griffith; (3) John; (4) Elinor, *m.* 1st, Sir Robert Salisbury; 2ndly, Thomas Needham of Poolpark, co. Derby [brother to Robert, 1st Viscount Kilmorey [I.]], and had (with possibly others by 1st husband) (i.) Sir Robert Needham of Poolpark, who *m.* Mary, da. and h. of [——] Hartop of Surrey, and had issue; (ii.) Richard Needham of Poolpark; (iii.) Arthur Needham of Cambridge; (iv.) Thomas Needham of London; (v.) Francis Needham of London; (vi.) Elizabeth Needham, living 1633; (5) Mary, *m.* Sir John Bodwell, co. Carnarvon; (6) Elizabeth. See Archdale's " Lodge," iv. p. 221, and Brydges' " Collins," v. p. 193. The latter was apparently identical with Ann, the only da. mentioned by Brydges, who *m.* Lewis Baillie, Bishop of Bangor, ancestor of the Baylys, *alias* Pagets, Marquises of Anglesey. *Ex inform.* G. D. Burtchaell, Esq.

TABLE XLVII.—Barbara Constable, *m.* as 1st wife, Sir Thomas Metham of Metham, *de jure* 15th Baron Stapleton (1313) [E.], who was killed *ex parte regis* at the battle of Marston Moor, 2 July 1644, and had issue with a son Thomas, who *d.s.p.*, *v.p.* 2 das. and co-h.'s, viz. Katherine, *m.* Edward Smith of Ashe, and *d.s.p.s.* ; and Barbara, who *d.* before 1630, having *m.* Thomas Dolman of Pocklington, co. York, by whom, who *d.* 1639, she had issue a son, Robert Dolman of Pocklington, *de jure* 16th Baron Stapleton [E.], *b.* 1626; *d.* 1694, whose son and h. Robert Dolman of Pocklington, *de jure* 17th Baron Stapleton [E.], *d.s.p.* 1730. He was succeeded by Robert Dolman of Helmsley, s. and h. of William Dolman of Reading, which William is said to have been younger brother of the *de jure* 17th Lord Stapleton. Robert Dolman of Helmsley, and in 1730 of Pocklington, who if a nephew of his predecessor will have been *de jure* 18th Baron Stapleton [E.], was father of a s. and h., Robert Dolman of Pocklington, M.D. (*d.* at Liege 14 Feb. 1792), whose son Thomas Dolman of Pocklington claimed to be, and who, if the above descent is correct, was undoubtedly *de jure* 20th Lord Stapleton. He *d.* at St. Omer 1842, leaving an eldest s. and h., John Thomas Dolman of Pocklington and Souldern House, co. Oxford, M.D., who petitioned the Crown for a confirmation of his right to the Barony of Stapleton. The petition was referred to H.M.'s Attorney-General, but no further proceedings were taken. John Thomas Dolman was *b.* 10 May 1811, and *d.* 15 Mar. 1867, having *m.* 25 Oct. 1836, Ann Helen, da. of Samuel Cox of Eaton Bishop, M.D.; she *d.* 21 Dec. 1891. He had issue (1) Marmaduke Francis Cox Dolman [? *de jure* 22nd Baron Stapleton], *b.* 29 Jan. 1839; *d.s.p.* 16 Aug. 1889; (2) the Rev. George Dolman, Catholic Priest at Banbury, and who, if a descendant of the above-named Barbara Metham, is now *de jure* 23rd Baron Stapleton (1313) [E.]; and (3) Mary Helen Alicia, who *m.* 24 June 1857, the Hon. Bryan John Stapleton (whose father, Lord Beaumont, is a co-h. to the said Barony of Stapleton), and has issue (see p. 85, Nos. 351–367). Since the claim was advanced by Thomas Dolman of Pocklington, however, doubts have arisen as to the exact relationship between the Robert Dolman of Pocklington, who *d.* 1730, and his successor; and the Rev. George Dolman, to whose courtesy the Editor is much indebted, writes:—

"With regard to the uncertainty of our descent from the Metham family, the case seems to be this :—The will of Robert Dolman (proved 1730) mentions his ' cousin' Robert, son of William Dolman of Reading, as succeeding to the Pocklington estates. When the claim was first put forward my grandfather then was advised that the word ' cousin,' as applied to Robert (of Helmsley), might reasonably be taken as meaning ' nephew,' in which case, of course, his father William would have been brother of the testator, and therefore equally descended from the Metham family. However, a few years afterwards, when I was only a child, a Mr. Paver discovered somewhere in Yorkshire what purported to be a copy of the will of Robert Dolman (proved 1730), and on the back of this copy it is stated (in what would seem contemporary writing) that the Robert to whom the estates were left was descended from a *junior* branch of the Dolmans of Pocklington—that is, from the *second* son of the Squire of Elizabeth's days. (I have not a copy of the Pedigree with me, but this Squire, who married, I think, a Vavasour of Spaldington, had five sons, the second being, I think, Philip.) Now supposing this statement on the copy of the will to be correct, it is quite clear that the existing Dolmans are not descended from the Methams, although equally representing the family of 'Dolman of Pocklington.' As the original claim rested on an uncertainty, viz., that Robert Dolman of Helmsley was nephew of Robert, who died 1729, and as there now seems reason to believe that this was not the case, I think the claim may now be looked upon as abandoned. Of course the antiquaries were unaware of the fact stated on the copy of will of 1730, and consequently they deemed this claim to be tenable. In conclusion, I may add that Robert Dolman, who died 1729, left a sister who married a Mr. Killingbeck, whose descendants may still be found in the Anne and Charlton families ; at least that is my impression."

The Editor knows nothing of the copy of the will alleged to have been discovered by Mr. Paver, but the original is at York, and Col. Philip Saltmarshe of Saltmarshe, junr., who has gone into the subject, remarks :—

" Robert's will, dated 21st January 1729, prov. 11th May 1730, only deals with personalty, and runs as follows : ' To my sister, £40 p. a. for life ; *to John, the youngest son of William Dolman, late of Reading, in the county of Berks*, £400.' (This is in the exact wording of the will.) Then legacies to the Cholmeleys, and Grimstons, Ralph Crathorn of Ness being executor and residuary legatee of the personalty. The relationship to William Dolman or his son is not mentioned. Of course the presumption is (1) that the landed property was settled, (2) that John had an elder brother. The will of Robert Dolman who died in 1694 is unfortunately missing, or would probably help us. Thomas Dolman's (father of the above) will is dated August 1639, and refers to the settlement of the landed property made on him, his wife Barbara and heirs, by his father, Sir Robert Dolman, but does not give the limitation. This is all one can find out from public records, but I presume that before Mr. Thomas Dolman claimed the barony (1835–1840) he had better proof among his title-deeds, which no doubt he parted with when he sold his estates. Burke (writing in 1851) and Sir Nicholas Harris both thought the claim a good one. I think any one vitally interested in the case could, if he took the trouble, prove William Dolman's descents from the registers of Reading, Badsworth, and Pocklington, or from the title-deeds of the present owners of the Dolman property. I took up the question merely as an adjunct to the history of the Methams." Numerous collateral descendants exist of the Robert Dolman who succeeded to Pocklington in 1730, failing whom the Barony of Stapleton would now be sisted in the heirs of Mrs. Killingbeck, who, of course, are undoubtedly descended from Sir Thomas Metham and Barbara Constable his wife.

P. 89, line 15, for "*m.* Feb." read "*m.* 24 Jan."; and for "D'Oyley" read "D'Oyly."

P. 188, line 2, for "Barnham" read "Barham."

P. 198, line 49, add after "issue" 1*c* to 5*c*.

1*c*. Frederick Theodore Bagshaw, Assoc. M.I.C.E. (*Inksten, Winnipeg, Canada*), *b.* Feb. 1860.

2*c*. Samuel Horace Bagshaw, Photographer (*Birtle, Canada*), *b.* July 1864 ; *m.* Elsie, widow of S. G. Breadfoot of Liverpool, da. of Capt. Turner.

Corrigenda and Addenda

3c. Frederick Charles Bentinck Bagshaw, of Boulton's Mounted Infantry (*Victoria, British Columbia*), *b.* Mar. 1867; *m.* 29 June 1888, Frances Ann, da. of Lieut.-Col. Robert Crawfurd, Rifle Brigade; and has issue (3 sons and 7 das.).

4c. Agnes Mary Bagshaw, *m.* Richard Clements Gould, of Corpus Christi Coll., Cambridge; and has issue (3 sons and 2 das.).

5c. Catherine Emma Bagshaw. [Nos. 7133a to 7133e.

Pp. 315–320. Sections 236–238, Nos. 23342–23536. See note above under Table XX.

P. 320, insert—

239. Descendants of EDWARD ROLLESTON of Toynton, co. Lincoln, and (on the death of his cousin Lancelot, *s.p.* 1685) of Watnall, co. Notts (see Table XVIII.), *d.* (–); *m.* [——]; and had (with possibly other) issue 1a.[1]

1a. *Christopher Rolleston of Watnall*, d. 21 Mar. 1736; m. *Hannah, da. of Samuel Holden of Aston, co. Derby*, d. 29 Ap. 1725; *and had (with other) issue* 1b *to* 2b.

1b. *Lancelot Rolleston of Watnall, High Sheriff co. Notts* 1743; d.s.p. 27 Ap. 1751.

2b. *Rev. John Rolleston of Watnall, for forty years Rector of Aston, co. Derby*, d. 30 June 1770; m. *Dorothy, da. of Sir Robert Burdett of Foremark, co. Derby*, d. 30 Oct. 1794; *and had issue (with 3 other sons)* 1c to 3c.

1c. *Lancelot Rolleston of Watnall, High Sheriff co. Notts* 1781; d. *unm.* 25 Ap. 1802.

2c. *Christopher Rolleston of Watnall, High Sheriff co. Notts* 1805; d. 3 Ap. 1807; m. *Anne, d. of Capt. Nicholas, R.N.*, d. 14 Feb. 1809; *and had issue* 1d to 3d.

1d. *Lancelot Rolleston of Watnall, Col. Royal Sherwood Foresters, M.P., J.P., D.L.*, b. 20 July 1785; d. May 1862; m. 1st, 17 Nov. 1808, *Caroline, da. of Sir George Chetwynd, 1st Bart.* [G.B.], d. 10 Mar. 1844; 2ndly, *Eleanor Charlotte, da. of Robert Fraser of Torbreck, co. Inverness*, d. June 1895; *and had issue* 1e to 7e.

1e. Lancelot Rolleston, J.P., High Sheriff co. Notts 1877 (*Watnall Hall, near Nottingham; Toynton, Lincoln; Wellow Hall, Ollerton*), *b.* 1847; *m.* 25 Feb. 1882, Lady (R.W. 1889) Charlotte Emma Maud, sister to Robert, 15th Earl of Carnworth [S.], da. of Col. the Hon. Robert Dalzell, C.B.

2e. Robert Sydney Rolleston, Comm. R.N., *b.* 1849.

3e. Henry Edward Rolleston, *b.* 1851.

4e.[1] *Caroline Jane Rolleston*, d. (? s.p.) 5 May 1858; m. 1st, *Lieut.-Col. J. Hancox, 7th Dragoon Guards*; 2ndly, as 1st wife, 20 Mar. 1849, Sir Richard Levinge, 7th Bart. [I.], M.P., d.s.p. 28 Sept. 1884.

5e.[1] Louisa Maria Rolleston, *m.* [——] Berens.

6e.[1] Charlotte Frances Rolleston, *m.* 1st as 1st wife, 11 Ap. 1840 (marriage dis.), Edward Heneage of Stag's End, Hemel Hempstead, M.P., *b.* 24 July 1802; *d.* 1880; 2ndly, H. Bromley; and had issue (at least) 1f.

1f. Frederick Heneage, R.A., *b.* 18—; *m.* Ann, da. of [——] Gordon; and has issue 1g.

1g. Arthur Heneage, R.A., *b.* 1881.

7e.[2] Eleanor Anne Rolleston, *b.* 1853; *m.* 14 Nov. 1878, Capt. John Robert Tennant (*Chapel House, near Skipton*), *s.p.*

2d. *Rev. John Rolleston, Vicar of Burton-Joyce*, d. 17 Nov. 1862; m. *Elizabeth,*

---

[1] Burke's "Landed Gentry," 1900, p. 1361.

724

Corrigenda and Addenda

da. of the Rev. Philip Smelt, d. 9 Ap. 1862; and had issue (several children, of whom) 1e.

1e. Christopher Rolleston, *m.* 1854, Catherine, da. of William Lislie, 10th Laird of Worthill, J.P., D.L.; and has issue (3 sons and 2 das.).

3d. Dorothy Rolleston, d.(–); *m. the Rev. William Tiffin, Rector of Matterson, co. Notts.* [Nos. 23536a–23536.

P. 331, line 16, for "Kilmarsh" read "Kelmarsh."

P. 331, line 45, for "6d" read "7d."

P. 331. Delete line 50 and read in place thereof—
"5d. Cicely Mary Godman, *m.* 1899, Alexander Edward of Sanquhar, Forres.
"6d. Mary Lisa Godman, *m.* 1899, George Broun Ibbetson."

P. 331, line 51 (now 52), for "6d" read "7d."

P. 332, line 28, for "2b" read "3b"; and between lines 35 and 36, insert—
"3b. Josephine Champion de Crespigny."

P. 333. Section 250, add the following note :—

Beltz in his "Order of the Garter," p. 168, remarks: "We have not ascertained whether Margaret Pudsey left issue." This is quoted by G. E. C. in "The Complete Peerage," sub. Nevill vi. p. 13, note c, but in the "Abstract of the Pedigree of Field-Marshal George Henry de Strabolgie Neville Plantagenet-Harrison, Prince of Plantagenet, Duke of Lancaster," &c. &c. (? otherwise George Henry Harrison), as well as in that gentleman's "History of Yorkshire," 1879, i. p. 14, *et seq.*, she is said to have *d.* in 1610, leaving issue a da. and h. Margaret, who *m.* 1612 Peter Marley of Helagh-in-Swaledale, Lord of Hilton, near Staindrop, co. Durham, who was living 1639, being then seised of Barham House, co. York, in right of his wife, by whom she had issue a son John, who *d.v.p.* leaving (by his wife Elizabeth, da. and h. of John Coupland of Langdale, co. York) a son, Peter Marley of Eppleby, Barham House and Helagh, who *d.* 10 Ap. 1688, having *m.* Margaret (*bur.* 24 Feb. 1700), da. and h. of Francis Wodrove of Beamish, co. Durham, by his wife Margaret, da. and h. of Robert Widdrington of Widdrington, co. Northumberland, by his wife Ursula, youngest da. and co-h. of David Ingleby of Ripley, by his wife Lady Ann Nevill, *d.* 1615 (see p. 338, Section 263), youngest sister to Lady Margaret Pudsey, above mentioned, which last named Peter Marley had issue by the said Margaret Wodrove an only surv. son and h., John Marley of Eppleby, &c., *d.* 11 Aug. 1728, having *m.* Margaret, sister and h. of Richard Holmes of Stubb House, co. Durham, and had issue an only da. and h. Mary, *b.* 11 Ap. 1721; *d.* at Stubb House 10 Aug. 1798, who *m.* 13 Sept. 1743 the Rev. Cornelius Harrison of Darlington, M.A. (Camb.), *b.* 1701; *d.* 4 Oct. 1748, and had issue (with a da. Mary, wife of James Robson of Leeds) an only son, Cornelius Harrison of Stubb House, co. Durham, and of Bowes Hall and Eppleby, co. York, J.P., D.L., *b.* 17 Dec. 1744; *d.* 5 June 1806; *m.* 28 Aug. 1766, Ann, da. and h. of Philip Brunskell of Bowes, co. York, *d.* 9 Jan. 1784, and had issue (with a youngest son Thomas, who succeeded to all the family estates [which he alienated at his death, *s.p.s.* 1842, to the exclusion of the right heirs], and two das., Margaret, wife of John Stanton of Newcastle-on-Tyne [by whom she had issue Philip Holmes Stanton, h. to his uncle Thomas in 1842, and Mary Ann, wife of Edward Bilton of Newcastle, Merchant], and Penelope, wife of Samuel Rowlandson of London, Merchant [by whom she was mother of an only child, Ann Brunskell Rowlandson]), an eldest son and heir, Marley Harrison of Wharton, co. York, disinherited by his father, *b.* at Stubb House, 22 Feb. 1772, *d.* 14 July 1822, having *m.* 15 Sept. 1808 Margaret, youngest da. of Francis Hutchinson of Newsham and Earby Hall, co. York, and had issue seven children, one of whom was the above-named Field-Marshal G. H. de S. N. Plantagenet-Harrison, &c. &c., who was *b.* 14 July 1811.

Corrigenda and Addenda

P. 374, line 28, section 300. . Delete the words " if any."

P. 455. Section 384. Lady Catherine Brecknell (*née* Colyear) had one da., who *m.* a good many years ago the Rev. Talbot Greaves, half brother of the late Charles Sprengel Greaves, an eminent Q.C. of Mayfield, Staffordshire, and Ingleby Hill, Derby. They both *d.* without issue. *Ex inform.* the Hon. Alfred N. Curzon.

P. 460. Section 389. They had issue a son and da., who both *d.s.p.* " Dict. Nat. Biog."

INDEX OF NAMES

Index

728

Index

Index

732

Index

5 A

Index

735

Index

Index

Index

Index

Jndex

743

Index

744

Index

747

Index

Index

749

5 c

Index

Index

Index

Index

Index

761

Index

763

Index

Index

E. K., 32876, 33500, 45249, 45873; C. B., 4829, 16340, 20480, 27858, 39170; Mrs. C. G., 27855, 39167; E. B. N., 32875, 33499, 45248, 45872; Mrs. F. C. A., 43251, 43278; G. A. M., 4828, 16339, 20479, 27857, 39169; Mrs. G. E. B., 23784, 29047, 37931; G. M., 4831, 16342, 20482, 27860, 39172; Mrs. K. S., 32874, 33498, 45247, 45871; Maj. M. H., p. 352, 25752; P. H., 4830, 16341, 20481, 27859, 39171; R. O., 4827, 16338, 20478, 27856, 39168
Haller, Mrs. J. E. de, p. 595, 51520
Hallett, Mrs. C., 58848
Hallowes, Mrs., p. 210, 7474; A. W., p. 209, 7448, 7482; B., p. 209, 7447, 7481; Rev. B., p. 209, 7445, 7479; Rev. B. C., p. 208, 7430; B. J., p. 208, 7425; B. R., p. 210, 7472; D., p. 208, 7428; E. P. B., p. 210, 7485; Maj. F. W., p. 209, 7441, 7475; G., p. 208, 7427; G. F. B., p. 208, 7431; G. M., p. 208, 7423; Maj.-Gen. G. S., p. 210, 7470; H., p. 208, 7426; H. C., p. 208, 7424; Maj.-Gen. H. J., p. 210, 7471; J. C., p. 208, 7422; J. W., p. 209, 7443, 7477; K. B., p. 209, 7449, 7483; L., p. 208, 7429; M. C., p. 208, 7432; M. F., p. 209, 7444, 7478; R. B., p. 208, 7421; Maj. T. R. F. B., p. 208, 7420; W. A. T., p. 210, 7486; W. E., p. 209, 7442, 7476; W. H., p. 209, 7446, 7480
Hallward, Mrs., p. 197, 7099; Mrs. M. S., 35884; B. M., p. 198, 7104, 35889; D., 35893; H., p. 197, 7101, 35886; H. C., p. 197, 7102, 35887; Rev. J., p. 197, 7100, 35885; K. L., p. 198, 7107, 35892; M. E., p. 198, 7106, 35891; M. G., p. 198, 7105, 35890; W. T., p. 197, 7103, 35888
Hall-Watt, A. D., p. 502, 43968, 57796; Mrs. J. P., p. 502, 43966, 57794; R., p. 502, 43967, 57795
Halsey, Mrs., p. 379, 26871
Hambro, Mrs., p. 296, 14729; A. V., p. 296, 14736; C. J., p. 296, 14732; C. J., p. 296, 14730, 14733; Lieut. H. E., p. 296, 14735; Mrs. K. A., 8580, 35664, 51157; O., p. 296, 14737; R. E., p. 296, 14731, 14734; V. M., p. 296, 14738
Hambrough, B. W. J., p. 330, 24199, 39203;

D. A., p. 329, 24179; E. A., p. 330, 24180; M. E., p. 330, 24189; M. V., p. 330, 24181; O., p. 330, 24201, 39185, 39205; O. O. Le M., p. 330, 24183; Mrs. S. E. G., p. 715, 59184; S. M., p. 330, 24182; W. G., p. 330, 24200, 39204
Hamilton, 13th D. of, p. 371, 26676; M. of, 5911, 13064, 17306, 21436, 42941; Mrs., p. 147, 2179, 48181; Mrs., p. 358, 25924; Mrs., p. 359, 25962, 26187; Mrs., p. 414, 34310; A., p. 147, 2172, 48174; Maj. A., p. 358, 25926; A., p. 389, 32719, 45092; Mrs. A., 10303, 23669, 31191; A. A. J., 8912, 18849, 42464, 58915; A. C., p. 251, 9395; A. E. C., p. 389, 32720, 45093; Maj. A. F., p. 374, 26737; A. G., 5925, 13078, 17320, 18465, 21450, 22595, 42955; A. G. F., p. 251, 9393; A. H., Lieut. A. H. J., p. 146, 2161, 48163; Lord A. J., 5915, 13068, 17310, 21440, 42945; A. K., p. 389, 32710, 45083; Capt. A. M., p. 373, 26734; Lady A. P., 5917, 13070, 17312, 21442, 42947; A. P., p. 287, 11669; A. St. G., p. 146, 2164, 48166; B., p. 147, 2170, 48172; B., p. 147, 2171, 48173; B. L., p. 389, 32716, 45089; Capt. B. S. A., p. 373, 26730; Caroline, Lady, 30040; Hon. C., 14641; Lord C., 5916, 13069, 17311, 21441, 42946; C. A. L., p. 374, 26739; C. B., p. 374, 26738; C. C., p. 287, 11648; C. de C., p. 132, 1791, 47793; C. E., p. 251, 9387; C. E., p. 287, 11653; Lady C. E. B. 5913, 12512, 13066, 17308, 21438, 31891, 33870, 37999, 40153, 40928, 42943, 55442; C. H. A., p. 146, 2163, 48165; C. I. A., p. 287, 11670; Lord C. J., 5920, 15073, 17315, 21445, 42950; C. L., p. 389, 32712, 45085; C. P., p. 147, 2180, 48182; C. R., p. 389, 32705, 45078; Capt. C. R. S., p. 374, 26735; D. A., p. 146, 2167, 48169; D. A. L., p. 390, 32724, 45097; Maj. E. C., p. 389, 32714, 45087; E. de C., p. 132, 1793, 47795; E. C. D., p. 389, 32715, 45088; E. F., p. 185, 6644; E. G., p. 389, 32717, 45090; E. G., p. 389, 251, 9394; E. G., p. 389, 32711, 45084; E. H., p. 389, 32708, 45081; E. J., p. 287, 11647; E. L., p. 287, 11667;

E. M., p. 147, 2183, 48185; E. M., p. 374, 26736; E. M. M., p. 390, 32726, 45099; E. R. M., p. 389, 32722, 45095; Lady E. W., p. 473, 41676; Lord E. W., 5928, 13081, 17323, 21453, 42958; F. A., p. 389, 32707, 45080; Mrs. F. A. H., p. 287, 11662; F. C. E., p. 287, 11663, 11665; Rev. F. C. L., p. 146, 2169, 48171; F. F., 29954, 32727, 45100; Lord F. S., 5927, 13080, 17322, 21452, 42957; Hon. Lord G., 5923, 13076, 17318, 21448, 42953; Lieut. G. C., 5921, 13074, 17316, 21446, 30041, 42951; G. C. M., p. 390, 32723, 45096; G. de C., p. 132, 1792, 47794; G. E. F., 5929, 13082, 17324, 21454, 41677, 42959; G. F. C., p. 251, 9388; G. F. C., p. 389, 32706, 45079; G. T. E., p. 251, 9391; Lt.-Col. G. V., p. 287, 11651; Lady G. W. L., p. 622, 52918; H., 8911, 18848, 42463, 58914; Rev. H. A., p. 373, 26729; H. A., p. 147, 2181, 48183; Rev. H. B., p. 146, 2160, 48162; H. E. G., p. 287, 11671; H. F. T., p. 251, 9392; Mrs. H. R. G., p. 545, 49502, 52608, 57019; I., p. 287, 11649, 26732; I., 5922, 13075, 17317, 21447, 30042, 42952; J., 8645; J., p. 251, 9386; J., p. 251, 9385; Lt.-Col. J., p. 358, 25925; J. A., p. 373, 26731; J. B., p. 473, 41680; J. B., 5932, 13085, 17327, 21457, 42962; Rev. J. C., p. 146, 2162, 48164; J. G., 5930, 13083, 17325, 21455, 42960; J. G. P., p. 473, 41678; J. H., p. 251, 9089; J. M., 28120, 58871; Lady K., 5914, 12513, 13067, 17309, 21439, 31892, 33871, 38000, 40154, 40929, 42944, 53443; K. E. M., p. 147, 2182, 48184; K. M. A., p. 389, 32718, 45091; K. S., p. 374, 26740; L. B., p. 287, 11666; L. H. K., 8910, 18847, 42462, 58913; L. M., p. 389, 32713, 45086; L. M., p. 389, 32709, 45082; Hon. M. A., 14637; M. B., p. 473, 41679; Lady M. C., 18463, 22593; Lady M. C. R., 5912, 12511, 13890, 17307, 21437, 31890, 33869, 37998, 40152, 40927, 42942, 53441; M. E., 8646; M. E., p. 251, 9390; M. H., 2166, 26733, 48168; Lady M. L., 12733, 26423; M. L. E., Dcss. of, 12732; Mrs. M. W., 8909, 18846,

42461, 58912; R. A. B., 8644; R. A. G., p. 390, 32725, 45098; R. A. V., p. 389, 32721, 45094; Lieut. R. C., 5926, 13079, 17321, 18466, 21451, 23596, 42956; R. C. C., Mess. of, 12510, 31889, 33868; R. E., p. 287, 11664; Capt. R. E. A., 8643; Hon. R. G. A., 8642; R. H., p. 287, 11650; R. J., 5924, 13077, 17319, 18464, 21449, 22594, 42954; R. M., 28122, 58873; Hon. S. E., 14639; S. J., 8656; Hon. W., 14640; W. D., p. 146, 2165, 48167; W. J., p. 146, 2168, 48170; W. J.;L., p. 287, 11652; W. J. R., 28121, 58872
Hamilton-Dalrymple, Alice M., Lady, 11409, 12433, 36327; A. M., 11412, 12436, 36330; H. C., 11410, 12434, 36328; J., 11411, 12435, 36329; M., 11413, 12437, 36331; S., 11414, 12438, 36332
Hamilton-Gell, Mrs. E. L., p. 207, 7398
Hamilton-Gordon, Capt. D. G., 55658; Lieut. D. W., 55659; E. H., 55662; E. L., 55667; Lady E. S. A., p. 646, 35657; G. W., 55664; H., 55661; K. E., 55666; R., 55663; S., 55660; W. H., 55665
Hamilton-Hoare, H. N., p. 198, 7111
Hamilton-Russell, Hon. A., p. 492, 43151, 55801; A. G. L., p. 492, 43150, 55800; Hon. C. E., p. 492, 43149, 55799; Hon. E. S., p. 492, 43152, 55802; Hon. F. G., p. 492, 43148, 55798; Hon. F. R., p. 492, 43158, 55808; Hon. G. W., p. 492, 43147, 55797; Hon. M. H., p. 492, 43154, 55804; Lady M. R., p. 591, 51415, 55778, 58198
Hamlyn, Mrs., p. 351, 25731
Hamlyn-Fane, E. H., p. 351, 25730
Hammersley, Mrs., p. 294, 14668; Mrs., p. 378, 26841; Z. W., 46031, 47391
Hammet, Mrs. A., 14450, 55387; C. F. J., 14451, 55388; V. I. M., 14452, 55389
Hammick, Elinor, Lady, 13363; Capt. S. F., 8686
Hammond, Mrs., p. 465, 40839; A. C., p. 246, 9210; A. M., p. 246, 9208; F. A., p. 246, 9209; M. I., p. 246, 9219
Hampden, A. K. M., 10132, 43612; Mrs. C. E., 10129, 43609; G. C. E., 10131, 43611; M. R., 10133, 43613; Capt. O. R. L., 10130, 43610; S. H., Vctss., 23712, 28974
Hampson, D. F., 31303,

2993, 37434, 43752, 52758

Hecht, Mrs. A. I., 29134, 29549, 54875; C. F., 29135, 29550, 54876

Heigham, Mrs. I. G., 13314, 25718

Heinemann, Mrs. M., p. 223, 7977, 44719; P. D., p. 223, 7978, 44720

Helbert, A. B. C., p. 441, 35209, 35461; F. de C., p. 441, 35206, 35458; G. G., p. 441, 35207, 35459; H. B. de M., p. 441, 35214, 35466; L., p. 441, 35213, 35465; L. A. C., p. 441, 35208, 35460; R., p. 441, 35210, 35462; R., p. 441, 35211, 35463; V., p. 441, 35212, 35464

Hellmuth, Mrs. M. L., p. 647, 55743

Helmsley, Vct., 55675

Helyar, C. I., p. 356, 25859; C. J., p. 356, 25860; C. V. H., p. 356, 25856; K. C., p. 356, 25857; P., p. 356, 25858

Hemphill, Capt. F., 30082; M. C. A., 30083; S. C. J., 30081

Henderson, Mrs., p. 371, 26675; D., 45945, 47305; G., 45946, 47306; Mrs. L. M., 45943, 47303; W., 45944, 47304

Heneage, 1st B., 10, 37347, 44244, 54687; A., 22, 23536g, 54699; Sir A. C. F., 72, 24808, 54749; Hon. A. M., 17, 37354, 44251, 54694; Maj. A. R., 26,!54703; C. L. M., 73, 13349, 24809, 54750; E. H. F., 27, 54704; E. M., 28, 54705; F., 21, 23536f, 54698; Hon. F. C., 14, 37351, 44248, 54691; Hon. G. E., 11, 37348, 44245, 54688; Hon. G. M., 19, 37356, 44253, 54696; H. E. F., 25, 54702; Hon. H. G., 12, 37349, 44246, 54689; H. W. F., 24, 54701; J. E., 24812; J. F., 75, 24811, 54692; Louisa E., Lady, 13348; Hon. M. F., 15, 37352, 44249, 54692; Hon. M. J., 18, 37355, 44252, 54695; Hon. T. R., 13, 37350, 44247, 54690; W. R., 23, 54700

Henley, A., p. 359, 25935; A., p. 359, 25934; A., p. 360, 25964; A. C., p. 360, 25965; B. M., p. 479, 41833; C., p. 359, 25937; C. B., p. 479, 41826; E. M., p. 479, 41834; Capt. F. J., p. 359, 25936; G. A., p. 359, 25933; J. A., p. 358, 25929; J. C., p. 359, 25930; J. J., p. 358, 25928; M. A., p. 479, 41836; M. C., p. 479, 41835; M. M., p. 359, 25938; Rev. R. E., p. 479, 41825; V. K., p. 359, 25931

Henniker-Major, Hon. A. M. M., 4633, 16144, 18352, 20284, 22482, 27662, 38973; Hon. C. H. C., 4629, 16140, 18348, 20280, 22478, 27658, 38969; Hon. D. F. S., 4636, 16147, 18355, 28976; Hon. E. E. E., 4634, 16145, 18353, 20285, 22483, 27663, 38974; Hon. Mrs. F. E. H., 3675, 3682, 30988; Hon. G. A. G., 4630, 16141, 18349, 20281, 22479, 27659, 38970; Hon. J. E. de G., 4632, 16143, 18351, 20283, 22481, 27661, 38972; Hon. L. B. A., 4635, 16146, 18354, 20286, 22484, 27664, 38975; Hon. V. A., 4631, 16142, 18350, 20282, 22480, 27660, 38971

Henry, Mrs., p. 362, 26190; A. O., p. 469, 41493; E. B., p. 470, 41501; E. G., p. 469, 41494; Mrs. E. H. S., 29916, 30366; E. O., p. 470, 41498; F. T. C., p. 470, 41499; J. W., p. 470, 41500; M. E., p. 469, 41492

Hensley, Mrs. A. N. S., p. 318, 23433

Henty, Mrs. G. L. A. H. E., 28571

Hepburne-Scott, Lady A., 3824, 31397, 31566, 39663, 39828; A. N., 6911, 25293, 26054; E. C., 6915, 25297, 26058; Mrs. E. F., 6909, 25291, 26052; F. W., 3826, 31399, 31568, 39665, 39830; H. V., 6913, 25295, 26056; J. C., 3825, 31398, 31567, 39664, 39829; L. G., 3827, 31400, 31569, 39666, 39831; M. H. C., 3828, 31401, 31570, 39667, 39832; M. M., 6914, 25296, 26057; P. J., 6912, 25294, 26055; W. T., 6910, 25292, 26053

Herbert, Lord, 5988, 13141, 17383, 21513, 37819, 43018, p. 540, 49300; Mrs., 141; Hon. A. E. W. M., 13890, 58605; Lieut. A. H., 3787, 55260; A. H., 3797, 22936, 37699, 49152, 49219, 55270; Hon. Mrs. A. A. M., 43723; A. K. L., 3792, 55265; Hon. A. N. H. M., 13876, 13881, 58596; Hon. A. P. H. M., 13889, 58604; A. S., 13711; A. T., 13891, 58606; Mrs. B. A., 30650; Beatrice E., Lady, 30872; Lady B. F. G., 5990, 13143, 17385, 21515, 37821, 43020; Mrs. C., p. 560, 49908, 49987; D. M. E., 3784, 30652, 55257; E. J. B., 43724; Lady E. L. A., p. 402, 33794, 53366; E. R. H., 3783, 30651, 55256; Col. E. W., 3782, 55255; F. C., 3788, 55261; F. M. U., 43725; Lt.-Col. G. C., 3786, 55259; G. E., 13715; Lady G. O., 13915, 58630; G. R. A., 142, 13712, 41642; Hon. G. S., 5989, 13142, 17384, 21514, 37820, 43019, p. 540, 49303; Lady H. G., 3774, 6515, 17909, 22040, 25527, 35684, 55247, 58505; H. J., 3794, 22933, 37696, 49149, 49216, 55267; Mrs. K. E., 13710; L. E., 3796, 22935, 37698, 49151, 49218, 55269; Rt. Hon. Lady M., p. 184, 6512, 17906, 22037, 58502; M. G., p. 540, 49308; Lady M. H., 25524; Lady M. K., 5991, 13144, 17386, 21516, 37822, 43021, p. 540, 49306; Lady M. L., 3775, 6516, 17910, 22041, 25528, 55248, 58506; Lady M. L. E. S., 2720, 7757, 13887, 18554, 22684, 29401, 58602; Hon. M. R. H. M., 13677, 13882, 58597; N. I., p. 140, 2018, 13892, 33710, 48020, 54167, 58607; Hon. P., 5988b, 13141b, 17383b, 43018b, p. 540, 49302; P. H. C., 3785, 30653, 55258; P. M., 3795, 22934, 37697, 49150, 49217, 55268; S., p. 540, 49307; Mrs. S. A., 22932, 37695, 49148, 49215; Hon. S. C., 5988a, 13141a, 17383a, 21513a, 30873a, 37819a, 41018a, p. 540, 49301; Mrs. T. S., 41641; Lady V. A. M. C., 2721, 7758, 13888, 18555, 22685, 29402, 58603; V. I. J., 13714; Hon. W. H., 3793, 55266; W. [L. E., 3781, 55254

Heriot, Mrs., p. 296, 14726; J. E., p. 296, 14727; M., p. 296, 14728

Heron-Maxwell, A. W., 53141; B. E., 53168; C. M., 53141; Mrs. C. V., p. 694, 57720; E. J., p. 627, 53184; E. M., p. 627, 53180; H. A., p. 627, 53179; I. W., 53128; J. E., p. 627, 53189; J. E. B., p. 627, 53185, 57721; Sir J. R., 9th Bart., 53127; K. E., 53138; M., p. 627, 53188; M., 53139; M. A., p. 627, 53182; M. K. D., 53144; M. V., p. 627, 53187, 57723; N., p. 627, 53181; P., p. 627, 53183; P. A., p. 627, 53186, 57722; R. C., 53140; S. H. W., 53142; Maj. W. H. M., p. 627, 53178

Herries, 14th L., 10662, 11816, 24327, 35723, 38800, 37081, 48531; Angela M. C., Lady, 4038, 11214, 13843, 15548, 19688, 33838, 36133, 38416, 53410; D. C., p. 671, 56957; E. F., p. 671, 56958; Mrs. L. E., p. 671, 56954; R. S., p. 671, 56956; W. H., p. 671, 56955

Herron, Mrs., p. 401, 33582, 34718

Herschell, 2nd B., p. 315, 23361; Hon. A. F., p. 315, 23362; Hon. M. F., p. 315, 23363

Hertford, 6th M. of, 30375, 41132, 42084, 54929; M., Mcss., p. 323, 24010

Hervey, Mrs., 3486, 23070; Mrs., p. 473, 41669; A. L., 12518, 40934; C. A., 3490, 23074, 23246, 30279; C. G., 5406, 16926, 21056; D. E. F. C., 5403, 16923, 21053, 41670; D. F. A., 5402, 16922, 21052; Mrs. E. D., 23242, 30275; E. G., 3489, 23073, 23245, 30278; Lord F., 2579, 4772, 16283, 20423, 27801, 29260, 39113; Lieut. G. E. W., 3487, 23071, 23243, 30276; G. H. V. F. G., 5404, 16924, 21054, 41671; Mrs. M. E., 12517, 40933; Lady M. K. I., 2588, 4781, 16292, 20432, 27810, 29269, 39122; O. C. F., 5408, 16928, 21058; P. H. C., 5488, 23072, 23244, 30277; Lady S. C., p. 391, 33073, 45446, 49374; S. E., 5409, 16929, 21059; V. H. E., 5407, 16927, 21057; W. G. E., 5405, 16925, 21055

Hervey-Bathurst, A. C., p. 604, 51845; A. R., p. 604, 51844; C., p. 604, 51847; E. F., p. 604, 51846; Lt.-Col. L., p. 604, 51843; S. L., p. 604, 51843

Hesketh, C. M., 10334

Heskett, F., 47342; H. 45981, 47341; Mrs. N. B. D., 45980, 47344

Hewat, Mrs., p. 495, 43206; C., p. 495, 43208; E., p. 495, 43207

Hewson, Mrs. J. G. A., p. 96, 728, 44223

Heydt, A. von der, 12881; Mrs. A. H. von der, 12880

Heysham, B. F., 31048; Capt. C. A. J., 31049; L., 31052; M., 31050; N., 31051

Heywood, Mrs., p. 190, 6847; G. S. P., 10046, 43526; Maj.-Gen. J. J., p. 187, 6684; Mrs. M., 10045, 10099, 43525, 43579; M. B., p. 436, 35047, 35299; Mrs. M. F. H., p. 436, 35046, 35298; M. J., p. 436, 35051, 35303; O. F. E., p. 436, 35050, 35302; V. N. B., p. 436, 35048, 35300

Heywood-Lonsdale, Hon. Mrs., p. 237, 8709

Index

Index

Index

3ndex

782

Index

785

Index

Index

Index

797   5 I

Index

Index

⟨Index⟩

Index

Index

Index

Mrs. D., p. 502, 43984, 57812; D. E., 50339, 50542; E. F., 50342, 50545; F. C., 50336, 50539; F. E., p. 502, 43986, 57814; F. N.. P. 495, 43224; G., 3415, 37547, 37566; G. E., 50338, 50541; Mrs. G. L., p. 475, 41752; G. L., p. 502, 43985, 57813; Lieut. H., 3409, 37541, 57560; H. C., p. 503, 43989, 57817; Lieut. H. F. D., p. 258, 9745, 24980; N. G., 50341, 50544; Mrs. H. I., 29314; L. A., p. 503, 43991, 57819; L. W. N., p. 495, 43221; M. N., 50340, 50543; N. F., 50337, 50540; R. N., p. 495, 43220; W. O., p. 495, 43222

Thomson, Mrs., p. 313, 23319, 56462; Mrs., p. 424, 34647; Mrs., p. 224, 8013, 8070, 44754, 44812; Mrs., p. 228, 8136; Mrs., 4121, 15631, 19771, 38500; [——], 4122, 15632, 19772, 38501; [——], p. 434, 34650; A. M., p. 424, 34649; D. W., p. 424, 34648; E. A., p. 228, 8142; E. V., p. 228, 8139; F. M. G., p. 224, 8014, 8071, 44756, 44813; H. B., p. 228, 8137; Hon. Mrs. M. A., 31681, 31717, 39943, 39979; N. F., p. 228, 8141; T. W., p. 228, 8138; W. M., p. 228, 8140

Thornhill, A. H., p. 691, 57629; A. J., p. 691, 57623; A. M., p. 691, 57644; B., p. 692, 57661; C., p. 691, 57638; C. J., p. 691, 57635; C. M., p. 692, 57664; C. S., p. 691, 57631; D. M., p. 691, 57643; E. B., p. 691, 57628; E. H., p. 691, 57627; E. M., p. 692, 57660; F. E., p. 691, 57640; F. H. W., p. 691, 57624; F. W., p. 691, 57636; G. R., p. 691, 57642; H. E. B., p. 691, 57653; H. F. B., p. 691, 57654; Mrs. H. G., p. 691, 57648; H. J., p. 692, 57662; H. O'B., p. 692, 57656; J., p. 691, 57651; Maj. J. C., p. 692, 57655; J. E., p. 691, 57641; J. H., p. 691, 57637; J. I., p. 691, 57646; K. A., p. 692, 57657; L., p. 691, 57626, 57650; L. A., p. 692, 57677; M., p. 691, 57639; M., p. 691, 57645; N., p. 691, 57625, 57649; P. I. C., p. 692, 57658; R., p. 692, 57663; W. B., p. 691, 57652; W. D., p. 691, 57630

Thornton, Hon. Mrs., p. 324, 24039; A. L., 35898; Col. A. P., 52804; Rev. A. V., 35900; B. E., 35904; C. E. C., 52809; C. V., 52807; C. V., 52815; D. M., 35906; D. V., 52817; E., 35911; E. M. H., 35905; E. V. C., 52808; F. C., 35897; Maj. F. S., 52810; G. K., 52800; G. L., 52799; H. C., 35901; H. C., 35909; H. C., 52811; H. G., 35908; Rev. H. P., 35907; H. R. H., 52805; Rev. J., 52796; J., 52797; J., 52798; J. O., 52813; K., p. 324, 24040; L. E., p. 90, 504, 56208; Capt. L. H., 52802; Hon. Mrs. M. A., 43704, 55291; M. C., p. 90, 505, 56209; M. E., 35899; M. G., p. 324, 42041; M. N., 52812; N. H., 52816; N. S., 52803; R. H., 35903; R. H., 52801; R. T., 35902; Maj. S. V., 52814; W. H., 52806

Thornycroft, Mrs., 5145, 16655, 26795; A., 46308; C. E., 46299; C. M., 5146, 16656, 20796, 28270, 46300, 56103; Mrs. E. F. L., 28269, 56102; F. F., 5151, 16661, 20801, 28275, 46305, 56108; F. J. M., 5147, 16657, 20797, 28271, 36301, 56104; G. A., 5150, 16660, 20800, 28274, 46304, 56107; H. S., 46307; J. R., 46306; R. E. S., 5149, 16659, 20799, 28273, 46303, 56106

Thorold, A. H. p. 613, 52200, 57051; A. H. G., 12791; Alexandrina H. M., Lady, p. 613, 52197, 57046; D. M., p. 613, 52203, 57054; F. J. A., 12792; J. E., p. 613, 52199, 57050; Capt. G., p. 613, 52198, 57047; M., p. 613, 52201, 57052; M. C. A., 12794; Mrs. T. M., 12790; W. B. M. du Pre, 12793

Thorp, C. W., p. 615, 52244, 57095; E., p. 615, 52247, 57098; Mrs. E., p. 615, 52242, 57093; E. M., p. 615, 52248, 57099; J. B., p. 615, 52245, 57096; M., p. 615, 52246, 57097; R. G., p. 615, 52243, 57094

Thorpe, Mrs. E. C., p. 391, 33070, 45443, 49371; J. I. S., p. 391, 33071, 45444, 49372

Throckmorton, A. M. E., 7419, 10548, 11509; B. C. D. A., 7414, 10543, 11504; B. M. S., 7417, 10546, 11507; Capt. C. R. B., 7413, 10542, 11503; G. B. W., 7416, 10545, 11506; Lieut. H. J. A., 7415, 10544, 11505; I. G. M. P., 7418, 10547, 11508; J. P. H., 10549, 11510; M. E., 10550, 11511; Sir N. W., 9th Bart., 10540, 11501; Capt. R. C. A., 10541, 11502

Thuillier, G. F., p. 440, 35162, 35414; Mrs. H., p. 440, 35160, 35412; H. S., p. 440, 35161, 35413

Thunder, Mrs., p. 275, 10925; B. W., p. 275, 10927; C. J., p. 275, 10926; C. M., p. 275, 10929; M. A., p. 275, 10930; W. M., p. 275, 10928

Thurnall, Mrs. L. F., p. 255, 9675, 9866, 24910, 25101, 43800

Thursby, Mrs., p. 220, 7892; A. D., p. 220, 7893, 46854, 47051; A. D., 46907, 47104; A. H., 46898, 47095; A. W. C., 46900, 47097; C., 46889, 47086; Mrs. C. A., 46953, 47126; C. A. H., 46909, 47106; C. D., 46867, 47064; Comm. C. F., 46877, 47074; C. P., 46880, 47077; C. R., 46857, 47054; D. G., 46874, 47071; D. M., 46901, 47098; E. H., 46908, 47105; F., 46856, 47053; F. C. N. G., 46852, 47049; F. D., 46887, 47084; G. J., 46890, 47087; G. J., 29572, 29766, 51403, 54898, 58186; H., 46879, 47076; Rev. H. E., 46869, 47066; Rev. H. W. G., 46902, 47099; H. Z., p. 220, 7894, 46855, 47052; I. C. A., 46878, 47075; I. C. A., 46857, 47127; Capt. J. H., 46851, 47048; Sir J. O. S., 2nd Bart., 46888, 47085; K. G., 46873, 47070; Louisa H., Lady, 29571, 29765, 51402, 54897, 58185; M. C., 46894, 47073; M. E., 46894, 47091; M. E., 29573, 29767, 51404, 54899, 58187; M. H., 46871, 47068; M. V., 46875, 47072; N., 46853, 47050; Capt. P. C., 46906, 47103; P. C., 46881, 47078; P. H., 46899, 47096; R., 46858, 47058; S. G. D., 46866, 47063; S. J., 46872, 47069; S. S., 46865, 47062; W. L., 46870, 47067; W. L., 46895, 47092

Thursby-Pelham, Rev. A., 46945, 47118; A. H., 46946, 47119; D. H., 46955, 47128; E. E. A., 46950, 47123; E. A., 46949, 47122; H. C., 46948, 47121; H. C., 46951, 47124; J. A. H., 46943, 47116; J. F., 46947, 47120; M. A. N., 46944, 47117; N., 46952, 47125

Thynne, Capt. A. C., 18214, 22344; Rev. A. C., 18219, 22349; A. C. G., 18229, 22359; A. G., 18223, 22353; Lord A. G., 18191, 22321, 49413; Lady A. V., 18189, 22319, 49410; A. R., 18200, 22330, 26471; Lt.-Col. A. W., 18232, 22362; Lady B., 18194, 22324, 49416; B. E., 18241, 22371; Lieut. B. G. C., 18213, 22343; G. E., 18256, 22386, 38163; Lieut. D. G., 18224, 22354; Lady E. M., 18190, 22320, 49411; F. J., 18212, 22342; G. A. C., 18215, 22345; G. B., 18230, 22360; H. E. G., 18226, 22356; Lord H. F., 18195, 22325; I. C., 18218, 22348; J. A. R., 18197, 22327, 22468; J. C., 18233, 22363; J. G., 18221, 22351; K. A., 18240, 22370; Lady M. B., p. 541, 49412; M. C., 18238, 22368; M. C., 18217, 22347; M. E., 18222, 22352; M. E. G., 18231, 22361; M. G., 18228, 22358; M. H., 18258, 22388, 38165; M. S. H., 18216, 22346; O. St. M., 18199, 22329, 26470; R. C. S., 18257, 22387, 38164; R. G., 18225, 22355; Maj.-Gen. R. T., 18239, 22369; S. C., 18253, 22383; S. G., 18227, 22357; Capt. T. U., 18196, 22326, 26467; Lady U. F. I., 26466; Capt. U. O., 18198, 22328, 26469; W. F. G., 18220, 22350

Tidswell, A., 26674

Tierney, Mary, Lady, p. 584, 51194

Tighe, A. E., 32675, 45048; D. F. C., 32671, 45044; F., 32674, 45047; Lt.-Col. J. S., 32668, 45041; K. A. L., 25561; K. A. L., 32667, 45040; L., 32673, 45046; L. E., 32685, 45058; Hon. Mrs. L. J., 25168; M. C. H. M., 25170; M. M., 32676, 45049; N. U., 32672, 45045; R. H. M., 25169; S. D., 32692, 45065; W., 32670, 45043; W. S., 32669, 45042

Tilley, Mrs., p. 150, 1711, 7348, 47713; 49432

Tillyer, Mrs. F. A., p. 690, 57621

Timson, Mrs., p. 148, 2005, 48007; D., p. 140, 2007, 48009; F., p. 140, 2006, 48008

Tindall, Mrs., p. 340, 24708; E. W., p. 340, 24709; J. C., 9094, 19031, 42645, 58827, 59097; Mrs. M. C., 9093, 19030, 42644, 58826, 59096

Titchfield, M. of, 18057, 22187, 23867

Toler, Mrs. E. A., 12867

Tolhurst, Mrs. P., 158, 2470, 48466

Tollemache, 2nd L., 43392; A. D. E. S., 43302; Capt. A. E., 43298; Rev. A. E., 43432; Rev. A. F., 43297; A. F. C., 43253; A. G., 43435; A. H. W., 43254; A. M., 43414; A. M., 43369; Maj. A. S., 26490, 43368; Hon. A. W., 5239, 16749, 20889,

Index

Index

Index

Index

Jnder

G. E., 26611 ; K. C. O., p. 225, 8023, 44765 ; M. I., 29596, 29790, 54922 ; M. J., 29592, 29786, 43430, 54918 ; M. M. D., 13427, 49055 ; Lady M. S. F., 13422, 49050 ; P. A. E., p. 225, 8021, 44763 ; Lieut. R. A. L., 13424, 49052 ; Hon. Mrs. R. A. S. D., 26615 ; Hon. Mrs. R. C. E., 43426 ; R. O., p. 379, 26866 ; S. C. G., p. 225, 8024, 44766 ; S. M. S., 32471, 33628 ; Lt.-Col. T., 29588, 29782, 54914 ; T. D., 29589, 29783, 43427, 54915 ; U. M., 32473, 33630 ; V. D. P. S., p. 225, 8022, 44764 ; V. E. M., 32480, 33637 ; Rev. W. H., 29593, 29787, 54919

Wood-Acton, Mrs. L. C., p. 266, 9984

Woodgate, Mrs., p. 248, 9284 ; A. G. K., p. 151, 2269, 48271 ; B., p. 248, 9311 ; C. A. N., p. 247, 9262 ; D. M., p. 526, 47641 ; E. A., p. 526, 47642 ; E. F. S., p. 248, 7286 ; E. M., p. 248, 9310 ; G. H., p. 248, 9288 ; G. K., p. 248, 9303 ; H. C., p. 247, 9261 ; H. P., p. 151, 2270, 48272 ; I. M., p. 248, 9304 ; Mrs. K. E., p. 526, 47640 ; M. M., p. 248, 9290 ; M. V., p. 151, 2272, 48274 ; R., p. 248, 9289 ; R. S. M., p. 248, 9287 ; R. S. S., p. 248, 9285 ; S. G. C., p. 151, 2271, 48273

Woodruffe, Mrs., p. 252, 9405 ; H. A., p. 252, 9406 ; J. S., p. 252, 9407 ; M. E., p. 252, 9408

Woods, Mrs. E. A., p. 96, 718, 25341, 26102, 44213 ; E. W., p. 96, 720, 25343, 26104, 44215 ; G. G. B., p. 419, 34509 ; G. S., p. 419, 34511 ; Lieut. H. C., p. 96, 719, 25342, 26103, 44214 ; M. H., p. 419, 34510 ; Mrs. M. L., p. 419, 34508

Woolacott, Mrs. J. K., 45983, 47343

Woolryche-Whitmore, Mrs. B. A., 6757 ; F., 6759 ; P. M., 6758

Wootton, A., p. 411, 34195 ; A. G., p. 411, 34197 ; A. R., p. 411, 34206 ; C. A., p. 411, 34193 ; C. F., p. 411, 34200 ; E., p. 411, 34194 ; E. M., p. 411, 34201 ; H. F., p. 411, 34202 ; H. L., p. 411, 34198 ; H. M. F., p. 411, 34207 ; J. C., p. 411, 34199 ; J. C. F., p. 411, 34192 ; M. G., p. 411, 34196 ; M. O., p. 411, 34205 ; N. F., p. 411, 34203 ; R. M., p. 411, 34204

Worcester, M. of, 5046, 16557, 20697, 28171, 31758, 40020 ; Lord Bishop of, 25523, 41377, 41983

Workman, Mrs., p. 110, 1256

Worsley, Lord, 24616, 35679, 43815 ; A., p. 639, 53984, 57828, 57904 ; A., p. 639, 54007, 57927 ; A., p. 639, 54010, 57930 ; A. A., p. 639, 54001, 57921 ; A. B., p. 639, 53995, 57839, 57915 ; A. E., p. 717, 59230 ; A. M., p. 639, 54015, 57935 ; Mrs. A. M., p. 280, 11109, 11583, 48755, 58326 ; C., p. 639, 54009, 57929 ; C., p. 639, 54012, 57932 ; C. B., p. 717, 59238, 59240 ; C. E. A., p. 717, 59233 ; C. M., p. 716, 59214 ; D. A., p. 639, 54013, 57933 ; Rev. E., p. 717, 59228 ; E., p. 639, 54004, 57924 ; E. C., p. 639, 54000, 57920 ; E. D., p. 641, 54065 ; E. F., p. 639, 54014, 57934 ; E. G., p. 716, 59223 ; E. I., p. 638, 53982, 57826, 57902 ; E. M., p. 638, 53980, 57824, 57900 ; E. M., p. 717, 59239, 59241 ; F., p. 639, 54001, 57931 ; Capt. F., p. 641, 54055 ; F. F., p. 263, 9920, 54058 ; F. L. G., p. 716, 59224 ; F. M., p. 639, 53999, 57919 ; Capt. F. P., p. 263, 9922, 54060 ; F. R. C., p. 263, 9918, 54056 ; F. S., p. 716, 59213 ; Rev. F. W., p. 263, 9919, 54057 ; G. P. D., p. 716, 59217 ; G. T., p. 716, 59221 ; H. B., p. 716, 59222 ; Mrs. H. E., p. 717, 59237 ; H. E., p. 715, 59175 ; H. G., p. 642, 54078 ; Lt.-Col. H. G., p. 642, 54077 ; H. H. K., p. 717, 59231 ; H. M., p. 641, 54052 ; H. M., p. 642, 54075 ; H. M., p. 717, 59229 ; H. M. J., p. 717, 59235 ; J. F., p. 716, 59225 ; J. H., p. 642, 54076 ; J. N., p. 715, 59177 ; K. M., p. 717, 59236 ; K. P., p. 263, 9923, 54061 ; L., p. 639, 54002, 57922 ; L., p. 641, 54054 ; L. M., p. 715, 59186 ; M. C., p. 715, 59183 ; M. E., p. 263, 9921, 54059 ; M. L., p. 717, 59234 ; M. R., p. 639, 53985, 57829, 57905 ; M. R., p. 716, 59227 ; Rev. P. R., p. 642, 54073 ; Capt. P. W., p. 641, 54045 ; R. E., p. 716, 59226 ; R. H., p. 715, 59176 ; Lieut. R. H. W., p. 642, 54079 ; R. L., p. 717, 59232 ; R. Le G., p. 716, 59265 ; R. M. M., p. 641, 54064 ; R. P., p. 715, 59179 ; R. Le G., p. 716, 59216 ; R. S., p. 641, 54062 ; R. W., p. 642, 54074 ; R. W., p. 715, 59178 ; V., p. 638, 53983, 57827, 57903 ; V. G., p. 642, 54080 ; W. A., p. 638, 53979, 57823, 57899 ; Sir W. H. A., 3rd Bart., p. 638, 53978, 57822, 57898 ; W. H., p. 638, 53981, 57825, 57901 ; W. M., p. 641, 54053

Worthington, Mrs. M., p. 562, 49944, 51941 ; Lady M. G., 6621, 18016, 18527, 22146, 22657

Worthington-Eyre, Mrs., p. 147, 2188, 48192 ; F. M., p. 148, 2195, 48197 ; H. E., p. 148, 2192, 48194 ; L. G., p. 148, 2190, 48194 ; M. G., p. 148, 2193, 48195 ; O. G., p. 148, 2194, 48196 ; R., p. 148, 2191, 48193 ; W. S. E., p. 148, 2189, 48191

Wrangham, Mrs. A., p. 689, 57601 ; A. E. F., p. 675, 57190, 57609 ; Mrs. D., p. 697, 57949 ; Capt. D. F., p. 675, 57185 ; Lieut. D. G., p. 675, 57192 ; Mrs. E. A. F., p. 689, 57607 ; Mrs. F., p. 674, 57184 ; F. M., p. 675, 57193 ; G. W., p. 675, 57189, 57608 ; H. H., p. 675, 57187 ; J. D., p. 675, 57186 ; W. G., p. 675, 57188 ; W. J., p. 675, 57191

Wreford, Mrs. D. B. A., 52576

Wrey, Mrs., p. 133, 1808, 47810 ; Rev. A. B., p. 133, 1799, 47801 ; Rev. A. B. C., p. 129, 1675, 1873, 47677, 47875 ; A. C. F., p. 129, 1696, 1894, 47698, 47896 ; A. E., p. 129, 1684, 1882, 47686, 47884 ; A. H., p. 129, 1677, 1875, 47679, 47877 ; A. M., p. 129, 1682, 1880, 47684, 47882 ; B. A., p. 129, 1686, 1884, 47688, 47886 ; Rev. B. W. T., p. 129, 1688, 1886, 47690, 47888 ; C. E., p. 133, 1795, 1809, 47797, 47811 ; D. E. A. B., p. 133, 1798, 47800 ; D. E. B., p. 129, 1692, 1890, 47694, 47892 ; C., p. 129, 1678, 1876, 47680, 47878 ; E. C., p. 129, 1693, 1891, 47695, 47893 ; E. F., p. 133, 1802, 47804 ; E. H., p. 129, 1683, 1881, 47685, 47883 ; E. M., p. 129, 1694, 1892, 47696, 47894 ; F. A., p. 129, 1685, 1883, 47687, 47885 ; F. M. P., p. 128, 1674, 1872, 47676, 47874 ; G. E. B., p. 133, 1794, 47796 ; Rev. H. B., p. 129, 1689, 1887, 47691, 47889 ; H. B., p. 133, 1801, 47803 ; H. E. B., p. 129, 1691, 1889, 47693, 47891 ; H. S., p. 129, 1697, 1895, 47699, 47897 ; I. M., p. 129, 1687, 1885, 47689, 47887 ; K. A., p. 129, 1680, 1878, 47682, 47880 ; M. B., p. 129, 1695, 1893, 47697, 47895 ; M. C., p. 133, 1810, 47812 ; M. C. B., p. 129, 1690, 1888, 47692, 47890 ; P. B. S., p. 128, 1673, 1871, 47675, 47873 ; Sir (R) B. S., 10th Bart., p. 128, 1672, 1870, 47674, 47872 ; Lieut. R. C., p. 129, 1681, 1879, 47683, 47881 ; R. C. B., p. 129, 1679, 1877, 47681, 47879 ; Lieut. W. A. B., p. 153, 1800, 47802 ; W. B. S., p. 129, 1676, 1874, 47678, 47876

Wright, Mrs., p. 153, 2329, 48325 ; A. G. B., p. 703, 58078 ; C., 47266 ; Mrs. C. C., p. 703, 58077 ; E., 31342, 32177, 35797, 39608, 40439 ; H. H., 31340, 32175, 35795, 39606, 40437 ; Mrs. H. L., 47115 ; J., p. 278, 11081, 11555 ; Mrs. J. C., 47262 ; Mrs. M. H., 31339, 32174, 35794, 39605, 40436 ; Mrs. J., 12151, 14106, 14538, 54529, 55475 ; M. S., 31341, 32176, 35796, 39607, 40438 ; T., 47265

Wrightson, A. N., p. 155, 2352, 48348 ; C., p. 155, 2354, 48350 ; R. B., p. 155, 2351, 48347 ; R. F., p. 155, 2353, 48349

Wrottesley, 3rd L., 1001, 1181, 5575, 16969, 21099, 46423 ; Hon. C., 1005, 1185, 5579, 16973, 21103, 46427 ; E. A., 1216, 5610, 17004, 21134, 46458 ; Hon. E. H., 1004, 1184, 2791, 5578, 7829, 16972, 21102, 29473, 46426 ; Rev. F. J., 1214, 5608, 17002, 21132, 46456 ; F. J., 1217, 5611, 17005, 21135, 46459 ; Lieut. F. R., 1215, 5609, 17003, 21133, 46457 ; Hon. G., 1006, 1186, 5580, 16974, 21104, 46428 ; Lieut. E., 1191, 5585, 16979, 21109, 46433 ; M. E., 1192, 5586, 16980, 21110, 46434 ; Hon. V. A., 1002, 1182, 2790, 5576, 7827, 16970, 21100, 29471, 46424 ; Hon. W. B., 1003, 1189, 2791, 5577, 7828, 16971, 21101, 29472, 46425

Wyatt-Edgell, Mrs., 5546, 19230 ; C. S. C., 5548, 19232 ; L. P., 5549, 19233 ; M. R. A., 5547, 19231

Wyborn, Mrs. A., p. 549, 49579, 53345 ; C. F. B., p. 549, 49580, 53346

Wykeham, M., 359, 25932

Wyld, Mrs., 5430, 16950, 21080

Wylde-Browne, C. H. A., p. 526, 47633 ; C. J., p. 526, 47636 ; E. E., p. 526, 47638 ; F., p. 526, 47632 ; F. F., p. 526, 47622 ; Capt. G. H., p.